Special Edition

Using

Microsoft®
Word and
Excel 2000

Patrick Blattner
Ed Bott
Woody Leonard
Laurie Ulrich
Timothy Dyck
Bill Camarda

A Division of Macmillan Computer Publishing, USA
201 W. 103rd Street
Indianapolis, Indiana 46290

CONTENTS

Using Microsoft® Word and Excel 2000

Copyright© 1999 by Que® Corporation.

International Standard Book Number: 0-7897-1929-0

Library of Congress Catalog Card Number: 98-86993

Printed in the United States of America

First Printing: June 1999

01   00   99   4   3   2   1

Trademarks

Publisher
John Pierce

Development Editor
Susan Hobbs

Managing Editor
Thomas F. Hayes

Copy Editors
Julie McNamee
Margo Catts
Jill Bond

Indexer
Christine Nelsen

Layout Technician
Eric S. Miller

Cover Designer
Dan Armstrong

Copywriter
Eric Bogert

Book Designers
Lousia Klucznik
Ruth Lewis

CONTENTS

VII Creating and Modifying Charts

ABOUT THE AUTHORS

Ed Bott is a best-selling author and award-winning computer journalist with more than 12 years of experience in the personal computer industry. As senior contributing editor of *PC Computing* magazine, he is responsible for the magazine's extensive coverage of every conceivable flavor of Microsoft Windows and Microsoft Office. He also writes the magazine's monthly "NT Update" column. From 1991 until 1993, he was editor of *PC Computing*, and for three years before that he was managing editor of *PC World* magazine. Ed's collection of books (all published by Que) take up more than six feet of shelf space. Ed is a two-time winner of the Computer Press Award, and he and Woody won the prestigious Jesse H. Neal Award, sometimes referred to as "the Pulitzer Prize of the business press," in back-to-back years for their work on *PC Computing*'s Windows SuperGuide. He lives in an extremely civilized corner of the Arizona desert with his wife, Judy, and two amazingly smart and affectionate cats, Katy and Bianca.

Woody Leonhard describes himself as an "Office victim." With 15 (or is it 16?) computer books under his belt, Woody's seen parts of Office that would curl your hair. He runs the software company famous for "Woody's Office POWER Pack," the award-winning Office add-on that you'll find on this book's CD-ROM. He's the publisher of "Woody's Office Watch"—a (free!) weekly electronic newsletter that holds Microsoft's feet to the fire—and a contributing editor at *PC Computing* magazine, where he's been working with Ed for years. His writing has won six Computer Press Awards and, with Ed, two American Business Press Association awards. A Tibetan human rights activist, Woody lives on top of a mountain in Colorado.

Patrick Blattner has been using Excel for more than 12 years in corporate and private business. After graduating from Northeast Louisiana University, he started out in the contracting and gold-mining industry. He then branched off into product development where he received a United States Utility Patent (5,031,865) and set up manufacturing in China with international distribution. He's spent the last four years in interactive software development and is a member of The Academy of Interactive Arts and Sciences. Patrick currently works for the Walt Disney Company. He can be contacted at Patrick@Blattnerbooks.com or you can visit his site at www.Blattnerbooks.com.

Laurie Ulrich has been teaching computer classes for universities and corporate training centers for over 10 years. She also runs her own firm, Limehat & Company, Inc., an organization that specializes in technical documentation, software education, Web page design, and Web site hosting. Her firm's primary focus is helping businesses to make the most of their computer investment—by shedding their fears of computerization, and remaining on the cutting edge of business software. In the last two years, Laurie has been a contributing author on several books, and authored four of her own for Macmillan Computer Publishing: *Using Microsoft Word 97*, *Using Microsoft PowerPoint 97*, *The Microsoft Office 97 Productivity Pack*, and *The Complete Idiot's Guide to Running a Small Office with Microsoft Office*. One of her upcoming titles includes *Sams Teach Yourself Microsoft Office 2000 in 21 Days*.

Bill Camarda is author of 11 books, including the #1 selling *Special Edition Using Word 97*, Bestseller Edition (Que); *Microsoft Office Administrator's Desk Reference* (Que); and *Cheapskate's Guide to Bargain Computing* (Prentice Hall PTR). He is also a consultant and copywriter who specializes in working with leading technology companies, including IBM, AT&T, Bell Atlantic, Lucent Technologies, PC EXPO, and many others.

TELL US WHAT YOU THINK!

As the reader of this book, *you* are our most important critic and commentator. We value your opinion and want to know what we're doing right, what we could do better, what areas you'd like to see us publish in, and any other words of wisdom you're willing to pass our way.

As the Executive Editor for the General Desktop Applications team at Macmillan Computer Publishing, I welcome your comments. You can fax, email, or write me directly to let me know what you did or didn't like about this book—as well as what we can do to make our books stronger.

Please note that I cannot help you with technical problems related to the topic of this book, and that due to the high volume of mail I receive, I might not be able to reply to every message.

When you write, please be sure to include this book's title and author as well as your name and phone or fax number. I will carefully review your comments and share them with the author and editors who worked on the book.

Fax: 317-581-4663

Email: office@mcp.com

Mail: Executive Editor
          General Desktop Applications
          Macmillan Computer Publishing
          201 West 103rd Street
          Indianapolis, IN 46290 USA

INTRODUCTION

Funny how things change in less than a decade. Way back in the early 1990s—an eternity when measured in Internet time—Microsoft decided to bundle its most popular programs in a single package called Office. The individual programs that made up that first Office version had little in common except a few toolbar buttons and top-level menus. It was basically a four-for-one deal, crammed onto a foot-high stack of floppy disks.

Three versions later, Microsoft Office is the best-selling business application in the history of personal computing, with more than 70 million copies sold. In Office 2000, Microsoft has largely delivered on its promise to integrate the different programs that make up Office—toolbars don't just look alike, they use the exact same code, and when you learn how to customize one application you can generally transfer the same skills to other Office programs.

Integration and collaboration between applications is one of Microsoft Office's strong points. It offers incredible power by enabling the user to combine Word, Excel, PowerPoint and Access information into each program. Adding Web integration to this mix, and the sky's the limit for creating, editing, and sharing documents, information and data. This book offers ideas, methods, and practices to use Word and Excel not only as stand-alone applications, but in combination with other Microsoft programs.

To be productive with Office applications, you need a good reference book. This book takes the approach that Word and Excel are the workhorse applications of the Office Suite—the programs that most Office users depend on the most in their jobs. If you find that you spend most of your Office time with these two applications, then this book is probably the right book for you.

But, if you have never used Word or Excel before, this might not be the right book for you. This book does not cover the basics, such as typing and editing in Word, or data entry in Excel. This book is not designed for first-time users needing help with introductory steps. If you need a more in-depth look at Word, Excel, or other Office 2000 applications, please consider one of the other Que Office books, such as:

Special Edition Using Microsoft Office 2000

Special Edition Using Microsoft Word 2000

Special Edition Using Microsoft Excel 2000

Special Edition Using PowerPoint 2000

Special Edition Using Microsoft Access 2000

Special Edition Using Outlook 2000

Regardless of which Office or Office application book you choose, we know that you will find the *Special Edition Using* books about Office to be the most comprehensive and useful reference books available for these programs.

BUILDING SLICKER DOCUMENTS FASTER

CHAPTER 1

TEMPLATES, WIZARDS, AND ADD-INS

In this chapter

WHAT TEMPLATES ARE AND HOW THEY WORK

Templates are patterns for your documents. When you choose a template for your new document, you're telling Word what information—text, formatting, and graphics—you want to appear in that document automatically.

Of course, the more information you can automatically add to your new documents, the less you have to add manually. You can use templates to dramatically reduce the number of documents you create from scratch. Depending on your work, you might virtually eliminate them. Travel often? Create an expense report template. Provide a status report every month? Build a status report template with subheads for every topic you must cover, and links to Excel worksheets containing the raw data you're analyzing.

But slashing the time it takes you to create new documents is only half of what templates can do for you. That's because templates don't merely place information in new documents. They enable you to create custom editing environments for specific clients, projects, or companies. They store all the tools you and your colleagues need to edit specific documents as efficiently as possible, including *styles*, automated *macro procedures*, *AutoText* boilerplate text, and more.

To make the benefits of templates seem less abstract, consider the possible applications. You might, for example, build a template designed to streamline document creation for a specific client, project, or company. Your template could include the following:

- **All relevant styles.** As you will learn in Chapter 2, "Streamlining Your Formatting with Styles," you can create a system of styles that make it easy to make specific documents look consistent. You can store this system of styles in a template, making it easy to use when you need it.

- **All relevant boilerplate text (AutoText entries).** For example, your template can include contract clauses, marketing language, product names and descriptions that you often use in connection with a client, project, or company. You learn more about AutoText in Chapter 4, "Automating Your Documents: AutoCorrect, AutoFormat, AutoText, and AutoSummarize."

- **Macros that streamline tasks associated with specific documents.** For example, you might include a macro that opens a dialog box where users can define what elements should be included in a proposal.

- **New toolbars, menus, or menu items.** These items provide shortcuts for tasks associated with specific documents. For example, if your template helps a user run an electronic mail merge, it might include a toolbar that walks the user through each step of the process. In some cases, the toolbar might borrow buttons from Word's built-in Mail Merge toolbar, such as the Mail Merge Helper button. In other cases, the buttons might be attached to custom macros.

Templates such as these are extremely valuable to you, but they can be even more valuable to your colleagues and others who may be working on similar documents. The project at the end of this chapter walks you through the process of building such a template. But first, let's take time to examine the basics.

SELECTING A TEMPLATE FOR A NEW DOCUMENT

When you create a new document using the File, New dialog box (see Figure 1.1), you're actually choosing a template on which your document will be based. The default Blank Document template that most people use is based on Word's Normal template, an especially important Word template that you'll learn more about shortly.

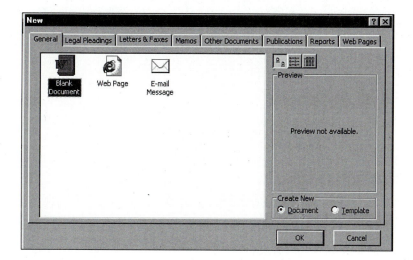

Figure 1.1
The choices in the New dialog box are templates that contain predefined text, formatting, and graphics.

USING WORD'S BUILT-IN TEMPLATE LIBRARY

Word comes with nearly 30 templates for the documents you're most likely to create. These templates can be used to create letters, faxes, memos, reports, résumés, Web pages, brochures, manuals, and many other documents.

Most of Word's templates actually contain their own directions on how to use them most effectively. For example, the Report templates explain how to insert your own company name, create consistent bulleted lists, and even how to *AutoFormat* a table consistent with the one already in the document.

Note

Later in this chapter, in the "Using Word Wizards" section, you'll learn more about the wizards that also appear in the New dialog box.

Wizards walk you step-by-step through the creation of letters, faxes, mailing labels, memos, résumés, Web pages, newsletters, legal pleadings, agendas, and several other types of documents.

To select a template, display the New dialog box, then click the tab containing the template you want and double-click the template. When you use some templates in Word 2000 for the first time, Word may need to install them before running them. If Word displays a dialog box asking permission to do so, click <u>Y</u>es.

Note

If you installed Word across the network, Word looks for templates in the network location you originally installed from. If you installed Word locally, Word prompts you to insert the Office 2000 or Word 2000 CD-ROM.

Tip #1

If you installed Microsoft Office 2000, you can open Word and a document based on a template of your choice, both at the same time. On the taskbar, click Start, New Office Document. Office displays a list of all the templates associated with Word (as well as other Office programs you may have installed). Double-click any Word template. (They're recognizable by their Word icons.)

THE NORMAL TEMPLATE: CRUCIAL TO ALL DOCUMENTS

No matter which template you choose for a specific document, one template is always open: the Normal template, stored as Normal.dot in Word 2000's template folder. Although the Normal template doesn't include any text, it does include the following:

- The 90+ built-in Word styles you learned about in Chapter 6.
- Word's built-in AutoText entries for letters and other business documents (see Chapter 8).

As you work, your new styles, AutoText entries, macros, and many other customizations are stored in the Normal template, unless you deliberately choose to save them elsewhere. Therefore, the longer you work with Word, the more valuable your Normal.dot file is likely to become.

Caution

This file is so important, it's the first target of many macro virus authors. Even if you don't back up your entire Word installation as regularly as you should, at least store a current copy of Normal.dot somewhere safe every couple of weeks.

Word looks for Normal.dot whenever it starts up. If Normal.dot is damaged, or renamed, or if Word simply can't find it in the template (or Workgroup template) folder you've specified in Tools, Options, File Locations, it simply creates a new one using Word's default settings. However, the new Normal.dot won't contain any of the styles, AutoText entries, or other customizations that you have added since installing Word.

You can generally use the Organizer to copy custom styles, toolbars, macros, and AutoText entries from the renamed Normal.dot to the new Normal.dot. (If your original Normal.dot was virus-infected, don't copy macros into the new one.) The Organizer is covered in Chapter 2, and is reviewed again later in this chapter, in the "Moving Elements Among Templates" section.

Note

While Word normally manages template files well on its own, if you want to copy templates amongst computers manually—or if you run into problems with a template—it helps to know where and how Office 2000 stores templates. Word recognizes four types of templates:

- **User-customized templates.** These are templates you create yourself. These are stored in one of two locations, depending on which version of Windows you're using, and how you've set it up. If you are running Windows 95 or Windows 98 without separate profiles for multiple users on the same computer, your custom templates are automatically stored in the \Application Data\Microsoft\Templates subfolder of your Windows folder. If you are running Windows 95, 98, or NT 4.0 with profiles, your user templates are stored in the \Profiles\[username]\Application Data\Microsoft \Templates subfolder of your Windows folder, where [username] is the name of the folder associated with your profile.

- **Custom workgroup templates.** These are templates stored in a special workgroup template folder (commonly established as a read-only shared folder on a network server). When Word finds templates stored here, these templates are displayed in the General tab of the New dialog box.

  (You can change the location where Word looks for user templates and custom work-group templates through the File Locations tab of the Tools, Options dialog box. When you make a change here, it affects all your Office applications.)

- **"Advertised" and Installed templates.** These are templates that come with Microsoft Office 2000; they are listed in the New dialog box the first time you open Word, whether or not they have been copied to your hard drive. If they have not been copied to your hard drive, you will be prompted to install them the first time you use them. These are stored in the following folder: c:\ \Program Files\Microsoft Office\Templates\[language id number], where [language id number] is different depending on your default language. The U.S. version of Microsoft Office uses 1033 as its ID number. You can have several separate folders, each containing Word's tem-plates for a specific installed language.

- **"Non-file-based" templates.** These are special templates used internally by Word to create some new kinds of documents; they do not correspond to separate physical files, but rather features directly built into Word.

Tip #2

Occasionally, a damaged Normal.dot may cause Word to crash upon startup. You can quickly narrow startup problems to two possible causes: a damaged Normal.dot or a damaged Registry data key. To do so, load Word bypassing these items:

1. On the Windows taskbar, click Start, Run.

2. Enter the following command:

   ```
   "C:\Program Files\Microsoft Office\Office\WinWord.exe" /a
   ```

   (If your Winword.exe file is in a different location, enter that path within quotation marks instead.)

3. Click OK.

If Word loads properly, you know you either have a damaged Registry key or a damaged Normal.dot. Try the following:

1. Using Windows Explorer, rename Normal.dot.

2. Start Word; it creates a new Normal.dot.

If Word now starts reliably, you can copy custom styles, toolbars, macros, and AutoText entries from the renamed Normal.dot to the new Normal.dot using the Organizer, as already mentioned. If Word still does not start reliably, either use Help, Detect and Repair to reinstall damaged files and Registry entries, or run the Windows installer and choose Repair to restore your original Word or Office Registry settings.

CREATING A NEW TEMPLATE

Now that you've learned what templates are and how to use the ones Word provides, it's time to start creating your own. Word gives you two ways to do so: from scratch, or by saving an existing document file as a template. Answer the following questions to decide which approach makes more sense:

- Do you already have a document that can easily be transformed into a template? For example, if you're creating a template for business proposals, have you made a proposal lately with which you're especially pleased? Would it be easy to edit the contents that are specific to one client or project, leaving "holes" for you to fill in custom information later? If the answers to these questions are yes, then it makes sense to open that file, make your changes, and save it as a template.

- Are you creating a template for a document for which there is no usable model? Then you may want to create it from scratch.

CREATING A TEMPLATE BASED ON AN EXISTING DOCUMENT

To create a template based on an existing document, follow these steps:

1. Open the existing document.

2. Edit the document to eliminate the specific references that you won't want to appear in other similar documents.

Tip #3

Before you delete these references, consider whether they're worth saving as AutoText entries. If you're building your template from a proposal you made to Alpha Corporation, you don't want all your Alpha-related experience to show up in proposals you might make to their fiercest competitor, Omega Corporation.

But you do want to have that boilerplate conveniently available as an AutoText entry the next time you make a proposal to Alpha.

3. Add any styles, AutoText entries, macros, toolbars, or keyboard shortcuts you want (or copy existing ones from other templates, using the Organizer).

4. Choose File, Save As.

5. Choose Template in the Save as Type drop-down box. When you do, Word changes the current folder to the one where it saves templates, typically \Windows\Application Data\Microsoft\Templates (see Figure 1.2).

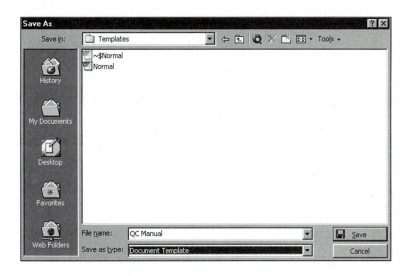

Figure 1.2
When you tell Word you want to save a template, it switches you to the folder where you currently save all templates.

6. Enter a name for the template in the File Name text box.

7. If you want to save your template in that folder, so it appears in the General tab of the New dialog box, click Save. If you want it to appear in a different tab in the New dialog box, double-click that folder and click Save.

You are not limited to using the folders Word automatically provides. For example, you might want to create a new folder that contains all the custom templates you provide for your company, and name that folder "Company Templates." Word makes this easy to do.

After you display the Save As dialog box and choose Document Template to save your template, click the Create New Folder button. The New Folder dialog box appears. Enter the name you want to use, and click OK. Word creates the new folder, and opens it. Make sure you've entered an appropriate filename for your template, and click <u>S</u>ave. Next time you open the New dialog box, your new folder will appear with its own tab, and if you click on that tab, you'll find an icon for the template you just saved.

Caution

Word's New dialog box only displays subfolders containing at least one template. If you create the folder but then do not save your template, the folder will not appear in the New dialog box.

Similarly, if you create the folder in Windows Explorer but fail to copy any files into it, the folder will not appear in the New dialog box within Word.

Tip #4

If you would like to use your revised template with one of Word's built-in wizards, the filename must include the word Fax, Letter, Memo, or Résumé, and you must save the template in the corresponding subfolder. For example, if you want to make a new memo accessible to the Memo Wizard, store it in the \Templates\Memos folder.

 If Word is saving document files as templates instead of DOC or HTML files, see "What to Do If Word Saves Files as Templates" in Troubleshooting at the end of this chapter.

CREATING A TEMPLATE FROM SCRATCH

You can also create a new template from scratch, much as you create a new document. To do so, choose <u>F</u>ile, <u>N</u>ew, and make sure Blank Document is selected in the General tab. Then, choose <u>T</u>emplate from the Create New section in the lower-right corner of the dialog box and click OK.

If you follow this procedure to create a template file, you can save the file as a template only, not as a Word document. Once you've done so, you can add content, styles, macros and other elements, and save the finished template as you would save any other template.

CREATING A TEMPLATE BASED ON AN EXISTING TEMPLATE

Sometimes you may not have a document that's an adequate model for a template, but Word just might. You can browse the tabs in the New dialog box to find out. Click on a template. In the Preview box, Word displays a thumbnail sketch of a sample document based on it.

If you find a template you'd like to use, click <u>T</u>emplate to indicate that you want to create a new template rather than a document. Then click OK. A new template opens, containing all the contents of Word's built-in template. Adjust it any way you like, and save it under a new name or in a different folder. If you change the document's formatting, consider changing its styles to match.

→ For more information about changing styles, **see** "Creating and Changing Styles," **p. 41**.

UNDERSTANDING THE RELATIONSHIP BETWEEN STYLES AND TEMPLATES

In Chapter 6, you learned how to create a set of consistent styles and store them in a template. The styles available to your current document depend on the templates open at the time. These templates are as follows:

- The Normal template.

- Whatever template you based the document on, if you based it on a template other than Normal.dot.

- Any other global templates that are currently loaded. Global templates are discussed in the following section. By default, no global templates other than Normal are loaded.

What if several templates are open, and each defines the same style differently? This happens often, even if you stay with Word's built-in styles. For example, Heading 1 is 14-point Arial Bold in the Normal template, but 10-point Arial Bold in the Contemporary Letter template. If you open a document based on the Contemporary Letter template, Word uses its styles, not those in any other template, global or otherwise.

If you change the styles in your document without storing those changes in a template, the document's revised styles override all the templates available to that document.

UNDERSTANDING GLOBAL TEMPLATES

Global templates are templates whose styles and other settings are available to all open documents. As already mentioned, Normal is a global template. However, you can add more global templates, either for your current session or permanently. You might load a global template in the following situations:

- When you want to make sure a set of macros, styles, or AutoText entries are available for use in all documents you plan to create during one session—but not necessarily for all sessions. For instance, if you are editing several sales proposals today, you may want to load a sales proposal template as a global template today, so you can have access to its special toolbars, shortcuts, AutoText entries, and macros. However, since you only edit sales proposals one day a week, you can avoid cluttering your editing environment with irrelevant tools and shortcuts, by not loading this global template on other days.

- When you want to make sure third-party macros are available to all your documents, without copying them into your Normal.dot template. (In fact, many third-party templates do not permit you to copy individual macros out of them.)

Global templates are also helpful when you want to distribute a set of customizations to others: You can build them into a template and instruct your colleagues how to load the template as a global template when they need these customizations.

LOADING A GLOBAL TEMPLATE FOR THE CURRENT SESSION

You can add a global template any time during the course of a session. Global templates are controlled in the Templates and Add-Ins dialog box (see Figure 1.3).

Figure 1.3
The Templates and Add-Ins dialog box enables you to add one or more global templates for use in all documents.

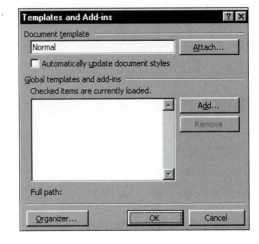

To add a global template, choose Tools, Templates, and Add-Ins, and click Add. Then, in the Add Template dialog box (see Figure 1.4), Word displays a list of the templates currently available in the Templates folder. Browse the list to select the template you want, and click OK.

Figure 1.4
The Add Template dialog box works much as the Open dialog box does; browse for the template you want, and click OK.

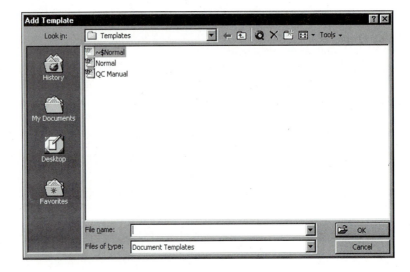

Tip #5	Templates can be stored anywhere on your hard disk, or on a networked hard drive. However, only templates stored in the Office 2000 Templates folder, one of its subfolders, or a networked folder designated as the Workgroup Templates folder, appear in the New dialog box. (Workgroup templates are covered later in this chapter.)

When you return to the Templates and Add-Ins dialog box, the additional template appears in the Global Templates and Add-Ins scroll box with a check mark next to it. It remains loaded until you uncheck the box or exit Word. The next time you restart Word, the template will be listed in the Global Templates and Add-Ins scroll box, but its check box won't be checked. In other words, it won't be loaded as a global template unless you return to Templates and Add-Ins and check the box.

 If you suddenly lose access to a template that was available before, see "What to Do If You Lose Access to a Template," in "Troubleshooting" at the end of this chapter.

LOADING A GLOBAL TEMPLATE PERMANENTLY

You often want to load the same global template automatically whenever you run Word. The easiest way is to copy the template into Word's Startup folder. In a typical installation of Microsoft Office 2000, this folder is \Windows\Application Data\Microsoft\Word. After you do so, the template loads automatically when you run Word, and stays loaded unless you uncheck its check box in Templates and Add-Ins.

Note	Why wouldn't you load a global template permanently? Conceivably, it might contain confidential information that you wouldn't want others to access routinely. More likely, you're simply trying to save memory and make sure Word starts as quickly as possible by not loading any more templates than necessary.

ATTACHING A NEW TEMPLATE TO AN EXISTING DOCUMENT

Every document has one template attached to it (except for documents created by wizards, which have a wizard attached to them, as you'll see later). Typically, the attached template is the one you used to create the document—whether you used the Normal template, another built-in Word template, or one of your own. However, in some instances, you may want to change the template associated with a document.

For instance, imagine your company, Acme Chocolate, has just been purchased by Intergalactic Candies. Intergalactic has different corporate design standards than Acme. However, it's quite likely that both companies use Word, and it's possible that both companies have Word templates codifying basic document formats such as headings and body text. If so, you may be able to redesign your documents to the Intergalactic standard simply by attaching the Intergalactic template to them.

Note

Of course, things aren't usually quite this simple. The style names you used at Acme may not be the same as those used by Intergalactic, or Intergalactic might not have a template containing all its styles. However, you can still create a new template that combines Intergalactic's formatting rules with the style names you've already been using, and achieve the same result.

To attach a different template to your document, choose Tools, Templates and Add-Ins, and click Attach. The Attach Template dialog box opens (see Figure 1.5). Browse to the template you want to attach, and click Open. If you want to update your existing document's styles to reflect those in the new template, check the Automatically Update Document Styles check box.

Figure 1.5
Select the template you want to attach, or browse to the folder containing it.

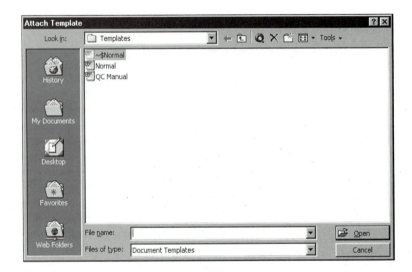

Tip #6

To automate the process of migrating from one document design to another, record a macro that changes the attached template to the new template and automatically updates the document's styles. Name the macro AutoOpen and store it in the Normal template. It will run every time you open a new document, changing the formatting of the document to reflect your corporate redesign.

Note

Sometimes you want to attach a new template but not update the styles. For example, you might be perfectly happy with your document's formatting, but you want access to a set of AutoText entries associated with a different template. In this case, attach the template, but do not check the Automatically Update Document Styles check box.

USING THEMES TO CHANGE THE STYLES IN YOUR TEMPLATE

In addition to templates, Word 2000 provides several dozen *themes*: sets of styles that you can copy into your current document, immediately giving it a different appearance. Themes are helpful for communicating the tone of your document. Although they're designed primarily for Web and intranet pages (or for Word documents viewed electronically), they can also be used for printed documents if you wish.

Word themes are purely concerned with the visual appearance of your document. In contrast to templates, themes do not include editing customizations, AutoText entries, macros, or other elements that may be included in templates. They do include

- Background colors and/or graphics (intended purely for online viewing; these backgrounds do not print)
- Formatting for *heading styles* and body text
- Formatting for *hyperlinks* and *table borders*
- *Custom bullets* and horizontal lines

Note

While you can switch among Word's themes, you can't change the contents of a theme. There is a workaround, however: You can create a document with a theme, change the styles in that document, and save the revised document as a template.

Note

If Theme is grayed out on the Format menu, you need to install the feature by running Maintenance Setup from the Office 2000 or Word 2000 CD-ROM. The Theme components are found in Office Tools, not in the Word section. You also need to choose which sets of themes to install: Typical Themes, Additional Themes, or both.

If you want to copy every Additional Theme to your computer, you need to choose Run from My Computer for each individual theme that is currently marked Install on First Run.

If you are in the process of running a wizard, such as the Web Page Wizard, you cannot install a new theme using the Windows installer.

Tip #7

If you've installed FrontPage 2000, which comes with Office 2000 Premium Edition, you can also use the themes provided by that program.

To apply a theme to your document, choose Format, Theme. The Theme dialog box opens (see Figure 1.6).

Figure 1.6
You can choose among several dozen predefined themes in the Theme dialog box.

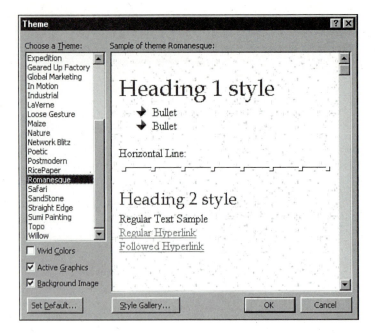

To select a theme, choose it from the Choose a Theme scroll box. You see a preview in the Sample scroll box, showing you how first- and second-level headings, text, hyperlinks, bullets, and horizontal lines will appear in your document if you choose this theme. You can also control three elements of your theme, through check boxes at the bottom-left corner of the dialog box:

- Vivid Colors tells Word to use brighter colors for text than it would normally.

- Active Graphics, which is turned on by default, tells Word to use animated bullets rather than regular graphical bullets. You won't see the difference until you load your page in a Web browser, however; Word does not display animated graphics.

- Background Image, also turned on by default, tells Word to include a background. If you do not want to include the background, you can clear this check box.

Figure 1.7 shows a document created with Word's Loose Gesture theme.

Caution

Note that some themes use fonts that may not be available to everyone who views your document as a Web page, especially those working on Macintosh computers and/or running Netscape Navigator rather than Internet Explorer.

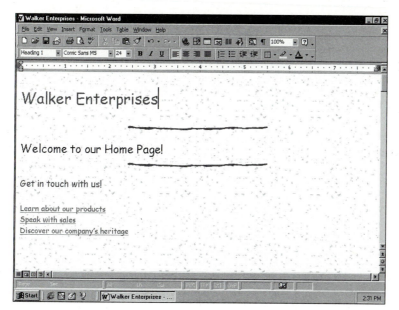

Figure 1.7
A Web page created with the Loose Gesture theme.

PREVIEWING NEW TEMPLATES WITH STYLE GALLERY

You may be interested in how your document would look if you used the styles from a different template. For example, in the Acme-to-Intergalactic example, you might want to know how easy it would be to simply apply Intergalactic's template to your current documents, and how much work you would still have to do manually.

To use Word's Style Gallery to preview what your document would look like (see Figure 1.8), choose Format, Theme, and click Style Gallery.

Next, select a template you would like to preview from the Template scroll box. Word then shows what your document would look like if it were using the styles in that template. If some styles only appear later in the document, you can use the scrollbar to move to any location you wish. If you would like to apply the styles in the new template you've chosen, click OK.

It's important to understand what Style Gallery doesn't do. The Style Gallery does not attach a different template to your document. Rather, it copies styles from that template into your document, where they override any formatting settings from the template that is attached.

By default, Style Gallery previews how your document would look if you changed its styles to resemble those in a different template. Sometimes, however, this doesn't give you enough information to decide whether you want to apply another template's formats. Possibly, you've just started editing your document, and haven't yet used the styles you're interested in previewing.

Figure 1.8
The Style Gallery enables you to preview how a document will appear with different style formatting.

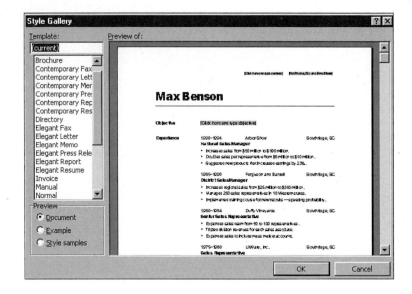

If you want to preview all the styles in a built-in Word template, you can ask Style Gallery to show you a sample document that uses all the styles in that template. With the Style Gallery dialog box displayed, choose Example. Figure 1.9 shows how Style Gallery displays an example of a Professional Letter.

Figure 1.9
Previewing an example document based on the Professional Letter template.

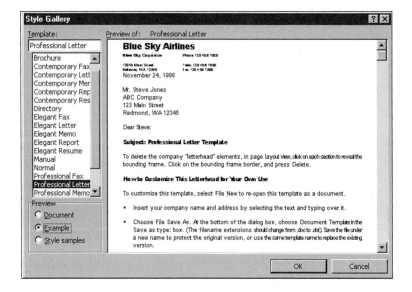

MOVING ELEMENTS AMONG TEMPLATES

In the "Keeping Track of Styles with the Organizer" section of Chapter 6, you learned that Word provides the *Organizer (page 249)* to help you move styles from one template (or document) to another. The Organizer doesn't just work with styles: it's Word's tool for moving a wide variety of elements between templates, including

- **AutoText entries** (boilerplate text and graphics; see Chapter 4)
- **Toolbars** (see Chapter 28)
- **Macro Project Items**

To use the Organizer, choose Tools, Templates and Add-Ins; then click Organizer. The Organizer appears, with the Styles tab displayed (see Figure 1.10).

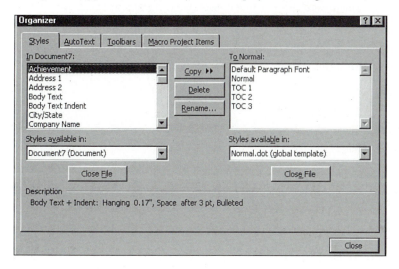

Figure 1.10
The Organizer can move styles, AutoText entrie, toolbars, and Macro Project Items between templates.

→ For more information on moving styles between templates, **see** "Keeping Track of Styles with the Organizer," **p. 51**.

If you have trouble copying elements between templates with the Organizer, see "What to Do If You Can't Copy Styles, AutoText Entries, Macros, or Toolbars," in "Troubleshooting" at the end of this chapter.

MANAGING TEMPLATES TO MINIMIZE YOUR WORK

You now understand the basics of using and creating templates. You're ready to plan a strategy for using templates to minimize your work and improve the efficiency of all your colleagues.

Note

Although our examples assume you're in a corporation or small business, you can follow the same steps to streamline document production even if you work solo.

PLANNING AND CREATING YOUR CUSTOM TEMPLATES

Start by giving some thought to the kinds of documents you create most—the ones where templates can give you the most "bang for the buck." As an example, assume you spend most of your time in Word creating

- Letters
- Memos
- Reports
- Fax cover sheets

Do you already have Word documents that are formatted essentially the way you want these documents to look in the future? If so, follow these steps to create templates from these documents:

1. Make sure you've used styles to define the different portions of each document.
2. Delete the elements that are specific to one document, such as the name of a memo's recipient.
3. Save the documents as templates. If you save the templates you expect to use most in the default Templates folder, they are instantly available when you display the New dialog box.

ORGANIZING YOUR CUSTOM TEMPLATES

The tabs of the New dialog box correspond to folders on your hard disk. Assuming you installed Office 2000 in the default location, the templates in the General tab are located in C:\Windows\Application Data\Microsoft, and each of the other tabs are subfolders beneath this folder.

This means you can reorganize your templates using Windows Explorer or Windows NT Explorer—even adding new subfolders if you need to. You see the results immediately in the New dialog box, as shown in Figure 1.11. Note that Word doesn't display empty template subfolders; you must store a template in the folder before that folder will appear in the dialog box.

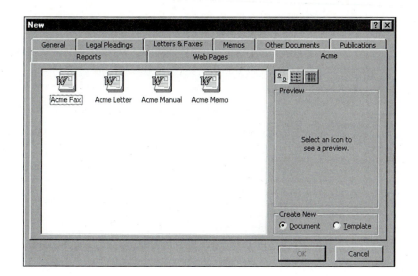

Figure 1.11
A customized New
dialog box displaying
templates specific to
the Acme Company.

It also means you should move or copy all the templates you use most into the General folder, for quicker access. If you manage the way members of your workgroup use Word, you can hide or delete the templates or folders you don't want used. For example, if you standardized on the Elegant family of templates for letters, faxes, and memos, copy those into the Templates folder, and consider moving the Letters & Faxes and Memos folder elsewhere on your hard drive so they don't appear in the New dialog box at all.

Think for a moment about how to name your most commonly used templates. Consider including your company's name (or an abbreviated version) in each of them, to make it obvious that these templates are customized to your company's needs.

If you don't have a model to work from, consider using Word's templates or wizards as the basis for your custom templates (possibly modifying them with new fonts, as discussed in Chapter 2). After you adapt them, save them as templates.

FURTHER AUTOMATING DOCUMENTS WITH TEMPLATES

Your templates are now model documents that contain all the text and formatting that is common to all the documents based on them. You've already saved yourself and your colleagues many hours. Your next step is to use the other capabilities of Word templates to build custom editing environments that make you (and your colleagues) even more efficient. To do this, you draw upon a variety of Word features:

- **AutoText entries** (Chapter 4)
- **Styles** (Chapter 2)
- **Custom toolbars and menu items**
- **Macros**

ADDING AUTOTEXT ENTRIES TO YOUR CUSTOM TEMPLATE

First, take a look at some documents you've already created, and identify blocks of copy that seem to reappear often. For example, many of your company's status reports might include a table that lists steps to be taken next. You can store a skeleton table as an AutoText entry. Then you can use the Organizer to copy this AutoText entry into your Report template.

Tip #8

> As you think about your documents, you might find elements that ought to be in them, but haven't been added. Now's a good time to create those elements. If you like, you can scour Word's built-in templates and wizards for ideas. An especially good source for business ideas is Word's Agenda Wizard.
>
> If you're using Office 2000, you'll also find that PowerPoint is replete with good ideas you can adapt. To find them, either run PowerPoint's AutoContent Wizard or review the templates in PowerPoint's File, New dialog box.
>
> After you create these elements, you should let people know about them. The easiest way is to include them on a custom toolbar so they're instantly obvious to anyone creating a document.

ADDING STYLES TO YOUR CUSTOM TEMPLATE

Next, consider which styles should be used in the documents this template is being created for. Create those styles, or copy them from documents that already contain them.

→ To learn more about moving styles between templates and documents, **see** "Keeping Track of Styles with the Organizer," **p. 51**.

ADDING CUSTOM TOOLBARS, MENU ITEMS, AND MACROS TO YOUR CUSTOM TEMPLATE

After you've created AutoText entries and styles, and copied them into the appropriate templates, you can move on to customizing Word's user interface. You can include custom menus and/or toolbars in a template. Then, whenever you or anyone else creates a document based on that template, these custom menus and toolbars are there to help.

You might create toolbar buttons that make it easier to insert the AutoText entries you've already provided. Or you might add Word features to your toolbars. For example, your Report toolbar could include a button that inserts an Executive Summary on the first page, using Word 2000's AutoSummarize feature.

→ To learn more about summarizing documents with Word's AutoSummarize feature, **see** "Working with AutoSummarize," **p. 106**.

The previous examples—adding AutoText entries and the AutoSummarize feature—require no *Visual Basic* experience. You can use Word's *Macro Recorder* to record inserting an AutoText entry in your document, and then use Word's Tools, Customize dialog box to add that macro to a toolbar. Adding AutoSummarize is even easier: The AutoSummarize command is already available through the Customize dialog box, so you don't have to record any macro at all.

If you're prepared to work in Visual Basic, you might, for example, include a button that automatically sends your fax cover sheet and an attachment to a specified list of fax numbers. Suddenly, a task that may have taken a half-hour can be performed in a minute or two. If you've never recorded macros or worked with Visual Basic, perhaps these examples will begin to give you a sense of their power.

Your letters, memos, faxes, and reports probably also have a good deal in common. For example, they may all draw upon the same address lists, and involve the same colleagues, suppliers, and customers. If so, you might create a menu with commands that apply to all your documents. Then, you can store this menu in a global template that always loads at startup, as mentioned earlier in this chapter.

→ To learn more about using global templates, **see** "Understanding Global Templates," **p. 11**.

Tip #9	As discussed later in this chapter, if your computers are networked, you can store your global template in a central Workgroup Templates folder that everyone can access. Then, when you make changes to this global template, you can store the new one in Workgroup Templates rather than copy it to everyone's computer.

After you're familiar with the Word features involved, you can create a preliminary version of all these templates in just a few hours, excluding Visual Basic programming. Try it out. If you're working as part of a team, share it with a few of your colleagues. Modify it as necessary. If you've chosen the right documents to automate, your time investment will pay for itself in just a few weeks—or possibly even a few days.

USING WORKGROUP TEMPLATES

One of the best ways to keep your entire workgroup or organization in sync is to use *workgroup templates*, which are stored centrally on a network server. All your users can share access to these templates at the same time. Better yet, you can centrally update and manage workgroup templates—eliminating the need to provide individual copies of your critical templates to every user.

Here are some of the ways you can use workgroup templates:

- Centrally store AutoText boilerplates you want everyone to use
- Provide a library of standardized documents built around the needs of your department or company
- Update everyone's user interface at the same time

You create a workgroup template the same way you create any other template. You then store it in a folder that each user's computer recognizes as the location for workgroup templates. It usually makes sense to mark workgroup templates as read-only, to prevent inadvertent or unauthorized customizations that affect everyone who uses them. To ensure that unauthorized individuals don't have access to them, consider storing them on a server with limited permissions.

Follow these steps to specify a workgroup template location on a specific computer:

1. Choose Tools, Options.

2. Choose the File Locations tab (see Figure 1.12).

3. In the File Types scroll box, click Workgroup Templates. (By default, no location is associated with workgroup templates.)

4. Click Modify. The Modify Location dialog box opens (see Figure 1.13).

5. Browse and select the folder you want to use.

6. Click OK twice.

Figure 1.12
You can establish or change the Workgroup Templates folder in the File Locations tab of the Options dialog box.

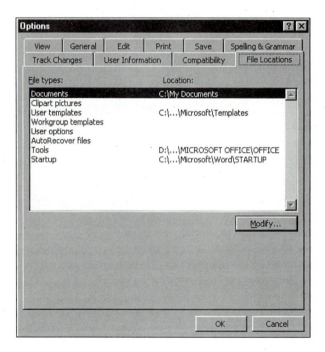

Tip #10

The procedure just described sets a workgroup template location for a single workstation. You can, however, specify a workgroup template location through the Office Profile Wizard so it applies to all users who are subject to the policies you create. Alternatively, you can give your users a file containing an *AutoOpen* macro that changes the workgroup template location; instruct the users to open the file to change the location.

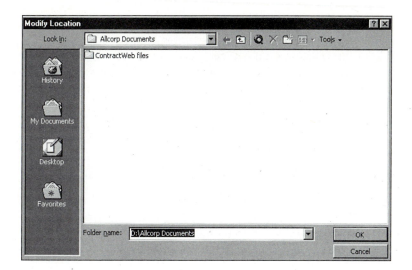

Figure 1.13
In the Modify Location dialog box, choose the folder you want to use.

After you establish a Workgroup Templates folder, any templates you save there automatically appear in the General tab of the New dialog box when users open a new file, just as if they were stored locally.

Caution

If the Workgroup Templates folder is temporarily inaccessible, the templates stored there will be absent when a user creates a new file. Users are dependent on your network to create documents based on those templates.

USING WORD WIZARDS

In addition to templates, Word provides a set of interactive *wizards* that enable you to walk through the construction of a document step by step, making choices about how it will be built. When you finish making the choices, Word creates the document for you. Then you only need to "fill in the holes" with your specific text and graphics. The document's structure and formatting are already in place, reflecting your choices.

WIZARDS INCLUDED WITH WORD 2000

Word 2000 includes more wizards than previous versions of Word. These include wizards for creating

- Agendas
- Calendars
- Envelopes
- Fax cover sheets
- Legal pleadings
- Letters
- Mailing labels
- Memos
- Newsletters
- Résumés
- Web pages

→ To learn more about creating Web pages with Word's built-in wizards, **see** "Creating a Web Site with Word's Web Page Wizard," **p. 1234**.

Note

Depending on how you originally installed Word, the first time you double-click on a Wizard to run it, you may be prompted to install it first—either from your CD-ROM or the original network location you installed Word from.

WALKING THROUGH A TYPICAL WIZARD

The best way to get the flavor for how wizards work is to walk through using one. To run Word's Résumé Wizard, choose File, New, click the Other Documents tab, and double-click Résumé Wizard.

The opening window of the Résumé Wizard appears. Along the left side, a subway-style map shows the entire process. A green square indicates where you are right now; you can click any other square to "hop" there. Four buttons along the bottom of the window also help you navigate through the wizard. Finally, if you click the Help button, the Office Assistant offers help about this wizard.

Tip #11

You don't always have to walk through every step of a wizard. After you've included all the information you want to include, click Finish. Word generates the document based on whatever information you've given it.

Click Next to get started. The wizard asks you to choose from Word's three built-in styles for résumés: Professional, Contemporary, or Elegant. These are the same three style options available in most of Word's templates and wizards, making it easy to build a consistent set of documents. Make a choice, and click Next.

The wizard next asks what type of résumé you want to create. You can choose an Entry-Level Résumé designed for individuals with little job experience; a Chronological Résumé that lists your work experience by date; a Functional Résumé that lists types of achievement; or a Professional Résumé, which is commonly used in several professions. Make your choice and click Next.

In the Address window, you're asked for the personal information that Word doesn't already know. If you entered your name when you installed Word, that name already appears in the Name text box. After you enter the personal information once, it appears automatically on this screen whenever you run the Résumé Wizard. When you're finished entering personal information, click Next.

In the Standard Headings window, Word displays a list of headings that are commonly included in Résumés. The ones already checked are most commonly included in the type of résumé you want to create. You can check or clear any of these check boxes. Click Next.

You may have experiences or qualifications that don't fit into typical categories used by résumés. For example, if you're new in the work force, you might want to mention Extracurricular Activities or Community Activities. If you are a professional engineer, you might have Patents and Publications to your credit. You can specify these in the Optional Headings window. When you're finished, click Next.

Now, in the Add/Sort Heading window Word gives you a chance to organize the headings you've chosen or add new ones that weren't included in previous windows. If you want to add a new heading, enter it in the Are There Any Additional Headings...text box, and click Add.

After you add any new headings, you can make sure your headings are organized the way you want. Select a heading in the These Are Your Résumé Headings text box, and click Move Up or Move Down to move it toward the top or bottom of your résumé. If you decide upon reflection that you don't want a heading—perhaps you don't have enough to include in it, or it's inappropriate for the specific job you're seeking—select it, and click Remove. When you're finished, click Next.

You're now in the final window of the Résumé Wizard. Here's your chance to review your work. You can click any box at the left edge of the window to view its current settings, or click Back repeatedly to move back through the wizard one screen at a time.

After you're satisfied, click Finish, and Word creates your document. You can see the results in Figure 1.14.

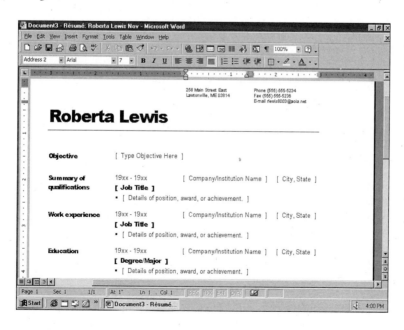

Figure 1.14
A sample résumé created by the Résumé Wizard.

All the text in the résumé that appears within brackets is text you need to replace. Simply click inside any set of brackets; Word selects the entire block of text contained there. Start typing, and Word enters your replacement information. When you've added all the information you want to include about yourself, save the file as you normally would.

Note

These clickable areas are actually MacroButton fields. You can use them whenever you're creating a document where you want others to add information in specific locations. You'll learn more about MacroButton fields in Chapter 18, "Automating Your Documents with Field Codes."

Caution

If you forget to replace one of these bracketed fields, the boilerplate text will print—making your omission painfully obvious to anyone who reads your résumé.

Because the Résumé Wizard stores the settings you enter in it, it's suddenly much easier to create a customized version of your résumé whenever you apply for a new job. You no longer have to create "one-size-fits-all" résumés for mass résumé mailings; you can target your résumés to the needs of specific employers.

Tip #12

If you especially like a document that results from working with a wizard, consider saving it as a template. That way, you always have access to a document that's well along the way to completion, without even having to run the wizard.

Tip #13

The next time you're searching for a job, consider using another Word feature along with the Résumé Wizard. AutoText entries are perfect for saving boilerplate content you can reuse in future personalized résumés and cover letters. For example, if you have language specifically written to highlight your qualifications as an administrative assistant, store that language as an AutoText entry, and reuse it the next time you apply for that position.

You can use the same approach with other Word wizards as well. For example, to create a boilerplate letter that can easily be combined with standard paragraphs of contract information, create a custom letter template with *AutoText entries*, and save it in the same sub-folder as the other Letter templates.

You can then use that letter template with the Letter Wizard, building the skeleton of a new letter document. Once you've created the new document, you can use the AutoText entries built into it to add the contract language quickly.

→ For more information on saving blocks of text for easy reuse, **see** "AutoText: The Complete Boilerplate Resource," **p. 87**.

UNDERSTANDING WORD ADD-INS

Templates and wizards are powerful, but if you want to customize your Word environment even more, you should know about add-ins. These are separate dynamic link libraries (.DLLs) that extend Word's capabilities, adding new features and custom commands. They're compiled, so they typically run faster than macros can. Like DLLs, they have access to the full capabilities of the Windows operating system. After they're built, they are renamed as .WLLs to indicate that they are Word linked libraries.

Other add-ins offer specialized capabilities to Word. For example, the EndNote Plus add-in from Niles & Associates (`www.niles.com`) enhances Word with extensive bibliographic reference capabilities. EndNote Plus has been purchased by more than 100,000 academic writers and researchers.

When you have an add-in, either follow the instructions that come with it, or install it the same way you install a global template. Choose Tools, Templates and Add-Ins; click Add. Then, in the Add Templates dialog box, select the add-in you want to load, and click OK.

Like global templates, add-ins normally don't load at startup unless you copy them to Word's startup folder or run a macro that loads them.

TROUBLESHOOTING

WHAT TO DO IF WORD SAVES FILES AS TEMPLATES

If Word only allows you to save files as templates, not as .DOC documents, your computer may be infected by a Word macro virus. Run recent antivirus software to eliminate the infection.

WHAT TO DO IF YOU LOSE ACCESS TO A TEMPLATE

If you suddenly lose access to a template that was always available before, check to see whether the corresponding template file (.DOT) has been moved. Also check to see whether you have lost access to the server where it is stored. If you have exited and restarted Word, also check to see whether the template is a global template that must be reloaded.

WHAT TO DO IF YOU CAN'T COPY STYLES, AUTOTEXT ENTRIES, MACROS, OR TOOLBARS

If the Organizer won't let you copy elements between templates or documents, there are a few possible causes. First, the destination template may be set as read-only. Second, it may be password protected. Third, it may be protected for tracked changes, comments, or forms, which means you can only change the file using those features unless you know the correct password. To determine the cause, open the template file for editing. (Don't open a new file based on the template—open the template itself.)

CHAPTER 2

STREAMLINING YOUR FORMATTING WITH STYLES

In this chapter

WHY STYLES ARE SO VALUABLE

Styles are one of Word's most powerful timesavers, for five important reasons.

First, styles can dramatically reduce the time it takes to format a document—often by 90% or more. Second, styles can also help you make sure all your documents look consistent, with very little effort on your part. Third, if you export your Word document to a *desktop publishing program*, most programs can use Word styles to help automate their work. Fourth, if you need to change the way your styled document looks, you need to change only a few styles, not hundreds of manual formats.

Finally, it's much easier to take advantage of Word's powerful automation and organization features if you use styles. For example, Word can automatically build and update a table of contents based on the styles in your document. Without styles, you would have to manually apply a field to every single item you want to include in your table of contents. In addition to tables of contents, Word styles make it easier to use all these features:

- **Web Publishing.** See Chapter 39, "Using Word to Develop Web Content," to learn how Word uses styles in pages saved in HTML as Web pages.
- **Outlining.** See Chapter 7, "Outlining: The Best Way to Organize a Document," to learn how styles enable you to easily outline and reorganize your document.
- **AutoFormat.** See Chapter 4, "Automating Your Documents: AutoCorrect, AutoFormat, AutoText, and AutoSummarize," to learn how styles enable you to format your document automatically, all at once.
- *AutoSummarize.* See Chapter 4 to learn how styles can help Word build an automatic summary of any document.
- *Outline Numbering.* See Chapter 7 to learn how styles enable you to apply automatic outline numbers to your documents and have Word track them automatically.
- *Tables of Figures.* See Chapter 9, "Tables of Contents, Figures, Authorities, and Captioning," to learn how styles enable you to build and update figure tables automatically.
- **Master Documents.** See Chapter 8, "Master Documents: Control and Share Even the Largest Documents," to learn how styles enable you to automatically divide a large document into several subdocuments for easy, team-based editing.

For all these reasons, styles are a great foundation for automating your document. Best of all, Word now makes styles very easy to use. (In fact, as you'll see later, Word's *automatic style definition* feature might enable you to get the styles you need with almost no effort on your part.)

Surprisingly, many Word users never bother with styles; they are comfortable with Word's easy manual formatting capabilities. Others use a few styles now and then, but don't take full advantage of them. If you fall into either category, this chapter can help you dramatically improve your productivity.

Tip #15

If you can't or won't format your document with styles, Word 2000 gives you an alternate way to get *some* of their automation advantages. As covered in Chapter 7, you can specify *outline levels* for individual blocks of text, and Word can use those outline levels rather than styles.

However, it's usually more work to create outline levels than styles; outline levels don't work with as many Word features as styles do; and you probably want the styles anyway for formatting reasons.

Note

Word 2000 also provides a new feature, Themes, which can help you establish a consistent format for your document quickly. Especially well-suited for Web pages, Themes contain formatting that visually communicates a wide variety of moods and messages, from the very informal "Loose Gesture" to the buttoned-down "Corporate."

When you choose a theme, Word changes the styles in your document to reflect the formatting in the theme, and (if you wish) also adds backgrounds, horizontal lines, and special graphical bullets. Themed documents are by definition HTML documents. If you select a theme for a Word document, Word converts your file to HTML. Before doing so, make sure anyone else who needs to work with your document can use it in HTML format.

Themes are covered in detail in the "Using Themes to Change the Styles in Your Template" section of Chapter 1, "Templates, Wizards, and Add-Ins."

WHAT STYLES ARE AND HOW THEY WORK

In Word, a style is a series of formats that can be applied all at once to one or more paragraphs, or one or more characters. Rather than apply formats one at a time by clicking toolbar buttons or using keyboard shortcuts or dialog boxes, you choose a style, and Word automatically applies all the formatting for you. If you want or need to change the appearance of your entire document, all you have to do is change the styles.

HOW STYLES AND TEMPLATES WORK TOGETHER

Styles are intimately linked to another Word feature, *templates*. As you learned in Chapter 1, templates are patterns for your documents, which can include many features, including styles, boilerplate text, manually formatted text, graphics, and custom automation tools such as macros and special toolbars.

When you store your styles in a template, the styles are immediately available whenever you create a document based on that template. By default, your styles are stored in the Normal template—which makes them available to every document you create. As you saw in Chapter 1, you can use templates to manage, organize, and distribute collections of styles—and this makes it easy to refine and standardize the look of all your documents.

→ For more information about working with templates, **see** Chapter 1, "Templates, Wizards, and Add-Ins," **p. 3**.

Word offers two kinds of styles: paragraph styles and character styles; both can be stored in your templates. Each type of style is covered next.

UNDERSTANDING PARAGRAPH STYLES

Paragraph styles control the formatting of entire paragraphs. Any manual formatting you can add to a font or paragraph can be included in a paragraph style. If you can find it in one of the following dialog boxes, you can add it to a paragraph style by choosing

- Format, Font (Font, Character Spacing, and Animation tabs)
- Format, Paragraph (Indents and Spacing, Line and Page Breaks tabs)
- Format, Tabs (tab stops, alignment, and leaders)
- Format, Borders and Shading (Borders and Shading tabs, but not Page Borders)
- Tools, Language, Set Language (the language in which text should be proofed)
- Format, Bullets and Numbering (Bulleted, Numbered, and Outline Numbered tabs)

UNDERSTANDING CHARACTER STYLES

Unlike paragraph styles, *character styles* can be built only from the text formatting options available in the Format, Font dialog box, from borders and shading, and from language formatting.

Chances are, you'll use paragraph styles much more often than character styles. Paragraph styles are easier to create, and they can do more. For certain purposes, however, character styles are indispensable.

For example, you might have a short block of text that must always be formatted in a specific way, such as a company name. With character styles, it's easier to make sure that this text is always formatted correctly to begin with, and remains formatted correctly as a document evolves.

Don't Overuse Multiple Styles

Avoid using too many typefaces, sizes, and font styles in the same document: This distracts from your message. Use the formatting in your styles to make headings and section titles easy to distinguish—in essence, making your document's outline and structure visible even to readers who see the document in print.

HOW PARAGRAPH AND CHARACTER STYLES INTERACT

Character styles are superimposed on paragraph styles. When character and paragraph styles conflict, the font specified in a character style takes precedence. However, if a character style does not specify a formatting attribute and the paragraph style does, the paragraph style is applied.

For example, imagine you have a paragraph style named Summary that specifies

12-point Times New Roman italic

Now, imagine you superimpose a character style named Smith, which specifies

14-point Impact

You get 14-point Impact just as your character style requests, but you'll also get italic because your character style hasn't expressed a preference and your paragraph style has. On the other hand, if your paragraph and character styles both specify italic, Word assumes you want to preserve some contrast between the two styles, and formats the text as not italic. Therefore, you can't count on a character style being absolute.

As is covered in the next section, "How Manual Formatting and Styles Interact," manual formatting of text overrides both paragraph and character styles.

HOW MANUAL FORMATTING AND STYLES INTERACT

Manual formatting is superimposed on both paragraph and character styles. As in the preceding example, however, Word seeks to maintain contrast. So, if you add italic formatting to a paragraph styled to use italic, Word displays non-italic text.

Tip #16

To see which formatting elements in a block of text have been created by styles and which have been created by manual formatting, press Shift+F1, and click the What's This mouse pointer on the text that interests you (see Figure 2.1).

To clear all manual formatting and character styles, leaving only paragraph styles, select text and press Ctrl+Spacebar.

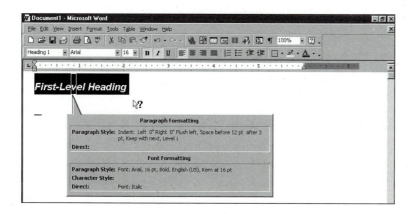

Figure 2.1
Displaying all the paragraph and font formatting associated with a block of text.

DISPLAYING STYLES WITH YOUR TEXT

Sometimes you might like to view the styles in your document as you work. For example, you may have a set of corporate styles you need to follow. Or, you might have styles that look similar to each other; viewing the style names helps you tell them apart.

Word's Style Area (see Figure 2.2) enables you to view style names alongside the text in your document. Style Area works only in *Normal view* and *Outline view*. To display a Style

Area, choose <u>T</u>ools, <u>O</u>ptions, View. Then, specify a *Style Area Width* greater than 0 inches. (The default setting, 0", means that Word displays no Style Area. That's why you may never have seen one.)

Tip #17

Try a measurement of 0.8 inches, sufficient to display most style names without reducing the editing area too much.

After you have a Style Area, you can resize it with the mouse. To do this, place the mouse pointer over the border of the Style Area. When the pointer changes to appear as vertical bars, click and drag the border to the width you want.

Figure 2.2
Word's Style Area, along the left side of this figure, enables you to view your styles and document at the same time.

Style Area

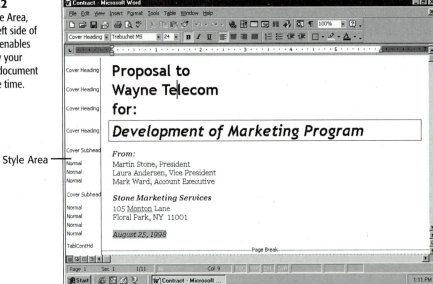

UNDERSTANDING WORD'S DEFAULT STYLES

You're using styles whether you know it or not.

Word actually contains more than 90 built-in styles. When you display a new document and begin entering text, Word enters the text using the Normal style, Word's standard style for body copy. (By default, Normal style is 12-point Times New Roman, left-aligned, single-spaced, with an outline level equivalent to body text.) Similarly, whenever you use automated features such as *AutoFormat*, Tables of Contents, or Indexes, Word applies built-in styles in many places to ensure overall consistency.

All these built-in styles are designed to work together, creating documents that are consistently formatted—if a bit on the ordinary side. They're all stored together in Word's *Normal template*, which means they are available to every document you create. And, as you'll see later, changing these built-in styles is the fastest way to change the overall look of all the documents you create.

In the next few sections, you'll learn how to make the most of these built-in styles—and you'll also learn techniques you can use with the styles you create.

APPLYING AN EXISTING STYLE

Because Word contains so many built-in styles, the fastest way to add styles to your document is to use the ones that already exist. To apply an existing style, select the text you want to style. Then click the arrow in the *Style box* on the Formatting toolbar, or press Ctrl+Shift+S (see Figure 2.3), and choose the style you want from the list that appears.

Figure 2.3
Choosing a style from the Style box on the Formatting toolbar.

In Word 2000, the Style box doesn't just list the available styles; it shows them formatted, so you can see what they look like before you apply them.

Note

While all of Word's built-in styles are available to all your documents, this may not be true of custom styles you create.

If you have stored custom styles in more than one template, the custom styles available for your use may vary depending on which templates are currently accessible to your documents. To learn more about controlling which templates are available to your documents, see "Attaching a New Template to an Existing Document," in Chapter 1.

SHORTCUTS FOR THE MOST COMMON STYLES

Five of Word's most widely used styles also have quick keyboard shortcuts:

Style	Keyboard Shortcut	Common Use
Normal	Ctrl+Shift+N	Body text
Heading 1	Alt+Ctrl+1	First-level headings
Heading 2	Alt+Ctrl+2	Second-level headings
Heading 3	Alt+Ctrl+3	Third-level headings
List Bullet	Ctrl+Shift+L	Bulleted lists

Sometimes you want to apply a different paragraph style to a block of text. You can always do so by selecting any part of the paragraph and choosing a new style from the Style box.

 Because many styles are heading styles, you often find yourself changing styles to change heading levels. One very effective way to make these changes is to switch into Outline view and use the Promote and Demote buttons on the Outlining toolbar (covered in detail in Chapter 15). If, however, you're just changing one or two headings, simply click the Style box, and use the up- or down-arrow keys to move to the style you want.

Tip #18

> Two additional keys allow you to change heading styles: Alt+Shift+Right arrow *demotes* the paragraph you've selected. For example, if you select a paragraph formatted as Heading 1, pressing Alt+Shift+Right arrow converts the paragraph to Heading 2 style.
>
> Conversely, Alt+Shift+Left arrow promotes the paragraph; for example, from Heading 3 to Heading 2.

Tip #19

> If you're sure of the style name you want to use, you can simply type it in the Style box. However, if you mistype, Word creates a new style formatted as your text already appears.

To minimize clutter, Word typically displays only seven built-in styles in the Style box of a new document: Normal, Heading 1, Heading 2, Heading 3, and three Table of Contents (TOC) styles. All the other styles built into Word are still available, however. If you want to apply a style that doesn't appear in the Style box, apply it from the Style dialog box (see Figure 2.4) as follows:

1. Select the paragraph(s) you want to modify.
2. Choose Format, Style.
3. Select All styles from the List box.
4. Select the style you want from the Styles box.
5. Click Apply. The style is applied to the current paragraph(s) you selected.

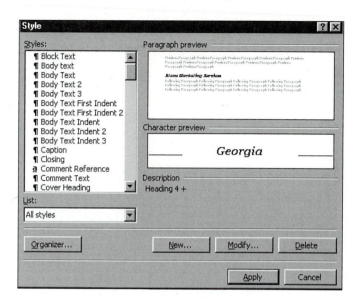

Figure 2.4
You can get more
control over styles
through the Style
dialog box.

APPLYING MULTIPLE STYLES AT THE SAME TIME

Maybe you'd rather not have your train of thought interrupted by stopping to apply styles as you write. If so, you can write your document the way you normally do and then have Word's *AutoFormat* feature apply the styles for you, using the built-in styles it recognizes.

Note

Or you can use AutoFormat As You Type to make similar changes as you type.

You learn more about AutoFormat and *AutoFormat As You Type* in Chapter 4, but briefly, Word can recognize the following elements and assign styles to them:

- **Headings.** If you enter one line of text without a period, ending with a paragraph mark, Word recognizes it as a heading and applies a heading style. If your headings are not already manually numbered or styled, Word typically uses Heading 1.

  If you have already formatted some headings, Word applies the next subordinate heading style beneath your headings. That's useful to know if, for example, only the name of your chapter uses Heading 1 style. Format that one line of copy manually, and Word automatically formats all the other headings it finds as Heading 2. This leaves you with fewer to correct manually.

- **Bulleted and numbered lists.** AutoFormat can recognize some lines of text as belonging to a bulleted or numbered list, and reformat those with built-in list styles. For example, if either AutoFormat or AutoFormat As You Type encounters paragraphs that begin with an asterisk and a space, it will reformat them as items in a bulleted list.

- **Body text.** AutoFormat takes the remaining paragraphs that it hasn't reformatted in any other way and formats them using Word's built-in Body Text style. Body Text style is identical to Normal style except that 6 points have been added after each paragraph to compensate for the extra paragraph mark AutoFormat automatically removes.

- **Letter elements.** Depending on where they appear in a letter, Word can recognize salutations, addresses, and other elements, and apply corresponding built-in styles.

To use AutoFormat to apply several styles at once, choose Format, AutoFormat, and click the Options button. Then, on the AutoFormat tab (see Figure 2.5), specify the types of styles you want Word to apply—Headings, Lists, Automatic Bulleted Lists, and/or Other Paragraphs (including Body Text, Inside Address, Salutation, and some other styles). These options are all in the Apply area of this tab; if you don't want Word to change any other document elements aside from these, clear the other check boxes. Click OK twice, and Word AutoFormats the document.

Figure. 6.5
If you want Word to apply styles automatically but make no other changes to your document, check the boxes in the Apply area of the Auto-Format tab, and clear the boxes in the Replace area, as shown.

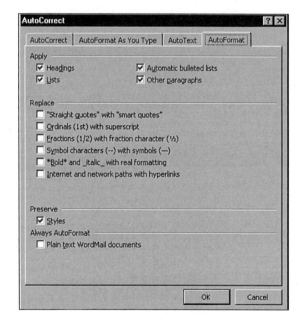

Word isn't perfect. Double-check the styles Word applies: You may have to do some tweaking. However, if your document's structure isn't too unusual, using AutoFormat can often save you a good deal of time.

CREATING AND CHANGING STYLES

Until now, you've learned how to use the existing styles Word provides. If you do nothing more than use Word's styles, your documents will look consistent; you will spend less time formatting them, and you'll have access to all the power of Word's automation features.

However, considering that Word is—by far—the world's most popular word processor, your documents will have a tendency to look a lot like everyone else's. Moreover, you might encounter situations where Word has no applicable built-in style. For example, Word doesn't have a built-in style for chapter summaries, or for tips, or for many other elements you find in this book.

For these reasons, you should know how to create new styles or change existing ones. Fortunately, Word makes this easy to do.

CREATING PARAGRAPH STYLES EASILY WITH STYLE BY EXAMPLE

The quickest way to create an entirely new style is to use Word's Style by Example feature, as follows:

1. Select and format a block of text the way you want it.
2. Click inside the Style drop-down box on the Formatting toolbar (or press Ctrl+Shift+S).
3. Type the new style name in the Style box and press Enter.

Note

When you create a style using Style by Example, the style is automatically stored in the template that is currently attached to your document. If you created the document based on the Blank Document template (Word's default setting), this means your custom styles will be stored in the Normal template. If you created the document using a different template, or if you have chosen a different template since you created the document, your new styles will be stored in that template.

To learn more about how styles and templates interact, see "Understanding the Relationship Between Styles and Templates," in Chapter 1.

DEFINING CHARACTER STYLES

Character styles can't be defined on the Formatting toolbar (although they can be selected from there after they've been defined). To define a character style, you have to venture into the Style dialog box:

1. Select and format a block of text the way you want it.
2. Select Format, Style.

3. Click New.

4. Enter a style name in the Name box.

5. Choose Character from the Style Type drop-down list. Figure 2.6 shows what the New Style dialog box may look like now.

6. Click OK.

7. Click Apply.

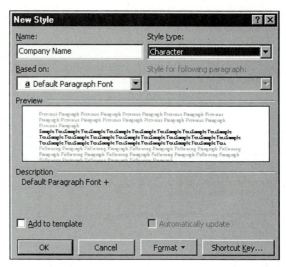

Figure 2.6

USING AUTOMATIC STYLE CHANGES

The same AutoFormat technology that enables you to create all your styles at the same time can also help you change existing styles automatically. For example, because Word can recognize a line of type as a heading, it can also recognize when you are formatting a line of type manually to look like a heading. It also can automatically transform your manual formatting into a heading style.

Automatic style definition is part of Word's AutoFormat As You Type feature. To use it, follow these steps:

1. Choose Format, AutoFormat.

2. Click Options.

3. Click the AutoFormat As You Type tab.

4. In the Apply As You Type area, specify the elements for which you want Word to automatically create styles: Headings, Borders, Tables, *Automatic Bulleted Lists*, and/or *Automatic Numbered Lists*.

5. Check the Define Styles Based on Your Formatting check box at the bottom of the dialog box.

6. Click OK.

7. Click Close.

After you turn on automatic style definition, pay close attention to it for a few days to make sure that it isn't creating styles you don't want. If the formatting in your documents starts changing in ways you don't like, turn the feature off.

→ For more information about enabling or disabling automatic style updates for specific styles, **see** "Enabling or Preventing Automatic Style Updates," **p. 47**.

CONTROLLING STYLES VIA THE FORMAT STYLE DIALOG BOX

Until now, this chapter has focused primarily on the quickest, easiest ways to create and use styles. However, Word provides some advanced style capabilities that aren't accessible from the Formatting toolbar or a keyboard shortcut. These capabilities can significantly improve your productivity if you spend a few minutes getting to know them.

Word's central control panel for creating and managing styles is the Style dialog box (refer to Figure 2.4). From here, you can

- **Apply an existing style to selected text.** You're most likely to use the Style dialog box to apply built-in styles that don't show up in the Style box on the Formatting toolbar. To apply an existing style, select it from the Styles list and click Apply.

- **Review your existing styles and delete any that no longer apply or are redundant.** To delete a style, select it from the Styles list and click Delete. However, you can't delete any built-in styles in Word's Normal template.

- **Create a new style.** As you've learned, you must use the Style dialog box to create character styles. However, you must also use the Style dialog box to create paragraph styles when you want to do any of the following:
  - Use advanced features such as Based On styles or Following Paragraph styles
  - Automatically update your document to reflect style changes
  - Add a style to a template, not just to your current document
  - Create shortcut keys for a style
  - Systematically establish the formatting and attributes for a style
  - Modify an existing style's attributes (or formatting)
  - Move styles among documents and templates, via the Organizer

Throughout the remainder of this chapter, you'll learn more about creating, modifying, and organizing styles, but first, here's a word about displaying them in the Style dialog box.

CHOOSING THE MOST CONVENIENT WAY TO LIST YOUR STYLES

In the Style dialog box, Word can list styles in the following three ways:

- **Styles in use.** Word lists only the styles you have already assigned to text in your document. You might use this list to make sure all the styles you've used are consistent with your corporate standards.

- **All styles.** Word lists every style in every currently open template, including the 90+ styles in the Normal template, plus any other styles you've added to it and any styles in any other template to which your document has access.

- **User-defined styles.** Word lists only the available styles you have created. You might use this list to manage a system of styles you've developed. Style systems are discussed in detail in the project at the end of this chapter.

CREATING A NEW STYLE USING THE NEW STYLE DIALOG BOX

As you've learned, you sometimes want to create a new style using the Style and New Style dialog boxes rather than Style by Example. Earlier in the chapter, you saw how to create a character style this way. Now you can take a closer look at several other options available to you.

First, choose Format, Style and click New to display the New Style dialog box. At the top, you see the style Name and Style Type boxes you encountered earlier. Enter the style name you want and choose either Paragraph or Character as your style type.

WORKING WITH BASED ON STYLES

Next, if you want, you can specify the existing style that your new style is to be based on. By default, most built-in Word styles are based on the Normal style, and unless you make a change, your new style is based on it also. Of course, Word uses the formats you specify, but where you do not specify a setting, Word makes assumptions based on the Normal style, which includes the following:

- Font: Times New Roman
- Size: 12-point
- Proofing Language: English (United States), unless you change the Regional Settings in the Windows Control Panel
- Character scale: 100%
- Alignment: Flush left
- Line spacing: Single
- Pagination: Widow/Orphan Control
- Outline level: Body Text

At times, you might have a different style you would like to use as the basis for your new style—one with formatting that closely resembles the style you are creating.

For example, you might want to base all your headings on your Heading 1 style. That way, if you change the font in Heading 1, all the other headings change automatically.

With the New Style dialog box open, click the Based On box, and choose the style you want to use as the basis for your new style. If you are working with a Paragraph style, you can choose from all the styles available to your current document.

If you are working with a Character style, your choices are more limited. They include several styles associated with Web pages, including Emphasis and Strong. These are styles that Web browsers such as Microsoft Internet Explorer and Netscape Navigator have long used to control the display of text on Web and *intranet* sites.

Tip #20

If the Based On style you want to use appears in the Formatting toolbar, here's a quicker way to get the same result:

1. Format a block of text using the Based On style.
2. Reformat the text to reflect any changes you want to make.
3. Click in the Style box.
4. Type the new style name and press Enter.

USING BASED ON STYLES TO TRANSFORM THE LOOK OF YOUR DOCUMENTS

Based On styles enable you to create a unique look for all your documents with little effort. All you have to do is change the Normal style, which underlies all Word's styles.

For example, if you're bored with Times New Roman, you can change the Normal style to a somewhat more interesting font, such as Garamond. That change cascades through all the styles that are based on the Normal style—except for those that already specify a different font, such as Arial.

Once you make a change such as this, you probably need to make a few other changes as well. Some of Word's styles, although they are based on Normal, also specify their own fonts. For example, Heading 1 uses the Arial font. Consider changing these styles to specify a font that complements the one you've now chosen for text.

Tip #21

If you choose a serif font for text, generally choose a sans serif font for some or all of your headings. Serif fonts have tiny tails at the ends of each letter to improve readability; sans serif fonts don't.

Serif and sans serif fonts complement each other well and often are used in combination to make book and newspaper designs more attractive. .

You should note one more thing about choosing fonts for your styles. Different fonts have different widths. Times New Roman is unusually narrow, which simply means that more words fit on a line when you're using it. If you choose a wider font, such as Bookman, you may find you've lengthened a long document by several pages.

CHOOSING A FOLLOWING PARAGRAPH STYLE

Think about your documents for a moment. In most cases, after you type a heading, you usually type body text. After you type the first element in a list, you usually type another list element. Word paragraph styles take advantage of this. When you specify a paragraph style, you can also specify the style that should be used in the paragraph that follows it .

By default, the Following Paragraph style is Normal. These steps show you how to specify a different one:

1. Open the New Style dialog box (refer to Figure 2.6).

2. Click in the Style for Following Paragraph drop-down box.

3. Choose the style you want to use.

4. When you're finished with the settings in the New Style dialog box, click OK.

After you've set a Following Paragraph style, Word applies it automatically as you work. When you press Enter at the end of one paragraph, Word applies the Following Paragraph style to the next paragraph.

CREATING STYLE FORMATS FROM THE NEW STYLE DIALOG BOX

You already know that you can quickly establish a style's formats using Style by Example. You might, however, want convenient, centralized access to every formatting option associated with a new style, so you can systematically create all your formatting at the same time. Word gives you that access.

With the New Style dialog box open, click the Format button. A list of formatting categories appears (see Figure 2.7). Choose the category you want, and a dialog box appears containing your choices. In most cases, this dialog box is identical to the one you would use elsewhere to create manual formatting. For example, clicking Font displays the Font tabbed dialog box with three tabs: Font, Character Spacing, and *Animation*.

You can now systematically walk through each dialog box, establishing the settings you want your style to have. This is a great way to make sure you don't forget an important setting that might be easy to overlook if you used Style by Example.

TEMPLATE OR DOCUMENT? WHERE TO STORE YOUR STYLES

By default, Word adds your new style to your current document only. If you change a built-in style, that change also applies in only your existing document. However, you sometimes want to make the style available for many documents. You can do this by adding the style to the template associated with the document in which you are working.

It's easy to add a style to a template. With the Style dialog box open, click New to create a new style. From the New Style dialog box, create the style settings you want. Then, check the Add to Template check box, and click OK.

It's not quite as easy to decide whether you should add a style to your template. Here's what you need to know. Unless you have chosen another template, you are probably working in the Normal template. If you add a new style to the Normal template, you make it available to every document you create.

If you change a built-in style, you likewise change it globally, meaning that it is changed for all documents using this particular style. Be careful not to introduce inconsistencies with existing documents that use Word's default styles.

→ To learn more about how templates and styles work together, **see** "Understanding the Relationship Between Styles and Templates," **p. 11**.

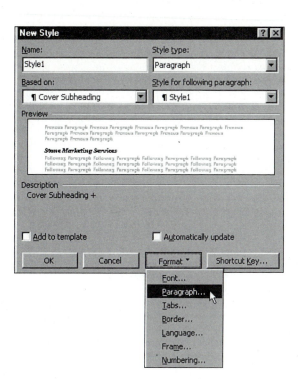

Figure 2.7
You can choose a category of formatting to apply by clicking the Format button in the New Style dialog box.

> **Caution**
>
> Because the styles in your document aren't included in your template unless you check the Add to Template check box, it's possible for different documents using the same template to have varying styles with the same style names.

> **Note**
>
> See the project later in this chapter for a quick and easy alternative: creating a separate template specifically for your new and revised styles.

ENABLING OR PREVENTING AUTOMATIC STYLE UPDATES

As you've learned, Word can create new styles automatically by transforming your manual formatting into styles as you type. If you want, Word can also change your styles automatically for you whenever you manually reformat them.

In some circumstances, this is a great shortcut, because you can manually reformat one line and your entire document is updated to match. However, it's not always appropriate. Imagine that one of your headings refers to the title of a book, which should be formatted in italic. If Word is automatically updating your styles, all the headings using this style change, even those that shouldn't be italicized.

Word enables you to specify which styles qualify for automatic updating. To set a new style for automatic updating, first create the style by clicking New in the Style dialog box. From the New Style dialog box, establish the style settings you want. Then, check the Automatically Update check box, and click OK.

If you want to automatically update a style that already exists, display the Style dialog box and click Modify. The Modify Style dialog box opens; check the Automatically Update check box, and click OK.

CHANGING STYLES

In the past few pages, you've learned how to create new styles. However, you can also make changes in existing styles. You can do so through the Style dialog box, or through the Style box on the Formatting toolbar.

CHANGING A STYLE THROUGH THE STYLE DIALOG BOX

If you want to systematically review and adjust the formatting of a style, use the Style dialog box. To do so, choose Format, Style. In the Styles list, choose the style you want to change, and click Modify.

The Modify Style dialog box opens (see Figure 2.8). As you can see, it looks much like the New Style dialog box. However, the existing style you've already chosen is listed in the Name box. The style's current settings are also listed in the Description area of the dialog box, and their appearance in your document is previewed in the Preview area.

As soon as you change a style, Word applies the change throughout your document anywhere you used the style—or anywhere you used a style based on it. If you add the changed style to a template, the change takes effect in all new documents based on that template.

However, the changes are not made automatically in existing documents. First, you have to save the changes by saving the template. Then, when you open an existing document based on that template, you have to tell Word that you want to update the styles.

To update styles based on the template, first open a document based on the template you've changed. Next, choose Tools, Templates and Add-Ins, and check the Automatically Update Document Styles check box. Click OK and Word reformats the document to reflect any style changes you saved in the template.

CHANGING A STYLE THROUGH THE FORMATTING TOOLBAR

If you want to make a simple change to a style, such as changing a font size or adding italics, use the Style box on the Formatting toolbar. Reformat the style as you want it to appear, click inside the Style box, and press Enter.

The Modify Style dialog box appears, as shown in Figure 2.9. (This is a different "Modify Style" dialog box than the one you accessed through Format, Style.) To change the style, make sure the Update the Style to Reflect Recent Changes button is selected, and click OK.

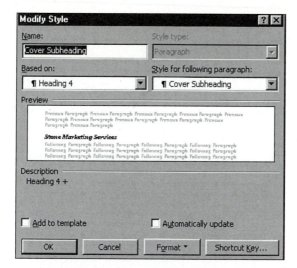

Figure 2.8
The Modify Style dialog box looks and works just like the New Style dialog box you've already seen.

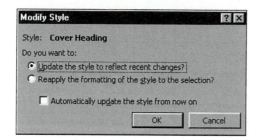

Figure 2.9
This dialog box confirms that you want to update a style.

You can also use this dialog box to eliminate manual formatting you've added to a block of text. Select the text, click inside the Style box, and press Enter. When the Modify Style dialog box appears, select Reapply the Formatting of the Style to the Selection, and click OK.

This technique only works with styles for which Automatically Update is turned off. If Automatically Update is turned on, the style will automatically be changed to reflect your formatting before you have a chance to instruct Word to do so. To learn how to turn off Automatically Update, see "Enabling or Preventing Automatic Style Updates," earlier in this chapter.

 If Word is changing styles on its own, in ways you don't like, see "What to Do If Styles Suddenly Change When You Don't Expect Them To," in "Troubleshooting" at the end of this chapter.

If styles you create appear different from the way you expect, see "What to Do If Styles Look Different Than You Expect," in "Troubleshooting" at the end of this chapter.

CREATING KEYBOARD SHORTCUTS FOR YOUR STYLES

Earlier, you learned that Word comes with built-in keyboard shortcuts for the three highest-level heading styles, Normal style, and List style. You may discover other styles, new or existing, that you find yourself using quite often. To assign a keyboard shortcut to any style, follow these steps:

1. Choose Format, Style.

2. If you are adding a keyboard shortcut to an existing style, click Modify. If you are creating the style, click New instead.

3. Click Shortcut Key. The Customize Keyboard dialog box opens (see Figure 2.10).

Figure 2.10
You can create a convenient keyboard shortcut for any style you expect to use often.

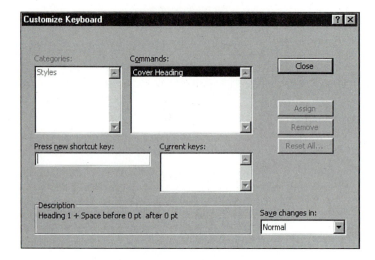

4. Press the keyboard shortcut combination you want to use. The combination appears in the Press New Shortcut Key box. If that combination is already in use, the current use is listed beneath the box where the keyboard combination is displayed.

5. If the combination you've chosen is acceptable to you, click Assign. If not, press another keyboard combination, and when you're satisfied, click Assign.

MANAGING STYLES

Before you start accumulating new and changed styles, you should give a little thought to how you'll manage them. Managing styles involves the following:

- Deciding which styles should be placed in templates, and organizing those styles in the templates associated with specific kinds of work

- Naming styles so you and your colleagues understand their purpose

- Occasionally moving styles or deleting styles you no longer use

You can perform some management tasks in the Style dialog boxes you've already studied. For other tasks, such as moving styles between templates, you use the Organizer, which is described later in this chapter.

How to Choose Style Names

Spend a few moments thinking about how to name your styles. Keep the following tips in mind:

- Name your styles based on their function, not their appearance. Don't name a style Arial 48 Bold; what if you decide to change its appearance someday? Rather, name it based on how you expect to use it—for example, Front Page Headline.

- Keep your style names as consistent as possible. Imagine you use a set of styles for only projects involving Omega Corp. Consider starting each style name with O. That way, they'll all be listed together—and you'll be less likely to inadvertently use them in projects that don't involve Omega.

Quick and Easy Style Names with Aliases

You've just seen some advantages to creating relatively long style names that clearly explain the purpose of each style. However, what if you also like to type your style names in the Style box to select them? It takes too long to type a long name, and if you make a mistake, Word creates a new style, which isn't what you want to happen.

You can have it both ways. Use *aliases*. An alias is an abbreviated style name that Word recognizes in place of the full style name. For example, if you have a style named Major Headline, you might want to use the alias MH.

To create an alias, display the New Style dialog box. Type the style's full name, add a comma, and then type your alias. For example, to create the style Document Summary and assign the alias DS at the same time, enter

```
Document Summary,DS
```

Both the full name and alias appear in the Style box, but you can select the style by typing only the alias.

Tip #22
You can create aliases for existing styles by adding them in the Name box of the Modify Style dialog box.

Keeping Track of Styles with the Organizer

The *Organizer* (see Figure 2.11) is Word's control center for copying, deleting, and renaming styles. To display the organizer, choose Format, Style and click Organizer. The Organizer opens with the Styles tab displayed.

Figure 2.11
You can use the Organizer to move styles between documents or templates.

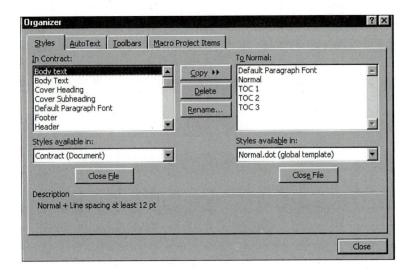

Tip #23

The procedures you'll learn for working with styles in the Organizer also work for moving AutoText entries, Toolbars, and Macro Project Items.

➔ For more information about working with AutoText entries, **see** "AutoText: The Complete Boilerplate Resource," **p. 87**.

When the Organizer opens, it displays two windows. The left window, named after the document that is currently active, lists all the styles contained in that document. The right window corresponds to the Normal template (NORMAL.DOT).

COPYING STYLES

When you open the Organizer, it is already set to copy styles from the current document to the Normal template. All you need to do is select the style you want to copy and click Copy (or press Enter). If you're not sure whether you want to copy a style, you can review the style's contents, which are displayed beneath its window.

You can also copy styles in the opposite direction, from the Normal template to the current document. Click a style in the right window. The arrow inside the Copy button switches direction, now facing the Document window.

Note

You'll often want to copy styles to different templates, not just different documents. To learn how, see "Working with Different Documents and Templates," later in this chapter.

If you copy a style to a destination that already has a style of the same name, Word displays a warning dialog box asking whether you're sure you want to do so. Click Yes to confirm; click Yes to All if you're sure you want to overwrite any other styles as well.

Tip #24

If you'd like to copy a style from one document to another, and the style name isn't already used by the destination document, try this shortcut. Select some text that's already formatted using the style and copy it. Then simply paste it into the other document.

The style comes along with it and is now listed on the Style box along with all other styles in this document. It'll still be there even after you delete the text associated with the style.

RENAMING STYLES

Sometimes you might want to rename a style. For example, you might be setting up several styles associated with a specific project and template, and you want them all to begin with the same letter or word. To rename a style, select it in the Organizer, and click Rename. Then, enter the new name in the Rename dialog box (see Figure 2.12) and click OK.

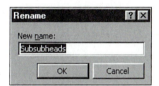

Figure 2.12
The Rename dialog box displays the current name, which can be edited or replaced as you want.

WORKING WITH DIFFERENT DOCUMENTS AND TEMPLATES

Until now, you've used the Organizer only to move styles between the current document and the NORMAL.DOT template. However, the Organizer can be used to move styles between any documents or templates. You simply need to place the appropriate documents or templates in the left and right windows. To do so, follow these steps:

1. Beneath either the left or right window, click the Close File button. The window becomes empty, and the button has changed to read Open File.

2. Click the Open File button. Word displays the Open dialog box, showing your current list of document templates stored in the Templates folder. If you want a template, navigate to it, select the template, and click Open. If you want a document instead, choose Word document in the Files of Type box. Then navigate to the document you want to use and click Open.

3. Repeat the same process in the other window to display the appropriate document or template there.

You can now copy, delete, or rename styles just as you've already learned in this chapter.

Tip #25

Because the Organizer's Open File button displays the same Open dialog box you normally use to open files, you have full access to the extensive file search capabilities.

Tip #26	If you're organizing a template with several specific styles, you can create all the styles in a new, blank document, delete the styled text, and save the remaining blank document as a template. Then, use that template whenever you want to access those styles.

Word Styles and Desktop Publishing Programs

If you export files for use in separate desktop publishing programs, most of these programs can recognize Word styles. The designer working with that software is likely to want to change the specific formatting associated with each style, but the styles themselves already exist, eliminating time-consuming "tagging."

Microsoft Publisher 2000 can import Word 2000 files directly; Adobe PageMaker can do so with an optional filter, currently available at www.adobe.com/supportservice/custsupport/download.html. At this writing, QuarkXPress provides a "beta test" version of its Word 2000/Word 97 filter at www.quark.com/files/xtquarkxts_40.html, but does offer a released version of a Word 6/95 filter.

No filter is perfect. Even the best of them don't support all of Word's myriad features. For example, PageMaker 6.5's Word filter doesn't support character styles. Instead, it reformats that text as if you had manually formatted it. However, it does a very nice job with paragraph styles.

For all these caveats, though, using Word styles in desktop publishing can still save significant time and money.

Troubleshooting

What to Do If Styles Suddenly Change When You Don't Expect Them To

Check in Format, Style, New Style to see whether Automatically Update is turned on for that style. If it is, Word may have misinterpreted a manual formatting change as an instruction to change the style. Clear the check box.

If this doesn't solve the problem, did you change a style on which other styles are based? If so, those styles change as well, sometimes unexpectedly.

If your styles are still changing improperly, is a template that your document depends upon missing? Assume your document uses a template stored on a network drive. If you open a Word document while the server is temporarily unavailable, Word may use styles with the same name from the Normal template stored on your hard disk.

What to Do If Styles Look Different Than You Expect

Perhaps you added manual formatting inadvertently, or imported text that already had manual formatting. Press Shift+F1 and click the text to see whether it has any unexpected manual formatting. If so, select the text and press Ctrl+Spacebar to eliminate it. Another possibility is that you have attached a different template to a document, or opened it as part of a master document that contains the same style names but formats those styles differently.

CHAPTER **3**

MAKING THE MOST OF WORD'S PROOFING TOOLS

In this chapter

USING AUTOMATIC SPELLING AND GRAMMAR CHECKING

By default, when you open a file in Word 2000, Word's new automatic language feature checks the text to determine which language you are writing in. It then runs a spell and grammar check on all sections that are written in languages for which it has proofing tools. Since you probably write most documents in your default language, Word typically proofs your entire document.

Word flags all possible errors with wavy underline marks, as shown in Figure 3.1. Potential spelling errors are marked with a red wavy underline—including words not in Word's dictionary, repeated words, apparent errors in capitalization, and combinations of words with the spaces missing. Word flags potential grammar errors with a wavy green line.

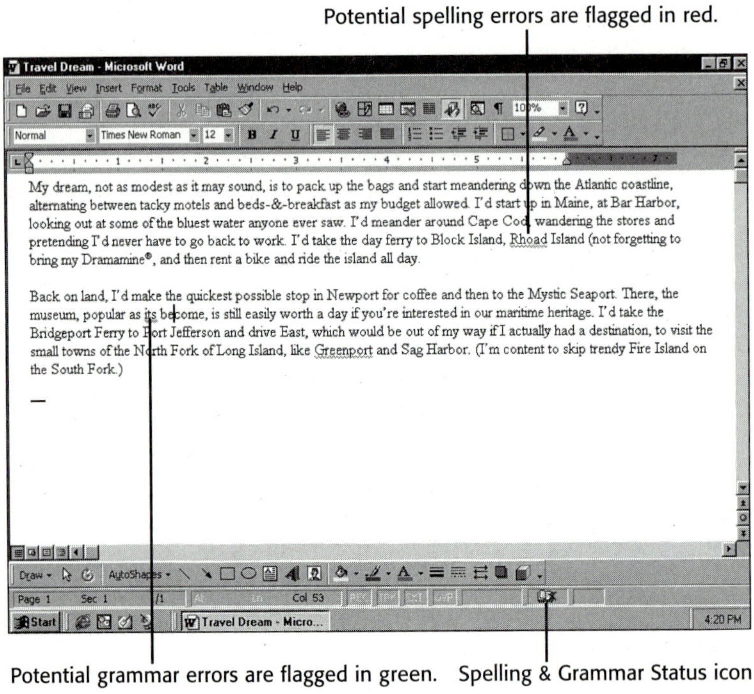

Potential spelling errors are flagged in red.

Figure 3.1
Potential spelling and grammar errors flagged automatically by Word.

Potential grammar errors are flagged in green.   Spelling & Grammar Status icon

To resolve an individual potential spelling error, right-click on the flagged word. A shortcut menu appears (see Figure 3.2), listing any suggestions Word may have about the correct spelling, as well as a set of choices that depend on the error Word has found. If Word has found a word that does not appear in its dictionary, your choices include

- **Ignore All.** Tells Word to disregard all occurrences of the spelling within the current document (and to stop displaying them with red underline).

- **Add.** Tells Word to add the spelling to your custom dictionary; after you add it, Word won't flag the spelling as an error anymore, in any document that uses the same custom dictionary.

- **A̲utoCorrect.** Enables you to select a way to correct your spelling and add it to your AutoCorrect file, so Word can automatically make the same correction every time you make this mistake from now on.

- **L̲anguage.** Enables you to mark the word as being in another language. If you have proofing tools installed for that language, Word uses those proofing tools automatically to check the word. If you do not have the appropriate proofing tools, Word will skip the word—in other words, the word will not be marked as a potential error.

- **S̲pelling.** Opens Word's spell checker dialog box, which may provide more alternative spellings than the shortcut menu, and can allow you to save a new word in a different custom dictionary, if you have one.

→ For more information about custom dictionaries, **see** "Custom Dictionaries for Custom Needs," **p. 63**.

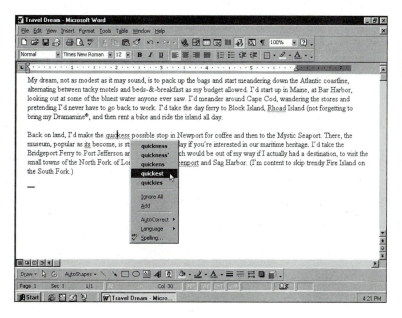

Figure 3.2
You can access Word's most commonly used proofing features from the Spelling and Grammar shortcut menu.

PART

I

CH

3

If Word shows a green wavy underline indicating a possible grammar error, right-click to see the grammar shortcut menu. Word may propose choices, as in Figure 3.3, or make general suggestions. You can also

- Instruct Word to Ignore the sentence
- Open the Grammar checker to see more options
- Choose About This Sentence to see more information about the potential error Word has flagged

Figure 3.3
In some cases, Word presents a specific suggestion for solving the grammar problem.

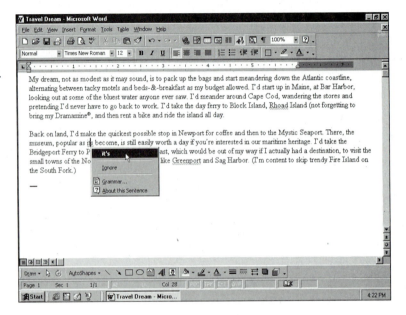

→ For more information about grammar checking, **see** "Checking Your Document's Grammar," **p. 67**.

You can also resolve errors without using the shortcut menu by simply editing the text. Word checks the word or sentence again as you move your insertion point away from it, and if the word is now spelled correctly or the sentence now uses correct grammar, the corresponding wavy underline disappears.

Tip #27

To quickly find the next spelling or grammar problem, double-click the Spelling and Grammar Status icon on the status bar, or press Alt+F7.

Note

In Word 2000, Microsoft has increased the size of the spelling dictionary, improved the spelling and grammar suggestions it offers, and attempted to reduce the number of "false positive" grammar errors that were reported in Word 97.

If you are upgrading from a version of Word earlier than Word 97, you will also notice several additional improvements. The Word spell checker now recognizes the names of all countries, United States cities over 30,000 in population, all Fortune 1000 companies, and a much wider selection of first names. By default, the spell checker no longer flags words in uppercase letters, words containing numbers, URLs, Universal Naming Convention names for network locations (such as \\server\sharename), email addresses, registered usernames, and organization information.

In addition, Word 2000's *AutoCorrect* feature has been enhanced to correct more of the most common spelling errors and typos writers make.

Together, all these improvements should mean that proofing will take significantly less time and cause much less aggravation than it once did.

DISABLING OR HIDING AUTOMATIC SPELLING AND GRAMMAR CHECKING

Automatic spelling and grammar checking isn't everyone's cup of tea. Many people appreciate the way it catches typos and other inadvertent errors as they make them—without going through the trouble of a formal spelling or grammar check. Others find it distracting and want to turn it off immediately—especially the grammar checker, which has improved but is still far from perfect. The feature also slows down Word slightly.

If you prefer not to use automatic spell checking or automatic grammar checking, you can easily turn off one or both of them. Choose Tools, Options, and click the Spelling & Grammar tab. Then, to disable automatic spell checking, clear the Check Spelling as You Type check box. To disable automatic grammar checking, clear the Check Grammar as You Type check box. When you're finished, click OK.

Tip #28

You can also display Spelling & Grammar options by right-clicking the Spelling & Grammar Status icon on the status bar, and choosing Options from the shortcut menu.

→ For more information about spelling options, **see** "Controlling Spelling Settings," **p. 62**.

Tip #29

In large documents with many potential errors, Automatic Spelling and Grammar Checking sometimes turn themselves off, displaying a prompt that they can no longer display wavy green or red lines in your document.

Another option is to enable Word to keep checking the document but prevent it from displaying the potential problems with red or green underlines. You can also do this from the Spelling & Grammar tab of the Options dialog box. Check the boxes Hide Spelling Errors in This Document and Hide Grammatical Errors in This Document.

Later, when you check the document's spelling or grammar using the Spelling and Grammar dialog box, the process goes faster because Word has already found the potential errors. Or, when you're ready, you can clear these check boxes and fix all your potential errors at once from within the document.

CHECKING SPELLING THROUGH THE SPELLING AND GRAMMAR DIALOG BOX

In addition to the streamlined spelling and grammar tools Word makes available through the shortcut menu, Word provides a powerful spelling and grammar checking dialog box that gives you even more options for fixing your current document—and improving the way you check future documents. To access it, click Spelling and Grammar on the Standard toolbar, or press F7.

The Spelling and Grammar dialog box opens, displaying the first potential error it finds (see Figure 3.4).

Figure 3.4
The Spelling and Grammar dialog box, showing a spelling error and offering suggestions.

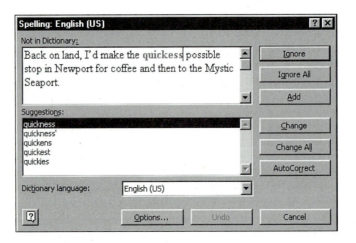

Note

Word displays both spelling and grammar errors in the Spelling and Grammar dialog box. If you want to check only spelling, clear the Check Grammar with Spelling check box.

The sentence containing the potential problem appears in the Not in Dictionary scroll box; the incorrect word appears in red. You now have several options:

- If one of the words shown in the Suggestions list is correct, click Change; Word changes the spelling to match that suggestion.

- If you want Word to change the spelling wherever it appears in the document, click Change All.

- If you want Word to add the correction to its AutoCorrect database, so Word can fix the error as soon as you make it from now on, click AutoCorrect.

- If the word is spelled correctly, and you want Word to add it to the custom dictionary (so the word will never be flagged as wrong again), click Add.

- If Word hasn't made any acceptable suggestions, but you know how to fix the error manually, edit the word in the Not in Dictionary scroll box, and click Change (or Change All or AutoCorrect).

➔ For more information about AutoCorrect, **see** Chapter 4, "Automating Your Documents: AutoCorrect, AutoFormat, AutoText, and AutoSummarize," **p. 75**.

No matter which option you choose, Word follows your instructions and automatically moves to the next potential error it finds. If you've chosen to proof only part of your document (by selecting that part of the document before running spell check), Word offers to proof the rest after it finishes. Otherwise, it reports that the spelling and grammar check is complete.

➔ For more information about proofing portions of a document, **see** "Proofing Only Part of a Document," **p. 61**.

➔ For more information about proofing portions of a document, **see** "Proofing Only Part of a Document," **p. 61**.

Tip #30

If a change you make to fix a word or syntax error affects surrounding text, you can edit any part of the sentence that appears in the Not in Dictionary scroll box—not just the incorrect portion.

Or, if you prefer, you can click inside the document and make your edits there. The Spelling and Grammar dialog box remains open. When you finish, click inside the dialog box and click Resume.

Why Proofreading Is Still a Necessity
Incorrect usage and misspellings are unprofessional. Unfortunately, running a spell check isn't enough to solve the problem: Proofread your documents manually, as well. For example, spell checkers—even those with associated grammar checkers, like Word's—often miss homonyms. If you misspell "sight" as "site," odds are Word won't flag the problem.

PROOFING ONLY PART OF A DOCUMENT

Word enables you to check your entire document or any part of it, including just a single word. If you don't want to check your entire document, select only the text you want to check—even if it's just a single word.

You can also tell Word to never proof a portion of your document. To do so, select the text you don't want proofed. Next, choose Tools, Language, Set Language. The Language dialog box opens. Check the Do Not Check Spelling or Grammar check box, and click OK.

This turns off both spelling and grammar: You can't tell Word to avoid spell checking part of a document while still grammar checking it (or vice versa).

UNDOING SPELLING OR GRAMMAR CHANGES YOU JUST MADE

 You can always undo your most recent spelling or grammar changes (except for adding words to a custom dictionary). From within the Spelling and Grammar dialog box, click Undo. If you've already finished spell checking, you can still click the Undo button on the Standard toolbar to undo one change at a time, starting with the last change you made.

REPROOFING A DOCUMENT YOU'VE ALREADY CHECKED

If you proof a document a second time, Word doesn't recheck the spelling of words (or the syntax of sentences) you already proofed. If you want Word to catch previously caught errors, reopen the Spelling and Grammar Options dialog box (either choose Tools, Options and click the Spelling & Grammar tab or click the Options button inside the Spelling and Grammar dialog box) and click the Recheck Document button. Word asks you to confirm that you want to recheck text you've already proofed; choose Yes.

CONTROLLING SPELLING SETTINGS

The Spelling & Grammar tab of the Options dialog box (see Figure 3.5) gives you extensive control over how you interact with Word's spell checker. You can display this dialog box by clicking the Options button in the Spelling and Grammar dialog box, or by choosing Tools, Options, and clicking the Spelling & Grammar tab.

You've already learned about the first two options in this dialog box: Check Spelling as You Type and Hide Spelling Errors in This Document. Word also offers you several additional controls:

- **Always Suggest Corrections.** Word's spelling suggestions are often inaccurate in highly technical documents or documents that contain a lot of arcane jargon. For such documents, to save time, you might want to disable Word's suggested spellings feature.

- **Suggest from Main Dictionary Only.** By default, Word looks in all open dictionaries to make suggestions about spelling changes. This can take time. It also means that Word may recognize as correct certain words that are actually incorrect when read in context. If you're sure your current document won't benefit from words you added to your custom dictionaries, check this box.

- **Ignore Words in UPPERCASE.** No spell checker understands all acronyms. Because most acronyms are all caps, you can tell Word not to flag words that are all caps. (This feature is turned on by default.)

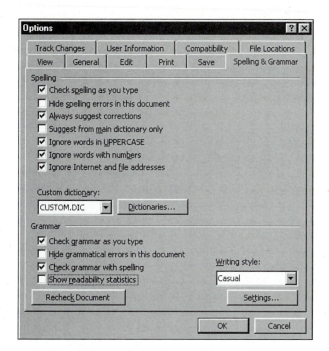

Figure 3.5
You can control the behavior of spelling and grammar from the Spelling & Grammar tab of the Options dialog box.

- **Ignore Words with Numbers.** Some product names combine words and numbers. Suppose that you sell a 686MX computer, a DX677 CD player, and a KFE100 fire extinguisher. Word might flag each of these as incorrect—a real problem if you're proofing a long price list. Therefore, by default, Word ignores word/number combinations.

- **Ignore Internet and File Addresses.** Until recently, most spell checkers have incorrectly flagged Internet file addresses such as the Web address www.microsoft.com or the filename c:\windows\system.dat. If you leave this check box checked, Word doesn't spell check addresses such as these.

The Spelling & Grammar tab can control one additional aspect of Word spell checking: custom dictionaries. These are covered next.

CUSTOM DICTIONARIES FOR CUSTOM NEEDS

When you use Word's spell checker to add words to your dictionary, Word stores these in a custom dictionary file called CUSTOM.DIC. It then consults CUSTOM.DIC whenever you run a spell check—thereby making sure that it doesn't flag words as incorrect that you indicated are accurate. If you wish, you can also create other custom dictionaries—up to ten—for special purposes. For example, if you do legal editing on only Tuesdays and Thursdays, you can maintain a legal custom dictionary and use it on only those days.

The following sections show you how to work with Word's custom dictionaries.

CREATING A NEW CUSTOM DICTIONARY

To create a new custom dictionary, choose Tools, Options, Spelling & Grammar, and click Dictionaries. The Custom Dictionary dialog box appears (see Figure 3.6), listing custom dictionaries that already exist. Dictionaries that are currently enabled—in other words, dictionaries Word is currently using in spell checking—appear checked.

Figure 3.6
The Custom Dictionaries dialog box shows the custom dictionaries being used during a spelling and grammar check.

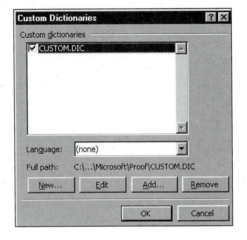

To create a new dictionary, click New. The Create Custom Dictionary dialog box opens, which is similar to a standard Save As dialog box. Enter a name for your dictionary and click Save. The dictionary now appears checked in the Custom Dictionaries dialog box. Note that words you add to custom dictionaries during a spell check are placed in whichever enabled custom dictionary is listed first.

DISABLING A CUSTOM DICTIONARY

From the Custom Dictionaries dialog box, you can also make a custom dictionary unavailable by clearing its check box. While the dictionary is unavailable, keeping it in the list allows you to make it available again without first browsing your system to locate it.

To make the dictionary disappear entirely from the list of dictionaries, select it and click Remove. Note that this doesn't erase the dictionary file; you can use the Add button to locate it, place it back on your list, and make it available again.

CHOOSING A CUSTOM DICTIONARY WHILE SPELL CHECKING

Suppose, during a spell check, that you find a word that you want to add to a custom dictionary other than the default CUSTOM.DIC file that Word normally uses. To select a different custom dictionary

1. Make sure the word you want to add appears highlighted in the Spelling and Grammar dialog box.

2. Click <u>O</u>ptions.

3. Click <u>D</u>ictionaries.

4. Select the custom dictionary you want to use, and make sure it is checked.

5. Click OK twice to return to the Spelling and Grammar dialog box.

6. Click <u>A</u>dd to add the word to the dictionary you've selected. Any additional words you add to the custom dictionary will be placed in the dictionary you've selected, until you choose a different one.

7. Continue checking spelling and grammar as usual. If you want to add words to a different custom dictionary, change the custom dictionary by following steps 1–5 again.

EDITING A CUSTOM DICTIONARY

While you're spell checking, it's easy to mistakenly add words to the custom dictionary that shouldn't be there. If you do enter words in a custom dictionary by mistake, however, it's easy to delete them. You can also manually add lists of words to a custom dictionary—you don't have to wait for them to show up in your documents. For example, you might want to add the last names of all the employees in your company or the company names of all your clients.

Word dictionary files are ASCII (text only) lists of words with a .DIC extension. When you open a custom dictionary, you can add as many words as you want—either manually, or by cutting and pasting them from another file. The only limitation is that you must save the file as Text Only (TXT) and place only one word on each line.

Word stores words in custom dictionaries in alphabetical order, with all capitalized words appearing before all lowercased words. However, you do not need to store your words in this order—you can insert them any way you want. Word reorganizes your list automatically the next time you add a word to this dictionary during a spell check.

To edit a custom dictionary, display the Spelling & Grammar tab of the <u>T</u>ools, <u>O</u>ptions dialog box; then follow these steps:

1. Click <u>D</u>ictionaries.

2. Select the dictionary you want to edit.

3. Click <u>E</u>dit.

4. Word displays a dialog box telling you that it must stop automatic spell checking, and that you'll have to re-enable it manually. Click OK to acknowledge this.

5. The dictionary opens in a new Word editing window.

6. Make your edits, and click the Save button on the Standard toolbar.

7. Choose <u>F</u>ile, <u>C</u>lose to close the dictionary file.

If you cannot edit your custom dictionary, see "What to Do If You Can't Edit Your Custom Dictionary," in "Troubleshooting" at the end of this chapter.

Caution

> When you edit a custom dictionary, Word turns off automatic spelling and grammar checking. After you close the dictionary file, you must turn these features on again. Do so by choosing Tools, Options, clicking the Spelling & Grammar tab, and placing checks in the Check Spelling as You Type and Check Grammar as You Type check boxes.

FLAGGING "CORRECT" WORDS AS POTENTIAL ERRORS

Occasionally, you might want to have the spell checker flag a word as a possible misspelling even though the word is in the dictionary. Imagine that you noticed you often mistype "liar" as "lira," both of which are spelled correctly. Because you write crime novels, not reports on European currency exchange, wouldn't it be nifty if the spell checker would always question lira as a misspelling, rather than assume that you know what you're doing?

You can't remove a word from Word's basic dictionary. You can, however, create a supplemental file called an *exclude dictionary*, which includes words you want to flag as problems even if they're spelled correctly.

Caution

> When you create an exclude dictionary, all your Office applications will use it, flagging the words in the exclude dictionary as possible errors even if they are actually correct.

Like custom dictionaries, exclude dictionaries are ASCII files with one word on each line. Exclude dictionaries use the same file name as the main dictionaries with which they're connected, except they have an EXC extension. They are stored in the same folder as the main dictionary.

If you're using the default dictionary for American English, the name of the exclude dictionary you create will be MSSP3EN.EXC.

In Office 2000, the default location for the exclude dictionary is the following path: <winversion>\<profile>\application data\microsoft\proof, where <winversion> is your main Windows folder, and <profile> is the user profile associated with this installation of Office. Since this is a different location from the location used by previous versions of Office, if Word is installed over an existing version, your preceding custom and exclude dictionary files will be copied to the new proof folder. To create an exclude dictionary, edit it manually and save it as Text Only with the correct name and extension in the correct folder. (Make sure Word doesn't append a TXT extension to the filename, or it won't work.)

Communicating with Word: Avoid Clipped Words

When working in an industry with its own jargon, it is easy to fall into the trap of using truncated or clipped words: saying "lab" instead of "laboratory," or "specs" instead of "specifications." When writing, use the formal word, unless you're positive the clipped version will be understood by your audience.

For instance, if you're communicating with a colleague in your laboratory, "lab" is acceptable; if you are communicating with a Congressman investigating your safety procedures, it isn't.

As clipped words are not abbreviations, they should not be followed by periods, nor preceded by apostrophes. Never use clipped "slang," like thru (through) and nite (night).

A CLOSER LOOK AT THE GRAMMAR CHECKER

Word's grammar checker, like all contemporary grammar checkers, follows rules that identify potential writing problems. Word's grammar checker has gradually been refined; however, it still cannot "understand" your documents, so it's best to have modest expectations.

On a good day, the grammar checker might pleasantly surprise you—catching things you would never have noticed. On another day, it may flag many "errors" that are, in fact, not errors at all. Later in this chapter, you'll learn to personalize the grammar checker to catch only the types of errors you actually make, with fewer false alarms.

CHECKING YOUR DOCUMENT'S GRAMMAR

As you learned earlier in this chapter, Word flags potential grammar problems as you work, displaying them with a green wavy underline. To get Word's suggestions, right-click anywhere in the underlined text. Word displays either potential solutions or a general description of what it thinks is wrong. For example, in Figure 3.7, Word recognizes that you've used the wrong word—"their" instead of "there."

Figure 3.7
Viewing Word's suggested solutions for a potential grammar problem. If you don't agree with Word's grammar checker, click Ignore, and the green wavy underline disappears.

If you want to take a closer look at your document's grammar, choose Grammar. The Spelling and Grammar dialog box opens, with the questionable phrase displayed in green (see Figure 3.8). The text box is named after the rule Word believes you have broken.

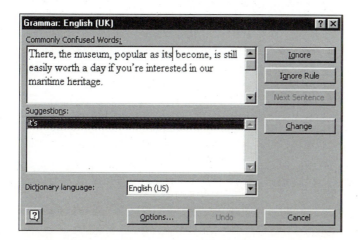

Figure 3.8
The Spelling and Grammar dialog box, displaying a potential grammar error.

Word displays possible improvements in the Suggestions scroll box. The category of problem it has identified appears above the flagged text. Often, none of Word's suggestions are ideal; you can then edit the text manually until the green wavy underlines disappear.

It's also possible that you won't agree there's a problem at all. To tell Word to ignore the sentence, click Ignore. To tell Word never to flag problems for the same reason it flagged this one, click Ignore Rule. To leave the sentence alone without making any decisions, click Next Sentence.

Word follows your instructions and moves to the next potential error it finds—either a spelling or a grammar error. If you've chosen to proof only part of your document, after Word finishes, it offers to proof the rest. Otherwise, it reports that it has finished proofing.

 If Word keeps checking grammar during a spell check even after you've turned it off, see "How to Completely Disable Grammar Checking," in "Troubleshooting" at the end of this chapter.

Avoiding the Passive Voice

Word's grammar checker is especially useful for detecting sentences written in a passive voice. In almost all cases, active voice is superior, for two reasons. First, passive voice is wordier and usually more convoluted. Second, it is often ambiguous and uninformative.

One key to avoiding passive voice is to avoid the use of the word "it" whenever possible. For example, don't say: "it has been reported." Rather, say "three of our top customers report."

STRATEGIES FOR MAKING GRAMMAR CHECKING WORK MORE EFFECTIVELY

Word's grammar checker contains 26 fundamental rules that it can check in your document, ranging from identifying the passive voice to recognizing cliches. Word has incorporated five writing styles into its grammar checker, which proof based on varying combinations of these rules. These five writing styles are: Standard, Casual, Formal, Technical, and Custom. For example, Word's built-in Casual style checks documents against only five rules, whereas Formal checks for 24 of 26 rules—excluding only gender-specific and first-person usage.

You can change the settings for any of these writing styles to apply a "mix and match" of grammatical rules to the grammar check of your document. Word provides a Custom writing style you can use to build the rules you want to use for the way you write.

One strategy for deciding how to deal with the grammar checker is to run a full grammar check on a few of your documents, noticing which type of errors you make most often, and then customize the grammar checker to flag only those errors. The grammar checker is especially good at catching passive sentences, subject-verb disagreements, incorrect punctuation, and cliches.

Tip #31

Writing style preferences are stored with *templates*, so you can set different preferences for different templates. Once you've done so, the appropriate settings are automatically used when you create a document based on the template.

> For example, you can make sure that contracts are proofed using the Formal style while your personal correspondence is proofed using Casual by selecting the correct template for each document.

→ For more information about creating templates, **see** Chapter 1, "Templates, Wizards, and Add-Ins," **p. 3**.

CHOOSING WHICH WRITING STYLE TO APPLY

The easiest decision you can make about grammar checking—aside from whether to use it at all—is which writing style to apply. To match Word's grammar checking style with the type of documents you create, choose Tools, Options; then click the Spelling & Grammar tab. In the Writing Style drop-down list box, choose Standard, Casual, Formal, Technical, or Custom; then choose OK.

CHOOSING WHICH RULES OF GRAMMAR TO APPLY

You can edit any of Word's five writing styles. You might generally like one of Word's existing writing styles, but you want to tweak it a bit. Or you might want to create your own Custom writing style from scratch. To edit a writing style, display the Spelling & Grammar tab of the Options dialog box, and click Settings. The Grammar Settings dialog box opens, as shown in Figure 3.9. Then, follow these steps:

1. In the Writing Style drop-down box, choose the writing style you want to edit. Notice that the Custom writing style highlights every potential problem except the use of first-person language.

2. Check the boxes corresponding to rules you want the grammar checker to enforce; clear the boxes corresponding to rules you want to ignore.

3. When you're finished, click OK.

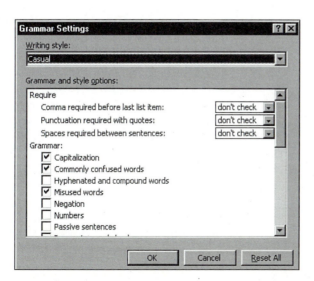

Figure 3.9
The Grammar Settings dialog box gives you control over how Word checks your grammar.

PART

I

CH

3

Tip #32

For an excellent explanation of Word's grammar and style rules, click the Office Assistant, and ask: "How do I set Grammar and Writing Style Options?"

If you later decide that you would prefer to use Word's default grammar settings, reopen the Grammar Settings dialog box, choose the writing style you want to reset, and choose <u>R</u>eset All.

ADDITIONAL GRAMMAR SETTINGS

Word's grammar settings include three settings you may be interested in even if you never use grammar checking for anything else. They are listed at the top of the Grammar and Style <u>O</u>ptions scroll box in the Grammar Settings dialog box:

- **Comma Required Before Last List Item.** Some individuals swear by serial commas; others swear against them. If you're a professional writer, you may find that some of your clients feel each way, making it very easy to make mistakes! You can instruct Word to make sure you always use a serial comma before last item a list, or make sure you never use one, or ignore the issue completely (don't check).

- **Punctuation Required with Quotes.** You can specify whether you prefer to place punctuation inside or outside your quote marks, or whether Word should ignore how you punctuate quotes.

- **Spaces Required Between Sentences.** If you are of a certain age, your typing teacher taught you always to place two spaces between sentences. Now, in this era of typeset and desktop published documents using attractive fonts, the standard has changed: You should generally use one space between sentences. You can use this setting to specify one or two spaces between sentences, or to instruct Word to ignore the issue altogether.

You might decide that one or more of these three settings are all the grammar you ever want to check. In that case, create a Custom Writing style with all the Grammar and Style Options boxes cleared, and with the settings of your choice for commas, punctuation, and spaces between sentences.

USING THE WORD THESAURUS

As you write, you may sometimes find yourself getting into a rut—using the same word or phrase repeatedly when another word might make your point more clearly. That's what a thesaurus is for. Word 2000 comes with a significantly enhanced thesaurus—one that you might find much more effective than the version you've used before.

To use the thesaurus, right-click on the word for which you would like to see synonyms (similar meanings), and choose S<u>y</u>nonyms on the shortcut menu (see Figure 3.10). Or, select the word and press Shift+F7. Select an option to use in place of the existing word.

Figure 3.10
Choosing a synonym from the shortcut menu.

Word may need to install the thesaurus the first time you use it.

If you don't like any of the options Word presents, and you want to explore more, choose Thesaurus from the shortcut menu. Word's Thesaurus dialog box opens, displaying a list of synonyms—often a longer list than the one you already saw (see Figure 3.11).

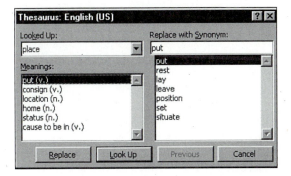

Figure 3.11
Looking up a synonym for a word.

If the word you want to look up isn't in the document yet, click on a blank area in the editing window, and press Shift+F7. Word displays the Thesaurus dialog box with all its text boxes empty.

The word you select appears in the Looked Up combo box. To the right, in the Replace with Synonym box, Word proposes the most likely equivalent term. The example in Figure 3.11 asks for synonyms for the word "place," and Word provides "put" as the most likely synonym. It also provides several additional alternatives in the Replace with Synonym scroll box. When you find the synonym you're looking for, select it, and click on the Replace button. Word substitutes the synonym for the original word in your document.

The thesaurus also enables you to find synonyms for the particular usage of a word that can be used in multiple senses. For example, in Figure 3.11, the word "place" can be used in several senses, which are listed in the Meanings box. If you want to use it as a noun ("That was a great place we had dinner.") you might select "location (n.)" in the Meanings box. When you do, new synonyms for "put" appear in the Replace with Synonym box to the right: "space," "spot," "area," and so on.

When Word presents a list of synonyms, you might decide you would like to review the meanings and synonyms of one of those words. To do so, select the synonym and then click the Looked Up drop-down list box. Sometimes you might follow a trail of several suggested replacements before arriving at the word you want.

If you want to return to a previous thesaurus request, you can. Click the down-arrow on the Looked Up drop-down list box to show all the requests you've made since opening the Thesaurus dialog box. Click on the word you want, and the synonyms for that word reappear.

FINDING ANTONYMS

In many cases, the Word thesaurus can show you antonyms (opposite meanings) of a word or phrase. Antonyms are followed by the word *Antonym* in parentheses. As with synonyms, you can select an antonym and click Replace to place it in your document.

WHEN WORD CAN'T FIND A SYNONYM OR ANTONYM

Sometimes Word can't find a synonym for a word. Then, in case you might have misspelled it, Word presents you with an alphabetical list of words with similar spellings. If you spelled the word wrong, you can pick the correct word from this list and search Word's thesaurus for its synonyms.

COUNTING A DOCUMENT'S WORDS, PAGES, LINES, AND CHARACTERS

Often, you need to count the words, characters, lines, paragraphs, or pages in your document. For example, in creating your document, you might have been given a word limit you aren't permitted to exceed. To get an accurate estimate of your document's current size, choose Tools, Word Count. Word reads your document and displays the Word Count dialog box (see Figure 3.12).

Figure 3.12
The Word Count dialog box.

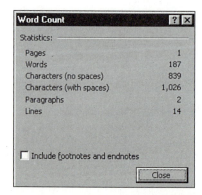

By default, Word does not include footnotes and endnotes in its count. If you want them included, check the Include Footnotes and Endnotes check box; Word recounts immediately.

Tip #34	Word displays an approximate character count in the status bar whenever it opens an existing document.
	You can also count words, characters, paragraphs, and sentences by running Readability Statistics, as discussed in the next section of this chapter.
	Counts of pages, paragraphs, lines, words, and characters are also available through the Statistics tab of the File, Properties dialog box.

Tip #35	You can't print the results from the Word count dialog box, but you can use the NumChars, NumPages, and NumWords fields to insert that information in your document.
	The project at the end of Chapter 18, "Automating Your Documents with Field Codes," shows how to build a cover sheet that includes this and other information at the beginning of any document you want.

DISPLAYING READABILITY STATISTICS

Sometimes word counts aren't enough: you want to know how readable your document is, and whether it is suitable for the audience that is to read it.

To display readability statistics, choose Tools, Options, and click the Spelling & Grammar tab. Check the Show Readability Statistics check box, and click OK. Then, check spelling and grammar in your document by pressing F7 or choosing Tools, Spelling and Grammar. Allow Word to check your document completely; at the end, it displays a dialog box similar to the one in Figure 3.13.

INTERPRETING READABILITY STATISTICS

The statistics listed in the Readability Statistics dialog box are based on an estimate of the number of words in an average sentence, and the average number of syllables in each word. The Flesch Reading Ease score in the Readability field of the dialog box rates text on a scale of 1 to 100; the higher the score, the more understandable the document. You should generally shoot for at least 60 points.

The Flesch-Kincaid Grade Level score rates text based on the average United States grade level of education needed to understand it. For example, a score of 7.0 means an average seventh-grader should understand the document. If you write a nontechnical document for a general audience, and it receives a score much higher than 8 or 9, consider editing to make the document simpler.

Figure 3.13
A sample Readability Statistics dialog box as it appears after checking spelling and grammar in a document.

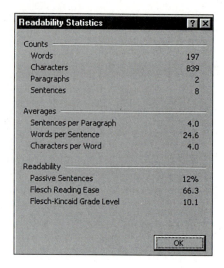

TROUBLESHOOTING

WHAT TO DO IF YOU CAN'T EDIT YOUR CUSTOM DICTIONARY

Two causes are possible. First, your custom dictionary might be empty: You can't edit it until it contains at least one word. Second, if you're running Word across the network, your network administrator may have set CUSTOM.DIC or its folder as Read Only. Ask permission to create your own local copy of CUSTOM.DIC and store it where you can access it.

HOW TO COMPLETELY DISABLE GRAMMAR CHECKING

You may have hidden grammar mistakes rather than disabled grammar checking. Or, you may have disabled Check Grammar as You Type. To completely disable Grammar Checking, choose Tools, Options, and click the Spelling & Grammar tab. Then, remove the checks from the Check Grammar as You Type and the Check Grammar with Spelling check boxes.

CHAPTER 4

AUTOMATING YOUR DOCUMENTS: AUTOCORRECT, AUTOFORMAT, AUTOTEXT, AND AUTOSUMMARIZE

In this chapter

AUTOCORRECT: SMARTER THAN EVER

Are you getting smarter as you get older? You are if you're using Word. With each new version, Word's AutoCorrect feature becomes more powerful. In Word 2000, unless you tell it otherwise, Word automatically corrects thousands of the most common spelling mistakes people make—even using suggestions built into the spell checker that it didn't use before. That's not all. Word performs the following tasks:

- Makes sure you start all your sentences with a capital letter
- Corrects words you inadvertently start with two capital letters
- Capitalizes days of the week, such as Tuesday
- Fixes things when you inadvertently press the Caps Lock key
- Replaces character strings such as (c) with symbols such as ©
- Replaces Internet "smileys" such as :) with Wingding symbols such as ☺

If you're using Word's default settings, this is all happening right now in the background; you haven't had to do a thing. You can take control of Word's AutoCorrect settings and make it back off on certain things, or stop correcting you altogether. Conversely, you can make it even smarter by adding your own entries. To control AutoCorrect, choose Tools, AutoCorrect to display the AutoCorrect tab of the AutoCorrect dialog box (see Figure 4.1).

Figure 4.1
From the AutoCorrect tab, you control AutoCorrect's overall behavior and specify which text elements it automatically corrects.

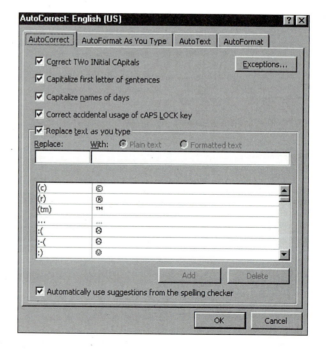

Tip #36	Three more of Word's automation features—AutoCorrect, AutoFormat, and AutoText—can also be controlled from the AutoCorrect dialog box. Rather than accessing this dialog box only when you want to make a single change, consider investing a few minutes in systematically adding entries to AutoCorrect and AutoText, and setting the AutoFormatting controls that make most sense for you.

By default, all of Word's AutoCorrect capabilities are selected. A couple of AutoCorrect options are so innocuous that few people want to turn them off. Capitalize <u>N</u>ames of Days automatically adds a capital letter at the beginning of the seven days of the week: Sunday, Monday, Tuesday, and so on. If you think about it, you'll rarely, if ever, want these words lowercased.

Note	This feature doesn't change day-of-the-week abbreviations such as Tues. or Thu.; it affects only days of the week that are fully spelled out.

Another option, Correct Accidental Usage of c<u>APS</u> L<u>OCK</u> Key, is designed for those times when your left pinkie finger inadvertently presses Caps Lock rather than A or Q at the left edge of your keyboard. If this happens part way into a word, Word recognizes you probably didn't mean it. Rather than letting you continue typing until you notice the problem, it turns off Caps Lock and changes the capitalization on all the letters it thinks you reversed. For instance, if you typed

`sPORTSMANSHIP`

Word will turn off Caps Lock and edit your text to read

`Sportsmanship`

Note	This feature never changes text you capitalized by pressing and holding the Shift key.

Communicating with Word: Replacing Clipped Words
Although you should never use the clipped form of a word in written communication, you often use it when you think of what you want to say. Using the AutoCorrect feature of Word, you can have Word automatically "professionalize" your written communications. Just have Word substitute the full word for the clipped version. For instance, have Word replace the word "spec" with "specification" and "specs" with "specifications."

AUTOCORRECTING ERRORS FLAGGED BY THE SPELL CHECKER

AutoCorrect AutoCorrect finds errors in two ways. First, it watches for errors flagged by Word's interactive spell checker. When an error is made, and Word is sure of the correct spelling, AutoCorrect fixes the error automatically. If Word is not sure of the correct spelling—for example, if several alternative words seem reasonable—AutoCorrect leaves the word unchanged.

PART

I

CH

4

Note

If you find AutoCorrect making spelling changes you disagree with, you can turn off this feature by choosing Tools, AutoCorrect, and clearing the Automatically Use Suggestions From the Spelling Checker check box in the AutoCorrect tab.

AUTOCORRECTING NEARLY 1,000 COMMON ERRORS

In addition to AutoCorrecting errors caught by Word's spell checker, AutoCorrect draws upon a database containing nearly 1,000 mistakes that writers tend to make most often. These errors fall into the following categories:

- **Spelling errors.** Word replaces *acheive* with *achieve*.

- **Common typos.** Word replaces *teh* with *the*.

- **Spaces left out between words.** Word replaces *saidthat* with *said that*.

- **Errors in usage.** Word replaces *should of been* with *should have been* and *their are* with *there are*.

- **Missing or incorrect apostrophes.** Word replaces *wouldnt* with *wouldn't* and *you;re* with *you're*.

- **Forgotten accent characters.** Word replaces *seance* with *séance*.

In addition, Word inserts a wide variety of symbols in place of the "fake" symbols that many writers use. For example, if you type (c), Word will replace it with ©. Word adds a list of Internet/email smileys. For example, Word replaces :(with the corresponding symbol from the Wingding font: L. The complete list of symbols AutoCorrect replaces is shown in Table 4.1.

TABLE 4.1 SYMBOLS AND SMILEYS WORD AUTOMATICALLY REPLACES

Text You Type	Symbol Word Inserts
(c)	©
(r)	®
(tm)	™
...	…
:(	L
:-(	L
:)	☺
:-)	☺
:-|	K
:|	K
<--	←
<==	←

Text You Type	Symbol Word Inserts
<=>	⇔
==>	→
—>	→

If you're simply not comfortable with Word changing your text, you can clear the Replace Text as You Type box, and Word will leave all your potential errors alone.

REMOVING AN AUTOCORRECT ENTRY

You might be comfortable with Word's AutoCorrect feature, but object to one or more of the replacements Word makes by default. For example, if you copy text formatted with the Wingding font into an email message, that text may not appear correctly when your recipient gets it. If you are a fiction writer using dialect, you don't want Word to clean up usage like "should of had." Or, perhaps you work for the CNA insurance company and want Word to stop changing your company name to "CAN."

To remove an AutoCorrect entry, choose Tools, AutoCorrect. In the Replace text box, type the entry you want to remove (or scroll to it in the list beneath the Replace text box); then click Delete.

The entry is removed from your AutoCorrect list. However, it remains in the Replace and With text boxes, so if you change your mind, you can click Add to put it back in your list.

Tip #37	If you save a Word file to text-only format, Word reverts the smileys to their original characters. For example, ☺ becomes :) again.

ADDING A NEW AUTOCORRECT ENTRY

Just as you can remove AutoCorrect entries you don't want, you can also add new, custom AutoCorrect entries that reflect the errors you make most often. To add a new entry, display the AutoCorrect tab by choosing Tools, AutoCorrect; then type the incorrect text you want Word to replace. In the With text box, type the text you want Word to insert. Click Add. The new entry now appears in the AutoCorrect list.

Tip #38	You can also add AutoCorrect entries while you're spell checking. In fact, that's a great time to do it, because that's when you systematically review documents and discover the errors you're most likely to make. Click the Spelling and Grammar button on the Standard toolbar to run Word's spell checker. Word displays your first error in the Spelling and Grammar dialog box. Select the replacement text you want to use; if you want Word to correct this error from now on, click AutoCorrect.
	You can also right-click an error within the document; select AutoCorrect from the shortcut menu, and select one of the choices Word provides (see Figure 4.2). Word then automatically corrects the mistake in the future.

Figure 4.2
You can add an AutoCorrect entry from the shortcut menu in any document.

→ To learn more about working with Word's spell check feature, **see** Chapter 3, "Making the Most of Word's Proofing Tools," **p. 55**.

Tip #39

A word doesn't have to be misspelled for you to ask Word to correct it. For example, if you constantly type manger rather than manager, you can tell Word to make the change automatically, even though manger is a perfectly legitimate word.

This is an example of why it's not enough to run a spell check on an important document: You have to actually read the document to make sure everything's okay!

CHANGING AN AUTOCORRECT ENTRY

On occasion, rather than delete an entry, you might want to change the replacement text Word uses. From within the AutoCorrect tab, scroll to the entry you want to change, and select it. The entry appears in the Replace and With text boxes. Enter the replacement text you prefer in the With text box, and click Replace.

USING AUTOCORRECT TO INSERT BOILERPLATE TEXT

Later in this chapter, you'll learn about AutoText, a powerful feature that enables you to manage boilerplate text and insert it into a document with just a few keystrokes. You can also use AutoCorrect this way—not to correct errors, but to insert large blocks of formatted or unformatted text automatically.

For example, ever since securities reform legislation passed Congress, it's common to see an extremely lengthy disclaimer appear in press releases and other documents, to the effect that "forward-looking statements" involve risks and uncertainties, and the company is not making an ironclad commitment that these predictions will come true. These statements can involve 100 words or more; you wouldn't want to constantly retype them, and your lawyers wouldn't want you to inadvertently leave something out.

Follow these steps to have AutoCorrect insert such a block of text automatically:

1. Select the text you want Word to add automatically. (You don't have to copy it.)

2. Choose Tools, AutoCorrect. The text you selected appears as Formatted Text in the With text box. If necessary, the text box expands to two lines to accommodate at least some of the additional text. The text appears with the same boldface, italic, or underline character formatting you applied in the document; this formatting will appear whenever Word inserts the AutoCorrect entry.

3. In the Replace text box, enter a distinctive sequence of letters that you wouldn't inadvertently use for any other purpose, such as dsclmr.

4. Click Add.

After you've added your AutoCorrect entry, every time you type dsclmr followed by a space, Word will automatically replace that word with the entire block of boilerplate text.

Tip #40

With the AutoCorrect dialog box open, you can enter as many new entries as you want. After you click Add to add an entry, type the next AutoCorrection you want in the Replace and With text boxes; then click Add again.

You can also use AutoCorrect to insert graphics or heavily formatted text. Follow the previous steps, selecting the graphics or formatted text before choosing Tools, AutoCorrect. A portion of your selected text or image will appear in the With box, as shown in Figure 4.3.

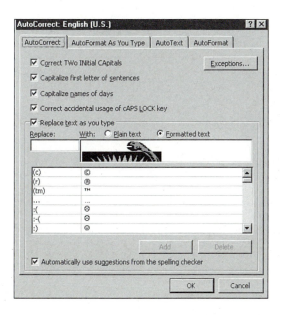

Figure 4.3
When you select an image and open AutoCorrect, part of the image appears in the With box.

Caution

Word doesn't limit the length of Formatted text you can place in an AutoCorrect entry, but it does limit Plain text (ASCII) entries to 255 characters and cuts off any text that extends beyond that.

Tip #41

Just as you can insert formatted text or images, you can also insert *fields* using AutoCorrect. For instance, you might want to use AutoCorrect to replace text with { INCLUDETEXT } fields that retrieve text from an external "source" file. When you change the text in that source file, you can update the document containing the fields, and the text in that document will be updated wherever it appears.

➜ For more information about working with fields, **see** Chapter 18 "Automating Your Document with Field Codes," **p. 555**.

USING AUTOCORRECT TO ADD DUMMY TEXT

Ever need to quickly add some generic or dummy text, just to get a feel for the formatting of a page? Word has a built-in AutoCorrect entry that'll do it for you. It enters paragraphs full of this classic sentence (carefully designed to use one of each letter in the alphabet): The quick brown fox jumps over the lazy dog.

To tell Word to insert a paragraph containing this sentence five times over, type =rand() and press Enter.

You can actually control how many times the sentence appears and how many paragraphs you get. Type =rand(p,s), where p equals the number of paragraphs and s equals the number of sentences. This works only when the Replace Text as You Type feature is turned on in the AutoCorrect tab.

AUTOCORRECTING INITIAL CAPS AND SENTENCE CAPITALIZATION

You might have noticed two more options in the AutoCorrect dialog box:

- **Correct TWo INitial CApitals.** If you place two capital letters at the beginning of a word, AutoCorrect makes the second letter lowercase.
- **Capitalize First Letter of Sentences.** If you start a sentence with a lowercase letter, AutoCorrect capitalizes it for you.

Most of the time, these features work as intended, fixing inadvertent mistakes. However, there are times you won't want Word to make these AutoCorrections. For example, say that you include an abbreviation within a sentence, and the abbreviation ends in a period, as follows:

Please contact Smith Corp. regarding their overdue invoices.

When AutoCorrect was first introduced in Word 6, it would see the period after "Corp.," see the space after it, and assume wrongly that the word "regarding" started a new sentence. Word 2000 (as well as Word 97 and 95) fixes this problem by enabling you to specify exceptions—words that AutoCorrect won't fix. In Word 2000, AutoCorrect contains a list of 115 common abbreviations. When Word sees one of these abbreviations, it doesn't assume that it has arrived at the end of a sentence, notwithstanding the period in the abbreviation.

If you use specialized abbreviations, such as those common in scientific or technical fields, you might want to add them to your Exceptions list. To do so, follow these steps:

1. Choose Tools, AutoCorrect.

2. Click Exceptions. The AutoCorrect Exceptions dialog box opens, as shown in Figure 4.4.

3. Click the First Letter tab.

4. Enter your new exception in the Don't Capitalize After text box.

5. Click Add.

6. Click OK.

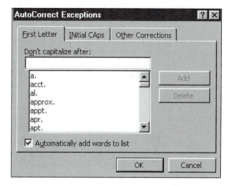

Figure 4.4

CREATING CAPITALIZATION EXCEPTIONS FOR PRODUCT NAMES, BRAND NAMES, AND ACRONYMS

As mentioned earlier, Word also automatically "fixes" words that start with two capital letters. No standard English words begin with two capital letters, so most of the time you'll want this. However, you may occasionally come across a product, brand name, or acronym that is capitalized oddly to attract attention. For example, the CompuServe online information service renamed itself "CSi." Word automatically corrects this to "Csi." You can create an exception for oddly capitalized words as follows:

1. Choose Tools, AutoCorrect.

2. Click Exceptions. The AutoCorrect Exceptions dialog box opens.

3. Click INitial CAps. The INitial CAps tab appears, as shown in Figure 4.5.

4. Enter your new exception in the Don't Correct text box.

5. Click Add.

6. Click OK.

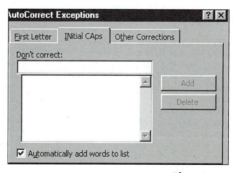

Figure 4.5

CREATING OTHER AUTOCORRECT EXCEPTIONS

Although many of the AutoCorrect exceptions you want to create are likely to fall into the First Letter and Initial Caps categories, what happens when you encounter an exception that doesn't? In Word 2000, for the first time, there's a solution—the Other Corrections tab. Follow these steps to create an exception that doesn't fall into the First Letter or Initial Caps categories:

1. Choose Tools, AutoCorrect.

2. Click Exceptions. The AutoCorrect Exceptions dialog box opens.

3. Click Other Corrections. The Other Corrections tab appears, as shown in Figure 4.6.

4. Enter your new exception in the Don't Correct text box.

5. Click Add.

6. Click OK.

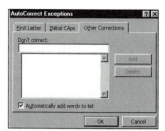

Figure 4.6

TELLING WORD TO CREATE EXCEPTIONS AUTOMATICALLY

Wouldn't it be nice if Word were smart enough not to make the same mistake twice? What if Word saw the fixes you made manually, and added them to its Exceptions list so you wouldn't be bothered again? It can, and it does.

If you check the Automatically Add Words to List check box in any of the three AutoCorrect Exceptions tabs, Word will watch as you work. If Word corrects an initial cap, first letter, or other word, and you immediately use the left-arrow key or the Backspace key to go back and type over the correction, Word adds your correction to the exception list.

> **Note**
>
> Word won't add a correction to the exception list unless you use the Backspace or left-arrow key to make the correction. Neither pressing shortcut keys nor using Undo will work.

> **Tip #42**
>
> Each tab of the AutoCorrect Exceptions dialog box has separate automatic exception controls. So, for example, you can tell Word to automatically add abbreviations to the list for First Letters, but not to the list of Initial Caps or Other Corrections.

BACKING UP AND RESTORING AUTOCORRECT ENTRIES

The longer you work with Word, the more entries you're likely to add in the AutoCorrect dialog box. If you get a new computer, can you move those entries with you? Or, can you share these entries with other users? Or, can you restore an AutoCorrect file that has somehow been damaged, preventing AutoCorrect (or Word itself) from functioning properly? Yes. Microsoft provides a special AutoCorrect utility to perform all these tasks.

The AutoCorrect utility is stored in the Macros9.dot template. This template does not install automatically as part of Word; it does not even install automatically the first time you need to use it. You must retrieve it from Microsoft's Office Web site, and copy it manually into your templates folder from the \Pfiles\Msoffice\Office\Macros folder on the Office 2000 CD-ROM.

Note

> If you are connected to the Web, choose <u>H</u>elp, Office on the <u>W</u>eb to access this macro.

 After you've done so, click the Open button to display the Open dialog box; choose Document Templates from the Files of <u>T</u>ype drop-down box; then browse to and open the Macros9.dot file. A Macros toolbar appears. Click Sample Macros and choose AutoCorrect Utility from the drop-down list of macros. The AutoCorrect Utility dialog box opens (see Figure 4.7).

Figure 4.7
From here, you can create a Word file containing your list of AutoCorrect entries, or transform such a list into a working AutoCorrect file.

To create a backup copy of your AutoCorrect file, click Backup. Word adds each AutoCorrect entry, showing its progress on the status bar. It then reformats the information into a three-column table, making the information easier to read and edit. This process may take a minute or two.

When Word finishes, it displays the Save As dialog box, suggesting "AutoCorrect Backup Document" as a filename. Click <u>S</u>ave to save the file in your My Documents folder.

Word AutoCorrect files are stored in special binary files with an ACL extension. To back up an ACL file, the AutoCorrect Utility translates it from ACL format into Word document format. To restore an ACL file, the AutoCorrect utility translates it back into the ACL format.

EDITING AN AUTOCORRECT BACKUP DOCUMENT

You can use Word to edit an AutoCorrect Backup Document to add or delete entries before restoring them to another computer. As shown in Figure 4.8, AutoCorrect Backup Documents consist of three-column tables.

PART

I

CH

4

Figure 4.8
An AutoCorrect Backup Document contains a three-column table that you can edit to add, change, or delete entries.

AutoCorrect Backup Document		
Name	Value	RTF
(c)	©	False
(r)	®	False
(tm)	™	False
...	...	False
abbout	about	False
abotu	about	False
abouta	about a	False
aboutit	about it	False
aboutthe	about the	False
abscence	absence	False
accesories	accessories	False
accidant	accident	False
accomodate	accommodate	False
accordingto	according to	False
accross	across	False
acheive	achieve	False
acheived	achieved	False

The first column, Name, includes the word or phrase you want to change. The second column, Value, indicates the word or phrase you want to use in its place. The third column, RTF, indicates whether the replacement text should be inserted as ASCII text or as formatted text. The default setting here is False. However, if you added text with formatting (as discussed in the "Using AutoCorrect to Insert Boilerplate Text" section), the RTF entry is True.

COPYING AUTOCORRECT ENTRIES TO AN AUTOCORRECT FILE

To copy an AutoCorrect Backup Document's entries into Word's AutoCorrect file, follow these steps:

1. Run the AutoCorrect utility (as described in "Backing Up and Restoring AutoCorrect Entries").

2. Click Restore.

3. Click Yes to confirm that you want to replace any current AutoCorrect entries with equivalent entries in the backup document. The Open dialog box opens.

4. Browse to and select the AutoCorrect Backup Document you want to use.

5. Click Open. Word begins adding AutoCorrect entries to the computer's ACL file. This may take a few minutes.

Communicating with Word: AutoCorrect Saves Time on Technical Writing

AutoCorrect is invaluable if you make extensive use of long words or complex phrases; for instance, if you use technical, scientific, or legal terms in your work. You can set up shortcuts for words, phrases, or even paragraphs you use often, and have AutoCorrect insert the lengthy text blocks automatically whenever you type the shortcut.

Simply type a few letters in the Replace text box of the AutoCorrect dialog box, and copy the lengthy word or phrase into the With text box. When choosing the few letters that will serve as your shortcut, make sure they are memorable, easy to type, and will not appear in your document except when you intend for AutoCorrect to replace them.

AUTOTEXT: THE COMPLETE BOILERPLATE RESOURCE

You've already seen how you can use AutoCorrect to enter large blocks of boilerplate text quickly. However, this isn't AutoCorrect's primary function. Another Word feature, *AutoText*, is designed specifically to help you manage and quickly insert boilerplate text. If you build a library of AutoText entries, you can dramatically reduce the amount of retyping you have to do. At the same time, you can help your colleagues build documents more quickly and more consistently. In other words, whether you're working on your own or in a corporate setting, AutoText offers enormous opportunities to improve productivity.

AUTOTEXT ENTRIES BUILT INTO WORD 2000

Word 2000 comes with dozens of built-in AutoText entries to help you streamline letters and other documents. The categories of entries and the text associated with each entry are listed in Table 4.2.

PART

I

CH

4

TABLE 4.2   WORD 2000'S BUILT-IN AUTOTEXT ENTRY TEXT

Category (Submenu)	Entry Text Options
Attention Line	Attention:; ATTN:
Closing	Best regards; Best wishes; Cordially; Love; Regards; Respectfully Yours; Respectfully; Sincerely yours; Sincerely; Take care; Thank you; Thanks; Yours truly
Header/Footer	–Page–; Author Page# Date; Created by; Created on; Confidential; Page # Date; Last printed; Last saved by; Filename; Filename and Path; Page X of Y
Mailing Instructions	CERTIFIED MAIL; CONFIDENTIAL; PERSONAL; REGISTERED MAIL; SPECIAL DELIVERY; VIA AIR-MAIL; VIA FACSIMILE; VIA OVERNIGHT MAIL
Reference Line	In reply to:; RE:; Reference
Salutation	Dear Mom and Dad; Dear Sir or Madam; Ladies and Gentlemen; To Whom It May Concern
Subject Line	Subject:

INSERTING AN EXISTING AUTOTEXT ENTRY

To use one of Word's entries—or any other entry you create—choose Insert, AutoText, and display the cascading menu containing the entry you want to use (see Figure 4.9). Click the entry, and Word inserts the corresponding entry text in your document.

Figure 4.9
Select an existing AutoText entry.

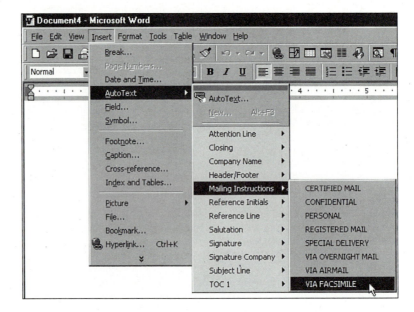

Tip #43

Some of Word's built-in AutoText entries insert not only text, but also fields that update themselves. For example, if you insert the Author, Page #, Date entry in your header or footer, Word enters three fields: the { AUTHOR } field, which reports the name of the author as it appears in your Properties dialog box; the { PAGE } field, which displays the current page number, and the { DATE } field that displays the current date. You can see sample field results for this AutoText entry in Figure 4.10.

Figure 4.10
You can get a footer containing Author, Page, and Date information by choosing it from the list of AutoText entries.

When you display a header or footer, the Header and Footer toolbar appears—including the Insert AutoText button, which lists all of Word's Header and Footer AutoText entries (see Figure 4.11), making them conveniently accessible.

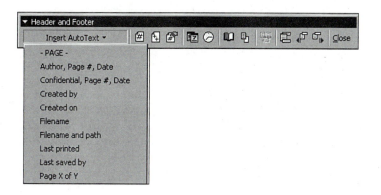

Figure 4.11
Choose an AutoText entry name for a header or footer.

Selecting AutoText entry names from menus and toolbars is especially convenient when you are inserting Word's built-in AutoText entries, because many of those entries are relatively long and easy to mistype. However, when you create your own entries, you'll typically use short, easy-to-remember names for your AutoText entries. If you remember the name of an AutoText entry (custom or built-in), you can use it in your document without working with menus. Just type the AutoText entry name and press F3. Word replaces the AutoText entry name you typed and inserts the longer text that is associated with the entry.

Caution

The AutoText entry must be separate from the text that precedes and follows it for Word to recognize it as an AutoText entry when you press F3. However, it can be within parentheses, or immediately before punctuation such as a period, colon, or semicolon.

WORKING WITH THE AUTOTEXT TOOLBAR

If you're planning to work with quite a few AutoText entries at the same time, you may want to display the AutoText toolbar (see Figure 4.12). This toolbar contains three buttons:

- The AutoText button, which displays the AutoText dialog box, where you can control all aspects of your collection of AutoText entries.

- A button that displays all your current AutoText entries, or those associated with the style you're currently using.

- A New button appears when you've selected text. Click it to display the Create AutoText entry you've already seen.

Currently available AutoText entries

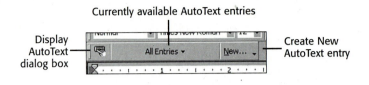

Figure 4.12
If you're working on many AutoText entries at the same time, display the AutoText toolbar.

Display AutoText dialog box

Create New AutoText entry

ENTERING AUTOTEXT ENTRIES EVEN FASTER WITH AUTOCOMPLETE

Imagine you have an AutoText entry, such as "dsclmr," that places your company's standard disclaimer clause in your document. As you've seen, if you want to use this entry, you can type dsclmr, press F3, and Word inserts the formatted text. But there's an even quicker way. As soon as you type the fourth letter in this (or any) AutoText entry, a *ScreenTip* appears showing all the text associated with the AutoText entry (or as much as will fit within the ScreenTip). You can see an example in Figure 4.13. If you are planning to use this AutoText entry, just press Enter and Word inserts *AutoCompletes* the entry at the current insertion point.

Figure 4.13
When you type the fourth letter of an AutoText entry, Word displays the first words of text associated with that entry as a ScreenTip.

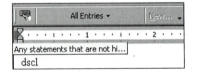

If you aren't planning to use the AutoText entry—for example, if you're typing another word that just happens to start the same way as an AutoText entry—just ignore the ScreenTip and keep typing.

Note

If you have two AutoText entries that start with the same four letters, Word doesn't display a ScreenTip until you've entered enough text for it to recognize which one you're most likely to want.

Tip #44

AutoComplete doesn't just work with AutoText entries; it also offers to complete months of the year, days of the week, and today's date. Be careful about using Word to AutoComplete today's date, however. If you're working past midnight, AutoComplete doesn't always notice that a new day has arrived.

Note

AutoText ScreenTips have a slight effect on your system's performance. If Word is running slowly, you might try disabling them. To do so, choose Insert, AutoText, AutoText; then clear the Show AutoComplete Tip for AutoText and Dates check box.

CREATING YOUR OWN AUTOTEXT ENTRY

Word's built-in AutoText entries are very handy, but you don't get the full benefits of AutoText until you start creating your own entries. There are several ways to create your entry. The quickest way is to select the text you want to transform into an AutoText entry, and press Alt+F3. You can also display this dialog box by choosing Insert, AutoText, New. Either way, the Create AutoText dialog box opens (see Figure 4.14).

Figure 4.14
One of the quickest ways to create an AutoText entry is to press Alt+F3 to display the Create AutoText dialog box.

Word automatically displays the first word or words in the text you've selected. Edit this text into a brief entry name you'll find easy to remember, and click OK. Now, the entry name appears in the AutoText cascaded dialog box with any other entries you may have added.

CONTROLLING WHICH FORMATTING IS INCLUDED IN AN AUTOTEXT ENTRY

If you want your AutoText entry text to include paragraph formatting, include in your selection the paragraph mark (¶) at the end of the paragraph containing that formatting.

AutoText entry text is stored with whatever character formatting you've applied with them. That saves you the trouble of duplicating complex character formats later. However, paragraph styles aren't saved unless you select a paragraph mark. When you do not select the paragraph mark, your AutoText entry text takes on the paragraph style of the surrounding text wherever you insert them.

UNDERSTANDING WHERE AUTOTEXT ENTRIES ARE STORED AND DISPLAYED

All Word's built-in AutoText entries are stored in the *Normal template*. New AutoText entries are stored in the *template* associated with the document in which you're working. In other words, if you are working on a document based on the Normal template, any AutoText entry you create manually is also stored in the Normal template.

Then, whenever you are working on a document based on the Normal template, you have access to all the AutoText entries you've stored in the Normal template, with one major exception. If your insertion point is currently within a block of text formatted in a custom *style*, and if that custom style has AutoText entries associated with it, Word displays only the entries associated with the custom style.

→ For more information about how Word displays AutoText entries based on specific styles, **see** "Adding New Categories of AutoText Entries," **p. 92**.

PART

I

CH

4

You can see this most easily when the AutoText toolbar is displayed. If you are currently working in text formatted in a custom style that has AutoText entries associated with it, that style's name appears in place of All Entries. When you click the button, you see only the entries associated with that style.

Tip #45	If you need access to an AutoText entry that isn't displayed, press Shift as you display the list of AutoText entries via either the AutoText toolbar or the Insert, AutoText cascaded menu. Or else click your insertion point in text formatted with any of Word's standard styles, such as Normal, Body Text, or any built-in *heading style (page 590)*.

SAVING AN AUTOTEXT ENTRY IN A DIFFERENT TEMPLATE

At times you might want to store AutoText entries in a template other than Normal. For example, your AutoText entries might be relevant only when you're creating a specialized kind of document, and you always use the same custom template to create that kind of document. Why clutter up the Normal template with AutoText entries you'll never use in the documents you create with Normal?

To create AutoText entries in another template, first create or open a document based on that template; then create the AutoText entry as you normally do.

CONTROLLING THE TEMPLATES IN WHICH AUTOTEXT ENTRIES ARE AVAILABLE

By default, Word makes available AutoText entries in all templates that are currently open. For example, if you are working in a file created by a template named SMITH.DOT, you have access to all AutoText entries stored in SMITH.DOT, as well as those in NORMAL.DOT—a global template that is always open. However, you might not want to see the more general AutoText entries you may have associated with NORMAL.DOT if you're using a customized template.

You can choose any open template and tell Word to display only the AutoText entries associated with that template. To do so, choose Insert, AutoText, AutoText. The AutoText tab of the AutoCorrect dialog box opens (see Figure 4.15). In the Look In drop-down list box, choose the template containing the entries you want to see, and click OK.

When you return to your editing window, you see that AutoText entries associated with other templates are no longer available from the AutoText menu. If you type them in your document and press F3 or use AutoComplete, nothing happens.

ADDING NEW CATEGORIES OF AUTOTEXT ENTRIES

You might want to add new categories of AutoText entries. That way, when you click Insert, AutoText, your new categories appear along with Word's built-in submenus. For example, imagine you work for the sales department of Acme Corporation; you might want to add a submenu called Acme Proposals that contains AutoText entries you can include in your sales proposals.

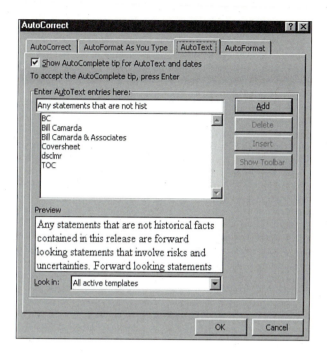

Figure 4.15
With the AutoText tab of the AutoCorrect dialog box, you can control which template's AutoText entries are active.

Word organizes AutoText entries in submenus, based on the styles with which they are associated. When you want to create a new submenu, you can use this to your advantage.

First, create a new style with the name you want to appear in your custom submenu. To do so, select a paragraph, click the drop-down style box, type the new name, and press Enter. Don't worry much about how your style is formatted. When you select an AutoText entry, it uses the surrounding formatting in your document, not the formatting associated with the style you've just created.

Next, enter the first block of text for which you want to create an AutoText entry and format the text using the style you just created.

Finally, create the AutoText entry using whatever method you prefer. Repeat the process for any other text you want to appear in the same submenu; make sure to format the text with your custom style before you create the AutoText entry.

After you do this, your new AutoText entries appear in their own submenu whenever you're working in the same template where you created them.

CREATIVE WAYS TO USE AUTOTEXT

You can use AutoText to store virtually anything you can place in a document, not just text. Here are some types of entries that you might want to store as AutoText:

- Your signature and the signature of anyone else for whom you prepare documents
- Your corporate logo

PART
I
CH
4

- Photos and drawings
- Complex *table formats*
- Complex field codes, such as customized *cross-references*

Tip #46

If you are creating a Web page, you can also store AutoText entries that place custom design elements or pieces of *HTML code (page 384)* into your document, such as customized bullets and borders.

PRINTING LISTS OF AUTOTEXT ENTRIES

The more you work with AutoText entries, the more you'll need to keep track of them. You've already seen how you can review your entire list of AutoText entries in the AutoText dialog box, and how you can move entries among templates with the Organizer. You might also want to print a list of entries associated with a specific template. To print the list of entries, first create or open a new document based on the template containing the entries you want to print. Choose File, Print. In the Print What drop-down box, choose AutoText Entries, and click OK.

CHANGING AN EXISTING AUTOTEXT ENTRY

You'll occasionally want to change an AutoText entry. To change an entry, follow these steps:

1. Insert the AutoText entry in your document.
2. Edit the AutoText entry to reflect your changes.
3. Select the entire AutoText entry.
4. Choose Insert, AutoText, AutoText to display the AutoText dialog box.

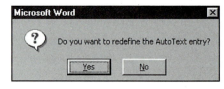

Figure 4.16

5. Select the name of the AutoText entry you want to change.
6. Click Add. Word displays a dialog box asking whether you want to redefine your AutoText entry (see Figure 4.16).
7. Click Yes.

Changing AutoText entries doesn't change any text you've previously inserted in a document using those entries. Unless, that is, you use the procedure discussed in the following section.

INSERTING AUTOTEXT ENTRIES THAT UPDATE THEMSELVES

After you enter text in your document using an AutoText entry, that text looks and behaves no differently than if you had typed it manually. But what if you could enter an AutoText entry that updates itself whenever the AutoText entry is updated? Imagine that your corporate lawyers change the boilerplate disclaimer language you've been using. Wouldn't it be great if your entire workgroup could have access to the new language immediately? And wouldn't it be even better if you could automatically update your existing documents to reflect the change?

You can. Rather than insert your AutoText entry using the methods discussed earlier, use an { AUTOTEXT } field. Follow these steps:

1. Choose Insert, Field. The Field dialog box opens.
2. Choose AutoText from the Field Names list.
3. Click Options. Word displays a list of all the AutoText entries currently available to you.
4. Select the entry you want to insert.
5. Click Add to Field.
6. Click OK.

If you display field results, your document looks exactly as if you had inserted the AutoText entry the normal way. If, however, you change the text (or other document elements) associated with this AutoText entry, Word can update the field the same way it updates any other fields.

PART

I

CH

4

Tip #47

Remember, you can update all the fields in your document by pressing Ctrl+A and then F9.

→ For more information about working with fields, **see** Chapter 18, "Automating Your Document with Field Codes," **p. 555**.

INSERTING AUTOTEXT OPTIONS WITHIN YOUR DOCUMENT

If you're setting up a document or template for others to work on, you can streamline their work by making it easy for them to choose the right AutoText entries wherever they're appropriate. You do this by inserting an { AUTOTEXTLIST } field at those places in your document where a choice needs to be made.

You can see { AUTOTEXTLIST } fields at work in Word's letter templates, which embed multiple options for Salutations and Closings directly in the documents they create. In Figure 4.17, if you right-click the word Sincerely, Word displays a list containing all Word's built-in choices for letter closings. As you can see in Figure 4.18, if you click the word once, a ScreenTip appears explaining how the { AUTOTEXTLIST } field works.

Figure 4.17
If you right-click the letter closing in a built-in Word letter template, you can choose from all Word's AutoText entries for letter closings.

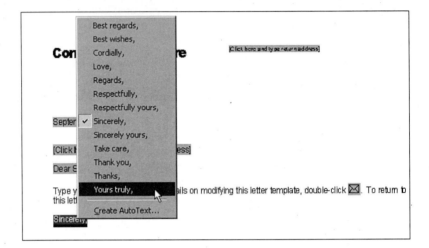

Figure 4.18
You can insert a ScreenTip that includes directions for anyone who single-clicks the { AUTOTEXTLIST } field you entered.

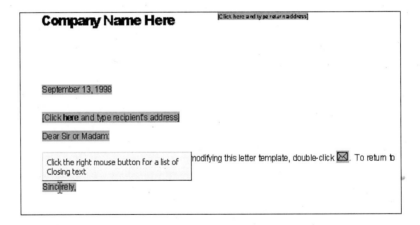

The syntax for an { AUTOTEXTLIST } field is as follows:

```
{ AUTOTEXTLIST "<LiteralText>" \s ["<StyleName>"] \t ["<TipText>"]]
```

"LiteralText" is the text you want to appear in the document before the user right-clicks it. It serves as the document's default text.

Tip #48

> For "LiteralText," use the text that's most likely to be the right choice. That way, users can often ignore the field.

The \s switch and "StyleName" tell Word to display all the AutoText entries associated with a specific style. You don't have to specify the same style in which the field result is formatted. You can choose any style currently available to the document.

If you like, you can ignore the \s switch and format the text using the style containing the AutoText entries you want to show.

The \t switch and "TipText" tell Word what information to display in the ScreenTip when a user hovers his or her mouse pointer over the field. If you don't include a \t switch, Word displays instructions similar to those you saw in Figure 4.17.

Tip #49

> Consider the many ways you could use { AUTOTEXTLIST }:
>
> - To choose different text in a proposal based on whether the project schedule is normal or rushed
> - To select one of several preformatted tables
> - To insert a signature from any one of several people
> - To choose the contents of a letter from a set of preestablished AutoText entries

→ For more information about working with fields, **see** Chapter 18 "Automating Your Document with Field Codes," **p. 555**.

AUTOFORMATTING: THE FASTEST WAY TO FORMAT

If you haven't bothered to format your document at all, or if you received it in ASCII (text-only) format via email, Word's AutoFormatting feature may be able to handle the formatting for you. Among the tasks AutoFormat can perform are

- Creating headings and lists, including bulleted lists
- Applying styles to many document elements
- Replacing ASCII text with custom symbols, including curly "smart quotes," fractions, ordinal numbers such as 1st and 2nd, em and en dashes
- Replacing Internet and network addresses with *hyperlinks* to the same addresses

To use AutoFormatting, choose <u>A</u>utoFormat from the F<u>o</u>rmat menu. The AutoFormat dialog box opens (see Figure 4.19).

Figure 4.19
You can tell
AutoFormat to refor-
mat anything it
pleases, or you can
review the results of
AutoFormat's handi-
work, one change at a
time.

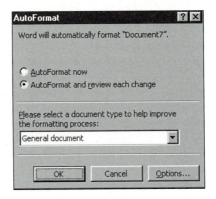

To give it a try, click OK, and Word reformats the entire document for you. Table 4.3 shows many of the changes Word can make.

TABLE 4.3 WHAT AUTOFORMAT CHANGES	
Whenever You Type the Following	**Here's How Word Changes It**
The following sequence: A number; followed by a period, hyphen, closing parenthesis, or > sign; followed by a space or tab; followed by text.	Word begins a numbered list.
The following sequence: An asterisk, one or two hyphens, or any of the following: >, -> —> ; followed by a space or tab; followed by text.	Word begins a bulleted list.
A symbol or inline picture, at least two spaces, followed by text or picture.	Word begins a bulleted list, using the symbol as the bullet.
At least three of the following characters in a row above a paragraph: - _ * ~ # .	Word places a border line above the paragraph. (AutoFormat As You Type only.)
Straight quotation marks: " or '.	Word replaces these with curly quotation marks (SmartQuotes).
The following fractions: 1/4, 1/2, or 3/4.	Word replaces these with fraction symbols: $\frac{1}{4}$, $\frac{1}{2}$, $\frac{3}{4}$.
Ordinal numbers: 1st, 2nd, 3rd, 4th.	Word replaces these with 1st, 2nd, 3rd, 4th.
Hyphens between text (for example, 28 - 56).	Word eliminates space surrounding hyphens; changes hyphen to en dash: 28–56.
Double hyphens surrounded by text.	Word changes hyphens to em dash (—).
Asterisk (*) followed by text and another asterisk.	Word removes asterisks; boldfaces remaining text (or uses other character formatting in Strong character style).

Whenever You Type the Following	Here's How Word Changes It
Underline (_) followed by text and another underline.	Word removes underlines; italicizes remaining text (or uses other character formatting in Emphasis character style).
Web address; for example, www.yahoo.com.	Word formats Web address as a hyperlink.
Plus sign (+) followed by hyphens, followed by another plus sign.	Word inserts a table, with one column per plus sign.
Formatted list item, followed by one of the following: . : - — ? ! followed by a space or tab; text.	Word applies the same formatting to the lead-in text in the next paragraph. In other words, Word assumes you are continuing a customized list. (AutoFormat As You Type only.)

If your document is a letter (or email), telling Word that helps it do a better job of AutoFormatting. In the AutoFormat dialog box, choose Letter or Email rather than General document.

Tip #50	If you choose Email, Word will (among other things) remove extra paragraph marks that often appear at the end of every line in email messages.

Tip #51	Sometimes it takes a couple of tries to get the best results from AutoFormat. Try running AutoFormat simply to get an idea of what AutoFormat does to your document. You may notice problems the first time around. Click Undo, and then (as is discussed in the next section) adjust AutoFormat options so Word doesn't make changes you don't like. Then run AutoFormat again.

If you want, you can AutoFormat only part of a document. To do so, select it before you choose Format, AutoFormat. Don't forget that tables have a separate set of AutoFormatting controls (choose Table, Table AutoFormat). The AutoFormat command discussed in this chapter doesn't touch the way your tables are formatted.

→ For more information about AutoFormatting tables, **see** "AutoFormatting a Table," **p. 133**.

CONTROLLING THE CHANGES AUTOFORMAT MAKES

You have a good deal of control over the changes AutoFormat makes. With the AutoFormat dialog box open, click Options. The AutoFormat tab of the AutoCorrect dialog box appears (see Figure 4.20). You can now clear any check boxes corresponding to document elements you want AutoFormat to leave alone.

Figure 4.20
In the AutoFormat tab, you can control the formatting changes that Word makes when you run AutoFormat.

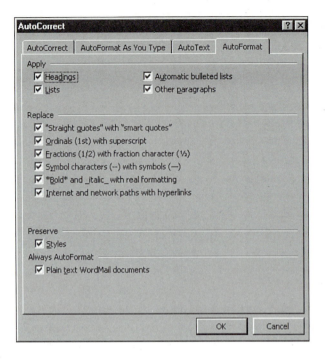

 If Word makes formatting changes you don't want, see "What to Do If Word Makes Formatting Changes You Don't Want," in "Troubleshooting" at the end of this chapter.

Here's a closer look at the document elements AutoFormat can change, along with some tips for making the most of AutoFormat:

- **Headings.** One of the best reasons to use AutoFormatting is to save time in transforming a text-only file into one that can benefit from Word's outlining. Before you try to add heading styles manually, consider clearing every box except Headings, and running AutoFormat to see how many headings it can format properly.

- **Lists.** With Lists checked, Word automatically starts applying Word's built-in list styles (List, List 2, List 3, and so on) to any list of consecutive lines separated by paragraph marks.

- **Automatic *Bulleted Lists*.** With this check box checked, Word automatically inserts bullets in place of the characters that are commonly used to substitute for bullets, such as dashes and asterisks.

- **Other Paragraphs.** By default, AutoFormat transforms all text formatted as Normal into other formats such as Body Text. In some cases, Word can recognize from the contents of text what the text is likely to be: For instance, it recognizes address lines and reformats them with the Inside Address style. However, for convenience and simplicity, you might prefer to keep all text other than headings formatted as Normal. Clear this check box if you do not want Word to change the styles associated with text paragraphs.

- **"Straight Quotes" with "Smart Quotes".** With this box checked, Word replaces straight up-and-down quotation marks and apostrophes with curly ones that look better. If you're exporting your document for use by another program, especially if you're crossing platforms (say, to the Macintosh or a UNIX workstation), make sure the other program can display SmartQuotes properly before using them.

Tip #52

If you're a writer, you might have one client that requires SmartQuotes and another that prohibits them. Sometimes you'll realize partway through a document that Word has been adding undesired SmartQuotes. You already know you can turn off SmartQuotes through the AutoFormat As You Type tab of the AutoCorrect dialog box, but what about the ones that are already in your document? Use Find and Replace to get rid of them.

First, choose Edit, Replace. Then, place a straight quote mark (") in the Find box and another straight quote mark (") in the Replace box. Choose Replace All. Word searches for both curly and straight quotation marks, and replaces them all with straight quotation marks.

- **Ordinals (1st) with Superscript.** Word recognizes typed ordinals (1st, 2nd, 3rd, and so on), and can automatically replace them with the more attractive 1st, 2nd, 3rd, and so on. This works with any number, but does not work with spelled out numbers such as "twenty-eighth."

- **Fractions (1/2) with Fraction Character ($^1/_2$).** By default, Word replaces 1/2, 1/4, and 3/4 with the better-looking symbol characters. Most fonts don't have symbol characters for other fractions, such as 1/8 or 3/16. If your document uses fractions that can't be reformatted, you may want to clear this check box to keep everything consistent.

- **Symbol characters (--) with Symbols (—).** When Word recognizes that you've typed characters that are typically used in place of symbols, such as two consecutive hyphens in place of an em dash (—), it can substitute the proper character automatically. As with SmartQuotes, if you're planning to export your Word document, make sure the program to which you're exporting it can handle the symbols correctly.

- ***Bold* and _Underline_ with Real Formatting.** Bold works just the way it's supposed to work. If you type an asterisk followed by text and another asterisk, Word eliminates the asterisks and formats the text as boldface. You might find the underline feature confusing; it formats text in italic, not as underline. "Pre-computer" style manuals instructed users to simulate italic on a typewriter by using underlining, but this can be confusing if you first learned how to create documents using PCs that created italic properly as a matter of course.

Note

In fact, there's something even more interesting going on here. Word is actually using the built-in character styles Strong and Emphasis, which are included in the HTML standards for Web documents. By default, Strong corresponds to boldface and Emphasis corresponds to italic type. If you really want underlining, you can change the Emphasis character style to underlining and this AutoFormat option gladly gives it to you.

PART
I

CH
4

- **Internet and Network Paths with Hyperlinks.** This is a welcome feature if you are creating an electronic document; it saves you the trouble of manually adding hyperlinks. It is not so welcome if you are creating a printed document, or if you are providing a disk file for use in another program, such as a desktop publishing program. Word replaces standard text with hyperlink fields which look different (they're blue and underlined) and act differently (they're *field codes*, which can't be understood by many programs to which you may be exporting your Word file). If this sounds like trouble, clear this check box.

- **Preserve Styles.** By default, if AutoFormat finds that you've formatted a paragraph with any style other than Normal, it leaves that paragraph alone. If you clear this check box, Word uses its judgment and reformats any paragraph it thinks necessary.

- **Plain Text *WordMail* Documents.** If you are on a network, and if you receive email, and if you have selected Word as your email editor through a Microsoft email client such as Outlook, checking this box tells Word to AutoFormat email documents that arrive as plain ASCII text. Checking this box doesn't affect any other text-only document, including those you retrieve as ASCII files from other email systems and display in Word via the File, Open dialog box.

AUTOFORMATTING INTERACTIVELY

You've already learned that you can run AutoFormat, undo the results if you don't like them, and then control the types of AutoFormatting Word applies through the AutoFormat tab of the AutoCorrect dialog box. You can also run AutoFormatting interactively and make decisions one at a time.

This gives you finer control over the AutoFormatting changes Word makes. However, because Word stops everywhere it changes an apostrophe into a SmartQuote or replaces spaces with tabs, this can be a very slow process. (There's no way to accept all the formatting changes of a certain type.) One approach is to first run AutoFormat automatically, selecting only the changes you're sure you would accept. Then, you can run AutoFormat again, this time interactively, using different settings that correspond to changes you'd like to accept or reject individually.

To AutoFormat interactively: Choose Format, AutoFormat. Then choose AutoFormat and Review Each Change and click OK.

Word AutoFormats the document and displays the AutoFormat dialog box (see Figure 4.21), from where you can review each change Word has made, in order to accept or reject that change.

Figure 4.21
From here, you can accept or reject all changes, review them one at a time, or display the Style Gallery.

The AutoFormat dialog box stays open as you move through the document. So before you start reviewing changes in detail, you might want to use the scrollbar and other Word navigation tools to get a rough idea about how close Word has come. If the document looks right on target, click Accept All. If Word's AutoFormatting is far from what you had in mind, click Reject All.

If Word landed somewhere in between, click Review Changes. The Review AutoFormat Changes dialog box opens (see Figure 4.22), describing the first change Word has made to your document. While this dialog box is open, Word also displays the text changes it made throughout your document, with revision marks. Insertions are marked in blue; deletions in red. If you prefer to see the document as it would look if all the changes were accepted, click Hide Marks. If you then want to take a closer look at a specific change, click Show Marks.

Figure 4.22
You can use this dialog box to move through your document to approve or reject individual changes.

To move toward the beginning of the document; click ← Find. To move toward the end, click → Find. Word selects the first AutoFormatting change it made. When you select a change, Word tells you what it changed—for example, it might say "Adjusted alignment with a tab."

USING STYLE GALLERY TO REFORMAT AUTOFORMATTED TEXT

The AutoFormat dialog box (refer to Figure 4.21) that appears after AutoFormat runs also gives you access to the Style Gallery. Using the Style Gallery, you can quickly reformat your styles to match the styles in a different template. Click Style Gallery to view it. Then, in the Template scroll box, choose a template containing formats you would like to view. If you prefer the formats associated with the template, click OK.

As is always the case when you use Style Gallery (see Figure 4.23), Word doesn't actually change the template associated with the document with which you're working. Rather, it changes the formatting associated with the styles in your current document to make the formatting look like the formatting in the template you chose.

PART

I

CH

4

Figure 4.23
You can quickly change the look of your AutoFormatted document through Style Gallery.

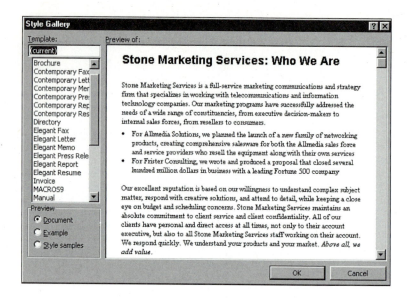

→ For more information on working with the Style Gallery, **see** "Previewing New Templates with Style Gallery," **p. 17**.

Because all Word's built-in templates are based on Times New Roman and Arial, most of Word's built-in templates don't radically change the appearance of your document. However, if you've created custom templates that use Word's built-in style names, Style Gallery enables you to apply those styles quickly to an AutoFormatted document.

USING AUTOFORMAT AS YOU TYPE

Word can also AutoFormat as you type, helping make sure your document is formatted properly as you work. In many (but not all) cases, the document elements Word reformats on-the-fly are similar to those you've already covered. In other cases, they are different. For example, by default, Word doesn't convert text that it identifies as headings into Heading styles while you work. Most people find that too distracting. On the other hand, you can ask Word to change headings if you like.

To control Word's on-the-fly AutoFormatting, choose Format, AutoFormat. Then choose Options. The AutoCorrect dialog box appears. Choose the AutoFormat As You Type tab (see Figure 4.24). Make any changes you want to these options, then click OK twice. (For explanations of the options here see the earlier discussion in "Controlling the Changes AutoFormat Makes.")

The following two differences are worth pointing out:

- **Borders**. Unlike regular AutoFormat, AutoFormat As You Type can transform rows of hyphens or underlines into true bordering.

- **Tables**. AutoFormat As You Type transforms a row of hyphens and plus signs into a table row, with one column for each plus sign.

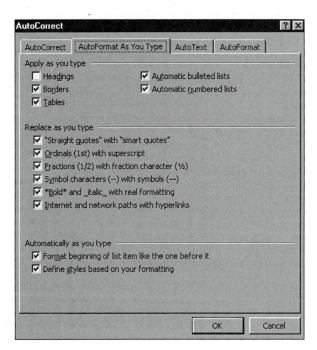

Figure 4.24
The AutoFormat As You Type tab enables you to control formatting changes Word makes while you work.

PART

I

CH

4

AUTOMATING FORMATTING FOR THE BEGINNING OF LIST ITEMS

When you are creating a list, you may occasionally format the first word or phrase in the list differently than you format the remaining text in each list paragraph. You can see an example of this in Figure 4.25. Word can recognize this specialized formatting and apply it to the new list items it creates each time you press Enter at the end of a list paragraph.

To activate this feature, check the Format Beginning of List Item Like the One Before It check box in the AutoFormat As You Type tab.

Caution

If you're creating a numbered or bulleted list, this feature doesn't deliver the results you want unless you also check the Automatic Bulleted Lists and/or Automatic Numbered Lists check boxes.

Figure 4.25
After you create specialized formatting to begin a list, Word can use that formatting in list items that immediately follow.

Word recognizes formatting you've applied to the first number in your list…

And also sees that you want the first phrase after the number to be italicized…

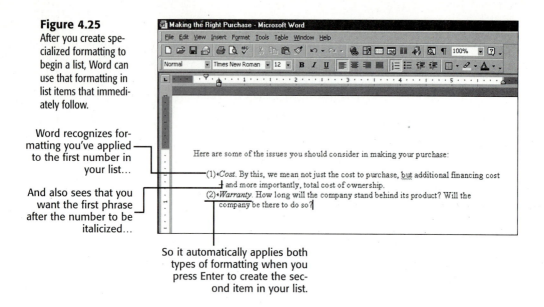

So it automatically applies both types of formatting when you press Enter to create the second item in your list.

USING AUTOFORMAT AS YOU TYPE TO GENERATE STYLES AUTOMATICALLY

If you can'tbe bothered with creating styles through the Style box, you can ask Word to watch you work and create the styles based on the manual formatting you apply. To turn this feature on, display the AutoFormat As You Type tab, check the Define Styles Based on Your Formatting check box, and click OK. Make sure the document elements you want to AutoFormat, such as Headings, are also selected. Then click Close.

After you've turned on automated style definition, you can see it at work. Open a new document; then type a line of text without placing a period at the end of it. Word interprets the fact that you haven't added a period as a cue that you're creating a heading. The line of text must also be at least 20% shorter than your current maximum line length, based on the type size and margins you're using. Format the entire paragraph, using any character or paragraph formatting you want; then press Enter. Now, if you click your insertion point back in the paragraph where you typed your heading, the Style drop-down list box displays the Heading 1 style. Any future paragraphs you format as Heading 1 will use the formatting you just created.

WORKING WITH AUTOSUMMARIZE

Who would have ever thought a computer could summarize your documents for you? Word can. *AutoSummarize* reviews the entire document, then scores each sentence based on a variety of factors, such as whether a sentence contains *keywords*—the words that are used most often throughout the document. The sentences that get the highest score are included in your summary.

Because Word can't understand the subtleties of your document, the results of running AutoSummarize are mixed—from good to terrible. In general, the more tightly structured your document is, the better chance you have of getting useful results. You also generally have better luck with documents that cover a few key topics in-depth, as opposed to documents that include just a paragraph or two on many disparate topics.

In general, AutoSummarize does a fair-to-good job on the following types of document:

■ Reports
■ Articles
■ Scientific papers
■ Theses

AutoSummarize does a poor job on the following document types:

■ Fiction
■ Most typical correspondence
■ How-to instructions (such as this book)

Of course, some documents, such as contracts, are just too important to rely on AutoSummarize; there's no alternative to reading every word.

On the other hand, there's no law that restricts you to summarize only those documents you create. Use AutoSummarize as a tool to deal with all kinds of information overload. It's like hiring your computer to skim for you. Run AutoSummarize on any long, well-structured document that can be opened and edited in Word—such as Web pages formatted in HTML—and you can quickly see whether the document is worth reading in its entirety.

PART
I

CH
4

Tip #53

AutoSummarize works a little bit better if you've installed the Find All Word Forms dictionary. By default, Find All Word Forms installs on first use, but only from the Find or Replace dialog box—in other words, if you run AutoSummarize and Find All Word Forms is not already installed, you will not be prompted to install it.

If you choose to install it as part of a maintenance install, you will find the feature in the Proofing Tools section of the Office Tools options in the Windows installer.

If you're creating an executive summary or abstract for a longer document, AutoSummarize rarely delivers perfection, but it often gives you a significant head start. Using the content AutoSummarize creates, you can fill in holes, polish and tighten the text, and make sure your summary reads smoothly—all in significantly less time than it would have taken you to create it from scratch.

To AutoSummarize your document, choose Tools, AutoSummarize. Word immediately builds a summary of your document, and stores it in memory pending your instructions. The AutoSummarize dialog box then opens (see Figure 4.26).

Figure 4.26
In the AutoSummarize dialog box, you specify where to place your summary, and how detailed you want it to be.

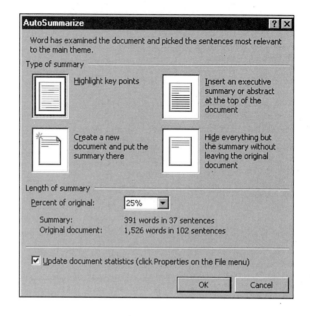

You now have the following four choices:

- **Highlight Key Points.** Without changing the contents of your document or creating a new document, Word applies yellow highlighting to the sentences it deems most important, as shown in Figure 4.27. The AutoSummarize toolbar appears in your document. Other, un-highlighted paragraphs appear in gray. You can drag the Percent of Original scrollbar to highlight more or less of the document; as you drag it, sentences are highlighted or highlighting is removed.

Figure 4.27
Using AutoSummarize to highlight the most important sentences in your document.

Highlight/Show Only Summary

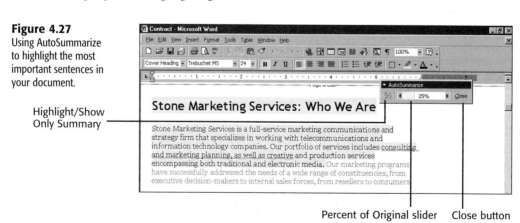

Percent of Original slider   Close button

Tip #54

Word highlights AutoSummarized text in yellow, so if you used yellow highlighting else-where in the document, you won't be able to tell the difference. Consider using a different highlight color in documents you plan to AutoSummarize using the Show Highlights Only feature.

- **Create a New Document and Put the Summary There.** Word creates a new docu-ment and places the summary there. This document has no link to the original docu-ment, so after the text has been inserted, there's no way to adjust it except for running AutoSummarize again. This option makes sense if you need to provide an executive summary or abstract, but you don't want to change the page numbering or contents of your original document.

- **Insert an Executive Summary or Abstract at the Top of the Document.** This copies the AutoSummarized text to the beginning of your document, where it can be edited and saved along with any other document contents. After you copy the text, you can't adjust the size or contents of the summary except through conventional editing techniques.

Tip #55

If you choose either of the preceding two options, consider increasing the percentage of sentences Word inserts in your summary, because it is easier to delete sentences from your summary later than to add more. You can change this value with the Percent of Original slider in the AutoSummarize dialog box.

- **Hide Everything But the Summary Without Leaving the Original Document.** This option makes no changes to the text in your current document; rather, it tem-porarily hides all the paragraphs that weren't selected to be part of the summary. In other words, your document looks as if it contains only the summary. If you print your document with only the summary showing, only the summary prints. However, when you click Close on the AutoSummarize toolbar, all the hidden text reappears.

You can also control what percentage of your document appears in the summary by enter-ing a value in the Percent of Original drop-down list box. You can enter any percentage. Or, using the options in the drop-down list box, you can choose a specific number of sen-tences or words. If you leave Word's default setting alone, Word creates a summary con-taining 25% of the original document. If you're creating an executive summary of a very long document, you may want to shrink it to 10–15%, or place a word limit, such as 500 words, to keep things manageable.

If you choose either Highlight Key Points or Hide Everything But the Summary Without Leaving the Original Document, you can toggle between these options using the Highlight/Show Only Summary button on the AutoSummarize toolbar. In other words, if you've chosen to hide the parts of your document not included in the summary, you can view them at any time by clicking the Highlight/Show Only Summary button.

If Word is not summarizing your document as you expect, see "What to Do If Word Doesn't Summarize Your Document," in "Troubleshooting" at the end of this chapter.

 If text in an AutoSummarized document seems to disappear, see "What to Do If Text Disappears from an AutoSummarized Document," in the "Troubleshooting" section of this chapter.

USING AUTOSUMMARIZE TO UPDATE FILE PROPERTIES

As you will learn in Chapter 38, "Sharing Files and Managing Word," you can use the Properties dialog box to track information about your document, making it easier to track and search for documents later. As you've seen, within the information that AutoSummarize generates about your document is a list of keywords. Of course, it also includes the summary itself. Because this information is already available, AutoSummarize offers to place it in your Properties dialog box.

When the Update Document Statistics check box is checked, as it is by default, Word inserts the top five keywords it finds in the Keywords text box in the Summary tab of the Properties dialog box. It also inserts the first few paragraphs of the summary itself in the Comments text box, also in the same tab.

Caution

When would you want to clear Update Document Statistics?

If you are already using Keywords or Document Contents information for another purpose, you don't want Word overwriting the information stored there. For example, you might have already specified keywords and used the { KEYWORDS } field to display those keywords in a cover sheet to your document. Unless you clear this check box, when Word displays your summary, it will also replace your keywords with the ones it thinks are most important.

TROUBLESHOOTING

WHAT TO DO IF WORD MAKES FORMATTING CHANGES YOU DON'T WANT

There are two places to control AutoFormatting, and it's very easy to get them confused. The settings in the AutoFormat tab are applied only when you run AutoFormat from the AutoFormat dialog box. The settings in the AutoFormat As You Type tab apply when you are editing a document—except they do not apply when you run AutoFormat from the AutoFormat dialog box.

The settings in each tab are similar but not identical. Changes you make to the settings in one tab are not automatically reflected in the other. As a result, it's all too easy to clear a check box in the AutoFormat settings tab and wonder why Word is still making AutoFormat changes automatically as you type—or vice versa. Make sure you've made your changes in AutoFormat As You Type. Also:

- If you tell Word not to replace symbol characters with symbols, and Word keeps inserting symbols, delete the symbol entries in the AutoCorrect tab (accessible through Tools, AutoCorrect).

- If Word is updating a style globally whenever you change it manually in one location, choose Format, Style, select the style, click Modify, and clear the Automatically Update check box.

- If you told Word you don't want it to automatically format headings as you type, and it keeps doing so, clear the Define Styles Based on Your Formatting check box in the AutoFormat As You Type tab of the AutoCorrect dialog box.

WHAT TO DO IF WORD DOESN'T SUMMARIZE YOUR DOCUMENT

AutoSummarize ignores the following: text formatted in a language other than English (assuming your user interface is set to English); text formatted as "no proofing," and text that appears inside text boxes, frames, and tables. In short documents, AutoSummarize may not display any sentences at all, unless you increase the Percent of Original setting in the AutoSummarize dialog box.

Word can prepare summaries of documents written in Chinese, French, German, Italian, Japanese, Korean, Brazilian Portuguese, Spanish, or Swedish, assuming the appropriate language files are installed. If a document contains text prepared in more than one language, AutoSummarize uses the language used most often in the document.

WHAT TO DO IF TEXT DISAPPEARS FROM AN AUTOSUMMARIZED DOCUMENT

If you run AutoSummarize using the Hide Everything But the Summary option and then save the file while only the summary is visible, Word applies hidden text formatting to all the text not included in the summary. Then, if you reopen the document, you won't see most of your text because it's now formatted as hidden text.

To see the missing text, choose Tools, Options, View, and check the Hidden Text check box. To eliminate the hidden text formatting that has made part of your document invisible, press Ctrl+A to select the entire document; choose Format, Font; click the Font tab; and clear the Hidden check box.

PART

I

CH

4

CHAPTER **5**

TABLES: ORGANIZING YOUR PAGES

In this chapter

TABLES: WORD'S ALL-PURPOSE SOLUTION FOR STRUCTURING INFORMATION

In Word, *tables* are collections of horizontal rows and vertical columns organized into individual cells, in which you can place text, numbers, graphics, *fields*, or other elements. Traditionally, tables were used primarily to display numbers, but you can use Word tables for any task that requires information to be displayed in a structured fashion. Use tables to

- Help build newsletters, brochures and other "desktop published" pieces where elements must be placed in specific locations on a page and kept there (see Chapter 14, "Word Desktop Publishing")

- Structure and organize Web pages (see Chapter 39, "Using Word to Develop Web Content")

- Write certain scripts that require audio/video directions to appear in one column with spoken narration in a second column (though this format is less common than it once was)

- Build forms that can be filled out electronically or on paper (see Chapter 17, "Creating Forms")

- Build databases that can be used for mail merging (see Chapter 6, "Using Mail Merge Effectively")

When you want a complex table to perform a complex task, Word 2000 provides more power and flexibility than any previous version. And when all you want is an old-fashioned row-and-column table for text or numbers, Word gets the job done quickly and simply.

WORD'S MULTIPLE APPROACHES TO CREATING A TABLE

Depending on the kind of table you want, and how you prefer to work, Word offers several approaches to drawing a table:

- If you need to create a simple table and you know how many rows and columns you need, but you don't need to control anything else, you can use the Insert Table button on the Standard toolbar.

- If you want to control the number of rows and columns, but you also want to control column width at the same time, choose T̲able, I̲nsert, T̲able to work from the Insert Table dialog box.

- If you prefer to draw your tables freehand, or if you need tables with varying row and column sizes, click the Tables and Borders button on the Standard toolbar, and use the tools on the Tables and Borders toolbar.

- If you already have information in tabular form, or you've imported information in a standard format such as "comma-delimited," use Word's Convert Text to Table feature, covered in the "Converting Text to Tables" section of this chapter.

- If you learned to create "fake tables" on a typewriter, using hyphens and plus signs, do the same thing in Word; when you press Enter at the end of the first line, Word transforms your typing into a real table.

The following sections cover each of these methods in more detail.

Communicating with Word: Planning Your Tables

Know how your table will be used before you format it. If your document will be published in a journal, magazine, or even a company brochure, find out what the publisher's needs are. Find out if the table will be a graphic element placed in the text before printing, or if it will be laid out as a table within the text. Many scientific journals ask that you include your tables on separate pages at the end of your manuscript one table per page.

Unfortunately, in certain cases, your publisher may not accept Word tables at all. In this case, use Word's Table, Convert, Table to Text feature to replace table cells with tabs or other document elements that the publisher can use. For more information, see the "Converting Tables to Text" section, later in this chapter.

CREATING NEAT ROWS AND COLUMNS WITH THE INSERT TABLE BUTTON

In many tables, each column is the same width, and each row is the same height. Word makes it extremely easy to create tables such as these. If you need to make modifications later—perhaps adjusting the width of just one column—it's easy to do so.

→ For more information about changing the width of a table, **see** "Controlling the Width of Columns," **p. 148**.

To create a table where each column is the same width and each row is the same height, follow these steps:

1. Click the Insert Table button in the Standard toolbar. A set of rows and columns appears.

2. Drag the mouse pointer down as many rows as you need. Word automatically adds rows as you drag. You see the number of rows highlighted as you go.

3. Still pressing the mouse button, drag the pointer across, covering as many columns as you need. Again, you see the number of columns highlighted (see Figure 5.1).

PART

I

CH

5

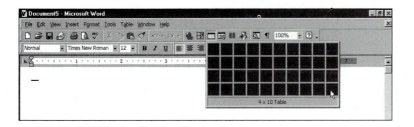

Figure 5.1
Clicking the Insert Table button displays a white grid of cells. Drag down and across to specify the number of rows and columns you want.

Tip #56

It helps to have a rough idea of how many rows and columns you'll ultimately need, but don't worry about it too much. After the table is created, it's easy to add and delete rows and columns.

4. When you are satisfied, let go of the mouse. Word creates a table, as shown in Figure 5.2.

Figure 5.2
When you release the mouse pointer, the table appears in your document.

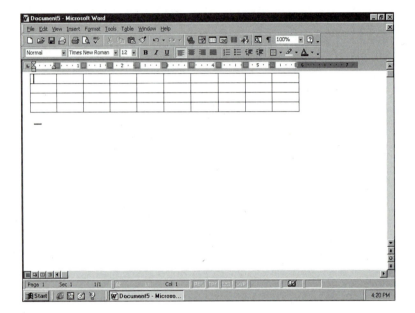

The higher the resolution of your monitor, the more rows and columns you can create using this technique.

Word sets the height of each row in your table to match the height of surrounding paragraphs. By default, this is 12-point (in other words, six lines to an inch). However, if your surrounding paragraphs use different line spacing settings, your tables match those instead.

Word sets the width of each column by calculating the width between the margins you've set, and dividing that width equally among the number of columns you specify.

CONTROLLING COLUMN WIDTHS WHEN YOU CREATE A TABLE

Although you can change the width of a column any time you want, sometimes you want to set widths precisely as you insert the table—or tell Word how to automatically set them for you. To do so, use the Insert Table dialog box, as follows:

1. Click in your document where you want the table to appear.

2. Choose Table, Insert Table, and the Insert Table dialog box appears (see Figure 5.3).

3. Specify the Number of Columns and Number of Rows you want in the table.

4. Next, specify column width, choosing one of three options:

- You can set a precise width to be used by all the columns in your table by clicking in the Fixed Column Width scroll box and entering (or scrolling to) the value there.

- You can choose AutoFit to Window, which adjusts the width of every cell based on the width of the screen of the individual viewing it. For example, if you change your monitor from displaying at 640×480 to 800×600, your cells widen. This feature works only with documents saved as Web pages and viewed from within Word or a Web browser.

- You can choose AutoFit to Contents, which enables Word to widen or narrow columns based on the contents you insert in them. Word adjusts the columns as you type within the cells. This feature works in regular Word documents as well as documents saved as Web pages.

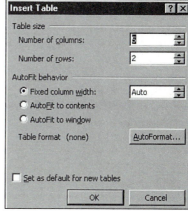

Figure 5.3

5. If you want to use one of Word's built-in AutoFormats to format your table now, click AutoFormat and work in the AutoFormat dialog box. (This feature is covered later in the chapter, in the section titled "AutoFormatting a Table.")

6. If the settings you've established reflect the way you'll usually want your tables to look, check the Set as Default for New Tables check box.

7. When you're finished, click OK. Word inserts your table into your document.

Note

After you create a table, it's easy to change its AutoFit setting. Select the table; choose Table, AutoFit; and choose whichever setting you prefer: AutoFit to Contents, AutoFit to Window, or Fixed Column Width.

Tip #57

Here's a quick way to AutoFit a column to its contents: Double-click the column boundary at its right.

DRAWING TABLES FREEHAND WITH WORD'S DRAW TABLE FEATURE

Word provides an even more intuitive way to insert tables: you can simply draw them with your mouse, much as you might draw them with a pencil on a piece of paper. Don't worry if you can't draw a straight line: Word straightens your lines for you.

Draw Table is ideal for creating tables that contain uneven columns or rows—similar to the table you see in Figure 5.4.

Figure 5.4
Using the Draw Table feature, you can easily create a table similar to this one.

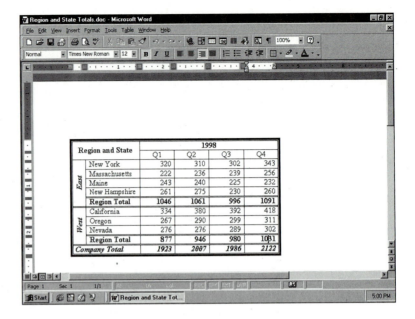

To draw a table, follow these steps:

1. Click the Tables and Borders button on the Standard toolbar. Word switches to *Print Layout view* if necessary, and displays the Tables and Borders toolbar. (Most of this toolbar's buttons remain gray until you create a table.) See Table 5.1 for a description of each button on the Tables and Borders toolbar.

2. Click in the document where you want to draw a table. The mouse pointer icon changes to a pencil.

3. Drag the mouse pointer down and to the right margin until the outline that you see while dragging appears to be the approximate size you want for the outside boundaries of the table.

4. When you release the mouse button, the insertion point appears inside the table, which looks like a box (see Figure 5.5).

You now have a table consisting of one large *cell* (the intersection of a row and a column). To create multiple cells that appear in rows and columns, you can draw additional columns and rows inside the original cell, roughly where you want them to appear. As long as you start or finish the lines near a cell border, Word automatically extends and straightens lines that you've drawn only part way.

Caution

If your lines come nowhere near an existing cell border, Word may insert a nested table instead—a second table within a table. Should this occur, click Undo.

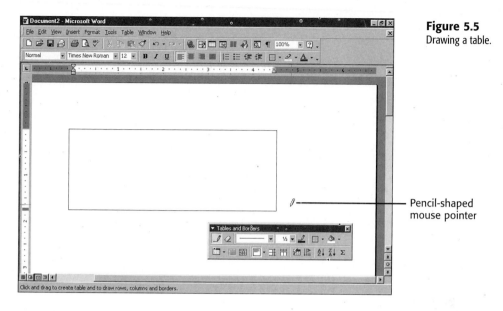

Figure 5.5
Drawing a table.

Pencil-shaped
mouse pointer

If you draw a line where you don't want one, click the Eraser button on the Tables and Borders toolbar, and drag across the line until it disappears.

You can also use Draw Table to draw diagonal lines that extend across an individual cell. To do so, click the Draw Table toolbar button, then click in one corner of a cell and drag to the other corner.

You might use diagonal lines to call attention to the fact that a cell contains no data, as shown in Figure 5.6. Notice that drawing diagonal lines does not actually divide a rectangular cell into smaller triangular cells: If you type in the cell, your text will overlap the diagonal line.

Region and State		1998			
		Q1	Q2	Q3	Q4
East	New York	320	310	302	343
	Massachusetts	222	236	239	256
	Maine	243	240	225	232
	New Hampshire	261	275	230	
	Region Total	**1046**	**1061**	**996**	**1091**
West	California	334	380	392	418
	Oregon	267	290	299	311
	Nevada	276	276	289	302
	Region Total	**877**	**946**	**980**	**1031**
Company Total		*1923*	*2007*	*1986*	*2122*

Figure 5.6
Creating diagonal lines in a table cell.

Diagonal lines in a table cell

PART
I

CH

5

When you finish drawing the table's rows and columns, click the Draw Table toolbar button again, and your mouse pointer reverts to its normal state. You can now edit or format the table as you wish (or work elsewhere in the document).

 Now that you have a table, you can polish it any way you want. For example, if you want several of your columns to be the same width, select them, right-click on them, and choose Distribute Columns Evenly from the shortcut menu. Or, after you enter text in a cell, you can turn that text sideways by clicking Change Text Direction on the Tables and Borders toolbar. Table 5.1 shows the options available on this toolbar.

TABLE 5.1   THE TABLES AND BORDERS TOOLBAR

Button	Function
	Draws a table.
	Erases borders in a table.
	Specifies the style of line used when drawing.
	Specifies the thickness of the line used when drawing.
	Specifies the color of the line used when drawing.
	Specifies where borders should appear around a cell, group of cells, or table.
	Specifies a cell shading color.
	Displays the Table shortcut menu, offering choices for inserting columns, rows, and cells, and controlling column width.
	Merges selected cells.
	Splits a selected cell into multiple cells.
	Enables you to choose the alignment of text in a cell or cells you select.
	Formats the rows you select with equal heights.
	Formats the columns you select with equal widths.
	Displays the AutoFormat dialog box, where you can choose how you want to automatically format the table.

Button	Function
	Changes the direction of text in a cell.
	Sorts selected entries in ascending order (A–Z).
	Sorts selected entries in descending order (Z–A).
Σ	Adds the values above or to the left of the cell containing the insertion point, and inserts the sum in the cell in which you've clicked.

Note

In addition to the Tables and Borders toolbar, you can find tools for working with tables in the Table menu; and in the Table shortcut menu that appears whenever you right-click inside a table (see Figure 5.7).

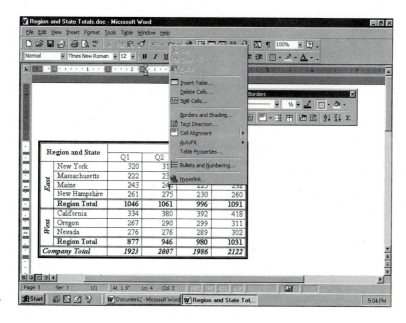

Figure 5.7
The Table shortcut menu appears whenever you right-click inside a table.

PART

I

CH

5

CREATING A TABLE FROM THE KEYBOARD

If you're more comfortable working with the keyboard, you can also type a pattern that represents the kind of table you want, with plus signs corresponding to cell borders and minus signs corresponding to units of width within a cell. Here is an example:

+-----+-----+-----+

After you type the line, press Enter. Word inserts a one-row table. Each cell is the same width as the number of dashes you typed between plus signs.

> **Note**
>
> If this feature does not work, turn it on in the AutoFormat As You Type tab of the AutoCorrect dialog box. Choose Tools, AutoCorrect, click the AutoFormat As You Type tab, check the Tables check box, and click OK.

CREATING SIDE-BY-SIDE TABLES

Occasionally, you may need to create tables that appear side-by-side on your page. In previous versions of Word, you could create the illusion of side-by-side tables by carefully setting manual borders, so there appeared to be gaps between tables located on the same lines. Now, Word can create side-by-side tables automatically, as shown in Figure 5.8.

Figure 5.8
An example of true side-by-side tables.

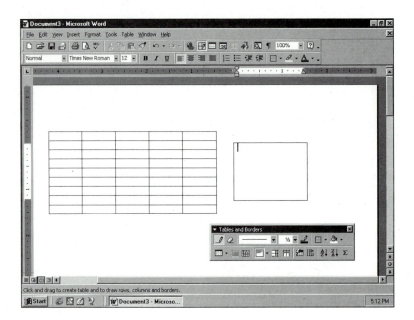

To create two tables on the same line:

 1. Insert the first table using Draw Table on the Tables and Borders toolbar, or the Insert Table dialog box (choose Table, Insert, Table).

> **Caution**
>
> Don't use the Insert Table button on the Standard toolbar: It uses up all the space between your left and right margins, leaving no room for another table.

 2. To the right of the existing table, use Draw Table to draw another table. Word inserts the table with an 0.5" border, and adds unbordered table cells between the two tables (creating the illusion of a second table but actually simply extending the first table).

If you create a side-by-side table next to a table that consists of only one row, Word 2000 actually extends the first table rather than create a new one—but makes sure there are no borders in the area between the two parts of the table. In other words, it fakes side-by-side tables just as you might have done manually in earlier versions of Word. The difference: Word 2000 does all the required bordering for you, automatically. You can see these "fake" side-by-side tables in Figure 5.9.

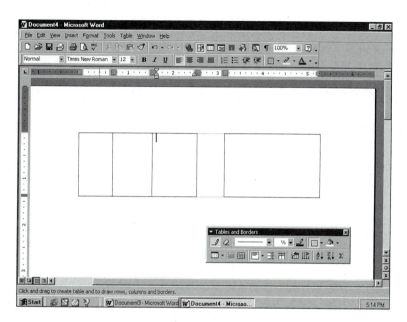

Figure 5.9
An example of "fake" side-by-side tables.

CREATING NESTED TABLES

In Word 2000, you can create tables within tables, called *nested tables*. This technique is primarily used in building Web pages. It can give you more control over the appearance of your table, by allowing you to more precisely control where information in your table appears. Sample nested tables are shown in Figure 5.10.

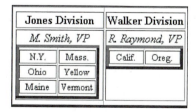

Figure 5.10
An example of nested tables.

To create a nested table within an existing table, first click inside the table where you want the nested table to appear. Then create a new table, using any of Word's table creation tools: the Insert Table button on the Standard toolbar, the Draw Table button on the Tables and Borders toolbar, or the Insert Table dialog box.

PART
I

CH
5

Caution

If you're concerned about how quickly your Web pages will display on browsers, use nested tables sparingly: They tend to display more slowly than ordinary tables. In particular, avoid creating very complex nested tables—especially, don't nest tables within other nested tables.

Tip #58

You can copy existing nested tables into Word from a Web browser, and edit them to meet your needs. Nested tables copy into Word 2000 with surprising fidelity.

EDITING IN A TABLE

After you create a new empty table, the next step is to put something in it—and that can be anything you want: text, graphics, you name it.

When Word creates a new table, it positions the insertion point in the table's first cell. Typing in a table is similar to typing anywhere else in a document, with a few significant exceptions. Unless you selected AutoFit to Contents when you created the table, when you reach the right edge of a cell, Word wraps text back to the left edge, as if you were at the end of a line. Also, some keystrokes behave differently within a table. In particular, pressing Tab within a table cell moves you to the next cell; if you need a real tab, you must press Ctrl+Tab.

You can enter paragraph marks or line breaks within a cell. These breaks add lines to the row the cell is in, and to all other cells in the same row, as shown in Figure 5.11.

Figure 5.11
Adding line breaks within a cell.

Paragraph marks —

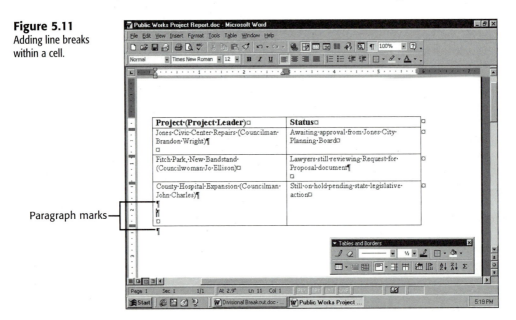

To move within the table, click the cell to which you want to go. Word also offers many keyboard shortcuts. For example, Tab moves you to the next cell; Shift+Tab moves you back. A complete list of keyboard navigation shortcuts appears in Table 5.2.

TABLE 5.2   KEYBOARD SHORTCUTS FOR NAVIGATING WITHIN TABLES

This Key	Moves the Insertion Point
Up arrow	Up one line within a cell. If at the top of a cell, up one cell. If already at the top of the table, moves one line above the table.
Tab	To next cell.
Shift+Tab	To preceding cell.
Down arrow	Down one line within a cell. If at the bottom of a cell, down one cell. If already at the bottom of the table, moves one line below the table.
Left arrow	Left one character within a cell. If at the beginning of a cell, moves to end of preceding cell.
Right arrow	Right one character within a cell. If at the end of a cell, moves to start of next cell.
Home	To beginning of current line in current cell.
End	To end of current line in current cell.
Alt+Home	To beginning of first cell in current row.
Alt+End	To end of last cell in current row.
Alt+PageUp	To beginning of first cell in current column.
Alt+PageDown	To beginning of last cell in current column.

Tip #59

Within tables, Word appropriates the Tab key for moving between cells. To actually set a tab within a table, press Ctrl+Tab.

PART

I

CH

5

CHANGING A TABLE'S STRUCTURE OR FORMATTING

As you begin to edit the contents of your table, you may find that you want to adjust its structure or formatting. This may include

- Changing the widths of columns, perhaps to accommodate more or less information than you originally anticipated, or to adjust Word's automatic settings.

- Changing the heights of rows, perhaps for aesthetic reasons, or to compensate for changes Word makes automatically when you enter larger or smaller text into table cells.

- Adding or deleting rows or columns, again to accommodate more information (or less).

- Merging two or more cells into one, perhaps to create complex table designs that are often used in forms.

- Splitting one cell into two or more.
- Changing the appearance of individual cells or the entire table.

As with other formatting tasks in Word, your first step is often to select the elements of the table you want to change. You need to know a few special techniques to select part or all of a table.

SELECTING PART OR ALL OF A TABLE

You can use the following techniques to select elements of a table:

- To select a column, move the mouse pointer over the top of the column. When the mouse pointer changes to a black arrow pointing downward, click the mouse. Or, click anywhere in the column you want to select, and choose Table, Select, Column.

- To select a row, move the mouse pointer to the left edge of the row. Click when the pointer changes to a black arrow pointing up and to the right. Or, click anywhere in the column you want to select, and choose Table, Select, Row.

- To select a cell, move the mouse pointer to the left boundary of the cell. When the pointer changes to a black arrow pointing up and to the right, click. Or, click inside the cell, and choose Table, Select, Cell.

- To select a block of cells, click in the top left cell you want to select, and drag the mouse pointer across all the other cells you want to select, highlighting them. Or select the first cell, row, or column you want to select, and press Shift as you select the last cell, row, or column you want to select.

- To select the entire table, hover the mouse pointer over the table or click anywhere inside it; a table selection icon appears at the top left corner of the table (see Figure 5.12). Click the table selection icon.

Figure 5.12
When you hover your mouse pointer over a table, a table selection icon appears at the top left of the table.

Table selection icon

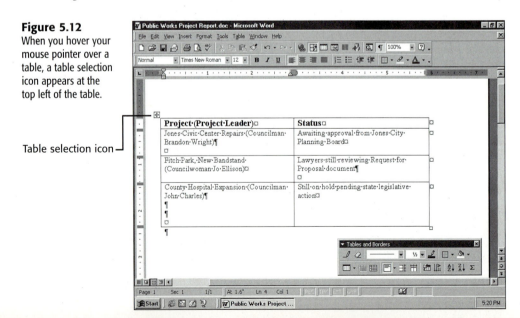

Tip #60

In Word 2000, you can move a table to another location on your page by dragging the table selection icon.

 If you try to move a table in Web Layout view (page 17)*, and Word snaps the table into a position you don't want, see "What to Do If Word Moves Tables into the Wrong Position," in the "Troubleshooting" section of this chapter.*

SELECTING PART OR ALL OF A CELL

Thus far, you've been learning to select entire cells, rows, columns, and tables. However, there are times you want to select only the text within a specific cell, not the entire cell. For example, if you copy an entire cell to another location in your document, you create a new one-cell table. Often, however, that's not what you intend: You want to copy the contents of the table cell, not the cell itself.

 Every cell in a Word table contains an end-of-cell marker; to avoid copying the cell itself, you must avoid copying this marker. To see end-of-cell markers in your table, click the Show/Hide Paragraph Marks button on the Standard toolbar. Figure 5.13 shows a table with end-of-cell markers displayed. As you type in a cell, the end-of-cell marker moves to stay just ahead of your typing.

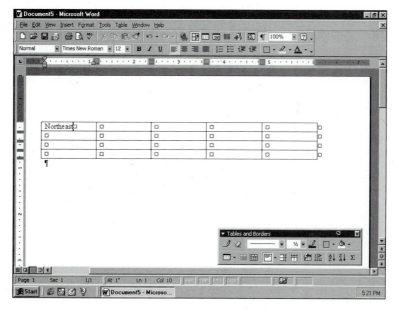

Figure 5.13
A table displaying end-of-cell markers.

PART

I

CH

5

Pay attention to end-of-cell markers when you format your tables. When an end-of-cell marker is selected, your formatting affects the entire table cell surrounding it. When an end-of-cell marker is not selected, your formatting affects only the text or graphics within that cell.

INSERTING ADDITIONAL ROWS, COLUMNS, AND CELLS

Often, you want to add a new row, column, or block of cells to your table. For example, in a year-to-date financial report, you might be called upon to add a column containing the latest month's results, or a row reflecting the addition of a new department or sales channel. Word makes such additions easy.

INSERTING NEW ROWS

To add a new row to the bottom of your table, position your insertion point in the last cell and press Tab. A new row appears in the same format as the preceding row.

 To add a new row anywhere else in your table, select the row where you want a new row to be placed. The standard Table toolbar button changes to an Insert Row button. Clicking the Insert Row button inserts a row above the row you selected. Alternatively, you can right-click on a table row, and choose Insert Rows from the shortcut menu.

Whichever method you choose, a new row appears, using the height, widths, and formatting of the row in which your insertion point is currently. Other rows are pushed down to make room.

If you want to insert a row below the one you've selected, choose Table, Insert, Rows, Rows Below.

Tip #61

You can insert several rows at the same time by selecting the same number of rows in the table, before you choose the menu command to insert rows. In other words, if you select six rows before choosing Table, Insert, Rows Above, Word places six empty rows above the rows you selected.

INSERTING NEW COLUMNS

 To add a new column within your table, select a column to the right of the location where you want your new column. The Insert Table button in the Standard toolbar changes to an Insert Column button. Click it, and the new column will be inserted; the other column widths are adjusted to compensate, so the entire table is no wider than it was before.

If you do not want to change the widths of existing columns when you insert a new one, use this procedure instead. If you want the new column to appear to the left of the column you selected, choose Table, Insert, Columns to the Left. If you want the column to appear to the right, choose Table, Insert, Columns to the Right.

A new column appears where you specified, and other columns are pushed to the right to make room. To add a new column at the right edge of your table, select the column at the far right of the existing table, and choose Table, Insert, Columns to the Right.

When you insert a new column, it takes the same formatting as the column you selected before inserting it.

Tip #62

You can insert several columns at the same time by selecting the same number of columns in the table, before you choose the menu command to insert columns. In other words, if you select three rows before choosing Table, Insert, Columns to the Right, Word places three empty columns to the right of the columns you selected.

Tip #63

Often, you'll want to insert a column containing a list of consecutive numbers, such as serial numbers. Use Table, Insert, Columns to the Left to insert a blank column. Then, with the blank column selected, click the Numbering icon on the Formatting toolbar.

INSERTING NEW CELLS

 You also can insert cells anywhere within a table. Select a cell adjacent to where you want your new cell to appear. The Insert Table button on the Standard toolbar changes to the Insert Cells button. Click it, and the Insert Cells dialog box appears, as shown in Figure 5.14.

Figure 5.14
Telling Word how you want it to insert cells.

PART

I

CH

5

Note

You can also display the Insert Cells dialog box from the Tables and Borders toolbar. If the Tables and Borders toolbar is displayed, you can display the Insert Cells dialog box by clicking the down arrow next to the Insert Table button, and choosing Insert Cells from the shortcut menu.

Tell Word where you want to move the cells you are displacing: Shift Cells Right or Shift Cells Down. If you are sure that is what you want, click OK in the dialog box to confirm. Some of the time, you may want to make further adjustments. For instance, you might really want to add an entire row or column, so Word also offers those options.

If you choose to Shift Cells Right or Shift Cells Down, Word shifts only these cells—leaving you with a table that has additional cells in some rows or columns, as shown in Figure 5.15.

Figure 5.15
A table with extra cells
in some rows.

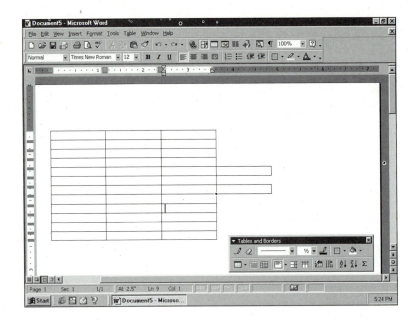

If you intend to perform calculations that use cell references in your table, be careful about adding or removing cells from rows; this can make it difficult to accurately identify cells in your formulas.

DELETING ROWS, COLUMNS, OR CELLS

Word 2000 has made it easier to delete portions of a table—or the entire table. Simply click one of the cells you want to delete, or (if you are deleting more than one row or column) select all the rows and columns you want to delete. Then,

- To delete the column in which your insertion point is, (or all the columns you've selected), choose Table, Delete, Columns.
- To delete the row in which your insertion point is, (or all the rows you've selected), choose Table, Delete, Rows.
- To delete the entire table, choose Table, Delete, Table.

To delete individual cells, select them; right-click; and choose Delete Cells from the shortcut menu. A dialog box appears, asking you how to adjust the table after deleting the cells (see Figure 5.16). Be aware that you can inadvertently create a lopsided table by deleting single cells, thereby leaving fewer cells in one row or column than are contained in the other rows or columns in the table.

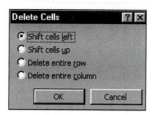

Figure 5.16
Choose the adjustment you want to make to the table's structure after you delete a single cell.

MERGING AND SPLITTING CELLS

Occasionally, you create a table with information in separate cells that you later decide should be merged into a single cell. You might, for example, realize there isn't enough width to create all the columns you wanted; but you do have room to extend the information vertically, in deeper rows.

Merging cells solves this problem. Select the cells you want to merge, and choose Table, Merge Cells; or from the Tables and Borders toolbar, click the Merge Cells button.

Word combines all the selected cells in each row into a single cell. The information that originally was in separate cells is separated with a paragraph marker within each new cell. The new cell is the same width as all the previous cells combined, and can be adjusted with any of Word's column width tools. The overall width of the row is not changed; nor are the widths of other cells in the same column that you did not select. Figures 9.17 and 9.18 show a typical before-and-after example of using Merge Cells.

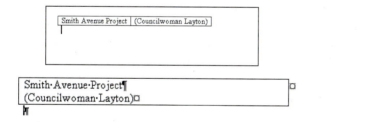

Figure 5.17
Cells before merging...

Figure 5.18
...and after merging.

Conversely, you may sometimes find that you need to split one table cell into two, perhaps to customize a *form* or some other complex layout. To do so:

1. Right-click inside the table cell you want to split.

2. Choose Split Cells from the shortcut menu. Word displays the dialog box you see in Figure 5.19.

3. In the Number of Columns scroll box, specify into how many columns you want to split the cell.

4. In the Number of Rows scroll box, specify into how many rows you want to split the cell.

5. Click OK. Word divides the cell you've chosen into the number of rows and columns you specified.

All the text that appeared in the original cell now appears in the first cell, unless one or more paragraph marks appeared in the original cell. In that case, Word will follow your paragraph marks, placing text after the first paragraph mark into the second cell; text after the next paragraph mark into the next cell, and so forth.

Figure 5.19
Use this dialog box to split cells in a table.

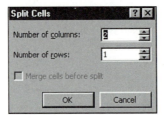

Tip #64

You can use this technique to quickly create an entire table with rows and columns of equal size. Use the Draw Table toolbar button to draw a large one-cell table, and use Split Cells to create the correct number of rows and columns.

CUTTING OR COPYING TABLE INFORMATION

To move or copy information from one cell to another, select the text and use standard drag-and-drop methods (drag to move, Ctrl+drag to copy) or use the Cut, Copy, and Paste commands. To replace the contents of the destination cell, select the entire source cell, including its end-of-cell marker. To retain the contents of the destination cell, select text but not the end-of-cell marker in the source cell.

If the text you move or copy contains character formatting, both the text and its formatting appear in the destination cell; however, you cannot move or copy any cell formatting, even if you include end-of-cell markers. Cell formatting includes borders, shading, text alignment, and text direction.

Note

In some earlier versions of Word, such as Word 95, copying the end-of-cell marker also copied cell formatting; in Word 2000 and Word 97, you cannot copy cell formatting.

You can also use standard drag-and-drop or Cut, Copy, and Paste commands to move entire rows or columns by selecting entire rows or columns before you move. When you move or copy a row or column, Word automatically overwrites the destination cells with the source information because the source selection contains end-of-cell markers.

COPYING A TABLE

After you have a table looking the way you want, you might want to copy it elsewhere in your document. To do so choose Table, Select, Table to select the table. Then copy and paste it using whatever copy and paste methods you prefer.

Tip #65

You can select a formatted table and store it as an AutoText entry, making it easy to insert anytime you want. Choose Table, Select, Table; then choose Insert, AutoText, New. Enter a one-word name for the AutoText entry in the Create AutoText dialog box, and click OK.

FORMATTING WITHIN A TABLE

When you create a table, it takes on the character and paragraph formatting of the paragraph preceding it. In other words, if the preceding paragraph uses Times New Roman 14-point type, double-spaced, so will your table unless you change it. You can change any of this formatting by using any of the character and paragraph formatting techniques discussed in previous chapters.

AUTOFORMATTING A TABLE

You can also automatically format your table by choosing from one of 42 prefabricated formats available through Word's Table AutoFormat feature.

Note

Most of these 42 AutoFormats were available in Word 97 as well, but Word 2000 adds three new Web formats, which display each cell in a table as an outline. Figure 5.20 shows a table AutoFormatted with the Web 1 style and displayed in Internet Explorer 5.0.

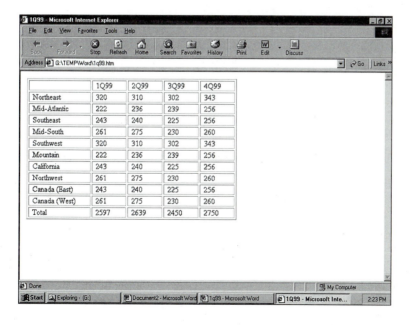

Figure 5.20
A table AutoFormatted in Word's Web 1 style and displayed in Internet Explorer 5.

To automatically format an existing table, place your insertion point anywhere inside the table and choose T<u>a</u>ble, Table Auto<u>F</u>ormat.

To AutoFormat a new table, choose T<u>a</u>ble, <u>I</u>nsert Table, set the number of rows and columns (and optionally the column width), and then click <u>A</u>utoFormat. In either case, the Table AutoFormat dialog box appears, as shown in Figure 5.21.

Figure 5.21
Choosing an auto-
matic table format
from the Table
AutoFormat dialog
box.

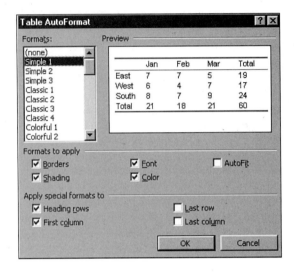

To choose a format, select it from the Forma<u>t</u>s list box. By default, AutoFormat expects to apply the <u>B</u>orders, <u>S</u>hading, and <u>F</u>ont elements from the built-in format. (<u>F</u>ont does not change your table's text font to Arial, as implied in the Preview, but it does add bold or italic as shown there.)

AutoFormat also expects to use AutoF<u>i</u>t to content, which shrinks or enlarges each column to fit the widest cell contained in that column.

You can turn off each of these features by clearing their check boxes. You also can add color in those Table AutoFormats that support it, by making sure the <u>C</u>olor box is checked (as it is by default). Twenty of the formats support color; some of the other formats use more intricate gray or black shading when you choose <u>C</u>olor.

Word's Table AutoFormats often include special formatting for Heading <u>R</u>ows, and for the First C<u>o</u>lumn. These are on by default. Word assumes you are actually putting something special in the top row and first column—such as headings. If you are not, you can turn this feature off.

 Alternatively, you might want the last row or column to contain special formatting; perhaps you're showing a total there. Check <u>L</u>ast Row or Last Col<u>u</u>mn to place special formatting there. Again, the Preview box shows you what to expect. When you have your AutoFormat the way you want it, click OK. (If you don't like the results, click Undo.)

ADDING TABLE BORDERS AND SHADING

Earlier, in "AutoFormatting a Table," you saw how Word's Table AutoFormat feature uses borders and shading to make tables easier to read and more attractive. You can format tables with borders and shading any way you want, calling attention to specific cells or headings.

Communicating with Word: Less Is More with Table Borders

Don't overdo borders and shading. For instance, if you have a table where all the cells contain approximately the same amount of text, try simply placing one horizontal line under the headings, and another at the end of the table. The white spaces formed by the cell padding can create the illusion of vertical lines separating the columns. This works best on tables when the cell contents within each column are relatively close to the same widths.

CONTROLLING THE BORDERS OF TABLES AND INDIVIDUAL CELLS

By default, Word inserts tables with an 0.5-point border around each cell. You can adjust or remove these borders, or specify which cells are bordered and which ones are not.

To work with the borders of a table, select the table (Alt+NumPad5), or select the cells for which you want to change bordering. Then, choose Format, Borders and Shading, and choose the Borders tab (see Figure 5.22). To add borders to specific cells, select them before choosing Format, Borders and Shading.

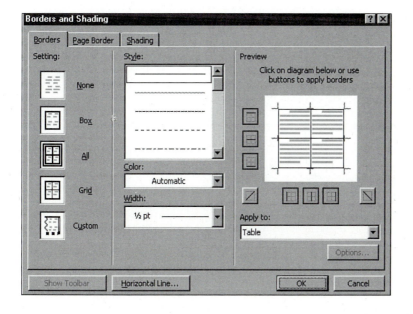

Figure 5.22
Working in the Borders and Shading dialog box.

PART

I

CH

5

Tip #66

In Word 2000, the Borders and Shading dialog box is also accessible by right-clicking on a table and choosing Borders and Shading from the shortcut menu.

Yet another way to reach this dialog box is to choose Table, Table Properties, click the Table tab, and click Borders and Shading.

At the left, Word presents the border approaches it expects you to use most often: None, Box, All, Grid, and Custom.

- All is the default setting: Word places a border at the top, bottom, left, and right of every cell you've selected.
- None clears all borders from the cells you've selected.
- Box places a border around the edges of the block of cells you've selected. If you select the entire table, a border appears around the outside edges of the table, but not around each individual cell.
- Grid places a 1 1/2-point border around the edge of the table, and a 3/4-point border around every cell.

The Grid and All boxes appear only if you choose multiple cells within a table and nothing else. If you choose one cell, or if you choose text inside and outside a table, the Shadow and 3-D boxes appear instead. Samples of Box, All, and Grid borders are shown in Figure 5.23.

Figure 5.23
Samples of each type of table border.

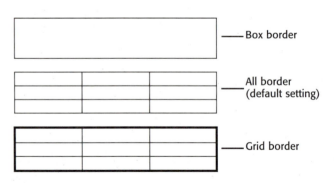

— Box border

— All border (default setting)

— Grid border

You can also individually control the left, right, top, and bottom borders of your table, or any cells within it. And in Word 2000, you can also add diagonal lines that cut across the entire table, or individual cells. To set or clear the border of one side of a table, click the edge you want to change in the Preview box. If you've chosen to set the border, after you select it, you can control its appearance through the other tools in this tab: Style, Color, and Width.

You also can choose a color for your border. Click on the Color drop-down box and select from the options listed there (see Figure 5.24), or click More Line Colors to create a custom palette.

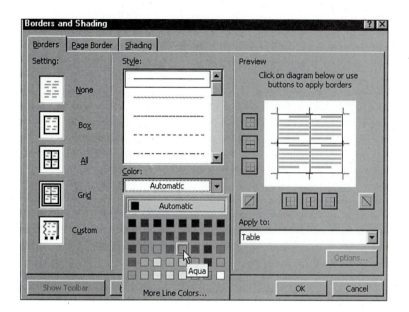

Figure 5.24
Choosing a line color.

Although Word has default settings for its boxes and grids, you can change them. To change the Box border, first select it, then choose a different border from the Line area.

To change the Grid area, first select it. To change the outside borders, choose a different border from the Line area. To change the inside borders of each individual cell, click in the middle of the thumbnail sketch, then choose a new border from the Line area.

PART

I

CH

5

Note

If you use tables without borders, you may find it difficult to recognize where one cell ends and another begins. Choose Table, Show Gridlines to display light gray lines that show the edges of each cell onscreen, but will not print.

CONTROLLING THE SHADING OF TABLES AND INDIVIDUAL CELLS

You also can create shading in part or all of a table. Select the cell or cells you want; then choose Format, Borders and Shading, and choose the Shading tab, as shown in Figure 5.25.

Figure 5.25
Creating shading for a
table or specific cells.

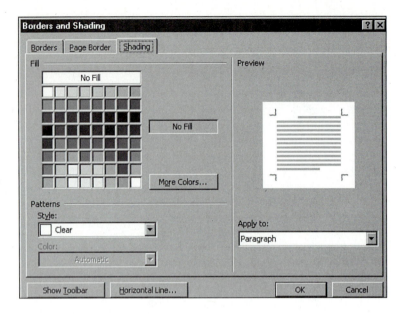

To choose a color, click the color in the Fill area; the name of the color appears to the right, and a sample of the color appears in the Preview area. If you cannot find a satisfactory color, click More Colors to choose a custom color.

→ For more information about creating custom colors, **see** "Controlling Colors," **p. 419**.

You can also superimpose a pattern over a color. To choose one, click the Style drop-down box. The patterns showing percentages (such as 5%, 10%, and so on) can be used to lighten the color you've selected. Additional patterns (such as Dk Horizontal and Lt Trellis) can be used as design elements.

Note

Be careful with shading. Text that is printed over shading is much less readable—especially text printed over patterns such as Dk Horizontal.

In general, unless the cell is intentionally left blank (as, for example, some cells on tax forms are), don't use more than 20% shading for text that is to be printed on a laser or inkjet printer.

The readability of shading depends on the quality of your printer. You can get away with darker shading if your text is sent to a Linotronic or other typesetting machine at 1,200 dots per inch. If you are working with a 9-pin dot-matrix printer, you might want to avoid shading altogether, or limit it to 10%, or you might want to boldface the text in a shaded area, so it stands out more.

If you are working on a Web page and you plan to add shading to individual cells, test the results on the browsers your site's visitors are likely to use. Some old browsers cannot recognize colors that are applied to only portions of a table.

CONTROLLING TABLE BREAKS AND TABLE HEADERS

Even after you create, edit, and format your table, you may need to take more control over it, and Word offers a variety of techniques for taking that control. For example, you can

- Split one table into two
- Control where page breaks appear within tables
- Set a header that appears on every page of your table, even though you entered it in your document only once
- Resize all the rows and columns in a table instantly

In the next few sections, you learn these techniques, which give you more control over your tables than you've ever had before.

USING SPLIT TABLE TO ADD SPACE ABOVE OR BETWEEN TABLES

Occasionally, you'll set up your entire table at the top of the page and then realize you need to add text before the table. You can't move your insertion point in front of the table. Even moving to the beginning of the document (Ctrl+Home) doesn't do it. Word's Split Table feature solves the problem. Click in the top-left cell of the table and choose Table, Split Table. Word adds a paragraph mark above the table and places the insertion point in that paragraph.

Similarly, what if you decide you'd really like to split the table into two tables so that you can place some text between them? Again, use Split Table. Click in the row you want to become the first row of the second table. Then choose Table, Split Table. Word divides the table into two tables and places the insertion point in a paragraph that appears between the two new tables.

Tip #67

You can also move the insertion point above a table by clicking the insertion point in the first cell, and pressing Ctrl+Shift+Enter.

PART

I

CH

5

SPECIFYING RECURRING HEADERS

What happens when you have a table that continues for several pages, and you would like each page to share the same headings? Use Word's Heading Rows Repeat feature to specify a heading row (or rows) that repeats on each page—appearing automatically after every page created by an automatic page break. Your heading row (or rows) must include the first row of the table.

To create a repeating heading row, select the row, you want to include in the repeating headers and choose Table, Heading Rows Repeat.

Another way to set a header row is to work from the Table Properties dialog box. Choose Table, Table Properties (or right-click on the table, and choose Table Properties from the shortcut menu). Click the Row tab; then, check the Repeat as Header Row at the Top of Each Page check box.

Tip #68

To tell whether a heading will repeat on multiple pages, select it and see whether Heading Rows Repeat is checked in the Table menu. To stop a heading from repeating, select it and uncheck Heading Rows Repeat in the Table menu.

You can see the repeated rows in Print Layout view or Print Preview.

PREVENTING ROWS FROM BREAKING ACROSS PAGES

In Word 2000, rows can easily break across pages, leaving hard-to-understand text (or blank space) on the following page. Such "widow" and "orphan" lines in tables can be hard for readers to understand, especially if you haven't bordered the cells in your table. Fortunately, you can select specific rows (or an entire table) and tell Word not to let them break across pages.

Right-click on the row you want to make sure remains intact on one page. (Or if you prefer, select several rows or the entire table, and then right-click.) Next, choose Table Properties from the shortcut menu, and click the Row tab. Clear the Allow Row to Break Across Pages check box, and click OK.

Now, if any of the rows you selected do not fit entirely on the first page, Word jumps all the contents of that row onto the next page.

Tip #69

If you don't mind breaking a table into two tables, you can separate the tables by inserting a manual page break (Ctrl+Enter) at the end of the row following where you want the break to be inserted.

The disadvantage: you can no longer use table selection, formatting, Header Rows Repeat, or sorting tools that assume you're working within a single table.

RESIZING YOUR TABLE AUTOMATICALLY

Often, you want to resize a table to fit a predefined space on a page. In earlier versions of Word, this required manual resizing of individual rows and columns. In Word 2000, you can resize every row and column in a single motion.

Hover your mouse pointer over the table you want to resize. At the bottom-right corner of the table, a square resize handle icon appears (see Figure 5.26). Drag the resizing icon until your table is the correct size. As you drag the icon, all column widths and row heights automatically adjust proportionally to the new size of the overall table. Text within the table automatically rewraps to reflect the new column widths and row heights.

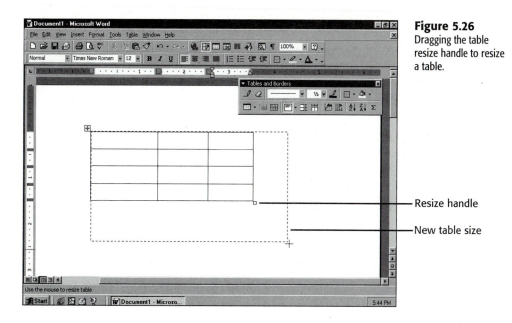

Figure 5.26
Dragging the table resize handle to resize a table.

Resize handle

New table size

 If Word is resizing your table when you don't want it to, see "What to Do If Word Resizes Cells Inappropriately," in the "Troubleshooting" section of this chapter.

WORKING WITH TABLE PROPERTIES

In Word 2000, Microsoft has delivered more control over tables than ever before—and brought it together in a single dialog box called Table Properties. From here, you can control all these options, and more:

- Table height and width
- The height of individual rows
- The width of individual columns
- The alignment of your table on a printed or Web page
- Whether text should wrap around your table, and if so, how it should wrap
- The vertical alignment of text within individual cells
- Whether a header row should repeat across multiple pages
- Cell margins, and whether any individual cells should have unique margins

The following sections walk you through the use of Table Properties—and in some cases, you show faster or easier ways to achieve the same goals.

PART

I

CH

5

SETTING THE PROPERTIES FOR AN ENTIRE TABLE

Word provides settings you can use to control the appearance or behavior of an entire table. To work with these settings, right-click on the table, and choose Table Properties from the shortcut menu. Then, click the Table tab, shown in Figure 5.27.

Figure 5.27
Controlling table settings that affect the entire table.

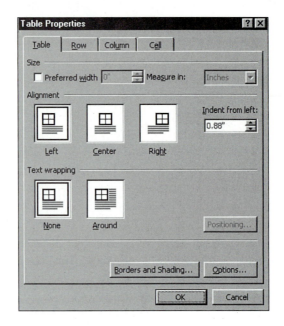

CONTROLLING THE PREFERRED WIDTH OF A TABLE

In Word 2000, you can specify a preferred width for your table—an overall table width that is to be used unless you choose other settings—or display the table on a browser or monitor that makes your preferred width impossible to use. To set a preferred width for the entire table, check the Preferred Width check box, and enter the width in the scroll box that appears next to it.

As with many measurement-related features in Word 2000, you can set your measurement either in Inches or in Percent—a percentage of the width of the screen. If you're creating a Web page, using percentages enables your browser to make adjustments so that your entire table is visible regardless of the browser or monitor being used by the person viewing it.

Caution

As you always should when creating Web pages, test your pages to see how they will actually display on the browsers and monitors you expect your site's visitors to use.

CONTROLLING THE ALIGNMENT OF A TABLE

By default, Word tables start at the left margin, but you can choose to start them anywhere on your page. If you're inserting a new table, you can use the Draw Table button on the Tables and Borders toolbar, and start drawing the table anywhere on the page. No matter how you insert the table, however, you can adjust its alignment any way you like, using the Alignment settings on the Table tab of the Table Properties dialog box.

To specify whether your table is left-aligned, center-aligned, or right-aligned on the page, click the sample table above the Left, Center, or Right windows. Or, to set a precise indentation from the left margin, enter the value in the Indent from Left scroll box.

Using an Indent from Left setting is often the best way to get precise control over alignment, because your table doesn't move unless you change the left margin. With centering, in contrast, your table adjusts every time the total width of all its columns changes, and in Word 2000, this tends to happen quite often.

Caution

These table alignment settings don't affect the alignment of text within each cell of a table. You can control horizontal text alignment using the same tools you use outside a table, including the Left Align, Center Align, and Right Align buttons on the Formatting toolbar.

And, as you'll see later in this chapter, you can control vertical alignment of text within a cell using the Cell tab of the Table Properties dialog box.

CONTROLLING TEXT WRAPPING AROUND A TABLE

In previous versions of Word, you couldn't wrap text around a table unless you used a complicated workaround, such as placing your table inside a text box. Now, you can treat a table the way you treat any other inline graphic—and run text around the table. To do so, display the Table tab of the Table Properties dialog box, and click the Around table sample.

After you click Around, the Positioning button becomes available. To adjust how text wraps around your table, click Positioning; the Table Positioning dialog box appears, as shown in Figure 5.28.

The Horizontal and Vertical controls specify where the table appears in relation to the surrounding text. By default, the table appears to the left of surrounding text, but you can choose Center or Right as well; these move the table to the center of the page or the right margin, respectively.

You can also choose Inside and Outside; these settings move the table to the inside or outside of the page, and then adjust the location of the table automatically if an odd-numbered page becomes an even-numbered page, or vice versa.

For example, in most books, page 1 is a right-hand page; choosing Outside would display the table toward the right edge of that page. However, if you edit the book so the table now appears on page 2, Word moves it automatically to the left edge of the page—and moves the surrounding copy to the right edge.

PART
I
CH
5

Figure 5.28
Controlling how text
wraps around a table.

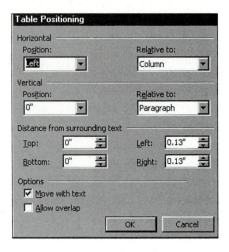

As you'll learn in Chapter 14, Word enables you to create multiple-column documents, where text snakes from the bottom of one column to the top of the next. This is a technique you might use in newsletters and magazines.

In one-column documents, of course, it makes no difference whether you measure a table from the margin of your current column or your page margin. In multiple column documents, however, there is a difference—and Word allows you to control the position of your table in reference to either the column margin or the page margin.

Use the Relative To drop-down box to specify what you want Word to measure your table's position against: Margin, Page, or Column.

CONTROLLING THE VERTICAL RELATIONSHIP OF A TABLE TO SURROUNDING ELEMENTS

The settings described cover the table's horizontal relationship to its surroundings; you can also control its vertical relationship. By default, the table and its surrounding text both start at the same point on a page, as shown in Figure 5.29. However, if you choose, you can specify that the table begin higher or lower by setting a different value in the Vertical Position combo box. For example, specifying 0.75" tells Word to insert 0.75" of the surrounding text before starting the table, as shown in Figure 5.30.

By default, this measurement is set off against the surrounding paragraphs of text, but you can tell Word to set the vertical position against the top or bottom page margin, or against the edge of the page itself. To do so, choose Margin, Page, or Paragraph in the Vertical Relative To scroll box.

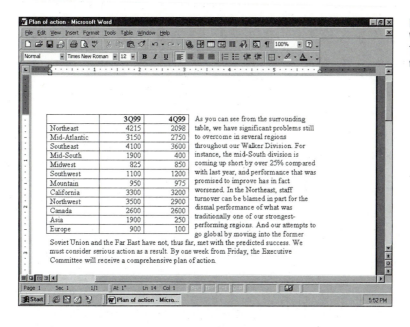

Figure 5.29
Word's default setting:
Table and text begin
together.

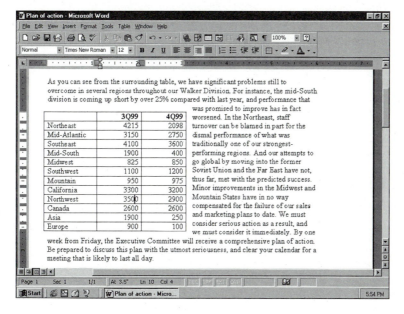

Figure 5.30
Using Vertical Position
to start a table lower
on the page than the
surrounding text.

CONTROLLING THE DISTANCE BETWEEN A TABLE AND SURROUNDING TEXT

By default, when you wrap text around a table, Word places no extra space above or below a
table; it places 0.13" to the left or right of the table. You can change each of these settings
by displaying the Table Positioning dialog box, and entering new values in the Top,
Bottom, Left, and Right scroll boxes.

SETTING DEFAULT MARGINS FOR ALL THE CELLS IN A TABLE

Each cell in a Word table has its own left, right, top, and bottom margins: the space between the edge of text and the border of the cell. (In an HTML document, this is known as *cellpadding*.) By default, the top and bottom margins of cells are zero; the left and right margins are 0.08". Similarly, Word does not typically provide for any spacing between cells.

It's unlikely that you'll need to change these margins in printed documents, but many Web designers need more control over cell margins and spacing—and Word 2000 provides that control. To control these settings, right-click on the table and choose Table Properties from the shortcut menu; click the Table tab; and click Options. The Table Options dialog box appears (see Figure 5.31).

Figure 5.31
Make changes to your table in this dialog box.

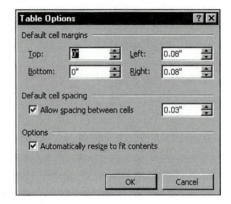

To change the default cell margins in your current table, enter new values in the Top, Bottom, Left, or Right scroll boxes. To change Word's default setting of no spacing between cells, check the Allow Spacing Between Cells check box, and enter a value in the scroll box next to it.

CONTROLLING THE HEIGHT OF ROWS

By default, when you create a table, Word uses a row height of "one line." "One line" starts out equal to one line in the preceding paragraph. As you work within the table, "one line" can grow or shrink depending on the type size you use on each row—and unless you divide cells vertically, when Word shrinks or enlarges a row's height, it does so for all the cells in the row.

Word provides several ways to change row height. The first involves simply dragging the row's borders where you want them. This is visual, and easy—but it works on only one row at a time, and unless your eye-hand precision is outstanding, it's also approximate. The second method takes you into the Table Properties dialog box, so it involves a few more steps, but it is highly precise and can control many rows (or an entire table) at once.

CHANGING A ROW'S HEIGHT BY DRAGGING ITS BORDERS

To change the height of one row within a table by dragging its borders, follow these steps:

1. In the table, point the mouse pointer to the bottom of the row you want to change. The mouse pointer changes to display vertical arrows (the Vertical Split Pointer, as shown in Figure 5.32).

2. Click and drag the row's border up or down to shrink or enlarge the row's height.

3. Release the mouse pointer when you're finished.

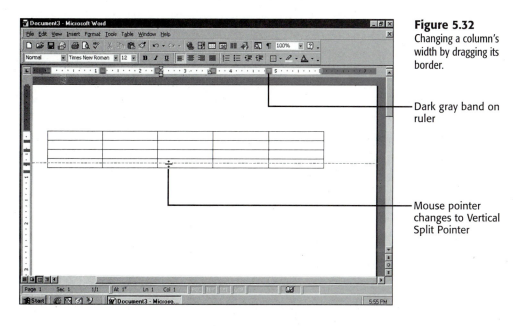

Figure 5.32
Changing a column's width by dragging its border.

Dark gray band on ruler

Mouse pointer changes to Vertical Split Pointer

PART

I

CH

5

Tip #70

You can also use the vertical ruler to move a row's border: Drag the dark gray band immediately to the left of the row you're adjusting.

Tip #71

If you want to see the exact measurements of rows or columns as you drag their borders, press the Alt key as you drag; the changing measurements will appear in the vertical or horizontal ruler.

CHANGING ROW HEIGHT THROUGH THE TABLE PROPERTIES DIALOG BOX

To change the height of table rows using the Table Properties dialog box:

1. Select the row or rows you want to adjust.

2. Choose Table, Table Properties.

3. Click the Row tab.

4. Check the Specify Height check box.

5. Enter the row height you want in the Specify Height scroll box.

6. In the Row Height Is drop-down box, choose whether Word must follow your row height Exactly, or whether Word can use your row height as a minimum (At Least).

7. If you want to control rows above the ones you selected, click Previous Row. If you want to control rows below the ones you selected, click Next Row.

8. When you're finished, click OK.

 If Word is only displaying part of the text in a table cell, see "What to Do If Word Cuts Off the Tops of Letters in a Table Cell," in "Troubleshooting" at the end of this chapter.

MAKING SURE SEVERAL ROWS HAVE THE SAME HEIGHT

Sometimes, you're not that concerned with the precise height of rows in a table, but you do want them all to have the same height, so the table looks as professional as possible.

 To accomplish this, first select the rows you want to adjust. Then, choose Table, AutoFit, Distribute Rows Evenly. (Or, if the Tables and Borders toolbar is displayed, click the Distribute Rows Evenly button.)

Word reformats the rows you selected so that they are all the same height. If the rows are empty, or have text that is all the same size, Word will distribute the rows so that they take up the same amount of height they did before; in short, if all the rows together were 3" high before, they will still be 3" high. However, if the rows contain text of differing sizes, Word will distribute the rows to reflect the largest text, so that no letters will be cut off in any row—even if this means some rows are much larger than necessary.

CONTROLLING THE WIDTH OF COLUMNS

Often, the column widths you set when you create your table need to be adjusted later, as you modify the content that goes into the table. For example, you may have created a descriptive first column followed by many shorter columns of numbers. Or, in a glossary, your first column might include just a word or a phrase, but your second column might include a detailed explanation.

Earlier in this chapter, you learned how to use *AutoFit* to enable Word to control your column widths. However, you sometimes need to control your column widths manually, and Word provides several ways to do so. As with rows, you can adjust column widths directly by dragging their borders, or via the ruler, or through the Table Properties dialog box.

CHANGING A COLUMN'S WIDTH BY DRAGGING ITS EDGE

The easiest way to adjust a column's width is usually to drag the edge of the column with the mouse pointer. To do so, position the mouse pointer anywhere on the column's right gridline or border. Next, drag the *gridline* or border left or right to the location you want, and release the mouse pointer.

Unless you're adjusting the last column in your table, the width of the following column changes to compensate for the widening or narrowing you've just done, so your overall table retains the same width. If you widen the last column, your table extends to the right. If you narrow the last column, the right edge of your table moves to the left.

CHANGING COLUMN WIDTH USING THE HORIZONTAL RULER

You also can change column width in the horizontal ruler. As you can see in Figure 5.33, when you are within a table, the table's column borders are shown on the horizontal ruler. You can change these column borders by positioning the mouse pointer on the border shown in the ruler (avoiding the indent markers) and dragging to the new border that you want. As you drag a column border, the new measurements are visible on the ruler. The columns that follow shrink or enlarge to compensate, unless you are changing the last column.

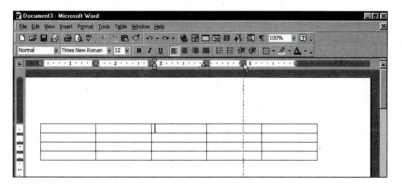

Figure 5.33
Changing a column's width with the horizontal ruler.

PART

I

CH

5

CHANGING COLUMN WIDTH THROUGH THE TABLE PROPERTIES DIALOG BOX

If you need more precise control over your column width, or if you want to change a column's width without changing the others, you need to work from the Table Properties dialog box. To change the width of columns using the Table Properties dialog box:

1. Select the column or columns you want to adjust.

2. Choose Table, Table Properties.

3. Click the Column tab.

4. Check the Specify Width check box.

5. Enter the Column Width you want in the Specify Width scroll box.

6. In the Column Width Is drop-down box, choose whether Word should measure your column width in Inches or as a percentage of the overall width of your table ("Percent of Table").

Note

> The Percent of Table setting is used primarily on Web pages, and enables your columns to adjust themselves automatically based on your other settings, and the monitor and browser being used to show your page.

7. If you want to control columns to the left of the ones you selected, click Previous Column. If you want to control columns to the right of the ones you selected, click Next Column.

8. When you're finished, click OK.

MAKING SURE SEVERAL COLUMNS HAVE THE SAME WIDTH

Sometimes, you're not that concerned with the precise width of columns in a table, but you do want them all to be the same width. To accomplish this, first select the columns you want to adjust. Right-click anywhere on the columns you selected, and choose Distribute Columns Evenly from the shortcut menu.

CONTROLLING THE PROPERTIES OF INDIVIDUAL CELLS

Just as Word gives you extensive control over the properties of tables, rows and columns, you can also control the properties of individual cells. These include

- The width of the specific cell
- The vertical alignment of text or other elements within the cell
- Whether the cell shares the same margins and wrapping options as the rest of the cells in the table

CHANGING A CELL'S WIDTH BY DRAGGING ITS EDGE

The easiest way to adjust a cell's width is to drag the edge of the cell with the mouse pointer. To do so, select the cell; then place the mouse pointer anywhere on the cell's right gridline or border. Next, drag the gridline or border left or right to the location you want, and release the mouse pointer.

Unless you're adjusting a cell in a column that's on the right edge of your table, the width of the adjacent cell changes to compensate for the widening or narrowing you've just done, so your overall table retains the same width.

If you're changing the last column, your cell "bulges outward" to the left or right, as shown in Figure 5.34. Be careful to make sure this is what you really intend: Often, it isn't.

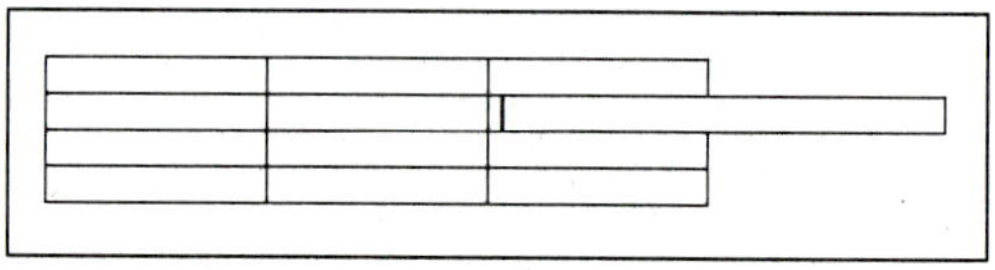

Figure 5.34
A cell that "bulges outward" from the rest of the table.

CHANGING THE WIDTH OF CELLS THROUGH THE TABLE PROPERTIES DIALOG BOX

Sometimes you need more precise control over the width of an individual cell (or cells). Or you want to adjust a block of cells at once, without changing entire rows or columns. Or you want to adjust one cell without also changing the adjacent cell.

In these cases, you need to work from the Table Properties dialog box. To change the width of cells using the Table Properties dialog box:

1. Select the cell or cells you want to adjust.
2. Choose Table, Table Properties.
3. Click the Cell tab.
4. Check the Preferred Width check box.
5. Enter the cell width you want in the Preferred Width scroll box.
6. In the Measure In drop-down box, choose whether Word should measure your column width in Inches or as a percentage of the overall width of your table ("Percent of Table").
7. Click OK.

CONTROLLING THE VERTICAL ALIGNMENT OF A CELL'S CONTENTS

By default, Word starts the contents of individual cells at the top left corner of the cell, but this may not always be what you want. For example, if some of the cells in a row are very deep, the result can be an imbalanced, unattractive design. You might want to vertically center the text in cells such as these, as shown in Figure 5.35.

Figure 5.35
Information vertically centered within cells in a table.

Word 2000 enables you to control both vertical and horizontal alignment at the same time. Select the cell or cells you want to adjust, right-click to display the shortcut menu, and click the right arrow next to the Cell Alignment command. Then, choose one of the nine options that appear (see Figure 5.36).

Tip #72

If you've displayed the Tables and Borders toolbar, you can get the same choices by clicking the Cell Alignment (Align Top Left) button.

Figure 5.36
Choosing a cell alignment from the shortcut menu.

CONVERTING TEXT TO TABLES

Sometimes you might need to convert text into a table format, or the other way around. For example:

- You might have an old table created using tabs; you now want to revise it, and it is easier to make the revisions by using tables.

- You might have a print merge or database file that was created or exported in tab-delimited or comma-delimited format.

- You might have text that you decide would simply look better in table format.

To create a table using existing text, first make sure the text contains a separator character Word can use to identify where it should start new table cells and rows. It's common for documents to use tabs or commas in locations where you'll want new cells; and to use paragraph marks in locations where you'll want new rows. However, as long as the document is consistent, Word lets you work with any separator characters that may be present.

Once you've checked the document, select the text you want to convert; then choose Table, Convert, Text to Table. The Convert Text to Table dialog box appears, as shown in Figure 5.37.

When the dialog box opens, Word shows you its best guess as to the Number of Columns required and how you want the text to be separated. If, for example, you have selected tabbed material, Word is likely to assume you want to Separate Text At Tabs. The result: Word starts a new cell every time it encounters a tab mark.

If the only breaks Word can find are paragraph marks, Separate Text At Paragraphs is likely to be marked; if you leave this marked, Word starts a new cell every time it encounters a paragraph mark. You can change the setting, choosing from Paragraph, Tabs, or Commas. Or, you can click the Other button, and enter whatever separator character you need in the text box next to Other.

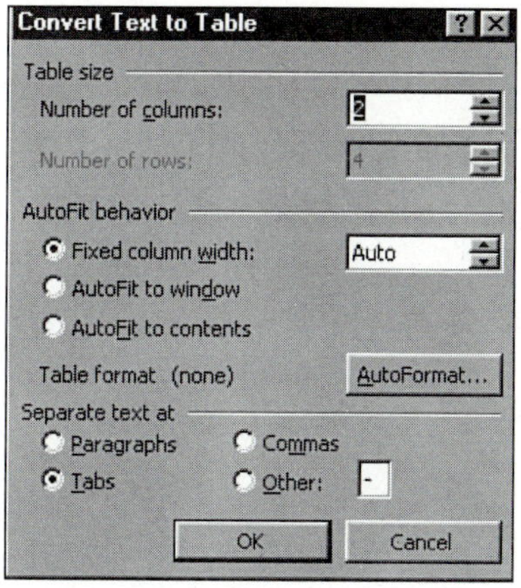

Figure 5.37
The Convert Text to Table dialog box gives you extensive control over how Word transforms text into a table.

SOME TIPS FOR BETTER TEXT-TO-TABLE CONVERSIONS

It is generally easier to convert text where tabs or commas split cells than where all you have is paragraph marks. First, much of the text you will want to reformat as tables was probably originally created with tabs. (Commas usually are used with exported database files.) A more important reason, however, is the difference in how Word handles the text-to-table conversion.

When you are converting from tabbed or comma-delimited material, Word recognizes a paragraph mark (or line break) as its cue to start a new row. Word also is smart enough to create a table that accommodates the line with the most commas or tabs. All this means you can easily convert long lists of text into tables.

However, if you choose paragraph marks, Word can no longer tell when to end a row. It places each paragraph (or each chunk of text ending with a line break) in its own row. The result is a one-column table.

If you have a table of moderate length, you can use Edit, Replace to swap all the paragraph marks (^p) in the selected text for tabs (^t). Then manually restore the paragraph marks where you want each row to end. Finally, use Table, Convert Text to Table.

If you are converting from tabbed text, whenever Word sees a tab, it places the text that follows the tab in a new cell to its right. Sometimes people use extra tabs (in the place of blank data) to make sure all the text lines up properly.

Extra tabs can create havoc when you convert from text to table, because Word will create unwanted empty cells. Of course, this does not happen if custom tabs are set, replacing the 0.5" default tabs.

If you are converting from comma-delimited text, be careful to make sure that your document contains commas only where you want cell breaks. Sometimes a comma is really just a comma. It is easy to be thrown off by city/state addresses (Fort Myers, FL would be split into two columns) and by numbers (1,000,000 would be split into three columns).

CONTROLLING WIDTHS AND AUTOFITTING IN THE CONVERT TEXT TO TABLE DIALOG BOX

Working from the Convert Text to Table dialog box, you can specify the column width manually by setting a Fixed Column Width. Or, if you prefer, you can specify one of Word's AutoFit options to enable Word to control your column widths. AutoFit to Window adapts your column widths depending on the display device and browser software with which your page is being displayed. AutoFit to Contents adapts the column's width based on the width of text in the column. You can also click AutoFormat to select an automatic table format from Word's AutoFormatting dialog box.

When you finish establishing settings, click OK, and Word converts your text to a table.

Tip #73

If you don't like the results of your text-to-table conversion, use Undo Text Table immediately. If you change your mind later, you can still revert to text by using Convert Table to Text, as described next. But you have to accurately specify whether Word should use paragraph marks, tabs, or commas to divide the contents of the table.

If you use tabs, you might also need to adjust the tab settings Word creates, which match the cell borders of the table you just eliminated.

CONVERTING TABLES TO TEXT

As you might expect, you can convert a table to straight text in paragraphs. To do so, follow these steps:

1. Select the entire table you want to convert.

2. Choose Tables, Convert Table to Text. The Convert Table to Text dialog box appears (see Figure 5.38).

3. In the Separate Text With area, choose one of the following options: Paragraph Marks, Tabs, Commas, or Other. If you choose Other, type the character you want Word to insert when it comes to the end of each row.

4. Click OK. Word converts the selected table into regular text, breaking at the separator you chose.

Figure 5.38

CALCULATING WITH TABLES

Basic tables look tantalizingly like spreadsheets. In fact, a Word table can actually be made to perform a wide variety of calculations. In this section, you'll learn how to use tables as if they were spreadsheets.

Note

If you find that Word's table calculation capabilities are not sufficient for your needs, or if your source data is already stored in an Excel worksheet, see Chapter 37, "Integrating with Microsoft Office," to learn how to embed Excel worksheet data and calculations in your Word documents.

ADDING A LIST OF NUMBERS USING AUTOSUM

Perhaps the most common calculation you'll want to perform in a table is to add a list of numbers, as shown in Figure 5.39. Word's AutoSum feature makes this extremely easy.

	3Q99	4Q99
Northeast	4215	2098
Mid-Atlantic	3150	2750
Southeast	4100	3600
Mid-South	1900	400
Midwest	825	850
Southwest	1100	1200
Mountain	950	975
California	3300	3200
Northwest	3500	2900
Canada	2600	2600
Asia	1900	250
Europe	900	100
Total		

Figure 5.39
A typical table that would benefit from Word's AutoSum feature.

 Place your insertion point in an empty cell beneath (or to the right of) the list. Then, from the Tables and Borders toolbar, click the AutoSum button. Word enters a field in the cell containing a { SUM } function that calculates all the cells above it, or to its left.

Because the calculation is entered as a field, it can be updated automatically after you change the numbers in the table. To update the calculation, select the field (or press Ctrl+A to select the entire document and update all its fields) and press F9.

 If AutoSum doesn't add all the numbers it should, see "What To Do If AutoSum Doesn't Add All the Numbers in a Row or Column," in the "Troubleshooting" section of this chapter.

CREATING MORE COMPLEX FORMULAS THROUGH THE FORMULA DIALOG BOX

Sometimes your calculation requires more than a simple sum, or you may want to control the way Word inserts a value into your table. For these purposes, choose Table, Formula.

The Formula dialog box appears, as shown in Figure 5.40. If you've opened the Formula dialog box while your insertion point is at the bottom or to the right of a list of numbers, the formula text box will already contain a formula such as =SUM(ABOVE) or =SUM(LEFT). If all you want to do is add the list of numbers, you can click OK and Word inserts the calculation field just as if you clicked the AutoSum button.

Figure 5.40
Creating a formula in
the Formula dialog
box.

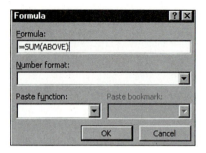

However, that's just the beginning of what you can do here. You can create fairly complex calculations, based on either values in the table or data that can be found elsewhere. You can also control the formatting of the values that result from your calculations. In the following sections, you'll learn more about the calculations you can perform within Word tables.

CREATING YOUR OWN FORMULAS

From within the Formula dialog box, you can write your own formula. Formulas that you create within this dialog box are placed in your document as fields, and can be updated the way other fields are updated: by selecting them and pressing F9.

Caution

In most cases, formulas will not update themselves automatically when the values they depend upon change. Therefore, don't assume a value is correct unless you know you have updated the field to reflect the latest information.

To make your formulas calculate the contents of other cells, you can use cell references, much like those in Excel. The top left cell in a table is called A1. Rows are numbered, columns are lettered. Accordingly, to subtract cell A1 from cell A2, use the following formula:

=A2-A1

To multiply cell A1 by cell A2, use the following formula:

=A1*A2

To divide cell A1 by cell A2, use the following formula:

=A1/A2

Word also offers a variety of functions that can be used in table formulas. These are available in the Paste Function box. See Table 5.3 for a brief description of what each function does.

TABLE 5.3   FUNCTIONS AVAILABLE IN TABLES

Function	Purpose
ABS	Displays the absolute value of a number or formula, regardless of its actual positive or negative value.
AND(x,y)	Used in logical expressions, AND returns the value 1 if both x and y are true, or the value 0 (zero) if either expression is false.
AVERAGE()	Calculates the average of a list of numbers that appear, separated by commas, in the parentheses.
COUNT()	Displays the number of items in a list. The list appears in the parentheses, with list items separated by commas.
DEFINED	Displays 1 if the expression x is valid, or 0 if x cannot be computed.
FALSE	Displays 0 (zero).
IF(x,y,z)	Evaluates x and displays y if x is true, or z if x is false. Note that x is a conditional expression, and y and z (usually 1 and 0 (zero)) can be either any numeric value or the words "True" and "False."
INT	Displays the numbers to the left of the decimal place in the value or formula x.
MIN()	Displays the smallest number in a list. The list appears in parentheses with its items separated by commas.
MAX()	Displays the largest number in a list. The list appears in the parentheses, with its items separated by commas.
MOD(x,y)	Displays the remainder that results from dividing x by y a whole number of times.
NOT (x)	Returns the value 0 (zero), meaning false, if the x is true, or the value 1, meaning true, if x is false. X is a logical expression.
OR(x,y)	Returns the value 1, meaning true, if either or both x and y are true, or the value 0 (zero), meaning false, if both x and y are false.
PRODUCT()	Displays the result of multiplying a list of values. The list of values appears in the parentheses, with the values separated by commas.
ROUND(x,y)	Displays the value of x rounded to y number of decimal places; x can be either a number or the result of a formula.
SIGN (x)	Displays the value 1 if x is a positive number, or the value –1 if x is a negative number.
SUM()	Returns the sum of a list of numbers or formulas that appear, separated by commas, in the parentheses.
TRUE	Displays 1.

PART
I

CH
5

Your formulas aren't limited to calculating numbers stored in the table in which you're working. You can include numbers from other tables in your document, or from anywhere else in your document. To use a number in a formula when it isn't in the table you're working in, first mark the number as a bookmark:

1. Select the number.

2. Choose Insert, Bookmark.

3. Type a one-word name in the Bookmark Name text box.

4. Click Add.

5. Click where you want to create the formula.

6. Choose Table, Formula.

7. Edit your formula.

8. When you get to the place in your formula where you want Word to reference the bookmark, choose the bookmark from the Paste Bookmark drop-down box. Word inserts the bookmark name in your formula.

9. Finish editing your formula if necessary.

10. Click OK.

Tip #74

If the "number" you select to bookmark is itself a formula, updating the entire document's fields will update both formulas. You can update all the fields in a document by pressing Ctrl+A, then F9.

→ For more information about bookmarks, **see** Chapter 11, "Footnotes, Bookmarks, and Cross-References," **p. 325**.

FORMATTING FORMULA RESULTS

Often, you'll create a formula that inserts an accurate value, but you'll want to format it differently from the default format Word may use. For instance, you may want to round the number at three decimal points, or present it as a percentage.

To control the format Word uses to insert a value it calculates, you can select a generic number format from the Number Format drop-down box. Table 5.4 lists the number formats and shows samples of the numbers they return.

TABLE 5.4   NUMBER FORMATS AND HOW THEY LOOK

Number Format	Sample
#,##0	12,580 or –12,580
#,##0.00	12,580.00 or –12,580.00
$#,##0.00;($#,##0.00)	$12,580.00 or ($12,580.00)
0	12580 or –12580
0%	12580% or –12580%
0.00	12580.00 or –12580.00
0.00%	12580.00% or –12580.00%

Tip #75

You can customize your number formats even further, using the Numeric Picture techniques covered in Chapter 18, "Automating Your Documents with Field Codes," in the section titled "Customizing Numeric Formats to Your Specific Needs."

QUICK AND EASY SORTING

Often, you'll want to sort items in a table—perhaps to alphabetize them, or to place them in numeric order, or to organize them by date. Word provides two sorting tools that make this easy:

- If you simply want to alphabetize a list, use the Sort Ascending or Sort Descending button on the Tables and Borders toolbar.

- If you want more control over how Word sorts your information, choose Table, Sort, and work from the Sort dialog box.

Tip #76

Although you're most likely to use sorting within tables, it works with any text in your document.

Tip #77

Some Word users like to organize documents in Outline view using Word's sorting feature. Start with a document that hasn't had outline numbering applied; then click Show Heading 1 to view only the highest-level headings, and manually assign numbers to them, based on the order you'd like them to appear in. Finally, select all the high-level headings (again, with nothing else showing), and click Sort Ascending on the Tables and Borders toolbar to arrange them in the order you want.

Now imagine you have a slightly more complex list, such as the list of customers in Figure 5.41.

Last Name	First Name	Phone
Smith	Robert	555-222-1800
Louisa	Mark	555-264-3720
Anderson	Kenneth	555-217-3420
Demby	Mark	555-264-3728
Alliana	Stuart	555-273-4120
Smith	Adrianne	555-296-1940
Talbot	Cari	555-802-4917
Schmidt	Fraser	555-497-1906

Figure 5.41
Sorting a list of customers.

Select the table and choose Table, Sort. The Sort dialog box appears, as shown in Figure 5.42. You can specify up to three levels of sorting. Imagine you have a table in which column 1 includes company names, column 2 includes cities, and column 3 includes names of sales representatives for these companies. If you have many contacts at some of the companies with which you do business, you might tell Word to sort first based on company names; after those are in order, to sort based on cities; and finally on the sales representatives' names.

Figure 5.42
Using the Sort dialog box to sort rows of a table.

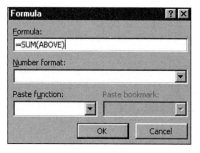

Word gives you a neatly ordered list of companies, in which each company's listings are sorted by city, and each company's city listings are sorted alphabetically by name.

You also can tell Word to sort a table alphabetically based on text, sort a field based on date order, or sort a field in numeric order. (These sorts can have different results.) You also can specify whether each sort should appear in ascending or descending order.

Often, you'll have a table with a header row that contains information you don't want to sort. To avoid sorting the top row, click Header Row.

Although the sorting options you've already learned will usually be all you need, occasionally you may need to refine your sorts even further. To do so, click Options in the Sort dialog box. The Sort Options dialog box appears (see Figure 5.43).

Figure 5.43
The Sort Options dialog box.

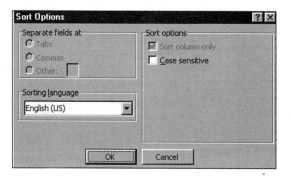

You might want to sort only the contents of a single column without also moving text in other columns. If so, choose Sort Column Only.

Normally, Word sorts are not case sensitive: march and March are listed next to each other. If you want Word to separate them, listing all capitalized words before lowercase words, choose Case Sensitive in the Sort Options box.

Finally, if you are sorting text that is not in a table or separated by paragraph marks, specify the separator you want Word to use in sorting the text. Other than paragraph marks, the most common separators are Tabs or Commas. However, if you want to use another character, you can enter that character in the Other text box.

TROUBLESHOOTING

WHAT TO DO IF WORD RESIZES CELLS INAPPROPRIATELY

Word 2000 automatically resizes cells as you type more information into them. This can be disconcerting, and can also result in table layouts you don't like. To turn this feature off, select the table, and choose Table, AutoFit, Fixed Column Width.

WHAT TO DO IF WORD MOVES TABLES INTO THE WRONG POSITION

If you're working in Web Layout view, when you move a table, Word may automatically snap it to the left or right of where you intend it to go. If this occurs, clear Text Wrapping for the table.

To do so, right-click on the table, choose Table Properties from the shortcut menu, and click the Table tab. Click None in the Text Wrapping area, and click OK.

WHAT TO DO IF AUTOSUM DOESN'T ADD ALL THE NUMBERS IN A ROW OR COLUMN

If you use AutoSum to add the contents of an entire column or row, you might find that AutoSum misses some of the numbers you want included. This occurs when blank cells appear in the row or column AutoSum is asked to add: AutoSum stops adding when it encounters a blank cell. Replace the blank cell with 0, and update the cell containing your AutoSum formula.

WHAT TO DO IF WORD CUTS OFF THE TOPS OF LETTERS IN A TABLE CELL

If you use the Exactly setting to set a row height shorter than the text in the row, Word cannot display all the text in the row, and cuts off some of the top. Instead, use the At Least setting, unless you have specific typographical or design reasons for setting exact measurements. If you must use Exactly, increase the size of the row.

A similar problem can occur—within or outside a table—when you set the line spacing of paragraphs to Exactly in the Format, Paragraph dialog box. (This sometimes can occur without your knowledge when you import a document from another word processing format.) Again, the solution is to use the At Least line spacing setting if at all possible; and if you must use the Exactly setting, to increase the value.

PART

I

CH

5

INDUSTRIAL STRENGTH DOCUMENT PRODUCTION TECHNIQUES

CHAPTER **6**

USING MAIL MERGE EFFECTIVELY

In this chapter

AN OVERVIEW OF WORD'S MAIL MERGE

Mail merge is the process of creating custom mailings (or other documents) that combine unique information with standard text to create a set of unique documents—typically, one for every recipient. Word's mail merge feature gives you the power to customize your message for just a few people—or for thousands at the same time.

To successfully run a mail merge, you need to understand two fundamental concepts. The first is this: You need a main document and a data source.

The *main document* contains the text that you want to remain constant. The main document also contains instructions about which changeable text Word should import and at which point it should import it. These instructions are called *merge fields*.

Your second file, the *data source*, contains the text that is to change from one form letter (or envelope or label or catalog page) to the next. Your data source file can consist of a table in a Word document, or it can be an Access database, Outlook address book, or Excel worksheet. It can also come from a variety of other sources, such as dBASE-compatible (DBF) database files.

→ For more information about using Access databases, **see** "Using an Access Database as a Data Source," **p. 184**.

→ For more information about using Outlook data sources, **see** "Using an Outlook Address Book as a Data Source," **p. 183**.

The second concept is this: Merging is a step-by-step process, much more so than many other tasks you perform in Word. Starting in the middle of the process can be confusing. The first part of this chapter walks you through the mail merge process for form letters and catalogs. The next walks you through the mail merge process for labels and envelopes.

No matter which type of mail merge you want to perform, however, you can start the process by displaying Word's Mail Merge Helper.

USING THE MAIL MERGE HELPER

To help organize and structure the mail merge process, Word provides the Mail Merge Helper, shown in Figure 6.1. The Mail Merge Helper guides you step by step through a mail merge. To open it, choose Tools, Mail Merge.

Note
If the Mail Merge command does not appear on the Tools menu, click the double arrow at the bottom of the menu and wait a moment until it appears.

Take a quick look around. The Mail Merge Helper shows the three main tasks you need to perform:

- Preparing a main document
- Preparing a data source
- Creating the settings for—and then actually running—your mail merge

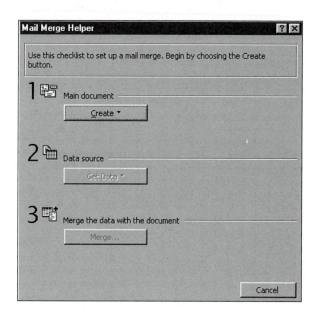

Figure 6.1
The Mail Merge Helper, as it appears when you begin a mail merge.

Only the tasks you're ready to perform are available. For instance, if you haven't prepared a main document and a data source, Word doesn't allow you to use the Merge button. Some buttons are grayed out, and others do not appear at all until you're ready to use them.

CREATING A MAIN DOCUMENT

Your first step in preparing a mail merge is to create your main document—the document that contains any boilerplate text that should appear in all your merged documents, as well as instructions about which kinds of information should be merged into them (*mail merge fields*). You can create one of four kinds of main documents:

- When you create a form letter, Word creates a new letter for each set of merge data.
- When you create envelopes, Word creates a new envelope for each set of merge data.
- When you create labels, Word creates new labels for each set of merge data.
- When you create a catalog, Word creates only one new document that contains all the merged data. Word repeats any standard text you add to the catalog main document for each set of data.

PART

II

CH

6

Note

To combine any type of standard text with unique information that is listed in a separate file, follow the instructions for form letters. You can use this basic process to create legal documents, contracts, and many other types of customizable documents. To print a list of information from a database, such as a parts list or a membership directory, follow the instructions for catalog main documents.

If you are working on a mailing that requires both a form letter and a set of envelopes or labels, create the form letter first, and use the same merge settings later to create your envelopes or mailing labels. This way, you can make sure you print corresponding labels or envelopes for each letter, and the labels or envelopes print in the same order. You don't have to re-create the settings from scratch: Word can retain them for you.

→ For more information about creating matching labels or envelopes after you finish creating your form letters, **see** "Printing Accompanying Envelopes and Labels," **p. 204**.

Tip #78

If you want to use an existing document as your main document, open it before you display the Mail Merge Helper.

To create a main document:

1. Choose Tools, Mail Merge to display the Mail Merge Helper.

2. In the Main Document section of the Mail Merge Helper dialog box, click Create. A list of options appears, as shown in Figure 6.2.

Figure 6.2
Choosing which type of main document you want to create.

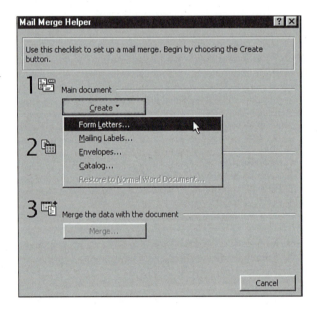

3. Choose the type of main document you want to create: Form Letters, Mailing Labels, Envelopes, or Catalog.

Note

The Catalog option merges all your data into a single document (rather than into separate letters, for example). This feature has many uses beyond catalogs: For example, it is ideal for creating membership directories and parts lists. It's also a great way to build a list of who you've already mailed to, for follow-up by telephone or other means.

4. You're now asked whether you want to build your main document from the document already displayed in your active window, or whether you want to create a new one (see Figure 6.3). (Note: Mail Merge isn't accessible—it's grayed out—if you don't have a document open.)

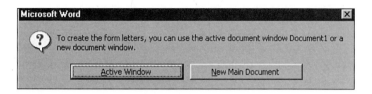

Figure 6.3
Specifying whether you want to use an existing main document or use a new, empty document.

If you've already opened the document you want to use as your main document, click Active Window; otherwise, click New Main Document. After you make your choice, Word adds a new button to the Mail Merge Helper: the Edit button.

5. Click Edit. The main document you just created appears on the drop-down list beneath the Edit button, along with the merge type; in this example, Form Letter. (If you're using a main document that's already been saved with a filename, that filename will appear instead of Document1.)

6. Select the main document from the Edit drop-down menu (see Figure 6.4). Word hides the Mail Merge Helper and displays, instead, your main document. If you chose New Main Document in step 4, the main document is blank. Word also displays the Mail Merge toolbar described in Table 6.1. (Some buttons are available and others are grayed out, depending on how far along you are in the merge process.)

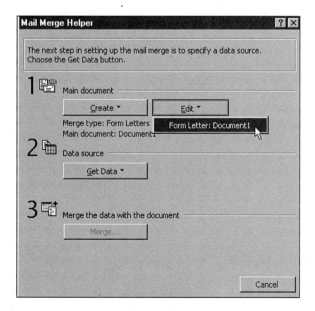

Figure 6.4
Select the main document from this menu.

PART
II

CH
6

TABLE 6.1 MAIL MERGE BUTTONS

Button	Name	Function
Insert Merge Field	Insert Merge Field	Places a merge field in the main document
Insert Word Field	Insert Word Field	Places a Word field in the main document to customize the document
« » ABC	View Merged Data	Shows what the main document would look like if it contained information from the data source in place of merge fields
⏮	First Record	Shows what the main document would look like if it contained information from the first record of the data source in place of merge fields
◀	Previous Record	Shows what the main document would look like if it contained information from the previous record of the data source in place of merge fields
1	Go to Record	Enables you to specify a record from the data source and see how your main document would look if it contained that record's data, in place of merge fields
▶	Next Record	Shows what the main document would look like if it contained information from the next record of the data source in place of merge fields
⏭	Last Record	Shows what the main document would look like if it contained information from the last record of the data source in place of merge fields
📋	Mail Merge Helper	Opens the Mail Merge Helper dialog box
📝	Check for Errors	Checks the merge for errors
📄	Merge to New Document	Performs the merge and places the results in a new document (or documents, depending on the type of merge you are performing)
🖨	Merge to Printer	Performs the merge and prints the resulting merged pages
📄	Mail Merge	Opens the Merge dialog box
🔍	Find Record	Enables you to search for a particular record in the data source document
📝	Edit Data Source	Reopens the Data Form dialog box so you can edit records in the data source document
—.	More Buttons	Adds or removes buttons from the Mail Merge toolbar

Communicating with Word: The Right Tone

Be careful to use the right tone for your audience in all your direct mail—and use Word's mail merge features to customize your letters for your audience as much as possible.

For instance, collection letters and overdue bills understandably tend to bring out the aggressiveness in many writers. But long-standing customers whose accounts are overdue for the first time do not deserve the same tough letter as constant deadbeats—and they are likely to be deeply offended if they receive such a letter.

Later in this chapter, you'll learn about merge fields that can be used to customize your letters precisely to the needs of your individual recipients.

BUILDING YOUR FORM LETTER OR CATALOG

If you've just created a form letter or a catalog, Word gives you two choices about what to do next. You can edit your main document to include the boilerplate text, graphics, or other elements you want to include in it. Or you can work on creating or choosing your data source. In most cases, you write or edit the main document first.

Note

> If you have created a main document for an envelope or a mailing label, you must work on your data source immediately, before you go any further. After you do so, you can set up your main document with the specific envelope or label formats it needs to follow. Mail merges for labels and envelopes are covered in more detail later in this chapter, in the section titled "Printing Accompanying Envelopes and Labels."

If you choose to write or edit your main document first, you should

- Create, edit, proofread, and polish the text of the letter.
- Leave placeholders where you're planning to add changeable data, such as locations where you expect to use your recipient's name and address. Figure 6.5 shows a main document with placeholders surrounded by square brackets. You can use any placeholder you like: You're simply reminding yourself where merge fields need to go later.
- Print a sample letter to make sure you've left enough room for your preprinted stationery (you should test this again later in the process, when you know exactly how much space your merged data uses).

Tip #79

¶

> You might want to display hidden characters such as spaces and paragraph marks by clicking the Show/Hide Paragraph Marks button on the Standard toolbar. Doing so makes it easier to insert merge fields within paragraphs, enabling you to see that there is precisely one space before them and one space after them.

 After you finish editing and formatting, save the main document. Click Save on the Standard toolbar, just as you would to save any document. If you need to quit working and want to resume working later, simply reopen the main document; Word recognizes that you are in the process of building a mail merge. To display the Mail Merge Helper again, click the Mail Merge Helper button on the Mail Merge toolbar.

Figure 6.5
A sample main document that includes placeholders for merge fields.

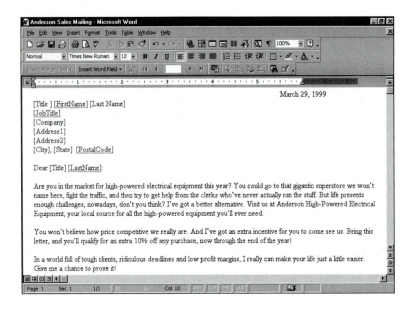

BUILDING YOUR MAIN DOCUMENT FOR ENVELOPES OR MAILING LABELS

You've seen that form letters contain boilerplate text that won't change from one merged document to another, and you've walked through adding that boilerplate text. However, if you are creating labels, or addresses for preprinted envelopes, you usually need to start working with your data source immediately, because these types of merge documents contain little or no boilerplate text or graphics.

No matter what merge type you're creating, you will at some point have to create your data source; doing so is covered next.

CREATING AND USING DATA SOURCES

You need to create or select a data source document to accompany your main document. Your data source must contain the information that changes in each of your merged documents. If possible, it should also contain headings or fields that identify each specific category of data, such as first names or zip codes.

Note

If your data source does not have usable headings or field names, you can create a separate header source document. This is discussed later in the chapter, in the section titled "Creating a Separate Header Source."

After you set up your data source, Word attaches the data source file to the main document, and you return to the main document to specify where each category of information goes.

The Mail Merge Helper provides tools to create a data source within Word. If you use these tools, Word builds a row-and-column *table* where the top row contains headings for each category of data, and the remaining rows each contain the information for one letter, envelope, label, or catalog entry. (In a Word table used as a data source, each row is called a *data record*.)

Note

If you already have a Word table containing the data you need, you can use that as your data source.

CHOOSING THE BEST DATA SOURCE

In addition to Word tables, many other types of files can act as a mail merge data source, including

- An address book from a personal information manager, such as a Microsoft Outlook Address Book
- A Microsoft Access table or query
- A Microsoft Excel worksheet
- A third-party database

In some cases, you won't have a choice about where your data comes from. In other cases, you may be in charge of organizing and managing the data as well as the mail merge process. In the latter situation, you need to decide which program makes the most sense to use for entering and managing the data you will merge with Word. Here are some rules of thumb you can use to make that decision.

Word tables lend themselves best to small mail merges, typically 100–200 data records or less. Of course, if your data is already stored in Outlook, Access, Excel, or a third-party database, it usually makes more sense to use your existing data source than to create a new one. If you're building a data source from scratch, however, consider these factors:

- **With which program are you most comfortable?** If you can achieve identical results with a program you already know as you can after investing many hours in learning a new program, consider using the program you already know.
- **How big is your database?** As your database grows—to many hundreds or thousands—it makes sense to use a dedicated database program such as Microsoft Access. If your database is very large—say, containing 100,000 records or more—consider migrating to an enterprise-scale database such as Oracle, Sybase, Informix, IBM DB2, or Microsoft SQL Server 7.0.
- **How else do you intend to use your data?** If you're sending a sales mailing to all your business contacts, and you plan to follow up with telephone calls, use a contact manager such as Microsoft Outlook or Symantec's ACT!.

PART
II

CH
6

■ **Where does your data come from?** If you input all your own data, Microsoft Word or Outlook may be all you need. If others help input your data, consider a database program such as Microsoft Access, which enables you to create forms that streamline and simplify the process. If your data is imported from another source, consider Excel or Access for their excellent data import and cleanup (parsing) capabilities.

Note

> If you have installed the proper converters, you also can use any of the following file types as a data source:
>
> • ASCII text files
> • Any Word for the Macintosh version 3.0–98 file
> • Any Word for DOS 3.0–6.0 file
> • Any WordPerfect version 6.x for Windows or WordPerfect 5.x for DOS file
> • Any Lotus 1-2-3 version 2.x–4.x file

In this chapter, you'll first walk through building a data source within Word, and then learn how to access data stored in Outlook and Access.

SOME CONSIDERATIONS IN CREATING ANY NEW DATA SOURCE

If you choose to create your own data source rather than use an existing one, here are some questions that can help you choose the right information to store there:

■ **Will you need to sort your data?** For example, you may want to sort mailing labels and/or envelopes by zip code, particularly if you are preparing a bulk mailing. In this case, be sure to create a separate merge field for the zip code. Do not include the zip code as part of the State merge field.

■ **Will some records contain more information than others?** For example, are some addresses three lines long while others are only two lines long? In these cases, create the data source document to accommodate the longest record. You can leave merge fields blank in a data source document. By default, blank merge fields do not create unattractive empty spaces in your merged documents.

■ **Will you need to use similar information in different ways?** For example, you may use the recipient's entire name and title in the inside address (for example, Ms. Mary Smith), but, later in the letter, address her directly (for example, Ms. Smith). If you need to use the same information in more than one way, break the information up into separate merge fields; for example, create merge fields for Title, First Name, and Last Name.

■ **Do you plan to use the data source document with more than one main document?** You might want to use a name and address data source document for a form letter and to produce corresponding mailing labels or envelopes. You can selectively choose which fields to merge into the main document; therefore, set up a single data source document that includes all the information you think you will need for all uses of that data source document.

CREATING A DATA SOURCE IN WORD

Word's Mail Merge Helper can help you walk through the process of creating a data source in Word. To create a data source in Word, first, click the Mail Merge Helper button on the Mail Merge toolbar to display the Mail Merge Helper. Next, click Get Data, and choose Create Data Source. The Create Data Source dialog box opens (see Figure 6.6).

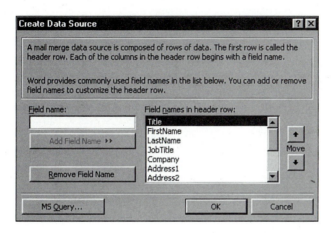

Figure 6.6
The Create Data Source dialog box displays the most frequently used categories of data.

CHOOSING CATEGORIES TO INCLUDE IN YOUR DATA SOURCE

Now that you've opened the Create Data Source dialog box, you can choose which types of data to include in your data source, or create your own new categories. As most database programs do, Word uses the term *fields* to describe types of data. The names of these fields will be stored in the first row of a Word table, called the *header row*.

> **Note**
> These are not the same fields described in Chapter 18, "Automating Your Documents with Field Codes." But, like those fields, they do offer a way for Word to include varying input in a document—in this case, the information contained in different records in your database.

When you create a new data source, Word automatically includes the types of information you're most likely to use when you merge letters, labels, and envelopes. These include

- Title (for example, Mr., Ms., Mrs., and so forth)
- FirstName
- LastName
- JobTitle
- Company
- Address1 (First address line)
- Address2 (Second address line)
- City
- State
- PostalCode (in the United States, corresponds to zip code)
- Country
- HomePhone
- WorkPhone

Note

One obvious field that's missing is email. Make sure to add this field if you plan to create merge letters for email (or follow up your letters via email). Similarly, if you plan to send broadcast faxes ("mass faxing"), make sure you include a field that contains fax numbers.

Caution

If you are creating a data source for sending faxes, and if you are using Symantec Fax Starter Edition as your fax software, make sure the fax numbers follow the strict format Word requires:

```
Fax@1 555 555-5555
```

If you are using Outlook as the source of your data, it's unlikely your entries are formatted properly. Here's a workaround that will work if you have access to Microsoft Excel. Using Outlook, export the records you want to fax to, in Excel format. Then open the new Excel file, and search/replace the phone numbers in the Fax column so that they are formatted appropriately. Save and close the file. Then, run Word mail merge, and choose the Excel file as your data source.

For more information on this, see Microsoft Knowledge Base articles Q195881 and Q189932.

Communicating with Word: Atomizing Your Fields

When you create your data source, break your information down to the smallest elements possible. This maximizes your flexibility in using the data. For example, "Dr. Frederick M. Banting" can be divided into a title, first name, last name, and middle initial.

This allows you to create text like "Dear Dr. Banting" from the same information you use to generate the name you place on your envelope. Otherwise, you might find yourself using stilted language like "Dear Dr. Frederick M. Banting," or else duplicating your efforts to create a new, appropriate data field when you need it.

Note

As you can see, Word assumes you're planning to track people: After all, that's who generally gets mass mailings. But you could equally well use this dialog box to set up categories for a catalog that includes products and their features and prices.

Your job now is to winnow out the categories you don't need, add new categories, and move the categories to match the order in which you want them.

To remove a category, select it in the Field Names in Header Row box, then click Remove Field Name.

To add a category, type a new category name in the Field Name text box, and then click Add Field Name. Each of these category names must be one word containing no more than 40 characters, with no spaces. The word must start with a letter, although you can include numbers afterward. You can use underscore characters to connect words, as in the following example:

```
Last_Called_When?
```

To move a category, select it in the Field <u>N</u>ames in Header Row box, and then use the up or down arrow to the right of the Field <u>N</u>ames in Header Row box to place it elsewhere in the list.

Tip #80	You don't have to reorder your fields unless doing so will make data entry more convenient later. Word inserts merge field data in your main document wherever you specify, regardless of the order in which the data appears in your data source.

SAVING YOUR DATA SOURCE

After you finish using the Create Data Source dialog box to set up fields, click OK. Word displays the Save As dialog box, prompting you for a filename. Type a name in the File <u>N</u>ame text box, select a destination folder if necessary, and click OK. This saves the data source file.

CHOOSING WHAT TO DO NEXT

You're now given a choice of what to do next. You can <u>E</u>dit Data Source—adding live data to your data source, such as the names and addresses of the people you want to receive letters. Or you can <u>S</u>et Up Main Document, which returns you to the main document you created earlier: You then add merge fields that tell it which categories of data in your data source to use when it runs the mail merge.

If you choose to set up the main document first, you can return to the data form later by choosing <u>G</u>et Data, <u>E</u>dit Data Source in the Mail Merge Helper. In fact, you can add records at any time by clicking <u>E</u>dit Data Source.

Whether you edit your data source now or later, of course, you need to provide data before you run your mail merge.

Tip #81	As you work on your data source, the main document remains open, in a separate Word window that you can access by clicking it in the taskbar. If you close your main document, you can reopen it whenever you're ready to work on it again, and Word will display the Mail Merge toolbar.

PART

II

CH

6

WORKING WITH THE DATA FORM

When you choose <u>E</u>dit Data Source, Word displays the Data Form dialog box shown in Figure 6.7. From here, you can enter data into your fields—such as the names and addresses of each person you want to receive your mailings.

When you open the data form for the first time, you see the first empty record. To fill in the record, click on the field you want to enter (or press Tab to move to it). Then start typing. To move from one field to the next, press Enter or Tab.

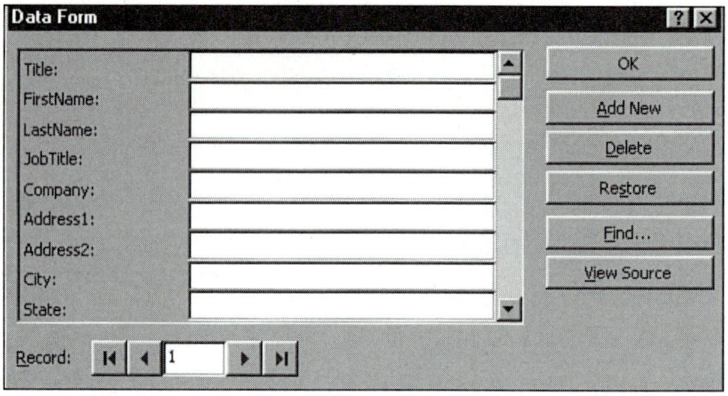

Figure 6.7
You can enter information for each data record in the Data Form dialog box.

Tip #82

If your insertion point is in the last field of a record in a data form, pressing Enter displays the next record. If you are in the last record of your database, pressing Enter creates a new record.

If you want to create another record after you finish entering the data in the current record, click Add New. A new blank record appears. If you don't like the edits you've made to the current record, click Restore to revert this record to its contents before you edited it (in this case, a blank record). If at some point you no longer need a record, click Delete to eliminate it.

Tip #83

As you edit your data form, keep in mind these pointers:

Don't duplicate information that is included as boilerplate text in the main document. For example, don't add a comma after the city, because then you have to add a comma after every city name. Plan to include a comma in the main document immediately after the City merge field.

Also remember that you can copy information from one field to another field (even on different records) by using the standard Windows keyboard shortcuts for Copy (Ctrl+C) and Paste (Ctrl+V).

Caution

You can't enter character formatting such as italic and boldface in a data form, and Word disregards any character formatting that may appear in records in an underlying Word table.

→ For more information about viewing the contents of an underlying data table in Word, **see** "Working with the Underlying Data Table and the Database Toolbar," **p. 179**.

Caution

Word's Undo feature isn't available from within the Data Form dialog box.

FINDING INFORMATION IN RECORDS

To move quickly among records, you can use the Record box, which always displays your current record (see Figure 6.8).

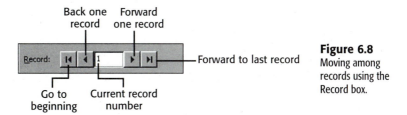

Back one record — Forward one record

Forward to last record

Go to beginning — Current record number

Figure 6.8
Moving among records using the Record box.

You can also search for specific information within the data form. To do so, click Find. The Find in Field dialog box opens, as shown in Figure 6.9.

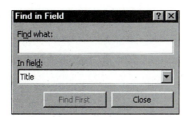

Figure 6.9
Finding specific data within a field.

Type the information you want to find in the Find What box. Specify the field you want Word to search in the In Field list box. Then click Find First. Word finds the first reference and displays the Find Next button. To find another reference to the same text, click Find Next.

WORKING WITH THE UNDERLYING DATA TABLE AND THE DATABASE TOOLBAR

The data form is only a friendly "front end" patched onto a standard Word table. Not surprisingly, you can do some things from the table that you can't do from the form.

Here's an example. As you just learned, you can locate text stored in a specific field using the data form's Find in Field dialog box. But if you work inside the table itself, you can use Word's standard Find and Replace dialog box to locate information anywhere in the table and to replace data anywhere you need to do so. (Suppose an area code has changed: It is a lot faster to make changes in the table than in the data form.) Viewing the table is also the only way you can see your data in tabular format, with many records showing at once.

To work in the underlying data table, click View Source from the Data Form dialog box. The table appears, along with the Database toolbar (see Figure 6.10).

PART

II

CH

6

Figure 6.10
The underlying database table and the Database toolbar.

Database toolbar ⟶

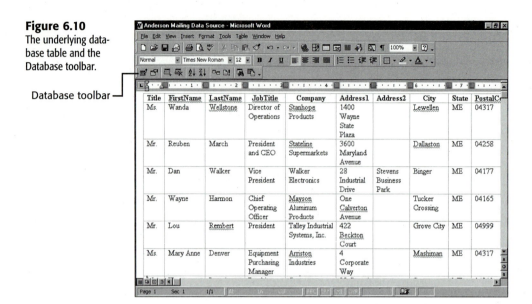

As you can see, the table may be too wide for your screen, and even so, many words may wrap, making them harder to read. The aesthetics leave plenty to be desired, but all your information's there.

Tip #84

> You can format and print the data source table the same way you would any other table. It still functions as a data source. You can also use Word's table features (such as the Table shortcut menu) to edit the table. You can, for example, use Delete Column to get rid of a field you no longer need.

The Database toolbar, meanwhile, contains the shortcut buttons you're likely to need while you work on the data source table. These are listed in Table 6.2.

Tip #85

> If you plan to work at length in the source table, consider turning off Automatic Spell Checking. It probably will report many names, street addresses, cities, and other data as incorrectly spelled, because these are not included in Word's dictionary. To turn off Automatic Spell Checking, choose Tools, Options; click the Spelling & Grammar tab; and clear the Check Spelling as You Type check box.

➜ For more information about automatic spell checking, **see** "Using Automatic Spelling and Grammar Checking," **p. 56**.

TABLE 6.2   DATABASE TOOLBAR BUTTONS

Button	Name	What It Does
	Data Form	Returns you to the data form, where you can edit a record
	Manage Fields	Adds/deletes a database field
	Add New Record	Adds a new record to a database at the insertion point
	Delete Record	Deletes a selected record from a database
	Sort Ascending	Sorts records in A to Z and/or 0 to 9 ("ascending") order
	Sort Descending	Sorts selected records in Z to A and/or 9 to 0 ("descending") order
	Insert Database	Gets information from elsewhere and places it in the current document
	Update Field	Updates the results of fields you select
	Find Record	Locates a specific record in a mail merge data source (opens the Find in Field dialog box)
	Mail Merge Main Document	Switches to the main document

A few of these buttons bear special mention. For example, the Manage Fields button enables you to insert, delete, or rename fields. It opens the dialog box shown in Figure 6.11, which works as the Create Data Source dialog box does, except that you can also choose an existing field and rename it. The Add and Remove buttons do the same thing as inserting a table row or selecting a row and deleting it.

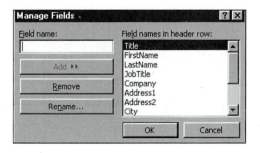

Figure 6.11
The Manage Fields dialog box enables you to add, delete, or rename fields "on the fly."

PART
II

CH

6

Sort Ascending and Sort Descending sort rows, based on the contents of the first column. These buttons ignore the first line, which contains Word's field headings.

Tip #86 · You can also use Word's Table, Sort feature to sort the contents of data tables.

→ For more information about sorting the contents of tables, **see** "Quick and Easy Sorting,"
p. 159.

 If Word keeps telling you that your data source is a main document, see "What to Do If Word Confuses Your Data Source with Your Main Document," in the "Troubleshooting" section of this chapter.

INSERTING EXTERNAL RECORDS INTO A DATA SOURCE

The Insert Database button imports data from other files into your existing Word data source. When you click it, the Database dialog box appears, as shown in Figure 6.12. Click Get Data; then browse the Open Data Source dialog box, choose the data source you're looking for, and click Open. After you've done so, the other buttons in the Database dialog box become available.

Figure 6.12
The Database dialog box.

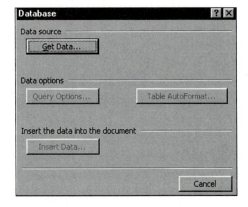

Next, you need to specify which database records you want to import, and how you want to import them. In the Database dialog box, click the Insert Data button. The Insert Data dialog box opens (see Figure 6.13).

Figure 6.13
Using the Insert Data dialog box to control which data to insert.

If you know which records you want to import, enter the numbers in the From and To text boxes. If you want every record, click All. If you want the information you're importing to update automatically if it changes in the source file, check the Insert Data as Field box. When you're finished, click OK, and Word imports the data.

If you chose Insert Data as Field, the imported information is stored in your data source in the form of { DATABASE } fields. As long as the source database still exists in the same location, you can click the Update Fields button to update your data source file any time you want.

OPENING AN EXISTING WORD DATA SOURCE

The previous sections focused on creating and building a new data source based on a Word table. But in many cases, all the information you need for your mail merge already exists. In this section, you learn how to use a table in an existing Word document as your data source. Then, you learn how to use Microsoft Outlook and Microsoft Access files as your data sources.

 After you've created a main document, display the Mail Merge Helper dialog box by clicking the Mail Merge Helper button on the Mail Merge toolbar. Click Get Data, and choose Open Data Source. The Open Data Source dialog box appears; browse to and select the file containing your data source, and click Open.

USING AN OUTLOOK ADDRESS BOOK AS A DATA SOURCE

Many Word users have stored hundreds or thousands of contacts in Microsoft Outlook, which they use to track contacts, tasks, schedules, email and other aspects of their business relationships. Word makes it easy to use Outlook contact information as the data source in a mail merge.

 To do so, first create your main document. Next, click the Mail Merge Helper button on the Mail Merge toolbar to display the Mail Merge Helper. Click Get Data, and click Use Address Book. The Use Address Book dialog box opens (see Figure 6.14). Choose the Outlook Address Book you want to use, and click OK.

Note

You can also choose from other MAPI-compliant address books stored on your computers, such as those from Schedule+ or the Corel Address Book that accompanies Corel WordPerfect Office.

PART

II

CH

6

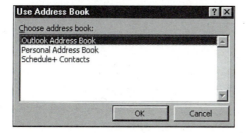

Figure 6.14
Choosing among the address books stored on your computer.

Word attaches the Outlook database as your data source, and tells you to add merge fields from that database to your main document. Click Edit Main Document to return to the main document and add merge fields.

→ For more information about adding merge fields, **see** "Specifying Fields to Merge into Your Main Document," **p. 186**.

USING AN ACCESS DATABASE AS A DATA SOURCE

If you creating a large mailing, it's likely your information is stored in a powerful relational database program like Microsoft Access. In this section, you walk through using an Access database as a mail merge data source. Before you start, create your main document. You may also want to open your Access database and review it to see which tables contain the data you need, or whether any preexisting queries already select the precise records you need. After you've done so, follow these steps:

1. Click the Mail Merge Helper button on the Mail Merge toolbar to display the Mail Merge Helper.

2. Click Get Data.

3. Click Open Data Source. The Open Data Source dialog box opens.

4. In the Files of Type drop-down box, choose MS Access Databases.

5. Browse to, and select, the database you want to use. The Microsoft Access dialog box opens (see Figure 6.15).

6. In the Tables In scroll box, choose the table that contains the data you need.

7. If you (or a colleague) have already built queries in Access that return the records you want, click the Queries tab. The Queries tab opens (see Figure 6.16). In the Queries In scroll box, choose the query you want.

8. Click OK.

Figure 6.15

Figure 6.16

Word attaches the Access database as your data source, and tells you to add merge fields from that database to your main document. Click Edit Main Document to return to the main document and add merge fields.

→ For more information about adding merge fields, **see** "Specifying Fields to Merge into Your Main Document," **p. 186**.

CREATING A SEPARATE HEADER SOURCE

Suppose you're using an external data source, such as a Word table or Excel worksheet, or data downloaded from a mainframe computer—but the first row of the data source contains data rather than merge field names. Or, what if you plan to perform many different mail merges with the same main document, but each one uses a different data source—and while the data sources contain similar information, they use different field names?

Because you need consistent field names to perform a mail merge, you have a problem—and Word provides a solution. You can create a separate header source document that Word can use rather than search for headers in your data sources.

A header source document is a Word document consisting of a table with one row: the header row that contains the merge field names you want to use in your main document. To create a header source document, follow these steps before you choose a data source in the Mail Merge Helper:

1. Display the Mail Merge Helper dialog box. (If you're working in the main document, you can do so by clicking the Mail Merge Helper button on the Mail Merge toolbar.)

2. Click Get Data, and choose Header Options.

3. Click Create. (If you've already created a header source document as part of another mail merge, choose Open to use it.)

4. The Create Header Source dialog box opens. This dialog box closely resembles the Create Data Source dialog box you saw in Figure 6.6.

5. To edit the field names you want to include in your header source document, follow the steps discussed in the "Creating a Data Source in Word" section earlier in this chapter.

6. When you finish editing, click OK. Word displays the Save As dialog box.

7. In the File Name text box, enter a name for your header source document, and click Save.

After you've created or selected a header source document in the Mail Merge Helper dialog box, choose the Get Data button again, and this time, choose either Create Data Source or Open Data Source. By following these steps, you attach both a header source document and a data source document to your main document.

Note

When you create a header source document, keep the following points in mind:

- The number of merge field names in the header source document must be equal to the number of data fields in the data source document.

- Merge field names in the header source document must appear in the same order as the corresponding information in the data source document.

- Merge field names in the header source document must match the merge field names you have included in the main document.

SPECIFYING FIELDS TO MERGE INTO YOUR MAIN DOCUMENT

Thus far, you've followed these steps:

- You created or selected a main document.
- You inserted the boilerplate text that is to appear in every form letter (or catalog entry).
- You inserted placeholders where you plan to insert merge fields that tell Word which data to incorporate in each customized letter (or other merge document).

Now it's time to replace those placeholders with actual merge fields that tell Word what data to pluck from your data source and where to put it. To insert a merge field, follow these steps:

1. Display the main document. If you've been viewing the data source document, click the Mail Merge main document button. If necessary, reopen the main document.

2. Click to place the insertion point where you want a merge field to appear. (If you created a form letter and used placeholders, select the first placeholder.)

3. Click the Insert Merge Field button on the Mail Merge toolbar. Word displays the merge fields available to your main document (see Figure 6.17). These are the same merge fields that appear in the data source or heading source document you've chosen.

Figure 6.17
Use this list to insert merge fields.

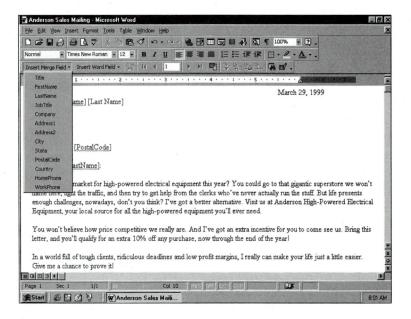

4. Choose the merge field you want to insert. Word places the merge field in your document at the location of the insertion point. If you selected a placeholder, Word replaces the placeholder with the merge field.

5. Format your merge field using any character formatting you want to apply to your merged text when you run your merge.

6. Repeat these steps for each merge field you need to place in your document.

7. Save the main document.

Note

If you are using an address book as a data source, only a subset of the address book's fields may be used in your mail merge.

If you need a field that cannot be used, you can export your data from the address book to a CSV file, and then use the CSV file as your data source; or else set up the mail merge from within the program that created your address book, such as Outlook or Schedule+.

If you prefer, you can also export to Microsoft Excel and use an Excel worksheet as your data source.

Each merge field starts and ends with chevron symbols: <<>>. You can't insert a merge field from the keyboard: You have to use the Insert Merge Field button. Place each of your merge fields in the correct location. Don't forget to include spaces between merge fields if they are separate words. And remember the punctuation that needs to appear in the finished document. Look, for example, at this standard letter introduction:

```
Mr. Thomas Walker
Vice President
Walker Corporation
Suite 48032 Industrial Drive
Mission Hills, ND 45881

Dear Mr. Walker:
```

Figure 6.18 shows the merge fields required to achieve this result.

Tip #87

At this point, you can perform your merge—especially if you don't want to customize your merged documents. So, if you're ready to merge, skip to "Preparing to Merge" later in this chapter.

Or if you'd like to preview your merge before running it—usually a good idea—see "Previewing Your Mail Merge from Within the Main Document," later in this chapter.

PART

II

CH

6

Caution

When you run a mail merge, Word disregards any character formatting in your data table. To include character formatting, format the merge fields when you enter them in your main document.

Figure 6.18
A typical form letter containing merge fields.

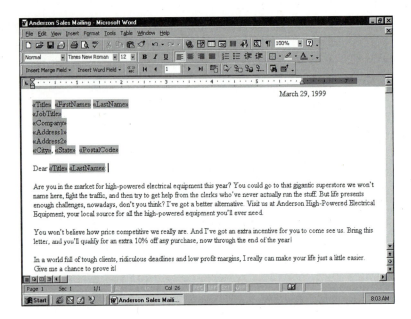

Tip #88

In addition to adding character formatting to a merge field, you can also add *general field switches* that define how text, values, or dates will be formatted in your document.

For instance, let's say you're sending a mass mailing that thanks the recipient for being a loyal customer, and includes a field listing how many purchases she has made in the current year. In our example, you're retrieving that value from a database where it is stored as a numeric integer:

23

But you'd like it to appear spelled out as text in your letter:

twenty-three

To do so, right-click on the merge field that corresponds to the value, and choose Toggle Field Codes from the shortcut menu. You should now see a field similar to this:

{ MERGEFIELD Purchases }

Now modify the field using the * Cardtext formatting switch Word provides to turn a number into text:

{ MERGEFIELD Purchases * CardText }

→ For more information about using field switches to control the appearance of text, dates, and values, **see** "A Closer Look at Field Formatting," **p. 574**.

CUSTOMIZING MERGED DOCUMENTS WITH WORD FIELDS

In many mailings, every form letter is alike, except for a personalized name, address, and salutation (Dear Mr. Jones). However, in other mailings you may want to customize your form letters further, varying your message depending on the individual recipient. In still other cases, you may want to skip certain recipients altogether, while still retaining them in your data source. Word provides a set of special fields that can be used to customize your letters in ways like these.

→ For more information about Word fields in general, **see** Chapter 18, "Automating Your Documents with Field Codes," **p. 555**.

These mail merge fields provide many ways in which you can customize a merge. To insert any Word field, place the insertion point in the main document where you want the field to appear, click the Insert Word Field button (see Figure 6.19), and choose a Word field.

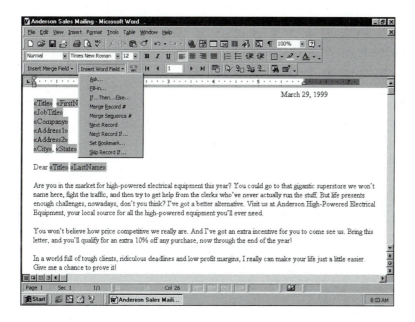

Figure 6.19
Nine Word fields are especially well-suited for customizing mail merges.

Table 6.3 lists the Word fields available from the Insert Word Field toolbar button, and briefly describes what they do. Many of these fields are discussed in more detail in the following sections.

TABLE 6.3	WORD FIELDS ESPECIALLY WELL-SUITED FOR MAIL MERGE
Field	**What It Does**
Ask	Asks the user for input and assigns that input to a *bookmark (page 727)*. With the Set and/or { REF } fields, you can use that bookmark throughout your document.
Fill-in	Asks the user for input at each new mail merge document and places that input in the document.

continues

PART

II

CH

6

TABLE 6.3 CONTINUED

Field	What It Does
If...Then...Else...	Specifies text to print if a certain condition is met, and different text or alternate merge field otherwise.
Merge Record #	Inserts the number of your data record in your main document.
Next Record	Tells Word to print the next record without starting a new page. Often used with labels.
Next Record If...	Starts the next record on the same page only if certain conditions are met. This command is a leftover from very old versions of Word; using Query Options, as discussed later in this chapter, accomplishes the same task with more flexibility.
Set Bookmark...	Marks text as a bookmark that you can insert repeatedly throughout a document.
Skip Record If...	Skips printing the current record if a specified condition is met. This command is a leftover from very old versions of Word; using Query Options, as discussed later in this chapter, accomplishes the same task with more flexibility.

Tip #89

These fields can be used in any type of mail merge main document. Some, such as Ask and Fill-in, are available in any Word document.

You can also use other Word fields to customize your form letters. For example, using { DATE } can enable Word to insert the current date into your letters.

Or, you can use Word formula fields to perform calculations. For example, perhaps you're sending a letter confirming a customer order. You can use merge fields to place dollar amounts for each item in your letters, and use the *AutoSum* button on the Tables and Borders toolbar to insert a formula field that tallies the value of all those items.

USING THE FILL-IN FIELD

Perhaps the most straightforward Word field is Fill-in. When you insert a Fill-in field, Word stops before printing each document and asks the user for input to place in the location specified by the Fill-in field.

To insert a Fill-in field, click on Insert Word Field and choose Fill-in. The Insert Word Field: Fill-in dialog box opens (see Figure 6.20).

In the Prompt box, insert the question you want to ask whomever is running the mail merge—for example, "How big a discount for this customer?"

If you want the same text in every letter, check the Ask Once check box. Then, after the user inserts the information once, Word repeats that information in all letters that the mail merge generates.

Figure 6.20
Use the Insert Word Field: Fill-In dialog box to create the Fill-in field.

To specify default text that prints unless you choose different text for a specific letter, type the default text in the Default Fill-in Text box.

When you (or a colleague) start the merge process, Word displays a Fill-in dialog box that displays the question or information you supplied when you created the Fill-in field, and prompts you to type information (see Figure 6.21).

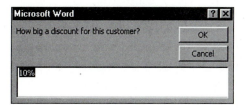

Figure 6.21
A sample Fill-in prompt dialog box.

USING THE ASK FIELD

The Ask field takes this concept of requesting user input one step further. Rather than place your response directly in text, the Ask field transforms your response into the contents of a bookmark. Wherever you place that bookmark in your text, these contents appear. Therefore, Ask is ideal for inserting the same text repeatedly throughout a letter.

After you click Insert Word Field and choose Ask, type the name of the bookmark you want Word to create (see Figure 6.22). The bookmark's name can be up to 40 characters long but cannot include spaces. In the Prompt text box, type the text you want Word to display when it prompts you for the bookmark. In the Default Bookmark Text box, type the information you want Word to include in the main document when you type nothing in the Ask dialog box that appears when you start the merge process.

All Ask does is create a bookmark; it doesn't place anything in your letter by itself. You have to place a bookmark field wherever you want the text. You can insert this field manually before you use the Ask field. First, press Ctrl+F9 where you want the bookmark to appear. Field brackets appear. Then, type the bookmark name between the field brackets; for example, { offer }.

Figure 6.22
Inserting an Ask field.

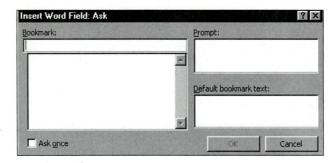

The Ask field also displays a prompt during the merge so that you can add personal notes to clients or add other information that is not suitable to store in a data source. As with the Fill-in field, the prompt appears each time Word merges a new data source document record with the main document unless you instruct Word otherwise.

Tip #90

The information you supply when you include an Ask field can be used in other fields; for example, if you supply a number as the response to an Ask field, you can later use that number as a basis of comparison in an If...Then...Else... field.

USING THE IF...THEN...ELSE... FIELD

The If...Then...Else... field uses the following syntax: If such-and-such happens, Then do this; Else do something different. You can use this field (especially in conjunction with other merge fields and Word fields) to customize the text of each letter, based on any attribute of the recipient you choose.

Suppose, for example, that some of your form letters go to recipients in Tampa, while others go to recipients in Orlando. If you're asking your recipient to make an appointment, you may need to provide different phone numbers for Tampa and Orlando residents to call. In this case, you could use an If...Then...Else... statement to tell Word which phone number to include if the city is Tampa and which phone number to include if the city is Orlando.

To create an If...Then...Else... field:

1. Click your insertion point at the place in the document where you want the customized text to appear.

2. Click Insert Word Field, and choose If...Then...Else.... The Insert Word Field: IF dialog box opens (see Figure 6.23).

3. In the Field Name list box, choose the field you want Word to use when making the comparison.

4. In the Comparison list box, choose the comparison operator; for example, whether you want text inserted only if a value is Greater Than the value found in the field. You can choose from the following comparisons: Equal to, Not equal to, Less than, Greater than, Less than or equal, Greater than or equal, Is blank, or Is not blank.

5. Unless you've chosen Is blank, or Is not blank, you also need to fill in the Compare To box. Enter the number or text you want Word to search for in the selected field.

6. In the Insert This Text box, type the text you want Word to insert if the comparison is true.

7. In the Otherwise Insert This Text box, type the text you want Word to insert if the comparison is false.

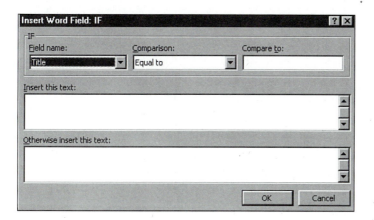

Figure 6.23
You can use this dialog box to build an If...Then...Else... field.

Tip #91

If you edit the field directly (by right-clicking it in the document and choosing Toggle Field Codes, then entering text and field codes within the field brackets that appear), you can gain even more control of your If...Then...Else... field.

For example, you can insert an INCLUDETEXT field as either the Then or Else value, and the INCLUDETEXT field can retrieve a large block of text from the source document you choose. In fact, the source document INCLUDETEXT brings into your merge document can even have its own merge fields, as long as they access the same data source.

This technique makes it convenient to create mail merges that send two entirely different letters to two categories of recipients: for example, those who are on time with their payments, and those who are late.

PART
II

CH
6

USING THE SET BOOKMARK FIELD

The Set Bookmark field (which actually inserts a field simply called "Set") sets the contents of a bookmark, much as you've already seen Ask do. But there's one big difference: The user isn't prompted for the contents of these bookmarks during the mail merge. Rather, you set the contents of the bookmark ahead of time. You can then include the bookmark in another field, such as an If...Then...Else... field.

To create a { SET } field in your main document, click the Insert Word Field button, and choose Set Bookmark. The Insert Word Field: Set dialog box opens (see Figure 6.24).

Figure 6.24
You can define a bookmark in advance using the Insert Word Field: Set dialog box.

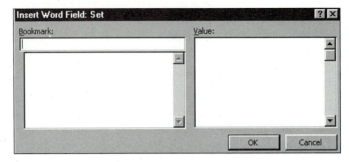

In the Bookmark text box, type the name you want to give to the bookmark. In the Value text box, type the text you want the bookmark to represent. To print the information, you must insert a Ref or Bookmark field in the document or include the bookmark in an Ask or If…Then…Else… field.

USING THE MERGE RECORD # AND MERGE SEQUENCE # FIELDS

Sometimes, in a direct mail campaign, you want to include a unique serial number on each letter you send; it's a quick way for recipients to identify themselves. Word provides two ways to include such a serial number: the Merge Record # and Merge Sequence # fields. The distinction between these fields is subtle: Both generate a unique number in each merged document. However, the number they generate may be different.

Merge Record # returns a record number based on the number of the first record in your data source that you actually used in your merge. So if you created a merge that ignored the first five records in your data source, your first letter would display the number 6.

Merge Sequence # always inserts the number 1 in the first merged letter (or other document) you create; the number 2 in the second letter, and so forth—incrementing each additional letter by 1.

Tip #92

You can use Mergerec inside a formula field to generate numbers from any starting point you want. For example, if you want your first letter to be numbered 101 instead of 1, insert the following field:

```
{ 100 + { MERGEREC } }
```

USING THE NEXT RECORD AND NEXT RECORD IF FIELDS

When you choose Next Record from the Insert Word Field list, you instruct Word to merge the next data record into the current document, rather than start a new merged document. Word automatically does this when you are setting up a mailing label, envelope, or catalog, but it's rarely needed in form letters.

INCLUDING OTHER TYPES OF FIELDS

The Mail Merge Helper toolbar supplies most of the fields you need when you create a merge, but there are a few less common fields you can use in a merge. You can see these fields if you choose Insert, Field and click Mail Merge in the Categories list (see Figure 6.25).

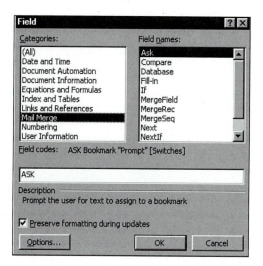

Figure 6.25
The Mail Merge fields available through the Field dialog box.

➜ For more information about working with fields, **see** Chapter 18, "Automating Your Documents with Field Codes," **p. 555**.

Some of the fields that appear in the Field Names list might seem familiar, and, in fact, they are the same as the fields just discussed in the preceding section. For example, the { ASK } field performs exactly the same function as the { ASK } field covered earlier in this chapter.

A few additional fields in the Field dialog box, however, didn't appear in the Word Field list: { COMPARE }, { DATABASE }, and { MERGEFIELD }.

When you use the Compare field, Word looks at two values and displays the result 1 if the comparison is true or 0 (zero) if the comparison is false.

The Database field helps you insert the results of a query to an external database in a Word table. The Database field contains all the information needed to connect to a database and perform a query using Structured Query Language (SQL), a standard query language used by many contemporary databases. When you want to query the database again—to get the most up-to-date information—you simply update the field by selecting it and pressing F9.

The Insert Database button on the Database toolbar, discussed earlier in this chapter, inserts a Database field.

PART

II

CH

6

Finally, MergeField is used automatically by Word whenever you insert a merge field from the Insert Merge Field button on the Mail Merge toolbar. If you insert a merge field corresponding to the Title field in your database, Word inserts the following field code:

```
{ MERGEFIELD Title }
```

Because Word inserts Mergefields automatically when you use the Mail Merge toolbar, you'll probably never have to insert one manually. But it helps to recognize them in case you ever have to troubleshoot the behavior of a field in a mail merge main document—or adjust its *numeric formatting*.

PREPARING TO MERGE

 Now that you've edited your main document, set up your data source, and placed merge fields in your main document, you're nearly ready to run your merge. If you're in the main document, click on the Mail Merge button on the Mail Merge toolbar to display the Merge dialog box, as shown in Figure 6.26. (You can display the same dialog box by displaying the Mail Merge Helper dialog box and clicking Merge in step 3.)

Figure 6.26
You can prepare and manage your merge from the Merge dialog box.

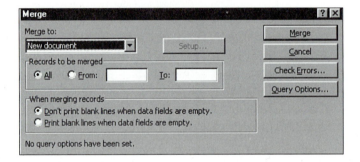

From here, you can make key decisions about how to run your merge, including where to merge (to a new document, your printer, or email); which records to merge; and how you want to handle empty data fields. You can also:

- Use Word's Check Errors feature to test your merge for potential problems
- Use Word's Query Options feature to refine the way you choose records to be merged

The following sections walk you through each of these decisions.

HANDLING BLANK LINES

By default, Word doesn't print blank lines in empty data fields. Why not? Some letters have two-line addresses; others have only one. Some recipients might have titles; others might not. Leaving a blank line in an address or other field is a dead giveaway of a computer-generated letter.

On the other hand, you might want the blank line to appear. Perhaps you're printing a form, and you want the reader to know that the information is incomplete. (Maybe you want the reader to complete it.) In such a situation, you want to choose Print Blank Lines When Data Fields Are Empty.

CHOOSING THE RECORDS TO MERGE

Word gives you exceptional control over which records you include in a mail merge. You can choose a set of records to merge, or you can set up detailed filtering criteria to select records that match your criteria.

 For example, suppose you know that you want to merge the 5th through the 10th records from the data source document. Click Start Mail Merge to display the Merge dialog box. Then, in the Records To Be Merged text boxes, insert the corresponding record numbers.

Sometimes this option is helpful, but much of the time, you don't know exactly which records you want to merge. And if you do know, chances are those records aren't part of a consecutive range such as "From 10 to 20." For more complex record selection problems, click Query Options. The Query Options dialog box opens, as shown in Figure 6.27.

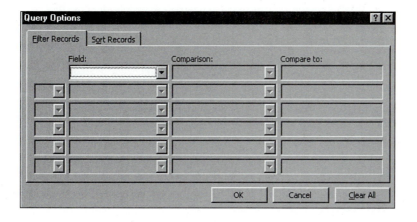

Figure 6.27
Use the Filter Records tab to specify criteria for Word to use when selecting records to merge.

The Filter Records tab enables you to choose which records to print based on detailed criteria you specify. First, you tell Word the field on which you want to base your selection. Then you tell Word which comparison to make to decide whether to include a record. You can make several kinds of comparisons:

- Equal To
- Not Equal To
- Less Than
- Greater Than
- Less Than or Equal To
- Greater Than or Equal To
- Is Blank
- Is Not Blank

Caution

You can't use Microsoft Query to select Outlook contact records based on fields in each record. You can, however, achieve the same result if you create your mail merge in Outlook—or if you export selected Outlook records to a file that can be read by Word as a data source, such as a CSV file.

In most cases, you not only must provide a comparison, but you also must tell Word what it needs to compare the text or number. ("Equal to what?") Here are a few examples of how filtering records works, first in English, and then in Word's query language.

To print letters for all records where the company name is AT&T, enter the following:

Field:	Comparison:	Compare To:
Company	Equal to	AT&T

To print letters for all records where the order size is less than $1,000, enter the following:

Field:	Comparison:	Compare To:
Order Size	Less than	$1,000

To print a letter for every record except those that don't have a name:

Field:	Comparison:
Name	Is not blank

Note

The last example does not require you to enter anything in the Compare To box.

Using the list box at the left, which specifies And by default (but also can specify Or), you can make up to six comparisons at the same time in the same query. Here's an example that uses the And operator.

To print a letter for all records where Postal Code is greater than 11700 but less than 11999 (thereby printing only letters addressed to Long Island, New York):

	Field:	Comparison:	Compare To:
	Postal Code	Greater than or Equal	11700
And	Postal Code	Less than or Equal	11999

Here's another example, this time using the Or operator. To print a letter for all records where the addressee's company is AT&T, IBM, or General Electric, enter the following:

	Field:	Comparison:	Compare To:
	Company	Equal to	AT&T
Or	Company	Equal to	IBM
Or	Company	Equal to	General Electric

If you tell Word to print only records that meet one condition and another condition, you almost always get fewer records than if you select records that meet one condition or the other (and you never get more records).

The order in which you use the Ands and Ors makes a difference in the records Word prints. Word performs each operation in order, and the result from one operation is used when it performs the next operation.

For instance, suppose Word sees this query:

	Field:	Comparison:	Compare To:
	Job Title	Equal to	Vice President
Or	City	Equal to	Cincinnati
And	Title	Equal to	Mr.

Word finds all the vice presidents in your database, and adds to it everyone from Cincinnati. Having done this, Word next subtracts all the women. But swap things around a bit, and it's a different story:

	Field:	Comparison:	Compare To:
	Job Title	Equal to	Vice President
And	Title	Equal to	Mr.
Or	City	Equal to	Cincinnati

Word first finds all the vice presidents in the list, next excludes the women vice presidents, and then adds anyone from Cincinnati, without regard to gender.

Tip #93   If you create a set of filtering rules that doesn't seem to work properly, you can start over again by choosing Clear All.

SORTING MERGED RECORDS

You may also decide that you want to produce your merged documents in a specific order. For example, you can often lower the cost of a mass mailing by bundling letters going to the same zip code, which is practical only if you print your letters in zip code order.

To control the order in which your records print, display the Query Options dialog box and click the Sort Records tab (see Figure 6.28).

In the Sort By list box, you choose a field upon which to base your sort. You also can choose whether to sort in ascending or descending order. *Ascending* sorts from 0 to 9 and then from A to Z (in other words, any entries starting with a number appear before entries starting with a letter). *Descending* sorts from Z to A and then from 9 to 0; in other words, letters appear before numbers.

You can sort up to three levels. Word first sorts by the field you choose in the Sort By box. Next, Word sorts by the field in your first Then By box. If you've specified another Then By field, Word then sorts by that field's contents.

Figure 6.28
Controlling the order in which your records print.

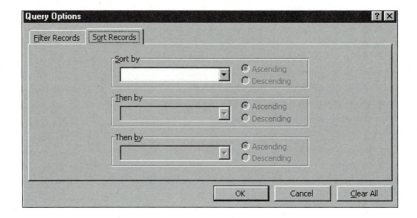

In essence, Word uses the second and third fields as "tie-breakers": if it finds two or more records that meet the same criterion, it looks for the next criterion and then the third to determine which order to use. So, for example, you might sort your letters first by zip code and then alphabetically by last name; all letters to the same zip code would be printed together, but within each zip code, the letters would be alphabetized.

PREVIEWING YOUR MAIL MERGE FROM WITHIN THE MAIN DOCUMENT

Before you actually merge, you can preview sample merged documents onscreen by clicking the View Merged Data button on the Mail Merge toolbar in the main document. When you click this button, Word replaces the merge fields in the main document with the first record in the data source document that meets your Query Options criteria (see Figure 6.29).

Figure 6.29
You can preview merged documents before actually merging.

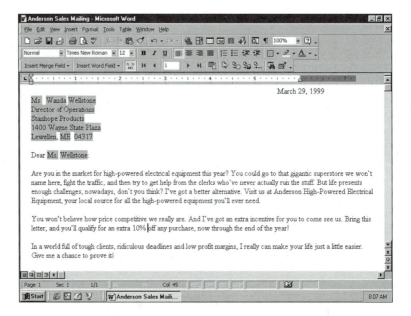

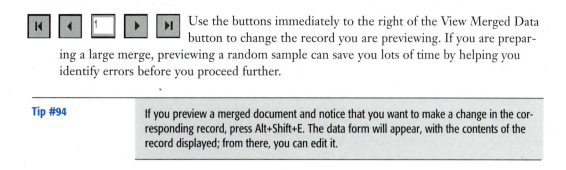 Use the buttons immediately to the right of the View Merged Data button to change the record you are previewing. If you are preparing a large merge, previewing a random sample can save you lots of time by helping you identify errors before you proceed further.

Tip #94

If you preview a merged document and notice that you want to make a change in the corresponding record, press Alt+Shift+E. The data form will appear, with the contents of the record displayed; from there, you can edit it.

Caution

Don't edit the contents of an address book with the data form. Use the program that created the address book, such as Microsoft Outlook.

→ For more information about editing records using data forms, **see** "Working with the Data Form," **p. 177**.

CHECKING YOUR MAIL MERGE FOR ERRORS

As the preceding section described, you can preview individual form letters (or other merged documents) by clicking View Merged Data while your main document is displayed. But in a large mailing, it may be impractical to check every document individually, and it's all too easy to miss potentially disastrous problems, such as discrepancies between merge fields in the main document and field names in the data source, or incorrect sort order.

That's where Word's Check Errors feature comes in. To run error checking, first display the Merge dialog box. (From within the main document, click the Mail Merge button. From elsewhere, display the Mail Merge Helper and click Merge in Step #3.) Next, click Check Errors. The Checking and Reporting Errors dialog box appears (see Figure 6.30).

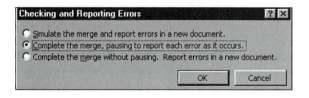

Figure 6.30
Choosing how you want Word to check and report on potential errors in your mail merge.

PART
II

CH

6

You have three choices. The first and third choices list your errors in a new document, named Mail Merge Errors1. The middle choice runs the merge, displaying a dialog box onscreen if an error occurs.

Figure 6.31 displays the most common error Word can find: an invalid merge field. This often occurs when you enter merge fields, and later change your data source. If the new data source includes different field names from those you used originally, Word can't find the information it needs to include in your merged documents.

Figure 6.31
Word can identify invalid merge fields as you check a merge for errors.

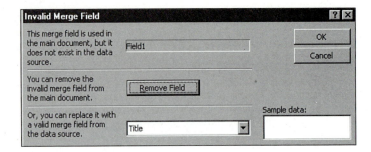

When the Invalid Merge Field dialog box appears, you can click Remove Field to remove the field from your main document. Word continues checking for errors immediately without asking you to confirm the change.

CHOOSING WHERE TO MERGE

 The last step before running your merge is to decide where you want the merged output to go. You can make your choice in the Merge To drop-down box of the Merge dialog box. You have three choices:

- **New Document.** Word places all the merged documents in a single new document. If you are creating form letters, this document is named Form Letters1; if you are creating catalogs, it is Catalog1; and so forth. *Continuous section breaks* (section breaks that don't also include page breaks) separate each merged document from the one that follows. After you merge the documents, you can review them one more time, make any manual customizations you like, and then print the letters.

- **Printer.** Word displays the Print dialog box, where you can establish any printer settings you need. For example, you can choose a different printer from the Name drop-down box, or set the Number of Copies to print more than one set of letters. When you establish all the settings you want, click OK, and your merged documents print.

- **Electronic Mail.** As discussed in the next section, you can send your customized letters to email addresses rather than postal addresses. If your computer has a faxmodem, you can also send custom "broadcast" faxes.

SPECIAL CONSIDERATIONS FOR BROADCAST EMAIL OR FAX

If your computer has a MAPI-compatible email or fax program, such as Outlook, Schedule+, Microsoft Exchange, Symantec WinFax Pro, or Microsoft Fax, you can use the Mail Merge Helper to create broadcast email or faxes.

Caution

If you plan to use broadcast fax or email, make sure you understand the legal restrictions, and be sensitive to the attitudes of your recipients.

To successfully merge to either email addresses or fax numbers, you must include them as merge fields in the data source document. However, you do not need to include these merge fields as part of your main document. After you've done so, follow these steps:

1. Open the Query Options dialog box, and click the Filter Records tab (refer to Figure 6.27).

2. Set up a filter criteria that chooses the Email or Fax field in your data source, and uses the comparison "Is Not Blank." This ensures that you generate merged documents for only users who have an email address or fax number. If you use a fax number, make sure to format it correctly, as discussed earlier in this chapter.

Tip #95

If, later on, you want to send postal mail to those you cannot reach via fax or email, return to this dialog box and reset the comparison to "Is Blank." That way, you generate a list of recipients who do not have fax numbers or email addresses.

To open the Query Options dialog box, click the Mail Merge button. Then, click the Query Options button and choose the Filter Records tab.

3. Click OK to display the Merge dialog box again.

4. Open the Merge To list box and choose Electronic Mail. The Setup button appears.

5. Click Setup. The Merge To Setup dialog box appears (see Figure 6.32).

Figure 6.32
Use this dialog box to tell Word where to look for the email addresses or fax numbers you want to use.

6. In the Data Field with Mail/Fax Address drop-down box, select the merge field containing the email addresses or fax numbers you want to use.

7. If you are sending email, enter a subject line in the Mail Message Subject Line text box.

8. If you are sending email, Word incorporates the text of each message into the body of the message by default, eliminating formatting. If all your recipients have Microsoft Word, you might consider checking the Send Document as an Attachment check box; this way, they receive a formatted document. If you are sending a fax, always select Send Document as an Attachment.

9. When you're finished, click OK.

PART

II

CH

6

Tip #96

If you're not sure whether your recipients can read a file formatted as a Microsoft Word file, consider sending a file formatted as Rich Text Format (RTF)—a format that can be imported by nearly all competitive word processing software.

RUNNING THE MERGE

By now, you should have completed all the steps involved in preparing your mail merge. Here's a checklist. Have you...

- Created your main document?
- Created or selected your data source?
- Made sure your data source contains data?
- If necessary, created a header source document?
- Inserted all appropriate merge fields in your main document?
- Inserted any Word fields you might need in your main document?
- Set your query options to specify which records to print, and in what order?
- Specified how you want to handle blank lines?
- Specified where you want to output your merged document?
- Previewed your merge and checked it for errors?

If you've done all that, you have only one thing left to do: Click <u>M</u>erge, and Word runs your merge.

 If you find that merge fields are printing instead of the information contained in the corresponding fields, see "What to Do When Merge Fields Print Instead of Information from the Corresponding Records," in the "Troubleshooting" section of this chapter.

PRINTING ACCOMPANYING ENVELOPES AND LABELS

You can print matching envelopes or labels for your merged letters by using the same data source with the same selection and sorting options. Word makes this easy.

To print labels or envelopes to accompany form letters, first set up all the merge options for your form letters, especially the query options. Then run the merge to generate your form letters.

When you're sure your merge ran correctly, open your main document (it is usually still open, and listed on the Windows taskbar). Click the Mail Merge Helper button on the Mail Merge toolbar to display the Mail Merge Helper.

Next, click <u>C</u>reate, and choose <u>M</u>ailing Labels (or <u>E</u>nvelopes). Word asks whether you want to <u>C</u>hange Document Type or create a <u>N</u>ew Main Document. Choose <u>C</u>hange Document Type.

Click Setup. If you've chosen to create a label, the Label Options dialog box appears. If you've chosen to create an envelope, the Envelope Options dialog box appears. Choose which kind of label or envelope you want to use, from which tray of your printer you want to print your labels or envelopes, and bar coding and other options if applicable. Finally, click OK.

PRINTING ENVELOPES THAT DO NOT ACCOMPANY FORM LETTERS

To print envelopes when you have not already run a mail merge to create form letters, follow these steps:

1. Choose Tools, Mail Merge.
2. Choose Create; then choose Envelopes.
3. Choose New Main Document.
4. Choose Get Data. Select or create a data source, as discussed earlier in this chapter.
5. Set up your main document for envelopes by choosing Set Up Main Document from the Mail Merge Helper dialog box. The Envelope Options dialog box appears.
6. Establish your envelope settings and click OK.
7. The Envelope Address dialog box opens. Create your envelope address by choosing merge fields from the Insert Merge Field box, as if you were working directly in a main document.
8. If you also want to add a POSTNET bar code to streamline mail handling, choose Insert Postal Bar Code. The Insert Postal Bar Code dialog box appears.
9. To add the postal code, specify which of your merge fields contain the zip code and the street address. Click OK.
10. Choose Mail Merge from the Tools menu. Then, in the Mail Merge Helper screen, choose to Edit your main document. Your envelope appears in Print Layout view.
11. If necessary, move the frame that contains your delivery address merge fields.

    Notice that the return address is that shown in Tools, Options, User Information. If you don't need a return address, select and delete it. If the name and address are wrong, you can edit them.

12. Click the Mail Merge button on the Mail Merge toolbar, and prepare your merge. Along the way, set Query Options, check errors, and establish other settings, as discussed elsewhere in this chapter.
13. Run your merge.

PART
II
CH
6

PRINTING LABELS THAT DO NOT ACCOMPANY FORM LETTERS

To print labels when you have not already run a mail merge to create form letters, follow these steps:

1. Choose Tools, Mail Merge.

2. Choose Create; then choose Mailing Labels.

3. Choose New Main Document.

4. Choose Get Data. Select or create a data source, as discussed earlier in this chapter.

5. Set up your main document for labels by choosing Set Up Main Document from the Mail Merge Helper dialog box. The Label Options dialog box appears.

   You can choose a standard label or define a custom label here, and also specify how you want your label to print. (Chapter 4 covers the Label Options dialog box in-depth.)

6. Click OK. The Create Labels dialog box opens.

7. Create your label address by choosing merge fields from the Insert Merge Field box as if you were working directly in a main document.

8. If you also want to add a POSTNET bar code to streamline mail handling, choose Insert Postal Bar Code.

9. To add the bar code, specify which of your merge fields contain the zip code and the street address. Click OK.

 10. If you want to check the formatting of your labels, display the Mail Merge Helper and choose Edit Main Document. Your label fields appear in Normal view. Note that you see the fields, not the finished mail merge.

11. Click the Mail Merge button on the Mail Merge toolbar, and prepare your merge. Along the way, set query options, check errors, and establish other settings, as discussed elsewhere in this chapter.

12. Run your merge.

TROUBLESHOOTING

WHAT TO DO IF WORD CONFUSES YOUR DATA SOURCE WITH YOUR MAIN DOCUMENT

Chances are you were viewing the data source document when you reopened the Mail Merge Helper, so your data source document was accidentally chosen as the main document. Switch to the data source document and follow the procedure described previously to convert the data source document to a Normal Word document. Save the data source document and close it. Then, open the document you want to use as a main document, use the Mail Merge Helper to create the main document and then attach the data source document using the Get Data button in the Mail Merge Helper dialog box.

WHAT TO DO WHEN WORD DISREGARDS CHARACTER FORMATTING IN YOUR DATA SOURCE

Mail-merged information takes on the formatting of the merge field in the main document; any formatting you apply in the data source document is ignored. Format your merge fields in the main document to make merged data appear the way you want. You may also be able to use formatting switches available to Word fields to achieve the formatting you're looking for.

→ For more information about using field switches to control the appearance of text, dates, and values, **see** "A Closer Look at Field Formatting," **p. 574**.

WHAT TO DO WHEN YOU WANT TO TRANSFORM A MAIN DOCUMENT INTO AN ORDINARY WORD DOCUMENT

If you no longer want to use a main document in mail merges, but Word keeps prompting you to locate a data source when you work with the main document, do the following: In the main document, open the Mail Merge Helper. Choose the Create button, and then choose Restore to Normal Word Document.

WHAT TO DO WHEN YOU WANT TO USE MAIN DOCUMENTS FROM OLDER VERSIONS OF WORD

You automatically can use main documents you created in Word 97 or Word 95 (Word 7.0). If the main documents are attached to data source documents, you also can use main documents created in Word 6 for Windows and Word 2 for Windows. If the main documents contain a DATA field that identifies the data source document, you also can use main documents created in Word 1 for Windows, Word for the Macintosh, or Word for MS-DOS.

WHAT TO DO WHEN MERGE FIELDS PRINT INSTEAD OF INFORMATION FROM THE CORRESPONDING RECORDS

Adjust your Print options: They're probably set to print field codes rather than field results. Choose Tools, Options, and click the Print tab. Then, remove the check from the Field Codes check box in the Include with Document section.

WHAT TO DO WHEN YOUR MERGED DOCUMENTS CONTAIN BLANK LINES YOU DON'T WANT

Sometimes you can solve this problem by clicking the Merge button to display the Merge dialog box, and clicking the Don't Print Blank Lines When Data Fields Are Empty option button. If blank lines are appearing where you've used an If, Ask, or Set field, try to insert the field within an existing paragraph, not in its own paragraph. If your document format won't allow this, format the paragraph mark as hidden text.

Then, before you print, make sure hidden text doesn't print. Choose Tools, Options; click the Print tab; clear the Hidden Text check box; and click OK.

Another way to print text inserted by an If field as a separate paragraph is to insert the paragraph mark directly into the field code that generates the text, surrounded by quotation marks.

→ For more information about creating and editing field codes manually, **see** "Inserting a Field Using Field Characters," **p. 56**

PART

II

CH

6

WHAT TO DO IF ELECTRONIC FAX DOESN'T APPEAR IN THE "MERGE TO" OPTIONS

First, check to make sure you are using MAPI-compatible fax software. Also, if you are running Microsoft Mail as your email system, edit the [EFAX Transport] section of your MSMAIL.INI file to include this statement:

```
LocalFax=1
```

Make sure to save the file as text only.

WHAT TO DO IF YOU GET ERROR MESSAGES WHEN MERGING TO FAX

In your data source, make sure you've formatted your fax numbers properly, as in the following example (include the brackets):

```
[FAX:2065550187]
```

If this doesn't work, and you are running Windows 95 with Microsoft Mail, follow the steps in "What to Do if Electronic Fax Doesn't Appear in the 'Merge To' Options."

Tip #97

If you find yourself having mail merge problems not covered here, call Microsoft's Fast Tips hotline at (800) 936-4100, and ask to receive Knowledge Base article Q162210, which contains an extensive list of potential problems with Word mail merge, and Microsoft articles that contain the solutions.

CHAPTER

7

OUTLINING: THE BEST WAY TO ORGANIZE A DOCUMENT

In this chapter

THE BENEFITS OF OUTLINING

Word's outlining feature gives you a quick and convenient way to organize (and reorganize) any document or Web page. The larger your documents, the more valuable you will find the organizing capabilities that outlining provides. As you'll see, with outlining it's easy to view your document at a very high level, then drill down to any specific element that needs attention, and move large blocks of text easily. In other words, you can see the forest and the trees—and work with both.

Communicating with Word: Use Outlining to Make Things Easier

Use outlining to plan your document before you start to write. First, brainstorm—and enter the content you want to include in rough form. Then, use Word's outlining tools to reorganize the text, decide what should be emphasized and which areas are minor details subordinate to more important points.

Organize your sections by heading and then support them using the subheadings. Traditionally, the first paragraph under a heading should introduce the subject or focus for that heading, and the subheadings should provide an argument to support the heading. Under each subheading, introduce your argument in the first paragraph, and then provide evidence to it. The last paragraph should often summarize the evidence, and restate the argument. After the last subheading is complete, as the last paragraph in the section, draw together each subheading and restate the purpose you outlined in the first paragraph. This purpose is your focus for the section, and by following this format, you will focus your reader's attention and deliver a more compelling argument.

THE ROLE OF HEADING STYLES IN OUTLINING

Outlining works seamlessly with the heading styles you may already have inserted in your documents. Or, if you haven't applied heading styles, Word can add them for you automatically, while you work on your outline. Each heading style corresponds to a specific outline level in your document: Heading 1 corresponds to the first level of your outline, Heading 2 the second level, and so forth.

You can't change the outline level associated with a built-in heading style though, as you'll see later in this chapter, you can assign any outline level you want, from 1 to 9, to other styles, and use those styles as the basis for your outline. This was not possible in versions of Word prior to Word 97.

→ For more information about assigning outline levels to styles, **see** "Applying Outline Levels to Specific Text," **p. 225**.

Tip #98

As you've already learned, after your heading styles are in place, you can use them to automate many Word features. Later in this chapter, in the section titled "Using Word's Automatic Outline Numbering," you'll discover one of the best of these features: Word's simple, quick Outline Numbering feature. You'll learn how Word can instantly number all your headings and subheads—and keep them numbered properly, come what may.

CREATING A NEW OUTLINE

An outline is embedded in every document you create, but unless you deliberately look for it, you might never realize it because Word treats an outline as just another way to view a document. This means you don't have to actively create an outline to get one. It also means that when you do want a polished outline, you can simply refine the one that's already built into your document.

 Outlines can be created in two ways. The first is to work from scratch. Open a new blank document, and click the Outline View button to display it in Outline view (see Figure 7.1).

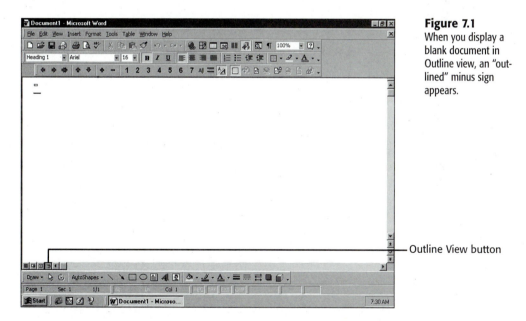

Figure 7.1
When you display a blank document in Outline view, an "outlined" minus sign appears.

Outline View button

You can create an outline from scratch if you're starting a major new project, such as a book or manual, and you don't yet have any text. Working from scratch is convenient because you don't have to worry about moving existing blocks of text or reorganizing material that should have been handled differently from the outset. You can organize the document the best way right from the beginning. If you're leading a team of writers, you can divide your outline into sections and delegate each part.

PART

II

CH

7

Tip #99

With Word's closely related *Master Documents* feature, you can divide the document into subdocuments, assign each subdocument to a different writer, and then edit and manage all the subdocuments together, as if they were still part of one longer document.

Tip #100

Use Outline view in connection with Word's *Track Changes* and *Versions* tools to streamline the process of getting your outline approved.

The second way to create an outline is to do nothing at all. Work as you normally do. Apply heading styles as part of the formatting you ordinarily would perform. Then, whenever you're ready, switch to Outline view; Word displays your existing document as an outline. Figure 7.2 shows a typical document displayed as an outline: Each first-level heading appears furthest to the left, with second-level headings and body text subordinate to it. As you can see, this only works if you use heading styles; without them, this document would appear as a one-level outline, with no apparent structure or organization.

Figure 7.2
Whenever you're ready, click the Outline View button to display your document as an outline.

First-level heading ⌐
Second-level heading ⌐

- ○ **Project specifications**
  - □ Please quote this project based on the following specifications:
  - ○ *Quantity*
    - □ 300 packages
  - ○ *Pages/Sheets*
    - □ 64 sheets printed one side
  - ○ *Colors*
    - □ One color (black)
  - ○ *Fulfillment and Other Services*
    - □ Collated, hole-drilled and shrinkwrapped together with one diskette, to be provided
- ○ **Optional Line Items**
  - □ Please include *as a separate line item* packaging 200 of these to be mailed to 200 separate domestic locations via US Mail, and packaging the remaining 100 in one package for mailing to one additional location. Do not include postage.
  - ○ *Deliverable*
    - □ Electronic files will be provided to you in Word 6/95 format, with all required fonts.
  - ○ *Schedule*
    - □ We will deliver this project to you in one week. We require finished printed pieces in 72 hours.
  - ○ *Other required information*
    - □ Please state your required schedule for fulfillment.
    - □ Please state any subcontractors you intend to use on this project.
    - □ Please state the name, phone number and E-mail address of your company's contact on this project.

Tip #101

If you want the organizational benefits of outlining but you don't like the appearance of Word's heading styles, change the formatting associated with the heading styles.

To do so, format some text with the heading style; then manually reformat it as you wish. Click in the Style box on the Standard toolbar, and press Enter. The Modify Style dialog box appears; specify that you want to Update the Style to Reflect Recent Changes, and click OK.

Your style changes will be reflected in all views within this document, including Outline view. Repeat the process for each heading you intend to use.

To learn more about formatting text with an existing style, **see** "Applying an Existing Style," **p. 37**.

If you want to copy only the headings from one document to another, see "How to Copy Only a Document's Headings Without Copying All the Subordinate Text" in the "Troubleshooting" section of this chapter.

UNDERSTANDING OUTLINE VIEW

Soon, you'll learn techniques for polishing your outline to make sure your document is actually structured the way you want. First, however, you notice three things about Outline view:

- **Each paragraph has a symbol to its left.** These symbols tell you what you need to know about the paragraph's relationship to surrounding text:
  - A plus sign (+) tells you the paragraph has subordinate text. This text may consist of lower-level headings, paragraphs formatted in styles that Word does not recognize as a heading or outline level, or both.
  - A minus sign (–) tells you the paragraph has no subordinate text. In other words, the paragraph has a heading style or outline level, but no subheads or body text are beneath it.
  - A small square tells you the paragraph is body text.

- **Paragraph formatting, such as indents and line spacing, disappears.** In fact, Word grays out the Format, Paragraph menu command, so you can't use it to add new paragraph formatting. In its place, Word displays its own outline indenting to make it obvious which paragraphs are most important (for example, which appear at the highest level of your outline) and which are subordinate.

- **The Outlining toolbar appears.** This toolbar contains all the tools you need to edit and manage your outline.

Tip #102

You can use keyboard shortcuts or the Increase Indent and Decrease Indent buttons on the Formatting toolbar to set standard indents without changing the outline level of your heading. You can also right-click to access a shortcut menu that includes some formatting controls (see Figure 7.3).

PART
II

CH
7

Figure 7.3
Right-click anywhere in Outline view to see its shortcut menu.

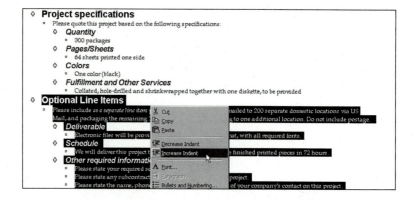

Tip #103

You can switch back and forth between views at any time. You might use Outline view whenever you're organizing your document, Normal view when you're editing content, and *Print Layout view* whenever you're primarily concerned about graphics and the appearance of your pages.

If you're working in Normal view, and you decide to change a heading level, you might want to switch into Outline view so you can quickly change all the subordinate headings at the same time.

USING THE OUTLINING TOOLBAR

Take a closer look at the Outlining toolbar (see Figure 7.4), which includes Word's tools for organizing and managing your outline. These buttons fall into the following three categories:

- Tools for increasing or decreasing the relative importance of paragraphs (Promote, Demote, and Demote to Body Text)
- Tools for moving paragraphs up or down in the document (Move Up, Move Down)
- Tools for controlling which paragraphs display and how they look (Expand, Collapse, Show Heading 1 through 7, Show All Headings, Show First Line Only, and Show Formatting)

Figure 7.4
The Outlining toolbar appears only when you are working in Outline view; you can't display it anywhere else.

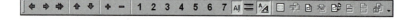

The Master Document tools at the right side of the Outlining toolbar are covered in Chapter 8, "Master Documents: Control and Share Even the Longest Documents."

Nearly all these buttons also have a keyboard shortcut equivalent, as listed in Table 7.1.

TABLE 7.1 KEYBOARD AND TOOLBAR SHORTCUTS FOR WORKING IN OUTLINE VIEW

Task	Keyboard Shortcut	Toolbar Button
Promote paragraph	Alt+Shift+Left arrow	
Demote paragraph	Alt+Shift+Right arrow	
Demote to body text	Ctrl+Shift+N	
Move selected paragraph(s) up	Alt+Shift+Up arrow	
Move selected paragraph(s) down	Alt+Shift+Down arrow	
Expand text beneath heading	Alt+Shift++ (plus sign)	
Collapse text beneath heading	Alt+Shift+- (minus sign)	
Expand/collapse all text or headings	Alt+Shift+A	
Toggle character formatting	/ (on numeric keypad)	
Toggle to display only first line of body text	Alt+Shift+L	
Show only Level 1 headings/text	Alt+Shift+1	
Show all levels through [a number]	Alt+Shift+[number from 1 to 7]	

Tip #104

The Promote, Demote, Demote to Body Text, Move Up, and Move Down keyboard shortcuts work in every view, not just Outline view. It's a very quick way to change heading styles or move paragraphs.

PART

II

CH

7

It's helpful to understand what the Outlining toolbar buttons and symbols don't do, so you don't make the common mistakes that trip up many first-time outliners:

- The right arrow button does not insert a tab, even though it looks as if it might. It does indent text much as a tab does. Remember: the right arrow key demotes a paragraph by one heading and/or outline level.

- The numbered buttons do not specify heading or outline levels. They simply control how many levels you can see at the same time.

- The plus and minus buttons do not increase or decrease the importance of selected text. Rather, they hide or display all the subordinate text and headings beneath the paragraph you've chosen.

  Similarly, the plus and minus symbols next to each paragraph say nothing about the heading level associated with the paragraph. All they tell you is whether the paragraph has text subordinate to it. It's common to have two headings next to each other, both formatted in the same style, but one adorned with a plus sign and the other a minus sign.

ADDING NEW SUBHEADINGS

Now that you've taken a tour of Word's outlining tools, it's time to start using them. If you open a blank document and switch to Outline view, Word typically displays a minus sign. This indicates that, for the moment at least, no text is subordinate to the line in which you are working.

If you start typing the first line of an outline, Word formats your text as a first-level heading, using the Heading 1 style. If you finish your paragraph and press Enter to start a new one, Word creates a new paragraph, also with the Heading 1 style. You can see this in Figure 7.5, which shows an outline with style names displayed in the *Style Area*.

Note

To set a Style Area, choose Tools, Options; click View, enter a value in the Style Area Width spin box, and click OK.

Figure 7.5
If you press Enter after creating a first-level heading in Outline view, Word starts another first-level heading.

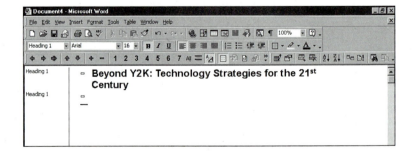

Note

> In this respect, Word behaves differently in Outline view than in other views. Elsewhere in Word, if you press Enter to create a new paragraph after a heading, Word assumes you want to create Normal text—text formatted with the Normal style. (That's what Word's built-in Heading style settings tell it to do.) However, people rarely create text in Outline view, so Word assumes that you're creating an outline and want another heading like the one you've just finished.

PROMOTING AND DEMOTING HEADINGS

 Often, you don't want another heading at the same level as the one you've just completed. Instead, you want a subordinate heading or body text. To demote any heading by one level, position your insertion point anywhere in the paragraph, and click Demote or use the keyboard shortcut Alt+Shift+Right arrow.

When you demote a heading, Word indents it, and also changes the heading style. For example, if you demote a first-level heading, Word changes the style associated with it to Heading 2. If the heading contains text, the character formatting also changes to reflect the new style.

 Of course you can promote subordinate headings as well; click the Promote button or Alt+Shift+Left arrow. Again, Word changes the style and formatting as well as the indentation.

DRAGGING HEADINGS WITH THE MOUSE

You can also drag a heading to a new level. Click the outline symbol next to the heading; your mouse pointer changes to a crosshair and Word selects the heading and its subordinate contents. Then drag the mouse to the right. The mouse pointer changes to a horizontal double-arrow, and you'll see a gray vertical line that moves as you jump from one heading level to the next (see Figure 7.6). When you've arrived at the heading level you want, release the mouse pointer.

Tip #105

> If you want to move a heading by several levels, it's often quicker to change the style instead. For example, to move a heading from second to sixth level, choose Heading 6 in the Style drop-down list box.

PART

II

CH

7

Figure 7.6
You can drag a paragraph left or right to a new heading level.

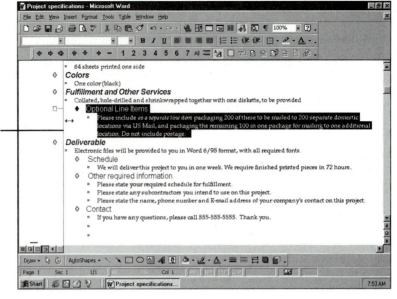

Vertical line indicates level to which selected text is being moved.

DEMOTING TEXT TO BODY TEXT

 To demote any heading to body text, click Demote to Body Text or press Ctrl+Shift+N. Word reformats that text in the Normal style, and displays the small square Body Text symbol next to it. When you finish a paragraph of body text, you can start a new one by pressing Enter; another Body Text symbol appears to the left of the new paragraph.

Tip #106

In most cases, it's inconvenient to edit your whole document in Outline view, but you might have some ideas you'd like to jot down while you're organizing a new document in Outline view. Click Demote to Body Text in a new paragraph and start typing.

Note

Word uses the term "body text" to refer to two different things: a style and an outline level. As you'll see, this can cause confusion for the unwary.

Some people format all body text using Word's Body Text style rather than the Normal style. In fact, Word often makes this change automatically when you run *AutoFormat*. However, Normal and Body Text are two different styles. In particular, Body Text adds 6 points of space after each paragraph, and Normal does not.

Surprisingly, when you use Demote to Body Text, you reformat text with the Normal style, not the Body Text style (though this does apply the Body Text outline level). As a result, if your document utilizes the Body Text style, but you also click Demote to Body Text in Outline view, you may inadvertently introduce small formatting inconsistencies.

If you want to standardize on the Body Text style rather than the Normal style, spend five minutes recording a quick *macro* that replaces the Normal style with the Body Text style throughout your document.

PROMOTING OR DEMOTING SEVERAL HEADINGS AT THE SAME TIME

If you select one heading and promote or demote it, nothing changes elsewhere in your document. That might be just fine with you. Often, however, when you promote or demote a heading, you want all your subordinate headings to be carried along with it.

Word makes this easy to do. Rather than select the paragraph, click the outline symbol next to it. This selects both the current paragraph and all the paragraphs subordinate to it. In Figure 7.7 you can see a first-level heading that has been selected along with the second-level heading and subordinate body text beneath it.

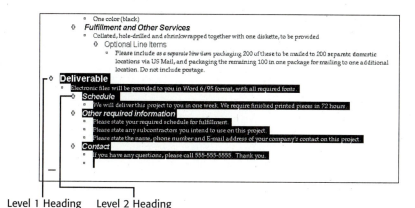

Figure 7.7
Clicking the outline symbol next to a paragraph selects the paragraph and all the subordinate headings and body text beneath it.

Level 1 Heading   Level 2 Heading

Figure 7.8 shows what happens after you click Demote. The second-level head is now a third-level head; the third-level head is now a fourth-level head, and so on. Text formatted in nonheading styles does not change, however, regardless of which headings it is subordinate to. To transform body text into a heading, you have to select it and promote it.

Tip #107

Just as you can demote a heading to body text, you can also promote body text to a heading by selecting it and clicking Promote. Doing so transforms body text into a first-level heading formatted with the Heading 1 style; if necessary, you can then click Demote once or more to transform the text into a lower-level heading.

You can promote several consecutive paragraphs of body text at once, as long as your selection doesn't contain any headings. Select all the paragraphs, and click Promote.

Figure 7.8
After you click
Demote, all the
selected heading lev-
els are demoted, but
text formatted with
other styles does not
change.

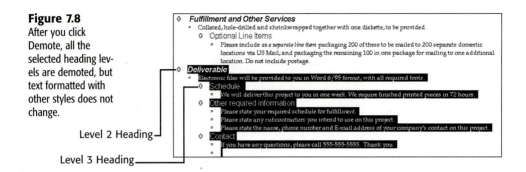

Level 2 Heading
Level 3 Heading

MOVING PARAGRAPHS WITHIN AN OUTLINE

As you organize your outline, you might find a heading or a block of text that you would like to move toward the front or rear of the document. Word's Cut and Paste tools work within Outline view. However, if you are simply moving a heading or text by one (or a few) paragraphs, there's a quicker alternative.

Place your insertion point in the paragraph you want to move, and click the Move Up or Move Down button on the Outlining toolbar. The entire paragraph moves. If you want to move more than one paragraph, select them all before clicking Move Up or Move Down.

If you're moving text farther than a paragraph or two, there's a quicker solution: drag and drop it. Click the Outline symbol next to a paragraph. Your mouse pointer changes to a crosshair. Drag the mouse up or down. The pointer changes to a vertical double-arrow, and a gray horizontal line appears, moving as you jump from one paragraph to the next (see Figure 7.9). When you arrive at the location you want, release the mouse pointer.

Figure 7.9
Dragging text up or
down in Outline view.

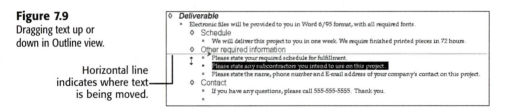

Horizontal line
indicates where text
is being moved.

Tip #108

The technique you've just learned works if you're moving just one paragraph (and its sub-ordinate contents). However, what if you want to move several consecutive paragraphs that all share the same heading level?

First, select all the paragraphs. Next, press Alt and click the Outline symbol next to the first paragraph. Finally, drag the paragraphs to their new location.

Tip #109

Here's another quick way to organize a long document in Outline view:

1. Click Show Heading 1 to display only first-level headings.
2. Manually enter heading numbers to reflect the order in which you want the first-level headings to appear. (Don't use any of Word's automatic numbering features.)
3. Press Ctrl+A to select all the first-level headings.
4. Choose Table, Sort.
5. Click OK. Word sorts the headings in number order—thereby reorganizing the entire document at the same time.

CONTROLLING YOUR OUTLINE VIEW

You've already heard that Word's outlines enable you to "view the forest and the trees." In fact, you can control the exact level of detail you view at any time. It's as if you could not only view the forest or the trees, but also specific leaves, branches, trunks, individual trees, or groups of trees as well.

DISPLAYING ONLY SELECTED HEADING LEVELS

Imagine you're reviewing a complex document with several levels of headings. You might want to start by looking at the document at a very high level—viewing only first-level headings. Click Show Heading 1 on the Outlining toolbar, and Word hides all paragraphs except those formatted as first-level headings (see Figure 7.10). The gray underlining beneath these headings tells you they have subordinate text you aren't seeing.

Figure 7.10
A document showing only first-level headings.

After you're satisfied with the high-level organization of the document, you can drill deeper; click the Show Heading 2 button to view both first-level and second-level headings, click 3 to view the first three levels of headings, and so on.

Tip #110

Displaying only one or two levels of headings can make it much easier to find a distant location in a large document. After you find it, you can click its heading and start editing there—in Outline view or any other view you choose.

PART

II

CH

7

Tip #111

Word supports nine outline levels, but the Outlining toolbar doesn't contain Show Heading 8 and Show Heading 9 buttons. To display eighth-level headings, press Alt+Shift+*. To display ninth-level headings, press Alt+Shift+(.

Alternatively, you can click Show All Headings twice. The first click displays all headings and body text, including Heading 8 and Heading 9. The second click hides the body text but leaves all nine heading levels visible.

If you often work with eighth and ninth level headings, you can add the ShowHeading8 and ShowHeading9 commands to the Outlining toolbar, from the Commands tab of the Tools, Customize dialog box.

DISPLAYING THE ENTIRE DOCUMENT, INCLUDING BODY TEXT

At some point, you may want to view the entire document, including body text. Click the Show All Headings button, and the entire document appears, appropriately indented and marked with outlining symbols.

DISPLAYING ONLY THE FIRST LINE OF BODY TEXT

Sometimes headings aren't enough to tell you the gist of a paragraph, but displaying entire paragraphs takes up so much space that you can lose track of the document's structure and context. Word allows you view the first line of text in every paragraph of body text.

 To do so, first click Show All Headings to display all heading and body text. Next, click the Show First Line Only button. Word displays the first line of text in every paragraph in the document (see Figure 7.11). Ellipses (…) indicate where body text has been cut off.

Figure 7.11
Show First Line Only shows the first line of every paragraph, giving you a better idea of the paragraph's contents.

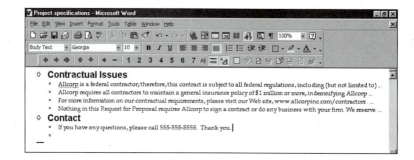

Note

Show First Line Only displays the first lines of paragraphs only if they would otherwise have been displayed in full. For example, if you have clicked Show Heading 3 to show only the first three levels of headings, Show First Line Only won't display any body text.

HIDING CHARACTER FORMATTING

You've already learned that Word hides paragraph formatting while you're working in Outline view. However, it displays font (character) formatting. If your headings are especially large, or if they are formatted in display typefaces, you might find that character formatting makes working with your outline difficult.

 To display text without displaying its formatting, click the Show/Hide Formatting button on the Outlining toolbar. You can see the results in Figure 7.12.

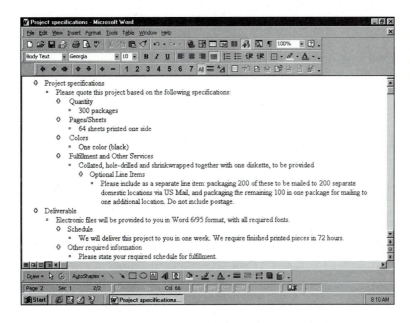

Figure 7.12
Word can display all outline headings and body text as unformatted text.

Tip #112

If Word displays unformatted text that is too small to read, use the Zoom control on the Standard toolbar to enlarge it.

EXPANDING/COLLAPSING HEADINGS

Sometimes you want to focus on a specific section of your document and review it in much greater detail than the rest. You can double-click the Outline symbol next to any paragraph, and Word displays all the headings and body text subordinate to it. Word calls this *expanding* the heading. Double-click again and Word hides the subordinate contents. Word calls this *collapsing* the heading.

 You can use the Expand and Collapse toolbar buttons on the Outlining toolbar to precisely control the detail at which you view a section of a document, so you can better understand how that section is organized, and make appropriate changes to either structure or text.

For instance, imagine all headings and body text are currently displayed, but you want to view one paragraph at a higher level—with only its first- and second-level headings visible, not lower-level headings or body text.

Click the paragraph you want to adjust to select it. Next, click Collapse to hide all body text. Only headings remain visible. Click Collapse again to hide the lowest heading level subordinate to the paragraph with which you are working. Keep clicking Collapse to hide heading levels until you've reached the level you want.

Tip #113

If you have a Microsoft IntelliMouse or a compatible mouse with a wheel, you can expand or collapse selected paragraphs using the wheel between the two mouse buttons as follows:

1. Click the Outline symbol you want to expand or collapse.
2. Press and hold Shift. Roll the wheel forward to expand the selected text one level at a time; roll it back to collapse it one level at a time.
3. When you're at the level you want, release the wheel.

NAVIGATING AN OUTLINE DOCUMENT WITH DOCUMENT MAP AND BROWSE OBJECT

Word's Document Map (see Figure 7.13) makes it easier to navigate through complex outlined documents. Document Map compiles all your headings (and text to which you've assigned outline levels) in a separate window.

Figure 7.13
Document Map compiles all your headings and outline levels in a separate window to the left of your document.

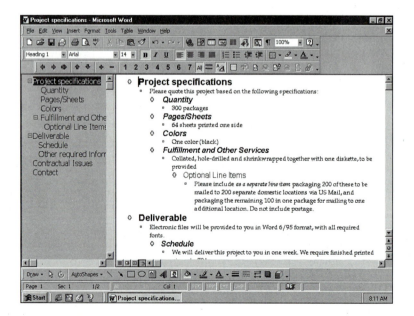

To see the Document Map, click the Document Map button on the Standard toolbar, or choose <u>V</u>iew, <u>D</u>ocument Map. After Document Map opens, you can click any entry and move to the corresponding location in your document.

You can also use Word's Browse Object feature to move quickly from one heading to the next.

To set Word up to browse headings, first click the Select Browse Object button beneath the vertical scrollbar. With the Browse options displayed, choose Browse by Heading. The Previous Heading/Next Heading double-arrow buttons turn blue. Then, click Previous Heading to find the preceding heading, or click Next Heading to find the next one.

APPLYING OUTLINE LEVELS TO SPECIFIC TEXT

Throughout this chapter, you've seen that when you change the level of a heading in Outline view, Word also reformats the heading using the appropriate heading style. Fourth-level paragraphs are automatically formatted in Heading 4 style, and so on. Any heading levels you apply anywhere in Word automatically correspond to outline levels in Outline view.

In Word 95 and earlier versions of Word, using heading styles was the only way to define outline levels. Heading 1 was a first-level heading by definition; Heading 2 a second-level heading, and so on. But there were some problems with this approach.

For example, what if you want to organize the levels of your document using different style names than the heading names Word provides? By default, Outline view displays any style name other than Heading 1–9 at the level of body text. What if you have titles, subtitles, or other elements that should appear at a higher level in your outline?

Or what if you have blocks of body text that you would like to be included in the first level of your outline? This text is important, but it's still body text; you don't want to format it using the Heading 1 style.

Word's outline levels solve the problem. You can use them to format any paragraph for any of nine levels of importance (or format it as Body Text, which is the least important of all). Then, when you work in Outline view, those paragraphs are displayed based on their outline level, regardless of their style.

To format one or more paragraphs with an outline level, first select the paragraphs. Choose F<u>o</u>rmat, <u>P</u>aragraph. In the <u>O</u>utline Level drop-down list box, choose the outline level you want: Level 1 through 9 or Body Text. Click OK.

Note

You cannot change the outline levels associated with Word's built-in heading styles.

Tip #114

You might find you always want text formatted in one of your custom styles to be treated as a first-level outline element. In that case, modify the style to include Outline Level 1 as one of its attributes.

→ For more information about changing the paragraph formatting in a style, **see** "Controlling Styles via the Format Style Dialog Box," **p. 43**.

PRINTING YOUR OUTLINE

Occasionally, you might want a printed copy of your outline. For example, you might need approval for an outline before proceeding to draft your entire document.

To print an outline, first display your document in Outline view. Next, display the elements of your outline that you want to print. For example, specify how many levels of headings you want, and whether you want to collapse or expand any parts of your document. Finally, click the Print button on the Standard toolbar.

Tip #115

Word doesn't provide an easy way of copying outline headings only into a new document. One workaround does the job as long as you're careful. First, save a copy of your file. Then, find all text formatted using the Normal style, and replace it with nothing at all. Repeat the process with each style in your document that uses the Body Text outline level. (The fewer styles that appear in your document, the less time this will take.)

To replace text formatted in a specific style with no text at all, follow these steps:

1. Press Ctrl+H or choose Edit, Replace to display the Find and Replace dialog box.
2. Enter ^? in the Find What text box.
3. Click More to make sure all the Find and Replace options are available.
4. Click Format, Style.
5. In the Find Style dialog box, choose whichever style you want to eliminate (such as Normal or Body Text) and click OK.
6. Make sure the Replace With text box is empty, and click Replace All.

The result is a document containing only text formatted as headings, and text formatted with styles that use outline levels other than those you deleted.

 If Word prints pages with uneven page breaks, see "What to Do If Manual Page Breaks Print from Outline View," in the "Troubleshooting" section of this chapter.

USING WORD'S AUTOMATIC OUTLINE NUMBERING

Have you ever had to number the headings in a document—and then change the numbering every time you add or move one of them? In this section, you'll learn how to let Word insert and manage all your heading and outline numbering for you.

Word includes seven built-in outline numbering schemes that can handle many of the documents and Web pages you're likely to create. To use one of them, first select the paragraphs you want to number. If you want to add numbering throughout the document, press Ctrl+A to select the entire document. Right-click in the editing window, and choose Bullets and Numbering from the shortcut menu; then click the Outline Numbered tab (see Figure 7.14).

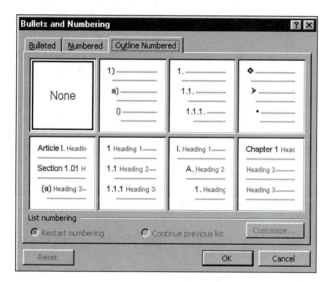

Figure 7.14
The Outline Numbered tab gives you seven standard choices from which to select; or select one and click Customize to adapt it to your needs.

Caution

If you want to number only headings, not paragraphs of body text, be sure to use one of the numbering schemes in the bottom row of the Outline Numbered tab. The schemes in the top row number both headings and body text.

Choose the scheme you want; then click OK. Figure 7.15 shows outline numbering applied to a sample document.

Figure 7.15
Outline numbering
based on the second
numbering scheme in
the bottom row of the
Outline Numbered
tab.

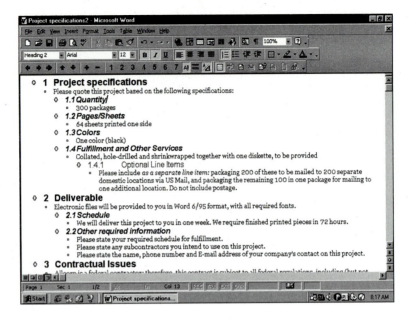

CREATING CUSTOMIZED OUTLINE NUMBERING

If you're in a position to decide how you want your outline numbering to appear, try to use one of Word's defaults; it saves you some trouble. However, your document may require a numbering scheme that isn't one of Word's default settings. That's where Word's extensive Outline Numbering customization capabilities come in handy.

To customize outline numbering, right-click in the editing window and choose Bullets and Numbering from the shortcut menu; then click the Outline Numbered tab.

Select the numbering scheme closest to the one you want, and click Customize. The Customize Outline Numbered List dialog box opens (see Figure 7.16). In the Preview box, you can see how the entire outline numbering scheme behaves; any changes you make are shown there immediately.

CHOOSING THE OUTLINE LEVEL YOU WANT TO CUSTOMIZE

You can customize each of Word's nine levels of outline numbering separately. Choose the level you want from the Level drop-down list box at the top left. Word displays the current settings for the level you've selected. These settings vary not just based on outline level, but also based on the scheme from which you chose to start.

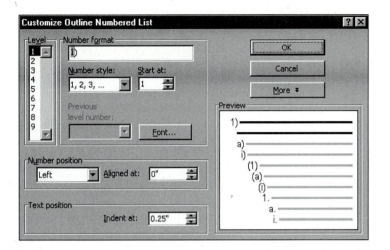

Figure 7.16
In the Customize Outline Numbered List dialog box, you can change and preview virtually any aspect of a numbered list.

Tip #116

It's easy to forget in which level you're working. While you're customizing your outline numbering, glance at the Level drop-down list box every now and then to make sure you're customizing what you think you're customizing. Or if you prefer, check in the Preview box; the currently selected level is displayed in black while others are displayed in light gray.

CHOOSING TEXT TO ACCOMPANY YOUR LETTERING OR NUMBERING

In the Number Format text box, you can specify the text or symbols you want to appear before or after the number or letter Word inserts next to your heading or paragraph. You do this by editing the text surrounding the grayed-out number or letter. For instance, in the example shown in Figure 7.16, Word adds a closed parenthesis mark. You might want to place an open parenthesis mark before the number as well, so Word inserts numbers as (1) rather than 1).

CHOOSING A PATTERN FOR YOUR NUMBERING OR LETTERING

You can't use the Number Format text box to control the automatic lettering or numbering that Word adds to your document. Rather, you select the lettering or numbering pattern you want Word to choose from the Number Style scroll box. Word 2000's lettering and numbering schemes include the following:

- 1, 2, 3,...
- I, II, III,...
- i, ii, iii,...
- A, B, C,...
- a, b, c,...

- 1st, 2nd, 3rd,…
- One, Two, Three,…
- First, Second, Third,…
- 01, 02, 03,…

Word also includes several bullet styles from which you can choose, or you can choose New Bullet to select a different bullet character from the Symbol dialog box.

Tip #117   You can also choose no lettering and numbering at all. If you choose (none) in the Number Style scroll box, Word only inserts the text you enter in the Number Format text box. Imagine you're writing the feature description of a product, and you want to add a word like NEW! before every second-level heading in your document. You could use this feature to do so.

CHOOSING A NUMBER OR LETTER FROM WHICH TO START

By default, Word assumes you want your numbering to start at 1 and your lettering to start at A, but that won't always be the case. For example, if you're contributing the fourth chapter of a book, you might want your first-level heading to start with the number 4. In the Start At scroll box located to the right of Number Style, choose the number you want to appear next to the first heading of the current level.

INCLUDING A PREVIOUS OUTLINE LEVEL WITH YOUR NUMBERING

It's common to see documents that include multilevel numbering like that shown in the following examples:

1.A.

4.4.2.

II.C.

You can instruct Word to insert numbering such as this. To do so, in the Previous Level Number drop-down list box (located beneath Number Style), choose the level of outline numbering that you want to appear next to your lower-level headings or paragraphs. For example, if your first-level headings are numbered (1), (2), (3), and you want your second-level headings to be numbered (1A), (1B), (1C), and so on, select Level 1 in the Previous Level Number box.

Notice that Word doesn't add the surrounding text you included in the Number Format text box for the preceding heading level; just the letter or number itself. Otherwise you could easily wind up with ((1)A) or something equally unattractive.

Note

Because there is no level prior to Level 1, the Previous Level Number drop-down list box is grayed out when you're customizing Level 1 headings.

CUSTOMIZING FONT FORMATTING

You can spice up your outline numbers with almost any character formatting you like. From the Customize Outline Numbered List dialog box, click Font. The Font dialog box opens. You can choose any character formatting, spacing, or animation.

Note

Every font formatting option you normally have is available for numbered headings with two exceptions: You cannot use the Outline or Small Caps text effects.

CUSTOMIZING THE POSITION AND ALIGNMENT OF OUTLINE NUMBERS

Some of Word's built-in schemes left-align all outline numbers, regardless of levels. Other schemes indent outline numbers; the deeper the outline level, the greater the indent. You might want to change these built-in settings. For example, you might like everything about a scheme except the way it indents paragraphs.

Outline numbering alignment is controlled from the Number Position drop-down list box in the Customize Outline Numbered List dialog box. You can choose to left-align, center, or right-align outline numbers. You can also specify against what the outline numbering is aligned. The Aligned At scroll box specifies how far from the left margin the alignment point is. For example, if you choose Centered as the number position, and you choose 1" as the Aligned At location, your outline number is centered over a point 1" from the left margin.

Note

The Aligned At setting doesn't control whether the entire line is left-aligned, centered, or right-aligned. It only controls how the outline numbering within the line is aligned.

Remember, you have to change the number position separately for each outline level you expect to use.

To see the effect of these changes in your document, switch to Normal or Print Layout view; changes are not accurately reflected in Outline view.

CUSTOMIZING THE POSITION AND ALIGNMENT OF TEXT NEAR OUTLINE NUMBERS

You can also control the distance between the end of Word's automatic outline number and the start of the paragraph's text. To do so, enter a setting in the Indent At scroll box, in the Text Position area of the Customize Outline Numbered List dialog box.

The Indent At setting is measured from the left margin. If the Indent At setting is very small, it may have no effect on the first line of a paragraph, because the outline number itself already extends beyond the indent. (Word doesn't overlap an outline number on top of paragraph text.) Indent At behaves as a hanging indent. In Figure 7.17, you can see first-level headings that are left-aligned at 0.25" with text indented at 1.5".

Figure 7.17
The first-level headings in this sample are left-aligned at 0.25" with text indented at 1.5".

0.25" left-alignment

1.5" indent

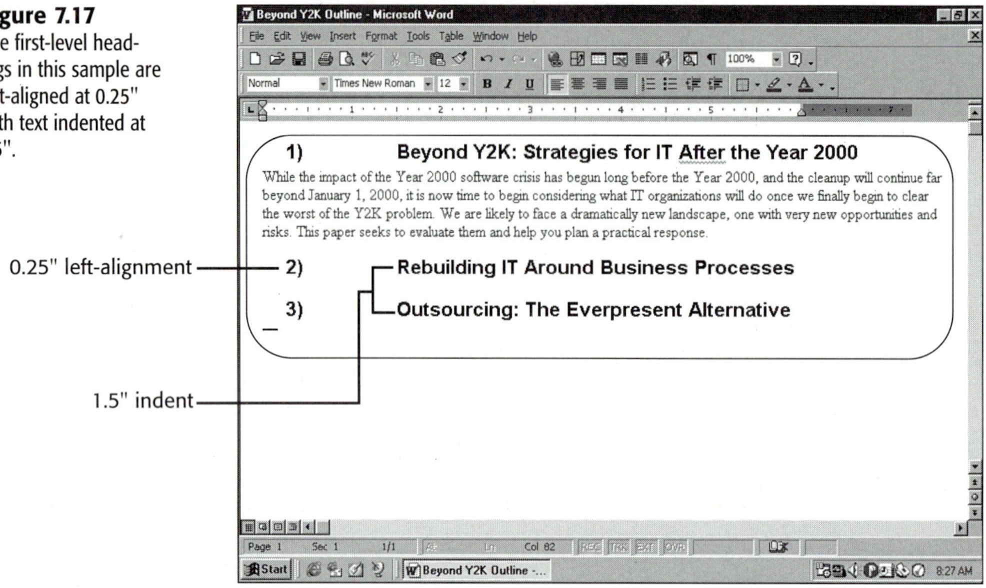

ADVANCED OUTLINE NUMBERING OPTIONS

Some outline numbering customizations are rarely used, but when they're needed, they're needed very badly. You can control these by clicking More in the Customized Outline Numbered List dialog box. More options appear (see Figure 7.18).

LINKING AN OUTLINE LEVEL TO A STYLE

The Link Level to Style drop-down list box in the Customize Numbered List dialog box enables you to attach any style to an outline numbering level. That way, whenever you enter or format a paragraph using that style, Word automatically includes numbering, just as it includes all the other formatting associated with the style.

CHOOSING A SPACER CHARACTER

The Follow Number With drop-down list box in the Customize Numbered List dialog box enables you to choose the noneditable character that Word places between your outline number and your paragraph text. By default, Word uses a tab, but you can change this to a space, or instruct Word not to insert a character at all.

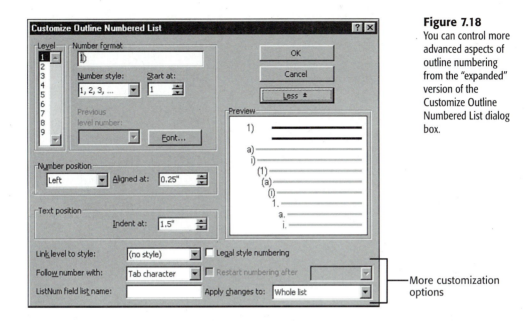

Figure 7.18
You can control more advanced aspects of outline numbering from the "expanded" version of the Customize Outline Numbered List dialog box.

PLACING TWO OUTLINE NUMBERS ON THE SAME LINE

In some documents, notably contracts, you may be required to include two outline numbers on the same line, as in the following example:

Article I.

Section 1.01 (i)

(ii)

Word lets you do this, although it's a little involved. You use the ListNum Field List Name drop-down list box, an advanced outline number customization feature. You also have to use the ListNum field.

First, set up your headings as you normally would. Then, place your insertion point where you want the first extra heading to appear, and do the following:

1. Choose Insert, Field.

2. Select ListNum from the Field Names box (see Figure 7.19).

3. Enter a name in quotation marks and click OK. Word can use this list name to recognize which fields you want to include in a specific sequence. For example, all fields named

   ```
   {LISTNUM "Sequence1"}
   ```

   are included in the same sequence, while all fields named

   ```
   {LISTNUM "Sequence2"}
   ```

   are included in a different sequence.

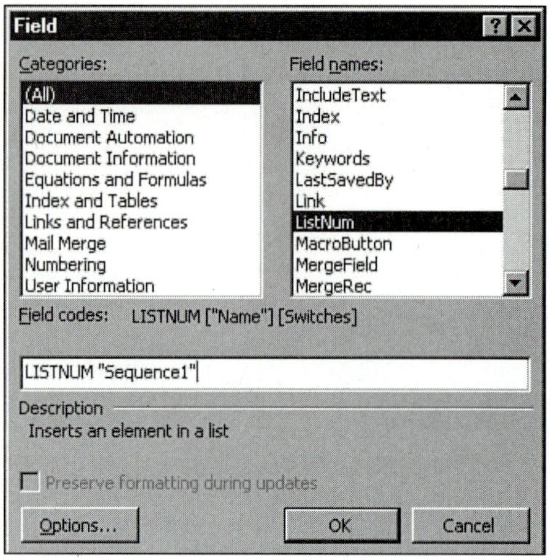

Figure 7.19
Setting up a
{ LISTNUM } field in
the Field dialog box.

4. Select the entire field, and copy it to every other location where you want a heading just like it.

If you view the field results, you can see that you've now added a basic heading, such as a)

Follow these steps to attach all the headings in the same sequence to a level in your outline numbering scheme, so they look exactly as you want them to:

1. Choose Format, Bullets and Numbering, Outline Numbered.
2. Extra headings are most commonly used with the Section and Article scheme (the scheme on the bottom row at the left). Select this scheme and click Customize.
3. Click More to display the advanced options.
4. Make sure you're working at the level you want and that the Number Format settings are the way you want them.
5. In the ListNum Field List Name drop-down list box, enter the same word you used in your ListNum field. In the example, that would be Sequence1.
6. Click OK.

You now have normal outline numbering as well as an extra outline number that uses the Number format of the level immediately beneath the first outline number. In other words, if the outline number you applied through Format, Bullets and Numbering is formatted as Level 1, the outline number you applied through Insert, Field is Level 2.

→ To learn more about working with fields, **see** Chapter 18, "Automating Your Documents with Field Codes," **p. 555**.

APPLYING LEGAL STYLE NUMBERING

Some legal documents must utilize Arabic numbering (1, 2, 3...) throughout. For example, even though Word's numbering scheme for legal documents may specify that Articles use Roman numerals in some levels (for example, Article I, II, and so on), this may not be appropriate for your document. You could change every level's Number style to Roman numerals individually. However, Word 2000 provides a shortcut; you can simply check Legal Style Numbering in the Customize Outline Numbered List dialog box and Word does it for you.

INCREMENTING LIST NUMBERS IN A SPECIFIC LEVEL

By default, Word restarts numbering whenever an item in a list follows an item one level above it. You can see this behavior in Figure 7.20.

Figure 7.20
By default, Word restarts numbering whenever a lower list level follows a higher list level.

Numbering reverts to 1 after first-level heading.

However, if you clear the Restart Numbering After check box near the bottom of the expanded Customize Outline Numbered List dialog box, Word continues to increment the numbers from where they left off (see Figure 7.21).

In Word 2000, you can also choose which level of heading you want to trigger the restarting of numbering. This choice can be different for each outline level. To change the outline level that triggers renumbering:

1. Make sure you're working in the outline level you want to change. (This feature is unavailable if you're working in Outline Level 1.)
2. Make sure the Restart Numbering After check box is checked.
3. Choose the level you want from the Restart Numbering After drop-down box.
4. Click OK.

PART
II

CH
7

Figure 7.21
Clearing the Restart Numbering After check box instructs Word to keep incrementing lower-level headings rather than restart them at 1.

Numbering continues to increment from 1.4 to 2.5.

SPECIFYING WHERE YOUR CHANGES SHOULD APPLY

By default, if you make changes anywhere in the Customize Outline Numbered List dialog box, they apply globally to the entire document as soon as you click OK to exit. However, you might have a portion of a document that you want to treat differently. You have more additional options, available through the Apply Changes To drop-down list box:

- Choosing Current Paragraph tells Word to apply changes only to the paragraph where your insertion point is currently located.

- Choosing This Point Forward tells Word to apply your changes to the rest of your document, starting at the insertion point.

- Choosing Selected Text tells Word to apply your changes only to paragraphs that are currently selected (or to the current paragraph, if no text is selected).

TROUBLESHOOTING

WHAT TO DO IF YOUR OUTLINING TOOLBAR DISAPPEARS

First make sure you're in Outline view by clicking the Outline View button on the status bar. If the Outlining toolbar is still not visible, choose View, Toolbars, Outlining to display it.

HOW TO COPY ONLY A DOCUMENT'S HEADINGS WITHOUT COPYING ALL THE SUBORDINATE TEXT

You can't, but here's a workaround that accomplishes the same goal. Insert a table of contents in your document that does not contain page numbers. Select it, and press Ctrl+Shift+F9 to convert it into text. You can now cut and paste it to any location or document you want.

WHAT TO DO IF MANUAL PAGE BREAKS PRINT FROM OUTLINE VIEW

One problem with printing outlines is that Word leaves manual page breaks in—and these can create pages that only have a few headings on them. The only way to avoid this is to temporarily remove the page breaks. You can do so by using Edit, Replace to replace page breaks with no text at all. (Entering ^m in the Find What box tells Word to search for a page break.)

 Print the document; then click Undo to restore the page breaks.

Alternatively, save a copy of the document, delete the page breaks, and print from the copy.

HOW TO NUMBER HEADINGS, BUT NOT BODY TEXT

Outline Numbering has been redesigned to number body text paragraphs as well as headings by default. However, if (in the Outline Numbered tab of the Bullets and Numbering dialog box) you choose a numbering scheme that includes the word "Heading," Word only numbers headings.

CHAPTER **8**

MASTER DOCUMENTS: CONTROL AND SHARE EVEN THE LARGEST DOCUMENTS

In this chapter

The Advantages of Master Documents

Often, you need a way to edit parts of a document—while still staying in control of the whole document. *Master documents* give you that flexibility. A master document is, in essence, a gathering place for multiple smaller documents—called *subdocuments*—each of which can be developed and edited separately, by separate users on separate computers.

After you've created a master document, you can reopen it any time you want, displaying all the subdocuments together. This gives you a quick, efficient way to see how all the components of your document relate to each other, even if individual subdocuments have been heavily edited by your colleagues since you viewed them last. You can use Word's navigation tools as if you were working with a conventional document rather than a collection of documents. You can also handle all the tasks that generally should be performed on the entire document at the same time, such as:

- Ensuring consistent formatting throughout
- Spell checking and ensuring consistent spelling of specialized terms
- Building an *index* and *table of contents*
- Reorganizing the document, moving large blocks of text among chapters
- Printing

→ To learn more about creating a table of contents in a master document, **see** "Creating a Table of Contents, Index, or Cross-References for a Master Document," **p. 257**.

The master document doesn't merely gather the subdocuments in one place: It integrates them, enabling you to set unified styles and document templates that can apply to every subdocument. Using master documents thereby helps you maintain visual consistency throughout large documents, even if many authors are contributing to them.

No matter what formatting is attached to styles in your subdocuments, when those subdocuments are displayed as part of a master document, they all use the formatting associated with styles in the master document's template. So if you stay with a basic set of headings and other styles, you're virtually assured of consistent formatting.

In addition, when you display subdocuments as part of a master document, all cross-references, footnotes, outline numbers, and page numbers are automatically updated to reflect the new location of the subdocument within the larger document. In fact, master documents behave very much like regular Word documents. You can format them, save them, and print them just as you would any other document.

Master documents are extremely helpful in organizing complex projects. As you'll learn later, you can organize the project in a Word outline, divide the project into subdocuments, and delegate those subdocuments to your colleagues as needed.

There's one final benefit to using master documents. Because Word usually works faster when editing smaller documents, working in subdocuments rather than a much larger main document can significantly improve Word's performance during mundane editing tasks.

CHOOSING HOW TO CREATE A NEW MASTER DOCUMENT

If you've learned how to use outlines, you're halfway toward understanding master documents, too. Master documents closely resemble outlines, and you control them in *Outline view*, using the buttons on Word's Outlining toolbar. The primary difference: You're outlining material that comes from several documents rather than one.

→ To learn more about outlining, **see** "Creating a New Outline," **p. 211**.

You can create master documents in two ways:

- You can do it from scratch, by outlining your document and then dividing it into subdocuments.

- You can make existing documents part of your master document.

Whenever possible, you're better off creating your master documents from scratch. It's quick, easy, and you have total control over all the subdocuments you create. If you start from scratch, it's also much easier to maintain consistency throughout the editing process. Here's why:

- You usually don't have to worry about users working from different templates. All your subdocuments automatically share the same *template*, so they share the same *styles*, *AutoText entries*, and *macros*.

- You don't have to worry about tracking the locations of your subdocuments. You can just place them all in the same folder on your local hard disk or shared network drive, and tell people to leave them there.

- You usually don't have to worry about people inadvertently editing the wrong version of the file. There is only one: the subdocument you created.

However, you may not always have the luxury of starting from scratch. You may be asked to build upon existing text—updating it, including new topics, broadening coverage with new chapters. So Word makes it very easy to incorporate existing documents in your master document.

You may also find yourself taking a hybrid approach: outlining the entire master document from scratch; then inserting existing documents where they exist, and reorganizing the master document to reflect contents you already have.

Finally, remember that a master document can contain anything a regular document can, while containing subdocuments at the same time. So you might choose to create and edit some of your text in your master document, and use subdocuments for only the chapters others are creating.

CREATING A NEW MASTER DOCUMENT AND SUBDOCUMENTS

In this section, you'll learn how to create a master document from scratch, by building an outline and dividing your document into subdocuments.

Note

A master document is simply a document that contains subdocuments, so adding subdocuments to any document transforms it into a master document.

 Start by opening a blank document and clicking the Outline View button on the status bar (or choosing <u>V</u>iew, <u>O</u>utline). Word switches into Outline view, and displays the Outlining toolbar, which includes both outlining tools and master document tools.

Note

In some previous versions of Word, you were required to select Master Document view to work with master documents. In Word 2000, master document tools are now built into Outline view, and the Master Document view menu item has disappeared from the View menu.

 Nevertheless, you may find it more convenient to work with your master documents if you switch into Master Document view (by clicking the Master Document View button on the Outlining toolbar). Doing so makes the borders between your subdocuments easier to see and use.

Figure 8.1 shows the master document tools at the right side of the Outlining toolbar. You'll find tools for inserting, removing, and managing the subdocuments that are the components of a master document. Each tool is explained in Table 8.1.

Figure 8.1
The Master Document toolbar includes Word's tools for managing subdocuments and master documents.

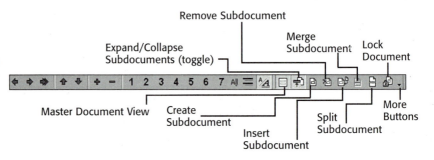

Note

The Master Document toolbar buttons appear grayed out if all your subdocuments are collapsed, or if they are expanded but locked to prevent them from being edited.

TABLE 8.1   MASTER DOCUMENT BUTTONS ON THE OUTLINING TOOLBAR

Button	Name	What It Does
	Master Document View	Toggles between Master Document View and displaying subdocuments as sections within the same document
	Expand/Collapse Subdocuments	Toggles between showing all the contents of a master document and showing hyperlinks in place of subdocuments
	Create Subdocument	Creates a new subdocument from selected text, or creates multiple subdocuments from text selections that incorporate several headings of the same level
	Remove Subdocument	Eliminates a subdocument and places its text in the master document
	Insert Subdocument	Inserts an existing document as a subdocument in the current master document
	Merge Subdocument	Combines two or more subdocuments into one
	Split Subdocument	Divides one subdocument into two, at the insertion point
	Lock Document	Toggles between locking and unlocking a subdocument

CREATING SUBDOCUMENTS

Now that you've opened a new document and displayed it in Outline view, you can create and organize the outline of your document, using Word's outlining tools, just as you would if you weren't intending to create a master document.

After you have the outline the way you want it, you can divide it into subdocuments. If you set up your document properly, Word can organize your entire document into subdocuments with one click. Of course, it's also easy to set up individual subdocuments manually, if you prefer.

Tip #119	If your outline needs to be approved, get the approvals you need before you divide it into subdocuments—and especially before you delegate those subdocuments to individual contributors.

Caution

> When Word creates subdocuments, it places continuous section breaks between them. Therefore, once you've established subdocuments, you need to be aware of how each section handles *headers*, *footers*, and page numbering. It's usually best to establish these settings globally for your whole document before you divide the document into subdocuments.
>
> Since the section breaks Word inserts are *continuous section breaks*, you may want to add manual page breaks at the end of each section in order to start the next section on a new page.

CREATING MULTIPLE SUBDOCUMENTS AT THE SAME TIME

The quickest and most intuitive way to set up subdocuments is to create an outline where every first-level heading—in other words, every paragraph formatted with the Heading 1 style—corresponds to a new subdocument.

For example, if you're writing a manual or book, you might format chapter titles with the Heading 1 style, so each subdocument you create corresponds to a separate chapter. Of course, these subdocuments contain all the headings and body text subordinate to the Heading 1 paragraph with which they start.

Caution

> It's equally important to not use Heading 1 style for any block of text you don't want set apart in its own subdocument.

 To create a subdocument for every Heading 1 style in your document, click Show Heading 1 to display only first-level headings. Next, press Ctrl+A (or choose Edit, Select All) to select the entire document. Finally, click the Create Subdocument button on the Master Document toolbar.

Word divides the entire document into subdocuments automatically, starting each new subdocument at the point where it finds another paragraph formatted as Heading 1. The first time you save the document after dividing it, each subdocument will be saved with a different name. Once you divide the documents, the text is stored in each subdocument, rather than the master document.

→ To learn more about how subdocuments are saved, **see** "Saving a Master Document," **p. 250**.

Tip #120

> You can collapse or expand subdocuments by clicking Ctrl+\. This is the only master document tool with a corresponding keyboard shortcut.

CREATING MULTIPLE SUBDOCUMENTS FROM LOWER-LEVEL HEADINGS

Although you're most likely to use Heading 1 styles as the dividing lines between your subdocuments, you can divide subdocuments by lower-level headings as well, in order to share smaller chunks of your document for editing by colleagues. You can select any group of headings, as long as

- Your selection includes more than one heading of the same level.
- The first heading in your selection is styled with the heading level you want to use as your dividing line between subdocuments.

When might you divide a document based on lower-level headings? Imagine you're making a sales proposal that covers a wide range of products, each of which is to be covered in only a page. You can create subdocuments for second- or third-level headings corresponding to each product.

Tip #121	After you create these small, modular subdocuments, you can insert them in future documents as well. As your products are updated, have your product managers revise and re-save their subdocuments. You can then include these subdocuments in future proposals and be assured that you're including the most current information about each product. You might even record macros that automatically insert each subdocument, and attach these macros to a special toolbar, so your salespeople can insert current information about any specific product with a single click.

CREATING A SINGLE SUBDOCUMENT

You don't have to create multiple subdocuments at the same time. You can create a subdocument from any block of text that includes at least one heading. To do so, select the text you want to incorporate in a subdocument. After the text is selected, click Create Subdocument.

Tip #122	Usually, the quickest way to select text for inclusion in a subdocument is to click the outline symbol next to the highest-level heading you want to use. Word then selects all text subordinate to that heading.

TAKING A CLOSER LOOK AT SUBDOCUMENTS

Within the master document, Word marks the subdocuments you create in two ways (see Figure 8.2). First, text in a subdocument is surrounded by a thin, gray border. Second, a subdocument icon appears to the top left of the first heading in the subdocument.

In Master Document view, you can select the entire subdocument by clicking this subdocument icon. You can open the subdocument in its own editing window by double-clicking the subdocument icon. Later in this chapter, you'll learn more about organizing, formatting, and editing subdocuments.

Figure 8.2
Text that has been selected as a subdocument is bordered with a gray rectangle; a subdocument icon also appears to its top left.

Marker for section break

Subdocument icon

Subdocument border

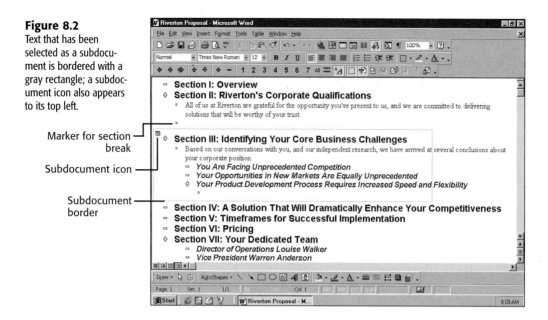

When Word creates subdocuments, it separates them by adding continuous section breaks, which are section breaks that start the next section on the same page. If you switch to Normal view (see Figure 8.3), you can see the section break markers. You can delete them without damaging your subdocuments, but in general you should leave them alone.

Figure 8.3
In Normal view, Word separates subdocuments with section break markers.

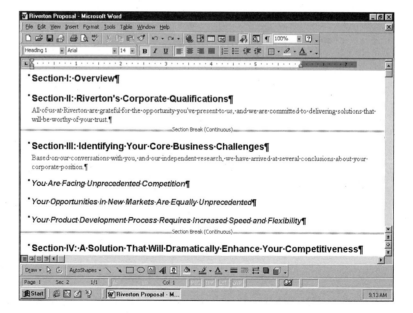

TRANSFORMING AN EXISTING DOCUMENT INTO A MASTER DOCUMENT

Until now, this chapter has discussed creating a new master document from scratch. However, what if you already have a document you want to turn into a master document? Follow these steps:

1. Open the document and choose <u>V</u>iew, <u>O</u>utline to display it in Outline view.

2. Use Word's outline tools to organize the document, if necessary. Ideally, arrange the document so that each first-level heading corresponds to one of the subdocuments you want to create. If the document hasn't used heading styles, consider using Find and Replace, or possibly AutoFormat, to insert them.

 3. Create your subdocuments. You can create them one at a time by selecting text and clicking Create Subdocument. Or if you've been able to organize your document by first-level headings, select the entire document and click Create Subdocument to create all your subdocuments at the same time.

ADDING AN EXISTING DOCUMENT TO A MASTER DOCUMENT

What if you have a document you would like to add to an existing master document? (Or what if you would like to add your document to a conventional document, thereby turning it into a master document?)

 First, open the master document and click Expand Subdocuments. Next, click in the master document where you want to insert your subdocument, and click Insert Subdocument. The Insert Subdocument dialog box opens (see Figure 8.4). Browse to select the document you want, and click <u>O</u>pen.

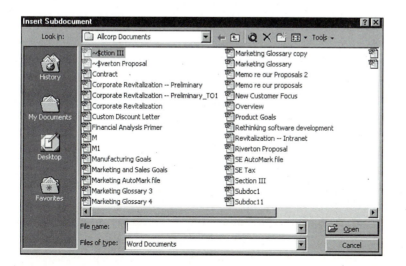

Figure 8.4
The Insert Subdocument dialog box enables you to make any document part of your master document.

Note

After you expand subdocuments, the toolbar button changes to the Collapse Subdocuments button. Click this button when you need to collapse the subdocuments again.

Word inserts the subdocument into your outline at your current insertion point. If any text is formatted with styles that have the same names as those in your master document, those styles are displayed to match the rest of your master document.

SAVING A MASTER DOCUMENT

You can save a master document the same way you save any other Word file: by clicking the Save button, pressing Ctrl+S, or choosing File, Save.

When you save a master document that contains new subdocuments, Word creates new files for each subdocument, and stores them in the same folder as the master document. Word automatically names your subdocuments, using the first letters or phrase at the beginning of each subdocument. If the names of more than one subdocument would be identical, or if another identical filename already exists in the same folder, Word adds a number to distinguish them. For example, if the subdocuments all start with the word Chapter, they would be named

```
Chapter1.doc
Chapter2.doc
Chapter3.doc
```

Caution

Double-check the filenames Word chooses to make sure they're appropriate. If you save a subdocument named Section 1 to a folder that already has a file named Section1, Word renames your file Section2. Then it'll name your Section 2 subdocument Section3. The result could be very confusing.

If Word ever chooses a subdocument name that you don't like, open the subdocument from within the master document, choose File, Save As, and rename it. The master document will now contain the renamed file.

If you're working on a subdocument from within a master document, and that subdocument already has a name, when you click Save, Word saves it using its existing name. Word also saves other subdocuments that are open within the same master document.

To avoid this problem, consider setting up a new folder that will contain both your master document and your subdocuments.

→ To learn more about working with subdocuments from within a master document, **see** "Editing a Subdocument from Within the Master Document," **p. 251**.

After you create and save a subdocument, Word stores its contents in the subdocument—not in the master document. This has two important implications: First, as you'll see shortly, it means you (or a colleague) can edit a subdocument without opening the master document. You simply open the document as you normally would. Assuming nobody else is using the file, nothing tells you you're working on a subdocument rather than a normal document. Second, it means that if you delete a subdocument, move it, or rename it—without informing the master document—it will disappear from the master document.

Caution

> Users who don't realize they are working on subdocuments can cause problems for others who are responsible for managing a master document containing those subdocuments. For example, a user may rename a file or save it somewhere else, and suddenly, a gap appears in the master document. Or worse, the user renames the file, but the old version of the file stays in the master document (since a link to that file still exists)—and nobody ever realizes there's a newer, revised version.

SAVING MASTER DOCUMENTS AS WEB PAGES

If you create a master document in Word's DOC format, and then resave the master document as a Web (*HTML*) page, Word saves each subdocument as a Web page. Word gives you a choice about how it does this:

- Word can overwrite your existing DOC file in HTML format (while still retaining the DOC extension). This eliminates the possibility that a user might edit the wrong file, since only one file exists—but before you post the file to your Web server, you may have to change its extension to HTM or HTML.

- Or, Word can create a copy of your DOC file with an HTM extension, leaving the original DOC file on your hard disk (but linking to the HTM file rather than the DOC file). This gives you a convenient backup; but you run the risk that users may open the wrong file if they are not working from within the master document.

To save a master document as a Web page, open it and choose File, Save as Web Page. Click Save. Word displays the dialog box shown in Figure 8.5.

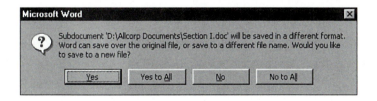

Figure 8.5
Controlling the way Word resaves subdocuments in HTML format.

- If you choose Yes, Word resaves a copy of the first subdocument with the HTM extension, and asks the same question again about the next subdocument.

- If you choose Yes to All, Word resaves a copy of every subdocument with the HTM extension.

- If you choose No, Word saves the subdocument in HTM format, but retains the DOC extension (copying over the existing DOC file, and deleting it). It then asks the same question again about the next subdocument.

- If you choose No to All, Word saves all the subdocuments in HTM format, but retains the DOC extension (copying over each existing DOC file, and deleting it).

For any subdocuments containing images, Word also creates a separate folder containing corresponding GIFs or JPGs, as well as an XML file listing the images included.

The master document itself is also saved as a Web page, containing hyperlinks to each subdocument. (In essence, you're saving a document as a miniature Web site.)

→ For more information about XML and how Word uses it, **see** "The New Technologies Used in Word 2000 Web Pages," **p. 1254**.

OPENING A MASTER DOCUMENT

After you create, save, and close a master document, you can open it the same way you open any other document. When you first open a master document, however, rather than headings that correspond to the top-level headings of each subdocument, you see *hyperlinks* that show the name and location of each subdocument in your master document (see Figure 8.6).

 If you prefer to see formatted headings and text rather than hyperlinks, click Expand Subdocuments. You can then use Outlining toolbar buttons like Show Heading 1 and Show Heading 2 to control how much detail you see in your subdocuments.

Figure 8.6
When you reopen a master document, you see hyperlinks to each subdocument contained in it.

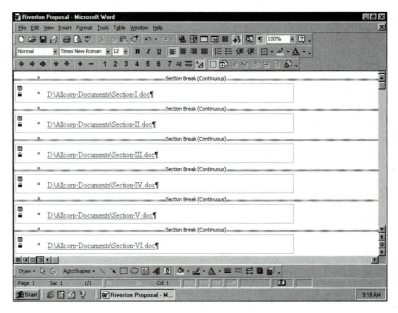

EDITING A SUBDOCUMENT FROM WITHIN THE MASTER DOCUMENT

After you've opened the master document, you can either edit individual subdocuments from within the master document, or you can display only the subdocument for editing.

To display an individual subdocument for editing, click on the hyperlink. The subdocument now appears in its own window. Section breaks appear at the end of the document, as discussed earlier. In Word 2000, the original master document remains open even while you're editing a subdocument this way. You can view the original master document at any time by clicking its separate icon in the taskbar (see Figure 8.7).

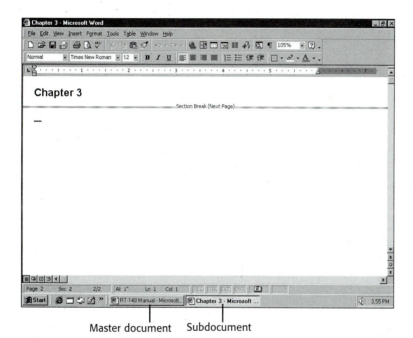

Figure 8.7
You can switch from a subdocument to a master document by clicking on the master document's icon in the taskbar.

Master document   Subdocument

Note

Hyperlinks in a master document change color from blue to magenta after you click them once. However, once you close the master document, they revert to blue the next time you open it. Moreover, if you edit and save a subdocument, its hyperlink also reverts to blue.

Sometimes, you may prefer to edit a subdocument with the rest of the master document's contents visible. For example, you may want to move text from one subdocument to another, or to create references to text in another subdocument. To view the contents of the entire master document, click Expand Subdocuments, then use Word's Outlining toolbar buttons to focus in on the specific areas of text you want to edit.

No matter how you open a subdocument, you're not limited to viewing and editing it in Outline view. Select whatever view makes the most sense for the editing you need to do.

EDITING SUBDOCUMENTS OUTSIDE THE MASTER DOCUMENT

 As you've learned, you don't have to open a master document to edit one of its subdocuments. You can open the subdocument directly, by using the Open dialog box or by double-clicking on its icon in Windows Explorer. If you're using master documents to manage a document with several authors, this is how your colleagues typically open the subdocuments you delegate to them.

Here's a general rule of thumb: Open subdocuments separately when you intend to make changes that affect only the subdocument. For example, it's fine to open the subdocument separately if you plan to do any of the following:

- Edit text within the subdocument
- Create footnotes to appear at the bottom of the page or at the end of the subdocument
- Create temporary headers or footers that you only want to print from within the subdocument
- Check spelling within the subdocument
- Print only the subdocument

Tip #123

For example, you might add a subdocument footer that includes the words PRELIMINARY DRAFT. This footer prints whenever you open the subdocument on its own. However, the official footer you establish for final documents appears instead whenever the subdocument is printed from the master document.

On the other hand, if you plan to make organizational, formatting, or editing changes that affect the entire document, open the subdocument from within the master document.

Caution

Never rename or move a subdocument that you've opened outside the master document. Word has no way of tracking the change. The next time you open the master document, the renamed or moved subdocument will be missing.

To rename or move a subdocument, open it from within the master document; choose File, Save As; enter the new name or location in the Save As dialog box, and click Save.

Note

If you have both a subdocument and its master document open, you cannot edit the subdocument's text in the master document: You will find it locked. You must click the subdocument icon on the taskbar and edit the subdocument directly.

STYLE BEHAVIOR IN MASTER DOCUMENTS AND SUBDOCUMENTS

If you open a subdocument from within a master document, the subdocument utilizes all the styles stored in the master document's template. If you open it separately and make style changes or apply a different template, your subdocument reflects those style changes as long as you're editing it outside the master document. However, if you save it, open the master document, and reopen the subdocument, you'll find that the master document's styles now take precedence wherever they conflict. If you insert an existing document into a master document, and the existing document is based on a different template, once again the master document's template takes precedence.

If you create a new style within a subdocument, and later open that subdocument from within the master document, your new style is listed in the master document as well. However, if the style is based on a style which looks different in the master and subdocuments, text formatted with the new style may also look different depending on whether you're working on it in the master document or in a separate subdocument editing window.

Because this is complicated, here's an example.

Imagine that you're working in a subdocument that appears in its own editing window. You create a style named BookText, and base it on the Normal style (which by default, is 12-point Times New Roman). You add the extra formatting you want BookText to include: a first-line 1/2" indent, and 8 points after each paragraph.

You now close the subdocument, and open the master document that contains the subdocument. When you do so, the BookText style appears in your list of styles. Text formatted in the BookText style still has a 1/2" indent and 8 points after each paragraph. However, in our example, your master document uses a different version of the Normal style, calling for text to be displayed in 11-point Georgia (instead of Times New Roman). Since your BookText is based on the Normal style, it now also displays in 11-point Georgia.

In other words, the elements you add to a style remain intact regardless of whether you display the text from within a master document or as a separate subdocument. However, where elements are based on another style, Word looks for that style in different places depending on how you are displaying the text. If you are displaying it as part of the master document, Word uses the underlying styles from the master document. If you are displaying it as a subdocument, in its own editing window, Word uses the underlying styles from the subdocument.

→ To learn more about based-on styles, **see** "Working with Based On Styles," **p. 44**.

REORGANIZING A MASTER DOCUMENT

All the outlining skills you learned in Chapter 7, "Outlining: The Best Way to Organize a Document," come in especially handy when you need to reorganize a master document. Display your document in Outline view, and click Expand Subdocuments to view all the contents of your subdocuments. Now you can use Word's Outlining toolbar and keyboard shortcuts to rearrange any elements of your master document.

MOVING AN ENTIRE SUBDOCUMENT

You might decide that you want to move an entire subdocument to a different location in your master document. First, use Word's Outlining and Master Documents toolbar buttons to display the portions of the master document you need to see in order to know exactly where you want to move the subdocument. Next, click the subdocument symbol to select the entire subdocument (see Figure 8.8).

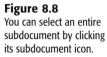

Figure 8.8
You can select an entire subdocument by clicking its subdocument icon.

Subdocument icon —

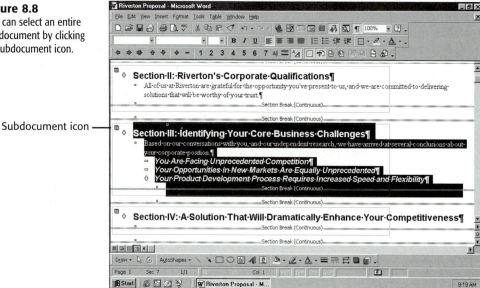

Now you can perform any of the following actions:

■ Move the subdocument intact to another location in your document. Drag the subdocument into the empty space between two other subdocuments. (By default, when you create subdocuments, Word leaves one paragraph of body text between them, just for this purpose.)

■ Move an entire subdocument into another subdocument, by using the Move Up or Move Down buttons. You get the same result as you would by merging subdocuments: You now have one subdocument containing both chunks of text.

Note

If you use Move Up/Move Down to move a subdocument into another subdocument and then move it back out, the text is placed in the master document. It is no longer a separate subdocument. You have to click Create Subdocument to make it a subdocument again—or click the Undo button until you revert back to where you were when you started.

- Use drag and drop to move an entire subdocument into another subdocument. This behaves differently than Move Up or Move Down. Now the subdocument where you've dropped the file contains its own subdocument. You're likely to use this feature only in exceptionally complex documents, where you may delegate a large section to someone who will in turn delegate smaller portions to others.

As you move subdocuments or the elements within them, a gray line appears, showing where your selected text will land if you release the mouse button.

Tip #124

If you move a subdocument to the wrong place, click Undo to move it back, and try again.

MOVING PARTS OF SUBDOCUMENTS

 When it comes to moving or reorganizing individual headings and subordinate text, there's no difference between master documents and conventional documents. First, display your master document in Outline view and click the Master Document View button to access all your outlining and master document tools.

 Now you can click on a heading to select all the text subordinate to it—or select just one paragraph. You can then use cut and paste, drag and drop, or the Move Up/Move Down buttons and keyboard shortcuts to move your selected text anywhere in the master document. It all works—whether your destination is in the same subdocument, a different subdocument, or in the master document itself.

SPLITTING A SUBDOCUMENT INTO TWO

Sometimes as you develop a large document, the contents of one subdocument may grow larger than you expected. Or, perhaps, your company might reorganize, and two people may have to divide responsibility for a chapter that was previously assigned to one individual. You might also discover that part of a chapter requires someone else's specialized knowledge.

 In short, there are many reasons you might decide that one subdocument needs to be split into two. To split a subdocument, first display the subdocument's contents from within the master document. Next, click your insertion point where you want to split the subdocument. Finally, click Split Subdocument.

You now have two subdocuments; the second contains all the text that originally followed the insertion point in your first subdocument.

COMBINING MULTIPLE SUBDOCUMENTS

Alternatively, you might find that you need one person to handle multiple subdocuments. In that case, you can combine two or more subdocuments into one, as follows:

1. Open the document and display it in Master Document view.

 2. Click Expand Subdocuments.

3. Make sure the subdocuments are adjacent; use Word's outlining tools to move them if necessary.

4. Click the subdocument icon next to the first subdocument you want to combine.

5. Press Shift and click the subdocument icon next to the last subdocument you want to combine. You have now selected the first and last subdocuments, and any subdocuments in between.

6. Click Merge Subdocument. The first of the subdocuments you selected now contains all the text that previously appeared in all the individual subdocuments you selected.

Note

You can't combine subdocuments if they're marked with a padlock icon. Locking and unlocking subdocuments is discussed later in this chapter.

Caution

The other subdocuments you merged into the first subdocument no longer appear as separate subdocuments within your master document. However, they still exist as separate files on your hard disk. Either delete or move these "stranded" files, so nobody edits them, mistakenly believing they are working on the current version of the document.

REMOVING A SUBDOCUMENT

Sometimes you want to keep the information contained in a subdocument, but you no longer want to store it in a separate subdocument. Possibly your colleague has finished with it, and you would like to move it back into the master document, so you'll have one less subdocument to manage.

 Follow these steps to eliminate the subdocument while moving its contents to the master document. First, click the subdocument icon to select the entire subdocument you want to convert. Next, click the Remove Subdocument button. The subdocument no longer appears in the master document, and all of its text is copied into the master document, from where it can be edited.

Caution

The original subdocument file remains on disk after you remove a subdocument. If you no longer need it, you may want to move or delete it.

Tip #125

If you want to eliminate the text from your document entirely, click the subdocument icon and press Delete.

Tip #126

You can eliminate all subdocuments at the same time by pressing Ctrl+A to select the entire document, and then clicking Remove Subdocument. This copies all the contents of your subdocuments into your master document file, and eliminates hyperlinks to subdocuments.

CREATING A TABLE OF CONTENTS, INDEX, OR CROSS-REFERENCES FOR A MASTER DOCUMENT

From within your master document, you can create tables of contents and indexes that reflect the contents of all your subdocuments. Follow these steps:

1. Open the master document, display it in Outline view, and click the Master Document View toolbar button.

2. Click Expand Subdocuments to make the contents of all subdocuments visible.

3. Position your insertion point where you want to create your table of contents, index, or cross-reference.

4. Follow Word's procedures for inserting an index, table of contents, or cross-reference. You can work from the Insert, Index and Tables or Insert, Cross-Reference dialog boxes; or insert index fields directly by pressing Alt+Shift+X and working from the Mark Index Entry dialog box; or enter fields directly by pressing Ctrl+F9 and editing the text between the field brackets.

You can enter your fields in the master document, in a subdocument displayed in the master document, or in a subdocument displayed in its own editing window.

Caution

If you open a subdocument using File, Open rather than open it from within the master document, any table of contents, index, or cross-reference you create won't reflect the contents of the master document.

→ For more information on creating tables of contents, **see** "Quick and Easy Tables of Contents," **p. 266**.

→ For more information on creating indexes, **see** "Creating a New Index Entry," **p. 300**, and "Compiling Your Index," **p. 307**.

→ For more information on building and using cross-references, **see** "Working with Cross-References," **p. 341**.

PRINTING MASTER DOCUMENTS AND SUBDOCUMENTS

You print master documents and subdocuments the same way you print any other documents. You can click the Print button on the Standard toolbar to get one complete copy of whatever master document or subdocument you're working in. Or you can choose File, Print to display the Print dialog box and select printing options manually.

In general, what you see is what you print:

- If you click Expand Subdocuments and then print a master document in Normal view, Word prints the entire master document, including all subdocuments. All styles, headers/footers, and page numbering are defined by the master document, not by individual subdocuments.

- If you print a master document with hyperlinks showing, the hyperlinks print rather than the document text. It's a handy way to get a list of your subdocuments, complete with their drive and folder locations.

- If you print a master document from Outline view, Word prints whatever headings and body text are currently displayed; for example, if you collapse part of the master document or display only the first line of body text paragraphs, only the elements that appear onscreen print.

- If you double-click a subdocument icon in a master document and display a subdocument in its own window, clicking Print prints only the subdocument—using the master document's styles and template.

- If you open a subdocument without first opening the master document, the subdocument prints as if it were an independent document—using its own styles and template.

WORKING WITH OTHERS ON THE SAME MASTER DOCUMENT

You've learned that master documents can simplify collaboration. You can delegate parts of your document for others to edit while working on other elements yourself; then when you're ready, you can review and edit the document as a whole.

By default, Word gives you complete access to any subdocument of which you are the author (assuming that subdocument is stored in a folder you have rights to access). Word gives you more limited access to subdocuments you did not author.

Note

Word determines who the author is by looking in the Author field of the File, Properties dialog box. How does the name of the author get there in the first place? It comes from the information you gave Word when you installed it (or changes you've made since in the User Information tab of the Tools, Options dialog box).

To make sure your colleagues have priority in accessing the documents for which they're responsible, you can enter their names in the Properties dialog box of each subdocument. Remember that if you give other users priority over yourself, you won't be able to edit their submissions until they finish working and close the files.

If you did not author a subdocument, you may find that it is locked when you try to open it. You can tell that a subdocument is locked when a small padlock icon appears beneath the subdocument icon (see Figure 8.9).

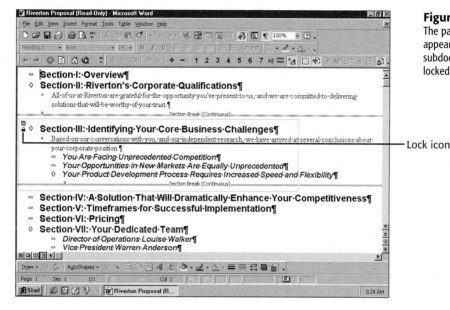

Figure 8.9
The padlock icon appears whenever a subdocument is locked.

Lock icon

When you first open a master document, displaying subdocuments as hyperlinks, all subdocuments are locked, no matter who authored them. If you click Expand Subdocuments, the Lock icons disappear, except in the following cases:

- If someone else is already working on his or her subdocument, Word displays a message offering to create a copy on which you can work. (If you create a copy, the word Copy appears in the title bar of the document you create.) Alternatively, you can wait until the first user has finished, and then open the original subdocument.

- When the subdocument's author saves it as Read-Only Recommended, using the check box in the Save Options dialog box. When you try to open a Read-Only Recommended file, Word displays a dialog box asking, in effect, whether you want to respect this preference. You can click No, and edit the document.

- When the subdocument's author has established a Password to Modify, also using options in the Save Options dialog box. You can read this subdocument, but you can't edit it without knowing the password.

■ When the subdocument is stored in a shared folder to which you have only Read-Only rights. Again, you can read the file, but you can't edit it unless you convince your network administrator to upgrade your rights. The words Read Only appear in the title bar of a read-only document.

If a subdocument is locked, you can attempt to unlock it as follows:

1. Open the master document, display it in Outline view, and click the Master Document View button.

2. Click Expand Subdocuments. (Until you expand your subdocuments, they're all locked.)

3. If the subdocument you want to edit is still locked, click anywhere in it.

4. Click the Lock Document button on the Master Document toolbar.

If the document remains locked, you may need to contact the individual using it, and ask him to close the document. A last resort is to copy the contents into another document, add that document as a subdocument, and remove the subdocument that caused the problem.

INSERTING FILES RATHER THAN USING MASTER DOCUMENTS

If you need to include the contents of multiple Word files in a single document, and you don't need the flexibility that master documents give you, Word offers another option: the Insert File feature. With Insert File, you simply browse to another Word file and insert its contents into the Word file you have open. You can do one of the following:

■ Insert the contents without establishing a link—essentially copying an entire document into your file, without going through the trouble of opening the file and selecting all its text

■ Insert the contents as a link, so that changes to the original file can automatically be reflected in the file you're working in

Follow these steps to use Insert File:

1. Click where you want to insert a file.

2. Choose Insert, File. The Insert File dialog box appears (see Figure 8.10).

3. Browse to the file you want to insert, and select it.

4. If you simply want to insert the file's text without creating a link, click the Insert button. If you prefer to create a link, click the down arrow to the right of the Insert button, and choose Insert as Link.

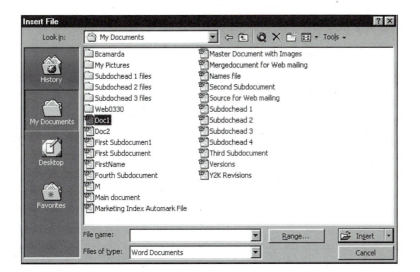

Figure 8.10
The Insert File dialog box looks much like the Open dialog box, with these differences: You can only select one file at a time and you can select a range of cells in an Excel worksheet.

Note

If you're inserting a file that isn't a Word 2000 or Word 97 file (for example, a file from an older version of Word or a competitive word processor), Word attempts to convert it first. If the file can be converted, Word inserts it. If not, Word displays an error message.

If you insert the file using a link, Insert File actually inserts an INCLUDETEXT field in your document that includes a reference to the document you inserted. As with master documents, you can reflect the latest information in the source document, though the process is slightly less automatic. You have to select the field and press F9 to update it, just as you would with any other Word field.

→ For more information on how fields work and how you update them, **see** "Understanding Fields," **p. 556**, and "Updating Your Fields," **p. 568**.

Insert File also lets you build tables of contents, indexes, and cross-references that take into account the text from another document. One major difference, however, limits the usefulness of Insert File: You can't click the field to open and edit the file you've inserted.

Tip #127

You can, however, edit the text you've inserted. After you do, you can press Ctrl+Shift+F7 to update the source document so it reflects your edits.

USING INSERT FILE TO INSERT PART OF A DOCUMENT

You can also use Insert File to insert part of any document into your current document. For example, you might want to quote a portion of a current price list. Inserting part of a document is a two-step process.

First, open the source document that contains the text you want to insert, and do the following:

1. Select the text you want to insert.

2. Choose Insert, Bookmark.

3. In the Bookmark Name text box, enter the name of a bookmark that you want to associate with this text. (Keep it short so you'll remember it.)

4. Save and close the document.

Next, open the destination document where you want to insert the text, and do the following:

1. Place your insertion point where you want to insert the text.

2. Choose Insert, File.

3. Select the document containing the source text.

4. In the Range text box, enter the name of the bookmark you've just inserted in the source document.

5. Click OK.

The source document's bookmarked text will appear in the destination document. Afterward, you can update the destination document to reflect any changes in the source document by selecting the field and pressing F9.

Tip #128

Other valuable field shortcuts include
- Temporarily preventing changes to the field by pressing Ctrl+F11
- Allowing changes again by pressing Ctrl+Shift+F11
- Transforming the field into text by pressing Ctrl+Shift+F9–thereby permanently preventing automatic updates.

Caution

You can't update the text if the source document is moved, or if it is edited to eliminate the bookmark.

→ To learn more about working with bookmarks, see "Using Bookmarks," **p. 338**.

TROUBLESHOOTING

WHAT TO DO IF WORD WON'T SAVE A MASTER DOCUMENT

Word's capacity for managing subdocuments varies with the number of files and programs you have open, how much memory your computer has, and other factors specific to your system. It is possible to run out of resources while you're trying to save a master document.

If Word won't save a master document,

- First, cancel the save; close any other open programs and files, and try again.
- If this doesn't work, convert some subdocuments into text in the master document by selecting them and clicking Remove Subdocuments. Then try saving again.

If you find that your system can't support the master document you're trying to create, you have some alternatives. One is to use Word's Insert File feature, covered earlier in the "Inserting Files Rather than Using Master Documents" section of this chapter.

A fallback position is to use Office 2000 Binders, which enable you to group many documents together for printing or distribution, but don't offer the editing and management capabilities of Word master documents, and do not allow you to build a unified table of contents or index for all subdocuments at once.

WHAT TO DO IF YOUR SUBDOCUMENTS DISAPPEAR

Did you click the Show All Headings button (or any of the other Show Headings buttons on the Outlining toolbar) while only hyperlinks were displayed in your master document? Word thinks you want to see only headings and body text, and it can't find any—all it can see is hyperlinks. First, click Expand Subdocuments, and then click Show All Headings.

TABLES OF CONTENTS, FIGURES, AUTHORITIES, AND CAPTIONING

In this chapter

TABLES OF CONTENTS

If you've ever had to prepare a table of contents manually, you'll appreciate how thoroughly Word automates the process. Word can do in moments what used to take hours.

In the next few sections, you'll learn the quickest ways to compile tables in your documents. You'll learn a few tricks for getting your tables of contents to look exactly the way you want them to, when Word doesn't do the job as automatically as you might like. You'll even learn how to instantly create a table of contents that appears in a frame on a Web page—a task that previously required painstaking HTML coding.

Communicating Effectively with Word: Use Tables of Contents Liberally
Tables of contents are such a convenient navigation tool, so you should look for opportunities to use them, even in documents that aren't required to have them. Your readers will thank you.

QUICK AND EASY TABLES OF CONTENTS

Sometimes you need a table of contents but you don't especially care what it looks like. If you used heading styles in your document, you can have your table of contents in less than 60 seconds.

To create a default table of contents, click where you want it to appear. Choose Insert, Index and Tables, click the Table of Contents tab (see Figure 9.1), and click OK.

Figure 9.1
From here, you can control all aspects of your table of contents's appearance—or simply click OK to get a default table of contents using heading styles.

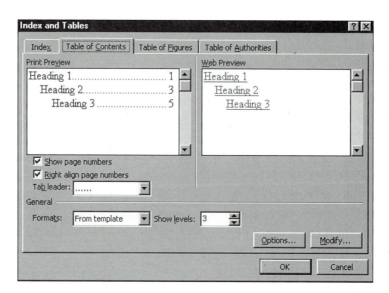

Word inserts a table of contents based on the first three heading levels in your document, using the built-in table of contents styles in your current template, with a dotted-line tab leader and right-aligned page numbers. If you already inserted specially formatted page numbers in your document, such as page numbers that include chapter numbers, those appear in your table of contents.

In short, you now have Word's default table of contents (see Figure 9.2). If that isn't enough for you, the rest of this section shows how to change Word's default settings to get the exact table of contents you have in mind.

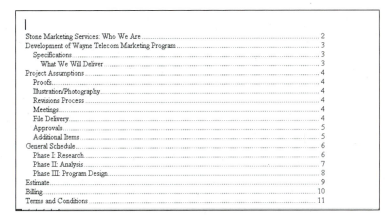

Figure 9.2
A sample table of contents built with Word's default styles and settings, and displayed in Normal view.

PART
II

CH

9

Tip #129

When you work in Normal or Print Layout view, table of contents entries act as hyperlinks even though they appear as regular text. You can click on any table of contents entry to move to the corresponding location in your document.

If you display your page in Web Layout view, the table of contents entries also look like Word hyperlinks—in other words, they appear as blue, underlined text. However, the page numbers disappear (because page numbers are largely irrelevant on Web sites).

When Word inserts a table of contents in your document, it's actually inserting a TOC field with the specific instructions you gave Word about how to build the table of contents. Later, you learn a little more about this field, so you can manually control some aspects of your tables of contents that can't easily be controlled through the Table of Contents tab of the Index and Tables dialog box.

→ For more information about controlling tables of contents with TOC fields, **see** "Creating a Table of Contents for Part of a Document," **p. 278**.

Tip #238

Before you compile a table of contents for a printed document, take these steps to make sure you get an accurate one:

1. Double-check to make sure you've used heading styles for all the headings you want Word to include in your table of contents. As you'll see later (in the section titled "Changing the Styles Word Compiles in Your Table of Contents"), you can include other styles and text in a table of contents if you're willing to invest a little extra time. But it's simplest to stay with headings.

2. Make sure you properly set margins and other section formatting that can affect page count.

3. Make sure hidden text is actually hidden. (When displayed, hidden text appears with a thin dotted underline. To hide it, click on the Show/Hide Paragraph Marks button on the Standard toolbar.)

4. Make sure your document is displaying *field results (page 998)* rather than the fields themselves. If you see codes within brackets, press Alt+F9 to display field results throughout the document.

5. Unless you have fields you do not want to update, update all your field results as follows: Press Ctrl+A to select the entire document, and then press F9.

CREATING TABLES OF CONTENTS IN WEB FRAMES

As you learned in Chapter 10, "Using Word to Develop Web Content," Word makes it easy to create *frames* that divide Web pages into sections that can be browsed independently. One common Web design technique involves using one frame as a table of contents, which remains displayed as the user navigates the site. Each item in the table of contents is displayed as a *hyperlink* that the user can click to display the corresponding location in another frame. Traditionally, creating tables of contents in frames has been a labor-intensive, complex process. In Word 2000, it's simple—again, assuming you build your table of contents from heading styles. When you're ready to create your table of contents, choose Format, Frames, Table of Contents in Frame. Word creates a new frame at the left side of the screen, and inserts table of contents hyperlinks corresponding to any heading in your document based on a heading style from Heading 1 through Heading 9. Figure 9.3 shows an example.

After you create a frame containing a table of contents, you can format it as needed. For example, you might want to consider

- Adding a company logo and a heading at the top of the Table of Contents frame
- Increasing the size of the hyperlinks (10-point Times New Roman by default)
- Deleting low-level headings (such as headings built from third- or fourth-level heading styles, or lower) if they make the table of contents too cumbersome, or too lengthy to fit on a single screen

- Editing some of your hyperlinks for brevity and clarity. Headings that work very well in print, or at the top of a page, may be too long or formal to attract clicks on an intranet or Web site. Figure 9.4 shows how the table of contents created in Figure 9.3 has been adapted for more effective Web use.

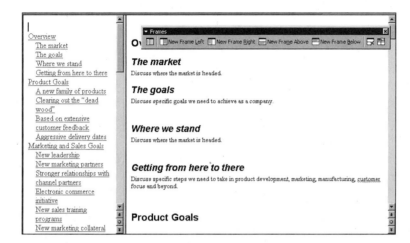

Figure 9.3
Word inserts table of contents hyperlinks in a new frame at the left side of the screen.

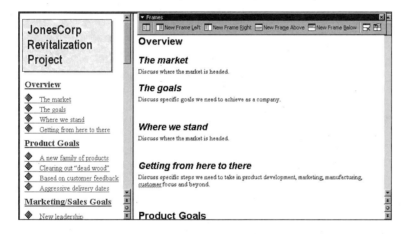

Figure 9.4
Editing and formatting a table of contents for more effective Web use.

Caution

Be careful not to overuse frames, or to create frames that take up too much screen "real estate"–leaving too little space for the content you want to communicate.

You can find a more detailed discussion of the advantages and disadvantages of frames in Chapter 40.

Note

When you use Format, Frames, Table of Contents in Frame, Word inserts a separate { HYPERLINK } field for each line of the table of contents, placing these hyperlinks in a new left frame.

On the other hand, if you have a Word document that contains a table of contents, and you save that table of contents as a Web page, the table of contents will remain a single TOC field, and they will remain in the same location where you originally placed them. If you created the TOC using default settings, the page numbers and leader lines will disappear when displayed as a Web page. However, if you display the Web Page in Print Layout view, or resave it as a printed document, the page numbers and leaders will reappear.

FORMATTING YOUR TABLE OF CONTENTS

Sometimes the default table of contents format Word applies isn't appropriate for your document. If so, you have two choices:

- Try out one of the six additional table of contents formats Word provides.
- Adapt Word's built-in table of contents styles to your specific needs.

CHOOSING ONE OF WORD'S BUILT-IN FORMATS

Word offers six built-in table of contents formats for use in printed documents: Classic, Distinctive, Fancy, Modern, Formal, and Simple. One of these might do the job if you don't have sophisticated requirements or a set of graphics standards with which to comply. (In truth, none of Word's built-in formats are especially classic, distinctive, fancy, modern, or formal, though Simple is reasonably simple.)

To try out a built-in format, first choose Insert, Index and Tables, Table of Contents. Next, choose the format in the Formats scroll box. In the Print Preview box, Word shows a generic table of contents for a printed document that uses this format. In the Web Preview box, you can see how the same format looks displayed on a Web or intranet site.

If you like what you see, click OK, and Word builds a table of contents that follows the format you've chosen.

BUILDING YOUR OWN TABLE OF CONTENTS FORMAT

The appearance of your table of contents is defined in part by the formatting of nine built-in styles, TOC 1 through TOC 9. If you are building a document that uses custom fonts and formatting throughout, it's likely that you'll want to adapt Word's built-in TOC styles as well. Word's Index and Tables dialog box includes a <u>M</u>odify option, which connects you to Word's Style dialog boxes where you can change these styles.

→ **See** "Creating and Changing Styles," **p. 41**.

Working through Word's nested Style dialog boxes can be time consuming, however. There's a quicker way to change your TOC styles:

1. Choose <u>I</u>nsert, In<u>d</u>ex and Tables.

2. Choose the Table of <u>C</u>ontents tab.

3. Click OK to insert a table of contents in your document. Don't worry about how it looks just yet.

4. After the table of contents is inserted, select any first-level TOC entry formatted with the TOC 1 style. Be careful not to select the entire table of contents.

PART

II

CH

9

Tip #130	It's often easiest to navigate and select text from within a table of contents by using keyboard shortcuts such as the arrow keys and Ctrl+Shift+Left arrow (to select words to the left) or Ctrl+Shift+Right arrow (to select words to the right).
	If you left-click in a table of contents, as you may have done in previous editions of Word, Word will jump to the location corresponding to the table of contents listing you clicked on. Alternatively, you can right-click in the table of contents, and press Esc to hide the shortcut menu that appears, while leaving your insertion point in the table of contents.

Tip #131	Sometimes, Word doesn't let you select the first line of a field result without selecting the entire field (for example, the entire table of contents). There are two workarounds.
	If your table of contents includes several lines formatted as TOC 1, select one from the middle (instead of the beginning) of your table of contents.
	If your table of contents only has one line formatted as TOC 1, do the following. First, right-click after the first character in the first line, press Esc to hide the shortcut menu, and press Enter. Now, you can select the new second line, reformat it, and then edit it to place the first character back where it belongs.

5. Reformat the TOC 1 entry the way you want it to look.

6. Repeat steps 2–3 for each additional TOC style in your table of contents.

If you used Word's default settings, which capture only heading levels 1 through 3 in a table of contents, you have to reformat only two more styles: TOC 2 and TOC 3. As you change each style, Word immediately updates all the TOC entries that use the same style to reflect the new formatting.

Caution

After you have the TOC styles you want, don't choose another format in the Table of Contents tabbed dialog box. By default, Word doesn't just reformat your table of contents; it reformats your custom styles with the built-in formats you just chose.

(This automatic style updating won't occur if you clear the Automatically Update check box in each style's Modify Style dialog box, available through Format, Style.)

CREATING TABLES OF CONTENTS WITHOUT PAGE NUMBERS

Occasionally, you might want to compile printed tables of contents that do not include page numbers. For instance, many people insert tables of contents without page numbers as a way to generate a quick hard-copy document outline for use in a meeting.

To tell Word not to include page numbers in a printed table of contents, display the Table of Contents tab, clear the Show Page Numbers box, and click OK.

Tip #132

If you print your table of contents from Web Layout view, it prints without page numbers whether or not you clear the Show Page Numbers check box.

CHANGING THE ALIGNMENT OF PAGE NUMBERS

Word includes page numbers in all its built-in table of contents formats designed for printing. In most cases, those page numbers are right-aligned, as shown earlier in Figure 9.2. However, you can tell Word to place the page numbers next to the table of contents entries rather than right-align them.

To tell Word not to right-align page numbers in a table of contents, display the Table of Contents tab, clear the Right Align Page Numbers check box, and click OK.

CHANGING THE TAB LEADER USED IN A TABLE OF CONTENTS

In printed documents, if you create a table of contents based on the TOC styles in the Normal template (for example, if you use the From template format in the Table of Contents tabbed dialog box), Word inserts a *tab leader (page 96)* on each line (refer to Figure 9.2). By default, this tab leader is a series of dots that runs from the end of the table of contents text entry to the page number.

Note

Tab leaders disappear in Web Layout view.

You can change the tab leader, or eliminate it altogether. Display the Table of Contents tab, and choose the leader you want in the Tab Leader drop-down list box. Word offers dots, dashes, and solid underlines—or you can choose (none) to show no leader.

CHOOSING THE NUMBER OF LEVELS IN YOUR TABLE OF CONTENTS

By default, Word builds tables of contents from the first three heading levels. In other words, it collects all text formatted with the Heading 1, Heading 2, and Heading 3 styles, and incorporates that text in the table of contents.

Of course this means your table of contents doesn't include Heading 4 through Heading 9 text. This may be a problem, especially if you used Heading 1 as only a chapter heading. In that case, your table of contents has only two levels to cover everything important that's going on within your chapters.

Tip #133	One way to avoid this problem is to format chapter headings using Word's Title style instead of the Heading 1 style.

You can tell Word to place from one to nine levels in a Word table of contents. To do so, first display the Table of Contents tab of the Index and Tables dialog box. Choose a number from 1 to 9 in the Show Levels scroll box, and click OK.

Word builds the table of contents using all the outline levels you've selected. For example, if you set Show Levels to 5, your table of contents would be built from headings formatted as Heading 1, Heading 2, Heading 3, Heading 4, and Heading 5.

You've just learned how to control the number of levels included in your table of contents. But, in the example described earlier, for instance, you may not want Heading 1 included at all—because you've used it as a chapter title, not a subheading. Word allows you to specify exactly which styles Word looks for when it builds your table of contents—and in the next section, you'll learn how.

CHANGING THE STYLES WORD COMPILES IN YOUR TABLE OF CONTENTS

Sometimes you want to compile tables of contents based on styles other than Heading 1 through Heading 9. Word enables you to pick any styles you want and choose the order in which they'll be placed in your table of contents. Display the Table of Contents tab, and click Options. The Table of Contents Options dialog box opens (see Figure 9.5).

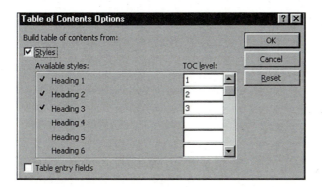

Figure 9.5
The Table of Contents Options dialog box lets you specify what styles and table entry fields Word compiles into your table of contents.

Check marks appear next to all styles that are already in your table of contents. If you want to remove a style, delete the number in its corresponding TOC Level box. To add any style that's already in your document, click its TOC Level text box and enter a number from 1 to 9 there. More than one style can share the same level.

When you're finished, click OK to return to the Index and Tables dialog box. If your other settings are the way you want them, click OK again to compile your table of contents.

Note

Because you can only choose from styles that already exist in your document, make sure you've added all the styles you want before building your table of contents.

Note

If you decide to revert to Word's default styles (Headings 1 through 3), click the Reset button in the Table of Contents Options dialog box.

WHEN YOU CAN'T USE STYLES: TABLE OF CONTENTS ENTRY FIELDS

On occasion, you might want your table of contents to include entries that aren't associated with styles at all. For example, you might want the first sentence of each chapter to appear in your table of contents, but you might prefer not to create a separate style for the paragraphs where these sentences appear in your document. You might prefer to create at least some of your table of contents entries without using styles in a few other situations:

- You'd like to include an entry that paraphrases text in your document rather than repeat it precisely.
- You'd like to include only one entry formatted with a given style, not all of them.
- You'd like to suppress page numbering for selected table of contents entries, but not for all of them.

You can use Table Entry fields to instruct Word to include any text in a table of contents. It's a two-step process. First, insert the fields in your document, and then instruct Word to use them in building the table of contents by checking the Table Entry Fields check box in the Table of Contents Options dialog box. The following two sections walk you through the process.

→ See "Inserting a Field Using Field Characters," p. 566.

STEP 1: INSERTING TC FIELDS *TC fields* are markers that Word can use in compiling a table of contents. You can place a TC field in any location in your document for which you want a table of contents entry. When Word builds the table of contents, it creates the entry by including

- Entry text you've specified within the TC field
- A page number corresponding to the location of the TC field in your document

¶ You can insert TC fields through the Insert, Field dialog box. You can also enter them directly into your document by pressing Ctrl+F9 to display field brackets and entering the syntax between the brackets. However, if you work within field brackets, make sure to toggle the Show/Hide Paragraph Marks button, because TC fields are immediately formatted as hidden text that isn't otherwise visible for editing. Using Insert, Field is a little easier, especially if you're not accustomed to working directly with fields. But working with field brackets is quicker—especially if you're inserting multiple TC fields in your document.

PART

II

CH

9

Tip #134

If you often insert fields, add the Insert Field command to the Text shortcut menu, as follows:

1. Choose Tools, Customize, and click the Toolbars tab.

2. Check the Shortcut Menus check box in the Toolbars scroll box. The Shortcut Menus toolbar is displayed.

3. Click the Commands tab in the Customize dialog box.

4. Click Insert in the Categories scroll box.

5. In the Commands scroll box, choose Field and drag it to the Text command on the Shortcut Menus toolbar. A cascaded menu appears.

6. Drag Field to the Text submenu, and drag it across to place it where you want it on that menu.

7. Click Close on the Customize dialog box.

The command now appears on the shortcut menu that appears when you right-click on an empty space in your editing window.

Caution

If you use brackets, you must press Ctrl+F9 to create the brackets: You can't just type bracket symbols on the keyboard.

Tip #135

Here's a workaround you can use to keep TC fields (and other hidden fields) visible while you're working on them.

After you enter field brackets, type an unusual character, such as ^, before you enter the letters TC. Word won't recognize that you're creating a hidden field. Create all your fields this way, and with your field codes displayed, use Word's Replace feature to replace all the ^ characters with no text. Word now recognizes the fields as hidden, and hides them all (unless you've set Word to display hidden text).

TC fields use the following syntax:

```
{ TC "Words you want to appear in table of contents" [Switches] }
```

In other words, immediately after the field name TC, enter the text you want Word to place in your table of contents, within quotation marks. Then follow it with one or more of these *switches (page 1006)*:

Switch	What It Does
\l Level	Specifies which level of your table of contents to use. If no switch is included, Word assumes Level 1. Example: { TC "Continental League" \l 3 } tells Word to insert a third-level entry consisting of the words Continental League and formatted using the TOC 3 style.
\n	Tells Word not to include a page number for this entry. Example: { TC "Bonus Coverage" \n } tells Word to include the words Bonus Coverage in the table of contents, but not to include the page number on which the field appears.
\f Type	Specifies which list of figures in which to include this entry. Type corresponds to any character of the alphabet; all TC fields that use the same character compiled together. Example: { TC "Mona Lisa" \f m } tells Word to include a table of figures entry named Mona Lisa whenever a table of contents is compiled from all the TC fields that use the \f m switch. The field { TC "Warhol" \f x } would not be included in the same table of figures, because a different letter—x, instead of m—has been used. This switch is only used for tables of figures, not for tables of contents.

→ To learn more about tables of figures, **see** "Building Tables of Figures," on **p. 289**.

Here are two more examples:

Sample Field	What It Does
{TC "Marketing Reorg" \l 2 }	Inserts a second-level table of contents entry Marketing Reorg (including page numbers).
{ TC "Smith" \l 1 \n }	Inserts a first-level entry Smith, with no page number.

Tip #136   After you have the TC syntax correct, you can copy TC fields wherever you need them, changing only the elements that need to change, such as the text that Word will place in the table of contents.

STEP 2: TELLING WORD TO USE YOUR TC FIELDS   After you enter TC fields wherever you need them, choose Insert, Index and Tables to reopen the Table of Contents tab. Click Options to view the Table of Contents Options dialog box. Next, check the Table Entry Fields check box.

If you want your table of contents to be built from TC fields only, clear the Styles check box. Click OK to return to the Table of Contents tab; click OK again to compile the table of contents.

UPDATING A TABLE OF CONTENTS

Your table of contents entries are likely to change after you first create your table of contents. Perhaps edits or margin changes will affect your page numbering. Possibly new headings will be added to your document, or you may be called upon to reorganize existing headings. Or maybe you've used Word's outlining tools to change heading levels. Whatever the reason, you may need to update your table of contents to reflect changes in your document. Follow these steps:

1. Right-click on the table of contents, and choose Update Field from the shortcut menu.

2. Choose whether you want to update only page numbers or the entire table (see Figure 9.6). If you update the entire table, you lose any manual formatting or editing you've done within it. However, you may have no choice if you've added or reorganized headings; these changes aren't reflected if you update only page numbers.

Figure 9.6

Tip #137

What if you've done extensive formatting and editing in your table of contents? It seems a shame to lose all that work for just one or two new headings. You don't have to. You can patch your table of contents to reflect the new headings. Click where the new heading should appear in your table of contents, and type it in manually.

Even better, use Word's Cross-Reference feature twice—first to insert the heading text, and then again to insert the page reference. You may also have to manually apply the heading style that corresponds to the heading level you want, and polish up the formatting to make sure it matches its surroundings.

As a result, you have a cross-referenced field that updates just as the rest of the table of contents does. Everything works fine—unless you forget to tell Word to update the entire table rather than just page numbers. (That's what Undo is for!)

→ To learn more about cross-references, **see** "Working with Cross-References," **p. 341**.

ADDING A SECOND TABLE OF CONTENTS TO YOUR DOCUMENT

You might want to add a second table of contents to your document. What kind of documents have two tables of contents? It's increasingly common for how-to manuals and books (such as this book) to have a high-level, "at a glance" table of contents, as well as a more detailed, conventional table of contents that goes several levels deep into the document.

You might also want to insert separate tables of contents for each major section of a book, as well as an overall table of contents in the front. Whatever your reason, adding a second table of contents is easy to do.

After you insert your first table of contents, click where you want the second one to appear; establish its settings in the Table of Contents tab; and click OK. Word asks if you want to replace your existing table of contents. Click No, and the second table of contents appears.

Tip #138

If you need more than two tables of contents, you can add them by following the same procedure described here. Once you have two tables of contents, each one can be updated separately (and, in fact, updating one doesn't automatically update the other).

CREATING A TABLE OF CONTENTS FOR PART OF A DOCUMENT

The procedure you've just learned works fine most of the time. For example, it's perfect for including a second high-level table of contents that includes only one or two heading levels. But what if you want to insert a table of contents for only part of a document? Use a TOC field.

As you learned earlier, when Word inserts a table of contents, it's actually inserting a TOC field with switches that correspond to the choices you made in the Table of Contents dialog box. However, you can do a few things with the TOC field directly that you can't do through a dialog box, and compiling a table of contents for only part of a document is one of them.

First, select the part of the document for which you want to create a table of contents. Next, *bookmark* it. To do so, choose Insert, Bookmark, enter the name of the bookmark, and click Add.

Now that you have a bookmark, insert a TOC field where you want your table of contents to appear. Include the \b switch and the bookmark name. Here's a bare bones example:

```
{ TOC \b Jones }
```

Tip #139

The TOC field has many switches. Follow these steps to get the exact partial table of contents you want without learning them all:

1. Create and insert your table of contents the conventional way by making choices in the Table of Contents tab of the Index and Tables dialog box.
2. Right-click in the table of contents, and choose Toggle Field Codes from the shortcut menu.
3. Click inside the field code, next to the right bracket.
4. Type \b followed by the name of the bookmark.
5. Right-click on the field and choose Update Field from the shortcut menu.

Tip #140

If you're sure that nothing will change in your table of contents except page numbers, there's an easier way to get a partial table of contents. Insert a table of contents the way you normally would, and just edit out the entries you don't need.

Alternatively, you can copy the entries you want and paste them beneath the table of contents; then delete the original table of contents. The entries paste into the document as hyperlinks, formatted with blue underlining. You can reformat them as needed; they will still update correctly when your page numbers change.

After you do this, remember to update only page numbers, not the entire table.

PART
II
CH
9

BUILDING TABLES OF CONTENTS FROM MULTIPLE DOCUMENTS

It's common for large documents to be composed of multiple smaller documents that need to be brought together into a single table of contents. The easiest way to do this is to work with Word's master document feature, discussed in Chapter 8, "Master Documents: Control and Share Even the Largest Documents."

First, display your document in Outline view and set up your subdocuments (or insert subdocuments using documents that already exist). Place your insertion point where you want the table of contents to appear. Next, choose Insert, Index and Tables. If the Office Assistant asks whether you want to open all subdocuments before continuing, choose Yes. (If you don't, Word doesn't include the missing subdocuments in your table of contents.) The Index and Tables dialog box opens. Establish the settings you want for your table of contents, and click OK. Word inserts your table of contents at the insertion point.

Note

In Outline view, your table of contents appears as 10-point body text. To view your table of contents as it will print, choose Print Layout view. To view your table of contents as it would appear on the Web, choose Web Layout view.

INCLUDING TABLE OF CONTENTS ENTRIES FROM ANOTHER DOCUMENT

Although master documents are usually the best way to build tables of contents incorporating several documents, you may occasionally want to make reference to a table of contents in another document without using master documents. For instance, you might be sending a memo summarizing the contents of a document now being developed.

Word provides a special field, the Referenced Document (RD) field, for tasks such as these. Using the RD field to build a table of contents is a two-step process: First you create the RD field, specifying which file you want to reference. Next, you insert your table of contents.

Note

When you build a table of contents with the RD feature, Word incorporates entries from both the referenced document and your current document. The entries associated with your referenced document are located as if the entire referenced document was located at the spot where you inserted the RD field.

As discussed earlier in this chapter, one easy way to enter a field such as RD is to press Ctrl+F9 to display field brackets and enter the syntax between the brackets. Before entering text, be sure to click the Show/Hide Paragraph Marks button on the Standard toolbar to display hidden text. RD fields are invisible, and if you don't display hidden text, Word hides them as soon as you enter the letters RD within the field—even before you finish editing the field!

RD fields use the following syntax (notice the double backslashes in the pathname):

```
{ RD "c:\\folder\\filename.doc" }
```

If the file you want to reference happens to be in the same folder as your current document, you can simply specify the filename, as follows:

```
{ RD "filename.doc" }
```

> **Caution**
>
> Whether you use a full pathname or reference a file in the current folder, if you move the referenced file, the link will be lost.
>
> One exception: If you reference a file in the current folder, and move both the file you're working on and the file you're referencing, the link remains intact as long as both files are in the same folder.

Now that you've entered the RD field, you can insert your table of contents the way you normally would: Click in the document where you want it to appear; choose Insert, Index and Tables, choose the Table of Contents tab; establish the settings you want; and click OK.

> **Note**
>
> When you use the RD field for applications like the ones discussed earlier, you may want to make some changes to Word's default settings in the Table of Contents tab.
>
> For example, if you are summarizing another document's table of contents and you want only high-level headings to appear, adjust the Show Levels spin box to 1 or 2. In many cases, your readers don't need to know the page numbers of the referenced document, and you can also clear the Show Page Numbers check box.

Figure 9.7 shows an RD field and TOC field in a memo; Figure 9.8 shows the corresponding field results. Note that the table of contents has been manually reformatted to fit with its surroundings.

 If your table of contents contains the words `Error! Bookmark not defined` *after you update it, see "How to Fix Update Problems in Tables," in "Troubleshooting" at the end of this chapter.*

If your table of contents displays incorrect page numbers, see "How to Fix Incorrect Page Numbers in Tables," in "Troubleshooting" at the end of this chapter.

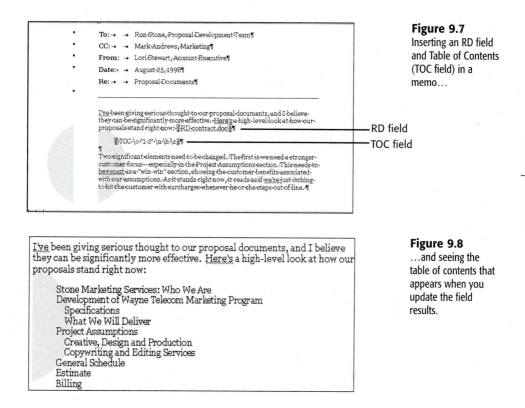

Figure 9.7
Inserting an RD field and Table of Contents (TOC field) in a memo…

RD field
TOC field

PART
II

CH

9

Figure 9.8
…and seeing the table of contents that appears when you update the field results.

INTRODUCING TABLES OF FIGURES AND CAPTIONS

Often, you want other tables in your document besides a table of contents. For example, you may want a table that compiles all the figures in your document, or all the equations, or for that matter, all the Word tables. You can build tables such as these in much the same way you've just learned how to build tables of contents.

However, Word contains a few extra tricks that might make your life even easier. For example, it can automatically insert captions for you—and then build your table of figures from the captions it has inserted. The next sections review Word's powerful captioning features. After you understand captioning, you learn how to compile your captions into tables of figures—or any tables you like.

INSERTING CAPTIONS: AN OVERVIEW

You can't have a table of figures if you don't have any figure captions to compile into your table. So your first step is to get some figure captions into your document and let Word know that they're figures. There are three ways to do that.

You can insert your figure captions manually, using a style that you won't use for anything except captions. Word has a built-in style, Caption, that's perfectly suited for this purpose. You also can use Word's Caption feature. Or, best of all, you can tell Word to automatically insert a caption whenever it sees you inserting something that ought to be captioned.

USING WORD'S CAPTION FEATURE

To use Word's Caption feature to streamline captioning, first click where you want a caption to appear. Then, choose Insert, Caption to display the Caption dialog box, as shown in Figure 9.9. Word displays its default caption, Figure 1, in the Caption text box. If you want to add a description of the figure, you can type it after the figure number, click OK, and Word inserts the entire caption at your insertion point.

Figure 9.9
The Caption dialog box enables you to enter specific caption information while Word handles boilerplate text and automatic caption numbering.

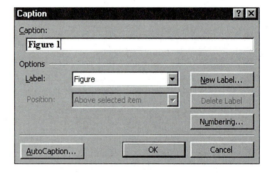

Tip #141

If you insert new captions or move existing ones, Word automatically renumbers all the captions for you whenever you display the document in Print Preview, print the document, or update your fields. To see the new numbering right away, choose Edit, Select All (or press Ctrl+A) to select the entire document. Then right-click on a field and choose Update Field (or press F9) to update all your fields.

If you already have a table of contents, you'll be asked whether you want to update the entire table or only page numbers. Remember to choose Update Page Numbers Only if you've added custom formatting to your table of contents that you don't want to lose.

CREATING CAPTIONS FOR OTHER DOCUMENT ELEMENTS

What if you aren't creating captions for figures? If you're creating captions for equations or tables instead, choose Equation or Table in the Label drop-down list box. If you're creating another element, such as a photo or map, you can create a special label by clicking New Label. The New Label dialog box opens (see Figure 9.10). Type your label and click OK.

The new label now appears in the Caption text box, and it is added to the list of available labels for future use. If you decide you no longer need it at some point, click Delete Label to eliminate it.

Figure 9.10
If you're creating captions for something other than a Figure, Table, or Equation, enter your custom label in the New Label dialog box.

PART
II
CH
9

CHANGING THE SEQUENCE WORD USES TO NUMBER CAPTIONS

By default, Word numbers captions with Arabic numbers (1, 2, 3...). However, you can change this. In the Caption dialog box, click Numbering; the Caption Numbering dialog box opens (see Figure 9.11). In the Format drop-down list box, choose a new sequence, such as capital letters or lowercase Roman numerals. Click OK.

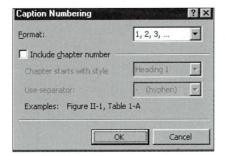

Figure 9.11
The Caption Numbering dialog box enables you to change the sequence Word uses to number captions, or to add a chapter number to your caption numbers.

ADDING CHAPTER NUMBERS TO YOUR CAPTIONS

Often, you want your captions to include chapter numbers as well as sequence numbers, like the captions in this book. You should know that Word's "official" approach to inserting chapter numbers is surprisingly complex, and it makes sense only if you have multiple chapters in your document. If you are editing a document that contains only one or a few chapters (even if it's part of a larger book), skip to the "Easier Ways to Add Chapter Numbers" section for some quicker ways to accomplish this!

Word connects chapter numbering in captions with the Outline Numbering feature. That means you have to insert outline numbers in your document before you can get chapter numbers in your captions. If you don't, you're likely to encounter the bewildering message box shown in Figure 9.12.

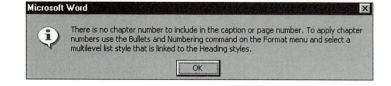

Microsoft Word
There is no chapter number to include in the caption or page number. To apply chapter numbers use the Bullets and Numbering command on the Format menu and select a multilevel list style that is linked to the Heading styles.
OK

Figure 9.12
Word doesn't want to insert chapter numbers in your captions because you haven't inserted outline numbers throughout your document.

→ **See** "Using Word's Automatic Outline Numbering," **p. 227**.

By connecting captions to chapter numbers, Word can use { STYLEREF } fields that look for the most recent example of a style, and borrow the text they need from there. This way, Word knows when a caption should read Figure 1.1 and when it should read Figure 2.1.

This is a hassle, especially if you weren't intending to use outline numbering, but go along with it—for now.

STEP 1: SET UP YOUR DOCUMENT FOR OUTLINE NUMBERING Start by using Word's outlining tools to make sure you used heading styles throughout your document. This doesn't work if you simply use outline levels; you have to use the heading styles Heading 1, Heading 2, Heading 3, and so on. Set aside one heading level—typically Heading 1—specifically for your chapter names. Figure 9.13 shows how your first-level headings should look in Outline view.

What the Court Says - Microsoft Word
First-level headings
Style area displaying style names
Heading 1 What the Court Says: A Topic-By-Topic Review of American Constitutional Law
Heading 1 The Foundations of Constitutional Law
Heading 2 The Constitution: A Living Legacy
Heading 2 A Document That Transcended Its Time and Place
Heading 3 The Articles of Confederation
Heading 3 The Constitutional Convention
Heading 3 The Federalists and the Anti-Federalists: A Very Close Call
Heading 1 The Bill of Rights
Heading 2 Freedom of Speech
Heading 2 Freedom of Religion
Heading 2 Freedom of the Press
Heading 2 Freedom of Association
Heading 2 The Second Amendment and Gun Control
Heading 1 Cruel and Unusual Punishment
Heading 2 The Death Penalty
Heading 1 Personal Privacy

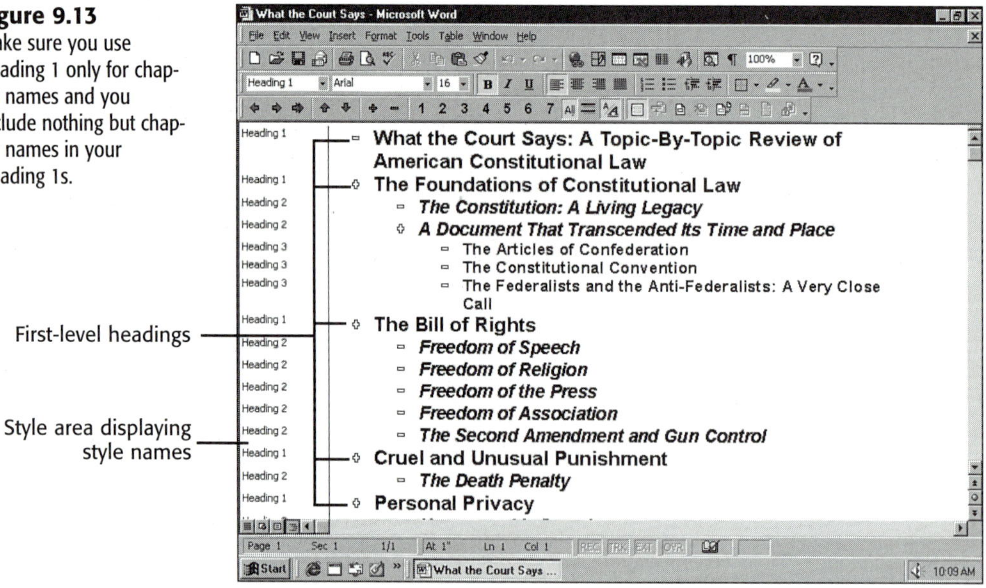

Figure 9.13
Make sure you use Heading 1 only for chapter names and you include nothing but chapter names in your Heading 1s.

Tip #142

To display the styles used in a document (as shown in Figure 9.13), choose Tools, Options, View; set Style Area Width to a width wide enough for all your styles to be visible, such as 0.8".

STEP 2: INSERT YOUR OUTLINE NUMBERING   Next, insert your outline numbering, as follows:

1. Select the entire document (or at least all sections where you want to add captions).

2. Choose Format, Bullets and Numbering.

3. Choose the Outline Numbered tab.

4. Select a heading numbering scheme from the bottom row of four options. (If you choose from the top row, Word numbers all your paragraphs, not just headings, so your figure numbers won't match your chapter numbers.)

5. Click Customize to make any changes to your outline numbering scheme, or just click OK to insert the outline numbers.

STEP 3: INSERT YOUR CAPTIONS   Now that you have outline numbers in your document, follow these steps to insert your captions:

1. Place the insertion point where you want your first caption.

2. Choose Insert, Caption.

3. In the Caption dialog box, add any information you want to your caption. If necessary, add a new label.

4. Click Numbering. The Caption Numbering dialog box opens.

5. Check the Include Chapter Number check box.

6. Choose Heading 1 in the Chapter Starts with Style drop-down list box. (This example assumes that chapter numbers are formatted with Heading 1 style—and, as already discussed, they are the only text formatted with that style.)

7. In the Use Separator drop-down list box, choose the separator character you want from the following selection: a hyphen, period, colon, em dash, and en dash. Separator characters appear between the chapter number and figure number, as in the following examples: 1.1, 1-1, 1:1.

8. Click OK twice.

The caption appears in your document, containing the number of the current chapter. Underneath the hood, here's what's happened. Word has inserted a { STYLEREF } field that searches toward the beginning of the document for the first Heading 1 style. When a Heading 1 style is found, the text formatted in that style is displayed as the field result.

PART

II

CH

9

Tip #143

If you've gone through all this, and then decide you don't want outline numbers after all, here's a possible solution. When the document is absolutely finished, select it all (Ctrl+A). Then follow these steps:

1. Press Ctrl+Shift+F9 to *unlink (page 1011)* all the fields in your document, so none of them will update ever again. (This affects all fields, including the fields that track caption numbering within the chapter—so be careful!)

2. With the entire document selected, choose Format, Bullets and Numbering, Outline Numbered. The Outline Numbered tab appears.

3. Choose None and click OK. The outline numbers disappear, but the captions stay the way they were.

EASIER WAYS TO ADD CHAPTER NUMBERS

Boy, that was hard work. Isn't there an easier way? You'd better believe it. You really don't have to include outline numbering to get chapter numbers in your captions.

ADDING CHAPTER NUMBERS TO CAPTIONS IN ONE-CHAPTER DOCUMENTS   Consider the easiest case: a document containing only one chapter. Maybe you've been asked to write Chapter 12 of a book. You're not working from within someone else's master document (or, if you are, they aren't requiring you to use Word's outline numbering approach to captions).

Follow these steps to insert chapter numbers:

1. Use Word's Insert, Caption feature to insert captions without chapter numbers.

2. Choose Edit, Replace and then use Word's Find and Replace feature to search for all references to the word "figure" that are styled using the Caption style, and replace them with "figure" followed by your chapter number and whatever separator character you want to use. You can search for a style by clicking the Format button in the Replace tab, clicking Style, and choosing the style for which you want to search.

→ **See** "Creating and Changing Styles," **p. 41**.

CREATING CUSTOM CAPTION NUMBERING FOR ALL YOUR DOCUMENTS   You can go a step further and create a chapter numbering solution you can reuse in all your documents, no matter how many chapters they contain—without ever using outline numbering unless you want. Follow these steps:

1. Select the chapter number anywhere in your document and format it with a new character style through the New Style dialog box (see Figure 9.14), accessible through Format, Style. For this example, name the character style Chapnum.

→ **See** "Understanding Character Styles," **p. 34**.

2. Use Insert, Caption (refer to Figure 9.9) to insert a caption that doesn't contain a chapter number.

Figure 9.14
Creating a character style named Chapnum in the New Style dialog box.

3. If you wish, reformat the caption to your tastes, and update the caption style to reflect your changes. After you reformat the caption, click in the Style drop-down box, press Enter, and click OK in the Modify Style dialog box that appears.

> Figure { styleref chapnum } 1

Figure 9.15

4. Click where you want the chapter number to appear within your caption.

5. Press Ctrl+F9 to insert field brackets.

6. Type the following within the field brackets (see Figure 9.15):`styleref chapnum`. Inserting a STYLREF field that will look fo rtext you formatted in a unique character style.

> Figure 1 1|

Figure 9.16

7. Press F9 to update the field. It should now display the chapter number to which you applied the character style (see Figure 9.16). After you update the STYLREF field, it should display the chapter number.

8. Manually enter any separator characters you need (see Figure 9.17). In this example a period is added to separate the chapter number and figure number.

> Figure 1.1

Figure 9.17

9. Create an *AutoText entry (page 303)* based on your caption. To do so, select the caption, choose Insert, AutoText, New, type a entry name such as fig (see Figure 9.18), and click OK. Finally, make the entire caption an AutoText entry so it's easy to reuse.

Figure 9.18

Now, whenever you start a new document that you want to contain automatically numbered captions, do this: First, type the chapter number and mark it as a bookmark named chapnum. Then, wherever you want to insert a caption, type the AutoText entry and press F3 to turn it into a complete caption.

AUTOMATING CAPTIONS

You can take Word's captioning feature one giant step further. Word can automatically add captions any time you add specific graphics or other elements to your document. To use Word's AutoCaption feature, choose Insert, Caption to display the Caption dialog box. Then, click AutoCaption. The AutoCaption dialog box opens (see Figure 9.19).

Figure 9.19
From the AutoCaption dialog box, you can tell Word which document elements to caption automatically, which label to use, and where those captions should appear.

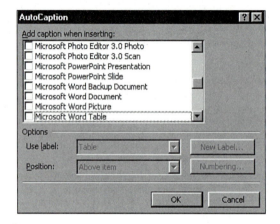

In the Add Caption When Inserting scroll box, you see a list of document elements. This list varies depending on the software installed on your computer; it includes (among other things) files from all the programs you own that are OLE (Object Linking and Embedding) servers.

Check the box next to every item you would like Word to caption. Then, specify the label you want to use (or create a new label, if you wish). In the Position drop-down list box, choose whether you want your caption to automatically appear below or above the item you insert. If you want to change automatic caption numbering, click Numbering and make your changes in the Caption Numbering dialog box you learned about earlier.

If you choose, whenever you check a box to automatically caption another type of document element, you can also click New Label to customize the text of the caption that will accompany that specific element. These customized labels are attached to the document's current template, which means that you can associate different caption text with the same file types if you work with a document attached to a different template.

When you finish, click OK in the AutoCaption dialog box. Word begins adding captions automatically whenever you insert a document element you told it to caption.

BUILDING TABLES OF FIGURES

Now that you understand captions, it's time to discuss ways you can compile those captions into tables of figures. First, choose Insert, Index and Tables, and click the Table of Figures tab (see Figure 9.20).

> **Note**
>
> Tables of "figures" can list a range of document elements: images, equations, row-and-column tables, and many others.

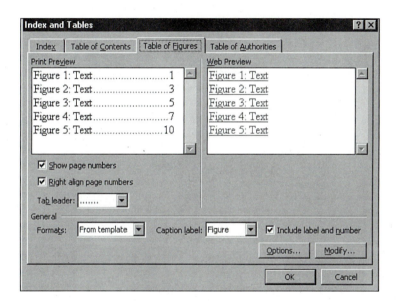

PART
II

CH
9

Figure 9.20
The Table of Figures tab offers many of the same options as the Table of Contents tab.

The Table of Figures tab looks quite similar to the Table of Contents tab you learned about earlier in this chapter. For example, you can choose whether page numbers should appear in your table, and if so, whether they should be right-aligned or appear next to the caption text. If you right-align your figure listings, you can choose a tab leader. You can also choose from five formats: Classic, Distinctive, Centered, Formal, and Simple.

You can see the effects of any change you make in two separate preview boxes: Print Preview shows how your table of figures will appear in a printed document, and Web Preview shows how it will appear on an intranet or Web site.

> **Note**
>
> Although these formats complement the Table of Contents formats with the same names, they're not identical. As with tables of contents, you can see what a format will look like in the Preview box.
>
> When you choose a Table of Figures format and click OK, Word inserts the table in your document. Word applies its built-in Table of Figures style, after changing the style to reflect the format you chose.

Each table of figures Word compiles is based on one set of captions in your document. In other words, if you created some captions using the Table label, and others using the Figure label, each set has to be compiled separately into its own table of figures—but then, that's what you probably want.

In the Caption Label drop-down list box, choose the type of captions you want to compile. If you want to include the labels and numbers as well as the caption text, check the Include Label and Number check box; otherwise, clear it. If you're now satisfied with your table, click OK and Word inserts it in your document. Figure 9.21 shows a default table of figures using the built-in styles in the Normal template.

Figure 9.21
The default table of figures.

Figure 1. Typical network hub. 3
Figure 2. Network routers. 7
Figure 3. The architecture of the Internet. 9
Figure 4. Configuring an IP client workstation. 10
Figure 5. How IPv6 changes typical IP networks. 15

BUILDING TABLES OF FIGURES FROM A DIFFERENT STYLE

Until now, you've learned how to build tables of figures by telling Word to collect the contents of every figure formatted with the Caption style. Because Word automatically uses the Caption style for all the captions it creates, you're in good shape as long as you use Word's automatic captioning feature. But what if you would like to compile a table from text formatted in a different style?

Choose Insert, Index and Tables, then choose the Table of Figures tab displayed, and click Options. The Table of Figures Options dialog box opens (see Figure 9.22).

Figure 9.22
In the Table of Figures Options dialog box, you can choose another style from which to build your table—or, as you'll see later, you can choose a set of table entry fields.

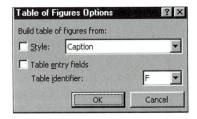

To choose another style, check the Style check box, and select the style from the drop-down box next to it. Click OK to return to the Table of Figures tab, and click OK again to insert the table in your document.

BUILDING TABLES FROM FIGURES WITH DIFFERENT STYLES

Occasionally, you might want to create a table of figures based on document elements that don't share a common style. For example, you might want a table of figures that contains all the quotations in your document. Because those quotations appear within paragraphs of various types scattered throughout your document, you can't compile them into a single figure table based on one style.

Earlier in this chapter, you learned about TC fields, which Word can use to build tables of contents without using styles. TC fields come to your rescue again now. You learned several procedures for inserting TC fields (or any other field). Either refer to the earlier discussion, or follow this procedure:

1. Choose Insert, Field.
2. Choose TC from the Field Names scroll box.
3. In the Description text box, enter the text you want to appear for this reference when the table of figures is compiled. Be sure to place the text within quotation marks.
4. After the close quotation mark, enter \f followed by a letter of the alphabet that will identify all entries for this table of figures.
5. Click OK.

Continuing with the quotation example discussed in the "Building Tables from Figures with Different Styles" section, imagine your document has a quotation by Alvin Toffler. You might enter the TC field:

```
{ TC "Toffler" \f q }
```

Then, later, you come across a quotation by Tom Peters you'd like to flag:

```
{ TC "Peters" \f q }
```

Because they both use the \f q switch, you can compile them by following these steps:

1. Choose Insert, Index and Tables, Table of Figures to display the Table of Figures tab.
2. Click Options to display the Table of Figures Options dialog box.
3. Check the Table Entry Fields check box.
4. Choose Q (or whatever letter you've inserted after \f in your TC fields) in the Table Identifier drop-down list box.
5. Click OK twice.

As shown in Figure 9.23, Word builds a table of figures which contains the names of all the people you've quoted, and the page numbers where the quotes may be found.

Great Quotes from This Month's Edition of *Business Smarts*	
Toffler	1
Peters	5
Covey	8
Blanchard	10
Ziglar	12
Robbins	13

Figure 9.23
Word built this table of notable quotables from a series of TC fields that all used the \f q switch.

INTRODUCING CITATIONS

If you're responsible for preparing legal documents, you know that special techniques are required to insert and track *citations*, which are references to cases, statutes, or other legal documents. Word streamlines both marking citations and collecting them into tables of citations, called *tables of authorities*.

Tip #144

If you prepare legal documents, you may be interested in the Legal Pleading Wizard, which streamlines the process of creating reusable document templates that follow the requirements of the courts you work with.

To work with the Legal Pleading Wizard, choose File, New; click the Legal Pleadings tab; and double-click the Pleading Wizard icon.

MARKING CITATIONS

There's nothing unusual about entering the text of your citations: You simply type them as you normally would, wherever they are needed in your document. Commonly, in the first reference to a citation, you'll enter the long (full) version, which typically includes case numbers, dates, and other essential information. In later references, you'll usually enter a short version, which typically includes only the name of the case.

The next step is to mark the citations you've entered, so that Word can compile them into a table of authorities. Select the first long citation in your document, and press Alt+Shift+I to open the Mark Citation dialog box (see Figure 9.24).

Figure 9.24
You can insert and manage citations in a legal document through the Mark Citation dialog box.

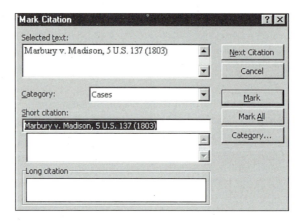

Tip #145

If you use Mark Citation extensively, you can add it to your Insert menu through the Tools, Customize dialog box, as covered in the " Adding a Command to a Toolbar" section of Chapter 28, "Customizing Word."

Your citation appears in the Selected Text box. Edit and format it so it looks the way you want it to appear in your table of authorities. Your citation also appears in the Short Citation text box. Edit the short citation so it matches the short citations you've placed in your document. Typically, this means deleting everything except the case name.

Because some tables of authorities are organized by category (for example, cases in one table, statutes in another), choose a Category from the drop-down list box. Word includes seven built-in categories: Cases, Statutes, Other Authorities, Rules, Treatises, Regulations, and Constitutional Provisions. If you need to create a table of authorities for a different category, you can create the category yourself. Word provides nine generic categories, numbered 8 through 16, which you can rename any way you like. Follow these steps to create a custom category:

1. In the Mark Citation dialog box, select one of the numbered categories.
2. Click Category. The Edit Category dialog box opens (see Figure 9.25).
3. Enter the new name in the Replace With text box.
4. Click Replace.
5. Click OK. You return to the Mark Citation dialog box with your new category already selected.

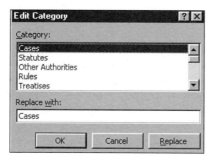

Figure 9.25
You can add up to nine custom categories of citations using the Edit Category dialog box.

You've now prepared your citation for marking. If you want to mark only the long citation you've already selected, click Mark. If you want Word to search your entire document and mark all references to the same citation, long and short, click Mark All.

Now that you've marked all references to the first citation, you can move on to the next. Click Next Citation. Word searches your document for the next block of text it thinks might be part of a citation. For example, Word flags the abbreviation v. and the phrase In re, both commonly used in case names. Word also flags the symbol § that often appears in statute citations.

If Word has flagged a citation you would like to mark, click the document, and select the entire citation. Open the Mark Citation dialog box; the citation you selected appears in both the Selected Text and Short Citation text boxes. You can then edit and mark it following the steps you've already learned.

Note

When you mark a citation, Word inserts a TA (Table of Authorities) field in your document. This field stores the information that will be compiled when you create your table of authorities. For long citations, the TA field looks like this:

```
{ TA \l "Marbury v. Madison, 5 U.S. 137 (1803)" \s "Marbury v.
Madison" \c 1 }
```

As you can see, the TA field for a long citation includes both the detailed text of the long citation and the abbreviated version Word uses to search for short citations. The Mark Citation dialog box doesn't let you edit a long citation after you've marked it, but if you need to, you can edit the field directly.

For short citations, the TA field looks like this:

```
{ TA \s "Marbury v. Madison" }
```

Word inserts TA field codes formatted as hidden text. If you press Alt+F9 to toggle field codes and you still don't see your TA field codes, click the Show/Hide Paragraph Marks button on the Standard toolbar to display them.

ADDING MORE CITATIONS LATER

Imagine you've already marked the citations in your document, and you return to add new citations—either long citations, or additional references to short citations you've already marked elsewhere. To mark them, just press Alt+Shift+I to open the Mark Citation dialog box, and click Next Citation; Word searches for the first citation it hasn't already marked. If Word doesn't find one of your new citations, select it yourself and then press Alt+Shift+I; the citation is displayed in the Mark Citation dialog box when it opens.

COMPILING TABLES OF AUTHORITIES FROM CITATIONS

After you've created your citations, you can compile them into tables of authorities. Choose Insert, Index and Tables, and click the Table of Authorities tab (see Figure 9.26).

Figure 9.26
The Table of Authorities tab of the Index and Tables dialog box gives you extensive control over how your tables of authorities compile.

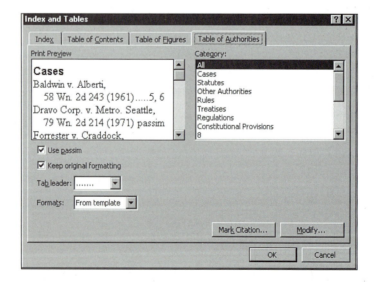

If you've used tables of contents or figures, this dialog box certainly looks familiar. By default, Word builds your table of authorities from styles in your current template. Or you can choose from one of four formats: Classic, Distinctive, Formal, and Simple. You can also specify the tab leader to use—or no tab leader at all. A default table of authorities is shown in Figure 9.27.

Cases
Bond v. Floyd, 385 U.S. 116 (1966) 8
Cohens v. Virginia, 19 U.S. 264 (1821) 13
Marbury v. Madison, 5 U.S. 137 (1803)....................................... 20
Martin v. Hunter's Lessee, 14 U.S. 304 (1816) 23
United States v. Nixon, 418 U.S. 683 (1974)............................... 30

Figure 9.27
A default table of authorities using the built-in styles in Word's Normal template.

Caution

Word's built-in Tables of Citations formats meet the requirements of most courts and jurisdictions, but it never hurts to compare your table of authorities with similar documents the court has accepted, or conceivably to double-check with the court clerk if you're not sure.

Tip #146

You can also click Modify on the Table of Authorities tab to change the TOA Heading style Word uses to build tables of authorities—but as discussed in the table of contents section of this chapter, it's faster to reformat and update the styles in your document.

By default, Word includes every citation in your table of authorities. If you want a separate table for one category of citation, choose it from the Category drop-down box located on the Tables of Authorities tab.

It's common practice, when listing citations that appear repeatedly in a legal document, to substitute the word passim for the multiple page references. By default, Word substitutes passim whenever you have at least five references to the same citation. To display the actual page numbers instead, clear the Use Passim check box on the Tables of Authorities tab.

Many citations contain complex character formatting, especially boldface, italic, and underlining. By default, Word carries that formatting into your table of authorities. However, you can tell Word not to do so by clearing the Keep Original Formatting check box on the Tables of Authorities tab.

TROUBLESHOOTING

HOW TO FIX UPDATE PROBLEMS IN TABLES

It's common for the words Error! Bookmark not defined to appear in a table in place of page numbers. If this occurs, it's possible that you deleted one or more headings or TC entry fields from your document and then updated the table of contents using the Update Page Numbers Only option. You have three options:

- Restore the heading in your document.
- Delete the offending line from your table of contents manually.
- Update the table of contents, and when Word displays the dialog box asking whether you want to update the entire table, choose the Update Entire Table option (thereby also removing any manual formatting or editing you may have added).

Another possibility: You may have separated the table of contents from the material it was built from. For example, you may have copied the table of contents into another document; or you may have built a table of contents in a master document and broken the links to the subdocuments.

To create a separate document that contains only a table of contents, while preserving the accurate page numbering:

1. Choose File, Save As to make a separate copy of your document.
2. Working in the duplicate file you just created, select your table of contents.
3. Press F9 to update your table of contents.
4. With the table of contents still selected, press Ctrl+Shift+F9. This eliminates the underlying TOC field but retains all the text it displayed, including page numbers.
5. Delete everything else in the duplicate document except the table of contents.

→ For more information about managing links between master documents and subdocuments, **see** Chapter 8, "Master Documents: Control and Share Even the Largest Documents," **p. 239**.

HOW TO FIX INCORRECT PAGE NUMBERS IN TABLES

Occasionally, tables may contain incorrect page numbers. This may be caused by

- Hidden text that was visible when you last updated your table of contents
- Changes in margins or other document elements that affect page numbering

Make sure your document looks exactly as it should when you print it; then select the table of contents and press F9 to update it. Unless you've removed or added headings or TC entries, choose Update Page Numbers Only when asked how you want the table to be updated.

HOW TO ELIMINATE BODY TEXT IN TABLES OF CONTENTS

Occasionally, tables of contents may incorrectly include paragraphs of text from your document. If this occurs, search for the paragraph and make sure it is not formatted with a heading style, or formatted with an outline level other than Body Text.

Often, this problem occurs when you place a line break (Shift+Enter) between a heading and the following paragraph, instead of a paragraph break (Enter).

→ For more information about outline levels, **see** "Applying Outline Levels to Specific Text," **p. 225**.

If you must format paragraphs in an outline level other than Body Text, but you still do not want them in your table of contents, one workaround is to delete them manually from your table of contents after you build it. Remember that when you update your table of contents, you must choose Update Page Numbers Only instead of Update Entire Table; otherwise the paragraphs will reappear.

PART

II

CH

9

CHAPTER **10**

BUILDING MORE EFFECTIVE INDEXES

In this chapter

HOW WORD INDEXES WORK

Word's indexing features are intended to automate those aspects of indexing that a computer is smart enough to do on its own, and streamline those for which there's no substitute for your human judgment.

Building an index with Word is a three-step process. First, you mark your index entries—either one by one, or a batch at a time. Next, you tell Word which types of entries to include in your index and how to format the index. Then there's the easy part—actually compiling the index.

Note

In general, compiling your index should be one of the last things you do with your document. Indexing last reduces the number of times you have to rebuild your index. It also tends to increase the quality of your index because you have access to the entire, final document while you're making decisions about how individual entries should be handled.

If you are indexing multiple documents—such as chapters in a book—you may want to build a mini-index to view all your index entries for one chapter, before you start to work on the next. By doing so, you can improve the consistency of the index entries you create, and minimize the amount of index editing you'll have to do later.

To create an index for a single chapter, open the file containing that chapter, and insert the index using the procedure described later in this chapter, in the "Compiling Your Index" section. Select the index; press Ctrl+Shift+F9 to unlink the index field and convert it into ordinary text. Then cut it from the document and paste it into a blank document that you can print or view for reference while working on other chapters.

→ For more information about working with field codes, **see** Chapter 18, "Automating Your Documents with Field Codes," **p. 555**.

CREATING A NEW INDEX ENTRY

The quickest way to mark an index entry is to select it and press Alt+Shift+X. Alternatively, you can choose Insert, Index and Tables; click the Index tab; and choose Mark Entry. Either way, the Mark Index Entry dialog box opens (see Figure 10.1). The text you've selected appears in the Main Entry text box. In some cases, that text serves perfectly well as your index entry.

 If you're satisfied with your entry, click Mark. Word inserts an { XE } *field code* in your document that contains the text of your entry. Because the field code is hidden text, you don't see it unless you display hidden text by clicking the Show/Hide Paragraph Marks button on the Standard toolbar.

In many other cases, you want to modify the entry. You can do so directly, in the Main Entry text box. Since the entry appears highlighted when the text box opens, you can replace it by simply starting to type your new entry. Or if you only want to edit the entry slightly, click in the box and start editing text.

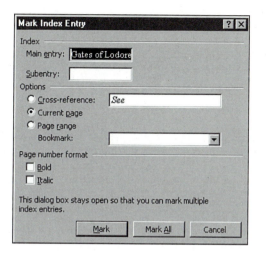

Figure 10.1
You can control all elements of your index entries through the Mark Index Entry dialog box.

PART

II

CH

10

Tip #152

You can include symbols and other nontypable text as part of the text you select, and it will be included in your index entry as it appears in your document.

You can also select a picture and create an index entry for it, but you will have to specify text for the entry: Word will not insert a picture in an index.

IDEAS FOR IMPROVING YOUR INDEX ENTRIES

Often, simply copying text from your document doesn't give you an index entry that's as useful as it could be. Here are some ideas you can use to build better index entries:

- Switch last and first names, so your main entry reads Gerstner, Lou rather than Lou Gerstner.

- Spell out and explain abbreviations, using the most familiar version first, so references to PCI boards appear as PCI (Peripheral Component Interconnect). Consider "double-posting" acronyms like these, so a second entry in the index would say "Peripheral Component Interconnect, see PCI." To learn how to create index entries that use syntax like this, see "Creating Cross-Referenced 'See' Index Entries," later in this chapter.

- Change word forms for consistency or simplicity, so your entry reads "law" rather than "legalities." Avoid multiple entries that might confuse the reader, such as separate entries for "installing," "installations," and "install procedures."

- Make sure your index entries are clear and concise. Avoid vagueness, and avoid words like "understanding" or "using" that are implied with every entry.

- Avoid adjectives, especially at the beginning of index entries. Readers are much less likely to look up an entry such as "multiple tables" than they are to look up "tables" and find "multiple" as a subentry beneath it.

- Make sure your index reflects the level of your audience, with simpler entries for audiences new to the subject matter, and more complex entries for readers who already have a substantial base of knowledge to draw upon.

Note

> You can edit field codes after you insert them, by inserting your cursor directly in the { XE } field code, and using any of Word's text entry or editing features, including cut, copy, and paste.

After you mark the index entry, the dialog box remains open. If you want, you can create a second entry in the same location. This is called *double-posting*, and it reflects the fact that different readers will look in different places in your index for the same information. In professional indexing, double-posting is widespread, and even *triple-posting*—three different entries for the same location in the document—can be common.

Whether you double-post or triple-post, the Mark Index Entry dialog box stays open, assuming you'll want to create another entry. To create another entry elsewhere in the document, click the document, select the text you want to index, then click again in the Mark Index Entry dialog box. The text you've selected now appears in the Main Entry text box.

You can move throughout the document this way, using Word's navigation tools, creating entries as you go. When you're finished, click Close and the Mark Index Entry dialog box closes.

Note

> When you use the Mark Index Entry dialog box, you are inserting an { XE } field in your document. If you are planning to do quite a bit of indexing, you might want to dispense with the dialog box altogether, and create a *macro* that inserts an { XE } field in your document and positions your insertion point at the appropriate location within it.
>
> To create such a macro, follow these steps:
>
>
>
> 1. Make sure the Show/Hide Paragraph Marks icon on the Standard toolbar is toggled on; if it isn't, click it. ({ XE } field codes are invisible unless you show them, and this is usually the easiest way to do so.)
> 2. Choose Tools, Macro, Record New Macro.
> 3. In the Record Macro dialog box, assign the macro a name, such as IndexEntry.
> 4. Click Keyboard, choose a keyboard shortcut for the macro, such as Alt+X, and click Assign.
> 5. Click Close. The Macro Recorder begins working.
> 6. Press Ctrl+F9 to insert field brackets.
> 7. Type the following between the field brackets:
>   XE " "
> 8. Press the left arrow key once to position the insertion point between the field brackets.
> 9. Press the Stop Recording button on the Stop Recording toolbar.
>
> Now, every time you need to enter an index entry, you can simply press Alt+X and type the entry between the quotation marks.
>
> For more about entering index entries directly in field codes, see "Creating Subentries," later in this chapter.

Tip #153

If you plan to create an index entry that doesn't use any of the words in the surrounding text, don't select any text before pressing Alt+Shift+X. The Mark Index Entry dialog box appears with no text already present in the Main Entry or Subentry text boxes.

While it's convenient to display the Mark Index Entry dialog box with text already present, many professional indexers find it quicker to type the entry they want than it is to edit the text Word inserts automatically.

Tip #154

You can apply boldface, italic, or underlining to any index text you enter in the Mark Index Entry dialog box. Simply select and format all or part of the text. This enables you to create index entries for book titles that require italics. It also helps you call attention to special aspects of an entry, as in the following example:

```
Rubin, Robert, quoted, 307
```

Within the Mark Index Entry dialog box, you can select text and press Ctrl+B to boldface it, or Ctrl+I to italicize it. This saves you the trouble of editing or formatting field codes in your document.

While these two formats are probably the most common in indexes, others—such as superscript, subscript, and underlining—can be applied if needed just as easily with their usual keyboard shortcuts.

You might also set aside boldface to call special attention to exceptionally detailed discussions of a topic.

If you plan to create many index entries, and you prefer to use the Mark Index Entry dialog box rather than entering the entries directly into field codes, it may be worth your time to create a toolbar button that displays the Mark Index Entry dialog box. Drag Mark Index Entry (under Insert) from the Commands tab of the Customize dialog box to your favorite toolbar.

Tip #155

Adding a toolbar button for Mark Index Entry actually causes a new toolbar button to appear, containing the words Mark Index Entry. If the toolbar button is too wide for you, right-click it while the Customize dialog box is displayed, click the Name command, and edit the name. (You might shorten it to XE, the name of the field code it inserts.) When you're finished, close the Customize dialog box.

Tip #156

> Because index entries are fields, you can also insert them from the Insert, Field dialog box, which contains detailed instructions for building proper field syntax. You might want to create your index entry field from here when you know you need to use complex switches or parameters—especially if you are creating an index entry field you plan to copy throughout the document.
>
> For instance, if you want to insert an index entry field that displays text in place of a page number, you can build it in the Field dialog box by clicking Options, choosing the \t switch, and entering the text. (The text should appear in quotation marks.)

MARKING MULTIPLE ENTRIES AT ONCE

If you want, you can tell Word to mark all references to specific text. Follow these steps:

1. Select the text you want to index. Unlike marking single entries, you can mark multiple entries only if you select text before you open the Mark Index Entry dialog box.

2. Press Alt+Shift+X; the Mark Index Entry dialog box opens.

3. Edit the Main Entry box to reflect the exact entry you want. Word will mark all locations in your document where it finds the text you originally selected, not the edited version in the Mark Entry box. In other words, the index entry will reflect your edits within the Mark Index Entry dialog box, but the references will point to locations where the original text appeared.

4. Choose Mark All.

While this procedure marks every instance of a specific word or phrase, the "Automating Indexing with Index AutoMark Files" section of this chapter shows how to mark every instance of many different words or phrases at the same time.

Caution

> So you can see the index entries you're placing in your document, Word displays hidden text after you enter your first index entry—not just field codes, but also other document text you may really want to stay hidden! When you're finished marking index entries, you need to rehide this hidden text manually, by clicking the Show/Hide Paragraph Marks button on the Standard toolbar. Make sure to re-hide hidden text before you compile either an index or a table of contents. If you don't, your page numbering is likely to be incorrect.
>
> The Show/Hide Paragraph Marks button also displays other types of hidden text. If you find this annoying, an alternative is to choose Tools, Options; display the View tab; clear the All check box, and check the Hidden Text check box. Now, hidden text is displayed, but other elements—such as paragraph marks and dots corresponding to spaces between words—remain hidden.

FORMATTING PAGE NUMBERS AS BOLD OR ITALIC

Earlier, you learned that you can format a specific index entry as boldface or italic. Many indexers prefer to call attention to some entries by boldfacing or italicizing the page numbers associated with the entry. For example, it's common to italicize page numbers associated with entries that refer to photos rather than body text.

Formatting the text of an index entry doesn't affect the formatting of the page number. If you want to add formatting to a page number, check the <u>B</u>old or <u>I</u>talic check box in the Mark Index Entry dialog box.

CREATING SUBENTRIES

Often, it's not enough to create an index entry. You might also want a subentry that gives your readers a better sense of what they'll find. Subentries are typically used when you expect to make several references to an item in your index, and each reference covers significantly different points, as in the following index excerpts:

```
Brinkley, J.R.
     goat gland prostate surgery, 24
     medical license suspended, 32
     XER radio station, 27
Bryan, William Jennings
     Cross of Gold speech, 106
     Scopes trial prosecuting attorney, 148
     Spokesman for Florida real estate, 127
```

PART

II

CH

10

To create an index entry that contains a subentry, either select text to be indexed or click where you want the index entry to be placed; then click Alt+Shift+X to display the Mark Index Entry dialog box again. Enter or edit your main entry, being careful to be consistent about how you create main entries you expect to use more than once. Then, enter text in the <u>S</u>ubentry text box as well, and click <u>M</u>ark.

Tip #157

It's sometimes quicker to enter a subentry in the Main <u>E</u>ntry box. To do this, type the main entry followed by a colon. Type the subentry in the same text box. Don't add a space between the colon and the subentry unless you want Word to use the space when it alphabetizes your subentries (placing subentries that begin with a space before those that don't).

Including the entry and subentry on the same line is especially convenient when you are using the same index entry for several different blocks of text, because you can copy the entry into the Clipboard and paste it into the Main <u>E</u>ntry text box for each entry you want to create.

Tip #158

If you prefer to work with { XE } fields directly, you can also copy an entire { XE } field and paste it anywhere you need the same index entry.

Note

If the text of your index entry contains a colon or quote marks, Word inserts a \ before the character in the field to avoid confusion with subentries, which also use colons.

CREATING MULTILEVEL SUBENTRIES

In some respects, building an index isn't much different from creating an outline; you might want more than two levels of index entries. Occasionally, you find an index entry fits most naturally as a subentry to another subentry. Here's an example:

```
Procter & Gamble
    Peanut Butter, 47
    Soap, 113-122
            Camay® brand, 116
            Ivory® brand, 113-117
                    Repackaging, 114
            Oil of Olay® brand, 118
            Safeguard® brand, 120
            Zest® brand, 122
```

To create a multilevel subentry, press Alt+Shift+X to display the Mark Index Entry dialog box. In the Main Entry text box, enter each level of entry and the subentry, all separated by colons. Don't leave space between levels. For example,

```
Procter & Gamble:Soap:Ivory® brand:Repackaging
```

Word supports up to seven levels of index entry, though it's unlikely you'll ever need more than three or four.

CREATING CROSS-REFERENCED "SEE" INDEX ENTRIES

By default, Word includes a page number along with each index entry: the page number where it finds the { XE } field when it compiles the index. This is how Word behaves when the Current Page option button is selected in the Mark Index Entry dialog box. Sometimes, however, you don't want a page reference. Instead, you want to refer people to a different index entry, as in the following examples:

```
AMEX, See American Stock Exchange
```

```
Family and Medical Leave Act, See also Parental leave
```

To create a cross-reference in your index, set up the rest of the entry as you normally would; then click the Cross-Reference option button and enter the cross-reference text you want to include, next to the word "See."

Tip #159

Because page numbers aren't displayed for cross-references, it doesn't matter where you add them. You can create cross-references hundreds of pages from the text you are indexing or referencing. This is helpful if you think of something that you want to cross-reference which isn't related to the part of the text you are currently working on—or which appears in a separate chapter file you may not have access to yet.

Note

There are two different types of references used within indexes and they are easy to confuse. "See" references should be used to lead the reader to a reference when the topic is indexed under another main entry. For example, if you have chosen to index all of the vocalists mentioned in a document under "Singers" and not under "Vocalists," you might include "Vocalists, See *Singers*" to redirect readers if they look up Vocalists. A "see" reference is most commonly used for acronyms and synonyms.

The other type of reference, a "See also" reference, is used to direct readers to related subject matter. So along with the subentries for singers under "Singers," you might also include a subentry "See also *choruses*."

Note

You don't have to use the word "See," which Word provides as a suggestion. You can edit or replace it if you prefer a different way of referring to other index entries.

These cross-references are unrelated to the automated cross-references you can place throughout your document via the Insert, Cross-Reference dialog box covered in Chapter 11, "Footnotes, Bookmarks, and Cross-References."

SETTING PAGE NUMBERS FOR MULTIPLE-PAGE INDEX ENTRIES

Sometimes you want to create an index entry for a discussion that stretches across two or more pages. Word makes this easy: first you create a *bookmark* corresponding to the block of text you want to index; then you specify the bookmark as part of the index entry.

To create the bookmark, select the text for which you want to create the entry and choose Insert, Bookmark. Then enter a name for the bookmark and click Add.

Now, build the index entry using the bookmark:

1. Click Alt+Shift+X to display the Mark Index Entry dialog box.
2. Enter the main entry and/or subentry text you want.
3. Click the Page Range button.
4. Choose the appropriate bookmark from the Bookmark drop-down list.
5. Click Mark.

→ For more information about using bookmarks, **see** Chapter 11, "Footnotes, Bookmarks, and Cross-References," **p. 325**.

COMPILING YOUR INDEX

Now that you've learned how to create index entries, you can move on to compiling them. To prepare your index for compilation, place your insertion point where you want the index (typically at the end of the document). Then, choose Insert, Index and Tables, and click the Index tab (see Figure 10.2).

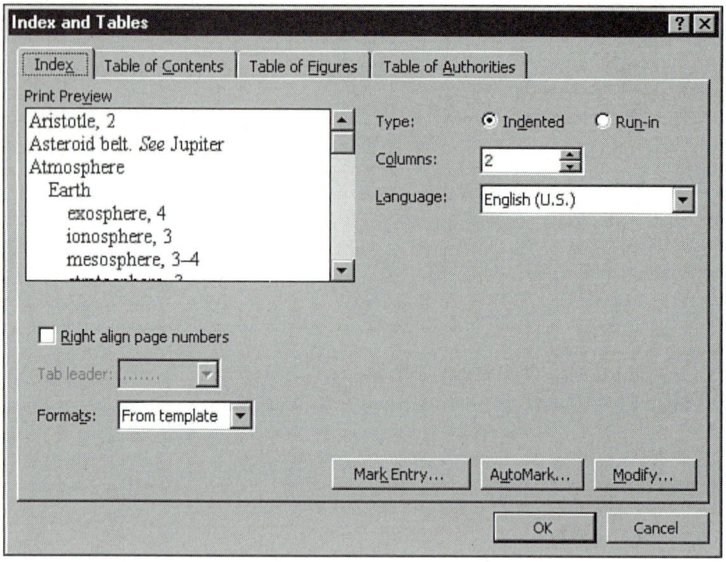

Figure 10.2
You can control nearly all aspects of compiling an index through the Index tab of the Index and Tables dialog box.

If you've read the coverage of tables of contents in Chapter 17, "Tables of Contents, Figures, Authorities, and Captioning," you see some familiar elements in this dialog box. For instance, as with tables of contents, Word's default format for indexes is From Template, which means it uses the Index styles built into any template you're using.

Word also provides several more formats: Classic, Fancy, Modern, Bulleted, Formal, and Simple. If you've chosen one of these formats for your table of contents, you should probably choose the same format for your index for a consistent look. When you change a format (or make most other changes), Word shows what you can expect in the Print Preview box.

After you've finished making changes throughout the Index tab of the Index and Tables dialog box, click OK. Word inserts an index in your document. Notice that the index appears in a section of its own. Word places the index in its own section because most indexes use a different number of columns than the surrounding text. You can see a default Word index in Figure 10.3.

Tip #160

Because the index is contained in its own section, you can create a separate header or footer for it, or customize its page numbering.

Tip #161

Unlike the From Template format, all of Word's alternative index formats, with the exception of the Simple format, also add headings for each letter of the alphabet. A sample index formatted with the Fancy format is shown in Figure 10.4. If you want headings like these, use any of the alternative formats except Simple.

Accessibility, 1
Adaptability, 2
Adaptive systems theory, 3
Adoption cycle, 4
    Early adopters, 4
Advertising, 5
    Agencies, 5
Aided recall, 6
American Management Association, 7
American Marketing Association, 8
Antitrust issues, 9
    IBM, 9
    Microsoft, 9
Arbitron, 10
Area of Dominant Influence, 11
Auction sites, 12
    Onsale, 12
    Surplus Auction, 12
Auctions, 13
Audience measurement, 14
    Arbitron. See Arbitron
    Nielsen. See Nielsen
Audit Bureau of Circulation (ABC), 15
Audits, 16
Awareness, 17
Baby-boom marketing, 18
Bait-and-switch techniques, 19. See also Federal Trade
    Commission

Channels, 45
Chaos, 46
    In Marketing, 46
    In mathematics, 46
    In science, 46
Churn, 47. See also Loyalty programs
Clipping services, 48. See also Public relations
Cluster analysis, 49. See Claritas
Clustering, 50
Collateral materials, 51
    Brochures, 51
    Data sheets, 51
    White papers, 51
Communications planning, 52
Comparative advertising, 53
Consumer goods, 54
Consumer marketing, 55
Consumer price index, 56. See Inflation, effects of
Contests, 57
Cookies, 58
    on Web sites, 58
    Snackwell® repositioning, 58
Cooperative advertising, 59
Copy testing, 60
Copywriting, 61
Couponing, 62
Credit cards, 63
Cross-tabulations, 64

Figure 10.3
An index built using Word's default settings.

A

Accessibility, 1
Adaptability, 2
Adaptive systems theory, 3
Adoption cycle, 4
    Early adopters, 4
Advertising, 5
    Agencies, 5
Aided recall, 6
American Management Association, 7
American Marketing Association, 8
Antitrust issues, 9
    IBM, 9
    Microsoft, 9
Arbitron, 10
Area of Dominant Influence, 11
Auction sites, 12
    Onsale, 12
    Surplus Auction, 12
Audience measurement, 14
    Arbitron. See Arbitron
    Nielsen. See Nielsen
Awareness, 17

Channels, 45
Chaos, 46
    In Marketing, 46
    In mathematics, 46
    In science, 46
Churn, 47. See also Loyalty programs
Clipping services, 48. See also Public relations
Cluster analysis, 49. See Claritas
Clustering, 50
Collateral materials, 51
    Brochures, 51
    Data sheets, 51
    White papers, 51
Communications planning, 52
Comparative advertising, 53
Consumer goods, 54
Consumer marketing, 55
Consumer price index, 56. See Inflation, effects of
Contests, 57
Cookies, 58
    on Web sites, 58
    Snackwell® repositioning, 58
Cooperative advertising, 59
Copy testing, 60
Copywriting, 61
Couponing, 62
Credit cards, 63
Cross-tabulations, 64

B

Figure 10.4
In this index built with Word's Fancy format, each letter that contains an index entry has its own heading. Word skips letters without index entries.

CHANGING INDEX FORMATTING

The *Normal template* contains nine index levels, all formatted as 12-point Times New Roman, with each level indented 0.17 inches more than the level before it. If you want to change these formats manually, follow these steps:

1. Insert an index in your document.

2. Manually reformat one index entry based on the Index 1 heading (including the paragraph mark at the end of the entry). By default, Word immediately reformats all entries based on the Index 1 style.

3. Repeat step 2 for each index style you want to modify.

 If you reformat an index entry, but Word doesn't reformat the others consistently, see "What to Do If Word Doesn't Reformat All Index Entries Consistently," in the "Troubleshooting" section of this chapter.

CREATING RUN-IN INDEXES

If you're short on space, you may want to create a run-in index, such as the one shown in Figure 10.5. Often, using the Run-In option can shorten your index by as much as 30–40%. The more subentries you use, the more space you save. To create a run-in index, click the Run-In button in the Index tab.

Figure 10.5
Using the Run-In option can substantially reduce the number of pages required for your index.

Typical run-in index entry

Accessibility, 1
Adaptability, 2
Adaptive systems theory, 3
Adoption cycle, 4; Early adopters, 4
Advertising, 5; Agencies, 5
Aided recall, 6
American Management Association, 7
American Marketing Association, 8
Antitrust issues, 9; IBM, 9; Microsoft, 9
Arbitron, 10
Area of Dominant Influence, 11
Auction sites, 12; Onsale, 12; Surplus Auction, 12
Auctions, 13
Audience measurement, 14; Arbitron. *See* Arbitron; Nielsen. *See* Nielsen
Audit Bureau of Circulation (ABC), 15
Audits, 16
Awareness, 17

Churn, 47. *See also* Loyalty programs
Clipping services, 48. *See also* Public relations
Cluster analysis, 49. *See* Claritas
Clustering, 50
Collateral materials, 51; Brochures, 51; Data sheets, 51; White papers, 51
Communications planning, 52
Comparative advertising, 53
Consumer goods, 54
Consumer marketing, 55
Consumer price index, 56. *See* Inflation, effects of
Contests, 57
Cookies, 58; on Web sites, 58; Snackwell® repositioning, 58
Cooperative advertising, 59
Copy testing, 60
Copywriting, 61
Couponing, 62

CREATING INDEXES IN DIFFERENT LANGUAGES

You may need to index a document written entirely, or in part in a language that uses accented letters such as À, Ë, or Ñ (for example, French, German, or Spanish). These accented letters generally require custom alphabetization according to the rules of the language; if you simply work in English, they will be alphabetized incorrectly.

If you have installed Office 2000's Multilanguage support, you can choose which language's rules to use in your index.

To do so choose Insert, Index and Tables and choose the Index tab. Then select a language from the Language drop-down box, make any other setting changes you need, and click OK to compile your index.

RIGHT-ALIGNING PAGE NUMBERS IN AN INDEX

Except for Word's Formal index style, all Word's built-in index styles place the page number next to the end of the index entry text. If you prefer to right-align the page numbers (see Figure 10.6), check the Right Align Page Numbers check box in the Index tab.

A

Accessibility	1
Adaptability	2
Adaptive systems theory	3
Adoption cycle	4
Early adopters	4
Advertising	5
Agencies	5
Aided recall	6
American Management Association	7
American Marketing Association	8
Antitrust issues	9
IBM	9
Microsoft	9
Arbitron	10
Area of Dominant Influence	11
Auction sites	12

Sampling	44
Channels	45
Chaos	46
In Marketing	46
In mathematics	46
In science	46
Churn	47. *See also* Loyalty programs
Clipping services	48. *See also* Public relations
Cluster analysis	49. *See* Claritas
Clustering	50
Collateral materials	51
Brochures	51
Data sheets	51
White papers	51
Communications planning	52
Comparative advertising	53
Consumer goods	54
Consumer marketing	55
Consumer price index	56. *See* Inflation, effects of

Figure 10.6
This index is styled in the Classic format, and uses right-aligned page numbers with a dot leader.

If you choose to right-align page numbers, Word also lets you select the Tab Leader that Word is to use between the entry text and the page numbers: either a dotted, dashed, or solid line.

CONTROLLING THE NUMBER OF COLUMNS IN AN INDEX

By default, Word creates two-column indexes. Most books use two-column indexes, and in most cases, so should you. However, you may occasionally want to change this setting, especially if

- You're using a relatively wide page size
- You're using relatively small type for your index entries

Word builds indexes of up to four columns. Enter the number of columns you want in the Columns list box of the Index tab.

ADDING CHAPTER NUMBERING TO YOUR INDEX

If your document has multiple chapters, each renumbered from the first page of the chapter, you probably want an index that includes chapter numbers with each listing, as in the following example:

```
Van Diemen's Land (Tasmania), 4-2, 12-29, 14-10
```

Word automatically includes chapter numbering in your document if you have used Word's page numbering feature (Insert, Page Numbers) to insert chapter numbers in your header or footer. In the previous example, the separator character which separates the chapter number from the page number is a hyphen. However, when you establish your page numbers, you can choose a period, colon, em dash, or en dash instead, and the separator character you choose will apply in your index as well.

Caution

To use Word's page numbering feature to insert chapter numbers, you have to first use Outline Numbering. This issue is discussed at length in Chapter 9.

BUILDING INDEXES FROM MULTIPLE DOCUMENTS

You may be called upon to create an index that includes entries from multiple documents. As with tables of contents (covered in Chapter 9), you have two alternatives:

- You can incorporate each document in a *master document*, expand all the *subdocuments* to make them visible in the master document, and then insert your index. Word searches each subdocument for index entries and incorporates them in an overall index. This approach takes a bit more time to organize up front, but gives you more control over how your documents work together. You can learn more about master documents in Chapter 8, "Master Documents: Control and Share Even the Largest Documents."

- You can use { RD } fields to incorporate other documents into your indexes without using master documents. This approach can make for smaller, more manageable files, but it doesn't do anything to help you standardize styles, headers, footers, or page numbers throughout a large document.

Caution

Whether you use master documents or { RD } fields, be careful that documents which are part of your index remain where Word can find them. If you don't, some of your index entries may disappear when you update your index. Worse, if an old version of the original file remains in its original location while an updated version is stored elsewhere, you may find yourself generating an inaccurate index.

{ RD } fields make no provision for moved documents; you must remember to edit the fields manually. However, if you need to move a subdocument in a master document, you can do so—as long as you move it from within the master document:

1. Open the master document.

2. Display the master document in Outline view.

3. Click the *hyperlink* associated with the document you want to move. The document opens in its own window.

4. Choose File, Save As. The Save As dialog box opens.

5. Browse to the location where you want to save the subdocument, and click Save. The next time you open the master document, Word will look in the file's new location.

BUILDING AN INDEX IN A MASTER DOCUMENT

To build an index in a master document

1. Switch to Outline view.

2. Open (or create) your master document, and click Expand Subdocuments on the Master Document toolbar to display all its contents. (If you don't, Word builds your index without the index entries contained in those subdocuments.)

3. Insert your index entries as appropriate, if you haven't already done so.

4. Click your insertion point where you want the index to appear.

5. Choose Insert, Index and Tables.

> **Note**
>
> If you didn't expand the subdocuments as directed in step 2, Word will prompt you asking if you want to expand the subdocuments. You need to click Yes for Word to include the index entries for the subdocuments. If you click No, Word will create an index but it will not include entries from the subdocuments.

6. Click the Index tab, and establish the index settings you need there.

7. Click OK. Word inserts your index at the insertion point. If you already have an index, Word offers to replace it.

USING { RD } FIELDS TO INCLUDE INDEX ENTRIES FROM OTHER DOCUMENTS

When you incorporate index entries using an { RD } field, the page numbers Word places in the index are those in the referenced document. You need to make sure the numbers are sequenced as you want them, and do not overlap page numbers in other documents included in your index. One solution is to use chapter numbers in your index, as discussed in the "Adding Chapter Numbering to Your Index" section, earlier in this chapter.

After you've made sure the page numbering in your referenced document is appropriate, follow these steps to incorporate the { RD } field:

1. Click the Show/Hide Paragraph Marks button on the Standard toolbar to display hidden text. As mentioned in Chapter 17, { RD } fields are invisible, and unless you display hidden text, Word hides them even before you finish editing them.

2. Press Ctrl+F9 to insert an empty field code in your document.

3. Between the two field brackets, enter RD followed by the complete pathname of the file you want to reference. Use double backslashes in the pathname, as follows:

```
{ RD "c:\\folder\\filename.doc" }
```

4. Click where you want to insert your index.

5. Choose Insert, Index and Tables.

6. Choose the Index tab.

7. Establish the index settings you want.

8. Click OK.

CHANGING THE FORMATTING OF YOUR INDEX

You've already seen that you can choose among six basic formats for your index, or use the *styles* built into Word's Normal template (styles Index 1 through Index 9). You can easily change the formatting of individual levels within your index, and with a little more effort, you can store your new formats in the Normal template for use in other indexes you create later.

To reformat your index, first insert it into your document. Next, select a paragraph in your index that uses the style you want to change, for example, Index 1, Index 2, and so forth. Reformat it; Word automatically reformats all the other paragraphs in your index that use the same style.

The formats are now stored in your document. To copy them into a template—such as the Normal template, which defines styles for most Word documents—use the *Organizer*:

1. Choose Format, Style.

2. Click the Organizer button.

3. In the left window (the window with your filename), select the styles you want to copy.

4. Look at the right window to make sure it displays the styles in the template you want to use. If it does, click Copy. You may be asked to confirm that you want Word to overwrite existing styles in the target template; choose Yes.

Note

If you want to store your index styles in a different template than the one Word displays, click Close File in the right window; then click Open File, browse to the template you want, and choose Open.

REVIEWING AND UPDATING THE CONTENTS OF YOUR INDEX

What if you make content changes in your document after you create your index (as is nearly inevitable)? You can update your index by clicking anywhere in it and pressing F9; or by right-clicking on the index and choosing Update Field from the shortcut menu.

Tip #162

Often it's easier to select the entire document (Ctrl+A) and press F9. That way, you update all your other fields at the same time—making sure the page numbering in your index is accurate and up to date.

You should update your index, of course, any time you make significant changes in your document. However, you should also walk through your index systematically after you create it for the first time, to fix the corresponding entries that aren't quite right, and then update the { XE } fields to fix the problems you found. For example, you should look for the following:

- Redundant entries that use slightly different variations on a word, or duplicate entries for a word in capitalized and lowercase form

- Better ways of organizing high-level concepts

- Misspellings

Caution

Make sure that you fix errors in your index by fixing the individual { XE } index entry fields, not by editing the compiled index itself. If you edit the compiled index, the next time you update it, your edits will be removed. Moreover, by editing your index manually, you may inadvertently introduce page numbering errors.

Caution

Word's spell checker does not check spellings in a compiled index. This isn't a problem if you stick with index entries based exactly on text in the document, which can be proofread. However, if you heavily edit your index entries, you may want to proofread them separately.

There are two workarounds, neither of them ideal. First, you can wait until your index is absolutely final, select the index, and press Ctrl+Shift+F9 to unlink the index field. This changes the index field into text which can be proofread. However, you can no longer update the index—a potential disaster if page numbers start changing again. You'll have to delete the entire index, insert a new one, and start over again with editing and spellchecking it. (Before you unlink your index, make a backup copy of your document.)

Or, you can click the Show/Hide Paragraph Marks button on the Standard toolbar to display all the index entry { XE } fields within your document, and then run a spell check on the entire document. That spell check also checks the contents of your index entry fields.

The best way to review an index is to open a second window on your file and set up Word so you can view the index in one window while you view the document in another. To do so, follow these steps:

1. Open the document containing the index. (It should be the only document you have open.)

2. If your { XE } index entry fields are not visible, click the Show/Hide Paragraph Marks button on the Standard toolbar to make them visible.

3. Switch to Normal view if you aren't already there.

4. Choose Tools, Options, View, and check the Wrap to Window check box if it isn't already checked. This ensures that you can see all your text no matter how narrow your windows are.

5. Create a new window and arrange the two windows so that you have a narrow window for the index column and a wider window for the document as shown in Figure 10.7.

Figure 10.7
Setup to review an index alongside the document being indexed.

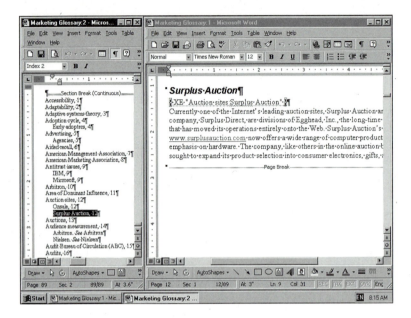

Now you can move through the index one item at a time; whenever you find an item that needs changing, click in the window that displays the document, navigate to the { XE } field code that caused the problem, and edit it. When you're finished, click in the index (or select the entire document) and press F9 to update the index.

AUTOMATING INDEXING WITH INDEX AUTOMARK FILES

Earlier, you learned how to mark all the references to specific text in a document at the same time, by selecting the text, pressing Alt+Shift+X to display the Mark Index Entry dialog box, and clicking Mark All. You can go much further than this, telling Word to automatically mark (AutoMark) all references to many different words and phrases at the same time.

To do so, you first create a special file called an *Index AutoMark file*. Then you tell Word to use that Index AutoMark file to identify text for AutoMarking and to specify what each automated index entry will say. In a moment, you'll walk through AutoMarking a document, but first, you should decide whether AutoMarking is the best alternative.

PART

II

CH

10

> **Note**
>
> Index files built with AutoMarking are sometimes confused with *concordances*. Traditionally, a concordance is an alphabetical listing of every word in a text, showing the context in which every occurrence of the word appears. An AutoMarked index is usually built only from words selected for their relevance.

IS AUTOMARKING WORTH YOUR TIME?

To decide whether it will really save time to build and use an Index AutoMark file, scroll through your document looking for elements that lend themselves to automatic indexing. Names of any kind are excellent candidates, including people's names, product names, and brand names. Also, look for words and phrases that are

- Typically used in a context that you want to index.
- Used consistently throughout your document.
- Important enough to index. Look for words that are relevant, specific, and that Word can find. Avoid words that are so common as to appear in your index on every page.

Don't be surprised if you find that an Index AutoMark file handles only a quarter or a third of the index entries you need to create. If it can do even that much, however, it still saves you quite a bit of time in indexing a large document. Of course, you can still manually mark additional items by using the techniques discussed previously. But you can use AutoMarking to handle the mind-numbing, repetitive aspects of indexing, leaving you with the more interesting entries—the ones that require judgment.

CREATING AN INDEX AUTOMARK FILE

 To create an Index AutoMark file, click New on the Standard toolbar to display a new blank document. Then insert a two-column table. You can do so in several ways; the easiest is to click the Insert Table button, drag across the matrix to create a two-column table, and release the mouse button.

Now start adding entries. In the left column, type words or phrases for which you want to search. In the right column, type the entry the way you want it to appear in your index, including colons and subentries where needed, as discussed earlier in the "Creating Subentries" section of this chapter. You can also boldface or italicize an entry in the right column, and Word will format it to match when you compile your index.

If you don't enter anything in the right column, Word creates an entry using the text in the left column.

Because indexing is case sensitive, make sure your left column includes all variations of words that might appear both uppercase and lowercase. However, make sure you standardize on either lowercase or uppercase for the right column, so Word doesn't generate duplicate entries you don't want. Also make sure you capture all forms of a word, such as explode, exploding, and explosion.

Some people find it easier to set up the editing window so the Index AutoMark file appears at the left and the document to be indexed appears at the right. You learned how to do this in the discussion of updating indexes, earlier in this chapter. If both documents are visible, it's easy (and more accurate) to copy entries from one to the other.

When you finish adding entries, save and close the file.

USING THE INDEX AUTOMARK FILE FOR AUTOMARKING

To create an Index AutoMark file, follow these steps:

1. Open the document you want to index, if it isn't already open.

2. Choose Insert, Index and Tables, and display the Index tab.

3. Click AutoMark. Word displays the Open Index AutoMark File dialog box, which looks just like a standard Open File dialog box.

4. Browse and select the Index AutoMark file you just created.

5. Click Open. Word inserts index entries wherever you told it to.

Tip #163

If you create an AutoMark file that will have value in many documents, consider recording a macro for running that file, and giving the macro a keyboard shortcut or toolbar button. If you wish, you can include index entries that only appear in some of your documents, but should be marked wherever they do appear. Doing so enables users to build detailed preliminary indexes even if they have no indexing expertise at all.

PLACING MORE THAN ONE INDEX IN A DOCUMENT

Occasionally, you might want to include more than one index in your document. For example, you might want a separate index for all quotes in your document. Using the method that follows, Word enables you to create as many different indexes in the same document as you need. First, create a bookmark that covers all the text you want to incorporate in one of your indexes. To do this, select the area of your document for which you want to create a separate index and choose Insert, Bookmark. Then enter a name for the bookmark (in this example, we use Index2 although you can use any name you want) and click Add.

Now, position your insertion point where you want to create your index, and follow these steps:

1. Press Ctrl+F9 to insert a set of field brackets.

2. Within the field brackets, enter the following text:

```
INDEX \b Index2
```

This field tells Word to create an index covering only the block of text corresponding to the bookmark named Index2.

3. Press Ctrl+A to select the entire document.

4. Press F9 to update all the fields, including the { INDEX } field you just entered.

In this example and some that follow, other switches you might need have been excluded for simplicity. The best way to edit the { INDEX } field code is to first use the Index tab of the Index and Tables dialog box to create as many settings as possible, and then display the field code to add the settings you can't make elsewhere.

INDEXING ONLY SELECTED LETTERS OF THE ALPHABET

If your index is especially large, you may want to split it into two or more indexes to improve Word's performance. You might, for example, create one index that covers letters A through M and another for N through Z.

Tip #164

Even if Word is performing perfectly well, you might occasionally want to compile an index based on only part of the alphabet for review purposes. Large indexes require careful review; you might ask one reviewer to handle letters A through M and another reviewer to handle N through Z.

To create an index covering only some letters of the alphabet, follow these steps:

1. Create all your index entries as you normally do.

2. Insert the index into your document the way you normally do.

3. Right-click anywhere in the index, and choose Toggle Field Codes to display the field code rather than the field result.

4. Add the following to your { INDEX } field code:

```
\p n--z
```

Notice the double hyphens. In this example, you've told Word to compile the index from N to Z. Of course, you can substitute any letters you like.

Double-check to make sure that your partial indexes are picking up every letter you expect them to. Some users have reported that Word 2000 starts partial indexes one letter later than it should.

COMPILING AN INDEX WITH ONLY THE ENTRIES YOU SELECT

Word indexes typically contain all the index entries you selected. However, you can create custom indexes that only contain the items you specify. For example, you might be forwarding a large document to a reviewer with expertise about one specific topic. If you create a custom index, you can call attention to the pages that contain information you want reviewed. That saves the reviewer time. It might also discourage the reviewer from slowing you down with gratuitous comments about other areas of the document!

 Assuming you've already indexed the document, click Show/Hide Paragraph Marks to display hidden text, including the contents of your { XE } index entry fields. Now, in each entry you want to appear in your specialized index, add the \f switch, a space, and any letter of the alphabet except *I*. (You can also use numerals and any symbol characters that appear in the ANSI character set. However, in most situations the 25 characters and 10 numbers 0 through 9 should provide you more than enough custom indexes without resorting to ANSI codes.) Word interprets *I* as a direction to include an entry in the default index. Use the same letter in every entry you want to compile together. So, for example, you might have an index entry that reads

```
{ XE "Year 2000 Crisis" \f r }
```

Tip #165

Does marking entries for a special index sound like a lot of work? Here's how to streamline it. With all the field codes visible, use Word's Edit, Replace dialog box to add the \f r switch to all identical fields at once.

In the preceding example, you might include the following in the Find What box

```
XE "Year 2000 Crisis"
```

and add the following in the Replace With box:

```
XE "Year 2000 Crisis" \f r
```

Then click Replace All, and Word fixes them all at the same time. You can use this technique any time you need to make a global change in many fields at the same time.

After you finish customizing your index entries, create and insert your index the way you normally do. Click anywhere inside the index and press Shift+F9 to view the { INDEX } field code. Click inside the field code and add the same switch at the end. For example,

```
{ INDEX \f r }
```

Then update the index by any means you choose (such as right-clicking the field and choosing Update Field). This will insert the updated custom index and return to the view of the index rather than the { INDEX } field code.

USING { INDEX } FIELD CODES TO CONTROL OTHER INDEX FORMATTING

You've already seen how manually editing an { INDEX } field code can enable you to create partial indexes based on letters of the alphabet or specific index entries. Occasionally, you may have to use other { INDEX } field switches to generate index formatting you can't get any other way.

CREATING SEPARATOR CHARACTERS

The \d switch sets the separator character that Word places between chapter numbers and page numbers in index entries. By default, Word uses a hyphen, as in the following example:

```
Hedge funds, 3-8, 5-6
```

However, it's not uncommon to use colons or other characters:

```
Derivatives, 4:6, 9:12
```

You can separate chapter numbers from page numbers with any character. You can even use several characters (up to five). Within your { INDEX } field, add the \d switch and a space. Then add quotation marks containing the characters you want to use, as in the following example:

```
{ INDEX \d ":" }
```

→ Creating chapter numbers in Word is not straightforward; **see** "Adding Chapter Numbers to Your Captions," **p. 283**.

CREATING SEPARATOR CHARACTERS FOR PAGE RANGES

Just as you can create separator characters that go between chapter numbers and page numbers, you can also create *separator characters* that go between the numbers in ranges of pages. By default, Word uses an en dash, as in the following example:

```
Process reengineering, 62-68, 104-113
```

Use the \g switch to change the separator. The syntax is exactly the same as for the \d switch. For example, to use a colon as a separator, enter the following:

```
{ INDEX \g ":" }
```

CONTROLLING THE APPEARANCE OF ALPHABETICAL HEADINGS

Earlier, you saw that Word can insert headings before the index listings associated with each letter of the alphabet using special index formats in the Index tab of the Index and Tables dialog box. You can use the \h switch in the { INDEX } field to control the appearance of these headings. You're most likely to use this switch in two ways: to insert a blank line rather than a heading between letters, or to lowercase the letters in your headings for design reasons.

To insert a blank line, edit your existing { INDEX } field code to include the following:

```
\h " "
```

Be sure to include the space between the quotation marks. Even though Word's Help file says this isn't needed, Word will not insert a blank line without the space.

To lowercase your headings, edit the \h switch in your existing { INDEX } field code to include the following:

```
\*lower
```

For example, if your current field code reads

```
{ INDEX \h "A" \c "2" }
```

you would then edit it to read

```
{ INDEX \h "A" \*lower \c "2" }
```

You can also use the \h switch to custom design your own heading styles with special symbols or characters before or after the letter in the heading. To do this, enter the characters you want along with the letter A between quotes after the \h switch, like this:

```
{ INDEX \h "***A***" \c "2" }
```

This inserts three asterisks before and after each heading letter. In place of asterisks, you can use any symbol character in a normal text font except for letters of the alphabet. This feature will not properly generate characters from fonts such as Symbol or Wingdings, however.

TROUBLESHOOTING

WHAT TO DO IF CHAPTER NUMBERING IS INCORRECT IN INDEXES BUILT WITH MASTER DOCUMENTS

Sometimes, indexes in master documents don't show chapter numbers when they're supposed to, or they refer to Chapter 0 rather than the correct numbers. You may have included chapter numbering in your subdocuments but not in your master document, or vice versa. It must be turned on in both locations. To do so

1. Insert *outline numbering* in each subdocument if it is not already present. (Choose Format, Bullets and Numbering, click the Outline Numbered tab, choose one of the available sequences, and click OK.)

2. Add chapter numbering to each subdocument, through the Insert, Page Numbers, Format dialog box. (To do this, you must tell Word which style is used for chapter numbers throughout your document—a fairly complex procedure that is explained in the "Adding Chapter Numbers to Your Captions" section of Chapter 9.)

3. Open the master document and click Expand Subdocuments to display all your subdocuments.

4. Choose Format, Bullets and Numbering, click the Outline Numbered tab, choose a heading numbering sequence for the master document, and click OK.

5. Rebuild the index.

WHAT TO DO IF PAGE NUMBERING IN YOUR INDEX IS INCORRECT

Make sure to hide the hidden text in your document before building the index. Also, select the index and rebuild it (by pressing F9) after you create tables of contents and other document elements that affect page numbering.

→ For more information about using outline numbering throughout your documents, **see** "Using Word's Automatic Outline Numbering," **p. 227**.

WHAT TO DO IF WORD DOESN'T REFORMAT ALL INDEX ENTRIES CONSISTENTLY

Make sure automatic style updating is turned on for this style. Follow these steps:

1. Choose Format, Style.
2. In the Styles scroll box, choose the style with which you're having problems. (If it does not appear, choose All Styles from the List drop-down box.)
3. Click Modify. The Modify Style dialog box opens.
4. Check the Automatically Update check box.
5. Click OK and Close.

PART

II

CH

10

CHAPTER 11

FOOTNOTES, BOOKMARKS, AND CROSS-REFERENCES

In this chapter

USING FOOTNOTES AND ENDNOTES

Footnotes and endnotes are notes that provide more information about specific text in your document. In Word, *footnotes* appear at the bottom of your current page. Notes compiled at the end of a document—or at the end of a section—are called *endnotes*. Both footnotes and endnotes are equally easy to insert—and easy to work with after you add them. You can use them both in the same document.

Word can automate the most annoying aspects of managing footnotes and endnotes: sequencing and placing them properly. When you use Word's footnote and endnote features, you get extensive flexibility over your footnotes and endnotes. Of course, you can control the text that appears in your footnotes and endnotes—and how that text is formatted. But you can also control

- Where your footnotes appear on your page, and exactly where your endnotes are placed at the end of your document
- How your footnotes and endnotes are sequenced
- What kind of footnote or endnote marks (called *note reference marks*) you use
- How footnotes are separated from other text on your pages

By using Word's controls, you can customize your footnotes or endnotes for any type of document, including specialized documents such as legal documents, which may have very strict footnote or endnote requirements.

Communicating with Word: A Second Good Reason to Use Footnotes
Footnotes and endnotes are often used to cite references or sources of information. It is important to give due credit for the information—not only for ethical reasons, but because the original source could be in error. If you cite the reference, you give your reader an opportunity to check the source and evaluate its credibility.

INSERTING FOOTNOTES AND ENDNOTES

To insert a standard footnote, place your insertion point where you want the footnote mark to appear, and press Alt+Ctrl+F. Word inserts a *note reference mark* containing a number. If this is the first footnote in your document, the number is 1; if you have already inserted footnotes, Word uses the next number after your last footnote, using the sequence 1, 2, 3, and so on.

To insert a standard endnote, place your insertion point where you want the endnote mark to appear, and press Alt+Ctrl+D. Word inserts a note reference mark containing a lowercase letter. If this is the first endnote in your document, the letter is "i"; if you have already inserted endnotes, Word uses the next letter after your last endnote, following the sequence i, ii, iii, and so on. Later, you'll learn how to change this sequence if you want.

Note

If you use footnotes and endnotes a lot, you can add them to the shortcut menu that appears when you right-click on text in your document. To do so,

1. Choose Tools, Customize, and click the Toolbars tab.
2. Check the Shortcut Menus check box in the Toolbars scroll box. The Shortcut Menus toolbar appears.
3. Click the Commands tab, and choose Insert from the Categories scroll box.
4. In the Commands scroll box, click on the command you want to add; in this case, either Footnote or Insert Endnote Now.
5. Drag the command to the Text button on the shortcut toolbar; drag down to choose the shortcut menu you want to use (Text); then drag across the cascaded menu, and release the mouse pointer where you want the command to appear.
6. Click Close in the Customize dialog box.

In *Normal view*, when you insert a footnote or endnote, Word also displays the *note pane*. Figure 11.1 shows how this note pane looks immediately after you insert your first footnote. Figure 11.2 shows how it looks immediately after you insert your first endnote.

PART

II

CH

11

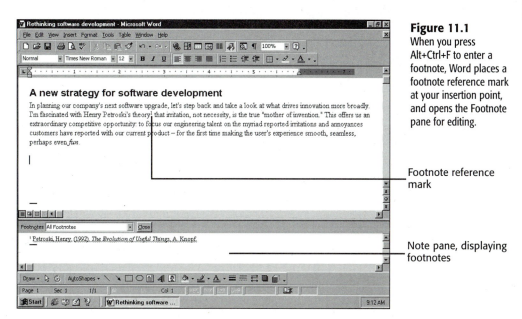

Figure 11.1
When you press Alt+Ctrl+F to enter a footnote, Word places a footnote reference mark at your insertion point, and opens the Footnote pane for editing.

Footnote reference mark

Note pane, displaying footnotes

Figure 11.2
When you press
Alt+Ctrl+D to enter an
endnote, Word places an
endnote reference mark
at your insertion point,
and opens the Endnote
pane for editing.

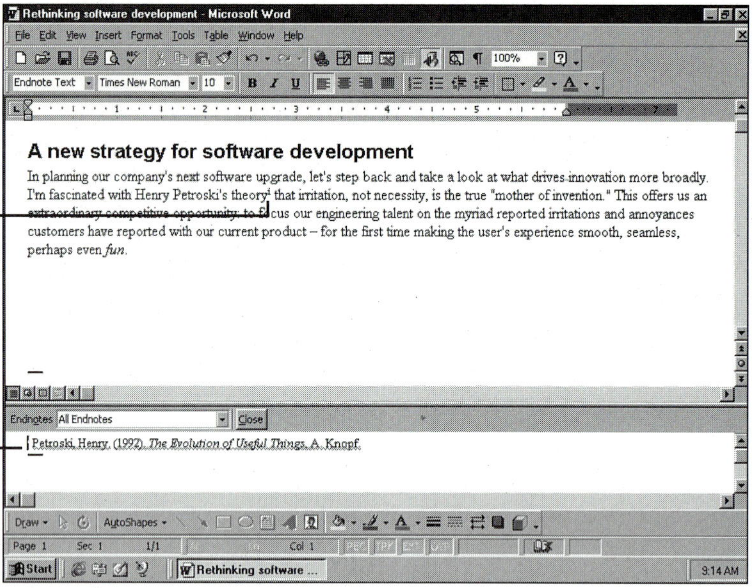

Endnote reference
mark

Endnote pane

In *Print Layout view*, there is no separate note pane (see Figure 11.3). You simply edit footnotes wherever they are located on the page—typically beneath a footnote separator line that stretches about one-third of the way across the page.

If you're creating endnotes, it is usually best to work in Normal view. If you create an endnote in Print Layout view, Word moves you to the list of endnotes at the end of the document or section. You can edit the endnote there, but you can't see the document text to which it relates.

Tip #168

You can move to a footnote or endnote's location in the document and close the note pane at the same time. Just double-click the reference mark in the pane.

EDITING FOOTNOTES AND ENDNOTES

Within the note pane, you can edit or format text in most of the ways you're familiar with. You can even add images or tables. A few of Word's features are off limits, but not many. For example, you can't use Word 2000's drawing tools, or insert *comments* or *captions*. You can't create *multiple columns*, either, but *multicolumn tables* are a possible work-around.

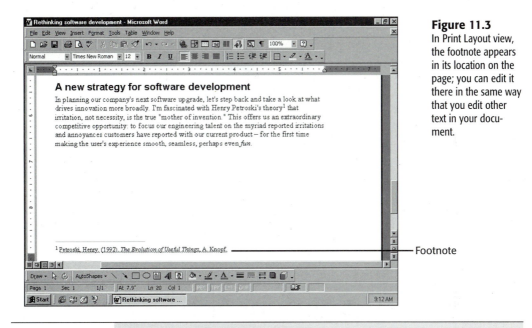

Figure 11.3
In Print Layout view, the footnote appears in its location on the page; you can edit it there in the same way that you edit other text in your document.

Footnote

PART

II

CH

11

Tip #169

In case you ever need to insert a drawing in a footnote or endnote, here's how.

Create the drawing in Word's editing window, copy it to the Microsoft Paint applet, and save it as a bitmapped image there. You can then place it in your Footnote pane just as you would any other bitmapped image: by clicking in the Footnote pane; choosing Insert, Picture, From File; browsing to the image file; and choosing Insert.

→ For more information about using Word's Drawing tools, **see** Chapter 13, "Drawing in Word," **p. 401**.

If you are working in your document and you want to edit the text associated with a footnote or endnote, double-click its note reference mark. The note pane opens, displaying the corresponding note. In Normal view, you can also view the note pane by choosing View, Footnotes. If you prefer to view endnotes, you can choose All Endnotes from the drop-down box within the note pane (see Figure 11.4).

Figure 11.4
Use the drop-down box to switch from viewing footnotes to viewing endnotes.

Tip #170

If you don't need to *edit* the text of a note, but you would like to *see* it, hover your mouse pointer over the accompanying note reference mark in your document. The mouse pointer changes shape to resemble a piece of note paper; then a *ScreenTip* appears displaying the contents of the note (see Figure 11.5).

Figure 11.5
Hover your mouse pointer over a note reference mark, and Word displays the note's contents in a ScreenTip.

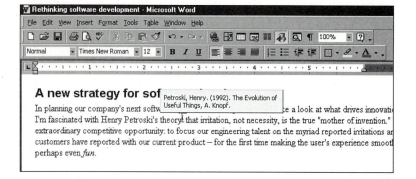

If you're working in a document with many footnotes or endnotes, you might want to view more than those that appear in the size of the default note pane. To adjust the size of the note pane, place the mouse pointer over the border until it changes to double vertical arrows (see Figure 11.6). Drag the border up or down to resize the pane.

Figure 11.6
Resizing a note pane by dragging its top border.

Resize pointer

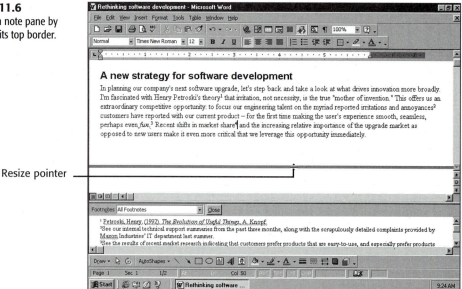

CUSTOMIZING YOUR FOOTNOTES AND ENDNOTES

Word gives you total control over the appearance, sequence, and location of footnotes and endnotes. In the next few pages, you'll learn how to change each of Word's default settings, beginning with the change you're likely to make most often: customizing the character Word uses as its note reference mark.

INSERTING A CUSTOM MARK

In documents where you have only a few footnotes or endnotes, you may want to use a *custom mark*—a special character that appears in place of the number or letter Word normally uses as a note reference mark. Follow these steps to create a custom mark:

1. Place your insertion point where you want the footnote or endnote.

2. Choose Insert, Footnote. The Footnote and Endnote dialog box appears, as shown in Figure 11.7. (If Footnote does not appear in the Insert menu, wait a moment until Word displays its full menus.)

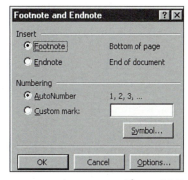

Figure 11.7

3. Choose Footnote or Endnote to specify what kind of note you're creating.

4. Click in the Custom Mark text box and enter the character(s) you want to use in your note reference mark. (You can insert up to ten characters in a note reference mark.)

5. Click OK.

Tip #171

If you want to change an existing note reference mark into a custom mark, select the mark in your document before you follow these steps.

Tip #172

You can use custom marks in documents that also use conventional note reference marks. When Word numbers the conventional note reference marks, it skips any custom marks in your document.

You can't edit a note reference mark directly; you must create a custom mark (or change Word's automatic numbering sequence, as you'll learn about shortly).

USING SYMBOLS FOR YOUR CUSTOM MARKS

You might want to use a symbol as your note reference mark, such as † or ‡. If so, follow steps 1, 2, and 3 from the preceding section; then click the Symbol button in the Footnote and Endnote dialog box. The Symbol dialog box appears (see Figure 11.8). Choose the symbol you want to use and click OK. The symbol you chose now appears in the Custom Mark box. Click OK to finish creating the footnote or endnote.

Figure 11.8
Choose a symbol from the Symbol dialog box. To choose from a different character set, select another symbol font (such as Wingdings) from the Font drop-down box.

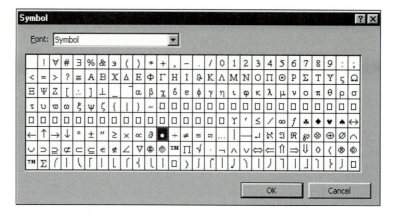

CONTROLLING FOOTNOTE NUMBERING AND LOCATION

As you've seen, Word automatically numbers footnotes using the sequence 1, 2, 3.... Word also assumes that you want your footnotes to number consecutively throughout your document, beginning with the number 1. Finally, Word assumes you want your footnotes to appear at the bottom of each page. You can change each of these default settings.

To control footnote numbering and location, choose Insert, Footnote, and click Options. The Note Options dialog box opens. To control footnotes, choose All Footnotes if it isn't already chosen (see Figure 11.9). To control endnotes, choose All Endnotes (see Figure 11.10). As you can see, both tabs are quite similar.

Figure 11.9
You can control footnote numbering and location through the All Footnotes tab of the Note Options dialog box.

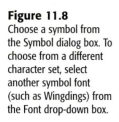

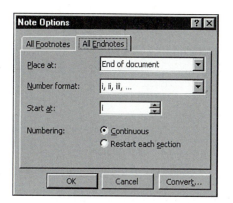

Figure 11.10
If you want to control endnotes, choose the All Endnotes tab instead.

Note

Any changes you make in the Note Options dialog box affect *all* your footnotes or endnotes—both the ones you *will* insert and the ones you've *already* inserted.

→ If you need to create multiple footnotes that share the same footnote number and refer to the same text, **see** "Cross-Referencing a Footnote or Endnote," **p. 345**.

CONTROLLING WHERE FOOTNOTES OR ENDNOTES APPEAR   In the Place At drop-down box within the Note Options dialog box, you can control where your footnotes or endnotes appear.

If you're working with footnotes, your choices are Bottom of Page (the default setting) or Beneath Text. If you choose Beneath Text, your footnotes are placed directly underneath the last line of text on each page. This means the location of footnotes can vary, depending on how far down the page your document text extends.

If you're working with Endnotes, your choices are End of Document (the default setting) or End of Section. If you choose End of Section, all the endnotes in each section are compiled after the last line of that section.

CONTROLLING THE NUMBERING SEQUENCE OF FOOTNOTES AND ENDNOTES   If you allow Word to automatically sequence your footnotes or endnotes (rather than manually creating custom marks yourself), Word gives you control over the numbering and lettering sequences it uses. You can specify the sequence through the Number Format drop-down box in the Note Options dialog box. Your choices are the same whether you're working with footnotes or endnotes. They are

> 1, 2, 3...
>
> a, b, c...
>
> A, B, C...
>
> i, ii, iii...
>
> I, II, III...
>
> *, †, ‡, §...

The last option inserts a series of the most commonly used footnote symbols. After you go past four footnotes or endnotes, Word "doubles up" the characters. The reference mark associated with footnote #5 is **; footnote #6 is ††, and so on. Then, after you go past eight footnotes or endnotes, Word "triples up" the characters, and so on.

Note

You can't set Word to automatically use a single custom character repeatedly in all your footnotes or endnotes, but you can insert the same custom mark manually every time you add a footnote or endnote.

Controlling the Starting Number of Footnotes or Endnotes   Word assumes that you want your footnotes to begin numbering with 1 and your endnotes to begin numbering (or, perhaps, lettering) with i. You might, however, be creating a chapter of a book that already contains footnotes or endnotes. You know that several notes appear before yours. To start with a different number (or letter), select it in the Start At spin box.

Note

The letters or numbers in the Start At spin box change, based on the Number format you've chosen. If you enter a different number, letter, or symbol in the Start At spin box, and later change the Number format, your starting number automatically changes to the corresponding number or letter in the new sequence.

Restarting Numbering for Each Section or Page   By default, Word numbers footnotes or endnotes sequentially through the entire document. However, you might want your notes to begin numbering again with 1 (or whatever starting number you've chosen) at the beginning of each new document section. If so, click the Restart Each Section button on the All Footnotes or All Endnotes tab.

If you're working with footnotes, you have an additional option: to restart footnote numbering with each new page. To choose this option, click the Restart Each Page button.

Converting from Footnotes to Endnotes (and Vice Versa)   Occasionally, you might start out creating footnotes and later decide that you want endnotes instead. Or perhaps you start out with endnotes and discover that your client, publisher, or organization prefers footnotes. You can convert between footnotes and endnotes whenever you want; you can even swap endnotes and footnotes at the same time.

To convert all your footnotes or endnotes at once, choose Insert, Footnote, and click Options. Choose Convert. The Convert Notes dialog box opens (see Figure 11.11). Select one of the available options, and click OK.

Figure 11.11
You can convert all footnotes to end-notes, all endnotes to footnotes, or swap footnotes *and* end-notes at the same time.

When you convert footnotes to endnotes, or vice versa, Word correctly renumbers them, taking into account any notes that already exist. For instance, if you convert two footnotes to endnotes, and you already have one endnote, Word will correctly sequence all three end-notes, from i to iii.

To convert only one footnote to an endnote (or vice versa), display the note in the Footnote or Endnote pane, right-click on it to display the footnote shortcut menu and choose Convert to Endnote (or Convert to Footnote).

WORKING WITH FOOTNOTES AND ENDNOTES: A CLOSER LOOK

You've already learned that you can edit any footnote or endnote in the note pane. The note reference mark in your document and the text of your footnote or endnote are con-nected. Whenever the note reference mark moves in your document, the footnote/endnote text moves with it. This means you can

- Duplicate a footnote by selecting, copying, and pasting the note reference mark.
- Move a footnote by cutting and pasting (or dragging and dropping) the note reference mark.
- Delete a footnote by deleting the note reference mark.

Of course you don't have to cut, copy, paste, or delete only the note reference mark; chances are you'll also be editing related surrounding text at the same time. The note refer-ence mark moves with the surrounding text. Whenever you move, copy, or delete a note reference mark, Word automatically updates the numbering of all the footnotes or endnotes in your document.

Caution

If you delete text that includes a reference mark, you delete the accompanying footnote or endnote as well.

Communicating with Word: Formatting Your Footnotes Correctly for Publication
Before creating references in footnotes or endnotes, make sure you are formatting them appropriately. *The Chicago Manual of Style* details the conventional approach for citing sources, but if your document will be published, make sure you contact your publisher in advance to learn its requirements. These requirements can vary widely, depending on your field and your publisher.

PART

II

CH

11

NAVIGATING AMONG FOOTNOTES AND ENDNOTES

You've already learned that you can double-click any note reference mark to display the note pane. Whenever you click inside a footnote or endnote in the pane, Word also displays the corresponding location in the main document.

You can move among notes in the main document without opening the note pane. To move to a specific footnote, press F5 to display the Go To tab of the Find and Replace dialog box. Choose Footnote in the Go To What scroll box; then, in the Enter Footnote Number text box, enter the footnote number you want to view, and click Go To.

Follow these steps to move from one footnote or endnote to the next:

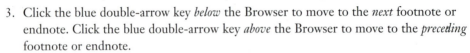

1. Click the Select Browse Object button (see Figure 11.12).

2. Click Browse by Footnote or Browse by Endnote (see Figure 11.13).

3. Click the blue double-arrow key *below* the Browser to move to the *next* footnote or endnote. Click the blue double-arrow key *above* the Browser to move to the *preceding* footnote or endnote.

Figure 11.12
Working with Select Browse Object.

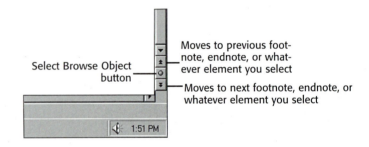

Select Browse Object button

Moves to previous footnote, endnote, or whatever element you select

Moves to next footnote, endnote, or whatever element you select

Figure 11.13
Using Select Browse Object to move between footnotes or endnotes.

Browse by endnote   Browse by footnote

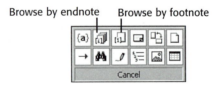

REFORMATTING FOOTNOTES AND ENDNOTES

Word builds footnotes using two built-in styles: Footnote Text for the contents of the footnote, and Footnote Reference for the reference mark (as it appears in both the document and the Footnote pane). For endnotes, Word uses Endnote Text and Endnote Reference. This means you can create a document where all footnotes use one set of formatting instructions, and all endnotes use a different set of formatting entirely.

Follow these steps to change the appearance of either footnotes or endnotes by changing their associated styles:

1. Select footnote or endnote text, or a note reference mark that you want to change.

2. Reformat the footnote or endnote text or note reference mark to appear the way you want all similar text or reference marks to look.

3. Click anywhere inside the Style drop-down box on the Formatting toolbar.

4. Press Enter. Word displays a dialog box that asks whether you want to change the style or revert selected text to the style that already exists.

5. Choose Update Style to Reflect Recent Changes.

6. Click OK.

→ To learn more about creating styles easily, **see** "Creating Paragraph Styles Easily with Style by Example," **p. 41**.

CONTROLLING FOOTNOTE AND ENDNOTE SEPARATORS AND NOTICES

By default, Word separates footnotes from the text of your document by inserting a line roughly one-third the width of a standard page margin. This is called the footnote or end-note *separator*.

If a footnote is so long that it must jump to the next page, Word separates it from the text on that page as well, using a footnote or endnote *continuation separator*. By default, this is a line that extends across the entire width of the page. You can see examples of both in Figure 11.14.

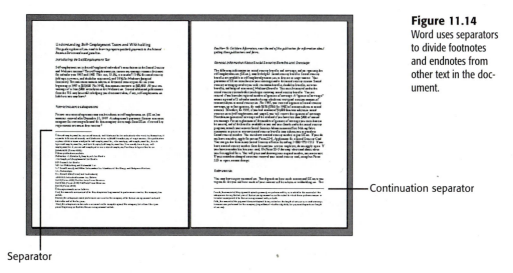

Figure 11.14
Word uses separators to divide footnotes and endnotes from other text in the document.

Continuation separator

Separator

You can change the appearance of either the separator or the continuation separator. You can also edit them to include text. To do so, first display the Footnote or Endnote pane by double-clicking on any footnote or endnote reference mark in Normal view. From the Footnotes or Endnotes drop-down box in the notes pane, select the element you want to edit. The current setting appears; typically either a short or long line. Edit the element to include the text, underlining, and/or formatting you want, and click Close.

Tip #173	If you want, you can also add text that tells users a note is jumping to the next page. With the Footnote pane open, choose Footnote Continuation Notice. (Or with the Endnote pane open, choose Endnote Continuation Notice.) Then enter and format the text you want. Click Close. By default, there is no Footnote or Endnote Continuation Notice.

Tip #174	Visit Microsoft's Web site (choose Help, Office on the Web) and download the MACROS9.DOT template, which contains a series of helpful macros, including a wizard that will help you create footnotes in the official Modern Language Association format. If you work extensively with footnotes, you might consider a third-party bibliographic database product, such as ProCite 4.0 (www.risinc.com) or Endnote 3.0 (www.endnote.com). Both products include sophisticated "Cite while you Write" Word macros that streamline complex footnoting.

 If Word won't print endnotes on a separate page, see "What to Do If Word Won't Print Endnotes on a Separate Page," in the "Troubleshooting" section of this chapter.

 If Word superimposes footers on top of footnote text, see "What to Do If Word Prints Page Footers On Top of Footnote Text," in the "Troubleshooting" section of this chapter.

 If Word won't delete reference marks, see "What to Do If Word Won't Delete Footnote or Endnote Reference Marks," in the "Troubleshooting" section of this chapter.

USING BOOKMARKS

When you're working in a long or complex document, you often want a quick way to move back to a specific location—without having to remember page numbers, headings, or exact search text. That's where Word's *bookmarks* feature comes in very handy.

Bookmarks are even more valuable than they appear. Word itself uses bookmarks to track blocks of text it needs to know about. By using the bookmarks you create, Word can

- Compile *index entries* that span multiple pages (see Chapter 9, "Tables of Contents, Figures, Authorities, and Captioning")

- Build formulas that include references to numbers elsewhere in a document (see Chapter 5, "Tables: Organizing Your Pages")

- Create *custom properties* that reflect the changing contents of a document

- Manage internal *cross-references*

- Ask users for input and then display that input throughout the document (discussed later in this chapter)

- Build *hyperlinks* that connect to specific locations in external documents or the current document (discussed later in this chapter)

- Mark locations for later retrieval by a *field* or macro

→ For more information about working with field codes, **see** Chapter 18, "Automating Your Documents with Field Codes," **p. 555**.

INSERTING BOOKMARKS

Follow these steps to insert a bookmark:

1. Select the text you want to associate with a bookmark, or click in your document at the location where you want to create a bookmark.

2. Choose Insert, Bookmark. The Bookmark dialog box opens (see Figure 11.15).

3. Enter a bookmark name. Bookmark names must begin with a letter, and can't include spaces or most punctuation—though they can include underscore characters (_). They cannot exceed 40 characters.

4. Click Add.

PART

II

CH

11

Figure 11.15

VIEWING BOOKMARKS IN YOUR DOCUMENT

You may at some point want to view the borders of the bookmarks in your document. (For example, you may be editing text that you suspect is near the boundary of a bookmark. You may want to know whether the text you add or delete is part of the bookmark.) To view the bookmarks in your document, choose Tools, Options, View, check the Bookmarks check box, and click OK. Text you bookmarked is now displayed within dark gray or black non-printing brackets, depending on your computer and video card (see Figure 11.16).

Figure 11.16
Dark gray brackets mark the boundaries of book-marks within your document.

Nonprinting bookmark brackets

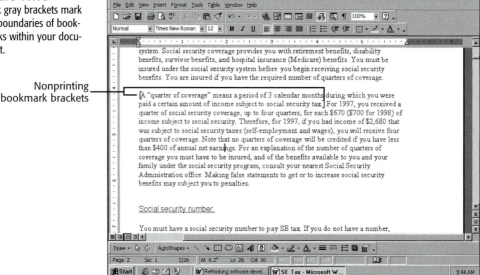

If you edit text that appears entirely within bookmark brackets, the bookmark will encompass all the text as you've edited it. However, if you cut text from within the bookmarks, and paste that text outside the bookmarks, that text will no longer be encompassed by the bookmarks.

FINDING BOOKMARKS

There are two ways to find a bookmark after you've created it:

■ You can choose Insert, Bookmark, select a bookmark, and click Go To.

■ You can press F5 (or double-click on the page number in the status bar) to display the Go To dialog box. Then, choose Bookmark in the Go To What scroll box, select a bookmark name from the Enter Bookmark Name text box, and click Go To.

In both cases, when you go to a bookmark, Word selects all the text contained in the bookmark.

MOVING FROM ONE BOOKMARK TO THE NEXT

To browse your bookmarks, choose Insert, Bookmark to display the Bookmark dialog box; then sort your bookmarks by Location. One at a time, click each bookmark in the list and click Go To. The Bookmark dialog box remains open as you work (although you may want to drag it out of your way).

DELETING BOOKMARKS

Perhaps you created a bookmark temporarily, to track specific text while you were focusing on one element of your document. Now you'd like to delete the bookmark so it no longer clutters up your bookmark list. To delete a bookmark, choose Insert, Bookmark; select the bookmark; click Delete; and click Close.

> **Note**
>
> If you delete all the text associated with a bookmark, the bookmark is deleted automatically.

WORKING WITH CROSS-REFERENCES

Cross-referencing is a great way to help readers find relevant material scattered throughout a long document. However, many writers avoid manual cross-referencing, because it is extremely difficult to manage and update. Every time you edit your document and change its page numbering, who'll go through the entire document and fix every cross-reference?

Word will. Word 2000 automates cross-references, making them exceptionally convenient and flexible. And if there's a cross-referencing task Word won't handle by itself, chances are you can still make it happen with field codes.

→ For more information on working with field codes, **see** Chapter 18, "Automating Your Documents with Field Codes," **p. 555**.

You insert nearly all your cross-references through the Cross-Reference dialog box. To display it, choose Insert, Cross-Reference. (If Cross-Reference does not appear in the Insert menu, wait a moment until Word displays its full menus.) The Cross-Reference dialog box is shown in Figure 11.17.

Figure 11.17
The Cross-Reference dialog box can insert virtually all your cross-references.

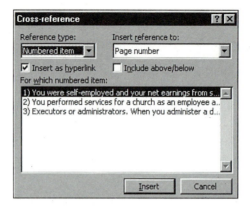

This deceptively bare-looking dialog box packs quite a wallop: You can create cross-references to nine different elements of your document and customize the contents of any of them. More specifically, you can create cross-references to the following document elements.

Note

In these examples, the underlined text represents examples of text Word can insert as a cross-reference.

- Headings you formatted using one of Word's built-in Heading styles. (Example: "For more information about Honus Wagner, see Baseball in the 1920s.")
- Numbered items (paragraphs and/or headings) you numbered using Word's *Outline Numbering* feature. (Example: "See Section I.2.a.")
- Bookmarks you created anywhere in your document. (Example: "See coverage on page 133.")
- *Footnotes* or *endnotes*. (Example: "See Footnote 7.")
- Equations, Figures, and Tables for which you created captions using Word's Caption feature (Example: "See Table 3.2: 1999 Quarterly Results.")

Tip #175

If you use Heading Styles and *AutoCaptions*, you make it much easier to create cross-references based on headings and captions.

To understand cross-referencing, it helps to first understand the steps involved in creating any cross-reference. After that, take a closer look at the cross-references you're most likely to create: headings, bookmarks, footnotes, and figures.

CREATING A CROSS-REFERENCE

Whenever you create a cross-reference from the Cross-Reference dialog box, you follow these steps:

1. Choose the specific element you want to reference from the Reference Type drop-down list box. For example, if you chose Footnote as your reference type, you now choose the specific footnote you want to use.

2. From the Insert Reference To drop-down box, choose which aspect of the document element you want to reference. For example, if you're referencing a footnote, do you want your reference to include the footnote number, the page number on which the footnote appears, or something else? The options available to you depend on the reference type you choose.

3. Make one or two more decisions about your footnote. Should it appear as a hyperlink that readers can click and jump to? If so, check the Insert as Hyperlink check box. Should it include the word "above" or "below"? If so, check the Include Above/Below check box. You'll learn more about these options later.

4. Click Insert to place the cross-reference in your document.

The next section takes a closer look at some of the cross-references you'll use most.

CROSS-REFERENCING A HEADING OR BOOKMARK

Headings are natural reference points within a document. They stand out due to size and formatting, so they're easy for your reader to find. Moreover, they define important topics in your document that are often worth referencing. Sometimes, though, you'll want to cross-reference a block of text that doesn't correspond neatly to a document heading. For example, you might want to refer to an anecdote that was covered elsewhere in a different context; the anecdote may not have been important enough to warrant its own heading.

To cross-reference a block of text that is not a heading, first select it and use Insert, Bookmark to create a bookmark. Creating bookmarks is covered in more detail earlier in this chapter.

→ For more information about inserting a bookmark into your document, **see** "Inserting Bookmarks," **p. 339**.

After you create a bookmark (or identify a heading you want to cross-reference), follow these steps to build your cross-reference:

1. Place your insertion point where you want the cross-reference to appear.

2. Add any text you want to appear next to your cross-reference. For example, if you plan to tell readers "see page 32," enter the words:
   ```
   see page
   ```

3. Choose Insert, Cross-Reference.

4. Choose Heading or Bookmark as the Reference Type. Whichever selection you make, Word lists all the available choices currently in your document (in other words, all the available headings or bookmarks).

5. In the For Which Heading or For Which Bookmark box, select the heading or bookmark you want.

6. In the Insert Reference To drop-down box, choose the aspect of the heading or bookmark you want to reference. The following options are available:

   - If you choose Heading Text or Bookmark Text, Word inserts the entire text of the heading or bookmark.

   - If you choose Page Number, Word inserts the page number on which the heading appears.

   - If you choose Heading Number, Word inserts the heading number that appears in your document, but only if you already inserted heading numbers with Word's Outline Numbering feature.

   - If you choose Heading Number (No Context), Word inserts an abbreviated heading number, if you're in the same section as the text you're referencing. For example, if you're in section 6.F, and you insert a cross-reference to heading 6.C, Word inserts the reference C rather than 6.C. You might use (No Context) if you think it would be redundant to include the section number. This setting has no effect if you cross-reference a document element elsewhere in your document. For example, if you're in section 6.F and you insert a cross-reference to heading 3.L, Word inserts 3.L no matter what—never just L.

   - If you choose Heading Number (Full Context), Word inserts a full heading number, even if you're in the same section as the heading you're referencing.

   - If you choose Above/Below, Word inserts the word *above* or *below* in your cross-reference, depending on whether you're placing your cross-reference before or after the text you're referencing. If you move either the cross-reference or the reference text, Word can automatically adjust—switching "above" to "below," or vice versa, if needed.

7. Clear the Insert as Hyperlink check box if you do not want the cross-reference to appear as a hyperlink.

8. Click Insert. The cross-reference appears in your document.

Tip #176

To really help readers find their way to your cross-reference, consider using two cross-references near each other: one that references the heading text, and another that references the page number. You can see how this works in the following example (both references are underlined):

For more information, see <u>The Retreat at Dunkirk</u>, page <u>146</u>.

Tip #177	You may sometimes create a complex cross-reference that you expect to reuse throughout your document. In other words, you expect to repeatedly reference the same text in the same way. If so, insert the cross-reference, select it, and create an AutoText entry based on it. Then you can simply insert the AutoText entry wherever you need the cross-reference.

→ For more information about working with AutoText, **see** "AutoText: The Complete Boilerplate Resource," **p. 87**.

CROSS-REFERENCING A FOOTNOTE OR ENDNOTE

You may at times want to cross-reference a footnote or endnote. To do so, follow these steps:

1. Place your insertion point where you want the cross-reference to appear.

2. Choose Insert, Cross-Reference.

3. Choose Footnote or Endnote as the Reference type. All the headings in your document appear in the For Which Footnote (or For Which Endnote) scroll box.

4. Select the footnote or endnote you want.

5. In the Insert Reference To drop-down box, choose the aspect of the footnote or endnote you want to reference. The following options are available:

   - If you choose Footnote Number (or Endnote Number), Word inserts the number of the footnote or endnote.

   - If you choose Page Number, Word inserts the page number where the footnote began.

   - If you choose Above/Below, Word inserts the word *above* or *below* in your cross-reference, depending on where the referenced text appears.

   - If you choose Footnote Number (Formatted) or Endnote Number (Formatted), Word inserts the number, formatted as if it were another footnote (or endnote) in your document. This enables you to create multiple footnotes or endnotes that refer to the same footnote text and use the same footnote or endnote number, as is often required by scientific journals. Since you're actually inserting a cross-reference that *resembles* a footnote, not a "true" footnote or endnote, the numbering of the other footnotes and endnotes in your document isn't affected.

6. Clear the Insert as Hyperlink check box if you do not want the cross-reference to appear as a hyperlink.

7. Even if you chose an element other than Above/Below in step 5, you can still tell Word to include the word *above* or *below* in your cross-reference by checking the Include Above/Below check box.

8. Click Insert. The cross-reference appears in your document.

PART

II

CH

11

CROSS-REFERENCING A FIGURE (OR OTHER CAPTIONED ITEM)

If you place a figure in your document, it's likely you'll want to cross-reference that figure in text somewhere nearby. If you created the figure using Word's caption or *AutoCaption* feature, you can easily insert the cross-reference using the Cross-Reference dialog box as well. To cross-reference a figure, table, or equation you've already captioned, follow these steps:

1. Place your insertion point where you want the cross-reference to appear.
2. Choose Insert, Cross-Reference.
3. Choose Figure, Table, or Equation as the Reference Type. All the corresponding elements in your document appear in the For Which scroll box.
4. Select the appropriate figure, table, or equation.
5. In the Insert Reference To drop-down list box, choose the aspect of the figure, table, or equation you want to reference. The following options are available:

    - If you choose Entire Caption, Word inserts the entire text of the caption, including its label and figure number.
    - If you choose Only Label or Number, Word inserts the label and figure number, for example, Figure 1.1.
    - If you choose Only Caption Text, Word inserts the text of the caption, excluding label and figure number.
    - If you choose Page Number, Word inserts the number of the page where the figure, equation, or table appears.
    - If you choose Above/Below, Word inserts only the word *above* or *below*, depending on the figure's location relative to the cross-reference.

6. Clear the Insert as Hyperlink check box if you do not want the cross-reference to appear as a hyperlink.
7. If, in step 5, you chose Page Number, you can ask Word to include the word *above* or *below* in your cross-reference by checking the Include Above/Below check box.
8. Click Insert. The cross-reference appears in your document.

CUSTOMIZING CROSS-REFERENCE FIELDS

When you insert a cross-reference, you're actually inserting a *field*. In most cases, Word inserts a { REF } field, with the following exceptions:

- If you create a cross-reference to a page number, Word inserts a { PAGEREF } field.
- If you create a cross-reference to a footnote or endnote, Word creates a { NOTEREF } field.

You can see some examples of these fields in Figure 11.18.

Note

Word also places a hidden bookmark at the location containing the material you're cross-referencing. That's why, if you toggle a cross-reference to view the underlying field code, you'll see something like

```
{ REF _Ref392747853 \h }
```

The long string of letters and numbers is the name of the hidden bookmark for which the { REF } field looks. If you want to see the hidden bookmarks in your document, choose Insert, Bookmark, and check the Hidden Bookmarks check box. After you display hidden bookmarks, you can select one of them and click Go To; Word takes you to the corresponding location in your document.

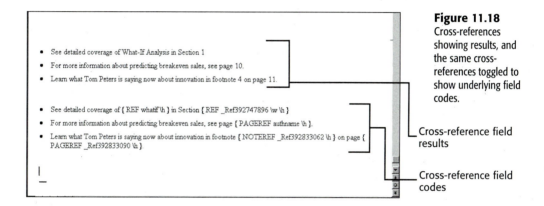

Figure 11.18
Cross-references showing results, and the same cross-references toggled to show underlying field codes.

Cross-reference field results

Cross-reference field codes

Why do you care that cross-references are really fields in disguise? There are three reasons:

- You can update a cross-reference just as you would update any other field: by selecting it and pressing F9.

- There are a few "off-the-beaten-track" tricks you can use in formatting cross-references—tricks that aren't available through the Cross-Reference dialog box. For example, you've seen that you can insert a reference to a heading number such as *Section 4.8.2.2*. You might want your reference to exclude the word *Section*, even though it appears in the automated heading numbering you placed in your document. You can arrange this by editing the field to include the \t switch. Or you can use one of the standard formatting switches available to most fields, such as * Upper, which formats the cross-reference in ALL CAPS.

→ For more information about using switches in field codes, **see** "Using Switches to Change a Field's Behavior," **p. 564**.

■ If a cross-reference isn't working correctly, you can occasionally troubleshoot it by viewing the field's contents. For example, you may occasionally see this message: `ERROR! Bookmark not defined.`

If you do, you can click inside the message and press Shift+F9 to toggle the field code. After you see which bookmark the field code is looking for, you can determine whether this bookmark has inadvertently been deleted from your document.

LINKING CROSS-REFERENCES TO THE CONTENT THEY REFERENCE

By default, Word inserts cross-references into your document as links, which means that if you click a cross-reference, Word jumps to the spot in the document you cross-referenced. If you do not want to insert a cross-reference as a link, clear the Insert as Hyperlink check box in the Cross-Reference dialog box. Note that Word doesn't format linked cross-references any differently than the surrounding text; they are not blue and underlined, like true hyperlinks. This is true even if you display your document in *Web Layout view (page 17)*—and even if you re-save the document as a Web page. In fact, the only difference between a linked cross-reference and one that isn't is the presence of an \h switch in the underlying field code.

Tip #178   If you *do* want to insert a blue underlined hyperlink that will be visible to people reading your document in electronic formats, choose Insert, Hyperlink.

You can add hyperlinking to a cross-reference by manually adding the \h switch, or remove it by deleting the \h switch.

Because hyperlinks look like ordinary text, there's little reason not to format cross-references as hyperlinks. Even if you're creating a document for print, leaving Insert as Hyperlink checked makes it easier for you to move to the text you're referencing, making sure your references are accurate and read as they should.

AUTOMATING REFERENCES WITH THE { ASK } AND { REF } FIELDS

You've learned that you can create a *bookmark* and use it to create a cross-reference. After you do this, Word can place the text you bookmarked in many locations throughout your document, wherever you insert a cross-reference to that bookmark.

Sometimes, however, you'll want to repeat text throughout your document, but you don't have an existing bookmark to work with. In fact, you don't know what text you want to repeat yet. What then?

USING THE { ASK } FIELD TO CREATE REFERENCES THAT REFLECT USER INPUT

Imagine the following scenario: You have a standard boilerplate letter, as shown in Figure 11.19 As you can see, this letter offers a discount to a specific customer. What if you want to offer an extra-large discount to a specific customer? You can set up the letter to request input from whoever is preparing the letter. Word stores that information as if it were a bookmark, and then inserts it anywhere your cross-reference looks for that bookmark.

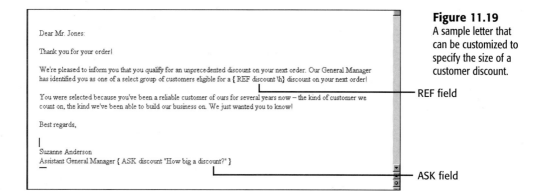

Figure 11.19
A sample letter that can be customized to specify the size of a customer discount.

REF field

ASK field

To create a reference that reflects user input, follow these steps:

1. Press Ctrl+F9 to display field brackets.

2. Enter an { ASK } field that requests input and stores it in a bookmark. In the following example, the bookmark is named *discount*; the text in quotes is what appears in the dialog box that requests input from the user:

   { ASK discount "How big a discount?" }

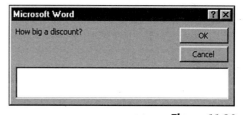

Figure 11.20

3. Select the field and press F9 to update it. Figure 11.20 shows the dialog box that appears.

4. Enter sample input in the dialog box and click OK. (You must do this because the { ASK } field doesn't create the bookmark until you provide input.)

Now that you've created the { ASK } field and provided it with sample input, you can create your cross-reference.

PART

II

CH

11

Choose Insert, Cross-Reference, and follow the steps described earlier to create a reference to a bookmark. Use the bookmark name you specified in the { ASK } field. Next, click Insert to place the cross-reference in your document. Repeat steps 1–3 to insert another identical cross-reference anywhere you want the same information to appear.

You're done—except for one thing. You can't always rely on other users to press F9 and display the dialog box you created for them. However, you can do it for them by recording a simple macro that consists of just two commands:

- Press Ctrl+A (or Edit, Select All) to select the entire document.
- Press F9 to update all fields (or right-click on a field and choose Update Field from the shortcut menu).

If you plan to reuse the same letter over and over again, name the macro AutoOpen. It runs—and displays the dialog box—every time you open the document. If you plan to save the letter as a template and create new letters based on it, name the macro AutoNew, and store it with the new template. It runs every time you create a new document based on that template.

USING FIELDS TO CREATE "SMART" CROSS-REFERENCES

Until now, you've been using { ASK } and { REF } fields to enable users to customize letters one at a time. What if you could set up a cross-reference that would automatically know for what discount each customer was eligible, based on some other piece of information you provide, such as the size of the order they placed? You can, though it takes a little doing.

In this example, assume that customers who place orders larger than $10,000 are eligible for a discount of 10% on their next orders. Customers with smaller orders aren't eligible yet, but they will be if they reach the $10,000 threshold—and you'd like to encourage them to do so.

First, create an { ASK } field, as you've already learned how to do. This { ASK } field asks a user to specify the dollar value of a customer's orders to date. After the user responds, the information is stored in a bookmark named dollarvalue:

```
{ ASK dollarvalue "Value of customer's orders to date?" }
```

Tip #179

As discussed earlier, you can write a quick and easy *macro* that updates fields automatically when you open this document, so the dialog box requesting user input appears automatically.

Now that you've captured the value of a customer's order in a bookmark, you can use an { IF } field to show Word what decisions you want it to make—and what text you want it to place in your letter as a result. A generic { IF } field uses the following syntax:

```
{ IF test "DoIfTrue" "ElseDoThis" }
```

At the heart of an { IF } field is a test. You specify a condition, and Word sees whether that condition has been met. For example, the test might include a formula that asks, "Has the customer ordered at least $10,000 worth of merchandise?"

To create a formula such as this, first create a bookmark for the location in your document that contains the value you want to test. Often, you'll want to bookmark a table cell. In the following example, you create a bookmark named dollarvalue and used it in a formula that serves as the test:

```
IF dollarvalue >=10000
```

Next, the { IF } field specifies the text you want Word to insert if the condition has been met. In this example, you use the following text, surrounded by quotation marks:

```
"You've just qualified for a 10% discount on your next order! Thanks for being
such a great customer!"
```

Finally, the { IF } field specifies the text you want Word to insert if the condition has not been met. Again, this text should appear in quotation marks.

```
"Qualify for a 10% discount when you place $10,000 in orders! You're well on your
way!"
```

Now build the { IF } field by putting all three components together: the test, the text that should appear if the test comes back "true," and the text that should appear otherwise:

```
{ IF dollarvalue >=10000 "You've just qualified for a 10% discount on your next
order! Thanks for being such a great customer!" "Qualify for a 10% discount when
you place $10,000 in orders! You're well on your way!" }
```

After Word knows the size of the order, it also knows what text to add to the letter.

You might want to place the same text in several locations throughout your document, or perhaps on an accompanying envelope stored as page 0 of the same file. That's the easy part. Select the entire field (or field result) and mark it as a bookmark. In this example, the bookmark is named discount. Insert a cross-reference to the bookmark anywhere you want the text to appear.

TROUBLESHOOTING

WHAT TO DO IF WORD WON'T PRINT ENDNOTES ON A SEPARATE PAGE

By default, Word places endnotes on the same page as the last text in the document. If you want them on a separate page, you have to add a manual page break (Ctrl+Enter).

WHAT TO DO IF WORD PRINTS PAGE FOOTERS ON TOP OF FOOTNOTE TEXT

This may happen if both the *page footer* and footnote text exceed five lines and a section break appears on the same page. If you can't remove the section break, add some blank lines above the footnote text in the Footnote pane.

WHAT TO DO IF WORD WON'T DELETE FOOTNOTE OR ENDNOTE REFERENCE MARKS

You may have deleted the footnote text in the Footnote pane, but you also must select and delete the footnote reference mark in the document.

WHAT TO DO WHEN YOU CAN'T FIND THE HEADING YOU WANT TO CROSS-REFERENCE

Check: Did you format it with one of Word's built-in heading styles (for example, Heading 1 through Heading 9)? If not, do so. If you can't (or don't want to), select it as a bookmark and cross-reference it the same way you would cross-reference any other bookmark.

WHAT TO DO WHEN CROSS-REFERENCES IN A MASTER DOCUMENT RETURN ERROR MESSAGES

Make sure the subdocuments to which your cross-references refer haven't been removed from the document. Make sure they are available and open.

PART III

THE VISUAL WORD: MAKING DOCUMENTS AND WEB PAGES LOOK GREAT

CHAPTER 12

GETTING IMAGES INTO YOUR DOCUMENTS

In this chapter

OPPORTUNITIES TO USE GRAPHICS EFFECTIVELY

Every year, your documents must compete for attention in an increasingly sophisticated visual environment. Using Times New Roman and Arial fonts isn't enough anymore: today's best documents are visually rich, incorporating high-quality graphics and a variety of other visual techniques. This chapter focuses on Word's powerful capabilities and resources for importing and utilizing graphics—along with some "do's and don'ts" for using graphics effectively.

Before going further, you may find it valuable to perform a brief inventory of your graphics resources and the opportunities you may have to improve your documents through the use of graphics.

- Do you create reports that include numbers presented in tabular form? Consider adding or substituting charts (as covered in Chapter 15, "Using Graphs to Make Sense of Your Data—Visually").

- Can you more effectively promote your corporate identity by adding your corporate logo to more of your forms and documents?

- Do you create documents that would benefit from directly relevant photographs? For example, if you appraise real estate, would it improve your reports to include scanned photos, or photos taken on a digital camera?

- Would it save you time to send documents by fax directly from your computer, rather than print them on stationery? If so, consider creating stationery *templates* that incorporate your logo and scanned digital signatures that can easily be imported into your documents.

- Are your newsletters and other customer communications too "gray"—all text and headlines, with no visuals to keep your reader's attention? Consider using digital *clip art*—preexisting images stored in a computerized format that can be used in Word. As you'll see, Word comes with an extensive library of digital clip art, with much more available on the Web and through low-cost CD-ROMs.

If any of these scenarios sound familiar, you can benefit from a better understanding of how to use graphics in your documents. It's no longer a purely aesthetic issue: It's now directly related to your competitiveness.

MANAGING CLIP ART THROUGH CLIP GALLERY 5.0

Microsoft Word and Office come with an applet that serves as a central clearinghouse for managing your clip art: Clip Gallery 5.0.

If you've used Clip Gallery in a previous version of Word or Office, you'll find that it's been completely revamped. It now looks and behaves much more like a Web browser. For instance, you choose images by clicking on hyperlinks, and can click Forward or Back buttons to view clips you've seen before.

Although Clip Gallery offers better tools than it did before, its core capabilities remain much the same as in Word 97. Clip Gallery does the following:

- Provides quick access to artwork (and multimedia clips) based on categories and keywords—either built-in or those you add yourself
- Enables you to import thumbnails of clip art from other sources so you can view and manage them from a central source
- Provides a Web connection that gives you access to additional clip art on Microsoft's Web site

Clip Gallery stores "thumbnail" versions of each image in an index that also contains pointers to the actual image, as well as information about the image that can be used to locate it. The images themselves stay where they were originally stored—either on your hard drive, a CD-ROM, or on a network location.

Caution

If you move an image from its original location, you'll need to tell Clip Gallery where to look for it next time.

Note

Clip Gallery was previously called Clip Art Gallery, but it can now store multimedia as well as traditional clip art, so Microsoft changed the name.

Word and Office come with their own clip art library; if you have purchased a version of Office containing Microsoft Publisher, this library contains well over 10,000 images. To view any of these images, and to use them in your document, first place your insertion point where you want the image to appear. Then, choose Insert, Picture, Clip Art. Clip Gallery appears, as shown in Figure 12.1.

Note

If you install Clip Gallery on a computer that ran an older version of Microsoft Office, the first time you open Clip Gallery it will index the clips that were installed with the prior version. This can take quite a while—often as much as a half hour or more, depending on the number of clips it finds.

As Clip Gallery indexes these clips, a progress bar indicates how much further it has to go. If you wish, you can click Postpone at any time to delay the indexing until the next time you use Clip Gallery. However, if you do this, you won't see thumbnails of the images you postponed indexing, and any searches you perform within Clip Gallery won't find these images until you do index them.

Clip Gallery indexes not only clip art associated with Microsoft Word and Office, but also clip art associated with other Office-compatible applications.

PART
III

CH
12

Figure 12.1
Clip Gallery displays
dozens of categories of
clip media.

Show all
categories

Copy   Paste

Click here to shrink
the window.

Return to the
preceding
window.

Go forward to the next
window.

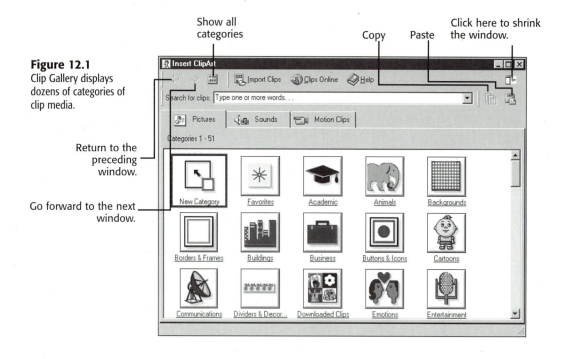

Tip #182

You might want to display Clip Gallery full-screen, so that you can see more categories and images. To do so, click the Maximize button (the second button from the right on the title bar).

Conversely, if you're planning to insert more than one image in your document, you may wish to keep Clip Gallery open, but make it as small as possible. To do so, click the Change to Small Window button. Clip Gallery shrinks, as shown in Figure 12.2.

You can then click the taskbar to switch between Clip Gallery and your document. Most of your document remains visible even when Clip Gallery is open.

SELECTING AN IMAGE WITH CLIP GALLERY

Clip Gallery gives you several ways to select an image. For instance, you can scroll through the 51 categories of images it provides until you find a category that matches the image you're looking for. After you find the most appropriate category, click its hyperlinked category name. Clip Gallery displays all the images that fit into the category. You can now scroll through the images and select the one you want.

When you're finished working within a specific category, you can view all the categories again by clicking the Back button, clicking the All Categories button, or pressing Alt+Home.

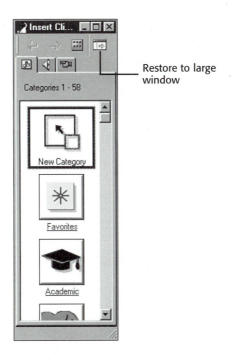

Figure 12.2
Clip Gallery displayed
in Small Window
format.

Restore to large
window

INSERTING AN IMAGE WITH CLIP GALLERY

After you find the image you want, here's how to insert it into your document. First, click
on the image. A series of options appears to its right (see Figure 12.3).

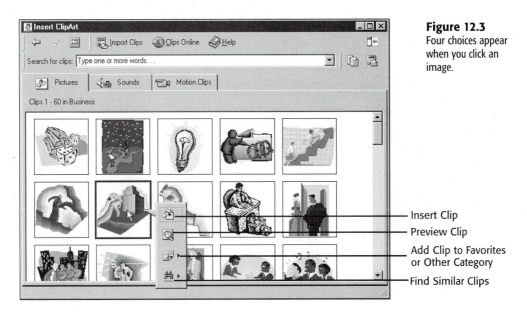

Figure 12.3
Four choices appear
when you click an
image.

Insert Clip
Preview Clip
Add Clip to Favorites
or Other Category
Find Similar Clips

PART

III

CH

12

If you would like to take a closer look at the image, click the Preview Clip magnifying glass button. A larger version of the image appears (see Figure 12.4). When you're finished viewing the clip, click the Close button in the Preview window. If you're ready to insert the image, click the Insert Clip button (the top button).

Figure 12.4
Choosing Preview Clip displays a somewhat larger version of the image you're considering.

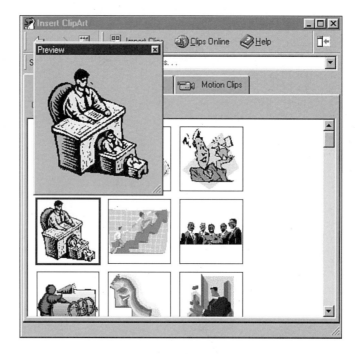

If Clip Gallery can't find the file for the indexed image you've chosen to insert or preview, Clip Gallery displays a dialog box similar to the one shown in Figure 12.5.

Figure 12.5
Clip Gallery displays a dialog box when it can't find a clip you're trying to insert or preview.

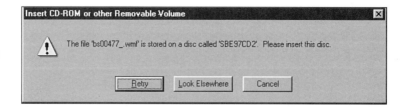

If, as in the example shown, the image is stored on a CD-ROM that isn't currently in your CD-ROM drive, insert the disc and choose Retry.

If the image has been moved elsewhere, click Look Elsewhere and the Cannot Locate Clip dialog box appears (see Figure 12.6). To point Clip Gallery to the location where you've moved the file, click Update Location; then browse to the location and click OK. If the clip is no longer available on your system or network, click Remove This Clip. To ignore the problem and try to find another clip, click Cancel.

Figure 12.6
From the Cannot
Locate Clip dialog
box, you can identify
a new location where
the clip can be
found, or remove it
from the index.

Note

In addition to the options that appear when you click on an image in the Clip Gallery, you also have access to a shortcut menu that appears when you right-click an image. From the shortcut menu, you can Insert, Copy, Paste, or Delete an image. You can also

- Choose Select All to select every image in the category you've displayed.
- Choose Recover to recover the Clip Gallery database, as is covered later in this chapter in the "Restoring or Compacting a Clip Gallery Database" section.
- Click Clip Properties to view information about the clip you've selected, as is covered later in this chapter, in the "Working with an Image's Properties" section.

INSERTING SOUNDS AND MOTION CLIPS

Office 2000 comes with small libraries of MIDI (MID) audio files and animated GIFs that you can also insert in your documents.

Note

MIDI files are computer-generated (rather than recorded) music files. They are designed to be very small for quick playback, but generally sound a bit tinny and artificial compared with audio files created by recording actual music.

Note that MIDI files used on Web sites are not streamed: They must be downloaded in their entirety before they start playing. In many cases, streamed audio formats such as RealAudio and Microsoft NetShow are superior for Web use. However, these cannot be created or managed through Office 2000.

Note

Animated GIFs are GIF files that contain several versions of an image. When a Web browser loads an animated GIF, it plays each image in turn, presenting an animated effect. Animated GIFs are used widely in Web banner advertising.

Word does not support animated GIFs: If you insert one in your document, you see only the first image in the series, not the animated effect. If you have PowerPoint 2000, which does support animated GIFs, you can preview your animated GIFs there.

To insert a MIDI audio file, first display the Clip Gallery. Next, click the Sounds tab, browse to the file you want, and follow the steps listed in the preceding section, "Inserting an Image with the Clip Gallery." If you preview an audio file, Clip Gallery opens the Windows Media Player to play it (see Figure 12.7).

Figure 12.7
Previewing an audio file with the Windows Media Player.

To insert an animated GIF, click the Motion Clips tab, browse to the file you want, and once again follow the steps listed in the previous section. If you preview an animated GIF file, Clip Gallery opens the Microsoft GIF Player applet to play it.

After you've inserted an animated GIF file in your Word document, it appears as a static image. However, if you save the document as a Web page and display it from within a Web browser, the animation will work. Once you've inserted an audio file in your Word document, it will appear as a loudspeaker icon (for WAV files) or a score sheet icon (for MIDI files). You can double-click the icon to hear the audio.

MAKING YOUR FAVORITE CLIPS EASIER TO FIND

If you find an image (or other clip) you especially like, you may want to reuse it often. Chances are, you'd rather not have to search for the same image over and over again. You can place a copy of the image's thumbnail sketch in Clip Gallery's Favorites category, so you'll always know where to find it. Or, perhaps, you'd like to copy the thumbnail sketch into a different category containing other images you use often. For example, you might have a set of product photos you reuse in many of your documents.

Wherever you'd like to copy the thumbnail, here's how. First, click the image thumbnail. Click the Add Clip to Favorites or Other Category button. In the box that appears (see Figure 12.8), choose the category into which you'd like to copy the thumbnail. Favorites is the default category, but you can choose any other category from the Add Clip to the Following Category drop-down box. Finally, click Add.

Figure 12.8
Specifying in which category you want an image to appear.

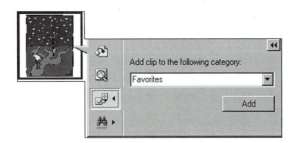

FINDING SIMILAR CLIPS TO THE ONE YOU'VE SELECTED

Often, the clip you select is close to what you want, but not exactly what you want. In this case, you may want to search for similar clips. Within Clip Gallery, first click to select the image that seems close to what you're looking for. Second, click the Find Similar Clips button. Clip Gallery displays a box that enables you to choose how to search for similar clips.

- If you click the Find Best Matching Clips *hyperlink*, Clip Gallery searches for all the clips it believes most resemble the image you've selected, based on the keywords associated with the image you've selected.

- Or, you can search for clips with a specific keyword by clicking the keyword from the Or Search for Clips with Keyword scroll box.

Clip Gallery displays all the images it finds that meets your search criteria. You can then scroll through them, previewing and inserting them using the techniques described previously in the "Inserting an Image with the Clip Gallery" section.

USING CLIP GALLERY'S SEARCH FOR CLIPS FEATURE

Clip Gallery's Search for Clips feature enables you to search for an image without bothering to scroll through Clip Gallery's 51 categories. In the Search for Clips combo box, enter one or more *keywords*—words that describe the image you're looking for—and press Enter. Clip Gallery displays the clips that fit your description. You can now choose one and insert it into your document, as covered earlier, in the "Inserting an Image with the Clip Gallery" section.

To give you an example of how Clip Gallery uses keywords, the Office 2000 image database contains a picture of children running into an old-fashioned schoolhouse. The following keywords are connected to this image:

PART

III

CH

12

academic	leaves
autumn	people
back to school	person
buildings	school bells
children	schoolhouses
education	schools
facilities	seasons
fall	students
kids	teachers
leaf	wmf

Tip #183

To see all the keywords associated with a specific image, right-click on its thumbnail, choose Clip Properties from the shortcut menu, and click the Keywords tab. For more information about working with keywords, see "Adding or Removing Keywords from a Clip's Properties," later in this chapter.

Tip #184

You can also use keywords to search for all images with a specific file format. Simply enter the file format's extension, such as GIF or JPG, in the Search for Clips combo box.

WORKING WITH AN IMAGE'S PROPERTIES

Like Word document files, each image in the Clip Gallery database has a set of properties that contain information about the image. You can control some of these properties to make images easier to find and use. To view an image's properties

1. Browse to and select the image in Clip Gallery.
2. Right-click on the image; the Clip Gallery shortcut menu appears (see Figure 12.9).

Figure 12.9
Working with the Clip Gallery shortcut menu.

3. Choose Clip Properties. The Clip Properties dialog box opens (see Figure 12.10).

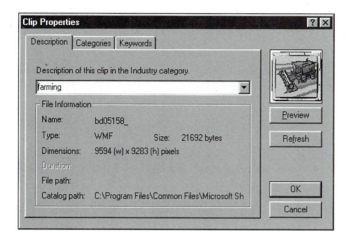

Figure 12.10
The Clip Gallery dialog box, with the Description tab displayed.

VIEWING AND EDITING FILE DESCRIPTIONS

In the Description tab of the Clip Properties dialog box, Word lists the filename, file format, and (in most cases) the size of the file. It is helpful to know this information for a variety of reasons. For instance, large files may take longer to display and print, and can slow down Word's editing.

Note

Most of the image files that come with Office 2000 are in the WMF (Windows Metafile) format. When you save a Word document as a Web page, WMF files are converted to GIF files, which use compression, and are commonly 50–75% smaller.

Tip #185

If you need to include many large graphics files in your document, you may wish to use Word's Picture Placeholder feature to show blank boxes rather than pictures while you edit the document's text. This can make Word run quite a bit faster. To do so, choose Tools, Options, and click the View tab. Check the Picture Placeholders check box, and click OK.

Each image file in the Clip Gallery database can contain a brief description that appears as a ScreenTip when you hover over the image. You can edit that description in the Description of This Clip combo box.

Tip #186

The ScreenTip also displays a file's format, so you don't need to enter the Clip Properties dialog box to discover it.

PART

III

CH

12

ADDING OR DELETING FILE CATEGORIES

As you've already learned, each image in the Clip Gallery database is listed under one or more categories. You can control the categories under which an image is listed. To do so

1. Browse to and select the image in Clip Gallery.
2. Right-click on the image; the Clip Gallery shortcut menu appears.
3. Choose Clip Properties. The Clip Properties dialog box opens.
4. Click the Categories tab (see Figure 12.11).
5. To associate an image with an additional category, check the check box next to the category's name. To disassociate an image from a category, so that it will not appear when you look for images in that category, clear the check box.
6. When you're finished making changes, click OK.

Figure 12.11
Changing the categories associated with an image.

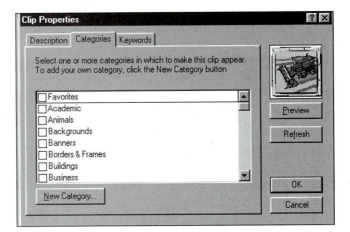

Note

You'll use this feature quite often when you insert new images from sources other than Microsoft, because these images rarely have category information that Clip Gallery can import.

ADDING A NEW CATEGORY

Sometimes you need to add a new category. For example, you might want to set up a category for images specific to your company: corporate logos, photos of your products, images you regularly reuse in your newsletters, and so forth.

To set up a new category, display the Categories tab of the Clip Properties dialog box, and then click New Category. The New Category dialog box opens (see Figure 12.12). Enter the name of the new category and click OK. The category appears checked in the currently selected image's list of categories, and you can also use it when assigning new clip properties to existing clips.

Figure 12.12
Adding a new category in Clip Gallery.

ADDING OR REMOVING KEYWORDS FROM A CLIP'S PROPERTIES

You can also add or remove keywords associated with a clip. To do so, right-click on the clip and choose Clip Properties to display the Clip Properties dialog box. Then, click the Keywords tab (see Figure 12.13).

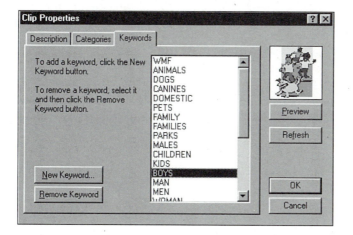

Figure 12.13
The Keywords tab of the Clip Properties dialog box.

PART

III

CH

12

To add a keyword, click New Keyword, type it in the New Keyword text box, and click OK. To remove a keyword, choose it in the Keywords scroll box and click Remove Keyword.

RENAMING OR DELETING CATEGORIES

You've already learned how to browse images by category and assign images to new categories. At some point, however, you may find that you want to manage your categories. For example, you may find that you have more categories than you can easily work with, or you may have created categories you no longer need. Or perhaps you may need to rename a category—maybe your company has merged or been renamed, and the old category name is no longer appropriate.

To perform any of these tasks, right-click on the category in Clip Gallery. A shortcut menu appears (see Figure 12.14).

Figure 12.14
Working with the Clip Gallery shortcut menu.

Note

If you want to manage categories, but specific images from within a category are displayed instead of all the categories, click the All Categories button or press Alt+Home.

To rename a category, click <u>R</u>ename Category, enter the new name in the Rename Category dialog box, and click OK.

To delete a category, click <u>D</u>elete Category; then click OK to confirm that you want to delete the category.

Caution

Deleting a category doesn't delete the clips included in that category. However, if a clip isn't indexed under any other category, you'll be able to find it only via keywords or by description. If you usually search for clips via category, you'll never find it again.

RETRIEVING ADDITIONAL IMAGES FROM MICROSOFT'S WEB SITE

If you can't find an acceptable image by searching the images that come with Office 2000, it's quite possible you can find the image you want on Microsoft's Web site. If you're running Clip Gallery on a computer that's connected to the Internet, here's how to find out:

1. Choose Insert, Picture, Clip Art to display the Clip Gallery.

2. Click Clips Online.

3. Clip Gallery displays a dialog box that tells you it's possible to browse a special Web page to view more images. If you wish, check the Don't Show This Message Again box to avoid seeing this dialog box in the future. Click OK.

4. Your Web connection loads. (If you normally must follow a dial-up sign-on sequence to get on the Web, you'll have to follow it here, as well.) As soon as you're connected, Microsoft's end-user license agreement appears in your Web browser. Read the agreement and click Accept. The Microsoft Clip Gallery Live Web page appears (see Figure 12.15).

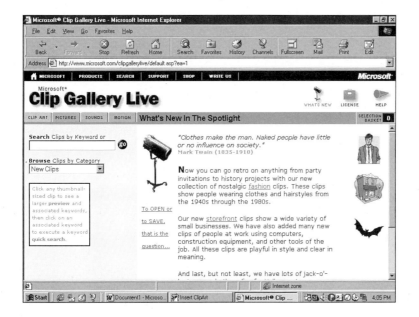

Figure 12.15
Microsoft's Clip Gallery Live Web page.

PART

III

CH

12

5. You now have several ways to search for the clip(s) you want:
   - If you want to search by keyword, enter the keyword in the Search Clips by Keyword text box, and click Go.
   - If you want to see all the clips in a specific category, choose the category in the Browse Clips by Category drop-down box and click Go. The default setting, New Clips, shows all the clips that have recently been added by Microsoft.
   - You can also read the front page of Clip Gallery Live, which usually includes hyperlinks to new seasonal clips, or other clip libraries that are of special interest.

6. Clip Gallery Live displays the clips you've selected (see Figure 12.16). To preview a clip, click on it; a larger version of the image then appears on the left side of the window. The keywords associated with the image appear to the right of the preview image.

Tip #187

If you want more images associated with a specific keyword, click on the keyword, and Clip Gallery Live will display all the online images containing that keyword.

7. To download the clip immediately, click the animated down arrow next to the clip. If you're prompted to choose between saving to disk or opening the files immediately, choose to open the files. Word retrieves the image and its associated database information. You can then view the clip by choosing the Downloaded Clips category in the Clip Gallery application.

Figure 12.16
Clip Gallery Live displays the clips you've selected.

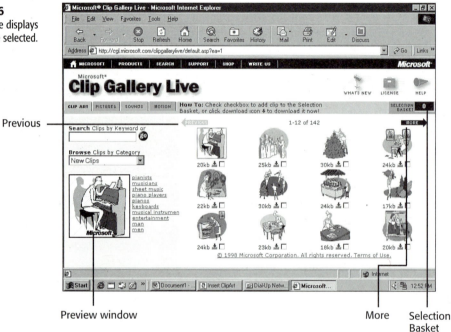

You can also download several files at once. To select files for downloading, check their check boxes. When you've selected all the files you want, click the words SELECTION BASKET. Clip Gallery Live displays a window containing thumbnails of the files you've selected (see Figure 12.17). Next, click Download.

Clip Gallery Live reports the number of files you've chosen and how long it expects your download to take at 28.8Kps (see Figure 12.18).

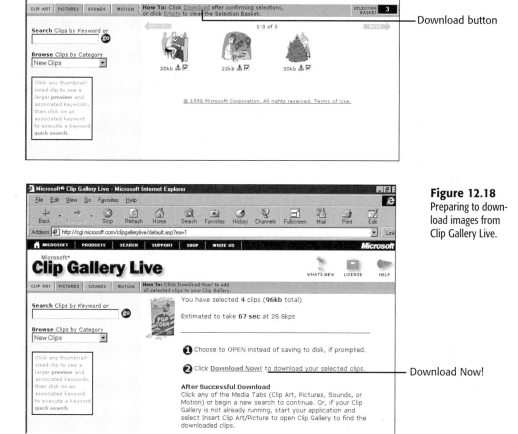

Figure 12.17
This window shows all the images in your selection basket.

—Download button

Figure 12.18
Preparing to download images from Clip Gallery Live.

—Download Now!

Click Download Now!. If you're prompted to choose between saving to disk or opening the files immediately, choose to open the files. Thumbnails of each clip are copied into their appropriate categories as well as the Downloaded Files category in Clip Gallery. Each file's keywords are also retrieved, so the images can be found in future searches you perform with Clip Gallery. The files themselves are also downloaded.

Note

In Windows 95 and Windows 98 (running without profiles), the files are stored in the C:\Windows\Application Data\Microsoft\Media Catalog\Downloaded Clips folder. In Windows NT 4.0, by default, they are stored in the C:\Winnt\Profiles\<*username*>\ Application Data\Microsoft\Media Catalog\Downloaded Clips folder.

If you are using Windows 98 with profiles, the folder will be the same as Windows NT uses, except that it will be placed in your Windows folder instead of the Winnt folder.

Note

If, at any point in this process, you're prompted whether to save or open the files, choose Open.

Caution

Even if you installed Office on a drive other than Drive C, your media clips—as well as Word templates and many other personal customizations (such as your Outlook database)—are stored within your Windows or Winnt folder on Drive C.

This has two implications: First, you may run out of space on Drive C sooner than you expect, which can cause unreliable or slow system performance. Second, if you're in the habit of backing up only your data folders, make sure you also back up the folder that contains the customizations.

Under Windows 95 or 98 running without profiles, this folder is typically C:\Windows\ Application Data\Microsoft. Under Windows NT, the folder is C:\Winnt\Profiles\ <*username*>\Application Data\Microsoft. Under Windows 98 running with profiles, the folder is typically C:\Windows\Profiles\<*username*>\Application Data\Microsoft.

RESTORING OR COMPACTING A CLIP GALLERY DATABASE

Clip Gallery's keywords, categories, descriptions, and image thumbnails are stored in a database. As time passes, it is possible for this database to become corrupted. Failing that, Clip Gallery may start to run very slowly as you add many more images. Clip Gallery provides database recovery tools that can sometimes fix these problems. To work with these tools, right-click on any category, and choose Recover from the shortcut menu. The Clip Gallery Database Recovery dialog box appears (see Figure 12.19).

Figure 12.19
The Clip Gallery
Database Recovery dialog
box.

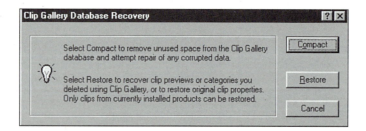

To squeeze unused space out of the Clip Gallery database, so that it will run faster (and to attempt repair if your database is damaged), click Compact.

To tell Clip Gallery to search your drive for installed clip art so that it can restore clip previews or categories you've removed, click Restore. The Clip Gallery Restore dialog box opens (see Figure 12.20). Here, you can specify what elements you want to restore to their original settings: categories, clips, and/or properties such as keywords and category assignments.

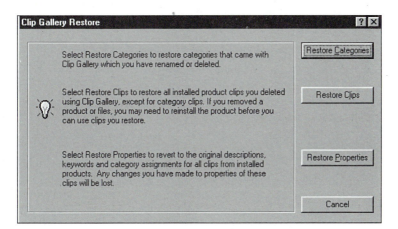

Figure 12.20
Choosing which elements of the Clip Gallery database you want to restore.

OTHER CLIP ART CD-ROMS

Inexpensive CD-ROMs have revolutionized the clip art industry, transforming clip art from a scarce commodity to an item that should rarely cost you more than a fraction of a penny per image. If the images you need can't be found on your Office CD-ROM or Microsoft's Web site, consider these clip art products:

- Macmillan's Imagine It! 555,000 (www.notalentrequired.com).
- Corel Gallery 1,000,000 (www.corel.com)
- ClickArt 200,000 Image Pak (www.broderbund.com)
- IMSI MasterClips 1,000,001 (www.masterclips.com)

These products change rapidly, so check the Web sites for the latest information.

Note

> Images from third-party CD-ROMs or Web sites don't import into Clip Gallery automatically, but you can import them by following the steps in the "Adding Your Images to the Clip Gallery" section, later in this chapter. Or you can use them directly, using Insert, Picture, From File. This technique is discussed in "Inserting Pictures Directly, Without Clip Gallery," later in this chapter.

OTHER WEB-BASED IMAGE RESOURCES

If you can't find the image you need on the CD-ROM or at Microsoft's site, don't despair. There are literally thousands of Web sites dedicated to graphics and clip art. Looking for the right image on the Web might seem like trying to find a needle in a haystack, but luckily there are some excellent "needle finders" available: specialized areas of Web search engines that focus on identifying images.

Most search engines work in a fashion similar to the Clip Gallery keyword search: Type a word or phrase into the search text box and press the Search (or Go!, Find It!, and so on) button. In a few moments, your search results are returned as a list of Web linked addresses. If you see something promising, click the link and check it out.

Searching with only the keyword has a major drawback, though, when you're looking for clip art: You'll usually be forced to sift through many unrelated links. A number of the search engines have special tools to help you to limit your search to only graphics. The following list outlines how some of the search engines work:

- AltaVista (www.altavista.com) enables you to limit right in the Search text box the keyword search to a graphic. For example, if you type "image:mars" in the Search text box, you'll get a list of available NASA photographs. This technique works not only on AltaVista but also on other search sites that use the AltaVista core search engine.

- HotBot (www.hotbot.com) includes a Media Type panel where you can check off graphics, video, audio, or whatever type of clip you're seeking. You can even have it hunt for specific file extensions such as GIF or JPG.

- Image Surfer (ipix.yahoo.com) is Yahoo!'s dedicated graphics search engine. You can do a keyword search or browse the categories (Arts, Entertainment, People, and so on) and subcategories. Click a link and you get a screen similar to the one in Figure 12.21.

- Lycos (www.lycos.com) has a special Pictures and Sound category that searches its multimedia database for clip art, photographs, and more.

After you've located your image, how do you bring it onto your system? If you're getting your images from a clip art collection, chances are the files are already stored in a compressed format designed for downloading, such as the ZIP format.

Figure 12.21
Yahoo!'s Image Surfer provides links to image databases, organized by categories.

With most images, you click the filename and the download process begins; your browser opens a Save As dialog box to enable you to save the file to a special location or give it a different name. After the download starts, another dialog box opens and displays the progress of transfer.

You can also download any graphic you see on the Web. Move your mouse pointer over an image and right-click. You get a shortcut menu where one of the options is Save Image As (or Save Picture As). This menu choice opens a regular Save As dialog box. From there, you browse to the folder, name the file, and click Save; the image downloads onto your hard drive.

Caution

> Be sure you read the copyright information associated with each collection. Many, but not all, images are free to use privately. Most ask to be contacted by you if you're using their artwork for a profit-making venture.

ADDING YOUR IMAGES TO THE CLIP GALLERY

If you retrieve third-party images and use them regularly, consider adding them to the Clip Gallery so that you can access them from the same source—and with the same search techniques—as you can your Microsoft image library. To import other clips into Microsoft Clip Gallery:

1. Choose Insert, Picture, Clip Art to display the Clip Gallery.
2. Click Import Clips. The Add Clip to Clip Gallery dialog box opens (see Figure 12.22).

PART
III

CH
12

Figure 12.22
Adding a clip to the Clip
Gallery.

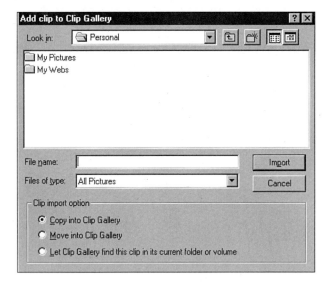

3. Browse to and select the clip you want to import. Remember that you can select multiple clips by pressing the Ctrl key while you click on each clip. You can select all the clips in a folder by pressing Shift, selecting the first clip, and (with Shift still pressed) selecting the last clip.

4. By default, Clip Gallery creates a pointer to the image's current location. If you expect the image to be unavailable at that location the next time you need it, click the Copy Into Clip Gallery button to copy the image onto your C: drive. (Otherwise, Clip Gallery copies only thumbnails into its database.)

5. When you've selected all the files and settings you need, click Import. Clip Gallery begins importing files, and displays the Clip Properties dialog box (see Figure 12.23). Here, you can

   • Enter descriptions, categories, and keywords for your clips one at a time, as discussed earlier in this chapter, in the "Working with an Image's Properties" section.

   • Click Skip This Clip to import the clip without any keywords or custom categories. Clip Gallery places a thumbnail of the clip in the Clip Gallery, but without any categories, and without any keywords except for its file format. (This option does not appear if you select only one clip for import.)

   • Create settings for this clip, and check the Mark All Clips with the Same Properties check box to apply the same settings to all the clips you're importing. (This option also does not appear if you select only one clip for import.)

6. When you finish establishing the properties of each clip, click OK.

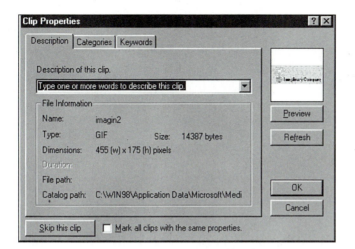

Figure 12.23
Assigning properties
to a clip you're
adding.

Note

Word can import and convert 17 different graphic file types. Of those 17 types, the following can be imported directly, without a special filter:

Installed automatically:

BMP	Windows Bitmap
EPS	Encapsulated PostScript
GIF	Graphics Interchange Format (Web graphics)
JPG	JPEG File Interchange Format (photos for the Web)
PCT	Macintosh PICT
PCX	PC Paintbrush
TIF	Tagged Image File Format

Installed on first use:

EMF	Windows Enhanced Metafiles (and Compressed Windows Enhanced Metafiles)
CDW	CorelDRAW
CGM	Computer Graphics Metafile
DRW	Micrografx Designer/Draw
DXF	AutoCAD Format 2-D
PCD	Kodak PhotoCD
TGA	Targa
WPG	WordPerfect Graphics
PNG	Portable Network Graphics (new Web image format, only beginning to be widely supported)
WMF	Windows Metafiles (and Compressed Windows Metafiles)

PART
III

CH
12

Caution

If you plan to save your document back to Word 6/95 format, be aware that EMF, PNG, and JPG files will be converted to WMF format—which in many cases can enlarge your files dramatically.

INSERTING PICTURES DIRECTLY, WITHOUT CLIP GALLERY

There's no law that says you must use Clip Gallery every time you want to import a picture. If you intend to use an image only once, it's often faster to insert the image directly into your document. To do so, first choose Insert, Picture, From File. Browse to, and select, the image file you want to use. The Preview window at the right side of the screen shows a large preview of the image (see Figure 12.24). When you're satisfied with the image you've chosen, click Insert.

Tip #188

If you prefer to insert only a link to the original image, click the down arrow next to the Insert button, and choose Link to File. The image will still appear in your document, but your document will be smaller because it doesn't contain the actual image. The image is automatically updated whenever you open your Word document or edit the graphic while the Word document is open. However, if the image is moved, the image will no longer appear.

You can also choose Insert And Link, which creates a link and also inserts the actual image.

Figure 12.24
When you use Insert Picture to select an image, it's previewed in the Preview window.

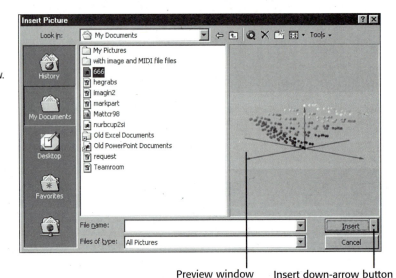

Preview window   Insert down-arrow button

If Word doesn't recognize the file type you're importing, see "What to Do When Word Doesn't Recognize the File Type You've Tried to Import," in the "Troubleshooting" section of this chapter.

INSERTING CLIP ART AS AN OBJECT

In some cases, you will want to insert an image that you created in a graphics program. However, you may also want to edit that image after you've inserted it into Word. To insert an image in a form that can easily be edited by the original graphics program, insert it as an object, as follows:

1. Choose Insert, Object.

2. Click the Create from File tab (see Figure 12.25).

3. Click Browse.

4. In the Browse dialog box, browse to and select the image file you want to insert.

Tip #189

To preview the image, click the down arrow next to the Views button and choose Preview.

---

5. Click Insert.

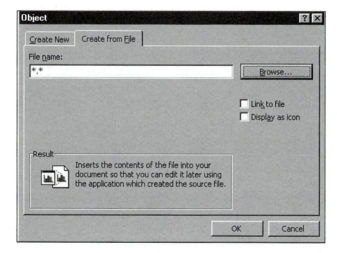

Figure 12.25
Using the Create from File tab to insert an image as an object.

Note

Word also gives you the option of displaying an icon in place of the object; the default icon corresponds to the program your computer uses to edit the object. To display an icon in place of an image, click the Display as Icon check box in the Create from File tab of the Object dialog box. When you do, the Change Icon button appears; you can click this button to select a different icon for your image.

INSERTING CLIP ART FROM A SCANNER OR DIGITAL CAMERA

Word 2000 enables you to insert images directly from a scanner or digital camera, without using an additional applet such as Microsoft Photo Editor. To do so, Word utilizes the scanner or digital camera drivers you've already installed. To place a picture from a scanner or digital camera, follow these steps:

1. Place your insertion point in the document where you want the image to appear.

2. Make sure your scanner or digital camera is properly connected. If you're using a scanner, place the printed image on the scanner.

3. Choose Insert, Picture, From Scanner or Camera. The Insert Picture from Scanner or Camera dialog box appears (see Figure 12.26).

4. If you have more than one scanner and/or digital camera available, choose the source from the Device drop-down box.

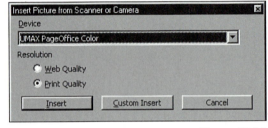

Figure 12.26

5. If you intend to use your scanned image on a Web or intranet site, choose Web Quality. Word scans your image at a lower resolution that is usually sufficient for onscreen display. If you plan to use the image in a printed document, use Print Quality. Word scans the image at higher resolution, creating a significantly larger file.

6. Click Insert. Word captures the image and places it in your document.

Caution

Word only works with scanners and digital cameras that support the industry-standard TWAIN interface. In addition, you must install the device's driver, connect the device, and turn it on before using Word's Insert Picture from Scanner or Camera feature.

Tip #190

If you plan to edit the document later, using an image editor such as Microsoft PhotoDraw 2000 or Adobe Photoshop, choose Print Quality. This gives you a higher quality image to start with, and you can use the image editor to prepare a lower-resolution Web file later, after you've refined the image.

CUSTOMIZING SCANNER OR DIGITAL CAMERA SETTINGS

The Web Quality and Print Quality options are "lowest-common-denominator" options that take care of many of your basic image capture needs. But if you need more precise settings, you can access your own scanner or digital camera's driver and use whatever settings are available there.

To do so, follow steps 1–4 in the preceding section. Then, with the Insert Picture from Scanner or Camera dialog box open, click <u>C</u>ustom Insert. Your device's settings dialog box opens; this dialog box will vary depending on the scanner or camera you own. Establish your settings there and click Scan (or OK).

EDITING CLIP ART TO SERVE YOUR NEEDS

Regardless of how you've inserted images into your documents, you may need to modify them to serve your needs more effectively.

At the least, you'll probably need to reposition and perhaps resize your clip art to integrate it into your document. However, you can do much more. Graphics can be *cropped*, brightened, recolored, and even redrawn. You can also adjust how graphics work with other page elements. The following sections teach you all you need to know to edit the graphics you insert into Word documents.

UNDERSTANDING VECTOR AND BITMAPPED GRAPHICS

To better understand the ways in which graphics can (and cannot) be edited, it helps to understand the difference between two types of graphics files: vector and bitmap.

A *vector-based graphic* is composed of points and lines that are described in space, for example, "a perfect circle with a diameter of one inch, filled with a bright yellow color and outlined with a 1-point wide black solid line." Complex vector-based drawings are composed of layers and layers of such objects and lines.

Because the graphic is described rather than exactly plotted (like the bitmapped image), it is said to be *scalable*—which means that it can be resized without losing quality. For example, if the image described above were edited to be double its original size, the description of the elements would likewise double, such as: "a perfect circle with a diameter of two inches, filled with a bright yellow color and outlined with a 2-point wide black solid line." This ensures that the image's quality remains constant despite the rescaling.

Also, in most cases, these layers and lines can be edited—so you can make minor or major adjustments to the content of an image. For example, if a piece of clip art contains a photo of a dog with a veterinarian, you may be able to edit out the veterinarian by removing the lines and fills in the image that comprise the veterinarian.

→ For more information about editing vector-based clip art, **see** Chapter 13, "Drawing in Word," **p. 401**.

Typical vector file types include Windows Metafiles (WMF), Computer Graphics Metafiles (CGM), CorelDRAW (CDR), and Encapsulated PostScript (EPS). Vector files are produced by programs such as Adobe Illustrator, CorelDRAW, and Microsoft Draw.

Bitmap images, on the other hand, are display-resolution dependent. Bitmapped images are made up of a multitude of colored dots (commonly called pixels). When you resize or zoom in on a bitmapped image, each pixel is magnified and the overall picture is blurred, if not made unrecognizable. The effect is similar to a tile mosaic where each tile is one color—if

PART

III

CH

12

you stand too close, you can't see the whole picture. However, bitmapped images can contain millions more colors than vector-based images and the smooth shading of color can fool the eye into perceiving additional resolution.

Bitmap images are typically used for photographs and background images. The main file types are Windows bitmap (BMP), Graphics Interchange Format (GIF), and Joint Photographic Experts Group (JPG). GIF and JPG are the two most commonly used formats on the Web, so if you copy a graphic from a Web site, it's likely to be in one of these two bitmap formats.

POSITIONING AND SIZING IMAGES

Before you insert an image, you position your insertion point where you want the image to appear. Still, it's likely that you'll have to make adjustments to the image's size or position after it is placed in your document. The next few sections show you how.

RESIZING IMAGES USING SIZING HANDLES

The easiest way to resize an image is by dragging its edges to match the size and shape you want. To do so, click the image once to select it. A box appears around the image with eight sizing handles (see Figure 12.27). The different handles have different effects:

- Dragging the corner handles resizes your image diagonally, making it wider and taller (or narrower and shorter) at the same time. By default, the aspect ratio of the image remains the same—so the image doesn't appear oddly stretched in any direction.

- Dragging the middle handles resizes the object only vertically (using just the top and bottom handles) or horizontally (using the handles on the side). Of course, this does change the aspect ratio—stretching the image out of its original proportion.

Figure 12.27
Selecting and dragging an image.

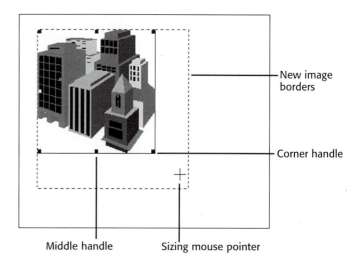

New image borders

Corner handle

Middle handle   Sizing mouse pointer

Tip #191

Generally, vector graphics look better after being enlarged or stretched than do bitmap graphics; with bitmaps, the stretching can introduce unattractive roughness into the image.

Note

The size of the image Word inserts depends on the size of the original image. For example, if your original image is 200 pixels high and 300 pixels wide, the inserted image will also be 200×300 pixels. Often, this means you will want to reduce the size of the image once you've inserted it, to accommodate text and graphics in a layout that gives appropriate importance to each.

RESIZING IMAGES PRECISELY, USING FORMAT, PICTURE

Word also has a way for you to resize an image more precisely than you can by dragging its edges by hand. If you want to resize an image while retaining all its contents, use the Size tab of the Format Picture dialog box.

Note

If you want to resize an image by cutting out (cropping) parts of it, see the section later in this chapter, "Cropping an Image."

To resize an image precisely, right-click on the image and choose Format Picture from the shortcut menu. Next, click the Size tab (see Figure 12.28).

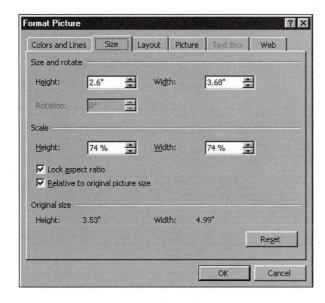

Figure 12.28
Resizing images through the Size tab of the Format Picture dialog box.

In the Height scroll box (in the Size and Rotate area), enter the exact height you want the picture to be. When you do so, the value in the Width scroll box changes as well. In other words, by default, Word retains the picture's aspect ratio—its proportions.

Alternatively, you can resize an image by scaling it up or down. To do so, enter a new value in the Height scroll box in the Scale area. Again, the value in the accompanying Width box changes proportionally.

If you want to stretch an image out of proportion, clear the Lock Aspect Ratio check box before you make changes in the height or width scroll boxes.

Tip #192

Even if the Lock Aspect Ratio check box is cleared, you can still use sizing handles to stretch an image proportionally if you need to do so. Select the image, press and hold the Shift key, and drag the corner sizing handles. Word resizes the image proportionally as you drag its borders. Release the mouse pointer; then release the Shift key.

Note

Notice that the Rotation scroll box is grayed out. Rotation is available for only those images you create in Word using Word's AutoShape and WordArt drawing tools. These tools are covered in Chapter 13, "Drawing in Word."

WRAPPING TEXT AROUND YOUR IMAGES

After you've placed an image in your document, and sized it appropriately, the next thing to control is how text flows around that image. In Word, this is called *text wrapping*.

In Word 2000, pictures are placed "in line with text" by default. That means a picture, no matter how large, acts just like any other character of text you might insert. Figure 12.29 shows how this works.

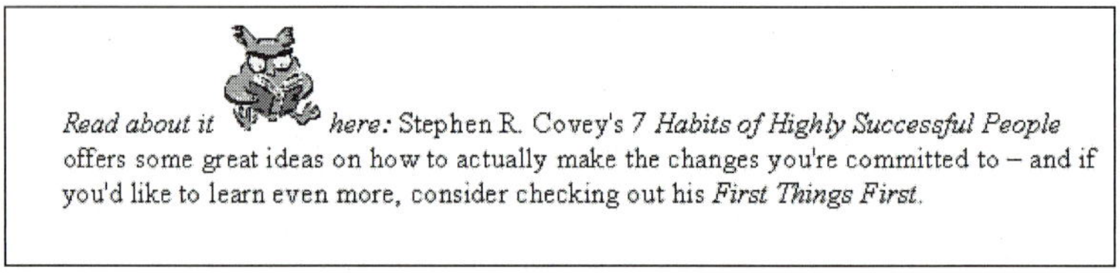

Figure 12.29
Graphics placed "inline," such as this one, are placed just as if they were characters in text.

Read about it ✎ here: Stephen R. Covey's *7 Habits of Highly Successful People* offers some great ideas on how to actually make the changes you're committed to – and if you'd like to learn even more, consider checking out his *First Things First*.

Note

This is a change from Word 97's default "float over text" behavior, which many users found confusing.

You can access Word's most widely used wrapping alternatives by clicking the Text Wrapping button on the Picture toolbar (see Figure 12.30).

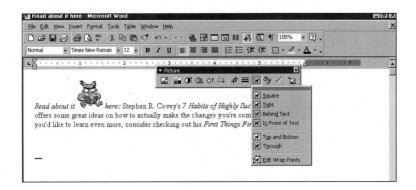

Figure 12.30
Setting wrapping with the Text Wrapping toolbar button.

The options that appear in the Text Wrapping toolbar work as follows:

- **Square.** This option wraps text to the left and right of the bounding box that contains the picture. If the picture is inserted at the left margin, Square wraps to the right only.

- **Tight.** This option wraps text so that it follows the left and right edges of the actual image, not just the bounding box.

- **Behind Text.** Choosing this option enables text to be superimposed on the picture. This is the setting normally used with watermarks.

- **In Front of Text.** With this option selected, the picture is superimposed on top of the text. With many graphics, this makes the text unreadable. In other cases, such as GIFs with transparent backgrounds or text created with WordArt, the text can still show through. Use this option sparingly, however, because even when the text is visible, it is often difficult to read.

- **Top and Bottom.** Choosing this option prevents text from wrapping around the image; the text instead jumps from above the image to below it.

- **Through.** Same as Tight, but without a fixed outer wrapping boundary. This option lets text fill gaps in the image (if there are any). Use Edit Wrap Points to allow more or less text in each gap.

- **Edit Wrap Points.** This enables you to wrap text around any corner or edge of an image, as discussed in the next section.

SETTING PRECISE TEXT WRAPPING WITH EDIT WRAP POINTS

The final text wrapping option available through the Text Wrapping button is called Edit Wrap Points. This option enables you to control precisely where text wraps to refine your page layout—for example, to accommodate a long word that would otherwise wrap oddly. If you click Edit Wrap Points, all the edges of the image are highlighted. Figure 12.31 shows the wrap points in a vector image. (In a bitmap image, the only wrap points are the edges of the bounding box.)

PART
III

CH
12

Figure 12.31
Dragging wrap points to customize the way text wraps around and through an image.

Wrap point

Dragging a wrap point

When wrap points are displayed, you can click and drag any small square to adjust the edge of the image Word recognizes for text wrapping. When you're finished editing wrap points, click outside the image to deselect it.

Note

Changes you make to Edit Wrap Points don't change the actual content of the image.

SETTING TEXT WRAPPING FROM THE FORMAT PICTURE DIALOG BOX

Word's "one-click" toolbar options are all you need in most cases. But you can get even more control through the Layout tab of the Format Picture dialog box (see Figure 12.32). Select your image, right-click and choose Format Picture from the shortcut menu, and click the Layout tab.

Figure 12.32
Adjusting wrapping styles and horizontal alignment.

Once you've displayed the Layout tab, follow these steps to control the layout of your image:

1. Choose the wrapping style you want: In Line with Text (the default setting), Square, Tight, Behind Text, or In Front of Text.

2. If you choose a setting other than In Line with Text, you can also choose where you want the text to wrap: to the Left, Center, Right, or Other.

3. For even more control, click Advanced to display the Advanced Layout dialog box. There, in the Text Wrapping tab, you can control whether text wraps on both sides of your image and exactly how far from the image the text appears.

4. If you want to control any of the following, work from the Picture Position tab:
   - The alignment of your image
   - How images fit into a book layout (for example, whether they always appear nearest the spine or the edge of the page)
   - The absolute position of an image on a page
   - Whether images should move when text moves

CROPPING AN IMAGE

Cropping means cutting away a portion of an image. Images are typically cropped to eliminate extraneous elements, to focus the reader's attention on a particular area, or simply to make the graphic fit on a page. When you use Word 2000's cropping tools, you actually hide part of the image you're cropping, which means you can restore it later if need be.

Word provides two ways to crop an image: through the Crop tool and through the Format Picture dialog box. To use the Crop tool, first display the Picture toolbar. To do so, select the image. If the Picture toolbar doesn't appear, choose View, Toolbars, Picture (see Figure 12.33).

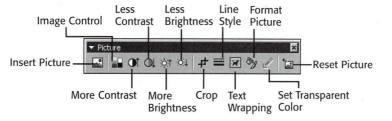

Figure 12.33
Display the Pciture toolbar to show Word's Picture tools.

After the Picture toolbar is displayed, click on the image to select it. Next, click the Crop button on the Picture toolbar. Then, click and drag any sizing handle on the edges of the image. The handles enlarge or shrink the borders of the image just as they do with resizing.

Figure 12.34 shows a picture being cropped.

Figure 12.34
Cropping can hide unwanted sections of a graphic.

To reveal a cropped section of a picture, reverse the process. Follow these steps:

1. Select the graphic.

2. Click the Crop tool from the Picture toolbar.

3. Click a sizing handle and drag away from the picture to "uncrop" the image, displaying the parts of the image that were hidden when it was originally cropped.

Tip #193
> Just as you can precisely resize an image using the Format Picture dialog box, you can crop an image "by the numbers." Select your image and then choose Format, Picture to open the dialog box. Click the Picture tab. In the Crop From section, change the values in the Left, Right, Top, and/or Bottom boxes.

RECOLORING WHOLE IMAGES

Most clip art today is produced in color. Word 2000 enables you to convert any image from full color to a *grayscale* image consisting of levels of gray, or to straight black and white. You can also adjust the brightness and the contrast of an image to de-emphasize it or make it stand out even more. Finally, Word includes a default watermark setting that converts your picture to one that works well behind text. Change your image in any of these ways:

1. Click the image to select it.

2. Display the Picture toolbar if it isn't already displayed.

3. Click the Image Control button.

4. Make a choice from the drop-down list that appears. Word eliminates or softens the colors in your picture, displaying it as you've requested:

   - Automatic uses the same colors as your original image. Use it to reset the colors, if necessary.

   - Grayscale converts colors to their gray equivalent, preserving relative contrast and brightness.

- Black & White changes multicolored images to two colors. It is useful for creating high-contrast line art.
- Watermark sets Brightness to 85% and the Contrast to 15%. This usually results in an image that is visible, but which can underlie text without interfering with its legibility.

Note

The same settings are available through the Color drop-down box in the Picture tab of the Format Picture dialog box.

Figure 12.35 shows the effect of converting a colored graphic with the Watermark setting.

Tip #194

To create a true watermark, which always appears behind the text in the document, also click the Text Wrapping button on the Picture toolbar and choose Behind Text. You learned about text wrapping options earlier in this chapter, in the "Wrapping Text Around Your Images" section.

Figure 12.35
A watermark is a faded version of a graphic, which enables you to super-impose legible text over it.

PART
III

CH
12

Caution

Watermarks don't automatically appear on every page in your document. To place a watermark on every page, not just the current page, you must insert the watermark image in your header or footer.

CONTROLLING IMAGE BRIGHTNESS AND CONTRAST

You may sometimes wish to brighten or darken an image, or adjust its contrast. You can do so from the Picture toolbar; or if you need more precise control, you can use the Format Picture dialog box. First, select the image you want to adjust.

 To brighten the image, click the More Brightness button, or to darken the image, click the Less Brightness button. Each time you click the button, Word adjusts the image's brightness by 3%.

 To sharpen the image's contrast, click the More Contrast button, or to reduce the contrast, click the Less Contrast button. Each time you click the button, Word adjusts the image's contrast by 3%.

 If you need more precise control, select the image and click Format Picture. In the Picture tab, enter precise values in the Brightness or Contrast scroll boxes. Click OK to see the results.

MINIMIZING GRAPHICS FILE SIZE

How big can a Word document with graphics be? The answer is "very." Some images, especially high-resolution bitmapped photographs, can be over a megabyte by themselves. It's easy to imagine how large a file with many images can get. This can be a problem: Larger files tend to run more slowly, and less reliably. One way to keep file sizes manageable is to include links to graphics, rather than graphics themselves. By linking, you ensure that updates to the image in its source program are reflected in your Word document.

To insert a link to a picture rather than the picture itself, follow these steps. Choose Insert, Picture, From File; then browse to and select the picture you want. Click the drop-down arrow next to the Insert button, and click Link to File.

ADDING ALTERNATIVE TEXT TO YOUR IMAGE

If you're creating Web pages, you should always include alternative text that can appear in place of images. Alternative text appears in the following circumstances:

- When a Web page is displayed in a browser with images turned off (to increase speed)
- When a Web page is displayed in a browser customized for an individual with a visual disability (the alternative text can be read aloud by the computer, whereas an image cannot)
- When an image cannot be accessed from the Web server
- In Internet Explorer, as a ScreenTip that can be used to explain an image

To create alternative text, right-click on an image, choose Format Picture from the shortcut menu, and click the Web tab. The Web tab of the Format Picture dialog box appears (see Figure 12.36).

Figure 12.36
Entering alternative text for an image included on a Web page.

In the Web tab's Alternative Text box, enter the descriptive text. Though the dialog box is quite large, it's usually best to keep the text as concise as possible. If the alternative text is associated with a navigation button or other graphical element, make sure readers know what clicking the button will do. When you're finished, click OK.

INTRODUCING WORDART

Clip art that combines text and graphics falls into a special category. Many logos include the name of a company or a special phrase and it's obviously impossible to find ordinary clip art that matches your company's name or trademarked tag line. Word provides a wonderful program for creating fancy text objects: WordArt.

With WordArt your text can have added dimension, color, and style. Best of all, your WordArt creation is completely customizable—even if you want to change the words you've inserted. WordArt can also be used to generate key words to highlight a particular section of a document, or to create a headline in a brochure, such as "Sale!" or "New!"

Fancy WordArt text objects are ideal for custom uses such as newsletter banners. However, it's best to use them sparingly so that you can achieve maximum impact without compromising the readability of your document.

Note

WordArt objects work much like other objects, such as drawing objects. You can resize them by selecting them and dragging their resizing handles; you can also drag them to new locations.

Unfortunately, they also have the drawbacks of other Word objects: They cannot be checked for spelling, nor can their text be located through Find and Replace.

INSERTING A WORDART OBJECT

To create a WordArt object, follow these steps:

1. Choose Insert, Picture, WordArt. The WordArt Gallery appears (see Figure 12.37).

Figure 12.37
The WordArt Gallery offers 30 customizable preset designs.

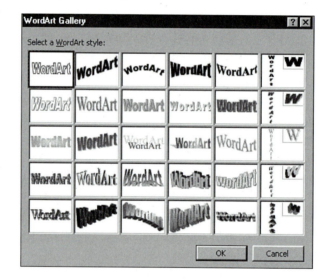

2. Double-click any of the 30 preset designs. The Edit WordArt Text dialog box opens (see Figure 12.38).

3. Type in your text to replace the "Your Text Here" phrase.

4. Make any font changes you want, and click OK. WordArt creates your object with sizing handles around it and opens the WordArt toolbar.

When you're finished, you can click outside of the WordArt object to return to the regular document. Later, you can change the text in your WordArt object by double-clicking it to reopen the Edit WordArt Text dialog box.

Tip #195

If you select a word or phrase prior to starting the WordArt process, your text automatically appears in the Edit WordArt Text dialog box.

Figure 12.38
Editing the text that will appear in your WordArt object.

MODIFYING YOUR WORDART OBJECT

It's easy to modify a WordArt object after you've created it. You can either try different pre-set effects through the WordArt Gallery or combine a preset with one of 40 different shapes. Your new shape can then be stretched, resized, and rotated. Experimentation with the various shapes is the best way to understand what generates the best look for your particular WordArt object. Often, trying to achieve one effect leads you to a completely unexpected, but attractive, result.

To modify your WordArt object, first select it. This typically displays the WordArt toolbar (see Figure 12.39); if the toolbar doesn't appear, choose View, Toolbars, WordArt.

CHANGING WORDART CONTENT AND STYLING

 If you're not satisfied with the content or the appearance of the WordArt image you already have, you can use the WordArt toolbar to change it entirely. Click the Edit Text button to return to the Edit WordArt Text dialog box and change your text, or click the WordArt Gallery button to choose a different pre-styled effect.

ADJUSTING THE SHAPE OF A WORDART OBJECT

If you are reasonably satisfied with your WordArt image, you can use the WordArt toolbar to make adjustments to get exactly the effect you're looking for.

 For instance, to change the shape into which your WordArt object is warped, select your WordArt object; then click the WordArt Shape button (see Figure 12.40), and select one of the 40 available shapes.

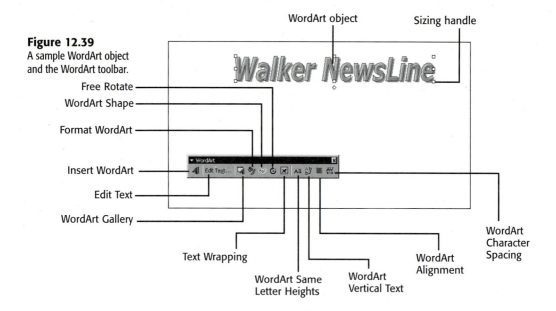

Figure 12.39
A sample WordArt object and the WordArt toolbar.

WordArt object

Sizing handle

Free Rotate

WordArt Shape

Format WordArt

Insert WordArt

Edit Text

WordArt Gallery

Text Wrapping

WordArt Same Letter Heights

WordArt Vertical Text

WordArt Alignment

WordArt Character Spacing

Figure 12.40
Click the WordArt Shape button to choose from 40 shapes for your text.

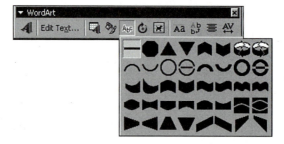

ROTATING A WORDART OBJECT

You can also rotate WordArt objects to any angle you wish. Click the Free Rotate toolbar button; the object's selection handles change to green circles, and your mouse pointer changes to resemble the Free Rotate icon (see Figure 12.41). Click on a selection handle, and drag the object to the angle you want. When you're satisfied, click the Free Rotate button again to finish.

Caution

Free Rotation stays on until you click the Free Rotation button again.

Figure 12.41
Rotating a WordArt image.

USING VERTICAL TEXT IN A WORDART OBJECT

 WordArt offers several options for adjusting text. For example, you can stack letters on top of each other by clicking the WordArt Vertical Text button (see Figure 12.42).

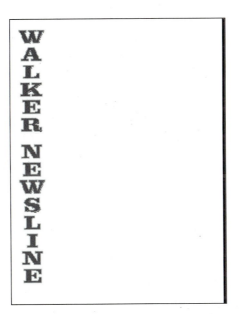

Figure 12.42
Stacking the text in a WordArt image.

PART
III

CH
12

Tip #196   You can create columns of text in a WordArt object. When you enter the text for your WordArt object, place a paragraph mark at the end of each word or phrase you want in a separate row. Then, after you display the WordArt object, click the Vertical Text button.

USING WORDART'S SAME LETTER HEIGHTS OPTION

 You can also click WordArt's Same Letter Heights to make your lowercase letters as large as your capital letters.

Tip #197

> The Same Letter Heights tool, like all the WordArt toolbar formatting options, affects the entire WordArt object and can't be selectively applied to one word or a part of a phrase. To achieve that result, you need to create two (or more) WordArt objects, applying the Same Letter Heights formatting to only the object or objects you wish. If you then want to group the objects together so you can treat them as a single object, click all the objects by using Select Objects from the Drawing toolbar. Finally, click the Draw button and then the Group button.

ALIGNING OR STRETCHING YOUR WORDART TEXT

You can align or stretch your text using the options that display when you click the WordArt Alignment button (see Figure 12.43). Table 12.1 takes a closer look at the options available to you.

Figure 12.43
Aligning the text in a WordArt image.

TABLE 12.1   WORDART ALIGNMENT OPTIONS

Button	Name	Description
	Left Align	Paragraphs are aligned to the left edge of bounding box.
	Center	Paragraphs are centered in bounding box.
	Right Align	Paragraphs are aligned to the right edge of bounding box.
	Word Justify	Word justifies paragraphs to the edges of the bounding box by stretching the spaces between words. If there is only one word on a line, the letters are spaced out equally.
	Letter Justify	Word justifies paragraphs to the edges of the bounding box by spacing the letters and the spaces between words equally. Single-word lines are treated the same as with Word Justify.
	Stretch Justify	Word justifies paragraphs to the edges of the bounding box by stretching the letters and the spaces between words equally.

ADJUSTING LETTER SPACING IN WORDART TEXT

As with regular Word text, you can tighten or loosen the letter spacing of text in WordArt objects. Normal spacing is 100%; condensed or tighter spacing is less, and expanded or looser spacing is more.

With regular text, letter spacing moves the letters closer or farther apart. WordArt works differently. Here, letter spacing narrows or widens the characters themselves.

 To alter a WordArt object's spacing, click the WordArt Character Spacing button. WordArt provides five preset values (Very Tight, Tight, Normal, Loose, and Very Loose) as well as a Custom box. You can also fit characters such as "A" and "V" more tightly together by enabling the Kern Character Pairs. Figure 12.44 contrasts the two preset extremes, Very Tight and Very Loose.

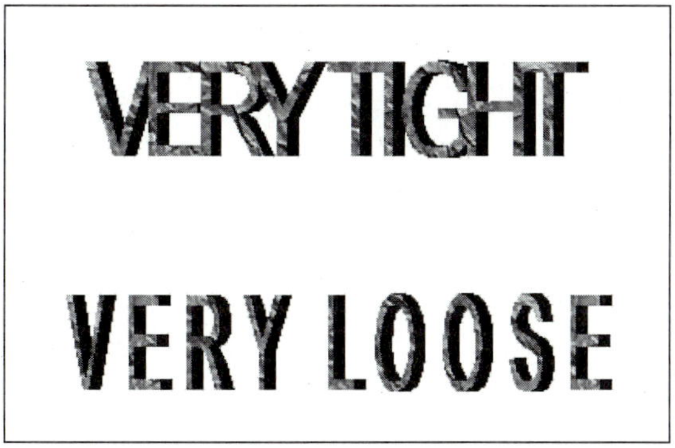

Figure 12.44
Controlling the letter spacing of text in a WordArt image.

ADJUSTING A WORDART OBJECT WITH THE ADJUSTMENT HANDLE

Besides the square sizing handles that accompany most Word objects, WordArt objects also have additional adjustment handles that appear as yellow diamonds (refer to Figure 12.39). These adjustment handles control the intensity of the effect induced on a WordArt shape.

Depending on the form of the shape, dragging an adjustment handle may have different effects. For example, in a shape with a curved bottom, the adjustment handle alters the degree of the curve. In a shape that fades at the right, the adjustment handle moves the vanishing point.

USING THE FORMAT WORDART DIALOG BOX

Much like other Word objects, WordArt objects have a Formatting dialog box that brings together many of their formatting options (see Figure 12.45). To view this dialog box, select the object and click Format WordArt on the WordArt toolbar (or right-click on the object and choose Format WordArt from the shortcut menu).

PART
III

CH
12

Figure 12.45
Using the Format
WordArt dialog box.

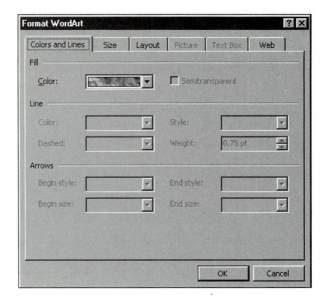

Many of the elements in this dialog box, such as Size and Layout, are similar to those you learned about in the discussion of the Format Picture dialog box, earlier in this chapter. Two options are worth pointing out, however:

- In the Colors and Lines tab, you can change the fill color, line color, and line weight of your WordArt object.
- In the Web tab, Word automatically inserts a copy of the same text that appears in your WordArt object, so viewers can see the text even if they cannot see the formatting.

TROUBLESHOOTING

WHAT TO DO WHEN WORD DOESN'T RECOGNIZE THE FILE TYPE YOU'VE TRIED TO IMPORT

Make sure that you have installed the necessary graphics filter. The easiest way to do this is to choose Insert, Picture, From File to open the Insert Picture dialog box. Next check the list of filters in the Files of Type box. If the filter you need is not listed, run Setup again and install the filters you need.

If the file you need is not supplied by Microsoft, but you can still open it with another graphics program, you have two choices. First, after opening the file in a drawing program, select the graphic, copy it, and paste it into your Word document. The graphic becomes a Windows metafile (.wmf). If you later resave the Word document as a Web page, the graphic is resaved as a JPG.

Alternatively, open your image file in the program that created it, copy it to the Clipboard, switch to Word, and choose Edit, Paste Special. Then choose the format in which you want the file to be pasted; for example, choose the original format so the original drawing program can continue to edit the image.

Yet another option is to open the file in another graphics program, and then resave it in a format that can be imported into Word.

WHAT TO DO WHEN A FILE THAT SHOULD CONTAIN GRAPHICS DISPLAYS ONLY TEXT

First, check the View tab of the Options dialog box—the Picture Placeholders options might be enabled. When enabled, Picture Placeholders shows all graphics as an empty box; this is intended to speed up the display for graphic-intensive documents. Choose Tools, Options, and click the View tab. If the Picture Placeholders box is checked, click to clear it. While you're on the Options dialog box View tab, double-check the Drawings check box. If this is not selected, you won't see any of the drawing objects—including text boxes. To see all your graphics, check the Drawings box and clear the Picture Placeholders one.

If this doesn't work, check whether the images were incorporated in your document as links. If so, it's possible that the document or linked images have been moved, breaking the links. Choose Edit, Links; then click the Change Source button. Browse to the new location of the linked files, select them, and click Open.

PART

III

CH

12

CHAPTER **13**

DRAWING IN WORD

In this chapter

When to Use Word's Drawing Tools—And When Not To

In the preceding chapter, you learned how to import graphics that already exist into Word. But what if the graphic you want doesn't exist? Often, you can create it yourself, using Word's drawing tools.

It's helpful to understand what Word's drawing tools can do well—and what they can't do well. In the following scenarios, Word's drawing tools can be invaluable:

- When you need to create a simple flowchart or organizational chart (But also keep in mind that Word and Office also come with Microsoft Organization Chart 2.0, an applet designed specifically for creating organizational charts.)

- When you need to annotate text or other elements in your document with arrows, lines, or *callouts*

- When you need starbursts and other shapes for an advertisement or flier

- When you need to create a simple room or office design with prefabricated shapes

- When you need to edit a vector image you already have (such as a WMF clip art file), especially to delete an element you don't want to include

- When you need to create an image that can be built from simple, regular shapes such as rectangles and circles

In short, Word's drawing tools are very well-suited for solving a wide variety of specific business problems. But they're less well-suited for projects where superb aesthetics are required, such as the following:

- When you need to create a complex freehand illustration, such as a sketch of a scene or a person

- When you need to create an image with absolutely precise coloring (Word gives you quite a bit of flexibility, but what you see onscreen may not be precisely what you get in a printed document—Word isn't designed to perform professional-quality color matching.)

- When you need to create a "painted" bitmapped drawing (However, as you'll see, Word can save its line-and-fill drawings to GIF or JPG bitmap formats for use on the Web.)

Tip #198

Chances are, you already own at least two programs for working with bitmapped images:
- Microsoft Paint, which comes with Windows 95, 98, and NT.
- Microsoft Photo Editor, which comes with Word and Office 2000.
- If you have Office 2000 Premium Edition, you also have the new PhotoDraw 2000.

USING WORD 2000'S DRAWING TOOLBAR

To draw in Word, first display the Drawing toolbar. To do so, either click the Drawing button on the Standard toolbar or choose <u>V</u>iew, <u>T</u>oolbars, Drawing. The Drawing toolbar appears at the bottom of the Word application window (see Figure 13.1).

Figure 13.1
The Drawing toolbar centralizes all of Word's tools for drawing objects.

The Drawing toolbar brings together all of Word's tools for drawing. Some of these tools—such as callouts—are valuable even if you never create an image from scratch. Table 13.1 presents an overview of each button and what it does.

TABLE 13.1   DRAWING TOOLBAR FEATURES

Button	Name	Description
Draw ▾ ⇱ ⟳	Draw	Contains editing controls for manipulating drawing objects.
⇱	Select Objects	Enables the selection of one or more drawing objects.
⟳	Free Rotate	Enables click-and-drag rotation of any drawing object.
AutoShapes ▾	AutoShapes	Contains the library of automatic shapes, including lines, basic shapes, block arrows, flowchart elements, stars and banners, and callouts.
＼	Line	Enables you to click and drag a line.
↘	Arrow	Enables you to click and drag an arrow.
▭	Rectangle	Enables you to click and drag a rectangle.
◯	Oval	Enables you to click and drag an oval.
▤	Text Box	Enables you to click and drag out a text box.
𝐀	WordArt	Starts the creation of a fancy text object.

continues

TABLE 13.1 CONTINUED

Button	Name	Description
	Insert Clip Art	Displays the Clip Gallery for inserting clip art.
	Fill Color	Controls the color, pattern, or effect inside a drawing object.
	Line Color	Controls the color, pattern, or effect of a drawing object's border.
	Font Color	Controls the color of selected text.
	Line Style	Enables quick formatting for a line's thickness and style.
	Dash Style	Enables quick formatting for a line's appearance.
	Arrow Style	Enables quick selection from a variety o arrowhead styles.
	Shadow	Controls shadow appearance for any drawing object.
	3D	Controls the 3D appearance for any drawing object.

→ The WordArt and Text Box features are not discussed in this chapter, but you can find information about them in Chapter 12 and Chapter 14, respectively.

UNDERSTANDING HOW WORD DRAWINGS WORK

Before you start working with Word's drawing tools, it helps to understand how Word drawings work.

Word drawings are vector drawings, which means that they are composed of lines and shapes. These lines and shapes, which Word calls *drawing objects*, can be edited separately or grouped to be edited together. They can also be layered, so that some components of your drawing appear "on top of" others. You'll learn how to use the grouping and layering tools later in the chapter; for now, it's just important to know they exist.

→ For more information about vector drawings and how they compare to bitmapped drawings, **see** "Understanding Vector and Bitmapped Graphics," **p. 381**.

What does it mean to you that Word drawing objects are made of lines and shapes? For one thing, it means you can often edit drawings to remove elements you don't need, and add elements you do want. Take a look at Figure 13.2, a Windows Metafile taken directly from Office 2000's clip art library. This would be a great image for a home inspector's ad. But, because it's layered, you can get rid of the house, leaving just the detective. And that opens up all kinds of possibilities, as shown in Figure 13.3.

Figure 13.2
A sample image, made up of many objects and layers.

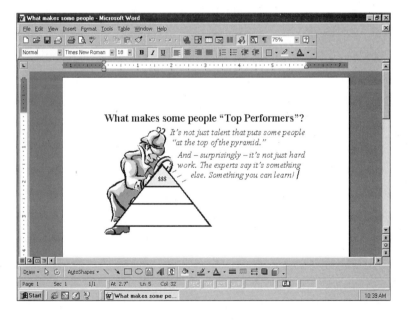

Figure 13.3
How the image might be edited for another use.

Now that you have a taste for how Word's drawing tools work and what you can do with them, it's time to start actually using them.

DRAWING LINES AND OTHER BASIC SHAPES

The simplest objects of a Word drawing are lines and basic shapes. You'll often find simple elements such as these at the heart of even complex drawings. In the next few sections, you'll learn how to create these graphical elements using Word's drawing tools.

DRAWING A STRAIGHT LINE

To draw a straight line in Word, click on the Line button on the Drawing toolbar; the mouse pointer changes to crosshairs. Next, click in the editing window where you want to begin the line, and drag the mouse pointer to where you want the line to end (see Figure 13.4). Release the mouse pointer, and a line appears selected in your document.

Figure 13.4
Dragging the mouse pointer to draw a line.

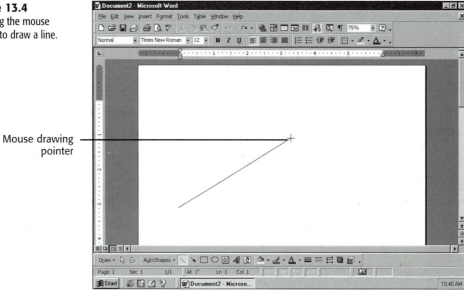

Mouse drawing pointer

Note

If you aren't in Print Layout view, Word switches you there when you click the drawing tool you want to use.

CHANGING THE APPEARANCE OF A LINE YOU'VE DRAWN

After you've created a line, you may want to make adjustments to it. For example, you may want it to be thicker or narrower than Word's default 3/4-point line. Or you may want a dotted line rather than Word's default solid line. To change a solid line to a dotted or dashed line, select it by clicking on it. Then, click the Dash Style button on the Drawing toolbar (see Figure 13.5).

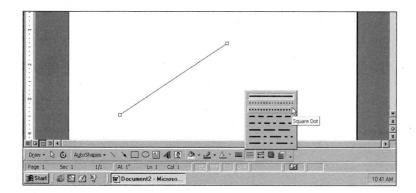

Figure 13.5
Choosing a dotted or dashed line using the Dash Style button.

 To change the thickness of a line, select the line and click the Line Style button (see Figure 13.6).

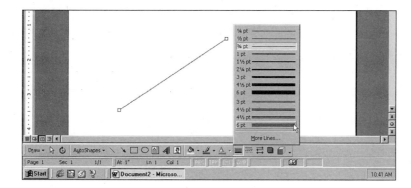

Figure 13.6
Choosing a thicker or narrower line using the Line Style button.

If none of Word's built-in line styles suffice, click More Lines to display the Format AutoShape dialog box (see Figure 13.7).

Each type of Word shape has its own Format AutoShape dialog box, where you can control elements such as color, thickness, size, and *text wrapping*. Format AutoShape dialog boxes are very much like the Format Picture dialog boxes you learned about in Chapter 12, "Getting Images into Your Documents." A few points about the Colors and Lines tab are especially worth mentioning:

- From the Color drop-down box, you can choose one of 40 built-in colors; click More Colors to choose a custom color, or choose Patterned Lines to select a pattern for your line or arrow.

- From the Weight text box, you can set your line to be as thick or as narrow as you wish. If you use the built-in spin controls, you can set the weight in increments of 0.25 points. If you enter the value directly, you can use increments of 0.01 points.

- The Style drop-down box contains the same options as the Line Style button on the Drawing toolbar. The Dashed drop-down box contains the same options as the Dash Style button on the Drawing toolbar.

- You can use the Size tab of the Format AutoShape dialog box to set an exact height, width, and angle of rotation for your line or shape.

- In the Web tab, you can type alternative text that appears on Web pages when your shape cannot be displayed.

Figure 13.7
The Colors and Lines tab of the Format AutoShape dialog box.

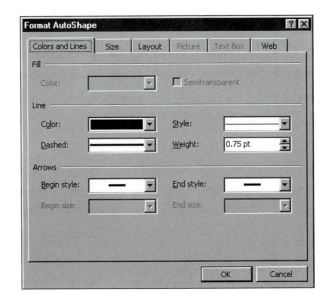

> **Note**
>
> The dialog box shown in Figure 13.7 appears whether you're working with a line or an arrow.

→ For more information about the Format Picture dialog box, **see** "Resizing Images Precisely, Using Format, Picture," **p. 383** (chapter 12); "Setting Text Wrapping from the Format Picture Dialog Box," **p. 386**; and "Adding Alternative Text to Your Image," **p. 390**.

DRAWING ARROWS

You've already learned how to draw a line. Wouldn't it be neat if that line had an arrow at the end of it? Then you could draw a pointer to anything you wanted.

 To insert Word's default arrow, click the Arrow button on the Drawing toolbar; the mouse pointer changes to crosshairs. Click where you want the arrow's "tail" to begin, then drag it to where you want its "arrowhead" to appear, and release the mouse pointer.

Sometimes, you may want to format your arrow differently. For example, Word's default arrow may not be readable if it points into a dark background. Or you may want an arrow that points in both directions, to emphasize that two elements on your page are connected.

Word provides a library of arrows from which to choose, and if these aren't enough, you can create your own. To use one of Word's built-in arrows, first insert either an arrow or line. (You can turn a line into an arrow following the same steps for changing an arrow.) Next, with the arrow selected, click the Arrow Style button (see Figure 13.8), and click on a style. The line or arrow is reformatted as you specified.

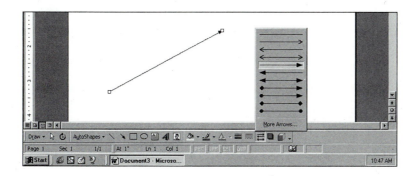

Figure 13.8
Displaying Word's basic arrow styles by clicking the Arrow Style button.

If none of Word's standard arrow styles meet your needs, choose More Arrows. The Format AutoShape dialog box appears (you saw this dialog box in Figure 13.7). Here, you can choose among a wide variety of thicknesses, styles, and sizes.

DRAWING RECTANGLES AND OVALS

Drawing basic squares, rectangles, and ovals works much the same way as drawing lines. Click the Rectangle or Oval button; then click in the document. Next, drag the mouse pointer to set the shape's borders. Release the pointer, and the shape appears in your document.

Tip #199	If you want an exact square or circle, click the Rectangle or Oval button and press Shift while you drag the mouse.
	You can also use the Shift key to make straight lines that are precisely horizontal, vertical, or diagonal. If you press Shift while you drag the Line tool, you're limited to increments of 15°.

Tip #200	To enter text in a shape such as a rectangle or oval, right-click on it and choose Add Text from the shortcut menu. This transforms the shape into a text box and displays a cursor inside it. You can then type or format the text.
	Text boxes are covered in more detail in Chapter 14, "Word Desktop Publishing."

PART

III

CH

13

Note

If you simply want to place a box around a block of text, don't bother with Word's drawing tools. Just select the text and click the Outside Border button on the Formatting toolbar.

AUTOSHAPES: WORD'S LIBRARY OF PREDRAWN SHAPES

Squares, circles, lines, and arrows are nice—but for those of us who aren't professional artists, they don't go nearly far enough. We need a whole library of shapes that arrive in our documents perfectly drawn—and Word delivers with seven categories of *AutoShapes*:

- Lines—This category includes Word's tools for creating freeform shapes and "scribbles."

- Basic Shapes—This category includes a collection of 2D and 3D shapes, lightning bolts, suns, moons, hearts, smiley faces, and other commonly used shapes.

- Block Arrows—This category includes a series of 2D and 3D arrows that are fancier than the arrows covered earlier, and can be filled with colors, patterns, or gradients.

- Flowchart—This category includes a collection of the 28 symbols most commonly used in building flowcharts.

- Stars and Banners—This category contains starbursts and other objects ideal for newspaper advertising and fliers.

- Callouts—This category combines text boxes and arrows, making it possible to annotate anything on a page in a single step.

- More AutoShapes—Word 2000 provides additional AutoShapes, scattered throughout its clip art library. When you choose this option, the Clip Gallery appears, displaying both AutoShapes and other images.

These AutoShapes can be resized, rotated, flipped, colored, and combined with other shapes (or your basic ovals and rectangles) to make more intricate shapes. Many AutoShapes have an adjustment handle you can use to change the most prominent feature of a shape— for example, you can enlarge or shrink the point of an arrow.

To use an AutoShape, click the AutoShapes button on the Drawing toolbar, choose the category you want to use (see Figure 13.9). Then, click in your document and drag the AutoShape to the proportions you want.

AutoShapes ▾

Tip #201

If you find yourself accessing one AutoShape menu repeatedly, you can "tear off" the menu and put it anywhere on your screen for immediate access.

Click AutoShapes from the Drawing toolbar. Select one of the categories, such as Lines or Callouts. Highlight the bar on the top of the submenu and that submenu becomes an independent toolbar that you can reposition (see Figure 13.10). When you finish working with the AutoShapes menu, click the Close button.

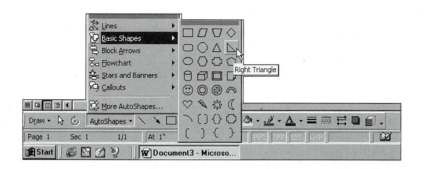

Figure 13.9
AutoShapes contain over 100 predefined graphic shapes.

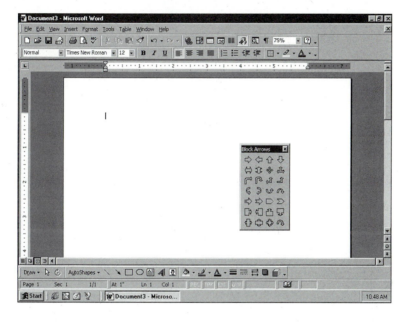

Figure 13.10
Creating a floating toolbar from one of the AutoShapes categories.

The following sections show you AutoShapes at work in a variety of applications, and give you a feel for how you might use them most effectively.

SETTING AUTOSHAPE DEFAULTS

Often, it can take some effort to get an AutoShape formatted just the way you want it. After you've done so, you may want all the AutoShapes you create to use the same formatting. If so, right-click on the shape you've formatted and choose Set AutoShape Defaults from the shortcut menu.

Caution

Setting AutoShape defaults changes the formatting of all the AutoShapes you create from now on—not just AutoShapes identical to the one you formatted. In other words, if you choose Set AutoShape Defaults with a rectangle selected, your new defaults will affect circles, callouts, flowchart shapes, and any other AutoShape you create.

PART

III

CH

13

USING WORD'S STARS AND BANNERS AUTOSHAPES

Stars and Banners AutoShapes (see Figure 13.11) are ideal for retail advertising and fliers, but might also have uses in newsletters and company publications. Be careful how you use them, though: They can be a bit garish.

Figure 13.11
Stars and Banners
AutoShapes available in
Word.

Figure 13.12 shows a typical application for AutoShape starbursts: a sales flier. Notice the gray gradient added for visual interest. This was created by right-clicking on the AutoShape, choosing Format AutoShape from the shortcut menu, clicking the Colors and Lines tab, clicking Color, clicking Fill Effects, and choosing a one-color horizontal gradient. You'll learn more about these formatting options later in the chapter.

Figure 13.12
An AutoShape starburst
used as part of a sales
flier.

MAKING FLOWCHARTS WITH WORD'S AUTOSHAPE FLOWCHART AUTOSHAPES

Word's library of 28 Flowchart AutoShapes (see Figure 13.13) is sufficient for a wide variety of flowcharting tasks. In fact, you may find that you'll be able to do all you need with a small fraction of them. Several of the most commonly used flowchart icons are listed in Table 13.2.

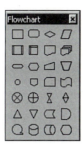

Figure 13.13
Flowchart
AutoShapes available
in Word.

TABLE 13.2   COMMONLY USED FLOWCHART ICONS

Icon	What It Represents
	A process
	An alternative process
	A point where a decision must be made
	A point where preparation is required
	A manual operation that must be performed
	A document is generated
	Many documents are generated

Among the tasks you may be able to perform with Word's flowchart AutoShapes are

- Simple process descriptions and business process reengineering
- Charting for ISO quality management
- Planning a small- to moderate-sized project
- Planning a small- to moderate-sized Web site

Figure 13.14 shows a sample flowchart created with Word's flowchart, text box, and arrow tools.

PART

III

CH

13

Note

If you find that Word's flowchart tools are insufficient to meet your needs, two popular (but expensive) alternatives are the drawing program Visio 5.0 (Visio Corporation), and Microsoft Project, Microsoft's project management software. Less costly alternatives include Flow! Express and Turbo Project Express from IMSI, and Project Manager Pro from The Learning Company.

Figure 13.14
A sample flowchart describing the processing of customer orders.

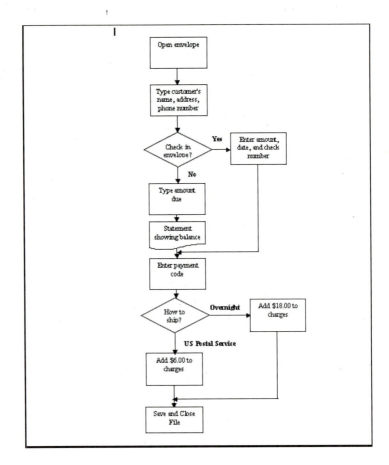

USING CALLOUTS

What do you do if you need to annotate a visual element of your document, such as a logo or photograph? Use callouts. A *callout* combines an arrow with a text box in which you can type. Clicking AutoShapes, Callouts displays 20 different types of callouts (see Figure 13.15).

Figure 13.15
Word's library of 20 pre-formatted callouts.

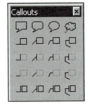

To use one of Word 2000's Callout Autoshapes, follow these steps:

1. From the Drawing toolbar, click the AutoShapes button.

2. Choose Callouts, and then select the particular callout you want to insert. The pointer changes into a small crosshair.

3. If you want to use one of the line callouts, click the subject of your callout first, and then hold down the mouse pointer while you drag away from it to the point where you want the callout box to appear. Release the mouse pointer. Word inserts both a line (called a *leader*) and a text box where you can enter the text of your callout. An insertion point flashes within the text box.

   If you want to use one of the four rectangular or nonline callouts, click where you want to place the callout, and then hold down the mouse pointer to enlarge it. You can move the pointer by clicking and dragging its yellow diamond adjustment handle after placing the callout.

4. Type your text and apply any formatting.

5. If necessary, resize the callout box by clicking and dragging any of the sizing handles.

6. You can adjust the placement of the leader by clicking the yellow diamond adjustment handle at the end of the line, as seen in Figure 13.16. Some callouts have two or three adjustment handles, enabling you to manipulate the angles of the line that stretches between the callout and the element you are calling attention to.

7. Click anywhere outside the callout box to return to the regular document.

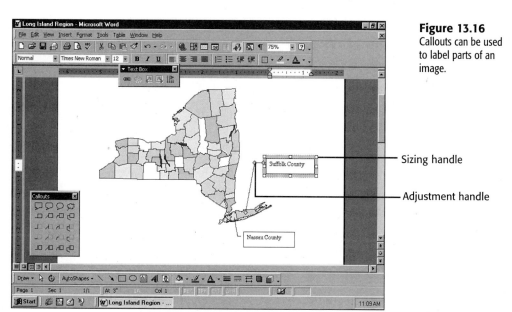

Figure 13.16
Callouts can be used to label parts of an image.

PART

III

CH

13

Tip #202

Callout lines and boxes can also be formatted. To format them, right-click the callout and choose Format AutoShape from the shortcut menu. Go to the Text Box tab, where you can manually adjust the size of the callout text box, if necessary. Click the Format Callout button at the bottom of the dialog box. Select the options you want from the Format Callout dialog box and click OK when you're done. Note that the Format Callout option is not available for callouts that use nonline leaders, such as comic-strip style "thought balloons."

 If text disappears from a text box when you shrink it, see "What to Do If Words Disappear from a Drawing Object," in the "Troubleshooting" section of this chapter.

USING MORE AUTOSHAPES TO CREATE ROOM DESIGNS AND OTHER DRAWINGS

In addition to the six categories of AutoShapes you've already learned about, Word 2000 adds a separate library called More AutoShapes. Among its contents are outlined images of

- Furniture such as desks, chairs, and lamps, used for drawing simple office layouts
- Electronic appliances, such as computers, telephones, and CD players
- Widely understood symbols, such as padlocks and puzzle pieces

To display the More AutoShapes library, click AutoShapes on the Drawing toolbar and choose More AutoShapes. The More AutoShapes window appears (see Figure 13.17).

Figure 13.17
The More AutoShapes window contains many additional widely used symbols.

Tip #203

More AutoShapes displays all of the clip art contained in the Clip Gallery—not just outlined AutoShapes. If you choose an image that isn't an outlined AutoShape, you may not be able to convert it into a text box or manipulate it in other ways available to AutoShapes.

The More AutoShapes window works exactly like the Clip Gallery. To insert an image, click where you want it to appear, display the More AutoShapes window, and click on a category. Then, click to select an image (see Figure 13.18) and click the Insert Clip button.

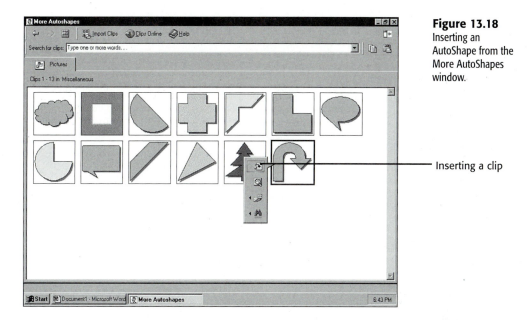

Figure 13.18
Inserting an AutoShape from the More AutoShapes window.

Inserting a clip

→ For more information about the Clip Gallery, **see** "Managing Clip Art Through Clip Gallery 5.0," **p. 356**.

FREEHAND DRAWING

Although Word gives you a large number of preset shapes to choose from, sooner or later you are likely to need a graphic that can't be found even in the AutoShapes library.

In that event, the Drawing toolbar gives you access to three freehand drawing tools. You can choose from a tool that creates curves, one that uses a combination of straight lines and freehand drawing, and one that relies entirely on freehand drawing.

The freehand drawing tools are all located under the Lines submenu of the AutoShapes button (see Figure 13.19). (Lines also contains a basic Line tool, a regular Arrow tool, and a Two-Headed Arrow tool along the top row of the submenu. You create any of these shapes by clicking and dragging.)

PART

III

CH

13

Figure 13.19
Options on the
AutoShape Lines sub-
menu.

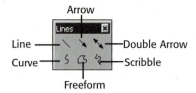

Line and Arrow work just like the Line and Arrow tools covered earlier in this chapter, in the "Drawing Lines and Other Basic Shapes" section. Double Arrow works just like the Arrow tool, except that it creates an arrow with arrowheads at both ends. The other three tools—Curve, Freeform, and Scribble—are covered in the next three sections.

DRAWING CURVES

You use the Curve tool to achieve a smooth-turning line or shape. After selecting the Curve tool, click where you want your shape to start and move the mouse—a line follows your movement. Click again where you want the line to begin to curve. Continue clicking and moving the mouse to build your shape. Press Esc or double-click where you want the shape to stop. To close a shape, click your starting point instead.

Tip #204	Freehand drawings can use Fill and Line options just like any other drawing object. You can even fill a shape that isn't closed. When you do, Word draws an imaginary straight line between each end of your curve, and fills the contents that would be within the closed curve if you had actually drawn that straight line.

Note	You can't convert a closed freehand shape to a text box, so you can't add text inside it, except by superimposing a separate text box on top of it.

DRAWING FREEHAND WITH THE FREEFORM TOOL

The Freeform tool enables you to create an object made of straight lines and freehand drawing. After selecting Freeform from the Lines submenu, you can draw freehand by clicking, holding down the mouse button, and dragging the mouse. A freehand line follows as you drag. You can keep drawing until you're finished, or click once to pause while you figure out where to continue the freehand line. When you're finished, press Esc or double-click to end the freehand line. Or, if you want to close the shape, click on its starting point.

Tip #205	You've just about finished your freehand drawing masterpiece and you click in the wrong place, placing a line where you don't want it. Press Backspace and your most recent step is erased, just like a mistyped character. In fact, you can keep pressing Backspace to delete all your points, one by one.

DRAWING FREEHAND WITH THE SCRIBBLE TOOL

The final freehand tool is known appropriately as the Scribble tool. This is a complete free-hand drawing mode: Click it, click in the document, and start dragging. Word inserts lines as you drag, until you release the mouse pointer. Because your mouse isn't a very precise input tool, drawings you make with the Scribble tool are likely to look, well, scribbled.

CONTROLLING COLORS

Without color, all the drawing objects you create are merely outlines. Word enables you to choose from a full range of colors—including shades of gray—to fill your objects, change your borders, and modify your text. In addition, you can fill your shapes with multicolor gradient blends, preset textures, and even user-selectable pictures.

Caution

If you're working with a printer that can reproduce only grayscale, like most laser printers, be careful of using colors without enough contrast to reproduce well. A color you choose may work well on the screen but be unreadable or indistinguishable from others when printed. It's a good idea to always print a test copy when working with color.

CHANGING FILLS AND LINE COLORS

Shapes you create with Word's drawing tools (except for lines and arrows) have two parts that can be colored. Although the interior fill color is the most obvious, you can also control the border color separately. The only difference is that with bordering lines you don't have access to some of Word's niftier multicolor possibilities, such as gradients.

The easiest way to change a fill or line color is by clicking the correct button on the Drawing toolbar. Both the Fill Color and Line Color buttons have option arrows that open a similar Color menu with 40 color swatches and extended options. Click any of the onscreen colors to change either the fill or line color of your selected drawing object. Clicking the No Fill or No Line options makes those respective choices transparent.

If you choose More Fill Colors from the Fill Color button, or More Line Colors from the Line Color button, the Colors dialog box appears (see Figure 13.20). This dialog box has two tabs: Standard and Custom. The Standard tab displays a default color palette in a hexagon shape, as well as a 16-step grayscale blend between black and white.

If your color palette is set to 16- or 32-bit color (also called High Color or True Color), you can use the Custom tab shown in Figure 13.13. Click anywhere in the Hue area on the left to choose a basic color, then select its intensity by clicking the Luminance strip on the right. The Red-Green-Blue and Hue-Saturation-Luminance values change as you select different colors.

Figure 13.20
Choosing a color from the Standard color palette.

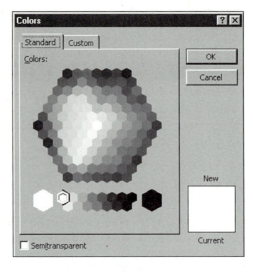

Figure 13.21
You can choose from 16 million colors through the Custom tab of the Colors dialog box.

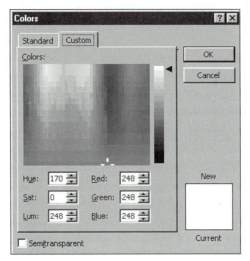

Tip #206

If you've worked hard to get a color just the way you want it, and you want to use the same color in another drawing object, here's a shortcut.

Select the shape whose color you want to match. Click Format Painter on the Standard toolbar. Click the second shape. The lines and colors on the first shape now appear on the second.

ADDING FILL EFFECTS TO YOUR SHAPES

You can add some pretty fancy backgrounds to the shapes you create with Word's drawing tools. These include gradients, textures, patterns, and even pictures. Word refers to these backgrounds as *fill effects*. To add a fill effect to a shape, first select the shape. Then, click the down arrow next to the Fill Color button on the Drawing toolbar, and click Fill Effects. The Fill Effects dialog box appears; from here, you can work with all of Word's fill effects.

USING GRADIENTS

To work with gradients, choose the Gradient tab of the Fill Effects dialog box (see Figure 13.22) to select—or custom-blend—a special gradient. You can choose whether your gradients should contain one color or two; if you choose two colors, you can specify which colors you want. You can specify how the gradients change: from top to bottom (Horizontal), from left to right (Vertical), diagonally, or from the corner. Try experimenting. Each of these options offers a different, interesting effect.

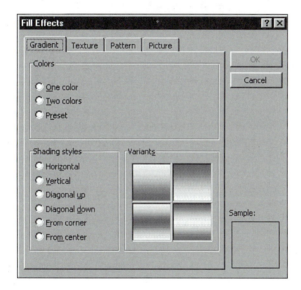

Figure 13.22
Choosing a gradient from the Gradient tab of the Fill Effects dialog box.

You can also choose from among a series of preset gradients, designed to communicate a certain mood. These include Early Sunset, Horizon, Desert, Rainbow, Calm Water, Gold, Brass, Chrome, and several others.

PART

III

CH

13

Tip #207

Gradients and textures can help you design attractive, consistent navigation buttons for use on Web pages. Figure 13.23 shows two examples. The one at left uses the Gold preset gradient. The one at right uses the Canvas texture available through the Texture tab of the Fill Effects dialog box (discussed shortly).

Figure 13.23
Sample Web navigation buttons created with gradients and textures.

USING TEXTURES

Word also provides 24 textures you can place in a shape you've created. To browse them, click the Texture tab of the Fill Effects dialog box (see Figure 13.24). Click a texture, and click OK. Figure 13.25 shows an advertisement that uses the water droplets texture in a thought-balloon callout.

Figure 13.24
Choosing a texture from the Texture tab of the Fill Effects dialog box.

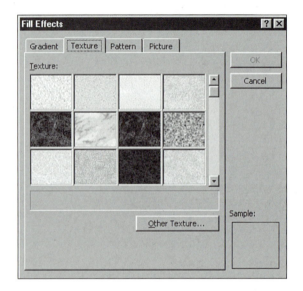

USING PATTERNS IN YOUR SHAPES

Word also provides 48 patterns you can use in any shape you create. As with other fill effects, be careful—lest you create a garish effect. Used with care, though, patterns can add visual interest, and help you call attention to specific elements of your drawing.

To browse Word's patterns, display the Fill Effects dialog box and click the Pattern tab.

By default, patterns are displayed in black and white, but you can choose from Word's entire color palette for both the background and foreground colors. Click the down arrow beneath Foreground or Background to change the color; an updated sample appears at the right.

Figure 13.26 shows one of Word's built-in clip art images, made more striking through the use of a white-on-black pattern.

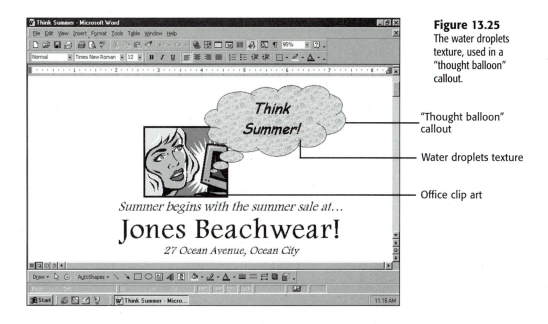

Figure 13.25
The water droplets texture, used in a "thought balloon" callout.

"Thought balloon" callout

Water droplets texture

Office clip art

Figure 13.26
Using a pattern to add drama.

INSERTING PICTURES IN YOUR SHAPES

Thus far, you've learned how to make your shapes more attractive using gradients, textures, and patterns. When even these options aren't sufficient, Word also allows you to insert pictures in shapes. To insert a picture into a shape, follow these steps:

1. Select the shape.

 2. Click the down arrow on the Fill Color button and choose Fill Effects.

3. Click Picture to display the Picture tab of the Fill Effects dialog box (see Figure 13.27).

Figure 13.27
The Picture tab of the Fill Effects dialog box.

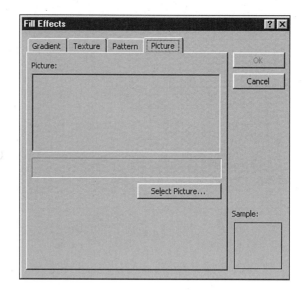

4. Click Select Picture. The Select Picture dialog box opens.
5. Browse to and select the picture you want.
6. Click Insert, and click OK.

The picture appears in your document. Figure 13.28 shows images used within striped right arrows found in the Block Arrows AutoShapes submenu.

Figure 13.28
Using pictures within striped right arrows.

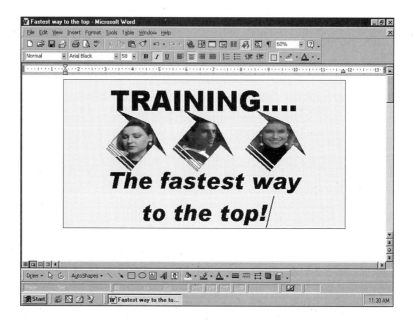

ADDING DEPTH TO YOUR GRAPHICS

Word 2000 includes two effective tools to make your graphics appear to leap off the page. Any drawing object—including lines, freeform drawings, or clip art—can now cast a shadow, in almost any direction and any color. Shadows help separate a graphic from its background on the page. The second depth-defying tool enables all drawing objects (with the exception of clip art) to extend into the third dimension; it's appropriately called 3D. Both tools are available through the Drawing toolbar.

> **Caution**
>
> You can't apply shadowing and 3D to the same object. If you apply a shadow effect to an object formatted as 3D, the shadow replaces the 3D effect.

USING SHADOWING

You can instantly add a 50-percent gray drop-shadow to the border of a line or shape. The shadow appears on any side of an object, appears on top of the object, or surrounds the object like a picture frame. As shown in Figure 13.29, drop-shadows add an interesting three-dimensional effect to lines, rectangles, ovals, and other shapes.

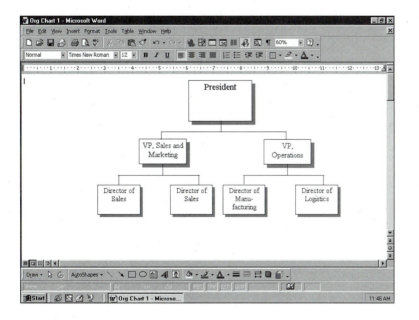

Figure 13.29
An example of using shadows to make a box stand out on the page.

 To add a drop-shadow, first select the object you want to shadow. Next, click the Shadow button on the Drawing toolbar, and choose from among the 20 preset shadows displayed in Figure 13.30. If you want to adjust the shadow's position and color, select Shadow Settings. The Shadow Settings toolbar appears; there, you can select the settings you want.

Figure 13.30
Choosing a shadow from the list of shadows available.

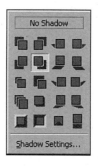

If you don't like the way the shadow looks, you can choose a different shadow. Or if you decide that you really don't want a shadow after all, select the shape and choose No Shadow from the Shadow palette to remove the shadow.

You can change the shadow's style settings by choosing the Shadow Settings command on the Shadow palette. The Shadow Settings toolbar appears, as shown in Figure 13.31.

Figure 13.31
You can control a shadow's settings from the Shadow Settings toolbar.

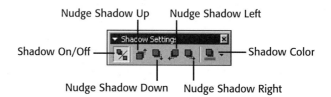

From this toolbar, you can choose several options to change the look of a shadow. To add or remove a shadow, click the Shadow On/Off button. You can even move the shadow a little bit at a time in a particular direction. Choose Nudge Shadow Up, Nudge Shadow Down, Nudge Shadow Left, or Nudge Shadow Right.

To change the color of the shadow, click the Shadow Color drop-down arrow and select the color of your choice (see Figure 13.32). Clicking Semitransparent Shadow makes the shadow partially see-through. Clicking More Shadow Colors displays the Colors dialog box: From there, you can choose from a wider set of colors or create a custom color.

Figure 13.32
Choosing a different shadow color from the Shadow Settings toolbar.

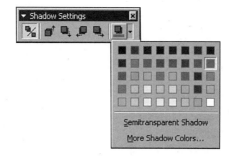

The Shadow Color settings include a special Semitransparent Shadow option that enables text to be seen through the shadow. When combining text and an object's shadow, however, it's usually a better idea to move the object behind the text via the Order command (covered later in this chapter).

Tip #208	Two shadow styles create an embossed or engraved look by eliminating the outline of the object. If you choose either of these (Shadow Styles 17 and 18, the first and second styles in the fifth row of options), and then pick another shadow style, you must re-apply the border. To do this, click the Line Style button from the Drawing toolbar and select one of the presets. (The default is 3/4 pt.)

USING 3D EFFECTS

Word 2000's 3D tool goes beyond shadowing, enabling you to give a two-dimensional drawing object apparent depth by extending its edges and rotating it to any angle.

This technique of expanding the edges is called *extruding*. You can control both the depth of the extrusion and the direction. What makes the extrusion look three-dimensional is the use of a computer-generated light source that creates an illusion of light and shadow. Word 2000 even gives you control over the direction and intensity of the light. Finally, you can choose from four different surface types: Wireframe, Matte, Plastic, or Metal.

 The 3D tool works much like the Shadow tool. Select a drawing object and click the 3D button from the Drawing toolbar. Choose any of the 20 preset 3D effects. Figure 13.33 shows what four standard 3D styles look like when applied to the same object.

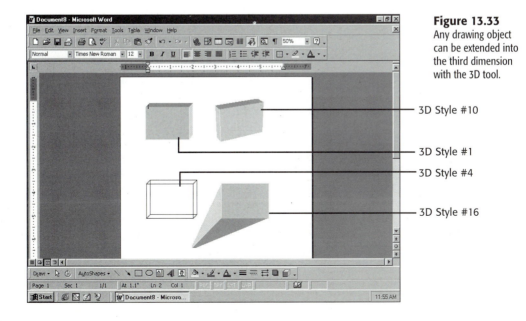

Figure 13.33
Any drawing object can be extended into the third dimension with the 3D tool.

3D Style #10

3D Style #1

3D Style #4

3D Style #16

PART
III

CH
13

After you have applied a basic 3D style, you can adjust the settings by selecting the 3-D Settings option from the 3D menu. Table 13.3 outlines the options available to you.

TABLE 13.3   3D SETTINGS

Button	Name	Description
	3D On/Off	Enables or disables the 3D effect.
	Tilt Down	Each mouse click moves the object down five degrees. Shift+click moves the object in 45-degree increments. Ctrl+click moves the object in one-degree increments.
	Tilt Up	Each mouse click moves the object up five degrees. Shift+click moves the object in 45-degree increments. Ctrl+click moves the object in one-degree increments.
	Tilt Left	Each mouse click moves the object five degrees to the left. Shift+click moves the object in 45-degree increments. Ctrl+click moves the object in one-degree increments.
	Tilt Right	Each mouse click moves the object five degrees to the right. Shift+click moves the object in 45-degree increments. Ctrl+click moves the object in one-degree increments.
	Depth	Controls the size of the extrusion. There are six preset values (including Infinity) and a Custom option.
	Direction	Controls the direction of the extrusion. There are nine preset values, and Parallel or Perspective options.
	Lighting	Controls the direction and intensity of the light. There are nine preset directions and three preset intensities.
	Surface	Controls the reflectiveness of the extruded surface. Surface types include Wireframe, Matte, Plastic, and Metal.
	3D Color	Controls the color of the extrusion. Displays the color palette; choosing More 3D Colors displays the Colors dialog box.

The depth of your 3D object is expressed in point size—the preset values include 0 pt. (no extrusion), 36 pt., 72 pt., and so on. Think of the depth as how thick your object appears; a depth of 72 pt., makes your object an inch thick. (There are 72 points in an inch.)

In addition to the Custom option, which enables you to enter your own depth value, there is an Infinity alternative. Selecting Infinity causes your object to extrude to its *vanishing point*—a term used in perspective drawing to indicate the place where all lines meet.

Perspective also comes into play when selecting the direction of your 3D object. You can choose between Parallel and Perspective style for any direction. Perspective uses the vanishing point when drawing the extrusion, whereas Parallel continues all edges in their original direction. In general, Perspective gives a more three-dimensional appearance.

Note

3D effects do have limitations. You can use them only on AutoShapes (which include WordArt), and, to a limited degree, text boxes. Although you have access to the full range of 3D options with text boxes, only the frame around the text is affected, not the text itself. Consequently, only the effects in which the face of the drawing object does not tilt (such as 3D Style 1) work well.

Note

You may find that many of these adjustments are overkill for the types of 3D objects you need to create. You may also find that many of the combinations available to you do not generate realistic 3D objects. Here are a few tips that may help:

- If you want to enter text inside the 3D object, consider setting lighting to come through the object (using the middle setting of the nine available lighting settings), rather than from above, below, or the side of the object. This will give you a white background to enter text in.

- Make sure the object and its 3D background have significant contrast; this does not always happen by default. This may mean setting the 3D color to black or another dark color.

- The higher the depth setting you use, the stronger the 3D effect will be. Be careful that the "third dimension" of depth that you create does not visually overpower the first two dimensions.

EDITING OBJECTS IN A WORD DRAWING

When you have a line, rectangle, circle, or other AutoShape in your document, you must first select the object to work with it. Lines and shapes are selected when you first place them in your document. After that, you can select a line or shape at any time by clicking on it. When the object is selected, small square boxes called *sizing handles* appear at the ends or corners of the shape.

You can select more than one object at a time. To do so, select the first object; press Shift and select each additional object you want. Release the Shift key; the objects remain selected, and you can format them together.

MOVING, RESIZING, OR DELETING A SHAPE

After you select a shape, you can

- Move the shape by dragging it
- Shrink or enlarge the shape by clicking on a sizing handle and dragging it
- Delete the shape by pressing the Backspace or Delete key

PART
III

CH
13

SELECTING MULTIPLE DRAWING OBJECTS AT ONCE

Most of your original drawings—and virtually any piece of editable Office clip art—will contain more than one shape. You'll often want to select many shapes in a drawing at the same time. You can do so in two ways.

 First, you can click the Select Objects button on the Drawing toolbar and drag the pointer across all the drawing objects you want to select. The Select Objects pointer selects only objects that are entirely within the area you select—if a corner peeks off to the side, that object won't be selected. Figure 13.34 shows a simple drawing with all its different objects selected.

Note

If you are selecting objects in clip art that you've inserted, first right-click the clip art and choose Edit Picture from the shortcut menu, so you can edit it.

Figure 13.34
A drawing with all its objects selected.

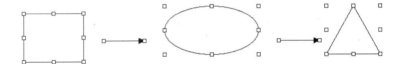

Or, you can select an object, press the Shift key, and select another object. Both objects remain selected. As long as you keep the Shift key pressed, you can keep selecting more objects in your drawing.

GROUPING AND UNGROUPING

At some point, you might have several shapes and lines you'd like to move, format, or delete together. For example, if you're building an organization chart, you might need to move half the boxes an inch to the left to make room for a new division. Or your boss says he'd like to see all the VPs in red and salespeople in blue.

You've already learned that you can select many objects at once by dragging the Select Object pointer around them, or by selecting the objects one at a time with the Shift key pressed down. However, if you do this, it's easy for the individual images to get separated.

If you group the images you're using, they stay together no matter what. To do so, select the objects you want to group, right-click on one of them, and choose Grouping, Group from the shortcut menu. Notice that selection handles now surround the group of objects, not each individual object, as shown in Figure 13.35. You can now work with all the objects as if they were one object.

If you later need to edit one of the grouped objects, you'll need to separate ("ungroup") it from the rest. If you are editing an object in a piece of clip art, first right-click on the clip art and choose Edit Picture from the shortcut menu. Then, whether you are editing clip art or a drawing you created, right-click on the object, and choose Grouping, Ungroup. Once you've done so, you can click the Select Object button, and drag the Select Object pointer across the individual objects you want to work with.

Tape dispenser is part of the image, but not part of the selected group.

Paperclips and thumbtack are grouped.

Figure 13.35
When grouped objects in a drawing are selected, one set of handles surrounds them all.

If a set of objects have ever been grouped, Word remembers how they were grouped even after you ungroup them. To regroup a set of objects as they were before being ungrouped, right-click on one and choose Grouping, Regroup from the shortcut menu.

LAYERING YOUR DRAWING

Each drawing object you create is placed in an individual layer. By default, your text layer is on the bottom. Every time you add another object, it is drawn in the layer on top of the previous object. The stacking order becomes noticeable when objects overlap each other—the object last drawn is on top and obscures a portion of any objects that were drawn earlier.

You can move objects to a different position in a stack, much as you might reshuffle a deck of cards. This is referred to as changing the stacking or *Z-order*. (In describing coordinates on paper, X refers to the horizontal, Y, the vertical, and Z, the depth.) For example, you can move objects up or down within a stack one layer at a time, or you can move them to the top or bottom of a stack in one move. Naturally, this means that you don't have to draw the bottom object first—you can always move it later. Because text is on its own layer, Word has two special commands for moving an object behind or in front of text.

PART
III

CH
13

Tip #209

One way to find an object on a page is by using the Tab key. Click your top object. Press Shift+Tab to select the object below the current one; press Tab by itself to select the object above the current one. Continue pressing the keys until your object is highlighted.

To change the Z-order of any object, click the Draw button on the Drawing toolbar and choose Order. The Order submenu appears, giving you several choices. For example, you can move an object to the front or back, forward or back one layer, or in front or behind text.

ROTATING ILLUSTRATIONS

Word offers features for rotating shapes and illustrations. To turn an image 90 degrees to the left or right, click the Draw button on the Drawing toolbar, and choose Rotate or Flip; then choose Rotate Left or Rotate Right.

 To rotate an image to any angle, click the Free Rotate button on the Drawing toolbar (or click Draw and then choose Rotate or Flip, Free Rotate). Green rotation handles appear on the object you selected. Click and drag the handles to the position you want; then click the Free Rotate button again to turn rotation off.

Tip #210	You can't use these tools to flip or rotate pictures or clip art—only drawing objects. Moreover, if you are using a fill effect, such as a gradient, pattern, picture, or texture, the fill does not flip or rotate with your object. To achieve these effects, it's best to use an outside graphics program and insert your altered image.

USING THE GRID TO LINE UP OBJECTS

Word 2000 automatically divides pages into an invisible grid, with each square in the grid set to 0.13" by 0.13". By default, objects you draw are lined up against the nearest gridlines, making it much easier to align multiple objects consistently. This automatic feature is called Snap to Grid.

You can adjust the increments used by Word's grid, up to a fineness of 0.01". You can turn the grid off, make the gridlines visible, or even specify where on the page you want the grid to begin.

To access the Grid controls, click the Draw button on the Drawing toolbar. Choose Grid to open the Drawing Grid dialog box (see Figure 13.36). You can input new values for both the Horizontal Spacing and Vertical Spacing by either typing in the values directly or using the spinner arrows.

The Horizontal Spacing controls the amount of horizontal space between vertical gridlines, and the Vertical Spacing controls the amount of vertical space between horizontal gridlines.

The two Snap options can be used either independently or together. If you have Snap Objects to Grid checked, objects will always settle their upper-left sizing handles at the intersection of two grid lines. If you have Snap Objects to Other Objects checked, objects will always settle their upper-left sizing handles with each other. If both are checked, Snap Objects to Other Objects overrides Snap Objects to Grid.

In Word 2000's *Print Layout view*, you can also display grid lines onscreen to help you design pages more precisely. To do so, check the Display Gridlines on Screen box. Then set values in the Horizontal Every and Vertical Every scroll boxes. The lower the values you set, the finer the gridlines. Figure 13.37 shows a page with horizontal and vertical gridlines.

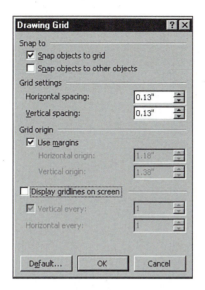

Figure 13.36
Controlling how the grid behaves and appears.

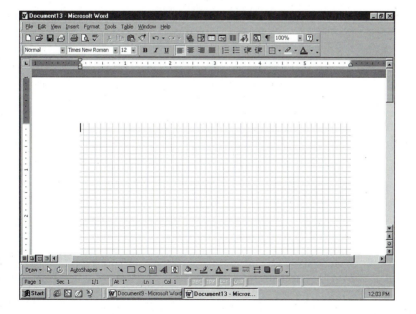

Figure 13.37
Displaying gridlines on your page.

Note You can turn off the Snap to Grid option temporarily by pressing Alt while moving your drawing object.

Nudging an Object

If you've ever tried to use your mouse to position an object just right there, you'll appreciate Word's nudging feature. Although the mouse is great for quickly moving an object around a page, it isn't the world's best when it comes to precise placement. You can move your object in increments as small as one pixel at a time using the Nudge option found under the Draw button of the Drawing toolbar. You can nudge an object in any direction—Left, Right, Up, or Down.

The distance the object moves depends on your Grid options; if you have Snap Objects to Grid selected, a nudge moves your object one grid measurement. If this Snap option is not enabled, your object moves one pixel in the chosen direction.

Tip #211	You can also nudge any selected object by selecting the object and pressing any arrow key. Using this technique, your object always moves one pixel at a time in the direction you've chosen. (If you have Snap Objects to Grid enabled, pressing the arrow key nudges the object one unit of grid space, instead of one pixel.)

Aligning and Distributing Drawing Objects

In addition to precise positioning of an object on the page, Word also offers *relative positioning*. A drawing object can be aligned relative to another object or to the page itself. This means that two or more objects can be lined up along any of their edges or centers. They can also be centered on the page or aligned along the edge of the page. Furthermore, you can have Word evenly space your objects across (or down) the page. All in all, a tremendous amount of power is packed under the Align or Distribute commands, accessed by clicking the Draw button on the Drawing toolbar.

To align objects, first select the objects you want to align. You can do this by either clicking the Select Objects button on the Drawing tool and dragging a marquee around the objects you want to select, or by pressing Shift while you click each object.

Next, click Draw, Align or Distribute from the Drawing toolbar. Then, from the Align or Distribute submenu, select one of the following:

- **Align Left.** Aligns selected objects along the left edge of the object farthest to the left.
- **Align Center.** Aligns selected objects along the vertical center of the selected objects.
- **Align Right.** Aligns selected objects along the right edge of the object farthest to the right.
- **Align Top.** Aligns selected objects along the top edge of the highest object.
- **Align Middle.** Aligns selected objects along the horizontal center of the selected objects.
- **Align Bottom.** Aligns selected objects along the bottom edge of the lowest object.

You can also center a drawing object on the page. To do this in Word 2000, click D<u>r</u>aw, <u>A</u>lign or Distribute from the Drawing toolbar and then click Relative t<u>o</u> Page. After this feature has been enabled, all align or distribute commands use the page as a super object that controls the positioning. This means that if you have Relative t<u>o</u> Page checked and choose Align Center, your selected object(s) is centered horizontally on the page; Align Middle moves your objects to the vertical center of the page.

You might not think you need the distribute commands until you use them once—but after you understand what they can do, you'll use them all the time. When objects are distributed, they are arranged evenly with an equal amount of space between them, either horizontally or vertically. If you select three objects, click <u>A</u>lign or Distribute, and choose Distribute <u>H</u>orizontally, Word spaces the objects evenly, using the outside objects as boundaries. If Relative t<u>o</u> Page is enabled, Word uses the edges of the page as its boundary.

You often use the align commands and the distribute commands one after another. Figure 13.38 shows a typical three-step process. First, you create the objects, roughing out the placement. Next, you choose Align Top to line up the objects. Finally, after checking Relative t<u>o</u> Page, you select Distribute <u>H</u>orizontally to arrange the objects across the page.

Step #1: Create the objects.

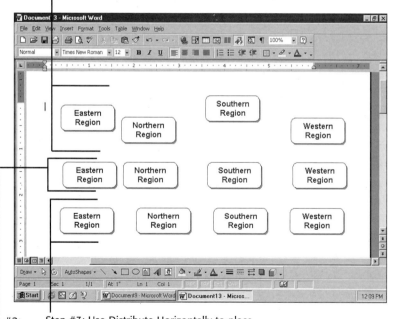

Figure 13.38
The Align and Distribute tools are used to achieve an even, balanced look.

Step #2: Use Align Top to align the objects' heights.

Step #3: Use Distribute Horizontally to place the same amount of space between objects.

PART

III

CH

13

TROUBLESHOOTING

WHAT TO DO IF WORDS DISAPPEAR FROM A DRAWING OBJECT

Text within drawing objects is not automatically resized to fit; you have to either reduce the size of the text or enlarge the drawing object by clicking and dragging the sizing handles. To adjust text placement, you have to use all the formatting options at your disposal to get the effect you want—the alignment buttons, paragraph marks, tabs, nonbreaking spaces (Ctrl+Shift+Space), and so on—to move the text where you want it.

WHAT TO DO IF DRAWINGS DON'T APPEAR IN PRINTED DOCUMENTS

First, make sure you're not printing in Draft mode. Choose Tools, Options, click the Print tab, and then clear the Draft Output check box. Also in the same tab, check the Drawing Objects check box, if it is not already checked.

Finally, some printers have settings that override the Word 2000 options. Check your printer settings by choosing File, Print, and then clicking the Properties button on the Print dialog box.

WHAT TO DO IF YOU WANT TO CENTER ONLY SOME OBJECTS ON THE PAGE

Centering only some of the objects on a page can be tricky. A common problem is mistakenly leaving the Relative to Page option on the Align or Distribute menu checked. Because you have to click the Draw button each time you change one of these options, it's easy to forget. If you're doing a lot of work with aligning or distributing, you can separate the menus by clicking and dragging the bar across the top of the Align or Distribute submenu. Drag it to a convenient place on your screen, and then you have one-click access to all the commands, including Relative to Page.

If you make a mistake in centering an object, click Undo to eliminate your change and try again.

CHAPTER **14**

WORD DESKTOP PUBLISHING

In this chapter

WORD 2000: *ALMOST* A FULL-FLEDGED DESKTOP PUBLISHING PROGRAM

What program comes with the capability to create multicolumn layouts, smoothly import any kind of graphics, use slick design techniques such as drop caps, even embed fonts for delivery to a typesetting machine? Hint: It's the same program that provides built-in brochure and newsletter designs, custom fonts, clip art images, and drawing and font effects software. Yes, Word 2000 does all that.

Word isn't quite a full-fledged desktop publishing program. But if you know your way around Word, you can create a pretty fair newsletter or brochure. In the preceding two chapters, you've learned about many of the features you can use to build visual documents, including

- Importing graphics (Chapter 12, "Getting Images into Your Documents")
- Creating text-based graphics with WordArt (Chapter 12)
- Scanning graphics or acquiring them with a digital camera (Chapter 12)
- Controlling text wrapping and other aspects of picture formatting (Chapter 12)
- Drawing with Word's drawing tools (Chapter 13, "Drawing in Word")
- Editing elements into and out of existing images (Chapter 13)
- Using prefabricated AutoShape images (Chapter 13)
- Working with colors, patterns, and fill effects (Chapter 13)
- Using shadowing and 3D (Chapter 13)
- Controlling layers and grouping in drawings (Chapter 13)
- Working with the drawing grid (Chapter13)

You also learned some other valuable techniques earlier in this book:

- Formatting characters and paragraphs
- Using styles to build consistent visual documents
- Using templates to automate the production of visual—and other—documents
- Using tables as a layout tool

Note

And in Chapter 15, "Using Graphics to Make Sense of Your Data–Visually," you'll discover one additional Word tool for bringing visuals into your documents: Microsoft Graph.

In this chapter, you'll learn about several more features that you can use in any document—but that lend themselves especially well to newsletters, brochures, and other traditionally "desktop published" documents.

Tip #212	To use most of the techniques in this chapter, you'll want to switch to Print Layout view, if you aren't there already.

WHEN TO USE WORD—AND WHEN *NOT* TO

Should you use Word as a desktop publishing program, or should you use a different piece of software designed specifically for the purpose?

Consider using Word if

- You're creating a fairly simple publication, especially one that can be built from one of Word's built-in *templates* or *wizards*.
- You expect to customize your documents and need access to Word features such as *mail merge* to do so.
- Your desktop-published document links to other documents stored on your computer, such as Excel worksheets.
- You want to do it yourself and you already know how to use Word.
- You don't have access to desktop publishing software.

Consider using a dedicated desktop publishing program if

- Your publication will require the use of full-color photography, and will be printed professionally—in other words, not on a desktop printer (Word does not support four-color separations, a requirement for high-fidelity color reproduction).
- Your layouts will be especially complex or precise.
- You will be delegating your project to a professional designer, or you already have and know how to use a desktop publishing package well.

Tip #213	Even if you export your Word documents to a desktop publishing program, include styles as you work; these can easily be imported into most leading desktop publishing programs.

PART

III

CH

14

Note

If you need a professional desktop publishing program, but you're worried about the complexity, or reluctant to invest a sizable amount of money, consider Microsoft Publisher, which is bundled with every version of Office 2000 (except for the Standard Edition).

Publisher 2000 is an easy-to-learn program with all the bells and whistles necessary to output a wide range of publications. Publisher comes with a variety of templates and wizards that make it easy to produce everything from a newsletter to a business form, change color schemes quickly, even repurpose printed materials for the Web. Publisher also supports four-color separations for professional color printing.

Just as Word uses text boxes, Publisher makes extensive use of text frames (and, for graphics, picture frames). As a result, much of what you learn in this chapter is applicable in Publisher.

Not only does Publisher import Word files, it also enables you to set Word as your primary editor—so you can do all your extensive editing in the familiar Word environment, while you benefit from Publisher's more sophisticated layout capabilities.

PLANNING YOUR DOCUMENT

Before you start using Word's desktop publishing tools, consider quickly sketching out a preliminary layout by hand, especially if you're using any kind of graphic such as logos, clip art, or photographs. Getting your ideas on paper, even roughly, can give you a better idea of what size your images should be, how large you can make your headings, and how much room you'll have for your basic text.

Communicating with Word: Support the Key Message

When you plan a document, you must first ask: What is the key message you're trying to communicate? Make sure the headlines, graphics, and choice of typography work together to support that message. For example, don't use the Comic Sans typeface to promote investment services.

When you are putting together a larger publication, such as a newsletter or quarterly report, it's best to gather all your materials before you begin designing the document. One of the biggest problems you'll have as a layout artist is getting the text to fit within a specific number of pages. Whether you have too much text or too little, it is much easier to make it fit when you have all the pieces. If you must lay out a document without all the elements in hand, use rectangles and text boxes that are approximately the same size as placeholders. This gives you a truer picture of how your text is going to fit.

Tip #214

If you want to see how text will flow around a picture or an AutoShape, but don't have the text yet, you can use Word's built-in text generator. Place your insertion point where you want the text to start, type =Rand(),and press Enter. Word inserts three paragraphs. Each paragraph contains the same sentence repeated three times: "The quick brown fox jumps over the lazy dog."

If you need more or less than three paragraphs, you can also specify the exact number of paragraphs, and the number of sentences in each paragraph, using the =Rand() function. The syntax is

=rand(p,s)

where p equals the number of paragraphs, and s equals the number of sentences in each paragraph.

Tip #215

Keep all the files for a project together. Create a single folder to hold the document itself, any subsidiary Word files, plus all the pictures, graphs, and anything else you may need to assemble and maintain the document.

One final word about planning your document: moderation. When you're choosing fonts, font sizes, and styles for your publication, select the smallest number of options that can do the job. Two fonts and three different font sizes are adequate for a great number of publications. An advertisement or other document with too many changes in fonts and/or font sizes is difficult to read and detracts from your message. Just because you can change fonts every letter doesn't mean you have to.

QUICK AND EASY BROCHURES WITH THE BROCHURE TEMPLATE

Word includes a handy template for creating trifold brochures, the kind that are printed on the front and back of plain sheets of paper (8.5" × 11", or A4), then folded twice.

Tip #216

You aren't limited to using the built-in template of course if your printer can handle 8.5" × 14" paper, consider printing a four-column brochure, assembled by folding three times.

The built-in Brochure template includes most of the standard brochure features: columns, graphics, headlines, and advanced paragraph formatting. Besides providing a tool that can make your brochures shine even if you have no layout talent, the Brochure template also offers a tutorial on useful techniques.

To create a brochure, choose File, New, and click the Publications tab. Double-click on the Brochure icon. You'll get a complete brochure, with pictures in appropriate places, various text samples, and hints for making changes (see Figure 14.1).

PART

III

CH

14

Figure 14.1
Creating a new brochure from the built-in template.

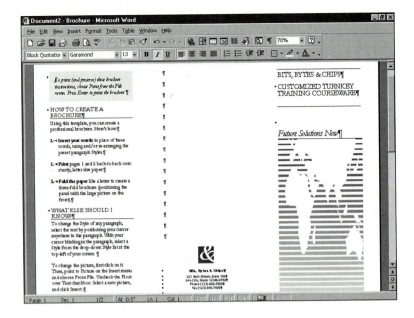

Tip #217

Print the brochure template before you start changing it. The template is full of tips and instructions on how to create a brochure.

Start by modifying the brochure in ways that will apply to all the brochures you might want to make: Change the business name, address, tag line, logo, and so on.

Tip #218

As soon as you've completed these general changes, save a copy of the brochure. That way, in the future, you don't have to start all over again with Word's "generic" template.

Each of the different brochure elements, such as main headings, body text, cover title and subtitle, numbered lists, and the return address, are set in a particular style, so it's easy to quickly modify the overall look of the newsletter.

→ For more information about working with styles, **see** Chapter 2, "Streamlining Your Formatting with Styles," **p. 31**.

To customize the brochure, follow the tips in the template to replace the placeholder text; change the formatting of styles, individual paragraphs, or blocks of text; and to replace the pictures in the template with those of your own devising.

Communicating with Word: Less Is More
Don't try to squeeze too much in. Readers turn off too dense layouts; white space makes any document more inviting, and gives the eye a place to rest. Word's nicely designed three-panel "Slim-Jim" brochure template contains space for only about 650 words.

To replace a picture, click to select it; then use one of Word's Insert, Picture tools to choose a new picture that replaces it.

For example, if you want to use a picture from the Clip Art Gallery, choose Insert, Picture, Clip Art; browse to the picture, click to select it, and click the Insert Clip icon. Word replaces your picture with the new one. You may need to resize the picture to better fit the needs of your brochure.

→ For more information about inserting images into your document, and resizing them after you insert them, **see** Chapter 12, "Getting Images into Your Documents," **p. 355**.

Tip #219

> For many people, the hardest part of creating a trifold brochure is getting the back sheet printed correctly—on the proper side of the paper, and rightside up instead of upside down. Invariably it will take several tries to get it correct. When you've finally figured out the right way to do it, take a heavy marker and put a big arrow on the brochure, indicating which side goes up, and which edge goes into the printer first. Then put that brochure in a sheet protector, and attach it firmly to your printer.

WORKING WITH MULTIPLE COLUMNS

One of the hallmarks of newsletters and other desktop-published documents is the use of multiple "newspaper-style" columns, where text snakes from the bottom of one column to the top of the next column.

Word gives you extensive control over columns. You can create uneven columns, specifying exact widths for each and the amount of white space that appears between the columns. You also can add a new column to existing columns. If columns are turned on for more than one page, Word can flow text from the bottom of the last column on one page to the top of the first column of the next page. To help you refine your layouts, Word can also draw vertical lines between each column—although you can't control the placement or formatting of those lines.

Tip #220

> If you need to set up a column layout for part of a page, where specific text, graphics, or other elements must remain in a rigid location and not move as you edit them, use Word tables (see Chapter 9).

CREATING MULTIPLE COLUMNS THE EASY WAY

 If you want to create multiple columns of the same width, click on the Columns toolbar button. (If you want to create multiple columns for only part of the document, select the text you want to split into columns, and then choose the Columns toolbar button.)

When you choose Columns, a box appears, displaying four columns. Click on the box and drag across until the number of columns you want is highlighted (see Figure 14.2). Then release the mouse button. Word applies the columns either to your entire document or, if you have selected text, to only that text. Word also displays your document in Print Layout view, so the columns are immediately visible. You can, however, switch back to Normal (or another) view and work there, if you choose.

Figure 14.2
Selecting columns from the Standard toolbar.

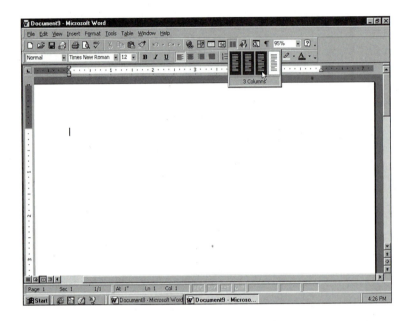

If you're creating multiple columns for only a portion of your document, Word inserts section breaks before and after the text you've selected.

Note

Although the Columns button displays four columns when you open it, you can use it to create up to six columns. Just click on the right-most column (number four), and drag to the right.

Tip #221

The Column button is great for making quick headings that span your columns. Select the text that you want to spread across your columns and click the Column button (see Figure 14.3).

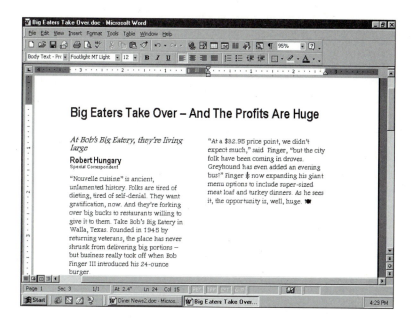

Figure 14.3
You can use the Column button to make any text span your columns.

GETTING MORE CONTROL THROUGH THE COLUMNS DIALOG BOX

You may want more control than the Columns button can give you. You might want columns of different sizes, for example. You might want to change the exact spacing between individual columns, or add a line between columns. To do any of these things, choose Columns from the Format menu. The Columns dialog box opens (see Figure 14.4).

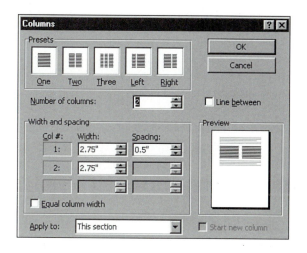

Figure 14.4
Working in the Columns dialog box.

PART
III

CH
14

Columns comes with five preset column formats: basic <u>O</u>ne column, T<u>w</u>o-column, and Three-column formats, as well as two-column formats in which the <u>L</u>eft or <u>R</u>ight column is smaller.

The width of your columns depends on your left and right margins; the wider the margins, the narrower the columns will be. If you choose one of the unequal width presets, <u>L</u>eft or <u>R</u>ight, the "named" column is set to a little less than one-half the width of the other column. For example, on a page with 1-inch left and right margins and two columns, selecting the <u>L</u>eft preset makes the left column 1.83" and the right column 4.17" with a .5" space in-between; selecting the <u>R</u>ight preset switches the widths of the columns.

The gutter between your columns is controlled by the <u>S</u>pacing measurement. Generally, it's a good idea to keep your spacing between .25" and .5". (Word's default setting is 0.5".) You might want to use a larger measurement if you are also using the Line <u>B</u>etween check box to place a vertical line between each column, or if you intend to use the empty space for figures.

You also can specify the number of columns directly, using the <u>N</u>umber of Columns spin box. Word won't create columns narrower than 0.5", so if you're using Word's default formatting of 1.25-inch left and right margins on an 8.5" page, you can specify up to 12 columns—realistically, less, because you inevitably need at least a little space between the columns for readability.

Note

Left-aligned text can often remain readable with slightly narrower space between columns than justified text.

Check Line <u>B</u>etween to tell Word to place a line between each column.

Note

Word does not add space between columns to compensate when you add a line between columns. If your space between columns is narrower than 0.5", check to make sure the line you've added does not overlap the text to its right.

In the <u>A</u>pply To box, choose whether you want your column settings to apply to This Section, the Whole Document, or from This Point Forward. If you choose This Point Forward, Word inserts a section break at your insertion point unless you're already at the start of a new section. If you've selected text before opening the Columns dialog box, your choices here are Selected Text or Whole Document, if the document only has one section; the choices are Selected Text or Selected Sections, if the document has more than one section.

As already mentioned, if you create columns for selected text, section breaks are added before and after the text. As you make changes, Word shows their effects in the Preview box of the Columns dialog box.

Note

> Columns of unequal width—your first column being narrower than your others, for example—are used to add more visual variety to a large-format publication, such as a newsletter. There are no hard and fast rules for sizing your columns, other than to be sure that your text can still be read easily. If a large number of the lines in your column end in hyphenated or broken words, your column is too narrow.

CHANGING COLUMN WIDTHS WITH THE RULER

Once you've created columns, you can adjust column width and the space between columns by hand, using the ruler.

If all your columns are of the same width, you can use the ruler to increase or decrease the width of all the columns (and thus the space between columns) at the same time. If you start out with columns that are all the same width, you'll end up with columns that are all the same width.

If your columns are of different widths, you can use the ruler to change the width of each column individually. In this case, as you widen or narrow a column, the space between that column and the next increases or decreases to compensate.

Note

> Changing column widths with the ruler does not affect overall page margins.

To change column widths with the ruler, make sure you're in Print Layout view, and that the ruler is visible (View, Ruler). If all the column widths are equal, click and drag the column marker on the ruler (see Figure 14.5) to make adjustments—a ScreenTip will tell you if you're working with the Left or Right Margin of the column.

If the column widths are unequal, you can drag the Left or Right Margin markers to adjust the column widths; the width of the gutter between the columns increases or decreases, as you would expect. If the column widths are unequal, though, you have one additional column marker available, called Move Column. If you click and drag on the Move Column marker, the width of gutter stays the same, while the widths of the columns to the left and right of the gutter get adjusted.

PART
III

CH
14

Click the left or right margin and drag to a new column width.

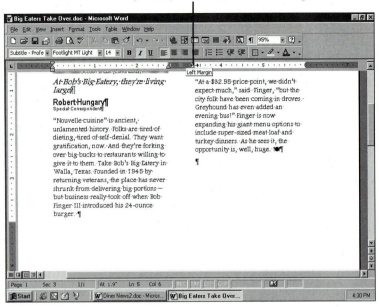

Figure 14.5
The ruler can be used to adjust column widths quickly.

Tip #222	If you hold down the Alt key as you drag a column marker, Word will show you precise measurements for column and gutter widths, in the ruler area.

Tip #223	After you've moved your columns to a new place, you can use the Undo/Redo buttons to toggle between two different widths for your columns. It's a quick way to compare two choices.

Note	You can't drag one column marker into the space reserved for another column. If you need to widen a column beyond the space currently available for it, you must first narrow an adjacent column to make more room for it.

GETTING MORE CONTROL OVER INDIVIDUAL COLUMN WIDTHS

You can set precise column widths in the Columns dialog box (refer to Figure 14.4). Choose Format, Columns to display the dialog box. If your current settings are for columns of equal width, clear the Equal Column Width check box. This enables you to work on any column listed in the Width and Spacing area.

For each column, set Width and Spacing. (You can move from one box to the next by pressing Tab.) If you have more than three columns, a scroll bar appears to the left of the Col # list. Use it to scroll to the columns you want to set.

STARTING A NEW COLUMN

Sometimes, as you edit your document, you'll realize you need to change the number of columns that appear from your insertion point onward. For example, your document might consist of only one column for the first several pages, but you now need to enter material that should be formatted in three columns. There are two ways to change the number of columns in a document from the insertion point onward:

- Select Format, Columns, apply the column settings to This Point Forward, and check the Start New Column box that appears at the bottom right of the dialog box.

- Insert a column break by choosing Insert, Break. Then in the Break dialog box (see Figure 14.6), click the Column Break option in the Break Types section and click OK.

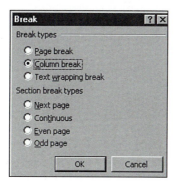

Figure 14.6
Inserting a column break in the Break dialog box.

Tip #224

If you're having trouble seeing where to insert column breaks, you can see—and edit—the whole page at the same time by clicking the arrow next to the Zoom control and selecting Whole Page.

REMOVING COLUMN BREAKS

You remove column breaks just as you would a manual page break. The easiest way to see the break is to switch to Normal view by choosing View, Normal. Then select the Column Break line. Press Delete to remove it.

Tip #245

If you don't want to switch to Normal view to delete the column break, place your insertion point in front of the line that starts the new column. Then, press Backspace to remove the column break.

PART

III

CH

14

EVENING YOUR COLUMNS

Sometimes you want to balance your columns so that the text is spread evenly over all your columns. This choice can be made for aesthetic ("It just looks better") or practical ("I couldn't follow the article before") reasons.

Balancing your columns isn't always easy to do in a way consistent with your paragraph pagination commands. For example, if you've specified that two paragraphs must stay together (Keep With Next), you limit Word's capability to move a few lines around to even things out.

Word does provide an easy solution, however: Use a continuous section break at the point where you want the column to end. Word will then end the section wherever necessary to balance the columns. Follow these steps:

1. Create your columns, if you have not already done so.

2. If necessary, switch to Print Layout view by choosing View, Print Layout.

3. At the end of the text that you want to balance, click to place the insertion point.

4. Choose Insert, Break.

5. From the Break dialog box, select a Continuous Section Break.

6. Click OK to close the dialog box.

 If you've tried using a continuous section break, but can't tell where one section stops and the next one starts, see "How to Tell Where One Section Stops and the Next One Begins" in the "Troubleshooting" section of this chapter.

USING DROP CAPS

Word can easily create large initial capitals, more commonly known as *drop caps*, that give your documents a distinct, magazine-style appearance. Drop caps work extremely well in newsletters, particularly those formatted with columns.

Drop caps are so named because usually the first letter or word of a paragraph, formatted in all capitals, is "dropped" into the paragraph so that the first two or three lines are pushed to one side. Figure 14.7 shows an example of a drop cap.

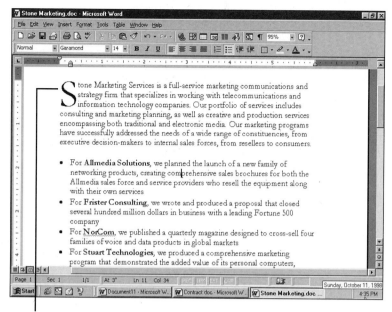

Figure 14.7
A drop cap adds visual spice to a page.

Drop cap

Follow these steps to add a drop cap to any paragraph:

1. Highlight the letter(s) or word(s) you want to convert to a drop cap.

2. Choose Format, Drop Cap. The Drop Cap dialog box appears (see Figure 14.8).

3. Select the position in which you want your drop cap to appear. Click either Dropped or In Margin.

4. Next you can select a different font for the drop cap by clicking the arrow next to the Font text box.

5. To change the size of the drop cap, enter a new value in the Lines To Drop text box.

6. To alter the amount of space between the drop cap and the surrounding text, enter a new value in the Distance From Text box.

7. Click OK to see the result.

Word makes your drop cap by putting your selected text into a frame. To alter your options and get a different look, click the frame with the drop cap and select Format, Drop Cap again. To remove a drop cap, click the frame, select Format, Drop Cap, and choose None.

PART

III

CH

14

Figure 14.8
Working in the Drop
Cap dialog box.

Drop caps are one of the few remaining Word features that use old-fashioned Word frames rather than text boxes. To format a frame, select it and choose Format, Frame. The Frame dialog box appears (see Figure 14.9). Here you can specify the following settings for the drop caps frame:

- Whether text wraps around the frame or not
- Horizontal and vertical positioning
- Width and height of the frame (not the letter itself)
- Whether the frame moves with text or locks (anchors) in place

You can also add borders or shading to a frame by right-clicking on it and choosing Borders and Shading from the shortcut menu.

Figure 14.9
Formatting the frame
surrounding a drop
cap.

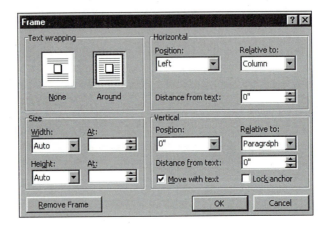

Tip #226

> A classic designer's trick is to pick a font for the drop cap that's from a different typeface than the one used for the body of the paragraph. For example, if your paragraph is in a serif font such as Times New Roman, use a sans-serif font such as Arial for your drop cap.

INSERTING SYMBOLS AND SPECIAL CHARACTERS

Often, you'll want to use characters other than those shown on a standard keyboard. In some cases, you'll need foreign language characters such as é or ñ. In other cases, you may need special characters, such as the section character §, which is often used in legal documents. In still other cases, you may want to use special-purpose symbols, such as the No Smoking icon available on Microsoft's free Webdings font. Finally, you may want to use symbols as decoration to spruce up newsletters and other documents. In the next few sections, you'll learn how to access symbols like these and use them most effectively.

WORKING WITH SYMBOLS

In Chapter 12, you learned how you can use WordArt to transform ordinary text into attractive artwork. But often you can achieve surprisingly attractive results simply by using characters in the fonts already installed on your computer.

Sometimes it's the small touches that make the difference—like settling on a "slug" that you'll use at the end of every article. Slugs, as shown in Figure 14.10, tell the reader that the article ends here—and if you pick the right one, they also add a touch of attractiveness and professionalism.

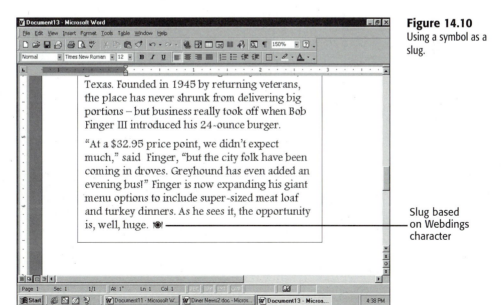

Figure 14.10
Using a symbol as a slug.

Slug based on Webdings character

PART

III

CH

14

Word's tool for accessing symbols and other special characters is the Symbol dialog box. In addition to selecting symbols and other characters one at a time, the Symbol dialog box also enables you to set up a variety of shortcuts for characters you use often. Follow these steps to insert a symbol:

1. Place your insertion point where you want the special character to appear.

2. Choose Insert, Symbol. The Symbol dialog box opens (see Figure 14.11).

Figure 14.11
The Symbol dialog box shows you all the characters in the font you've selected.

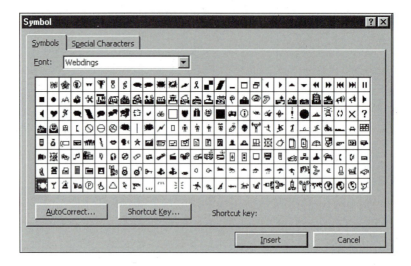

3. To preview a symbol at larger size, click it (see Figure 14.12).

4. To select a character or special symbol from a different font, click the arrow next to the Font text box and choose a font from the drop-down list.

5. When you're ready to insert a character, select it and click Insert. The Symbol dialog box remains open in case you want to enter more characters.

Figure 14.12

➔ To learn how to create a keyboard shortcut for symbols you reuse often, **see** "Creating a Keyboard Shortcut for a Symbol or Special Character," **p. 455**.

Tip #227

Enter all the characters you think you'll need, even if you have to move them later. It's easier to cut and paste characters in your document than to reopen and relocate characters in the Symbol dialog box every time you need one.

6. When you finish working in the Symbol dialog box, click the Close (×) button.

Tip #228
> In Windows 95 and NT 4.0, most of the interesting symbol characters were located in the Wingdings and Symbol fonts. If you've installed either Windows 98 or Internet Explorer 4.0 or later, you have three more fonts to choose from: Wingdings 2, Wingdings 3, and Webdings. Unless you specifically bypassed it, Office 2000 and Word 2000 automatically install Internet Explorer 5, so chances are very good you have these fonts.

WORKING WITH SPECIAL CHARACTERS

Traditionally, typographers have improved the look of documents by turning to some characters that do not appear on typewriter keyboards, such as copyright and registered trademark symbols, em dashes (—), and en dashes (–). By default, Word's AutoFormat As You Type feature adds many of these characters automatically.

→ For more information about AutoFormat As You Type, **see** Chapter 4, "Automating Your Documents: AutoCorrect, AutoFormat, AutoText, and AutoSummarize," **p. 75**.

Sometimes, however, you may need to add characters such as these directly. To do so, choose Insert, Symbol, click the Special Characters tab (see Figure 14.13), then double-click the symbol you require.

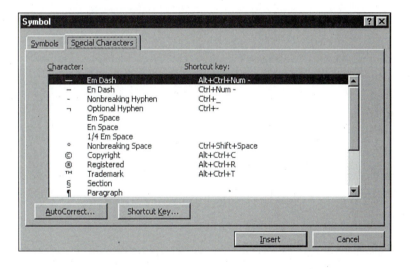

Figure 14.13
Entering a special character through the Special Characters tab of the Symbol dialog box.

CREATING A KEYBOARD SHORTCUT FOR A SYMBOL OR SPECIAL CHARACTER

Several special characters have keyboard shortcuts assigned to them. It pays to become familiar with these keyboard shortcuts: They can save you a lot of time.

However, many special characters don't have keyboard shortcuts—and neither do symbols you entered in the Symbols tab. If you expect to make extensive use of one of these characters, it might be a good idea to create a custom keyboard shortcut for it. To do so, follow these steps:

PART
III

CH
14

1. Choose Insert, Symbol.

2. Locate and select the character in either the Symbols or Special Characters tab.

3. Click Shortcut Key. The Customize Keyboard dialog box opens (see Figure 14.14).

4. Press the shortcut key combination you want to use. If that combination is already assigned, Word tells you so; try another combination.

5. When you've chosen a combination you want to use, click Assign.

6. Click Close twice.

Figure 14.14
Assigning a shortcut key to a symbol or special character.

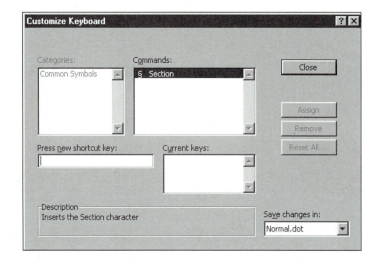

After you've created the shortcut key, you can insert the corresponding symbol at any time, by clicking where you want it to appear, and then pressing the shortcut key.

USING TEXT BOXES

Normally, when you work in Word, your text adjusts up, down, or sideways when you make other editing changes. But sometimes you want something—text, a graphic, a table, or some other document element—to stay put, no matter what.

Or perhaps you want to include sidebar or pullquote text in your document, and make sure the other text flows around it (see Figure 14.15). Or, perhaps you want to create copy that flows between one location and the next—as you would if you were producing a newsletter with a story that "jumped" from one page to another. You might want an address block on the back cover, or a form that recipients could return. These are some of the many valuable uses for Word's text box feature.

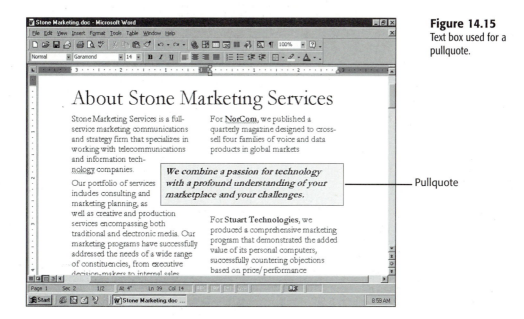

Figure 14.15
Text box used for a pullquote.

Text boxes are free-floating objects, independent of your regular document. You can specify precise locations and sizes for text boxes, as well as borders, fills, and other formatting.

Tip #229

In Word 2000, you can also wrap text around tables, so you can sometimes use tables rather than text boxes for sidebars and similar applications.

This is a valuable alternative whenever you have a multiple-column document and you need to call attention to information that is tightly structured, such as a row-and-column set of names, products, or financial results.

INSERTING A TEXT BOX

To insert a text box, follow these steps:

1. Choose Insert, Text Box. Your pointer becomes a small crosshair and Word switches to Print Layout view if you aren't already in that view.

2. Click where you want the upper-left corner of your text box to appear.

3. Drag out a rectangle matching the size and shape you want your text box to have.

4. Release the mouse button. Word displays a text box with shaded borders, as shown in Figure 14.16.

PART

III

CH

14

Figure 14.16
A typical text box, selected.

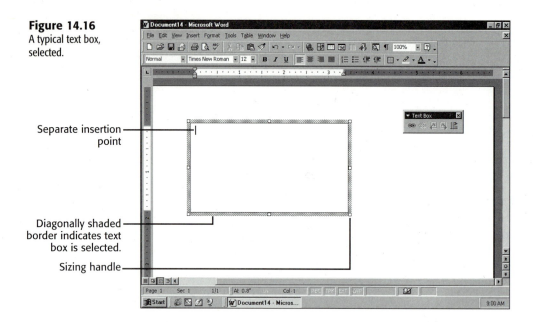

Separate insertion point

Diagonally shaded border indicates text box is selected.

Sizing handle

Your text box has its own insertion point; you can now enter text in it. You can also insert graphics, tables, fields, or virtually anything else Word can place in a document, with the following exceptions:

- Page and column breaks
- Comment marks
- Footnotes and endnotes
- Indexes and tables of contents (note that although entries for your index and table of contents can be placed in text boxes, Word won't find them when it compiles your index and table of contents)
- Columns
- Drop caps

Note　You can use frames for these tasks, as is covered in the following section.

When a text box is selected (refer to Figure 14.16), it has a special diagonal-line border with eight sizing handles around it. The text box also has its own ruler settings, which enable you to set tabs independently from the rest of the document. You can deselect the text box by clicking outside it.

Tip #230

If you're not sure how large you want your text box to be, you can use Word's default size. Choose Insert, Text Box; when you see the pointer become a small crosshair, just click once. A default text box appears. You can later size it as needed using the sizing handles.

Caution

Text boxes can be a bit tricky to delete. After you've selected one, click the border of the text box again. The border changes from a diagonal to a dot pattern. Then press Delete, and the text box disappears.

 When you create a text box, Word displays the Text Box toolbar. The Change Text Direction button can turn text in a text box sideways. As you click, the direction toggles; first to the right (read top to bottom), then to the left (read bottom to top); then back to normal (read left to right). You can't turn text upside down, nor can you turn only some of the text in a text box—it's all or nothing.

Tip #231

Using text boxes can add a bit of extra work, because you have to worry about how they're positioned and formatted. For example, default text boxes have 0.75-point borders that you may not want. If you get a text box formatted perfectly, and want to use it as a pattern for others you create, right-click to select it, and choose Set AutoShape Defaults.

CONVERTING TEXT BOXES TO FRAMES

In Word 6 and Word 95, many of the tasks now performed by text boxes were performed by frames. Frames were largely abandoned in Word 97. They still exist in Word 2000, but are rarely used. (These frames should not be confused with the new Web frames feature, which you can use to structure Web pages. Although the names are identical, the concepts are completely different.) Use a frame if

- You want to insert text or graphics that contain comments, or refer to footnotes or endnotes.
- You want to insert certain fields, including AUTONUM, AUTONUMLGL, and AUTONUMOUT (used for numbering lists and paragraphs in legal documents).

Word also ignores certain fields if they are placed in a text box; these fields are recognized if they are placed in a frame instead. They are: TC (Table of Contents Entry), TOC (Table of Contents), RD (Referenced Document), XE (Index Entry), TA (Table of Authorities Entry), and TOA (Table of Authority). If you would like to create an index or table of contents entry in a text box, use a frame instead.

Because frames are rarely used, there is no built-in menu command for creating them. To create a frame, follow these steps:

PART

III

CH

14

1. Insert a text box, as described in the previous section.

2. Choose Format, Text Box.

3. Click the Text Box tab.

4. Click Convert to Frame.

5. Click OK to confirm.

6. Unless the Office Assistant has been disabled, it appears, offering to add a Frame command to the Insert menu. If you plan to use many frames, choose Yes.

OTHER TYPES OF TEXT BOXES

Word text boxes aren't limited to rectangles. As you learned in Chapter 20, Word provides over 100 AutoShapes that enable you to include practically any shape in your document, from flowchart symbols to starbursts to cartoon-style callouts. You can easily transform any of these to a text box (except for lines and arrows, which lack an inside area where text could be entered). Follow these steps:

1. Click the Drawing button on the Standard toolbar (or choose View, Toolbars, Drawing) to display the Drawing toolbar.

2. Click AutoShapes on the Drawing toolbar, and select an AutoShape.

3. Your mouse pointer changes to a crosshair; drag the shape to the size and proportions you want.

4. Right-click the shape to display the shortcut menu.

5. Select Add Text. Word displays an insertion point inside it (see Figure 14.17), so you can type your text.

Figure 14.17
An AutoShape, formatted and converted into a text box, displaying text.

NEW
FOR '99!

Editable area

Note	

Although the AutoShape itself can be irregular, the area in which you can edit text is still rectangular, fitting entirely inside the AutoShape. This means your editing area can be much smaller than you expect.

Note

If you rotate the AutoShape, the text will not rotate with it.

FORMATTING YOUR TEXT BOX

By default, text boxes are surrounded by thin (.75 point) black lines; their interior is white (but not transparent). Text boxes are also set to appear in front of text, which means that they will obscure text behind them.

All these settings can be changed, using essentially the same techniques that were covered in Chapter 20 for formatting pictures with the Format, Picture dialog box. To reach text box formatting controls, select a text box and choose Format, Text Box. Or select the text box, right-click, and choose Format Text Box from the shortcut menu.

Either way, the Format Text Box tabbed dialog box opens, as shown in Figure 14.18.

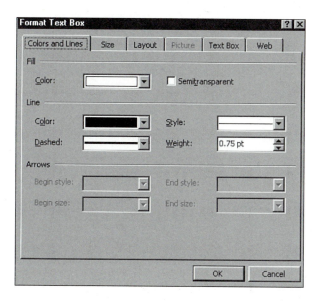

Figure 14.18
The Format Text Box dialog box.

- In the Colors and Lines tab, you can control the Fill Color that appears within a text box, and the Line Color, Style, and Weight that appear at the edge of the text box.

→ For more information, **see** "Changing the Appearance of a Line You've Drawn," **p. 406**.

- In the Size tab, you can control the size, rotation, and scale of the text box.

→ For more information, **see** "Resizing Images Precisely, Using Format, Picture," **p. 383**.

- In the Layout tab, you can control text wrapping, the precise position of a text box on a page, and how (or whether) the text box moves if surrounding page elements move.

→ For more information, **see** "Setting Text Wrapping from the Format Picture Dialog Box," **p. 386**.

PART

III

CH

14

- In the Text Box tab (see Figure 14.19), you control the internal Left, Right, Top, and Bottom margins of the text box; the default settings are 0.1" at the left and right, and 0.05" at the top and bottom.

Figure 14.19
Controlling the margins of a text box.

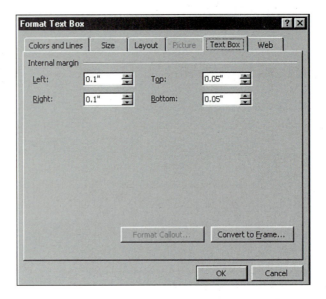

- Finally, in the Web tab, you can specify Alternative Text that will appear in Web browsers when the text box itself does not appear. If your text box contains text, Word automatically uses that text as the alternative text.

→ To learn more about using alternative text on Web pages, **see** "Adding Alternative Text to Your Image," **p. 390**.

Tip #232   You can also format text inside a text box using any of Word's Font and Paragraph formatting tools, or use tools on the Drawing toolbar, such as Fill Color, Line Color, Shadow, and 3D (see Chapter 21).

LINKING TEXT BOXES

If you've ever tried to create a newsletter, you know that it can be difficult to manage the "jumps" from one page to another within an article—especially if you're still editing that article. You may have found yourself moving small chunks of copy manually from one page to the next—and then having to do it again after you made more edits.

With Word's linked text box feature, that's no longer necessary. As you edit an article to become longer or shorter, the contents of each linked text box can adjust accordingly—automatically.

Linked text boxes were traditionally found only in dedicated desktop publishing applications such as Adobe PageMaker and Microsoft Publisher. Using text boxes, you may be able to publish many documents in Word that you once could create only with desktop publishing software.

Follow these steps to link one text box to another:

1. Create at least two text boxes.
2. Select the first text box.
3. Click the Create Text Box Link from the Text Box toolbar. The pointer changes to an upright pitcher (see Figure 14.20).
4. Move through the document until you find the second text box. Note that when you are over a text box available for linking, the upright pitcher changes into a pouring pitcher (see Figure 14.21).
5. Click the second text box.

You can now create another text box and link it to the second box by again following steps 2 through 5. You can either create and link all your text boxes ahead of time—when you are designing your newsletter—or add your boxes and link them as needed.

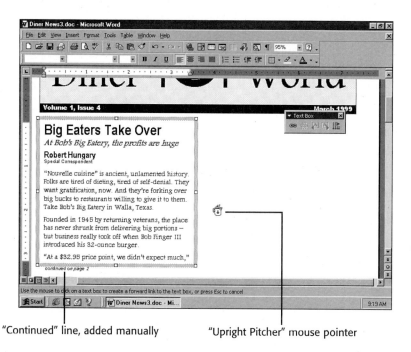

Figure 14.20
After you click the Create Text Box Link button, the mouse pointer changes to an upright pitcher shape.

"Continued" line, added manually   "Upright Pitcher" mouse pointer

Figure 14.21
When you're over a linkable text box, the pitcher mouse pointer changes to a pouring pitcher shape.

"Pouring Pitcher" mouse pointer

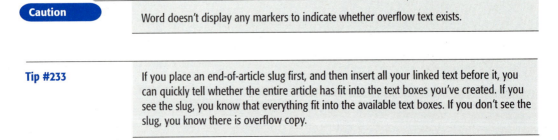

You can create links between as many text boxes as you want. Then, if you start entering text in the first text box and run out of room, the text flows into the next text box, and continues flowing from one linked text box to the next. If there's not enough text to fill them all, the text boxes at the end of the chain remain empty. If you have too much text to fit in all the text boxes, the excess text will run below the borders of the last text box. You may notice part of a line of text, depending on how the last text box has been sized.

Caution

Word doesn't display any markers to indicate whether overflow text exists.

Tip #233

If you place an end-of-article slug first, and then insert all your linked text before it, you can quickly tell whether the entire article has fit into the text boxes you've created. If you see the slug, you know that everything fit into the available text boxes. If you don't see the slug, you know there is overflow copy.

You can format the contents of all linked text boxes at the same time. Press Ctrl+A within one text box, to select all the text in all text boxes linked to it. (Conversely, if you press Ctrl+A to select all text outside a text box, no text inside any text box is selected.)

After you've linked text boxes, you can easily move from one text box to the next by clicking the Previous Text Box or Next Text Box buttons on the Text Box toolbar. You can also break links between text boxes whenever you want, as covered in the next section of this chapter.

You can have multiple articles running through separate sets of links. From a practical point of view, you don't want to do this with every item in your newsletter; it makes the articles too hard to follow.

BREAKING LINKS BETWEEN TEXT BOXES

 Occasionally you need to break a link between text boxes—maybe you need to reflow some text and start over or perhaps the wrong text boxes were linked. Whatever the reason, it's simple to break a link between two text boxes. Select the text box where you want the text to end, then click the Break Forward Link button on the Text Box toolbar.

If you break a link between two text boxes (say, "Text Box A" and "Text Box B"), all the links connecting after the second text box (Text Box B) are also lost.

When you break a link, all the text that previously appeared in the linked text box is now stored with the previous text box. Of course, the excess text that had appeared in the text box you've now unlinked will not be visible in the previous text box unless you expand that text box or reformat the text to make it smaller.

FOLLOWING A LINK

After your text boxes are linked, you can follow the links, forward or backward. When you have finished editing a story or article, it's good practice to follow your text through all the linked boxes to make sure it looks the way you want it to. Linked text boxes are very susceptible to widows (the last line at the bottom of a text box by itself) and orphans (the first line at the top of a text box by itself).

To follow a series of linked text boxes, select the first text box, then

- To move to the next linked text box, click the Next Text Box button.
- To move to the previous linked text box, click the Previous Text Box button.

You can also move from one text box to another using Word's arrow navigation keys. However, you cannot select text from two text boxes at the same time.

Linked text boxes must stay within one document: You can't link a text box to another in a separate file. Nor can you link text boxes between subdocuments when you're using a Master Document structure.

Tip #234

To add a continued line, as in Figure 14.20, place a small text box directly beneath the main one, type and format the continued line, then select both (Shift+click) and group them (right-click, Grouping, Group). The same technique can be used at the top of the next text box ("continued from" in a text box above them).

TROUBLESHOOTING

HOW TO TELL WHERE ONE SECTION STOPS AND THE NEXT ONE BEGINS

Continuous section breaks can be a little tricky. Unless you change the number of columns after a continuous section break, or put some sort of "spacer" between the section above and the section below, a reader might not even notice that there is a break. So, for example, if you have a three-column list of the names of full-time employees, balanced with a continuous section break, followed by a three-column list of part-time employees, it will be exceedingly difficult to tell where the full-timers end and the part-timers begin.

One way to force a visual separation is to select the first line following the continuous section break. (In this example, you'd create a blank line after the last full-time employee, and before the first part-timer, and select it.) Click the Column button on the toolbar and select 1 Column. That makes the blank line span the entire width of the page—giving a visual cue that one list has ended, while another has begun.

CHAPTER 15

USING GRAPHS TO MAKE SENSE OF YOUR DATA—VISUALLY

In this chapter

UNDERSTANDING GRAPHS AND CHARTS

If a picture is worth a thousand words, it's easily worth a thousand numbers. Tables or columns of numbers often appear dry, uninteresting, and difficult to understand—but a chart that shows a graphical representation of the same information can impart instant understanding. It can enable you to see both individual data points and patterns, so you can spot developing trends you'd never notice just by looking at numbers. It can consolidate facts that communicate the big picture more clearly. Not least, well-designed charts make documents look better.

> **Note**
>
> If you'd like to know more about communicating effectively and honestly with charts, graphs, and statistics, consider these two classic books:
>
> *The Visual Display of Quantitative Information*, Edward R. Tufte, Graphics Press.
>
> *How to Lie With Statistics*, Darrell Huff, Irving Geis, W.W. Norton & Co.

To help you include dynamic graphs in your documents, Word 2000 calls upon Microsoft Graph 2000 whenever you ask to create or insert a chart.

You can create many different types of charts with Graph 2000. All of them, however, have one thing in common: a *data source*. Your source data can be on the same page, elsewhere in the same document, in another Word file, or in a file created in Excel or some other program.

→ For more information about building charts in Word that use Excel data, **see** "Establishing a Link with Microsoft Excel," **p. 495**.

A HIGH-LEVEL LOOK AT CHARTING IN WORD

Here's a high-level overview of the process of creating a chart in Word, using Graph 2000:

1. Select the values in your Word document that you want to graph. (As you'll see, this step is optional; you can enter your source data directly in a Microsoft Graph *datasheet*. However, in most cases you'll already have created the data you want to graph; you may as well use that data rather than start from scratch.)

2. Choose Insert, Picture, Chart to run Microsoft Graph. Graph inserts a basic chart in your document, immediately beneath the source data.

3. Right-click on the chart, and choose Chart Type from the shortcut menu.

4. Set the Chart Type—in other words, tell Word what kind of chart you want.

5. Set Chart Options: what elements you want the chart to include, such as titles, gridlines, legends, and data labels.

6. Format the chart and its elements, selecting fonts, colors, backgrounds, and other attributes.

7. Take another look at the chart and make any changes you want, using Graph's editing, formatting, and drawing tools.

8. Click outside the chart area to return to Word.

The following sections take a closer look at each step of the process.

Note

Microsoft uses the terms graph and chart interchangeably throughout Microsoft Graph. This chapter does as well.

CREATING DATA TO BE GRAPHED

The easiest way to create data in Word for charting by Microsoft Graph is to first enter your data in a Word table, as shown in Figure 15.1.

	1Q99	2Q99	3Q99	4Q99
New York	750	772	784	779
California	886	911	937	958
Texas	456	512	528	556
Florida	398	433	465	499

Figure 15.1
Creating data for charting.

To create a chart from a table, first select the information in your table that you want to chart. Next, choose Insert, Picture, Chart.

Word inserts a 3D column chart based on your data, below your table, in a floating frame—as shown in Figure 15.2. Graph 2000 toolbars and menus temporarily replace the Word 2000 ones. The datasheet window opens.

To return to your regular document, click anywhere outside the chart frame.

Chart menu

Standard toolbar

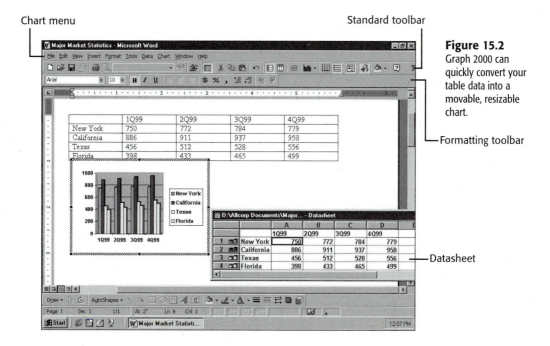

Figure 15.2
Graph 2000 can quickly convert your table data into a movable, resizable chart.

Formatting toolbar

Datasheet

TIPS FOR SELECTING WHICH DATA TO INCLUDE

To get a chart that says what you want to say, you must select the correct information from your data source. Here are some tips to keep in mind:

- Include at least one header row or column in your selection.

- If your table includes a cell, row, or column that contains totals, you may not want to select those totals, unless they measure an average rather than a quantity. Otherwise, including totals can skew the scale of your graph, making all the other data points look small in relation to the data point or points that contain the total. If you're creating a pie chart, exactly half the pie will contain your total. This is probably not the result you had in mind.

- Select only the data and headings you need. In particular, avoid selecting the table's overall title. If your first selected row or column does not have heading information, Graph 2000 doesn't read your selection properly and the result is a generic chart with dummy data.

MAKING YOURSELF AT HOME IN MICROSOFT GRAPH

When Word inserts a chart based on your information, it selects the chart. As long as the chart or any part of it is selected, you are working in Microsoft Graph. (If you click outside the chart, you have to double-click the chart to return to Microsoft Graph.)

Look around to get comfortable in your chart editing environment.

The menus on the menu bar and the buttons on your Standard and Formatting toolbars now reflect Microsoft Graph's commands rather than Word's (refer to Figure 15.2). Using these toolbars and menu commands, you can

- Format the chart or elements of it.
- Change the data that the chart graphs.
- Add or change elements of the chart, such as *data points*, *legends*, or *data labels*.
- Add a background pattern, shading, or a picture to the chart—or to individual chart elements or to the chart's background.

Note

The first time you run Graph 2000, it displays a one-line toolbar combining the most commonly used toolbar buttons from its Standard and Formatting toolbars. Most users want to display both complete toolbars to get access to all the menu commands. This chapter refers to buttons on the full toolbars whenever they provide the fastest way to get the job done.

To view the full toolbars, click on the toolbar handle at the left of the Formatting toolbar and drag it beneath the Standard toolbar.

Many of these toolbar buttons should be familiar to you as they are the same as buttons on the Standard and Formatting toolbars in Word. A few of the toolbar buttons shown in Figure 15.2 come in especially handy later, when you start formatting and editing elements of your chart. For example, the Chart Objects drop-down list box enables you to select a specific chart element so that you can format or edit that element. You'll find it especially helpful when you need to select a chart element that's difficult to click on, such as a thin gridline.

 The Import File button enables you to open a Microsoft Excel or other file and add information from that file to the chart you already have open. The Chart Type button gives you a quick way to switch among the most popular types of charts.

 And, on the Formatting toolbar, the Currency Style, Percent Style, Increase Decimal, and Decrease Decimal buttons give you a quick way to make sure your axes and other chart elements display numbers formatted as you like. All of these buttons are discussed later and shown later in this chapter in the section "Formatting Data in the Datasheet."

Caution

If you use Undo, be aware that Graph 2000's Undo button enables you to undo only your last action—not any of the last 100 or more actions, as in Word.

CHOOSING AMONG WORD'S EXTENSIVE SELECTION OF CHARTS

By default, Graph 2000 displays your information in its default chart format: a 3D column chart using standard colors against a gray background with gridlines and a legend. Graph's default chart makes sense in many situations, but you'll often want something else.

Graph 2000 gives you plenty of choices. For openers, you can choose between 18 different chart types, most with five to eight different variations or sub-types. From there you can modify every feature of the chart—titles, legends, grids, data series, size, placement, and wrapping—and you can use Word 2000's enhanced fill and color capabilities to include gradients, textures, and patterns.

Your first decision, however, must be to determine what kind of chart you want. Microsoft Graph chart types include

 ■ **Column charts.** Each data point corresponds to a vertical line; each series of data uses vertical lines of the same color.

 ■ **Bar charts.** This is probably the most popular type of chart. It shows data as a series of horizontal bars. Bar charts can be used effectively with three or four series of data over a period of time (such as monthly sales figures from four different regions).

 ■ **Line charts.** Line charts are almost always used to display changes in data over time. You can display the changes over time in one data series, or many. Several styles of line charts are available, including stacked and unstacked options. Stacked charts show the lines above one another; unstacked charts do not.

Note

A *data point* is a single piece of data, such as the sales associated with one product in one month. A *data series* is a set of related data, such as the sales associated with one product in each month of the current year.

■ **Pie charts.** This type of chart is particularly useful for showing the relationship or degree of relationship between numeric values in separate groups of data.

■ **Scatter charts.** These help you identify patterns or trends and determine whether variables depend on or affect one another.

■ **Area charts.** This chart shows data as areas filled with different colors or patterns. Area charts are best suited for charts that don't have large numbers of data points and that use several data series. They look particularly dramatic in 3D form.

■ **Doughnut charts.** This is basically a pie chart but with more flexibility—and a hole in the middle. Each ring of the doughnut chart represents a data series. Use this chart to compare the parts to the whole in one or more data categories.

■ **Radar charts.** This chart resembles a cobweb and shows changes in data or data frequency relative to a center point. Lines connect all the values in the same data series.

■ **3D Surface charts.** This chart resembles a rubber sheet stretched over a 3D column chart. 3D surface charts can help show relationships among large amounts of data. Colors or patterns delineate areas that share the same value. Use this chart for finding the best combinations between two sets of data.

■ **Bubble charts.** These are similar to an XY scatter chart. The bubble size is a third value type that is relative to the x-axis and y-axis data. Use this for depicting the relationship between two kinds of related data.

Word 2000 also provides three variants: cylinder charts, pyramid charts, and cone charts. You can use these just as you use bar or column charts, except that the data points are displayed as cylinders, pyramids, or cones.

Caution

Not every set of data can be used with every chart type. Worse, in some cases, you can chart the data, but the results are misleading or incomprehensible. After you create a chart, read it carefully to make sure it communicates what you have in mind.

Communicating with Word: Tips for Choosing the Right Chart

Choose the right type of chart for your data to help ensure your point comes across as you intended. If you have data that is continuous, such as time, or concentrated data, you should use a scatter or XY plot. If your data is categorical, such as the number of red cars versus the number of blue cars, you can use a larger variety of charts such as the bar chart and the column chart.

The main difference between the types of data is if you have measurements on a continuous scale, then the intervals between your measurements do not have to be equal and may even be impossible to make equal. The scatter or XY plot takes the variable intervals into account. The bar chart and column charts will plot the data using equal intervals.

CHANGING CHART TYPE WITH A SINGLE CLICK

To select a different chart type from the one Graph has used to build your chart, first make sure Graph is open. If Word's menus and toolbars appear rather than Graph's, double-click anywhere in your chart to activate Graph.

 Then, right-click on the chart and choose Chart Type from the shortcut menu. Next, choose one of the 18 chart types that appear (see Figure 15.3). Word replaces your chart with its default version of the chart type you selected.

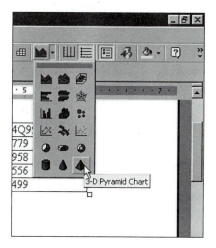

Figure 15.3
Choosing a new chart type from the Standard toolbar.

TAKING MORE CONTROL OVER CHART TYPES

Choosing a chart with the Chart Type toolbar button is quick—but what if you aren't satisfied with the default chart it places in your document? Change it, with Word's extensive tools for selecting and adjusting chart types. Follow these steps:

1. Either choose Chart Type from the Chart menu, or (with Microsoft Graph open) right-click in a blank part of the chart area and choose Chart Type from the shortcut menu that appears. The Chart Type dialog box appears (see Figure 15.4).

2. From the Standard Types tab of the Chart Type dialog box, click any of the Chart types in the left column to see the corresponding Chart Sub-Types on the right. Use the scroll button to see additional selections. Select the desired sub-type.

3. To see how your data looks using the chart type you've selected, click the Click and Hold to View Sample button.

4. When you're finished, click OK.

CHANGING YOUR DEFAULT CHART TYPE

As you've learned, Word's default chart type is a 3D bar chart. However, you might prefer to use a different standard or custom chart type as your default for all charts from now on.

Figure 15.4
Changing the type of standard chart you use.

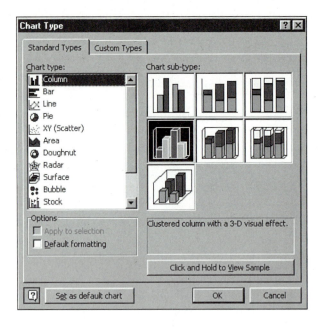

Caution

Some users find that Microsoft Graph's 3D effect can distort their data, or that its charts do not reproduce well on low-end printers. In addition, most technical users avoid 3D charts based on less than three sets of data.

To choose a different default chart, right-click on your chart and choose Chart Type from the shortcut menu. In the Standard Types tab of the Chart Type dialog box, select the chart type and sub-type you want as your new default. (Later, you'll learn about custom chart types; you can use one of these, also, by choosing it from the Custom Types tab.) Click Set as Default Chart, and click OK.

Now every time you create a chart, Graph 2000 uses your new default.

CHOOSING FROM WORD'S LIBRARY OF CUSTOM CHARTS

In addition to Word's standard charts, you can choose from 20 built-in custom charts already formatted and ready to use. If you find one you like, you'll save the time and effort of formatting your charts one element at a time.

To choose a custom chart from within Microsoft Graph, right-click on a chart and choose Chart Type from the shortcut menu. Click the Custom Types tab, shown in Figure 15.5. Select the chart type you want. In the Sample box, Word displays a preview of how your data will appear if you choose this chart. Finally, click OK.

→ To create your own user-defined chart, **see** "How to Create a Custom Chart," **p. 487**.

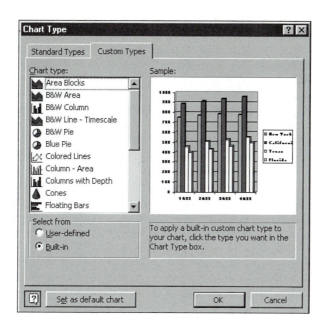

Figure 15.5
You can choose from
a full range of graphs
and their sub-types
from the Chart Type
dialog box.

WORKING WITH CHART OPTIONS

Now that you've decided what type of chart to create, you can set a wide variety of options for your chart. For example, you may want to annotate the chart with a title, a legend, and titles for each individual chart axis, depending on the number of axes the chart has. All these elements become part of the chart, and if you resize or move the chart, they are resized or moved as well.

Before you start working with chart options or with chart formatting, however, it's helpful to take a look at the elements that can appear in charts, and the nomenclature Graph uses to describe these elements—which may not always be familiar.

INSPECTING A CHART

Figure 15.6 shows a typical 3D column chart. This chart's elements include the plot area (the main part of the chart), which is bounded by the axes: the x-axis, y-axis, and (in some three-dimensional charts) a z-axis.

Tip #237

If you're not sure where a chart element is, or what it's called, move the mouse pointer of an element on the chart. Word displays a ScreenTip that shows you the name of the chart element you're pointing to.

Within the plot area, the chart depicts one or more data series, each representing a row or column of data from your Word table or other source. The individual bars, columns, or other elements representing each data point within the data series are called *data markers*.

Figure 15.6
A typical Microsoft
Graph 3D column
chart.

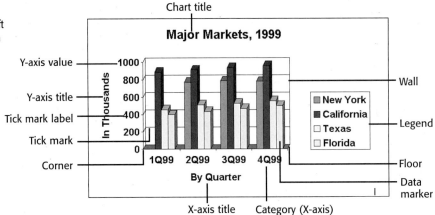

The plot area can also contain several optional text elements, such as *axis titles* that describe what each axis is measuring, and *data labels* that show the exact values (or names) for each data marker. *Gridlines* help the eye keep track of multiple lines.

A *chart title* appears at the top of the chart. In this example, the y-axis is the scale Microsoft Graph uses to generate the chart. This is true with most charts, with the notable exception of pie charts. If all your data points are between 0 and 500, for example, Graph places 0 at the bottom of the scale and 500 at the top.

Each increment on the y-axis is called a *tick mark*. Graph also features a y-axis title that you can use to tell your audience what you're measuring. Some examples might be

    Profit, in millions of dollars

    Commissions, by percentage

    Hard disk speed, in milliseconds

    Land, in square miles

The x-axis normally tells which data series is being measured. Often, the y-axis displays the passage of time. For example, it might show four quarters in a year, or monthly results. Or, it might also show results from various locations or divisions.

By default, Graph displays each data series in a different color, with like information displayed in the same color. Graph generally maintains contrast between adjacent bars, pie slices, and so on. This contrast enables you to understand the data clearly, even when it's printed in black and white. As you'll see later, however, you can change color, add patterns, or change the background Graph normally uses.

In 3D charts, such as the one shown in Figure 15.6, Graph also includes a wall, corner, and floor. These make up the 3D background to the "room" where the chart appears. Walls and floors can each be formatted separately.

Finally, most charts (except those that use only one data series) also contain a *legend*—an explanation of what each color or pattern represents. Graph inserts a legend by default.

SETTING CHART OPTIONS

To control the options available for your specific chart, select the chart and choose Chart Options from the Chart menu. Or, right-click on an empty area within the chart and choose Chart Options from the shortcut menu. The Chart Options dialog box appears, as shown in Figure 15.7.

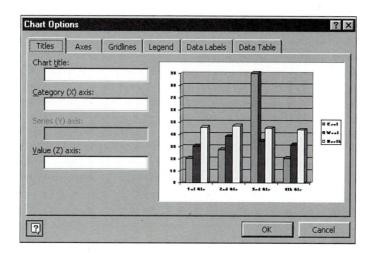

Figure 15.7
You can control the elements included in your chart through the Chart Options dialog box.

Keep in mind that the options available to you depend on the chart you've chosen. For example, a column chart has two axes that can be titled, whereas a radar chart has none. Most charts have gridlines; pie charts and doughnut charts do not.

Some controls are available no matter what kind of chart you have, however. For example, you can always specify a title for your chart in the Titles tab, or a legend in the Legend tab.

As you work in the tabs of the Chart Options dialog box, you can see the effects of your changes in a preview that appears on the right side of the dialog box.

The next few sections discuss each chart option available through the Chart Options dialog box.

INSERTING TITLES FOR YOUR CHART AND AXES

To add a title to your chart, display the Chart Options dialog box and select the Titles tab. Graph displays title options, as shown earlier in Figure 15.7. Here, you can specify which titles you wish to add: a Chart Title, and in most cases, titles for at least one axis. Type the titles in the text boxes, and click OK. Graph now displays the titles in the chart, inserted as text boxes.

You can now edit or format the titles manually by clicking inside the title you want to edit. As you edit and format the title, you have access to Standard toolbar buttons such as Cut, Copy, and Paste; and Formatting toolbar buttons such as Font, Font Size, Bold, Italic, and

Underline. These work just as they do in Word. To move any title, click it once to highlight its text box, and then click and drag the borders of the box.

→ For more information about formatting chart elements, **see** "Formatting Chart Elements," **p. 482**.

Caution

Any text in a chart automatically resizes when the overall chart is resized. This can lead to undesirable results. To turn off automatic resizing, right-click inside the title and choose Format Chart Title from the shortcut menu. Then, in the Font tab of the Format Chart Title dialog box, clear the Auto Scale check box.

CONTROLLING AXES

By default, Graph displays tick mark labels about each axis of data it is graphing. You can use the Axes tab of the Graph Options dialog box to hide tick mark labels for some of the axes in your chart, or to change the labels displayed on your chart's primary axis.

To hide the tick mark labels associated with any axis, with Microsoft Chart open, right-click on the chart, and choose Chart Options from the shortcut menu. Click the Axes tab (see Figure 15.8), and clear the check box next to the axis beside which you don't want to display tick mark labels. Click OK.

Figure 15.8
Controlling how axes display through the Chart Options dialog box.

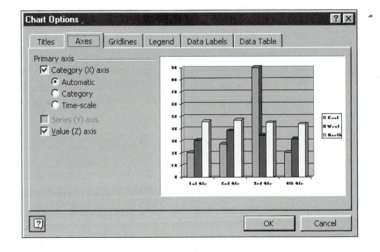

To change the contents of your primary axis tick mark labels, right-click on the chart and click the Axes tab. Make sure the Primary Axis is checked; then click the Automatic, Category or Time-Scale button, and click OK.

CONTROLLING GRIDLINES

Gridlines can make your chart more readable—or, if you overdo them, they can make your chart more obscure. Graph 2000 gives you complete control over the gridlines along each axis. You can easily turn them on or off, or format them any way you like.

To enable or disable a gridline, click its corresponding button in the Standard toolbar. The Value Axis Gridline button controls horizontal lines; the Category Axis Gridline button controls vertical lines.

If you want more control over your gridlines, choose the Gridlines tab in the Chart Options dialog box (see Figure 15.9).

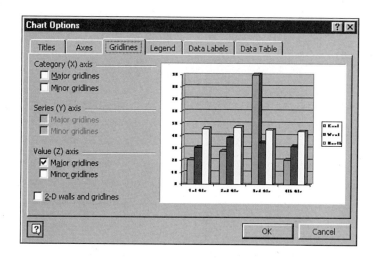

Figure 15.9
Controlling gridlines through the Chart Options dialog box.

By default, Graph places gridlines perpendicular to the data being charted, at the same points where values are shown along the axis. For example, if you create a bar graph where the columns appear horizontally, the value axis is the x-axis, and the gridlines are displayed vertically from that axis. However, you can add gridlines for another axis, as shown in Figure 15.10.

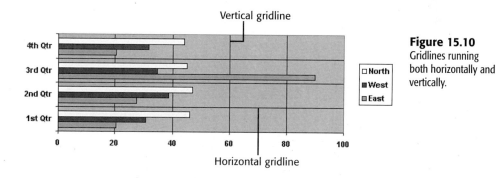

Figure 15.10
Gridlines running both horizontally and vertically.

Gridlines placed at the same points as values are called *major gridlines*. If you want additional gridlines to appear between major gridlines, add *minor gridlines*. By default, Word does not display gridlines parallel to the data being charted (in other words, on another axis). But you can add these as well—both major and minor gridlines.

INSERTING A LEGEND

 Legends are used to explain the color or pattern conventions used in a chart. You can turn a chart's legend on or off by clicking the Legend button on the Graph 2000 toolbar. Or, if you want to specify where the legend appears in your chart, display the Legend tab of the Chart Options dialog box (see Figure 15.11).

Figure 15.11
You can place a legend to the left, right, top, or bottom of the chart.

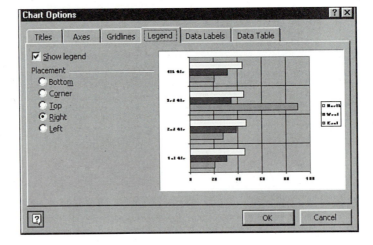

Check the Show Legend check box to place a legend in your chart; then choose Bottom, Corner, Top, Right, or Left to specify where the legend appears. (If you choose Corner, the legend appears at the top right of the chart object.)

Tip #238	After you place the legend in your chart, you can drag it anywhere you want.

ADDING OR CHANGING DATA LABELS

By default, Graph inserts a chart without including the specific values or names associated with each data point. However, if your readers need to know specific values or names, you can add them. Right-click on a data marker, choose Format Data Series from the shortcut menu, and click the Data Labels tab (see Figure 15.12).

You can display either the value associated with each selected data series or data point (Show Value), or the name of that data series or data point (Show Label). For pie charts, you also have the option of displaying a percentage (Show Percent). If you already have data labels and want to remove them, choose None.

The data labels that Graph inserts in your chart are linked to the headings of the columns and rows displayed in the datasheet that Graph creates from your source data. Therefore, if you change the headings in your datasheet, Graph updates the label on your chart— whether or not you change the headings in your source document.

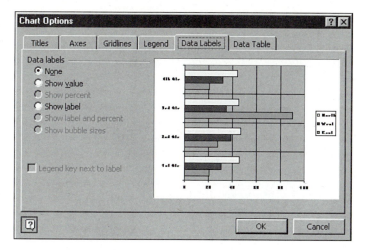

Figure 15.12
Inserting data labels
through the Chart
Options dialog box.

 If data labels disappear when you resize your chart, see "What to Do If Your Chart Loses Data Labels After Resizing," in the "Troubleshooting" section of this chapter.

ADDING DATA TABLES

You can use *data tables* to make sure readers not only get the visual gist of the chart, but also see the actual data on which it is based.

Data tables can be especially helpful if your data comes from a source other than the Word document where you are placing the chart. You can see an example of a data table in Figure 15.13.

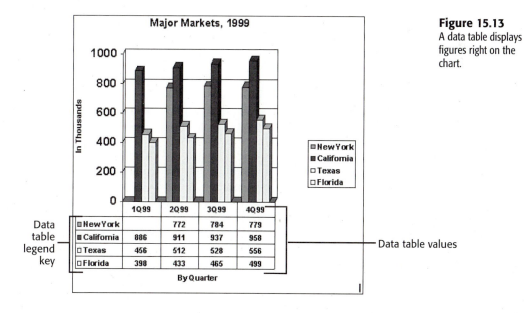

Figure 15.13
A data table displays
figures right on the
chart.

To insert a data table in your chart, click the Data Table button on the Standard toolbar. You can also insert a data table through the Chart Options dialog box. Right-click on the chart, and choose Chart Options from the shortcut menu. Click the Data Table tab (see Figure 15.14), check the Show Data Table check box, and click OK.

Figure 15.14
Setting up a data table through the Chart Options dialog box.

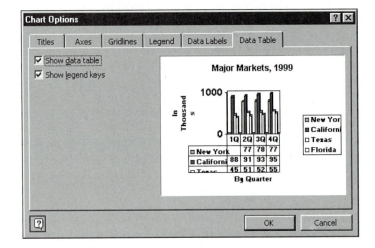

The default data table includes *legend keys* next to its headings (refer to Figure 15.13). Legend keys give you the same color and pattern information you would normally place in a legend—so you don't need to use both. However, if you don't want to include the color and pattern information, you can clear the Show Legend Keys check box in the Data Table tab of the Chart Options dialog box.

FORMATTING CHART ELEMENTS

Any element of a chart that you can insert, you can also format.

In some cases, as mentioned earlier, you can format a chart element directly. For example, you can select text in a title and apply font formatting to it. You can also move elements, such as your chart's legend or plot area, by dragging them with the mouse.

However, in most cases you'll work with dialog boxes to access the formatting controls you need. To format a chart element, double-click on it; or right-click on it and choose the format command that appears at the top of the shortcut menu.

For example, if you right-click on your chart's title, the Format Chart Title command appears, and if you select it the Format Chart Title dialog box appears—which contains tabs for formatting the Patterns, Font, and Alignment of text in the title (see Figure 15.15).

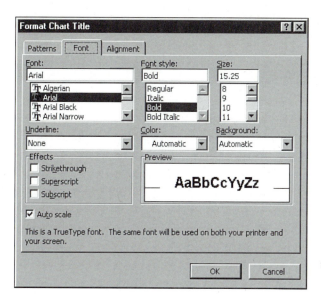

Figure 15.15
The Format Chart Title dialog box is an example of the dialog boxes available for formatting individual chart elements.

Tip #239

If you're having trouble precisely positioning the mouse pointer on the chart element you want to click, you can select it from the Chart Objects drop-down box on the Standard toolbar (see Figure 15.16).

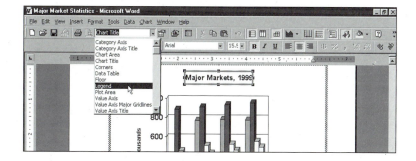

Figure 15.16
Selecting a chart element from the Chart Objects drop-down box.

Table 15.1 lists the chart elements that can be formatted, and the formatting categories available to you through that chart element's Format dialog box.

TABLE 15.1   CHART ELEMENTS AND AVAILABLE FORMATTING

Chart Element	Available Formatting
Axis	Patterns, Scale, Font, Number, Alignment
Chart Area	Patterns, Font

continues

TABLE 15.1 CONTINUED

Chart Element	Available Formatting
Chart Title	Patterns, Font, Alignment
Data Labels	Patterns, Font, Number, Alignment
Data Points	Patterns, Data Labels, Options
Data Series	Patterns, Axis, Y Error Bars, Data Labels, Options (varies with chart type)
Data Table	Patterns, Font
Error Bars	Patterns, Y Error Bars
Floors	Patterns
Gridlines	Patterns, Scale
Legend	Patterns, Font, Placement
Legend Entry	Font
Plot Area	Patterns
Trendline	Patterns, Type, Options
Walls	Patterns

WORKING WITH PATTERNS

In Chapter 13, "Drawing in Word," you learned how to use Word's backgrounds and fill effects in your document. Many of these features are available in Graph 2000, as well. For example, as listed in Table 15.1, nearly all the elements in a Microsoft Graph chart contain patterns. You can adjust these patterns using the same color and fill effects available to drawing objects in Word.

→ For more information on working with fill effects, **see** "Controlling Colors," **p. 419**.

In addition to colors, you can also give your charts textures, patterns, and gradient fills; you can even fill an element with a picture of your own choosing. To give a chart element a different fill color or effect, follow these steps:

1. Right-click on the chart object you want to format, and choose the Format option on the shortcut menu. The appropriate Format dialog box opens.

2. If necessary, click the Patterns tab.

3. To choose a standard color, click one of the color swatches in the Color section. For additional color options, click the More Colors button.

4. To choose one of the enhanced effects (gradients, textures, patterns, or picture), click Fill Effects. Choose the appropriate tab and fill effect.

5. Click OK.

Figure 15.17 shows a chart that makes heavy use of gradients: Each data series is formatted with a one-color fill effect that is dark at the base and gradually lightens as you move up. The Chart Area uses a similar gradient, except that it's dark at the top and light at the bottom.

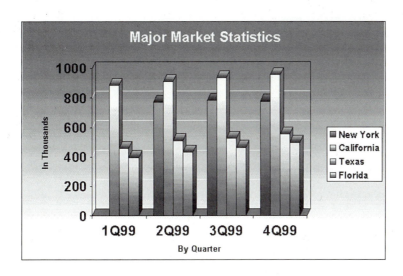

Figure 15.17
Adding textures and fill effects to a chart is an easy way to make it look more interesting.

Typically, when you start adding textures such as these to the background, you have to adjust text fonts and other elements as well. In this example, the chart title has been formatted in white type, and the legend is formatted with a white background to make it easier to read against the gray background of the chart area.

Caution

Be aware that many of the color schemes Microsoft Graph proposes may not reproduce with sufficient contrast on a black-and-white printer.

Tip #240

You can select an individual element of a data series and reformat it for emphasis, without changing the other elements. To do so, double-click on the data point. The Format Data Point dialog box opens, containing formatting controls that affect no other data point except the one you selected.

ADDING CALLOUTS WITH GRAPH'S DRAWING TOOLS

As you learned in Chapter 13, callouts can be used to call attention to specific text or graphics in your document. You can also use callouts to comment on charts you produce in Graph 2000, as shown in Figure 15.18. The tools and the techniques are the same. As in Word, Graph's callout feature can be found on a special Drawing toolbar.

Figure 15.18
Callouts enable you to emphasize and comment on your Graph 2000 chart.

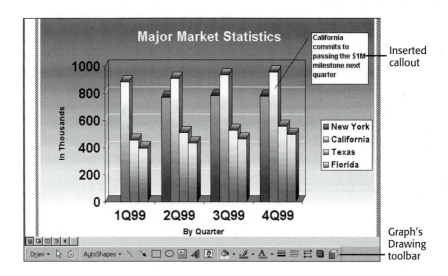

Inserted callout

Graph's Drawing toolbar

To place a callout in your Graph 2000 chart

1. Click the Drawing button on the Standard toolbar (or choose View, Toolbars, Drawing).
2. Click the AutoShapes button on the Drawing toolbar.
3. Select Callouts and then choose a callout to insert. The pointer changes into a small crosshair.
4. Click your callout's subject first and then, holding down the mouse button, drag to your callout location. Release the mouse button.

   An insertion pointer appears in the callout box.
5. Input your text and apply any formatting desired.
6. If necessary, resize the callout box by clicking and dragging any of the sizing handles.
7. If you wish, adjust the placement of the leader by clicking the yellow diamond adjustment handle(s).
8. Click anywhere outside of the callout box to return to the chart.

→ For more information about working with callouts, **see** "Using Callouts," **p. 414**.

Tip #241	Of course, you can use Graph's other Drawing tools to add text boxes, arrows, and any other shape that might clarify your chart's contents.

CREATING A CUSTOM CHART TYPE

Earlier, you learned that you can use the Chart Options dialog box to choose from two sets of built-in charts: Standard Types and Custom Types. Custom chart types are similar to templates in Word: They bring together a collection of styles and settings you can use over and over again.

Each custom chart type is based on a standard chart type and may contain additional formatting and options, such as a legend, gridlines, data labels, a secondary axis, colors, patterns, fills, and placement choices for various chart items.

Now that you've learned how to customize a chart's elements and formatting, you may wish to create your own custom chart. To do so, you can start from one of the custom charts Microsoft provides, or build your own from scratch.

HOW TO CREATE A CUSTOM CHART

You create a custom chart by first creating an example. Format a chart as you want it, complete with specific fills, typefaces, chart options, and colors. After you've built your "model," follow these steps to build its settings into a reusable custom chart:

1. Right-click on the chart, and choose Chart Type from the shortcut menu.

2. When the Chart Type dialog box opens, click the Custom Types tab.

3. Click the User-Defined radio button in the Select From section.

4. Click the Add button. The Add Custom Chart Type dialog box opens (see Figure 15.19).

5. Type the name for this new chart type in the Name text box. If you like, you can also type a brief description in the Description text box. This section could include when the chart was previously used, what it is to be used for, who created it, and so on.

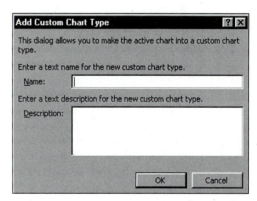

6. Click OK on both the Add dialog box and then the Chart Type dialog box.

Figure 15.19

HOW TO USE A CUSTOM CHART YOU'VE CREATED

After you've created a custom chart, here's how to use it:

1. Insert a chart in your document.

2. With Microsoft Graph open, choose Chart, Chart Type.

3. Click the Custom Types tab.

4. Click the User-Defined button.

5. In the Chart Type scroll box, select the name of the chart you created. A thumbnail of your chart appears in the preview section. Note that it may not be perfectly representative of how your data will ultimately look.

6. Click OK. Word reformats your chart based on your custom chart type.

HOW CUSTOM CHART TYPES CAN SUPPORT YOUR CORPORATE DESIGN STANDARDS

If you're working in a large office, you may want to standardize on a set of custom chart types that reflect your company's design standards. Word and Graph provide several ways to share custom chart types.

The first is to have each user open a document that contains the chart you want, select the chart, and store the format as a custom format—using the procedure previously described in "How to Create a Custom Chart."

A second alternative is to embed your custom charts in a template you can distribute or place in the workgroup templates folder.

In most cases, however, the best alternative is to copy the file Grusgral.gra, which stores custom charts, to each computer you want to have access to them. In Word 2000 running on Windows 98 or 95, this file is typically stored in the folder C:\Windows\Application Data\Microsoft\Graph. In Word 2000 running on Windows NT 4, this file is typically stored in the C:\Winnt\Profiles folder, in the \Application Data\Microsoft\Graph sub-folder of whichever profile is associated with your user logon.

Copying this file to another computer makes its custom charts available to that user.

Caution

If you copy your Grusgral.gra over a user's existing Grusgral.gra file, you will delete any custom charts they have created. Ideally, create and store your custom charts before you install Microsoft Word or Microsoft Graph on your colleagues' computers—in other words, before your colleagues have had time to create their own custom charts.

CREATING A CHART FROM SCRATCH

You don't have to have an existing table in your document to build a chart. You don't even need a pre-existing data source. You can open Graph 2000 using a set of dummy (fake) data, and then replace that data with your real data.

To do so, place your insertion point where you want the chart to appear. Then choose Insert, Picture, Chart. The default chart uses dummy values to create a two-series 3D column chart.

WORKING IN THE DATASHEET WINDOW

Alongside the chart is a datasheet window containing the dummy data, as shown in Figure 15.20. The datasheet looks much like a basic spreadsheet, except that you can enter only numbers and letters in it—it cannot handle formulas. The only purpose of the datasheet is to control the data that creates a chart in Microsoft Graph.

When you first insert a chart, the datasheet appears in a separate window near the chart. You can toggle the datasheet on or off by clicking the Datasheet button on Microsoft Graph's Standard toolbar.

Column heading   Active cell

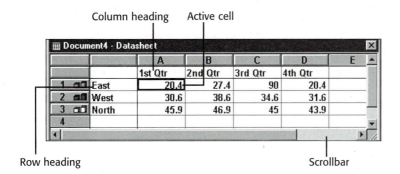

Row heading   Scrollbar

Figure 15.20
A datasheet accompanying a Microsoft Graph chart.

If you create your chart from data in a Word document, that data appears in your datasheet when you open it. To change a value, click in its cell and enter the new value. When you change a value in the datasheet, the chart reflects the change immediately.

Caution

Remember that changes you make in the datasheet are not automatically reflected in the table or other data source from which you may have built the chart. To link the values in your document to the contents of your chart automatically, see "Establishing an OLE Link Between Word and Graph," later in this chapter.

Notice that each row of the datasheet also contains a *data series graphic*: a chart icon showing the color and pattern of the corresponding data series as it now appears in the chart.

If you've ever worked in a spreadsheet program such as Excel, you'll be comfortable working in the datasheet. Here are some brief pointers on datasheet editing:

- To clear any section of the datasheet, select an area by clicking and dragging over it and then press Delete.

- You can quickly select the entire sheet by clicking the unmarked button at the upper-left corner of the columns and rows.

- To overwrite any existing data, just click the cell and input your new value or label.

- To edit existing data without retyping it, double-click in the cell, or select the cell and press F2.

- After entering any new values or labels, you must confirm them by pressing Enter, Tab, or any arrow key, thereby moving out of the present cell.

- Graph 2000 reserves the first column and row for data series labels (except in xy scatter and bubble charts, where the first row or column contains values). No matter how far you scroll to the right, the first column remains visible; no matter how far you scroll down, the first row remains visible. This way, you can always see your headings.

- If your label or data is too wide to fit in the width of the column, you can adjust the column by clicking and dragging the line on the right between the column headings. When your pointer is positioned correctly, it changes into a double-headed arrow.

When a column is too narrow to properly display a value, Graph shows a series of symbols (for example, "#####") until the column is widened.

■ You can exclude a data series from the chart without erasing it by double-clicking the corresponding row or column heading. The row or column turns a light gray to indicate that it is inactive. To activate it again, double-click it.

 If you need a hard copy of your datasheet, see "How to Print a Copy of Your Datasheet," in the "Troubleshooting" section of this chapter.

MOVING DATA IN THE DATASHEET

Datasheet contents can be cut and pasted like most other elements in Word. To highlight a cell on the datasheet, click it once. From there, Cut, Copy, and Paste work as they do in Word.

You can also drag and drop your cells to replace one value with another. To drag and drop a cell, position your pointer on the black border around a selected cell, then click and drag your cell to a new location. Release the mouse button. If the new location already contains a value, Graph asks you to confirm that you want to replace it.

> **Caution**
>
> If you find that the drag-and-drop feature is not working, it may have been disabled. With Graph open, choose Tools, Options, and click the Datasheet Options tab. Make sure the Cell Drag-and-Drop check box is checked.

FORMATTING DATA IN THE DATASHEET

Graph enables you to apply formats in your datasheet. Most of these formats—including font format, cell alignments, and column width—are available simply to help you make your datasheet more readable. They are not reflected in either your chart or your Word document. You can access these by choosing Format, Font or Format, Column Width, or by clicking buttons on Graph's Formatting toolbar.

However, one set of formatting options is reflected in your chart: Number formats. You have two ways to specify how numbers are formatted in your charts. The quickest way is to use the five number-related toolbar buttons on Graph's Formatting toolbar:

 ■ **Currency Style.** This button adds a leading currency symbol. In the U.S., this means that the figure 1234 is shown as $1,234.00.

 ■ **Percent Style.** This button displays the value times 100, followed by a percent sign. To depict 50%, the value would need to be .5.

 ■ **Comma Style.** This button adds a thousands separator, a decimal separator, and decimals to two places. If applied to the value 1234, the number displays as 1,234.00.

 ■ **Increase Decimals.** This button is used with the previous styles. Each time you click this button, one additional decimal place is shown in your chart.

■ **Decrease Decimals.** This button is used with the previous styles. Each time you click this button, one fewer decimal place is shown in your chart.

For more complex number formatting, right-click on a number in an individual cell, and choose <u>N</u>umber from the shortcut menu. This opens the Format Number dialog box (see Figure 15.21).

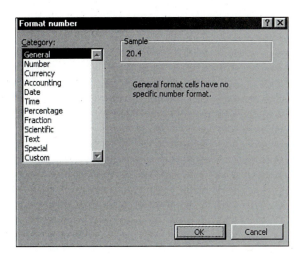

Figure 15.21
Using the Format Number dialog box to control the formatting of numbers in a datasheet.

Here, you can choose from a dozen format categories, including Currency, Accounting, Date, Time, Percentage, and Scientific. In each category are numerous subcategories detailing different options involving negative numbers and other choices. You can also use a Custom category to construct your own formatting option by entering your choice in the <u>T</u>ype text box.

→ For more information about creating custom number formatting, **see** "Customizing Numeric Formats to Your Specific Needs," **p. 577**.

UPDATING YOUR DATA

After you've created your chart, the datasheet is your main conduit for altering the data figures. As noted previously, you can also link your chart to your in-document table using a process described later in this chapter. In the Datasheet window, click the value you want to update.

As in spreadsheet programs such as Microsoft Excel, a single click of a cell—the box formed by the intersection of column and row—selects it, just as if you had double-clicked a word in the regular document. Type in your new number and the old number is replaced. You can move from cell to cell by pressing Tab, Enter, or any of the arrows. After you enter a new value, the chart updates when you confirm your entry by moving out of the cell.

USING TRENDLINES

Spotting trends is a major use of charts and data. Graph 2000 uses formulas developed through the study of regression analysis to create *trendlines*.

Trendlines extend the actual data forward to predict a possible course. You can also test your trend analysis by extending the data backwards and comparing it against actual figures.

Trendlines can be used in a variety of chart types: unstacked area, bar, column, line, stock, xy (scatter), and bubble charts. However, you cannot add trendlines to a 3D, stacked, radar, pie, or doughnut chart. If you have trendlines in place and you convert your chart to one that does not support trendlines, the trendlines disappear.

It's easy to add a trendline to your chart. Choose Chart, Add Trendlines. (If Add Trendlines is not active, then your chart type doesn't support this option.) The Add Trendline dialog box opens, as shown in Figure 15.22.

Figure 15.22
Choose a trend analysis from six different formulas.

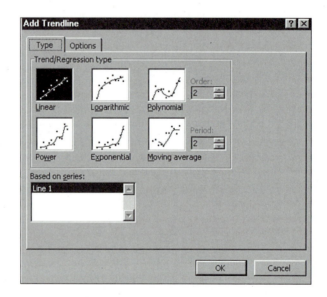

On the Type tab, you can choose from six different Trend/Regression formulas: Linear, Logarithmic, Polynomial, Power, Exponential, and Moving Average. After you've chosen a formula type for your trendline, click the Options tab of the Add Trendline dialog box. Here, you can give your trendline a custom name and set the number of periods your trendline is to forecast both forward and backward.

After you set these options, your chart will contain a trendline similar to the one in Figure 15.15. You can change the color, style, and weight of the trendline (and reset any of the previously chosen options, as well) by selecting the line and clicking the Format button on Graph's Standard toolbar.

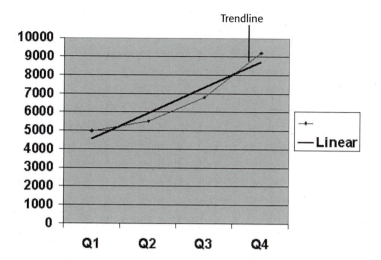

Figure 15.23
Trendlines predict
future developments
based on current
data.

USING ERROR BARS

Error bars show degrees of uncertainty relative to each data marker in a series. They're often used in engineering applications. They're also commonplace in polling and market research, where they're used to visually represent the potential error in a survey. (If you hear that a poll is accurate to within plus or minus three percent, you can represent that statistical statement with error bars.)

Error bars display as small T-shaped lines, upright to show error in the positive range and inverted to show error in the negative range. Error bars can be added to data series in area, bar, column, line, xy (scatter), and bubble charts. To add error bars to your chart, follow these steps:

1. Select the data series to which you want to add error bars.

2. Choose Format, Data Series.

3. In the Format Data Series dialog box, click the Y Error Bars tab shown in Figure 15.24. (If you are working with xy [scatter] and bubble charts, your dialog box will also have an X Error Bar tab.)

4. In the Display section, choose between these options: Both, Plus, Minus, or None.

5. In the Error Amount section, choose between Fixed Value, Percentage, Standard Deviation(s), or Standard Error. You can enter values for all but Standard Error.

6. Click OK when you've completed your choices. The error bars appear in your chart, as shown in Figure 15.25.

Figure 15.24
Setting error bars in the Format Data Series dialog box.

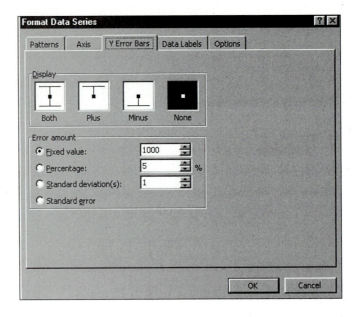

Figure 15.25
Error bars depict the potential error amounts relative to each data marker.

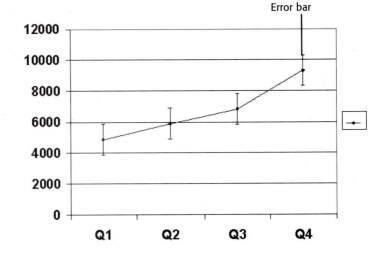

REVISING CHARTS AUTOMATICALLY

Earlier, you learned that charts created from Word tables are no longer connected to those tables: Changes you make in the datasheet aren't reflected in the source data. Of course, this may not be ideal: You may well want to maintain one consistent set of data that appears in both your data source and your charts. Moreover, you don't want to keep rebuilding and reformatting the same chart as you update it; you simply want the data to change—automatically.

The next two sections show you how to build enduring links between your charts and your data source—first using Word data, and then using data from an Excel worksheet.

ESTABLISHING AN OLE LINK BETWEEN WORD AND GRAPH

If you want tight and permanent links between your chart and your Word document, so that the chart changes whenever data changes in your document, you can establish an OLE link between the Word document's original chart data and the contents of the chart itself. Here's how to do this:

1. Select and copy the Word data you want to graph. (You could also copy data from another document, an Excel worksheet, or another OLE-compliant source.)

2. Choose Insert, Picture, Chart to open Microsoft Graph. Graph opens with dummy (fake) data in its datasheet.

3. If the datasheet does not appear, click the Datasheet button on Microsoft Graph's Standard toolbar to display it.

4. Click your insertion point in the top-left cell of the datasheet.

5. Choose Edit, Paste Link.

6. Word asks you to confirm that you want to replace the dummy data currently in your datasheet. Click OK.

7. Graph displays the chart, as well as the datasheet window containing the data you pasted.

When you establish the link in this way, the accompanying graph is automatically updated whenever you make changes to the Word table.

Not only can you change the data figures of your chart, you can also change the column or row headings. The chart is updated as soon as you confirm your entry by pressing Tab or otherwise moving from the cell.

You can even add a data series through a linked table, by adding another row or column in the table. Graph creates a new entry in the chart's legend and fills in the information as it is entered.

Tip #242	If you no longer want the link, you can break it. Double-click on your chart to open Microsoft Graph and choose Edit, Links. In the Links dialog box, click the Break Link button, and click OK.

ESTABLISHING A LINK WITH MICROSOFT EXCEL

The process for linking a chart with Excel (or any other compatible program) is basically the same as the one described previously for linking a table and chart in the same document. You select and copy the information in Excel, switch to Word and insert a chart, if one is not already in the document. After selecting the datasheet in Graph 2000, you choose Edit, Paste Link.

However, because you are working with two separate files now, the updating is not instantaneous unless Excel is open, Word is open, and you've double-clicked on your chart to open Microsoft Graph.

After you have changed, saved, and closed your Excel file, you can update your chart by opening your Word document and double-clicking the chart to invoke Graph 2000. The same holds true if your source data is in another Word document or a file created by another program, such as Lotus 1-2-3.

Tip #243

If you don't want to link your data to an external file, you have another option: simply import it. Open Graph by double-clicking your chart. Choose Edit, Import File and select the file from the dialog box. You can then choose to import either the entire sheet or a selected data range.

Caution

If you create a live link to an Excel worksheet (or other data source), be careful not to move the source file, or Graph may not be able to update it properly.

TROUBLESHOOTING

WHAT TO DO IF YOUR CHART LOSES DATA LABELS AFTER RESIZING

If you find that when your chart is reduced the text disappears, the font size is probably too small to display properly when the labels are aligned horizontally. You can either enlarge the chart by clicking and dragging the sizing handles or by double-clicking the axis. Then from the Alignment tab of the Format Axis dialog box, switch to a vertical or angled text.

HOW TO PRINT A COPY OF YOUR DATASHEET

You can't print the datasheet directly in Graph 2000. You can, however, include a data table in your chart. Click the Data Table button on the Graph 2000 toolbar to do this. (For more information, see "Adding Data Tables" earlier in this chapter.)

Another option is to copy the information where it can be printed. Click the Select All button in the datasheet (the gray cell at the top left of the datasheet). Click Copy. Click outside the chart and click New in Word to open a new document. Click Paste to place the datasheet's information there. You can convert the information into table format by choosing Table, Convert, Text to Table. In the Convert Text to Table dialog box, make sure that Tabs are selected in the Separate Text At section. Click OK.

THE CORPORATE WORD

CHAPTER **16**

MANAGING REVISIONS

In this chapter

AN OVERVIEW OF WORD'S TEAM WRITING TOOLS

Nowadays, few documents of any size are written entirely by one individual. In the corporate setting, most documents must be shepherded through a hierarchy; increasingly they must also be reviewed by cross-functional teams. Even freelance writers, of course, face the sharp red pencils of editors—often, more than one.

Word can't do much to make the substantive aspects of the review process easier. But it can work absolute wonders for the logistics of document review. If your review needs are especially simple, Word's Highlighting tool might be enough—just as it might have been enough for you in high school! For more complex reviews, Word offers the following tools:

- A Comments tool that enables reviewers to annotate your document with suggestions and recommendations without actually changing the text of the printed draft
- A Track Changes tool that helps you keep track of all the changes made by multiple reviewers, and then evaluate, incorporate, or reject them one at a time—or all at once
- A Protect Documents feature that enables you to prevent changes to your document except for annotations or tracked changes
- A Reviewing toolbar that brings all Word's reviewing tools together in one convenient location
- A Versioning feature that enables you to maintain multiple versions of a document in a single file
- Close integration with Microsoft Outlook to help you send file attachments to reviewers and track their progress

USING THE HIGHLIGHTER

Word's simplest reviewing tool is the Highlighter, which works just like the highlighting pen you might have used in high school. For the most informal reviews, where all you need to do is call attention to text, rather than make detailed comments about it, the Highlighter may be all you need.

Note

For any more complex reviews, Track Changes makes it easier to track, accept, and reject specific changes made by multiple reviewers. If you want to annotate a block of text with a suggestion or question, use Word's Comments tool.

To highlight one block of text, select it and click the Highlight icon on either the Formatting or Reviewing toolbar. By default, your text is highlighted in see-through yellow. Figure 16.1 shows highlighted text in a document.

— Highlights

Figure 16.1
Highlighted text.

If you plan to highlight several blocks of text, click the Highlight button before you select any text. Then select the first block of text; Word highlights it. Select another block of text; Word highlights that one, too. Word keeps highlighting text you select until you press Esc or click the Highlight button again.

If you prefer to use a color other than yellow, click the down arrow next to the Highlight button; a choice of 15 colors appears (see Figure 16.2). Select the color you want to use; this becomes the default color for all highlighting you do until you change it again.

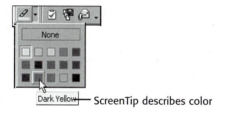

— ScreenTip describes color

Figure 16.2
Changing the default highlight color.

Tip #244

Consider giving different members of your workgroup different highlighting colors. Or consider standardizing colors for each type of change that must be made: for example, use blue for text that may have to be removed later, green for text that needs a technical review, and so on.

Tip #245

You may find that some highlight colors that are acceptable for online reading are too dark when you print them. Moreover, even if the highlighted text doesn't print too dark to be readable, you may simply not want any highlighting to appear in drafts that you print. To hide the highlighting both onscreen and in printed copies, choose Tools, Options and, on the View tab, clear the check box marked Highlight. From that point on, highlighting is invisible in the document, and does not appear when printed. To reverse the effect, simply recheck the box.

CHANGING THE COLOR OF HIGHLIGHTED TEXT

What if you've added yellow highlighting throughout your document and then decide your highlights should be a different color? Or what if someone else has reviewed the document using yellow highlights and you would like to reserve yellow highlighting for yourself—displaying your colleague's highlights in another color, such as blue? You can use Word's Replace tool to change all the text highlighting in your document (no matter what color it is) to a different highlight color that you can specify. To do so, follow these steps:

1. Change the highlight color to the one you want.
2. Choose Edit, Replace.
3. Make sure there's no text in either the Find What or Replace With text box.
4. Click the Find What text box.
5. If the Search Options portion of the dialog box is not visible, click More to display it. Then click No Formatting if it is not grayed out.
6. Click the Format button, and choose Highlight from the menu that appears.
7. Click the Replace With text box.
8. Repeat steps 5 and 6.
9. Choose Replace All. Word replaces all the existing highlights in your document with new highlights in the color you've just specified.

REMOVING HIGHLIGHTING FROM YOUR DOCUMENT

To remove highlighting throughout a document, press Ctrl+A to select the entire document, click the down arrow next to the Highlight button, and choose None.

HOW HIGHLIGHTS APPEAR ON WEB PAGES

When you save highlighted text as part of a Web page, Word stores the highlighting as part of Cascading Style Sheet information that can be understood by Microsoft Internet Explorer 3.0 and higher, as well as Netscape Navigator/Communicator 4.0 and higher. Earlier browsers may disregard the highlighting.

WORKING WITH COMMENTS

It's a classic problem: How do you make (or invite) comments in a document without introducing text changes that have to be undone later? The solution is Word's Comments tool (called Annotations in Word 95 and earlier versions).

With Comments, you have a way of annotating your document that doesn't get in your way while you edit and format your document. Then, when you're ready, your inserted comments are easy to view, print, and resolve. To insert a comment, either click where you want your comment to appear, or select the text that relates to the comment you want to make, then press Alt+Ctrl+M, or click the Insert Comment button on the Reviewing toolbar. (You can also choose Insert, Comment.)

A pale yellow comment mark appears in your document, containing your initials (as stored in the Tools, Options, User Information tab). If you selected a block of text for comment, the entire block of text now appears in pale yellow.

The dotted line beneath the comment mark is your cue that comments are hidden text; they appear only when your document is set to show hidden text. To hide comment marks, click the Show/Hide Paragraph Marks button on the Standard toolbar or choose Tools, Options, View; clear the All check box and make sure the Hidden Text check box is also cleared.

Tip #246	You can also use Comments to create notes to yourself about facts that need checking, additional text that needs to be added, and other unfinished business.

The comment mark also contains a number; each time another comment is added to the document, the number increments. This helps reviewers keep track of individual comments.

When you insert a comment into a document, the Comments pane opens (see Figure 16.3). This pane works in much the same way as the Footnote and Endnote panes covered in Chapter 11, "Footnotes, Bookmarks, and Cross-References." You can type your comment next to the comment mark in the Comments pane. If you want, you can leave the Comments pane open as you navigate through the document, inserting comments wherever necessary.

Word 2000 also inserts a hidden { PAGE } field above each comment in the Comments pane. When you print comments (as discussed later in the "Printing Comments" section), this page numbering is automatically updated to reflect any edits you may have made in the document, and page numbers are printed above each comment. After you print the page numbers for the first time, they become visible in the Comments pane. You can also display them without printing them, by selecting the comments (click in the Comments pane and press Ctrl+A) and updating the field codes (F9), or by checking the Field Codes check box in Tools, Options, View.

Figure 16.3
You can type your comments in the Comments pane.

Comment mark in document

Comment mark in comments pane

Comments pane

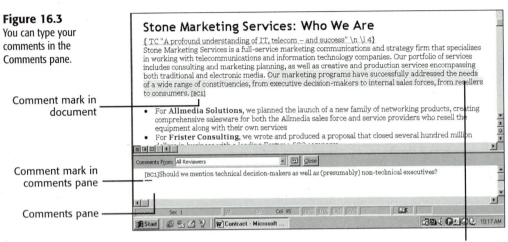

Highlighted comment

Occasionally you may want to make the same comment in several places. (For example, the writer whose draft you're reviewing may have made the same error repeatedly.) Insert the comment and edit the text in the Comments pane. Then select and copy the comment mark and paste it wherever you want the comment to appear.

Tip #247

If you turn on Track Changes before you start making comments, your comments are also tracked as changes, making it easier for the document's author to resolve both comments and proposed revisions at the same time. In particular, you make it possible for the author to combine your comments with the tracked changes and comments made by others, using the Merge Documents feature.

You'll learn more about tracking changes later in this chapter, in the "Working with Track Changes" section. You'll learn more about merging documents later in this chapter, in the "Merging Revisions" section.

INSERTING COMMENTS FROM MULTIPLE REVIEWERS

Several people can use Word's comments feature to annotate the same file. Word automatically places each reviewer's initials in her comment marks if her initials appear in the User Information tab. To check that your correct initials appear there, choose Tools, Options, and click the User Information tab.

Tip #248

> If you're using someone else's computer to make comments on a document, change the User Information to make your initials appear in future comment marks. This doesn't change comment marks that already appear in your document.
>
> Remember to change the User Information back when you're finished.

INSERTING VOICE COMMENTS

Occasionally, you might want to insert a brief audio comment in a file. For example, there may be a point you find it hard to explain in writing, but easy to explain verbally. Or you may have a digitized quote you would like to include. If you have a microphone and a sound card, Word makes it easy to add an audio comment. Even if your computer isn't audio equipped, you can insert WAV audio files you may have acquired elsewhere.

To record your own audio comment, follow these steps:

1. Choose Insert, Comment (or click the Insert Comment button on the Reviewing toolbar). The Comments pane opens.

2. Click the Cassette Tape icon at the top of the Comments pane. The Windows 98 or Windows NT Sound Recorder applet opens (see Figure 16.4).

3. Click the Record button and speak.

4. When you finish speaking, click Stop.

5. Choose Exit & Return from the File menu.

 If the cassette icon is grayed out, preventing you from using it, see "What to Do If the Voice Comment Recorder Cassette Icon Is Grayed Out," in the "Troubleshooting" section of this chapter.

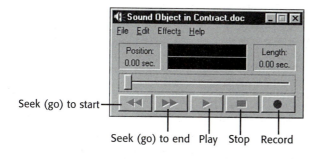

Figure 16.4
The Windows 98 (or Windows NT) Sound Recorder opens whenever you want to insert an audio comment.

Tip #249

> You can edit your sound file while Sound Recorder is open. For example, you can choose Edit, Insert File to insert another audio file into the comment. Or you can play your recorded file to the point where you made your most important point, and choose Edit, Delete Before Current Position to edit out everything that came before it.

Tip #250	You can include text along with an audio comment. Just enter it alongside the Speaker icon in the Comments pane.

Audio comments appear in your document as small Speaker icons (see Figure 16.5). To listen to an audio comment, double-click the icon. To edit the comment, right-click icon; the shortcut menu appears. Choose Wave Sound Object, Edit, and the Sound Recorder applet opens.

Figure 16.5
The Speaker icon signifies an audio comment; double-click the speaker to hear it.

Caution	Make your audio comments brief. Audio can quickly balloon the size of your files, reducing performance and straining your network.
	Of course, your reviewer needs a sound card and speakers to hear your audio comments.

LIMITING REVIEWERS TO USING ONLY THE COMMENTS FEATURE

As you've learned, one of the main benefits of Word's Comments feature is that it prevents reviewers from cluttering up a document with text that must simply be deleted later. You can go beyond inviting reviewers to use Word's Comments feature. You can set up your document so they can do nothing but make comments. Follow these steps:

1. Choose Tools, Protect Document. The Protect Document dialog box opens (see Figure 16.6).

2. Choose Comments.

3. If you want, enter a password that readers must know to do anything beyond inserting comments. (The password option is disabled for HTML documents.)

4. Click OK.

Figure 16.6

If you choose to enter a password, you are asked to enter it again in the Confirm Password dialog box. Do so, and click OK. Remember that Word passwords are case sensitive.

Note	If you do not use a password, when a reviewer opens the document he or she will still be restricted to making comments only. However, choosing Tools, Unprotect Document unlocks the document for any kind of editing.

Tip #251

If you forget your password, you can press Ctrl+A to select the entire document, Ctrl+C to copy it, and Ctrl+V to paste it into another file.

The result is a new file, unprotected by a password, which contains all your text, including fields. This file will not include any macros, keyboard assignments, custom style definitions, or toolbars stored within the original document. It also may not be attached to the same template, so AutoText entries, keyboard assignments, style definitions, macros, and tool-bars stored in the old template won't necessarily be available in the new document. The new document might not have the same paper size or margins, or feed from the same printer paper bin. Still, most of the formatting will come across intact.

VIEWING AND EDITING COMMENTS

So you've sent your document around for review, and you now have more comments than you know what to do with. Word makes it easier than ever to read, edit, and delete your comments. You can review all your comments systematically, in the Comments pane. Or you can review them more informally, in the editing window.

Tip #252

Before you start, consider saving a version of your file that contains all the comments as inserted by your reviewers. That way, you have a complete record of your document as it appeared before you decided what to do about each comment.

To save a version, choose File, Versions, and click Save Now. You'll learn more about versioning later in this chapter, in the "Using Word's Versioning Feature" section.

REVIEWING COMMENTS IN THE COMMENTS PANE

To review comments in the Comments pane, choose View, Comments to display the Comments pane. By default, Word displays all the comments made by all your reviewers. In some instances, you might want to review all the comments made by a single reviewer, or walk through the document one reviewer at a time. To view the comments made by only one reviewer, select the reviewer's name from the Comments From drop-down list box, as shown in Figure 16.7.

Figure 16.7
Choosing whose comments to view.

Whenever you click a comment within the Comments pane, Word displays the correspond-ing text in your document—making it easy to see to which text a reviewer is reacting. If a reviewer has suggested language you would like to use in your document, you can select it from the Comments pane and copy it into your document. More likely, you will want to edit a comment before incorporating it; nearly all Word's editing tools are available in the Comments pane.

When you finish working in the Comments pane, click Close or press Alt+Shift+C to close it.

If your document contains many comments, you might want to enlarge the Comments pane by dragging its top border higher in the editing window.

REVIEWING COMMENTS IN THE DOCUMENT WINDOW

Occasionally, when you notice the presence of a comment, you might be curious about it—but you might not want to bother opening the Comments pane. (Maybe you're busy doing something else, and you don't want to get too involved in reviewing comments just now, but you suspect you shouldn't wait to find out what your reviewer has said about this block of text.)

To view the contents of a comment, hover the mouse pointer anywhere in the comment. The comment's highlighting turns a deeper shade of yellow, and a ScreenTip appears, showing the full name of the reviewer and the contents of the comment.

Tip #253	You can use Edit, Find to locate specific text in a comment. In fact, Find searches comments, even if the Comments pane is closed and the comment marks are hidden in your document.

Note	If ScreenTips don't appear when you hover your mouse pointer over a comment or a tracked change, choose Tools, Options, View, and make sure the ScreenTips box is checked.

USING THE COMMENT SHORTCUT MENU

Right-click anywhere in the comment, and a shortcut menu appears (see Figure 16.8). To edit the comment, choose Edit Comment; the Comments pane appears. To delete the comment, choose Delete Comment.

Figure 16.8
You can edit or delete any comment using the Comments shortcut menu.

Caution

If you delete the comment marker, or all the document text that surrounds a comment marker, the comment is deleted as well.

MOVING FROM ONE COMMENT TO THE NEXT

You've already seen that you can click a comment in the Comments pane to move to it in the document. There's a more systematic way to review comments, however. Choose View, Toolbars, Reviewing to display the Reviewing toolbar. Then, move from one comment to the next, using the Previous Comment and Next Comment buttons. Each time you click the button, Word displays the next or preceding comment along with the ScreenTip detailing the reviewer's name and what he or she had to say.

Tip #254

You can also move among comments by using Word's Browser feature. Click the Browser (*Select Browse Object*) button beneath the vertical scrollbar; then choose Browse by Comment. After you select Browse by Comment, you can use the up-double-arrow and down-double-arrow buttons to move to the Previous Comment or the Next Comment.

If you want to walk through the document, resolving comments by a specific reviewer, you can do so with the Go To tab of the Find and Replace dialog box, as follows:

1. Press F5 to display the Go To tab (see Figure 16.9).
2. Choose Comment in the Go to What scroll box.
3. Choose the reviewer's name in the Enter Reviewer's Name box.
4. Click Next to move to the reviewer's next comment (or click Previous to move to the preceding comment).
5. When you're finished, click Close.

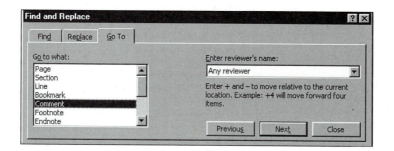

Figure 16.9
Moving among comments in the Go To tab of the Find and Replace dialog box.

Tip #255

> You don't have to enter a reviewer's name in the Enter Reviewer's Name box. If you want to view a specific comment, enter the comment number. If you want to jump ahead (or back) a specific number of comments, enter a positive or negative number with the corresponding plus or minus sign. For example, enter +3 to jump ahead three comments or −2 to jump back two comments.

PRINTING COMMENTS

Comment marks and comment highlighting do not normally appear in your printed document. If you want comment marks to appear in a printed document, choose Tools, Options, click the Print tab, check the box marked Comments, and click OK.

Although the comment marks appear wherever you placed them, the comments themselves appear at the end of the document. If you want, you can run a separate print job that prints only the comments by choosing Comments in the Print dialog's Print What drop-down box.

Word prints comments with associated page numbers that are updated to reflect your latest edits in the document. The { PAGE } *fields* Word inserts into the Comments pane are updated automatically when you choose to print—even if you've cleared the Update Fields check box in the Print tab of the Options dialog box.

HOW COMMENTS APPEAR ON WEB PAGES

When you save comments as part of a Web page, Word stores the comments as part of Cascading Style Sheet information that can be understood by Microsoft Internet Explorer 3.0 and higher, as well as Netscape Navigator/Communicator 4.0 and higher.

Internet Explorer 4.0 (and higher) displays comments as ScreenTips that appear when you hover the mouse pointer over them. Netscape Navigator 4.0 (and higher) displays the comment marks in the document, and places the comments themselves at the bottom of the Web page, much like footnotes (see Figure 16.10).

Note

> You might save documents containing comments as Web pages if
> - You've standardized on HTML as your primary document format.
> - You're setting up these documents for interactive review in a Web folder on a server running Office Server Extensions and some of your users don't have Internet Explorer 5.0.

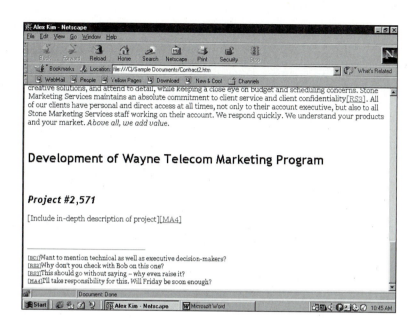

Figure 16.10
Displaying comments on a Web page in Netscape Navigator.

WORKING WITH TRACK CHANGES

Comments are invaluable when you or your reviewers want to make observations about the text in a document. But when it comes to line-by-line editing changes, Word offers a better tool: Track Changes (called Revision Marks in Word 95 and earlier versions).

With Track Changes turned on, you edit a document normally, and Word keeps track of all the text you add and delete. Then, you (or your colleague) can walk through the changes—deciding which to accept, which to reject, and which to modify.

The quickest way to start tracking changes is to double-click the TRK button in the status bar, or press Ctrl+Shift+E. If the Reviewing toolbar is open, you can also click the Track Changes button. (When Track Changes is on, you can use any of these methods to turn it off.)

No matter which procedures you use to turn Track Changes on, Word starts tracking changes in your document as follows:

- New text you add appears in red, with underlining. (Word may select a different color if you aren't the first person to review the document.)

- Existing text you delete remains visible, but is formatted in red with strikethrough applied. You can see an example in Figure 16.11.

- New text you add and then delete doesn't appear in the document at all.

- Wherever an editing change is made, a vertical line appears in the document's left margin, as in Figure 16.11. This makes it easier to find and focus on changes, especially in printed documents.

Tip #256	You can control which margin contains the vertical line that points out changed text. If you want the line in the right margin, choose Tools, Options, and on the Track Changes tab, set the Changed Lines/Mark box to read Right Border.
	While you might think that setting this Changed Lines/Mark box to read Outside Border would, in fact, force the vertical lines to the outside border, it doesn't. ("Outside Border" usually means the left margin on even-numbered pages and the right margin on odd-numbered pages.) If you want the vertical lines to appear on the outside border, you must also tell Word that you want different headers and footers on odd and even pages.
	To do that, choose File, Page Setup, click the Layout tab, and check the box marked Headers and Footers/Different Odd and Even.

Figure 16.11
With Track Changes turned on, new text is underlined, and deletions are marked with strikethrough character formatting.

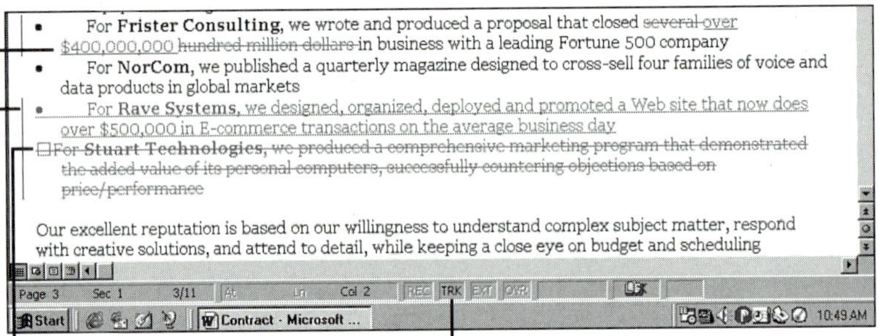

Inserted text —

Changed line —

Deleted text

TRK button on status bar

TRACKING REVISIONS IN THE BACKGROUND

If you're making extensive, line-by-line revisions, you may quickly find all these marks distracting. If so, you can hide them while you continue to mark the document. The document will be much more readable, and Word will continue to store the revisions in the background.

Choose Tools, Track Changes, Highlight Changes. The Highlight Changes dialog box appears (see Figure 16.12). Clear the Highlight Changes on Screen check box, and click OK. Assuming the Track Changes While Editing check box is checked, Word continues to mark all the changes in your document, but you don't see the change marks unless you check this check box again.

Note	When you clear the Highlight Changes on Screen check box, your document looks as it would if every change you made was accepted.

CHOOSING WHETHER TO PRINT REVISIONS

By default, Word reflects Tracked Changes when you print your document. If the Highlight Changes on Screen box has been checked, and the changes are visible onscreen, the change marks are visible in the printed document. If you've hidden the changes, you don't see the change marks; the document prints as though the changes had been accepted.

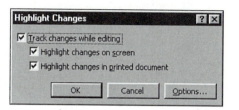

Figure 16.12
From the Highlight Changes dialog box, you can control whether changes are visible and whether they print.

If you want to see the change marks while you work, but you don't want to see them in your printed document, clear the Highlight Changes in Printed Document check box in the Highlight Changes dialog box. The printed document still reflects the changes, but the change marks aren't visible.

OPTIONS FOR CONTROLLING THE TRACK CHANGES FEATURE

As you've learned, Word marks the first reviewer's insertions as red underlined text, the first reviewer's deletions as red strikethrough, and adds change bars on the outside border of your page wherever a revision has been made. These are default settings; you can change them if you want. For example, you have the following options:

- If your document already contains extensive underlining, you might want to distinguish change marks with double underlining.

- If you don't want Word to automatically assign new colors to each reviewer, you can specify the color a reviewer will always use.

- If you want to see a reviewer's additions, but you're not very interested in what a reviewer has deleted, you can format deletions as hidden text rather than strikethrough.

- If you want to see where a reviewer has changed formatting, you can specify a color and mark for formatting changes.

- If you print interim drafts for distribution in three-hole binders, you can specify that change lines always appear on the right margin, making them easier to see. Or, if you print documents on both sides of the paper, you can specify that change lines always appear at the outside margin, away from the hole-punch. (See the preceding tip for an important quirk regarding vertical lines in the outside borders.)

You can control all these aspects of Track Changes through the Track Changes dialog box (see Figure 16.13): choose Tools, Options, Track Changes (or Tools, Track Changes, Highlight Changes, Options).

SPECIFYING HOW INSERTIONS AND DELETIONS ARE MARKED

To change the mark that Word applies to text inserted while Track Changes is turned on, choose a new Mark in the Inserted Text area; in addition to the default underline, your choices are bold, italic, double-underline, and none.

Figure 16.13
You can control the colors used in the review process through the Track Changes tab.

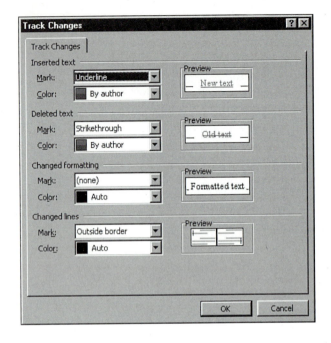

To change the mark associated with deletions, choose a new Mark in the Deleted Text area. In addition to the default strikethrough, you can choose hidden text—or you can tell Word to insert a ^ or # placeholder symbol in place of the text you deleted. This shows that text has been deleted, but doesn't clutter up the screen with hard-to-follow strikethrough marks. This technique is widely used in legal documents. Word continues to track the changes as it normally would, and if you restore the default settings for Deleted Text, the missing text will reappear with strikethrough text.

When you change a mark—or any other setting in this dialog box—Word displays a preview to the right of the area in which you're working.

Note

The new settings you establish in the Track Changes tab are global, and apply not only to the current document but to any others you open and use while these settings are in place.

SPECIFYING HOW WORD ASSIGNS COLORS TO REVIEWERS

By default, Word assigns colors to reviewers automatically. If Word runs out of colors, two reviewers have to share a color.

This system usually works well. However, you might want to permanently assign colors to individual members of your team, so you can tell at a glance who made each revision—especially if you're looking at a document printed on a color printer. Although Word can't assign a specific color to a specific reviewer, it can assign a specific color for all changes tracked on a specific computer. Follow these steps:

1. Choose Tools, Options, Track Changes to display the Track Changes tab.

2. In the Color drop-down box (in the Inserted Text area), choose a color. Or, if you prefer that reviewed text appear in the same color that Word uses by default for other text in the document, choose Auto.

3. In the Color drop-down box (in the Deleted Text area), choose a color—typically the same color you just chose for inserted text. Again, if you prefer that reviewed text appear in the same color that Word uses by default elsewhere, choose Auto.

4. Click OK.

SPECIFYING HOW FORMATTING CHANGES ARE MARKED

Word 2000's Track Changes feature can track some formatting changes as well as content changes. When you make a character formatting change to bold, italic, or underline, or a paragraph formatting change to bullets or numbering, Word inserts a vertical line in the outer margin, just as it would if you made a text change. If you change the font, font size, color, or paragraph alignment, no vertical line will appear. Even more strangely, a border applied to characters is shown as a change, whereas a border applied to a paragraph is not.

By default, Word does not apply a change mark to indicate where the formatting change was made. The rationale is simple: Change marks appear as formatting. Users might find it hard to tell which formatting has been applied by the reviewer and which is part of the change mark itself.

Unfortunately, the result can be even more confusing. If you review a document that contains tracked formatting changes, the vertical lines tell you that changes have been made, but you have no way to tell what those changes were.

If this proves troublesome, you can specify a change mark and a color for Word to use whenever it tracks a formatting change. Choose Tools, Options, and on the Track Changes tab pick the change mark (bold, italic, underline) in the Changed Formatting/Mark box, and the color in the Changed Formatting/Color box. Word indicates formatting changes in the colors you chose.

SPECIFYING THE APPEARANCE OF CHANGED LINES

As you've learned, Word inserts a black vertical line at the outside border of any line that contains a tracked change. This is called a *changed line*. To control changed lines, open the Track Changes tab, as described in the preceding section. Then follow these steps:

1. Select a Mark in the Changed Lines area (Outside border, Left border, Right border, or None).

2. Select a Color in the Changed Lines area.

3. Click OK.

LIMITING REVIEWERS TO USING ONLY THE TRACKED CHANGES FEATURE

Earlier in this chapter, you saw how to protect a document for comments, preventing reviewers from doing anything except adding comments. You can also protect a document for tracked changes. When you do, Word lets reviewers edit the document any way they want, but marks all the changes they make using the Track Changes feature—giving you an audit trail. To protect a document for Tracked Changes, choose Tools, Protect Document. Click the button marked Tracked Changes, and add a Password if you like.

As with protecting a document for comments, if you don't use a password, users can turn off Track Changes by choosing Tools, Unprotect Document.

QUICK AND EASY TRACKING CHANGES WITH THE COMPARE DOCUMENTS FEATURE

Imagine you've asked someone to review a document, but you forgot to turn on Track Changes first. Have you forever lost the chance to see where changes were made and systematically resolve them? No!

If you have a copy of the document in its original form (before the reviewer edited it), you can use Word's Compare Documents feature. When you're finished, you have a document that includes change marks wherever additions, deletions (and optionally, formatting changes) were made—just as if the edits were made with Track Changes enabled. Follow these steps:

1. Open the document where you want the change marks to appear.
2. Choose Tools, Track Changes, Compare Documents. The Select File to Compare with Current Document dialog box opens. This dialog box has the same features as a standard Open dialog box.
3. Browse to select the file you want to compare with the one you already have open.
4. Click Open. Word now compares the two documents and inserts change marks wherever they differ.

> **Caution**
>
> Compare Documents can occasionally deliver misleading results. For example, if you reorganize your document by moving large blocks of text, those blocks appear as large deletions and equally large insertions. Within those blocks of text, you don't have any way to tell whether additional copy edits were made. (You have the same problem in a document you marked with Track Changes.)

Track Changes and Compare Documents are like oil and water: Don't mix them. Say you start with a document and you send a copy of it off to Editor A, then you turn on Track Changes and send another copy off to Editor B. When the changes come back, you might be tempted to run Compare Documents on Editor B's "tracked" document, comparing it with the one returned by Editor A.

If you run Compare Documents and either of the documents has tracked changes, Word warns you "The new document already has changes. Word may ignore some existing changes. Compare anyway?" You can go ahead and run Compare Documents, but you need to be cautious of the results. The reasons are simply logistical. Say you have a sentence in the original document that was deleted in the "tracked" document, but altered in the "compare" document. What can Word tell you? In practice, Word shows the sentence as deleted, but that doesn't accurately reflect the changes contained in the "compare" document. Stuck between a rock and a hard place, Word does the best it can.

MERGING REVISIONS

You've already seen one scenario for reviewing a document; you send a file to one reviewer who makes changes and then forwards it to another reviewer who makes changes that are recorded in a different color, and so on. When everyone's finished, the changes are returned to you in one rainbow-colored document.

In today's fast-paced business world, however, you may not have time to wait for each person to review a document consecutively. You may have to send a separate copy of the document to each reviewer and receive separate marked-up copies in return. You can use Word's Merge Documents feature to integrate all those changes into a single document, where you can resolve them all at once in an organized fashion.

Follow these steps to merge revisions from several documents into a document you already have open:

1. Choose Tools, Merge Documents. The Select File to Merge Into Current Document dialog box opens; it looks just like the standard Open dialog box.

2. Browse to select the document you want to merge.

3. Click Open.

4. Repeat steps 1–3 for each additional document with revisions you want to incorporate.

Caution

The Merge Documents feature only merges tracked changes; it does not integrate any other difference that may exist between two documents. If you want to merge the complete contents of two documents (other than tracked changes), use Insert, File.

Word gives you a warning if there are differences in the two documents that aren't officially "tracked" changes. Even so, Word still lets you merge them. If you do merge two documents with changes that aren't officially "tracked," the resulting document will not include any of those changes.

 If you merge documents, but Word doesn't display change lines in the resulting file, see "What to Do If Word Doesn't Display Change Lines in a Merged Document," in the "Troubleshooting" section of this chapter.

RESOLVING PROPOSED CHANGES

No matter how you get change marks into your document, the real beauty of Word's Track Changes feature comes later, when you see how easy it is to resolve the changes your reviewers have proposed.

Proposed changes can be resolved in three ways: using the Reviewing toolbar (choose View, Toolbars, and check the item marked Reviewing), using the Accept or Reject Changes dialog box (choose Tools, Track Changes, Accept or Reject Changes; see Figure 16.14), or by right-clicking on the change and choosing the appropriate option from the context dialog box. In general, the context box is limited but fast; the Reviewing toolbar is quick and has more options; and the dialog box gives you the most choices of all—and more information.

Figure 16.14
With the Accept or Reject Changes dialog box open, you can move through your document, resolving one proposed revision at a time.

RESOLVING INDIVIDUAL CHANGES

Before you start resolving changes, you might want to press Ctrl+Home to move to the beginning of the document.

To navigate through the document, you have three choices:

- You can scroll to whichever change concerns you. Let your mouse hover over the change. In most cases, you'll see a ScreenTip (see Figure 16.15) advising you of the person who made the change, when it was made, and what the change entailed (for example, Inserted or Deleted).

Figure 16.15
If you hover your mouse pointer above a tracked change, Word displays a ScreenTip.

- If the Reviewing toolbar is visible, you can click on the Next Change (or Previous Change) icon. Word will move to the next (or previous) change and select it.

- If the Accept or Reject Changes dialog box is visible, you can click on the (backward or forward) Find buttons.

PART

IV

CH

16

Note

> The Accept or Reject Changes dialog box gives you more control than the Reviewing toolbar. For example, you can control how your document looks while you're reviewing changes. If you click the Changes with Highlighting button, you see all the change marks in your document. If you click Changes Without Highlighting, you see the document as it would look if you accepted all the changes.

After the change has been identified, you can accept or reject it by

- Right-clicking on the change and choosing Accept Change or Reject Change
- Clicking on the Accept or Reject buttons, on the Reviewing toolbar

- Clicking the Accept or Reject buttons in the Accept or Reject Changes dialog box

Of course you can edit the selected text, or just ignore the change by moving on, using any of the three navigation techniques discussed earlier.

Tip #257

> You don't have to resolve all your changes at the same time; you can leave some unresolved until you get more information or speak to the right person. You might want to insert a comment reminding yourself why a change is still unresolved.

You can always undo a change you just accepted, rejected, or edited by clicking the Undo button on the Standard toolbar. In addition, the Accept or Reject Changes dialog box has its own Undo button.

ACCEPTING OR REJECTING ALL CHANGES AT THE SAME TIME

It's unlikely, but you may occasionally be able to resolve all your revisions at the same time. Perhaps you (or your boss) make an executive decision to disregard all the wrong-headed comments provided by someone in another department. With the Accept or Reject Changes dialog box open, click Reject All to reject them all at the same time. Your document now appears as though no comments had ever been made. If you think better of this, click Undo.

Conversely, on rare occasion, you may want to accept all the comments that have been made about your document, by all of its reviewers. Or, perhaps, only one individual has reviewed the document, but he or she is so important that you have no choice but to accept their comments. Click Accept All; the revision marks all disappear and the tracked changes slip seamlessly into your document as if they'd been there all along.

HOW TRACKED CHANGES APPEAR ON WEB PAGES

When you save Tracked Changes as part of a Web page, Word stores the comments as part of *Cascading Style Sheet* information that can be understood by Microsoft Internet Explorer 3.0 and higher, as well as Netscape Navigator/Communicator 4.0 and higher.

As in Word documents themselves, additions are displayed with colored underlining and deletions are displayed as colored strikethrough text. Earlier browsers may not display the tracked changes.

 If Word won't let you accept or reject changes, see "What to Do If Word Won't Let You Accept or Reject Changes," in the "Troubleshooting" section of this chapter.

 If Tracked Changes aren't displayed in your document, and you've already checked to make sure Highlight Changes on Screen is checked in the Highlight Changes dialog box, see "What to Do If Tracked Changes Aren't Visible in Your Document," in the "Troubleshooting" section of this chapter.

USING WORD'S VERSIONING FEATURE

Many Word users are in the habit of using File, Save As to save a new copy of every new draft they create. By doing so, they not only make sure of having a recent backup in the event of disaster, they also create an audit trail that helps identify when a critical change was made in case it is questioned later.

Nothing has changed the need for storing backups, but Word now has a more convenient, reliable way of providing that audit trail. You can now store each new version of your document in the same file, so that older versions can't get easily lost, misplaced, or confused with the current version.

Follow these steps to save a new version of an existing file:

1. Choose File, Versions.
2. The Versions dialog box opens (see Figure 16.16).

Figure 16.16
Click Save Now in the Versions dialog box to save a new version of your document in the same file.

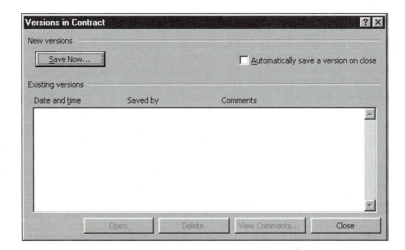

3. Click Save Now. The Save Version dialog box opens (see Figure 16.17). (You can also save a new version by clicking the Save Version button on the Reviewing toolbar; the Save Version dialog box appears.)

4. Enter comments on the version, such as whose changes it reflects, or why the new version was created. (Don't worry about entering the current date and time, or your own name—Word has already done that for you.)

5. Click OK. Word saves a new version of the document in the same file as the original.

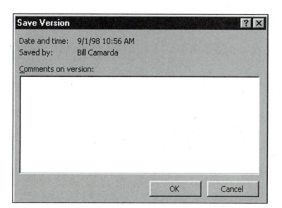

Figure 16.17
In the Save Version dialog box, enter detailed comments about why this draft was created, and/or whose comments it reflects.

Caution

If you save a file containing multiple versions using a format other than Word 2000/Word 97, the older versions will be lost. If you need to save the current version in an older format, first use File, Save As to make a copy of the file; then resave the copy in the older format you need. All the versions will, of course, remain in your original file.

Note

In a file containing multiple versions, Word's document statistics apply to the current version only.

WORKING WITH MULTIPLE VERSIONS OF A FILE

After you've created one or more additional versions of a file, a Versions icon appears at the far right of the status bar (see Figure 16.18). To work with your versions, you can double-click this icon, or choose File, Versions. This reopens the Versions dialog box. In Figure 16.19, you can see how this dialog box looks after several versions of a document named Contract.doc have been created.

To open any version, select it and click Open. To delete an old version, select it and click Delete; Word asks you to confirm the deletion and reminds you that you can't undo this action.

Figure 16.18
The Versions icon in the status bar indicates that a file contains multiple versions.

Versions icon

Figure 16.19
The Versions dialog box provides several new options after you have versions from which to choose.

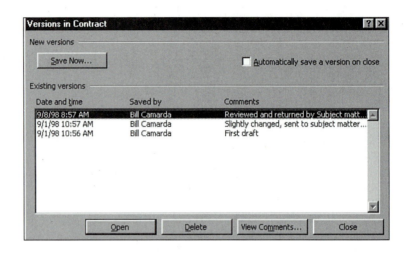

Tip #258

If you're planning to send a document out for review, you may want to delete all old versions to make sure reviewers see only the current one. (Or better yet, use File, Save As to create a new copy of the file and then delete the unwanted versions from the copy only.)

In the Versions dialog box, you can already see the first few words of comments about the file; if you want to see more, click View Comments. You can't edit comments made about a version that was saved previously; the comments are read-only.

SAVING A VERSION AS A SEPARATE FILE

When you open an older version of a file, Word displays the document in a separate editing window, which splits the screen as shown in Figure 16.20. Notice that the version you opened has a save date in its title bar—a gentle reminder that you're not working with the current version.

If you make changes to the older version, Word won't save it in the same file any longer. When you choose Save, Word displays the Save As dialog box, and shows the filename as it appears in the title bar with the version creation date. When you click Save, you get a new file containing only the version you edited.

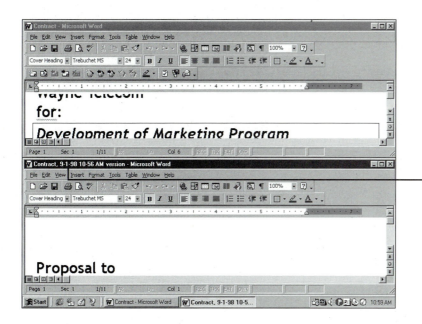

Figure 16.20
If you open an older version, Word displays a new editing window and displays the version's creation date in the title bar.

The older version's name includes its creation date.

Tip #259

Unfortunately, you can't use Word's Compare Documents feature to compare two versions of a document within the same file. You can work around this limitation, however, by saving each version you want to compare as a separate file, and then choosing Tools, Track Changes, Compare Documents.

→ For more information about comparing two documents, **see** "Quick and Easy Tracking Changes with the Compare Documents Feature," **p. 516**.

AUTOMATICALLY SAVING NEW VERSIONS

You may want to save a "snapshot" of your document each time another editor or reviewer finishes with it. To do so choose File, Versions and in the Versions dialog box, check the Automatically Save a Version on Close check box.

Tip #260

Word offers another (also imperfect) way of tracking how much a document has been worked on. Choose File, Properties, Statistics to display the Statistics tab of the Properties dialog box. Here, you can see how long the current document has been open and how many times it has been saved. Of course, if you save a document often, you might get a revision number in the hundreds.

VERSIONING AND WEB PAGES

Versioning is not available if you are editing a Web page. In addition, if you save an existing file in HTML (Web page) format, only the current version appears in the new HTML file. Word warns you that the older versions will be lost, and offers to create a backup copy (see Figure 16.21). Click Continue to save the backup copy and create a new Web file with only the current version.

Figure 16.21
Word warns you that Web pages can't include versions, and offers to store a backup DOC file at the same time it creates the Web page.

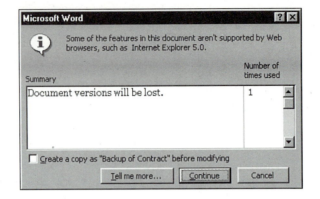

STREAMLINING THE REVIEW PROCESS WITH MICROSOFT OUTLOOK

Few things in life generate quite as many loose ends as reviewing a large document. To resolve an outstanding issue, you might realize you need to speak with a colleague, do some more research, check with the lawyers, run a search on the Web, or think something through in more detail. If you use the Microsoft Outlook personal information manager, it's very easy to create a new task associated with your current document and include it on your list of tasks to perform.

To create a new task, first save your current file, and click your insertion point in the paragraph you're concerned with. Choose View, Toolbars, Reviewing to display the Reviewing toolbar. Then, click the Create Microsoft Outlook Task button. Microsoft Outlook's Task dialog box opens (see Figure 16.22).

The following list points out some important elements of Outlook's dialog box, and some of the ways you can use it.

- The task is named after your Word file. You can edit the task name in the Subject text box.
- You can specify all kinds of information about your task, including a due date, start date, and reminder notification.
- The large text box at the bottom of the Task dialog box contains the first few lines of text from the paragraph where your insertion point appeared when you clicked the Create Microsoft Outlook Task button. This text gives you some context to help you remember what task you set up for yourself. You can edit the text to make it even clearer.
- The text box also contains a shortcut to your Word document. In the future, if you're working in Outlook, you can double-click the shortcut icon any time you want to open the Word document.

When you finish creating the task, click Save and Close; Word enters the task on your Task List (see Figure 16.23).

Save and Close button   Word document icon   Name of task

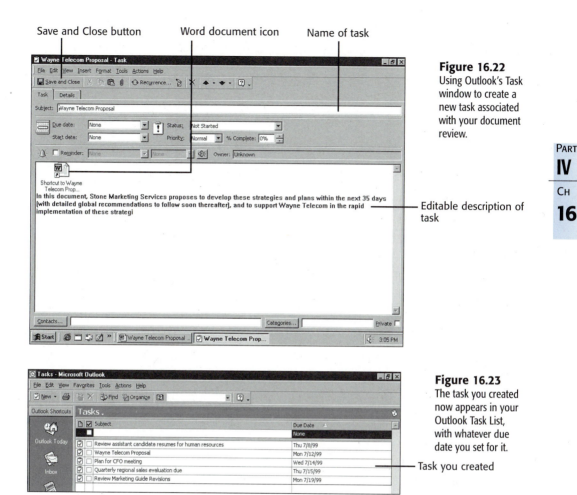

Figure 16.22
Using Outlook's Task window to create a new task associated with your document review.

Editable description of task

Figure 16.23
The task you created now appears in your Outlook Task List, with whatever due date you set for it.

Task you created

→ For more information about using Outlook and Word together, **see** "Using Outlook with Word," **p. 1176**.

ASSIGNING A REVIEW TASK TO SOMEONE ELSE

It's all well and good to assign a task to yourself, but your review process is likely to turn up tasks that someone else needs to perform.

If your colleagues also use Outlook 2000, and you can send email to each other, you can easily transform the task you created into an email message that can be sent to someone else. Because the task already includes a shortcut to your file, this is an exceptionally easy way to transmit a file for review, providing the file is accessible over the network.

Start by saving your Word file—and if you want, clicking your insertion point in the paragraph with which you're concerned. (If you don't, Outlook leaves the description blank, but you can always add your own.)

Click the Create Microsoft Outlook Task button on the Reviewing toolbar to display the Task dialog box (refer to Figure 16.22). Now, choose Actions, Assign Task. In the To text box, enter the name of the person you're delegating the task to. Outlook changes the Task window to an email window (see Figure 16.24).

Figure 16.24
If you click Assign Task, Outlook displays this email window, where you can delegate the task to someone else.

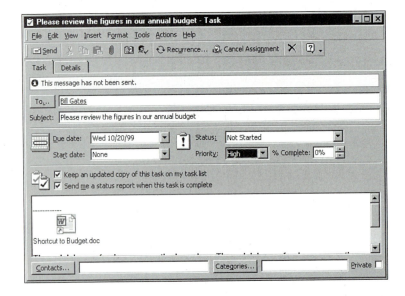

If you want to keep the task on your Task List as well, check the Keep an Updated Copy of This Task on My Task List check box. If you want to receive an emailed status report when your colleague finishes the task, check the Send Me a Status Report When This Task Is Complete check box. When you're finished, click Send to send an email message consisting of the task you've just delegated.

TROUBLESHOOTING

WHAT TO DO IF THE VOICE COMMENT RECORDER CASSETTE ICON IS GRAYED OUT

Check to make sure your computer has a sound card, and that the sound card is configured properly. You can check on this by clicking Start, Control Panel, double-clicking on the System applet, and clicking the Device Manager tab. Look to see whether a sound card is listed. If it has an exclamation point next to it, it is not configured properly; try reinstalling the driver or checking for resource conflicts.

WHAT TO DO IF WORD DOESN'T DISPLAY CHANGE LINES IN A MERGED DOCUMENT

Make sure you turned on Highlight Changes on Screen in the Tools, Track Changes, Highlight Changes dialog box. If change lines don't appear, it's possible you forgot to turn on Track Changes. Starting from your original (unchanged) file, use the Compare

Documents feature (Tools, Track Changes, Compare Documents) to mark all differences between your original and the file you sent out for review. Then use the Merge Documents feature (Tools, Merge Documents) to integrate each reviewer's set of changes into the original file, including the set of changes you just created using Compare Documents.

What to Do If Word Won't Let You Accept or Reject Changes

Most likely, your document is still protected for tracked changes. If so, choose Tools, Unprotect Document. If you're asked for a password, enter it. If you don't have the password, you may not be authorized to accept or reject changes.

What to Do If Tracked Changes Aren't Visible in Your Document

If you've already checked to make sure the Highlight Changes on Screen check box is checked in the Highlight Changes dialog box, it's possible that your changes are formatted in hidden text; click the Show/Hide Paragraph Marks button on the Standard toolbar to check.

CHAPTER **17**

CREATING FORMS

In this chapter

WORD'S FORMS CAPABILITIES: AN OVERVIEW

Word's sophisticated forms capabilities permit you to streamline a variety of business tasks that once required paper forms. You can create forms that enable users to choose among lists of options; forms that provide online help; even forms that guide users from start to finish. Best of all, users can fill in these forms without changing the underlying form itself. And if you're networked, you can use your network server or *intranet*—rather than some distant warehouse—as your central repository for forms.

WHEN TO USE WORD, WHEN TO USE ANOTHER TOOL

As you'll discover, building a printed or electronic form in Word 2000 is relatively easy. However, there may be times when it makes more sense to use another tool:

- Forms built in Word can perform calculations, but if your forms require extensive, complex calculations that go far beyond simple arithmetic, consider building them in Microsoft Excel rather than Word.
- Forms built in Word can transfer their data to a database such as Microsoft Access, but if integrating the information in your forms into a database is your central goal, consider building the forms in Access rather than Word.
- If the users who will fill out your online forms do not have access to Microsoft Word or Office, consider creating Web-based forms that can be accessed from a browser. Alternatively, consider using a traditional forms program such as FormTool 97 or FormFlow.

Note
> The tools Word provides for building Web forms—available through the *Control Toolbox toolbar*—can also be used in standard Word forms.

APPLICATIONS FOR WORD'S FORMS FEATURE

You can use Word's forms feature to build three types of forms:

- Printed forms that will be completed with a typewriter or a pen.
- Standard electronic forms that will be filled out in Word by users whose responses are limited to specific areas and types of information.
- Guided electronic forms where you display a series of questions and the forms can fill themselves in as the user provides answers.

In addition to fairly obvious applications such as questionnaires and surveys, forms can also be used in more traditional word processing functions such as automated document production. Lawyers use forms to fill out contracts, whereas bankers use them to complete loan applications.

In fact, Word's forms feature can help you build any document that is largely repetitive except for small areas of specific, individual information.

BUILDING THE SKELETON OF YOUR FORM

Whether you ultimately want your forms to be used as hard copy or online, the first step is the same: creating a template containing the "shell" of the form. The shell is the text, layout, and formatting elements that remain constant whenever the form is used. To create a template from scratch, choose File, New, click Template in the Create New area of the dialog box, and click OK.

> **Note**
>
> If you originally created a printed form in Word, and you now want to turn it into an electronic form that can be filled out from within Word, open the original Word file and resave it as a template.

After you create your template (or save an existing document as a template), you can use all Word's editing, formatting, and drawing tools, just as if you were creating any other kind of document. Most forms make very heavy use of the following features:

- Tables (see Chapter 5, "Tables: Organizing Your Pages")
- Text boxes (see Chapter 14, "Word Desktop Publishing")
- Borders and shading

Leave empty spaces (or placeholder characters such as &&&&) for the areas of the form you want users to fill in. Later, you'll learn how to use form fields that transform those empty spaces with interactivity and automation, enabling users to enter information more quickly and accurately. Figure 17.1 shows the skeleton of a form with all structure, text, and graphics in place.

> **Note**
>
> Your form template should also contain any *macros* and *AutoText* entries you can create to streamline filling out the forms later.

 If you can't edit a form one of your colleagues has created, see "What to Do If Word Won't Allow You to Edit an Existing Form," in the "Troubleshooting" section of this chapter.

After you've built the skeleton for your form, make sure you save it as a *template*, under a new name, preferably a descriptive one. If your organization numbers its forms, you might include the new form number in the name.

Figure 17.1
The skeleton of a form, awaiting the use of form fields.

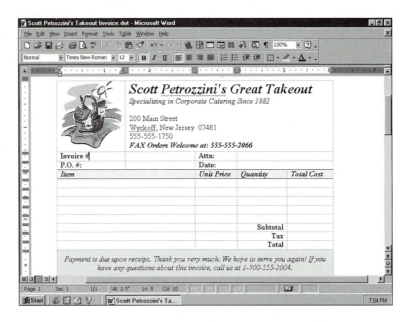

By default, Word saves all templates in the Templates folder; saving your file here makes it appear in the General tab of the New dialog box. You can also save it in any of the Templates subfolders, such as Letters & Faxes, Memos, Publications, and so on, which correspond to the other tabs of the New dialog box.

To enable users to access the form easily across a network, store it in a location to which they have access, such as the Workgroup Templates folder set up on your network. Of course, no matter how you choose to distribute your electronic forms, you should password protect them so they cannot be changed without authorization.

→ For more information on placing templates in a folder shared by an entire workgroup, **see** "Using Workgroup Templates," **p. 3**.

Note

If you have a form that you want everyone to fill in, you can send the template as an attachment on your electronic mail network. (Remember to add instructions on what to do with the form.)

Outlook 2000 has its own form-generating capability, and if you need strong email support, consider building the form with Outlook 2000, instead of Word 2000.

If you happen to be using Microsoft Exchange or another MAPI- or VIM-compatible email system, sending forms is especially easy. Word has already added two commands to your File menu: Send and Add Routing Slip. Send is ideal for sending the template to one or two individuals. Add Routing Slip makes it easy to send the template to as many people on the network as necessary—either one at a time or all at once.

When you want to edit the form again, you must open the template itself, not a document created from the template. To make sure that you're doing so, change the Files of Type to Document Templates in the Open dialog box.

➔ For more information about working with templates, **see** Chapter 1, "Templates, Wizards, and Add-Ins," **p. 257**.

ADDING INTERACTIVITY WITH FORM FIELDS

So far, you've only seen how to use Word's editing and formatting tools to create a document that resembles a form. In the rest of this chapter, you learn how to add interactivity and automation to your form with *form fields*. Form fields are special document elements that make it possible to fill out the form more easily and quickly, and to use the form's information after it's there.

WORKING WITH THE FORMS TOOLBAR

Word 2000 has grouped the essential commands for creating and editing a form together in the appropriately named Forms toolbar. Enable this toolbar as you would any other: Choose <u>V</u>iew, <u>T</u>oolbars, and then choose Forms from the submenu.

PART

IV

CH

17

> **Note**
>
> In Word 2000, displaying the Forms toolbar is the only way to work with form fields.

As with any other toolbar, you can drag it to any screen edge, if you want to, so that it doesn't interfere with your work.

Nine buttons appear on the Forms toolbar.

- Text Form Field inserts a text form field where users can enter text, numbers, symbols, and spaces. You can also use text form fields to make calculations based on entries that users make in other form fields.

- Check Box Form Field inserts a check box in your document; users can either check the box or leave it unchecked.

- Drop-Down Form Field inserts a drop-down form field that gives a user a list of alternatives; the user is limited to choosing one of those alternatives.

- Form Field Options is used to specify the detailed settings for any form field after you've inserted it.

- Draw Table displays the Tables and Borders toolbar, which contains buttons the form designer can use to build tables more easily, and activates the Draw Table tool.

- Insert Table inserts a table with a specific number of columns and rows, all of them the same height and width. This is the same Insert Table button that appears in the Standard toolbar.

➔ To see how to draw or insert tables, **see** "Word's Multiple Approaches to Creating a Table," **p. 114**.

- Insert Frame includes a free-floating box in the form that you can format with a precise size and location. (Insert Frame does not insert text boxes.)

- Form Field Shading toggles your form's text, check box, and drop-down fields between medium gray shading and no shading.

- Protect Form enables you to protect all areas of a form from change, except for those that users are intended to fill in.

Tip #261

As you build your form, you'll often want to use Protect Form to toggle between protecting the form (which shows how it will look and act when users work with it) and unprotecting the form, so you can make changes to it.

INSERTING A TEXT FORM FIELD

When it comes to basic forms, by far the most common type of entry is plain text. Very few forms do not, at a minimum, gather your name and address—and most require everything from your email address to your hat size. Text form fields are the workhorses of forms.

To enter a standard text form field, display the Forms toolbar, position your insertion point where you want the field to appear, and click the Text Form Field button. You've just inserted a text form field; it appears shaded in your document.

If form fields seem to disappear while you're trying to work with them, see "What to Do If Form Fields Disappear," in the "Troubleshooting" section of this chapter.

If you see codes like { FORMDROPDOWN } where you expect to see elements like drop-down boxes, see "What to Do If You See Field Codes Such as { FORMDROPDOWN }," in the "Troubleshooting" section of this chapter.

The generic 1/2" wide Text Form Field button you've just placed in your document enables users to insert any text, of any length. But you may want to restrict what users can enter here—and give them some help in entering the information you need.

You control the options associated with a text form field through the Text Form Field Options dialog box, shown in Figure 17.2. This dialog box can be reached in two ways. You can select the field you want to edit and click the Form Field Options button on the Forms toolbar, or you can right-click on the field and click Properties from the shortcut menu that appears.

PLACING A NUMBER, DATE, OR TIME IN A TEXT FORM FIELD

The first aspect of the text form field you can control is whether it should contain text. You can use the Type drop-down list box in the Text Form Field Options dialog box to specify several alternatives, including

- **Regular text.** The default setting; users can enter anything they like.
- **Number.** This setting restricts entry to numbers only; if a user enters a character other than a number, the form stores the number zero instead.

- **Date.** This setting restricts entry to a valid date or time. An error message appears if the user enters something else.

- **Current Date.** This setting inserts a { DATE } field. The field is updated when the document is first opened or created, and afterward in accordance with the traditional Word field updating rules.

→ For more information on the { DATE } field, **see** Chapter 18, "Automating Your Documents with Field Codes," **p. 555**.

- **Current Time.** This setting inserts a { TIME } field.

→ For more information on the { TIME }, field **see** Chapter 18, "Automating Your Documents with Field Codes," **p. 555**.

- **Calculation.** This setting tells Word you want the field to perform a calculation. As you'll see later in this chapter, in the "Using Calculations in Text Form Fields" section, if you use this setting, you have to create the equation as well.

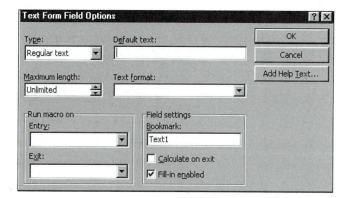

PART

IV

CH

17

Figure 17.2
From the Text Form Field Options dialog box, you can control the behavior of a text form field.

SETTING DEFAULT INFORMATION FOR YOUR TEXT FORM FIELD

In many text form fields, users want to insert the same information most of the time. You can automatically provide this information, which then appears in the form unless the user changes it.

To specify default information, display the Text Form Field Options dialog box, and enter the information in the Default Text text box. You can enter text, numbers, symbols, or spaces. The information will appear in the form as you typed it; the user can type over it to replace it with new information.

Note

This option is unavailable if you choose Current Date, Current Time, or Calculation as the type of information that should appear in the field.

If your users are not familiar with Word forms, you may need to to provide instructions that let the user know he or she can change this information.

CONTROLLING THE LENGTH OF USER INPUT

Many forms are designed to restrict the number of characters a user may enter in a specific area. For example, if your users are entering Social Security numbers, you should limit the number of digits to nine; any more digits than that, and the input is incorrect. You can set the length of a text form field in the Maximum Length scroll box in the Text Form Field Options dialog box.

CONTROLLING CAPITALIZATION IN TEXT FORM FIELDS

Most of the text formatting you apply to form fields is done the same way as other text formatting: by manually applying it to characters or paragraphs, or by using *styles*. However, the Text Form Field Options dialog box does enable you to control the case to be used in regular text entries. Make sure Regular Text is selected in the Type drop-down box; then choose Uppercase, Lowercase, First Capital, or Title Case from the Text Format drop-down box.

USING NUMERIC FORMATS IN TEXT FORM FIELDS

As you've already learned, you can limit a text form field to one of several types of information. One of the most useful types of information available to you is Number.

Specifying that data be entered as a number takes you one small step toward ensuring data integrity. Nobody can fill in alphabetical characters, for example, in a field that requires a dollar amount.

After you choose Number, you can also specify the format in which the number appears. Make a choice from the Number Format combo box. Then, even if the user enters a number in a different format, Word automatically changes it to be consistent with all the other forms you're collecting.

Note
Some elements of the Text Form Field Options dialog box change their names depending on the type of information you choose to include in your text form field.

In the sample invoice shown in Figure 17.3, text form fields have been added to each table cell beneath Unit Price. These text form fields have been set to appear in dollars-and-cents format.

Tip #262
You can go beyond standard numeric formats by adding a *numeric picture* in the Number Format combo box. The numeric picture ###.#, for example, tells Word to round off any entry to tenths.

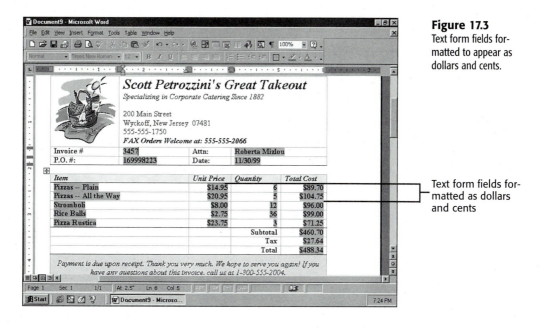

Figure 17.3
Text form fields formatted to appear as dollars and cents.

Text form fields formatted as dollars and cents

USING TIME STAMPING IN TEXT FORM FIELDS

Another useful option is *time stamping*. You can create a text form field that automatically displays the date and time when the form was filled out. Alternatively, you can specify that it always displays the current date or current time.

You can choose a date/time format from the Date Format combo box, or use Word's date/time picture feature to create your own. Later, when users work with this form, they can't change the date; Word sets this information automatically.

→ For more information about formatting date/time pictures, **see** "Formatting Dates and Times in Field Results," **p. 580**.

Caution

Remember that a user can still circumvent your date and time settings by resetting the system clock, thereby making it appear that a form was filled out sooner than it really was.

Caution

When you're creating or editing your form, get in the habit of protecting your document before you test your changes. Otherwise, selecting the form field and then entering some text will over-write any default value you have established for the field. To quickly lock and unlock your form, use the Protect Form button on the Forms toolbar.

Other features of the Text Form Field Options dialog box are covered later in the chapter. In particular, adding Help Text is covered in the " Adding Help to Your Forms" section, and running macros is covered in the "Running Macros from Form Fields" section.

USING CALCULATIONS IN TEXT FORM FIELDS

In Chapter 5, you learned that Word can perform simple calculations within tables, much as a spreadsheet program such as Excel can. Forms can especially benefit from this capability. For example, you can create invoices that calculate totals based on how many of each item someone orders, and how much each item costs.

Use the Text Form Field Options dialog box to build calculations. First, choose Calculation as the Type of data you want to insert. To the right of the Type drop-down box, the Expression text box appears. An equal sign is placed in the text box. (All formulas in Word begin with an equal sign.) You can now use any of Word's basic calculation techniques. The following tips may be helpful.

To specify values in table cells, you can specify the table cells. The first row of a table is row 1. The first column of a table is column A. The cell at the top left of a table, therefore, is cell A1. To add the contents of cells A1 and A2, enter

```
=A1+A2
```

Because every form field has a corresponding bookmark, you can also use bookmarks, such as

```
=Quantity_1+Quantity_2
```

You can also use any of the 18 functions Word provides. The simplest are SUM for addition and PRODUCT for multiplication. For example, to add the numbers in cells B1 and B2, enter

```
=SUM(B1,B2)
```

Or, to add all the numbers above your current cell, enter

```
=SUM(ABOVE)
```

To multiply the numbers in cells B1 and B2, enter

```
=PRODUCT(B1,B2)
```

→ For more information about working with formulas, **see** "Calculating with Tables," **p. 154**.

USING CALCULATE ON EXIT TO AUTOMATE YOUR CALCULATIONS

If you've ever worked with a spreadsheet program such as Excel and then had to do calculations in a Word table, you've probably wished that Word could automatically recalculate formulas every time a value was changed. With the Calculate on Exit feature for form fields, Word can recalculate specific form fields whenever a user makes a change to a value they depend upon. Calculate on Exit works when you click or tab away from the form field that contains this setting. (You don't have to wait until you exit Word or close the document.)

To use Calculate on Exit

1. Click the Text Form Field button on the Forms toolbar to place text form fields where you want to enter your numbers. Make sure you insert a form field for the total.

2. In all but the final form field (where the total is to appear), first change the Type from Regular Text to Number in the Text Form Field Options dialog box. Next, check the Calculate on Exit check box. If you like, you can also change the Number Format. Note the name of each form field in the Bookmark text box.

3. In the text form field that is to display the total, first change the Type to Calculation. Next, put your formula in the Expression text box. You can refer to the other form fields through their bookmark names. A typical formula that adds the three form fields above would read "=SUM(TEXT1,TEXT2,TEXT3)". Do not select the Calculate on Exit option for this final form field box.

4. After you close the text form field dialog boxes, lock the form by clicking the Protect Form button on the Forms toolbar.

Now any time you enter a number into your form fields, the formula will automatically recalculate.

ADDING CHECK BOX FORM FIELDS

Check boxes are a handy way to enable users to select one or more options that are not mutually exclusive. Rather than having to type a phrase like "Yes, I agree" or "No thanks, I'm not interested," your respondents can use check boxes to quickly indicate preferences or (by omission) rejections among a series of elements.

Check boxes are generally used when it doesn't matter how many of the items in a group your user can select. For example, a check box is the method of choice when you see the phrase "Check all that apply" in a survey or questionnaire. Figure 17.4 shows an example of how check boxes might be used.

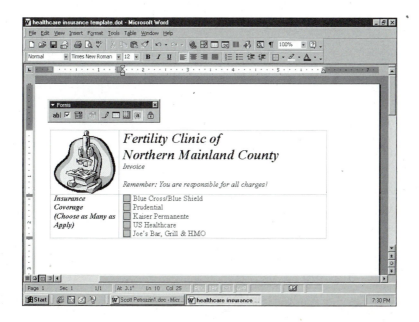

Figure 17.4
An example of how check boxes can be used in a form.

To insert a check box, place your insertion point where you want the check box to appear, and click the Check Box Form Field button on the Forms toolbar.

By default, Word displays boxes unchecked. If you want a box to appear checked, or to change other options associated with a check box, display the Check Box Form Field Options dialog box, shown in Figure 17.5.

Figure 17.5
Controlling the behavior of a check box form field.

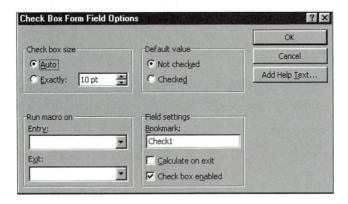

Note

To display the Check Box Form Field Options dialog box, select the check box form field you just created, and click Form Field Options on the Forms toolbar; or right-click on the form field and choose Properties from the shortcut menu.

To specify that a check box appear checked by default, choose Checked in the Default Value area. While you're here, you may want to consider some other settings as well.

Tip #263

Whether you prefer a default setting of Checked or Not Checked, there may be times when you want to prevent users from changing the default. For instance, you might want to include a check box in your form to indicate that you plan to make an option available in the near future, but prevent the user from checking the box until the option becomes available.

To prevent the user from changing the setting you specify, clear the Check Box Enabled check box in the Field Settings area.

By default, Word keeps your check box the same size as the text that follows it; if that text changes size, so does your check box. The Check Box Form Field Options dialog box, however, enables you to change the size of the check box without changing the size of any surrounding text. For example, you could enlarge a box for emphasis.

To specify the precise size of a form field check box, choose the Exactly option button in the Check Box Size area. Then, enter the new size in the spinner box.

Later, after you protect the form and make it available to users, they will see a square shaded box. To check it, they can click it once, or press either the spacebar or the X key. The same techniques uncheck a box that's already checked.

ADDING DROP-DOWN FORM FIELDS

Often, you'll want to give users a specific set of options from which to choose—and prevent them from entering any other alternative. For example, you might create a form that asks your telephone customer service representatives to specify which product family a caller is calling about. Word's drop-down form fields enable you to do this.

 To add a drop-down form field to a form, display the Forms toolbar and click the Drop-Down Form Field button. If that's all you do, however, your form will contain a drop-down form field with no options. You can supply the options by displaying the Drop-Down Form Field Options dialog box (see Figure 17.6).

Note

To display the Drop-Down Form Field Options dialog box, select the drop-down form field you just created, and click Form Field Options; or right-click on the form field and choose Properties from the shortcut menu.

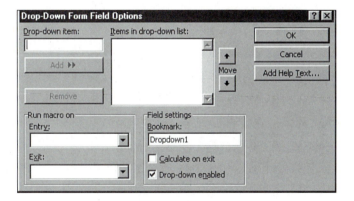

Figure 17.6
Creating options for a drop-down form field.

After the Drop-Down Form Field Options dialog box is open, you need to populate the drop-down list with items that will be available to your form's users. One by one, type the items in the Drop-Down Item box, and click Add. If necessary, select items you need to move and click the Move Up or Move Down arrows.

Word treats the first item in your list as your default choice—it's the one that appears selected when the user opens the form, as shown in the sample in Figure 17.7.

Figure 17.7
Sample use of a drop-down form field.

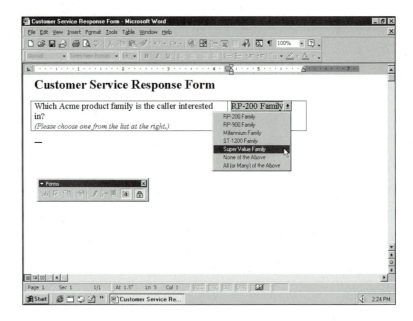

Suppose you no longer need one of your options, perhaps if you've discontinued a product. You can delete the option from your form by selecting it and choosing Remove.

As with check box form fields, there may be times when you want to specify choices, but not allow users to access them. Perhaps you plan to make the choices available later, but for the time being users are stuck with your default option. To disable the drop-down list box while still displaying the default option, clear the Drop-Down Enabled check box.

FORMATTING YOUR FORM FIELDS

 You can format form fields just as you would any other text characters. For example, you can make text and drop-down form fields bold, italic, or underline; change the font name or size; and so on. The field itself retains the same gray shading. You can toggle this gray shading on and off with the Form Field Shading button on the Forms toolbar. Most of the formatting you add—especially font formatting—isn't evident unless text is in the field.

Adding formatting such as boldface to text and drop-down fields is a good way to make it easier for users to see the information they (or others) have inserted in the form.

Note

The form must be unprotected for you to change the formatting of a form field.

Caution

When applying font formatting in a form, make sure you use fonts that will be available on all the computers using your form. Otherwise, Windows may substitute fonts that look unattractive or are difficult to read.

> Of course, this isn't a problem if you use basic Windows fonts such as Arial or Times New Roman. However, if you want to use more interesting fonts, here's an option: choose Tools, Options, Save, and check the Embed TrueType Fonts check box. Word actually stores a copy of the font in the template. (This option is not always the best choice, however. A template that includes the font is larger and a bit slower, and some fonts cannot be embedded this way due to manufacturer restrictions.)
>
> To discover whether a font contains embedding restrictions (and to learn more about the detailed characteristics of a font), download the ttext add-in from Microsoft's Web site, at http://www.microsoft.com/typography/property/property.htm.

REMOVING A FORM FIELD FROM YOUR FORM

To remove a form field from your document, first select it. The field turns a darker shade of gray than normal. Now, press Delete.

Note

> If your document is protected, you must first unprotect it. Choose Tools, Unprotect Document, or click the Protect Form button on the Forms toolbar.

ADVANCED FORM FIELD FEATURES

Word provides some powerful form field automation options that are available to you regardless of the types of form fields you're using. These include

- Adding help to your forms, including anything from a simple message in the status bar to a more detailed message that appears when the user presses F1.

- Associating form fields with *bookmarks*.

- Running macros when users enter or exit a form field. This means your form can help complete itself, based on the specific entries the user makes.

ADDING HELP TO YOUR FORMS

If you're in charge of helping people fill out their forms, you can cut down dramatically on the support you need to provide by adding built-in help to your online forms. Word's built-in help for forms can provide more detailed explanations than your form itself may have room for. You can use it to elaborate on the options you're offering, the information you want to collect, or how to use the form itself.

Note

> You should give at least basic help in the form itself, where the help is visible for people who don't know how to look for it. Include language such as this:
>
> ```
> To get help about any item, move to it with the mouse or the key-
> board and press F1.
> ```

To add help text, create the form field, right-click on it, and choose Properties; its Form Field Options dialog box appears. Click Add Help Text. The dialog box shown in Figure 17.8 appears.

Figure 17.8
In the Form Field Help Text dialog box, you can specify where help comes from, where it appears, and what it says.

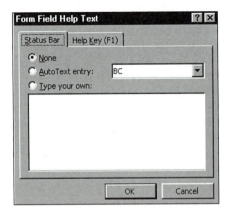

You now have two choices to make: where your help message appears, and where its contents come from. If you want help to appear in Word's status bar, click the Status Bar tab. If you want it to appear when the user presses F1, click the Help Key (F1) tab.

Note

You can create both kinds of help, by placing entries in each tab, as discussed in the next section, "Using Both Forms of Help Together."

No matter which tab you choose, you have the same two sources for your help text:

- An existing AutoText entry (choose it from the AutoText Entry drop-down box, which lists all AutoText entries available to the template you're working in)
- New text (type it in the Type Your Own text box)

Chances are, most of the time you will use Type Your Own rather than a preexisting AutoText Entry—if for no other reason than that they are conveniently stored in this dialog box where they can be easily revised as needed.

Caution

If you do want to use an AutoText entry, be aware that neither the status bar nor these Help dialog boxes can contain graphics, even though they can be stored in AutoText entries.

When you finish creating help, click OK.

USING BOTH FORMS OF HELP TOGETHER

You don't have to choose between offering help in a dialog box or in the status bar. For example, you might provide abbreviated help in the status bar, ending the status bar message with "Press F1 for more help." When the user presses F1, Word displays more detailed information in a special Help dialog box. (Status bar help is limited to 138 characters; help presented in a dialog box can be up to 255 characters in length.) Figure 17.9 shows how both kinds of help can complement each other in this fashion.

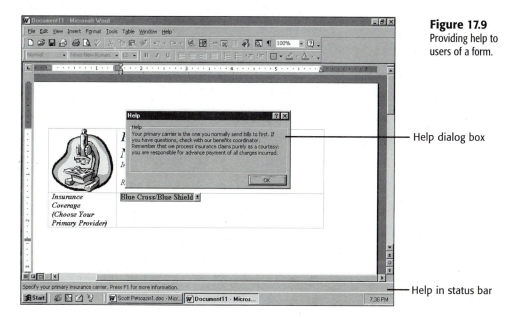

Figure 17.9
Providing help to users of a form.

Help dialog box

Help in status bar

Some users provide simple instruction on using the form in the status bar and provide background about how to interpret the form's questions in the dialog box.

For example, in a travel reimbursement form, the status bar might say "Enter total airline ticket cost," whereas the F1 key might display a summary of the company's travel reimbursement policies.

RUNNING MACROS FROM FORM FIELDS

You can instruct Word to run a macro whenever a user enters or leaves a field. In either case, you can select from macros available in your current document or template.

Tip #264	If you already have a macro you want to use, copy it to your form template using the *Organizer*.

An example of how you might use this feature is shown in Figure 17.10. In this example, a macro, PrintForm, has been recorded. PrintForm sends the form to a user's default printer. Whenever a user tabs to—or clicks in—the CLICK TO PRINT field, the file prints automatically.

Figure 17.10
Creating a form that includes a Print button.

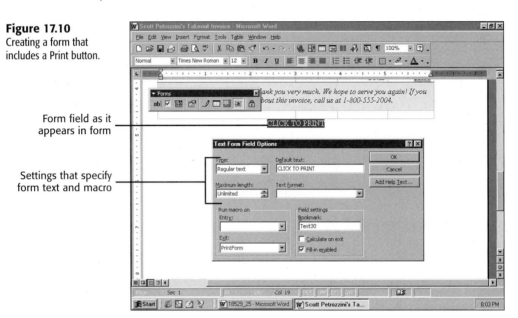

Form field as it appears in form

Settings that specify form text and macro

Every form field is automatically assigned a bookmark name. This means it is easy to create Word macros that check the current contents of a bookmark, and based on what they find there, place corresponding contents in other fields. For example, when a user inserts a name, the macro can automatically look up that name in a database and insert the corresponding company and address. Or, when the user checks a check box, the macro can enable other form fields that were previously grayed out.

After your macro is written, linking it to a form field is straightforward. First, double-click the field to which you want to attach the macro. Second, in the Run Macro On section, choose between Entry or Exit (you can do different macros for each, if you like). Third, select the macro from those listed. Click OK and you're finished. As always, make sure to lock the document using the Protect Form button on the Forms toolbar after you make your changes.

SETTING TAB ORDER FOR YOUR FORM FIELDS

Word enables you to control the tab order of the fields in your form, making it easier for users to navigate through your form—and making them more productive. By default, tab order follows the placement of form fields on the page, starting with the form field closest to the top left of the page. From there, tabbing continues from left to right and down.

However, this may not be the best order for your form. For example, you may want users to answer all questions in a square area of the form before they answer questions to the right. Also, form fields in frames may not tab in exactly the order you desire. You can force Word to go where you want by using the On Exit Macro function. To build the macro you need to know the bookmark name of the form field to which you are tabbing. Double-click the form field and note the name in the Bookmark text box. Then choose Tools, Macro, Macros, and select Create. Be sure to put the macro in the form template on which you are working. In the Visual Basic editor, type

```
Selection.Goto What:=wdGoToBookmark, Name:="FormFieldName"
```

where "FormFieldName" is the bookmark name of your form field.

When creating macros to alter the tab order, it's good to change the bookmark names of the form fields so that they're meaningful. "MaritalStatusBox" is far easier to remember than "Checkbox97". Similarly, name your macros so that you can identify them by sight, for example, "GotoMaritalStatus" rather than "Macro103".

CONVERTING ELECTRONIC FORMS TO PRINTED FORMS

It's common to create forms that will be used both from within Word and in printed versions. Word delivers "What You See Is What You Get" formatting, so your forms appear in print exactly as they do onscreen. (There is one exception: The gray rectangles that mark form fields onscreen do not appear in print.)

Having said this, the art of creating an easy-to-use printed form varies slightly from the techniques you need for electronic forms. Keep these pointers in mind:

- When they're working in Word, users can enter large amounts of data even in a tiny text form field (as long as you haven't limited the maximum length of their entries). Of course, this isn't true in print. Make sure you leave sufficient space in your design for users to enter all the text they need to enter.

- You need to remove drop-down fields (so that defaults are not printed in your form, preventing users from making other choices). Then you need to reformat your forms so that users can see a list of the choices from which you want them to select.

- You may need to enlarge Word's default check boxes to make them easily visible and usable in print.

- If you're designing a form that will be filled out on a typewriter, make the font size 12 or 10 points. The type elements for most typewriters are usually one of these two sizes and it makes aligning the responses much easier.

- The Drawing toolbar enables you to create a variety of shapes perfect for forms: straight lines, arrows, boxes, circles, and numerous AutoShapes. Moreover, they can all be independently positioned and aligned.

- A table is an easy way to create a series of evenly spaced lines. You can turn off all but the bottom border and set the table height to be exactly a certain point size. The Forms toolbar has both Insert Table and Draw Table buttons.

- If you need to position an element of the form precisely, use a frame or a text box. To insert a frame, click the Insert Frame button on the Forms toolbar and drag the mouse pointer until you reach the approximate size you need. Then you can refine the size and position by right-clicking on the frame and choosing Format Frame from the shortcut menu.

- Rather than use check box form fields, consider creating your check boxes through Format, Bullets and Numbering. Select the hollow square check box bullet. You can select any other symbol as a check box by clicking the Customize button on the Bullets and Numbering dialog box and then selecting the Bullet button. Click the Font button to change the bullet's size. Turn off your check list by clicking the Bullet button on the Formatting toolbar.

WORKING WITH PROMPTING FORMS

Word enables you, the form creator, to ask users a series of questions, and to automatically fill out their forms based on the answers. This technique is very useful when it comes to filling out a contract or other document that has a lot of boilerplate text surrounding a few changing entries. To build a form that prompts the user, follow these steps:

1. Click where you want the form field response to appear, then choose Insert, Field to open the Field dialog box.

2. From the Categories list, select Mail Merge.

3. From the Field Names list, select Fill-In.

4. Click in the box after the field code { FILLIN }, and type the prompt you want the user to see. Be sure to include it in quotes (see Figure 17.11).

5. To insert any default placeholder text, click the Options button. From the Options dialog box, select \d; click Add to Field, and type your default text, again in quotes (see Figure 17.12). Click OK to close this dialog box.

6. If you want to preserve any formatting the user adds to text when they fill out the form, instead of removing that formatting when the form field is updated, check the Preserve Formatting During Updates check box.

7. Click OK when you have finished.

8. Word displays an example of what your prompt will look like (see Figure 17.13). Click OK.

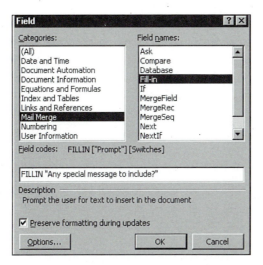

Figure 17.11
You can choose the Fill-In field from the Field dialog box, and insert the prompt within quotation marks.

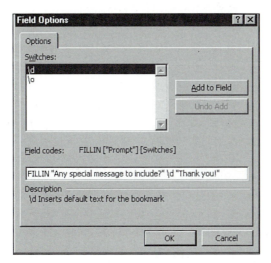

Figure 17.12
Adding default text that should appear in the text box users see.

After you protect and save the template, Word runs through the prompts one by one when you create a new form based on it. When all the prompts have been answered, the text is inserted into the proper places and this part of your document is complete.

 If Word won't permit you to use symbols or other special characters in your { FILLIN } dialog boxes, see "How to Use Symbols in { FILLIN } Dialog Boxes," in the "Troubleshooting" section of this chapter.

Figure 17.13
Fill-In fields enable users
to complete their forms
by answering questions
in dialog boxes.

Text you added
with the \d switch
appears selected —
when the dialog
box is displayed.

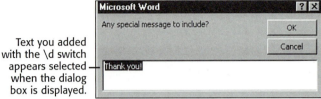

PROTECTING AN ENTIRE FORM

Word gives you extremely tight control over the changes that can be made to a form. When
you protect a template, a user can't make any changes in documents based on that template,
except where you've inserted form fields. In fact, a form doesn't behave like a form until
you protect it.

When you protect a form, some form fields that provide specific information can't be
changed either. In a text form field that makes a calculation, for example, the user can't
override the calculation. And, as you've seen, unchecking the Enabled check box in the
Options dialog box also prevents a user from making changes in that field.

To protect a form, first open the form and then choose Tools, Protect Document. The dialog box shown in Figure 17.14 appears.

Figure 17.14
Protecting a form.

If you want, you can add a password. Including one probably makes sense if your form is to
be used in a large organization where someone might feel like editing it inappropriately.
(You don't want sabbaticals in Tahiti added to your benefits option form.)

Unlike protecting an entire document, form passwords don't encrypt the document. Users
can still open a password-protected form template; they just can't unprotect and edit it.
When a user does try to unprotect such a document, the Unprotect Document Password
dialog box opens, as shown in Figure 17.15.

All the usual password safeguards apply. Choose a password you'll remember but nobody
else can figure out. Don't write it down and leave it in an obvious location. And remember,
after you create and confirm a password, you have no way to unprotect the document without the password.

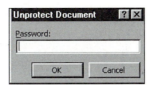

Figure 17.15
The Unprotect
Document Password
dialog box.

To remove a password, first open the document (using its password). Then unprotect it using the Unprotect Document option on the Tools menu. Then protect it again by choosing Protect Document from the Tools menu. Choose Forms in the Protect Document dialog box. No password appears in the Password box. If no password is what you want, click OK. When you save the file, it no longer requires a password. (If you want a new password, type it and confirm it. After you save the file, the new password goes into effect.)

PROTECTING A SECTION OF A FORM

Word enables you to divide your document into multiple *sections* and protect only one section. This enables users to edit at will elsewhere in the document—but when they come to the section you've set up as a form, they're restricted to making changes in only the contents of form fields.

To protect only a section of your form document, start by separating your document into sections using Insert, Break. If you don't want extra page (or column) breaks in your form, choose Continuous.

Then, to protect a specific section

1. Choose Tools, Protect Document.

2. Click the Forms button if it isn't already selected.

3. Click Sections. (If the Sections button is not available, either Forms is not selected or you don't have any section breaks in the document.) The Section Protection dialog box opens (see Figure 17.16).

4. Clear sections you do not want to protect; check sections you do want to protect.

5. Click OK when you're finished and OK again to close the Protect Document dialog box.

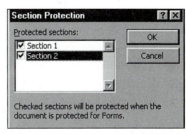

Figure 17.16

FILLING IN ONLINE FORMS

To fill in an online form, create a new document based on the template that contains the form. Each form field is shaded in gray. The first field is shaded in deeper gray; that's where your insertion point is.

Unless you specified a short maximum length for your field, the gray area extends as you type. If the field is located in a text cell, the text simply wraps when you reach the end of a cell.

After you fill in a form field, press Tab or the down-arrow key: Both move you to the next form field in which you might make an entry. Word skips over form fields that it automatically calculates and fields in which you disable user input.

Table 17.1 shows Word's editing and navigation keys for editing forms. As you can see, some keys work a little differently in forms compared with other documents.

TABLE 17.1   WORD'S FORM EDITING COMMANDS

To Do This	Use This Key or Combination
Move to the next editable field	Tab or down arrow
Move to the preceding editable field	Shift+Tab or up arrow
Show the contents of a drop-down list	F4 or Alt+down arrow
Move up or down in a drop-down list	Up arrow or down arrow
Make a selection in a drop-down list	Enter
Mark or unmark a check box	Spacebar or X
Show help for a form	F1 (if you specified that Word display a dialog box to show help; otherwise, help appears in the status bar)
Insert a tab	Ctrl+Tab

SAVING ONLY THE DATA IN A FORM

One of the key reasons for using a form is to collect data. Data is best accessed through a database where it can be sorted, filtered, and output in various forms. Word gives you an easy method to extract the information from a filled-out form without having to reenter it into a database: You can save only the data in a form. To do so

1. After your form has been filled out, click the Save button on the Standard toolbar.

2. In the Save As dialog box, choose Tools, General Options.

3. In the Save (Options) dialog box, check the Save Data Only for Forms check box and click OK. The file type changes to Text Only.

4. Choose a filename and folder location for your file. Click Save.

Tip #265

> If you want to save all your forms as data-only, you can choose Tools, Options, click the Save tab and then enable the Save Data Only for Forms check box.

When Word saves just the form data, it uses comma-delimited fields. You might be familiar with the concept of a comma-delimited field if you've worked with mail merges. The information from each field is placed in quotes and separated by commas. For example, one data file might look like this: "John","Johnson","123 Somter Street","Avery","SC","29678". The data appears in the tab order you specified.

This file format is used for both text form fields and drop-down form fields. Information returned from a check box form field is handled slightly differently. A checked box shows up as a 1, whereas an unchecked box is a 0. Neither appears in quotes.

Tip #266

> You can also print just the data from the form; use this feature when you want your data to appear on preprinted forms. To set this up, choose Tools, Options. On the Print tab, check the box next to Print Data Only for Forms. The data prints in the same location on the page as it does onscreen.

PART

IV

CH

17

After you have saved your forms as data, the information can be imported into an existing database in a program such as Microsoft Access. Almost any database program can read comma-delimited fields saved in a text file. If you speak *VBA (Visual Basic for Applications)*, you can write a macro to append the information in each form into one master file to make importing even easier.

PRINTING ONLY THE DATA IN FORMS

Just as you might sometimes want to save only the data in forms, occasionally you might want to print only the data in a form. For instance, your form may be many pages long; you might want to have a quick printed record of your responses without printing the whole form. To print only the data, choose Tools, Options. On the Print tab, check the box marked Print Data Only for Forms.

TROUBLESHOOTING

WHAT TO DO IF WORD WON'T ALLOW YOU TO EDIT AN EXISTING FORM

The original designer of the form has probably protected it from changes. To unprotect the form, choose Unprotect Document from the Tools menu. If your colleague has created the form with a password, you need to know the password to gain access.

The sections "Protecting an Entire Form" and "Protecting a Section of a Form," earlier in this chapter, cover protecting and unprotecting forms in more detail.

WHAT TO DO IF FORM FIELDS DISAPPEAR

Check to make sure your forms are locked. If the form isn't locked, selecting a form field for entry is just like highlighting a word or a block of text; the next character you enter erases whatever is selected if you have Typing Replaces Selection enabled (Tools, Options, Edit). Always keep your Forms toolbar open and available when you are creating or editing a form. It's much easier to remember to click the Protect Form button than it is to choose Tools, Protect Document.

WHAT TO DO IF YOU SEE FIELD CODES SUCH AS { FORMDROPDOWN }

If you see field codes such as { FORMTEXT }, { FORMCHECKBOX }, or { FORM-DROPDOWN } instead of the corresponding text boxes, check boxes, or drop-down boxes in your document, clear the Field Codes check box in the View tab of the Tools, Options dialog box.

HOW TO USE SYMBOLS IN { FILLIN } DIALOG BOXES

If you use the { FILLIN } field for prompting your users, you have to take extra steps to use certain characters in your prompt. For example, let's say you wanted your prompt to say: "Type "M" or "F" in the box." If you put that sentence next to the { FILLIN } field as is, Word sees only the first pair of quotes and your prompt would read: "Type". You must preface the quote with a backslash character to have it appear correctly. Therefore the proper form field line would read:

```
FILLIN "Type \"M\" or \"F\" in the box."
```

Notice that the backslash goes before each quote, not just each quote pair. Similarly, if you ever want to have a backslash appear in your Fill-In prompt, you must use an extra back-slash before it. For example:

```
FILLIN "Name the file to be stored in c:\\Invoices\\1997."
```

CHAPTER **18**

AUTOMATING YOUR DOCUMENTS WITH FIELD CODES

In this chapter

UNDERSTANDING FIELDS

A *field* is a set of instructions that you place in a document. Most often, these instructions tell Word to find or produce some specific text and place that text where you have inserted the field. In other cases, fields may be used to mark text, such as index entries, which you want Word to keep track of. In a few cases, Word fields can also tell Word to take an action that doesn't place new visible text in your document, such as running a *macro* that saves a file.

Using fields, you can delegate many details of assembling a document to your computer. For instance, suppose that your document contains figures and tables that need to be numbered consecutively. You can do this manually—and redo the numbering every time you insert or delete a figure or table. Or you can use a *field code*, and let Word track it all for you.

Word disguises many of its field codes behind friendly dialog boxes. For example, when you insert a *cross-reference*, *numbered caption*, or *table of contents*—or tell Word to insert a date and time that can be updated automatically—you're inserting a field code. But it still makes sense to become acquainted with the underlying field codes themselves. You can do many things by editing field codes that Word hasn't yet built into neat and clean dialog boxes.

Fields come in several categories:

- *Result fields* give Word instructions about what text to insert in your document.
- *Marker fields* mark text so Word can find it later—for example, to compile into an index or table of contents.
- *Action fields* take a specific action; for example, to run a macro.

Each of these categories are covered next.

WHAT RESULT FIELDS DO

Fields that specify instructions that Word can use to determine which text to insert in your document are called *result fields*, and the information they generate is called *field results*. These field results can come from many sources, including the following:

- Information stored in the document's Properties or Statistics dialog boxes (such as the author's name)
- Information Word calculates from sources you specify, such as adding a column of numbers
- Information Word requests later
- Information Word produces based on what it finds in your document (such as page counts)
- Information found in other files
- Information found elsewhere in your document

Because your document stores the field instructions, not the actual information, Word can update the field results with new information whenever a change in your document calls for it. That's the magic of field codes—they handle the details you might easily forget.

 If Word is failing to update fields properly, see "What to Do When a Field Won't Update Properly," in the "Troubleshooting" section of this chapter.

WHAT MARKER FIELDS DO

Some fields simply mark text, so that you (or another field you've inserted in your document) can find it later. For example, the TC field marks entries that later can be compiled into tables of contents.

WHAT ACTION FIELDS DO

Finally, some action fields tell Word to perform a specific action that doesn't place new visible text in your document. For example, the { MACROBUTTON } field places a button in the text. When you press it, Word runs a macro you've specified in your field code.

FIELDS THAT MIGHT ALREADY BE IN YOUR DOCUMENT

You've come across several field codes already, although you may not have realized it. When you place the date, time, or page number in a header or footer, and instruct Word to updated it automatically, Word places a { DATE }, { TIME }, or { PAGE } field code rather than text in the document. Whenever you update your fields, Word then checks your computer's built-in clock and updates the date and time to reflect what it finds there.

You can insert many fields quite easily if you use the specific Word menu commands, toolbar buttons, or dialog boxes, rather than inserting them directly as field codes. Table 18.1 lists these commands, buttons, and dialog boxes, and the field codes that correspond to them.

 If Word is failing to update a date or time field properly, see "What to Do When a Field Won't Update Properly," in the "Troubleshooting" section of this chapter.

Even if you enter a field code using a menu command, you might still want to edit it later for precise formatting. But that's still easier than creating it from scratch.

PART

IV

CH

18

TABLE 18.1   MENU COMMAND SHORTCUTS FOR SOME FIELDS

This Field Command...	Corresponds to This Menu Command
{ BARCODE }	Tools, Envelopes and Labels, Options
{ BOOKMARK }	Insert, Bookmark
{ DATE }	Insert, Date and Time
{ HYPERLINK }	Insert, Hyperlink

continues

TABLE 18.1   CONTINUED

This Field Command...	Corresponds to This Menu Command
{ INCLUDEPICTURE }	Insert, Picture, From File
{ INCLUDETEXT }	Insert, File
{ INDEX }	Insert, Index and Tables, Index tab
{ LINK }	Edit, Paste Special (Paste Link)
{ NOTEREF }	Insert, Footnote
{ PAGE }	Insert, Page Numbers
{ REF }	Insert, Cross-Reference
{ SEQ }	Insert, Caption
{ SYMBOL }	Insert, Symbol
{ TIME }	Insert, Date and Time
{ TOA }	Insert, Index and Tables, Table of Authorities tab
{ TOC }	Insert, Index and Tables, Table of Contents tab
{ XE }	Mark Index Entry (Alt+Shift+X or Insert, Index and Tables, Index, Mark Entry.
={ FORMULA }	Table, Formula

VIEWING FIELDS

Rarely do you see the fields in your document—what you see is the information the fields find or create. Sometimes, however, you do want to see the underlying field codes. For example, you might want to edit a field so that it presents different information, or presents it in a different format. Or maybe a field isn't behaving the way you expect, and you want to troubleshoot it.

To view a field code, click inside it and press Shift+F9. To view all the field codes in your document, press Ctrl+A to select your entire document, and then press Shift+F9. Or choose Edit, Select All, then right-click on a field and choose Toggle Field Codes from the shortcut menu.

Or, choose Tools, Options, then choose the View tab. Check the Field Codes box in the Show area.

CONTROLLING HOW FIELD CODES APPEAR IN YOUR DOCUMENT

By default, field codes are shaded in gray when you select them. This shading doesn't appear in Print Preview, nor does it print. You can control how your field codes are shaded from the View tab of the Options dialog box. In the Field Shading list box, you can choose Never (in which case your field codes are never shaded, even when selected) or Always (field codes always shaded, even when you haven't selected them).

When you need to see at a glance where all your field codes are (for instance, if you've extensively cross-referenced your document and you want to see where your cross-references are), choose Always. Conversely, if you're working in *Print Layout view* and you want to see exactly how your printed document will look—without being distracted by shading that won't print—choose Never.

VIEWING FIELD CODES AND FIELD RESULTS AT THE SAME TIME

You might occasionally want to view the field codes and the field results at the same time. You might, for example, want to check whether you've formatted a field the way you want. Open a second window on the same document (Window, New Window), and adjust the windows so they appear as shown in Figure 18.1. In one window, choose Tools, Options, View. Check the Field Codes check box. Your screen displays field codes in one window and field results in the other.

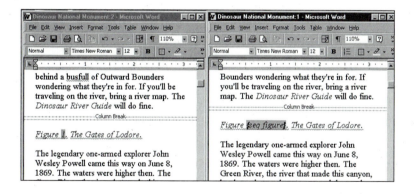

Figure 18.1
Displaying field codes in one window and field results in another.

PART

IV

CH

18

INSERTING A FIELD USING THE FIELD DIALOG BOX

Although you can enter a field into your document directly, most people prefer to use the Field dialog box. Unless you're creating a very simple field, or one with which you're especially familiar, working within the Field dialog box makes it easier to create field syntax Word understands, and it reduces your chances of making a mistake. Choose Insert, Field to display the Field dialog box (see Figure 18.2).

Figure 18.2
The Field dialog box
lists all available fields,
by category.

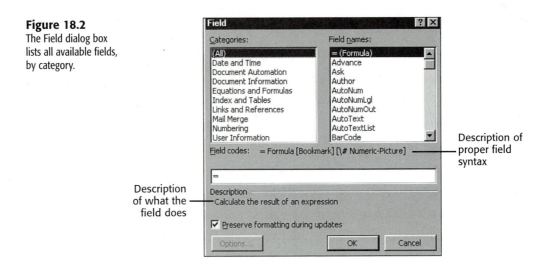

Description of
proper field
syntax

Description
of what the
field does

→ For more information about entering a field directly, **see** "Inserting a Field Using Field Characters,"
p. 566.

You can select the field code you want from a list of available fields in the Field Names box.
Or, if you already know which field you want, you can type it directly into the text box. If
you do type the field, unless you're creating a formula, delete the equal sign that appears in
the File Names box.

If you're not sure of the name of the field code you want, select a category of fields from
the Categories list, and Word lists your choices for you. Word organizes its field codes into
nine categories, listed in Table 18.2.

TABLE 18.2   WORD'S FIELD CATEGORIES AND WHAT THEY COVER

Field Category	What It Covers	Which Fields Are Available
Date and Time	Fields that include the current date or time, or the date or time that an event relevant to your document took place (for example, the last time you saved or printed)	{ CREATEDATE }, { DATE }, { PRINTDATE }, { SAVEDATE }, {TIME }
Document Automation	Compares values and takes an action (for example, runs macros, jumps to new locations, or sends printer codes)	{ COMPARE }, { DOCVARIABLE }, { GOTOBUTTON }, { IF }, { MACROBUTTON }, { PRINT }

Field Category	What It Covers	Which Fields Are Available
Document Information	Inserts or stores information about your document	{ AUTHOR }, { COMMENTS }, { DOCPROPERTY }, { FILENAME }, { FILESIZE }, { INFO }, { KEYWORDS }, { LASTSAVEDBY }, { NUMCHARS }, { NUMPAGES }, { NUMWORDS }, { SUBJECT }, { TEMPLATE }, { TITLE }
Equations and Formulas	Creates and calculates the results of formulas; inserts symbols	{ = (FORMULA) }, { ADVANCE }, { EQ }, { SYMBOL }
Index and Tables	Creates entries for, or builds, indexes and tables of contents, figures, and authorities	{ INDEX }, { RD }, { TA }, { TC }, { TOA }, { TOC }, { XE }
Links and References	Inserts information from elsewhere in your document, from AutoText entries, or from other documents and files	{ AUTOTEXT }, { AUTOTEXTLIST }, { HYPERLINK }, { INCLUDEPICTURE }, { INCLUDETEXT }, { LINK }, { NOTEREF }, { PAGEREF }, { QUOTE }, { REF }, { STYLEREF }
Mail Merge	Specifies information to be used in a Word mail merge, such as information from a data source	{ ASK }, { COMPARE }, { DATABASE }, { FILLIN }, { IF }, { MERGEFIELD }, { MERGEREC }, { MERGESEQ }, { NEXT }, { NEXTIF }, { SET }, { SKIPIF }
Numbering	Numbers your document's pages or sections, inserts, information about your document's page numbers or sections, or inserts a bar code	{ AUTONUM }, { AUTON }, { UMLGL }, { AUTONUMOUT }, { BARCODE }, { LISTNUM }, { REVNUM }, { SECTION }, { SECTIONPAGES }, { SEQ }
User Information	Stores your name, address, or initials, or inserts them in a document or envelope	{ USERADDRESS }, { USERINITIALS }, { USERNAME }

Tip #268

Notice the Preserve Formatting During Updates check box. If you mark this box, and you later make manual formatting changes to your field's contents, Word doesn't eliminate those manual formatting changes when it updates your field. For example, if you insert a field with this box checked, and later format the field result as boldface, Word will retain the boldface. If you clear this box before you enter the field, Word will eliminate the boldface.

As you'll see later, checking Preserve Formatting During Updates is equivalent of adding the * MERGEFORMAT switch to your field. Word adds this switch by default when you enter a field using a dialog box other than the Field dialog box.

 If Word is failing to update the contents of a field properly, see "What to Do When a Field Won't Update Properly," in the "Troubleshooting" section of this chapter.

After you select a Field Name, the field name appears in the text box. In certain cases, that's all the editing you need to do: You can simply click OK, and Word inserts a field that does what you want. For example, if you want Word to insert the user's name, and you don't need to change the way the field results are capitalized, choose the { USERNAME } field and click OK.

Note

Word inserts field names as All Caps for clarity, but field names aren't case sensitive: They work even if you lowercase them. Word also adds an extra space after the opening bracket and before the closing bracket, so field codes inserted by Word look like this:

```
{ FILENAME }
```

More often, however, simply creating a field that consists of the field name won't accomplish what you intend. You'll find that you need to refine the field, by adding either text or "switches" that modify the field's behavior. To discover the syntax Word expects you to use, look at the generic syntax Word displays in the Field dialog box, just above the text box where you type your field instructions (refer to Figure 18.2). After you know what syntax to use, you can enter the correct text and switches in the text box in the Field dialog box.

Of course, there's a bit more to field syntax than this. The next two sections take a closer look at the syntax you might need to add to your fields, and how you can do it.

Note

The Field dialog box helps you enter the proper syntax for a field. Later in this chapter, in the "Inserting a Field Using Field Characters" section, you'll learn the techniques and detailed syntax needed to build fields manually, without working in the Field dialog box.

Tip #269

To get online help about a specific field, select it in the Field dialog box, click the "?" help icon, and then click the "?" mouse pointer anywhere in the Field Names scroll box. Word's Help system will open, displaying the help page associated with the specific field code you've selected.

WHAT GOES INTO A FIELD

You already know that every field has a name. Most fields also require additional field instructions. Two of the most common field instructions are arguments and switches; these are covered next. More complex field instructions are covered later in the chapter, in the section "A Closer Look at Field Instructions."

USING ARGUMENTS TO GIVE WORD ESSENTIAL FIELD INFORMATION

In the example discussed earlier, you used { USERNAME } without any additional field instructions to insert the name of a user. When Word encounters this field, it inserts the username it finds stored in the User Information tab of the Options dialog box.

However, you can also use a { USERNAME } field to place a new name in the document and then permanently store that name in the User Information tab, where it can be used later for other purposes. If this what you want to do, you have to tell Word what name to use. The syntax is as follows:

```
{ USERNAME "Robert Smith" }
```

In this example, the field instructions in quotation marks after USERNAME are a simple example of an *argument*. Arguments are text, numbers, or graphics that help a field decide how to act, or what information to insert. Arguments should always be enclosed in quotation marks.

Note

Word correctly recognizes one-word arguments without the quotation marks, but it's best to get in the habit of using quotation marks all the time.

Note

Once in awhile, you may need to tell Word that you actually want real quotation marks to appear in the document. To indicate this, use backslashes, as in the following example:

```
{ TITLE "Start \"Loafing\" Around" }
```

This begs the question: What if you need to specify a document path, which already uses backslashes? (This might be necessary if you were using an { INCLUDEPICTURE } field to insert a picture stored in a different folder on your drive or network.) The answer: Use *two* backslashes wherever you would otherwise have used one:

```
{ INCLUDEPICTURE "c:\\reports\\image12.jpg" }
```

By using quotation marks around the filename, you make sure Word can read any filename, even a 32-bit Windows "long filename" that may consist of several separate words.

PART
IV

CH
18

USING SWITCHES TO CHANGE A FIELD'S BEHAVIOR

Another important type of field instruction is called a *switch*. Switches change the behavior or formatting of a field, and can be of two types:

- *General switches* determine behavior like how Word should capitalize your field results or what numeric formats it should use.

- *Field-specific switches* change field behaviors that are unique to the field with which you're working.

Switches in field codes are easily recognized, because they begin with a backslash. Most fields use general switches; the only exceptions are { AUTONUM }, { AUTONUMLGL }, { AUTONUMOUT }, { EQ }, { GOTOBUTTON }, { INCLUDEPICTURE }, { MACROBUTTON }, { RD }, { TC }, and { XE }. Some fields use both kinds of switches; others use only one kind.

Tip #270	It's easiest to enter switches by choosing them from the Field Options dialog box, available by clicking Options in the Field dialog box. This is covered in the "Specifying Field Options" section later in this chapter.

FIELD-SPECIFIC SWITCHES AT WORK: TWO EXAMPLES

The following two examples show field-specific switches at work. In the first example, the { FILENAME } field places the current document's filename in the document. The field-specific \p switch tells Word to insert the document's location on your hard drive or network as well. Make sure to add a space between the field name and the switch, as shown here:

```
{ FILENAME \p }
```

The following field code uses both an argument and a field-specific switch. In this example, the { TC } field inserts a table of contents entry; the argument within quotation marks is what the entry will say; the \n switch indicates that Word shouldn't include a page number.

```
{ TC "Discover the latest in sports marketing" \n }
```

GENERAL SWITCHES AT WORK: THREE EXAMPLES

You can use general switches to make sure that the text entered in your document by field codes looks correct in the context where you're using it—no matter where the text originally came from, or how it was generated. Here are three examples.

In the first example, a document's title is being inserted using the { TITLE } field code. The * Upper switch ensures the title will be inserted as all caps:

```
{ TITLE \* Upper }
```

Note

Make sure to place a space between * and the word you choose to follow it.

Note

Fields that allow you to choose capitalization typically offer four choices:

* Upper	Use all caps throughout inserted text
* Lower	Use lowercase throughout inserted text
* FirstCap	Capitalize first letter only
* Title Case	Capitalize first letter of each inserted word

In the second example, you're using the { NUMPAGES } field to insert the number of pages in your document. However, you would like the information to appear as text, not as a number:

```
{ NUMPAGES \* CardText }
```

In this example, if the { NUMPAGES } field finds that your document has 28 pages, it will insert twenty-eight.

Here's one more example: using a { SAVEDATE } field to insert the date a document was most recently printed. The \@ "d-MMM/yy" switch has been used to format the date as follows: 4-Mar-99.

```
{ SAVEDATE \@ "d-MMM-yy" }
```

Tip #271

Formatting switches like these can also be used with Mail Merge fields to control the appearance of form letters, labels, envelopes, and catalogs you create. To learn more about mail merge, see Chapter 6, "Using Mail Merge Effectively."

SPECIFYING FIELD OPTIONS

By now, you're probably wondering how to find out which switches can be used with which fields. Choose a field in the Field dialog box, and click Options. The Field Options dialog box opens, as shown in Figure 18.3.

PART

IV

CH

18

Figure 18.3
Field Options lists all field-specific switches associated with the field you've selected, plus general switches that affect field appearance.

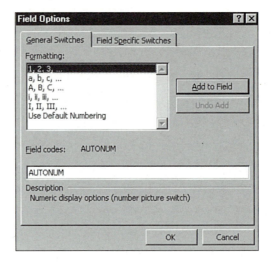

If at least two tabs appear, as in Figure 18.3, you can specify either general switches or field-specific switches. If only one tab appears, you're limited to the switches listed there.

To add a switch, select it from the scroll box that lists all available switches, and click Add to Field. The switch appears in the text box.

Note

If you've been editing text associated with the field code, make sure your insertion point is located where it needs to be. Remember that you need to leave space between the field name and the switch and between the switch and any text that modifies it.

Some switches require you to add more information. For example, if you're using the { SEQ } field to create a sequence of numbers—perhaps figure references—you can use the \r switch to tell Word to reset numbering to a specific number. This is invaluable if your document is to be inserted after another document that already contains sequential figure numbers. However, Word can't read your mind. After \r, you have to specify the starting number you want, as in the following example:

```
{ SEQ figure \r 6 }
```

After you finish, click OK to return to the Field dialog box, and click OK again to insert the field into your document.

INSERTING A FIELD USING FIELD CHARACTERS

Sometimes you know exactly what kind of field you need, and the field you need is a very simple one. For example, if you want to insert a page count within your document text, the field you need is simple:

```
{ NUMPAGES }
```

In such a case, why bother with dialog boxes? Enter the field directly into your document. To do so, press Ctrl+F9. Word places two curly brackets around your insertion point, and colors them gray to indicate that you're in a field (see Figure 18.4). These curly brackets are called *field characters*.

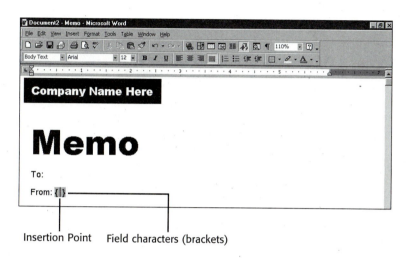

Figure 18.4
When you press Ctrl+F9 to insert a field, the field appears as two curly brackets; by default, these are highlighted in gray.

Insertion Point   Field characters (brackets)

Note

You can't insert field characters by pressing the curly bracket keys on your keyboard; you must press Ctrl+F9. However, you can customize a menu, toolbar, or shortcut menu to include a command for inserting field brackets. In the Customize dialog box, select the command InsertFieldChars and drag it to the toolbar or menu you want.

You can then type field names and any kind of field instructions inside the brackets. You can also cut and paste text into a field code from outside. Conversely, you can also cut or copy text from within field brackets to a location outside the field brackets. Keep the following syntax points in mind:

- You must leave one blank space after the left field bracket and before the right field bracket.

- After the first space, enter the field name; you can enter it in uppercase, mixed case, or lowercase.

- Leave one space between the field name and any switch.

- Leave one space between a switch and any parameters associated with that switch.

- If the field refers to a filename or specific text, enclose the filename or text in quotation marks.

Tip #272

Whenever you create a complex field instruction you might reuse, make it an AutoText entry. Then you have to enter it correctly only the first time; you can just copy it from then on.

Tip #273

If you're creating a complex field, you might find it more convenient to edit the field code's text outside field brackets; then click Cut, press Ctrl+F9 to create field brackets, and click Paste to place the text between the field brackets.

UPDATING YOUR FIELDS

One of the best things about fields is that you can update them automatically. F9 is the magic key:

- To update a single field, place your insertion point within it and press F9.

- To update more than one field, select the block of copy that contains all the fields you want to update and press F9. Or, after you select all the fields, right-click on one of them and choose Update Field from the shortcut menu.

- To update all the fields in a document, press Ctrl+A and then press F9. In a long document, this can take a little while. If necessary, you can stop the process by pressing Esc.

- When you insert a field using Ctrl+F9, Word doesn't update the field until you press F9.

Note

Updating with F9 doesn't affect the following fields: { AUTONUM }, { AUTONUMLGL }, { AUTONUMOUT }, { EQ }, { GOTOBUTTON }, { MACROBUTTON }, and { PRINT }.

 If Word is failing to update fields properly, see "What to Do When a Field Won't Update Properly," in the "Troubleshooting" section of this chapter.

UPDATING FIELDS WHEN YOU PRINT

By default, Word does not update fields when you print a document. For many users, this makes sense: They want to stay in control of when their fields update, and not have Word do it for them without warning. However, if you want to make sure your printed document always reflects the most current information available, you may want Word to always update fields before printing. To instruct Word to do so, choose Tools, Options, and click the Print tab. Then, check Update Fields in the Printing Options area.

LOCKING FIELDS TO PREVENT THEM FROM UPDATING

Suppose you want to temporarily prevent a field from being updated, even as you update fields surrounding it. For instance, suppose that you've prepared a report which uses an { INCLUDETEXT } field to display first-quarter results stored in a table in another document. One of these days, you might update the source table. But that doesn't mean you'll necessarily want the numbers in your executive report to change. If they did, your written analysis and the figures in the document wouldn't match.

To prevent a field from updating, you can *lock* it. First, place your insertion point in the field (or select text that includes several fields). Then, press Ctrl+F11 or Alt+Ctrl+F1. When you try to update this field, Word displays a message that the field is locked and cannot be updated.

To *unlock* a field so that it can once again be updated, place your insertion point in the field and press Ctrl+Shift+F11 or Alt+Ctrl+Shift+F1.

UNLINKING FIELDS TO REPLACE THEM WITH THEIR CURRENT VALUES

You might decide you never want to update a field. For example, you've absolutely finished your document, and you're exporting it to a desktop publishing program that doesn't recognize Word field codes. Word lets you permanently replace the field codes with the most recently updated field results. This is called *unlinking*. To unlink one or more fields, select them and press Ctrl+Shift+F9.

PART

IV

CH

18

Tip #274	To be sure the unlinked information is up to date before you unlink the field, first select it, and then press F9 (or right-click and choose Update Fields) to update it.

Note	Unlinking a field prevents an action field from working, but has no effect on a marker field. For example, if you unlink all the fields in your document, you can still build an index based on { XE } index entry fields you inserted earlier.

Caution	Except for marker fields, after you unlink a field, the field is gone forever (unless you click Undo immediately, or close the document without saving changes). If you have *any* reason to suspect you might someday need the document automation provided by the field, save a duplicate copy of the file with all fields still in place.

SHORTCUTS FOR WORKING WITH FIELDS

Word provides a variety of shortcuts for working with fields and navigating among them. These include shortcut menus, keyboard shortcuts, *Select Browse Object*, and Find/Replace/ Go To. These techniques are covered in the following sections.

USING WORD'S FIELD SHORTCUT MENU

When you right-click on a field, the Field shortcut menu appears (see Figure 18.5). This includes two of the most common tasks you might need: <u>U</u>pdate Field and <u>T</u>oggle Field Codes (*toggling* a field switches between displaying the field code and the field results).

Figure 18.5
The shortcut menu appears when you right-click inside a field.

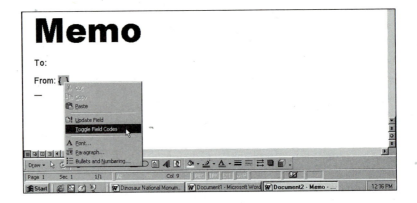

WORD KEYBOARD FIELD SHORTCUTS

You've already learned some of Word's keyboard shortcuts for inserting and managing fields, such as Ctrl+F9 for inserting field brackets in your document. All Word's relevant keyboard shortcuts are collected in Table 18.3.

TABLE 18.3   KEYBOARD SHORTCUTS FOR WORKING WITH FIELDS

Task	Key Combination	What It Does
Insert Field	Ctrl+F9	Inserts field characters { } so you can manually insert a field name and instructions
Update Field	F9	Produces a new field result
Go to Next Field	F11	Moves to next visible field
Go to Previous Field	Shift+F11	Moves to preceding visible field
View/Hide Field Code	Shift+F9	Toggles between displaying field codes and their results
Lock Field	Ctrl+F11	Prevents a field from updating until you unlock it
Unlock Field	Ctrl+Shift+F11	Enables a locked field to be updated again

Task	Key Combination	What It Does
Unlink Field	Ctrl+Shift+F9	Replaces a field with its most recently updated results, eliminating the field code
Update Source (works with IncludeText field only)	Ctrl+Shift+F7	Updates selected text in another document that is linked to the current document by an IncludeText field
Perform Field Click (works with MacroButton or GoToButton fields only)	Alt+Shift+F9	Performs whatever actions you've programmed into a MacroButton or GoToButton field
Insert Date Field	Alt+Shift+D	Inserts Date field with default format (in the U.S., 06/02/99)
Insert Page Field	Alt+Shift+P	Inserts Page field with default format (1, 2, 3...)
Insert Time Field	Alt+Shift+T	Inserts Time field with default format (in the U.S., 04:29 PM)

FINDING AND REPLACING FIELD CONTENTS

PART
IV
CH
18

Whenever the contents of field codes are displayed (as opposed to field results), you can use Edit, Replace to change those contents. This is invaluable if you ever need to change many field codes at once.

For instance, imagine that your document contains several { USERINITIALS } field codes, each designed to insert the user's initials in the document. Your department has grown; some people now share the same initials. You might decide to replace these fields with { USERNAME } fields which display the user's full name instead.

To display all field codes in your document, press Ctrl+A to select the whole document. Then, press Shift+F9 to display field codes. Now you can choose Edit, Replace to specify the changes you want to make.

Word's Replace feature is also ideal if you want to change the formatting of a specific kind of field that recurs throughout your document. For example, if your field is full of date fields, and you would like those date fields to also display the time, you could replace

M/d/yy

with one of Word's built-in date/time display options:

M/d/yy h:mm am/pm

Then, when you update your fields, all references to dates will also show times.

If Word is failing to update fields properly, see "What to Do When a Field Won't Update Properly," in the "Troubleshooting" section of this chapter.

Note
Some fields, such as index entries and table of contents entries, are automatically formatted as hidden text. As long as they are hidden, Word's field navigation and Find/Replace
tools skip them. To show these hidden fields (and other hidden text in your document),
choose Tools, Options, click the View tab, and check the Hidden Text button.

MOVING AMONG FIELDS

Word offers shortcuts for moving among fields. F11 moves to the next field and selects it;
Shift+F11 selects the preceding field. Here's another way to move among fields: Click
Word's Select Browse Object button, and choose Browse by Field.

A CLOSER LOOK AT FIELD INSTRUCTIONS

Earlier in this chapter, you learned about *field instructions*: information that can be included
with a field to adjust the way it behaves and the way it displays data in your document. You
also learned about two of the most common types of field instructions: arguments and
switches. Now you'll discover the power of two more kinds of field instructions:

- Bookmarks enable your fields to work with blocks of text stored anywhere in your current document or even in another document.

- Expressions enable you to build formulas into your field codes and have Word automatically update calculations just as a spreadsheet can.

CREATING FIELDS THAT CAN WORK WITH BLOCKS OF TEXT

In Chapter 11, "Footnotes, Bookmarks, and Cross-References," you learned that bookmarks are markers you can place anywhere in a document to identify a location or text
you've selected. You can add a bookmark to some fields, thereby telling Word to go to
that location or to use the bookmarked text for some purpose. For example, the following
{ REF } field tells Word to insert text about Jones that you've bookmarked elsewhere in the
document:

```
{ REF jones }
```

Note
Bookmark names can be only one word, so you don't have to insert quotation marks when
you insert a bookmark name in a field.

Or what if you don't want the bookmarked text to appear, but you would like a cross-reference to the page number where the bookmarked text can be found? Use { PAGEREF }:

```
{ PAGEREF jones }
```

Note

You can build this type of field using Insert, Cross-Reference, and then create an AutoText entry to quickly reuse it.

If you use the Field dialog box to create a field that uses a bookmark, click Options: The Field Options dialog box displays a list of the bookmarks in your current document. Choose one, and click Add to Field. If necessary, you can then continue to edit your field. When you're finished, click OK to insert it in your document.

You can also insert bookmark names manually; in fact, this is your only option if you are using { INCLUDETEXT } to insert text bookmarked in another document.

EXPRESSIONS: CREATING FIELDS THAT CAN CALCULATE

Expressions are field instructions designed to calculate—and to automatically update calculations when necessary—just as a spreadsheet program would.

The most basic Word expressions start with the = symbol. For example, if you enter the field

```
{ =24-8 }
```

Word displays the value 16.

Of course, this is a trivial example of what Word expressions can do. The real benefit of expressions is that you can base them on other information in your document—and when that information changes, the expression updates its results automatically. For instance, the field code

```
{ =joesales - bobsales }
```

tells Word to look for a bookmark named bobsales, which already contains a value, and subtract it from another bookmark named joesales, which also contains a value.

You can use the { IF } field to tell Word to display one kind of information if it finds one mathematical result, and different information otherwise. { IF } follows this syntax:

```
{ IF FirstExpression Operator SecondExpression TrueText FalseText }
```

In other words, you compare one value with another, and take one action if the resulting statement is true, another if it is false.

Consider the joesales/bobsales example. After you create the { =joesales - bobsales } field, you can bookmark it and name it joevbob. Now, you can build a field that pats Joe on the back if he outsells Bob. If not, it gently exhorts him to do better:

```
{ IF joevbob >0 "Congratulations, Joe, you're salesperson of the month!" "FYI,
you're #2 this month." }
```

Tip #275

If you're working within a table, you can also use cell names (A1, A2, and so on) in place of bookmarks, so a table can perform many of the tasks of a spreadsheet.

Tip #276

If you want to reference one or more cells in another table, first select that table and bookmark it. Next, including the bookmark name in your formula alongside the cell reference. For instance, to include a reference to cell A4 in a table you've bookmarked as Table5, enter

```
(Table5 A4)
```

as in the following formula:

```
=0.6*(Table5 A4)
```

A CLOSER LOOK AT FIELD FORMATTING

Earlier in this chapter, in the "Using General Switches to Customize How Field Results Appear" section, you learned the basics of using switches to control how field results display in your document. However, many Word users have discovered they need even more control. In this section, you'll learn some advanced techniques for controlling how field results appear.

Suppose you've made an important point somewhere in a large report. It's so important, you've formatted it in boldface for emphasis. Now you'd like to use a field to insert that phrase into your executive summary. But in that context, where everything's important, you don't want it to be boldfaced. Well, you could insert the field result and reformat it manually—but it would then revert to the bold formatting anytime you updated your fields. Or you could lock that field—but if you ever want to update the substance of the field, then what? Obviously, neither of these solutions are ideal. Fortunately, Word provides field formatting switches that can do the job.

If you use a field that consists of only the field name, such as { NUMCHARS }, controlling the formatting of your field results is easy. Format the first character of the field name to look as you want your text to look. If you want bold italic text, your field should look like this:

```
{ NUMCHARS }
```

If the field also contains instructions, again format the first character of the field name the way you want it. Then, add the following switch to the end of your field code:

```
\* charformat
```

For instance:

```
{ INCLUDETEXT "report.doc" \* charformat }
```

One more alternative is to manually format your field result, and instruct Word not to change the formatting no matter what. You do this with the * MERGEFORMAT switch. If you look at the fields Word inserts, you'll find that Word often inserts * MERGEFORMAT automatically.

There's only one catch to using * MERGEFORMAT. When you do, Word counts words and takes their formatting literally. If you've formatted the fourth and fifth words in your field result as bold italic, then those words will always be bold italic—even if the field result changes and the fourth and fifth words happen to change. Let's say the field you insert consists of the following:

> According to Yankelovich, cohort marketing techniques can help you craft messages that address the emotional needs of the generation you need to reach.

Later, you edit the source copy a bit. You could wind up with something like:

> Yankelovich cohort marketing techniques can help you craft messages that address the emotional needs of the generation you need to reach.

This literalism means you should use * MERGEFORMAT only when changing field results aren't likely to introduce a problem.

FORMATTING FIELD NUMBERS

You can use * CHARFORMAT and * MERGEFORMAT to format numbers as well. But numbers present some unique issues. What if a number should read one way in one location, and a different way where a field inserts it? Or what if you need your field to return a number in an unusual format, or with an unusual alignment, or in an unusual sequence?

In fields that typically return numbers, Word offers a wide variety of built-in number formatting options through the Field Options dialog box. And you can customize these options even further if you need to.

Figure 18.6 shows the Field Options dialog box for the { SECTION } field, which inserts a document's current Section number. Two types of number formatting options are available here:

- The options in the Formatting scroll box represent sequences of numbering that you can use; Word inserts these with the * switch.
- The options in the Numeric Formats scroll box represent formats you can use; Word inserts these with the \# switch.

The following sections take a closer look at each type of switch.

Figure 18.6
The { SECTION } field offers different kinds of number formatting in the Formatting and Numeric Format scroll boxes.

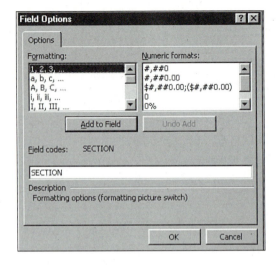

USING WORD'S BUILT-IN NUMBER SEQUENCES

Word provides several built-in sequencing options for the numbers that appear in field results. For example, you can format them as Roman numerals, convert them to words, or display them in a currency format such as you might see on a check or purchase order. Table 18.4 lists the choices Word offers.

TABLE 18.4   NUMBER SEQUENCES PROVIDED BY WORD

Sequence	Switch	What It Does	Example
1, 2, 3, …	* Arabic	Default format uses Arabic numbers	27
a, b, c, …	* alphabetic	Converts number into corresponding lowercase letters, "doubling up" letters after the 26th letter	aa
A, B, C, …	* ALPHABETIC	Converts number into corresponding uppercase letters, "doubling up" letters after the 26th letter	AA
i, ii, iii, …	* roman	Converts number into lowercase Roman numerals	xxvii
I, II, III, …	* ROMAN	Converts number into uppercase Roman numerals	XXVII

Sequence	Switch	What It Does	Example
1st, 2nd, 3rd, …	* Ordinal	Converts number to follow ordinal sequence	27th
First, Second, Third, …	* Ordtext	Converts number to text that follows ordinal sequence	twenty-seventh
One, Two, Three, …	* Cardtext	Converts number to text that follows cardinal sequence	twenty-seven
hex, …	* Hex	Converts number to hexadecimal	1B
Dollar Text	* DollarText "check" format	Converts number to and 00/100	Twenty-seven

As an example, if you want your field to report the section number as "three" rather than "3," you can select the A, B, C,… sequence from the Formatting scroll box, and click Add to Field. Your field now reads as follows:

`{ SECTION \* alphabetic }`

Or you could use a { REVNUM } field to insert a sentence such as

`NOTE: This is the fifth revision`

where the word "fifth" was generated by the following field:

`{ REVNUM \* OrdText }`

USING WORD'S BUILT-IN NUMERIC FORMATS

What if you're perfectly happy with plain old Arabic numbers (1, 2, 3…), but you need to control how many digits appear or where decimal points or commas or used, or you want to display a dollar sign before your field result? The options in the Numeric Formats scroll box enable you to control these and other elements.

When you choose one of these numeric formats, and click Add to Field, Word inserts a \# switch and places the numeric format in quotation marks. For example, the following field inserts the file size, in megabytes (the \m switch specifies megabytes). The \# switch at the end of the field tells Word to display fractions to two decimal points:

`FILESIZE \m \# "#,##0.00"`

CUSTOMIZING NUMERIC FORMATS TO YOUR SPECIFIC NEEDS

Word's built-in numeric formats are likely to be sufficient to handle many of your fields, but sometimes you have to create your own:

- You may need to create a numeric format for an expression. Oddly, Word does not enable you to use the Field Options dialog box to do so; you must do so manually.

- You may need a format Word does not provide, such as a field result with three decimal places, or a field result that formats numbers with a foreign currency symbol such as £ or ¥.

Tip #277

To insert a symbol into a dialog box such as the Field dialog box, insert it into your document using the Insert, Symbol dialog box; cut it into the Clipboard; open the dialog box where you want to paste it and click Ctrl+V to paste it.

For situations where you cannot use a built-in format, you must create the format manually. Word calls this *painting a numeric picture*.

Here's a simple example. Suppose that you're using fields to set up a list of numbers. If you use Word's default format, they look like this:

318.8

15.96

29

18.223

That's sloppy—and if you choose to right-align your numbers you're no better off:

318.8

15.96

29

18.223

You would prefer that each field result use the same number of decimal places, so they line up nicely when right-aligned:

318.800

15.960

29.000

18.223

Tip #278

In some cases, you can achieve the same result using a *decimal tab*.

To create a numeric picture Word can use to create field results with three decimal places, you can use two of Word's built-in placeholders: # and 0. Within a numeric picture, the # symbol tells Word: If there's no number in that location, insert a blank space. The 0 symbol tells Word: If there's no number in this location, insert a 0.

Therefore, to get the cleaned-up list, use the following switch with each field:

`\# "###.000"`

> **Note**
>
> Quotation marks are optional unless you're combining the number with text.

> **Note**
>
> A numeric picture using # or 0 placeholders rounds off a fractional number that requires more digits than you allowed. For example, the field code { =1/3 \# "##".} by default displays the result 0.33.

Table 18.5 describes several placeholders and other characters you can use in numeric formats.

TABLE 18.5   CHARACTERS YOU CAN USE IN NUMERIC PICTURES

Character	What It Does	Sample Usage	Sample Field Result
[No switch]	Enters the value in the default format	{= 1/4}	0.25
#	Substitutes a blank space where no number is present, rounds off extra fractional digits	{=1/3 \# "$#.##"}	$ .33
0	Substitutes a zero where no number is present	{=1/4 \# "00.000"}	00.250
$	Places a dollar sign in your field result	{=1/4 \# "$#.00"}	$0.25
+	Places a plus or minus sign in front of any field result not equal to zero	{=1/4 \# "+#.##"}	+.25
–	Places a minus sign in front of negative numbers (leaves positive numbers alone)	{= 1/4 \# "–#.##"}	–.25

continues

TABLE 18.5   CONTINUED

Character	What It Does	Sample Usage	Sample Field Result
.	Inserts a decimal point	{=1/4 \# "#.#"}	0.3
,	Inserts a comma separator (note: also use at least one 0 or #)	{=8500/2 \# "#,0"}	4,250
;	Enables you to specify more than one option for displaying numbers, depending on whether the numbers are positive, negative, or zero (options should be specified in the order shown: positive, then negative, then zero)	{revenue-expenses \# "$###.00; ($###.00); 0"}	$250.00 or ($250.00) or 0 depending on actual field result
x	If placed on the left, truncates digits to its left, if placed on the right, truncates digits to its right	{4875 \# "#x##"}	75
"text"	Includes text or symbols in numeric picture; place the entire numeric picture in double quotation marks, and the text in single quotation marks	{= "#### 'lira'"}	3472 lira

FORMATTING DATES AND TIMES IN FIELD RESULTS

As with numbers, you can format dates and times in many different ways. Usually, the quickest way to format date and time is to create your field with Insert, Field; the Field Options dialog boxes have most of the formats you need. However, as with numbers, you may occasionally need a specialty format.

The date-time switch is \@. Similar to what you've already seen with numbers, \@ creates a date-time picture—a model of how your dates and times should look. This date-time picture is usable with the following fields: { CREATEDATE }, { DATE }, { PRINTDATE }, { SAVEDATE }, and { TIME }.

You can use the characters in Tables 18.6 and 18.7 in date-time pictures. You can also add separators, such as colon (:), dash (-), or slash (/).

In date/time formatting, a character's meaning can change depending on its capitalization and the number of times you repeat the character. For instance, if you capitalize M in a date-time field, Word interprets that as *month*; lowercase m is recognized as *minute*.

TABLE 18.6   CHARACTERS YOU CAN USE IN DATE FORMATTING

Character	What It Does	Sample Usage	Sample Field Result
No switches (Default { DATE } field)	Inserts default date format	{ DATE }	7/6/99
M	Month in numeric format, 1–12	{ DATE \@ "M" }	7
MM	Month in numeric format, adding a zero to months that have only one digit	{ DATE \@ "MM" }	07
MMM	Month as three-letter abbreviation	{ DATE \@ "MMM" }	Jul
MMMM	Month, spelled out	{ DATE \@ "MMMM" }	July
d	Day of month in numeric format, 1–31	{ DATE \@ "d" }	6
dd	Day of month in numeric format, 01–31	{ DATE \@ "dd" }	06
ddd	Day of week, as three-letter abbreviation	{ DATE \@ "ddd" }	Thu
dddd	Day of week, spelled out	{ DATE \@ "dddd" }	Thursday
y	Year (last two digits)	{ DATE \@ "y" }	99
yy	Year (all four digits)	{ DATE \@ "yy" }	1999

Note

In Word 2000, whether your field result displays a two-digit year ("01") or a four-digit year ("2001"), Word is storing the true four-digit year—so you shouldn't have a Year 2000 problem in your calculations. For more details on how previous versions of Word have handled calculations involving dates, see `www.microsoft.com/technet/topics/year2k/product/product.htm`.

TABLE 18.7   CHARACTERS YOU CAN USE IN TIME FORMATTING

Character	What It Does	Sample Usage	Sample Field Result
No switches (Default { TIME } field)	Inserts default time format	{ TIME }	12:15 PM
h	Hour, based on a 12-hour clock running from 1 to 12	{ TIME \@ "h" }	8
hh	Hour, based on a 12-hour clock running from 01 to 12	{ TIME \@ "hh" }	08
H	Hour, based on a 24-hour clock running from 0 to 23	{ TIME \@ "H" }	17
HH	Hour, based on a 24-hour clock running from 00 to 23	{ TIME \@ "HH" }	06
m	Minute, running from 0–59 (must use lowercase m)	{ TIME \@ "m" }	3
mm	Minute, running from 00–59 (must use lowercase m)	{ TIME \@ "mm" }	03
AM/PM	Morning/afternoon data in the format AM or PM	{ TIME \@ "h:mm AM/PM" }	9:30AM
am/pm	Morning/afternoon data in the format am or pm	{ TIME \@ "h:mm am/pm" }	9:30am
A/M	Morning/afternoon data in the format A or P	{ TIME \@ "h:mm A/P" }	9:30A
a/p	Morning/afternoon data in the format a or p	{ TIME \@ "h:mm a/p" }	9:30a

Now for a couple of examples. Suppose you want to automate the creation of a list of daily specials for your restaurant. You want a field that automatically inserts the correct day of the week in the following sentence:

```
Welcome! Here are our specials for today, Saturday:
```

You can build a { DATE } field that displays only the day of the week (not the month or date):

```
{ DATE \@ "dddd" }
```

Or perhaps you need to abbreviate the current month and day, but you don't need to include the year at all:

```
Mar 27
```

Use the following field:

```
{ DATE \@ "MMMM d" }
```

NESTING FIELDS

Sometimes, the best way to have one field's results affect another field is to *nest* the first field inside the second. This may sound abstract, but it is immensely useful.

To nest a field, first press Ctrl+F9 to create the field, and edit the field as much as possible. Then, place the insertion point where you want the nested field to appear. Press Ctrl+F9 to insert a new field within your existing field. A sample (and simple) nested field appears below:

```
{IF {DATE \@ "d-MMM"}="15-Apr" "Have you paid your taxes or asked for an extension
yet?" "Don't forget: tax preparation today can save you money when April 15 rolls
around!"}
```

In this example, the { IF } field checks the date returned by the{ DATE } field. If the date and format match 15-Apr, Word inserts: "Have you paid your taxes or asked for an extension yet?" If Word finds another date, it inserts: "Don't forget: tax preparation today can save you money when April 15 rolls around!"

Here's a detailed example of how you can use nested fields to ask a user for an article name and then place that article name in the Summary Info tab of the Properties dialog box. After it's stored there, it can automatically be inserted anywhere else in the document you like, using another field.

Start by inserting a { SET } field, which sets a bookmark on the text that follows it. Call the bookmark Articlename:

```
{ SET ARTICLENAME }
```

Normally, the bookmark name would be followed by text. However, in this case, there is no text yet: You need to ask the user for it. You can use a nested { FILLIN } field that displays a dialog box asking the user to key in text:

```
{ SET ARTICLENAME { FILLIN "What is the article title?" } }
```

Next, create another nested field that stores Articlename in the Title box of the Properties dialog box. This field also places the data in your document. You might use it in a document header or footer to automatically place your document's title there:

```
{ TITLE { REF articlename } }
```

Using this nested-field technique, you can ask a user for any information and automatically place that information in the Properties dialog box, where other fields can retrieve it and place it anywhere in the document you want.

TROUBLESHOOTING

WHAT TO DO WHEN A FIELD WON'T UPDATE PROPERLY

First, try to update the field manually. Click inside it and press F9. If the information doesn't update

1. Check to make sure there really is new information available to replace the old information. For example, if a { FILESIZE } field doesn't change, make sure the size of your file on disk has actually changed (this field's value won't change until you resave the file after adding or removing characters or other document elements).

2. Check to make sure the field isn't locked. In some cases, Word beeps when you try to update a locked field. If you don't have sound enabled, try unlocking the field by selecting it and pressing Ctrl+Shift+F11. If the field still won't update, press Shift+F9 to view its contents. Delete the following characters if you find them present:
   \ !

If your field is contained in a text box, note that Word does not select text boxes when you select the text that surrounds them, or even if you select the entire document. To update a field code within a text box, select that text individually, and press F9.

If you select text and press Shift+F9, but the field doesn't appear, it's possible the field has been unlinked (replaced with ordinary text) or that it was never a field in the first place. For example, if you use Insert, Date and Time to enter the current date, but you leave the Update Automatically check box cleared, Word inserts the date in the form of text, not a field.

FORMATTING AND PRINTING EXCEL WORKSHEETS

CHAPTER **19**

FORMATTING WORKSHEETS

In this chapter

WHY CHANGE THE FORMATTING?

You could build an entire workbook with no special formatting at all. Excel's default styles, fonts, alignments, and other settings for text and numbers are sufficient for the legible and accurate display and printing of worksheet data. As Figure 19.1 shows, a worksheet needs no special formatting to display text and numbers legibly.

Figure 19.1.
Excel's default font is 10-point Arial, a very generic font that works for most basic text requirements.

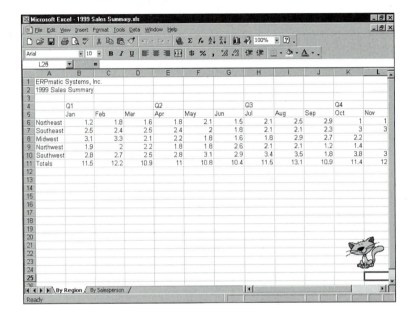

Many worksheets are never formatted, changed, or improved visually, because their users don't require any formatting to make the worksheets more interesting or informative. An equal number of worksheets, however, are formatted—different fonts applied, colors used, alignments changed, and titles dressed up—to make the data more interesting and easier to read. Figure 19.2 shows the same worksheet as shown in Figure 19.1, but some formatting has been applied. It's not hard or even time-consuming to apply this kind of formatting.

Note

It's important to understand that two different types of formatting are at work in any Excel worksheet: the visual formatting, which includes font choices, color, alignment, and so on; and the number formatting, which specifies how Excel stores, displays, and calculates the dates and numbers within a worksheet. Number formatting in Excel is not so much a matter of how the numbers look as how they work. Formatting numbers is discussed in the following chapter.

Even a small amount of formatting can make a worksheet easier to interpret—the formatting is used to draw the reader's eye to important information. Worksheets that will be published for customers, reports, or an Internet or intranet site will be much better received if they have a more polished, visually appealing look.

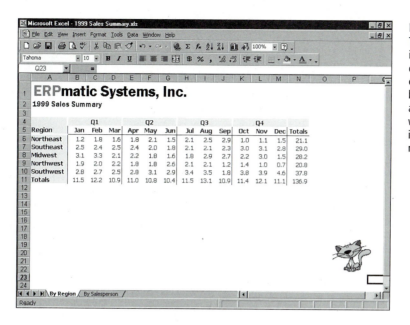

Tip #281

If you want readers to understand the overall content of the worksheet, see what information is being stored, and go right to the bottom line, make column headings and titles stand out through use of boldfacing or by applying a dynamic font, and draw attention to the bottom line—totals and the results of important formulas.

PART
V

CH
19

USING THE FORMATTING TOOLBAR

Excel's Formatting toolbar offers the most common tools used for changing the appearance of text. Table 19.1 shows the tools that change the appearance of text.

TABLE 19.1. TEXT FORMATTING TOOLS ON THE FORMATTING TOOLBAR

Button	Name	Method of Use/Formatting Effect
Tahoma ▼	Font	Click the down arrow to see a list of fonts. Select a font from the list to apply to the selected cell(s), or text or numbers within a cell.
10 ▼	Font Size	Click the down arrow to see a list of point sizes for the selected cell(s), or text or numbers within a cell. The larger the point size number in the Font Size box, the larger the text will be.

continues

TABLE 19.1 CONTINUED

Button	Name	Method of Use/Formatting Effect
B	Bold	Click the Bold button once to boldface the selected cell content, or selected text or numbers within a cell. If the selection is already bold, clicking this button removes the bold format.
I	Italic	Like the Bold button, the Italic button works by clicking it to apply the format. You also can click this button to remove italic formatting from a selection.
U	Underline	Click the Underline button to apply an underline to selected cell(s) or text or numbers within a cell. The underline spans spaces between words. Click the button again to remove the format. This is different from applying a bottom border to the entire cell, a technique discussed later in this chapter.
(align left icon)	Align Left	Text is left-aligned by default. You can apply this alignment to numeric content as well by selecting a cell or cells and clicking the Align Left button.
(center icon)	Center	Useful for titles and column headings, centering cell content creates equal space to the left and right of the content in each selected cell.
(align right icon)	Align Right	Numbers are right-aligned by default. You also can apply right alignment to text. This format is especially effective for row headings.
(merge and center icon)	Merge and Center	Used primarily for worksheet titles, this button enables you to center text in a single cell that spans multiple columns.
A	Font Color	Change the color of the cell content. Click the button to see a palette of 40 different colors, and click one of the colors to apply it to the selected cell(s) or text or numbers within a cell.

The remaining tools on the Formatting toolbar are for number formatting, and their formats do more than change the appearance of the cell content. The Borders and Fill Color tools are discussed later in this chapter.

Tip #282

When you're formatting a worksheet, it may be easier for you if you display the Formatting toolbar on its own. Choose Tools, Customize, click the Options tab, and turn off the Standard and Formatting Toolbars Share One Row option. Click Close to apply this change to the application window. This will give you full access to all of Excel's text formatting tools. Another method is to drag the Formatting toolbar by its move handle (the vertical bar at the left end of the toolbar) and position the toolbar floating or docked at any side of the window. Dragging the toolbar in this way also turns off the option in the Customize dialog box.

When applying formats from the toolbar, most tools toggle—one click to apply the format, a second click to remove it. For those that aren't toggles (alignment, color, Merge and Center), use the Undo button or press Ctrl+Z to remove the format.

Tip #283

You can add buttons to the Formatting toolbar to make quick formatting easier. Two good button choices are the Increase Font Size and Decrease Font Size buttons—click them to change the selected text/numeric font size in small increments.

To find out more about number formats, see Chapter 1, "Modifying Numbers and Dates."

USING THE FORMAT CELLS DIALOG BOX

For more control and a preview of the formatting tools' effects before you apply them, you can use the Format Cells dialog box, opened by choosing Format, Cells or right-clicking a cell or selection and choosing Format Cells from the context menu. (Be sure to have the cells you want to format selected before opening the dialog box.)

The Format Cells dialog box contains six tabs, two of which apply to worksheet text:

■ **Alignment.** Change not just the horizontal alignment (left, center, right) that you can adjust quickly from the toolbar, but the vertical alignment (top, center, bottom, and justified), and the orientation of the text (see Figure 19.3). You can rotate text up to 180°, an especially effective format for long column headings. You can also stack the text, useful for printing column headings vertically.

The Text Control settings on this tab also enable you to make selected cells' text wrap within the cell, shrink to fit the current cell dimensions, or merge the selected cells into one cell.

PART

V

CH

19

Figure 19.3.
Change the position of cell content with the Alignment tab's tools.

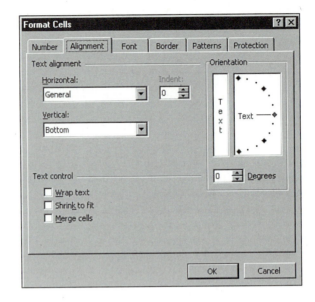

■ **Font**. Choose a font, size, style, and color for the selected cells' text. You can see a preview before applying the formats to the worksheet, as shown in Figure 19.4.

Note

The Underline options include double and single accounting-style underlines.

Figure 19.4.
Test drive font formats with the Font tab's Preview box.

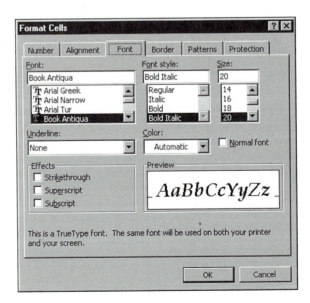

After making changes to the formats with one or both of these tabs, click OK to apply the changes to the selected cell(s) in the worksheet. You can undo any formatting by choosing Edit, Undo, or pressing Ctrl+Z.

Tip #284	If you can no longer Undo the formatting, select the cells that you want to "unformat" and choose Edit, Clear, Formats. The selected cell(s) revert to default formats.

CHANGING THE FONT, POINT SIZE, AND FONT STYLES

The default font in Excel—Arial, 10 points—is an effective generic font. It's available on virtually anyone's computer, and it's highly readable. Although you can format specific cells and cell ranges for visual impact, most users leave the majority of their cells, especially those containing numbers, in this default font. There's nothing wrong with that. But one of the simplest—and fastest—ways to dress up the worksheet and simultaneously draw attention to the more important text and numbers within the sheet is to make subtle changes to the font in certain areas of the worksheet. Fonts and font styles (bold, italic, and so on) can be applied with the Formatting toolbar or the Format Cells dialog box.

Tip #285	Avoid formatting entire columns or rows unless you plan to use all the cells. Excel must store the information for the thousands of cells involved in such formatting, which can enlarge the file size unnecessarily.

Caution	Make sure that you use only fonts that are installed on all of the other computers that will view your workbook. When Excel calls for a font that isn't installed, Windows replaces it with some other font, producing potentially unattractive results. For example, the title "ERPmatic Systems, Inc. 1999 Sales Summary" in Figure 19.2 is in Franklin Gothic Demi. On a computer that doesn't have this font installed, the text appears in Arial (but the Font drop-down box still says Franklin Gothic Demi). If you aren't certain what fonts are installed on your audience's computers, stick with Arial, Times New Roman, Garamond, and Courier New. These fonts are safe, if unexciting, bets because they come with Windows.

PART

V

CH

19

CHANGING THE FONT

The fastest way to change the font for a particular cell or range—including noncontiguous ranges—is to select the cell(s), click open the Font box on the Formatting toolbar, and click the font you want. Office 2000 shows each font's appearance (not just the name) in the drop-down list, as shown in Figure 19.5. TrueType fonts are indicated with a double T icon; printer fonts have a printer icon. (For more details on using fonts and printing with Windows, consult your Windows documentation.)

Figure 19.5.
The Font list shows the available fonts installed on your computer.

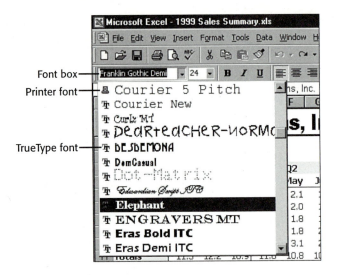

Font box

Printer font

TrueType font

If scrolling the list is too cumbersome, you can type the font's name in the Font box, although this technique works only when you know the font's exact name—if you want the Zurich XBlk BT font, you have to type it just like that. If you don't remember the exact name, you can click the arrow at the end of the Font box and type the first letter of the font you want, to jump to that part of the list. When you select a font in the list, it replaces whatever appears in the Font box.

Tip #286

You can control whether to view font styles with their names. Choose Tools, Customize, click the Options tab, and select or deselect List Font Names in Their Font. If you have a slower PC, you might find that deselecting this setting will make the Font box work faster. Because this is an Office setting, changing it in one program changes it for all Office programs.

SETTING THE POINT SIZE

Measurements in typography are expressed in *picas* and *points*. There are six picas in an inch and 12 points in a pica, which means that there are 72 points in an inch.

Although many typographical measurements are absolute, font measurement is slippery. The size of type is measured in points—say, 11-point Times New Roman or 24-point Arial Black. This is a measurement from the top of an *ascender* to the bottom of a *descender* in the font. The letter d has an ascender—the *stem* that rises above the *bowl*, or round part, of the d. The letter g has a descender—that is, the stem that extends below the bowl of the g. If you superimpose a Times New Roman d over a Times New Roman g, the number of points between the top of the ascender and the bottom of the descender is the font's point size. Unfortunately, one 12-point font may not look to be the same size as another 12-point font.

Compare Arial to Times New Roman at the same point size. Arial appears to be much larger than Times New Roman. That's because your eye determines the "size" by looking at everything but the ascenders and descenders.

> Having a sense of this measurement will help you lay out a worksheet, and set up print areas that fit on a page without sacrificing legibility.

You can specify the desired point size for cells and ranges. The default point size is 10, which provides decent readability in the default Arial font. However, many users prefer titles to be larger, footnotes to be relatively tiny, and so on. The Size box, located next to the Font box on the Formatting toolbar, is a drop-down list that you can use to select the point size, or you can just type the desired point size (see Figure 19.6). Typing the point size offers the advantage of being able to specify a point size that isn't included in the list of default point sizes for that font—even in-between point sizes such as 10.5. However, keep in mind that this option isn't useful if your printer can't size the font to that specification.

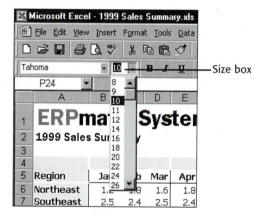

Figure 19.19.
Select or type the desired point size.

Size box

PART
V

CH

19

If you apply a larger point size, Excel automatically adjusts the height of the row to accommodate the new setting. The opposite isn't true, however; applying a smaller point size doesn't automatically reduce the row height unless you apply the point size to the entire row.

ADDING FONT STYLES

Now that you have the right font and point size in place, you may want to apply one or more *font styles* (also called *character styles*) to add emphasis to the text or numbers in the cell. The choices are reflected on the Formatting toolbar: bold (**B**), italic (*I*), or underline (U), as shown in Figure 19.7. Select the character(s) or cell(s) to which you want to apply the font style, and click the appropriate buttons. You can combine two or more font styles for additional emphasis.

Figure 19.7.
The Formatting tool-bar provides font style buttons for quick application.

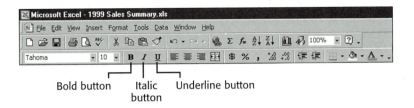

Bold button   Italic button   Underline button

Tip #287

Some fonts offer special bold and italic styles that are "true" italics and bolds. Clicking the Bold or Italic buttons causes Windows to create a bold or italic version of the font. True italics and bolds generally look better than their created counterparts. For example, the Franklin Gothic Demi font (look back to Figure 19.2) also came with Franklin Gothic Heavy and Franklin Gothic Book variants. Book is essentially the normal typeface, whereas Demi is bold and Heavy is very bold.

You also can use shortcut keys to apply the font styles. Press Ctrl+B for bold, Ctrl+I for italic, or Ctrl+U for underline. The same shortcut keys toggle to remove the designated font style.

FORMATTING INDIVIDUAL CHARACTERS

Although you most likely will change the font, point size, or character style for entire cells, you can format individual characters, words, numbers, sentences, and so on within a cell. Simply select the character(s) and apply the formatting as desired.

You also can reverse the formatting for individual characters within a cell. If you have for-matted a particular cell as bold, for example, you can make one or more characters "not bold" by selecting those characters and clicking the Bold button to remove the boldfacing.

If you increase the point size for individual characters, Excel adjusts the row height to accommodate the new point size, just as if you had changed the entire cell.

RESETTING EXCEL'S DEFAULT FONT

If you don't like Arial as the default Excel font, or you prefer a larger font (you probably wouldn't want a smaller font for the default), you can change the default setting.

To reset Excel's default font and font size, follow these steps:

1. Choose Tools, Options. The Options dialog box opens.
2. Click the General tab.
3. Adjust the Standard Font setting and/or the Size setting as needed (see Figure 19.8).
4. Click OK to apply the changes.

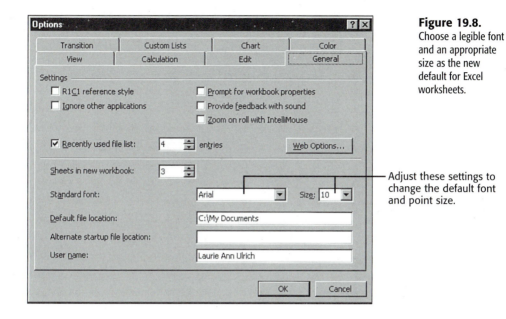

Figure 19.8.
Choose a legible font and an appropriate size as the new default for Excel worksheets.

Adjust these settings to change the default font and point size.

This change doesn't affect any open workbooks (it's not retroactive), and you must restart Excel before the changes can take effect.

 You can change the default font for just the active workbook. See "Changing the Default Font for the Active Workbook" in the Troubleshooting section at the end of this chapter.

Caution

Make sure you've selected a legible alternative for the default font—one that all users of your workbooks will have on their computers, and that can be read easily when printed, photocopied, and faxed. Also, choose a font that won't clash with any other fonts your organization uses in its letterhead or publications.

PART
V
CH
19

WORKING WITH STYLES

Styles are collections of formats, designed to make several formatting changes at once through the application of the style to a cell or range. For example, the Normal style—the default style that's applied to all new Excel content—consists of specific font, alignment, border, pattern, and other settings. To work with styles, choose Format, Style to open the Style dialog box shown in Figure 19.9.

Figure 19.9.
View the style
defaults and edit
them as needed.

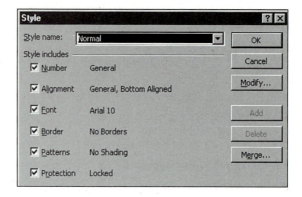

Normal is the only default style that includes all these settings. The other default styles specify only the number format and the alignment and placement of additional characters such as dollar signs, decimal points, and commas, as shown in the following list:

- **Comma and Comma (0).** These two styles add commas to numbers over 999.99. The Comma style displays two decimal places; Comma (0) displays none.

- **Currency and Currency (0).** These two styles add punctuation and currency symbols to match the regional settings for your computer. (Use the Regional Settings option in the Windows Control Panel to change the default monetary symbol, its position, and other currency properties as needed.) By default, Currency style for U.S. users displays two decimal places, commas for dollar amounts over $999.99, and the U.S. dollar sign ($). Currency (0) displays no decimal places.

- **Percent.** Displays the number with a percent sign (%). Percent amounts should be entered as decimals: .15, for example, is displayed as 15%.

The Comma, Currency, and Percent styles can be applied to selected cells by clicking the appropriate button on the Formatting toolbar: Comma Style, Currency Style, and Percent Style, respectively.

Tip #288

Changing the number of decimal digits for cells formatted with Comma style or Currency style doesn't change the style to Comma (0) style or Currency (0) style. If you want to use either of the (0) styles, you must apply that style to the cell(s) with the Style dialog box. As a faster method, you can add the Style box to a toolbar and use it to apply styles.

EDITING THE DEFAULT STYLES

You can edit the default styles in the current workbook to apply the attributes you want. You might want cells formatted in Currency style to have a different background color, for example, so that they're more noticeable (or less). Changes to styles apply in the current workbook only.

If you want to change the default styles permanently or create new styles that will apply to new workbooks, see "Creating Permanent Styles" in the Troubleshooting section at the end of this chapter.

To edit a style, follow these steps:

1. Choose Format, Style. The Style dialog box appears.

2. In the Style Name list, select the style you want to edit.

3. In the Style Includes section of the dialog box, turn any of the elements on or off by clicking the check boxes.

4. Click the Modify button to specify the settings for the selected options. This action opens the Format Cells dialog box, as shown in Figure 19.10.

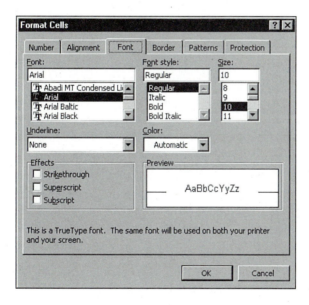

Figure 19.10.
You can change the font and alignment settings for the style, apply borders, add patterned or solid colored fills, or choose from a variety of number formats.

5. Using one or more of the six tabs in the Format Cells dialog box, select the new settings for the style.

6. Click OK to close the Format Cells dialog box and return to the Style dialog box.

7. Click OK. Excel immediately updates any cells with that style to reflect the formatting changes.

CREATING AND APPLYING CUSTOM STYLES

If you use Microsoft Word, you may already be comfortable with the process of creating custom styles to use for headings, bulleted lists, and so on. Excel's styles are comparable to those in Word, and offer just as many formatting possibilities. A common use for Excel styles is to create a certain "look" for worksheet titles used for a particular business. For worksheets disseminated outside your division or company, specific design standards may have been set up that require worksheets and charts to look alike. (In such circumstances, custom styles may already have been set up by someone else in your company. See the next section for details on how to combine those styles with yours.)

You create custom styles in either of the following ways:

- Design the style "from scratch" in the Style dialog box and Format Cells dialog box.
- Select a cell that already contains the formats you want to make into a named style, and use it as an example to establish the settings for the new style.

The methods are almost identical and are closely related to the technique for editing a default style. Follow these steps:

1. If you're creating a style by example, select a cell that uses the formats you want. If not, skip this step, or select any cells to which you want to apply the new style you're creating.
2. Choose Format, Style to open the Style dialog box.
3. Type a name for the new style in the Style Name box.
4. Select any settings you want in the Style Includes section of the dialog box.
5. Click the Modify button to open the Format Cells dialog box, and make any necessary changes. Then click OK to return to the Style dialog box.
6. If you want to apply the style immediately to the selected cells, click OK. If you just want to add the style to the list of styles without applying it, click Add. You can then close the dialog box with the Close button, or continue adding styles before you click the Close button.

To apply a style, select the cell(s) you want to format with the style, choose Format, Style, select the style in the Style Name list, and click OK.

MERGING STYLES FROM ONE WORKBOOK TO ANOTHER

The Merge button in the Style dialog box enables you to select another open workbook and merge any styles from that workbook with those in the active workbook. This feature saves time and effort by enabling you to create or edit styles in one workbook and then use them in other workbooks. For businesses with a standard set of styles, this feature also helps ensure consistency.

Merging the styles from one workbook to another overwrites existing styles with the same name (such as the default Normal style). Excel asks you to confirm this overwrite, but only once—you must either confirm or deny the overwrite for the entire set of styles.

To merge styles, follow these steps:

1. Open the source workbook containing the styles you want to merge.

2. Open or create the target workbook.

3. In the target workbook, choose Format, Style.

4. Click the Merge button to open the Merge Styles dialog box (see Figure 19.11).

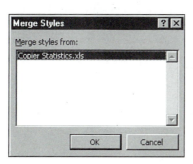

Figure 19.11.
Choose another open workbook's styles to merge with those in the current workbook. This helps create consistency throughout workbooks and their worksheets.

5. In the Merge Styles From list, select the source workbook whose styles you want to merge with the active workbook.

6. Click OK. Excel asks you to confirm that you want to merge styles that have the same name. This process will overwrite all existing styles with the same name.

7. Click Yes if you want to overwrite all existing styles with those in the source workbook. Click No if you don't.

8. Click OK or Close to exit the Style dialog box.

PART
V

CH
19

Caution

Merging styles can't be undone with Undo. Therefore, it's a good idea to review the styles in the workbook with which you want to merge like-named styles before performing the merge, and save the workbook before performing the merge. These extra steps can save you unexpected and potentially undesirable results (and enable you to go back to pre-merge status) should any of the formats be inappropriate for the current workbook. If you don't like the results, just close the workbook without saving, and reopen the saved version.

KEEPING WORKSHEETS LEGIBLE

Regardless of the method of applying fonts, font sizes, and formats, you'll want to make sure that these changes have the desired effect—to improve the overall appearance of the worksheets. Improving the overall appearance includes increasing (or at least not decreasing) legibility.

Caution

When you increase font sizes for numeric content for the first time, the column width adjusts automatically. Row height adjusts automatically to accommodate increases in both numeric and text content. If you adjust columns and rows manually, however, you'll have to continue to do so as changes are made to the font size, or use the AutoFit command to return to automatic adjustment.

Tip #290

Don't let the worksheet develop a cluttered look by allowing the gridlines to confine text and numbers, especially where you've applied elaborate fonts. Allowing some "breathing room" for worksheet content makes it easier to read and more pleasant to look at. Either turn off the gridlines if they're not needed (choose Tools, Options, click the View tab, and deselect the Gridlines option), or adjust the column width and row height to accommodate the size of cell contents.

If you have graphics software programs, games, and so on installed on your computer, you're likely to have a lot of fonts. Fonts also can be purchased on CD-ROM or downloaded from the Web and installed on your computer. A large selection of fonts certainly gives you a lot of choices when applying fonts to titles and column headings, or to important information to which you want to draw special attention. Don't let a variety of fonts lure you into one of the most common formatting mistakes, however. Don't create a circus-like atmosphere in your worksheets. Generally limit yourself to two or three fonts on one worksheet, and use fonts consistently throughout a workbook to maintain a visual theme among the worksheets.

Caution

Practical experience says it's best not to install more than 600 fonts on your computer. You might hear elsewhere that you should install no more than 1,000 fonts. Whatever the number, after you exceed it, you run the risk of experiencing system errors and of some programs not running properly.

CHOOSING COMPLEMENTARY FONTS

Following are some basic rules for the use of fonts in any business application, regardless of how creative the environment:

■ Fancy or artistic fonts (also called *display fonts*) are best used sparingly. Avoid using more than one display font in any worksheet, and restrict usage to short titles for best readability. Figure 19.12 shows a worksheet with too many artistic fonts in use.

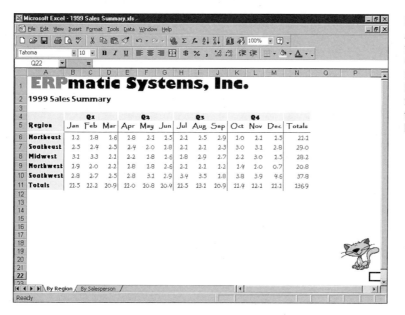

Figure 19.12.
A worksheet suffering from creeping fontitis. Compare this with Figure 19.2. Which looks more readable? Stick with two or three simple fonts for best results.

■ Generally avoid using more than one serif or sans serif font in the same worksheet. Having one serif and one sans serif font in the same worksheet is effective, as these types of fonts complement each other. Having two or more of either type can create visual havoc. When you combine serif and sans serif fonts, use one type for headings and the other for data, as Figure 19.13 shows.

A serif font (Charter) creates a dignified look for labels.

A sans serif font (Arial) works well with numbers.

Region	Q1			Q2			Q3			Q4			Totals
	Jan	Feb	Mar	Apr	May	Jun	Jul	Aug	Sep	Oct	Nov	Dec	
Northeast	1.2	1.8	1.6	1.8	2.1	1.5	2.1	2.5	2.9	1.0	1.1	1.5	21.1
Southeast	2.5	2.4	2.5	2.4	2.0	1.8	2.1	2.1	2.3	3.0	3.1	2.8	29.0
Midwest	3.1	3.3	2.1	2.2	1.8	1.6	1.8	2.9	2.7	2.2	3.0	1.5	28.2
Northwest	1.9	2.0	2.2	1.8	1.8	2.6	2.1	2.1	1.2	1.4	1.0	0.7	20.8
Southwest	2.8	2.7	2.5	2.8	3.1	2.9	3.4	3.5	1.8	3.8	3.9	4.6	37.8
Totals	11.5	12.2	10.9	11.0	10.8	10.4	11.5	13.1	10.9	11.4	12.1	11.1	136.9

Figure 19.13.
The simplicity of a sans serif font is appealing when used with a more complex serif font.

Serif fonts have a flourish on the ends of the letters, as you see in the text of this paragraph. The term comes from *seraphim* (Latin for *angels*), and is applied to text with small "wings" on the ends of characters. *Sans serif* means "without serif," or no wings. Times New Roman (Word's default font) is a serif font, and Arial (Excel's default font) is sans serif.

SIZING FONTS

Choosing the appropriate size for fonts depends on two things—legibility and printing needs. Obviously, having fonts that are too small can make worksheets hard to read. On the other hand, small fonts can help to fit more of the worksheet on one page. The goal is to find a happy medium—the size of font that's easy to read but isn't so big that the worksheet requires an inordinate number of pages to print in its entirety.

For most worksheets, 10- or 8-point text is large enough to be read, but not so large that you waste paper. Column headings and row labels can be 12 or 14 points, and worksheet titles can be any size that seems appropriate.

Font size figures into the guideline of two or three fonts per worksheet. Arial 10 and Arial 12 are two fonts. Figure 19.14 uses five fonts: 24-point Franklin Gothic Demi, 12-point Franklin Gothic Demi, 10-point Tahoma Bold, 12-point Tahoma Bold, and 10-point Tahoma. You could consider "ERPmatic Systems" to be a logo, reducing the font count by one. This user made a judgment call that the grand sales total needed to be especially highlighted, and used 12-point Tahoma Bold to accomplish the emphasis.

Figure 19.14.
Use font sizes as well as different fonts to format the worksheet's overall appearance.

ERPmatic Systems, Inc.
1999 Sales Summary

Region	Q1			Q2			Q3			Q4			Totals
	Jan	Feb	Mar	Apr	May	Jun	Jul	Aug	Sep	Oct	Nov	Dec	
Northeast	1.2	1.8	1.6	1.8	2.1	1.5	2.1	2.5	2.9	1.0	1.1	1.5	21.1
Southeast	2.5	2.4	2.5	2.4	2.0	1.8	2.1	2.1	2.3	3.0	3.1	2.8	29.0
Midwest	3.1	3.3	2.1	2.2	1.8	1.6	1.8	2.9	2.7	2.2	3.0	1.5	28.2
Northwest	1.9	2.0	2.2	1.8	1.8	2.6	2.1	2.1	1.2	1.4	1.0	0.7	20.8
Southwest	2.8	2.7	2.5	2.8	3.1	2.9	3.4	3.5	1.8	3.8	3.9	4.6	37.8
Totals	11.5	12.2	10.9	11.0	10.8	10.4	11.5	13.1	10.9	11.4	12.1	11.1	136.9

Tip #291

The user might have done equally well to use shading to put a colorful background behind the total instead, as Figure 19.15 shows. Bright yellow makes an excellent shade, by the way—not only does it display well, but it prints on a black-and-white printer as a shade of gray that doesn't interfere with text that appears on it. For more information about shading, see "Applying Borders and Shading," later in this chapter.

Figure 19.15.
Highlighting is a viable alternative to adjusting font size when you want to emphasize something, such as this grand sales total.

ERPmatic Systems, Inc.
1999 Sales Summary

Region	Q1			Q2			Q3			Q4			Totals
	Jan	Feb	Mar	Apr	May	Jun	Jul	Aug	Sep	Oct	Nov	Dec	
Northeast	1.2	1.8	1.6	1.8	2.1	1.5	2.1	2.5	2.9	1.0	1.1	1.5	21.1
Southeast	2.5	2.4	2.5	2.4	2.0	1.8	2.1	2.1	2.3	3.0	3.1	2.8	29.0
Midwest	3.1	3.3	2.1	2.2	1.8	1.6	1.8	2.9	2.7	2.2	3.0	1.5	28.2
Northwest	1.9	2.0	2.2	1.8	1.8	2.6	2.1	2.1	1.2	1.4	1.0	0.7	20.8
Southwest	2.8	2.7	2.5	2.8	3.1	2.9	3.4	3.5	1.8	3.8	3.9	4.6	37.8
Totals	11.5	12.2	10.9	11.0	10.8	10.4	11.5	13.1	10.9	11.4	12.1	11.1	136.9

Highlighted cell

FORMATTING TITLES WITH MERGE AND CENTER

The worksheet title is usually the first thing someone notices when viewing a worksheet. The title normally tells the reader what sort of information will be found in the worksheet or what purpose the worksheet serves.

Making the title stand out is important for worksheets that will be published—on paper or on the Web. This chapter has discussed applying various formats to enhance worksheet text, and certainly those formats will be applied to the title. However, to place the title above and across the width of the worksheet is a popular effect, requiring use of Excel's Merge and Center tool. The Merge and Center effect is frequently enough to make titles stand out, even if no other special formatting is applied to the title text.

To center the title across the worksheet, follow these steps:

1. Assuming the title is in cell A1 or a cell to the left of and above the worksheet or a portion thereof, select the title and the blank cells to its right, as shown in Figure 19.16.

2. Click the Merge and Center button on the Formatting toolbar. The cells are merged into one cell, with the title centered across the cells (see Figure 19.17).

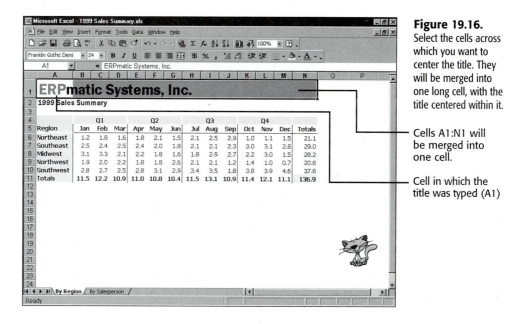

Figure 19.16.
Select the cells across which you want to center the title. They will be merged into one long cell, with the title centered within it.

Cells A1:N1 will be merged into one cell.

Cell in which the title was typed (A1)

PART

V

CH

19

Figure 19.17.
Keep the title visually separate from the rest of the worksheet content through the use of Merge and Center. (Merge and Center was applied to the subtitle, too.)

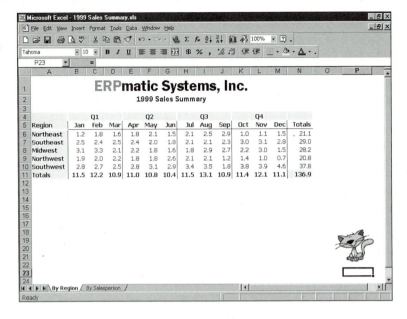

 If you select the whole row and then click Merge and Center, you'll get a surprise. See "Where Did the Worksheet Title Go?" in the Troubleshooting section at the end of this chapter.

ADJUSTING ALIGNMENT WITHIN CELLS, COLUMNS, AND ROWS

By default, Excel aligns text to the left, and numbers to the right. You can change the alignment of cell content by changing the number formats for numeric data, or by selecting a new alignment.

Why would you change cell alignment? The motivation is normally aesthetic, as changing alignment helps to change the worksheet's overall appearance and can help to set certain cells apart, such as column headings (see Figure 19.18).

Figure 19.18.
Centering the Q1, Q2, Q3, and Q4 headings helps make clear which months belong to which quarter. Right-aligning the month headings, however, makes clear their relationship with the numbers below.

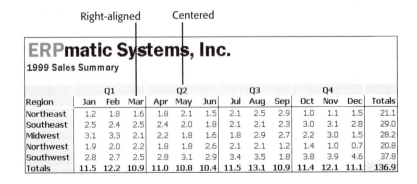

For more information about applying number formats, see Chapter 1.

ALIGNING CELL CONTENT

To change the alignment of a single cell or any range of selected cells, you can use the Formatting toolbar or the Format Cells dialog box (choose Format, Cells or right-click the cell or range and choose Format Cells; then click the Alignment tab). The dialog box gives you more options for changing the cells' alignment, as described in the following list:

- **Horizontal.** This option in the Format Cells dialog box gives you choices ranging from General (meaning that alignment will be dictated by the type of content—text will be left-aligned, numbers right-aligned) to Center Across Selection.

Tip #292

Center Across Selection is nearly the equivalent of the Merge and Center button on the Formatting toolbar, but not quite. If you use Merge and Center to place a title across A1:A5, clicking A1 selects the entire merged "cell" A1:A5. If you use Center Across Selection, clicking A1 just selects A1. Center Across Selection doesn't actually merge the cells; it just visually moves the title across the selection. The text remains in the first cell.

Center Across Selection is the way earlier versions of Excel handled centering titles. With Excel 97 came the Merge and Center feature, but it had a big drawback: You couldn't insert columns within a merged area, which was one of the reasons Microsoft kept the old Center Across Selection option. Excel 2000 has corrected this problem.

- **Vertical.** This setting enables you to align cell content to the top, middle, or bottom of a cell. By default, cells are bottom-aligned.

You can use the Decrease Indent and Increase Indent buttons to change the horizontal position of cell content within the cell. Before or after entering content into the active cell, click the Increase Indent button to move the content to the right, in small increments. To move the content to the left, click the Decrease Indent button.

ROTATING AND WRAPPING TEXT

The Alignment tab in the Format Cells dialog box also gives you access to tools for rotating text to any angle you need, and for choosing whether or not text will wrap in a cell.

Used primarily for column headings, the Orientation feature enables you to drag the wand to any position on the semicircle or enter a specific number of degrees of rotation for the text (see Figure 19.19). However, some fonts don't look very good when rotated, as Figure 19.20 shows. When you rotate text, be sure it's readable.

Wrapping text is frequently a better option than rotating it when you want it to fit a particular column width. Choosing Wrap Text enables you to type a phrase, sentence, paragraph, or more into a cell and have it wrap within the cell's current width. The cell grows taller to accommodate the wrapping text. You can also force Excel to wrap the text in the cell as you type—press Alt+Enter at the point where you'd like the text to wrap onto the next line. This is handy when you want line breaks to occur at specific points.

Figure 19.19.
Placing column headings on an angle reduces the need for wider columns.

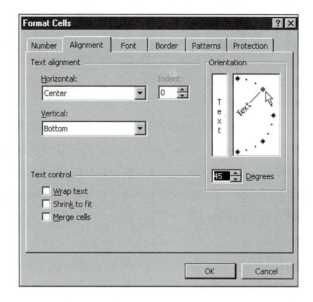

Figure 19.20.
Some fonts are hard to read when rotated. Notice how rotating the text also angles other cell formatting, such as shading.

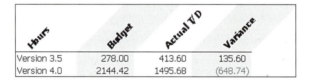

The Shrink to Fit and Merge Cells options are tools that give you more control over text placement. Shrink to Fit makes the text (or numbers) reduce in point size so that it fits in the cell's current dimensions. (Note that this can sometimes make cell entries unreadably tiny.)

Use Merge Cells to make one large cell out of two or more contiguous cells. You can do this before or after the selected cells have content.

Tip #293

Merged cells in conjunction with a centered horizontal alignment is equivalent to the function of the Merge and Center button.

Tip #294

Like fonts, alignment effects should be kept to a minimum. Using too many different alignments in a single sheet can be distracting for the reader.

APPLYING BORDERS AND SHADING

Using borders and/or shading in worksheets is an effective method for enhancing and improving a worksheet's appearance and highlighting important information.

Figure 19.21 shows a worksheet with borders and shading applied for both cosmetic and functional reasons.

Region	Q1			Q2			Q3			Q4			Totals
	Jan	Feb	Mar	Apr	May	Jun	Jul	Aug	Sep	Oct	Nov	Dec	
Northeast	1.2	1.8	1.6	1.8	2.1	1.5	2.1	2.5	2.9	1.0	1.1	1.5	21.1
Southeast	2.5	2.4	2.5	2.4	2.0	1.8	2.1	2.1	2.3	3.0	3.1	2.8	29.0
Midwest	3.1	3.3	2.1	2.2	1.8	1.6	1.8	2.9	2.7	2.2	3.0	1.5	28.2
Northwest	1.9	2.0	2.2	1.8	1.8	2.6	2.1	2.1	1.2	1.4	1.0	0.7	20.8
Southwest	2.8	2.7	2.5	2.8	3.1	2.9	3.4	3.5	1.8	3.8	3.9	4.6	37.8
Totals	11.5	12.2	10.9	11.0	10.8	10.4	11.5	13.1	10.9	11.4	12.1	11.1	136.9

Shading to highlight the major column and row headings

Thin borders to separate the quarters of the year

Thick border to separate column headings from data

Figure 19.21.
Use borders and shading to draw attention to specific numbers or to create a barrier between sections in a worksheet.

Don't have a color printer? It's still worthwhile to add color to worksheets. Whether you're publishing the worksheet to the Web or simply sending it to another user to view onscreen, the use of color is never wasted. Even a black-and-white printout is enhanced by the use of color, as the colors are translated into subtly varying shades of gray.

USING BORDERS EFFECTIVELY

By default, worksheet gridlines don't print. This means that borders added to cells in a worksheet are the only lines that appear on the hard copy. You can turn gridlines on when you print, but with proper use of borders, your printouts will be much cleaner and more effective.

What purpose do borders serve? Borders draw attention, and borders create separations. Consider the following uses:

- Add a double border under the last number in a series of numbers to be totaled.
- Insert a border under the worksheet title.
- Use inside borders within a block of cells to create a visual table.
- Placing a full border around a single cell draws attention to a grand total or other important number.

To apply a quick border, you can use the Borders button on the Formatting toolbar. Follow these steps:

1. Select the cell or cells to which you want to apply a border.
2. Click the down-arrow button to the right of the Borders button to display a drop-down palette of border styles.
3. Choose one of the 12 border options from the Borders palette.

PART
V
CH
19

Notice that the button face changes to display the border style you selected. If you make another selection in the worksheet and click the button (instead of clicking the down arrow to display the list), Excel applies the border style shown on the button face to the new selection.

The Borders button applies thick, thin, or double lines to any cell or group of cells you select. If you want more variety, use the Borders tab in the Format Cells dialog box, as described in the following steps:

1. Select the cell or range of cells to be bordered.

2. Choose Format, Cells or right-click the range and choose Format Cells to display the Format Cells dialog box.

3. Click the Border tab.

4. In the Border box, click the sides around the word Text to indicate on which side of the selected cell(s) you want borders applied, or click the buttons that surround the box to choose which sides to border. If you have multiple cells selected, as in Figure 19.22, the word Text appears twice, and you can click the Inside button or click between the two words to insert borders between cells.

Figure 19.22.
The Border box serves as a tool for previewing borders as well as applying them.

Click the border buttons or click within the box to add or remove borders.

Click these preset buttons for instant, simple borders.

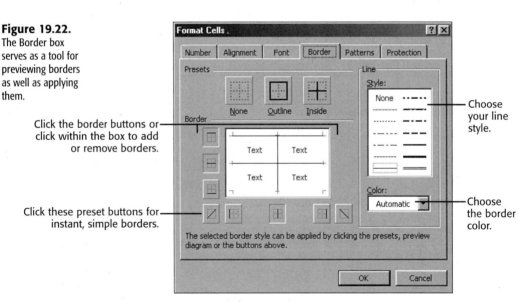

Choose your line style.

Choose the border color.

5. Choose a line style, and if desired, a color for the border(s).

6. Click OK to apply the border(s) to the selected cell(s).

Tip #295

To remove borders, select the cell(s), click open the Borders button, and select the No Border option in the upper-left corner of the palette.

USING COLORS, PATTERNS, AND TEXTURED FILLS

Shading cells can mean more than simply applying a shade of gray behind the cell content. Excel gives you 56 different solid colors and 18 different pattern fills to add visual interest and excitement to your worksheets.

To apply colors and patterns to selected cells, follow these steps:

1. Select the cell(s) and choose Format, Cells.
2. Click the Patterns tab (see Figure 19.23).

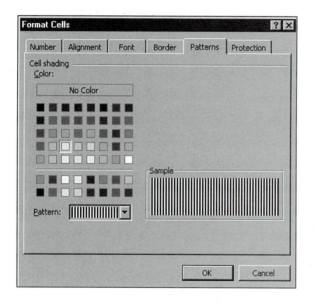

Figure 19.23.
Choose a color, a pattern, or both, and preview the selection in the Sample window.

3. To add color, click a solid color from the Color palette.
4. If desired, open the Pattern list box and choose a pattern. You can combine color and pattern by choosing a color and then a pattern, or vice versa.

Tip #296

If you choose both a color and a pattern, the pattern will appear in black on top of the selected color. You can make a number of nice combinations by experimenting.

5. Click OK to apply the color and/or pattern to the selection.

To apply a fill color quickly, select the cell or cells to be colored, and click the Fill Color button on the Formatting toolbar. Choose one of the 40 colors on the palette.

To remove both fill color and pattern, select the cell(s), click open the Fill Color list, and choose No Fill on the palette. To remove one or the other, open the Format Cells dialog box, click the Patterns tab, and click No Color in the Color list or Solid in the Pattern list.

Caution

Be careful when choosing a fill color or pattern. Dark colors can make cell content difficult to read (requiring you to change the text color to white or yellow), and patterns can render the cell completely illegible. If you choose a light text color, be aware that text may be illegible when printed on a black-and-white printer. A good rule of thumb is to choose colors (for background and text) that will work in the majority of viewing and printing scenarios—don't create problems for yourself by applying formatting that requires very specific display or printing configurations.

Tip #297

If you're using Excel to create a fill-in form, using patterns in empty cells can tell the user not to use those cells, or simply create a visually interesting separation between parts of the form.

COPYING FORMATS WITH THE FORMAT PAINTER

 Imagine you've formatted the column headings in one section of a worksheet with a different font, larger point size, a shaded background for the cells, and a thick border under the headings. That's four different formats you've applied. If you decide that you want the headings throughout the worksheet (or throughout the whole workbook) to look the same way, use the *Format Painter* to copy them from the section you've formatted to other sections you want formatted in the same way.

Tip #298

Another method is to create and apply styles for the headings. See the earlier section "Working with Styles" for details.

You can use the Format Painter to copy formats to one other location, or to several locations. To use the Format Painter, follow these steps:

1. Select the cell(s) containing the formatting you want to copy. These are the sample cells.

2. Click the Format Painter button. The mouse pointer changes to include a paintbrush symbol (see Figure 19.24).

3. Click on a single cell or drag through a range of cells that you want to format like the sample.

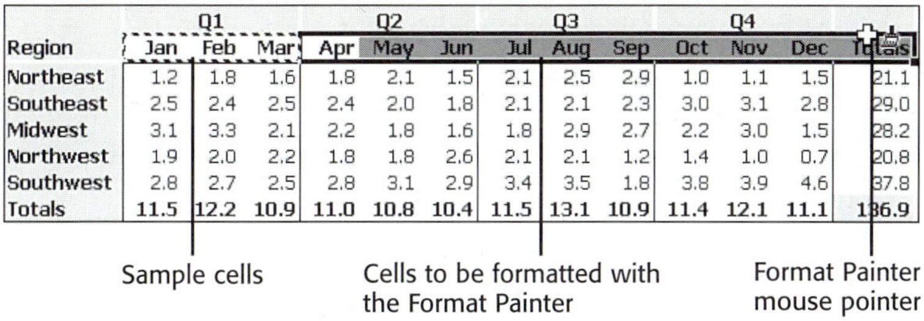

Figure 19.24.
Copy the formats (but not the content) from cell to cell with the Format Painter.

Sample cells

Cells to be formatted with the Format Painter

Format Painter mouse pointer

Tip #299

To copy the sample format(s) to several noncontiguous locations throughout the worksheet or workbook, double-click the Format Painter button. Doing this leaves the tool "turned on" until you click the button again to turn it off.

USING AUTOFORMAT TO ENHANCE YOUR WORKSHEETS

If you'd rather not spend your time selecting fonts and choosing when and where to apply shading and borders, let Excel make these choices for you. Excel's *AutoFormat* feature offers a series of preformatted effects that you can apply to any range of cells within a worksheet.

To use AutoFormat, follow these steps:

1. Select the range of cells you want to format, keeping the following rules in mind:
   - You must have two or more contiguous cells selected in order to use AutoFormat.
   - AutoFormat can't be applied to multiple ranges.

2. Choose Format, AutoFormat.

3. Select a format from the list of samples (see Figure 19.25).

   Clicking the Options button displays a list of the formats that will be applied with the selected AutoFormat. You can deselect any of the options you don't want AutoFormat to apply.

4. Click OK.

Caution

If you've already sized columns and rows before using AutoFormat, deselect the Width/Height option. AutoFormat sizes the columns and rows to fit the widest/tallest entry, which may result in a cramped or crowded look for the worksheet.

In some cases, the size and content of the selected range and the AutoFormat you chose don't match—for example, a border might be applied indicating a total where you don't have one. If this occurs, simply remove the offending formatting effect or use Undo to remove the AutoFormat. At this point, you can reapply the AutoFormat, and choose not to apply the borders (or whatever format didn't work well with the selected cells).

PART
V

CH
19

Figure 19.25.
By default, the AutoFormat's fonts, sizing, shading, and borders will be applied as shown in the sample.

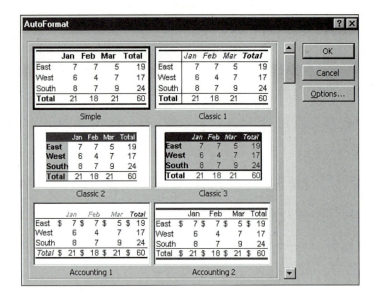

Note

If you find that you're turning off more than one or two of the formats to apply, this can be an indication that AutoFormat isn't appropriate for the currently selected range. Although AutoFormat is a time saver, it may not be the best formatting solution in every situation.

TROUBLESHOOTING

CHANGING THE DEFAULT FONT FOR THE ACTIVE WORKBOOK

How can you change the default font for the active workbook only?

Display the workbook whose default font you want to change. Choose Format, Style to open the Style dialog box, select the Normal style in the Style Name list, and click the Modify button to open the Format Cells dialog box. Click the Font tab, if necessary, and change the font as needed. Choose OK twice.

CREATING PERMANENT STYLES

I want to use styles I've created or modified in other workbooks. How do I do that?

Open the workbook whose styles you want to save permanently. Then open a new workbook and merge the styles to the new workbook. In the new workbook, choose File, Save As. In the Save As Type list, choose Template (*.xlt). In the File Name box, assign the file-name book. Store the file in the XLStart folder.

WHERE DID THE WORKSHEET TITLE GO?

I selected a row and clicked the Merge and Center button to merge the cells and center the title. Now I can't find the title, although it still appears in the Formula bar.

A common error when centering a title across the columns of a worksheet is selecting the entire row that contains the title. If you do this and then click the Merge and Center button, you'll merge all 256 cells of that selected row into one cell, and center the title across those 256 cells. Be sure to select only the cells that span the worksheet or a major portion of it.

PART
V

CH
19

CHAPTER **20**

MODIFYING NUMBERS AND DATES

In this chapter

APPLYING COMMON NUMERIC FORMATS FROM THE TOOLBAR

Numeric formatting changes the appearance of your numbers, converting them to currency, percentages, dates, and so forth. While this formatting may seem purely cosmetic, it also serves an important purpose in defining the nature of your numbers (do the sales figures represent dollar volume or number of units sold?). It also helps ensure that your numbers appear in a digestible format (reducing the number of decimals displayed in a percentage, for example) that doesn't crowd or complicate your worksheet unnecessarily.

The most commonly applied number formats are applied directly from the Formatting toolbar, and each is described in Table 20.1.

TABLE 20.1.   NUMBER FORMATTING TOOLS

Button	Name	Formatting
$	Currency Style	Converts numbers to currency, adding dollar signs to the left of the number, and adding two decimal places to the right. Commas are used as a thousands delimiter.
%	Percent Style	Used for numbers that are the result of a formula that results in a percentage, this tool converts numbers from decimals to percentages, such as from .05 to 50 percent.
,	Comma Style	Use this tool to add commas to your numbers in excess of 999. A comma and two decimal places to the right are added to the number.
+.0 .00	Increase Decimal	Even if your decimals are currently zeros, this tool will add more of them. You can view a number to an unlimited number of decimal places with this tool, clicking once per desired decimal displayed.
.00 +.0	Decrease Decimal	If you've used the Increase Decimal tool and merely want to reverse your action or just want to see fewer numbers to the right of the decimal point, click this button. As you remove decimal places, numbers to the left of the removed numbers round up as required. For example, 5.682 becomes 5.68, then 5.7, and then 6 if the Decrease Decimal button is clicked three times.

These buttons apply the default settings for each of these number formats. It is important to note that no matter what you do to the appearance of the format of your numeric content, the entire number you typed in is being stored and used by Excel. Remember that your formats merely adjust the way the number looks in the worksheet. You can customize the way each format is applied by using the Format Cells dialog box (see the following section).

Note

Scientific format allows you to display a shortened version of a number with many decimal places. This is useful for displaying scientific notation, as might a chemist entering the data on amounts of certain elements found in a sample compound. You can enter the number as it is (such as 2.3987900109299) or type the scientific format in (2.3E+12). You can also apply the Scientific format from the Format Cells dialog box—the category is found on the Number tab.

APPLYING BUILT-IN FORMATS

For many worksheets, Currency and Percentage formats will suffice. However, by using the Comma Style and Increase/Decrease Decimal buttons, a sufficient degree of customization is available through the toolbar should the defaults be inappropriate for a particular worksheet.

Should you need to use any additional number formats or want to adjust your defaults automatically, follow these steps:

1. Select the cells you want to format.

2. Choose Format, Cells or right-click the selection and choose Format Cells from the shortcut menu. The Format Cells dialog box opens.

3. Click the Number tab (see Figure 20.1).

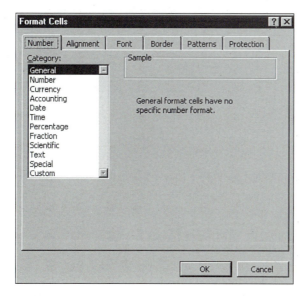

Figure 20.1.
There are 12 number-formatting categories available, most of which have their own set of options.

PART

V

CH

20

4. Select a Category by clicking the category name in the list.

5. For each category except General and Text, a different set of options appears. Figure 20.2 shows the settings for the Number category.

6. Select the appropriate settings for any options you want to customize, and click OK.

Figure 20.2.
Apply the Number format when your numeric data will require decimal places (or zeros after the decimal point) or commas.

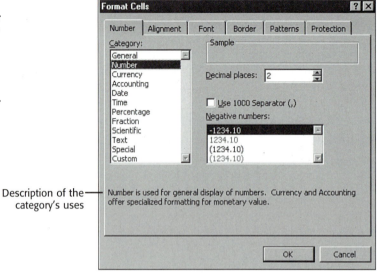

Description of the category's uses

Your settings for the selected category apply only to the selected cells. To quickly apply numeric formats to all the numbers in the entire worksheet, you can select the entire worksheet before using the Format Cells dialog box. Be careful to apply only formats that will affect purely numeric content (no date formats), so that your text entries are not visually changed. If any unwanted results occur in a few cells throughout the worksheet, you can always reformat those cells later.

WORKING WITH CURRENCY

Currency is probably the most common numeric format applied in Excel worksheets. Many of the numbers you'll enter into your worksheets represent money, and you want that to be obvious to the people who view your worksheets.

Applying the Currency format is quick and easy, requiring only that you select the cells to be formatted, and click the Currency button on the Formatting toolbar. If, however, you want to customize the way your currency looks in the worksheet, you'll need to follow these steps:

1. Select the cells you want to format as currency.

2. Choose Format, Cells.

Tip #300

If you've already applied the Currency format to your cells through the toolbar, you can follow these steps to customize the way the Currency category is applied to your previously formatted cells.

3. Click the Number tab.

4. Select Currency from the Category list.

5. Adjust the number of Decimal places as needed. You can type the number into the spin box, or use the triangles to increase or decrease the number.

6. Select a Symbol. If a U.S. dollar ($) symbol isn't appropriate (it's the default), scroll through the list and choose the monetary symbol to match the desired currency.

7. Choose how you want to see your Negative numbers displayed.

Tip #301

If you don't have a color printer, displaying your negative numbers in red (without parentheses) can make it hard to tell negative numbers on a printout. If you prefer red negative numbers and also want to be able to print on a black-and-white printer (without adjusting your print settings), choose the option to also add parentheses to red negative numbers.

---

8. View the Sample, which displays the content from your selected cell or the first cell in your selected range.

9. Click OK to apply your Currency settings and close the dialog box.

Figure 20.3 shows a worksheet with currency applied to the column totals from Jan through Jun. The format has been customized to show no decimals.

Caution

When you choose to reduce the number of displayed decimal places, Excel rounds the displayed numbers up where needed. For example, 7.68 becomes 7.7 with one decimal place, and 8 with none. This can result in the appearance of numbers that don't equal your total where a SUM has been used. Don't worry! Your totals (and all other formulas that use the rounded cell content) are correct—Excel is using the number you entered; it's merely displaying it rounded.

Converting to Euro Dollars

Excel 2000 supports the Euro dollar, the European Union's new currency. Unlike yen or pounds sterling, which are built into Excel, the Euro dollar requires enabling an add-in. Choose Tools, Add-Ins, and select Euro Currency Tools from the list of available add-ins. If you didn't install the add-ins when you installed Office 2000, selecting the add-in from the Add-Ins dialog box will spawn a series of dialog boxes that take you through the process of installing them. Once invoked, this add-in will place a Euro Dollar button on your Formatting toolbar.

PART
V

CH
20

FORMATTING FOR PERCENTAGES

The Percentage format normally is applied to the results of a formula that calculates a percentage. The format can be applied from the toolbar or the Format Cells dialog box, in which you can customize the way the format is applied.

Figure 20.3.
Currency formatting adds the currency symbol you use and lines up amounts in neat columns.

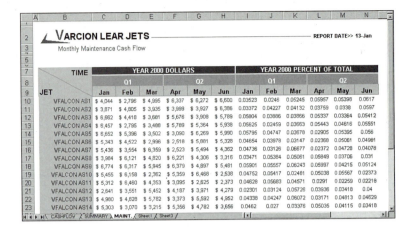

If you need to customize the Percentage format, choose F̲ormat, C̲ells, and in the Number tab, click the Percentage C̲ategory (see Figure 20.4).

Figure 20.4.
The Percentage format works best with numbers expressed as decimals or with numbers that are actually a calculated percentage.

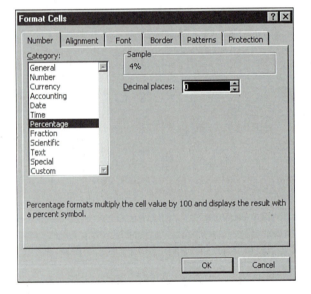

Your only Percentage format option is to adjust the number of decimal places added to the number. The default is two, and for most situations, this is appropriate. Figure 20.5 shows analysis to the right with calculated percentages, formatted in Percent Style.

Caution

If you apply the Percentage format to a number that isn't a calculated percentage, your results can be inappropriate. For example, in a cell containing the typed number 10, the 10 will change to 1000%.

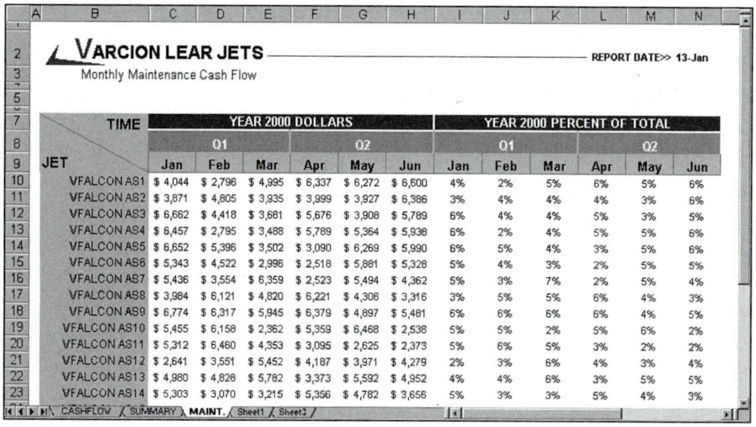

VARCION LEAR JETS — REPORT DATE>> 13-Jan

Monthly Maintenance Cash Flow

JET / TIME	YEAR 2000 DOLLARS						YEAR 2000 PERCENT OF TOTAL					
	Q1			Q2			Q1			Q2		
	Jan	Feb	Mar	Apr	May	Jun	Jan	Feb	Mar	Apr	May	Jun
VFALCON AS1	$ 4,044	$ 2,796	$ 4,995	$ 6,337	$ 6,272	$ 6,600	4%	2%	5%	6%	5%	6%
VFALCON AS2	$ 3,871	$ 4,805	$ 3,935	$ 3,999	$ 3,927	$ 6,386	3%	4%	4%	4%	3%	6%
VFALCON AS3	$ 6,662	$ 4,418	$ 3,681	$ 5,676	$ 3,908	$ 5,789	6%	4%	4%	5%	3%	5%
VFALCON AS4	$ 6,457	$ 2,795	$ 3,488	$ 5,789	$ 5,364	$ 5,938	6%	2%	4%	5%	5%	6%
VFALCON AS5	$ 6,652	$ 5,396	$ 3,502	$ 3,090	$ 6,269	$ 5,990	6%	5%	4%	3%	5%	6%
VFALCON AS6	$ 5,343	$ 4,522	$ 2,996	$ 2,518	$ 5,881	$ 5,328	5%	4%	3%	2%	5%	5%
VFALCON AS7	$ 5,436	$ 3,554	$ 6,359	$ 2,523	$ 5,494	$ 4,362	5%	3%	7%	2%	5%	4%
VFALCON AS8	$ 3,984	$ 6,121	$ 4,820	$ 6,221	$ 4,306	$ 3,316	3%	5%	5%	6%	4%	3%
VFALCON AS9	$ 6,774	$ 6,317	$ 5,945	$ 6,379	$ 4,897	$ 5,481	6%	6%	6%	6%	4%	5%
VFALCON AS10	$ 5,455	$ 6,158	$ 2,362	$ 5,359	$ 6,468	$ 2,538	5%	5%	2%	5%	6%	2%
VFALCON AS11	$ 5,312	$ 6,460	$ 4,353	$ 3,095	$ 2,625	$ 2,373	5%	6%	5%	3%	2%	2%
VFALCON AS12	$ 2,641	$ 3,551	$ 5,452	$ 4,187	$ 3,971	$ 4,279	2%	3%	6%	4%	3%	4%
VFALCON AS13	$ 4,980	$ 4,828	$ 5,782	$ 3,373	$ 5,592	$ 4,952	4%	4%	6%	3%	5%	5%
VFALCON AS14	$ 5,303	$ 3,070	$ 3,215	$ 5,356	$ 4,782	$ 3,656	5%	3%	3%	5%	4%	3%

CASHFLOW / SUMMARY / MAINT. / Sheet1 / Sheet3

Figure 20.5. Percentage calculations that result in long numbers with many decimal places can be quickly converted to manageable numbers with the Percent Style format.

For more information on creating formulas (for calculating percentages and other operations), see Chapter 24, "Constructing Excel Formulas."

FORMATTING THE DATE AND TIME

Dates and times are normally included in worksheets for information, for calculation, or both. By default, Excel converts typed dates as shown in Table 20.2.

TABLE 20.2. DEFAULT DATE FORMATS

Typed Content	Default Result
4/7/66	4/7/66
4/7	7-Apr
April 7, 1966	7-Apr-66

If you want to have your typed dates formatted differently, follow these steps:

1. Select the cells that contain or will contain dates to be formatted.

Tip #302

If the cells that you want to format are scattered throughout your worksheet, use the Ctrl key to select them as a group before applying the format.

2. Choose Format, Cells.
3. Click the Number tab, and select the Date Category.
4. Select one of 15 date formats in the Type list.
5. After viewing the Sample, click OK.

The Time Category settings are very similar, and eight Type options are available. Table 20.3 shows the Excel defaults for times as you type them into your worksheet cells:

TABLE 20.3. DEFAULT TIME FORMATS

Typed Content	Default Format
1:50:15	1:50:15
1:50 am	1:50 AM
1:50 a	1:50 AM
1:50 p	1:50 PM

The Type list contains formats in a 12- and 24-hour clock, with or without seconds, and with or without the date accompanying the time.

Note

If you'll be using your time entries in formulas, it will be easier to use the time in your formula if you apply a 24-hour format.

Tip #303

The 24-hour clock starts at 0:00:01 and ends at 24:59:59. To figure out the 24-hour equivalent of a 12-hour-based time, add 12 if the time is PM. For example, 1:00PM is 13:00 in a 24-hour format. AM times are the same in both 12- and 24-clocks.

WORKING WITH DATES IN 2000 AND BEYOND

A source of concern among many users is how computers will deal with dates in and beyond the year 2000. Excel 97 and Excel 2000 were both designed to effectively deal with this issue, with some further enhancements added to the 2000 edition of Excel.

First, you don't need to worry about entering a date for 2000 or 2001 and having Excel interpret it as a date in the year 1900 or 1901. If you enter 5/28/19, Excel assumes you mean May 28, 2019. Second, you can choose from two date systems, each enabling you to successfully calculate dates after 1999:

- **The 1900 Date System.** The first date is 1/1/1900 (serial value 1) and the last is 12/31/9999 (serial value 2958525).
- **The 1904 Date System.** The first date is 1/2/1904 (serial value 1) and the last date is 12/31/9999 (serial value 2957063). (This choice is available for compatibility with output from Macintosh versions of Excel. The Mac uses the 1904 date system.)

To change your date system (it's 1900 by default), choose Tools, Options, and in the Calculation tab, click the 1904 Date System check box.

Excel 2000 offers an additional tool for making it clear which 00 year you're referring to—1900 or 2000—by giving you the option to display dates as four digits (regardless of their entry as two or four digits). To display your dates as four digits, choose one of the formats that show four-digit years, such as 3/14/1998, 14-Mar-1998, or March 14, 1998.

CREATING CUSTOM FORMATS

If Excel's built-in formats don't match what you're looking for, you can create a custom format. For example, say you want a date to show the weekday, month, date, and year, such as "Saturday, January 16, 1999." Or, say you want to make sure that if a number is less than 1, that Excel omits the zero to the left of the decimal point. In both cases, you create a custom format.

To create a custom format, you type a string of *formatting codes* (also simply called *codes*) that Excel interprets. Here are the details:

1. Select the cell(s) to format.

2. Choose Format, Cells, click the Number tab, and choose the Custom Category.

3. In the Type field, type your custom format. In the list box below the Type field, you can choose a custom format upon which to base yours. For example, you can type **dddd**, **mmmm dd**, **yy** to represent day-of-week, month, day, year, such as Tuesday, January 19, 1999. The rest of this section explains how to develop custom formats.

4. Click the OK button. Excel formats the cell(s) using your custom format, and adds your custom format to the list of available custom formats so you can use it again later.

The difficult part of this task is knowing what codes to type in step 3. The codes can be broken down into two groups: *date and time* codes and *number and text* codes.

WORKING WITH DATE AND TIME FORMATTING CODES

For custom date and time formats, type combinations of codes as Table 20.4 shows. For example, "dddd, mmm d, yyyy" changes 2/2/99 to Tuesday, February 2, 1999.

TABLE 20.4.   DATE AND TIME FORMATTING CODES

Code	Meaning
d	Day, from 1 to 31.
dd	Day, from 01 to 31.
ddd	Three-letter day of week, such as Tue.
dddd	Day of week, such as Tuesday.
m	Month, from 1 to 12; or minute, from 1 to 60.
mm	Month, from 01 to 12; or minute, from 01 to 60.

continues

TABLE 20.4. CONTINUED

Code	Meaning
mmm	Three-letter month, such as Aug.
mmmm	Month, such as August.
yy	Two-digit year, such as 99.
yyyy	Four-digit year, such as 2001.
h	Hour, from 0 to 23.
hh	Hour, from 00 to 23.
s	Second, from 0 to 59. Follow with .0 or .00 to add tenths or hundredths of a second, respectively.
ss	Second, from 00 to 59. Follow with .0 or .00 to add tenths or hundredths of a second, respectively.
AM/PM	AM or PM, as appropriate.
am/pm	am or pm, as appropriate.
A/P	A or P, as appropriate.
a/p	a or p, as appropriate.

Note

If you use one of the AM/PM, am/pm, A/P, or a/p codes, Excel formats time on a 12-hour clock. If you omit these codes, Excel formats time on a 24-hour clock.

Figure 20.6 shows a custom date format that shows a four-digit year followed by a two-digit month.

Figure 20.6.
Type your custom format in the Type box.

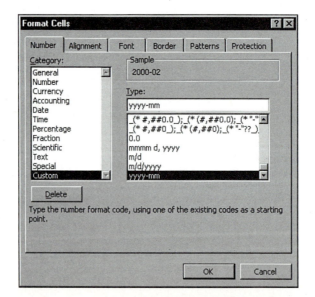

Tip #304

You can add a left and right bracket around any time or date code to make Excel show elapsed time. For example, if cell A1 contains 8/12/2001 10:15 and cell A2 contains 8/13/2001 9:42, and cell A3 contains =A2-A1, formatting cell A3 with [h]:mm:ss shows you how many hours, minutes, and seconds elapsed between the two dates.

Working with Number and Text Formatting Codes

Creating custom number formats can be more challenging, because Excel gives you lots of flexibility. Table 20.5 shows the codes available for formatting numbers and text.

TABLE 20.5.   NUMBER AND TEXT FORMATTING CODES

Code	Meaning
0	Digit placeholder. Use this code to ensure that the correct number of digits appears in a value. For example, if a cell contains .15 and you apply the format 0.000 to it, the cell will read 0.150. If the cell contained .15548, the 0.000 format would make it read 0.1555.
?	Digit placeholder. This is similar to the 0 placeholder, but places spaces instead of zeros on the right of the decimal point. 0.??? applied to a cell containing .21 would yield 0.21.
#	Digit placeholder. This is similar to the 0 placeholder, but does not pad a value with extra zeros. Use this placeholder mostly to show where to place commas. For example, #,### applied to a cell containing 123456789 yields 123,456,789.
.	Decimal point. Used in conjunction with other codes to signify decimal point placement. For example, 0.### applied to a cell that contains .1236 displays 0.124.
%	Percent symbol. This code multiplies the value by 100 and appends the percent symbol. Applying % to a cell containing 13 yields 1300%.
/	Fraction format. Use this code with the ? code to display numbers in fraction form. For example, applying ??/?? to a cell that contains 1.315 yields 96/73. Applying # ??/?? to the same cell yields 1 23/73. The more places you allow in the fraction, the more accurate it is. So ?/? applied to a cell containing .270 yields 2/7, while applying ??/?? yields 11/40.
,	Thousands separator, as well as rounding and scaling agent. When you surround a comma with #s, 0s, or ?s, the comma separates hundreds from thousands, thousands from millions, and so on. So #,### places a comma every third digit. When you place one comma at the end of a format, Excel rounds the number and displays it in thousands. When you place two commas at the end of a format, Excel rounds the number and displays it in millions. For example, #,###,###, displays 123456789 as 123,457 and #,###,###,, displays 123456789 as 123.

PART

V

CH

20

continues

TABLE 20.5.   CONTINUED

Code	Meaning
E+ E- e+ e-	Scientific notation. Use these formats in conjunction with ?, #, and 0 to cause numbers to display in scientific notation. For example, #.## e- ## applied to a cell that contains 545678132 displays 5.46 e 8. Also, E- and e- display - before negative exponents but no sign before positive exponents. E+ and e+ display - before negative exponents and + before positive exponents.
( ) $ - + / space	Literals. Excel places these characters directly into the value.
\	Literal interpreter. Precede any character with the backslash, and Excel places that character directly into the value. For example, \t inserts the character t (but not the backslash) into the format. (To insert several characters in a row, use "text", described below.)
_	Space inserter. This character leaves space equivalent to the width of the next character, to help you align elements. For example, _m leaves a space equal to the width of the m.
"text"	Literal string. For example, "Part No." inserts the text Part No. into the cell.
*	Repeater. Repeats the next character until the column is filled. Use only one asterisk per format.
@	Text placeholder. If a cell contains a text value, this character tells Excel where to show it. For example, if a cell contains the text "check," "Customer paid by "@"." displays Customer paid by check.
[color]	Color. Applies the specified color to the text. For example, [Red]#,###.## applied to a cell that contains 43567.4 displays 43,567.4 in red.

If a cell could contain a positive value, a negative value, zero, and/or text, you can apply a different format for each. Just write multiple formats, separating each with a semicolon. If you write two formats, the first applies to positive and zero values and the second applies to negative values. If you write three formats, the first applies to positive values, the second to negative values, and the third to zero. If you write four formats, they apply to positive, negative, zero, and text values, respectively. For example, you might write this format:

```
#,###; [red]#,###; "No balance"; "Note: "@
```

If the cell contains 2340, it displays 2,340. If the cell contains -4211, it displays 4,211 in red. If the cell contains zero, it displays No balance. If the cell contains the text "Non-negotiable," it displays Note: Non-negotiable. You might find it easier to use conditional formatting, described in the next section, to handle these kinds of situations.

CONDITIONAL FORMATTING

Most formatting is performed by you, selecting a cell or cells, and clicking the appropriate buttons or using a dialog box to execute your commands and customized options. You can, however, let Excel carry out your commands automatically by setting conditional formats.

Conditional formatting requires that you create a set of criteria, much like entering search criteria for a database. Using expressions such as "equal to" or "greater than" (expressed as = or >), you choose formats to apply to cells that contain text or numbers that match your criteria.

This can be a very useful tool, enabling you to apply visual formatting throughout a worksheet or an entire workbook, with one simple set of commands. To apply conditional formatting to your data, follow these steps:

1. Select the range of cells that you want to include in your conditional formatting.

Tip #305

If you want the search for your conditional formatting criteria to encompass the entire worksheet, click the Select All button, located in the corner of the worksheet headings, between the column heading buttons and row heading buttons.

2. Choose Format, Conditional Formatting.

3. In the Conditional Formatting dialog box, choose between Cell Value Is and Formula Is (see Figure 20.7). Cell values can be text or numbers you typed into the cells, or the results of formulas.

Compress Dialog button reduces dialog box to give you access to the worksheet for selecting cells.

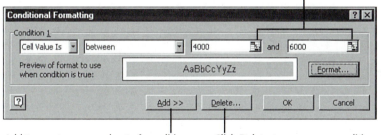

Figure 20.7.
Choose which conditions Excel should look for in your cells, and then which formats to apply.

Click Add to create a second set of conditions.   Click Delete to remove a condition.

4. Select an operator, or expression, such as equal to or greater than. You can choose from eight options.

5. Click the Compress Dialog button to access your worksheet, and click in a cell that contains the value you want Excel to search for and format. The cell address appears in the dialog box (see Figure 20.8).

Tip #306

If you aren't sure where the conditional value is in your worksheet, you can type a value into the box.

Figure 20.8.
When you click in a cell, the cell address appears in the dialog box. The dollar signs indicate that all other cells should be compared to the contents of this one cell.

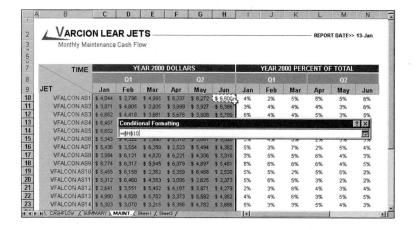

6. Click the Format button to establish the visual formatting for the cells that meet your criteria. The Format Cells dialog box opens, as shown in Figure 20.9, and you can assign a font style, color, or background shading to any cells that meet the defined conditions (click OK to return to the Conditional Formatting dialog box).

Figure 20.9.
When applying font formats, you cannot change fonts, but you can choose a style (such as bold or italic) or color. You also can apply borders or shading to the cells that meet your conditions.

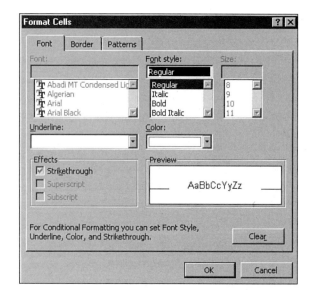

7. If you want to set up second or third sets of conditions, click the Add button.

8. After setting all your conditions and formats, click OK.

After you've set conditional formatting in a worksheet, any cells that you fill with content that matches the conditions you set will be formatted per your conditional formatting instructions. This will continue until you delete the instructions.

Figure 20.10 shows a worksheet formatted with cash flows that fall between $4,000 and $6,000 per month.

Cells containing values that meet the defined condition appear with the formatting you assigned.

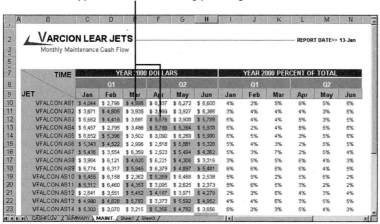

Figure 20.10.
Use conditional formats to call out numbers that meet certain criteria.

To delete the conditions from your worksheet (removing all formatting applied through conditional formatting and ending the continued application of your conditional formats), follow these steps:

1. Select the entire worksheet by clicking the Select All button.

2. Choose Format, Conditional Formatting.

3. Click the Delete button in the Conditional Formatting dialog box.

4. In the Delete Conditional Format dialog box that appears, place a check mark next to any conditions you want to delete (see Figure 20.11).

Figure 20.11.
Choose the conditions you no longer want to apply.

PART

V

CH

20

5. Click OK to return to the Conditional Formatting dialog box.

6. Click OK to remove the formatting applied through the deleted condition and close the dialog box.

Figure 20.12 shows a worksheet formatted with Conditional Formatting to show all the maintenance numbers that fall between $4,000 and $6,000, and those that don't. To help you or your intended audience understand the meaning of the conditional formatting, consider adding a legend to the worksheet. The formatting legend helps those who view the file onscreen or on paper understand how to interpret the formatting on this and any similarly formatted worksheets.

Formatting legend

Figure 20.12.
Be sure to include the formatting key in your print area when you print the worksheet, so others will know how to interpret the information.

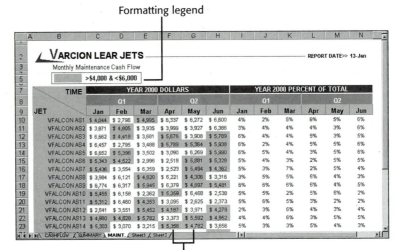

Conditional formatting applied a shaded
background to these cells.

TROUBLESHOOTING

FORMATTING FORMULAS AS TEXT

I applied the text format to a cell that contains a formula. Why did other cells immediately display the #VALUE error?

If you apply the Text format to a cell that contains a formula, Excel recognizes the cell's contents as text—not as a formula. So, if cell A1 contains a formula formatted as text, and cell A2 contains a formula that references cell A1, then cell A2 will display the #VALUE error.

The only way around this is to never apply the text format to cells that contain formulas.

GETTING ELAPSED TIME

I'm trying to get elapsed time in minutes, but Excel says the custom format I've created is in error. I've typed [mm:ss]. What am I doing wrong?

In all elapsed-time formats, you place the square brackets around only the first code. Change this format to [mm]:ss and it will work fine.

CHAPTER **21**

USING EXCEL'S DRAWING TOOLS

In this chapter

INTRODUCING THE DRAWING TOOLBAR

The *Drawing toolbar* is available through Excel, Word, and PowerPoint and offers the same set of tools in each application. The Drawing toolbar tools enable you to add shapes, lines, text boxes, artistic text, and clip art to your Office documents and manipulate them in terms of their size, placement, and colors.

Tip #307

Be aware that while not all of the drawing tools and commands available are covered in this chapter (nor are they all typically used in an Excel worksheet context), they are worth exploring on your own, if only to improve your use of them with Word and PowerPoint. In addition, the PhotoDraw application, shipped with the Professional and Premium editions of Office 2000, gives you even more tools for manipulating graphics, as well as retouching photographs.

Note

This chapter covers the basic uses of drawing objects, AutoShapes, and so on. For more advanced uses of the drawing tools, see Chapter 29, "Formatting Charts," Chapter 30, "Professional Charting Techniques," and Chapter 22, "Professional Formatting Techniques."

The use of drawing objects, shapes, colors, and so on is governed by the capabilities of your equipment. If you plan to create elaborate designs on your worksheets, keep in mind that you'll need a monitor, printer, and/or projection system capable of handling graphics at that level.

You can also use the Insert, Picture command to insert graphic images such as scanned photographs and logos. Several of the Drawing toolbar's tools can be used to affect placement and appearance of these items. This capability can enhance a product listing (with pictures of the products) or a financial report on a particular division (with a photo of the location).

Why add shapes, lines, and clip art to your Excel worksheets? In many worksheets, you can use shapes and lines to draw attention to or explain important cells or to add visual interest. Using clip art can add a message in the form of a picture, the image emphasizing the point made by your worksheet's data. Figure 21.1 shows a worksheet that contains drawn shapes, lines, and clip art.

Caution

It is very likely that if you're creating a worksheet, the thrust of the document is the numbers, not the look of the worksheet. Make sure that your graphic elements don't obscure the information that you're trying to convey.

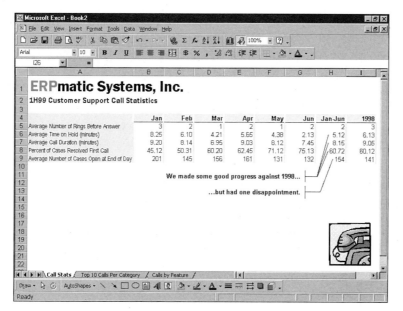

Figure 21.1.
Callouts, lines, and clip art, when used effectively, can make your worksheets more informative and interesting for your readers.

Table 21.1 describes each of the Drawing toolbar's tools.

TABLE 21.1. THE DRAWING TOOLBAR

Button	Name	Button Function
Draw ▾	Draw	Click this button to display a menu of commands that enable you to manipulate the placement of and relationship between your drawn objects.
▷	Select Objects	Use this arrow tool to click on drawn objects. Using this tool tells Excel that you're dealing with your drawn objects and not the worksheet's cell content.
⟳	Free Rotate	Click this tool and then the object you want to rotate, and drag the object's handles in the direction you want to spin the object.
AutoShapes ▾	AutoShapes	Click this button to display a list of AutoShape categories, such as Basic Shapes and Flowchart. From these categories, choose shapes from a palette of drawing tools.
╲	Line	Use this tool to draw straight lines of any length. You can later format the lines to varying lengths and styles, as well as add arrowheads to make the line point to something.
↘	Arrow	If you know your line will be an arrow, draw one using this tool. You can later select arrowheads for one or both ends of the line.

continues

PART
V

CH

21

TABLE 21.1. CONTINUED

Button	Name	Button Function
	Rectangle	This tool enables you to draw simple rectangles and squares.
	Oval	Draw elliptical shapes and true circles with this tool.
	Text Box	When you need a text object that can be placed on top of your cells anywhere on the worksheet, use this tool to create the box and type the text.
	Insert WordArt	Create artistic text headlines and banners with this tool. The WordArt program, with its own toolbars and menus, opens to give you the ability to create text objects with a wide variety of color, shape, and fill options.
	Insert Clip Art	Click this button to view and insert objects from a categorized list of clip art images that were installed with Office 2000. The Office 2000 also contains extra clip art images that you can add from the CD as needed—navigate to your CD-ROM drive to access them.
	Fill Color	Choose from a palette of solid colors to fill your drawn shape.
	Line Color	Click the button to display a palette of colors that you can use to color your line, arrow, or the outline of a shape.
	Font Color	Apply a color to text box text or to text within your worksheet cells.
	Line Style	Choose from various line weights and styles for double and triple lines.
	Dash Style	If you want your line to be dashed, dotted, or a combination thereof, click this button and select a style from the palette.
	Arrow Style	Turn a simple line into an arrow or change the arrowheads on your existing arrow line. Choose from 10 styles.
	Shadow	Choose from 20 shadow settings, each with a different light source and angle. Applying a shadow gives your object depth, and it can be applied to shapes or lines.
	3D	Apply up to 20 3D effects to your shapes. Unlike a shadow, which merely repeats the object in a flat 2D state behind the original, 3D settings add sides and depth to your object, and shade the sides for a true 3D effect.

You can display the Drawing toolbar by right-clicking any existing toolbar and choosing Drawing from the list, or by choosing View, Toolbars, Drawing.

Tip #308

You can turn your Drawing toolbar (or any toolbar, for that matter) into a floating toolbar by dragging it from the edge of the window onto your worksheet area. Click the left edge of the toolbar and drag the entire toolbar out onto the worksheet. After you release your mouse, the toolbar appears with its own title bar, which you can use to move the floating toolbar anywhere you want it onscreen.

When using the Drawing toolbar, keep the following concepts in mind:

- The Drawing toolbar's drawing tools (Line, Arrow, Rectangle, Oval, and all of the AutoShapes) work by clicking them and then drawing the associated shape or line.

- Each time you click and then use a drawing tool, the tool turns off as soon as the object is created. To draw another one, you must reclick the tool.

Tip #309

To avoid having to reclick a drawing tool to draw another shape, double-click the drawing tool (Line, Arrow, Rectangle, Oval), and you can draw an infinite number of objects with that tool. To turn off the tool, click it again.

- Buttons with a down arrow (triangle) display a palette or menu when you click the down arrow (see Figure 21.2).

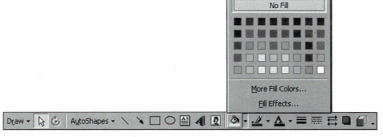

Figure 21.2.
Click the down arrow to the right of the color tools to see a palette of available colors. You also can access tools for more colors and fill effects.

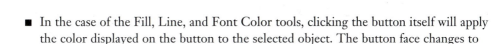

- In the case of the Fill, Line, and Font Color tools, clicking the button itself will apply the color displayed on the button to the selected object. The button face changes to show any new color you select from the palette.

- The Line, Dash, and Arrow style tools display a palette although there is no triangle on/next to the button (see Figure 21.3).

- The Draw and AutoShapes buttons display a menu and submenus/palettes as opposed to performing a task or applying a format (see Figure 21.4).

PART
V

CH
21

Figure 21.3.
Choose a line style from the palette that appears when you click the button. The style will apply to the selected object.

Figure 21.4.
Choose a Draw command to affect the placement of your drawn objects or their relationship to other shapes and lines.

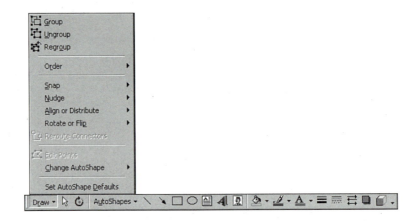

Caution

Drawn objects float over the worksheet content. Be careful to place them so that they don't obscure something important—they're intended to enhance your worksheet, not compete with it.

CREATING DRAWN SHAPES AND LINES

Drawing any shape or line is a simple process—click the tool and then move your mouse onto the worksheet. You'll notice, as shown in Figure 21.5, that your mouse pointer turns into a crosshair.

Crosshair mouse pointer

Figure 21.5.
The crosshair mouse pointer indicates that you're in drawing mode.

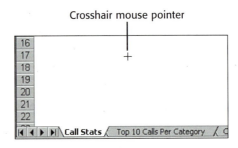

To draw the object, point, click, and drag your mouse diagonally away from your starting point. The farther you drag, the larger the object (or longer the line) becomes. The angle at which you drag will affect the dimensions of drawn shapes, determining their width and height (see Figure 21.6)

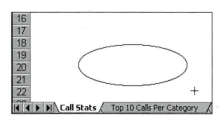

Figure 21.6.
You can see the shape's overall dimensions onscreen as you draw it.

Tip #310

If you want your drawn shape to have equal width and height (to make perfect squares or circles, for example), press the Shift key as you draw the shape.

When using the Shift key as you draw a shape, be sure to release the mouse before you release the Shift key or you'll lose your shape's equal width and height.

As soon as you release the mouse, your shape appears onscreen, with handles on its sides and corners, as shown in Figure 21.7. You can use these handles to resize the shape. Handles will be discussed later in this chapter.

Default white fill

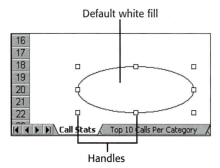

Handles

Figure 21.7.
A selected drawn object will have handles on its perimeter, enabling you to resize the object horizontally, vertically, or both.

As you draw your shapes and lines, Excel names and numbers them, and these names/ numbers appear in the Name Box at the left end of the formula bar (see Figure 21.8). You can rename these objects by selecting and replacing the automatic name with any text you desire.

PART

V

CH

21

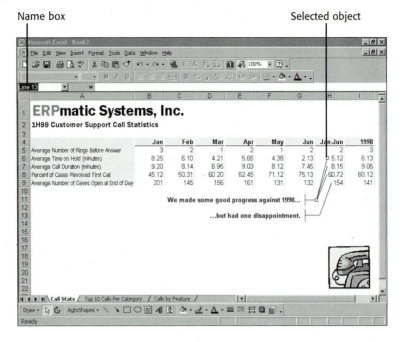

Name box   Selected object

Figure 21.8.
You can rename Line 13 to Average Time on Hold Reduced to make it clear what this line means and where it belongs.

Renaming your shapes and lines makes it easier to differentiate between them. When you choose to rename them, make the name indicative of the purpose and/or placement of the object.

DRAWING RECTANGLES AND OVALS

Rectangles and ovals are the most commonly used shapes and, therefore, are represented by buttons on the main Drawing toolbar. Access other shapes, such as triangles and stars, through AutoShapes.

Because rectangles and ovals are so commonly used, you'll find many uses for them in even the simplest worksheet. Following are some of those uses:

■ Place a rectangle between sections of your worksheet, acting as a visual separator. By using this technique (instead of adding color to the blank cells), you can more easily resize the rectangle to meet the needs of your changing worksheet and the size of its sections.

■ Place a rectangle or oval behind your worksheet content to draw attention to the worksheet content on top. (Remember to use the Shift key while drawing a rectangle to make it a perfect square and while drawing an oval to make it a perfect circle.) Using an oval can be especially effective in this situation, as it doesn't look like you've merely colored in your cells. You'll find out more about how to do this later in this chapter.

Tip #312

The Excel 2000 Drawing toolbar also gives you a quick way to create a circle or square without actually drawing the shape:

1. Click the Rectangle or Oval tool on the Drawing toolbar.

2. Click anywhere on your worksheet. A square or circle (depending on which tool you used) is inserted, with a white solid fill.

3. Continue to click and place shapes as you need them—place as many squares and/or circles as you need on the worksheet.

CREATING LINES AND ARROWS

Use the Drawing toolbar's Line and Arrow tools to add borders, underlines, directions (for flow charts or to visually link two sections of a worksheet, for example), or to connect a text box or clip art image to worksheet content to which it relates. Figure 21.9 shows an arrow pointing from one section of a worksheet to another.

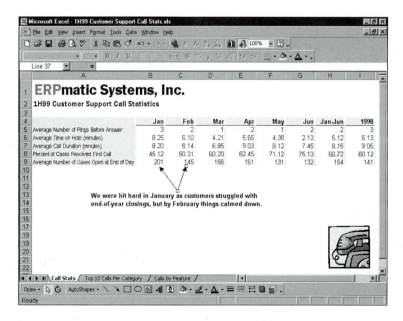

Figure 21.9.
Show direction, flow, or merely a relationship by pointing from one object to another.

You can draw lines at any angle, although pressing the Shift key as you drag and position the line will help you to place it at a 45- or 90-degree angle. After you draw a line, you can move it or resize it. You also can add arrowheads to the line at one or both ends.

Arrows have an arrowhead at the end by default. Also by default, your arrows point in the direction they were drawn. In Figure 21.9, both arrows were drawn from bottom to top, so the top end of the arrow has the arrowhead, pointing up. Although you can change the arrow's direction and arrowhead style later, it's easier to draw it in the proper direction first.

WORKING WITH AUTOSHAPES

Whether you're an artist with pen and paper or using Excel to create your art for your worksheets, you'll find that using the Drawing toolbar's AutoShapes tool will make it easier to draw polygons and other complex shapes than to create them with freehand line drawing tools or connected straight lines. There are seven AutoShapes categories, found by clicking the AutoShapes button on the Drawing toolbar:

- **Lines.** Choose one of six line types, from straight to squiggle, with or without arrowheads, as shown in Figure 21.10.

Figure 21.10.
Lines for every purpose—from straight directional lines to curved or freehand lines—are available.

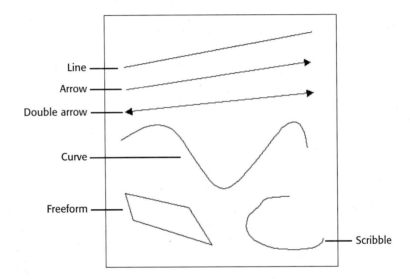

- **Connectors.** Create lines that connect one shape or line to another, with the connections highlighted by small boxes. Choose from nine connector types (see Figure 21.11). Select the connector type you want, click at the place you want the connector to begin, and drag to the place you want it to end. The connector snakes around as needed to connect the objects. You can click and drag the diamond-shaped handles to adjust a connector's shape. When you move an object to which a connector is drawn, the connector remains connected to the object, resizing itself as needed, as Figure 21.12 shows.

- **Basic Shapes.** Choose from 32 shapes, everything from triangles to hearts, from lightning bolts to crescent moons. The last seven of these shapes are a series of brackets and parentheses.

- **Block Arrows.** There are 28 arrows: straight, curved, bidirectional, and some that contain a box with an arrow melded into one shape. These are great for flow charts or any graphical depiction of a process or order of operations.

Selected connector

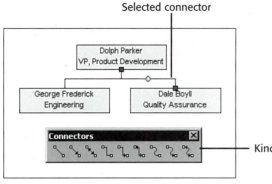

Figure 21.11.
Choose the connection type you need for making separate straight or curved lines meet.

Kinds of connectors available

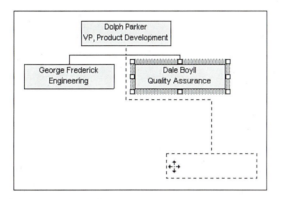

Figure 21.12.
When you move a connected object, the connector adjusts automatically.

■ **Flowchart**. If you're familiar with flowcharts and which shapes to use to indicate which point in a process, you'll find these symbols very useful (see Figure 21.13). You also can use them as simple geometric shapes.

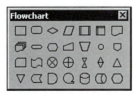

Figure 21.13.
Use these familiar flowchart shapes to describe a procedure.

Tip #313

You can use connectors between shapes in your flowchart. That way, if you need to rearrange the flowchart, the connectors move with the flowchart shapes.

■ **Stars and Banners**. A total of 16 stars, sunbursts, explosions, and banner styles are available (see Figure 21.14).

PART

V

CH

21

Figure 21.14.
These shapes are not for conservative worksheets.

- **Callouts.** A combination of a text box and a line that points from the text box to another item (worksheet content or another drawn object), callouts are effective tools for drawing informative attention to something on your worksheet that needs further explanation. Figure 21.15 uses callouts to highlight important information. Choose from 20 callout styles. The next section, "Creating Callouts," explains callouts in more detail.

Figure 21.15.
Callouts emphasize and explain by combining text with a pointing line.

- **More AutoShapes.** Click this option to open a new window, displaying a list of 55 shapes—line drawings (see Figure 21.16). (This window is essentially the Clip Gallery window. It operates the same way.)

Figure 21.16.
Click a shape and then click the Insert Clip button that appears in the shortcut toolbar.

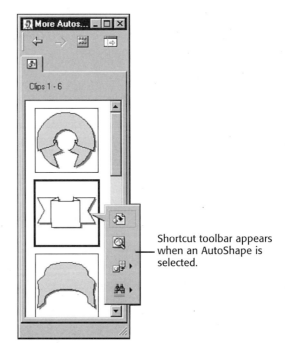

Shortcut toolbar appears when an AutoShape is selected.

After selecting the shape, follow these steps to create your AutoShape:

1. Move your mouse pointer onto the worksheet (note that the pointer has turned into a crosshair).

2. Click and hold the mouse button to establish your starting point for the shape.

Tip #314

If you want your AutoShape's width to match its height, hold down the Shift key as you drag to draw the shape.

3. Drag diagonally away from your starting point, dragging until your shape is the desired height and width.

Tip #315

If you're using the Shift key to achieve an object of equal height and width, be sure to release the mouse button and then the Shift key when you've completed your shape.

After drawing your shape, you can resize and move it as needed. If you need to delete the shape, click once on the shape to select it, and press the Delete key.

CREATING CALLOUTS

A *callout* is a combination of a drawn box and a line that points from the box to another object—part of the worksheet or even another drawn object. The box in the callout is a *text box*, a rectangle with an active cursor. You can type as much or as little text as you need into the text box, and you can move the callout as a unit, or move the box and line independently. Figure 21.17 shows a callout in a worksheet, used to explain data within the worksheet cells.

To create a callout, follow these steps:

1. Display the worksheet onto which you want to place the callout.

2. Click the AutoShapes button, and choose Callouts from the pop-up menu.

3. Choose a callout style by clicking a callout in the palette. When you move your mouse onto the worksheet, it changes to a crosshair.

4. Starting next to the item to which the callout points, drag diagonally until the callout is the appropriate size (see Figure 21.18).

5. As soon as a cursor appears in the text box portion of the callout, type your callout text (see Figure 21.19).

PART

V

CH

21

Line component of callout that points to item

Figure 21.17.
Make your paren-
thetical statements
or explanations with
a callout.

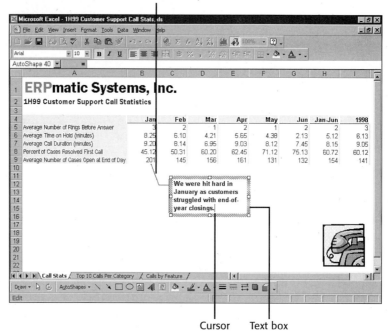

Cursor   Text box

Figure 21.18.
You can move and
resize your callout
after creating it, but
try to get the approxi-
mate size and posi-
tion from the start
through careful
dragging.

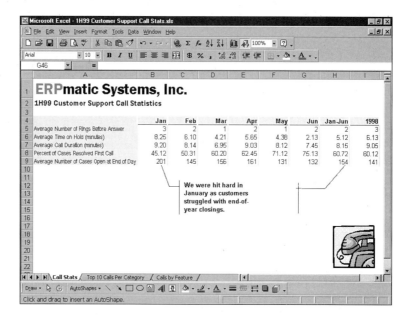

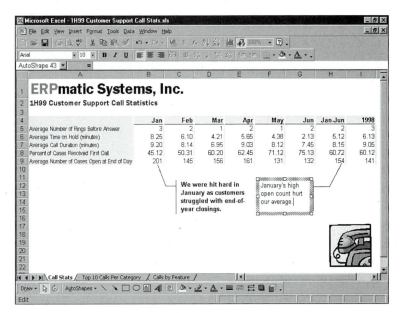

Figure 21.19.
The callout box text you type will follow your worksheet defaults for font and size. The installed default is Arial, 10 points. However, you can format callout text as you like.

When typing callout text, there is no need to watch the right margin within the text box. Type as you would in a table cell—the sides of the box will confine the text, causing it to wrap as you type. You need only press Enter if you want to create a new paragraph or type a list within the callout text box.

USING THE AUTOSHAPES LINE TOOLS

The AutoShapes Lines palette contains three straight-line tools and three curved-line tools. The first three, for drawing simple straight lines, single-headed arrows, and double-headed arrows, are drawn by clicking and dragging the mouse to create a line, as discussed earlier in this chapter. The last three enable you to draw with the mouse, creating s-curves, freeform shapes, and scribbled lines.

You'll use these tools to create lines that wrap around sections of your worksheet or to create shapes that can't be found through the other AutoShapes categories.

Tip #316

Using the Freeform and Scribble tools requires some mouse control, so don't be surprised if your first attempts to use it don't result in the precision you're looking for.

DRAWING CURVES WITH THE AUTOSHAPE LINES TOOL

To create a line with the Curve tool, follow these steps:

1. Click the Curve tool, and move your mouse onto the worksheet.

2. Click to create your starting point, and drag to draw a line.

3. Click again to make the line curve, moving your mouse to adjust the curve of the line (see Figure 21.20).

Figure 21.20.
Your second click creates the curve, and the depth of the curve is determined by the distance you drag your mouse.

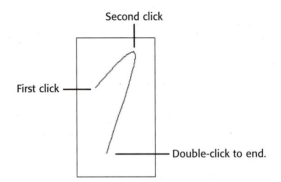

4. For a simple curve, double-click to end the line.

5. To continue creating waves or curves on a continued line, continue to click and move the mouse, creating curves, waves, or loops as required.

6. Double-click to stop the line and turn off the tool.

Note

Simple S-curves or arcs are the most common use of the Curve tool in an Excel environment. Typical worksheets don't require use of wavy or excessively curved lines. For an exception to this rule, see the section "Creating Visual Effects and Professional Pointing Devices" in Chapter 22, "Professional Formatting Techniques."

DRAWING FREEFORM SHAPES

While elaborate or wild shapes don't normally have a place in an Excel worksheet, you may need to create a shape that isn't found within the other AutoShape categories. You can use the Freeform tool in one of two ways:

- Click and drag the mouse, keeping the mouse button depressed as you draw a freeform shape with no straight sides. Come back to your starting point to create a closed shape (see Figure 21.21). By default, closed shapes are given a solid white fill.

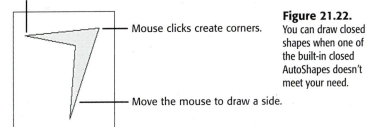

Figure 21.21.
Draw amoeba-like shapes with the Freeform tool.

■ Create a polygon with straight sides by clicking and moving the mouse. Click again to create a corner, and move the mouse again to create a second side. Continue this process until you return to your starting point, creating a closed shape that can be filled with color (see Figure 21.22).

Finish at the beginning to close the shape.

Mouse clicks create corners.

Move the mouse to draw a side.

Figure 21.22.
You can draw closed shapes when one of the built-in closed AutoShapes doesn't meet your need.

Tip #317

By default, all closed shapes will be filled with white. Choose No Fill from the Fill Color button on the Drawing toolbar to keep your drawn shape from obscuring worksheet content.

 If the object you draw prints across two pages, see "Drawn Object Prints Across Two Pages" in the Troubleshooting section at the end of this chapter.

USING THE SCRIBBLE TOOL

The Scribble tool enables you to draw on your worksheet. Using this tool requires great mouse control in order to create legible or recognizable shapes. Unlike the Freeform tool, you need not close the shape—your scribbles can be curved or jagged lines (see Figure 21.23). To use the Scribble tool, click it, click and hold the mouse button on the worksheet, and drag to create your shape.

PART
V

CH

21

Figure 21.23.
Draw on your work-
sheet with the
Scribble tool.

EDITING THE POINTS OF A SCRIBBLE, CURVE, OR FREEFORM SHAPE

It's challenging to draw good freehand shapes with the mouse. Fortunately, Excel includes the Edit Points command. It changes a line or polygon created with the Scribble, Curve, or Freeform Shape to a series of points you can drag to reshape the object. To adjust the shape of a freehand line or freeform polygon:

1. Select the object.
2. Choose Draw, Edit Points. The object's points become visible.
3. Drag the points to adjust the shape.

Figure 21.24 shows a freeform shape with its points visible.

Figure 21.24.
This freeform shape
has four points.

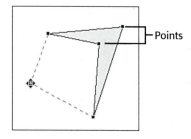

Points

There are four kinds of points:

- **Auto Points** are the simplest kind of point. All you can do with an Auto Point is drag it to a new location. Points in curves are Auto Points by default. You can change any point to an Auto Point by right-clicking it and choosing AutoPoint from the pop-up menu.

- **Straight Points** are never created automatically; you must convert a point to a Straight Point by right-clicking it and choosing Straight Point from the pop-up menu. The line through which a straight point runs is smoothly and equally curved.

- **Smooth Points** are never created automatically; you must convert a point to a Smooth Point by right-clicking it and choosing Smooth Point from the pop-up menu. A smooth point creates gradual transitions along the line that flows through it.

- **Corner Points** create abrupt transitions in lines that flow through them. The Scribble tool always creates Corner Points. You can change any point to a Corner Point by right-clicking it and choosing CornerPoint from the pop-up menu.

All points but Auto Points display *vertex handles* when you select them. Click and drag a vertex handle to adjust the way the line flows through the point. Figure 21.25 shows the same shape as Figure 21.24, except the upper-right point has been converted to a Smooth Point and one of its vertex handles is being adjusted.

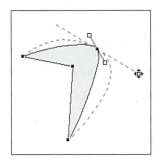

Figure 21.25.
Dragging a point's vertex handle lets you make fine adjustments to a shape.

ORDERING, GROUPING, MOVING, AND RESIZING DRAWN OBJECTS

After you draw lines and shapes on your worksheet, you'll probably want to move them around a bit so they line up just right, adjust their size, and even resolve unintended overlap of objects. Several techniques will help you.

CHANGING THE ORDER OF OVERLAPPING DRAWN OBJECTS

The objects you draw, if overlapping, will stack in the order in which they were drawn— first drawn on the bottom, last drawn on the top. Because you may not draw things in the order you need them to appear in overlapped groupings, you may want to change this order.

To restack your overlapping objects, follow these steps:

1. Click on the object that you want to move up or down in the stack of drawn objects. Figure 21.26 shows an object that is partially obscured by another object.

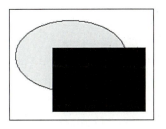

Figure 21.26.
If a buried object belongs on top, change its order in the stack.

2. Choose D<u>r</u>aw, O<u>r</u>der, and select the command that matches your needs—moving the item to the very top or bottom, or moving it up or down one layer in the stack. Your choices are

- Bring to Fron<u>t</u>. Takes the object from wherever it is in the stack and puts it on top of all other objects on the worksheet. This, of course, only affects items on top of which you later place the object.

- Send to Bac<u>k</u>. Places the selected object on the bottom layer of all drawn objects, but it remains above the worksheet content layer.

- Bring <u>F</u>orward. To move items one layer at a time (from fourth in the stack to second, for example), choose this command.

- Send <u>B</u>ackward. Move the selected object down toward the bottom, one layer at a time.

3. The object remains selected in its new stacking order, as Figure 21.27 shows. If moving one layer at a time (Bring <u>F</u>orward or Send <u>B</u>ackward), you can repeat the command until the object is where it belongs.

Figure 21.27.
Selecting the oval
and choosing D<u>r</u>aw,
O<u>r</u>der, Bring <u>F</u>orward
places it on top of the
rectangle.

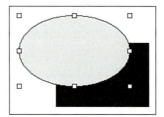

GROUPING DRAWN SHAPES AND LINES

After you've painstakingly aligned two or more objects in relation to one another, you don't want to accidentally move one of the objects out of place, changing its relative position. Or, perhaps you want to move the objects, but you want to move them as a group, so their relative positions remain unchanged. To accomplish this, the objects must be selected and grouped, so that Excel sees them as one unit.

To group two or more drawn shapes and/or lines on your worksheet, follow these steps:

1. Click on the first item in your group (the order in which you click the items is immaterial).

2. Press and hold the Shift key.

3. One at a time (with the Shift key still pressed), click on the other objects you want to include in the group. When the entire group of objects is selected (handles appear around each one of them, as shown in Figure 21.28), choose D<u>r</u>aw, <u>G</u>roup.

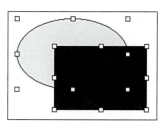

Figure 21.28.
As you build your group, handles appear on or around each selected item.

Once grouped, the entire group of items has one set of handles, as shown in Figure 21.29.

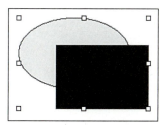

Figure 21.29.
One set of eight handles surrounds the entire group, even if the items in the group are scattered around a large area of the worksheet.

> **Note**
>
> Grouping is not the same as selecting multiple items for quick recoloring or resizing. Grouped objects remain a unit, even after you deselect them. If you click again on any item in the group, the entire group is selected.

You can ungroup your items at any time by selecting the group (click on any one item in the group) and choosing Draw, Ungroup. Use the Regroup command to put any one selected item back in a group with the items with which it was formerly grouped.

MOVING AND RESIZING DRAWN SHAPES AND LINES

Rarely are the shapes and lines you draw perfect from the start—you'll probably need to tweak them a bit, making them bigger, smaller, taller, wider, and/or moving them to a new spot on the worksheet.

Before you make any changes to the shapes and lines you've drawn, you must select them by clicking once on the object. You know an object is selected when you see handles appear on its perimeter, as shown in Figure 21.30.

PART

V

CH

21

Although a circle/oval doesn't technically have corners, it has corner handles.

Figure 21.30.
Handles appear on all four corners and in the middle of each side.

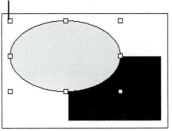

MOVING A SHAPE OR LINE

After you select a shape or line, follow these steps to move it:

1. Point anywhere on the shape or line (not on a handle). The pointer changes into a four-headed arrow (see Figure 21.31).

Figure 21.31.
Watch for the mouse pointer to turn into a four-headed arrow, indicating that you're in move mode.

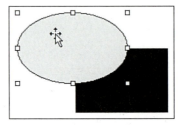

2. Click the mouse and drag the object to a new location. A dashed-bordered "ghost" of the object will follow your mouse movements, as shown in Figure 21.32.

Figure 21.32.
The object remains in its original location until you release the mouse at the desired new location.

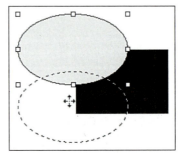

3. When the object is where you want it to be placed, release the mouse button.

RESIZING A SHAPE OR LINE

Making a shape larger or smaller or adjusting the length of a line requires dragging the object's handles. With regard to shapes, the handle you choose to drag from will determine the manner in which the shape is resized (see Figure 21.33).

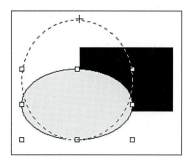

Figure 21.33.
For very specific sizing needs, you may need to drag from more than one handle, adjusting width first, and then height to achieve a shape that's "just right."

- Drag from a top or bottom side handle to make an object taller or shorter.
- Drag from a left or right side handle to make an object wider or narrower.
- Drag from a corner handle to adjust the width and height of your object at the same time.
- Dragging away from the center of an object makes it bigger. Dragging toward the center makes it smaller.

Note

If you want to maintain the object's current width-height proportions (also known as its *aspect ratio*), press and hold the Shift key as you resize. Release the mouse button first, and then release the Shift key when you have achieved the size you want.

Resizing lines and arrows requires dragging one of the two handles that appear when the line/arrow is selected. To make the line longer, drag away from the center of the line. To make the line shorter, drag toward the line's current center. Figure 21.34 shows a line being made longer, increasing its reach.

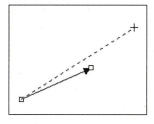

Figure 21.34.
Drag one of your line's handles to a point farther away from its current position, making the line longer.

Note

You can spin an arrow to make it point in another direction. Click and drag the handle on the end that has an arrowhead, and drag clockwise (or counterclockwise) until the arrow points in the desired direction. This is especially helpful when the object to which the arrow points has been moved.

NUDGING DRAWN OBJECTS INTO PLACE

If you're especially precise, you'll appreciate that Excel lets you nudge any object into place, one pixel at a time (or one grid point at a time, if Snap to Grid or Snap to Shape is turned on, as described in the next section). Here's how to nudge objects:

1. Select the object(s) you want to nudge.

2. Choose D̲raw, N̲udge, and then choose the direction you want to nudge the object(s): U̲p, D̲own, L̲eft, or R̲ight.

3. Keep nudging until the objects are where you want them.

Tip #318

If you are going to do a lot of nudging, tear off the D̲raw, N̲udge submenu and let it float on your screen. That way, the nudge controls are always ready.

USING THE GRID AND OTHER OBJECTS TO LINE UP DRAWN OBJECTS

The intersections of the cell boundaries in your worksheet make a *grid* by which Excel can align drawn objects. You can turn on *Snap to Grid*, which lets you move and resize objects so that they always *snap* to the grid. You can also turn on *Snap to Shape*, which lets you move and resize an object so that, if another object is nearby, it snaps to the other object. To turn on Snap to Grid, choose D̲raw, S̲nap, To G̲rid. To turn on Snap to Shape, choose D̲raw, S̲nap, To S̲hape.

FLIPPING AND ROTATING DRAWN OBJECTS

You can flip and rotate drawn objects using the tear-off menu available when you choose D̲raw, Rotate or Flip. Table 21.2 explains the commands.

TABLE 21.2. THE ROTATE OR FLIP COMMANDS

Button	Name	Button Function
	Free Rotate	Click this tool and then the object you want to rotate, and drag the object's handles in the direction you want to spin the object. Figure 21.35 shows an object after this button was clicked.
	Rotate Left	Rotate the selected object 90 degrees counterclockwise.

Button	Name	Button Function
	Rotate Right	Rotate the selected object 90 degrees clockwise.
	Flip Horizontal	Flip the selected object along its horizontal axis.
	Flip Vertical	Flip the selected object along its vertical axis.

Mouse pointer shows you're rotating.

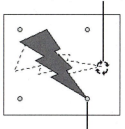

Click and drag a rotate handle.

Figure 21.35.
When you choose to free-rotate an object, click and drag one of the four rotation handles.

FORMATTING DRAWN OBJECTS

After you've created a shape or line, you ean change just about anything about it—its color, size, and relationship to the worksheet in which it resides. In addition, you can protect it from changes and specify how it will be represented on a Web page while the Web page loads.

To access these formatting tools in one dialog box, select the object (a shape or line), and choose Format, AutoShape. The Format AutoShape dialog box opens, as shown in Figure 21.36.

The dialog box is divided into the following five tabs:

■ **Colors and Lines**. Choose the Fill and Line (outline) color for shapes, or just apply a Line format to lines and arrows. The same line and arrow styles you access through the Drawing toolbar are available here.

Note

To let anything that appears behind your shape–cell content or other shapes–show through the shape, click the Semitransparent option in the Format AutoShape dialog box. Found in the Colors and Lines tab, the option makes the object slightly see-through, as Figure 21.37 illustrates.

PART

V

CH

21

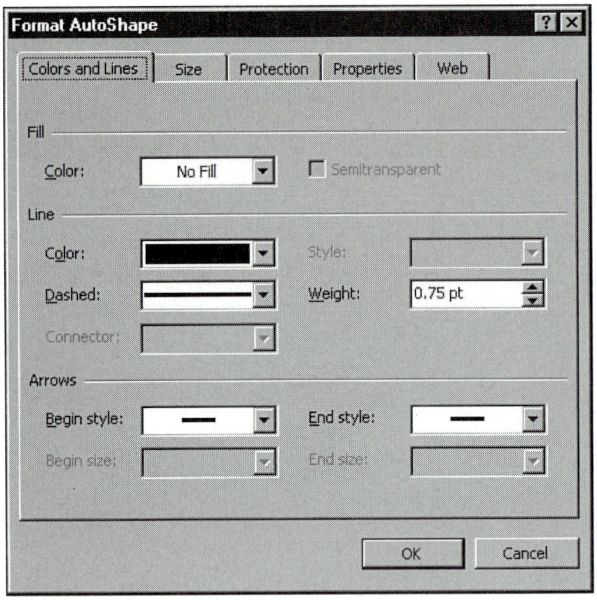

Figure 21.36.
The Format AutoShape dialog box offers one place to find many tools for manipulating your shapes and lines.

Format AutoShape

| Colors and Lines | Size | Protection | Properties | Web |

Fill

Color: [No Fill ▼]   ☐ Semitransparent

Line

Color: [⬛ ▼]   Style: [▼]

Dashed: [▼]   Weight: [0.75 pt ▲▼]

Connector: [▼]

Arrows

Begin style: [— ▼]   End style: [— ▼]

Begin size: [▼]   End size: [▼]

[OK]   [Cancel]

Figure 21.37.
The rectangle shows through the oval because the Semi-transparent option was set for the oval.

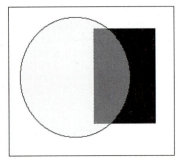

- **Size.** Adjust the Height, Width, and Rotation of your shape or line, as well as its scale (see Figure 21.38). You can increase your object's size by any percentage; numbers lower than 100% reduce it and greater than 100% make it larger.

Tip #319

Click the Lock Aspect Ratio option to ensure that when you increase the Height, the Width adjusts to keep the object's current proportions.

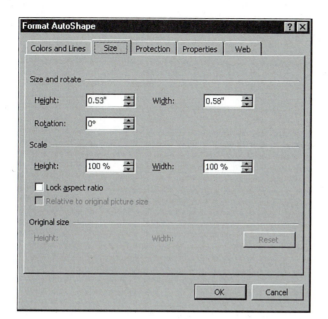

Figure 21.38.
More exact than the mouse, this dialog box can be used to enter precise measurements for your AutoShape.

Note

You also can use the Free Rotate tool to adjust the rotation of your AutoShape with the mouse. Click the shape/line and then the Free Rotate tool. Drag the green handles in a clockwise or counterclockwise direction.

- **Protection**. If your worksheet is protected, you can lock your selected shape, preventing it from being moved, resized, or in any way reformatted (see Figure 21.39). To protect your worksheet, choose Tools, Protect Sheet.

- **Properties**. This tab lets you control how Excel moves and sizes objects as you adjust cells (see Figure 21.40). Click the option that makes sense for your intended or potential worksheet modifications. Also, check or uncheck the Print object check box to control whether the object appears when you print the worksheet.

- **Web**. If you will publish your worksheet as a Web page, type the text that you want to appear in place of the AutoShape on your Web page (see Figure 21.41). This text will appear as the page loads through your browser, or in the event that the AutoShape is missing or the user has images turned off in the browser.

APPLYING SOLID COLORS AND FILL EFFECTS

When you need only apply a fill color to your shape, it may be easier to use the Fill Color tool on the Drawing toolbar. With your shape selected, click the triangle to the right of the Fill Color tool, and choose from a large palette of colors (see Figure 21.42).

PART
V

CH
21

Figure 21.39.
Click the Locked option to protect your selected AutoShape from inadvertent changes or deletion.

Figure 21.40.
Leaving the default option (Move and Size with Cells) turned on will save your moving and resizing your AutoShape when your worksheet is reformatted.

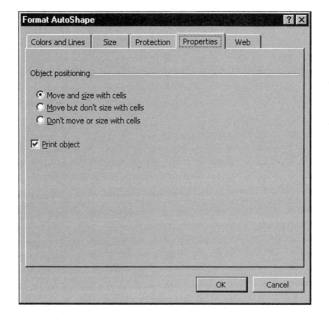

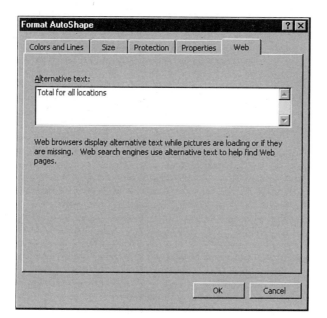

Figure 21.41.
If your worksheet will be part of a Web page, you'll want to add text to represent your AutoShape while the page loads onscreen.

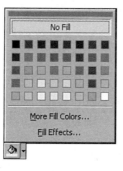

Figure 21.42.
Choose a solid color that will complement other colors you're using in the worksheet.

Not only does this tool give you quick access to a spectrum of solid colors with which to fill your AutoShape, it gives you access to a variety of fill effects, such as the following:

- **Gradient.** Choose Qne or Iwo Colors, or from a series of Preset gradient effects (see Figure 21.43). Apply a Shading Style and choose from four Variants to customize the way the gradient is applied to your shape.

PART

V

CH

21

Figure 21.43.
Apply a gradient when a subtle shading effect is desired.

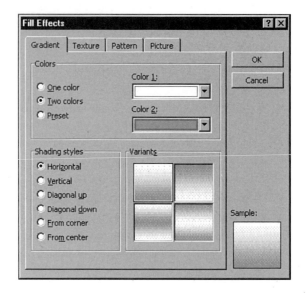

■ **Texture**. Choose from 24 textures, ranging from White Marble to Paper Bag (see Figure 21.44). Select a texture that matches the tone of your worksheet, and that won't overwhelm your worksheet content or other drawn shapes.

Figure 21.44.
Textures are especially effective when your worksheet is viewed onscreen.

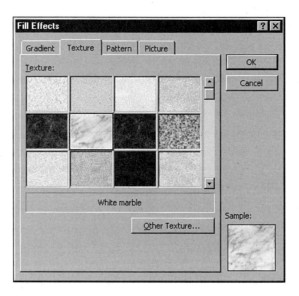

■ **Pattern**. Select one of 42 two-color patterns, and choose a Foreground and Background color for it. View the Sample to be sure that you've chosen complementary colors (see Figure 21.45).

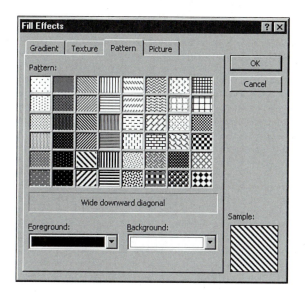

■ **Picture.** Use any photographs or clip art images you have on your computer, by clicking the Select Picture button. Browse to the graphic file you want to work with, and see it used as the fill for your AutoShape.

Caution

Using Picture fills can increase your workbook file size significantly. Avoid using this type of fill effect whenever small file size is important to you in order to accommodate limited hard drive space, or when files will be transmitted via modem or on disk.

APPLYING COLOR TO LINES AND ARROWS

To quickly apply a color to your lines, arrows, or the outline of an AutoShape, click the Line Color button on the Drawing toolbar. The color displayed on the button at that time will be applied to your selected shape or line. If you want to choose from a palette of 40 colors, click the triangle to the right of the Line Color tool (see Figure 21.46).

Tip #310

To choose from an entire color wheel representing hundreds of colors, click the More Line Colors command on the Line Color tool menu.

If you want to apply a patterned line style, click the Patterned Lines command in the Line Color menu. Choose from 42 two-color patterns, and select the Foreground and Background colors for the patterns.

PART

V

CH

21

Figure 21.46.
Choose a color that won't clash with your other lines, colors used to fill worksheet cells, or the fill colors of your AutoShapes.

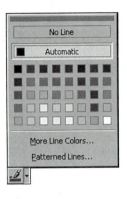

A line pattern is a very subtle effect (if not wasted) when applied to a thin line.

APPLYING LINE AND ARROW STYLES

No matter how your line was created—with the Line, Arrow, Curve, or Scribble tools—you can change its appearance. You also can apply Excel's line-formatting tools to the outline of shapes, using dashes, dots, and/or varying line widths to change the appearance of your AutoShape.

To format your line, select it and use one or more of the following tools:

■ **Line Style**. Choose from lines of varying widths, or make your line double or triple (see Figure 21.47).

Figure 21.47.
Applying a thick line style will make your drawn object stand out.

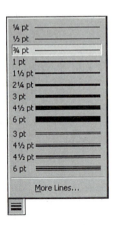

■ **Dash Style**. Make a rectangle look like a coupon, or indicate a tentative relationship between sections of your worksheet with a dashed or dotted line (see Figure 21.48).

Figure 21.48.
Dashes, dots, or a combination thereof can create an interesting border or make a line less obtrusive in your worksheet.

■ **Arrow Style**. Choose from arrowheads, circles, diamonds, or combinations thereof for one or both of your line's endpoints (see Figure 21.49).

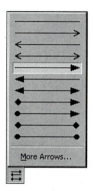

Figure 21.49.
Change a simple line into a pointer by adding an arrowhead.

WORKING WITH SHADOWS AND 3D EFFECTS

Applying a shadow or 3D effect to AutoShapes will make them appear to lift off the worksheet, whether viewed onscreen or on paper. Use them to create the look of depth and weight. Following are the options from which you can choose:

■ **Shadow**. Click this tool and choose from 20 shadow styles for your selected object. The shadow style implies a light source, a direction from which light is shining on your drawn object, as Figure 21.50 shows.

Figure 21.50.
The most subtle visible shadow generally gives the best effect.

■ **Shadow Settings**. Click this option to turn your shadow on or off, nudge the shadow up, down, left, or right, and choose a color for your AutoShape's shadow.

PART
V

CH
21

■ **3D**. This tool redraws your object as a 3D shape, with sides and a gradient fill on the top and sides (to imply a light source). Choose from 20 effects (see Figure 21.51).

Figure 21.51.
Use the 3D effect sparingly on your worksheets–its dynamic results can be overwhelming if applied too often within one sheet.

■ **3-D Settings**. Click this button to view a toolbar that enables you to adjust your 3D settings to meet your specific needs, as shown in Figure 21.52.

Figure 21.52.
Adjust the tilt, depth, angle, and light source for your 3D effect with the 3-D Settings toolbar.

CREATING TEXT BOXES

Text boxes are rectangles with text in them—the text and the box float on top of your worksheet, hopefully placed so as not to obscure worksheet content. Figure 21.53 shows a text box on a worksheet, used to display background information on a section of the worksheet's data.

To create a text box, click the Text Box tool and draw a rectangle the size you'll need for the text you'll be typing inside it. If you aren't sure how much room you need, draw the box and then resize it after you've started typing your text.

Tip #312

> To create a quick text box on a chart, select the chart and just start typing. When you've finished typing the text, press Enter. Excel creates the text in a text box and displays it on the chart. You can resize and format the text box and text as desired.

ENTERING TEXT

As soon as you release the mouse after drawing your text box, a cursor appears in the box. You can begin typing immediately. Be sure to allow the text to wrap naturally, using the sides of the box to control the text flow. Don't press Enter unless you want to create a paragraph or type items in a list.

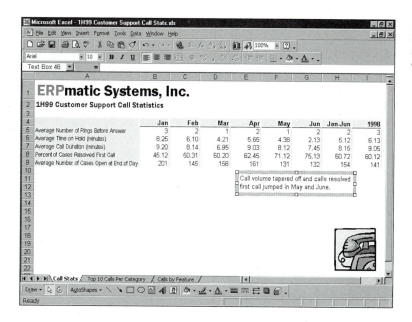

Figure 21.53.
Use your text box to
explain or support
worksheet data.

Tip #313

While typing, you can use the Backspace and Delete keys to edit your text box content, as
well as use the mouse to select text for replacement/deletion.

Note

As you begin to type and your text wraps, you may notice that the text doesn't flow legibly.
If this happens, widen the box by dragging a left- or right-side handle away from the center of the box. Drag in small increments, checking your results between adjustments.

FORMATTING TEXT IN A TEXT BOX

You can format text box text with the Font and Size tools on the Formatting toolbar, or
through the Format AutoShape dialog box. To open this dialog box, select your text box,
and choose Format, Text Box. A series of eight tabs is offered, each one enabling you to
customize the way text looks and relates to the text box itself. Four of the tabs will look
familiar—you've seen them in the Format AutoShape dialog box. The three that pertain to
text box content are described here:

- **Font**. Choose a Font, Font style, Size, and Color for your text (see Figure 21.54). A
  Preview box enables you to see a sample of your formatting before you apply it to the
  text box text.

PART

V

CH

21

Figure 21.54.
Choose a font and size that will be legible in your text box, avoiding elaborate fonts or point sizes that are too small to read.

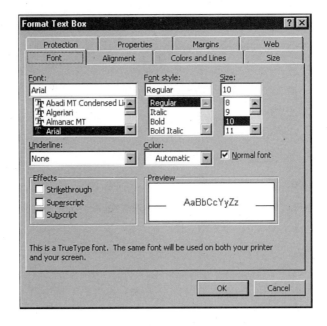

- **Alignment**. Select a <u>H</u>orizontal and/or <u>V</u>ertical alignment for your text (see Figure 21.55). You also can choose an orientation for the text, changing the direction in which the text prints.

Figure 21.55.
If your text box contains a short phrase or single word, center it horizontally and vertically.

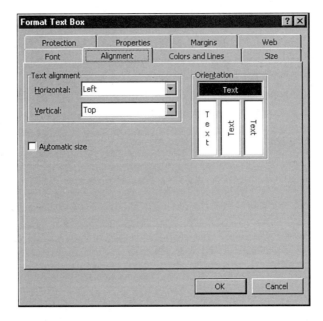

■ **Margins**. If you'd like to create some distance between the outline of your text box and its text content, increase the margins. Click the Margins tab and enter a small measurement in inches (don't type the inch marks), such as .01 for one-tenth of an inch (see Figure 21.56). Enter the measurement into the Left, Right, Top, and/or Bottom boxes, and click OK to apply them.

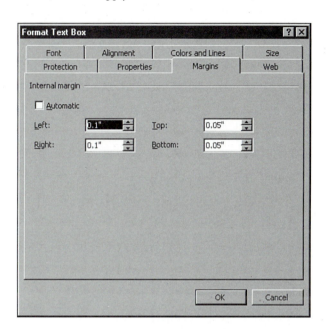

Figure 21.56.
Use very small increments to establish a margin between the text box borders and the text within the box.

Tip #314

To return your text box to its original size (after resizing it), click the Automatic Size option on the Format AutoShape dialog box's Alignment tab.

USING WORDART TO CREATE ARTISTIC TEXT

Use WordArt for creating artistic text for a worksheet title, dynamic label, or simply a text-based graphic, used anywhere in your worksheet. Figure 21.57 shows a WordArt object used as a worksheet title.

PART

V

CH

21

Figure 21.57.
Choose a WordArt style that matches the tone of your worksheet.

WordArt —

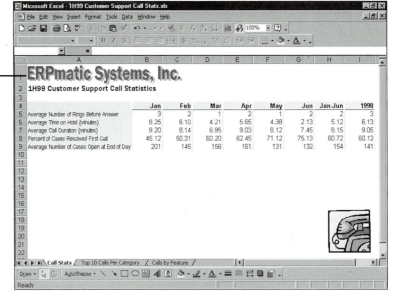

> **Caution**
>
> Although it's a lot of fun to experiment with WordArt's stranger options, remember that you want WordArt—any graphic, for that matter—to enhance your message, not detract from it. Use WordArt conservatively and sparingly in your worksheets.

To create WordArt, follow these steps:

1. Click the WordArt button to display the WordArt Gallery (see Figure 21.58).

Figure 21.58.
Choose a style for your WordArt object, selecting colors, shapes, and an overall look to match your worksheet.

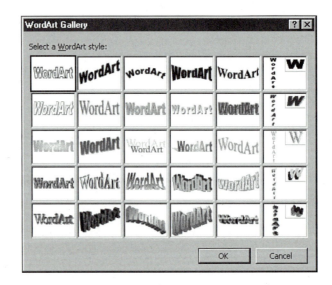

2. Choose a WordArt style by double-clicking one of the samples.

3. Type your text in the Edit WordArt Text dialog box (see Figure 21.59).

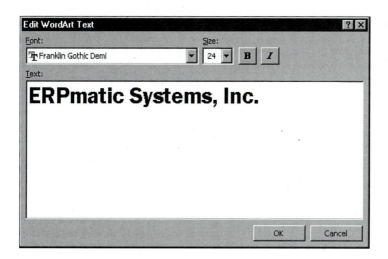

Figure 21.59.
Replace the sample text with your text—single words and short phrases work best as WordArt.

4. Choose a Font, Size, and apply Bold or Italic formatting if desired.

5. Click OK.

Your WordArt object is created and appears onscreen with handles on its perimeter. The WordArt toolbar appears, offering the tools described in Table 21.3:

TABLE 21.3. THE WORDART TOOLBAR

Button	Name	Function
	Insert WordArt	Creates a new WordArt object, starting the process of creating an object all over again. This button doesn't affect the selected WordArt object.
Edit Text...	Edit Text	Use this button to reopen the Edit WordArt Text dialog box. Edit the text within the dialog box and click OK to return to the object with the text edits reflected.
	Word Art Gallery	To choose a different WordArt style, click this button to redisplay the Gallery.
	Format WordArt	Open a four-tabbed dialog box, enabling you to adjust the fill and size of your WordArt.
	WordArt Shape	Each WordArt style applies a shape to the text—arches, curves, and so forth. Click this button to choose a new shape for your text.
	Free Rotate	Use this button to spin your WordArt object clockwise or counterclockwise, changing its degree of rotation onscreen.

PART
V

CH
21

continues

TABLE 21.3.   CONTINUED

Button	Name	Function
	WordArt Same Letter Heights	If your text combines upper- and lowercase characters, make them all the same height with this button.
	WordArt Vertical Text	Change the orientation of your WordArt text to vertical, stacked text.
	WordArt Alignment	Align your WordArt text to the left, right, center, or by the Word or Letter. You also can Stretch Justify the text to spread out across the width of the object area.
	WordArt Character Spacing	Spread your characters out within each word in your WordArt object, or bring them close together. Choose from five spacing options, plus a custom percentage setting.

You can move and resize a WordArt image like any drawn object—point to it and drag it to a new location, or use one of its handles to make it larger or smaller. To remove your WordArt object, click it once, and press Delete. To change the angle of the WordArt text, drag the yellow adjustment handle.

INSERTING CLIP ART IMAGES

 The capacity to add clip art images from the Drawing menu is new to Office 2000. In previous versions of Office, you could insert clip art by selecting Insert, Picture, Clip Art (and you still can use this method in Office 2000), but having an Insert Clip Art button on the Drawing toolbar certainly makes this process faster and easier.

To insert clip art from the toolbar, follow these steps:

1. Click the Insert Clip Art button.
2. From the Insert Clip Art dialog box, select one of the 58 category buttons in the Pictures tab (see Figure 21.60).

Note

If you aren't sure which category to select, type keywords in the Search for Clips box and press Enter. Your keywords will be compared to stored keywords that accompany each clip art image. Images matching your keywords will be displayed.

3. An array of clip art images for the selected category appears. Click the image you want to use. (If you don't like any of the images, press Alt+Home to redisplay the categories.)
4. From the shortcut toolbar, click the Insert Clip button (see Figure 21.61).

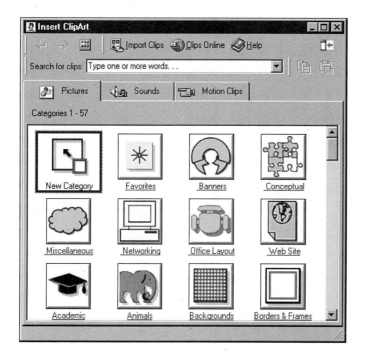

Figure 21.60.
Scroll through the category buttons to find one that seems applicable to your worksheet.

Insert Clip   Preview Clip

Figure 21.61.
You also can preview your image in a full-size preview window by clicking the Preview Clip button.

PART

V

CH

21

| Note | You also can right-click the image you want, and choose Insert from the shortcut menu. |

After it is inserted, you can resize a clip art image by dragging its handles or move it by pointing to the image and dragging it to a new location on the worksheet. To delete a clip art image, click once on the image to select it, and then press Delete.

TROUBLESHOOTING

DRAWN OBJECT PRINTS ACROSS TWO PAGES

I drew a callout on my worksheet. But when I print the sheet, part of the callout is cut off and appears on a second page. Why?

You let the callout extend beyond a page break. It's easy to ignore the dashed lines that indicate the edge of a page's print area. Try moving and/or resizing the callout until it fits.

DRAWN OBJECTS AND EXCEL FILE SIZES

I added clip art to one of my workbooks, but it made the file so large it takes forever to email it to someone over my dialup Internet connection. Is there clip art available that doesn't take up so much disk space?

It is challenging to find "lean" clip art and photographs. The more elaborate an image, the more data it adds to the workbook file, increasing its size. You can use image-editing software to crop photographic images to reduce their size. You can also use image-editing software to convert bitmapped, nonphotographic images to use a smaller number of colors—for example, reducing a 16-bit color image to a 256-color image reaps a tremendous savings in file size. However, some images don't look right when you reduce the number of colors. Finally, the World Wide Web is rich with sites that offer clip art. You may be able to find something out there that will be attractive, effective, and economically sized. (Bear in mind that much clip art available on the Web is copyrighted.)

CHAPTER 22

PROFESSIONAL FORMATTING TECHNIQUES

In this chapter

COMBINING EXCEL'S TOOLS FOR INNOVATIVE FORMATTING

The formatting possibilities are becoming endless with every new edition of Excel. Using the tools properly is the key to separating average formatting from professional-looking formatting. Because Excel is used across business environments of all types, think in terms of how you can apply formats from other industries to your current situation or business.

One of the first things I did to learn professional techniques in presenting information was surround myself with articles, magazines, and periodicals from all walks of life. Because there are so many demonstrations in different literature around us every day, I started to apply techniques I was seeing in newspapers, magazines, and just about any other piece of literature I could get my hands on. This chapter presents some of the possibilities I've discovered; however, don't limit yourself to my examples. Take these examples and build from them or apply them in new ways to fit your environment or business.

COMBINING DRAWING TOOLS WITH CHARTS AND WORKSHEETS

Understanding how and when to use tools, as well as how to combine tools to create dramatic effects, can enhance your charts, worksheets, and tables. The difficulty is that no set rule exists to help you decide which tools to combine, or even how to combine them. This chapter attempts to show you some ideas on how to effectively combine tools to enhance your information. Start by picking up magazines, newspapers, and periodicals to get ideas for presentations, and then visualize which tools it would take to re-create the presentation shown in the literature.

For the most part, there are very few presentations that you can't re-create with all of the tools available in Excel. The drawing tools, particularly, offer a wide variety of opportunities for improving your charts and worksheets—making them more understandable and simultaneously more interesting. Chapter 21, "Using Excel's Drawing Tools," provides details on the types of tools available and how to work with them. The following sections of this chapter take off from those basics, combining drawing objects in unique and sometimes unexpected ways to give your worksheets and charts a polished look.

LAYING A CHART ON A BEVEL

You can lay charts on bevels to give them a "raised-off-the-surface" look. The next time you look through one of the top financial publications, chances are you'll see this technique in use. It works especially well for onscreen presentations, but also can look great in print. Notice that in Figure 22.1 the chart is actually lying on the bevel and the chart area is filled with the same fill as the background of the sheet. The plot area is formatted white.

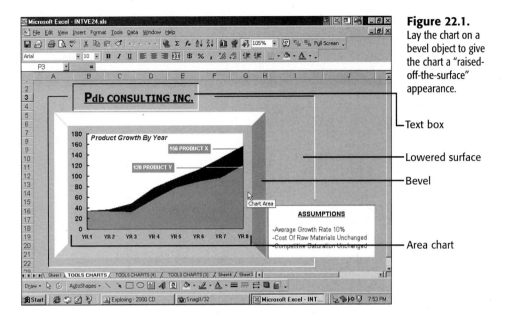

Figure 22.1.
Lay the chart on a bevel object to give the chart a "raised-off-the-surface" appearance.

Text box

Lowered surface

Bevel

Area chart

To lay a chart on a bevel, perform the following steps:

1. On the Drawing toolbar, click the AutoShapes button, select Basic Shapes, and click the Bevel tool (fourth row, second from the right), as shown in Figure 22.2.

2. Drag the bevel object to size it so that its raised portion approximately matches the height and width of the chart (see Figure 22.3).

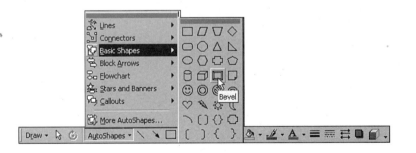

Figure 22.2.
The bevel is found on the AutoShapes button under Basic Shapes.

3. Adjust the degree of the beveling (the raised portion of the bevel object), if desired, by dragging the yellow sizing handle.

4. Drag the chart over the surface of the bevel. (If necessary, right-click the bevel and select Order, Send to Back to bring the chart to the front.)

5. Drag the chart to fit the size of the surface of the top of the bevel, as shown in Figure 22.4.

Figure 22.3.
Size the bevel to an adequate size for the chart.

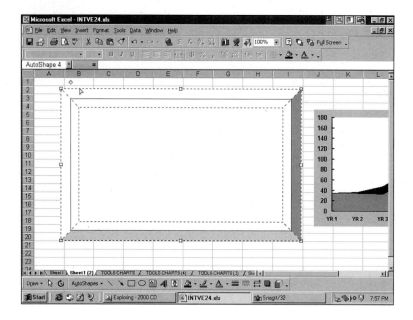

Figure 22.4.
Lay the chart on the bevel and drag the chart size to fit the top surface so that the lines and corners meet.

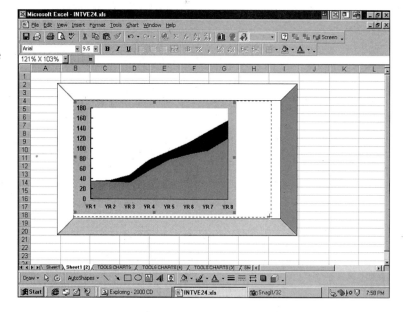

6. Format the chart area as gray.

7. Select and format the plot area as white.

8. Select the entire worksheet by clicking on the Select All button in the upper-left corner of the worksheet frame.

9. Apply a light gray fill.

CREATING A PRESENTATION ON A FILLED BEVEL

You can use Excel's drawing tools to become creative and effective at presenting information other than in chart format. In Figure 22.5, for example, I've filled a bevel object with gray, and used text, rectangles, and lines from the Drawing toolbar. As you can see, visual presentations aren't limited to just charts. In this example, I've created the measuring boxes in conjunction with color or grayscale to show the amount of coverage—white being minimal, gray being average, and black being extended.

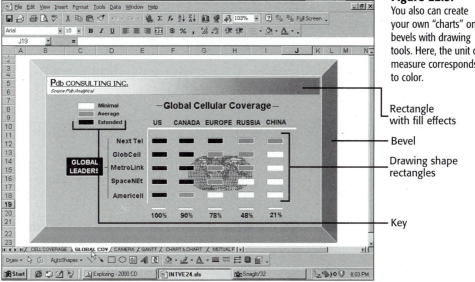

Figure 22.5.
You also can create your own "charts" on bevels with drawing tools. Here, the unit of measure corresponds to color.

Tip #315

> After you lay out all the elements of the drawing, select them all, click the Draw button on the Drawing toolbar, and choose Group to group all the pieces into one "picture" that you can move, copy, or resize as desired.

To further prove how this is just simple drawing tools placed on a larger drawing tool, all the objects in Figure 22.6 have been selected. Here you can clearly see how everything is placed in a chart fashion, without actually being a chart. After you create one box and format it to fit the legend, just copy and paste the legend boxes in the intersecting paths of the "chart"—for example, where CANADA and GlobCell intersect. The globe in the background is just a picture pasted on the bevel.

→ To learn more about inserting pictures with charts, **see** "Adding Pictures and Shapes to Charts," **p. 920**

Figure 22.6.
Notice how the three drawing tools—text box, line, and rectangles—are all that's used to create this "chart" on the bevel.

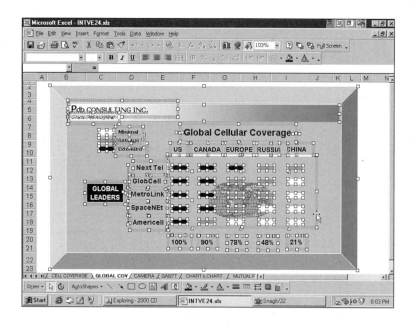

After creating the drawing, make sure that it looks substantial when printed by adding a title, subtitle, and possibly a footer. Often, without a heading of some kind, the presentation can lose impact. In Figure 22.7, the heading has been placed on the left side with a bold Arial font of 26 points, and a CONFIDENTIAL footer on the left side to balance out the printed sheet.

Figure 22.7.
Provide a substantial title to the sheet for an effective presentation that stands out.

Custom heading—

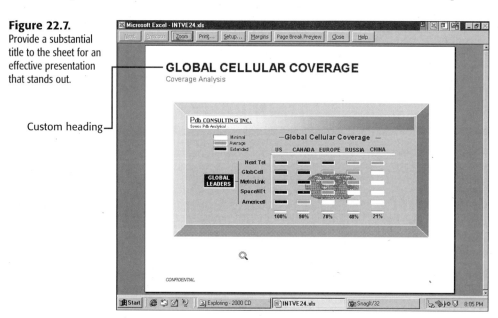

DRAWING TOOL COMBINATIONS

Figure 22.8 shows how you can marry the worksheet, drawing tools (on and off the chart), and text.

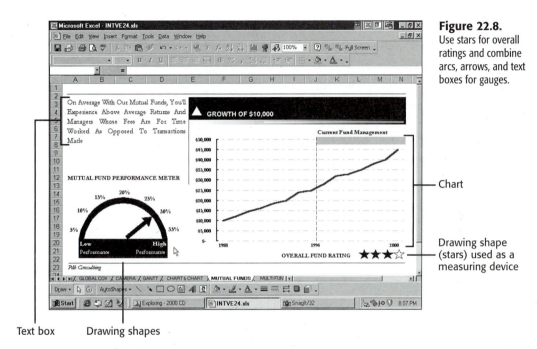

Figure 22.8.
Use stars for overall ratings and combine arcs, arrows, and text boxes for gauges.

Chart

Drawing shape (stars) used as a measuring device

Text box   Drawing shapes

The performance meter consists of four drawing tools placed together to create the meter (see Figure 22.9). The tools are a text box formatted with a black fill and white text, an arrow from the block arrows set on the Drawing toolbar, and a block arc (found on the Basic Shapes submenu from the AutoShapes button). Use the yellow sizing handle to size the thickness of the arc.

By utilizing fills appropriately, you can place stars side by side and use the fill as indication of achievement against overall industry standards (see Figure 22.10). In this example, the fund rating is three out of four stars.

Figure 22.9.
Combine several drawing tools to create measuring pictures and devices. Here, a performance meter gives additional information on the fund's performance over time.

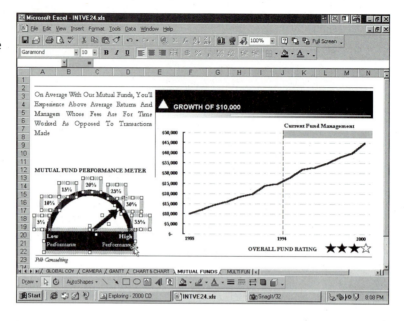

Figure 22.10.
Add drawing tools to the chart to further call out the important aspects of the fund's performance.

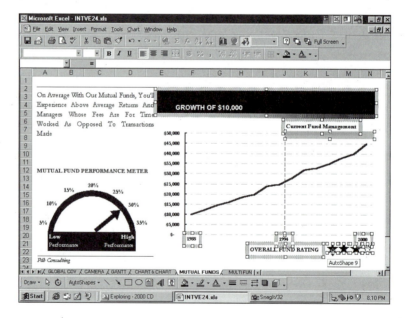

PROFESSIONAL TABLES

Not only can you apply drawing tools to charts to enhance the chart and display additional information, you also can create *multiple-dimension tables* (tables with views that show depth of coverage, or a view that adds a third dimension). These tables can convey massive amounts of information in a small space. If you have multiple bits of information that fall into one category, for example, you could add multiple columns to give the table the appropriate headings, and break out the elements to the lowest level of detail. You also could create a multiple-dimension table that includes all the elements or detail in minimal worksheet space.

The following sections describe how to work with these custom tables.

MULTIPLE-DIMENSION TABLES

A multiple-dimension table uses *inclusion tables* (tables that either include or exclude features on a single line item) to provide another dimension to a list or table. For the example in Figure 22.11, you have cartridge types that are coded and priced at a certain amount. You also want to show the different products across the market that the cartridge works with, as well as the total units sold and sales for the line item. This can be accomplished by using a multiple-dimension table.

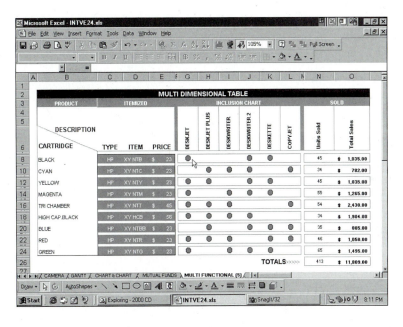

Figure 22.11.
A multiple-dimension table enables you to create lists or tables with the addition of a third dimension—in this case, the inclusion chart. The chart specifies which product works with the different products on the market.

Use the Merge and Center button on the Formatting toolbar to align and center the titles of the different table or list elements, and fill with different colors to separate the title levels (see Figure 22.12).

Figure 22.12.
Merge and center the title across several columns of information.

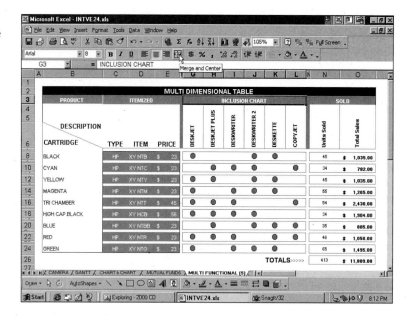

Notice in cell B6 that an "elbow" effect has been created, combining the heading for row 6 (DESCRIPTION) and column B (CARTRIDGE) in a single cell, with a dividing line between the two headings. To create this effect, follow these steps:

1. Select the cell in which you want to create the "elbow" heading.

2. Align the cell text to the left.

3. Type the row heading first. Then hold down the Alt key and press Enter to create blank lines between the row heading and the column heading. Figure 22.13 shows that Alt+Enter was pressed two times to create two blank lines between the headings (look at the Formula bar). Then type the column heading to complete the elbow text.

4. Place the insertion point in front of the row heading and add three or so blank spaces. This moves the row heading to the right, allowing for a diagonal line to fit between the two headings.

5. Adjust the column width and row height as necessary to achieve the effect.

6. Insert the diagonal line, applying a light gray line color (see Figure 22.14).

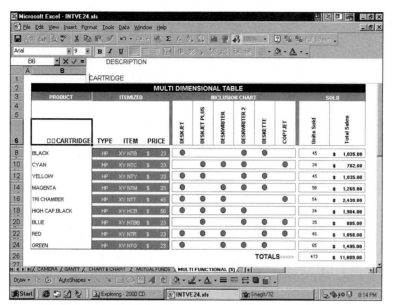

Figure 22.13.
To create the "elbow" effect, type the row heading, press Alt+Enter, and type the column heading.

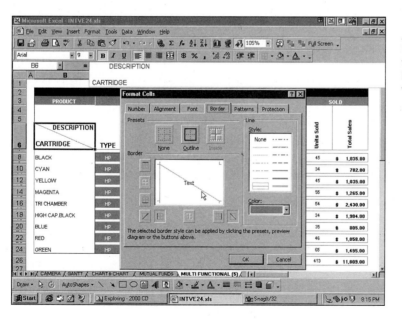

Figure 22.14.
Apply the diagonal line to show separation between the horizontal and vertical headings.

TWO-DIMENSION TABLES

You can add a second dimension to a single cell and give it more than one value or meaning (see Figure 22.15). Notice the use of a legend to call attention to the symbol meanings. By adding the second dimension to the table, you do two things: eliminate countless headings across the columns, and optimize worksheet real estate. You can use this in conjunction with charts or for presentations, optimizing advertising space to show the cost of your current products and how they work with other products in the marketplace.

Figure 22.15.
Add a second dimension to a single cell to give the cell multiple values.

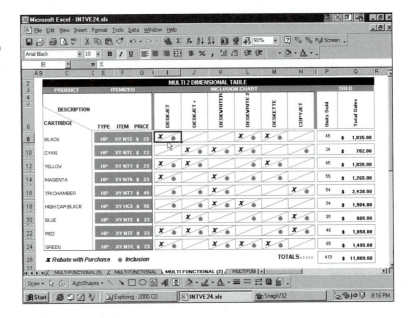

To add the second dimension to the table, simply apply a diagonal line through the cell (see Figure 22.16). You can apply an X in the cell and use a drawing tool such as an ellipse or circle for the second cell value. (You create a circle by holding down the Shift key as you create an ellipse.)

Tip #316

A top vertical alignment should be used to properly position the X in the cell.

After you have the proper alignment in the cell, copy the cell and paste it into the other cells that apply. Excel pastes the value and the drawing object in the same alignment. To establish the proper alignment the first time, it helps to zoom in on the cell with the Zoom feature and position the object in the most logical place, as shown in Figure 22.17.

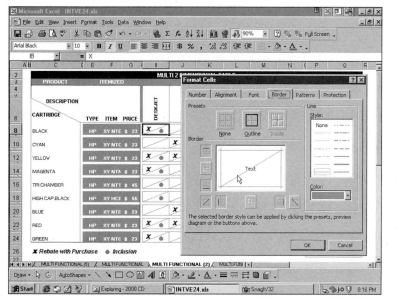

Figure 22.16.
Apply the diagonal line to the cell from the Border tab in the Format Cells dialog box.

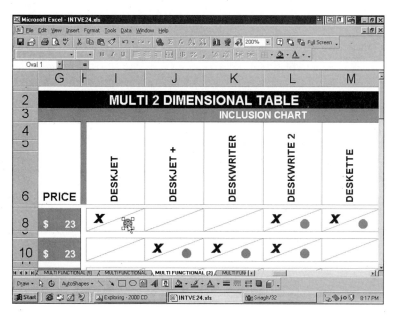

Figure 22.17.
Align the values and objects; then simply copy the cell and paste to a new location. The identical alignments are re-created.

THREE-DIMENSION TABLES

Now that you have the concept from the two-dimension table, take on a three-dimension table. Because it can get crowded and cluttered, however, you might want to consider a new format to the cell. Notice the pyramid approach used in Figure 22.18. This provides a raised 3D effect and separates the multiple dimensions within a single cell.

Caution

Be careful not to get too carried away with using multiple dimensions. I've seen situations using seven and eight drawing shapes, which ultimately loses the audience due to too much cross-referencing.

Figure 22.18.
Create three dimensions in a single cell and apply a pyramid effect to separate the dimensions and raise the cell from the surface.

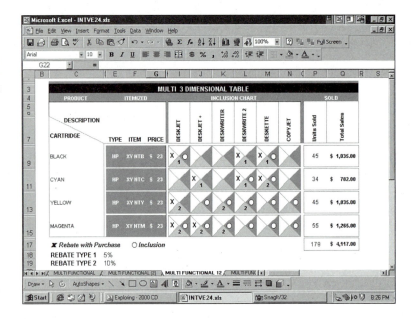

You can create a pyramid effect in several ways. One is to use the bevel tool discussed earlier. Press and hold down the Shift key while drawing the bevel to create a perfect square. Then use the yellow sizing handle and drag it to the center, thus creating the pyramid. Apply the objects to the bevel object's surface to add dimension.

Another way is to use the Isosceles Triangle tool. Follow these steps:

1. Make sure that the cell is rectangular and place an X and borders in the cell. Click the AutoShapes button on the Drawing toolbar, select Basic Shapes, and click the Isosceles Triangle tool (see Figure 22.19).

2. Draw the triangle over the cell so that the edges meet, as shown in Figure 22.20.

3. Format the triangle by selecting Format, AutoShape and give it a fill color of light gray, with no line color (see Figure 22.21).

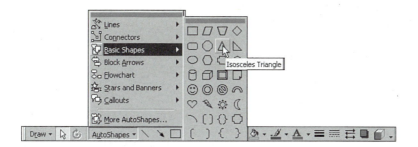

Figure 22.19.
Choose the Isosceles Triangle shape to create the pyramid.

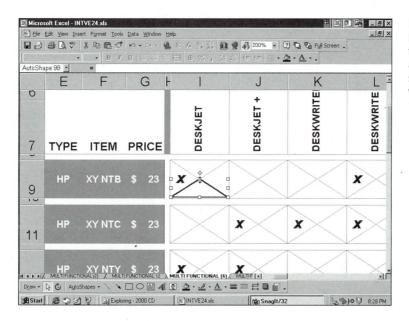

Figure 22.20.
Drag the triangle over the cell so the corners and lines meet. A square bevel also works well.

4. Create a copy of the triangle (pressing Ctrl+D when the triangle is selected is a quick method). Then format the copy with a darker shade of gray, flip it to the left, and place it in the right quadrant of the cell (see Figure 22.22).

Note

To flip an object, select it, click the Draw button on the Drawing toolbar to display the pop-up list, select Rotate or Flip, and then select the direction you want to flip from the submenu.

5. Apply circles, triangles, and numbers to the quadrants, along with the legend to illustrate the third dimension. You may need to use the BRING TO FRONT and SEND TO BACK commands to position everything correctly.

Figure 22.21.
Format the triangle with a light gray fill. You also can remove the border by choosing No Line for the Color option in the Line section of the dialog box.

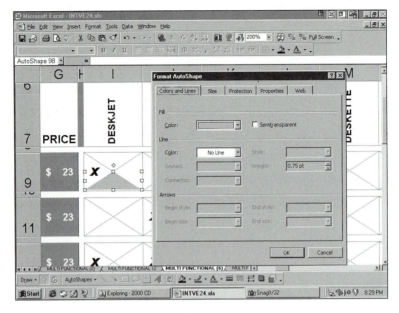

Figure 22.22.
Fill and flip the second triangle and size it to the right quadrant of the cell.

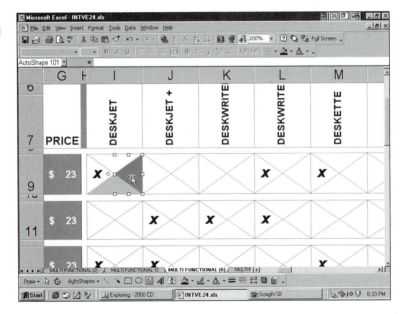

FOUR-DIMENSION TABLES

Add the fourth dimension to "round out" the quadrants. In Figure 22.23, all four quadrants are used to illustrate the products that intersect with the product type, the rebate, the rebate type, and the increase or decrease from previous rebate. Remember that you can apply the objects simply by copying a cell and pasting it into another cell. The units sold are actual numbers in cells, with a circle object copied and pasted in the cell, similar to how the other objects were placed, copied, and pasted.

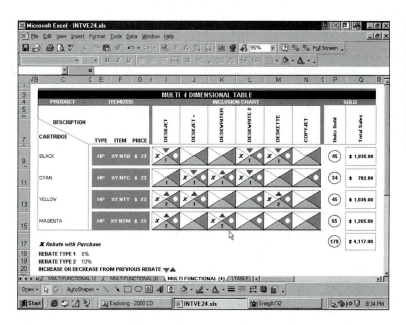

Figure 22.23.
By applying a fourth dimension, you can fully utilize the real estate of the worksheet. This works well for onscreen presentations, when you need to say a lot within a small space.

Caution

To avoid resizing later, all rows and columns that will use the quadrant effect should be sized to match the original, before copying the quadrants into place.

ORDER OF OCCURRENCE TABLES

When selling product in distribution channels, you ultimately will be looking for sales within specified periods of time, as well as lifetime sales. In addition, you probably will want to do comparative analysis among your various products.

Suppose that you have two products in the marketplace for the year and both have sold the same number of units. After further analysis of the products, you see that one product has been in the distribution channel two months longer, thus giving you a different perspective on the sales figure. Being able to create tables in order of occurrence will help give you visual understanding of the performance of your products.

Look at the two examples in Figures 22.24 and 22.25. Figure 22.24 is categorized in a random fashion that provides no real picture of the products' life spans. Figure 22.25 shows how the proper approach to setting up a table can take on a whole new meaning and help you to a better understanding of your products' sales and life spans.

Figure 22.24.
A random table without proper organization gives no real picture of the order of occurrence.

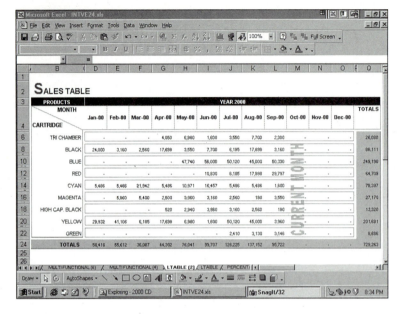

Figure 22.25.
Sales in order of occurrence gives you visual understanding of distribution in the sales channel.

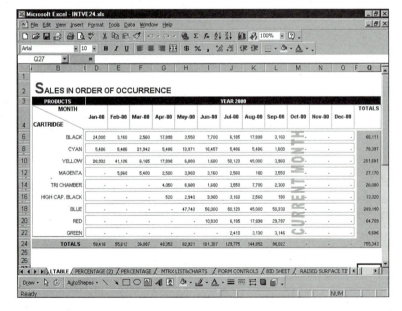

As mentioned before, make sure when setting up to print that you establish a prominent title, and balance the printed sheet with footers, as shown in Figure 22.26.

PERCENTAGE TABLES

Standard grids and tables often can take on a cumbersome, scrunched appearance that's difficult to look at, to say the least. The two tables in Figures 22.27 and 22.28 contain the same information; however, Figure 22.28 is formatted as a percentage table, meaning that the percentage is below the number it represents, and a space is applied between the percentage and the next row of information. To distinguish the percentages, making them easy to find, box the percentage and leave the currency number freestanding above the box. To make the look cleaner and more professional, you can add spaces between the totals at the bottom and the right for separation, and shade the totals.

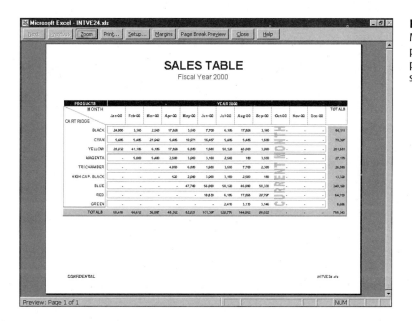

Figure 22.26.
Make sure you add prominent titles to the page and balance the sheet with footers.

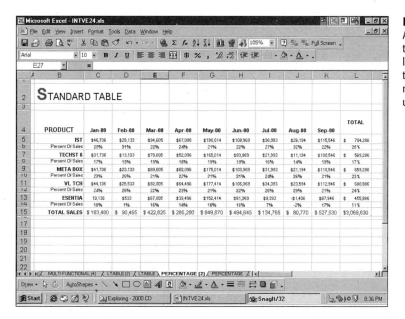

Figure 22.27.
A standard table can take on a scrunched look, making it difficult to view and even more difficult to understand.

Figure 22.28.
A formatted percentage table, with the percentage boxed off below the number it represents, helps the audience draw conclusions and ultimately makes the numbers easier to understand.

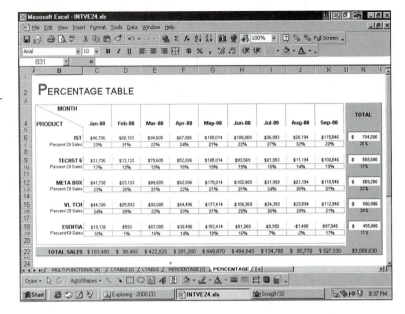

CREATING RAISED TIMELINES

When displaying a sequence of events in which the events continue over time, raised-surface timelines can create an impact and make the timeline instantly discernible (see Figures 22.29 and 22.30). If you're in marketing, for example, and want to create a presentation that displays the marketing sequence of events, a visual timeline can be an effective tool.

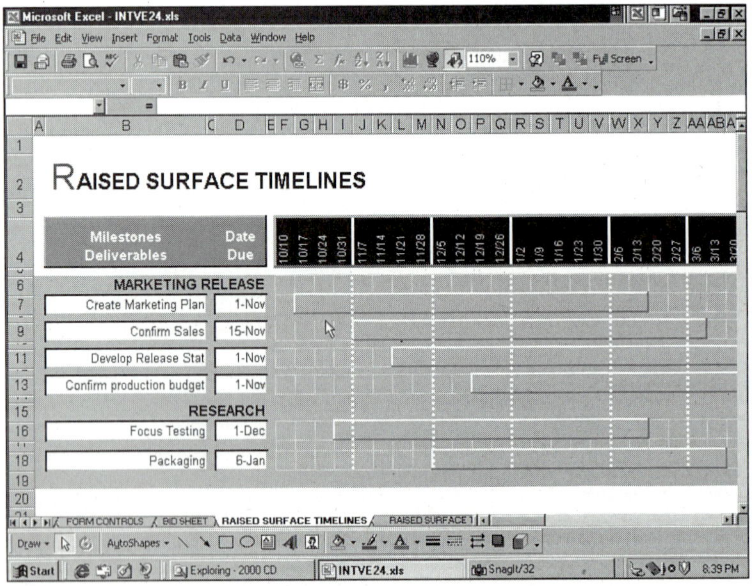

Figure 22.29.
Create raised-surface timelines to show events that occur over time.

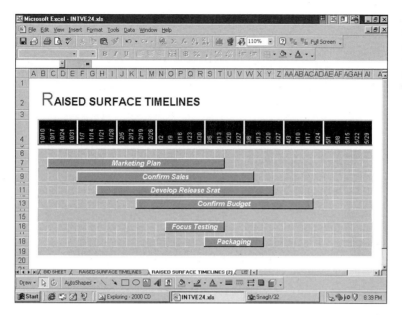

Figure 22.30.
When space is critical, create timelines with the process or name on the timeline.

To create a raised surface, follow these steps:

1. Select a range of cells (see Figure 22.31).

2. Choose Cells from the Format menu or right-click the selection and choose Format Cells from the context menu. The Format Cells dialog box opens.

3. Select the Border tab.

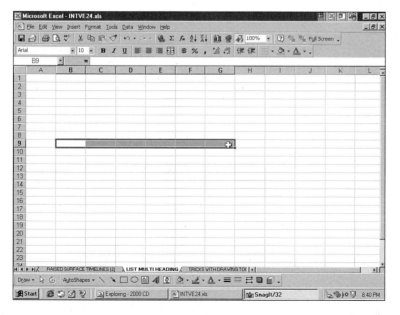

Figure 22.31.
When selecting the range of cells you want to raise from the surface, stay at least one column and row away from the edge of the worksheet, or the raised-surface effect loses impact.

4. Select a semi-bold solid line in the Style box. Make sure the line is a dark color.

5. Place dark lines on the bottom and the right sides of the preview in the Border box (see Figure 22.32).

Figure 22.32.
To create a raised surface, set the bottom and right line styles to dark, and the top and left to light.

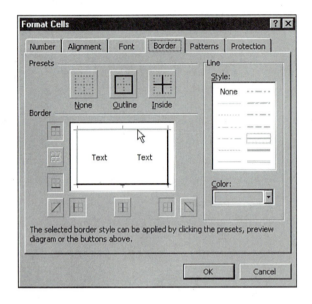

6. Change the color selection in the Color box to a light gray.

7. Place a light gray line on the top and on the left side in the Border box.

8. Select the Patterns tab and choose a fill color. (In most cases, I use gray because it prints better.) The result is shown in Figure 22.33.

Figure 22.33.
The final result of changing the external border styles is this raised effect.

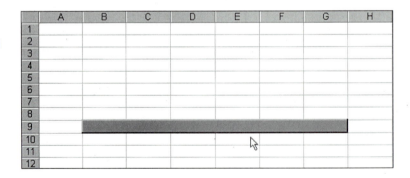

Note

To create a sunken effect, place dark lines on the top and left sides of the region, and light lines on the bottom and right sides of the outer perimeter only.

To apply text to the bar, select the bar, click the Merge and Center button, and then type the text. To move the bar, insert or delete cells to the left or right of the bar.

CAPTURING A DYNAMIC PICTURE FROM ANOTHER WORKSHEET

The *Camera* option in Excel is a unique tool few people know how to use, but I've found that this tool can be priceless. Suppose that you have a worksheet formatted to suit your presentation, and need to include something from another sheet. If you copy and paste, the data from the other sheet would be mixed into the current formatted sheet. The Camera tool can solve this problem by "taking a picture" of the data on the other sheet that you then can place in the target worksheet, without worrying about the data being combined.

In the example in Figure 22.34, notice that the Gantt chart appears to have different formatted columns and headings. That's because it's actually a linked object. It comes from a different sheet and sits on the surface of this sheet, but isn't really part of it. When it's changed on the original sheet, the link causes it to update automatically on the current sheet.

Tip #317

Obviously, you can reproduce this trick with OLE, but using the Camera makes Excel create the linking formula for you and reduces the number of steps involved.

To access the Camera, right-click any toolbar and choose <u>C</u>ustomize to open the Customize dialog box. Click the <u>C</u>ommands tab, if necessary. Under Categories, choose Tools, and then scroll the Comman<u>d</u>s list until you see the Camera option (see Figure 22.35). Drag the Camera button to the desired toolbar and drop it in place.

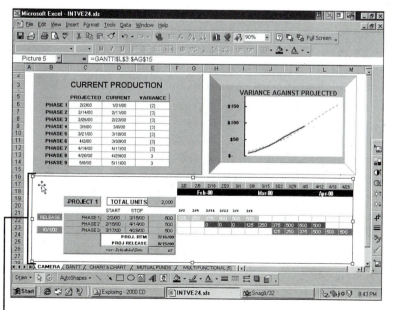

Figure 22.34.
The Camera tool enables you to take pictures of one worksheet and place them on a different sheet. The picture doesn't disturb the target sheet because it's really an object that floats on top of the sheet.

Notice the sizing handles and the mouse pointer. This "chart" is actually a linked object.

Figure 22.35.
Select the Camera icon and drag it to a toolbar.

To use the Camera tool, follow these steps:

1. Select the region you want to "photograph," as shown in Figure 22.36.

Figure 22.36.
Select the region for which you want to take a picture.

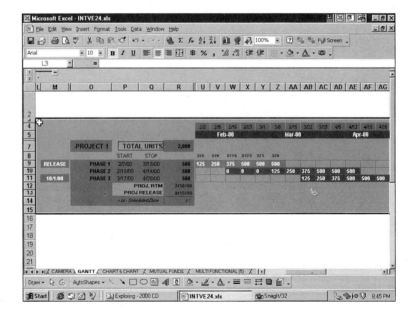

2. Click the Camera button to copy the picture (see Figure 22.37). The mouse pointer changes to display a crosshair.

Figure 22.37.
When you click the Camera button, it copies the selected region.

3. Select the final destination of the picture and place the crosshair where you want the upper-left corner of the picture (see Figure 22.38).

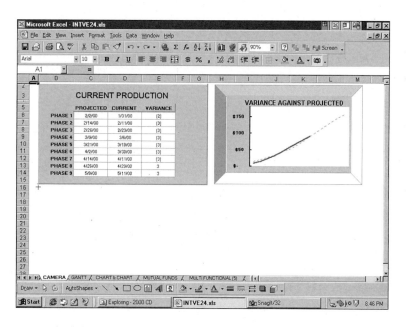

Figure 22.38.
Place the pointer where you want the upper-left corner of the picture.

4. Click to place the picture. Notice that the picture has a formula attached to it in the Formula bar, referencing the source sheet and region of the picture (see Figure 22.39).

Notice the formula for the picture in the Formula bar.

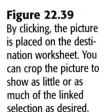

Figure 22.39
By clicking, the picture is placed on the destination worksheet. You can crop the picture to show as little or as much of the linked selection as desired.

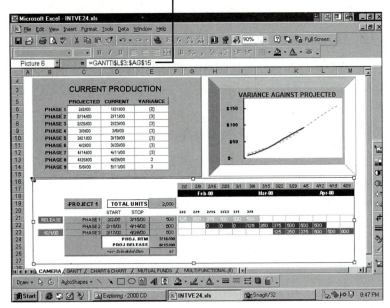

CREATING VISUAL EFFECTS AND PROFESSIONAL POINTING DEVICES

After you create worksheets, tables, presentations, and so on, you are likely to want to draw the reader's attention to an area of significance. What other choices do you have in addition to the (stale) straight arrow? One option is arrows that have more visual interest. If your chart has a breakeven point, for example, you can highlight it with an architectural arrow (see Figure 22.40).

Note

The connector AutoShapes can achieve a similar effect, although not with as dramatic a curve. Connectors aren't required to connect two other shapes; they can be used as stand-alone drawing objects. You also can use the arrows on the Block Arrows submenu of the AutoShapes button, but they're not quite as flexible as arrows you create yourself.

To create curved arrows like this, follow these steps:

1. Click the AutoShapes button, choose Lines, and select the Curve tool from the Lines submenu.

2. Draw the line up and to the right, click once, draw down, click once, and then draw back up and to the right, double-clicking to end the line (see Figure 22.41).

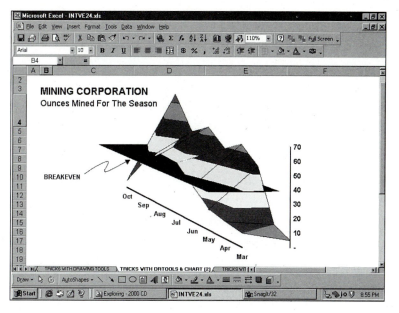

Figure 22.40.
Create arrows with interesting shapes as pointing devices for features of lists, charts, and tables.

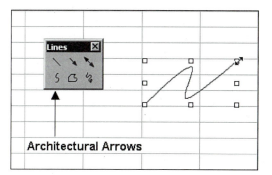

Figure 22.41.
Use the Curve tool to draw the architectural arrow.

Tip #318

Figure 22.41 shows the Lines palette as a floating toolbar. You can "tear off" any submenu or palette to a floating toolbar if the submenu or palette displays a small title bar at the top.

3. Format the curve to add the arrow by selecting the curved line and then choosing AutoShape from the Format menu or right-clicking the line and choosing Format AutoShape from the context menu. The Format AutoShape dialog box opens.

4. Add an arrowhead as shown in Figure 22.43, click OK, and then position and size the arrow as desired. You also can flip and rotate the line to point the arrow in any direction.

Figure 22.42.
Add the arrow to the
end of the curve.

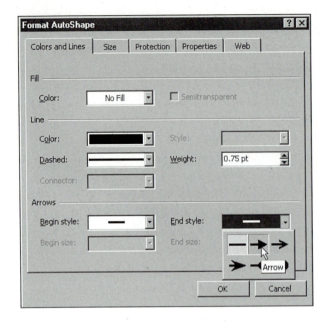

Tip #319

Another method for adding or changing arrow styles is to select the arrow and then click the Arrow Style button on the Drawing toolbar. Note that this method doesn't work for the block arrows.

SLICING THROUGH CHARTS WITH DRAWING TOOLS

Occasionally, you may find it useful to take a graphic to another plane. In Figure 22.43, the breakeven point of the 3D area chart was outlined with a freeform shape and then filled with black. To create effects like these, use the Freeform tool from the Lines submenu of the AutoShapes button on the Drawing toolbar.

Figure 22.44 shows the Freeform drawing tool being used to draw against the 3D chart for the slice effect. Click once to start the line, and again at each corner where you want the line to turn. When you reach the beginning corner, click again to close off the freeform object. Then apply a fill color or other formats to make the freeform object stand out.

Tip #320

Be sure that the lines of the freeform object are parallel to the chart's angles.

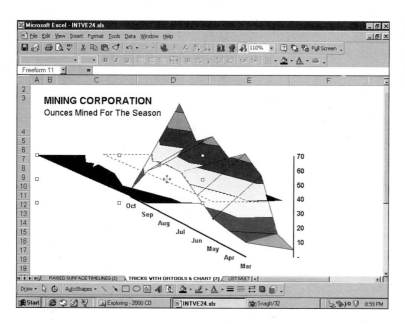

Figure 22.43.
The Freeform tool was used to create the slice through this 3D perspective chart.

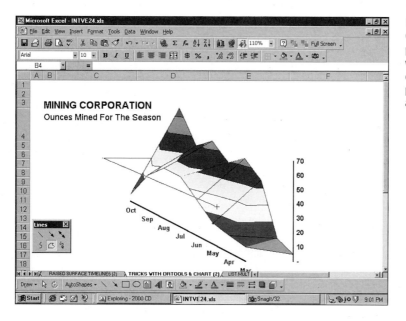

Figure 22.44.
Outline the breakeven points on the 3D chart with the Freeform tool, drawing the slice in perspective to the angle of the chart.

TROUBLESHOOTING

UNGROUPING GROUPED OBJECTS

I've inherited someone else's worksheet and Excel won't let me select a single object in what appears to be a group of objects.

The objects are probably grouped. Select the objects and click the Draw button on the Drawing toolbar. From the pop-up menu, select Ungroup.

CORRECTING THE SHADE OF CAMERA PICTURES

Excel gives the Camera picture a different shade than in the original worksheet.

Use the contrast controls on the Picture toolbar to adjust the shading of the picture.

CORRECTING COLOR PALETTE CHANGES

I have extensive formatting within a workbook, and at times when I open the workbook the colors change. Is there a solution to this problem?

The workbook file may be corrupted. If the workbook is small, you could copy each worksheet and paste it as values into a new workbook. If the workbook contains many sheets, however, that would be pretty complicated. Instead, choose Tools, Options to open the Options dialog box. Click the Color tab, select the color that appears to be wrong on the Standard Colors palette, and click the Modify button to open the Colors dialog box. On the Standard tab, replace the incorrect color in the Colors palette with the correct color, and click OK twice. The colors in the workbook should now reflect the modified color on the palette.

CHAPTER **23**

PRINTING EXCEL WORKSHEETS

In this chapter

PRINTING A WORKSHEET

While many worksheets will be viewed onscreen, the need to create tangible evidence of your spreadsheet content is undeniable. It's important to document your work as a backup, as well as for people with whom you share your work who might be without the use of or access to a computer. Some users find it easier to edit a worksheet on paper than onscreen, making notes and drawing on the worksheet to indicate changes in content, placement, and formatting. Printed worksheets also are handy for carrying to meetings, especially if you need to hand out copies to several people.

Printing your worksheet can be as simple as a click of a button, or it can be more complex, depending on what you want to print and how much control you want to have over the content and appearance of your printout. Excel gives you the tools for either approach, most of which can be accessed from within the Print dialog box.

Note

Charts can be printed with their worksheet content or on separate pages. For details, see the section "Printing Charts" in Chapter 27, "Building Charts with Excel."

 To print a single copy your active worksheet immediately, with standard Print options, click the Print button on the Standard toolbar.

To set Print options such as number of copies or which pages to print, choose File, Print. The Print dialog box opens, as shown in Figure 23.1.

Figure 23.1.
Use the Print dialog box to choose the printer, which pages, and the number of copies you want in your printout.

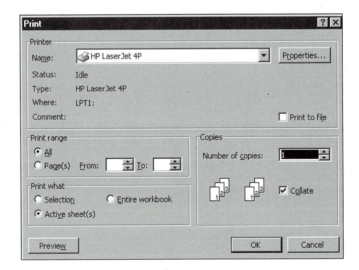

Tip #321

You also can invoke the print dialog box by pressing Ctrl+P.

The Print dialog box both gives and asks for information. It is divided into the following four main sections:

- **Printer**. Set the default or currently selected printer that will generate your print job. You can choose an alternate printer as needed.

  The selected printer's properties—its settings, options, and capabilities—are available through the Properties button found in the Printer section of the Print dialog box.

- **Print Range**. Choose to print all pages of your worksheet or a select few.

- **Print What**. A powerful section of the Print dialog box, this enables you to print the Active Sheet or Sheets (if you've grouped two or more sheets) or print the Entire Workbook. You also can print just a Selection, a single cell or a range of cells from within the active sheet, or a selected chart.

- **Copies**. Choose the Number of Copies of the selected pages, sheets, or workbook you'll need. By default, Collate is turned on, and in the case of printouts consisting of two or more sets of the selected pages, you'll want to leave it on. (Collate prints a document in its entirety before it prints the next copy of a document; if you clear the Collate check box, Excel prints the selected Number of copies of each page, and you'll have to collate the separate pages into complete document sets by hand.)

Tip #322

If you forgot to preview your worksheet before issuing the Print command, you can click the Preview button in the Print dialog box. To find out more about previewing before printing, see the section "Previewing the Print Job." [this chapter]

Detailed coverage of all the options found in the Print dialog box is provided throughout this chapter.

SELECTING A PRINTER

If you're on a network and have physical access through the network to more than one printer, you can choose an alternate printer before you begin your print job. If you're on a standalone computer but have more than one printer, you also can change printers before your printout is created.

To change printers, click the Name drop-down arrow in the Print dialog box to display a list of printers accessed by your computer and choose a different printer from the list, as shown in Figure 23.2.

You can click the Print to File check box in the Printer section of the Print dialog box to create a print job in the form of a computer file—the file then can be run through Windows Explorer, My Computer, or the Run command on the Start menu. By running the file, you will send the print job to the printer selected when the file was created. You needn't have Excel open to run the file.

Figure 23.2.
All your available printers are listed in the Name list.

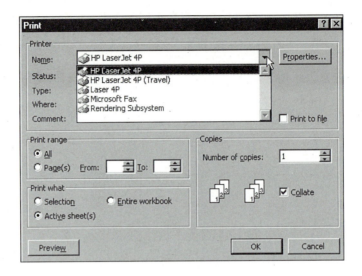

Tip #323

Be sure you've previewed and set up your worksheet to print exactly the way you want it to before you print it to a file, because when you print the file later, you won't have the opportunity to preview it or change print settings.

CHOOSING THE PRINT RANGE

Don't confuse print range with print area, which will be covered later in this chapter. A *print range* refers to the pages within your worksheet that will be printed—the physical pages, determined by page breaks (both naturally occurring and forced by the user) within the worksheet content. The *print area* is a manually defined range of cells that you select and designate as a range to be divided into pages and printed. Setting a print area is done before you use the Print dialog box, and is discussed in greater detail later in this chapter.

Tip #324

To quickly print a specific range of cells, select the range in the worksheet, and then click File, Print. In the Print dialog box, under Print What, click the Selection option, and then click OK.

Your print range choices are All or Page(s), the latter requiring a range (From and To) of page numbers be entered, as shown in Figure 23.3. To print a single page, enter that page number in both the From and To boxes. If you leave the default choice All selected, all the pages in defined print areas in the active worksheet will be printed; if you haven't defined print areas, everything in the active worksheet will be printed, including any empty rows and columns between ranges of data.

After you've set a Print range and any other options you want, send the file to the printer by clicking OK.

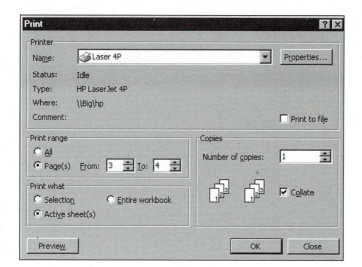

Figure 23.3.
If you don't want every page in your worksheet to print, select a range of pages by entering the From and To page numbers for your printout.

PREVIEWING THE PRINT JOB

What if you don't know how your worksheet has been broken into pages? While there are onscreen indications of page breaks, it can be hard to tell precisely where an integral section of information falls (see Figure 23.4). Excel's Print Preview feature lets you check your worksheet over before committing it to paper.

Other good reasons for previewing before printing are to check page headers and footers (make sure they're up-to-date and correct, and not overlapping the data area), and to make sure all the data is visible. Occasionally, numbers that are visible on your screen will be slightly too wide for the column on a printed page, and will print as ###### (before you waste time and paper, you can widen the column until all the numbers are displayed in Print Preview).

 To see what your printed page will look like, choose File, Print Preview, or click the Print Preview button on the Standard toolbar.

The Print Preview window shows you a small view of your first page, and a set of text buttons, as shown in Figure 23.5.

Use the Print Preview toolbar buttons to view subsequent and previous pages in your worksheet, and to alter the layout and appearance of your printout.

- **Next** and **Previous**. Use these buttons to move from page to page within your Preview.

- **Zoom**. If you need to be able to read your worksheet text, click the Zoom button to see a 100% view of your page. (Clicking the Zoom button is the same as clicking on the page with your mouse, which looks like a small magnifying glass when hovering over a page.)

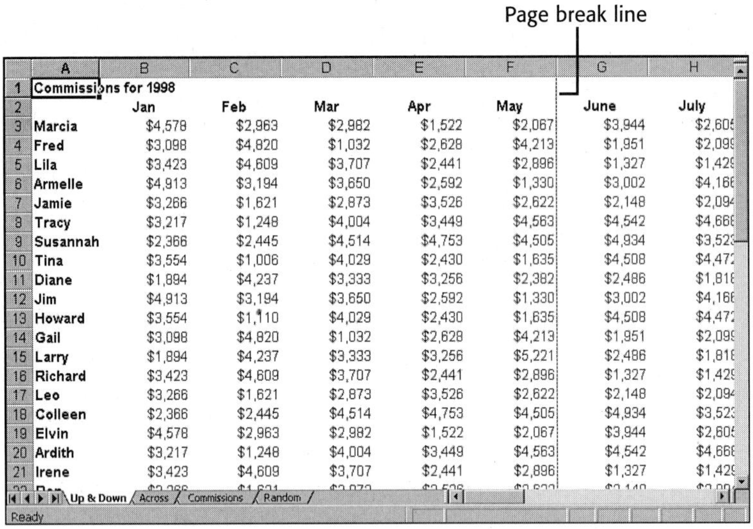

Figure 23.4.
Look for dashed vertical and/or horizontal lines on your worksheet, indicating page breaks.

Page break line

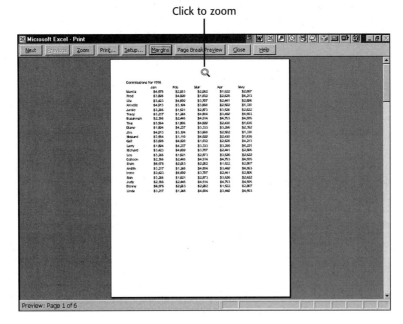

Figure 23.5.
A bird's-eye view of your worksheet through Print Preview makes it easier to see what changes you need to make before printing.

Click to zoom

- **Print**. This button opens the Print dialog box.
- **Setup**. This button opens the Page Setup dialog box (discussed later in this chapter).
- **Margins**. This button displays margin lines and column markers. You can use the mouse to quickly change margin and column widths by dragging the lines and markers.

> **Note**
>
> There are two sets of margins on your worksheet—the inner set are for the worksheet content, and the outer set (at the top and bottom) define the distance of your header and/or footer from the edge of the paper.

- **Page Break Preview**. To see and adjust how your page breaks were applied, click this button. This topic is covered in detail in the next section.
- **Close**. Click this button to return to your worksheet.
- **Help**. Click this button to access Print Preview-related help.

Tip #325

> Always look at a Preview of your worksheet before printing—you'll save paper by not printing things you don't want, and you'll save time by spotting and fixing problems before committing them to paper.

USING PAGE BREAK PREVIEW

As the data in your worksheet accumulates, it can exceed the size of a single page. The space allocated to a single page is determined by the size of your paper and the margins set within that page.

Page Break Preview gives you a big overview of how your worksheet breaks into pages. To enter Page Break Preview, choose View, Page Break Preview. Figure 23.6 shows the Page Break Preview of a four-page worksheet.

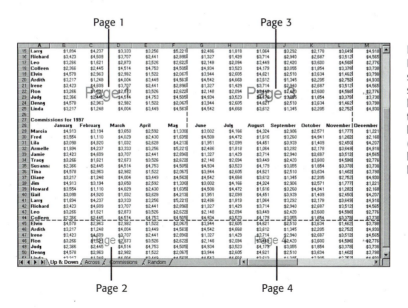

Page 1   Page 3

Page 2   Page 4

Figure 23.6.
Page Break Preview shows that this worksheet is not ready to be printed, because the pages break the lower table in half (the pages should break cleanly between the tables).

Tip #326

You also can see a Page Break Preview by clicking the Page Break Preview button in the standard Print Preview window of your worksheet.

To use Page Break Preview to adjust your page breaks, follow these steps:

1. Choose View, Page Break Preview. Page breaks appear onscreen as blue lines, running horizontally and vertically in the worksheet (see Figure 23.7).

2. Point to the page break that you want to adjust—you can adjust breaks side-to-side or up-and-down.

3. When your mouse pointer turns into a two-headed arrow, click and drag the page break borders to the desired location. Automatic page breaks (those that Excel sets using page margins) are broken blue lines; manual page breaks (those that you set) are solid blue lines.

Nonprinting page numbers   Page break border being adjusted

Figure 23.7.
A nonprinting page number appears on each page of the worksheet. Broken blue lines are automatic page breaks; solid blue lines are manual page breaks.

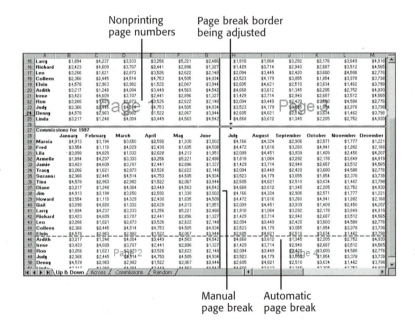

Manual page break   Automatic page break

4. Choose View, Normal to return to your worksheet.

Caution

If you drag any of the page breaks beyond the page margins while using Page Break Preview, Excel accommodates you by shrinking the printed text so that everything you want to print on a single page will be printed on a single page. This is a quick and convenient way to adjust page *scaling*, which is covered later in this chapter.

WORKING WITH PAGE SETUP OPTIONS

After you've created and formatted your worksheet, you'll need to set up the printed pages so they'll resemble what you created onscreen. To set ground rules for the layout, content, and output of your printed pages, click File, Page Setup to open the Page Setup dialog box.

Tip #327

If you're looking at the pages in Print Preview and decide to change the page setup, click the Setup button on the Print Preview toolbar to open the Page Setup dialog box.

In the Page Setup dialog box, you'll find these four tabs:

- **Page**. Adjust the orientation, scaling, paper size, and print quality of your printed output (see Figure 23.8).

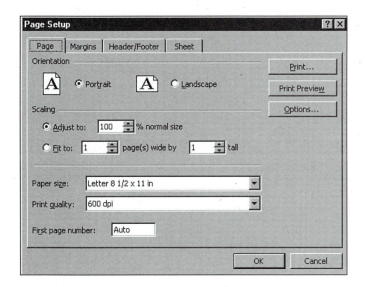

Figure 23.8.
Choose from four areas to control and adjust the appearance of your worksheet, both onscreen and on paper.

- **Margins**. While you can adjust them manually in Print Preview, this tab enables you to enter specific measurements for your margins (if you want margins identical side-to-side, it's easier to set them by measurement than by eye). You also can adjust your header and footer margins, and center the entire worksheet on the page both horizontally and vertically.

- **Header/Footer**. Click this tab to enter text or automatic entries into the header and/or footer of your worksheet printout.

- **Sheet**. This tab's settings enable you to choose a specific Print Area, set Print Titles for multiple-page worksheets, and choose the worksheet features (gridlines, column/row headings) that will be included in your printout.

Tip #328

From within any of the Page Setup dialog box tabs, you can preview the changes you've made by clicking the Print Preview button.

WORKING WITH ORIENTATION

Your worksheet orientation determines how your worksheet content will be applied to the paper. By default, your worksheet orientation is 8.5"×11" and Portrait. If your worksheet, or the portion of it you want to print, is wider than it is long, you can switch to Landscape orientation by clicking the Landscape option under Orientation (shown in Figure 23.8).

A worksheet like the one in Figure 23.9, which contains commissions figures for several salespeople, will be printed most effectively in Landscape, because the worksheet's layout is wider than it is tall. If you were to print that same worksheet in Portrait orientation, any month columns that exceed the 8.5" width (within set margins) would be printed on a second page (see Figure 23.10). Worksheet content that flows unnecessarily to a subsequent page should be avoided whenever possible because readers find it annoying to shift back and forth between two pages.

Figure 23.9.
Keep an "aerial view" of your worksheet in mind when selecting an orientation.

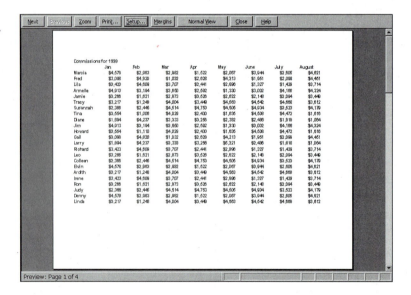

Tip #329

Sometimes, a switch to Landscape orientation doesn't create enough width for your worksheet. Consider using legal-size paper for 14" of printed width, or scaling the worksheet down to fit on a single page.

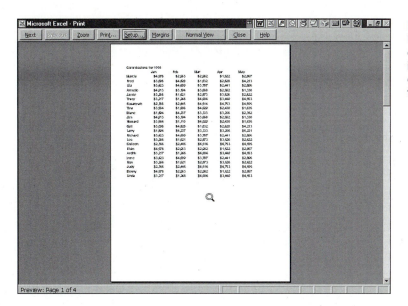

Figure 23.10.
For this data, portrait orientation is ineffective, as several of the columns don't fit on the page.

SCALING THE PRINTOUT

Another method of controlling the printed output of your worksheet is *scaling*. By scaling back, or shrinking, the size of your worksheet content—text, numbers, graphics—more of the worksheet fits on a page, thus reducing the number of pages in the entire printout. Reducing the number of pages, especially if it keeps as much of the worksheet as possible on one page, makes your printout easier to read.

To change the scale of your worksheet pages, follow these steps:

1. Choose File, Page Setup.

2. On the Page tab (shown in Figure 23.8), choose one of the following two scaling options:

   - **Adjust the percentage**. Use the spin box arrows to increase or decrease the percentage of original size or type a percentage. For example, reducing the number to 75% will give you 25% more worksheet on the page.

   - **Fit to a specific number of pages**. Your worksheet's pagination is based on the width and height of the worksheet. Choose how many pages wide and tall your printout will be. This is usually the most practical option—decide how many pages you want, and let Excel figure out the scale.

3. If you're finished setting up the page, click OK to close the Page Setup dialog box, or click Print to open the Print dialog box.

Tip #330	Before adjusting your page scaling, it's a good idea to preview your worksheet with Print Preview so that you can see the current pagination, especially when using the Fit To option. Fit To causes Excel to squeeze the worksheet into the specified number of pages, potentially resulting in print so tiny that you'll want to change the settings immediately.

CHOOSING A PAPER SIZE

The default paper size for your worksheets is letter size, 8.5"×11" Excel gives you eight additional choices, including four envelope sizes, on the Page tab of the Page Setup dialog box. To display the sizes, open the Paper size drop-down list, as shown in Figure 23.11.

Figure 23.11.
Letter and legal size paper are the most common selections for users in the United States.

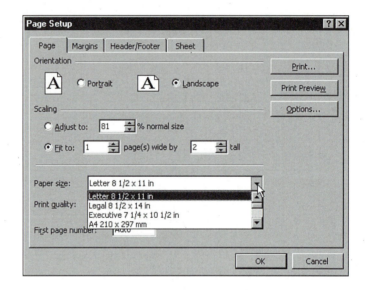

As you probably won't print your worksheets on envelopes, your main paper size options are as follows:

- Letter (8.5"×11")
- Legal (8.5"×14")
- A4 (210×297mm)
- Executive (7.25"×10.5")
- JIS B5 (182×257mm)

Note	A4 paper size is used primarily in Europe, and is slightly longer than Letter size. Be sure that the paper size you choose actually matches your paper so that none of your content is lost (prints off the page) or you fail to take advantage of the full paper size.

Bear in mind that you can adjust all the page setup options—changing orientation, scaling, and paper size—to meet the needs of your worksheet printout.

→ To find out more about changing orientation, **see** "Working with Orientation," **p. 714**

→ To find out more about scaling pages, **see** "Scaling the Printout," **p. 715**

ADJUSTING PRINT QUALITY

Print quality refers to the resolution of your printout and it's yet another option you can control on the Page tab. Click the Print Quality drop-down arrow to display a list of resolutions that reflect the capabilities of the printer or printers to which your computer can send output. If your printer is capable of 600 dpi (dots per inch) output, 600 and 300 (and perhaps 100 and 72, depending on your model printer) dpi output options will be offered in the list box. You cannot choose a dpi setting higher than your printer can handle.

PART

V

CH

23

Note

If you feel that your printer is capable of a higher dpi setting than is offered among your print quality settings, click the Options button in the Page Setup dialog box to view your selected printer's properties. (You can also use the Windows Control Panel to open the Printers window and check the Properties of your printer.) You may have the wrong driver set up for your printer or perhaps the settings for your printer have been changed from the default settings. Consult your printer's documentation before making any changes to the Properties settings.

Tip #331

Using a low dpi setting for draft prints can save printing time and toner or ink, with a result that's nearly as readable as a high dpi printout. When the worksheet is ready for a final print, switch the resolution to a higher resolution so it looks professional.

SETTING WORKSHEET MARGINS

The Margins tab in the Page Setup dialog box has options for setting specific numbers for your top, bottom, left, and right margins (see Figure 23.12). The default margins are 1 inch from the top and bottom, and .75 inch from the left and right.

To enter new margins for your worksheet, follow these steps:

1. Choose File, Page Setup.

2. Click the Margins tab.

3. In the Top margin box, type a new margin setting, or use the spin arrows to increase or decrease the number in .25" increments.

4. Set the Bottom, Left, and Right margins the same way.

5. Click OK to close the dialog box when you're finished, or Print to open the Print dialog box.

Figure 23.12.
While you can adjust your margins quickly from within Print Preview, this dialog box enables you to set more precise margins.

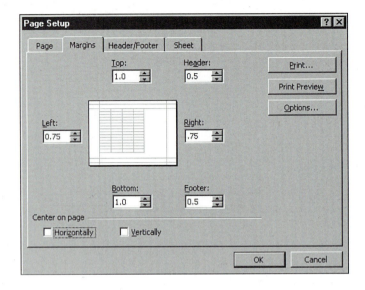

Tip #332

In addition to using the spin box arrows to increase or decrease the margin settings, you can use the up and down arrows on your keyboard to adjust the number in .25" increments.

SETTING HEADER AND FOOTER MARGINS

While in the Margins tab of the Page Setup dialog box, you'll notice that two additional spin boxes are offered. These settings let you control the placement of your header and footer content (if any) in relation to the edge of the paper. By default, these margins are set at .5 inch, just a half inch beyond the default top and bottom margins.

When setting new header and footer margins, keep your sheet margins in mind—if you've reduced your top and bottom margins to allow more worksheet content on the page, you'll have to reduce your header and footer margins, too. You need to reduce them enough so that they don't run into your sheet content, but not so much that they're off the page. Figure 23.13 shows reduced margins for the top, bottom, header, and footer on a worksheet. The header and footer margins are the topmost and bottommost margins on the page (if you point at a margin line and press the mouse button when you see the two-headed arrow, the status bar tells you at which margin you're pointing). The margins for the top and bottom of the data are the innermost margins.

To set header and footer margins, follow these steps:

1. Choose File, Page Setup, and click the Margins tab.
2. Type the Header setting you need, or use the spin box triangles to increment or decrement the measurement.

Header margin

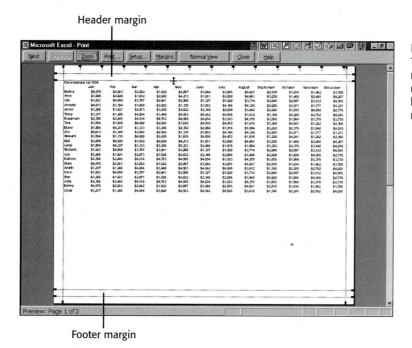

Figure 23.13.
Top and bottom margins of .5 inch require .25-inch header and footer margins.

Footer margin

3. Set the Footer margin the same way.

4. Click OK.

Note

Many worksheets don't require header or footer text—their content is either completely self-explanatory, or their use is informal. In any case, Excel inserts no header or footer content by default. Earlier versions inserted the worksheet name, but user requests resulted in Microsoft's deletion of that automatic insertion. The creation of header and footer content is covered later in this chapter.

→ To learn how to set header and footer text, **see** "Creating Headers and Footers," **p. 720**

CENTERING THE WORKSHEET ON THE PAGE

While technically unrelated to setting margins, the options for centering your worksheet on the page are found on the Margins tab. As shown in Figure 23.12, the Center on Page options are Horizontally or Vertically. You can select both options to place your worksheet in the actual center of the paper.

Caution

If your centering doesn't seem to work, check your margin settings. If your margins are not equal on opposite sides of the worksheet, your content will not appear centered on the page. You also may need to check your printer's settings; some printers have predefined margins on each side of the paper, and these settings may not be equal.

CREATING HEADERS AND FOOTERS

While not required for a worksheet printout, header and/or footer content can be very useful. Your worksheet already has space allocated for header and footer content, and you can use this space for information that will help your readers interpret your worksheet content. Figure 23.14 shows a worksheet with an informative header and footer.

Header

Figure 23.14.
Headers and footers are good places for company names and print dates.

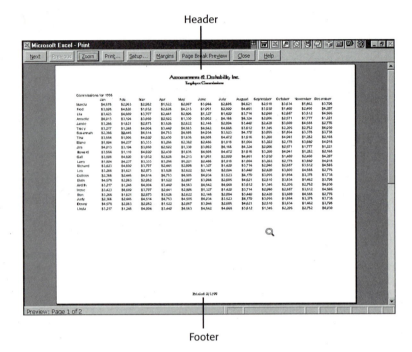

Footer

ENTERING HEADER AND FOOTER CONTENT

Headers are good places for information that identifies the document, such as a company name, department name, or report title. That kind of information can take up valuable screen space and interfere with data lists and tables if you place it on the worksheet; but, in a header, it appears where it's needed (on printed pages) and stays out of your way when you work with the data.

Footers are efficient places for automatic dates, times, and pages numbers. Automatic dates and times always print the date and time when the report was printed, so you know whether it's current, and page numbers tell you whether you've got the entire report. Like headers, footers place the information where it's needed (on the printed page) and out of your worksheet space.

Header and footer content can be totally automated. By clicking preset buttons, you can place the filename, worksheet name, current date, current time, page number, and total number of pages in the header or footer. Automated information is always correct and current, no matter what changes you make in the worksheet, and you can format it to be as elegant or mundane as you want.

To create header and/or footer content, follow these steps:

1. Choose File, Page Setup.
2. Click the Header/Footer tab, as shown in Figure 23.15.

Built-in headers   Header preview

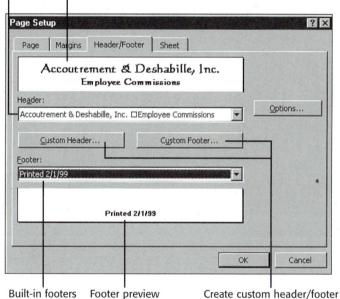

Figure 23.15.
You can choose built-in headers and footers, or create your own.

Built-in footers   Footer preview   Create custom header/footer

3. Choose from several built-in headers and footers in the Header and Footer drop-down lists, or follow steps 4-7 to create custom, formatted headers and footers.
4. Click the Custom Header button to open the Header dialog box, as shown in Figure 23.16.

Tip #333

The ampersand is a field code character, and won't appear in your header/footer text. To include an ampersand (like the one in Figure 23.16), type two ampersands.

---

5. Each of the three boxes represents a section of the header. Type your text and use the field buttons to create custom header content.
6. Click OK.
7. Back in the Page Setup dialog box, click the Custom Footer button, and repeat steps 5 and 6 if you want to create a custom footer.
8. Click OK to close the Page Setup dialog box.

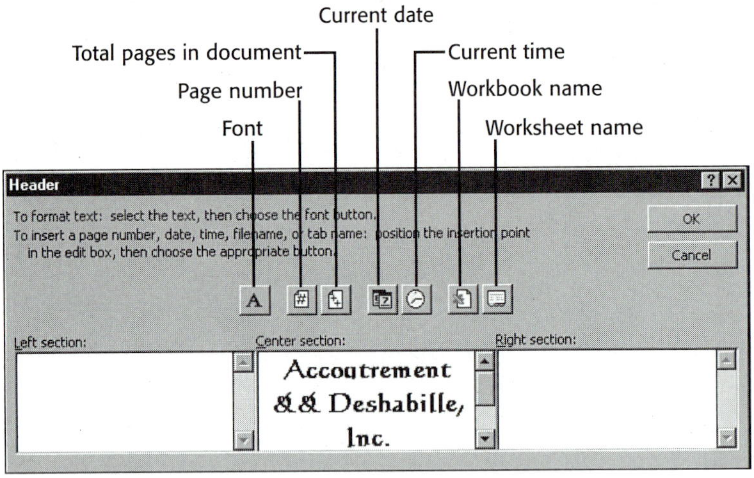

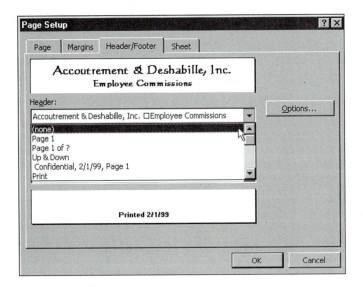

Figure 23.16.
Type your header text and/or click the field buttons to insert automatic content such as page numbers or the date.

Your header and/or footer will appear whenever you print that worksheet, but only for that worksheet. If your header or footer is tall, you'll need to reset page margins so it doesn't overlap the worksheet area. If you want to delete the header or footer completely, click (none) in the Header or Footer drop-down list (see Figure 23.17).

Figure 23.17.
To delete your header and/or footer completely, choose (none) from the built-in Header and Footer lists.

INSERTING HEADER AND FOOTER FIELDS

Some of the automatic information that you may want to add to your header and footer is available through buttons in the Custom Header and Footer dialog boxes (shown in Figure 19.16). The following table describes each button.

TABLE 23.1.   HEADER AND FOOTER FIELD BUTTONS

Button	Name	Code	Function
A	Font		Opens a Font dialog box, from which you can format selected characters in the header or footer.
	Page Number	&[Page]	Inserts the correct page number on each page of your printout.
	Total Pages	&[Pages]	Inserts the total number of pages in your printout.
	Date	&[Date]	Inserts the current date at the time of printing.
	Time	&[Time]	Inserts the current time at printing. This is especially useful in worksheets that are undergoing changes and updates on a daily basis—the time will help you be sure you have the most current copy.
	File Name	&[File]	Inserts the filename. If the file hasn't been saved, the default Book number will be inserted instead. If you subsequently save the file, the new filename will replace the default name.
	Sheet Name	&[Tab]	Inserts the sheet name. This is useful if you've named your worksheets.

PART
V

CH
23

Note

Use the Total Pages field button as an accompaniment to the Pages button. For example, type the word **Page**, and then click the Page Number button. Then type a space, type **of**, type another space, and then click the Total pages button. Your result looks like `Page 3 of 6`. This helps readers keep the pages in order and know immediately whether they're missing a page.

Caution

If it's important that a particular date be displayed in your header or footer, type the date rather than using the Date button. The Date button inserts the current date, which changes each time you open and print the file on a new date; but a date you type will remain the same, regardless of the date on which you print the file.

If you are inserting the current date or time, you are relying on your computer's system date and/or time (so keep in mind that your system clock needs to be correct).

Tip #334

You can type the automatic field codes yourself, if you want to, but the buttons are faster and foolproof.

WORKING WITH SHEET SETTINGS

The Sheet tab, shown in Figure 23.18, in the Page Setup dialog box gives you more control over what appears on your printout. The dialog box is divided into the following main areas:

- **Print Area**. Click the Collapse Dialog button to reduce the dialog box, enabling you to drag through a range of cells in your worksheet, selecting them as your print area. This is not the fastest way to set print areas, but if the Page Setup dialog box is already open, you can set and change print areas here.

- **Print Titles**. If your data requires multiple printed pages, you can end up without labels to identify the columns and rows in your pages; setting print titles ensures that all the data in the printed pages is identified.

- **Print**. Choose which elements of your worksheet to print or not print (Gridlines, Row and Column Headings, and Comments), and how your printout will be processed in terms of color (Black and White, Draft Quality).

- **Page Order**. Choose the direction Excel will take in paginating your worksheet.

Figure 23.18.
You can set print areas in the Page Setup dialog box.

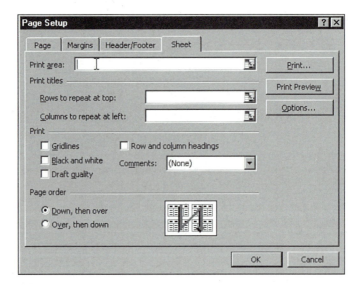

Tip #335 You can move from tab to tab in any dialog box by pressing Ctrl+Tab or Ctrl+Shift+Tab.

SELECTING A PRINT AREA

If you don't want to print the entire worksheet, you need to set a print area. There are three ways to do this:

- Select a range of cells and choose File, Print Area, Set Print Area. The selected range becomes your print area. To set multiple print areas, select the first range, then press

Ctrl while you select the remaining ranges, and then choose File, Print Area, Set Print Area. Each of the print areas will be printed on a separate page, and they'll all print the worksheet's header and footer.

- To print a specific range quickly without setting a more permanent print area, select the range to print, then click File, Print, and then choose Selection from the Print What section of the Print dialog box.

- Click File, Page Setup. In the Sheet tab, click in the Print Area box, and drag to select a range of cells (use the Collapse Dialog button if the box is in the way). To select multiple print ranges, you can type a comma between each print range (see Figure 23.19), or press Ctrl while selecting additional print ranges.

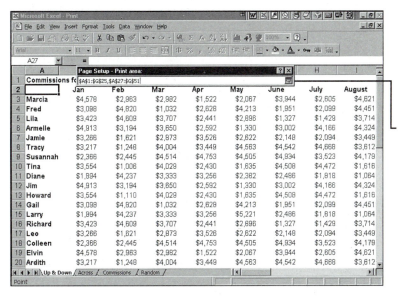

Figure 23.19.
Select multiple print areas by typing a comma between each range.

Click to expand the dialog box.

PRINTING TITLES AND ROW/COLUMN LABELS

If your worksheet is very large, some of your printed pages are not going to have the identifying row and column labels that a reader needs. For example, in the worksheet in Figure 23.20, page 1 shows both the month and employee name labels; for the rest of the pages, the data is meaningless. The solution is to set row and/or column labels as *print titles*, so that the data on every page is adequately identified.

Note

Print titles are not a replacement for headers and footers. A header or footer gets printed identically on every page of the document, but print titles print the row or column that corresponds to the displayed data on each page. You cannot use print titles to print identical information on each page.

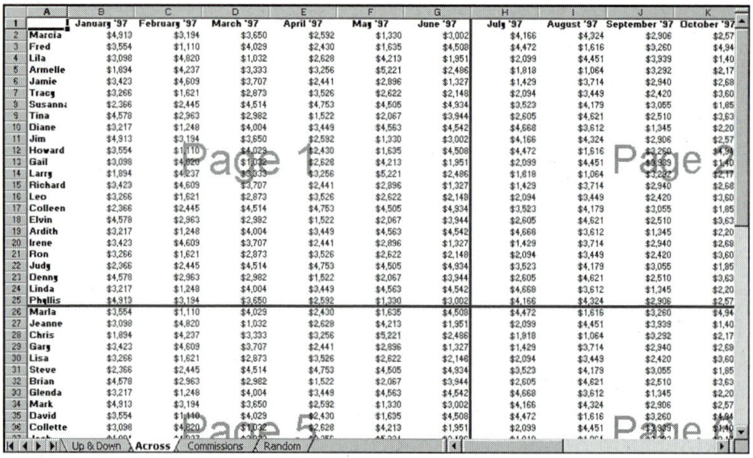

Figure 23.20.
Only page 1 has all
the identifying labels
it needs; the rest
of the pages need
column and/or
row labels.

To set print titles, follow these steps:

1. Choose File, Page Setup.

2. Click the Sheet tab.

3. Under Print Titles, click in the Rows to Repeat at Top box.

4. In the worksheet, click or drag the row selectors for the rows that contain the column labels. These rows are printed at the top of each page's data.

5. Click in the Columns to Repeat at Left box.

6. In the worksheet, click or drag the column selectors for the columns that contain the row labels. These columns are printed at the left side of each page's data.

7. Click OK to close the dialog box, or Print Preview to see the results.

Tip #336

Don't include the print title rows and columns in your print area, because, if you do, they'll be printed twice.

CHOOSING ELEMENTS TO PRINT

By default, your worksheet will print without gridlines. For many worksheets, this makes the data hard to read, especially if the worksheet is wide and the reader's eye must follow a row of data from left to right. If you don't want to format your data with borders (which look more professional but take more time), you can print the worksheet gridlines instead.

To print your worksheet gridlines (among other options), follow these steps:

1. Choose File, Page Setup.

2. Click the Sheet tab.

3. In the Print section of the dialog box, click to mark the check boxes next to Gridlines or Row and Column Headings. If you want to print worksheet comments, choose how you want them printed.

Comments are parenthetical references that you create and assign to a cell or range of cells. If you need to, you can choose to print them with your worksheet, choosing to have them appear at the end of the sheet or within the sheet, with the cells to which they refer.

4. Choose your color and print quality options (Black and White or Draft Quality).

5. Click OK.

Use the Draft Quality option if you want to create a quick printout that omits your graphic content. Use Draft quality for "rough" drafts or copies of your worksheet that will be edited. When you're ready to print a final copy that includes the graphic content, turn this option off.

DETERMINING PRINT ORDER

Use the Page order option buttons at the bottom of the Sheet tab to determine print order. Excel's default print order is down, then over. This order numbers multiple worksheet pages down the left side first, and then up to the top and down again (as shown in Figure 23.21). If your data looks better printed over, then down (as shown in Figure 23.22), you can switch the print order.

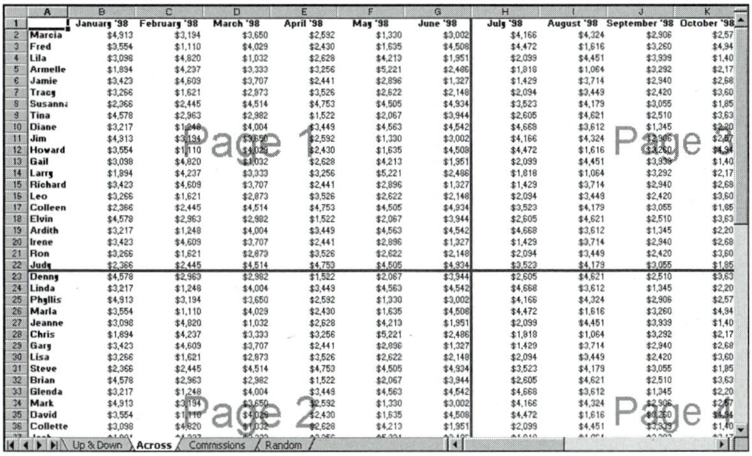

Figure 23.21.
This page order is down, then over.

Figure 23.22.
This page order is over, then down.

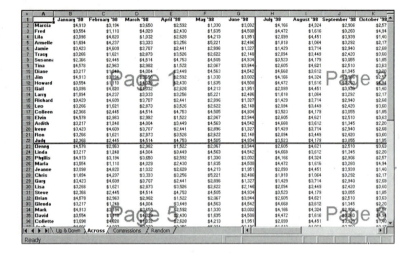

TROUBLESHOOTING

Printing problems are usually related to your printer rather than to the application through which you're printing (Excel, in this case). Some common printing problems and their potential solutions appear in Table 23.2:

TABLE 23.2. PRINTING PROBLEMS AND SOLUTIONS

Printing Problem	Possible Cause/Solution
One or two columns or rows flow onto a second or other unwanted subsequent page.	Too much data to fit on the page. Try reducing margins, or scaling the page to fit on a specific number of pages.
Printing takes too long.	A lot of graphic content—fonts, drawings, clip art. Increase the amount of memory in your printer or reduce the amount of graphic content in your worksheet, if possible. If you're on a network, try printing to a printer with more memory. If you have an ordinary laser printer, don't be surprised if it doesn't have enough memory to print even the smallest WordArt graphic.
Portions of your worksheet didn't print.	A print area has been defined that doesn't include the parts that are missing from your printout. Reselect the entire desired sections to print, and choose File, Print Area to reset. You can also redefine the print_area range name with an OFFSET formula so that the print area always fits the range (see Chapter 11, "Using Excel's Built-In Functions," to learn how).
Excel is ignoring the page breaks you set up.	Your Page Setup options may be in conflict with one another. Choose File, Page Setup, and on the Page tab, check the Fit To option, and specify the number of pages that your worksheet should print to.

If you're experiencing a lot of printing problems and none of the software-driven solutions seem to help, try reinstalling your printer driver. From the Start menu, choose Settings, Printers. Within the Printers window, double-click the Add Printer icon, and look for your printer's manufacturer and model. Follow the Add Printer procedure to install a new driver, which will appear as a copy of your original driver in the Printers window. You may need the original Windows 95/98 CD or disks in order to complete the process.

After the new driver is installed, delete the original icon for your printer so that your printer will utilize the newly installed driver, represented by the Copy icon. Restart your computer before printing again.

It's also a good idea to check your printer manufacturer's Web site periodically. Updated drivers are often available for free download.

USING FORMULAS AND FUNCTIONS

CHAPTER 24

CONSTRUCTING EXCEL FORMULAS

In this chapter

UNDERSTANDING BASIC FORMULA CONCEPTS

This chapter is about building your own mathematical formulas to calculate the data on a worksheet. Formulas, and the capability to build and edit them easily, are why you would want to use an electronic spreadsheet for storing and analyzing numeric data. Even if you're a mathematical genius, allowing Excel to do your calculations saves time, reduces the margin for error, and makes updating the results fast and easy. In addition, because numbers are stored in cells and you can refer to those cells in your formulas, the process of updating formulas with current data is automatic.

In Excel, you can write formulas from scratch or use a variety of automated features that write formulas for you. In this chapter, the focus will be on writing your own formulas to perform basic mathematical calculations in a worksheet; in Chapter 25, you'll use what you've learned about formula construction to write complex formulas that use *functions* to perform more intricate calculations.

There are a few basic concepts that you need to understand and remember when you write Excel formulas.

Tip #337	For users of other spreadsheet programs, such as Lotus 1-2-3, there are minor differences in how formulas are written. You'll want to learn how to write formulas the Excel way, but as an interim measure, you can tell Excel to accept formulas entered in Lotus 1-2-3 syntax: click Tools, Options, and on the Transition tab, check the Transition Formula Entry check box.

- All formulas begin with an equal sign (=).
- Formulas can use cell references and/or real numbers (called *constant values*) in their calculations.
- The mathematical operators Excel recognizes are + (addition), - (subtraction), * (multiplication), / (division), ^ (exponentiation), and % (percentage).
- You can add parentheses to control the order in which a formula carries out mathematical operations (when using parentheses, be sure you have complete sets of left and right parentheses).
- After a formula is entered, you'll see the formula in the Formula bar when the cell is active. The formula's result is displayed in the worksheet cell.
- When you edit a formula, you'll see the formula in both the Formula bar and the cell where you entered it, and you can edit the formula in either location.
- If you want to see all the formulas on your worksheet at once, instead of their results, you can switch the worksheet display. Press Ctrl+` (the grave accent in the upper left corner of your keyboard) to toggle between formulas and results, or click Tools, Options, and on the View tab, check the Formulas check box to show formulas (clear the check box to display results).

→ In addition to the mathematical operators, you can use Excel's built-in functions in formulas. **See** "Using Excel's Built-In Functions," **p. 759**

Note

If you use the Lotus 1-2-3 formula syntax (starting a formula with a plus [+] sign), Excel will change the syntax to begin with an equal sign after you enter the formula.

A formula can be as simple as =1+2. If you enter this formula into a worksheet, you'll get the result 3. But if you use cell references instead of values in your formulas, the formulas become much more flexible. For example, if you enter the value 1 in cell A1, and the value 2 in cell B1, you can write the formula =A1+B1 in any other cell, and the result will be 3. If you change the values in cells A1 and B1, the formula will continue to add the values in those cells and give you a correct result.

You can build on this principle by using cell references with other mathematical operators. For example, suppose you have a customer's invoice with a list of items and prices, and you want to add the sales tax to the subtotal. You can calculate the sales tax by multiplying the value in the subtotal cell by the sales tax. For example, in Figure 24.1, the tax rate is 5.5%, and the subtotal value is in cell E15. The formula =E15*5.5% in cell E16 calculates the correct tax whatever the subtotal.

PART

VI

CH

24

The formula appears in the Formula bar.

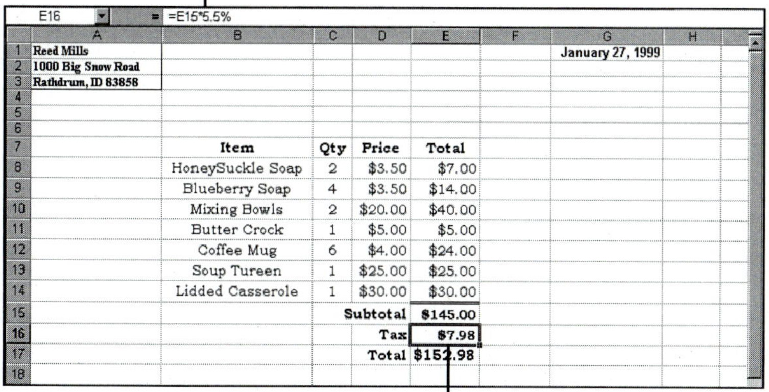

Figure 24.1.
This formula multiplies a cell reference (E15) by a constant value (5.5%).

The result appears in the cell.

USING AUTOSUM TO TOTAL COLUMNS AND ROWS OF DATA

Because the most common worksheet calculation is the totaling of data in a list or table, Microsoft created the AutoSum toolbar button. AutoSum writes a formula that uses the SUM function to sum the values in all the cells referenced in the formula, and it writes the formula rapidly. (You'll learn more about functions in Chapter 25.)

AutoSum attempts to guess which cells you want to use in your SUM formula. But if it guesses wrong, you can change the referenced range quickly while you enter the formula.

You can use AutoSum to write quick SUM formulas using only your mouse, and you can write SUM formulas all the way across the bottom or down the side of a table in two clicks of a mouse.

To use AutoSum, follow these steps:

1. Click in the cell where you want to display the formula result.

2. Click the AutoSum button on the Standard toolbar.

   Excel guesses which cells you want to include, and surrounds them with an animated border (as shown in Figure 24.2).

3. If the formula doesn't have an obvious row or column to sum, or if it guesses wrong, drag to select the cells you want to sum. The animated border surrounds all the cells you drag.

4. When the range is correct, press Enter (or click the Enter button, the green check mark left of the Formula bar) to complete the formula.

Figure 24.2.
When you click AutoSum, an animated border surrounds the cells included in the formula.

The Enter button on the Formula bar

The AutoSum button

The SUM formula appears in the Formula bar.

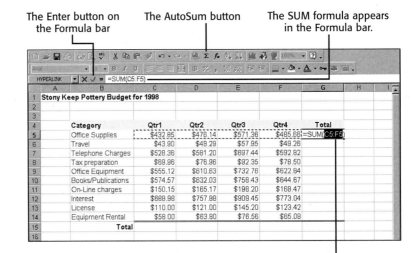

The SUM formula also appears in the cell.

If you want to write SUM formulas for several columns or rows in a table, follow these steps:

1. Drag to select all the cells that you want to display totals in, either across the bottom or down the right side of the table.

2. Click the AutoSum button.

   Each cell is automatically filled with a SUM formula that sums the contents of the column above it (as shown in Figure 24.3).

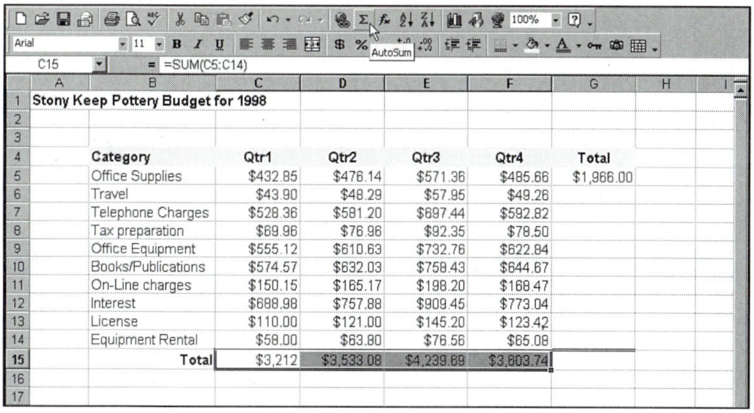

Figure 24.3.
If you select all the cells adjacent to a table, Excel knows which cells to sum.

EDITING FORMULAS

When you need to change a formula, either the calculation or the referenced cells, there are several techniques from which to choose: You can edit the formula in the Formula bar or in the cell.

To edit in the Formula bar, click the cell that contains the formula, and then click in the Formula bar. Use regular text-editing techniques to edit the formula—drag to select characters you want to change; then delete or type over them. Press Enter to complete the formula.

To edit the formula in the cell, double-click the cell. The cell switches to edit mode and the entire formula is visible (as shown in Figure 24.4). You can select and edit the formula just as you would in the Formula bar.

Tip #338 You can also press F2 to switch to edit mode for the selected cell you want to edit.

Note If, when you double-click the formula cell (or press F2), the cell references are selected but the cell doesn't change to edit mode, click Tools, Options, and click the Edit tab. Click the Edit Directly in Cell check box to turn it on, and then click OK.

Whether you edit a formula in the Formula bar or in the cell, the references in the formula are highlighted in color, and the corresponding cell ranges on the worksheet are surrounded by borders that are color-matched to the range references in the formula, as shown in Figure 24.4. Although you can't see the actual colors in this figure, the callouts point them out, and you'll experience similar color highlights on your own screen.

Figure 24.4.
Follow the colors to
locate the referenced
ranges.

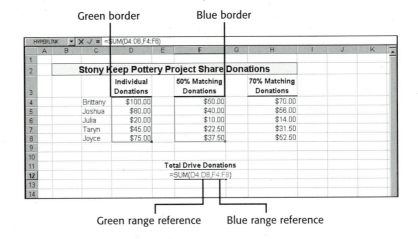

If you need to change the cell references so the formula calculates different cells, there are several techniques you can choose from. You can type new references, click and drag a new range on the worksheet, or use *range names*.

> **Note**
>
> To get out of a cell without making any changes, or to undo any changes you've made before you enter them, press Esc or click the Cancel button (the red X left of the Formula bar).

DRAGGING CELLS TO REPLACE A REFERENCE

A quick and direct way to add or replace a range reference is to select the range you want on the worksheet. To add a new range to the formula, click in the formula to place the insertion point where you want to add the new range reference; then use your mouse to drag and select the range you want. If you're adding a new reference to one or more existing references, type a comma to separate the references.

> **Tip #339**
>
> To add several separate ranges all at the same time, drag to select the first range; then press and hold Ctrl while you drag to select the remaining ranges. This maneuver inserts the commas between the separate range references for you.

If you want to replace a cell or range reference, double-click the reference to highlight it in the formula (see Figure 24.5). Then click and drag the replacement cell or range on the worksheet.

When you finish editing the formula, press Enter to complete the formula and close the cell.

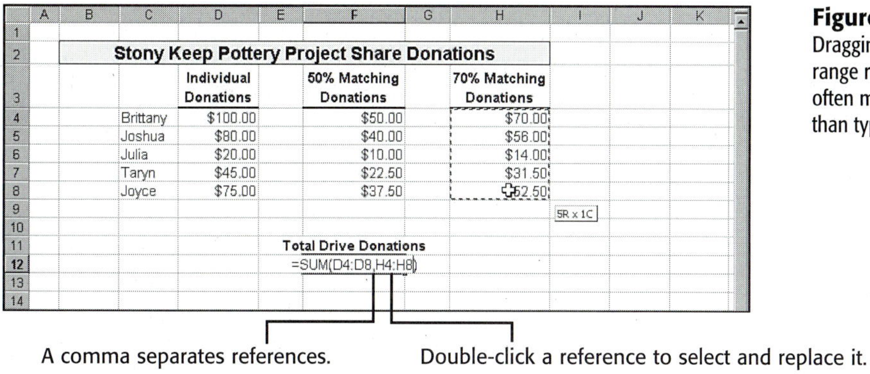

Figure 24.5.
Dragging to select range references is often more accurate than typing them.

A comma separates references.   Double-click a reference to select and replace it.

Tip #340

When you drag to select cells, a ScreenTip appears to tell you how many rows and columns you've selected.

Dragging a Range Border to Change a Reference

If you need to expand existing references (for example, if you added new columns or rows to a table and need to adjust the formula to include them), you can move or resize the colored range border to encompass the new cells. You can also move and resize the range border to reduce the range included in the formula.

To move a range border to surround different cells without changing its size, drag any side of the border. To expand or reduce the size of a range border, drag the *fill handle* to change the size of the range (see Figure 24.6).

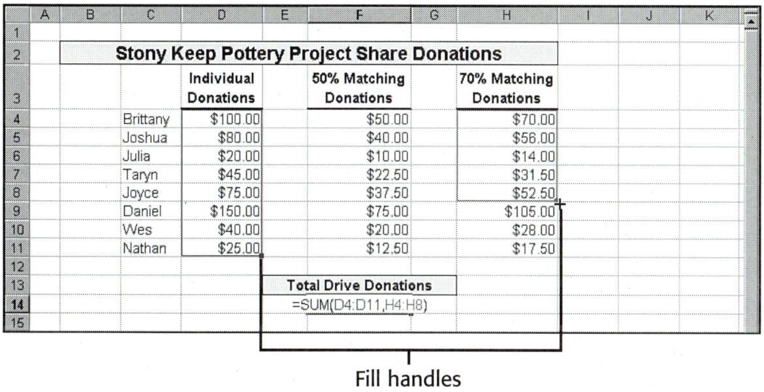

Figure 24.6.
You can edit a range reference by moving or resizing its colored borders.

Fill handles

TYPING REFERENCES DIRECTLY INTO A FORMULA

If you'd rather use your keyboard, you can type range references directly into the formula. Use common text-editing techniques to delete and replace characters in your references; be sure to use a colon to separate the upper-left cell reference from the lower-right cell reference in a range, and remember to separate range references with commas. If you need to reference ranges on other worksheets and other workbooks, the typing becomes a bit more complex; you'll learn about those later in this chapter, in "Referencing Other Workbooks and Worksheets."

TYPING A RANGE NAME INTO A FORMULA

If you named the ranges that you're using in formulas (a very efficient practice), you can type the range name in place of its reference.

It's useful to create range names that include some capital letters (such as Price or DecemberOrders), because the letter case will help you find misspelled range names. When you type a name into a formula, type it in all lowercase letters. If Excel recognizes the name, the characters will be converted to the case you created the name with; but if you mistype the name, the characters will remain lowercase and you'll get a #NAME? error. The lowercase name is your quickest clue to where the error is.

PASTING A RANGE NAME INTO A FORMULA

To be sure you don't misspell a range name when you add it to a formula (or if you don't remember exactly what the range name is), you can paste it from a list of all the range names in the workbook.

To paste a name into a formula, follow these steps:

1. Click in the formula where you want to paste the name.

2. Choose Insert, Name, Paste.

3. In the Paste Name dialog box (see Figure 24.7), click the name you want and click OK.

To replace a name with another name, double-click the name in the formula to select it, and then follow the preceding steps 2 and 3 to paste a new name in its place.

If you need to change the range that's calculated in the formula, don't change the formula; instead, change the definition of the range name. Click Insert, Name, Define, and in the Define Name dialog box, click the range name. In the Refers to box, change the range references, and then click OK.

Named range

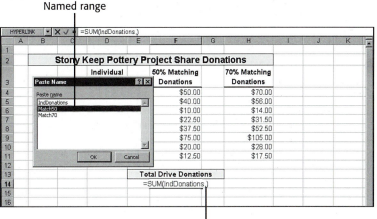

Figure 24.7.
Pasting a name prevents typing mistakes.

The pasted name will be inserted here.

→ To find out more about using named ranges in your formulas, **see** "Using Range Names in Formulas," **p. 806**

PART

VI

CH

24

WRITING MULTIPLE COPIES OF A FORMULA

Suppose you have a table similar to the one shown in Figure 24.8, and you need to add identical formulas at the end of each row. Instead of entering each formula individually, there are a couple of ways to create copies of your formula quickly. One method uses AutoFill to copy a formula into several more cells. Another method creates multiple copies when you enter the formula.

COPYING FORMULAS WITH AUTOFILL

When you copy a formula using AutoFill, each formula adjusts its references automatically so that the calculation is correct. For example, when you write a formula that sums the values in the four cells to the left (like the formula in Figure 24.8), each copy of the formula will sum the values in the four cells to its left. This works because the formula uses *relative references*.

→ To learn more about using relative references in your formulas, **see** "Using Relative, Absolute, and Mixed Cell References in Formulas," **p. 750**

To AutoFill a formula, follow these steps:

1. Enter your formula in the first cell (in this example, in the cell at the top of the column), as shown in Figure 24.8.

2. Select the formula cell. The active cell (or range) has a small black box in the lower-right corner called a *fill handle*.

3. Point the mouse at the fill handle; when the mouse pointer becomes a black cross, click and drag down to fill cells with copies of the formula (see Figure 24.8). You can use AutoFill to copy formulas in all four directions in your worksheet (up, down, left, and right).

4. At the end of range, release the mouse button. The cells you dragged are filled with copies of the formula, as illustrated in Figure 24.9.

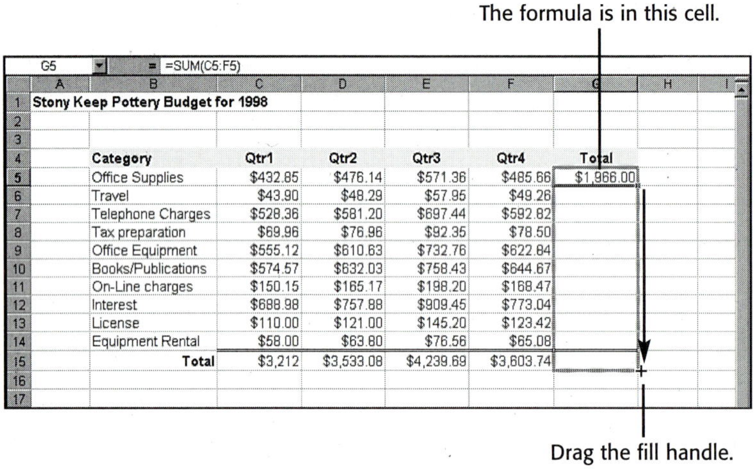

The formula is in this cell.

Figure 24.8.
When your mouse pointer is a black cross, you can drag to AutoFill the formula to adjoining cells.

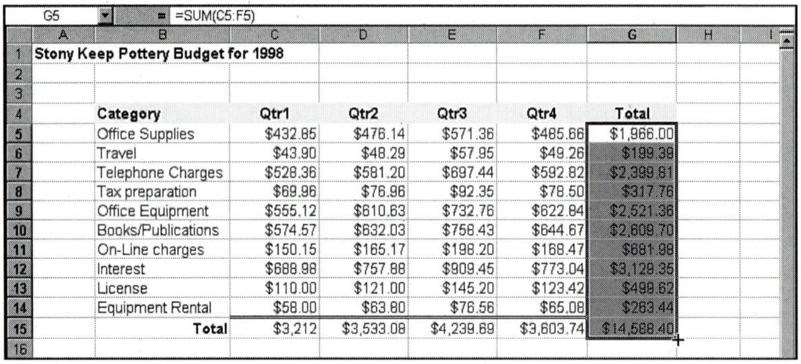

Drag the fill handle.

Figure 24.9.
When you release the mouse pointer, the cells are filled.

Tip #341

You can use AutoFill to fill out a table (for example, a loan payments table) by copying an entire row or column of entries and formulas. Select the range of cells you want to copy, and drag the fill handle on the lower-right corner of the range.

Also, if your table is extremely long, you can AutoFill an adjacent column by double-clicking the fill handle instead of dragging it.

ENTERING MULTIPLE FORMULAS ALL AT ONCE

If you've already entered a formula and need to copy it across a row or down a column, AutoFill is quickest. But to enter multiple copies of a formula even faster, enter them all at the same time.

To enter the same formula in several cells at once, follow these steps:

1. Select all the cells you want to enter the formula in (see Figure 24.10). They can be in a single row or column, or in noncontiguous ranges (press Ctrl to select noncontiguous ranges).
2. Set up your formula by whatever means you normally use, but don't press Enter when you finish.
3. When the formula is complete, press Ctrl+Enter. The formula is entered in all the selected cells simultaneously (see Figure 24.11).

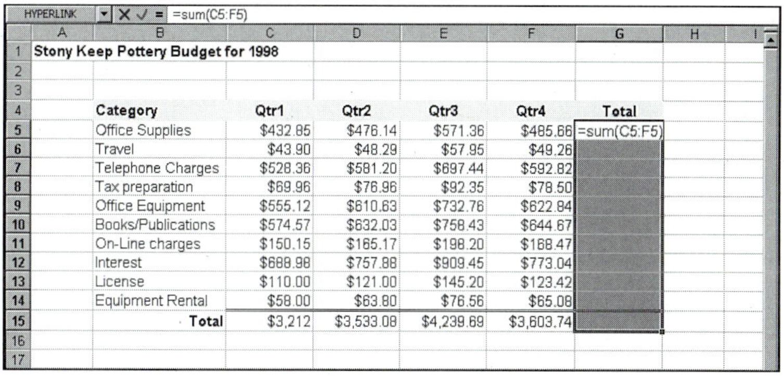

HYPERLINK =sum(C5:F5)

	A	B	C	D	E	F	G	H
1	Stony Keep Pottery Budget for 1998							
2								
3								
4		Category	Qtr1	Qtr2	Qtr3	Qtr4	Total	
5		Office Supplies	$432.85	$476.14	$571.36	$485.66	=sum(C5:F5)	
6		Travel	$43.90	$48.29	$57.95	$49.26		
7		Telephone Charges	$528.36	$581.20	$697.44	$592.82		
8		Tax preparation	$69.96	$76.96	$92.35	$78.50		
9		Office Equipment	$555.12	$610.63	$732.76	$622.84		
10		Books/Publications	$574.57	$632.03	$758.43	$644.67		
11		On-Line charges	$150.15	$165.17	$198.20	$168.47		
12		Interest	$688.98	$757.88	$909.45	$773.04		
13		License	$110.00	$121.00	$145.20	$123.42		
14		Equipment Rental	$58.00	$63.80	$76.56	$65.08		
15		Total	$3,212	$3,533.08	$4,239.69	$3,603.74		
16								
17								

Figure 24.10.
To enter multiple copies of a formula all at once, select all the cells first.

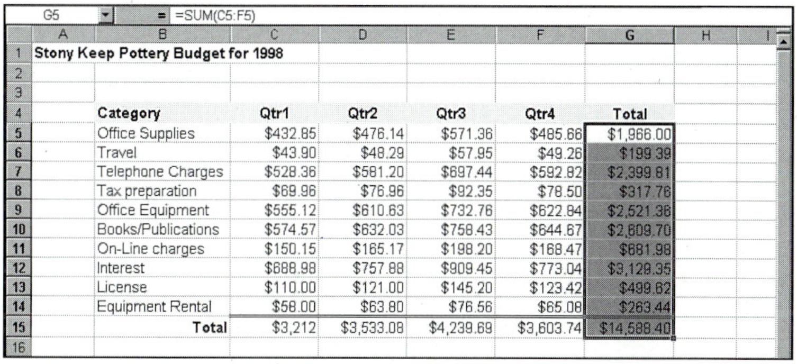

G5 =SUM(C5:F5)

	A	B	C	D	E	F	G	H
1	Stony Keep Pottery Budget for 1998							
2								
3								
4		Category	Qtr1	Qtr2	Qtr3	Qtr4	Total	
5		Office Supplies	$432.85	$476.14	$571.36	$485.66	$1,966.00	
6		Travel	$43.90	$48.29	$57.95	$49.26	$199.39	
7		Telephone Charges	$528.36	$581.20	$697.44	$592.82	$2,399.81	
8		Tax preparation	$69.96	$76.96	$92.35	$78.50	$317.76	
9		Office Equipment	$555.12	$610.63	$732.76	$622.84	$2,521.36	
10		Books/Publications	$574.57	$632.03	$758.43	$644.67	$2,609.70	
11		On-Line charges	$150.15	$165.17	$198.20	$168.47	$681.98	
12		Interest	$688.98	$757.88	$909.45	$773.04	$3,129.35	
13		License	$110.00	$121.00	$145.20	$123.42	$499.62	
14		Equipment Rental	$58.00	$63.80	$76.56	$65.08	$263.44	
15		Total	$3,212	$3,533.08	$4,239.69	$3,603.74	$14,588.40	
16								

Figure 24.11.
Press Ctrl+Enter to enter the formula in all the selected cells.

If you use range references in the formula, they'll automatically adjust to the correct references in each copy of the formula (see the section "Understanding Cell References" later in this chapter to learn more). If you use range names or worksheet labels in the formulas, each copy of the formula will find its correct range (but be careful using worksheet labels—they can be a bit unpredictable and tricky).

USING AUTOCALCULATE FOR QUICK TOTALS

Sometimes you need a quick and impermanent calculation—you need to know right now what your expense account entries add up to, or how many items there are in a list. You can use *AutoCalculate* to get quick answers.

To use AutoCalculate, select the cells you want to calculate. The answer appears in the AutoCalculate box on the Status bar (see Figure 24.12).

Selected cells

Figure 24.12.
Select two or more cells and see the automatic calculation of those entries displayed on the Status bar.

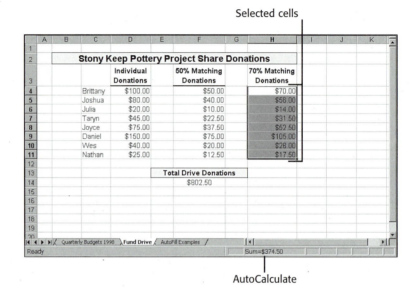

AutoCalculate

When you install Excel, AutoCalculate is set to calculate sums by default; but you're not limited to quick sums. You can also, for example, obtain a quick count of the items in a long product list or a quick average of your list of monthly phone bills. You can switch the calculation to Average, Count, CountNums, Max, or Min (or None to turn the feature off). To switch the calculation, right-click the Status bar (see Figure 24.13) and click the calculation you want on the shortcut menu.

Choose a calculation.

Figure 24.13.
Choose a different AutoCalculate function.

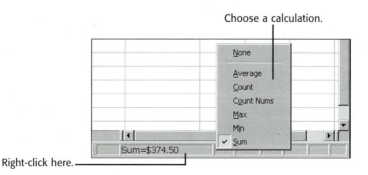

Right-click here.

Tip #342 | AutoCalculate retains whatever function you set until you change the function again.

AutoCalculate appears in the Status bar only when two or more calculable cells are selected. For example, if the AutoCalculate function is set to Sum and you select cells that contain only text entries, AutoCalculate won't appear (because there's nothing to sum).

AutoCalculate offers the following functions:

- **Average**—averages numeric values in the selected cells; ignores blank cells and nonnumeric values.

- **Count**—counts all entries, whether numeric, text, or logical; ignores blank cells.

- **CountNums**—counts only numeric values; ignores blank cells and nonnumeric values.

- **Max**—shows the single maximum numeric value in the selected cells.

- **Min**—shows the single minimum numeric value in the selected cells.

- **Sum**—sums numeric values in the selected cells; ignores blank cells and nonnumeric values.

PART
VI

CH
24

UNDERSTANDING FORMULA CONSTRUCTION

Earlier in this chapter, you began to learn about writing and editing formulas (writing simple formulas using both constant values and cell references, editing references, separating references with commas, and so forth).

In this section, you'll learn how to use arithmetic operators in your formulas, how to control the order in which Excel performs those operations, and how to fix error messages.

USING ARITHMETIC OPERATORS FOR SIMPLE MATH

To perform direct mathematical operations in a formula (as opposed to using *functions*, which you'll learn about in Chapter 11), you use arithmetic operators. *Arithmetic operators* in a formula tell Excel which math operations you want to perform.

A simple formula might consist of adding, subtracting, multiplying, and dividing cells. Excel can also perform exponentiation, so you can enter a number and exponent (such as 5^4, or 5 to the fourth power) and Excel will use the ultimate value of the exponent in the formula calculation. You can use percentages in a formula the same way—instead of entering 25% as a fractional value (25/100) or a decimal value (0.25), you can enter 25% in a formula; Excel will calculate and use its decimal value in the math operation.

Excel's arithmetic operators are detailed in Table 24.1.

TABLE 24.1. ARITHMETIC OPERATORS

Operator	Description
+ (plus sign)	Addition
- (minus sign)	Subtraction and Negation
* (asterisk)	Multiplication
/ (forward slash)	Division
^ (caret)	Exponentiation
% (percent)	Percentage

UNDERSTANDING THE ORDER IN WHICH EXCEL PERFORMS MATHEMATICAL OPERATIONS

If a formula performs more than one or two operations, you'll probably need to tell Excel in what order to perform those operations (or you may get a wrong answer).

For example, what's the answer to the equation 2+2*3? If you solve the equation left to right (perform the addition first, and then multiply), the answer is 12; but if you solve the equation using math rules (perform the multiplication first, and then the addition), the answer is 8. So how do you get Excel to solve the equation the way you want it solved, so you get the answer you want?

Excel follows standard math rules regarding which operations it performs first, next, and so forth; this is called the *order of operations*, and is shown as follows. To get the answer you want, you can use parentheses to divide the formula into segments and control the order of operations yourself.

- **Parentheses**. All calculations within parentheses are completed first.
- **Negation**. Making a number negative (such as −5) precedes any other operations, so that the negative value is used in the remaining calculations.
- **Percent**. Percentages (for example, 12%) are calculated next, so that the actual value (in this case, .12) is used in the remaining calculations.
- **Exponentiation**. Exponents (for example, 10^3 which means 10 cubed) are calculated next, so that the actual value is used in the remaining calculations.
- **Multiplication**. Performed after parenthetical operations and before all other calculations.
- **Division**. Follows any multiplication and is on the same level of precedence as multiplication.
- **Addition**. Performed after all divisions.
- **Subtraction**. Follows any additions and is on the same level of precedence as addition.

CONTROLLING THE ORDER OF OPERATIONS

Even though Excel follows a set order of operations when it calculates a formula, you can alter the order in a specific formula by using parentheses to break the formula into segments. Excel will perform all operations within sets of parentheses first, and you can use this to get exactly the order of operations you want.

If multiple operations are encased in multiple sets of parentheses, the operations are performed from inside to outside, then follow the order of operations, and then left to right. Table 24.2 shows results of rearranging parentheses within the same formula. Each parenthetical calculation is performed first; then the results of those first calculations are used for the second set of calculations, which follow the order of operations. All operations on the same level (in this case, all the additions) are then performed left to right.

TABLE 24.2. THE RESULTS OF REARRANGING PARENTHESES

Formula	Result
=(1+2)*3+4+5	18
=1+2*3+4+5	16
=1+2*(3+4)+5	20
=1+2*(3+4+5)	25
=(1+2)*(3+4)+5	26
=(1+2)*(3+4+5)	36

You must have balanced pairs of parentheses in any formula. If you forget a parenthesis, you'll see a message telling you there's an error. Sometimes Excel takes a guess at where you want the missing parenthesis (shown in Figure 24.14) and displays a prompt box. If the guess is right, click Yes; if it's wrong, click No and fix the formula yourself.

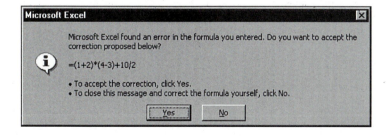

Figure 24.14.
Excel sometimes tries to guess what you want (but it may or may not guess correctly).

Tip #343

If your formula is long and contains many sets of parentheses, it can be difficult to find the missing parenthesis by eye. Instead, open the formula for editing, and use the arrow keys to move the cursor (the insertion point) through the formula one character at a time. Whenever the cursor moves over a parenthesis, both parentheses in the pair are momentarily darkened. If the parenthesis is not temporarily darkened when the cursor passes over it, that's the one that's missing a matching parenthesis for the set.

NESTING CALCULATIONS WITHIN A FORMULA

Some calculations are more complex than can be handled with isolated sets of parentheses; they require parenthetical sets that are *nested*, or contained within larger parenthetical sets. This isn't so common in simple mathematical formulas, but is very common when you use functions (which you learn about in Chapter 25).

Nested calculations use parentheses to force Excel to follow the order of operations that you want, even as it follows the standard order of operations. Figure 24.15 shows a simple example of the changes you can make by nesting parentheses within other parentheses.

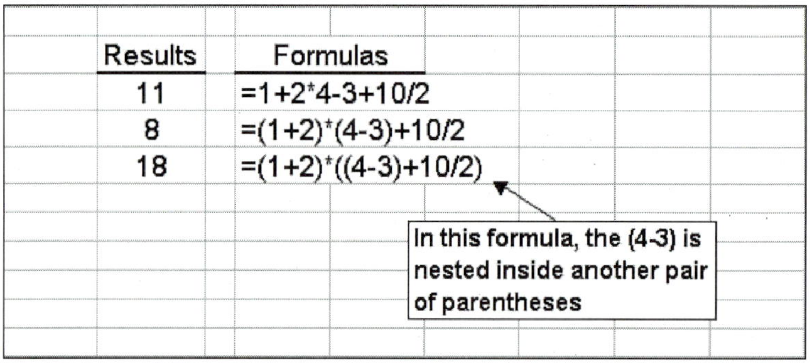

Figure 24.15.
Nesting parentheses within other parentheses alters the calculation even more.

Results	Formulas
11	=1+2*4-3+10/2
8	=(1+2)*(4-3)+10/2
18	=(1+2)*((4-3)+10/2)

In this formula, the (4-3) is nested inside another pair of parentheses

To simplify the principle: Excel calculates the innermost parentheses first, and then uses those quantities to calculate within the next outer level of parentheses, and so forth through all the nested levels. When all the parenthetical quantities have been calculated, Excel uses those quantities to calculate the formula by following the order of operations.

You'll see the real value of nested calculations in Chapter 25, where you learn about functions and how to nest them to make your worksheet work for you.

INTERPRETING FORMULA ERROR MESSAGES

When something prevents a formula from calculating, you'll see an error message instead of a result. The "something" might be a reference that was deleted from the worksheet, an invalid arithmetic operation such as dividing by zero, or a formula attempting to calculate a named range that doesn't exist.

Table 24.3 lists the error messages and their probable causes (some have several probable causes, and you must do some detective work to find the problem). But Excel has tools that can help you track down the source of an error.

TABLE 24.3.   ERROR VALUES

This Error	Means This	To Fix It, Do This
#####	The column isn't wide enough to display the value.	Widen the column.
#VALUE!	Wrong type of argument or operand (for example, calculating a cell with the value #N/A).	Check operands and arguments; be sure references are valid.
#DIV/0!	Formula is attempting to divide by zero.	Change the value or cell reference so that the formula doesn't divide by zero.
#NAME?	Formula is referencing an invalid or nonexistent name.	Be sure the name still exists or correct the misspelling.
#N/A	Most commonly means no value is available or inappropriate arguments were used.	In a lookup formula, be sure the lookup table is sorted correctly.
#REF!	Excel can't locate the referenced cells. (For example, referenced cells were deleted.)	Click Undo immediately to restore references and then change formula references or convert formulas to values.
#NUM!	Incorrect use of a number (such as SQRT(-1)), or formula result is a number too large or too small to be displayed.	Be sure that the arguments are correct, and that the result is between $-1*10^{307}$ and $1*10^{307}$.
#NULL!	Reference to intersection of two areas that do not intersect.	Check for typing and reference errors.
Circular	A formula refers to itself, either directly or indirectly.	Click OK and then look at the status bar to see which cell contains the circular reference. Use the Trace Precedents and Trace Dependents buttons on either the Circular Reference or Auditing toolbar to find the culprit references.

PART

VI

CH

24

LOCATING ERRORS IN FORMULAS

To locate the source of an error in a formula, begin by checking the formula itself for typing and spelling mistakes. The error may be in the formula, or it may be in a source cell that's referenced by the formula.

To locate the source of an error, follow these steps:

1. Click Tools, Auditing, Show Auditing Toolbar.

2. Click the cell containing the error.

3. On the Auditing toolbar, click the Trace Error button.

   If the error originated in a source cell rather than in the active cell, tracing arrows appear and guide you visually to possible sources of error (see Figure 24.16). Blue trace lines show referenced cells, and red trace lines lead to the cell that caused the error value.

   If no error-tracing arrows appear, the source of the error is in the formula itself. Use the information in Table 24.3 to find the problem.

   Even if there are no errors, you can trace the dependent and precedent cells in a formula by clicking the Trace Dependents and Trace Precedents buttons. Each time you click a Trace button, tracing arrows appear for the next level of precedents or dependents. The Remove Precedent Arrows and Remove Dependent Arrows remove the tracing arrows one level at a time.

The precedents for D8

Figure 24.16.
Tracing arrows show graphically where a cell's precedents and dependents are.

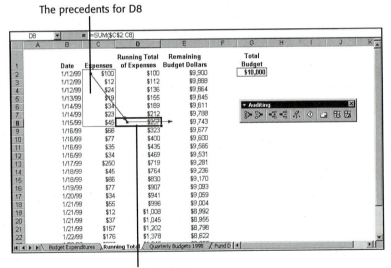

D8 points to its dependent.

USING RELATIVE, ABSOLUTE, AND MIXED CELL REFERENCES IN FORMULAS

Cells can have different types of references, depending on how you want to use them in a formula. Up until this point in the chapter, all the cell references written in the formula examples have been *relative* references. By default, Excel doesn't treat the cells you include in a formula as a set location. Instead, Excel considers the cells as a relative location. This type of referencing saves you from having to create the same formula over and over again. You can copy it and the cell references adjust accordingly. You saw this principle in action earlier in this chapter in the section on copying formulas ("Writing Multiple Copies of a Formula").

When writing AutoSum formulas, for example, formulas are written with relative references, and you can use AutoFill to quickly copy the formula to other cells. The copied formulas adjust themselves to the appropriate references. For example, if a relative reference in a formula refers to "the cell on my left," every copy of that formula refers to the cell on its left, no matter where you copy it.

Sometimes, however, you'll need to refer to the same specific cell on the worksheet in every copy of a formula. In a case like this, use an *absolute* reference. An absolute reference is fixed and never changes even if you move or copy the formula. Absolute references are denoted with dollar signs before the column and row address, such as $A$1.

PART

VI

CH

24

For example, suppose you have a departmental budget and you like to keep a running total of what you've spent and what remains available. Figure 24.17 shows a column of running totals and a column of remaining budget dollars. The formulas use both absolute references and relative references. The formulas in the Running Total of Expenses column each sum the range from cell $C$4 to the cell left of the formula. The formulas in the Remaining Budget Dollars column each subtract the cell to the left from the Total Budget (cell $F$4). As the list of expenses in the Expenses column grows, the formulas in the Running Total and Remaining Budget columns can be quickly copied down with AutoFill.

Each Running Total formula starts in $C$4....

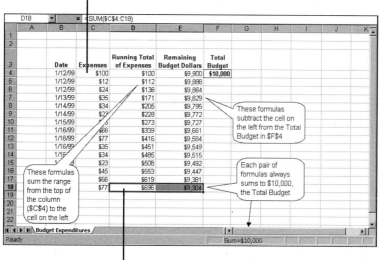

Figure 24.17.
Using absolute and relative references in the same formula enables you to create flexible lists.

...and sums down to its own row.

On occasion, you'll need a *mixed* reference. Mixed references can contain both absolute and relative cell addresses, such as $A4 or C$3. For example, if you want copies of a formula to refer to the value two columns left of the formula, but always in Row 3, you'd use a mixed reference with a relative column and an absolute row (such as A$3). Copies of the formula would always refer to a value in row 3, although which cell in row 3 would depend on where the formula was.

As mentioned previously, the default reference type is always relative, which means if you click and drag cells to add references to a formula, the references will be entered as relative. If you type them, you can type the dollar signs wherever you need to designate an absolute reference, but it's faster to type relative references and then change them to absolute or mixed.

You can quickly cycle through the reference types by pressing F4 on the keyboard. For example, if a formula uses the reference A1, pressing F4 will change the reference to $A$1, A$1, $A1, and A1 (in that order) with each press. Simply stop when the reference is the type you want to use.

To change the reference type, follow these steps:

1. Double-click the cell containing the formula (or select the cell and work in the Formula bar).

2. Within the formula, click in the cell reference you want to change (see Figure 24.18).

3. Press F4 until the reference changes to the type you want.

   Repeatedly pressing F4 cycles through all the possible reference types.

4. Press Enter to complete the change.

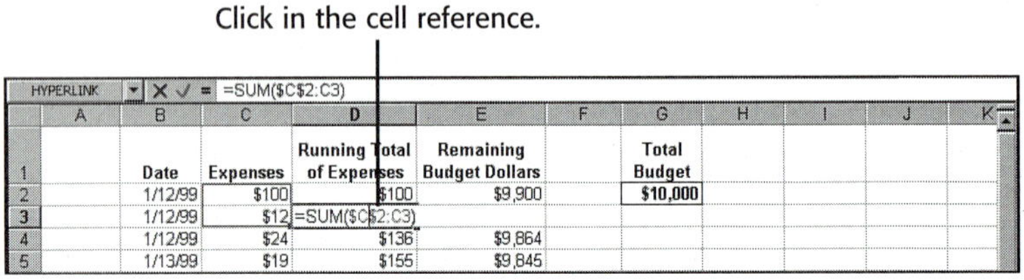

Click in the cell reference.

Figure 24.18.
To change the reference type, click in the cell reference; then, press F4.

REFERENCING VALUES IN OTHER WORKSHEETS AND WORKBOOKS

You can write formulas that calculate values in other worksheets and other workbooks, which is a common way to compile and summarize data from several different sources. When you write formulas that reference other worksheets and workbooks, you create links to those other worksheets and workbooks.

REFERENCING OTHER WORKSHEETS

Suppose you have a workbook that contains separate worksheets for each division in your company. You can combine data from each division's worksheet in a Summary sheet in that same workbook to compile and analyze data for the entire company. Formulas on the Summary sheet will need to reference data on the individual Division sheets (these are called *external references*). You can create external references by switching to the other worksheet and clicking and dragging the cells you want to reference, just as in a same-worksheet reference; the only difference is that the cells are located on a different worksheet.

To reference data from another worksheet in your formula, follow these steps:

1. Begin building the formula.

2. When you are ready to insert the reference from another worksheet, click the tab for that worksheet.

Tip #344

Sometimes it's easier to work in two windows, side by side on your screen. To open a second window, click <u>W</u>indow, <u>N</u>ew Window. Click <u>W</u>indow, <u>A</u>rrange, and in the Arrange Windows dialog box, click an arrangement (<u>T</u>iled always works well), and click OK. Finally, select the second worksheet in one of the windows.

3. Locate the cell that you want to reference, and click it. If you're referencing a range, drag across the range to select it. The sheet name and cell reference appear in the Formula bar, as shown in Figure 24.19.

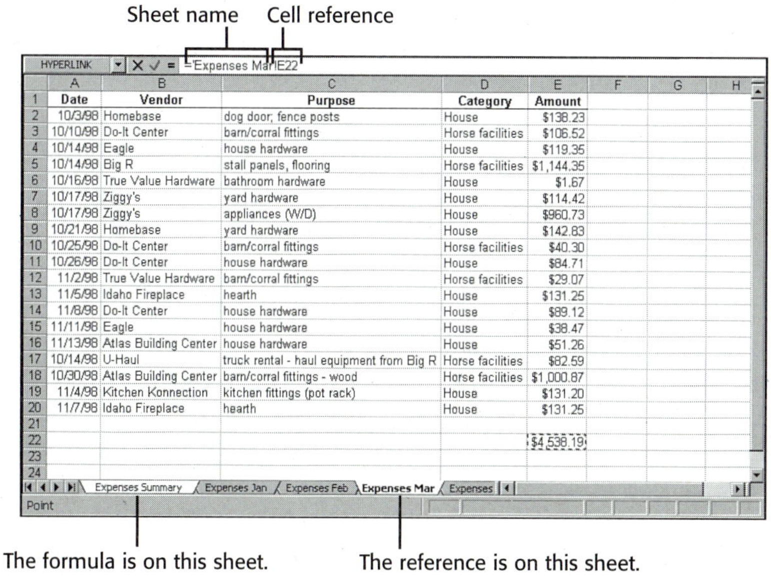

Sheet name   Cell reference

Figure 24.19.
An external worksheet reference is the sheet name, followed by an exclamation point, followed by the cell reference (which can be relative or absolute).

The formula is on this sheet.   The reference is on this sheet.

4. Continue building your formula by typing the remaining operators. If your formula requires cells from other worksheets (or from the original worksheet), repeat steps 2 and 3 to add them.

5. When the formula is complete, press Enter.

You can also enter external worksheet references by typing them. The syntax for an external worksheet reference is

`SheetName!CellReference`

If the sheet name contains spaces, enclose the sheet name in single quotes, like this:

`'Year End Summary'!CellReference`

If you change the sheet name after you've written formulas referencing it, no problem! Because they're in the same workbook, the formulas automatically update to show the current sheet name.

REFERENCING OTHER WORKBOOKS

If you need to reference data in another workbook (called a *source* workbook), you can write formulas with external workbook references. For example, employees in another city send you their Excel files with operational data for their division. The following steps show how to reference two additional workbooks. To write a formula using external workbook references, follow these steps:

1. Open the workbooks you want to use, including the source workbook(s) and the workbook in which you want to write the formula, and begin building your formula.

2. Click in one of the source workbooks, and click the cell you want to include in the formula.

   The cell reference is added to the formula, but because it's located in another workbook, the reference includes the workbook name and worksheet name, too (see Figure 24.20). The workbook name is in square brackets and is followed by the worksheet name; the worksheet name is separated from the cell reference by an exclamation point, like this:

   `[WorkbookName]WorksheetName!CellReference`

3. Continue building your formula by typing operators and clicking in other workbooks to enter the cell references.

4. Complete the formula by pressing Enter.

The formula in Figure 24.20 calculates the sum of the cells in the two source workbooks. All three workbooks are now linked by the formula.

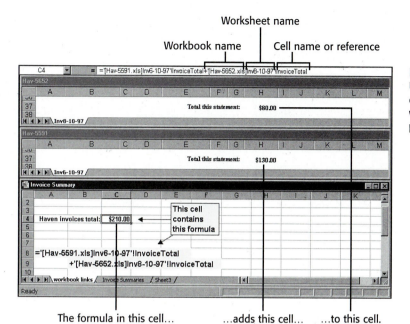

Worksheet name

Workbook name

Cell name or reference

Figure 24.20.
Using multiple windows is the easiest way to work in multiple workbooks.

The formula in this cell...   ...adds this cell...   ...to this cell.

You can also enter external workbook references by typing them. The syntax for an external workbook reference is

```
[BookName.xls]SheetName!CellReference
```

If the book name or the sheet name contains spaces, enclose the entire book-and-sheet reference in single quotes, like this:

```
'[North Division.xls]Year End Summary'!CellReference
```

UPDATING VALUES IN REFERENCED WORKBOOKS

The workbook that contains the formula is called the *dependent* workbook, and the workbook that contains the data being referenced is called the *source* workbook. If the values in the source workbooks change, the formula that references them can update its results automatically.

If the source workbook is open when you open the dependent workbook, the formula is automatically updated with no questions. If the source workbook is closed when you open the dependent workbook, you'll be asked whether you want to update all linked information (as shown in Figure 24.21).

Figure 24.21.
If a workbook contains formulas that reference data in other closed workbooks, you'll be asked whether you want to update when you open the workbook.

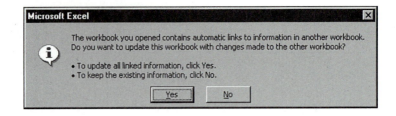

- If you click <u>Y</u>es, the formula is updated with current values in the source workbooks, even if those values have changed.

- If you click <u>N</u>o, the formula won't be updated with current values but will retain its previous values, which saves you time spent waiting for a large workbook to recalculate.

- If the source workbook has been deleted, moved, or you changed its name, you can click <u>N</u>o to retain the current values and rewrite the formula references, or click <u>Y</u>es and use the File Not Found dialog box to search for the source workbook in its new location. Searching for the file in the File Not Found dialog box is only a temporary fix; to permanently fix the link, you need to edit the links.

- To edit the links in a workbook, click <u>E</u>dit, Lin<u>k</u>s. In the Links dialog box, click <u>C</u>hange Source. In the Change Links dialog box, locate and click the name of the moved or renamed source workbook, and click OK. Click OK to close the Links dialog box, and the link is permanently fixed (until you move the source again).

Tip #345

If you don't want the formula to recalculate, ever, or be bothered by the links that need updating every time you open the workbook, you can break the link and save the current formula result as a value. Select the formula cell and copy it; then (with the cell still selected) click <u>E</u>dit, Paste <u>S</u>pecial. Click the <u>V</u>alues option, and click OK.

TROUBLESHOOTING

Formula errors are most often the result of a typo or the inclusion of a cell or range reference that doesn't contain appropriate values for the formula. Typos can include misspellings, missing or inappropriate operators, or missing parentheses. These rules may help you avoid formula errors:

- Type function names and range names in lowercase. You'll know immediately whether they're correct because Excel won't convert them to uppercase or proper case. Better yet, use the Paste Name and Paste Function dialog boxes to paste in the correct names.

- Watch out for range references that accidentally use a semicolon instead of a colon (better yet, click and drag to select cell and range references, because Excel won't enter a semicolon by mistake).

- Be sure that all nested functions, ranges, and arguments are held within a complete pair of parentheses, and that each left parenthesis has a matching right parenthesis.

- Don't type punctuation, such as dollar signs or commas, when you enter constant values into your formulas. For example, `=B7*$5,000` will result in an error message (the correct formula would be `=B7*5000`).

- If you want to break the link between worksheets or workbooks, you can find the linking formulas by searching the worksheet for an exclamation point. Click Edit, Find, type ! in the Find what box, be sure Formulas is selected in the Look in box, and then click OK. To break a link, copy the cell that contains the link; then right-click the cell and click Paste Special, click Values, and click OK.

CHAPTER 25

USING EXCEL'S BUILT-IN FUNCTIONS

In this chapter

UNDERSTANDING FUNCTIONS

Not all calculations are simple. Fortunately, with Excel's many functions, the program can handle just about anything you might throw its way.

Functions are built-in formulas that perform complex math for you. You enter the function name and any *arguments* (extra information) the function requires, and Excel performs the calculations. You saw the SUM function in action in Chapter 24, "Constructing Excel Formulas," and it's a simple, straightforward function that doesn't require any further elaboration. PMT (figures payments on a fixed-rate loan) and VLOOKUP (looks up a value in a table) are examples of common but more complex functions that I show you how to use in this chapter.

Tip #346	Many of the formulas you see in this chapter are written using cell or range names; if you need to learn more about naming cells and ranges, see Chapter 12, "Working with Named Ranges."

Excel comes with a slew of functions—some you use all the time, and some you'll be interested in only if you're an electrical engineer or nuclear physicist. Functions have specific names, such as SUM or AVERAGE or BETADIST, and function names must be spelled correctly or Excel won't recognize them; however, Excel provides dialog boxes that do the spelling for you and help you fill in the arguments each function requires.

Note	The more advanced (and less commonly used) functions are in the Analysis Toolpak. If you don't see the Analysis Toolpak add-in listed in the Add-Ins dialog box (open the Tools menu and select Add-Ins), you need to install the add-in from your Office 2000 or Excel 2000 CD-ROM.

BUILDING FUNCTIONS WITH THE PASTE FUNCTION DIALOG BOX

The easiest way to use a function in a formula is to use the Paste Function dialog box and the Formula Palette. These two integrated tools will walk you through the process of selecting and completing formulas using any of Excel's many functions.

To write a formula that uses a function, follow these steps:

1. Click the cell in which you want the results of the formula to appear.

2. On the toolbar, click the Paste Function button.

   The Paste Function dialog box appears (shown in Figure 25.1).

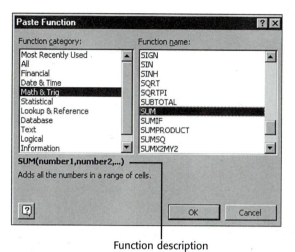

Figure 25.1.
The Paste Function dialog box briefly explains the selected function.

Function description

3. Click a category of functions, and then double-click the function you want to use from the list on the right. If you don't know which category to look in, click the All category and scroll through the alphabetical list of all functions.

The Formula Palette opens to help you complete the function (shown in Figure 25.2).

Arguments   Collapse Dialog button

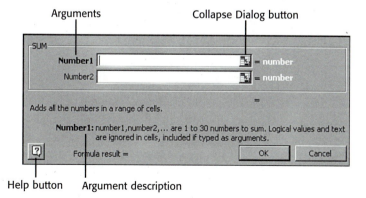

Figure 25.2.
The Formula Palette helps you fill in each argument.

Help button   Argument description

4. Click the top argument box and read the description of the argument to figure out what information is needed. (If this is the first time you've ever used the function, click the Help button for additional information about it.)

5. If the arguments call for cell references, click or drag worksheet cells to fill in arguments.

   To shrink the Formula Palette so that it doesn't cover worksheet cells you want to select, click the Collapse Dialog button at the right end of the argument and select the worksheet cells. Click the Expand Dialog button (at the right end of the collapsed argument box) to redisplay the Formula Palette and continue building your function.

6. When all the necessary arguments are added, click OK.

   The function is built and the formula is completed.

This is the basic procedure for using any function in a formula. Table 25.1 describes several of the most useful Excel functions.

Tip #348

After you type an equal sign, the Name box to the left of the Formula bar becomes a drop-down list of recently used functions. If you click a function in the list, the Formula Palette appears for that function.

Note

After you get comfortable with formulas, you can often write them faster yourself, but you must spell the function name correctly. Try this tip: Type the function name in lowercase letters. If it's spelled correctly, Excel converts it to uppercase after you press Enter. (For example, sum is converted to SUM.) If it's spelled incorrectly, Excel won't convert it to uppercase; that's your clue that it's the function name that's causing a #NAME? error.

TABLE 25.1.   USEFUL WORKSHEET FUNCTIONS

Function	Purpose
SUM	Add together the values in a selected range.
MIN	Find the minimum value in a selected range.
MAX	Find the maximum value in a selected range.
AVERAGE	Average the values in a selected range.
SUBTOTAL	Calculate the visible cells in a selected range; calculate filtered lists (11 calculations are available).
COUNT, COUNTA, and COUNTBLANK	COUNT counts the number of numeric entries in a range; COUNTA counts all the entries in a range; and COUNT-BLANK counts the blank cells in a range.
COUNTIF	Count all values that meet specific criteria.
SUMIF	Add together all values that meet specific criteria.

Function	Purpose
VLOOKUP and HLOOKUP	Find a value in a table.
INDEX and MATCH	MATCH finds the position of a value in a single row or column; INDEX finds a value in a table when the position of the value is known. Used nested in one formula, they look up values in a table, similar to VLOOKUP and HLOOKUP.
IF	Display a value that depends on criteria you set.
ISBLANK, ISNUMBER, ISTEXT	Return logical (TRUE or FALSE) information about the value in a cell (usually nested in another function).
AND, OR, NOT	Return logical (TRUE or FALSE) values depending on whether arguments meet formula criteria (usually nested in another function).
PMT	Calculate the payment for a loan.
NOW	Return the current date and time.
TODAY	Return the current date.
CONCATENATE	Join multiple cell values together in a single cell.
LEFT and RIGHT	Return a specific number of characters from the left or right end of a cell's value.
UPPER, LOWER, and PROPER	Convert text strings to all uppercase, all lowercase, or each word to proper case (lowercase with the first letter capitalized).
OFFSET	Return a range specified by its arguments.
RAND	Generates random numbers between 0 and 1 (generates a new random number each time the worksheet recalculates).
DSUM, DGET, and DAVERAGE	Some of the several D-functions, they return values from a specific table column that are based on criteria you set. DSUM returns the sum of items that meet the criteria (similar to SUMIF), DGET returns a single item, and DAVERAGE returns the average of items that meet the criteria.

WORKING WITH EXCEL'S MOST USEFUL FUNCTIONS

In this section, I show you examples of the functions in Table 25.1 (with the exception of the SUM function which you learned about in Chapter 24), with suggestions for using them in real-life worksheet situations. This short list of functions contains just a few of the hundreds of functions available in Excel. If you explore the list of functions in the Paste Function dialog box, you'll find functions that calculate sine, cosine, tangent, the actual value of pi, and functions for a lot of accounting and engineering equations, logarithms, and binomials.

If you want to use complex engineering and financial functions, you'll need to install the Analysis Toolpak. Click Tools, Add-Ins, mark the Analysis Toolpak check box, and click OK.

Tip #349

When you first write a formula, you want to test it to be sure that it's calculating properly (that is, you want to be sure you entered all the arguments correctly and the results are accurate). To test your formulas, enter *mock data* (phony numbers) in the worksheet. Use mock data that's simple: short text that's quick to type, and round numbers so that you can do the math in your head and know quickly whether the results are accurate.

→ To learn more about cell references, **see** "Using Relative, Absolute, and Mixed Cell References in Formulas," **p. 750**

→ To learn how to use the AutoSum button to quickly sum ranges, **see** "Using AutoSum to Total Columns and Rows of Data," **p. 735**

MIN

The MIN function

`MIN(number1,number2,...)`

returns the minimum, or lowest, value in a range of numbers. Of course, if your range is a single column of numbers, you can also find the smallest value by sorting or filtering the list. If your range is a large table of numbers, such as the one in Figure 25.3, the MIN function comes in handy.

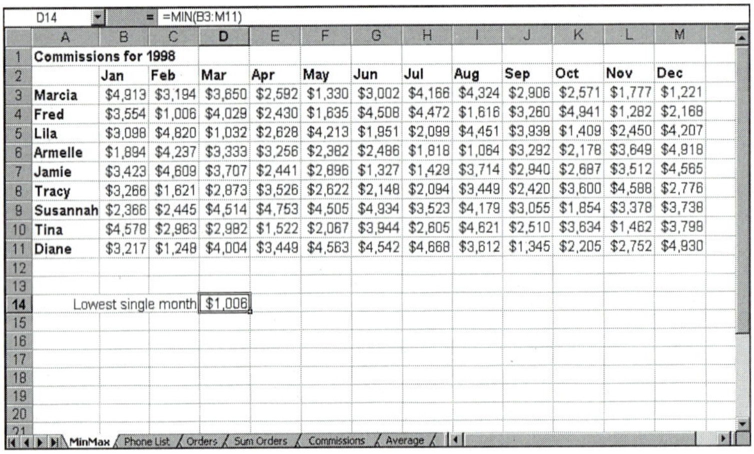

	A	B	C	D	E	F	G	H	I	J	K	L	M
1	Commissions for 1998												
2		Jan	Feb	Mar	Apr	May	Jun	Jul	Aug	Sep	Oct	Nov	Dec
3	Marcia	$4,913	$3,194	$3,650	$2,592	$1,330	$3,002	$4,166	$4,324	$2,906	$2,571	$1,777	$1,221
4	Fred	$3,554	$1,006	$4,029	$2,430	$1,635	$4,508	$4,472	$1,616	$3,260	$4,941	$1,282	$2,168
5	Lila	$3,098	$4,820	$1,032	$2,628	$4,213	$1,951	$2,099	$4,451	$3,939	$1,409	$2,450	$4,207
6	Armelle	$1,894	$4,237	$3,333	$3,256	$2,382	$2,486	$1,818	$1,064	$3,292	$2,178	$3,649	$4,918
7	Jamie	$3,423	$4,609	$3,707	$2,441	$2,896	$1,327	$1,429	$3,714	$2,940	$2,687	$3,512	$4,565
8	Tracy	$3,266	$1,621	$2,873	$3,526	$2,622	$2,148	$2,094	$3,449	$2,420	$3,600	$4,588	$2,776
9	Susannah	$2,366	$2,445	$4,514	$4,753	$4,505	$4,934	$3,523	$4,179	$3,055	$1,854	$3,378	$3,738
10	Tina	$4,578	$2,963	$2,982	$1,522	$2,067	$3,944	$2,605	$4,621	$2,510	$3,634	$1,462	$3,798
11	Diane	$3,217	$1,248	$4,004	$3,449	$4,563	$4,542	$4,668	$3,612	$1,345	$2,205	$2,752	$4,930
12													
13													
14		Lowest single month		$1,006									

Figure 25.3. The MIN function finds the minimum value in the selected table of data.

You don't need the Formula Palette for a simple function such as MIN; to write the function yourself, follow these steps:

1. Click the cell in which you want to place the formula.
2. Type `=`.
3. Type `min(`.
4. On the worksheet, drag to select the cells you want to search for a minimum value (in this example, the range B3:M11, all the numbers in the table).

5. Type).

6. Press Enter.

The minimum value in the worksheet table shown in Figure 25.3 is $1,006, and it would have taken a bit more time to find it yourself.

Tip #350

If your business requires monthly worksheets like the one in Figure 25.3, you could save yourself time by creating a template and including the MIN formula in it. When you open a copy of the template, the formula is already in place, and as you enter numbers, the formula finds the minimum value automatically.

Because the minimum value is the result of a formula, it continues to find the minimum value automatically, even if you change the numbers in the table.

MAX

The MAX function

```
MAX(number1,number2,...)
```

is the opposite of the MIN function and works exactly the same way. It finds the largest value in a selected range of cells. To write your own formula with the MAX function, you can follow the preceding procedure for the MIN function.

To write a MAX formula using the Formula Palette, follow these steps:

1. Click the cell in which you want to enter the formula.

 2. Click the Paste Function button.

The Paste Function dialog box appears (shown in Figure 25.4).

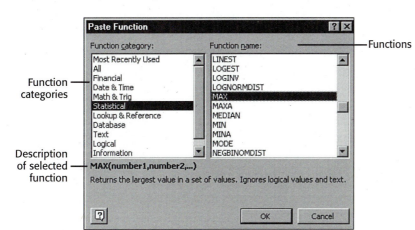

Figure 25.4.
The Paste Function dialog box helps you select and write a formula using any of Excel's many functions.

3. The MAX function falls under the Statistical category; click Statistical in the category list. (If you know the name of the function you want but don't know in which category to find it, click All.)

Tip #351

> When you use the MAX or MIN function to determine the highest or lowest value in a large table, you still have to search to find where that value is located among all those numbers. You can make it jump out visually by combining the MAX or MIN function with conditional number formatting, which formats the number in the table with any formatting you choose. To learn more about conditional formatting, see Chapter 7.

---

4. Locate the MAX function in the function name list and double-click.

5. In the Formula Palette, highlight or delete any value in the Number1 argument text box and enter the entire table range by dragging to select the cells. In this example, the table range is A2:M11, but I previously named this range Commissions, so when I select the range, Excel inserts the range name, shown in Figure 25.5.

Figure 25.5.
Using a range name such as Commissions, instead of cell references, makes the formula more understandable.

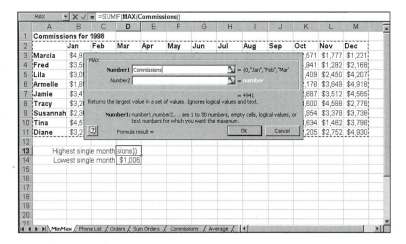

6. Click OK.

The formula is complete, and the maximum value in the range, 4941, is displayed (see Figure 25.6).

→ To learn more about conditional number formatting, **see** "Conditional Formatting," **p. 628**

AVERAGE

The AVERAGE function

```
AVERAGE(number1,number2,...)
```

is another common and easy-to-use function. It's as simple to write as the SUM, MIN, and MAX functions, so it's demonstrated here without using any dialog boxes.

The important thing to know about the AVERAGE function is that it gives a more correct result than you would get by adding cells and dividing by the number of cells. If you calculate averages by adding the cells together and then dividing by the number of cells, you'll occasionally get wrong answers because if a cell doesn't have a value in it, this method averages that cell as a zero. The AVERAGE function, however, adds the cells in the selected range and then divides the sum by the number of values; so any blank cells are left out of the calculation. (The comparison is shown in Figure 25.7. Cell comments show the formulas for each cell.)

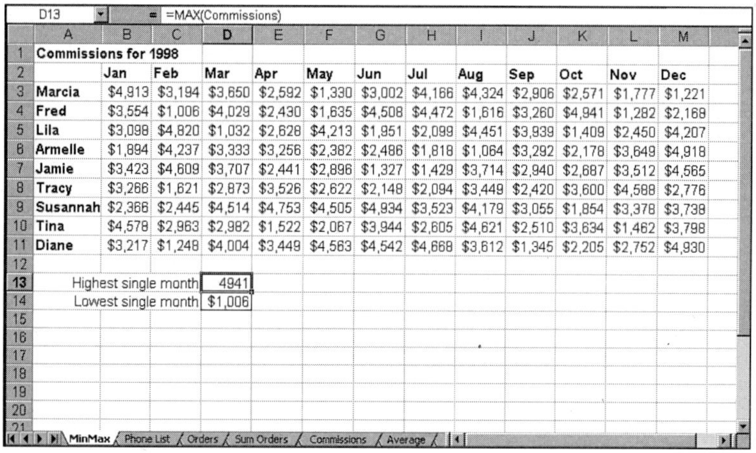

Figure 25.6.
Whether you use the Paste Function dialog box or write the formula yourself, the result is the same.

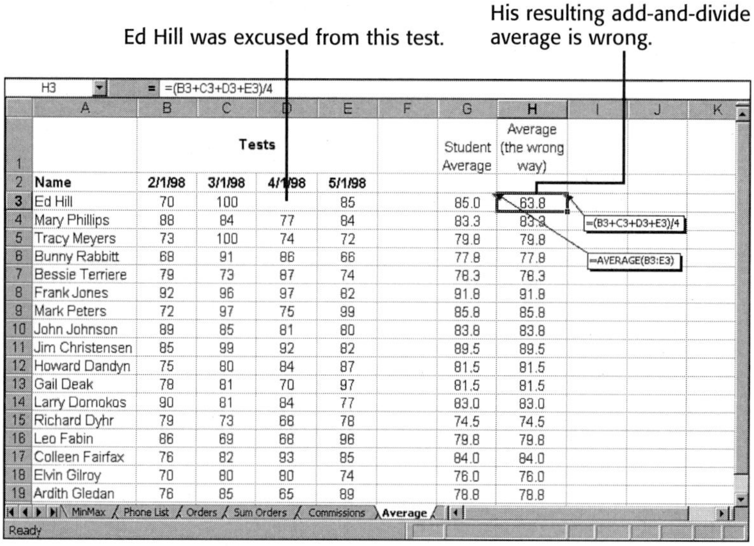

PART
VI
CH
25

Ed Hill was excused from this test.

His resulting add-and-divide average is wrong.

Figure 25.7.
Adding and dividing don't always give the correct average, but the AVERAGE function does.

To write a formula using the AVERAGE function, follow these steps:

1. Click the cell in which you want to place the formula.
2. Type =AVERAGE(.
3. In the worksheet, drag the range of cells you want to average (or type the range name).
4. Type a closing parenthesis,).
5. Press Enter.

SUBTOTAL

The SUBTOTAL function

SUBTOTAL(function_num,ref1,...)

is particularly useful for calculating values in a filtered list, because it calculates only the visible cells in a range. If you use the SUM or AVERAGE functions, the entire table is calculated rather than the records you display with a filter. If, however, you use the SUBTOTAL function, the formula calculates the filtered, displayed records only, rather than the entire table.

Note

If you use the AutoSum button to create a SUM formula when the table is filtered, a SUBTOTAL formula is created instead of a SUM formula, and the new SUBTOTAL function calculates a sum. If you want the SUBTOTAL function to calculate an average instead of a sum, you need to change the calculation argument in the SUBTOTAL function.

The SUBTOTAL function can calculate several different functions, depending on the arguments you enter. The function requires a number in the function_num argument that determines what specific calculation it performs. Table 25.2 shows the possible SUBTOTAL function_num arguments and their corresponding calculations.

TABLE 25.2. SUBTOTAL ARGUMENTS AND CALCULATIONS

This Argument	Performs This Calculation
1	AVERAGE (averages values)
2	COUNT (counts numeric values)
3	COUNTA (counts all values)
4	MAX (returns the maximum value)
5	MIN (returns the minimum value)
6	PRODUCT (multiplies the values and returns the product)
7	STDEV (calculates the standard deviation based on a sample)
8	STDEVP (calculates the standard deviation based on the whole population)
9	SUM (sums values)
10	VAR (calculates the variation based on a sample)
11	VARP (calculates the variation based on the whole population)

To illustrate how the SUBTOTAL function can be used, the next example sets up a SUBTOTAL formula that averages the filtered values in the Amount field of an expenses list. To write a SUBTOTAL formula, follow these steps:

1. Click a cell below the list in which you want to display the result of the formula, and click the Paste Function button.

Note

If you click a cell next to the list, the cell is probably hidden when you filter the list; a cell below the list is still visible during a filter.

2. In the All or Math & Trig category, double-click SUBTOTAL.

   The SUBTOTAL dialog box appears (shown in Figure 25.8).

Calculation argument   Range to calculate

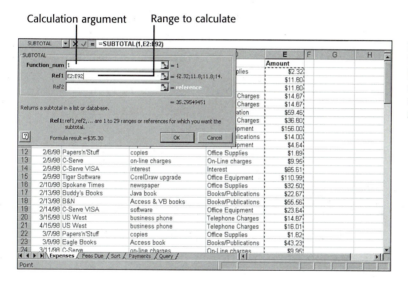

Figure 25.8.
This SUBTOTAL dialog box is set up to average whatever cells are displayed in the Amount column.

3. In the Function_num box, type 1.

   The argument 1 tells SUBTOTAL to calculate an average. For a different calculation, look up the argument in Table 25.2.

4. In the Ref1 box, enter the range to calculate (in this case, the range E2:E92, in the Amount column).

5. Click OK.

   The SUBTOTAL formula calculates an average for the Amount cells that are displayed. Figure 25.9 shows the SUBTOTAL formula and the list filtered for Sprint charges.

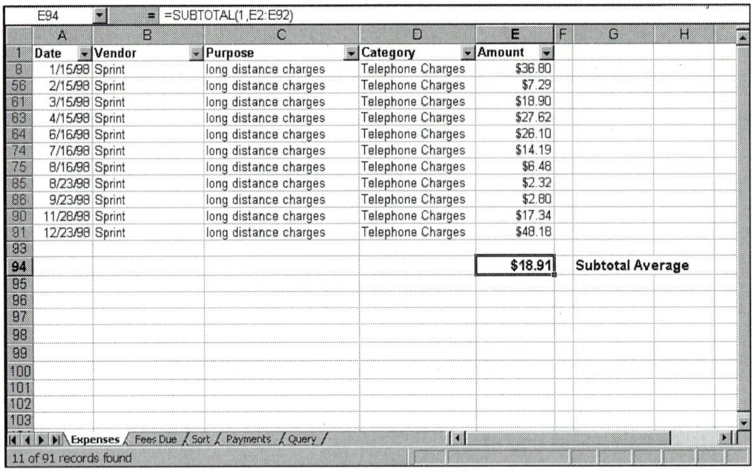

Figure 25.9.
Every time I change the filter, the SUBTOTAL formula recalculates an average for the displayed cells.

	A	B	C	D	E	F	G	H
E94		=SUBTOTAL(1,E2:E92)						
1	Date	Vendor	Purpose	Category	Amount			
8	1/15/98	Sprint	long distance charges	Telephone Charges	$36.80			
56	2/15/98	Sprint	long distance charges	Telephone Charges	$7.29			
61	3/15/98	Sprint	long distance charges	Telephone Charges	$18.90			
63	4/15/98	Sprint	long distance charges	Telephone Charges	$27.62			
64	6/16/98	Sprint	long distance charges	Telephone Charges	$26.10			
74	7/16/98	Sprint	long distance charges	Telephone Charges	$14.19			
75	8/16/98	Sprint	long distance charges	Telephone Charges	$6.48			
85	8/23/98	Sprint	long distance charges	Telephone Charges	$2.32			
86	9/23/98	Sprint	long distance charges	Telephone Charges	$2.80			
90	11/26/98	Sprint	long distance charges	Telephone Charges	$17.34			
91	12/23/98	Sprint	long distance charges	Telephone Charges	$48.18			
93								
94					$18.91	Subtotal Average		
95								
96								
97								
98								
99								
100								
101								
102								
103								

Expenses / Fees Due / Sort / Payments / Query /

11 of 91 records found

SUMIF

In the worksheet table shown in Figure 25.10, I want to know how much of the product named Celebes was sold in December.

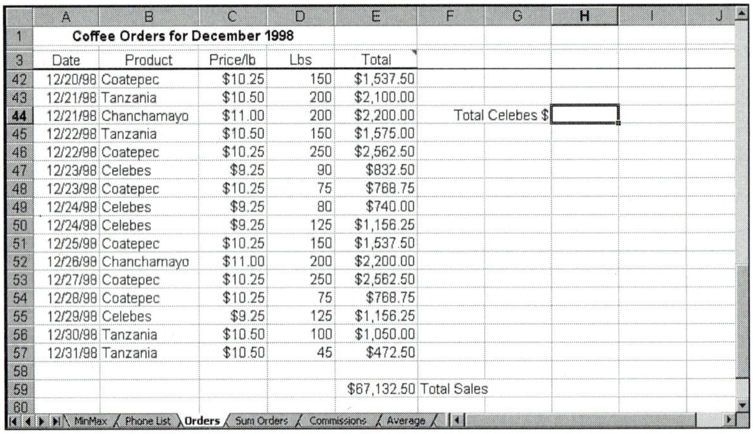

Figure 25.10.
For these December sales figures, I want to know the total revenues just for orders of Celebes coffee.

	A	B	C	D	E	F	G	H	I	J
1	Coffee Orders for December 1998									
3	Date	Product	Price/lb	Lbs	Total					
42	12/20/98	Coatepec	$10.25	150	$1,537.50					
43	12/21/98	Tanzania	$10.50	200	$2,100.00					
44	12/21/98	Chanchamayo	$11.00	200	$2,200.00	Total Celebes $				
45	12/22/98	Tanzania	$10.50	150	$1,575.00					
46	12/22/98	Coatepec	$10.25	250	$2,562.50					
47	12/23/98	Celebes	$9.25	90	$832.50					
48	12/23/98	Coatepec	$10.25	75	$768.75					
49	12/24/98	Celebes	$9.25	80	$740.00					
50	12/24/98	Celebes	$9.25	125	$1,156.25					
51	12/25/98	Coatepec	$10.25	150	$1,537.50					
52	12/26/98	Chanchamayo	$11.00	200	$2,200.00					
53	12/27/98	Coatepec	$10.25	250	$2,562.50					
54	12/28/98	Coatepec	$10.25	75	$768.75					
55	12/29/98	Celebes	$9.25	125	$1,156.25					
56	12/30/98	Tanzania	$10.50	100	$1,050.00					
57	12/31/98	Tanzania	$10.50	45	$472.50					
58										
59					$87,132.50	Total Sales				
60										

MinMax / Phone List / Orders / Sum Orders / Commissions / Average /

To find the answer, I use a SUMIF function

```
SUMIF(range,criteria,sum_range)
```

which sums values if they correspond to my criteria. (In this case, I write a formula that sums values in the Total column if they correspond to the value Celebes in the Product column.) A SUMIF formula can be written in one of two ways. You can use the Formula Palette, which is simpler and faster for single-criterion sums, or you can use the Conditional Sum Wizard, an add-in which is useful if you want to sum by two or more criteria. First, I'll show you how to write a simple SUMIF formula; then I'll show you how to use the wizard.

Note

If you want to use more than one criterion in your conditional sum formula (for example, how much Celebes and Tanzania were sold in December), using the Conditional Sum Wizard is easier.

To use the Paste Function dialog box to write a SUMIF formula, follow these steps:

1. Click the cell in which you want to place the formula; then click the Paste Function button.

2. In the All or Math & Trig category, double-click SUMIF.

   The Formula Palette for SUMIF appears (see Figure 25.11).

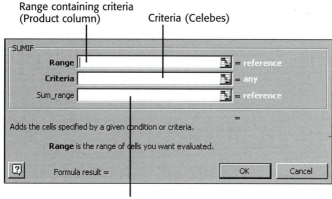

Range containing criteria
(Product column)   Criteria (Celebes)

Range containing values to sum (Total column)

Figure 25.11.
The Formula Palette makes the SUMIF function reasonably easy to write.

3. In the Range box, enter the range of cells that contains the criteria (in this example, the Product column, because it contains the Celebes criteria).

Note

My range entry, B:B, designates the entire column B as the range containing my criteria. It's important that there not be any other entries on the worksheet below this table, or the formula will calculate with those entries and get messed up. Also, the range reference B:B is a relative reference. If I wanted an absolute reference to column B, I'd type $B:$B.

You can drag the cells in column B (B3:B56), or you can enter the entire column (B:B), as I've done.

4. In the Criteria box, enter the criteria for which you want to sum values.

   - If it's a text string, as "Celebes" is, be sure to type quotation marks around it.

   - Alternatively, you can click a cell containing the entry Celebes, instead of typing the text string and quotation marks.

5. In the Sum_range box, enter the range of values you want to sum (in this example, column E, entered as the range E:E).

   Your SUMIF dialog box should look similar to the one in Figure 25.12.

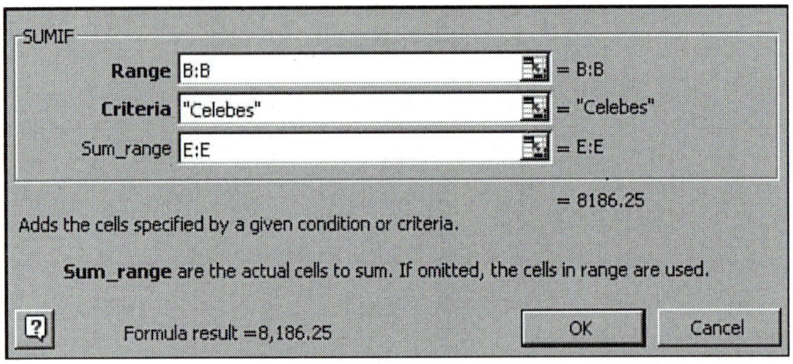

Figure 25.12.
The SUMIF dialog box, ready to sum only Celebes orders.

6. Click OK.

   The SUMIF formula is complete (as shown in Figure 25.13). To find the total for Tanzania, open the cell and edit the formula. Change "Celebes" to "Tanzania" and press Enter.

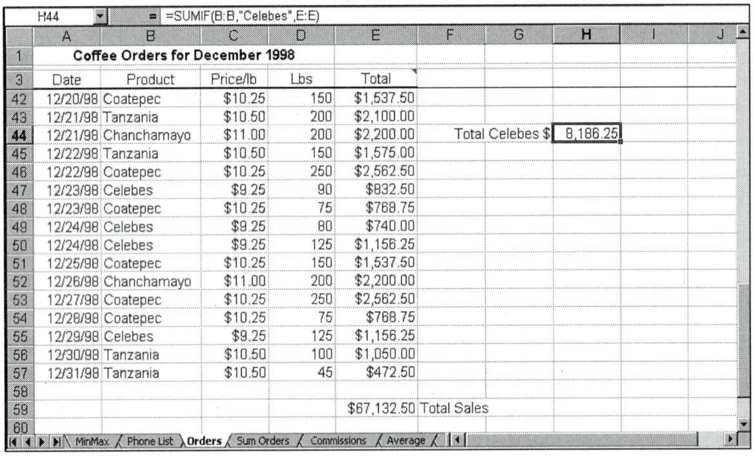

	A	B	C	D	E	F	G	H	I	J
1		Coffee Orders for December 1998								
3	Date	Product	Price/lb	Lbs	Total					
42	12/20/98	Coatepec	$10.25	150	$1,537.50					
43	12/21/98	Tanzania	$10.50	200	$2,100.00					
44	12/21/98	Chanchamayo	$11.00	200	$2,200.00	Total Celebes $		8,186.25		
45	12/22/98	Tanzania	$10.50	150	$1,575.00					
46	12/22/98	Coatepec	$10.25	250	$2,562.50					
47	12/23/98	Celebes	$9.25	90	$832.50					
48	12/23/98	Coatepec	$10.25	75	$768.75					
49	12/24/98	Celebes	$9.25	80	$740.00					
50	12/24/98	Celebes	$9.25	125	$1,156.25					
51	12/25/98	Coatepec	$10.25	150	$1,537.50					
52	12/26/98	Chanchamayo	$11.00	200	$2,200.00					
53	12/27/98	Coatepec	$10.25	250	$2,562.50					
54	12/28/98	Coatepec	$10.25	75	$768.75					
55	12/29/98	Celebes	$9.25	125	$1,156.25					
56	12/30/98	Tanzania	$10.50	100	$1,050.00					
57	12/31/98	Tanzania	$10.50	45	$472.50					
58										
59					$67,132.50	Total Sales				
60										

Figure 25.13.
Celebes orders totaled $8,186.25 in December.

The Conditional Sum Wizard is another way to get the same result, but you can switch the completed total to a different condition more easily. Instead of editing the formula, you type a different condition in the worksheet condition cell.

Note

> If you don't see the Wizard command on your Tools menu, or if you don't see the Conditional Sum command on the Wizard submenu, you need to install the Conditional Sum Wizard add-in. Click Tools, Add-Ins, mark the Conditional Sum Wizard check box, and click OK.

To use the Conditional Sum Wizard, follow these steps:

1. Click anywhere in the table.

2. On the Tools menu, point to Wizard, and click Conditional Sum.

   The Conditional Sum Wizard starts (shown in Figure 25.14). If the selected range is wrong, change it by typing new references or dragging the range on the worksheet.

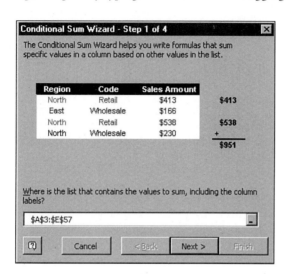

Figure 25.14.
The Conditional Sum Wizard assumes the table you clicked is the range you want.

3. Click Next.

4. In Step 2 of the wizard, choose the column you want to sum (in this case, Total) and the criteria.

   To set the criteria for this example, select Product, select =, and then select Celebes (shown in Figure 25.15).

5. Click Add Condition to add the condition to a list of conditions for the sum and then click Next.

6. In Step 3 of the wizard, you can choose to display just the sum or the sum and labels. Then click Next.

7. In the next few steps of the wizard, if you selected the "Formula and Conditional Values" option in Step 3 of the wizard, you can decide where the labels should be placed on the worksheet. In each step, click the wizard box and then click a cell on the worksheet for the criteria the wizard specifies; then click Next.

8. When you get to the last wizard step, click in the wizard box and then click the cell where you want the formula to be entered, and then click Finish.

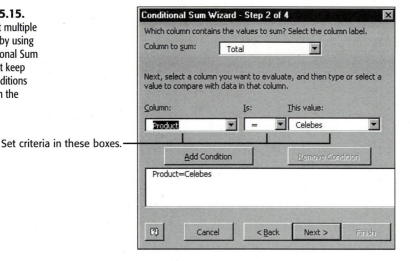

Set criteria in these boxes.

Figure 25.15.
You can set multiple conditions by using the Conditional Sum Wizard; just keep adding conditions to the list in the dialog box.

The wizard result is identical to the result of the SUMIF formula when you want to sum for a single condition (see Figure 25.16). The practical difference between a SUMIF formula you write and the SUMIF formula the wizard writes is that the wizard can use multiple conditions for selecting cells to sum, and the conditions can be changed by typing in the worksheet. For example, if you want to see the sum of Coatepec orders for December, replace **Celebes** in cell G46 with **Coatepec**.

	A	B	C	D	E	F	G	H	I	J
1	Coffee Orders for December 1998									
3	Date	Product	Price/lb	Lbs	Total					
41	12/20/98	Santo Domingo	$9.50	100	$950.00					
42	12/20/98	Coatepec	$10.25	150	$1,537.50					
43	12/21/98	Tanzania	$10.50	200	$2,100.00					
44	12/21/98	Chanchamayo	$11.00	200	$2,200.00		Total Celebes $	8,186.25		
45	12/22/98	Tanzania	$10.50	150	$1,575.00					
46	12/22/98	Coatepec	$10.25	250	$2,562.50		Celebes	$8,186.25		
47	12/23/98	Celebes	$9.25	90	$832.50					
48	12/23/98	Coatepec	$10.25	75	$768.75					
49	12/24/98	Celebes	$9.25	80	$740.00					
50	12/24/98	Celebes	$9.25	125	$1,156.25					
51	12/25/98	Coatepec	$10.25	150	$1,537.50					
52	12/26/98	Chanchamayo	$11.00	200	$2,200.00					
53	12/27/98	Coatepec	$10.25	250	$2,562.50					
54	12/28/98	Coatepec	$10.25	75	$768.75					
55	12/29/98	Celebes	$9.25	125	$1,156.25					
56	12/30/98	Tanzania	$10.50	100	$1,050.00					
57	12/31/98	Tanzania	$10.50	45	$472.50					
58										
59					$67,132.50	Total Sales				

Conditional Sum Wizard result SUMIF result

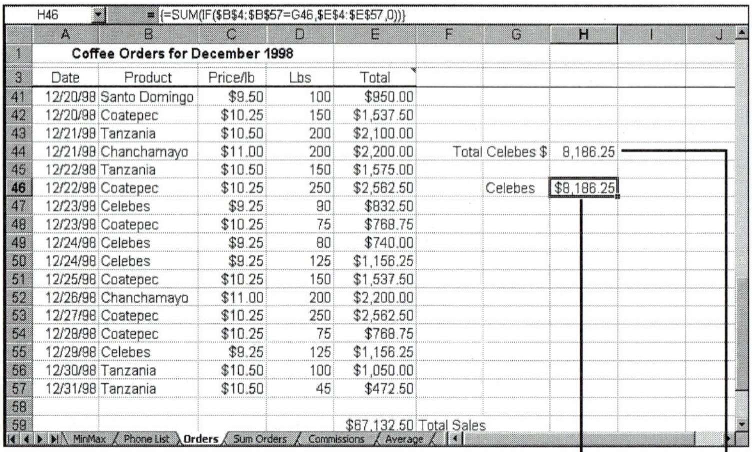

Figure 25.16.
The SUMIF function or the Conditional Sum Wizard: Use the wizard to sum for more than one category.

Tip #352

In a table like this one, you can also summarize amounts for each category by using Data Consolidation or worksheet Subtotaling.

COUNT, COUNTA, AND COUNTBLANK

These functions count the number of values in a range that meet each function's built-in criteria.

The COUNT function

```
=COUNT(range)
```

counts the number of numeric values in a range, and ignores all nonnumeric values and blank cells.

The COUNTA function

```
=COUNTA(range)
```

counts all values in a range that are not empty (if you need to count text values, use COUNTA).

The COUNTBLANK function

```
=COUNTBLANK(range)
```

counts all the cells in a range that are empty.

PART

VI

CH

25

These functions are most often used nested in other functions. The value returned by the nested function becomes the value used as another function's argument.

To write a formula using any of the COUNT functions, use the same procedures as for MIN, MAX, SUM, or AVERAGE. To use these functions nested in another function, insert the function (without its equal sign) in place of the argument whose value it supplies (you'll see an example of this in the OFFSET function, later in this chapter).

COUNTIF

The COUNTIF function

```
COUNTIF(range,criteria)
```

counts the number of values in a range that meet a specific criterion, such as "How many orders were there for Celebes coffee in December?"

Tip #353

> Another way to get a quick answer to this question is to filter the table to show only Celebes and then take a count of the orders by using AutoCalculate's COUNT function.

→ To learn about AutoCalculate, **see** "Using AutoCalculate for Quick Totals," **p. 744**
→ To learn about filters, **see** "Filtering a List," **p. 985**

The COUNTIF function works like the SUMIF function but without a wizard alternative (nor is there any need for one).

To write a COUNTIF formula, follow these steps:

1. Click the cell in which you want to place the result; then click the Paste Function button.

2. In the All or Statistical categories, double-click the COUNTIF function.

   The Formula Palette opens with the COUNTIF function arguments (shown in Figure 25.17).

Figure 25.17.
COUNTIF requires only a range to search and what to count in that range.

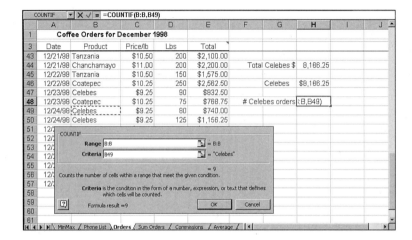

3. In the Range box, enter the range of cells to search (in this case, I've entered column B).

4. In the Criteria box, enter the criteria for counting cells (in this case, I've clicked cell B49, a Celebes entry, so the function counts all identical entries).

5. Click OK.

   The formula is complete (shown in Figure 25.18). I can find the average Celebes order by dividing the sum by the count.

Figure 25.18.
COUNTIF counts the number of Celebes orders in the list.

Number of Celebes orders in list

➔ To learn more about AutoFilter, **see** "Managing the List with AutoFilters," **p. 985**

VLOOKUP AND HLOOKUP

Sometimes you need to look up a value in another table. For example, in an invoice, you might want Excel to look up the state tax rate for the shipping address, or if you're a teacher keeping grade sheets, you might want Excel to look up the letter grades corresponding to your students' test score averages.

A good function for looking up values in another table is VLOOKUP

```
VLOOKUP(lookup_value,table_array,col_index_num,range_lookup)
```

(or its transposed equivalent, HLOOKUP)

```
HLOOKUP(lookup_value,table_array,row_index_num,range_lookup)
```

These two functions are quite similar, the only difference being that one works vertically (VLOOKUP) and the other works horizontally (HLOOKUP) in the table. I'll demonstrate VLOOKUP, and when you understand VLOOKUP, you'll be able to figure out HLOOKUP if you ever need it.

Write a VLOOKUP formula.

1. Create a lookup table that contains the values you want to look up (such as a state tax rate table or the letter grades table I use in this example).

   The table needs to be set up so that the values you are looking up (in this example, the test averages) are in the leftmost column (as shown in Figure 25.19) and sorted in ascending order. The table can have several columns in it, as long as the values you look up are on the left.

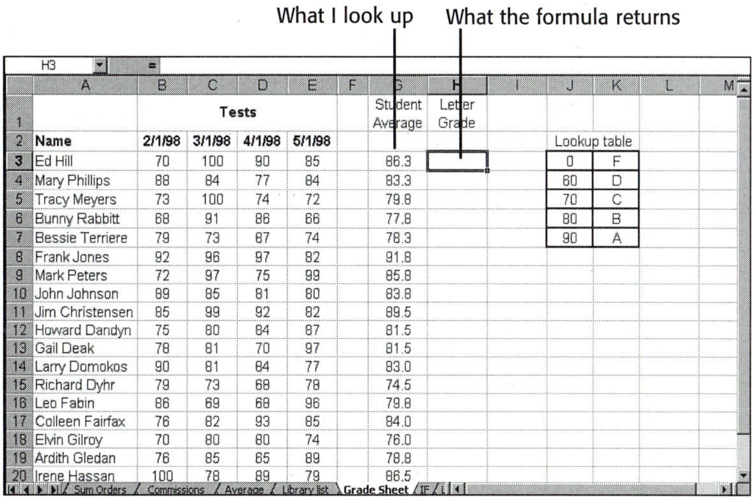

	A	B	C	D	E	F	G	H	I	J	K	L	M
1		Tests					Student Average	Letter Grade					
2	**Name**	**2/1/98**	**3/1/98**	**4/1/98**	**5/1/98**					Lookup table			
3	Ed Hill	70	100	90	85		86.3			0	F		
4	Mary Phillips	88	84	77	84		83.3			60	D		
5	Tracy Meyers	73	100	74	72		79.8			70	C		
6	Bunny Rabbitt	68	91	86	66		77.8			80	B		
7	Bessie Terriere	79	73	87	74		78.3			90	A		
8	Frank Jones	92	96	97	82		91.8						
9	Mark Peters	72	97	75	99		85.8						
10	John Johnson	89	85	81	80		83.8						
11	Jim Christensen	85	99	92	82		89.5						
12	Howard Dandyn	75	80	84	87		81.5						
13	Gail Deak	78	81	70	97		81.5						
14	Larry Domokos	90	81	84	77		83.0						
15	Richard Dyhr	79	73	68	78		74.5						
16	Leo Fabin	86	69	68	96		79.8						
17	Colleen Fairfax	76	82	93	85		84.0						
18	Elvin Gilroy	70	80	80	74		76.0						
19	Ardith Gledan	76	85	65	89		78.8						
20	Irene Hassan	100	78	89	79		86.5						

Figure 25.19. In my lookup table, the values I want to look up (test scores) are in the leftmost column (column J), and the table is sorted in ascending order.

Tip #354

> A lookup table can be on the same worksheet, another worksheet, or in another workbook. For example, if you need several identical worksheets that all look up values in the same table, you can create one table on its own worksheet and use that table in the VLOOKUP formulas on all the other worksheets.

For greater convenience, you can name the table and refer to it by name in the formula.

2. Click the cell in which you want the result to appear; then click the Paste Function button.

3. In the All or Lookup & Reference categories, double-click the VLOOKUP function. The VLOOKUP dialog box appears (shown in Figure 25.20).

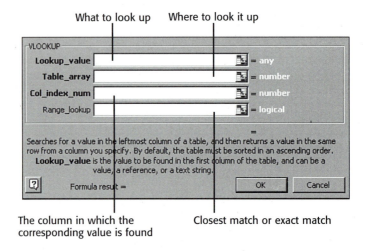

Figure 25.20.
The VLOOKUP dialog box is the easiest way to write the function until you become familiar with it.

What to look up   Where to look it up

The column in which the corresponding value is found   Closest match or exact match

4. Click the Lookup_value box and click the cell that contains the value you want to look up (in this case, the test average).

Note

> If you're using a range reference instead of a range name, be sure you change the range reference types to absolute (as I've done in Figure 25.21); otherwise, the lookup table range adjusts incorrectly in every copy of the formula. To change the reference type, open the formula, click the reference, press F4 to cycle through types, and press Enter to finish the formula. Better yet, name the lookup range—then if the range is moved for any reason, the formulas can still find it.

5. Click the Table_array box and drag to select the lookup table (or enter the range name if you named the table).

6. In the Col_index_num box, type the number of the lookup table column in which Excel is to find a corresponding value. Think of the table columns as numbered left to right,

starting with 1. In this example, the corresponding values (the letter grades) are in Column 2 of the lookup table.

7. In the Range_lookup box, decide whether you want to find the closest match or an exact match. For the closest match (which is appropriate in this case), leave the box empty. For an exact match (for example, in an unsorted list), type **false**.

In this case, each score you look up has a closest match, but probably not an exact match. The lookup table is sorted in ascending order, and VLOOKUP looks down the column for the closest match that's less than the test score value that it looks up.

For this example, the VLOOKUP dialog box should look like the one in Figure 25.21.

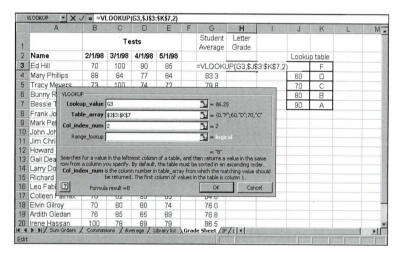

Figure 25.21.
The VLOOKUP dialog box is ready to look up a letter grade for the test score average.

PART
VI

CH
25

8. Click OK.

The VLOOKUP function looks up the score in the lookup table, finds the closest match, and returns the letter grade in the second column.

9. To copy the formula quickly down the side of the table, position the mouse pointer over the AutoFill handle and double-click.

Double-clicking the AutoFill handle works if the column is adjacent to the table, as shown in Figure 25.22. The formula is copied down the length of the table.

MATCH AND INDEX

The MATCH function

```
MATCH(lookup_value,lookup_array,match_type)
```

looks for a specific value in a single column or row, and returns a number that indicates the value's position in the list. The MATCH function is most often used in conjunction with other functions, such as INDEX (examples of the MATCH function alone and nested in an INDEX function are shown in Figure 25.23). The lookup_value argument is the value you are looking for; the lookup_array argument is the row or column being searched; and the match_type argument tells the function whether the row or column is sorted. The three match_type arguments are

- **0**—searches for an exact match; used in unsorted lists; returns #NA if an exact match isn't found.

- **1**—searches for the largest value less than or equal to the lookup_value; list must be sorted in ascending order. If omitted, the argument is assumed to be **1**.

- **-1**—searches for the smallest value greater than or equal to the lookup_value; list must be sorted in descending order.

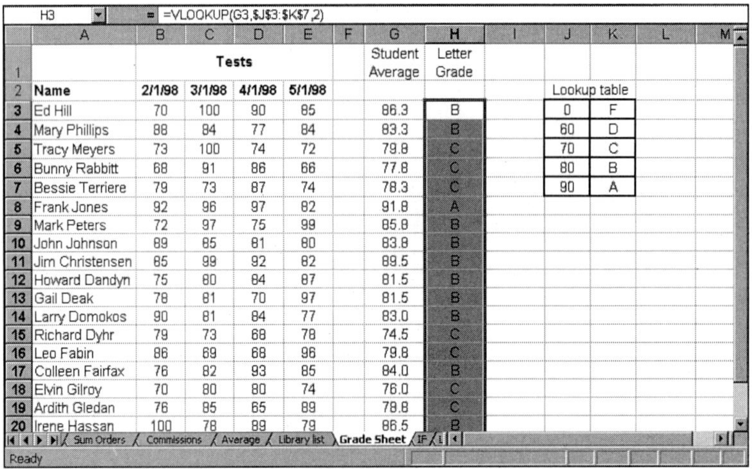

Figure 25.22.
AutoFill is the fastest way to copy the formula down the length of the table.

H3		=VLOOKUP(G3,$J$3:$K$7,2)											
	A	B	C	D	E	F	G	H	I	J	K	L	M
1				Tests			Student Average	Letter Grade					
2	Name	2/1/98	3/1/98	4/1/98	5/1/98					Lookup table			
3	Ed Hill	70	100	90	85		86.3	B		0	F		
4	Mary Phillips	88	84	77	84		83.3	B		60	D		
5	Tracy Meyers	73	100	74	72		79.8	C		70	C		
6	Bunny Rabbitt	68	91	86	66		77.8	C		80	B		
7	Bessie Terriere	79	73	87	74		78.3	C		90	A		
8	Frank Jones	92	96	97	82		91.8	A					
9	Mark Peters	72	97	75	99		85.8	B					
10	John Johnson	89	85	81	80		83.8	B					
11	Jim Christensen	85	99	92	82		89.5	B					
12	Howard Dandyn	75	80	84	87		81.5	B					
13	Gail Deak	78	81	70	97		81.5	B					
14	Larry Domokos	90	81	84	77		83.0	B					
15	Richard Dyhr	79	73	68	78		74.5	C					
16	Leo Fabin	86	69	68	96		79.8	C					
17	Colleen Fairfax	76	82	93	85		84.0	B					
18	Elvin Gilroy	70	80	80	74		76.0	C					
19	Ardith Gledan	76	85	65	89		78.8	C					
20	Irene Hassan	100	78	89	79		86.5	B					

Sum Orders / Commissions / Average / Library list / Grade Sheet / IF

Ready

The INDEX function has two syntaxes:

```
INDEX(array,row_num,column_num)
```

is the appropriate function for looking up a value in a single range, and

```
INDEX(reference,row_num,column_num,area_num)
```

is the appropriate function for looking up a value in multiple noncontiguous ranges. The INDEX function searches a range for a specific row and/or column position, and returns the value at that position. The only difference between the two forms of the INDEX function is that in the second form, INDEX can search multiple ranges, and you supply a number (1, 2, 3, and so forth) that tells the function which range to search. Examples of the INDEX function alone and with nested MATCH functions are shown in Figure 25.23.

MATCH and INDEX used together are similar to VLOOKUP, and useful for automating lookups on a worksheet. To write a nested INDEX/MATCH formula using the Formula Palette, follow these steps:

1. Set up input cells where you can type values for the MATCH functions (as shown in Figure 25.23).

2. Click in the cell where you want the result, and then click the Paste Function button.

3. In the Lookup & Reference category, double-click INDEX.

4. In the Select Arguments dialog box, select the upper row of arguments and click OK (the lower row is used for indexing multiple noncontiguous ranges). The Formula Palette opens.

5. In the Array argument, enter the name or range reference for the table where you want to look up a value.

6. Click in the Row_num argument, and then select MATCH from the drop-down function list at the left end of the Formula bar (if you don't see MATCH listed, select More Functions and then double-click MATCH in the Paste Function dialog box). The Formula Palette changes to MATCH, and the MATCH function is nested in place of the Row_num argument in the Formula bar.

7. Click in the Lookup_value argument; then click to select the row input cell in the worksheet.

8. Click in the Lookup_array argument; then type or drag to select the row where the MATCH function looks up the Lookup_value.

9. In the Match_type argument, type **0**.

10. In the Formula bar, type a comma between the two closing parentheses. The comma tells Excel you're not finished with the formula, and the Formula Palette returns to the INDEX function. The Row_num argument will be filled in with a nested MATCH function.

11. Repeat steps 6 through 9 to write a MATCH function for the column input.

12. Before you click OK, inspect the formula in the Formula bar. Excel may have entered an unnecessary comma between the two closing parentheses. Delete the comma in the Formula bar, and the Formula Palette returns to the INDEX function, fully filled in.

13. Click OK. The formula is entered, and returns the value found at the intersection of your two input cells. If you change the entries in the input cells, the INDEX/MATCH formula looks up the new values.

After you understand how the INDEX and MATCH functions work, you may find it easier to write them yourself without the Formula Palette.

Tip #355

If a formula is long and complex, write the nested functions separately, and then copy and paste the nested functions (without their equal signs) into the larger formula.

PART
VI

CH
25

Figure 25.23.
Nested together,
MATCH and INDEX
are useful for
automating lookups
in a worksheet.

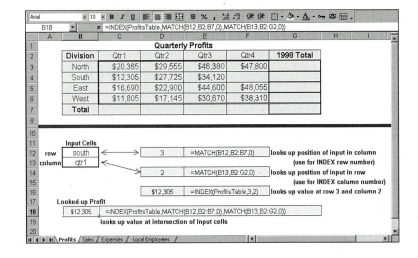

IF

The IF function

```
IF(logical_test,value_if_true,value_if_false)
```

is another way to determine a cell value based on criteria you set. The IF function works like this: IF a statement is true, THEN return this first value; OTHERWISE, return this second value. (Figure 25.24 shows several examples of the IF function in action.)

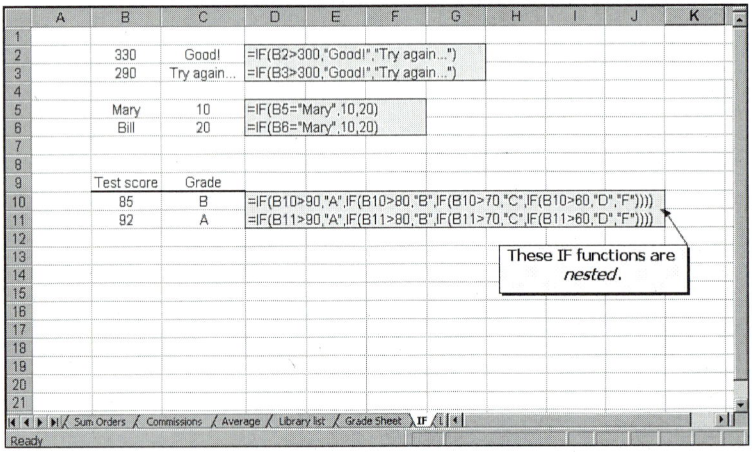

Figure 25.24.
You can use the IF
function in a lot of
creative ways. Each
formula in column C
is spelled out begin-
ning in column D.

As you can see in Figure 25.24, IF functions can be *nested* or combined within other IF functions to make them even more useful. In fact, any function can be nested in another function, up to seven levels deep, which enables you to be creative with worksheet calculations. After you get comfortable writing formulas, you'll probably find it easiest to write IF formulas manually, but you can also use the Formula Palette.

To write an IF formula using the Formula Palette, follow these steps:

1. Click the cell in which you want to place the result, and then click the Paste Function button.

2. In the Logical category, double-click the IF function. The Formula Palette appears.

3. In the Logical_test box, type the condition the function is testing for. For example, in Figure 25.23, the formula in cell C2 uses a logical operator (>) to test whether the value in B2 is greater than 300.

4. In the Value_if_true box, enter the value to return if the logical test result is true. For example, in Figure 25.23, the formula in cell C2 returns the text Good! if the value in B2 *is* greater than 300.

5. In the Value_if_false box, enter the value to return if the logical test result is false. For example, in Figure 25.23, the formula in cell C2 returns the text Try again... if the value in B2 *is not* greater than 300.

6. Click OK to complete the formula.

When you nest functions, each nested function takes the place of an argument. For example, in Figure 25.24, rows 10 and 11, each nested IF function takes the place of the value_if_false argument in the higher-level IF function, until the last and most internal IF function, which has a value_if_false argument of "F."

You'll find worksheet examples of the IF function with nested logical and information functions in the section "IF, Information, and Logical Functions."

PART

VI

CH

25

ISBLANK, ISNUMBER, AND ISTEXT

ISBLANK, ISNUMBER, and ISTEXT are called *information* functions, and are used nested in other formulas. Each of them returns either TRUE or FALSE, and the formula in which the function is nested uses that value to continue its calculation. You'll find the Information functions in the Information category in the Paste Function dialog box.

The ISBLANK function

`ISBLANK(value)`

tests whether a cell is empty, and if so, returns TRUE (if there is a value in the cell, it returns FALSE).

The ISNUMBER function

`ISNUMBER(value)`

tests whether a cell's value is numeric, and if so, returns TRUE (if the value is anything other than numeric, it returns FALSE). The value can be an entry or the result of a formula in the cell.

The ISTEXT function

`ISTEXT(value)`

tests whether a cell's value is text, and if so, returns TRUE (if the value is anything other than text, it returns FALSE). The value can be an entry or the result of a formula in the cell.

Used alone, information functions add little to a worksheet, but they're useful when nested in other functions and invaluable in programming procedures. You'll find worksheet examples of the IF function with nested information functions in the section " IF, Information, and Logical Functions."

AND, OR, AND NOT

AND, OR, and NOT are called *logical* functions, and are used nested in other formulas. Each of them returns either TRUE or FALSE, and the formula in which the function is nested uses that value to continue its calculation. You'll find the Logical functions in the Logical category in the Paste Function dialog box.

The AND function

```
AND(logical1,logical2,...)
```

tests whether *all* of its arguments are TRUE; if so, it returns the value TRUE (if any of its arguments are FALSE, it returns FALSE). In plain language, AND asks whether argument1 *and* argument2 *and* argument3 are TRUE—if so, it returns TRUE; if not, it returns FALSE.

The OR function

```
OR(logical1,logical2,...)
```

tests whether *any* of its arguments are TRUE; if so, it returns the value TRUE (if all of its arguments are FALSE, it returns FALSE). In plain language, OR asks whether argument1 *or* argument2 *or* argument3 is TRUE—if so, it returns TRUE; if not, it returns FALSE.

The NOT function

```
NOT(logical)
```

tests whether a criterion is *not* true. If the criterion is *not* true, the function returns TRUE; if the criterion *is* true, the function returns FALSE. For example, an IF formula that calculates a discounted subtotal in an invoice might read, "*If* the value in cell SubTotal is *not* greater than $500, then return the value in SubTotal; otherwise, return 90% of the value in SubTotal." This formula would look like this:

```
=IF(NOT(SubTotal>500),SubTotal,SubTotal*.9)
```

Of course, there are always other ways to write any formula, and another way might make more intuitive sense to you, but this example demonstrates how the NOT function works.

Used alone, logical functions add little to a worksheet, but they're useful when nested in other functions and invaluable in programming procedures. You'll find worksheet examples of the IF function with nested logical functions in the section "IF, Information, and Logical Functions."

IF, INFORMATION, AND LOGICAL FUNCTIONS

The Information and Logical functions become useful when they're nested in other functions, by providing the values TRUE and FALSE as arguments for those functions.

Figure 25.25 shows the ISBLANK, ISNUMBER, AND, and OR functions at work in a worksheet. Their TRUE and FALSE results are used as arguments in the formulas in Figure 25.26.

G3 =SUM(C3:F3)

Quarterly Profits

Division	Qtr1	Qtr2	Qtr3	Qtr4	1998 Total
North	$20,365	$29,555	$46,380	$47,800	$144,100
South	$12,305	$27,725	$34,120		$74,150
East	$16,690	$22,900	$44,600	$48,055	$132,245
West	$11,805	$17,145	$30,670	$38,310	$97,930
Total					

Function	Result	In plain language
=ISBLANK(F4)	TRUE	F4 is blank
=ISNUMBER(F4)	FALSE	F4 is a number
=AND(ISBLANK(E4),ISBLANK(F4))	FALSE	E4 is blank *and* F4 is blank
=OR(ISBLANK(E4),ISBLANK(F4))	TRUE	E4 is blank *or* F4 is blank

Profits / Nesting IS functions / Logical & Information / Sales / Expenses

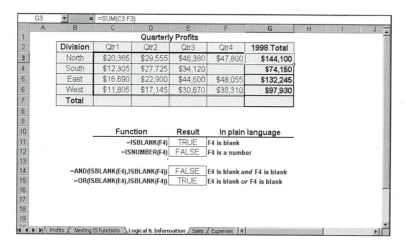

Figure 25.25. Logical and Information functions test cell values and return TRUE or FALSE.

In Figure 25.26, the Logical function ISNUMBER checks whether the cell values are numbers, and the AND function checks whether the cell values are *all* numbers. The If formula says, IF cell C3 *and* D3 *and* E3 *and* F3 are numbers, then sum their values, otherwise display the text "Data incomplete". The opposite formula, using OR and ISBLANK functions, gives the same results in this situation.

Quarterly Profits

Division	Qtr1	Qtr2	Qtr3	Qtr4	1998 Total
North	$20,365	$29,555	$46,380	$47,800	$144,100
South	$12,305	$27,725	$34,120		Data incomplete
East	$16,690	$22,900	$44,600	$48,055	$132,245
West	$11,805	$17,145	$30,670	$38,310	$97,930
Total					

These two formulas give the same results:

=IF(AND(ISNUMBER(C3),ISNUMBER(D3),ISNUMBER(E3),ISNUMBER(F3)),SUM(C3:F3),"Data incomplete")

=IF(OR(ISBLANK(C3),ISBLANK(D3),ISBLANK(E3),ISBLANK(F3)),"Data incomplete",SUM(C3:F3))

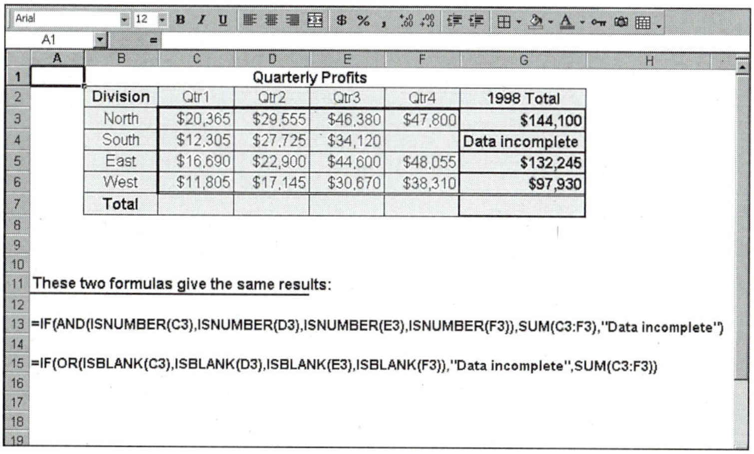

Figure 25.26. The TRUE and FALSE results from Logical and Information functions tell the IF formula what to do.

PMT

If you're shopping for a house, car, boat, or anything else that's expensive enough to require a loan, a key bit of information you want to know is the monthly payment. The PMT function

```
PMT(rate,nper,pv,fv,type)
```

figures it out for you quickly if you provide the annual interest rate, number of monthly payments, and total loan amount. (Figure 25.27 shows the PMT formula—in the Formula bar—filled out with the appropriate cells in the worksheet.) If you use cell references or named cells in the formula instead of numerical values, then you can experiment with the formula results by simply changing the input values on the worksheet.

Figure 25.27.
Use the PMT function to calculate how much of a loan you can afford.

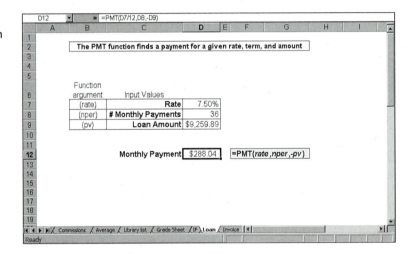

Two things to be aware of when you use the PMT function are

- Match the rate to the terms.
- The function calculates a negative payment.

If the interest rate is annual (as most are), and your payments are monthly, you need to divide the rate by 12 to make the rate and terms equivalent. It's easiest to divide the function argument by 12 (as shown in Figure 25.27), so you can enter an annual rate in the rate cell.

The PMT function calculates a negative payment for a positive amount, or a negative amount for a positive payment. To make the figures in the worksheet positive (which is what folks are accustomed to seeing), make the function's pv argument negative in the formula (as shown in Figure 25.27).

NOW AND TODAY

The NOW function returns the current date and time. The TODAY function returns the current date. They're useful to have in the corner of a worksheet so that you can always tell how current (or old) the information in a printed page is.

> **Note**
>
> If you want to see the serial number for a date, enter the date, and then format the cell as General. The serial numbers for dates begin with the number 1 on January 1, 1900; the serial number 100,000 corresponds to the date October 14, 2173. Time is determined by numbers on the right side of the decimal point in the serial number. For example, the decimal .5 corresponds to 12:00:00 noon.

> **Note**
>
> All the Office 2000 programs can format dates with four-digit years. If a two-digit year is from 00 through 29, the year is interpreted (and calculated) as 2000 through 2029. If the two-digit year is from 30 through 99, the year is interpreted (and calculated) as 1930 through 1999. If your data has dates that fall within the range 1900 through 1929, use four-digit years to keep your calculations correct.

PART
VI
CH
25

NOW and TODAY have no arguments; to write them, you type =now() or =today(), and press Enter. (Be sure you include the parentheses and don't type anything between the parentheses.) The resulting value is actually a serial number for the number of days since January 1, 1900. It's displayed as a date or time because the cell has a date or time format.

> **Tip #356**
>
> A quick trick to keep track of how long you've been working in a workbook uses a couple of NOW formulas. Pick two unused cells in the corner of the workbook, and enter the NOW formula in both of them. Copy one of the NOW formulas and paste it in place as a value. In a third cell, write a formula that subtracts the value cell from the active formula cell. Every time the workbook recalculates (or you press F9), the third cell shows the elapsed time since you wrote the formulas.

To learn more about converting formula results to values, see the later section "Converting Formula Results to Values." To learn more about formatting numbers, see Chapter 20, "Modifying Numbers and Dates."

LEFT AND RIGHT

Text functions such as LEFT and RIGHT

LEFT(text,num_chars)

RIGHT(text,num_chars)

seem rather pointless unless you have a real-life use for them; then, they're quite useful. The LEFT and RIGHT functions work similarly, except that LEFT forms a text string and RIGHT extracts the rightmost characters.

The list in Figure 25.28 is a stock list for a bookstore. The bookstore's owner wants to add a column of author codes that begin with the first three letters of the author's last name.

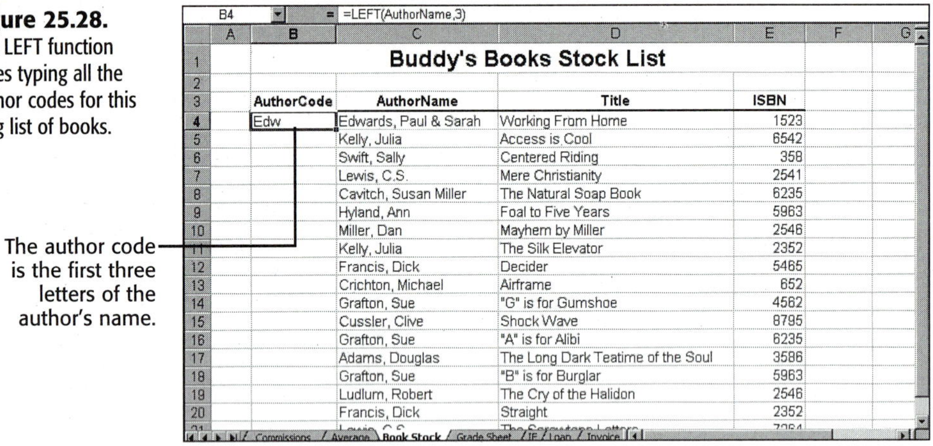

Figure 25.28.
The LEFT function saves typing all the author codes for this long list of books.

The author code is the first three letters of the author's name.

At this point, the LEFT function saves a lot of redundant typing.

To write a formula by using the LEFT function, follow these steps:

1. Click the cell where you want the result of the function (in this case, the book's author code) to appear.

> **Note**
> Remember, typing a function name in lowercase letters is a good way to catch spelling errors. If the function name is spelled correctly, Excel converts it to uppercase when you complete the formula.

2. Type =left(.
3. Click the cell containing the value from which you want to extract characters (in this case, the AuthorName cell next to the formula).
4. Type a comma (,), and then type the number of characters you want to extract (in this case, 3, for the leftmost three characters).
5. Type) and press Enter.

   The formula is complete, and it extracts the three leftmost characters in the AuthorName cell next to it.

6. Use AutoFill to copy the formula down the length of the list.

   As you can see in Figure 25.29, this saves a lot of typing.

Tip #357

To combine the extracted letters in the Author Code column with the numbers in the ISBN column (an industry code which specifically identifies each book), combine the text function with a concatenate function. In Figure 25.30, enter this formula in cell B4 and AutoFill it down the column: =LEFT(C4,3)&E4. (See the "Concatenate" section later in this chapter to learn more.)

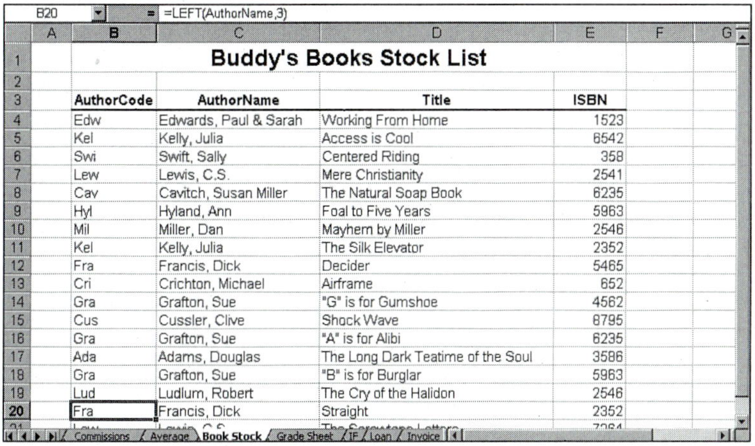

Figure 25.29.
After the formula is written using relative references, AutoFill copies the formula down the length of the table.

PART
VI
CH
25

The LEFT and RIGHT functions are also useful for creating an invoice numbering system, like the one in my invoice in Figure 25.30.

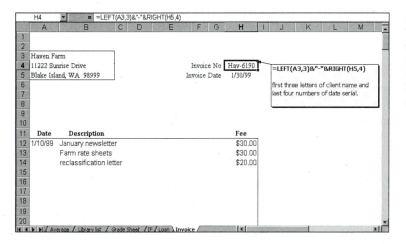

Figure 25.30.
The text functions work with the date serial number to help me create unique invoice numbers for good recordkeeping.

To create this unique numbering system for my invoices, I combined the date serial number in the Date cell with the LEFT and RIGHT functions, as described in the following steps:

1. Create a Date cell (in this case, cell H5) and a Client Name cell (in this case, cell A3).

2. Click the cell in which you want to display the formula result (in this case, the labeled Invoice No cell).

3. Enter the following formula:

```
=LEFT(A3,3)&"-"&RIGHT(H5,4)
```

This formula extracts the leftmost three characters from the Client Name cell (A3), joins or *concatenates* a dash character, and then extracts the rightmost four characters from the serial number in the Date cell (H5). In the next section, you learn more about concatenation. This makes the invoice number for each invoice unique. Because I save invoices by using the invoice number as a filename, I get a clue about how ancient or recent an invoice file is when I scan a list of filenames in a My Computer window.

CONCATENATE (&)

The CONCATENATE function joins together the displayed values in two or more cells. It can also join a text string to the displayed value in a cell.

Note

> Unlike most other functions, the CONCATENATE function name can be either spelled out (CONCATENATE) or abbreviated to an ampersand (&), which is much easier.

A situation in which the CONCATENATE function comes in handy is shown in Figure 25.31. I want to join the first and last name columns into a single column of full names. I can do this slowly and inefficiently by laboriously copying and pasting every name, or I can write a single CONCATENATE formula that AutoFill copies down the length of the FullName column.

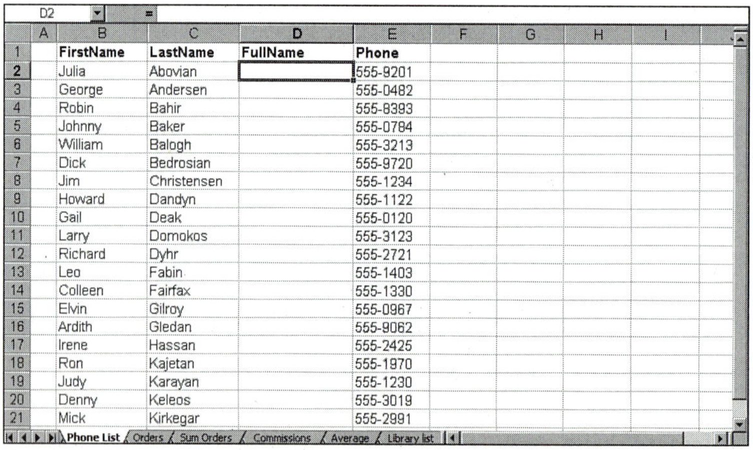

Figure 25.31.
To join each pair of names into a single cell, use the CONCATENATE function.

	FirstName	LastName	FullName	Phone
2	Julia	Abovian		555-9201
3	George	Andersen		555-0482
4	Robin	Bahir		555-8393
5	Johnny	Baker		555-0784
6	William	Balogh		555-3213
7	Dick	Bedrosian		555-9720
8	Jim	Christensen		555-1234
9	Howard	Dandyn		555-1122
10	Gail	Deak		555-0120
11	Larry	Domokos		555-3123
12	Richard	Dyhr		555-2721
13	Leo	Fabin		555-1403
14	Colleen	Fairfax		555-1330
15	Elvin	Gilroy		555-0967
16	Ardith	Gledan		555-9062
17	Irene	Hassan		555-2425
18	Ron	Kajetan		555-1970
19	Judy	Karayan		555-1230
20	Denny	Keleos		555-3019
21	Mick	Kirkegar		555-2991

To do this in your own worksheet, follow these steps:

1. Create a column in which the joined value will be displayed (in this case, the FullName column).

2. Type = and click the first cell to be joined (in this case, the FirstName cell in the same row).

3. Type &.

Note

If you later want to delete the original cells (in this case, the FirstName and LastName columns), convert the CONCATENATE formulas to values first, or you get a column full of #REF! errors because the cells to which the formulas refer are gone. To learn how to convert formula results to values, see the section "Converting Formula Results to Values" later in this chapter.

4. Insert a space between the two names by typing " " (two quote marks with a space between them).

5. Type & again.

PART

VI

CH

25

Tip #358

You can also join a text string such as Mr. to each cell value. To join, or concatenate, Mr. to the LastName values in Figure 25.31, click cell F2 and enter the formula ="Mr. "&" "&C2 (this formula joins Mr. and a space and the last name), and then use AutoFill to copy the formula down the list. (Of course, you'd have to edit the women's titles in this example, but it still saves time.)

6. Click the second cell to be joined (in this case, the LastName cell in the same row).

7. Press Enter to complete the formula.

The final formula is shown in Figure 25.32 in the Formula bar. The formula has been copied down the column.

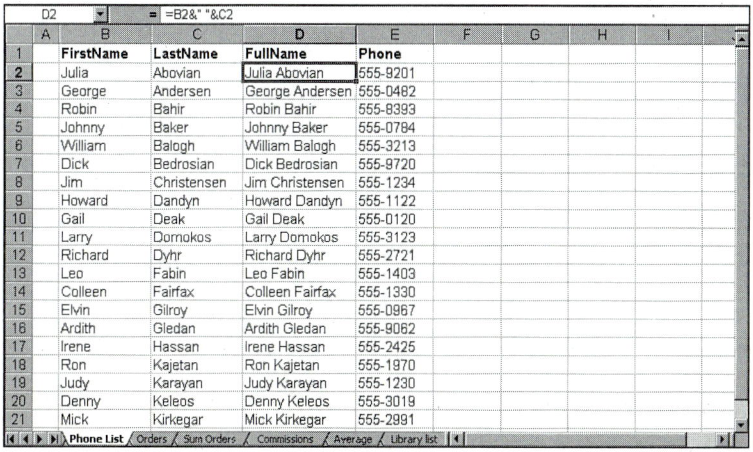

Figure 25.32.
CONCATENATE makes it easy to join cell values.

To learn how to convert formula results to values, see the later section "Converting Formula Results to Values."

Note

To separate a column of full names into separate first and last name columns, insert a new column to the right of the column you want to split. Then select the column and click Data, Text to Columns. Follow the steps in the Convert Text to Columns Wizard to split (or parse) the column into separate columns.

UPPER, LOWER, AND PROPER

The text functions UPPER, LOWER, and PROPER are useful for converting text strings in data that's been queried from external databases.

The UPPER function

```
UPPER(text)
```

converts all letter characters in a text string to uppercase (capital letters). The *text* argument can be a cell reference or a typed string of characters. Figure 25.33 shows an example of a column of names converted to uppercase by using the UPPER function.

The LOWER function

```
LOWER(text)
```

converts all letter characters in a text string to lowercase. The *text* argument can be a cell reference or a typed string of characters. Figure 25.33 shows an example of a column of names converted to lowercase by using the LOWER function.

Figure 25.33. The UPPER, LOWER, and PROPER functions change the letter case of text strings in the referenced cell.

D9 = =LOWER(C9)

	B	C	D	E
1	FullName	UPPER CASE	lower case	Proper Case
2	Julia Abovian	JULIA ABOVIAN	julia abovian	Julia Abovian
3	George Andersen	GEORGE ANDERSEN	george andersen	George Andersen
4	Robin Bahir	ROBIN BAHIR	robin bahir	Robin Bahir
5	Johnny Baker	JOHNNY BAKER	johnny baker	Johnny Baker
6	William Balogh	WILLIAM BALOGH	william balogh	William Balogh
7	Dick Bedrosian	DICK BEDROSIAN	dick bedrosian	Dick Bedrosian
8	Jim Christensen	JIM CHRISTENSEN	jim christensen	Jim Christensen
9	Howard Dandyn	HOWARD DANDYN	howard dandyn	Howard Dandyn
10	Gail Deak	GAIL DEAK	gail deak	Gail Deak
11	Larry Domokos	LARRY DOMOKOS	larry domokos	Larry Domokos
12	Richard Dyhr	RICHARD DYHR	richard dyhr	Richard Dyhr
13	Leo Fabin	LEO FABIN	leo fabin	Leo Fabin
14	Colleen Fairfax	COLLEEN FAIRFAX	colleen fairfax	Colleen Fairfax
15	Elvin Gilroy	ELVIN GILROY	elvin gilroy	Elvin Gilroy
16	Ardith Gledan	ARDITH GLEDAN	ardith gledan	Ardith Gledan
17	Irene Hassan	IRENE HASSAN	irene hassan	Irene Hassan
18	Ron Kajetan	RON KAJETAN	ron kajetan	Ron Kajetan
19	Judy Karayan	JUDY KARAYAN	judy karayan	Judy Karayan
20	Denny Keleos	DENNY KELEOS	denny keleos	Denny Keleos
21	Mick Kirkegar	MICK KIRKEGAR	mick kirkegar	Mick Kirkegar

Logical & Information / Sales / Expenses / Local Employees

The PROPER function

```
PROPER(text)
```

converts all letter characters in a text string to proper case (lowercase letters with initial capitals). The *text* argument can be a cell reference or a typed string of characters. Figure 25.33 shows an example of a column of names converted to proper case by using the PROPER function.

RAND

Some situations call for a table of random numbers to use as mock data, or a random assortment of items in a list. The RAND function generates random numbers between 0 and 1 each time the worksheet recalculates. An easy way to create a random sort order for a list is to add a column of RAND formulas to a list, and sort it repeatedly.

By nesting the RAND function in an INT formula (which returns whole numbers, or integers) and then multiplying by 10 or 100, you can create a table full of usable random numbers for mock data.

The RAND function takes no arguments. To fill a table with RAND formulas, select all the cells and type

```
=RAND()
```

Then press Ctrl+Enter to enter the formula in all the selected cells. A formula that generates random numbers between 0 and 1 to 15-digit precision is entered in the new column. Every time the worksheet recalculates, new random numbers are generated.

To freeze the random numbers, copy them and then paste them in place as values (see the section "Converting Formula Results to Values" at the end of this chapter).

To generate random numbers that are integers between 100 and 999, use this formula:

```
=int(rand()*100)
```

OFFSET

The OFFSET function

```
OFFSET(reference,rows,cols,height,width)
```

defines a range on a worksheet. The arguments in the function define the upper-left corner of the range, the number of columns in the range, and the number of rows in the range. You can use this function to write a formula that defines a *dynamic* worksheet range, a range that automatically changes its defined size to include all adjacent rows and columns. It uses nested COUNTA functions to tell the OFFSET function how many rows and columns to include in the range. Because it's a somewhat long and complex formula, you can save yourself time by *naming* the formula and then using the formula name in your worksheet (or as a source range for a print area, PivotTable, or chart).

To name a formula, click Insert, Name, Define, type a name in the Names in Workbook box, and type the formula in the Refers To box (as shown in Figure 25.34).

A simple OFFSET formula looks like the one I've laid out in Figure 25.34. To select the range, click in the Name box, type the name of the formula, and press Enter; or open the Edit menu, select Go To, type the name of the formula in the Reference box, and click OK.

Figure 25.34.
A simple OFFSET formula defines this worksheet range.

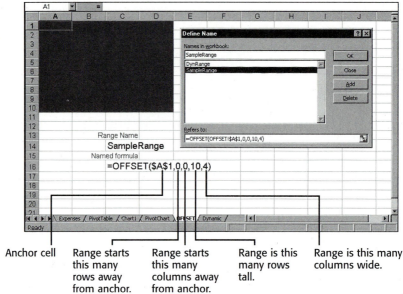

In Figure 25.34, I created a named formula, SampleRange, that defines the range I've colored in. If I filled the range with numbers, the formula =SUM(SampleRange) would sum all the numbers in the range. This named formula is a simple example of the OFFSET function. The range it defines is not *dynamic*; it's always the same size and location, just like a named range.

To make the range *dynamic*, I'll change the fourth and fifth arguments in the formula so that instead of the range being 10 rows tall and 4 columns wide, the range is as many rows tall as there are entries in column A and as many columns wide as there are entries in row 1. To do this, the formula nests a couple of COUNTA functions in the OFFSET function. (Figure 25.35 shows the dynamic range formula named DynRange.)

Note

For a dynamic range to work correctly, make sure that you have no entries in column A or row 1 other than those in the table because the dynamic range counts all the entries in the entire column and row.

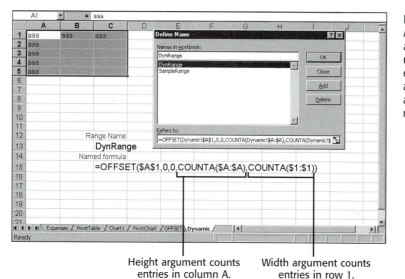

Figure 25.35.
A dynamic range always has as many rows as there are entries in column A and as many columns as there are entries in row 1.

Height argument counts entries in column A.

Width argument counts entries in row 1.

To create a dynamic range with a named formula, follow these steps:

1. On the worksheet where you want to create the named dynamic-range formula, choose Insert, Name, Define.

2. In the Define Name dialog box (shown in Figure 25.35), type a name for your dynamic-range formula under Names in Workbook.

Tip #359

When I write a long, complex formula like this, I find it easier to write it in a cell without an = because I can easily see and edit the entire formula and then copy the formula and paste it into the Define Name dialog box.

3. Type the OFFSET/COUNTA formula in the Refers To box.

4. Click OK.

Note

The formula name won't appear in either the Name box list or the Go To dialog box; however, both recognize the name, so if you type it in either the Name box or the Go To dialog box, the dynamic range is selected.

5. To test your dynamic-range formula, click the Name box (left of the Formula bar), type the formula name, and press Enter. If the formula is written correctly, the dynamic range is selected. (Be sure there are entries in column A and row 1 for the formula to count.)

If you're wondering where this is useful, you can use it to define a print area or a PivotTable source range in which the source range changes (you'll never have to redefine the source range).

→ To learn more about PivotTables, **see** "Using PivotTables and PivotCharts," **p. 1027**

To use your dynamic range in a PivotTable, type the range name in the Range box in Step 2 of the PivotTable and PivotChart Wizard. When you click the Refresh Data button, a dynamic-range PivotTable is updated with both changed data and newly added rows and columns.

To use your dynamic range in a print area, write the formula and name it Print_Area. Excel recognizes the name Print_Area (in fact, if you set a print area in a worksheet, and then choose Insert, Name, Define, you'll find the name Print_Area has been defined).

DSUM, DAVERAGE, AND DGET

The DSUM, DAVERAGE, and DGET functions are D-functions (they're located in the Database category in the Paste Function dialog box). They extract data from a table or list (called a database in the function arguments) based on criteria you set, similar to the SUMIF function but more flexible. They all work the same way and use the same arguments, but differ in what they return. In the D-functions, the argument *database* is the table or list you are extracting values from. The *field* argument is a column in the *database* table, and the *criteria* argument comes from a criteria range you set up on the worksheet.

The DSUM function

```
DSUM(database,field,criteria)
```

sums the numbers in the column (field) you specify that meet the conditions (criteria) you specify.

The DAVERAGE function

```
DAVERAGE(database,field,criteria)
```

averages the numbers in the column (field) you specify that meet the conditions (criteria) you specify.

You specify criteria by placing a criteria range on the worksheet (as shown in Figure 25.36). The criteria range can include any or all of the fields (columns) in the table, and must have labels identical to those in the table. The criteria range must have at least one row below the column labels.

The D-functions are like filters that calculate, and you can set up AND and OR criteria in your criteria range. To set up OR criteria (as shown in Figure 25.36), put the criteria on separate rows in the criteria range. To set up AND criteria (for example, to calculate records that show Tanzania in the Product field AND more than 100 in the Lbs field), put the criteria on the same row in the criteria range. When you change criteria in the criteria range, the D-functions recalculate automatically.

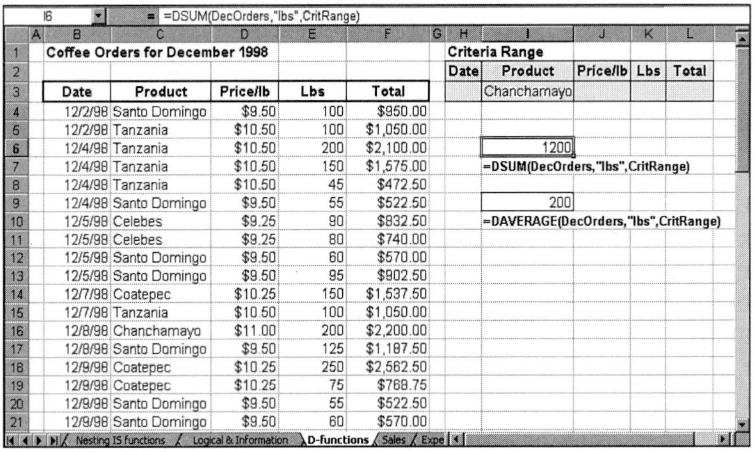

Figure 25.36.
These D-formulas calculate the sum and average of all records that have Chanchamayo OR Tanzania in the Product field.

The DGET function

`DGET(database,field,criteria)`

is just a bit different from the other D-functions. It extracts a single record that meets the conditions (criteria) you specify. If several records meet your criteria, you'll get a #NUM! error.

Figure 25.37 shows a DGET formula extracting a phone number from a list. The list, including heading labels, is named Contacts, and the criteria range is named PhoneCriteria. The DGET formula looks in the Contacts list, in the Phone field, for the record matching the criteria in the PhoneCriteria range.

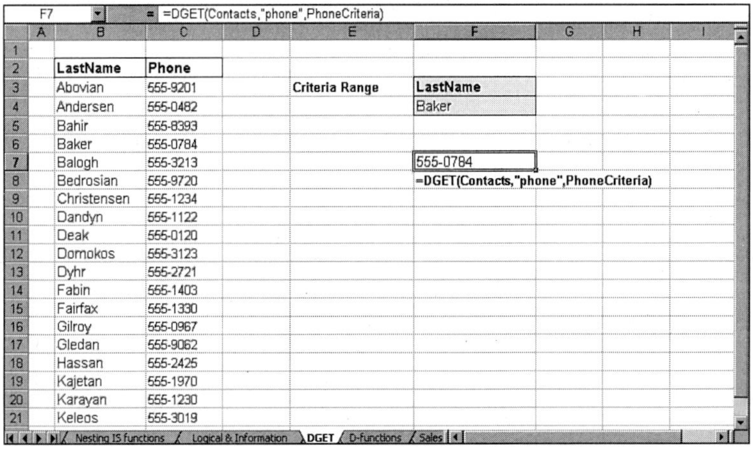

Figure 25.37.
The DGET function extracts a single record. If more than one record matches the criteria, the DGET function returns a #NUM! error.

CONVERTING FORMULA RESULTS TO VALUES

If you write a formula, such as a CONCATENATE formula, then delete the referenced cells that you no longer need on the worksheet, the formulas won't work any more. You can, however, convert the formula results to values so that you can delete the unnecessary source cells without changing the results that the formulas produced.

Another situation which calls for conversion is breaking a workbook or worksheet link. If you've written formulas that link workbooks or worksheets and you want to break the links because you don't need the links and don't want to be bothered with the update messages, you can break those links by selecting the cells with the linking formulas and converting them to values.

Yet another situation in which you might want to convert formulas to values is when you fill a table with mock data using RAND formulas, and you want the data to stop recalculating new random numbers.

Convert formula results to values.

1. Select the formulas.
2. Click the Copy button (or use your favorite copy method).
3. From the Edit menu, click Paste Special.
4. In the Paste Special dialog box (shown in Figure 25.38), click the Values option.

Figure 25.38.
Use the Paste Special dialog box to convert formulas to values; then you can delete the source cells without affecting the formula results.

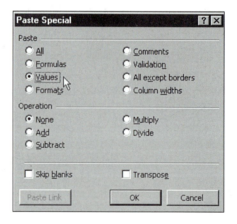

> **Note**
>
> In a worksheet like Figure 25.32, you might want to leave the last name column in place after you convert the concatenation formulas to values so that you can continue to sort the list by last name.

5. Click OK.

The formulas are replaced by their resulting values, and you can delete the source cells. If the moving border bothers you, you can remove it by pressing Esc.

TROUBLESHOOTING

If you build formulas by using the Paste Function dialog box and the Formula Palette, you'll have far fewer problems with your formulas. But when you get more comfortable with functions and start writing formulas by typing them yourself, here are some tips to help you avoid or fix problems.

- Be sure your parentheses are paired and balanced.
- Use the appropriate type of data in each function argument.
- Be sure all required arguments in the function have been filled in, and if you still don't get the results you expect, you may need to fill in optional arguments.
- Don't nest more than seven levels deep in any function.
- Make sure that any external references (to other worksheets or workbooks) are spelled correctly and in the correct syntax.
- Don't type punctuation such as dollar signs or commas in argument values—use plain numbers. (If you type a percent symbol or a caret symbol, Excel recognizes it as an arithmetic operator and uses it in the calculation.)
- See Table 24.3 in Chapter 24 for help with specific formula errors.

CHAPTER **26**

WORKING WITH NAMED RANGES

In this chapter

MANAGING NAMED RANGES

Named ranges, which represent a single cell or a range of cells, are a significant tool in your mastery of Excel. Moving from one location to another in a worksheet is made easier by range names, and finding a specific cell in a large or complex worksheet virtually requires them. But what else can they do for you? Assigning descriptive names to cells and ranges will save you a great deal of time when building formulas and functions, making it easier for you to remember what cell or range a formula refers to. As you build a worksheet, you should name significant ranges—important cells that contain information you'll want to find quickly or that you know you'll be using in formulas and functions.

If your Excel data is set up in a list or database format, for example, you could assign the name Database to the entire list, including the field names. This enables you to use the specified range name in Database functions that refer to the database. In addition, the Database range name is automatically updated to accommodate records that you add while using the data form.

As you modify or update your worksheets, you will occasionally find the need to rename, delete, or edit existing range names. Before you use range names in a formula or print a list of range names used in a worksheet, you'll want to ensure that they're up to date and relevant to your worksheet. Some simple worksheet maintenance will help you achieve that goal. Excel provides several commands and tools for helping you work with and manage the named ranges in your worksheets.

→ To learn more about Excel database design and using the data form, **see** "Using Excel As a Database Program," **p. 960**

RENAMING RANGES

Your list of named ranges will be only as static as your worksheet—as your worksheet grows and changes, be sure the named ranges remain relevant and complete. As you use your worksheet, you may find that the names you originally assigned are too short or vague (you aren't sure what they refer to) or too long (making them difficult to type into formulas).

To change the name of an existing range, follow these steps:

1. Choose Insert, Name, Define. The Define Name dialog box appears.
2. In the Names in Workbook list box, click the name you want to change. The name you select appears in the text box (see Figure 26.1).
3. Select the entire name in the Names in Workbook text box, then type the new name for the reference, and click the Add button.
4. Click the original name in the Names in Workbook list box, and then click the Delete button.
5. Click OK to close the Define Name dialog box.

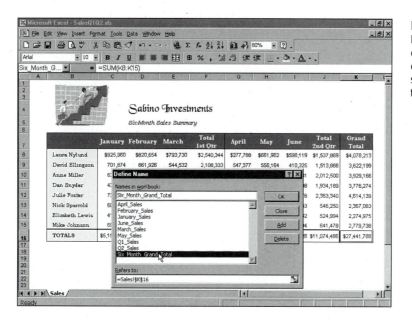

Figure 26.1.
Range names cannot contain spaces. You can use an underscore to show separations between words.

Tip #361

Keep your range names descriptive, yet short enough to remember them when you type them into formulas. Remember, you cannot use range names that are the same as cell references, such as Q4 or BL1999.

Caution

Excel enables you to give the same cell or range a new name without deleting the old one if you use the Insert, Name, Define method. When creating new ranges, ensure that the range doesn't already have another name—Excel will display only the first name assigned in the Name box. Check the Define Name dialog box to see whether you have any duplicates.

DELETING RANGE NAMES

When you copy or cut a named cell or range to the Clipboard, the range name moves with it when you paste the data. Cells that are dragged and dropped in another location take their names with them as well. If you delete named cells from one location and reenter them elsewhere, however, the names aren't transferred—they remain in their original location. In these instances, you may want to remove the old range name to avoid possible confusion.

To remove a range name that is no longer valid, follow these steps:

1. Choose Insert, Name, Define.
2. In the Names in Workbook list, click the range name you want to remove.
3. Click the Delete button; the name disappears from the list.
4. Click OK to close the Define Name dialog box.

If you delete the wrong range name, you can restore it if you click the Undo button immediately after you close the Define Name dialog box.

REDEFINING AN EXISTING RANGE NAME

What if the name is fine but the range it represents has changed? This is a common situation—imagine that your column of sales figures for the year now includes the first six months of the year, but when you named it, only the first three months of the year were entered. You need to extend the range to include an additional three months' worth of cells, but keep the name.

Figure 26.2 shows another instance of when you would want to redefine an existing range name. You've recently hired some new employees and need to redefine the range containing all of the records in the employee database. Updating the database range to include the new employees will enable you to include their records when performing salary subtotals by location, sorts, and other data analysis tasks.

Figure 26.2.
By entering the first and last cell addresses in the range, you can rebuild a named range from within the Define Name dialog box.

Name of the selected range

Current dimensions of the range

Rows that need to be added to the range

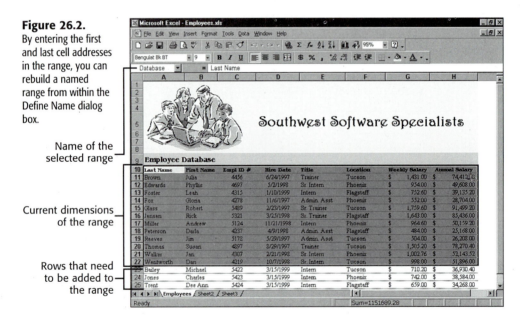

To redefine the boundaries of your named range, follow these steps:

1. Choose Insert, Name, Define.
2. Click once on the name you want to redefine.
3. In the Refers To box, edit the cell addresses (or use the Collapse Dialog button) to reflect your new range, as shown in Figure 26.3).
4. Click OK to close the dialog box and apply your changes.

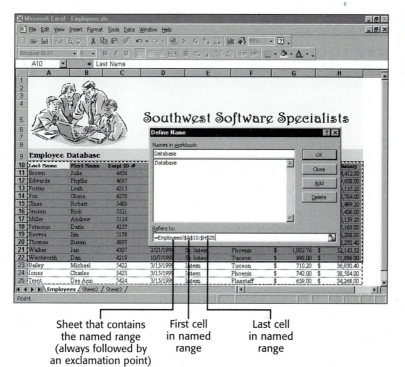

Figure 26.3.
Part of the range as it appears in the Refers To box is the name of the sheet on which the range is found.

Sheet that contains the named range (always followed by an exclamation point)

First cell in named range

Last cell in named range

Caution

Be careful when editing the range in the Refers To box—if you accidentally delete or move one of the symbols (parentheses, exclamation points, colon, dollar signs), your redefinition won't work. Excel will not warn you that you've made a mistake—your changes simply won't be applied.

If you've forgotten what a specific name in your worksheet refers to, you can click the name whose reference you want to check in the Names in Workbook list; then view the referenced cells in the Refers To box. You also could select the name from the Name box to see the range name highlighted in the worksheet.

All ranges you name in one worksheet of your workbook will be available in all sheets of that same workbook. As a result, you cannot use the same name twice in the same workbook, which is somewhat limiting—especially if you have similar information throughout your sheets.

Tip #362

Don't forget to add a sheet name followed by an exclamation point when creating single-sheet range names—it's key to Excel's interpretation of your range name as a single-sheet name.

USING RANGE NAMES IN FORMULAS

The benefits of naming ranges have been extolled throughout this chapter—navigation, editing, and explaining a worksheet's content is made easier through the use of named ranges. Probably the most significant benefit, however, is the use of named ranges in formulas. Rather than selecting a cell or range of cells (or typing their cell addresses) for use in a formula, you can select the named range from a list. This eliminates the margin for error (unless you named the range incorrectly) and makes it easier to edit a formula. The formula =(Sales_Total*Proj_Increase)*.85 can be easier to build than =(C8*M25)*.85 because you don't think of your numbers as C8 and M25—you think of them as what they are: your sales total and projected increase.

If you effectively name all the cells or ranges that you'll need to use in formulas, creating a formula can be as simple as shown in the following steps:

1. Click in the cell that will contain the formula.

2. Type an equal sign (and a function name, if applicable) to begin the formula.

3. Choose Insert, Name, Paste. The Paste Name dialog box displays.

4. Click the named range to use in your formula (see Figure 26.4) and click OK.

Figure 26.4.
The benefits of creative and relevant range names are reaped now—when you're selecting them for use in formulas.

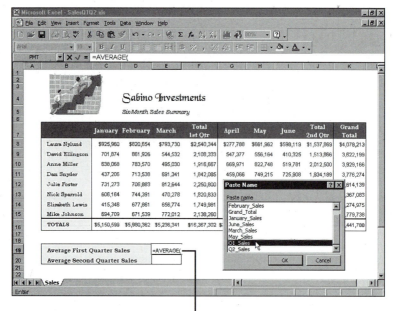

This cell will contain the formula.

5. If necessary, type the arithmetic operator.

6. Retrieve any other named ranges by repeating steps 3 and 4, as needed.

7. Complete your formula by adding any needed parentheses, and then press Enter (see Figure 26.5).

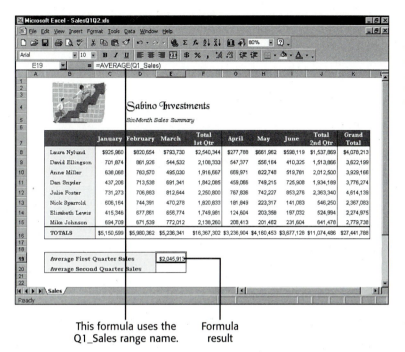

Figure 26.5.
A formula's construction is the same, whether or not named ranges are used. The names merely mask the cell addresses.

This formula uses the   Formula
Q1_Sales range name.   result

If you create your formulas by clicking in cells to add them to your formula, and if the cells have names, the names will be inserted into the formula automatically. On the other hand, if you type the cell addresses into the formula (rather than clicking the cells), names applied to those cells will not appear in the formula.

Tip #363

When using the Paste Function dialog box to create a formula, you can type range names directly into the argument boxes rather than selecting them (with the Collapse Dialog button) or typing cell addresses.

You can find out more about proper formula construction, with or without the use of named ranges, in Chapter 24, "Constructing Excel Formulas."

→ To learn more about using range names with complex formulas, **see** "Using Named Ranges in Long or Complex Formulas," **p. 1076**

PASTING NAMES INTO EXISTING FORMULAS

Using named ranges in your formulas does more than make your formula creation and editing process easier. It also makes it easier for another user (or you!) to see what your formulas actually do, as opposed to just seeing which cells they use in the calculation. When you first create a worksheet, you'll probably remember what everything in the formula represents. However, a week or a year from now, those formulas may seem a little obscure without named ranges.

If your formulas are currently based on cell addresses that you named after the formula was created, you can use the Insert, Name, Paste command to replace the cell addresses with range names. This command is also useful when correcting names that were mistyped in a formula.

Follow these steps to paste a range name in a formula:

1. Click in the cell that contains the formula.

2. In the Formula bar, select the cell address that will be replaced by a named range (see Figure 26.6).

Figure 26.6.
Edit your formula cell by cell, replacing cell addresses with named ranges.

Range to be replaced by new range name

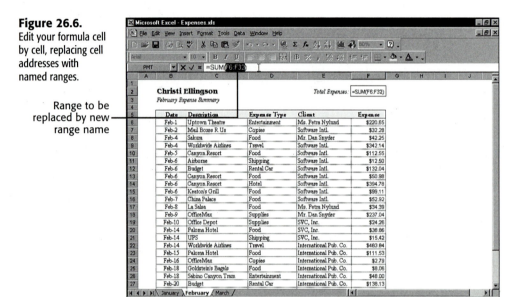

3. Choose Insert, Name, Paste. You also can type the range name if you're sure of its spelling.

4. Click the name you want to use, and click OK.

5. Press Enter to complete the formula (see Figure 26.7).

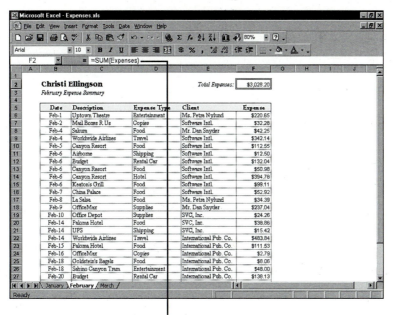

Figure 26.7.
The formula has been updated to include the new range name.

The formula now includes the "Expenses" range name.

REPLACING CELL REFERENCES WITH RANGE NAMES

If you build a formula after you've named all of your ranges throughout the worksheet, any named ranges used in the formula will appear by name in the formula. But what if you created the formula before creating or defining named ranges? Another method for updating your formulas to include range names is to use the Insert, Name, Apply command. This command provides additional options for inserting names in formulas other than the Insert, Name, Paste command that you read about in the preceding section.

To replace your cell addresses with names in an existing formula using the Apply command, follow these steps:

1. Select the formula that contains cell addresses you want to replace with named ranges.

2. Choose Insert, Name, Apply.

3. In the Apply Names dialog box, click the names you want to update in your formula (see Figure 26.8).

   You can click on as many names you want in the Apply Names list. Click the name a second time to deselect it if you make an error.

4. Click OK to apply the name(s) to your formula.

Figure 26.8.
Make use of your
named ranges by
updating formulas
built before the
names were created.

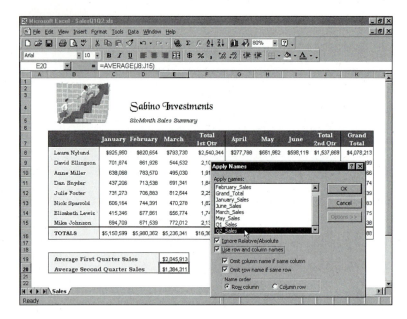

If you click the Options button in the Apply Names dialog box, the dialog box shows several ways Excel can apply your names to the selected formula. Table 26.1 lists the options for replacing cell references and explains their uses.

TABLE 26.1.   CELL REFERENCE REPLACEMENT OPTIONS

Apply Names Option	Description/Suggested Use
Ignore Relative/Absolute	If checked, this option ignores the absolute or relative reference status of the cells when inserting names. If you remove the check mark, absolute references will be replaced with an absolute reference name (including dollar signs), as will mixed reference cells.
Use Row and Column Names	If names for cells in the formula can't be found, column and row names will be used instead. The two Omit check boxes (for columns and rows) enable you to choose whether to use the column name, row name, or both.
Name Order	When applying names from column and row names, choose the order in which they're applied—Row Column or Column Row.

USING WORKSHEET LABELS IN PLACE OF RANGE NAMES IN FORMULAS

Excel provides a built-in shortcut that enables you to use existing column and row labels in worksheet formulas. This feature saves you the step of defining range names for use in formulas, as long as your worksheet is set up with labels at the top of columnar data and to the left of each row. Excel doesn't recognize these labels used in formulas by default.

You must first enable this feature by performing the following steps:

1. Choose Tools, Options; then click the Calculation tab.

2. In the Workbook options area, click the Accept Labels in Formulas check box to select it (see Figure 26.9).

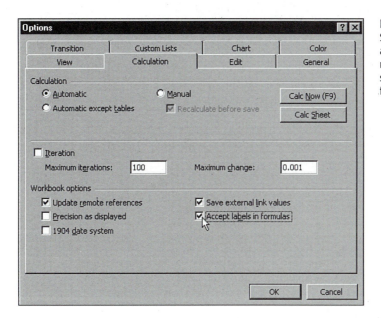

Figure 26.9.
Select this option to allow Excel to automatically accept worksheet labels in your formulas.

3. Click OK to close the Options dialog box, and accept your changes.

After you've enabled this feature by performing the preceding steps, you can use the row and column labels in formulas that refer to corresponding data. In Figure 26.10, for example, the formula =AVERAGE(January) was entered in cell C16. Although no range names have been set up in the worksheet, this formula produces the correct result because Excel is using the "January" label to determine which data to reference in the formula. After you enter the first formula, you can copy the formula across the row of cells; Excel adjusts the argument in the function to reflect data in the current column. If you copy the formula in cell C16 to cell C17, for instance, the formula in cell C17 appears as =AVERAGE(February).

Note

If you try using worksheet labels in formulas without first selecting the Accept Labels in Formulas option, your formula will result in the #NAME? error value.

For more information on the #NAME? error value, see "Avoiding the #NAME? Error Value" in the Troubleshooting section at the end of this chapter.

Figure 26.10.
If you use a work-sheet setup similar to this, you can save time by using row and column labels in formulas instead of range names.

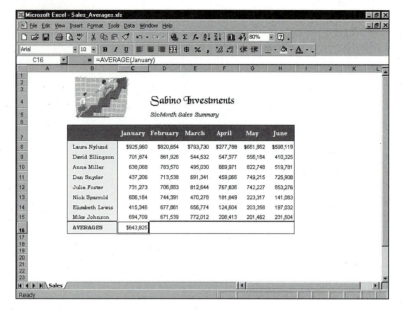

PASTING A LIST OF NAMED RANGES

You've named your ranges and used them in formulas, and they're a big part of your daily use of your worksheets. You use them to find cells, to quickly go to remote cells in your more complex worksheets. What more can named ranges do for you? If you'll be submitting the worksheet to other people in the form of a printout rather than an electronic file, the printout can be enhanced by including a list of your named ranges that shows the names and the cell addresses they represent.

In addition to helping others interpret your worksheet, appending your worksheet with a list of the named ranges used in that sheet can help you set up subsequent sheets that will be based on your current worksheet. That list of named ranges can save you from reinventing the wheel.

Tip #365

Display your formulas instead of their results in your worksheet cells, providing a map of your worksheet for use in developing a similar sheet or training someone in its use. Be sure to save this map with a different name to protect your working version of the worksheet.

To paste a list of named ranges in a worksheet, follow these steps:

1. Click in a cell at the end or bottom of the active area of your worksheet. You'll be pasting the list here, so it should be out of the way of your other data.

2. Choose Insert, Name, Paste. The Paste Name dialog box appears (see Figure 26.11).

3. Choose the Paste List button.

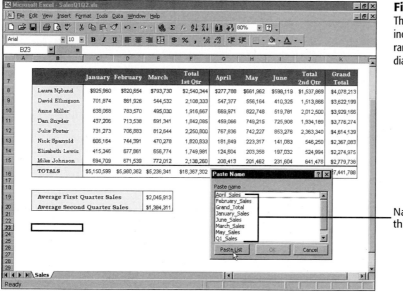

Figure 26.11.
The pasted list will include all the named ranges listed in the dialog box.

Named ranges in this workbook

The entire list of range names—for the entire workbook and any that you set up for one particular sheet—appear in a block of cells adjacent to the active cell (see Figure 26.12).

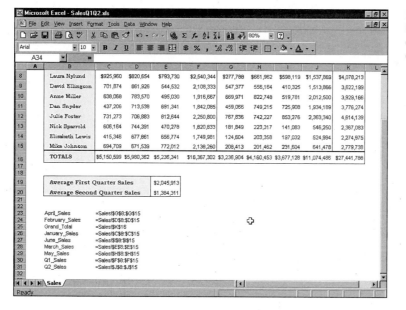

Figure 26.12.
Place the list outside of the worksheet's content.

When the worksheet is printed, you can print the list along with it, giving the recipient of the printout some idea of how you've structured the foundation of your worksheet. You also have a reference to use in building other worksheets based on this worksheet.

USING RANGE NAMES TO SPEED FORMATTING

Imagine that your workbook or worksheet contains many named ranges, and that several of those named ranges contain similar information. Perhaps you've named each of your individual months' sales totals or you've named each cell that contains summary information from your company's divisions.

These cells that contain similar information are likely to be formatted similarly as well, and Excel makes it easy to select these like ranges and apply formats to them all at once. To make a multiple-range selection, follow these steps:

1. Click the Name box drop-down list to display the list of named ranges in your worksheet.

2. Select one of the ranges you want to reformat; the named range is highlighted in the worksheet.

3. Press the Ctrl key and click the Name box drop-down list again to redisplay the list of names.

4. With the Ctrl key pressed, click another named range. This named range becomes highlighted as well.

5. Repeat steps 3 and 4 until all of the desired named ranges are highlighted onscreen.

6. Release the Ctrl key, and apply the desired formatting to the selected cells.

Tip #366   You can also use this multiple-range selection technique to select cells for editing or deletion.

TROUBLESHOOTING

AVOIDING THE #NAME? ERROR VALUE

I just typed a formula that included a range name from my worksheet, but when I pressed Enter, the label #NAME? appeared in the cell. What did I do wrong?

Ensure that you spelled the range name correctly. Although named ranges aren't case sensitive, you may have typed (or omitted) a punctuation mark that is part of the defined range name. Check the Name box to see whether the name you typed in the formula appears there. If it doesn't, it's possible that you deleted the range name or the cells that it once referenced. Create the named range again, and the #NAME? error message should disappear.

PART VII

CREATING AND MODIFYING CHARTS

CHAPTER 27

BUILDING CHARTS WITH EXCEL

In this chapter

AN OVERVIEW OF EXCEL CHARTS

Creating charts in Excel gives you the power to transform numbers into pictures that ultimately tell a story. All too often, charts are created "just because." But charts can be the basis of decision making in business; effective charts can ultimately express a business's current situation and future needs. In addition, charts presented and formatted properly can create impact. If done correctly, many charts can tell a story without any additional explanation.

Before creating a chart, ask yourself the question, "What story do I need to tell?" The answer(s) usually can help you to decide what type of chart you need, as well as how to present it effectively. Consider the following examples:

- **You want to show the sales force the results of the previous year's performance against projected performance for this year.** Use a combination clustered column to show the actual sales and a line chart to show the projected sales.

- **You need to project the number of employees needed for the next three years.** Use a stacked column chart to show the base number of employees, with the projected future numbers stacked on top of the base.

- **You need a presentation that shows current market share.** Use a pie chart and show the percentages as data labels.

CHART BASICS

Excel offers several ways to create charts. You can create a chart from the Insert menu with the Chart Wizard, from the toolbar with the Chart Wizard button, or by selecting the data and pressing F11 on your keyboard. You even can create a Microsoft Graph 2000 chart with the Insert, Object command.

You can embed your chart in the same worksheet with its source data or create the chart on a separate *chart sheet*. (By default, pressing F11 creates the new chart on a new sheet automatically.) See the later section "Choosing a Chart Location" for details on positioning charts.

Structuring Your Data for Automatic Charting

Excel makes it easy to create charts from information laid out in the proper manner. For example, structure your data in a simple grid, with titles along the left in the first column of the grid, and category information along the top in the first row. (Although category info certainly isn't a requirement, it's usually helpful in charts.)

Make sure that there are no blank rows or columns between the title and category headings and the body of the data, or Excel will plot the blank spaces. The cell where the headings cross—in the upper-left corner of the grid—should be blank.

If the data is formatted properly, as shown in later examples in this chapter, you can create an automatic chart instantly just by pressing F11. After you get the hang of the default Excel chart settings, you may find this feature to be a real time-saver.

By knowing all the chart elements and how to format your chart, you can create charts with visual impact rivaling that of drawing programs.

CHART TERMS

It's important for you to become familiar with the charting terminology. Then you can respond appropriately to the Chart Wizard prompts, and you'll know what to change when you want to edit a chart.

A basic chart offers a pictorial view of data, with the *Y-axis* (usually vertical) indicating the amount or quantity of the information in the chart, and the *X-axis* (usually horizontal) showing the categories. For example, the quarters in a year might be the category for a company or a division of a corporation.

Note

In a three-dimensional chart, Excel refers to the Y-axis as the *Z-axis*.

With multiple categories, a *legend* usually accompanies the chart. The legend provides a reference for the audience viewing the charted information, illustrating with text and a small sample of pattern or color exactly what category each pattern or color represents in the chart.

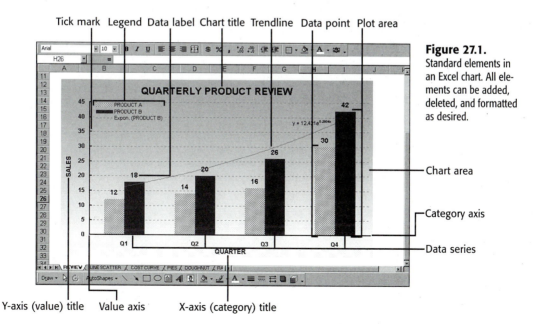

Figure 27.1.
Standard elements in an Excel chart. All elements can be added, deleted, and formatted as desired.

PART

VII

CH

27

Table 27.1 describes each basic chart element. In addition to these basic elements, certain chart types have other special features that we'll discuss later in the chapter.

TABLE 27.1. CHART ELEMENTS

Element	Description
Data point	The plotted value associated with the category.
Data labels	Text or values displayed at data points to indicate the specific value or category.
Data series	The plotted value range.
Chart title	The title associated with the chart.
Value axis	The (usually vertical) axis that shows the values by which the data series are measured.
Category axis	The (usually horizontal) axis that plots the categories of the data series.
Legend	A text-and-graphics description of the data series in a chart.
Tick marks	Separators on both the category and value axes. Tick marks act as guide markers for visual comparison.
Plot area	The area in which data series are plotted and graphed.
Chart area	The total area of the chart. All elements are included in the chart area.
X-axis (category) title	Describes the category of the plotted data.
Y-axis (value) title	Describes the value against which the data is plotted.
Z-axis (value) title	In 3D charts, displays the value of the plotted data.
Trendline	Marks the trend of the selected data series.
Series labels	Labels the category name of the data on the plotted chart.

Tip #368

Minimize clutter on the chart. Try to eliminate any information that just takes up space without really adding anything helpful for the chart's audience. If the chart's categories are obvious without the legend, for example, perhaps you can live without it. You probably don't need both data points and data labels. This chapter and the next three show alternative ways to construct charts, with creative uses of color, pattern, text, and drawing tools.

CREATING CHARTS WITH THE CHART WIZARD

The Chart Wizard enables you to create a chart, step by step, and provides options along the way to help you tailor the chart. You can always go back in and modify the chart after it's created, so don't worry if you've missed something. When creating the table that will be the source information for the chart, make sure that you've structured the data in a manner that Excel understands (see the earlier sidebar "Structuring Your Data for Automatic Charting"). For example, create the table with the title information in the left column and the category information across the top, or vice versa. Include the title and category information in the selection when creating the chart.

Setting Up the Source Table for a Chart

Don't include cells containing totals in the selection when creating the chart. Unless you're showing a graph with categories as a percent of the total, this will create a distorted view of the data.

It's also a good idea not to place data in the upper-left cell of the selection you want to plot. Excel may interpret the data below or to the left of the upper-left cell as a series and plot it.

Excel may plot row and column headings that are entered as numbers. For example, if you track sales over a period of years and enter year numbers for either the row or column headings, Excel will plot the years as numbers. One way to avoid this problem is to place an apostrophe (') in front of each heading that Excel may interpret as a number.

After creating the source table—including the title and category information—open the Chart Wizard. The wizard defaults to certain chart types if you don't make a specific chart type selection, so you essentially can click Finish in step 1 and the default chart will appear.

To create a chart with the Chart Wizard, simply follow these steps:

1. Create the table you want to chart.

2. Select the table (see Figure 27.2).

 3. Choose Chart from the Insert menu, or click the Chart Wizard button on the Standard toolbar.

4. Follow the steps in the Chart Wizard dialog boxes, filling in any details as needed. Click Finish when you're ready to create the chart.

The Chart Wizard button

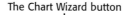

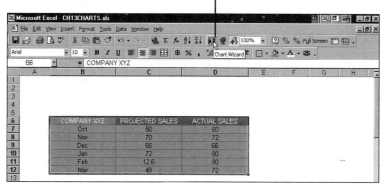

Figure 27.2.
The structure in which you create your table is important. For simplicity, it's best to create a table without empty cells.

Tip #369

Sometimes it's easier to dump a chart and start over than to fix it up. You may see immediately after clicking Finish that you should have selected more or different options in the Chart Wizard. Unfortunately, you can't undo a chart insertion. However, if the chart is embedded and still selected, you can just press the Delete key. If the chart is placed on a chart sheet, delete the new chart sheet. Select the table, click the Chart Wizard button, and then begin again.

Another option is to select the chart (if it isn't still selected), click the Chart Wizard button to open the Chart Wizard, change the settings, and then click Finish.

SELECTING THE CHART TYPE

The first step in creating a chart with the Chart Wizard is to select a chart type and sub-type. (See the later section "Excel Chart Types" for details.) To use one of the default chart types, click the Standard Types tab, scroll the Chart Type list as needed, and click the desired chart type. As shown in Figure 27.3, the sub-type list changes to provide variations of the chart type selected in the Chart Type list.

Figure 27.3.
The first step in the Chart Wizard gives you the opportunity to select the chart type and sub-type. You also can select a custom type.

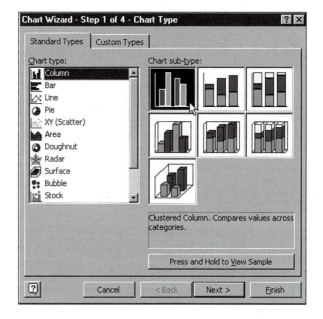

You can see a sample of the chart using the selected data by clicking and holding down the Press and Hold To View Sample button in the Chart Wizard dialog box under the Chart Sub-type list. Although this is a pretty tiny sample, it can help keep you from wasting time with a chart type that clearly won't give the audience the information you want to convey.

Clicking the Custom Types tab gives you an additional set of variations on the standard Excel charts (see Figure 27.4). For details on using custom charts, see the later section "Excel Chart Types."

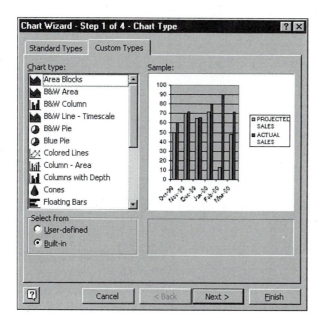

Figure 27.4.
The Custom Types tab enables you to select from predesigned custom charts or define your own by selecting User Defined in the Select From section of the dialog box.

After you make your selection, you can either go to step 2 of the Chart Wizard, or you can click Finish and Excel will select the default options for you.

SPECIFYING THE CHART SOURCE DATA

Although you'll typically select the data that you want to *plot* (display in the chart) before starting the Chart Wizard, you may decide after starting the wizard that you need to change the *data range* you selected. Or you may have forgotten to select the range before launching into chart creation. Step 2 of the Chart Wizard dialog box enables you to change the data range to be used in the chart (see Figure 27.5). The preview on the Data Range tab shows how the selected range will look in the chart. To adjust the range, change the settings shown in the fields on the Data Range tab.

PART
VII

CH
27

Figure 27.5.
Use the Data Range settings to change category orientation from rows to columns.

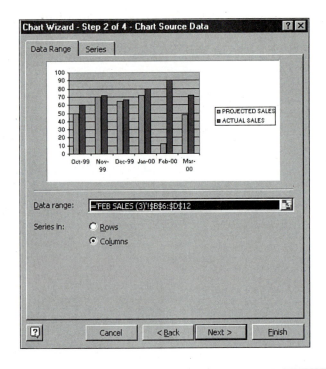

Tip #370

If you neglected to select a range before starting the Chart Wizard but left the cell pointer somewhere in the range you want, you may be surprised to see a preview of your chart in the Step 2 dialog box, with the appropriate data selected for you. If you formatted the data correctly (see the earlier section, "Chart Basics"), Excel can be pretty good at guessing exactly what you had in mind.

By default, a *data series* is one category of your table. By selecting one of the columns in the chart, you've selected a data series. You can change the *orientation* of the data from rows (the default) to columns. Figures 13.6 and 13.7, for example, show two different versions of the same chart in the preview window. In Figure 27.6, the data is plotted in rows; in Figure 27.7, the data is plotted in columns. If you change a series to plot from rows to columns, Excel changes the data from a clustered series with no spaces between the columns to individual columns. Excel usually plots the orientation of your data correctly, but if it's incorrect or not what you were expecting, you can change it in this dialog box.

If you are having problems selecting specific chart elements, see "Selecting Chart Element" in the Troubleshooting section at the end of this chapter.

On the Series tab, you can manipulate the series in a chart by either adding or removing a series of a chart (see Figure 27.8). For example, if you've selected the entire range of a table and decide you want to view one data series only (to focus the audience), you can remove the data series by selecting it and clicking the Remove button. Conversely, you can add a series to the chart by clicking the Add button, and then specify the details for the new series by using the other options on the Series tab.

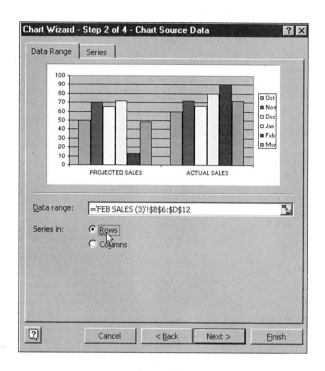

Figure 27.6.
When the Series In option is set to Rows, Excel plots each row as a data series, with each row heading appearing in the legend. The column headings appear as category labels along the X-axis of the chart.

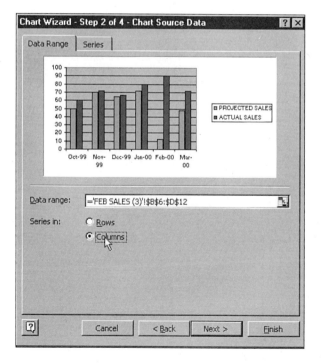

Figure 27.7.
Setting the Series In option to Columns plots each column as a data series, with each column heading appearing in the legend. Row headings now represent the categories that appear along the X-axis of the chart.

Figure 27.8.
The Series tab gives you the options of adding and removing data series. In addition, you can redefine the address from which Excel is retrieving names, values, and category labels.

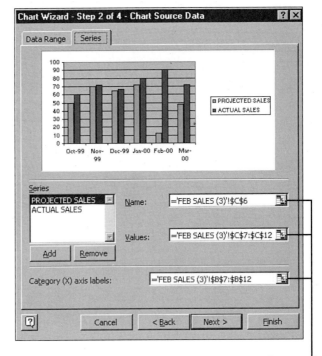

Collapse Dialog buttons

The options in this dialog box change depending on the type of chart and the series selected in the Series list box. The following list describes the available options:

- **Series, Add or Remove.** You can add a series to the chart by clicking the Add button and specifying the details. Remove a series by clicking Remove.

- **Name.** When you select a series in the Series list at the left side of the dialog box, this entry changes to show the address of the cell(s) containing the title for that series—for example, the name of a month or other time period, or the division or other category name used as a heading for that column or row.

  In Figure 27.8, for example, the series name (PROJECTED SALES) comes from the heading in cell C6 on the Feb Sales (3) sheet, as indicated in the Name box. Don't be thrown by the ='Feb Sales (3)'! designation; for dialog box options that list cell addresses, Excel lists the entire address, including the worksheet name. For example, if the worksheet name was Sales and the category title was in cell A2, the location formula would look like this: =Sales!$A$2. If the sheet name contains more than one word, Excel encloses it in single quotes (').

- **Values.** The Values box provides the address containing the values for the selected series. The values are the data used to build the columns. For some chart types, the Chart Wizard displays an X Values box and a Y Values box.

- **Category (X) Axis Labels.** This box shows the cell reference for the X-axis categories. In Figure 27.8, for example, the X-axis labels refer to the months listed in column B. As with the other options on this tab, you can select or type a different address or range for use as labels.

- **Second Category (X) Axis Labels.** Specifies the location of cell(s) containing the labels to be used for the second X-axis—for example, in stock charts or column-area custom charts.

If after completing your chart you want to add data labels to a series, see "Adding Data Labels" in the Troubleshooting section at the end of this chapter.

Tip #371

> If X-axis labels aren't located on a worksheet, you can type the labels in the Category (X) Axis Labels or Second Category (X) Axis Labels box, separating the labels with commas. Excel converts the labels to a formula, placing each label in quotes (") and surrounding all the labels with a set of braces ({ }).

- **Sizes.** In bubble charts, this option indicates the cell containing a value to indicate the size of bubble markers.

For options in which Excel lists a range, you can change the range if Excel hasn't guessed the address correctly. Select the option by clicking in the text box. Then use one of the following methods to change the range:

- Type the new range or name in the text box.
- Click outside the dialog box. Excel collapses the dialog box and enables you to select a new range.
- Click the *Collapse Dialog* button. This button squeezes the dialog box down to display just the option, as shown in Figure 27.9. Type or select the new range and then click the Collapse Dialog button again to return to the full-size dialog box.

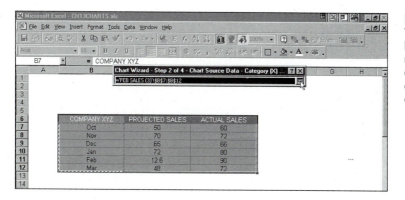

Figure 27.9.
The collapsed dialog box activates the range represented and enables you to drag over a new location on the worksheet.

PART
VII

CH

27

After you make your selections, you can either go back to step 1 of the Chart Wizard, go on to step 3, or click Finish and Excel will select the default options for you.

Tip #372	If your column or row headings tend to be long, use an abbreviated version for titles, legends, and so on in the chart. You can change these items when you finish the chart, or create the abbreviations in a separate area of the worksheet and change the settings in the Series tab of the Chart Wizard to refer to these special cells. On the other hand, if you tend to abbreviate column and row headings to squeeze as much information as possible into a worksheet, you can expand the titles and legends for use in charts.

 If you want to add a trendline to a data series, see "Adding a Trendline" in the Troubleshooting section at the end of this chapter.

CHOOSING THE CHART OPTIONS

Step 3 of the Chart Wizard dialog box enables you to tailor your chart in several ways. You can add and delete features at will; however, note that you must finish the chart before you can format the features added. (To learn about formatting parts of the chart, see Chapter 29, "Formatting Charts.") This dialog box also enables you to view the chart as you're adding the features to understand how the final chart will look with the changes you've made.

Caution	Keep the chart clean and drive home a point. Too much information on a chart detracts from the focus of the chart. All too often, people try to put everything on the chart; before long, the story they're trying to tell gets lost. Excel offers more features with each new edition of the program, but just because it's there doesn't mean you should use it. As a test, show someone the information and see whether they can grasp the point within five seconds—ultimately, that's all the attention time you'll get for your chart. For example, if you have five or six callouts on a chart with multiple colors, the reader will need several minutes just to read through the data.

CHART TITLES

The Titles tab of the Chart Wizard - Step 3 of 4 dialog box enables you to insert a chart title, name the category axis, and name the value axis, as shown in Figure 27.10. If you have a dual-axis chart, the dialog box also displays options for naming the second category (X) axis and (Y) axis. The preview in the dialog box adds the new title a few seconds after you stop typing or click another option.

For most charts, I recommend adding each of the elements listed in the Titles tab. The chart title represents the total picture of the information in the chart. In Figure 27.11, for example, an appropriate title that describes the information might be "Corporate Sales." This title clearly describes what the information represents. Keep the title short and to the point.

Tip #373	After you complete the Chart Wizard, add a subtitle to the chart if needed; for this example, "Projected Six Month" would clarify further the information contained in the chart.

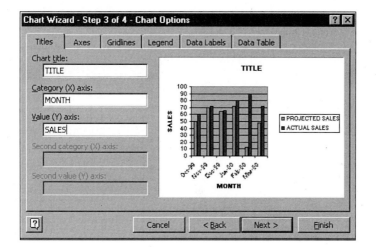

Figure 27.10.
The Titles tab enables you to add a chart title and provide titles for the chart's axes for easier reading.

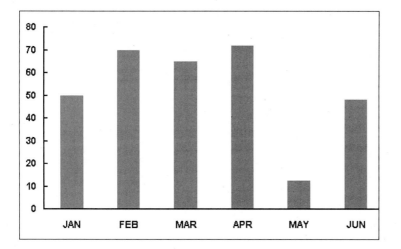

Figure 27.11.
A chart without a chart title and X- and Y-axis titles can draw blank stares.

I can't stress enough the importance of naming the value (Y) axis. All too often, I see graphs with no Y-axis title, and information that looks to be in the thousands of dollars can easily be misinterpreted as hundreds of thousands of dollars. In Figure 27.11, are you measuring sales in units or dollars? This should be part of the value (Y) title. In many cases, the category (X) axis title is self-explanatory; however, for consistency, it's good practice to name that axis as well. Without the titles, what's the story?

Figure 27.12 shows another version of the same chart, with titles added to clarify the information.

Figure 27.12.
With the proper titles in place, the chart now tells a clear story without any additional explanation.

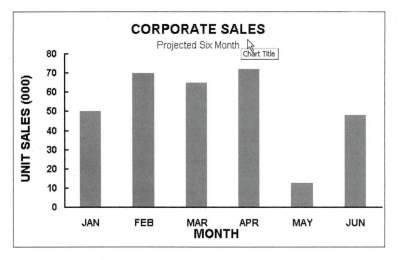

Tip #374

You can use the Display Units option in the Format Axis dialog box to specify what unit denomination you want to use, without adding a Y/Z-axis title. The advantage to using this feature is that Excel automatically changes the values on the Y/Z-axis to reflect whatever denomination you specify.

For example, if the source data contains values in millions, by default the scale values also appear in millions. However, if you specify millions for your display units, the word `Millions` will appear in the Y/Z-axis title and all scale values will be divided by one million. Thus 250,000,000 is displayed as 25 on the Y/Z-axis.

To specify a display unit, finish creating your chart. Then select the Y/Z-axis and choose Format, Selected Axis, or right-click the axis and select Format Axis from the context menu. In the Format Axis dialog box, click the Scale tab, and select the desired unit from the Display Units list box.

You may have noticed that the examples to this point use all uppercase letters for titles. Why? It's clean. The subtitle, on the other hand, should have initial caps, and you should drop the font size by two points to draw attention to the title first and subtitle second. The X- and Y-axis titles should be bold and two point sizes larger than the descriptions along the axis. (There's no absolute rule that says what's right and wrong, but experience has shown these practices to work well.)

Tip #375

Check the spelling! Misspelled titles will get far more attention than you'd like. Excel can spell-check these items for you after the chart is complete. With the chart selected, choose Tools, Spelling.

AXES

The Axes tab, as shown in Figure 27.13, automatically displays data with a time-scale format if the data is date formatted. By deselecting the Category (X) Axis option, you can remove the axis labels, as shown in Figure 27.14. If the Category (X) Axis option is selected, the selected radio button below the option indicates what the axis will display.

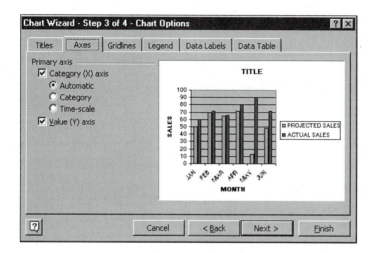

Figure 27.13.
The Axes tab enables you to show or hide values and text associated with the corresponding axis. You can also change the category axis to time-scale display.

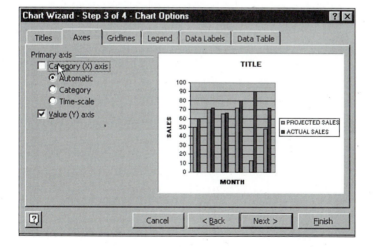

Figure 27.14.
By deselecting the Category (X) Axis option, you can hide the X-axis labels.

Figure 27.15 shows an example of time scale. When the Time-Scale option is selected on the Axes tab, Excel converts the category from a text format to a date format. (If your date text crosses over year thresholds, convert the date format to time scale.)

Caution

> If the date text isn't in a specific date format, Excel may not initially display the dates in the desired format. For example, if dates consist of month and year only (such as 5/98), Excel may initially display the dates as years only.
>
> You can change the date format after finishing the Chart Wizard. (To learn about formatting parts of the chart, see Chapter 29, "Formatting Charts.")

You also can add or delete the value (Y) axis. For example, if you're going to attach value labels to a data series, there's no need for the Y-axis.

Figure 27.15.
When the Time-Scale option is selected, Excel converts the text format to a date. If the date is formatted to show the month name in text, however, or you have data that crosses over years, you may want to convert the category to time-scale format to show the years.

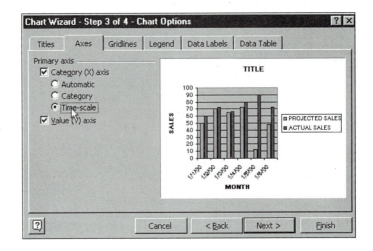

GRIDLINES

The Gridlines tab enables you to add major and minor axis gridlines (see Figure 27.16).

Figure 27.16.
The Gridlines tab enables you to apply vertical and horizontal gridlines to the plot area.

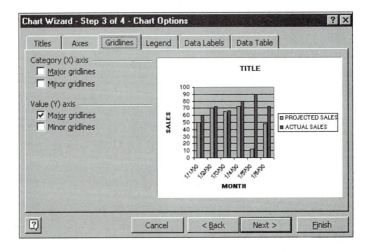

It's best to avoid gridlines to keep the chart clean. Normally, you would want to keep the major gridlines for the value (Y or Z) axis, but not apply additional gridlines. If formatted properly, however, gridlines can actually enhance and not detract from or clutter the chart.

Figure 27.17 shows major gridlines added to carry across and intersect the projected line when combining two chart types (this is a combination line chart and column chart).

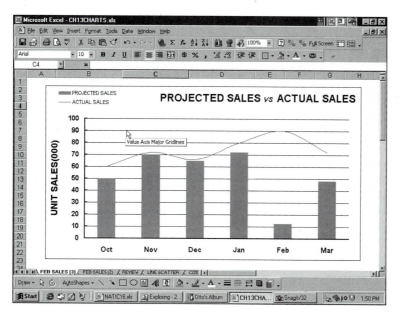

Figure 27.17.
By adding only major gridlines to a chart, and creating a lighter tone for the format of the gridlines, you can add organization without creating clutter.

In Figure 27.18, minor value gridlines and major category gridlines have been added to create a grid effect when showing incremental shifts. You also can lighten the grid effect by selecting the gridline and choosing Selected Gridlines from the Format menu. This example uses drawing tools to further illustrate the shift or decline over time on the chart.

→ To add drawing shapes to a chart, **see** "Enhancing Charts with Drawing Objects," **p. 901**

The last example, in Figure 27.19, uses white gridlines to carry across and highlight a specific month of data. Drawing tools were also added to the chart to call out the month increase.

LEGEND

The legend in a chart acts like a "map," with callouts to the different data series in a chart. If the chart consists of several categories, a legend is needed to pinpoint the pattern or color of each category. The Legend tab in the Chart Wizard dialog box enables you to apply or delete a legend (see Figure 27.20). You also can place the legend in different locations on the chart. Placement options just specify where the legend appears initially; you can move and/or resize the legend after the chart is created. For example, if you want the audience to focus on the chart itself, you may want to reduce the font size of the legend and place it in an inconspicuous place on the chart.

PART

VII

CH

27

Figure 27.18.
Minor value gridlines and major category gridlines can be used when highlighting incremental shifts where callouts are needed.

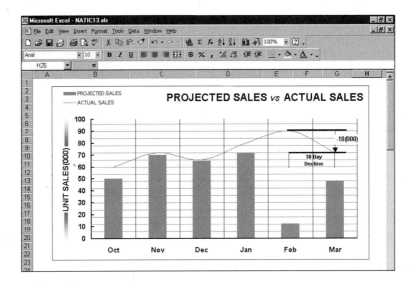

Figure 27.19.
The gridlines in this example are actually white, and a drawing tool rectangle sent to back was used to enhance the February sales increase. The chart area fill and the plot area fill are set to none.

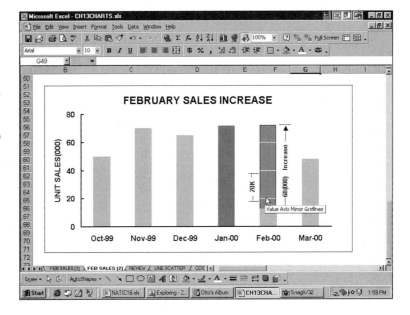

You can erase the borders of the legend to allow the legend to blend in with the rest of the chart. To erase the legend borders, select the legend after it's created on the chart (the sizing handles should be showing), choose Format, Selected Legend, and then set Border to None on the Patterns tab.

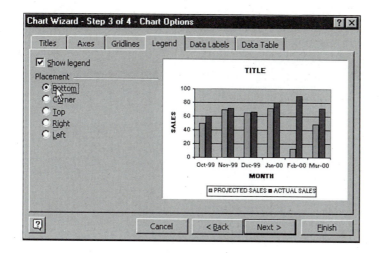

Figure 27.20.
The Legend tab enables you to delete the legend or place it in a different location on the chart.

Legends don't always have to be on the perimeter of the chart. Formatted properly, a legend can be placed within the plot area. Notice that in Figure 27.21 the legend actually sits better in the plot area than it would in any other region on the chart. This strategy also allows you to use the total landscape of the chart area.

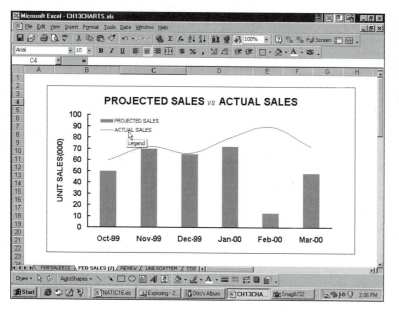

Figure 27.21.
By dragging the legend to the plot area and erasing the legend borders, you can take advantage of the total landscape of the chart area.

PART
VII

CH
27

DATA LABELS

The Data Labels tab in the Chart Wizard dialog box gives you the option of showing labels or values next to each data series in the chart (see Figure 27.22).

Figure 27.22.
The Data Labels tab enables you to attach labels or values to the data series.

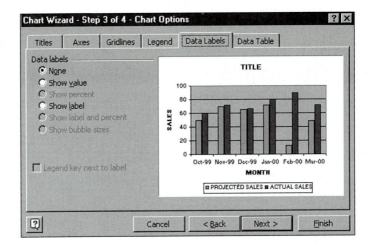

Figures 13.23 and 13.24 show examples of ways to use data labels. In Figure 27.23, notice how the data labels parallel the actual sales line. In Figure 27.24, by making the line white and adding the data labels, the months now represent the actual sales line.

Figure 27.23.
Data labels added to the actual sales line can distinguish the line or add more information.

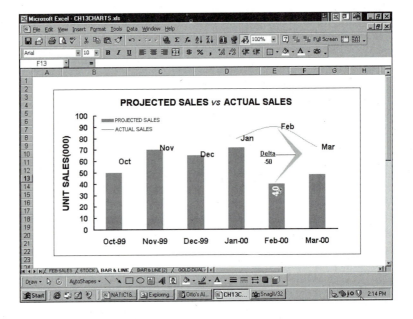

Tip #376

Data labels can even be used to create an entire chart. For example, you can completely eliminate the category axis and replace it with data labels, thus providing more landscape for callouts and text.

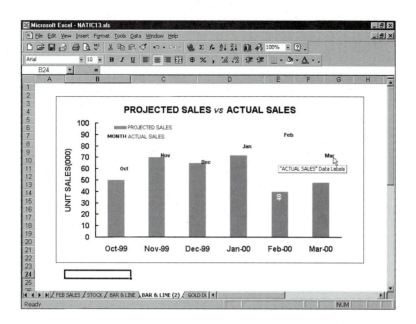

Figure 27.24.
Here the data labels take the place of the actual sales line in the chart.

DATA TABLE

The Data Table tab in the Chart Wizard dialog box enables you to place a table below the X-axis (see Figure 27.25). This feature aligns the numeric data under the corresponding data series. This is one way to display data labels without cluttering the plot area (see Figure 27.26). It's also a handy way to combine a chart and its data into a single compact form—for example, for embedding on a PowerPoint slide.

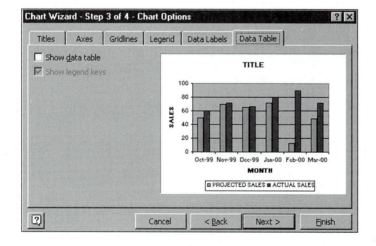

Figure 27.25.
The Data Table tab places data series values under the X-axis.

Figure 27.26.
Notice that the data table aligns directly below the categories.

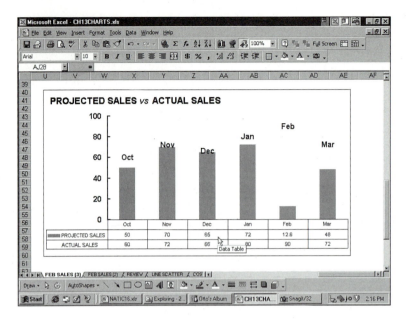

CHOOSING A CHART LOCATION

In step 4 of the Chart Wizard dialog box (the final step), you can use the following options to specify where you want to place the new chart (see Figure 27.27):

- As Object In. By default, this option embeds the chart in the worksheet containing the chart's source data (see Figure 27.28). You also can specify another sheet in the workbook by opening the drop-down list and selecting the sheet onto which you want to embed the chart.

Figure 27.27.
Specify whether you want to create the new chart as a chart sheet or embedded on a worksheet you select.

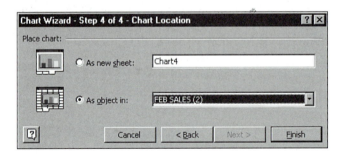

- As New Sheet. This option creates an independent *chart sheet* in the workbook (see Figure 27.29). With this option, the Chart Wizard automatically inserts a new sheet named Chart1. As with any other sheet tab, you can change this name to something more informative.

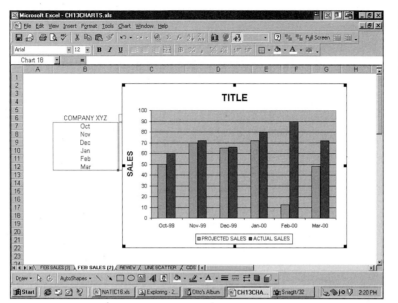

Figure 27.28.
This chart is embedded at your specified location within the worksheet.

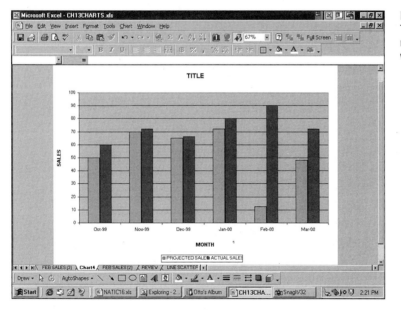

Figure 27.29.
The chart on a separate worksheet created within the workbook.

PART

VII

CH

27

Although it may seem minor, the placement of the chart on the worksheet is critical. When combining a chart with additional data or tables on worksheets, it's important to place the chart in a manner that makes sense to the reader. The following sections describe the considerations for each placement.

EMBEDDED CHARTS

There are many advantages to creating embedded charts:

- You can move and manipulate the size of the chart, as well as change locations by just cutting and pasting the chart.

- You can drag and size the chart and place it next to the source data. Changes in the data are immediately reflected in the chart, so you can experiment by watching the chart as you make changes.

- At times, you'll need to view multiple sets of chart information at once; with embedded charts, you can size and place all the info on the same sheet within a single window.

- An embedded chart enables you to easily print data and chart together.

- You can connect chart and data with drawing items and comments.

On the downside, an embedded chart is easy to delete accidentally when deleting rows or columns.

CREATING THE CHART ON A SEPARATE CHART SHEET

Creating a chart on a separate worksheet doesn't offer as many advantages as creating embedded charts:

- When displaying a chart on a chart sheet, movement of the chart is limited.

- A chart sheet isn't as convenient as an embedded chart for viewing the chart with the data. It requires extra steps to see data changes reflected in the chart.

And on the other hand:

- All the options for changing the chart's appearance are still available, except for being able to grab the chart itself and move it around the worksheet.

- A chart sheet gives the chart more room in the window so that you can view and edit it more easily.

- It makes for easy printing of the chart on its own page.

 If you want to move a chart from a sheet to an embedded chart, see "Changing a Chart Sheet to an Embedded Chart" in the Troubleshooting section at the end of this chapter.

EXCEL CHART TYPES

Excel offers a wide variety of chart types because certain data works better with some chart types than others. For example, if you're plotting sales figures over a period of months, it's better to use a clustered column chart or line chart than a radar chart. The different chart types and the data that works best with the charts can be confusing, so it's important to understand which is the best chart for the information. The Chart Wizard suggests a certain type based on the data, but that doesn't mean that the suggested type is the best type to represent the data.

At some point, you'll probably want to experiment with each chart type to see how it plots data. This section shows the types that probably will be most beneficial in real-world use. After you become familiar with the different charts and what they're best suited for, you can even combine chart types for complex charting.

The following sections explore the various chart types. Rather than showing the standard version of each chart type (you can see these in the Chart Wizard dialog boxes), I'll provide plenty of examples of how you can make your charts more interesting, readable, or effective with the special charting features available in Excel. These features are covered in detail in the next three chapters on charting (Chapters 28, "Modifying Excel Charts," 29, "Formatting Charts," and 30, "Professional Charting Techniques").

Tip #377

Excel charts can be created in two-dimensional (2D) or three-dimensional (3D) format. (Many supposedly 3D charts actually are just 2D charts with perspective added to give a 3D effect. A true 3D chart has three axes.)

If you're not sure whether you want your data portrayed in 2D or 3D, or you have already created a chart and want to experiment with a different look, then use the Chart Wizard to change the chart type or sub-type and watch the results in the preview window.

Caution

Adding a third dimension to a 2D chart makes it more visually interesting, but also can make it more difficult to understand or leave it open to interpretation. Frequent use of 3D charts also can dilute their effectiveness with your audience. Use 3D sparingly.

COLUMN CHARTS

A *column chart* has vertical bars and plots as separate points over time (noncontiguous). Column charts are good for showing value amounts and quantities over time (see Figure 27.30). I would suggest becoming familiar with this chart type—knowing it well can dramatically improve your communication of data to others.

In this example, I've separated the categories by displaying the value (Y) axis between categories on the X-axis. The method is simple: Right-click the X-axis, choose Format Axis, click the Scale tab in the Format Axis dialog box, and select the Value (Y) Axis Crosses Between Categories option. This actually is a good way to visually represent two distinct categories—by separating them with the value axis.

Another type of column chart is the *stacked column chart*. A stacked column chart would work well in the following situation: Your division must report personnel needs for the next two years to corporate headquarters, and a maximum headcount is in place that you can't exceed (see Figure 27.31). Notice that the additional personnel needed per department is called out in the dark stacked region, and a line chart is applied to show the maximum headcount per department.

Figure 27.30.
A column chart with the value axis repositioned.

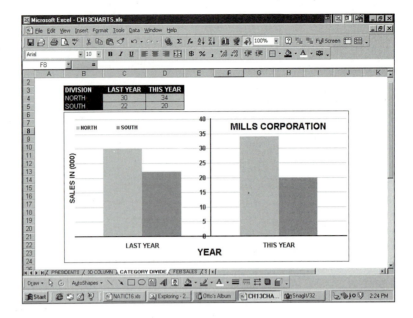

Figure 27.31.
A stacked column chart is a good way to show growth over current base. The use of drawing tools also can greatly enhance the story of the chart.

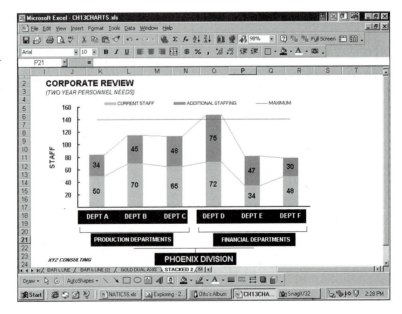

→ If you create 3D rather than 2D column charts, you have more formatting options to consider. For details, **see** "Formatting 3D Charts," **p. 910**

BAR CHARTS

A *bar chart* is similar to a column chart in that it plots bars as separate points; however, it plots the bars in a horizontal format. The bars can be placed side-by-side, as a cluster, stacked, or 3D. The bar chart was the original chart used for data display in the 1700s; the column chart came shortly after. When Excel plots a bar chart from your data, you'll notice that information normally viewed right-to-left translates to bottom-to-top.

→ To reverse a bar chart for top-to-bottom viewing, **see** "Changing the Series Order," **p. 875**

Bar charts are great tools for showing measurement, such as the percentage of a project completed (see Figure 27.32). In this example, an overlay effect helps pinpoint actual results against projected results.

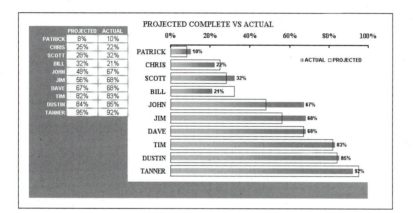

Figure 27.32.
A bar chart plots bars horizontally as separate points.

Bar charts originally were used to display events over time, and they're still great for that purpose, as shown in Figure 27.33. By adding a data label to the data series and applying no formats to the bars, the events become the chart. You can add drawing objects to further illustrate the point.

LINE CHARTS

Line charts serve well for measuring or plotting continuously over time. They make a good combination with column charts, or in multiple-line fashion. Line charts also are great for showing information that involves trends or change over time with one or two sets of data.

Tip #378

If you have more than two sets of data in a line chart, you'll need to be creative with line styles; otherwise, they start to blend together.

Figure 27.34 shows a typical line chart. Notice that the example shows the cost of a project to date against the projected cost.

Figure 27.33.
Use bar charts to illustrate events over time. By creating white borders and background on the bars and adding the data labels, the labels act as the chart.

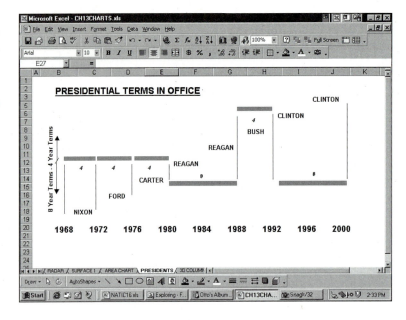

Tip #379

Think in terms of cumulative cost or production over time. If weekly values aren't combined, it may be difficult to see the visual impact of the total variance.

Figure 27.34.
Lines charts work well when showing variance analysis. Notice how drawing tools can be used as guide markers to the value (Y) axis.

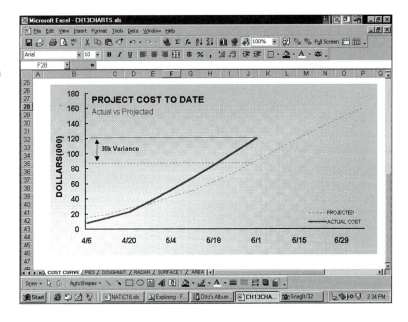

PIE CHARTS

Pie charts are used for showing a percentage of the whole. The pie chart types available are the standard 2D pie chart; exploded 2D pie; 3D pie; exploded 3D pie; *pie of a pie*, which extracts a subset of a pie slice; and *bar of a pie*, which extracts a subset of a pie and plots it as a stacked column chart.

One of the great features Excel offers with pie charts is that you can select the data point and drag it away from the whole pie, thereby *exploding* the slice—also called a *piece* or *wedge*—to highlight a certain data point.

Suppose that your company has been in business for 20 years and your market share was 20% twenty years ago. Now your market share has grown a single percentage point, to 21%, but in those twenty years, the value of that market share went from $20 million to $200 million. The 1% change would look very minor in some chart types. Shown in a pie chart, however, it's actually quite dramatic. Figure 27.35 shows this situation, using a combination of two pie charts of different sizes and a line chart. The line chart in the background displays the market over time. From this example, you can see how flexible combination charts can be.

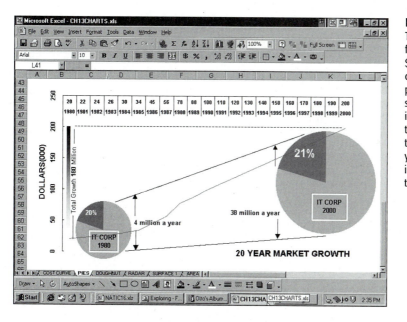

Figure 27.35.
The market grew from $4 million to $38 million; in this case, a single-digit percentage increase is substantial, considering the growth of the total market. By distorting the pie sizes, you create a visual image that represents the change in value.

PART

VII

CH

27

Tip #380

The key here is to understand that pies work well with market share, and line or bar charts work well with growth over time.

Tip #381

Visual distortions are best represented from smallest to largest, left to right.

If you need to plot several data series and insist on using a pie shape, I suggest using a doughnut chart (see the next section for details). Pie charts are designed specifically for one set of data, and doughnut charts are for two sets of data compared in pie form.

Caution

If you have more than 10 points of data in your data series, don't use a pie chart. With too much information, it's easy for the reader to become lost.

DOUGHNUT CHARTS

Doughnut charts are variations of pie charts. The difference is that doughnut charts are for multiple sets of data—sort of like plotting several pie charts against one another. One way to use a doughnut chart is to compare a fiscal year cycle of projected sales versus actual sales. The doughnut chart is a natural choice for this type of data because a year cycle is often thought of as a circle.

In Figure 27.36, the doughnut slice of actual sales takes up 60 percent of the doughnut's total area. If projected sales and actual sales were the same value, the slices of the doughnut would be equal in size.

The unit value associated with the 20 percent increase in actual versus projected sales is 25,000 units. I've called out this increase on the doughnut chart by using drawing tools.

Figure 27.36.
You can use doughnut charts to compare sets of stacked data or data sets over time.

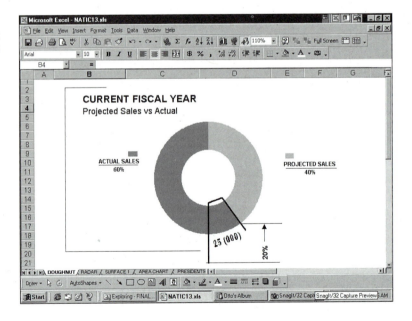

SCATTER CHARTS

Scatter charts are used for plotting data over uneven time intervals. This chart style is mostly seen in the scientific and engineering arenas. However, the use of scatter charts can definitely cross over into other areas, as shown in Figure 27.37. This chart shows scatter charts plotted against industry averages. The industry average is in the form of a line chart (unchanging), and the names of the students are plotted in scatter form against time and against the industry average.

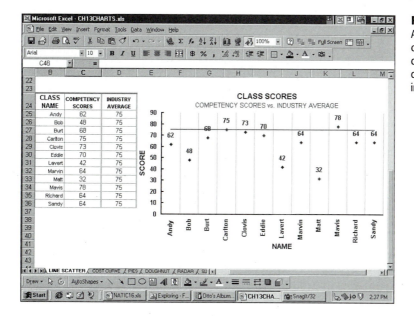

Figure 27.37.
A scatter chart for competency scores is combined with a line chart displaying the industry average.

Using the same approach, notice that Figure 27.38 has the same chart types, but the data is sorted from lowest scores to highest scores. When creating charts with random plotted points, a better approach may be to sort the information from smallest to largest so that the audience can grasp the information in a shorter period of time.

AREA CHARTS

Area charts are used much like line charts, in that area charts plot data over time in a continuous manner. The only difference is that the area is filled, hence the name area chart (see Figure 27.39).

Tip #382

When plotting multiple areas against one another on the same graph, consider using extreme differences in shading colors so the areas don't blend together. An example of this would be to use the lightest shade of gray first and then darker and darker as the layers get deeper.

Figure 27.38.
Sort the scores in the worksheet from smallest to largest before creating the chart. This way, it's easier to compare the class scores against the industry average.

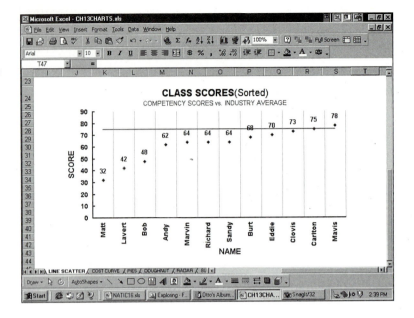

Avoid using more than five sets of data with this chart type. It's easy to lose the audience's focus if too much information is presented at once.

RADAR CHARTS

Radar charts show relationships between separate sets of data. The relationship is shown against the whole of a series, similar to the way a doughnut chart plots a data series against the whole of a series. Suppose that you want to compare the consumer spending in four categories of your market against your product distribution and focus. You can use a radar chart for market analysis in the form of a quadrant to analyze your current product focus against the consumer dollar spending, as shown in Figure 27.40. Radar charts help you to establish market comparatives for quick decision making, as well as refocus your audience's efforts and business strategy.

SURFACE CHARTS

Surface charts measure two changing variables in the form of a topographical map, providing a great 3D representation of the highs and lows. There are two types of surface charts, with two variations of each type. The *3D surface* provides variations in color, and the *3D wire frame* gives the topographical contour without color variations.

Assume that you have several variables that you want to display, such as time, profit, season, loss, breakeven, and so on. It can almost become confusing. However, with a 3D surface chart, you can measure certain sets of data and use drawing tools to analyze the rest. (Always think in terms of combining Excel's tools to enhance your graph. You'll run into situations that will practically require chart embellishment.)

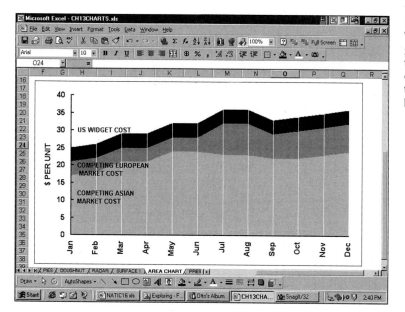

Figure 27.39.
When comparing global markets over time, area charts can effectively represent the differences between the markets.

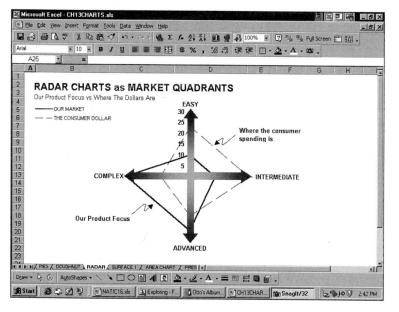

Figure 27.40.
Radar charts can be valuable tools in comparative analysis. This example helps the audience refocus its efforts and move its product focus closer to the consumer spending.

Figure 27.41 shows a surface chart and uses Excel's flexibility with drawing tools to tell the rest of the story. From this 3D view, you can see the average span of the season, the breakeven in mined ounces, and a profit scale above breakeven. There's a lot of information crammed into this small chart.

Figure 27.41.
You can use surface charts to show several levels of information that a two-dimensional chart would convey only with difficulty.

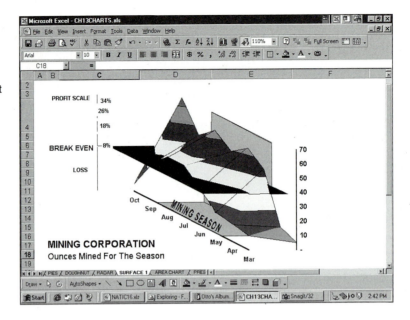

BUBBLE CHARTS

Bubble charts compare values in sets of three. The first two sets are actually used in the chart; the third value determines the size of the bubble markers. The bubble chart in Figure 27.42 represents the average ore mined per pod. In this example, you want to visually display the ounce concentration level per pod and show its respective location on the area map. If you have a picture of the map, you could paste it into the chart (in this case, however, it was drawn in). The highest concentration levels are formatted to be darker.

STOCK CHARTS

Stock charts are designed by default for the stock market and come in four varieties: high low close, open high low close, volume high low close, and volume open high low close. It might sound a little confusing; however, Excel indicates the order of the information in the chart sub-type in the Chart Wizard dialog box. For example, this type of chart can indicate the date and the high mark for the day, or the low mark and close for the day.

Often, you'll see *stock diaries* in publications that track information relative to the stock market's overall performance over the year or a specific period of time. The stock diary enables you to see the stock market's volume performance aligned against the high, low, and close for the specified period(s). You can create stock diaries in Excel as well. Notice the example in Figure 27.43, which consists of two charts: one for volume, and the other for the high, low, and close.

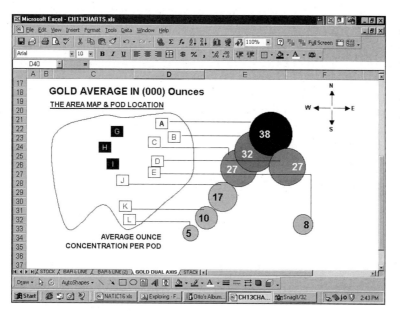

Figure 27.42.
The bubble chart example shows the ounce concentration per pod and its respective location on the mining grid or area map.

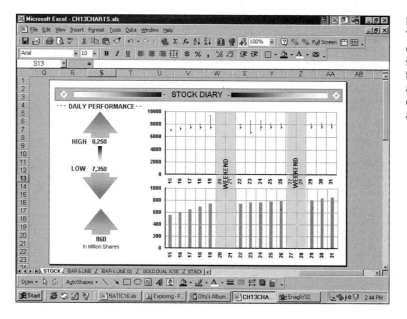

Figure 27.43.
You can create stock charts in Excel to measure performance over time. You also can align two charts, one over the other, to create a stock diary.

Rather than using two charts, you could plot this data on one chart with dual axes, but for simplicity it's easier to view it as two charts. Notice that I've aligned the two charts, used drawing tools to call out the key points for each day's performance, and blocked out the weekends.

Tip #383	Stock charts are also very handy for charting temperature variances for scientific or medical studies, crop yield projections, product analyses, and so on.

CYLINDER, CONE, AND PYRAMID CHARTS

Cylinder charts, *cone charts*, and *pyramid charts* are 3D charts with unique shapes. Where a standard column chart provides a rectangle effect in cluster column form, the cylinders, cones, and pyramids are shaped in the form of their names (see Figure 27.44). Sub-types include cluster column, stacked column, clustered bar, and stacked bar. If you like, you can create two forms of columns on the same chart—the example shows a column with a cylinder effect.

Figure 27.44.
A formatted cylinder chart can be great when a presentation is as much about the graphics as the supporting data.

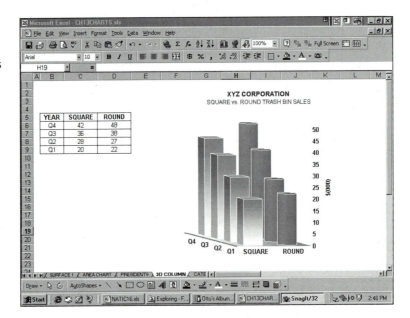

CUSTOM CHARTS

Excel offers many built-in custom chart types based on the standard chart types. Most of the custom chart types are formatted to add some pizzazz to a presentation or to put a little variety into a basic dull chart. To view what your data would look like as one of Excel's built-in custom chart types, select the Custom Types tab in step 1 of the Chart Wizard, or choose Chart Type from the Chart menu.

Chances are you probably won't use any of the custom types; however, they can provide ideas on how you can format your chart. Remember that charts are pictures that tell stories; it's easy to get carried away with all of the tools and formatting options in Excel. Be cautious; you can easily lose focus with too much on the chart at once.

CREATING A PERSONALIZED CUSTOM CHART

After formatting a chart, you can save the format as a custom type. You'll probably save several types of charts as custom types, so be sure that your title description fits the chart. To save charts as a custom type, follow these steps:

1. Select the chart you want to save as a custom chart.

2. Choose Chart Type from the Chart menu to open the Chart Type dialog box.

3. Click the Custom Types tab.

4. Select the User Defined option in the Select From section (see Figure 27.45).

5. Click the Add button to open the Add Custom Chart Type dialog box (see Figure 27.46).

6. Type a name for the new chart type and supply a description, if desired.

7. Click OK. The custom type now appears on the Chart Type list on the Custom Types tab. If you want this custom chart type set as the default chart type for use in Excel, click the Set as Default Chart button and respond Yes in the message box that appears.

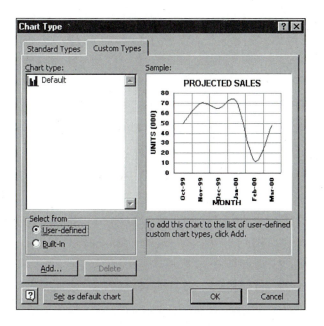

Figure 27.45.
The Custom Types tab in the Chart Type dialog box enables you to save a chart as a custom type.

PART

VII

CH

27

To delete a custom chart type, select it in the Chart Type list on the Custom Types tab, click the Delete button, and click OK when asked for confirmation.

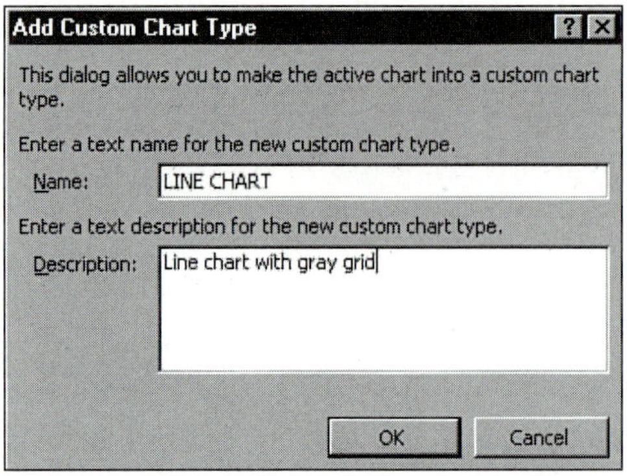

Figure 27.46.
Naming the custom
chart type.

Add Custom Chart Type

This dialog allows you to make the active chart into a custom chart type.

Enter a text name for the new custom chart type.

Name: LINE CHART

Enter a text description for the new custom chart type.

Description: Line chart with gray grid

OK | Cancel

PRINTING CHARTS

Before printing a chart, it's good practice to preview the chart (see Figure 27.47). You can preview a chart in the following ways:

- If you created the chart on a chart sheet, activate or select the chart sheet. Select Print Preview from the File menu; a preview of the printed chart appears onscreen.

- If the chart is embedded on a worksheet, select Print Preview to preview the entire worksheet with the chart on it.

- If the chart is embedded and you want to print just the chart, select the chart and choose File, Print Preview. Excel previews the selected chart and you can print it as you would a chart sheet.

Figure 27.47.
The Print Preview feature enables you to review the chart on the embedded worksheet before you print it.

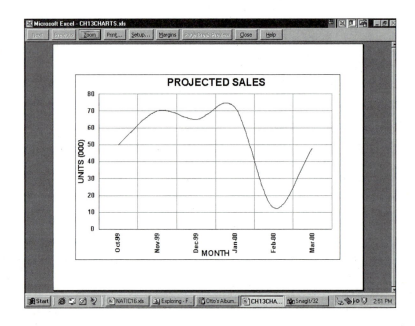

Whether you're printing on a color or a black-and-white printer (using *grayscale*), be sure to print a test copy and review it before distributing the chart. Remember that every printer is different, and that Print Preview shows you only Excel's projection of how the printout will look. If you create the chart in color but are printing in grayscale, the different colors on the chart may appear similar in shade when printed. Data series should stand apart from one another; be sure to use contrasting shades or switch from using color to using black-and-white patterns. Even when printing in color, be aware that color monitors and color printers don't "think" in the same colors. The colors may turn out to be more red, blue, and so on than you expected. Also note that the print quality of the printer, the paper, and the toner/cartridge/ribbon all affect the results you get.

When printing a chart on a chart sheet or printing a selected chart embedded on a work-sheet, you can click the Print button on the Standard toolbar to send the chart directly to the printer, using the default print settings. Note that Excel resizes the chart as necessary to occupy the whole sheet of paper; this may not be exactly what you had in mind. Using the File, Print command, on the other hand, displays the Print dialog box as usual, but the Print What section of the dialog box gives you only one option: Selected Chart. While an embedded chart is selected, you can't opt to print the worksheet with the chart. If you want both, cancel the dialog box, deselect the embedded chart, and then issue the Print command from the menu or the toolbar button.

TROUBLESHOOTING

SELECTING A CHART ELEMENT

Excel won't let me select a specific chart element.

Excel gives you two ways to select chart elements:

- Click the element so the selection handles are showing.
- Click open the Chart Objects button on the Chart toolbar and select the desired element from the drop-down list.

CHANGING A CHART SHEET TO AN EMBEDDED CHART

I can't move a chart sheet next to my data table.

Excel defaults to creating a chart as a worksheet, but you can change the chart worksheet to an embedded chart. Select Chart, Location to open the Chart Location dialog box. Select As Object In and use the drop-down list to specify the worksheet you would like the chart to be embedded in.

PART

VII

CH

27

ADDING A TRENDLINE

How do I add a trendline to a data series?

Trendlines can only be added to two-dimensional charts. To add a trendline, select the data series you want the trendline to represent. Choose Chart, Add Trendline to open the Add Trendline dialog box. On the Type tab, select the type of trendline you want and then choose OK.

ADDING DATA LABELS

The chart is complete, but I want to add data labels to a series.

Select the series of data for which you want to add labels. Then choose Format, Selected Data Series to display the Format Data Series dialog box. On the Data Labels tab, select the Show Label option. To add data labels to all the series at once, click anywhere in the chart and choose Chart, Chart Options to open the Chart Options dialog box. Click the Data Labels tab and select the Show Label option. Click OK.

CHAPTER **28**

MODIFYING EXCEL CHARTS

In this chapter

OPTIONS FOR IMPROVING YOUR CHARTS

After you create a chart, you probably will want to add information or change elements of the chart. Excel enables you to manipulate any part of the chart, as well as add elements to the chart. If you saved the chart as an embedded chart and now want to change it to a chart on a separate chart sheet, you can do that, too. Many times, however, you must go into an existing chart, delete a series of data, and replace it with data from a new location, or even change the chart type to give the chart a different look and feel.

Information in a newly created chart almost always will have to be modified to get your point across. The better you become at presenting information to achieve your goals, the better off you'll be.

Excel provides numerous tools and techniques to manipulate a chart to make it serve the specific needs of the audience. Some of these techniques are discussed in Chapter 29, "Formatting Charts," and Chapter 30, "Professional Charting Techniques." For now, it's important to learn the fundamentals of building and modifying charts. This section begins by discussing the fundamentals of adding information and changing existing information on a chart.

MOVING AND RESIZING EMBEDDED CHARTS

When an embedded chart is complete, you probably will want to move or resize the chart so that it fits better with the data on the worksheet.

To resize a chart, select the chart by placing the mouse pointer over the embedded chart and clicking. Small black boxes called *sizing handles* appear around the perimeter of the chart. Point to one of the handles. When the pointer changes to display a two-headed black arrow, drag away from the center of the chart to enlarge, or toward the center of the chart to reduce. While resizing, Excel displays a dotted box to give you an indication of the final size of the chart.

Tip #384	Dragging a corner handle resizes height and width simultaneously.

You may decide at some point that an embedded chart should have been placed in a different location: somewhere else in the current worksheet, on a different worksheet entirely, or on a separate chart sheet. Perhaps you chose the wrong option in the Chart Wizard, or you just changed your mind and want to move the chart from one place to another. As usual, multiple methods are available; the following methods are the easiest:

- Move the chart from one worksheet location to another with a quick cut-and-paste. Select the chart, cut it to the *Office Clipboard*, position the cell pointer in the new worksheet location, and paste the chart into place.

- To drag the chart elsewhere on the current sheet, select the chart so that the handles are visible. Then click somewhere in the chart area (a ScreenTip says Chart Area), but not on any of the individual elements of the chart—in other words, don't click the title, axes, and so on—and watch for the mouse pointer to display the typical selection arrow. Drag the chart to its new position, and drop it there.

- To move the chart from one worksheet to another or to a separate chart sheet, select the chart and choose Chart, Location to open the Chart Location dialog box. Specify whether you want to place the chart on a separate chart sheet or as an object in another worksheet in the current workbook (select from the drop-down list).

SELECTING PARTS OF A CHART FOR EDITING

It's very likely that you'll need to change particular aspects of a new or existing chart—removing a particular data marker, adding text boxes, adjusting line size and color, and so on. The first step to changing features within the chart is to select the chart so that the sizing handles are showing. After the chart is selected, place the mouse pointer over almost any item in the chart to display a *ScreenTip* that indicates which object on the chart you're pointing to. To select the specified object, click it.

Chart objects such as data series and data points are grouped; clicking any one selects the entire set. If you need to change a particular one of the set, click it a second time to display handles around that item alone. Don't double-click; just click once to select the set, wait briefly, and then click the individual item.

Tip #385	If the chart is small or somewhat crowded, you may find yourself squinting at the screen or increasingly frustrated as you attempt to click tiny elements in the chart. Instead, use the Zoom feature to enlarge the view so that you can see what you're clicking. If the chart is embedded, click outside the chart—anywhere in the worksheet—to enable the Zoom feature. Make your selections and changes, and then restore the original Zoom setting, if desired.

The Chart toolbar can be very helpful when you want to edit a chart—particularly if you're having difficulty selecting individual parts of a chart because you can't remember what they're called. Table 28.1 describes the buttons on the Chart toolbar. If the toolbar isn't displayed, right-click the menu or any toolbar and choose Chart from the context menu that appears.

TABLE 28.1. BUTTONS ON THE CHART TOOLBAR

Button	Name	Description
Chart Objects [Category Axis ▾]	Chart Objects	Displays a drop-down list of the objects and data points within the chart. Click the drop-down arrow and select the one you want from the list.
[icon]	Format *<object>*	Displays the Format dialog box for the selected object on the chart. (The ScreenTip name for this button changes to show the name of the selected object.)

PART
VII
CH
28

continues

TABLE 28.1.   CONTINUED

Button	Name	Description
	Chart Type	Displays a drop-down palette of chart types; click the type you want to apply to the current chart. The face of the button changes to show the last chart type selected.
	Legend	Toggles adding and removing a legend on the chart.
	Data Table	Toggles adding and removing a data table below the category (X) axis.
	By Row	Plots each row of data as a series in the chart.
	By Column	Plots each column of data as a series in the chart.
	Angle Text Downward	Changes the angle of selected text to 45 degrees downward. Use for data markers, axis labels, and so on.
	Angle Text Upward	Changes the angle of selected text to 45 degrees upward. Use for data markers, axis labels, and so on.

Tip #386   You can often save time by right-clicking the item in the chart and using the context menu rather than the main menu. You also can double-click the desired element of the chart to display the Format dialog box for that element.

CHANGING THE CHART TYPE

No matter how much time you spend deliberating before creating a chart about what type of chart to use, occasionally the result just isn't what you need. You can change the chart type very easily to some other type that works better for the data. Excel even lets you combine chart types by changing individual data series to a different type from the rest of the chart. For example, when comparing trends or different sets of data, it can be quite helpful to separate the data series with different chart types on the same chart to show distinct differences between two sets of information. Figure 28.1 shows projected sales in a line and actual sales in columns. In this example, displaying the projected sales as a line clearly emphasizes by how much sales fell short of projection.

The methods are basically the same for changing the chart type for the entire chart or for selected data series. The only difference is that if you want to change just a data series, you select the data series first. You can use any of the following methods to change the chart type:

- Choose Chart, Chart Type to open the Chart Type dialog box, and then select the desired chart type and sub-type (see Figure 28.2).
- Right-click any data point in the series (or anywhere else in the chart if you want to change the entire chart), and select Chart Type from the context menu to open the Chart Type dialog box. Change the settings as desired.

- Click the Chart Type button on the Chart toolbar, and select a new chart type from the displayed palette.
- Click the Chart Wizard button on the Standard toolbar to open the Chart Wizard - Step 1 of 4 - Chart Type dialog box. Select a new chart type and sub-type, and click <u>F</u>inish. This method changes the entire chart; it doesn't work for individual data series.

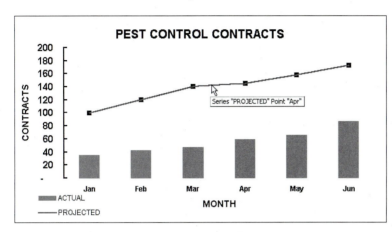

Figure 28.1.
The result of the changed series is in the form of a line chart.

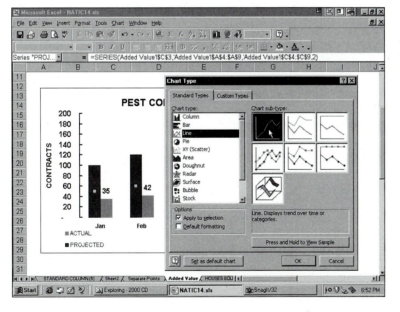

Figure 28.2.
Use the Chart Type dialog box to select a different chart type and sub-type.

Tip #387

The advantage of using the Chart Wizard to change the chart type for an entire chart is that you can use the Press and Hold to <u>V</u>iew Sample button to preview the data in the new chart format. This can save some steps if you need to try several chart types before you find the best type.

CHANGING A DATA SERIES

A *data series* is represented by the bars in a bar chart, the columns in a column chart, and so on. For example, if you have a column chart and a set of the individual columns is one color, all the columns of that color together represent a data series.

In addition to formatting data series by changing the color, pattern, and so on, you can add or remove data series in the chart, as described in the following sections.

SELECTING A DATA SERIES OR DATA POINT IN A CHART

To modify or format a data series in a chart, you first must select the data series by clicking any one of the data points (a column, bar, and so on) in the series. You'll notice three things:

- When the mouse pointer is placed over the data series, a ScreenTip displays a description of the series and the particular data point under the mouse pointer.

- When a data point is clicked, the whole series is selected, and the sizing handles show up on the data series as square dots.

- When a data series is selected, its corresponding data in the worksheet is surrounded by colored Range Finder boundary lines. A purple boundary surrounds the axis labels, a green boundary surrounds the series labels (the ones normally found in the chart's legend), and a blue boundary surrounds the data series entries.

You also can change an individual data point in a data series. With the series selected, click the point you want to change (see Figure 28.3). To change the value of the data point and its corresponding value in the worksheet—remember that the two are linked—select the data point in the chart and drag it to the desired value.

 If you want to change the chart type for a series, see "Changing the Chart Type of a Data Series" in the Troubleshooting section at the end of this chapter.

Figure 28.3.
By selecting a single data point in a data series, you can format or change the value of the data point.

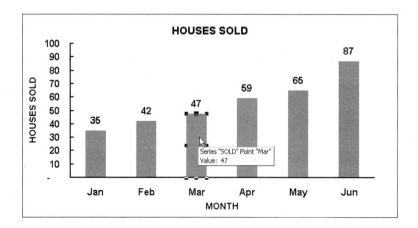

One reason you may want to change values this way is for visual emphasis. If you're trying to drive home a point and the actual value isn't static or exact, you may want to drag the value or data point to look a certain way (for example, very low or very high) as opposed to registering an exact value.

REMOVING A SERIES FROM A CHART

When displaying information with charts, you often want to analyze the information with and without different sets of data. For example, in a chart that shows actual versus projected sales for the year, you may want to display just the actual sales and then just the projections. To remove a data series from a chart, select the data series so that the handles are showing, and then press the Delete key, or choose Edit, Clear, Series. It's that simple.

ADDING OR ADJUSTING SOURCE DATA

Because business needs change, you may sometimes have to add data series to a chart—for example, to include a new division or product—or adjust existing data series or data points to include new information. You can build a new chart or just add data to the existing chart, as described in the following sections.

ADDING DATA POINTS OR DATA SERIES

Excel gives you the flexibility of adding data to a chart in several ways:

- Adjust the source data, as described in the following section.

- Select the chart and choose Chart, Add Data to display the Add Data dialog box (see Figure 28.4). Specify the range of the data you want to add. You can use the *Collapse Dialog button* to reduce the size of the dialog box, or just drag the dialog box out of the way to see the worksheet. When the range is correct, click OK. You also can use this method to add data from a different worksheet.

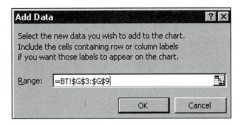

Figure 28.4.
Use the Add Data dialog box to add new series to an existing chart.

- Copy the data in the worksheet, select the chart, and paste the data into the chart. You can use the Paste command on the context menu; choose Edit, Paste; click the Paste button on the Standard toolbar; or press Ctrl+V. With the paste command, Excel selects the format for the new series automatically.

- If you want more control of how Excel pastes the new data, choose Edit, Paste Special to display the Paste Special dialog box, in which you can indicate how you want the new data to appear (see Figure 28.5).

Figure 28.5.
The Paste Special dialog box gives you options for plotting information as new points or in a new series, as well as by rows or columns.

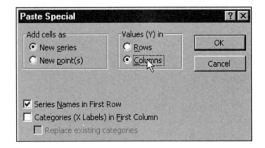

In the example in Figure 28.6, the new data is added as a series and plotted in the form of columns along the Y-axis—the same result as you would get with a simple paste. In Figure 28.7, on the other hand, the data is added as new points, thereby plotting the data separately, as a second category on the X-axis.

Figure 28.6.
The new information is pasted as a new series in columns.

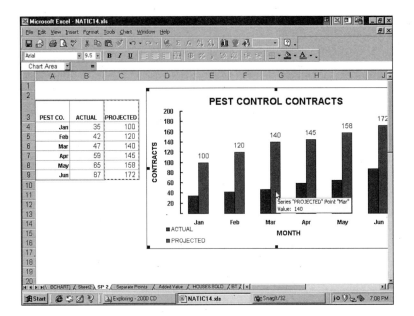

You can choose from the following options in the Paste Special dialog box:

- **New Series**. Adds the copied data to the chart as a new data series.

- **New Point(s)**. Adds the copied data to the chart as an additional data series along the same axis.

- **Rows** or **Columns**. Creates an additional data series from the contents of each row or column in the copied selection.

- **Series Names in First Row**. Uses the first row or column of the copied data as the label for the selected data series.

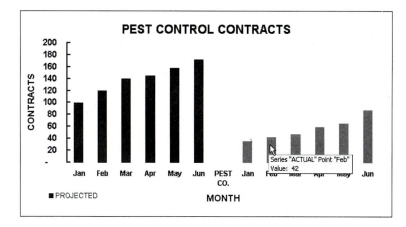

Figure 28.7.
The result of pasting information in as new points along the same category axis.

- **Categories (X Labels) in <u>F</u>irst Column**. Uses the first row or column of the copied data as category labels on the X-axis.
- **Replace Existing C<u>a</u>tegories**. Replaces the existing category labels with the category labels you want to paste in. For example, you could use this option to change existing labels January through December to 1 through 12.

Note — Choose <u>U</u>ndo if the results aren't what you had in mind.

- Use the drag-and-drop method to add data to a chart. Select the data you want to add. Move the mouse pointer over the edge of the selection until the pointer changes to an arrow. Click and drag the data anywhere inside the chart; then release the mouse button.

  If the data is on a different worksheet from the chart, hold down the Alt key and drag the data down to the tab for the worksheet containing the chart. When the destination worksheet appears, release the Alt key and drag the data into the chart.

  If the data is in a different workbook, open the workbook and use the <u>W</u>indow, <u>A</u>rrange command to display both workbooks onscreen. Display the worksheet containing the data and the worksheet containing the chart. Then select and drag the desired data from the source worksheet window into the chart. Data added from another workbook creates links to that workbook in the destination chart.

Note — You may be prompted with the Paste Special dialog box if Excel can't define the new data automatically.

Tip #388

Avoid adding too many data series to one chart. You can easily lose the point if too much information is presented at once. Another alternative is to create two charts and embed them on the same sheet, and then use drawing tools and/or text to help the reader compare them.

CHANGING THE DATA SOURCE

Sometimes you don't need to add a data series—just adjust some that are already included in the chart. You can change the source data for a chart in any of the following ways:

- Add data points or data series as described in the preceding section.

- With the worksheet data visible behind it, click an embedded chart (you may need to move the chart nearer to the source data for this method to work). Then drag the selection handles for the colored lines that surround the source data, headings, and labels. If the mouse pointer is an arrow, dragging moves the selection rectangle. If the pointer is a black cross, dragging expands or contracts the selection. As you adjust the colored lines, the chart changes to reflect the new selection.

- Select the chart, start the Chart Wizard, and click Next in the Step 1 of 4 dialog box. In the Step 2 of 4 dialog box, change the data source as needed; then click Finish.

- Select the chart and choose Chart, Source Data, or right-click the chart and choose Source Data from the context menu. The Source Data dialog box opens (see Figure 28.8). Select the Data Range tab. From here, you can change the absolute address from which the data is derived.

Figure 28.8.
The Source Data dialog box enables you to change the address of your chart data.

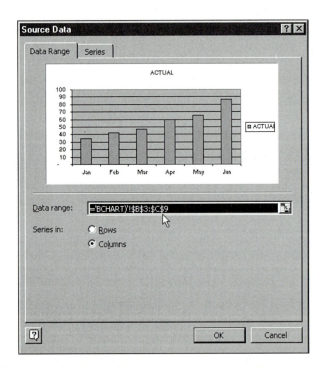

ADDING A SECONDARY AXIS TO THE CHART

More often than not, you'll run into a situation where you need to use a chart to compare two sets of data that are extremely different in value, such as unit output and dollars sold. One way to display this type of information is with a *secondary axis*. In most cases, the values would be extremely different, so you would want the units on one Y-axis, and the dollars represented on another Y-axis (see Figure 28.9).

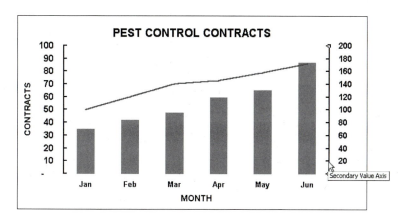

Figure 28.9.
Plotting series on two different Y-axes.

To create a dual-axis chart, follow these steps:

1. Select the data series that you want to plot on the secondary axis. In Figure 28.10, the dollar line is selected.

2. Choose Format, Selected Data Series to open the Format Data Series dialog box, as shown in Figure 28.11.

3. Select the Axis tab.

4. Under Plot Series On, choose Secondary Axis.

5. Click OK.

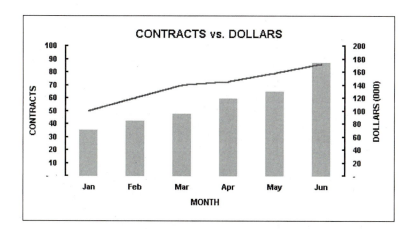

Figure 28.10.
In this example, the line chart will be plotted against the new secondary axis.

PART

VII

CH

28

Figure 28.11.
Use the Format Data Series dialog box to set up the secondary axis.

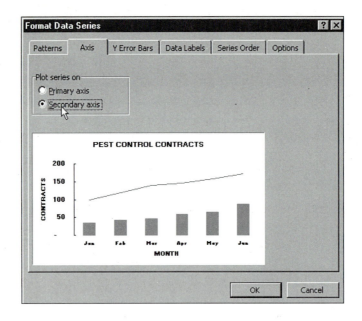

Tip #389 Use a secondary axis when you have two types of information with extremely different low and high values. If plotted on the same axis, the category with the lower values may not be visible.

VALUE AXIS SCALING

The *scaling* of the axes in a chart can control the chart's visual characteristics, and thereby the assumptions that the audience makes based on viewing the chart. The X- and Y-axes in a chart have different scaling options because they represent different things; usually, the X-axis represents categories of data, and the Y-axis represents the values corresponding to those categories. You can adjust the scale of the axes by constraining visual highs and lows: the place where the two axes intersect (called the *origin*), the maximum value displayed, and the unit iteration between values.

The following sections describe scaling the value axis; see the later section "Category Axis Scaling" for details on adjusting the X-axis.

CHANGING THE MAXIMUM, MINIMUM, AND TICK MARK VALUES

In Figure 28.12, the sales represented look quite substantial. If you want to make the bars appear smaller, you can change the scale of the axis to reduce the visual size of the columns. Increasing the maximum value of the Y-axis makes the columns look shorter; decreasing the maximum value makes them look taller. If the column value is 100, for example, and you set the maximum Y-axis value at 100, the column extends to the maximum height of the Y-axis, making it appear as if that data point is at peak value. Conversely, if you set the maximum value at 1000, the column value of 100 is only one-tenth the height of the Y-axis, minimizing the visual value of the column. In the example in Figure 28.13, the maximum value of the Y-axis is constrained to 100, and the column sizes appear less substantial in size, giving the change from this year to last year less impact than in Figure 28.12, in which the maximum value is 40.

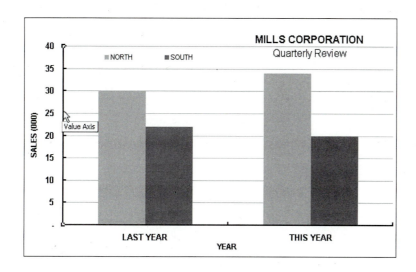

Figure 28.12.
By default, Excel places the origin at zero.

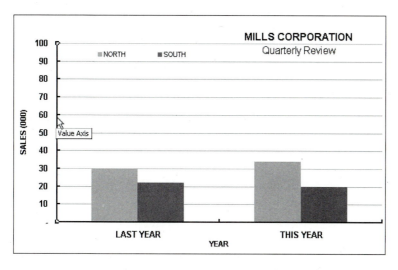

Figure 28.13.
By scaling the axis, you can control the visual size of the columns within the chart.

Caution

Obviously, skewing the visual elements in a chart also can skew the audience's perception of the chart's message. Be sure you understand exactly what information the chart is conveying.

If the maximum value is 10 and for some reason the value changes to 20, Excel automatically adjusts the value axis to accommodate for the increase in value. By changing the Maximum value setting on the Scale tab in the Format Axis dialog box, you can force Excel to use a particular maximum value you prefer (see Figure 28.14). For example, changing the maximum from the default of 40 to 100 for the chart in Figure 28.14 really diminishes the results visually.

Caution

When you set the maximum value, the Y-axis becomes static, showing plotted data series only to the maximum value that you specified.

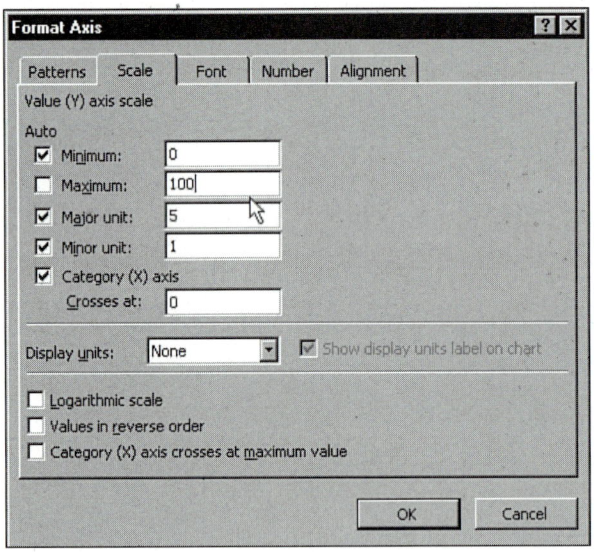

Figure 28.14.
The Scale tab in the Format Axis dialog box enables you to adjust the Y-axis scaling.

Figure 28.15.
The result of applying a maximum value to the chart is a reduced column visual.

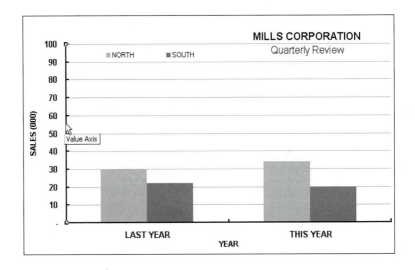

You also can use the settings on the Scale tab in the Format Axis dialog box to adjust the minimum unit to plot, as well as major and minor units that allow for interval adjustments. Suppose the Y-axis plots every 20 units, but you want it to plot every 10 units. Just change the Major Unit setting from 20 to 10. The Minor Unit setting controls the unit interval of the *tick marks* on the minor gridlines. To space minor gridlines over three ticks, for example, set the Minor Unit setting to 3. The gridlines will appear at every third tick mark on the value axis.

If you're using the Logarithmic Scale option, the default origin is at 1, and the Minimum, Maximum, Major Unit, and Minor Unit settings are calculated as powers of 10 for the value axis, based on the data range plotted in the chart.

RESIZING THE PLOT AREA

In addition to axis scaling, you can resize the *plot* area—changing the height or width—to change the visual message of a chart. Suppose a line chart shows a certain amount of growth over a period of time, and you want the increase to look much steeper or flatter. Narrowing or reducing the height of the plot area may give you exactly the look you want.

In Figure 28.16, for example, the chart on the left shows three different versions of a line chart—all of which represent the same value, plotted against the same Y-axis. The plot size in each case has been changed to give each line a different look. Figure 28.17 reverses this process; by adjusting the height of the plot downward, you can visually lessen the growth line.

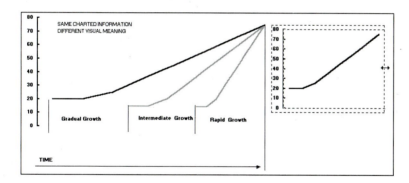

Figure 28.16.
By adjusting the plot area, you can change the visual steepness of a line chart. This can give a false sense of growth, but also help in providing the right look for the audience in a given situation.

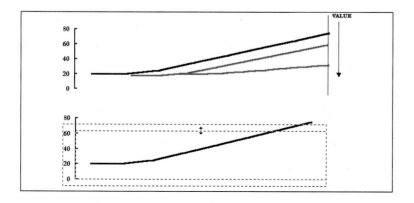

Figure 28.17.
You also can adjust the height to a level that reduces the steepness of the line (which "planes" or levels it out) by adjusting the plot area height.

PART

VII

CH

28

CHANGING THE ORIGIN

You can change where the category and value axis cross. By default, the value axis intersects the category axis at zero (the origin); however, you can adjust the origin by specifying the value at which you want the category axis to meet the value axis.

Suppose that you're showing scores in a competition for qualifying entrants for the current year and last year. The chart in Figure 28.18 shows a typical column chart setup (sometimes called a *waterfall chart*) that you might use. However, by moving the origin from 0 to 70, as shown in Figure 28.19, you can use the axis to display the breakeven point. In this case, 70 is the minimum qualifying score.

Figure 28.18.
A typical column chart, also called a *waterfall* chart. Notice that the origin is positioned at 0 in this example.

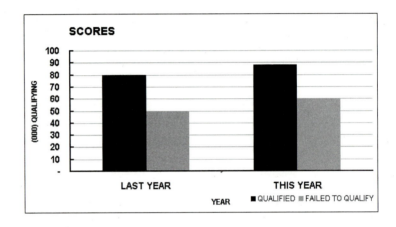

Figure 28.19.
The category axis now takes on two roles: the year and the minimum qualifying score.

This technique is useful for any kind of pass/fail data. Charts like this are often used to represent value indexes with healthcare coverage plans, or other industries comparing corporate plans and their measured coverage. Even though the index reads positive, by placing the category axis at a certain point along the value axis, any value that reads below the line is viewed as less coverage, poor in rating, and so on.

To change where the category axis meets the value axis, select the Y-axis and change the Crosses At setting on the Scale tab in the Format Axis dialog box.

Note

If you're using the Logarithmic Scale option, the default origin is at 1.

Tip #390

For an unusual look, you can set the X-axis to cross the Y-axis at the maximum value rather than the minimum value. Select the option Category (X) Axis Crosses at Maximum Value on the Scale tab in the Format Axis dialog box. Because this chart arrangement is more difficult for the audience to interpret, however, you may need to add more explanatory text.

CATEGORY AXIS SCALING

The category axis scaling options act much like the value axis scaling options described in previous sections. You can adjust the settings to help define the story you're using the chart to tell.

To access the category (X) axis settings, select the axis and choose Format, Selected Axis, or right-click the axis and choose Format Axis from the context menu. Either action opens the Format Axis dialog box. Click the Scale tab to display the scaling options for the X-axis. The following sections describe the options.

REPOSITIONING THE AXES

The Y-axis doesn't have to cross the X-axis at the corner of the plot area; you can reposition the Y-axis along the X-axis between categories. The example in Figure 28.20 shows a standard column chart. You could create more of a division between this year's numbers and last year's by positioning the Y-axis between the two sets of columns, as shown in Figure 28.21. In this example, you set the Y-axis to intersect at the second category of the X-axis.

PART

VII

CH

28

Figure 28.20.
Standard positioning
for the axes.

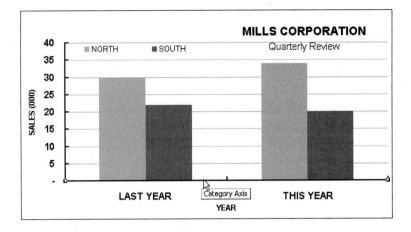

Figure 28.21.
Change the position
where the category
axis and value axis
cross to separate the
years.

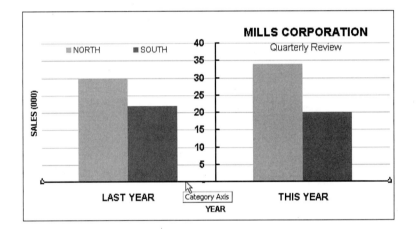

To change the position where the axes cross, change the setting for the option Value (Y)
Axis Crosses at Category Number (see Figure 28.22). Two other options also affect the
positioning of the Y-axes on the X-axis:

- **Value Y Axis Crosses Between Categories**. This option places the Y-axis at the edge
  of the category indicated in the box for the option Value (Y) Axis Crosses at Category
  Number. If this option is selected, data points are plotted between tick marks; if not,
  points are plotted at the tick-mark positions.

- **Value Y Axis Crosses at Maximum Category**. This option places the Y-axis after the
  last category on the X-axis.

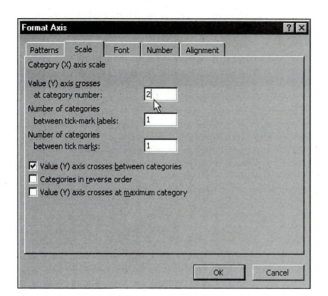

Figure 28.22.
Set the category number to move the value axis along the category axis.

CHANGING TICK MARKS AND LABELS

The option Number of Categories Between Tick-Mark Labels on the Scale tab specifies the frequency with which you want category labels to appear on the X-axis. For example, if a chart showing 40 years of sales figures displays a label for every year, you might decrease the number of labels so that they appear every fourth or fifth year, or just mark the decades.

The option Number of Categories Between Tick Marks specifies the number of categories you want to appear between each pair of tick marks. To place a minor tick mark between every category on the X-axis, set Number of Categories Between Tick Marks to 1.

Tip #391

> If category labels are long, or the chart includes quite a few labels, they can become too crowded on the axis to be easily readable. You can adjust the angle of the category labels by setting the *orientation* on the Alignment tab in the Format Axis dialog box.

CHANGING THE SERIES ORDER

By changing the series order, you can manipulate the set of data the viewers' eyes will see first. Why do this? It's really a form of advertising—if you want to get a point across without getting lost in a conversation about all of the other elements, you place the data in the most viewable place within a chart, which is the first series. Because people generally look at information from left to right or top to bottom, this will naturally allow you to flow into a discussion about which data set is most important in the chart. There are ways to draw focus using formatting that far outweigh series order, but series order is an important tool to gain control over the chart and the audience.

REVERSING THE CATEGORIES

Reversing the data series is a trick that comes in handy from time to time, particularly with bar charts. For example, if you create a bar chart with quarters, Excel plots the last series of quarters at the top (see Figure 28.23). Because we naturally view information in a top-down manner, you'll probably want to reverse the order in which the series are viewed, so that Q1 appears at the top of the chart and Q4 at the bottom (see Figure 28.24).

Figure 28.23.
The default category axis order clearly needs to be reversed because we view information from the top down.

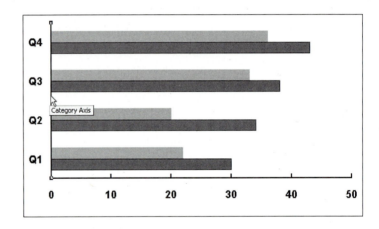

Figure 28.24.
Reversing the categories.

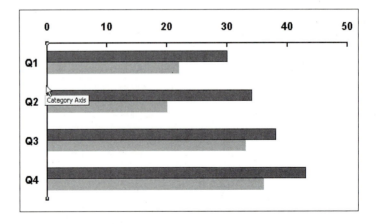

To display categories on the X-axis in the opposite direction, select the axis, open the Format Axis dialog box, click the Scale tab, and select the Categories in Reverse Order option (see Figure 28.25).

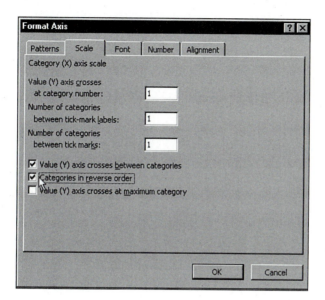

Figure 28.25.
The Format Axis dialog box enables you to reverse the order of the plotted data series.

REVERSING THE VALUES

Sometimes less is better. Using golf scores as an example, you might want a player with a lower score to have a more prominent column on a column chart. In this case, you would want to have zero or negative values at the top of the value axis and the largest number crossing at the category axis. In this reversed approach, the player with the lowest score would also be perceived as having the most prominent column on the chart. Selecting the Values in Reverse Order option on the Scale tab in the Format Axis dialog box for the value axis reverses the direction of values on scatter, column, and bar charts.

ADDING A TRENDLINE TO A DATA SERIES

Adding *trendlines* in Excel helps you understand where you've been and where you're potentially headed. Using *regression analysis*, you can plot trends against a data series and plot out periods of time going forward. You can even specify the number of periods for which you would like to project.

Note

Trendlines can only be added to certain types of charts: area, column, line, bar, and scatter.

To add a trendline to your chart, follow these steps:

1. Select the chart or select the data series to which you want to add the trendline.

2. From the Chart menu, choose Add Trendline to display the Add Trendline dialog box (see Figure 28.26).

3. From the Type tab, select the type of trendline you want to add.

4. Click OK.

Figure 28.27 shows a power trendline added to product B, showing the trend over fiscal quarters.

Figure 28.26.
The Add Trendline dialog box enables you to choose from six types of trends using regression analysis.

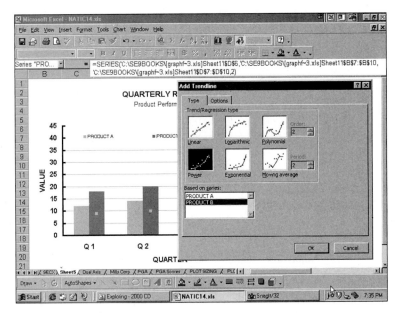

Figure 28.27.
By adding a trendline, you can graphically display the trend of a series of information.

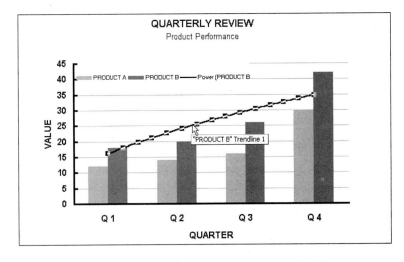

Table 28.2 describes the regression analysis trendline options available in the Add Trendline dialog box. The specific regression analysis equations and their explanations can be found by searching Excel's help for *Equations for calculating trendlines*.

TABLE 28.2. TRENDLINE SETTINGS

Option	Function
Linear	Inserts a linear trendline.
Logarithmic	Inserts a logarithmic trendline.
Polynomial	Inserts a polynomial or curvilinear trendline.
Power	Inserts a power trendline.
Exponential	Inserts an exponential trendline.
Moving Average	Inserts a moving average trendline. The number of points in a moving average trendline equals the total number of points in the series, minus the number you specify for the period.
Order	By entering a number in the Order box, you specify the highest polynomial order. The value is expressed as an integer between 2 and 6.
Period	By entering a number in the Period box, you specify the number of periods you want to use to calculate the moving average.
Based on Series	Selects the series in which the trendline will be displayed.

Caution

When you start to add elements to a chart, there's a point where you must begin subtracting elements to eliminate the clutter. Be cautious when adding trendlines; avoid making your chart more difficult to interpret.

FORMATTING THE TRENDLINE

As with many other chart elements, quite often you'll want to format the trendline to fit within the visual aspects of the chart you're creating. Excel offers many options to create the look and feel you need for the trendline to fit into the picture. By selecting or activating the trendline, you can format the trendline as you would any other element of the chart (see Figure 28.28).

To format a trendline, follow these steps:

1. Select or activate the trendline.
2. From the Format menu, choose Selected Trendline to open the Format Trendline dialog box.

PART
VII

CH
28

Tip #392

You can also double-click the trendline to access the Format Trendline dialog box.

Figure 28.28.
This trendline has a custom format.

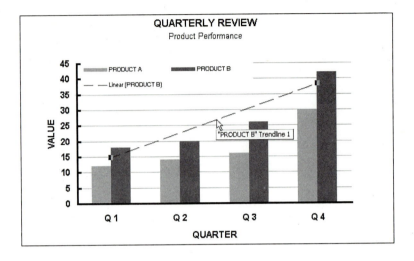

3. From the Patterns tab in the Format Trendline dialog box, select formatting options to create the desired visual effect (see Figure 28.29).

4. Click OK.

Figure 28.29.
On the Patterns tab, select the format style to apply to the trend-line.

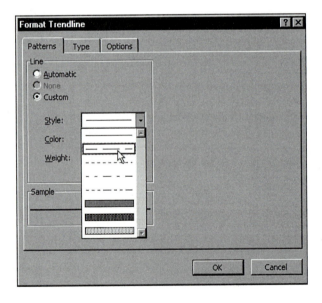

The following list describes some of the formatting options available for trendlines:

→ For details on using line formats in Excel charts, **see** "Formatting Lines: Axes, Tick Marks, High/Low Lines, and Error Bars," **p. 410**

- **Automatic.** Applies the default Excel settings to the selected line or object.

- **Custom.** Enables you to customize the style, color, and weight of the selected trendline.

- **Style**. Specifies a style for the selected line or border.

- **Color**. Designates a color for the selected line or border.

- **Weight.** Indicates the weight (thickness) of the selected line or border.

As you make selections, watch the Sample box to see how the line or border will look with the options selected.

TRENDLINE OPTIONS

The settings on the Options tab in the Format Trendline dialog box enable you to further customize a trendline (see Figure 28.30).

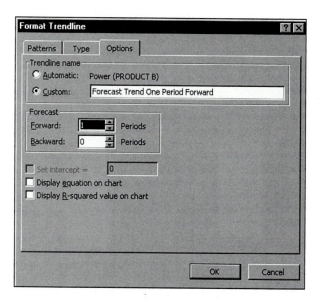

Figure 28.30.
The Options tab in the Format Trendline dialog box enables you to further customize the trendline with names and forecasting modes, as well as display the equations used.

The options are described in the following list:

- **Trendline Name**. Specify whether you want Excel to provide a name for the trendline, based on the trend chosen (Automatic), or select the Custom option and type your own name.

- **Forecast**. Use the options in this section to specify the number of periods to chart, going forward or backward. For example, based on the current or historical information from the charted series, Excel can plot out the trend of future periods (see Figure 28.31).

PART

VII

CH

28

- **Set Intercept = ___.** By setting the *intercept*, you specify where you want the trendline to meet the Y-axis.

- **Display Equation on Chart** and **Display R-Squared Value on Chart.** Use these options to post regression equations or R-squared values on the chart. If you have several scenarios of trendlines, for example, you may want to show the values for each trendline.

Figure 28.31.
The trendline forecast out one period.

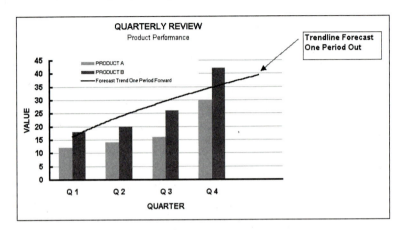

Tip #394	By default, trendlines are not the same color as the data series they're plotted against. Whenever possible, try to format the trendline to the color or shade of the series that the trendline represents. Doing this helps the audience to understand instantly which series the trendline is tied to, without additional explanation.

TROUBLESHOOTING

CHANGING THE MAXIMUM VALUE FOR THE VALUE AXIS

How can I make data appear smaller on the chart?

Select the value axis, choose Format, Selected Axis, select the Scale tab, and replace the Maximum value with a higher number.

CHANGING THE CHART TYPE OF A DATA SERIES

How do I change the chart type of just one of the data series in a chart?

Select the data series you want to change, choose Chart Type from the Chart menu, select the desired chart type, and click OK. Note that some chart types can't be combined, but Excel will warn you if you choose a chart type that won't work with the existing chart.

CHARTING DRAMATICALLY DIFFERENT VALUES ON THE SAME CHART

I have two data series on my chart with extremely different values. How do I compensate for this?

Use a secondary axis to plot one of the series. Select the data series to plot on the secondary axis. Then choose Format, Selected Data Series, click the Axis tab, and choose Secondary Axis.

CHAPTER **29**

FORMATTING CHARTS

In this chapter

AN OVERVIEW OF FORMATTING CHARTS

Formatting charts is as important as the data behind the chart. What you display says a lot about your skills and your ability to translate information to others. All too often, people clutter charts and the message gets lost in all the data. Because Excel offers such a wide variety of options, people want to use them all in graphic presentations. Actually, the less you try to cram onto the chart, the more easily understood your chart will be.

It's important to understand the characteristics and functions of the chart elements, as well as how to minimize or maximize their visual presence on a chart. You can format each chart element; understanding this, you can fade in and fade out elements. *Fading in* means darkening and *fading out* means lightening the element. An *element* is anything that can be selected on the chart with your mouse. Fading just adds or reduces emphasis on a chart element, and because all chart elements can be selected individually, you can create or take away emphasis on any element.

> **Note** Formatting options differ for different types of charts. For example, you can't format the axes of a pie chart, because it doesn't have any.

> **Tip #395** Use a standard format across all your charts. This will keep the focus on the information and away from trying to understand the new format with every chart presented. If the presentation is onscreen, the use of colors can be effective, but for most people, black and white is the standard form in which charts are presented.

FORMATTING LINES: AXES, TICK MARKS, HIGH/LOW LINES, AND ERROR BARS

Excel allows you to format just about any line element of a chart. The axes, for example, can be boldfaced and/or displayed with dots or dashes, colors, patterns, or different line weights. The same formatting options apply to high/low lines, tick marks, and error bars. Tick marks on the value or category axis can be removed from the axes altogether, placed inside the axes, crossed over the axes, or moved to the outside.

For radar charts, doughnuts, pies, and other nonrectangular charts, formatting options are available that don't apply to rectangular charts, such as *column charts* or *bar charts*. See the later section "Formatting Data Series" for details.

FORMATTING THE Y-AXIS, SECONDARY Y-AXIS, AND Z-AXIS

Formatting value axes in different ways can either draw attention to or away from the axes. Why would you want to change the format of the value axis? The default formats Excel chooses are fine; however, when presenting information, you might want to adjust the default formats for a more effective and clean presentation.

Tip #396	Format primary and secondary Y-axes to look at least somewhat alike, although the value, major units, and minor units may be extremely different.

Figure 29.1 shows the most common ways to format the value axis.

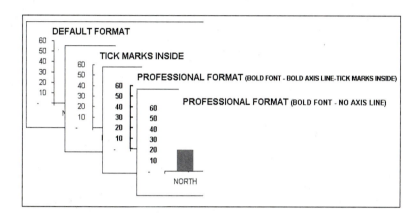

Figure 29.1.
These options are among the most common ways to format the value axis.

→ In most cases, you'll create a standard axis format that you'll use time and time again. Rather than reformatting repeatedly, you can save the chart as a custom type. For details, **see** "Creating a Personalized Custom Chart," **p. 853**

Tip #397	The default setting automatically places *tick marks* outside the axis. The tick marks generally reference the numeric or text value on the axis, so the general direction of the tick mark points to the number or text. However, considering the information you're referencing is usually on the inside of the plot area, you'll probably want to change the direction of the tick marks in most cases.

To format the Y-axis in the "professional" format shown in Figure 29.1, follow these steps:

1. Select the Y-axis so that the selection handles are showing.
2. From the Format menu, choose Selected Axis to display the Format Axis dialog box.
3. Select the Patterns tab.
4. Select the heavy weighted line, as shown in Figure 29.2.
5. Under Major Tick Mark Type, choose Inside.
6. Select the Font tab in the Format Axis dialog box.

Figure 29.2.
The Patterns tab in the Format Axis dialog box enables you to format the Y-axis line type and style, as well as customize the tick marks.

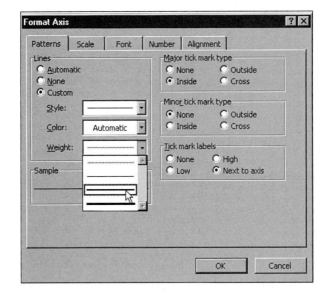

7. Under Font, choose Arial, as shown in Figure 29.3. (If Arial is your default font for Excel, this step can be skipped.)

Figure 29.3.
The Font tab in the Format Axis dialog box enables you to change the font type, style, and size.

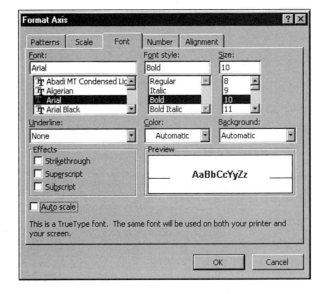

8. Under Font Style, select Bold.
9. Under Size, choose 10. (The size should be dependent on the size of the chart.)
10. Deselect Auto Scale.
11. Click OK.

Tip #398

The reason for deselecting the Auto Scale option is that you'll be changing the chart size on many occasions. If Auto Scale is selected, all the fonts on that axis will change proportionally when you size the chart. This generally is a time-saving issue only.

FORMATTING THE X-AXIS

Similar to formatting the value axis, formatting the category (X) axis can draw attention to or away from the axis. The number of categories ultimately dictates how you format the axis. For example, if you have several dates along the category axis, consider formatting the alignment vertically, so that Excel will wrap the text or change the number of labels displayed (see Figure 29.4). To make this type of change, use the *Orientation* settings on the Alignment tab in the Format Axis dialog box (see Figure 29.5). By aligning the information correctly and formatting the text size, you can usually keep all labels visible on the chart.

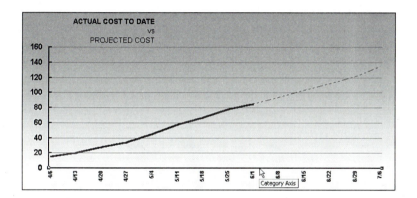

Figure 29.4.
This label orientation was changed to allow for a vertical view of the dates along the category axis.

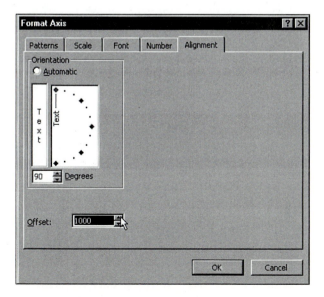

Figure 29.5.
You can change the orientation to vertical and offset the dates from the line or axis with the Offset option.

The <u>O</u>ffset option on the Alignment tab enables you to change the *offset*, which means how far the category labels are positioned from the line or axis. Usually Excel places labels next to the axis. By changing the offset, you can move the labels away from the axis, thus providing more room between the axis line and the labels. Figure 29.6 shows newly aligned axis labels; Figure 29.7 shows one way you can use the additional space between offset labels and the axis.

Figure 29.6.
The offset here has been set to its maximum value of 1000, moving the dates far away from the axis.

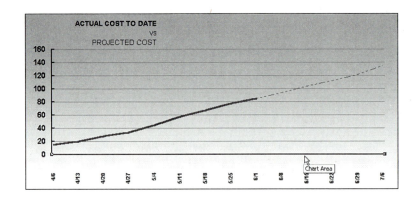

Figure 29.7.
The <u>O</u>ffset setting can give you additional room to apply elements to the chart between the axis and the labels.

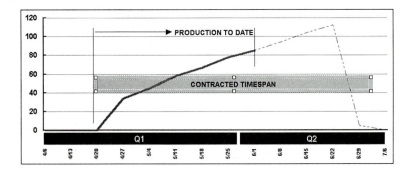

In addition to the alignment and offset, you can format the labels and axis in multiple ways. Figure 29.8 shows some of the most popular ways to format the axis.

The default setting automatically places tick marks outside the axis. If you only have a few categories on the X-axis, it's good practice to get rid of the tick marks altogether. Figure 29.8 shows only four categories, so you don't need guidelines to tell you where the categories separate—it's quite obvious. To remove the X-axis, tick marks, or tick mark labels from view, choose None for the appropriate option in the Format Axis dialog box (see Figure 29.9).

If you want to remove the axis, but keep the axis labels, see "Eliminating the Axis While Keeping Axis Labels" in the Troubleshooting section at the end of this chapter.

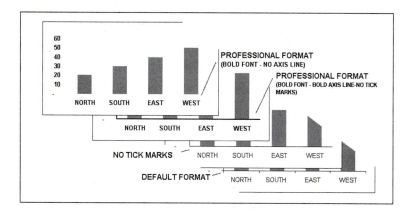

Figure 29.8.
Some common formatting options for the X-axis.

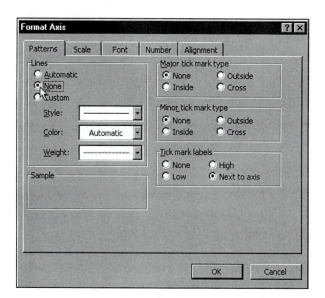

Figure 29.9.
The Patterns tab in the Format Axis dialog box enables you to choose multiple formatting combinations.

Looking at the final result of the X-axis in Figure 29.10, you can see how formatting the axis can provide a clean visual. The difference between the default chart format and the formatted axis is a much cleaner and more professional-looking chart.

FORMATTING AXIS LABELS

Besides changing the font style of the labels on an axis, you also can change the labels' number style and alignment. In addition, Excel enables you to display the units on the axis with different measurement units (see Figure 29.11).

Figure 29.10.
A comparison of the default chart and a chart with a formatted axis.

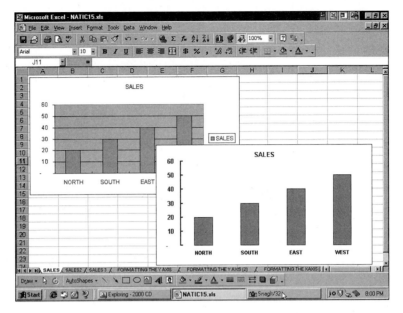

Figure 29.11.
Excel enables you to display units in the measurement amounts shown in the drop-down list.

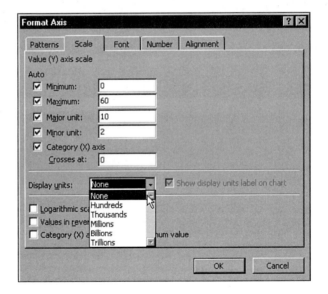

Figure 29.12 shows a comparison of some formatting options of the Y-axis labels. Because there are so many variations, these are just a few of the option combinations available. To create the combination of settings that you want, select the axis and then use the options in the Format Axis dialog box, on the Format menu, and on the Chart and Formatting toolbars.

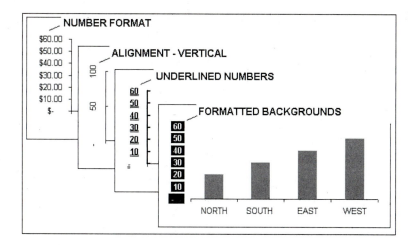

Figure 29.12.
A comparison of value formats on the Y-axis. Excel allows for multiple combinations.

Figure 29.13 shows some additional comparisons in formatting of the X-axis labels. Try to keep the labels as clean as possible, because the labels act as the reference point for the viewer. You'll notice that some of these label formats are combined with the X-axis line formats shown earlier (refer to Figure 29.8). When you start combining the formatting techniques shown, you become more effective in presenting the information.

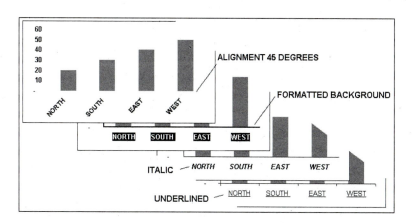

Figure 29.13.
A comparison of category formats on the X-axis. These are just a few of the formatting options available in Excel.

ADDING HIGH/LOW LINES

High/low lines generally are used for 2D stock charts that extend from the highest value to the lowest value in each category. High/low lines can help the chart reader distinguish the highs and lows of a data series. Figure 29.14 shows high/low lines as a guide from the lowest score to the highest score extending to the category axis. You can use high/low lines even if you're not creating a stock chart. (All options can cross over into other categories.)

Try to think out of the box when being creative with charts.) To add high/low lines, follow these steps:

1. Select the data series.

2. From the Format menu, choose Selected Data Series.

3. Select the Options tab in the Format Data Series dialog box.

4. Check the High-Low Lines check box.

Figure 29.14.
You can use high/low lines in other ways besides stock charts. Here, they serve as a guide to the category axis.

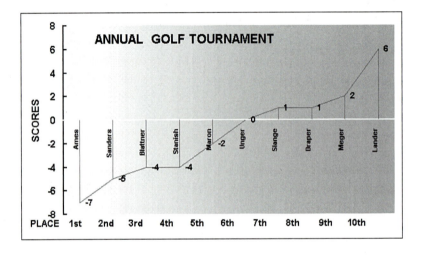

Want to format a single data point? See "Formatting a Single Data Point" in the Troubleshooting section at the end of this chapter.

ADDING ERROR BARS

The Y Error Bars tab in the Format Data Series dialog box enables you to show error amounts that you set, or you can use the standard error of the plotted values as the error amount for each data point. You most often see error bars associated with sample polls, where there's a possibility of error plus or minus. For example, a poll might indicate the number of people who drink milk on a daily basis, with a possibility of error plus or minus 3% from the results shown.

This option is not available for 3D charts (except for bubble charts), or for any pie, dough-nut, or surface charts.

X-axis error bars also are available with scatter charts and bubble charts, where you have values that are horizontal as well as vertical.

To access the Format Data Series dialog box, select the data series and choose Format, Selected Data Series (see Figure 29.15). Figure 29.16 shows error bars added to a typical sales chart. As Figure 29.17 shows, you can format the error bars, just like any other line in a chart. In this example, the error bars are simply boldfaced with the Bold button.

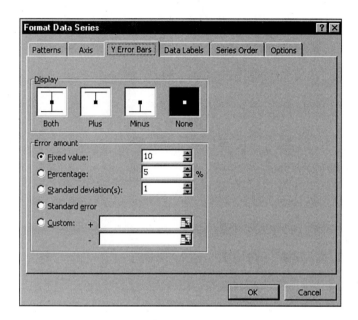

Figure 29.15.
Y error bars enable you to show plus or minus errors or deviations from the plotted data point.

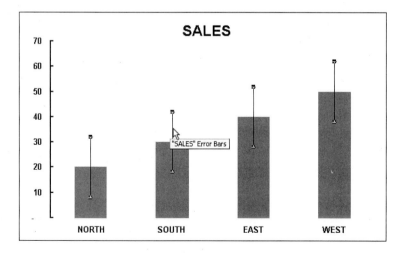

Figure 29.16.
Error bars can help the audience to see by what amount the results may be incorrect.

Figure 29.17.
Formatted error bars.
To format the error
bars, simply select the
error bars and select
Selected Error Bars
from the Format
menu.

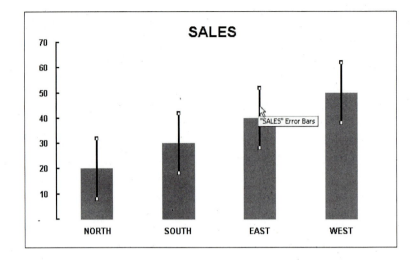

As with any element on the chart, by selecting the error bars, you can format them. The following list describes the options available on the Y Error Bars tab in the Format Data Series dialog box:

- **Both**. Displays both plus and minus error bars on the selected data series.
- **Plus**. Displays plus error bars.
- **Minus**. Displays minus error bars.
- **None**. Removes error bars from the selected data series.
- **Fixed Value**. Uses the value you input as the error amount.
- **Percentage**. Uses the percentage of each data point as the error amount.
- **Standard Deviation(s)**. Uses a fixed number of deviations from the mean of plotted values for the error amount.
- **Standard Error**. Uses the error of the values as the error amount for each data point.
- **Custom**. By typing a value in the plus (+) or minus (–) box or both, you set the error amount for each data point.

FORMATTING TEXT: DATA LABELS, TITLES, LEGENDS, AND TEXT BOXES

As mentioned earlier, all chart elements that can be selected also can be formatted. You can change the font, style, and color of the text as you would any other text in Excel. Simply select the text, title, legend, text box, and so on, and use the appropriate command on the Format menu, Formatting or Chart toolbar, etc.

For details on the techniques for formatting worksheets, see Chapter 19, "Formatting Worksheets."

The following sections provide some details on additional options for formatting the text in a chart.

ADDING AND FORMATTING DATA LABELS

Excel enables you to add information to a chart even after the chart is created. (I seldom get it right the first time.) You can add data labels to a series of data, or you can add data to a single data point.

PART

VII

CH

29

Tip #399

In many cases, you'll want to point out a certain figure or data point in your chart. In this case, you can add a data label or value to a single data point. To do this, select only the data point.

To add data labels to a chart, follow these steps:

1. Select the data series.

2. Choose Selected Data Series from the Format menu, or right-click the series and choose Format Data Series.

3. In the Format Data Series dialog box, click the Data Labels tab (see Figure 29.18).

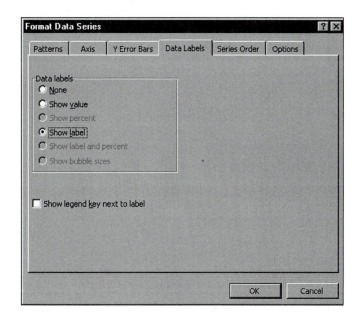

Figure 29.18.
To add labels or values to the desired data series, simply check the appropriate option under Data Labels.

4. Under Data Labels, select Show Label.

5. Click OK.

Tip #400

To add data labels to all data series at once, select Chart Options from the Chart menu to open the Chart Options dialog box. Click the Data Labels tab, select Show Label, and click OK.

After creating data labels, you may want to change the location and appearance of the labels to match the rest of the chart. You can format the data labels by selecting the data label as you would a data value. After the data label is selected, choose Selected Data Labels from the Format menu (or right-click the label and choose Format Data Labels); the Format Data Labels dialog box appears.

 If you want to add space between category labels and the axis line, see "Offsetting the Categories" in the Troubleshooting section at the end of this chapter.

As with other text options, you can use the settings on the Alignment tab to change the alignment and orientation of the labels; you also can adjust the label position in relation to the data series (see Figure 29.19). As shown in Figure 29.20, you can use the Font settings to apply particular font styles, change the color and background, and add effects. In this example, the labels will be formatted with a transparent (invisible) background and a white font, and then placed against dark columns in the data series (see Figure 29.21). Aligning the labels within the data series can give you more room on the chart to call out other points of interest.

Figure 29.19.
Excel enables you to align the data labels in several ways. Here, the label position is set to the inside end of the column and the orientation is at 90 degrees.

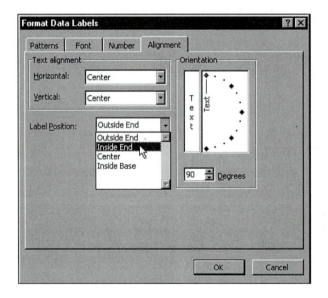

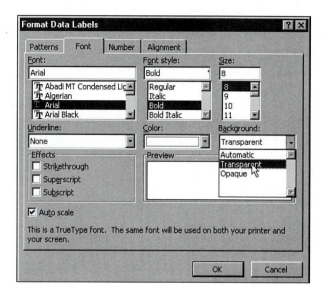

Figure 29.20.
When a label is placed in a dark filled column, create a white font and a transparent background to highlight the label.

PART
VII

CH
29

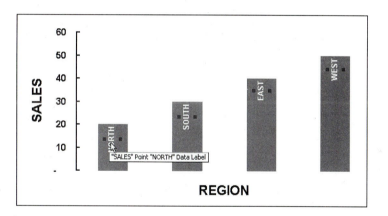

Figure 29.21.
By placing the data labels inside the columns, you can create more landscape on the chart.

Note

In most cases, you should stay away from getting too creative with your data labels. Remember, simple, clear, and concise is usually the best practice.

 If you want to remove the data label backgrounds, see "Eliminating Data Label Backgrounds" in the Troubleshooting section at the end of this chapter.

Moving or formatting a single data label is just as simple; after selecting the whole set of data labels, click the individual label you want to adjust. Then move the label as desired, or use the Format menu to make changes to that specific label.

ADDING AND FORMATTING CHART TITLES

Chart titles consist of the title of the chart, the title of the Y- or Z-axis, and the title of the X-axis. You can enter into a chart and add titles and elements using the Chart Options command on the Chart menu (see Figure 29.22).

Figure 29.22.
You can add chart titles from the Titles tab in the Chart Options dialog box.

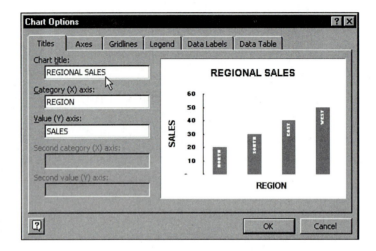

Tip #401

A very fast method to add a "title" is to select the chart, type the title text, and then press Enter. A text box will show up on the chart. You can select it and change the font style and size, and then place it in the desired location. Note that the text box doesn't contain the real title of the chart—for example, it doesn't show up in the Chart Options dialog box. This is just a quick way of creating text boxes in charts. This method also won't automatically resize the chart to accommodate the text. See the later section "Inserting and Formatting Text on a Chart" for details on working with text boxes.

When you have all the chart titles on the chart that you want, you'll probably want to change the size, font, style, or some other feature of the titles to fit your chart's appearance. Just select the title element and then choose Selected Chart Title from the Format menu, or right-click the title and choose Format Chart Title. The Format Chart Title dialog box opens, as shown in Figure 29.23. Select the font settings, effects, and alignment you want, and click OK.

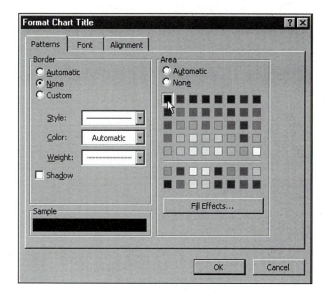

Figure 29.23.
Formatting the chart title. This example will show a black background and white text.

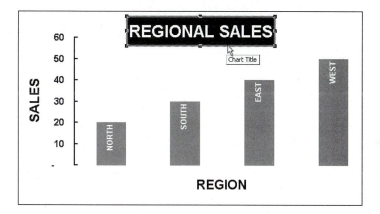

Figure 29.24.
Applying formats to the chart title can make it stand out from the other chart elements.

FORMATTING THE LEGEND

In most cases, you'll notice a legend takes up too much space in the chart. To move the legend, just select it and drag it to any location on the chart. Resizing is just as simple; click the legend and drag one of the handles toward the center of the legend.

INSERTING AND FORMATTING TEXT ON A CHART

Adding text to a chart is something you'll probably want to do on many occasions, not only for visual appeal (as shown in Figure 29.25), but also to call out certain aspects of your presentation. With proper formatting, adding text can be an effective way to help communicate your point.

Figure 29.25.
By adding text to a chart, you can call out certain aspects of the chart or just add a creative touch.

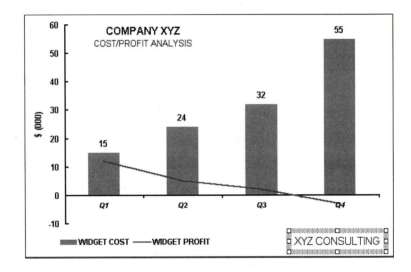

To add text to a chart, follow these steps:

1. Select the chart so the selection handles are showing.

2. Type in the Formula Bar the text you want to display.

3. Press Enter.

You format the text as you would any other chart element. Select the text box, and from the Format menu, choose Selected Object. The Format Text Box dialog box will appear with the font-formatting options available.

ENHANCING CHARTS WITH DRAWING OBJECTS

Adding drawing objects (generally called *shapes*) to a chart enables you to provide additional visual interest and clarify data within the chart. Figure 29.26 shows how you can effectively use some of the drawing tools in a chart. In this example, I've added the season across the charted time and applied the fiscal quarter names between the X-axis and its labels. For more information, see Chapter 30, "Professional Charting Techniques" and Chapter 22, "Professional Formatting Techniques."

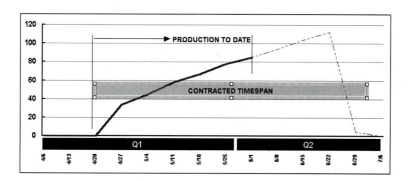

Figure 29.26.
You can add shapes to give several dimensions to your charts, including timelines and time spans that further tell the story of the chart.

Drawing objects are found on the Drawing toolbar, shown as shapes and AutoShapes. Table 29.1 describes some uses for the drawing tools available (see Figure 29.27).

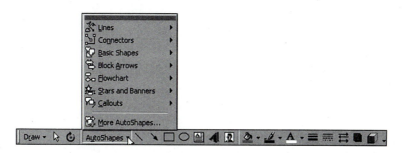

Figure 29.27.
AutoShapes enable you to further enhance charts, tables, and spreadsheets.

TABLE 29.1. SHAPES ON THE DRAWING TOOLBAR

Shape	Use
Lines	Used to point at or create specific cutoff points on a chart.
Connectors	Generally used for connecting shapes within flowcharts and can be used in Excel charts.
Basic Shapes	You can apply basic shapes (triangles, circles, squares, and so on) for creating visuals.

continues

TABLE 29.1.   CONTINUED

Shape	Use
Block Arrows	Used to point at relevant information in a presentation, or to indicate a rise or decline in numbers by connecting one data point to another.
Flow Chart	Can be added to graphic charts to further explain information plotted on the chart.
Stars and Banners	Used to create visual impact with a burst.
Callouts	Used to express ideas or call out points of interest. Points to specific information on the chart with a text message.
Boxes and Ovals	Used for creating legends, keys, and titles.
Lines and Arrows	Points to different elements on a chart in order to draw attention.

Applying shapes to a chart enables you to call out elements of the chart to create direct focus, or apply shapes to tell additional stories directly on the chart. After the chart is created, you can begin adding your drawing tools to the chart by selecting the chart and then selecting the drawing object you want to place on the chart. You can format the drawing objects as you would other elements of a chart—by selecting the element and choosing the desired option(s) from the Format menu. In Figure 29.28, for example, the organizational chart was created with text boxes and connectors. Figure 29.29 shows the individual drawing objects, selected to make them more visible.

Tip #404

Although some shapes are specifically designed to hold text (callout shapes, for example), you can convert almost any shape into a text box by selecting the shape and typing, or right-clicking the shape and choosing Add Text from the context menu.

Figure 29.28.
Understanding how to use shapes with charts can establish visual impact, as well as tell the story behind the picture.

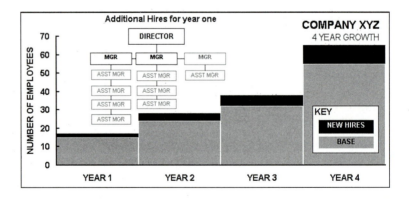

For details on working with the drawing objects, see Chapter 21, "Enhancing Your Worksheet with Excel's Drawing Tools." Chapter 30, "Professional Charting Techniques," also provides some helpful suggestions on ways to use shapes in charts.

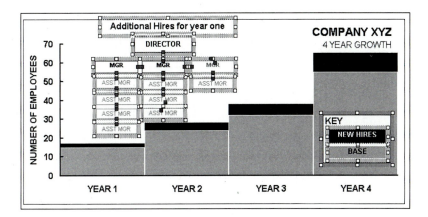

Figure 29.29.
The highlighted shapes placed on the chart were boxes with text typed in the boxes.

FORMATTING DATA SERIES

Probably one of the most important aspects of formatting a chart is the formatting of the data series. You either call attention to or away from a series by how it's formatted. In addition to using the chart options provided specifically for formatting data series, you can add colors, fill effects, patterns, and even pictures, as described in the later section "Changing the Border, Color, or Fill of a Chart Item."

By changing the overlap and gap-width settings for the data series in Figure 29.30, a "stacked column" step chart was created. For this chart, set the Overlap setting on the Options tab in the Format Data Series dialog box to 100 and the Gap Width setting to 0. What is the gap width and overlap? The *gap width* is the gap or space between the categories (for example, the sets of columns on a column chart). The *overlap* is the amount of overlap of the individual data series (the individual columns in a column chart, for example). You can lay the columns of one data series slightly over the next column data series by changing the gap width.

Note

If data series are stacked—for example, in a stacked column chart—there is technically only one column per category, so you would adjust gap width rather than overlap in this case. For charts with multiple series plotted separately, increasing the gap just changes the space between each category's group of columns.

Figure 29.30.
The <u>O</u>verlap and Gap
<u>W</u>idth settings can be
a powerful tool for
creating step charts.

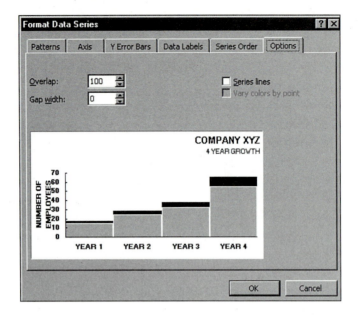

CHANGING THE SERIES ORDER

You can change the series order in the Format Data Series dialog box. Click the Series Order tab and specify how you want the series to move by clicking the appropriate button. In nonstacked charts, you can move data series left and right, forward or backward; stacked charts move series up and down. The preview in the dialog box shows the result you'll get. This feature is particularly useful with area charts, where a smaller set of data might be hidden when a larger set of data is positioned in front of it.

PLOTTING DATA ON THE SECONDARY AXIS

Use a *secondary axis* when comparing two sets of information that have totally different measurements, such as units sold for the year versus the revenue generated by those sales. If plotted on the same Y-axis, the chart could effectively diminish one set of values visually. For example, suppose that units sold for the year is 300, with revenue totaling $4 million. In this case, you might plot the dollars on the secondary axis. To add a secondary axis, use the Axis tab in the Format Data Series dialog box.

EXPLODING PIE SLICES

Quite often, you'll see pie charts that have *exploded* slices of the pie to make them more noticeable. For example, your pie chart shows the quarterly sales for the year, but each pie slice consists of seven products that make up that quarter's sales. By exploding the pie slice, you can display the values of the sales by product that create the total for the quarter.

To explode a slice, click the individual slice to display the selection handles; then drag it away from the center of the pie.

CHANGING THE DATA SERIES ANGLE IN PIE OR DOUGHNUT CHARTS

Sometimes you may want to rotate a pie or doughnut chart to place particular data series at specific positions in the chart. You can rotate the chart with the Angle of First Slice option on the Options tab in the Format Data Series or Format Data Point dialog box. Specify the setting for Degrees, watching the preview, until the chart is positioned as you want it.

FORMATTING A DATA POINT

Formatting an individual data point can be a great benefit in creating a focus. For example, if you have cost-to-date information in the form of a line chart as well as your projected future costs all in the same data series, you'll want to split the formatting of the line (see Figure 29.31). Notice the cost to date appears in bold, and the projected cost is a dotted line. When you receive the cost for the next week, you'll change the format from projected to actual by selecting the single data point and adjusting the format.

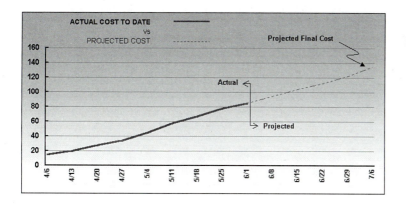

Figure 29.31.
By knowing how to format a single data series, you can create two stories on the same series.

To adjust the format of a single data point, perform the following steps:

1. Select the data series.
2. Select the data point.
3. Choose Selected Data Point from the Format menu.
4. Adjust the format as you would a series.
5. Click OK.

CHANGING THE BORDER, COLOR, OR FILL OF A CHART ITEM

You can format the backgrounds of the chart's data series, individual data points, plot area, chart area, and so on, by adding, altering, or removing borders and changing the color or fill effect used for the item. For example, a standard practice in formatting the background of the chart area is to create a black background with a white plot area. All the titles are converted to white with transparent backgrounds, as shown in Figure 29.32. You'll notice this standard approach to formatting in many publications and magazines.

Figure 29.32.
You can format the plot area in any shade available in Excel. This example uses a sharp contrast to the black chart area color.

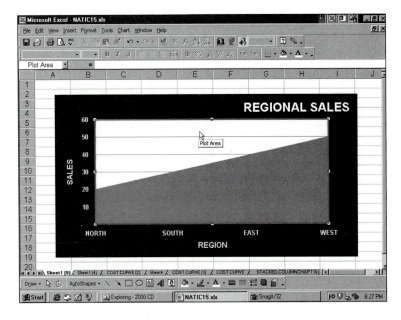

<table>
<tr><td>**Caution**</td><td>Formatting backgrounds can enhance the look of the overall chart; however, be careful not to overdo it. It's easy to get carried away and lose focus on what you actually want the picture to show.</td></tr>
</table>

<table>
<tr><td>**Tip #405**</td><td>One good practice for data series is to remove the standard borders on the series—unless the chart is a line chart, in which case this isn't an option.</td></tr>
</table>

To change the border or background of any chart item, select the item and use the Format menu to access the Format dialog box for that particular item. The options on the Patterns tab provide choices for borders, color, fill effects, and so on, as shown in Figure 29.33.

 If you want to create a chart without the chart borders, see "Eliminating Borders and Backgrounds" in the Troubleshooting section at the end of this chapter.

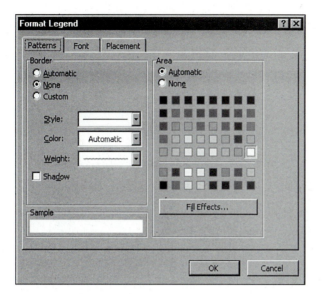

Figure 29.33.
The Patterns tab provides plenty of options for selecting just the right border, color, pattern, and so on.

FILL EFFECTS

Fill effects enable you to use shading, gradients, patterns, and pictures within a data series, plot area, drawing object, and so on. Fill-effect options enable you to get creative with every element on the chart. Figure 29.34 shows just a few of the different fill options you can use.

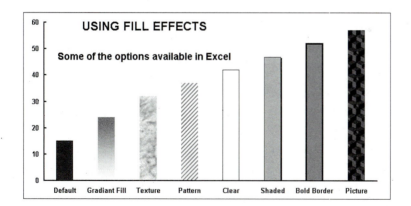

Figure 29.34.
Shown are some of the different fill effects you can use to give a custom look to your charts.

The fill in the Picture column is actually a picture, stacked and scaled, as shown in Figure 29.35. The following section describes how to use this feature.

Figure 29.35.
Using a picture as a fill effect.

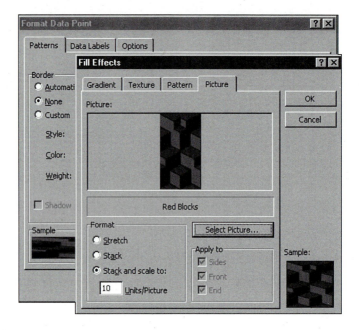

Now, notice the different fill on one column in Figure 29.36. This strong format draws the audience's eyes to the specific chart element you want them to notice.

Figure 29.36.
By applying a different format to one element, you call the attention of the audience to that element.

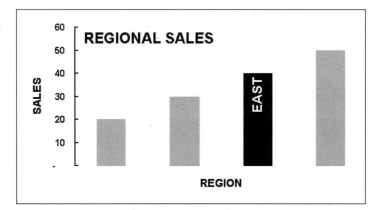

Caution

Be careful with fill effects! If you apply fills to too many elements of a chart, you can create confusion with all the colors and shades. One handy strategy is to apply fills only to every other series, with the remaining series using a solid background color.

To add a fill effect, click the Fi̲ll Effects button in the Area section of the Patterns tab. You can choose from four different types of fill effects: gradients, textures, patterns, or pictures.

→ To learn more about fill effects, **see** "Applying Solid Colors and Fill Effects," **p. 701**

Note
Gradient shades can be utilized to draw attention to or from a specified piece of data on the chart. As the gradient shade gets lighter, that's generally where the attention is drawn.

USING PICTURES AS BACKGROUNDS

The Picture tab in the Fill Effects dialog box enables you to apply a picture as a background (see Figure 29.37). You can use pictures in any of the standard picture formats: PCX, WMF, JPEG, GIF, and so on. Click the Se̲lect Picture button on the Picture tab, select the desired picture, and then adjust it as necessary, using the following options (see Figure 29.38). Note that some of the options may be disabled for certain picture formats.

- **S̲tretch**. Applies the picture and stretches it throughout the selected chart item.
- **Sta̲ck**. Stacks copies of the picture vertically and horizontally to fill the chart item.
- **Sta̲ck and Scale to**. Enables you to stack and scale the picture and adjust it to the size or units you select in the U̲nits/Picture box.
- **Si̲des**. Used for 3D charts, this option applies the picture to the sides of the data series.
- **Fro̲nt**. Used for 3D charts, this option applies the picture to the front of the data series.
- **E̲nd**. Used for 3D charts, this option applies the picture to the top end of the data series.

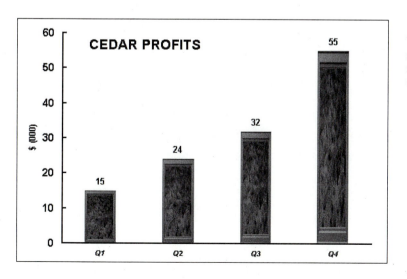

Figure 29.37.
The chart shows the selected picture stretched in the columns.

Figure 29.38.
The Picture tab enables you to insert a picture and scale or stack the picture based on the settings you determine.

 Does a chart seem to take forever redrawing when you change the underlying data? See "Reducing the Number of Units in a Picture" in the Troubleshooting section at the end of this chapter.

FORMATTING 3D CHARTS

Formatting 3D charts offers a few different options from 2D charts. On a 3D column chart, for example, you can format the front, side, and top of the column because Excel allows you to fill flat surfaces. Figure 29.39 shows the default format of a clustered column with a 3D effect. We'll use this as the starting point and walk through some of the important elements in formatting a 3D chart in the following sections. (For more information, see Chapter 30.)

Figure 29.39.
A 3D clustered column chart in default format.

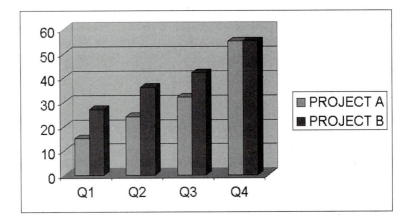

FORMATTING THE WALLS OF A 3D CHART

The walls of a 3D chart can be formatted in several ways, from erasing the walls completely, to applying fill effects. As usual with fill effects, you can apply gradients, textures, patterns, and pictures. As with all cautions on overdoing it, keep it simple and clean on these options. To format the walls of a 3D chart, follow these steps:

1. Select the walls of the 3D chart so the selection handles are showing at each corner of the wall.

2. Right-click and choose Format Walls, or choose Selected Walls from the Format menu.

3. The Patterns tab in the Format Walls dialog box enables you to apply fills to the area as well as outline the walls with border styles. To erase the walls, choose None under Area.

4. To get rid of the remaining gridlines, right-click the gridlines and choose Clear from the context menu, or select the gridlines and press Del.

You'll notice only the floor and axis are left. Many times, you'll find 3D charts work well as standalone charts, and you can get rid of a lot of the fluff that makes up the standard default chart.

FORMATTING THE FLOOR OF A 3D CHART

You format the floor of a 3D chart in a manner similar to that for formatting the other elements of the chart: Right-click and choose Format Floor, or select it and choose Selected Floor from the Format menu. The Format Floor dialog box appears, and the standard options on the Patterns tab become available.

Tip #406	In most cases, the floor of a chart isn't an area of focus, so sometimes it's helpful to eliminate the floor.

Fill effects work well on 3D chart floors because you can use a gradient fill to create a light-to-dark effect—for example, placing light colors closer to the audience and gradually darkening to very dark colors at the back.

FORMATTING THE DATA SERIES OF A 3D CHART

More options are available when formatting a data series in a 3D chart. For example, you can apply different column shapes to a column chart and adjust the depth to which the series reaches back into the chart. To use these 3D formatting features, follow these steps:

1. Select a data series on the 3D chart.

2. Choose Selected Data Series from the Format menu.

3. In the Format Data Series dialog box, select the Shapes tab (see Figure 29.40).

4. Select the desired column shape.

Figure 29.40.
The shapes available
enable you to format
the data series in the
picture shape you
select.

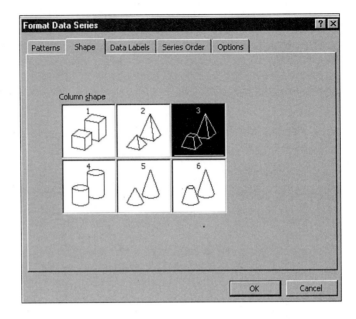

For a dramatic change in a column chart, choose a cone shape for one of the data series. Then, on the Options tab in the same dialog box, set the Gap Depth at 0, the Gap Width at 270, and the Chart Depth at 600, as shown in Figure 29.41.

Figure 29.41.
You can set the width
and depth to create a
dramatic effect for a
3D chart.

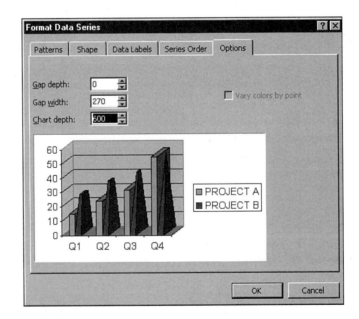

FORMATTING THE 3D VIEW

Now that you have the fundamentals of formatting the different elements of a chart, you can take the chart and create a view from any angle. By selecting the walls of a 3D chart, you can right-click to access the 3D view, or choose 3-D View from the Chart menu to access the 3-D View dialog box (see Figure 29.42).

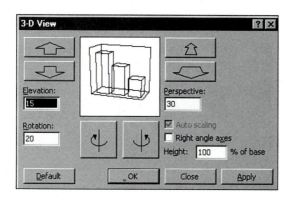

Figure 29.42.
The 3-D View options enable you to adjust the angle of the 3D chart as needed.

Options in this dialog box vary, of course, depending on the type of chart and the items in it, but the following list describes the major options:

- **Elevation**. Enables you to view the chart from a top-down manner, looking at the chart from above.
- **Rotation**. Changes the view in degrees, spinning the chart around the Z-axis.

Note
The arrows for elevation and rotation change the view from top down and right and left views of the 3D chart. Simply click on the appropriate arrow and see the chart angle in the preview window change.

- **Auto Scaling**. Available only when the Right Angle Axes box is checked, this option creates a right-angle proportion. Often, when charts are created in 3D, depending on how you're elevating and rotating the chart, the chart size is reduced.
- **Height % of Base**. Controls the Z-axis height relative to the length of the X-axis.
- **Right Angle Axes**. Independent of the chart rotation, this option sets right angles as opposed to seeing the chart in perspective view. Making sure the Right Angle Axes box is checked usually creates a more uniform look to your chart, because the lines are only displayed in a vertical manner.
- **Default**. Use this button when your adjustments to the chart view have left it a hopeless mess. Excel restores the default settings.

Tip #407

You also can adjust the plot view of a 3D chart with the mouse. Click the floor or wall of the chart to display the *sizing handles (page 382)*. Click on one of the corner handles at the corner of the floor (the ScreenTip displays Corners) and drag. You may need to click twice (not double-click) before you can drag successfully. The plot is replaced with a wire-frame image that you can drag to adjust the angle.

■ **Perspective.** This option is available only when the chart includes two or more sets of data that compare values across categories and series. Perspective view changes the horizontal view of the chart, making the chart appear closer or farther away. You can specify a particular Perspective setting, or use the arrow buttons above the option to make incremental adjustments. If the Right Angle Axes option is checked, perspective view becomes unavailable, because right angles allow for perpendicular lines and right angles only.

Caution

Charts in perspective view often take on a cluttered, unprofessional look, so use care when using angles other than right angles for 3D charts.

TROUBLESHOOTING

ELIMINATING THE AXIS WHILE KEEPING AXIS LABELS

Excel won't let me eliminate the axis line and keep the axis labels.

Select the axis and choose Format, Selected Axis to open the Format Axis dialog box. Click the Patterns tab, and choose None in the Lines section.

ELIMINATING BORDERS AND BACKGROUNDS

Why can't I chart information without the chart borders?

Select the chart and choose Format, Selected Chart Area. In the Format Chart Area dialog box, click the Patterns tab and choose None in the Border section. You also can choose None in the Area section to eliminate the area.

FORMATTING A SINGLE DATA POINT

Why does Excel make me format all of my data series at once?

You can format just one data point by selecting the data series and then clicking on the individual data point until handles are displayed around the single point. Then format this data point as you would format a series, using the Format options.

OFFSETTING THE CATEGORIES

I need to add space between category labels and the axis line.

The Offset feature enables you to move data labels away from the axis line. Select the axis and choose Selected Axis from the Format menu to open the Format Axis dialog box. Then adjust the Offset setting on the Alignment tab.

ELIMINATING DATA LABEL BACKGROUNDS

The colored background on my chart conflicts with Excel's data label colors.

Select the axis with the labels and choose Selected Axis from the Format menu. Select the Font tab in the Format Axis dialog box and choose Transparent under Background.

REDUCING THE NUMBER OF UNITS IN A PICTURE

Excel seems to take an eternity to redraw a chart that uses fill effects.

If you're using a picture with stacked units as a fill effect, and the number of units is fairly large, Excel may require additional memory and time to redraw the chart if you change the underlying data. You might be able to get away with a reduced number of repetitions, without changing the fill effect noticeably. Select the data point or series and open the Format Data Point or Format Data Series dialog box. Click the Fill Effects button, click the Picture tab, reduce the number in the Units/Picture box, and click OK.

CHAPTER 30

PROFESSIONAL CHARTING TECHNIQUES

In this chapter

FORMATTING CHARTS FOR A PROFESSIONAL LOOK

What are "professional" chart techniques? And who's to dictate what "professional" is? In my experience, professional techniques separate those who achieve and create impact from those who don't. To be able to say a thousand words with a single chart or a series of charts can be of extreme importance. There's a certain standard in the business world, as you may have noticed, but no one ever says what that standard is. Well, in this chapter, you'll learn some of those basic "professional" elements that can help you achieve greater impact with your charts. In addition, you'll learn some new ways to combine charts with their source worksheets.

This chapter reviews several distinctly different chart types. Learning ways to mix and match information will help you become more creative in utilizing the charting capabilities in Excel. I discuss such techniques as erasing borders and backgrounds, which is one of the key elements in being able to combine and manipulate information on worksheets with charts. Another way to combine tools in Excel is to use form controls. The best way I've found to use form controls with charts is when you have to continually extract cost-to-date information or production-to-date information. This technique is also described.

The key is understanding the tools in Excel—not only how to combine them, but combine them effectively. Because Excel offers more tools with each new edition, the learning curve never stops.

KEY ELEMENTS IN PROFESSIONAL FORMATTING

In Figure 30.1, some of the key elements in professional techniques are pointed out. Table 30.1 describes professional standard formats that will help you create more effective charts in the future. The cleaner, the better, in most cases.

Figure 30.1.
Standard professional formats can create clean, effective presentations without clutter.

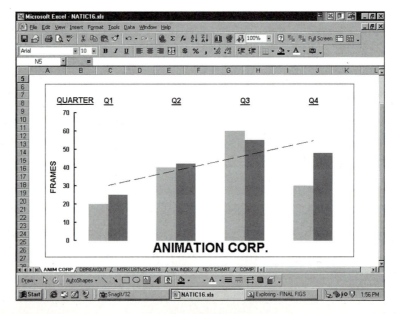

TABLE 30.1.   SUGGESTED FORMATS FOR STANDARD CHART ELEMENTS

Chart Element	Suggested Format
Chart title size	Standard chart title, 16 points
Chart title style	Bold
Y-axis title size	Standard Y-axis title, 12 points
Y-axis title style	Bold
Y-axis tick marks	Inside
Y-axis line style	Bold
X-axis title size	Standard X-axis title, 12 points
X-axis title style	Bold
X-axis tick marks	None
X-axis line style	Bold
Data series border	None
Data series (no emphasis)	Light fill
Data series (emphasis)	Dark fill
Trendlines	Same fill as the data series on which the trendline is based
Trendline style	Thin dotted
Legend border	None
Legend font style	Bold
Legend font size	Standard legend, 8 points
Legend placement	Bottom of chart

Tip #408

After you have a group of chart types that are formatted with the proper font sizes, axis thickness, and data series formats, save them as custom chart types to save future time and effort in reformatting.

Whenever possible, it's good practice to differentiate the data series with light and dark shades and create a spectrum of emphasis from light (least emphasis) to dark (most emphasis). The audience's attention is drawn toward bold and dark.

Tip #409

Excel offers so many options with callouts and drawing objects that it's easy to add elements and forget the focus. Objects such as bursts and stars can have appeal at times, but use restraint with fancy objects in charts. Don't use different font styles—keeping things constant creates a clean effect. Use consistent axis formatting; if you've created a bold Y-axis, also create a bold X-axis. A constant line size is a good practice.

ADDING PICTURES AND SHAPES TO CHARTS

You can enhance your charts with pictures, *AutoShapes* and *WordArt*. Figure 30.2 shows a column chart that could be improved by adding a picture to the background of the chart. To insert a picture, choose Insert, Picture, From File to display the Insert Picture dialog box, in which you can browse and select the desired picture (see Figure 30.3).

Figure 30.2.
From the Insert menu, Excel enables you to insert shapes, pictures, and WordArt.

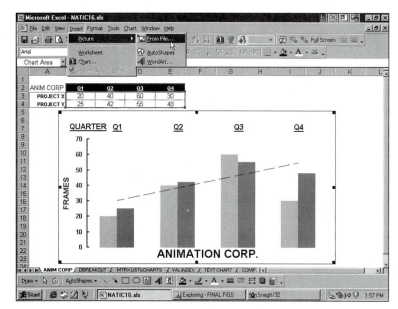

Figure 30.3.
Select the stored picture you want to embed in the chart, and then click Insert.

Tip #410

For increased flexibility, insert a picture into the worksheet, outside the chart. Outside inserts give you access to clip art and scanner images, which can still appear "in" a chart if you drag them onto the chart.

Note

Even with the chart selected, clip art can be inserted by using the ClipArt button on the Drawing toolbar.

After you select the picture and click Insert in the Insert Picture dialog box, the image appears with the Picture toolbar. This allows you to manipulate the picture's brightness, shading, and so on (see Figure 30.4).

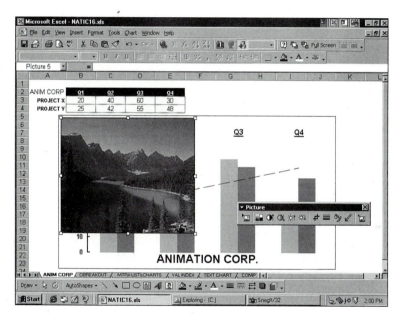

Figure 30.4.
By selecting the chart, you can insert a picture onto a chart and adjust the chart's characteristics with the Picture toolbar.

Table 30.2 describes the buttons on the Picture toolbar.

TABLE 30.2.   BUTTONS ON THE PICTURE TOOLBAR

Button	Name	Description
	Insert Picture from File	Displays the Insert Picture dialog box
	Image Control	Enables the image to be displayed as grayscale, black and white, or watermark

continues

TABLE 30.2. CONTINUED

Button	Name	Description
	More Contrast	Increases the distinction between light and dark areas of the picture, sharpening the image
	Less Contrast	Decreases the distinction between light and dark areas of the picture, reducing the sharpness of the image
	More Brightness	Lightens the image
	Less Brightness	Darkens the image
	Crop	Hides the edges of the selected picture (but doesn't remove them)
	Line Style	Changes the style of the lines or borders to make them heavier, lighter, and so on
	Format Object	Displays the Format Picture dialog box
	Set Transparent Color	Sets a pixel color within an inserted picture to transparent
	Reset Picture	Resets the picture to its original state

COMBINING CHARTS, PICTURES, AND DRAWING OBJECTS

Because Excel enables you to manipulate the backgrounds and styles of charts and their elements, you can combine charts with graphics, shapes, and worksheet elements. If you're in marketing or you plan to display your company's information in a presentation, for example, an image in the background of the chart can give it a certain look or feel. Figure 30.5 shows a chart/picture overlay. The chart in this figure doesn't have borders or backgrounds, and the line elements, numbers, and text have been formatted white with transparent backgrounds.

Tip #411

If you insert a picture into a chart and then drag the picture and size it to the chart, it covers the plot area that contains the data. Insert a picture onto a worksheet, and then size the chart and picture to the same size. Drag the chart over the picture and bring it to the front (right-click and select Bring to Front). Last, select the chart and remove the borders and backgrounds to make the chart transparent so that the picture shows through.

A faster (but less flexible) method is to select the chart area and access the Fill Effects feature. There you can insert a picture and have it appear as a background image without changing any other part of the chart. The drawback is that you can't format the inserted picture.

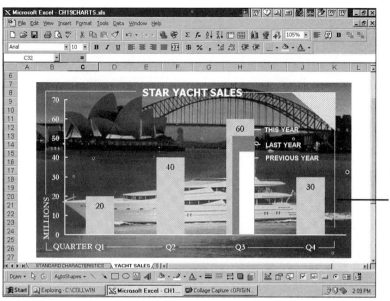

Figure 30.5.
Rather than inserting a picture into a chart, lay a chart on a picture and size the chart to the size of the picture. Select the chart and choose none for borders and backgrounds to make the chart transparent.

Chart has no background.

The Star Yacht Sales chart includes several drawing objects used to attain this professional look. Rectangles placed on the data point of Q3 allow for calling out previous years' performance without upsetting the original chart. Tricks like this create a nontraditional look. By using drawing objects over the column of Q3, it's easy to place emphasis in certain areas of the chart. Figure 30.6 shows all the drawing objects selected so that you can see the number of shapes involved in making this chart.

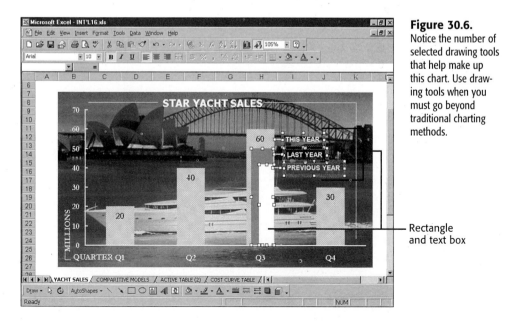

Figure 30.6.
Notice the number of selected drawing tools that help make up this chart. Use drawing tools when you must go beyond traditional charting methods.

Rectangle and text box

Drawing lines reversed to white create a border around the plot area, as well as an elbow connecting the X- and Y-axis titles. Inserting text to differentiate the Q3 performance difference in years calls the attention to Q3 as the high point.

To lay a chart over a picture, perform the following steps:

1. Paste a picture on a worksheet.
2. Place the chart over the picture.
3. Size the chart so that the chart completely covers the picture.
4. Choose Selected Chart Area from the Format menu.
5. Select the Patterns tab in the Format Chart Area dialog box.
6. Choose None in the Border area.
7. Choose None in the Area section of the dialog box.
8. Click OK.

   The chart appears with the picture in the background.

To format the text on the axis, follow these steps:

1. Select the axis.
2. Choose Selected Axis from the Format menu.
3. Choose the Font tab in the Format Axis dialog box.
4. Choose White from the Color drop-down list box.
5. Select Transparent from the Background drop-down list box (see Figure 30.7).
6. Click OK.

Figure 30.7.
To erase the background of fonts on the axis, select Transparent for the background.

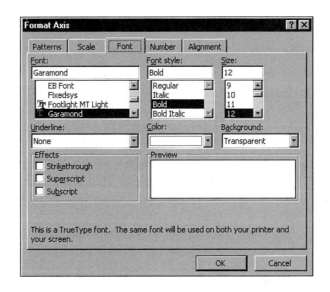

When using several layers of objects, charts, and text, you'll need to become familiar with such tools as the Bring to Front and Send to Back buttons. By selecting an object and choosing Bring to Front, the object is placed on top of all the objects layered. You can add toolbar buttons for the Bring to Front and Send to Back commands (see the following Tip), or you can select these commands from the context menu. For charts, right-click the chart and select Bring to Front or Send to Back. For drawing objects, right-click the object, select Order, and then select Bring to Front or Send to Back. If you have multiple layers of objects, you can use the Bring Forward or Send Backward command on the Order submenu to move the selected object forward or backward one layer at a time.

Tip #412

If you use the Bring to Front and Send to Back buttons often, add them to your Drawing toolbar. Right-click on the toolbar and select Customize to open the Customize dialog box. In the Categories list on the Commands tab, choose Drawing, and then scroll the Commands list to find the Bring to Front and Send to Back commands and drag them to the toolbar. Close the Customize dialog box when you're finished.

Another method is to open the Draw menu on the Drawing toolbar, select the Order option, and "tear off" the Order submenu as a floating toolbar with the Order buttons. You can use this toolbar as needed, or drag the buttons from the Order toolbar (hold down the Ctrl and Alt keys while dragging) to the desired position on any other toolbar.

ADDING A DRAFT STAMP OR WATERMARK WITH WORDART

You can create draft stamps or *watermarks* that you can place on charts or worksheets with WordArt. This is more of an aesthetic and formatting trick; however, it can add a nice touch for presentations. Figure 30.8 shows an example of a chart with a DRAFT stamp created with WordArt.

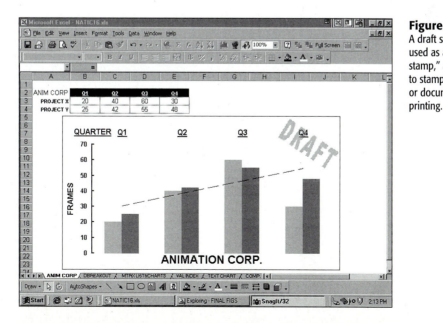

Figure 30.8.
A draft stamp can be used as an "onscreen stamp," as opposed to stamping a chart or document after printing.

Tip #413	With Excel's formatting capabilities, you can group objects with lines, creating stamps that show lines for signatures.

To create a transparent stamp, perform the following steps:

1. Click the WordArt button on the Drawing toolbar. Select the desired style for the text, as shown in Figure 30.9, and then click OK.

2. Type **DRAFT** in the Edit WordArt Text dialog box, as shown in Figure 30.10. Add boldface and/or italic, if desired, by clicking the Bold and/or Italic button.

Figure 30.9.
To create a transparent stamp, begin by selecting the WordArt style in the WordArt Gallery.

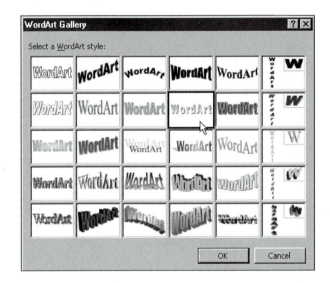

Figure 30.10.
Type the draft text in the Edit WordArt Text dialog box. You can capitalize it or use a combination of cases.

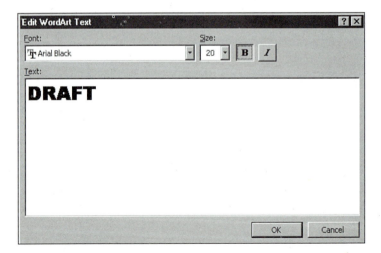

3. Click OK to close the dialog box and display the WordArt object in the chart.

4. On the Drawing toolbar, click the Shadow button and choose No Shadow (see Figure 30.11).

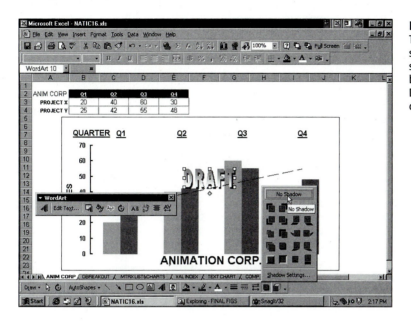

Figure 30.11.
To eliminate the shadow on WordArt, select the Shadow button on the Drawing toolbar and choose No Shadow.

PART

VII

CH

30

5. With the WordArt image still selected, choose WordArt from the Format menu.

6. In the Format WordArt dialog box, select the Colors and Lines tab.

7. Under Fill, choose Gray-25%.

8. Check Semitransparent.

9. Click OK.

10. Rotate the text as desired by clicking the Free Rotate button on the WordArt toolbar and then dragging the green rotate handles on the WordArt (see Figure 30.12).

ADDING CHARTS TO SHAPES

Not only can you place charts over pictures, but you can also place charts over drawing objects as shown in Figure 30.13. By creating a shape such as the 3D box shown, you can place a chart over the top of the box. Choose None for borders and areas as discussed in the previous example of Star Yacht Sales.

The arrows shown in this example are drawn from AutoShapes on the Drawing toolbar. The up arrow emphasizes the corrugate sales increase, and the down arrow emphasizes the chipboard decrease over the previous period. The arrow objects provide additional information that otherwise wouldn't be included in the chart.

Figure 30.12.
Rotate the text with the Free Rotate command from the WordArt toolbar.

Drag a rotate handle to change the position of the WordArt image.

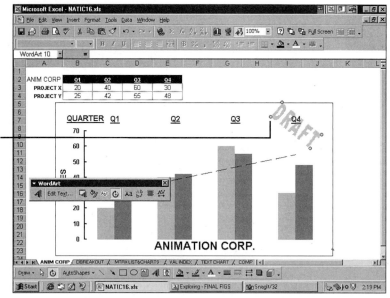

Figure 30.13.
By using fill effects, you can even create a gradient from the center of the pie to the edges.

Drawing tools

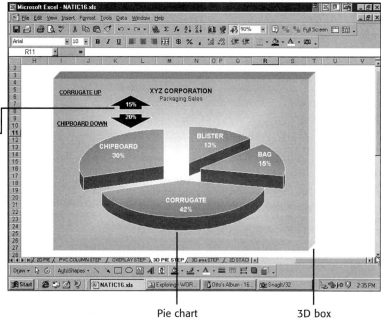

Pie chart   3D box

CREATING COLUMN DEPTH

After creating a default 3D column chart, you can either leave the chart in default format, or you can take advantage of Excel's depth options. By understanding the value of 3D elevation and rotation in Excel's 3D charts, you'll be able to add the right perspective to a chart and create emphasis on certain areas.

Caution

> Unless you have specific reasons to plot a chart in a 3D format, I suggest staying with 2D charts. A 3D chart may be more aesthetically pleasing, but remember that the audience should be able to determine what the chart says in seconds. If possible, use 2D charts.

By adding depth to a 3D column chart, you can dramatically change the shapes of the original columns, as shown in Figure 30.14. Applying gradient fills, drawing objects, and WordArt can further enhance the look of the chart.

3D box

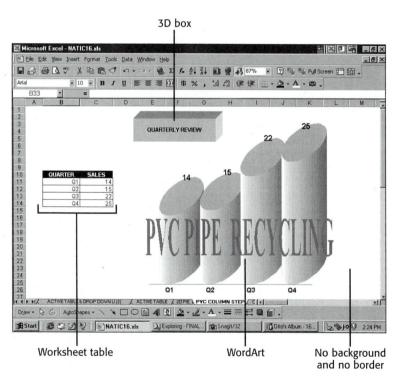

Figure 30.14.
Utilizing Excel's depth capabilities with 3D charts can give charts more appeal.

Worksheet table   WordArt   No background
                                          and no border

The following paragraphs highlight the important steps in creating a chart with depth and perspective similar to the chart shown in Figure 30.14. First, create a simple table like that in the figure. Then create an embedded 3D column chart from the table, using the Cylinder chart type instead of the standard 3D column to give the data series the oval shape.

To add the perspective and depth, follow these steps:

1. Right-click on the plot area of the chart.

2. Select 3-D View from the context menu to display the 3-D View dialog box.

3. Set the Elevation to 6 and the Rotation to 4. Be sure the Right Angle Axes option is checked (see Figure 30.15).

4. Click OK.

Figure 30.15.
Setting the elevation, rotation, and right angles of the 3D column chart.

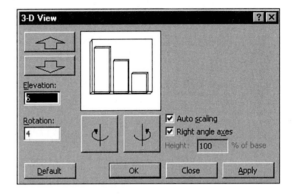

5. Select the data series.

6. From the Format menu, choose Selected Data Series to open the Format Data Series dialog box. Click the Options tab.

7. Set the Gap Depth at 0, Gap Width at 10, and Chart Depth at 960 (see Figure 30.16). These settings change the width of the columns, the depth to which the columns reach "back" into the chart, and the distance between the columns.

8. Click OK.

Figure 30.16.
The Options tab in the Format Data Series dialog box enables you to change the width and depth of the data series.

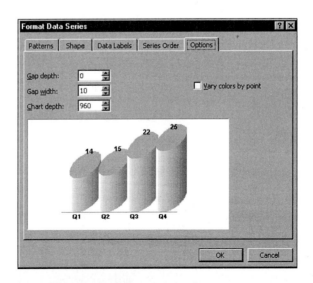

To add a 3D object as shown in the chart title (refer to Figure 30.14), select a drawing shape, draw the shape you want, and then select the 3-D button from the Drawing toolbar. Then apply the 3D perspective and depth you want.

To add the text, select the object and type the text you want. Excel automatically creates a text box that allows for text to be typed on the face of the 3D object.

 To add the WordArt, click the WordArt button on the Drawing toolbar and type the desired text. Place the WordArt over the chart. Right-click and select Bring to Front.

EXPLOITING THE SECONDARY AXIS, OVERLAP, AND GAP WIDTH

Occasionally, you may need to measure two sets of data in a chart. By understanding how to create an overlay, you can compare data more effectively. A simple column chart with overlays (such as the one in Figure 30.17) can compare this year versus last year, but what if you need to show the status on multiple projects for your weekly production meetings? This same approach in the form of a bar chart instead of the column chart could be used to show projected completion versus actual completion by this point in time (see Figure 30.18). The key elements in creating charts like this are to select one of the data series and give it a secondary axis. Then set the gap width and overlap, and set one of the data series fills to None.

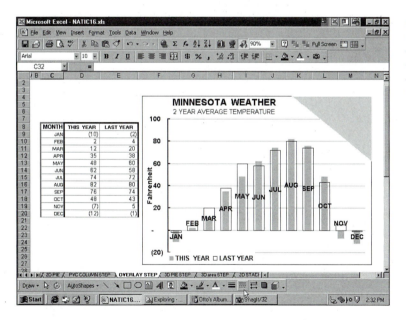

Figure 30.17.
By using the secondary axis and changing the overlap and gap width, you can create overlays.

Excel enables you to align the data series one over another. By eliminating the background of one of the data series, you can create this "thermometer" effect. To create a column chart with a thermometer effect as shown in Figure 30.17, follow these steps:

1. Start with a clustered *column chart*.

2. Select one of the data series.

Figure 30.18.
Using the same overlay approach, you can show projected versus actual on the same line.

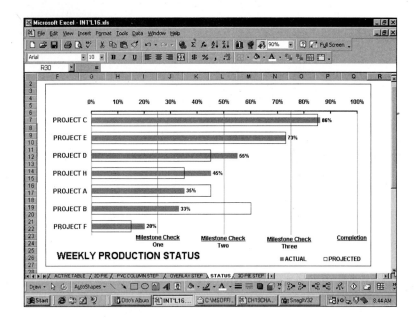

3. From the Format menu, choose Selected Data Series to open the Format Data Series dialog box.

4. Select the Patterns tab.

5. Under Area, choose None.

6. Select the Axis tab (see Figure 30.19).

7. Choose Secondary Axis.

Figure 30.19.
Create separation of the data series by plotting one of the series on a secondary axis.

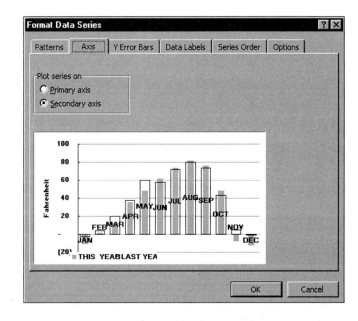

8. Select the Options tab (see Figure 30.20).

9. Set the <u>O</u>verlap to 0.

10. Set the Gap <u>W</u>idth to 50.

11. Click OK.

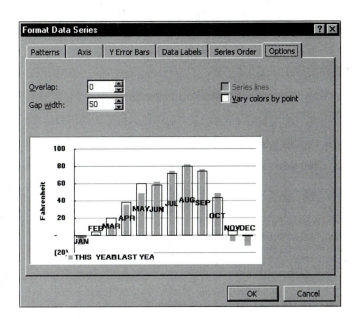

Figure 30.20.
Setting the overlap
and gap width.

Tip #414

To add the gray corner shown in Figure 30.17, select A<u>u</u>toShapes from the Drawing toolbar, and then select <u>B</u>asic Shapes. Select a triangle and draw it on your chart to the desired size. While the triangle is still selected, *flip* and position it to match the corner of the chart. Choose Dr<u>a</u>w from the Drawing toolbar, then Rotate or Fli<u>p</u>, and last Flip <u>H</u>orizontal or Flip <u>V</u>ertical as needed to position the triangle to match the corner. Place the triangle in the corner and fill with a desired fill.

PIE CHART TECHNIQUES

When creating pie charts, you'll want to bring focus to a certain category. You can focus the audience's attention on a certain pie slice in several ways. One is by formatting the slice to stand out. Another is by changing the angle of the first slice. The following sections describe these techniques.

→ To make a particular slice of the pie chart really noticeable, you can explode the slice. For details, **see** "Exploding Pie Slices," **p. 904**

SPINNING THE PIE CHART

Notice that Q4 in Figure 30.21 is angled to the top. This wasn't the default version of the chart. You can angle the first pie slice to make a particular slice appear on the top, side, and so on.

Figure 30.21.
You can "spin" a chart by changing the angle of the first slice.

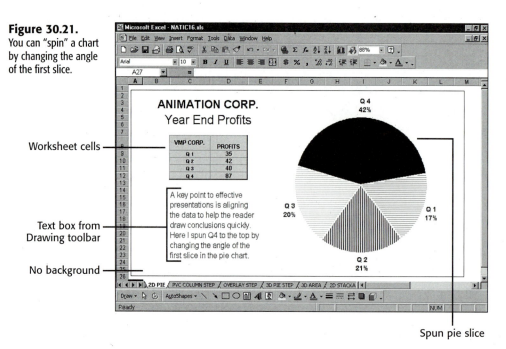

Worksheet cells

Text box from Drawing toolbar

No background

Spun pie slice

To change the angle of the first slice, follow these steps:

1. Select the data series that you want to adjust in the first slice of the pie.

2. From the Format menu, choose Selected Data Series to open the Format Data Series dialog box.

3. Choose the Options tab.

4. Using the spinner, select the desired angle.

5. Click OK.

To create a table on a chart as shown in Figure 30.21, select the chart and choose None under Area in the Format Chart Area dialog box. Drag the chart over a table and then deselect the chart. The table shows through the transparent chart area. You'll have to move and format the different elements of the chart to get the exact appearance you're looking for. It also helps to have the data behind the percentages on the pie.

ORGANIZING PIE CHARTS TO TELL A STORY

The organization of charts is extremely critical when it comes to helping the audience understand the point. Figures 30.22 and 30.23 show two versions of a pie chart showing expenses for a physician. In both cases, sorting the underlying data in ascending order gives the chart structure. In the second version, custom formats and titles are key elements in getting the point across, and the angle of the first slice is adjusted to create further structure. An additional table to the right of the pie chart provides related details.

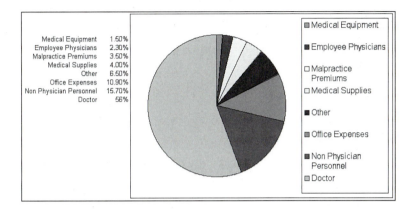

Figure 30.22.
With the data series sorted in order, this pie chart is clear and informative.

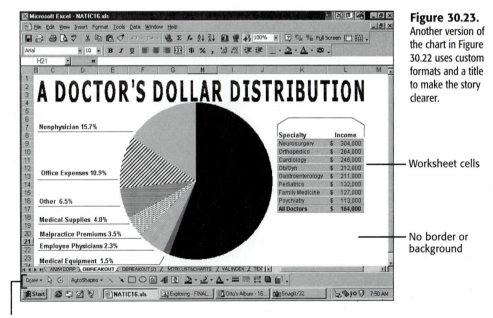

Drawing tools

Figure 30.23.
Another version of the chart in Figure 30.22 uses custom formats and a title to make the story clearer.

Worksheet cells

No border or background

USING FILL EFFECTS TO SHOW VARIANCE IN 3D CHARTS

One way to distinguish levels of data series is to apply a grade that reflects a series with colors or shades. Notice in Figure 30.24 that the different grades of stock are reflected by the gradient fills of the data series. Subtle visual tricks like these can work on the subconscious of the audience to help get the point across.

Figure 30.24.
Data series are formatted to reflect the series grade.

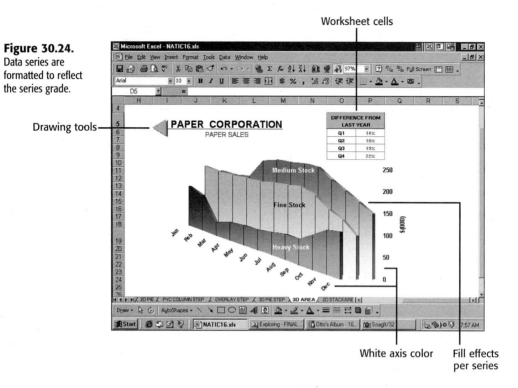

To create a 3D area chart with gradient fills that separate products, follow these steps:

1. Create a table that distributes the sets of data, as shown in Figure 30.25.

Figure 30.25.
This table distributes three sets of data over a period of time.

PAPER SALES

Month	Fine Stock	Medium Stock	Heavy Stock
Jan	136	125	90
Feb	135	128	80
Mar	138	135	30
Apr	142	182	40
May	146	195	45
Jun	155	200	46
Jul	160	208	52
Aug	168	212	58
Sep	158	195	59
Oct	138	180	80
Nov	125	165	102
Dec	100	150	108

2. Create an area chart with a 3D effect.

3. Right-click over the chart area and choose 3-D View.

4. Set the Elevation to 10 and the Rotation to 60.

5. Check the Right Angle Axes option.

6. Select the data series that you want to look heavy or dark. From the Format menu, choose Selected Data Series to display the Format Data Series dialog box.

7. Select the Options tab. Set the Gap Depth to 500 and the Chart Depth to 60. Select the Drop Lines option.

8. From the Patterns tab, choose Fill Effects to open the Fill Effects dialog box. Choose Two Colors (see Figure 30.26).

PART

VII

CH

30

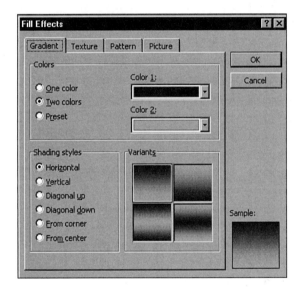

Figure 30.26.
Set the two-color gradients to reflect the grade of paper weight.

9. Choose Black for Color 1 and choose Gray-25% for Color 2.

10. Be sure that the shading style is Horizontal with the upper-left variant selected. Click OK twice.

11. Repeat the fill effect steps with each data series, selecting settings for medium and light shading.

12. Delete the chart wall, gridlines, and chart area.

To incorporate a table in the chart corner as shown, select the chart and be sure that Area is set to None on the Patterns tab in the Format Chart Area dialog box.

USING FORM CONTROLS WITH CHARTS

You might combine *form controls* and charts for several reasons. Based on a database from which the information is generated, you can use form controls to combine data into a single chart and make the chart active. (To learn more about combining charts with active tables, see Chapter 34, "Using PivotTables and PivotCharts," and Chapter 35, "Managing Data with Formulas and Form Controls.")

Figure 30.27 shows an example of a chart that uses option buttons to display the desired data. The user clicks the Wichita Plant button or the Middelton Plant button to change the displayed data in the chart. This combination of chart, tables, and form controls uses a formula to extract information from a large database and condense and display it in a small space. Form controls with charts can become powerful tools for accessing multiple data sets with just one click.

Figure 30.27.
Form controls can be a great way to access and view information that must be continually regenerated.

Option buttons ——

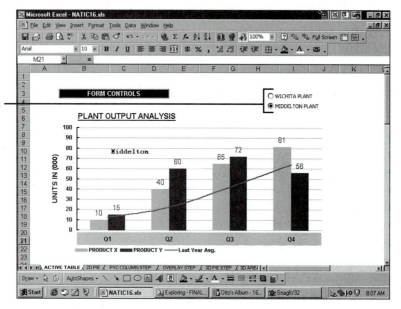

For this example, you create an active table that's derived from two separate tables. Using a simple IF statement, you then create the chart from the active table. Finally, the form control toggles the set cell referenced by the IF statement.

To access the form controls, right-click any toolbar and choose Forms, or select View, Toolbars, Forms.

To create an active chart with an option button, begin by setting up the information as described in the following steps:

1. Set up tables 1 and 2 as shown in Figure 30.28. These are the origin tables that the source table will reference.

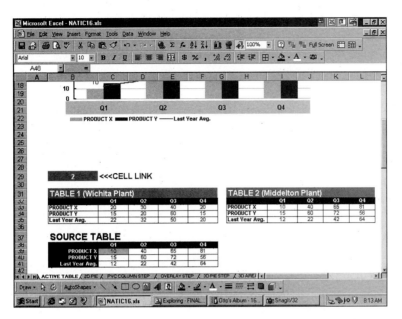

Figure 30.28.
It's important to set up the tables with the proper relative referencing.

2. Set up the source table, formatted identically to the origin tables.

3. Create the chart from the source table, and select it. (If you create the option buttons before selecting the chart, the buttons will be attached to the worksheet rather than the chart. Consequently, the buttons won't move with the chart.)

4. Draw an option button, right-click it, and then choose Format Control from the pop-up menu (see Figure 30.29).

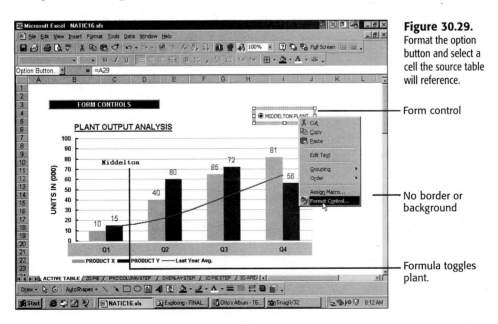

Figure 30.29.
Format the option button and select a cell the source table will reference.

Form control

No border or background

Formula toggles plant.

5. Select the Control tab in the Format Control dialog box (see Figure 30.30).

6. Type the address for the cell link (for this example, in cell B29).

7. Click OK.

Figure 30.30.
Format the control
and set the cell link
to the desired cell.

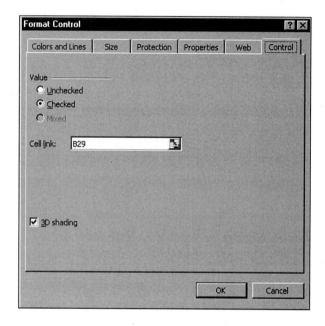

8. Select the option button and title the button.

9. Repeat steps 4 through 8 with the same cell link, but give the second option button a different name. To save time with the cell link and formatting, you can use Ctrl+D to duplicate the option button control. You still need to rename it, of course.

10. Now enter the formula. In this example, in cell C39 of the source table is the following formula: =IF($B$29=1,C33,I33). Drag and fill to the right and then down. The statement will fill to the right and down to mirror that of the two tables. This statement reads from the cell to which the option button is linked. If it's 1, the result is that of the first origin table (Wichita, in this example) or the second origin table (Middelton) if 2.

Notice in Figure 30.31 that when Middelton is selected, the source table values equal that of the origin table Middelton Plant. The chart changes to match.

To create a toggle name (such as Wichita or Middelton) that sits in the plot area, be sure you choose None for Area on the chart. Next, in a cell that won't get in the way of the data series, type a formula that references the cell link again. The formula in this example would reference the cell link B29 and reads as follows:

```
=If(B29=1,"Wichita","Middelton")
```

This basically says, if B29=1 then Wichita, else Middelton.

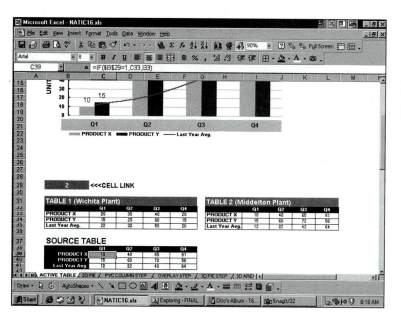

Figure 30.31.
When the formula from the source table references the cell link, the option buttons become actively integrated with the tables.

Tip #415

If you expect the chart to move at some point, don't use a cell in the background to represent the label. (Should the chart be moved or resized, a new cell would have to be used.) Chart titles and labels as well as text boxes (or any shape) can contain a reference to any cell on your worksheet. Place the preceding formula in any cell outside the chart area (maybe near the source table). Then select the chart and click on the Formula bar. Type an equal sign; then click or type the cell address containing the preceding formula, and press Enter. A text box will appear in the center of the chart. You can then move, size, and format the text box to your liking. Unlike using a cell directly, this text box will move and size with the chart.

Tip #416

You can add as many option buttons as you want and reference the same cell link. The number of the option button will continually increase, based on the number of option buttons you select and link.

If you don't anticipate moving or resizing a chart, you can create the option buttons on the worksheet behind the chart. Then eliminate the borders and the backgrounds in the chart by selecting None under Area on the Patterns tab in the Format Chart Area dialog box.

STACKING MULTIPLE CHARTS

If you have several bits of information to chart and are wondering how to effectively present it all together, the answer may be to separate the data into multiple charts and stack the charts. Because charts often are used to show historical information or projections over time, you can create multiple charts based on time frames, aligning the charts so each period of time appears directly above the next.

In Figure 30.32, the unit output chart has been aligned directly above the associated cost chart, and the fourth quarter has been highlighted to draw attention. You can stack two, three, or more charts in this manner to create comparisons of multiple groups of data. Why not place them on separate sheets? You can place each chart on its own sheet, but seeing how all the data correlates can provide conclusions you might not normally derive by reviewing the data separately.

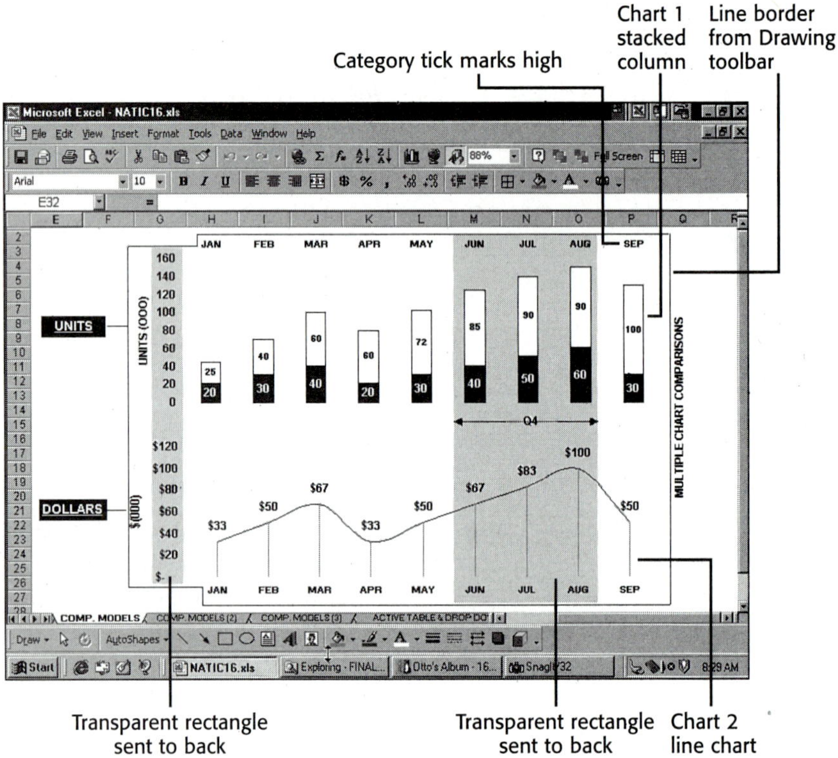

Figure 30.32.
Stacking charts can combine several bits of information on the same sheet, while still showing all the data at the same time.

After the charts are aligned, you can add drawing objects, such as lines and semitransparent boxes. The semitransparent box highlights the quarter and is sent to the back with the Send to Back command. Be sure you've selected None for chart fills so that the charts are transparent. Otherwise, the shape sent to the back will be covered by the chart's fill color.

CREATING COST AND PRODUCTION CURVES WITH CHARTS FOR VARIANCE

What is a *cost curve* or *production curve*? As process happens over time, cost accumulates over time, as do production, percentages, widgets, and so on. All too often, people have difficulty measuring and understanding how to view information over time, and especially being able to draw some relevant conclusion from the data. This section begins by establishing a table that provides projected weekly costs, and then, as the costs are incurred, applies that information as well (see Figure 30.33). By knowing how to lay out the underlying data, you can create charts that have meaning, instead of just graphic appeal.

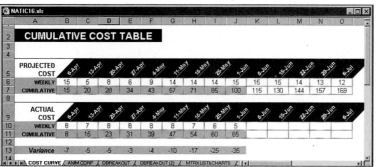

Figure 30.33.
By setting up a cost curve table in this fashion, you can establish a usable measuring tool in the form of a line chart that gives a visual of what has occurred over time.

As costs are incurred, you add that data to the actual weekly cost row. To automate the cumulative cost, sum the previous cumulative week plus the current week. (By doing this, you won't have to add up the cumulative every time a week's cost is input.) To display the data in chart format, select the date range and the cumulative projected/cumulative actual cost range, and then create the chart. Figure 30.34 shows a cost-curve line chart, displaying the variance between projected and actual costs. It's quick-hitting and easy to understand.

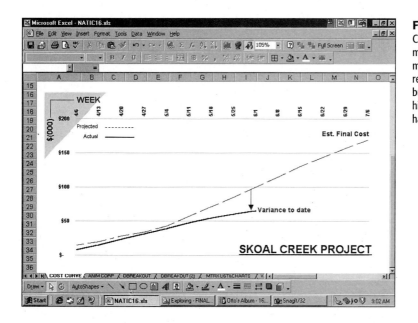

Figure 30.34.
Cost curves not only make for great measuring tools with regard to variance, but also show historically what has happened.

Production curves are created in similar fashion. Because production occurs over time as well, you can cumulate widgets, time, and so on. The key here is to understand that everything is measurable. If it isn't, either you're not accomplishing anything, or you're not creating anything.

To add the text as shown, select the chart, select the text box from the Drawing toolbar, and type the desired text.

To add lines or arrows for callouts, select the chart, select the Line or Arrow tool from the Drawing toolbar, and then draw the desired line. Adjust the position as necessary.

LINKING CHART TEXT TO WORKSHEET CELLS

When setting up workbooks that will be used by several people, you might want to link text or numbers from a cell in the workbook to a chart, so that when the chart is shown, it's representative of the worksheet. Suppose that you have a worksheet that performs many calculations and the chart is the outcome of the calculations, but is titled differently every time a calculation is done. In this case, you'll want to see a different title for each scenario or calculation. To link a cell to a chart, just select the chart and, in the Formula bar, type the formula =*cell*, substituting the cell reference for *cell*. When text or a number is generated in the cell, it shows up on the chart as well.

CHARTING HIDDEN DATA

You can maintain a chart's integrity even if you *hide* the data that the chart references. By default, Excel hides the information in a chart when the underlying data is hidden. Suppose that you created an outline that sums up the quarters under the months, as shown in Figure 30.35. If you hide the monthly data, as shown in Figure 30.36, the chart displays only the quarterly totals.

To plot nonvisible cells on the chart, perform the following steps:

1. Select the chart.
2. Choose Options from the Tools menu.
3. Select the Chart tab in the Options dialog box (see Figure 30.37).
4. Uncheck Plot Visible Cells Only.
5. Click OK.

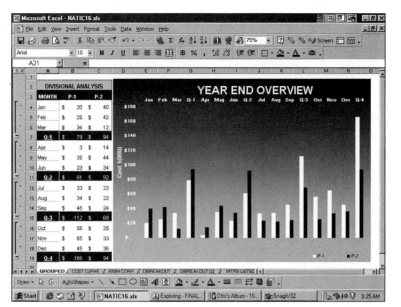

Figure 30.35.
A chart and its underlying monthly and quarterly data.

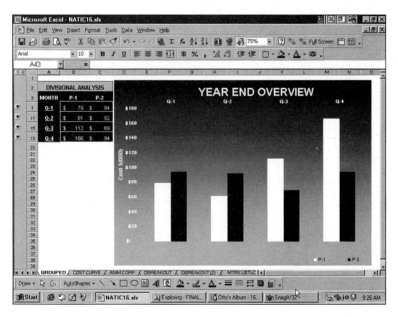

Figure 30.36.
Notice that only the visible cells are shown on the corresponding chart.

Figure 30.37.
Hidden cells remain plotted on the chart when the Plot Visible Cells Only option is unchecked.

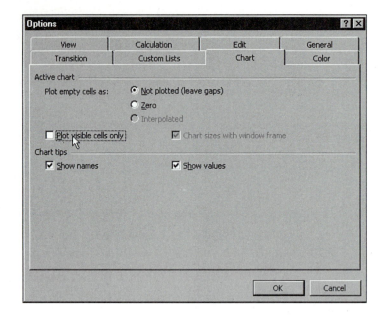

CREATING EFFECTIVE MULTIPLE-COMBINATION CHARTS

Multiple-combination charts are good for comparing two or more sets of data. Figure 30.38 shows the three sets of data used to create the chart in Figure 30.39. This example looks at the total contracted amount minus the monthly completed totals against the prior year's output. Charts can be a great way of showing depletion of total reserves.

Figure 30.38.
You can create multiple sets of data to establish a multiple-combination chart.

NATIC16.xls

GOLD MINING CORP

	CONTRACTED ORE TO MINE	ORE MINED	LAST YEAR
Jan	150	0	0
Feb	148	2	0
Mar	142	6	5
Apr	130	12	15
May	107	23	26
Jun	83	24	34
Jul	59	24	26
Aug	24	35	23
Sep	12	12	12
Oct	5	7	12
Nov	1	4	0
Dec	0	1	0

Sheet4 / GROUPED / COST CURVE / ANIM CORP

For this example, you start by establishing three sets of data as shown in Figure 30.39. The Contracted Ore to Mine data series reduces total quantity remaining from the monthly ore amounts mined. The third column represents last year's monthly output as a comparison to this year's quantities.

Bevel from Drawing toolbar

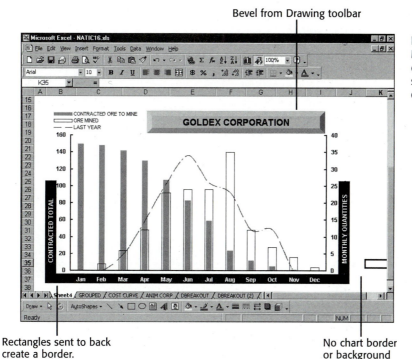

Figure 30.39.
Multiple-combination charts can separate several data series on the same chart.

PART

VII

CH

30

Rectangles sent to back
create a border.

No chart border
or background

You can create multiple-combination charts in more than one way:

■ Select the entire table and create a chart with the Chart Wizard, and then select each data series and change them independently by choosing Chart, Chart Type.

■ Paste the data separately.

After formatting a multiple-combination chart, save the chart as a custom chart type to avoid having to reformat each new multiple-combination chart you create.

VISUAL DISPLAY IN EXCEL

Visual display isn't limited to charts. Visual display can include words, objects, lists, or a combination thereof. Take sounds, for example. Although sounds aren't visual, audible sounds can create a sense of calm or urgency. Remember the theme from *Jaws* and how it created a sense of urgency? The same is true when thinking in terms of visual display. Soft pastel colors evoke a calm feeling, while bright or fluorescent colors can evoke urgency or attention.

You see this all the time in finance—illustrations shown in the red or in the black. We all know red is bad and black is good in finance, but because it's second nature, we don't think of it in terms of visual display. The same colors used in a different arena can have quite the opposite effect. Because I'm limited to displaying grayscale in this book, the visual display must be created primarily with structure and layout.

COMBINING CHARTS, WORKSHEETS, TEXT, AND TIME

Now that you have some of the basics in combining charts with worksheets, you can start to embed charts into worksheets and lists. You see this all the time in magazines and newspapers; however, many people use graphic programs to create these charts and marry them to the spreadsheet. With Excel's flexibility, you can start to create lists that measure visually. Take Figure 30.40, for example. This is a list of information that provides several vehicles of measure or value in the form of a chart, drawing tools or shapes, and finally words (see Figure 30.41). Combine these elements with a list of information, and now you have one line in a list that provides multiple angles or views on product or competition.

Start to think outside the box. Just because Excel is referred to as a spreadsheet program, don't allow that word *spreadsheet* to limit how you use Excel.

Figure 30.40.
By combining charts, drawing tools, and words with line-item information, you provide the audience with multiple views of the product or company.

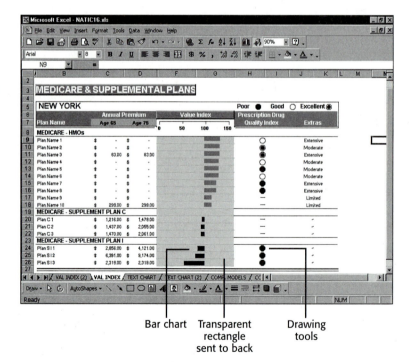

Bar chart   Transparent rectangle sent to back   Drawing tools

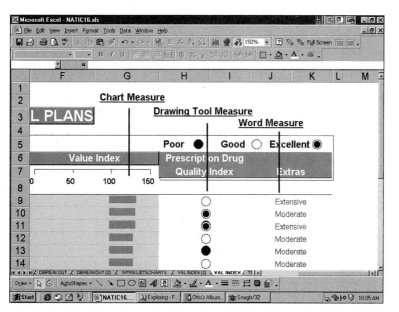

Figure 30.41.
You can create measuring tools from charts, drawing objects, and even words.

In Figure 30.42, I've removed the formatting to show how a bar chart was positioned on top of the grid. (Remove the borders and background fills to make the chart transparent.) In this example, I've constructed the chart to cross the X-axis at 100, so that the value index appears negative or less than average if the bar is to the left of 100.

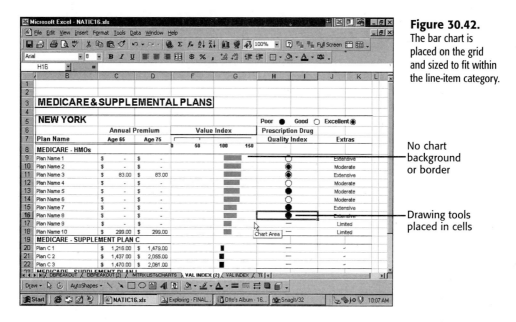

Figure 30.42.
The bar chart is placed on the grid and sized to fit within the line-item category.

No chart background or border

Drawing tools placed in cells

CREATING "CHARTS" WITHOUT CHARTS

Sometimes you run into situations where you have to represent data graphically, but a standard chart won't achieve what you need. You can visually display words, numbers, and time without using Excel's charting capabilities, but still creating the visual appeal of a chart with the proper layout and format. Figure 30.43 combines grid structure, fill colors, and text boxes to simulate a chart, visually demonstrating the profit/loss scenario per division over time. (The quality of this chart suffers a bit when the figure is reduced to fit within book margins. To see how the Divisional Analysis chart really works, review the file on the book's CD.)

This chart is created by setting up the grid to accommodate years from right to left. Then you align text boxes above or below the appropriate year in which the event or scenario takes place (see Figure 30.44).

Figure 30.43.
With the proper grid layout, fill colors, and text box placement, you can create charts without using Excel's charting capabilities, but rather tapping into its versatility of drawing tools and grid options.

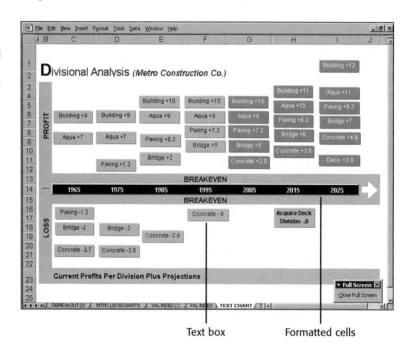

Text box   Formatted cells

EMBEDDING MULTIPLE CHARTS IN A MATRIX LIST

What is a matrix list? A *matrix* can be a table, a list, or anything that provides multiple values or scenarios that can intersect or create units of measure against the whole. In the example in Figure 30.45, each company has line items organized under its heading. The list reflects the four headings in cell B3. The embedded charts are placed within the line-item slot, next to the percentage of minority representation within the organization (see Figure 30.46). After you create the first one, copy and paste it to another location, and change the source data to reflect the line item it represents.

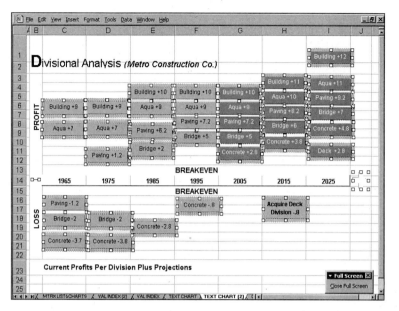

Figure 30.44.
The same chart, showing the drawing objects selected.

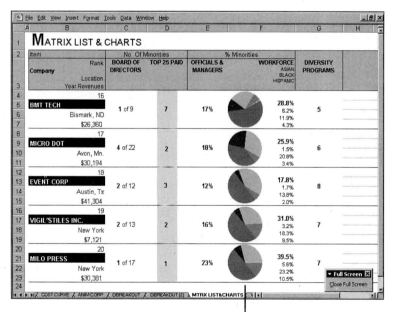

Figure 30.45.
You can combine a matrix list with multiple units of measure with charts to further explain the story.

Multiple pies sized and placed

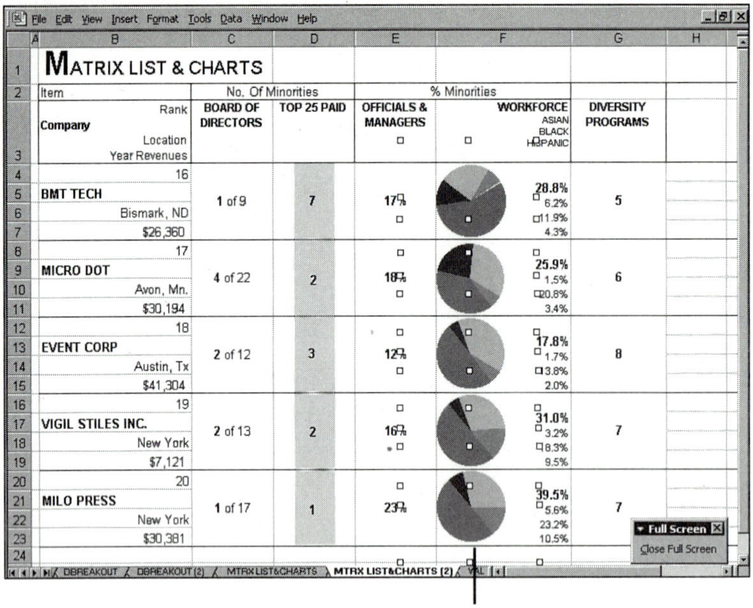

Figure 30.46.
Notice the list structure when formats are removed. The pie charts are sized and positioned along the left of column F for consistency.

No borders or backgrounds on pie charts

CREATING A CUSTOM L-BAR AXIS

Excel enables you to create custom axes, as shown in Figure 30.47. Eliminate the original axis and background of the chart and replace it with a transparent shape, such as the rectangle from the Drawing toolbar. After the rectangle is placed over the corresponding X and Y values, select a fill color on the Colors and Lines tab in the Format AutoShape dialog box, make the shape semitransparent, and then send the shape to the back, placing the object behind the values of the chart, and creating an *L-bar axis*.

BUILDING SINGLE-STACK CHARTS

Single-stack charts designed with text boxes and drawing tools can be extremely effective when showing percentages between categories, as shown in Figure 30.48. You'll often see charts of this nature when comparing industry categories. (If you have too many categories, however, the stacked chart can become cumbersome.) The borders and backgrounds were eliminated in this example. By eliminating these features, you can make chart stacks stand alone, and then use text boxes, callouts, and lines to finish the chart.

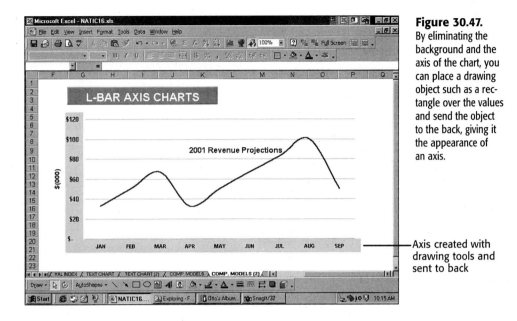

Figure 30.47.
By eliminating the background and the axis of the chart, you can place a drawing object such as a rectangle over the values and send the object to the back, giving it the appearance of an axis.

PART
VII

CH

30

Axis created with drawing tools and sent to back

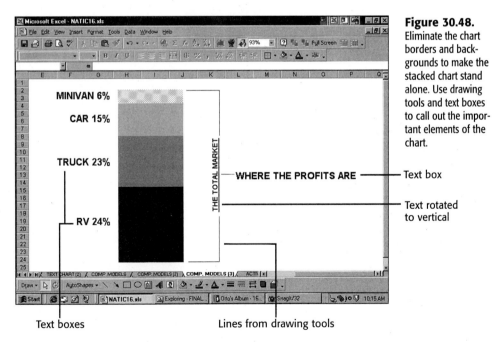

Figure 30.48.
Eliminate the chart borders and backgrounds to make the stacked chart stand alone. Use drawing tools and text boxes to call out the important elements of the chart.

Text box

Text rotated to vertical

Text boxes

Lines from drawing tools

CREATING LIFETIME PROFITABILITY/BREAKEVEN CHARTS

Lifetime charts are great for showing the profitability of a product over time. Notice in Figure 30.49 how you can view loss, breakeven, and profit, all in the same chart. For simplicity, you could also separate these items into individual charts, showing net units, total profits, and so on. It's important to understand the audience and intent of the chart when making those decisions.

Figure 30.49.
Use the line chart to establish lifetime profitability and break-even analysis charts.

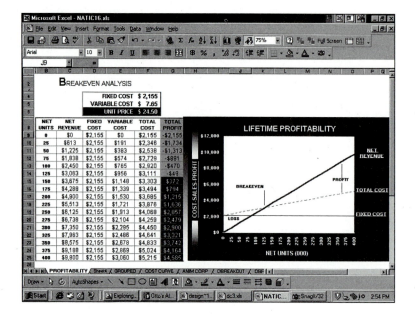

To set up a lifetime profitability chart, establish the table by following these steps:

1. Establish the net units in increments. In the example, the increments are set every 25,000 units in column B.

2. Set up the net revenue in column C, multiplying the net units by the unit price to calculate the net revenue.

3. Establish the fixed cost in column D. The example shows fixed cost of $2,155.

4. Apply the variable cost in column E. Multiply the variable cost rate by the net units in column B to calculate the variable cost in column E.

5. The total cost column in column F combines the fixed cost and variable cost to reach the total cost.

6. To create the chart, select the net units, net revenue, fixed cost, and total cost data from the table. (Select just these columns by holding down the Ctrl key as you click.)

7. Use the Chart Wizard to create a line chart.

8. In Step 2 of the Chart Wizard dialog box, select the Series tab and supply the Net Units range for the Category (X) Axis Labels setting.

9. Click Finish.

10. Select the net units data series in the chart and delete it. The net units is now the category (X) axis.

Tip #417

You can automate the Net Units column with a formula. For example, in another cell (let's say B6), type the increment number. In cell B10, type the following formula: **=$B9+$B$6**. Copy the formula down the column. This will enable you to quickly view interval changes in both the table and the chart by changing only cell B6.

TROUBLESHOOTING

MOVING CATEGORY LABELS

Excel won't let me place my category labels in a different location.

You can move the X-axis on a column chart to the top of the chart. Select the axis and choose Format, Selected Axis to open the Format Axis dialog box. On the Patterns tab, choose High under Tick Mark Labels.

INVISIBLE DATA SERIES

When I create a secondary axis for the second data series of my column chart, the columns are hidden behind the first data set.

Select the data series in front of the other data series, and choose Format, Selected Data Series to open the Format Data Series dialog box. On the Patterns tab, choose None under Area.

MOVING A CHART WITH OBJECTS

When I move or resize a chart, the drawing objects don't move with the chart and I have to move and realign them.

There are two ways to fix this problem. You can select all the objects (including the chart) and *group (page 529)* them. Or select the chart before you create an object, which makes Excel treat the object as part of the chart.

ALIGNING CHART LABELS WITH GRIDLINES

Excel doesn't allow me to align my chart labels to match the gridlines on the spreadsheet.

This can be tricky. Align the chart labels to match the gridlines as closely as you can. Then select the range of columns over the width of the chart and adjust the width to a larger size. Readjust the columns to a smaller size, and the category labels on the chart should then match.

PART **VIII**

ANALYZING AND MANAGING YOUR DATA

CHAPTER 31

SETTING UP A LIST OR DATABASE IN EXCEL

In this chapter

USING EXCEL AS A DATABASE PROGRAM

Although "number crunching" is Excel's primary purpose, the row-and-column format lends itself to creating and storing databases (called *lists* in Excel). Generally, a good rule of thumb is that if your list grows to more than 2,000 rows, you should store the information in a data warehouse or relational database. Whether you need to store a product catalog for quick lookups or employee information for use with your accounting software, you can create, edit, sort, analyze, and filter your data with the options on the Data menu.

This chapter begins discussion of data storage and analysis in Excel, with discussions of various methods of data entry and options for viewing, printing, and reporting on the list data. The following chapters explore additional options for sorting, filtering, grouping, consolidating, outlining, and auditing lists and tables; using tools and form controls to analyze data; and PivotTables, an important and useful feature of Excel for use in summarizing and manipulating the structure of your lists.

BUILDING AN EFFECTIVE LIST

Structuring a list is the most important part of the creation process because it ultimately determines what you'll be able to extract from the list and how effectively you can manage the list after it's created. Too much time is wasted in business today restructuring lists that were improperly set up.

Before you start to lay out a list, ask yourself the question, "What data will I need to compile after the list is created?" If you know what information you'll need to extract, laying out the list will become quite simple. In the list in Figure 31.1, for example, each category has its own heading—Date, Product, Process, and so on—and this data can be extracted as a whole or by individual categories.

When building the list, you can look at the list structure in terms of an outline—classify the outline from most important "topics" to least important. This provides a guideline in structuring the information. In Figure 31.1, the most important topic is product; the second is process.

In building the list, keeping things constant is extremely important. When you start to filter lists or extract information from lists with *functions* as discussed in later chapters, spelling and text case are critical.

Tip #418

How can you tell whether your list is structured effectively? As you check it over, ask yourself whether someone else could take over managing the list and understand its logic without assistance.

Field names in header row

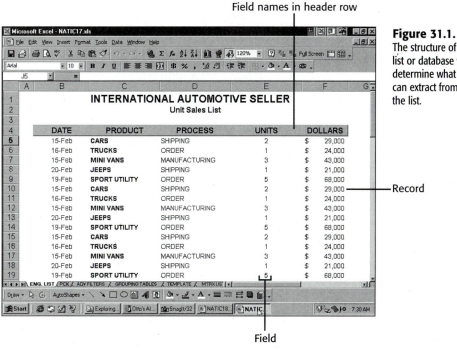

Figure 31.1.
The structure of a list or database will determine what you can extract from the list.

Record

Field

Excel lists are generally made up of a hierarchical structure. What does this mean? Well, think in terms of the lowest common denominator in your database or list. If you're setting up a list to track quantities or dollar amounts for the year by code, for example, the lowest-level item might be the actual cost or quantity, then the code, and finally the week or other timeline. The field names (headings) would be placed at the top of each field's column (working from right to left in this example), and beneath this header row would be the body of the list—the actual list data. The first field would be the week; second, the code; third, the cost or quantity. If you understand how to use PivotTables, you know the importance of information leveling.

Tip #419

Don't separate your list with blank columns or rows! Blanks create a mess when you try to manipulate data. Every level of information should have its own column, and there's no need to apply spacing between the rows. If you must add space between rows, use the row height feature to adjust the vertical size of each row.

Caution

Don't combine the names of employees, users, clients, and so on into a single cell. Separate first and last names so that each name has its own column for use in sorting the list by name or creating a PivotTable.

PART
VIII
CH
31

The following list summarizes some important list terminology:

- A *header row* at or near the top of the worksheet contains the field names for the list. This is not a requirement, but many list features won't work correctly (or at all) if the list isn't set up this way.

- *Field names* describe each category of data. These headings usually are positioned as column headings, but can take the form of row headings for lists in which the data is stored horizontally rather than vertically.

- Each cell containing data is called a *field*.

- Fields are combined into a single row or column that comprises all the data for that particular item or person. This group of fields is called a *record*.

- All the records in a database combine to form the *body* of the list.

Table 31.1 describes some suggested formats for the individual parts of the list. These formats will help create a clean, uncluttered list. When uppercase, lowercase, and initial caps are all used in the same list, the list is difficult to read. I would suggest following a standard format in all your lists. It's also good practice to create clean, short headings; the longer the heading, the more difficult the list is for others to review.

TABLE 31.1. STANDARD LIST LAYOUT

Item	Suggested Format
Horizontal field names	Bold type, uppercase, and 12-point font
Left column vertical field names	Bold type, uppercase, and 12-point font
Body text	Uppercase or initial caps and 10-point font, regular style
Font style	Arial, Tahoma, Courier, Garamond

By default, Excel 2000 extends the formatting of the list to any new list entries typed at the end of the list, including any formulas that are part of previous entries (assuming that at least three of the previous five entries used that formatting and/or formula, to establish a pattern for Excel to use). To turn off this feature—for example, if you want to customize certain types of entries within an individual list—choose Tools, Options, click the Edit tab, and deselect the option Extend List Formats and Formulas.

Tip #420

Maintain consistency in font style, upper- and lowercase, and initial caps. If you begin the body of your list with one initial style, maintain the same style throughout the list.

Don't enter multiple names and categories in one cell. If there's no consistency, rhyme, or reason to the body of a list, it becomes useless. If lists are set up properly, Excel can become a tool that solves problems for your business, not just a place to store numbers.

It's important to establish field names that match the category. Lists usually grow with time, and new field names are created as the list grows, so try to break down the description of the field name to its most detailed level from the beginning. Notice the headings in Figure 31.2.

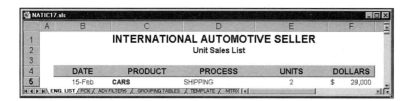

Figure 31.2.
Create field names that break down the description of the contents to the most detailed level.

The format for the body of the list (the actual data) is the most critical part of your standardization process. The data should maintain consistency with like or similar text formats and case. Consistency here will determine the manageability of the list.

In many cases, you'll inherit someone else's list and have to manipulate some of the current structure. Figure 31.3 demonstrates changing an existing list from lowercase to uppercase for consistency in this particular list. (You can change from uppercase to lowercase with the LOWER function.)

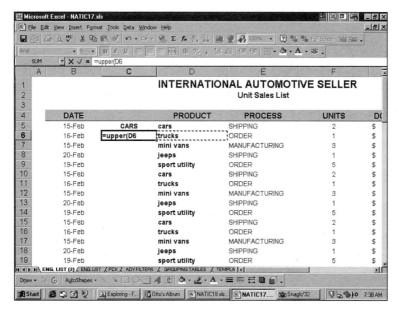

Figure 31.3.
You can use the UPPER function to convert lowercase text to uppercase, and the LOWER function to convert uppercase text to lowercase.

After you convert the lowercase entries to uppercase with formulas for this example, you'll want to return the converted—now uppercase—text to its original column. To do this, follow these steps:

1. Select the converted range (column of formulas).

2. Choose Edit, Copy.

3. Select the first cell in the range to paste.

4. Choose Edit, Paste Special.

5. In the Paste Special dialog box, select Values (see Figure 31.4). This option converts all the formulas to their resulting values.

6. Click OK. The values are copied to the target cells, as shown in Figure 31.5.

7. Delete the formula column.

Figure 31.4.
The Paste Special dialog box enables you to paste ranges of formulas as values.

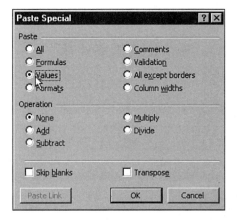

Figure 31.5.
After you convert the text from lowercase to uppercase and paste the converted text in the original column, you can delete the formula column.

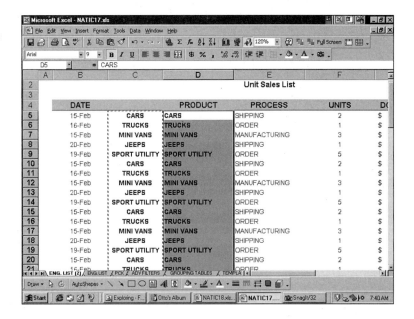

WORKING WITH THE DATA FORM

People who work with Excel on a regular basis usually are comfortable with the row-and-column structure and have no difficulty entering list data directly into the appropriate cells. However, the ongoing data entry and maintenance of a list might be handled by someone who is less familiar with Excel. For those users—and even experienced Excel users who prefer a simpler data-entry method—Excel provides the *data form*. The data form works like a dialog box; it floats over the worksheet and includes buttons and other form controls to enable the user to enter one record at a time into the list.

You also can use the data form to search for specific records in the list, using specified criteria, or even to delete records. *Filters* (covered in Chapter 32, "Using Excel's Data-Management Features") are more effective in scrolling for information, but if your list is quite long and you're searching for a specific element in the list, the data form works well in assisting you to find that particular line of information.

To use the data form, click anywhere in the list and choose <u>D</u>ata, <u>F</u>orm. Excel displays a data form, customized with the headings in the worksheet (see Figure 31.6). The data form displays the record count of the list and the scrollbar enables you to scroll the list, record by record, or many records at a time.

PART

VIII

CH

31

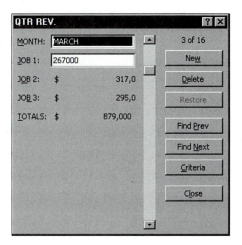

Figure 31.6.
Use the data form to enter or find records in a list.

To enter new records, click the Ne<u>w</u> button and type the information in the appropriate text boxes. (Notice that the record indicator in the upper-right corner of the dialog box changes to display the words New Record. The data form works as a multipurpose form for data entry, searching, and viewing the list; the message in the upper-right corner indicates how the form is currently being used.) Use the Tab and Shift+Tab keys, the underlined hotkeys, or the mouse to move from one text box to another. When the record is complete, press Enter or click the Ne<u>w</u> button to enter the new record at the end of the list and start another new record.

Tip #421

Unless the list is sorted chronologically or by a customized account or part number, you probably will want new records to be sorted from the end of the list to their appropriate positions alphabetically or numerically. See Chapter 18 for details on sorting and filtering lists.

Although the data form simplifies the process of entering list data, it doesn't offer the advantage of auto-repeating information you have already typed once. If your list includes the same information in multiple records—for example, each new employee record will list one of a set of five orientation and training classes—you probably won't want to type that information repeatedly when entering data. Enter the data directly into the cells—where you can take advantage of the copy and AutoComplete features—instead of using the data form, or skip those fields and enter that information later.

To find a specific record in a list, follow these steps:

1. Select the <u>C</u>riteria button (see Figure 31.7).

   Notice that the record indicator in the upper-right corner of the dialog box changes to display the word Criteria.

Figure 31.7.
Search for specific information within a list by typing the description in the corresponding text box.

2. Enter any known information from the record you're seeking and choose Find <u>N</u>ext or press Enter.

   The search function works like that in the Find dialog box; you can search for just the first few characters of an entry or type the whole entry.

Note

Typing the first few characters works only on nonnumeric data. To search for salaries, dates entered as dates, and so on, you must include the entire number or date.

Excel searches the list and finds the first record that matches the specified criteria. Note that searches are not case sensitive.

3. To continue searching, click Find Next again. To search in the reverse direction, click Find Prev. Note that either method continues searching from the previous record found, rather than starting at the top of the list.

When you reach the last record to match the specified criteria, Excel beeps if you try to continue searching in that direction.

4. To enter another set of criteria, click the Clear button and type the new criteria. To return to data entry, click the Form button.

VIEWING AND PRINTING THE LIST

The following sections provide a number of helpful suggestions for organizing the view of your list. Aesthetics aside, making your list worksheets attractive and readable can actually help with the data-entry process and make the list easier to use. And it's important that a list be understandable, especially when someone else has to use the list.

Caution

Don't get too carried away with these viewing options. As your data list grows, simple backgrounds and views become more desirable. The more complex the view, the less data you can see or comprehend onscreen.

KEEPING THE FIELD NAMES FROM SCROLLING

When scrolling lists in Excel, you'll notice that when you scroll down or across the list, headings and field names scroll off the screen. To keep the heading or field name onscreen as you scroll the body of the list, you can *freeze* the headings onscreen. Select the range below the heading or to the right of the headings and choose Window, Freeze Panes, as shown in Figure 31.8. In this example, rows 2 through 4 will remain onscreen as you work with the list. To unfreeze the panes, choose Window, Unfreeze Panes.

Splitting the window is much like freezing the panes, but the difference is the capability to intersect a row or column. For example, Figure 31.9 shows the same worksheet as in Figure 31.8, but with the window split, intersecting column D, meaning that the *split bar* splits right through the cell. Freezing panes freezes to the right or left, top or bottom of a cell. When panes are frozen, you can't move the frozen sections; you have to unfreeze the panes to adjust them. Split bars, on the other hand, can be dragged anywhere you like on the screen, which makes them more useful when working with lists.

Figure 31.8.
Freezing the pane enables you to scroll the body of the list while keeping headings or field names visible.

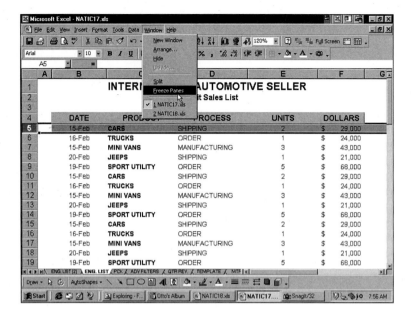

Split bar **Split box**

Figure 31.9.
Splitting the window is similar to freezing panes; however, with the split window, you can intersect a column or row, and also adjust it with your mouse.

You can split the window by selecting a row or column and choosing Window, Split. To adjust the split, simply drag the split bar to the desired location. Another way to split the window is to drag one of the split boxes by the scrollbars to the desired location. You can split the window both horizontally and vertically. To remove a split, double-click the split bar or drag it to the edge of the window.

ARRANGING MULTIPLE WINDOWS

When creating lists to store your data, you may need to work with several workbooks at the same time or multiple sheets within the same workbook. I often find myself doing this when I copy and paste information from one list to another, or when I write formulas that correspond from one workbook or worksheet to another.

Note

> When establishing multiple lists within a workbook, if possible, start your lists on the same line and cell. This helps in creating efficiencies in managing your workbook. Also try to make the lists as similar in type and style as possible for consistency within the workbook.

PART

VIII

CH

31

To view multiple windows or sheets at one time within the same workbook, perform the following steps:

1. Select one of the sheets in the workbook you want to view.

2. Select <u>W</u>indow, <u>N</u>ew Window. Excel adds a colon and the number 2 to the workbook title in the title bar of the second window and the number 1 to the title bar in the first window.

3. In the new window, select another sheet in the workbook.

4. Choose <u>W</u>indow, <u>A</u>rrange.

5. In the Arrange Windows dialog box, select the desired window arrangement. If you want to arrange only the windows showing the currently active workbook, be sure the <u>W</u>indows of Active Workbook option is checked (see Figure 31.10).

Figure 31.10.

6. Click OK.

Although Figure 31.11 seems to show two workbooks open, you actually are seeing two sheets within the same workbook. Any changes to either workbook are saved to the original workbook. In this example, the upper window and the lower window show two different worksheets in the same workbook.

Using the same method, you can view multiple workbooks or multiple windows showing the active workbook. When arranging multiple workbooks, be sure that the <u>W</u>indows of Active Workbook option in the Arrange Windows dialog box is not checked.

Figure 31.11.
By creating a new window in a workbook, you can view several pages of the same workbook at the same time.

A number after the workbook title indicates that you're viewing the same workbook in multiple windows.

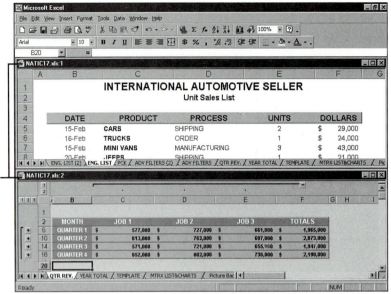

INSERTING DATA RANGES INTO A LIST

You probably are quite accomplished at cutting or copying a range and pasting it to an empty range. When working with lists, however, you may often need to paste cut or copied records between existing records. Rather than using a simple paste operation, use the Insert menu.

Tip #422

You can select multiple *noncontiguous* columns or rows and insert columns or rows between them. For example, you can select row 6 and row 8 at the same time and insert a row by selecting Cells or Rows under the Insert menu.

Figure 31.12 shows a selected group of records. In this example, the intention is to move the North Dakota records above the Minnesota records (assume that this list is not intended to be sorted alphabetically by project). To move these records, you would cut them from their current location and insert them above the Minnesota records. After cutting the North Dakota records, select the target range and choose Insert, Cut Cells. Excel repositions the existing data and inserts the cut cells (see Figure 31.13).

If you are inserting copied rather than cut cells, choose Insert, Copied Cells. The Insert Paste dialog box appears, as shown in Figure 31.14. Choose Shift Cells Down or Shift Cells Right to move the existing data in the target range out of the way of the incoming data.

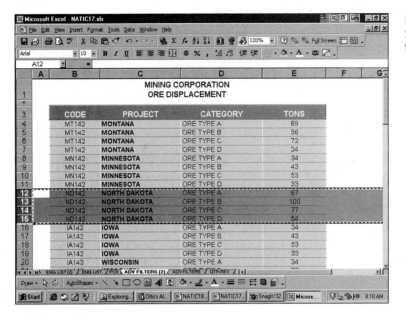

Figure 31.12.
Select and copy or cut
the source records.

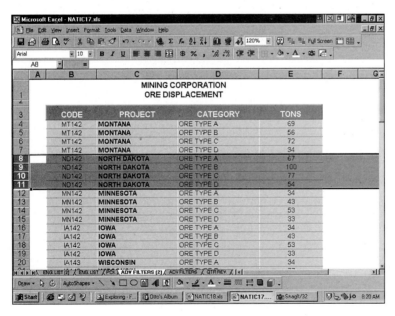

Figure 31.13.
The cut range is
pasted into place.

Figure 31.14.
In the Insert Paste dialog box, specify how you want the existing data to move.

Two drag-and-drop methods are also available:

- Position the mouse around the edge of the selection (just like the normal drag and drop), and drag the selection while holding down the Shift key. When the gray single-line-insert indicator appears in the desired location between rows/columns, release the mouse. The existing data is automatically shifted down/to the right, depending on the drag direction.

- Position the mouse in the same manner as the previous method, but drag with the right mouse button. When the gray border representing the data being moved is positioned in the desired location, release the mouse and choose Shift Down and Move (or Copy) from the shortcut menu.

Because Excel doesn't allow you to insert copies of noncontiguous selections, you can use this feature only for a contiguous selection. To enter list data from noncontiguous areas, use Edit, Paste. In Figure 31.12, for example, you could select all the ore type A projects, copy them from the list, and paste them in a new location. The projects would appear in the order copied, with no additional spaces between them.

ESTABLISHING CUSTOM VIEWS

Because lists grow in size and only a certain amount of information needs to be viewed at one time, Excel enables you to create *custom views* to look at just the relevant information defined by the user. You can even name the views to fit the situation. For example, Figure 31.15 shows a breakout by job and month, but you may be interested in only the high-level totals by quarter.

To hide the supporting information and show only the quarter totals, you can create a custom view. Follow these steps:

1. Establish the view you want saved as a custom view. In this example, you would hide rows 3 through 5, 7 through 9, and so on, until only the quarter totals are visible.

2. Choose View, Custom Views to open the Custom Views dialog box (see Figure 31.16).

3. Choose Add to open the Add View dialog box (see Figure 31.17).

4. Type a name for the new custom view.

5. Click OK.

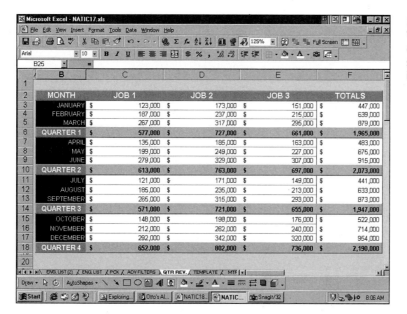

Figure 31.15.
You can create custom views to show only relevant information.

PART

VIII

CH

31

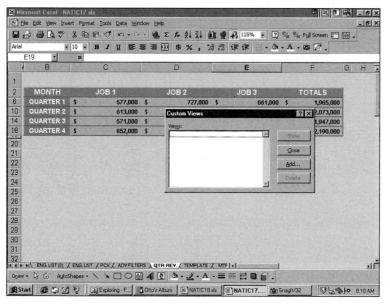

Figure 31.16.
The Custom Views dialog box enables you to add custom views.

Figure 31.17.
Provide a name for
the view. Keep it
as simple and
descriptive as
possible.

Custom views are saved with the workbook. To show your custom view at any time, open the workbook and select View, Custom Views. The Custom Views dialog box opens. Select the desired view and click Show. To delete a custom view, open the Custom Views dialog box, select the view name, and choose Delete. When prompted, select Yes to confirm that you want to delete the view.

Tip #423	Set up custom views in workbooks that are shared among multiple users. Each user can store his or her favorite view and print settings.

Custom views store the following information:

- Window size/position, including splits or frozen panes
- Hidden columns, rows, and sheets in the workbook
- Column-width settings
- Display options
- Selected cells, if any
- Filtered list criteria
- Page Setup settings

The Add View dialog box gives you the option of saving print settings, hidden rows, and filter settings. The last is an important issue for working with lists; see the next chapter for details.

CREATING CUSTOM REPORTS

Creating custom reports with Excel's *Report Manager* is similar to creating a custom view (discussed in the preceding section). Because the Report Manager basically consolidates all your named reports in one place, it's helpful when you create reports from different areas of a worksheet or even multiple worksheets in the same workbook. If you hide areas of the worksheet with a custom view for reporting purposes, for example, Excel remembers how that report was structured.

Note

You must define custom views before you can print multiple sets of data from the same worksheet; that is, sets that involve hiding rows/columns manually or via outlining and filtering. (The Report Manager doesn't store these settings directly.)

Report Manager is an add-in program that comes with Excel. If the Report Manager option doesn't appear on the View menu (you may need to wait a few seconds to see the full menu if you're using the personal menu feature), choose Tools, Add-Ins, select the Report Manager in the Add-Ins dialog box, and click OK. If prompted, indicate that you want to install the Report Manager immediately, and insert the Excel or Office CD used to install your software.

To add a report, follow these steps:

1. Choose View, Report Manager. In the Report Manager dialog box, click Add.

2. In the Add Report dialog box, provide a name for your custom report (see Figure 31.18).

3. Create a report by filling in the information in the dialog box. The following list describes the options:

   - **Report Name.** Creates a name for the custom report.

   - **Section to Add.** Enables you to select a section to add from the workbook to the report being created.

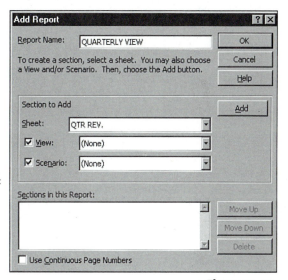

PART
VIII

CH
31

Figure 31.18.

   - **Sheet.** Enables you to select the sheet containing the data you want included in the section.

   - **View.** Selects a custom view from the selected sheet for the section that you want to add.

   - **Scenario.** Adds a named scenario to the report.

→ For details on using scenarios, **see** "Using Solver," **p. 1116**

   - **Add.** After you select your criteria, click Add to add it to the Sections in this Report list.

- **Sections in This Report.** Shows the sections in the report in the order that they will be printed (see Figure 31.19).

- **Move Up.** Adjusts the section order by moving the selected section up.

- **Move Down.** Adjusts the section order by moving the selected section down.

- **Delete.** Deletes the selected section.

- **Use Continuous Page Numbers.** When checked, uses continuous page numbers on printed reports, based on the order of the sections.

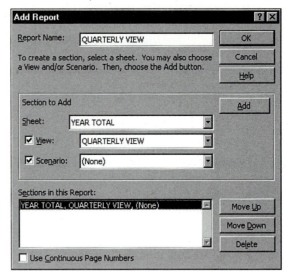

Figure 31.19.

Caution

Be selective when creating custom reports. It's easy to get carried away with saving and creating custom reports to the point where it can become confusing as to which report does what.

CHAPTER 32

USING EXCEL'S DATA-MANAGEMENT FEATURES

In this chapter

DATA MANAGEMENT IN EXCEL

Management of data in an Excel workbook shouldn't be time-consuming. This chapter discusses tools available within Excel that will enable you to manage both your time and data efficiently. From extracting information with formulas, to using built-in sorting and filtering tools created specifically for managing worksheet data and lists, to tracking changes in worksheets shared among multiple users, Excel gives you every option necessary to effectively use your time and get the most out of your Excel data. The last section in this chapter also covers a topic close to the heart of any information manager—preventing the loss of important data by protecting workbook contents.

USING CONDITIONAL FORMATTING WITH LISTS

Conditional formatting can be a great way to call out specific information within a list, or plot out timelines. The key when using conditional formats is to use a format to call out specific bits of information; for example, you can use it to call out "not to exceed" information or negative numbers.

The example in Figure 32.1 uses an interactive conditional format; when a state is entered in cell D3, the conditional format highlights the cells in the list that match the entry. When you enter a project name in this cell, the conditional formatting highlights the cells referring to that project within the list. Cell E3 contains a formula that then adds the numbers in column E (the Tons column) for the highlighted list entries. The key is to use the Excel tools in innovative ways to make your everyday tasks easier. By combining conditional formatting with a formula, a single entry in cell D3 yields two results: The specified project entries are highlighted in the list, and the tonnage for that project is totaled in cell E3. You can use up to three conditional formats within a list.

Figure 32.1.
By knowing how to use conditional formats, you can call out all references to the information entered in one cell.

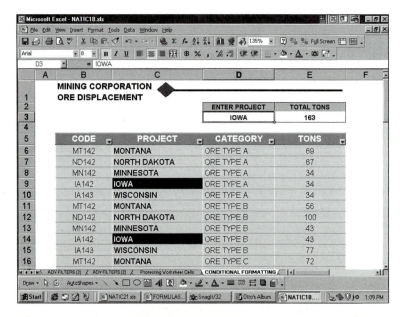

To create an interactive conditional format, follow these steps:

1. Select the list range to which you want to apply the conditional format.

2. Choose Format, Conditional Formatting.

3. In the Conditional Formatting dialog box, choose the first condition you want. For this example, you would choose Equal To from the middle drop-down list in the dialog box, as shown in Figure 32.2.

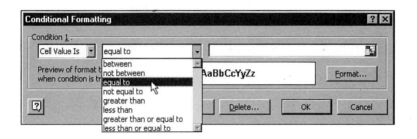

Figure 32.2.
Setting the condition.

4. In the remaining condition box, select the cell to which you want to link your condition (see Figure 32.3).

Figure 32.3.
To set a link for creating an interactive conditional format, enter the cell you want linked to your list.

5. Click the Format button in the Conditional Formatting dialog box.

6. Select the desired format from the three tabs in the Format Cells dialog box. For this example, I selected black shading on the Patterns tab, and made the text bold and white on the Font tab (see Figure 32.4).

7. Click OK. The format is shown in the preview window.

8. If desired, add more criteria by clicking the Add button to add another condition.

9. Make any desired changes and then click OK.

In the sample list, when you enter a project state, the condition applies itself to the list. Any entry in the Project column that matches the value entered in cell D3 will get the conditional formatting set in the Conditional Formatting dialog box (see Figure 32.5).

Figure 32.4.
Format the cells in the list that meet the conditional-formatting criteria.

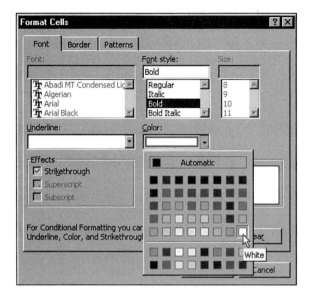

Figure 32.5.
When a project state is entered, the conditional format operates based on the trigger cell D3.

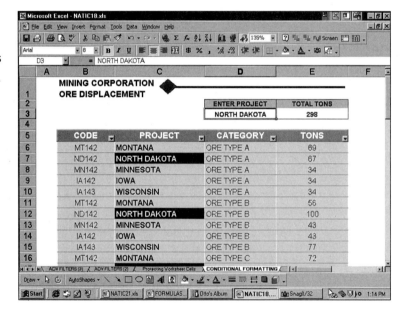

To understand how the formula in cell E3 works, look at the SUM(IF formula in the Formula bar in Figure 32.6.

Figure 32.6.
With a simple SUM(IF formula, you can add the entries that meet the condition.

The formula sums entries in the range E6:E25 only if the nested IF statement conditions are met. The conditions are that C6:C25 is equal to D3 (that is, the project name matches the entry in cell D3). Notice that the formula appears in braces ({}), indicating that it's an array formula. You enter array formulas by pressing Ctrl+Shift+Enter to activate the array.

> **Note**
>
> An *array formula* performs multiple calculations. The result can be a single result (as in this example) or multiple results. Because the values in the array formula (the *array arguments*) must refer to the same number of rows and columns, this type of formula works well for list data, in which each record has the same number of fields.

SORTING A LIST

After you create your list, you'll want to view your information in different ways. Excel enables you to sort information in multiple ways and even create custom sorts. To sort a list or database, select the information and choose <u>D</u>ata, <u>S</u>ort to open the Sort dialog box and specify your sort preferences (see Figure 32.7).

PART
VIII
CH
32

If you don't select anything before opening the Sort dialog box, Excel selects what it assumes is the list—all data contiguous to the active cell, minus the first row, which Excel assumes to be the header row. If your list contains possible blank lines or cells, select the list yourself before starting the sort process, or parts of the list may be excluded from the sort.

If the cell pointer is in a list with no (apparent) header row, Excel selects the No Header Ro<u>w</u> option. If the list appears to include labels, Excel chooses Header <u>R</u>ow and uses the labels as column indicators in the Sort By drop-down lists. When you manually select the data, the sensing feature is disabled. If the automatic selection includes your header row, specify the Header <u>R</u>ow option in the Sort dialog box to avoid sorting your field names with the rest of the list (refer to Figure 32.7). If you accidentally end up sorting the field names into the list, use Undo immediately after the sort process to restore the list.

> **Note**
>
> You can sort data in any column or row—it doesn't have to be a list. If you're just beginning a new worksheet, for example, you may start by entering a list of contact names, projects, inventory or catalog numbers, and so on. You can enter this information in random order and then sort it in the same way that you sort a list.

Figure 32.7.
Use the Sort dialog
box to specify the
way you want to sort
the list or selection.

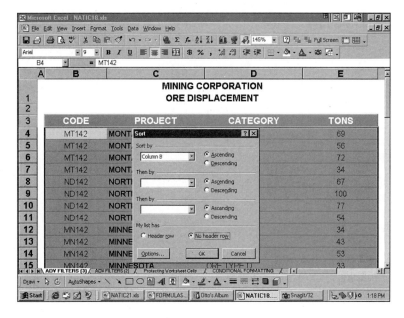

You can sort the list by up to three fields, in *ascending order* (0–9 and A–Z) or *descending order* (9–0 and Z–A). Excel can sort alphabetically, numerically, or by date. By selecting the Options button in the Sort dialog box, you can choose to sort left-to-right rather than the default top-to-bottom sort, in case your list has a horizontal rather than vertical orientation (see Figure 32.8). You can also make the sort case-sensitive—that is, sort such entries as *Oak* and *oak* separately because one is capitalized and the other isn't. In a case-sensitive sort, *Oak* would come before *oak* because capital letters are sorted above lowercase letters. (For details, see the later sidebar "Understanding Excel Sort Sequences.")

Figure 32.8.
The Sort Options dia-
log box enables you
to sort a list from top
to bottom or left to
right, depending on
your list setup.

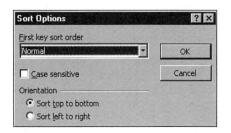

If your list is located contiguous to other data that isn't part of the list, or if you're sorting selected data that isn't part of a list at all, Excel may warn you that you may not have selected the entire list and ask whether you meant to include all the contiguous data (see Figure 32.9). The assumption is that the entire list is contiguous, and that nothing else is located next to the list.

Note

Excel does not always warn you about this, particularly if the list isn't the only data on the sheet.

Figure 32.9.
This dialog box indicates that the selection may not include the entire list.

If you meant to include all the contiguous data, accept the default setting, Expand the Selection; otherwise, choose Continue with the Current Selection.

Understanding Excel Sort Sequences

If you're unfamiliar with how computers "think," you may be surprised by the way in which Excel sorts your data. Excel sorts left-to-right, character-by-character, beginning with numbers first, then spaces, symbols, and finally letters. If your list contains names that include spaces, Excel may not sort them the way you would expect (or prefer). For example, consider the following list of names:

List	Sorted
McArdle	Mc Ardle
Mc Ardle	Mc Lean
McCandle	McArdle
Mc Lean	McCandle

Because Mc Lean includes a space, it falls before any names beginning with Mc that don't include a space. When sorting, Excel ignores apostrophes (in names such as H'ailea, for example), but sorts words with hyphens (–) to last position after the same word with no hyphen. For example, consider the following list of names that differ only in that one includes a space and one includes a hyphen.

List	Sorted
Barkley-North	Barkley North
Barkley North	BarkleyNorth
BarkleyNorth	Barkley-North

The name with the space comes first, followed by the one with no space, and last of all the name containing a hyphen.

You also may be baffled by sorts that include numbers with letters. If your part numbers run from B1 through B102, for example, this is how Excel sorts them:

B1
B10
B100
B101

continues

continued

```
B102
B11
B12
B13
B14
B15
B16
B17
B18
B19
B2
B20
B21
. . .
```

If you want the part numbers to sort correctly, insert zeros when numbering: B001, B002, and so on.

Excel uses the following sort sequence: 0–9 (space) ! " # $ % & ( ) * , . / : ; ? @ [\ ] ^ _ ` { | } ~ + < = > A–Z.

Blank cells or rows (depending on the sort selection) are sorted to the bottom of the list, whether you sort in descending or ascending order. When sorting values, note that FALSE comes before TRUE, and error values are all equal (but note that they appear in the original order in which they occurred). Ascending sorts place errors at the bottom; descending sorts place them at the top.

Based on custom lists you may have created, you also can define the first key sort order from the drop-down menu in the Sort Options dialog box.

Figure 32.10 shows the list sorted in ascending order by column D, CATEGORY.

Figure 32.10.
Based on the sort defined, Excel sorted the corresponding list by category in ascending order.

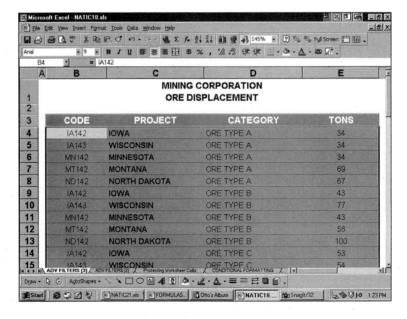

You can combine sorts to get the information the way you want it. For example, a common scenario would be sorting a customer list numerically by purchase, and then alphabetically by name, and perhaps including a third sort by contact name.

 The Sort Ascending and Sort Descending buttons on the Standard toolbar sort by the first column in any selection. If you select the whole list and want to sort based on the first column, this is a quick method. But don't select a single column (field) of your data for sorting without selecting the rest of the fields. Excel will sort that field only, separating those entries from the rest of the data in each record.

Because the Sort Ascending and Sort Descending buttons sort based on the position of the active cell, if you don't select any data—perhaps you merely clicked somewhere in the column by which you want the list sorted—the column containing the active cell becomes the sort key.

Reusing Sort Ascending and Sort Descending repeats any sorting options used previously.

FILTERING A LIST

Lists grow quickly, and soon locating a particular record in the list may take more time than you like. When you just want to view a particular record or records, *filtering* the list enables you to display only the selected information you want to see. The list itself is unchanged; you use the filter to specify exactly which data you want to see at that particular moment, and hide the remaining records. You can change the filter at any time to display a different set of records. The filtered records can be formatted, edited, and even charted. The active filter is saved with the workbook. (Note, however, that Excel allows only one list at a time to be filtered on a worksheet.)

Excel offers two types of filtering. An *AutoFilter* applies an automatic (simple) selection filter to the list, which you then can customize. An *advanced filter* enables you to specify more elaborate criteria for filtering.

PART

VIII

CH

32

Note

Filtering demonstrates a major reason for consistent data entry. Entries that are typed inconsistently (for example, *Evans' Plumbing* and *Evans Plumbing*) are treated as two different items by the filter. Excel will not treat them as one and the same.

Tip #424

The fastest method of filtering a list is to use the AutoFilter button. You can add this button to any toolbar, as described in Chapter 28, "Customizing Excel to Fit Your Working Style."

MANAGING THE LIST WITH AUTOFILTERS

To apply an AutoFilter to a list, select a cell in the list and choose Data, Filter, AutoFilter (see Figure 32.11). This command is a toggle; repeat it to turn off the AutoFilter at any time.

In a list with an AutoFilter, Excel displays arrow buttons for each entry in the header row (see Figure 32.12). These buttons activate pull-down menus that allow you to show individual records for viewing one at time or multiple records with the same entry in that particular field—for example, all records that list Minnesota as the project name or all records with ore type D as the category.

When you first set up an AutoFilter, Excel displays the AutoFilter buttons on the column headings but leaves the entire list displayed. To display a filtered list of records, use a button or combination of buttons. To display the records just mentioned, you would click the AutoFilter button in the PROJECT field name cell and select MINNESOTA, or use the CATEGORY button and select ORE TYPE D.

Figure 32.11.
AutoFiltering a list.

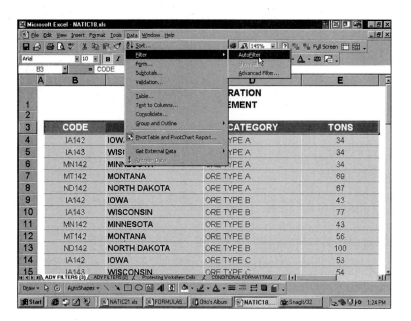

Using more than one AutoFilter button creates a combined filter. In the Mining Corporation example, selecting MINNESOTA in the PROJECT column narrows the displayed records to just those referring to the Minnesota project. If you then use the CATEGORY button to select ORE TYPE D, Excel displays only MINNESOTA records that list ORE TYPE D in the CATEGORY column, as shown in Figure 32.13. The arrows change color on the AutoFilter buttons that are currently in use—from black to blue.

The items at the top and bottom of the AutoFilter drop-down list provide special filtering options, as described in the following list:

- **(All).** Lists all the records in that category. Use this option to redisplay the entire list after filtering for selected records.

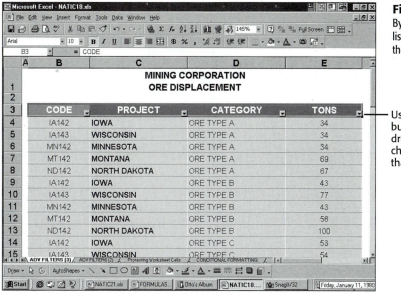

Figure 32.12.
By placing filters on a list, you can narrow the list to any level.

Use the AutoFilter button to open a drop-down list of choices for filtering that column.

Figure 32.13.
This AutoFilter combination displays only the single ORE TYPE D record for the MINNESOTA project.

- **(Top 10…).** Applies only to columns containing numbers or dates. Displays the Top 10 AutoFilter dialog box, in which you can specify that you want to see the records at the top or bottom of the list numerically (see Figure 32.14). You aren't limited to 10 records; you can specify that you want to see just the top or bottom (1) record, 50 records, or any number you prefer. To display the top or bottom 10% (or 15%, 50%, and so on) of your records, change the setting in the third combo box from Items to Percent.

Note

The Top 10 AutoFilter doesn't sort the displayed records, but you can select and sort them with the Data, Sort command if you want to see them in numeric order—for example, to list former employees in order by termination date.

- **(Custom…).** Displays the Custom AutoFilter dialog box, in which you can specify a more detailed filtering option. (See the next section for details.)

Figure 32.14.
Use the Top 10
AutoFilter dialog box
to display a selected
number of records.

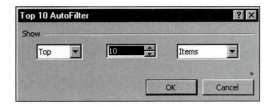

- **(Blanks)**. Displays the records containing blanks in a particular field (column). Use this option to find records that have missing entries.

- **(NonBlanks)**. Displays all records containing any entries in that field (nonblanks). Use this option to display only records for which entries have been made in that field—for example, a nonprofit organization may enter contributions for the current year in a particular column. Records with such listings could then be displayed, sorted, and merged with an end-of-year letter to donors regarding tax deductibility of contributions.

The (Blanks) and (NonBlanks) entries appear only if the column contains empty cells.

CREATING A CUSTOM AUTOFILTER

If the default AutoFilter doesn't provide enough options, you can create a *custom AutoFilter*. Follow these steps:

1. From the drop-down AutoFilter list, choose (Custom…), as shown in Figure 32.15.

Figure 32.15.
To create a custom
AutoFilter, select the
(Custom…) option.

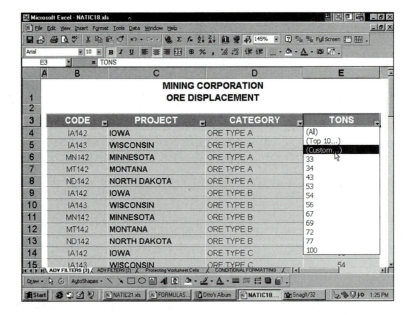

2. In the Custom AutoFilter dialog box, specify the custom criteria to use for filtering your list. Figure 32.16 shows the criteria for selecting records with values between two specified points—greater than 34 and less than 56.

3. Click OK.

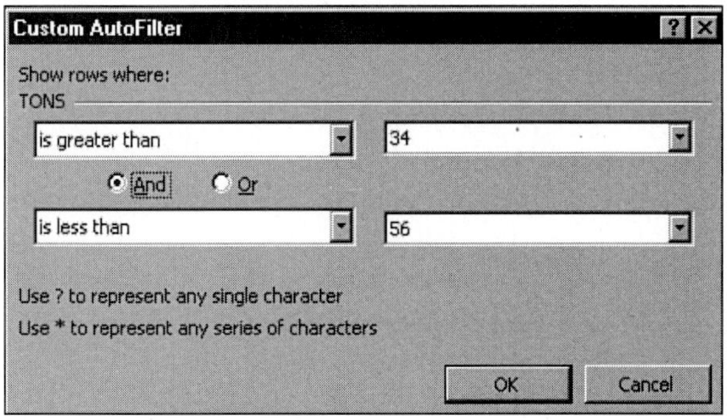

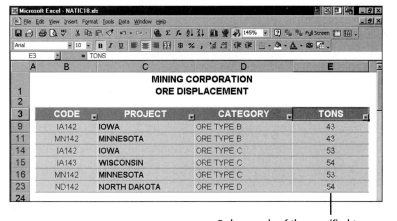

Figure 32.16.
The Custom AutoFilter dialog box enables you to display only records that meet the specified criteria.

Only records within the specified range show up in the filtered list (see Figure 32.17). You can customize the filtering even more by creating additional custom AutoFilters for other fields in the list.

PART

VIII

CH

32

Figure 32.17.
Only records matching the custom AutoFilter criteria are displayed.

Only records of the specified tonnage are shown.

To display more than one type of entry in a particular field—for example, to display entries for two different projects in the Mining Corporation list—enter the first criterion (the *comparison operator*) in the first set of boxes in the Custom AutoFilter dialog box; then enter the value criterion in the second set of boxes. Select the And button if you want the selected row(s) to meet both sets of criteria; select Or if you want records that meet either of the criteria. Figure 32.18 shows how to set the custom AutoFilter to display both the Minnesota and Wisconsin projects. For this example, you could use either contains or equals as the operator (see the following tip).

Figure 32.18.
Use the Or button if you want Excel to display records that meet either of the criteria in this dialog box.

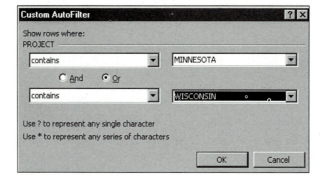

Tip #425

You can use wildcard characters to select records in which the entries vary by a single character (?) or multiple characters (*). To find entries that begin with the same character(s)—for example, anyone named *Smith, Smithe, Smythe,* and so on—search for records that contain *Sm**. To find records in which the apostrophe is missing from *Evans' Plumbing*, search for *Evans?Plumbing*, which would display the incorrect *Evans Plumbing* but not the correct *Evans' Plumbing*.

Be careful when using `equals` versus `contains` as the comparison operator. Using `equals` in the previous example will restrict the filter to names starting with *Sm*. Using `contains` will also filter *Desmond* and *Chism*, both of which contain the letters *sm*.

USING THE ADVANCED FILTER

An *advanced filter* is similar to a custom AutoFilter. The difference is that you create a *criteria range* outside the list—using the field names in the header row—and then specify the criteria on which you want to filter. Figure 32.19 shows the Mining Corporation list with a criteria range set up in D3:E4. Notice that the criteria range includes the column heading (field name) above the specified criteria. To use an advanced filter, your list must include field names for use in the criteria range. The worksheet also must include at least one blank row between the criteria range and the list.

The field names in the criteria range must match the field names in the list exactly, except for case (*Category* and *category* will both work, for example).

Tip #426

Copy the field names to the criteria range rather than typing them, to prevent errors.

Figure 32.19.
The criteria range determines the displayed entries in the list.

Tip #427

Prior to starting the advanced filter, select the list and assign it the range name Database. If you plan to extract filtered records to a different area of the worksheet, select that area also and give it the range name Extract. Excel automatically uses these named ranges in the Advanced Filter dialog box. The Criteria range name is automatically created/redefined each time you specify a criteria range, so there's no need to name this range yourself.

To create an advanced filter, follow these steps:

1. Create the criteria range, specifying the field names in one row and the desired criteria directly below. If possible, place the criteria range above the corresponding columns that you plan to filter for easy viewing of both.

2. To specify multiple criteria, add more rows to the criteria range.

3. When the criteria range is complete, click in the list and choose Data, Filter, Advanced Filter to open the Advanced Filter dialog box (see Figure 32.20).

4. Excel selects the list automatically if it's bounded by blank rows and columns. If the range in the List Range box is incorrect, specify the correct range.

5. Specify the criteria range.

6. Click OK to run the filter. Figure 32.21 shows the result in the Mining Corporation example.

PART
VIII

CH
32

Figure 32.20.
The Advanced Filter dialog box enables you to select the list range and criteria range.

Figure 32.21.
The results from the advanced filter match those specified in the criteria range.

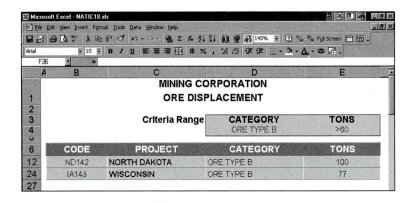

To show the entire list again, select Data, Filter, Show All.

Use the Advanced Filter when you need to do any of the following:

- Perform an Or condition across multiple fields.
- Specify more than two criteria in one field.
- Handle extremely complex criteria, requiring the use of functions/formulas, as well as multiple And/Or criteria in one filter.

You can change the entries in the criteria range at any point to display a different set of filtered records. The list responds automatically to the new specifications.

COPYING RECORDS TO A NEW LOCATION

When you use an advanced filter, you can specify a separate location where you want the filtered records copied; for example, to create a separate list of former clients. Select the Copy to Another Location option in the Advanced Filter dialog box and specify the target cell or range in the Copy To box. Excel will copy just the filtered records to the new location.

SELECTING UNIQUE RECORDS

If your list contains names or records that appear repeatedly, you may want to extract just the unique records. For example, in a list that includes state information, you might want to know how many states are represented in the list. To display only the unique records (a single record of each type), select the Unique Records Only option in the Advanced Filter dialog box. Excel hides all the duplicates.

PROTECTING YOUR DATA

Putting together an efficient worksheet—whether it contains simple tables, database lists, charts, or elaborate formulas and functions—requires some time and effort. All this work can be undone with a few keystrokes, however, by an inexperienced or inattentive user.

To prevent data disasters, Excel enables you to protect the workbook, worksheet, ranges, formulas, or single cells in a workbook. Note the following caution, however!

Caution

> Although you can protect cells within a workbook, if you have vital information hidden or protected, advanced Excel users can unprotect and disclose the hidden information. The only way to protect vital information is to protect the workbook, so a password is needed before a workbook is ever opened.

Excel provides multiple levels of protection to keep your data protected:

- The simplest method is to hide rows, columns, or even the whole worksheet or workbook. Of course, because Excel users learn quickly how to *hide* and *unhide* cells, hiding provides very little real protection.

- Locking cells prevents accidental or deliberate alteration or deletion of the locked cells. This technique is helpful for worksheets that will be used by one person or shared among only trusted users; unlocking cells is very easy (as described in the following section).

- Protecting the workbook with a password is the best method, but of course you must remember the password. Others should know the password as well, in case something happens to you.

The following sections provide details on these protection methods.

PROTECTING SELECTED WORKBOOK CELLS

The most common reason for protecting cells in a workbook is to prevent accidental deletion or alteration of information such as formulas, which provide vital calculations to the worksheet, workbook, or even other workbooks or documents.

Suppose you have a workbook like the one shown in Figure 32.22. As you can see from the [Shared] indicator in the title bar, this workbook is shared among multiple users, which makes it a prime candidate for unintentional changes. In this example, you might want to protect the formula cells in the range F4:F12, so that no one can edit or clear these cells accidentally.

Follow these steps:

1. Select the whole worksheet.

2. Choose Format, Cells to open the Format Cells dialog box.

3. Click the Protection tab and deselect the Locked option. (This option has no effect unless the worksheet is protected.) Deselecting the Locked option enables you to select a specific range or cell and then lock it.

4. If desired, hide the cell content or formula by checking the Hidden option at this time as well.

Figure 32.22.
To protect cells in a worksheet, unlock the worksheet and then lock the range containing the formulas.

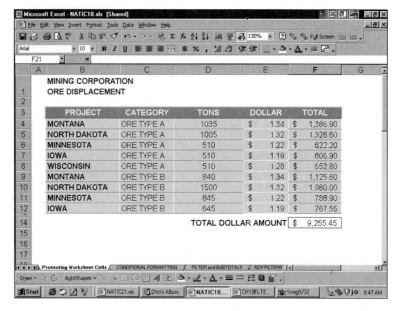

5. After making your selections, click OK.

6. Select the range you want to protect.

7. Choose F<u>o</u>rmat, C<u>e</u>lls to reopen the Format Cells dialog box.

8. Select the <u>L</u>ocked option on the Protection tab (see Figure 32.23).

Figure 32.23.
To protect the range of cells that contain the formulas, select the range and check the Locked option on the Protection tab in the Format Cells dialog box.

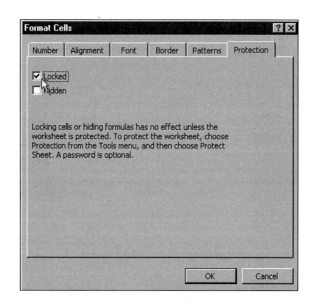

9. Choose Tools, Protection, Protect Sheet. The Protect Sheet dialog box appears and allows you to enter a password; however, the password entry is optional (see Figure 32.24).

Figure 32.24.
With password protection, you can make changes to the protected cells only if the worksheet password is entered and the cells are then unprotected.

HIDING FORMULAS

You can hide formulas within a workbook. To hide formulas, repeat the steps previously discussed; however, choose the Hidden option on the Protection tab in the Format Cells dialog box. Then reprotect the workbook with a password by choosing Tools, Protection.

PASSWORD-PROTECTING A WORKBOOK

You can apply a password to a workbook that will allow only users with the password to open and view the workbook. Password-protecting the workbook is the only fail-proof way of protecting vital information within a workbook. As mentioned previously in this chapter, advanced users can unprotect all other protection devices within Excel (very advanced users can even get past the workbook password, but this feature will provide enough coverage for most situations).

To protect the workbook so that a password is needed before the workbook is opened, follow these steps:

1. With the workbook that you want to password-protect onscreen and active, choose File, Save As.

2. In the Save As dialog box, click the Tools button to display the drop-down menu, and choose General Options.

3. In the Save Options dialog box, enter the password in the Password to Open box (see Figure 32.25). Without the password, the user will be unable to open the file at all.

4. If you want a separate password to be required for editing the file, enter that password in the Password to Modify box. With this option, the user may be able to open the file, but can't change workbook contents unless the password is entered.

   For additional protection, you can enter passwords in both the Password to Open and Password to Modify boxes.

PART
VIII
CH
32

Figure 32.25.
The Save Options dialog box enables you to apply a password to a workbook so that the workbook can be opened only after the password is entered.

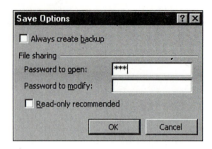

5. In addition to the password options, you can select the following settings:

   ■ **Always Create Backup**. Creates a backup copy of the file every time the file is saved. This is primarily a backup device in case a file is deleted or becomes corrupt.

   ■ **Read-Only Recommended**. When opening the file, the user is asked whether he or she wants to open the file as read-only. If Yes is selected, changes made to the file must be saved under a different name.

6. When the settings are complete, click OK.

7. In the Confirm Password dialog box, reenter the password to verify the correct password.

8. Click OK to close the Confirm Password dialog box and return to the Save As dialog box.

9. Specify a filename and path for the file, if necessary, and click Save.

10. Click Yes to replace the old version of the file with the new password-protected version (unless this is a first-time save or you're saving the file with a different name).

PROTECTING A SHARED WORKBOOK

If you have a workbook that's shared by many people, you'll find it helpful to use the *Track Changes* feature for tracking edits from the other users that occur within the workbook. Excel also enables you to share a workbook and track changes where the tracked changes can't be removed because a password is entered. If the workbook is shared, you first must remove the shared status of the workbook in order to proceed.

To protect and share a workbook with tracked changes, select Tools, Protection, Protect and Share Workbook to display the Protect Shared Workbook dialog box. Check the Sharing with Track Changes option, and enter a password if desired.

TROUBLESHOOTING

SELECTING A RECORD THAT APPEARS MULTIPLE TIMES IN A LIST

How can I filter a record that appears multiple times within a list?

Select the column range with the multiple records you want to filter. Then choose Data, Filter, Advanced Filter. In the Advanced Filter dialog box, check Unique Records Only. This will filter the list with the unique records that appear in the list.

PASTING CONDITIONAL FORMATS OVER MULTIPLE ROWS

When I create a conditional format in a row that equals a cell in that same row, how do I copy the conditional format down, equaling the corresponding cell in the same row pasted?

From the Conditional Formatting dialog box, select Cell Value Is, equal to, and then the cell in the corresponding row. Remove the dollar sign ($) in front of the row number to make it relative instead of absolute. Now the format will copy down, equaling a cell in the corresponding row.

PROTECTING VITAL INFORMATION

What's the best way to protect my data in Excel?

Save the workbook with a password! Choose File, Save As to open the Save As dialog box. Then open the Tools drop-down menu and choose General Options. From here, you have the option of protecting the workbook with a password.

PART

VIII

CH

32

CHAPTER **33**

OUTLINING, SUBTOTALING, AND AUDITING WORKSHEET DATA

In this chapter

ORGANIZING AND AUDITING YOUR DATA

As mentioned often in other chapters of this book, structuring the data in your workbooks is essential to using them effectively. Structure is particularly crucial if you plan to extract, chart, pivot, or create reports from the data. If the worksheet is put together randomly, without good planning, reorganizing it later can cost a lot of time and frustration. When a worksheet is well structured, on the other hand, you can take full advantage of Excel's data-management features to display, print, and report precisely what you want.

Chapter 32 describes the Excel options for *sorting*, *filtering*, and *protecting* your data. This chapter continues with data-management features by providing details on outlining and grouping, consolidating, and using data validation and auditing to help prevent, locate, and correct data errors.

GROUPING AND OUTLINING DATA

Outlining and *grouping* are two of Excel's data-management features. They're very similar. You can use grouping to effectively manage columns and rows with multiple levels of groups that display and hide information. Grouping data is different from outlining in that groups are defined to any depth, level, and location you want. An outline, on the other hand, is based on a structured list or table that has totals and subsets already built in.

> **Note**
>
> When structuring a workbook or database, don't move forward with the intention of just starting to create, and planning to incorporate the functionality as your needs grow. Outlines and groups are created from structure. If your list has no structure, your outline has little or no meaning for the user.
>
> To outline a list or table, I always work backward from the list and ask the question, "What information do I need to extract from the list?" If possible, write down the information and even how it's presented. This will help you work backward in planning the structure of the list.

Before launching into using the grouping and outlining features, you may want to create a custom toolbar for use with these features. Excel offers several very useful outlining and grouping toolbar buttons that can be added to any toolbar or used as a separate custom toolbar. The custom toolbar shown in Figure 33.1 includes buttons for creating, showing, and selecting visible cells in an outline or group. These buttons all come from the Data category on the Commands tab in the Customize dialog box. Another helpful item that you could include is the Group and Outline menu from the Built-in Menus category on the same tab.

Table 33.1 describes the buttons on this custom toolbar. (You can include the buttons on any toolbar, of course, but I've found it helpful to combine these functions in one place.)

Figure 33.1.
This custom toolbar shows tools in Excel useful for establishing outlines and managing the group and outline symbols.

TABLE 33.1. OUTLINING/GROUPING TOOLBAR BUTTONS

Button	Name	Description
	Show Outline Symbols	Shows the outline symbols along the rows and columns
	Group	Groups the selected rows or columns
	Ungroup	Ungroups the selected rows or columns
	Show Detail	Shows the detail by unhiding the hidden groups for the selected row or column
	Hide Detail	Hides the detail of the selected row or column
	Select Visible Cells	Selects or highlights only the visible cells

GROUPING DATA

If Excel data contains common attributes, you can *group* the data to make it more readable. In the table in Figure 33.2, for example, the common groups are the months and then the quarters. This *hierarchical grouping* can be done with days, weeks, months, quarters, and years. You also can reduce the list to lower levels, even minutes or seconds.

By creating a group, you can combine multiple rows or columns of information, enabling you to hide and show information with one click. To create a group, select the rows or columns you want to group and then choose Data, Group and Outline, Group. In the Group dialog box, specify whether you want to group Rows or Columns. (If you select the entire row/column, you won't get the Group dialog box; the grouping will occur automatically.) *Outline symbols* appear on the left side of the worksheet, as shown in Figure 33.3. By clicking the *outline buttons*, you can hide or display the selected information, as shown in Figure 33.4. Excel calls these techniques *collapsing* and *expanding* the group. An outline button with a plus sign (+) indicates that the group is collapsed to show only the totals. A minus sign (–) indicates that the group is fully expanded.

PART

VIII

CH

33

Figure 33.2.
The table shown is known as a *hierarchical table*. The months are grouped by their respective quarters.

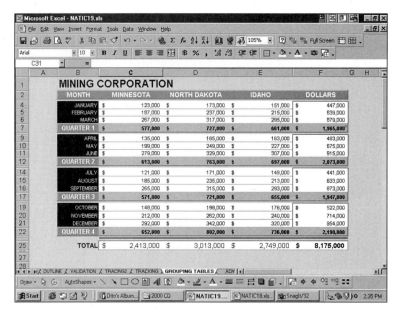

Figure 33.3.
After you create a group, you can hide the group by clicking on the outline buttons shown on the left side of the worksheet.

Clicking a button with a minus sign collapses the group.

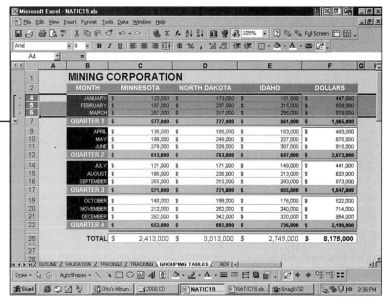

If you group the additional months (refer to Figure 33.2), you can show the quarters or the months by clicking the outline buttons. In addition, you can use the 1 and 2 buttons at the top of the outline area (to the left of the column headings) to control the level of the grouping displayed on the whole list. Click 1 to collapse the entire grouping to show only totals; click 2 to expand the list to show all the supporting rows. Your list may contain additional levels, in which case the buttons would be numbered 3, 4, and so on.

Clicking a button with a plus sign expands the group.   Rows 4–6 are collapsed to show only the total in row 7.

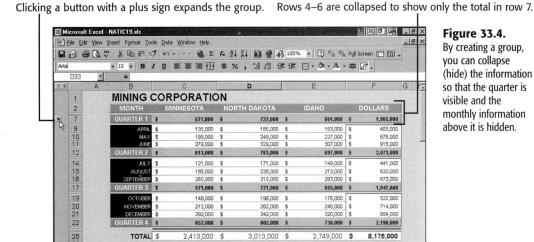

Figure 33.4.
By creating a group, you can collapse (hide) the information so that the quarter is visible and the monthly information above it is hidden.

Notice how effective grouping can be after the groups have been created (see Figure 33.5).

Not only can you group the rows but also the columns, as shown in Figure 33.6. By grouping the columns, you can collapse a view to the maximum—showing only totals—as in Figure 33.7.

Use these buttons to control the level of the grouping on the whole list.

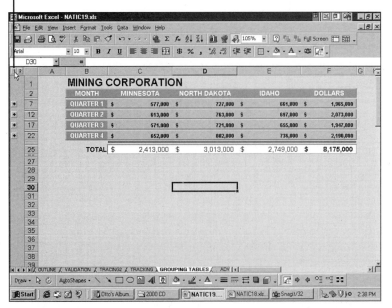

Figure 33.5.
Grouping the quarters enables you to view the summary of quarters, or the months if the groups are expanded.

PART

VIII

CH

33

Figure 33.6.
By grouping both rows and columns, you can collapse a list to show only totals.

The outline buttons for columns work in the same way as the buttons for rows, except that they collapse and expand columns.

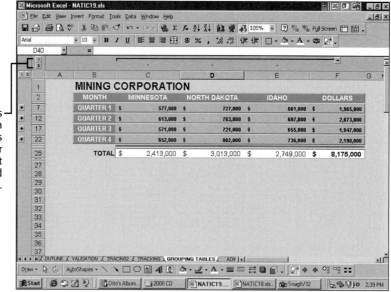

Figure 33.7.
The group now shows the lowest level of detail.

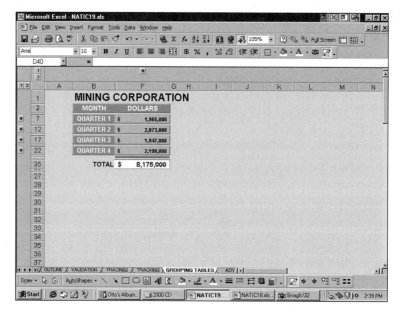

 Excel enables you to add layers of groupings as well. This further enhances the capacity to create hierarchical groups. Notice the additional outline button added to the rows in Figure 33.8. To add an additional layer to the group, select the rows you want to hide, and choose Data, Group and Outline, Group (or click the Group button). Excel applies the group symbols and buttons for the additional layer.

Another level of grouping has been added.

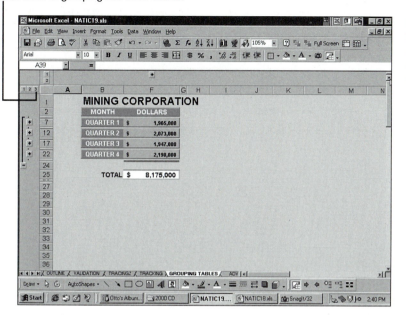

Figure 33.8.
Excel enables you to create groups of groups for multiple-grouping scenarios.

 After your list and groups are in place, you may want to restore the screen space lost to the outline symbols, while still keeping the grouping in place. Use the Show Outline Symbols toolbar button (refer to Table 33.1 in the preceding section) or press Ctrl+8 to hide and show the outline symbols. You also can turn the view of outline symbols off or on by choosing Tools, Options to open the Options dialog box, clicking the View tab, and selecting or deselecting Outline Symbols.

PART
VIII
CH
33

GROUPING SUMMARY TABLES

Now that you understand the basic logic of grouping, you can establish multiple summary tables on a single worksheet within a workbook and apply grouping symbols that apply to all the tables. If you have a workbook with several lists, for example, you might want to create one sheet that holds all your summary information. With this technique, you also can create custom views and reports easily and effectively. The key in creating summary tables on one worksheet with combined grouping is to establish similar setups for all the lists you plan to group. In Figure 33.9, for example, the geographic area tables are set up in similar fashion and the outline buttons apply to all.

The groups summarize the information in an effective manner, as shown in Figure 33.10, and can be managed on a single screen at the highest level (see Figure 33.11).

Figure 33.9.
By creating similar tables on a sheet within the workbook, you can apply groupings that apply to multiple tables.

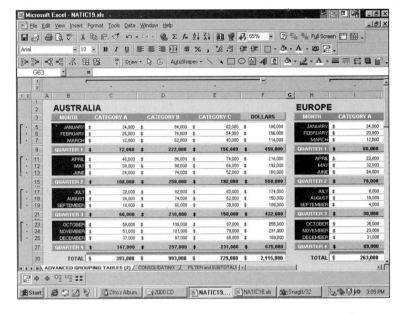

Multiple columns are collapsed.

Figure 33.10.
The groups are collapsed by column.

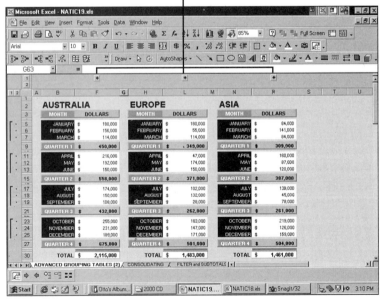

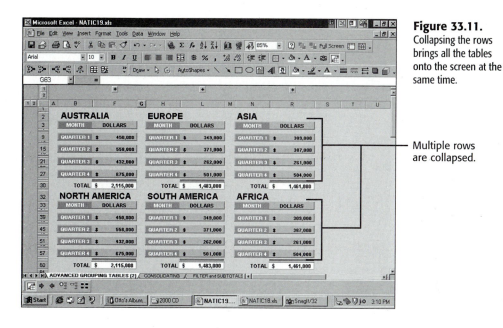

Figure 33.11.
Collapsing the rows
brings all the tables
onto the screen at the
same time.

Multiple rows
are collapsed.

GROUPING DATA WITH FORMATS

Not only is it important to create consistent structure within an Excel worksheet, it's also important to create formats that visibly tell the story of the worksheet. The lists in Figures 19.12 and 19.13 prove this point. Figure 33.12 is a sea of numbers. In Figure 33.13, the information is identical, but the story becomes clear. If you use structure and formatting well, the numbers can tell a story.

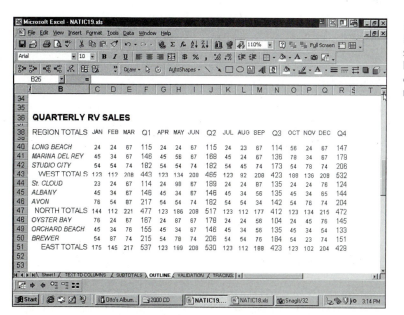

Figure 33.12.
Because this list has
structure but no
logical formatting,
deciphering the infor-
mation is difficult.

Figure 33.13.
The information is the same here as in Figure 33.12; however, the formatted list creates a story, and the structure of the list becomes visible.

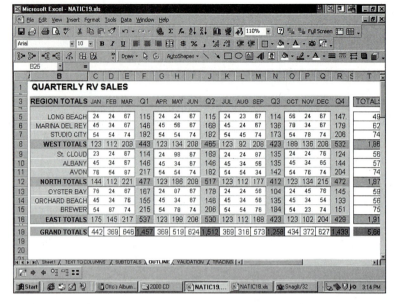

The structure of the list in Figure 33.13 follows simple guidelines. The timeline across the top of the worksheet shows column headings for months and quarter breaks. The city and region breaks are named vertically in the first column of the list. Notice that the spacing is minimized, but this layout still maintains a simple-to-follow grid by using formatting. The interior data has a white background; the remainder of the list is shaded, with the totals and their headings distinguished by boldfacing or a larger font.

→ To learn more about using formatting to distinguish parts of the worksheet, **see** "Combining Excel's Tools for Innovative Formatting," **p. 720**

OUTLINING DATA

Worksheet outlines use the same symbols as groups, but differ in that they're derived from a structured list, with no additional columns or rows. Based on the structure of the list in Figure 33.14, for example, it's easy to see where you can place outlining along the rows and columns. The list's critical information points are highlighted in the figure, with the first group symbol placed to group the first quarter.

To group selected columns or rows, choose Data, Group and Outline, Group, or click the Group toolbar button. The final result of the first level of groups is shown in Figure 33.15. Notice the second-level group in Figure 33.16—it groups the row's regions to roll up a grand total. Excel applies the level buttons to the highest roll-up level; the lower the outline level, the higher the button number.

Tip #428	You can group and ungroup a selection, respectively, by pressing Shift+Alt+right arrow and Shift+Alt+left arrow.

The first quarter is grouped.

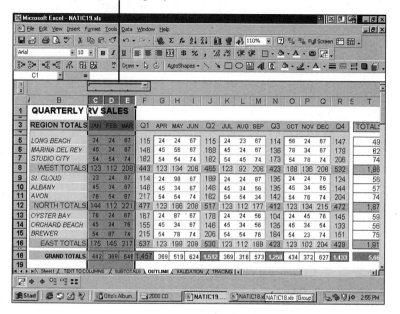

Figure 33.14.
The critical group points to keep visible here are highlighted (columns C through E). The groups are formatted to show the different levels of importance.

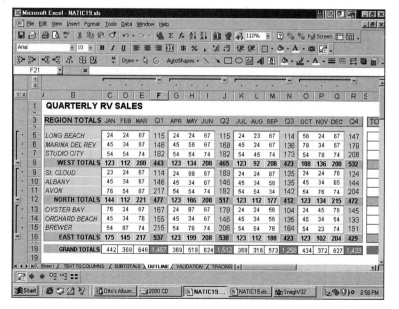

Figure 33.15.
The first level of groups applied in hierarchical fashion by quarters and regions.

PART

VIII

CH

33

Figure 33.16.
The second level group applied rolls up the list by regions. Notice the additional level button.

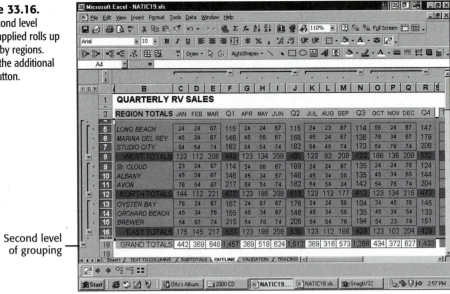

Second level of grouping

CREATING AN AUTO OUTLINE

Another way to outline a list is to use the *Auto Outline* feature. Auto Outline is a quick way to create an outline, but Excel first must understand the hierarchy of your list or database. You can apply all the groupings with one step if the list is structured in a manner that Excel understands. The information must be structured consistently throughout—for example, January, February, March, and then Q1 with no blank columns or rows as separators; then April, May, June, and Q2.

To create a multilevel Auto Outline, select Data, Group and Outline, Auto Outline. Excel applies outline symbols (see Figure 33.17). The active cell doesn't even need to be in the table/data set. You need only select the data if the worksheet includes more than one data set.

The Auto Outline feature depends on Excel's being able to detect the structure of your data automatically. If you get the error message `Cannot create an outline`, this means Excel doesn't see a logical structure to the data you're trying to outline. But you can place the outline symbols manually—to speed up the process, create the first outline, select the next range of data, and press F4 to repeat the last action.

CLEARING THE OUTLINE

To clear outline symbols, select the range of a single group or outline and use any of the following techniques:

- Choose Data, Group and Outline, Ungroup.
- Click the Ungroup button.

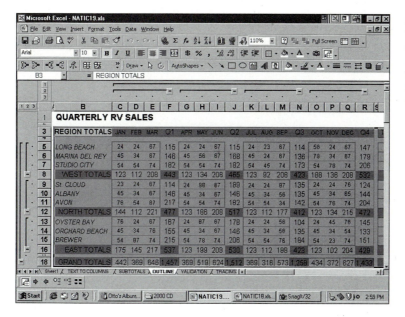

Figure 33.17.
The Auto Outline feature applies outline symbols to the list or table down to the lowest level defined by your list structure.

- Press Shift+Alt+left arrow.
- To eliminate all outlines at once, choose Data, Group and Outline, Clear Outline.

CHANGING THE OUTLINE SETTINGS

You can change the positioning of summary rows in the group or outline and apply Excel's built-in outline styles. Choose Data, Group and Outline, Settings to open the Settings dialog box. Specify whether you want summary rows placed below the detail and columns to the right of the detail (these are the default settings).

To apply Excel's built-in outline cell styles (RowLevel_1, ColLevel_1, and so on), select Automatic Styles in the Settings dialog box.

Clicking Create in the dialog box creates a new outline from the selected data with the settings you have specified in the dialog box. Clicking Apply Styles applies the settings to the existing outline.

CONSOLIDATING DATA

If you establish several lists or tables that have similar setups, you'll probably want to combine certain sets of data from these separate lists or tables into one consolidated list or table. Excel enables you to consolidate tables with the Consolidate command on the Data menu. Consolidation allows for analysis of the tables or lists with functions provided in the Consolidate dialog box.

PART
VIII

CH
33

The best way to consolidate a list or table is to set up a table that represents the format of the original tables, like the example shown in Figure 33.18. Consolidation isn't limited to a worksheet or a workbook—you can consolidate data from the same worksheet, a different worksheet in the same workbook, another workbook, or even from Lotus 1-2-3 files.

Figure 33.18.
When consolidating a list or table (as shown here in the range B21:F28), it's best to set up the consolidation destination with formats similar to those in the source tables.

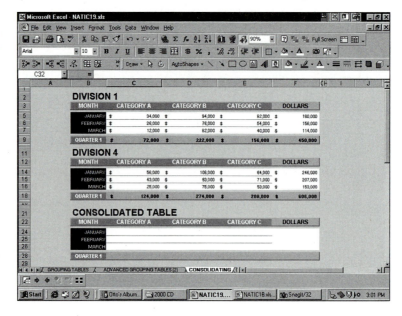

To create a consolidation table, follow these steps:

1. Select the destination for the consolidated data. In the example, the destination cell is C24.

Note

Don't select multiple cells as the destination unless you're positive that the consolidated data will fit within the selected area; although other existing cells won't necessarily be overwritten, Excel simply may fail to consolidate parts of the source tables.

2. Select Consolidate from the Data menu to open the Consolidate dialog box.

3. Select the type of analysis you want to perform from the Function menu.

4. Under Reference, select the first range you want to include for consolidation. To select the range in the worksheet itself, use the Collapse Dialog button or just drag the dialog box out of the way and click in the worksheet. If the worksheet uses named ranges, you can type the range names in the dialog box, which saves time in selecting.

   Consolidation ranges are often found outside the active sheet. You can easily activate another sheet in the current workbook to get to a range there. If the ranges are located in one or more other workbooks, however, open the workbook(s) before starting the consolidation command, and then use the <u>W</u>indow menu to switch to the desired workbook in order to access its ranges.

5. After you establish the range, click the <u>A</u>dd button to add the range to the All References box (see Figure 33.19).

6. If you want the consolidation table to be updated automatically when its source data is changed, select Create Links to <u>S</u>ource Data.

7. Click OK.

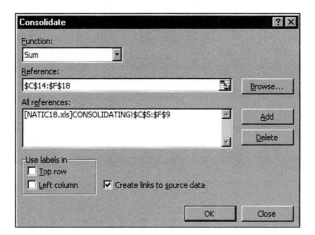

Figure 33.19.
This example uses the SUM function to total the figures for January through March and the quarterly total for Divisions 1 and 4.

The consolidated numbers in the example now reflect the addition of Division 1 and Division 4, as shown in Figure 33.20.

PART

VIII

Сн

33

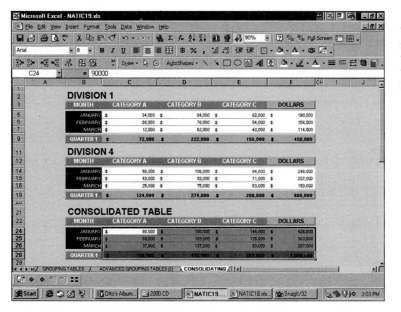

Figure 33.20.
The result of the consolidated divisions is the addition of the tables because the SUM function was used for analysis.

Tip #429

Although matching labels must be identical for the data to consolidate properly, sources that contain different column/row headings can easily be consolidated by using the Use Labels In options in the Consolidate dialog box. Let's say your sources have different row and column headings. You simply include those labels when selecting each source range, turn on both Top Row and Left Column in the dialog box, and both the labels and consolidated data appear in the destination range.

Excel enables you to change the function with which you analyze the data; just open the Consolidate dialog box again, change the setting in the Function box, and click OK.

Consolidation ranges are saved with the workbook, making the refresh process really easy. To refresh the consolidated table, just select the destination cell again (in this example, cell C24) and choose Data, Consolidate again. Verify or change the ranges to consolidate and click OK.

CREATING AUTOMATIC SUBTOTALS

Excel provides automatic subtotaling capability for use with any suitably organized data. Lists often lend themselves to subtotals because the most common question asked after filtering a list is, "How do I total just the visible cells?" In a *filtered* list, the Sub-totals command on the Data menu subtotals only the visible cells in the list. You can also use subtotaling for other calculations—using the functions COUNT, MAX, MIN, and so on.

Note

To subtotal a filtered list, begin by filtering the list, if desired. For any other kind of subtotaling, simply skip this step. The procedure is the same otherwise.

Tip #430

Because a list can vary in size and scope, create the subtotal for use as a quick reference in a place where it won't move and can remain visible at all times—for example, at the top of a list. When you filter the list, the subtotal remains in the same location, which enables you to view the subtotal without scrolling to the bottom of the list.

To add a subtotal to a list, follow these steps:

1. Sort the list (and filter it, if desired), and then select the records. The first sort key you use should be the one you plan to select in the At Each Change In drop-down list in the Subtotal dialog box (see step 3).

Tip #431

If your list is surrounded by blank rows and columns, Excel will select the data to subtotal automatically; you don't need to select it before beginning the subtotaling process. The active cell must be somewhere in the list when you start this process.

2. Choose <u>D</u>ata, Su<u>b</u>totals.

3. In the Subtotal dialog box, specify the subtotal criteria, function, and other settings you want to apply (see Figure 33.21):

- In the <u>A</u>t Each Change In box, select the heading that indicates when you want Excel to perform a subtotal—for example, at each change in state, employee name, client, and so on. If you want to subtotal grouped items, sort the list on the column you select here *before* you subtotal the list.

- In the <u>U</u>se Function box, select the function you want Excel to use for the subtotals.

- In the A<u>d</u>d Subtotal To list, select the column(s) that you want to subtotal.

- If you're performing a new subtotal function and want to replace the existing subtotals in the list, select Replace <u>C</u>urrent Subtotals.

- Select <u>P</u>age Break Between Groups if you want Excel to start each new sub-totaled group at the top of a clean page.

- If you want the subtotals and grand totals to appear below the data, select <u>S</u>ummary Below Data. If this option is deselected, Excel places the subtotals above the first entry subtotaled in each group and places the grand total (or grand average, grand min, and so on, depending on the function you selected) at the top of the column, just below the row of headings.

4. Click OK to run the totals.

The SUBTOTAL function uses the following syntax:

`SUBTOTAL(function_num,ref1,ref2,...)`

where `ref1`, `ref2`, and so on refer to the range(s) being calculated (up to 29 ranges), and `function_num` refers to a number from 1 to 11, with the following values:

Figure 33.21.

Reference No.	Function
1	AVERAGE
2	COUNT
3	COUNTA
4	MAX
5	MIN
6	PRODUCT
7	STDEV
8	STDEVP
9	SUM
10	VAR
11	VARP

To learn how to enter functions, see Chapter 25, "Using Excel's Built-In Functions." For a list of available Excel functions and their descriptions, see Appendix A, "Excel Function Reference."

Tip #432

You can build multiple layers of subtotals—using different functions and subtotaling different fields—by running the Subtotals feature multiple times and deselecting the Replace Current Subtotals option each time.

Notice that the original data is visible when the subtotal of the category is selected and the grand total of the subtotaled categories shown. You may want to delete the subtotaled records and place the Grand Total row above the category heading as shown in Figure 33.22. You probably will also want to change one aspect of the formula—subtotaling any record pulled from the range.

Figure 33.22.
By placing the subtotal above the row headings, you can view the grand total of the category filtered above the list. Change the subtotal formula's range to equal the full range of the list.

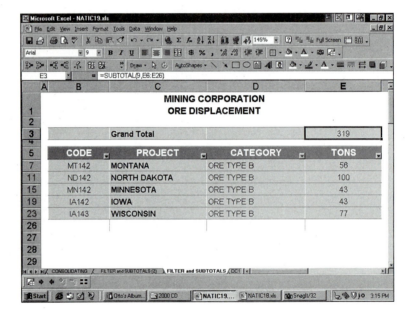

Follow these steps:

1. Select the subtotal cell with the formula in it. In the example in Figure 33.22, the formula cell is E3.

2. The specified range in the formula extracts to the end of the records selected. Change the maximum range to equal the last record in your list. (The last range in the Mining Corporation list is row 26.)

3. Press Enter after the formula has been modified. For this formula, notice that the function number in the subtotal formula is 9, which refers to the SUM function.

Note | Excel ignores any nested subtotals in the list, along with any hidden rows.

The Grand Total now reflects the displayed records only, in a physical location that remains unchanged. This works well when dealing with large amounts of information that must be called up and summed up at a moment's notice.

VALIDATING AND AUDITING DATA ENTRY

Somewhere along the line, the data in every Excel workbook came from a human being. The process may have included typing data directly, downloading from a network or the Internet, importing from a database or data warehouse, and so on, but every bit of data can eventually be traced back to someone "filling in the blanks." Everyone makes mistakes at least occasionally, and the most complex formula is useless if its source data is wrong. On the other hand, accurate source data isn't very helpful if the formulas aren't constructed in a way that returns appropriate results. How can you prevent data errors and incorrect formulas from creeping into your Excel workbooks?

Excel offers some special features for dealing with the possibility of error within a workbook:

- To prevent errors from being typed into a worksheet, the *data validation* feature enables you to provide some guidance for the person entering the data (that may even be you!). You can tell Excel to accept only certain kinds of entries within a cell—for example, numbers or dates within a certain range—and specify a message for the user with instructions on filling in the information. With this feature, you also decide how you want Excel to respond to noncompliance: Display an error message and refuse the entry? Accept the incorrect entry but warn the user that it's problematic?

- If invalid data already exists in the workbook, Excel can locate and circle those entries, using the same data-validation logic.

- To trace relationships between cells and formulas, you can use Excel's auditing feature to display the connection between formulas and their source cells (precedents) or between cells and their dependent formulas. You also can find the sources of error results in formulas.

The following sections describe these features.

As you might expect, Excel provides a special Auditing toolbar for these functions. You can turn on the toolbar from the Toolbars list on the Toolbars tab in the Customize dialog box. Table 33.2 describes the buttons on the Auditing toolbar.

PART

VIII

Ch

33

TABLE 33.2. AUDITING TOOLBAR

Button	Name	Description
	Trace Precedents	Shows the preceding formulas or cell references that contribute to the cell
	Remove Precedent Arrows	Removes the precedent auditing arrows
	Trace Dependents	Shows the cell references to which the current cell points
	Remove Dependent Arrows	Removes the dependent auditing arrows
	Remove All Arrows	Removes all auditing arrows
	Trace Error	Traces cells with error values
	New Comment	Applies a comment to a cell
	Circle Invalid Data	Circles data outside the parameters set by validation
	Clear Validation Circles	Clears the invalid data circles

DATA VALIDATION

For those who occasionally find that they have entered improper data, Excel has addressed this problem with data validation. Validation enables you to apply parameters to ranges or cells, keeping information within certain boundaries. For example, if your list applies to dates within a certain month only, you can specify parameters from the first of the month until month-end that allow the user to input only dates within that specified period of time. These parameters can be set up to prevent incorrect information completely, warn the user but allow the entry, and so on. (The next section describes how to come back and mark invalid data later.)

To apply validation parameters to a list, cell, or range, follow these steps:

1. Select the area where you want to apply validation. For a range in which you want date validation, for example, select the months, range of dates, and so on.

2. Choose Data, Validation.

3. If necessary, select the Settings tab in the Data Validation dialog box. In the Validation Criteria options, specify the parameters that will be acceptable when the user is entering data (see Figure 33.23).

This example shows dates applied between two specified date ranges; the Ignore Blank option is selected so that the user can either enter an acceptable date or simply skip specifying a date in the input range.

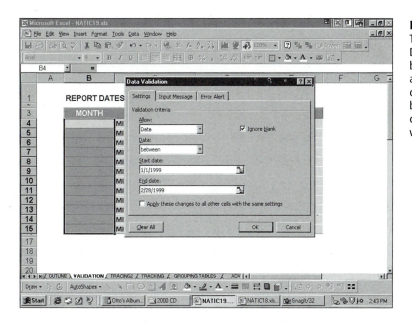

Figure 33.23.
The Settings tab in the Data Validation dialog box enables you to apply validation to dates, times, numbers, text, or even create a custom validation.

Similar to customizing options for filters in lists, you can specify several characteristics on the Settings tab. Under the Data option, you can make the dates equal to, greater than, less than, and so on. Excel allows for flexibility to fit your specific requirements, and the options on the Settings tab change to reflect the selected data.

PART

VIII

CH

33

4. (Optional) You can provide an input message to help the user to enter the correct data. Click the Input Message tab in the Data Validation dialog box, as shown in Figure 33.24. Whatever you specify in the Title box will appear in the title bar for the dialog box, and the Input message will be displayed in the box itself.

5. Next, specify what you want to happen if the user enters invalid data. Click the Error Alert tab (see Figure 33.25). Select a warning Style (the icon changes to match the style you select) and specify the Title you want the title bar of the message box to display. Finally, enter an Error Message to be displayed in the box.

6. After you enter all the information, click OK.

Figure 33.24.
Providing clues can help the user avoid making mistakes.

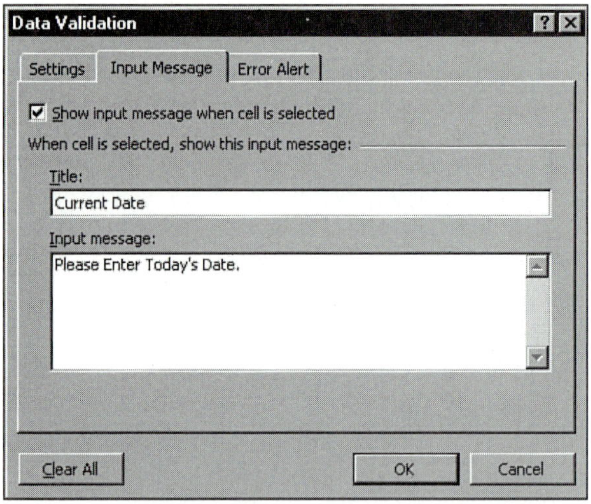

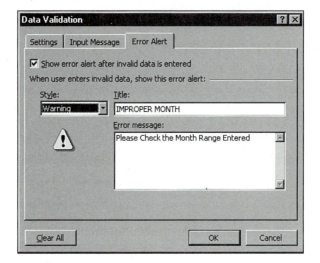

Figure 33.25.
The Error Alert tab lets you specify among three types of errors: Warning, Stop, and Information. You also can apply titles and text to the dialog box being created.

Figure 33.26 shows what happens when I apply a date that's outside the specified parameters for this example. I have the option of choosing Yes to accept the current date, No to correct the error, or Cancel to void the entry.

Note

Using the Stop style prevents users from entering invalid data.

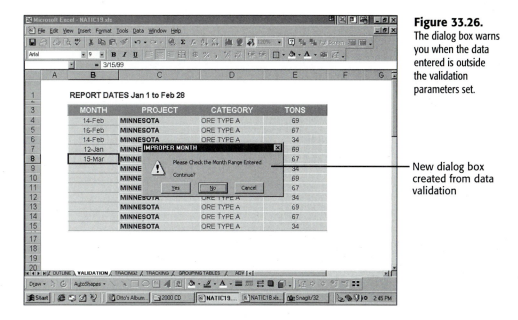

Figure 33.26.
The dialog box warns you when the data entered is outside the validation parameters set.

New dialog box created from data validation

You can change or remove the validation settings at any time by returning to the Data Validation dialog box. In most cases, you will just want to correct the settings, change the input or error messages, and so on. However, if you want to remove all the settings at once—all messages, alerts, and validation criteria, use the Clear All button at the bottom of the Data Validation box. (If you change your mind about this before closing the dialog box, clicking Cancel restores the settings.)

PART

VIII

CH

33

Tip #433

You can make one set of changes on the Settings tab and tell Excel to apply those new settings to other comparable validated cells. Select the option at the bottom of the tab, Apply These Changes to All Other Cells with the Same Settings.

CIRCLING INVALID DATA

Excel includes a special validation feature to find and mark invalid data that was previously entered. You might use this feature for a number of reasons:

- Data was entered before you instituted validation, and you want to go back and fix existing errors.

- The validation you have in place allows the user to enter invalid data after displaying a warning. (Sometimes you want to be able to enter invalid information, but have it verified, corrected, or approved later.)

- You want to change the validation conditions.

To audit the worksheet and quickly display a circle around information that doesn't meet the data validation conditions (up to 255 errors), click the Circle Invalid Data button on the Auditing toolbar. Excel circles the invalid data, as shown in Figure 33.27. If Excel finds 255 errors, you'll need to correct some of them and click the Circle Invalid Data button again before the program can mark any more.

Figure 33.27.
Excel circles all information that doesn't fall within the specified validation parameters.

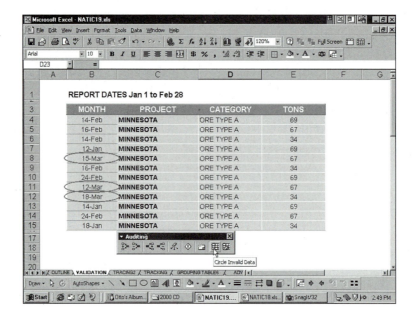

To remove the displayed circles, click the Clear Validation Circles button on the Auditing toolbar.

Tip #434

If validation wasn't applied to your list and you now want to highlight information that falls outside specified ranges, use *conditional formatting* and point to ranges and cells that establish parameters to meet your specifications.

AUDITING PRECEDENTS, DEPENDENTS, AND ERRORS

When inheriting a list of information or a workbook created by other users, the first thing you'll want to do is "check the wiring" of the workbook—how all the formulas and their data are connected. Excel's *auditing* feature can trace this information for you, as well as help you locate sources of errors returned by your formulas.

For each cell, auditing can trace the following information:

- If the cell contains a formula, auditing can trace its source cell(s), called *precedents*.
- If the cell contains data or formulas, auditing can trace any formulas that use the information from that cell, called its *dependents*.

- If the cell contains an error, auditing can trace the source of the error. For example, if a formula with a division operation returns #DIV/0, auditing can trace the source cell that either has no entry or contains a zero.

In each case, the relationships are pointed out with colored *tracer arrows*.

⚠️ *If the auditing menu commands or buttons are disabled, the tracer arrows may be hidden. See "Displaying Tracer Arrows" in the Troubleshooting section at the end of this chapter.*

Tip #435	You can't audit a protected worksheet. To remove protection, choose Tools, Protection, Unprotect Sheet. If your workbook has more layers of protection, however, you'll have to get through those layers before you can even access the worksheet. Chapter 32, "Using Excel's Data-Management Features," describes the various levels of protection available in Excel.

For example, if a cell contains a formula that sums a column of numbers, the formula's precedents would be the individual numbers being added. Each of those precedent cells would have the formula cell as one of its dependents. If that formula cell is itself included in a grand total somewhere else, the grand total would be a dependent of that formula cell.

The example in Figure 33.28 illustrates a simple scenario with a division formula. The formula divides the selling amount in column D by the number of units in column C for each row, as shown in cell E2. In this case, the worksheet shows several audits (the audited cells are shaded in the figure):

- Tracing the precedents for the formula in cell E4, Excel displays a blue arrow with origins in cells C4 and D4.
- Tracing the dependents of cell C8, Excel displays a blue arrow with the arrowhead in the single dependent formula cell E8.
- Cell D11 also has a single dependent, the formula in cell E11.
- The error in cell E14 is traced with a red arrow to its source, the empty cell C14.

If the information originates from or points to a different workbook or worksheet, the tracer arrow is black and the icon resembles a small worksheet.

To run or remove audits, you can use menu commands or the buttons on the Auditing toolbar, as described in the following list:

- **Trace a formula's precedents.** Select the cell containing the formula and choose Tools, Auditing, Trace Precedents or click the Trace Precedents button.
- **Trace a cell's dependents.** Select the cell and choose Tools, Auditing, Trace Dependents or click the Trace Dependents button.
- **Show multiple levels of precedents/dependents.** Repeatedly click the Trace Precedents or Trace Dependents button. If Excel beeps when you click one of these buttons, you have traced all levels of the formula, or you're trying to trace something untraceable (such as a graphic).

Figure 33.28.
By displaying precedents, dependents, and errors, you can quickly see relationships between cells.

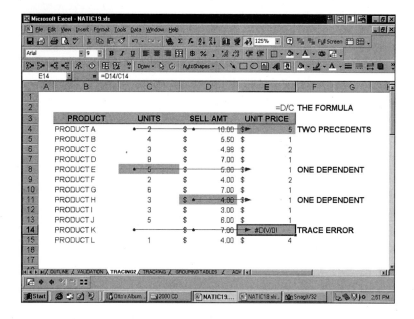

- **Track down the culprit cell leading to an error result.** Select the cell containing the formula with the error result and click the Trace Errors button or choose Tools, Auditing, Trace Errors. You may need to trace repeatedly to find all the errors involved.

- **Jump between dependents and precedents.** Double-click the tracer arrow. If the formula connects different workbooks, the workbook must be open to jump to it. If you jump to a different worksheet or workbook, Excel displays the Go To list; double-click the reference you want.

- **Remove tracer arrows.** To remove the tracer arrow from a cell to its dependents or precedents, select the cell and click the Remove Dependent Arrows or Remove Precedent Arrows button, respectively. To remove all tracer arrows, click the Remove All Arrows button on the Auditing toolbar or choose Tools, Auditing, Remove All Arrows.

Tracer arrows disappear when you save or close the workbook; you can't save an audit from one session to the next. Arrows also disappear if you insert or delete rows or columns, delete or move the cells involved in the formula, or change the formula itself.

TROUBLESHOOTING

DISPLAYING TRACER ARROWS

The Auditing toolbar buttons or menu options are unavailable.

If the worksheet isn't protected (you can't audit a protected worksheet), and the auditing features are unavailable, your Excel options are set up to hide graphical objects (which include tracer arrows). The auditing feature relies on tracer arrows to indicate errors, precedents, and dependents. To display the tracer arrows, choose Tools, Options to open the Options dialog box. Click the View tab, and select either Show All or Show Placeholders in the Objects section.

AUTO OUTLINE DOESN'T WORK

Why do I get the error message "Cannot create an outline"?

Excel understands only outlines that are set up consistently. Be sure you don't have inconsistent spaces between categories and totals, and that the rest of the list is organized in a consistent manner.

CHAPTER 34

USING PIVOTTABLES AND PIVOTCHARTS

In this chapter

UNDERSTANDING PIVOTTABLES

A *PivotTable* uses two-dimensional data to create a three-dimensional table—in essence, a summary table based on multiple conditions that have intersecting points. PivotTables are a great way to summarize large amounts of information in a small amount of space, with just a few short steps. They're interactive in that, after the PivotTable is created, you can drag a field to another location, thus *pivoting* the structure of the table with a single step.

PivotTables are often viewed as too complex to understand, but they're not that complicated if you think in terms of an automated summary table. You could write a formula to sum a quantity with multiple conditions, or you could use a PivotTable to summarize the data. Both are effective tools, but the advantage of the PivotTable is its flexibility to view the detail that makes up the total number.

PivotTables enable you to audit your data as well. If you must manage costs on a weekly basis—for example, costs of your employees and the hours they're generating—I'd strongly suggest using PivotTables. (See the later section "Managing Employee Hours and Costs with PivotTables" for specific details.)

It's important to note the new flexibility of PivotTables in Excel 2000. A PivotTable was a great way to summarize information in previous versions; however, it was so difficult to format and manipulate that it was easier to create your own tables and write formulas to extract the information. PivotTables are now a lot easier to format and can be utilized to their full potential. Your data sources for PivotTables can be queried through Microsoft Query if you're using a database or other data source.

The Excel list in Figure 34.1 shows the data for one division of a corporation. The structure of the list is important. In the example, there are three levels of information. The highest level of information being summarized is the mine site; the PivotTable will be based on the mine site. The next level is the code; the data will be organized and summarized by the code. The third level is the ore grade; the data will be structured and sorted based on the grade of the ore. To summarize this information, you could create a table manually and use formulas, or you could create a PivotTable that summarizes the information for you. The PivotTable in Figure 34.2 was created from this list. When you change the information in the list, you can use the Refresh Data command from the PivotTable toolbar to update the PivotTable.

In its typical form, a PivotTable is the intersection of two columns of data in your list, with one column of information listed down the left side of the table and the other column's information "pivoted" to list its elements across the top of the table. The intersection of the two becomes the summary data.

What's unique about PivotTables is the capacity to move fields by drag and drop. Excel summarizes the data in the new arrangement instantly. Figure 34.3 shows the same PivotTable as in Figure 34.2, but with the MINE SITE field dragged to the inside. When you move a field, the PivotTable *pivots* the data to accommodate the field's new location. You don't need to write new formulas or refilter the data because the PivotTable recalculates automatically when you rearrange the fields.

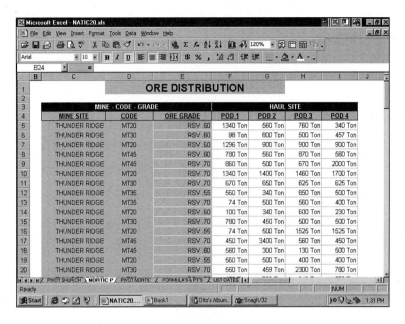

Figure 34.1.
A typical list of data organized by several categories.

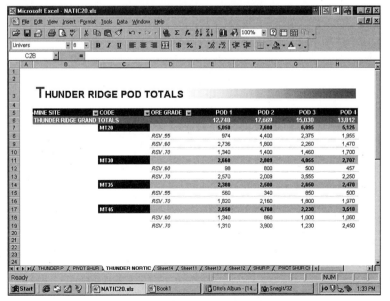

Figure 34.2.
A PivotTable quickly summarizes information in an interactive table.

Figure 34.3.
When you drag a field to a new location, the PivotTable pivots the information to reflect the data's new location.

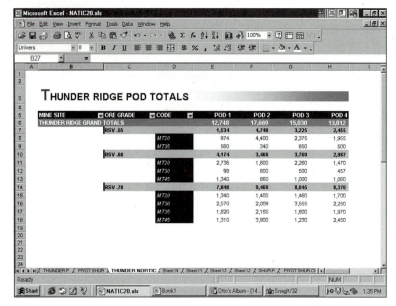

USING THE PIVOTTABLE AND PIVOTCHART WIZARD

You can use the PivotTable Wizard to create a new PivotTable or PivotChart, or to edit an existing PivotTable. (The difference between a PivotTable and a *PivotChart* is simply that one summarizes the data in the form of a table and the other in the form of a chart.) Like other wizards in Excel, the PivotTable Wizard walks you step by step through the process. The new PivotChart feature is also wizard-driven (see the later section "Creating PivotCharts").

To construct a PivotTable, follow these steps:

1. From the Data menu, select PivotTable and PivotChart Report.

2. In the Step 1 of 3 dialog box of the PivotTable Wizard, indicate the source of the data that you want to use in the PivotTable (see Figure 34.4). For the data source to be analyzed, you choose from four options:

   - **Microsoft Excel List or Database.** Uses data organized by row labels and columns on a worksheet. This is the default setting.

   - **External Data Source.** Created from a file or database outside the current workbook.

   - **Multiple Consolidation Ranges.** Creates a PivotTable or PivotChart from multiple Excel worksheets.

   - **Another PivotTable or PivotChart.** Creates a PivotTable or PivotChart from another PivotReport in the same workbook.

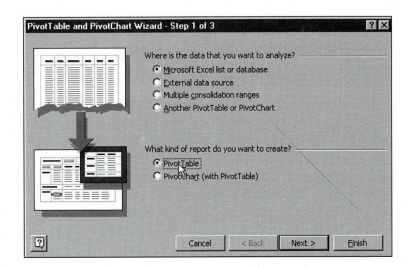

Figure 34.4.
Step 1 of 3 of the PivotTable Wizard enables you to choose from several data source options, as well as pivoting in the form of a table or chart.

3. Specify the type of PivotTable you want to create: a table or a chart. Then select Next.

4. In Step 2 of the PivotTable Wizard, select a data source if none is selected, or if the data is in a different workbook or range than the one shown in the dialog box (see Figure 34.5). Figure 34.6 shows the selected list I'm using for this example.

Caution

If you didn't select the data to be pivoted before starting the PivotTable Wizard, be sure to check the default range that Excel selects for accuracy.

Figure 34.5.
Step 2 of 3 of the PivotTable Wizard enables you to select a range and browse to a different document.

5. Step 3 of 3 of the PivotTable Wizard gives you multiple options to place and format your PivotTable (see Figure 34.7).

   The PivotTable can be placed on a new worksheet or on the existing worksheet next to the list; specify the location if you choose to place the PivotTable on the existing worksheet. You also can use the Layout and Options buttons to further specify the desired settings for the new PivotTable (see the following sections for details), or change these settings later, after creating the PivotTable or PivotChart.

6. When you're finished selecting the options you want, click Finish to create the table.

Figure 34.6.
This list will be summarized into a PivotTable.

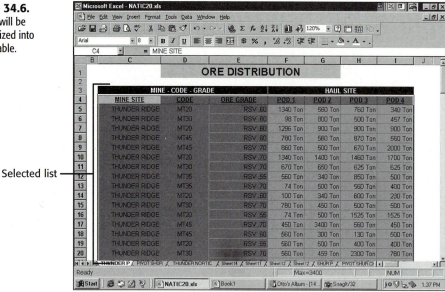

Selected list —

Figure 34.7.
Step 3 of 3 of the PivotTable Wizard enables you to establish the location of the PivotTable and also customize the format and other settings.

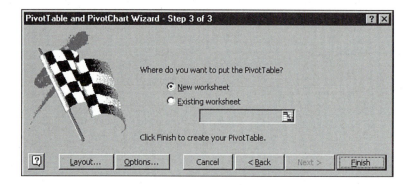

Note

If the active workbook contains at least one PivotTable, Excel enables you to create another PivotTable from that PivotTable by selecting Another PivotTable or PivotChart in Step 1 of the PivotTable Wizard. This saves on memory when creating large workbooks with multiple PivotTable reports.

LAYING OUT THE PIVOTTABLE

Clicking the Layout button in the Step 3 of 3 PivotTable Wizard dialog box displays the PivotTable and PivotChart Wizard - Layout dialog box shown in Figure 34.8. You can use this dialog box to control the view of data displayed in a PivotTable. The fields from the selected data appear on the right side of the dialog box. Select and drag the desired fields into the area in the center of the dialog box and drop them in the ROW, COLUMN, PAGE, and DATA sections of the dialog box to create the desired layout.

Note

The Layout dialog box is the way PivotTables were built in earlier versions. Microsoft kept this method in case users didn't like the new construction method, although usability studies rated the new method superior to the old layout design.

Tip #436

After a field is applied to a Row, Page, Column, or Data section, you can double-click the field to access and change the type of summary information, such as count, average, or sum. You can also customize the field name.

The following list describes the four areas that are available to apply fields:

- Page. Creates a drop-down menu above the table, enabling you to pull up a specified option, such as a selected division or country.
- Row. Applies a vertical format to the table, summarizing data from top down. The row drop area lists each item in the field down the left side of the PivotTable.
- Column. Applies a horizontal format to the table, summarizing the data from left to right; the column drop area lists each item in the field across the top of the PivotTable.
- Data. The data drop area is the summary of the numbers. This area adds, counts, or creates other analytical functions against the data dropped here. Double-click the field to access the desired function or summary type.

The following figures show the same data or list being summarized with different fields and layouts, to illustrate the change in PivotTable structure and analytical functions.

In Figure 34.8, the MINE SITE field is dropped into the page drop area. Figure 34.9 shows the resulting PivotTable.

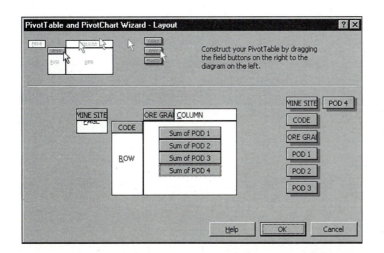

Figure 34.8.
Specifying the PivotTable layout with the wizard. In this example, I dropped the MINE SITE field into the page drop area.

PART
VIII

CH
34

Figure 34.9.
The PivotTable created from the layout in Figure 34.8.

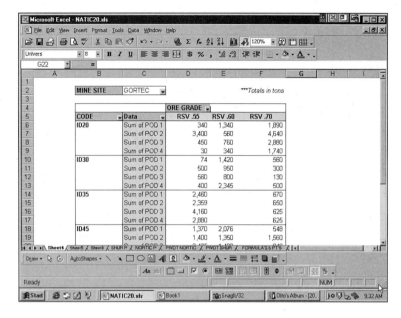

In Figure 34.10, the MINE SITE field is dropped into the row drop area. The result is a summary of the total tonnage for the pods in each mine site (see Figure 34.11).

Figure 34.10.
In this table, the MINE SITE field is dropped into the row drop area and will summarize the total tons for all the pods for each mine site.

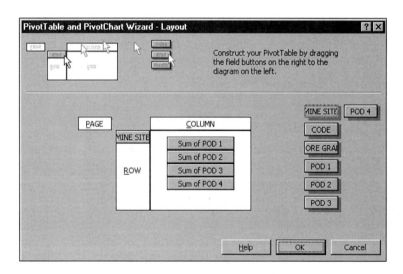

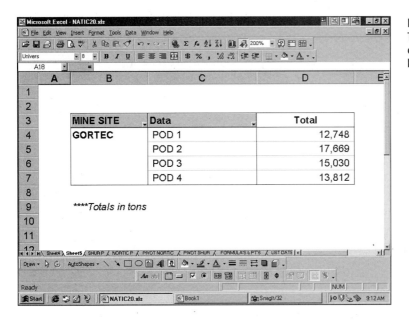

Figure 34.11.
The PivotTable created from the layout in Figure 34.10.

In Figure 34.12, fields are stacked in the row drop area, and the PivotTable will summarize the grades of ore by code. Notice the COUNT function applied to the CODE field in the data drop area. Figure 34.13 shows the result. The order of the ROW fields (from top to bottom) evaluates left to right in the PivotTable. The top ROW field in the Layout dialog box will be the leftmost field in the PivotTable.

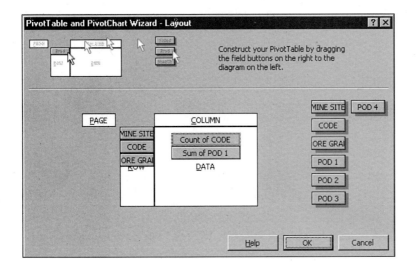

Figure 34.12.
With fields stacked in the row drop area, the PivotTable will summarize the grades of ore by code.

PART

VIII

CH

34

Figure 34.13.
The stacked field result summarizes by priority of the field dropped into the row drop area.

COUNT function

SUM function

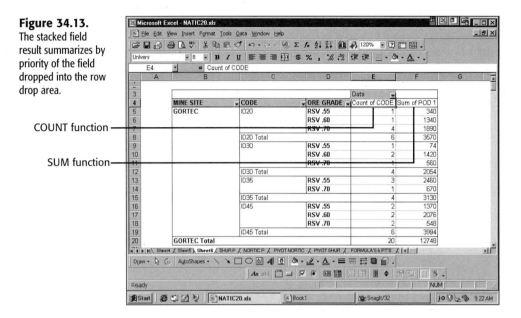

You can click <u>F</u>inish at any point in the PivotTable Wizard to create the PivotTable, and then use the new PivotTable toolbar to drag the fields to the drop zone areas on the PivotTable, as shown in Figures 34.14 and 34.15. This powerful new feature (which also can be used with PivotCharts) enables you to view fields in the drop area as soon as you add them to the PivotTable. In essence, it's an interactive PivotTable builder, with onscreen viewing as it happens (see Figure 34.16). If you don't like the result, drag the field off the table and replace it with another field from the toolbar.

Figure 34.14.
Start with an essentially blank PivotTable and then use the PivotTable toolbar to build the PivotTable.

Select a field and drag it off the toolbar onto the PivotTable.

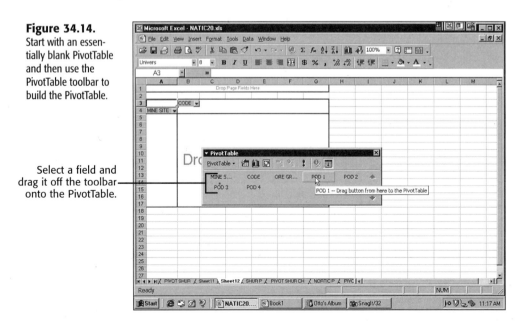

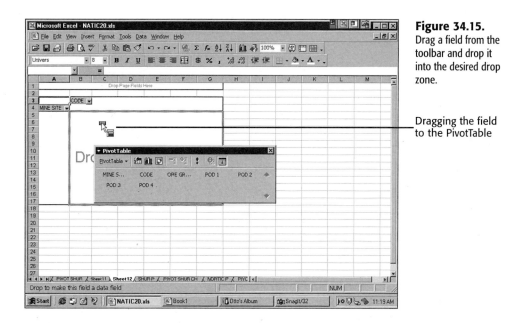

Figure 34.15.
Drag a field from the toolbar and drop it into the desired drop zone.

Dragging the field to the PivotTable

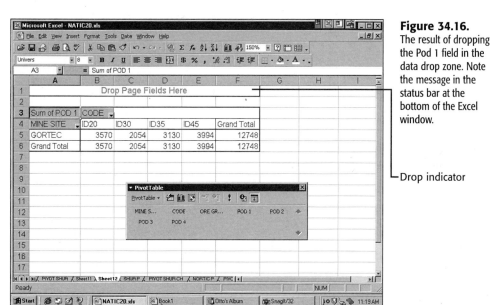

Figure 34.16.
The result of dropping the Pod 1 field in the data drop zone. Note the message in the status bar at the bottom of the Excel window.

Drop indicator

The function Excel chooses (COUNT, SUM, and so on) depends on the nature of the field you dropped. You can choose to apply different functions, such as averaging, showing the maximum or minimum, and so on. To change the function that Excel uses to summarize the data, double-click the field whose function you want to change in the DATA section of the PivotTable and PivotChart Wizard - Layout dialog box. The PivotTable Field dialog box opens; select the function you want to use (see Figure 34.17).

Figure 34.17.
The PivotTable Field
dialog box enables
you to change how
the data is analyzed.

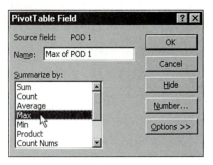

You can customize the summary functions by clicking the Options button to expand the PivotTable Field dialog box (see Figure 34.18). The additional options allow you to analyze data as percents of the total based on fields and base items. The *base field* is the comparison field in the custom calculation, and the *base item* is the field item in the custom calculation.

Figure 34.18.
Click the Options but-
ton in the PivotTable
Field dialog box to
further analyze fields
by base field and
item.

Extended options for analysis ⎯

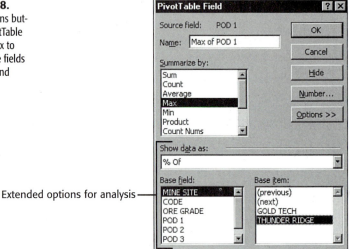

SETTING PIVOTTABLE OPTIONS

Clicking the Options button in the Step 3 of 3 dialog box for the PivotTable Wizard opens the PivotTable Options dialog box, in which you can further specify formats and data source options (see Figure 34.19). You can access this dialog box after completing the wizard by either clicking the PivotTable button on the PivotTable toolbar and selecting Table Options from the drop-down list, or by right-clicking a completed PivotTable and selecting Table Options from the context menu.

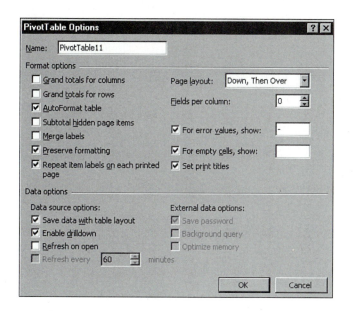

Figure 34.19.
You can customize
the PivotTable format
and data options.

The following sections describe the options.

NAMING THE PIVOTTABLE

The Name option in the PivotTable Options dialog box enables you to specify a name for the PivotTable. By default, Excel names new tables PivotTable1, PivotTable2, and so on, but you can type a different name. It's important to name the PivotTable something identifiable in case you have to start creating PivotTables from other PivotTables to save memory. If you haven't named your PivotTable, you'll find it hard to go back in and identify which PivotTable you want to re-create the PivotTable from. In a PivotChart, the name is still associated with the PivotTable report; changing it changes only the name of the PivotTable the chart is derived from.

ADDING TOTALS

The Grand Totals for Columns option in the PivotTable Options dialog box performs the analysis function and provides the grand totals for each column in the PivotTable. The Grand Totals for Rows option does the same for each row in the PivotTable. The default option selects the grand totals; however, I always deselect these two options because they clutter the PivotTable with too many totals.

If your PivotTable contains hidden fields, you may want those fields subtotaled, but without displaying the field contents. If so, select the Subtotal Hidden Page Items option in the PivotTable options dialog box.

APPLYING AUTOFORMATS

In previous versions of Excel, PivotTables were difficult to format and didn't allow for visual flexibility. Excel 2000 enables you to manipulate and format a PivotTable similar to the way in which you format worksheets—changing the font, point size, colors, and so on.

Excel automatically applies a preset *AutoFormat* to new PivotTables. If you prefer to select a different format, you can turn off the AutoFormat Table option in the PivotTable Options dialog box, or just change the format after creating the PivotTable.

 To change the AutoFormat applied to a PivotTable, choose Format, AutoFormat or click the Format Report button on the PivotTable toolbar (see Figure 34.20). In the AutoFormat dialog box, select the table style you prefer (see Figure 34.21).

Figure 34.20.
Rather than keeping the default format, you can apply a new AutoFormat to your PivotTable.

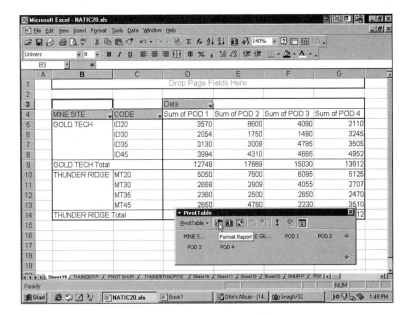

AutoFormats do more than apply the formats for color, font, and so on; they also adjust the fields and can pivot your information to display the information more effectively. After applying the new AutoFormat, if you don't like the result, just undo the change and try a different format. You can also manually reposition the fields after applying the AutoFormat, or repivot the fields.

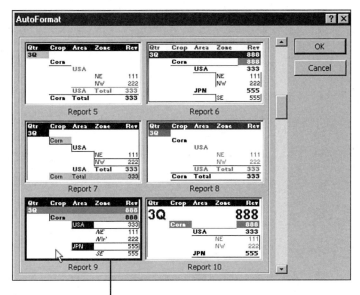

Figure 34.21.
In Excel, you can select from a variety of preset formats that can format and repivot the PivotTable.

Reports 1–10 also change field locations.

Figure 34.22 shows a PivotTable with a new AutoFormat applied. Notice the difference between the PivotTable in this figure and the one shown earlier (refer to Figure 34.20).

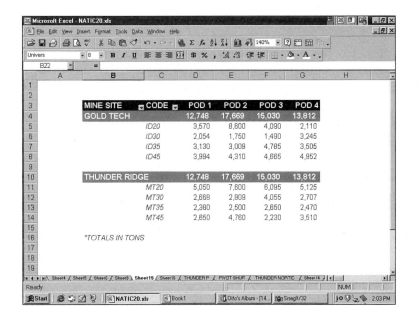

Figure 34.22.
With the right AutoFormat, the table format helps tell the story of the data.

PART

VIII

CH

34

An important improvement in Excel 2000 is Excel's capacity to preserve the formatting of a PivotTable when you refresh the data or change the PivotTable's layout. The Preserve Formatting option is selected by default in the PivotTable Options dialog box, but you can turn off this option if you prefer to revert to the original format.

Note

Manually applied inside borders (on right and left) are not preserved when the PivotTable is refreshed.

DISPLAYING LABELS

The Merge Labels option in the PivotTable Options dialog box enables you to merge column cells and row cells on the outer perimeter of the PivotTable. This is generally a formatting feature.

As with other printed reports, a PivotTable may run to multiple pages. Without labels for columns and rows, it can be difficult or impossible to determine what each individual item refers to. The option Repeat Item Labels on Each Printed Page in the PivotTable Options dialog box is set by default to repeat the item labels on each printed page. To print item labels on the first page only, deselect this option.

Another option in the PivotTable Options dialog box that relates to printing the labels is Set Print Titles. By default, this option is turned off. If you want to use the field and item labels in the PivotTable titles when printing the report, select this option.

Note

For most printed reports, you probably use the first few rows of the worksheet as the title and print it on the top of each page. If you use the field and item labels of a PivotTable as print titles, be sure to prevent repeating other columns and rows. Choose File, Page Setup, click the Sheet tab, and clear any settings in the Print Titles section.

CONTROLLING THE LAYOUT

By default, the field order in the PivotTable layout is down and then over, setting precedent for the vertical format. If you prefer that the order be over and then down, change the Page Layout setting in the PivotTable Options dialog box. One time you would want to change this format is when you're dealing with dates and you want a left-to-right precedent.

You can change the number of fields per column or row in the layout by indicating a specific number in the Fields per Column box in the dialog box. By default, the number is 0.

HANDLING ERRORS AND EMPTY CELLS

Two options in the PivotTable Options dialog box enable you to control what Excel displays in cells that don't display values as expected. The For Error Values, Show __ option enables you to specify a character or a blank in place of the error values; the For Empty Cells, Show __ option enables you to specify a character or a blank in place of the empty cells. For example, if you have a report that shows an #ERR message, you might find it helpful to point your attention to the errors by typing the phrase **missing name** in the box next to the For Error Values, Show __ option. This setup will display that phrase in every cell containing an error. In addition, you can apply *conditional formats* in order to apply colors to highlight the cells containing the phrase.

Leaving both options enabled with nothing in their text boxes will display the cells as blank in the PivotTable. Disabling the For Empty Cells, Show __ option will display a zero for empty cells in the PivotTable.

Tip #437	When enabled, this setting overrides the Zero Values option on the View tab in the general options dialog box for Excel (choose Tools, Options) for PivotTable cells only.

SOURCE DATA OPTIONS

The Data Options section of the PivotTable Options dialog box provides a number of helpful features. The following list describes these options:

- **Save Data with Table Layout.** Saves a copy of the data used from an external data source. Selected by default.

  This option isn't only for external data sources. Deselecting this option saves on the workbook's size but also forces you to manually refresh the PivotTable(s) when opening the workbook (unless the Refresh on Open option is enabled). With this option disabled, you can't work with PivotTables until they've been refreshed.

- **Enable Drilldown.** Shows the detail when a field is double-clicked. Selected by default.

- **Refresh on Open.** Refreshes the PivotTable when the workbook is opened. By default, this option isn't selected; I suggest selecting it for most cases.

- **Refresh Every __ Minutes.** Allows for automatic refreshing based on the minutes set. By default, this option isn't selected. This option is only available for PivotTables based on external data sources. (It really should appear under the External Data Options section of the dialog box.)

- **Save Password.** Saves the password associated with the external data source where the information is derived. This option is deselected by default; enabling this option compromises database security.

- **Background Query.** Runs the query in the background while allowing you to continue to work. Turned off by default.

- **Optimize Memory.** Optimizes and manages the memory when using PivotTables; however, this option slows down performance. By default, this option is not selected.

CREATING PIVOTCHARTS

Figures 34.23 and 34.24 show data that's structured with the same criteria as a PivotTable versus a PivotChart. When a PivotChart is created, Excel creates both a chart sheet and a PivotTable sheet within the workbook; because the chart information must be derived from a table, Excel automatically creates the table. The default action of the PivotChart feature is to create a chart as a worksheet, but you also can create an embedded chart on a worksheet in the last step of the PivotTable wizard or by selecting Location from the Chart menu and selecting the As Object In option after creating the PivotChart.

Figure 34.25 shows the difference between a PivotTable and a PivotChart: An embedded PivotChart has been formatted and placed on the same sheet as a formatted PivotTable. (Figure 34.26 shows the same worksheet, posted to a Web page. See the later section "Saving and Editing PivotTables in HTML Format" for details.)

PivotCharts can be formatted with worksheets to plot and show data in chart format and combined with other worksheet data, making this new feature flexible and powerful.

Figure 34.23.
A PivotTable based on a structured list.

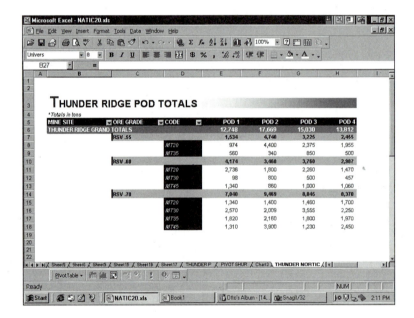

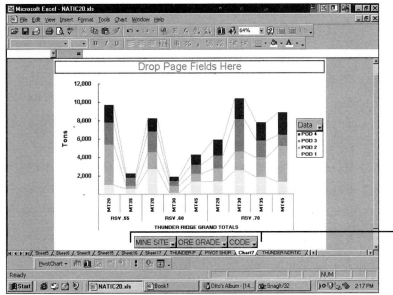

Figure 34.24.
A PivotChart based on the same structured list used in Figure 34.23.

These fields can be dragged.

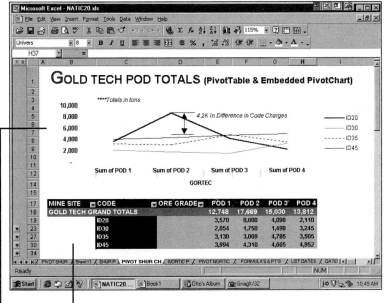

Figure 34.25.
PivotTable and PivotChart shown together in the worksheet. The field options on the PivotChart are turned off.

PART

VIII

CH

34

Embedded PivotChart   PivotTable

Figure 34.26.
With the Web Page Preview option, you can save the worksheet for Internet or intranet posting, keeping the formatting of the PivotTable and PivotChart intact.

Embedded PivotChart

PivotTable

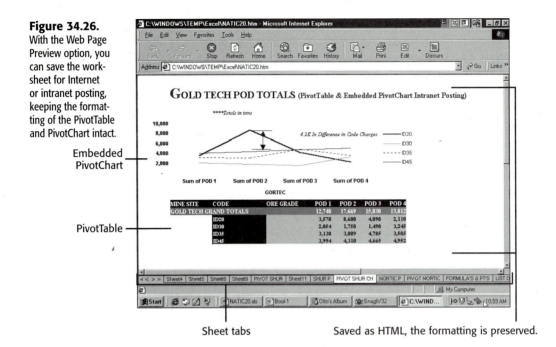

Sheet tabs

Saved as HTML, the formatting is preserved.

MODIFYING PIVOTTABLES AND PIVOTCHARTS

After you create a PivotTable or PivotChart, you can restructure the PivotTable or the PivotChart to look a different way by dragging and dropping fields, or by using the options on the menus or the PivotTable toolbar. You also can change the look or structure of the PivotTable with formatting options (see the earlier section "Applying AutoFormats"). Because of the new options available with PivotTables in Excel 2000, you can adjust and manipulate just about all aspects of the PivotTable or PivotChart. You can apply colored fills, borders, and font colors just as you would a regular table on a worksheet. PivotCharts are a bit more difficult to format because of sizing limitations on the plot area and legend locations, but for the most part, they're as flexible as charts created with the standard charting features.

USING THE PIVOTTABLE TOOLBAR

The PivotTable toolbar enables you to create a PivotTable layout by dragging the fields from the toolbar to the drop zones of the PivotTable. Table 34.1 describes the options available on the toolbar.

TABLE 34.1.   PIVOTTABLE TOOLBAR

Button	Name	Description
 PivotTable ▾	PivotTable	Drop-down menu with options for further PivotTable or PivotChart enhancement.
	Format Report	Opens the AutoFormat dialog box for use in formatting the PivotTable.
	Chart Wizard	Opens the Chart Wizard dialog box for use in formatting the PivotChart.
	PivotTable Wizard	Activates the PivotTable and PivotChart Wizard.
	Hide Detail	Hides the detail of a grouped range in a PivotTable.
	Show Detail	Displays the detail behind grouped ranges in the PivotTable.
	Refresh Data	Refreshes the data in the selected PivotTable.
	Field Settings	Allows for adjusting the summarization of the data in the field selected.
	Hide Fields/Display Fields	Hides/displays the field buttons on the toolbar or the outlines and labels in the PivotTable layout.

DRAGGING FIELDS IN A PIVOTCHART

PivotCharts offer the power of PivotTables and charts combined in one interactive surface. You can select and drag fields to new locations on the chart, and Excel will pivot the chart to correspond to the new field location. For example, dragging the field out of the drop zone in the PivotChart in Figure 34.27 eliminates the field and changes the chart to correspond to the new pivoted information, shown in Figure 34.28. Changes to the fields in the PivotChart also are reflected on the corresponding PivotTable.

ELIMINATING FIELD DATA

Clicking the arrow button shown on a field in the PivotChart or PivotTable displays a drop-down list from which you can select or deselect items (see Figure 34.29). The information will be removed from or added to the PivotChart or PivotTable (see Figure 34.30).

PART

VIII

CH

34

Figure 34.27.
You can select and move the fields in a PivotChart, just as in a PivotTable.

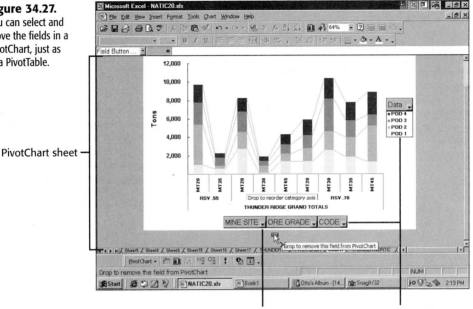

PivotChart sheet

Click the arrow buttons to display drop-down field lists.

PivotChart fields

Moved field location

Figure 34.28.
By dragging the field to a new location or the drop zone, you can restructure the chart with one move.

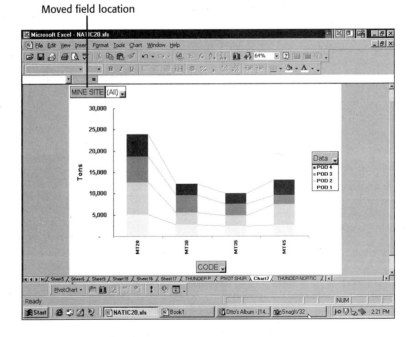

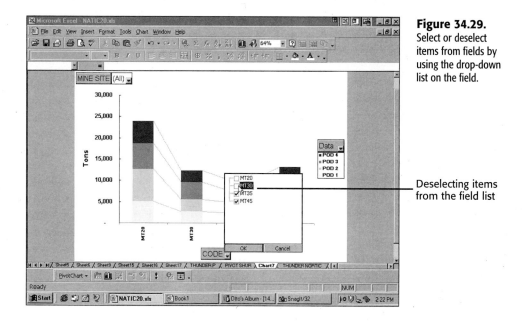

Deselecting items from the field list

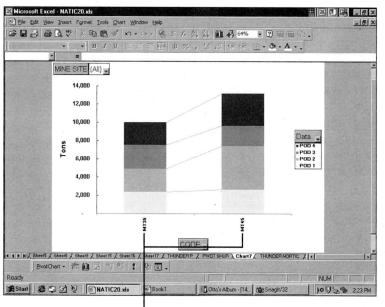

Figure 34.30.
By deselecting categories from fields, you can eliminate data sets with one click.

PART

VIII

CH

34

Only these two items are still selected.

SHOWING AND HIDING DETAIL

You can show detail behind a field by double-clicking the data of the field. If lower-level information exists behind the field, the Show Detail button on the PivotTable toolbar is enabled (see Figure 34.31). Select the category for which you want to show the detail; Excel will drill down (to show the detail that makes up the total number). For example, if you have employees' hours summed for the week and you double-click the total number, Excel shows all the weekly information that creates the total number (see Figure 34.32). In this case, I double-clicked the RSV .55 line to show the detail behind it.

After detail is added, double-clicking RSV .55 again will hide the detail, and another double-click will show it again (without the dialog box appearing a second time). Along the same line, if I double-clicked the ID20, code Excel would hide the ore grades for that item (again, no dialog box would appear) because the CODE field already has ore grade details showing.

If I clicked the field label ORE GRADE and used the Show Detail button on the PivotTable toolbar (double-click won't work here), I could add details for all of the ore grades at once.

Figure 34.31.
Excel enables you to drill down to show the detail that makes up the summary information in the PivotTable.

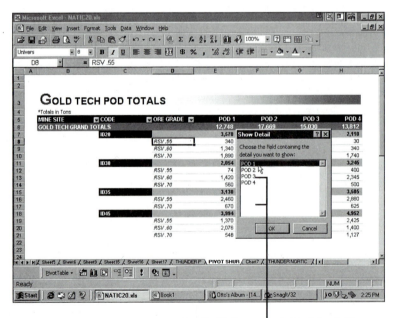

Detailed information behind the field

GROUPING PIVOTTABLE LEVELS

You can manage information in a PivotTable—much like that in a list—by *grouping* to roll up different levels of the PivotTable for various reports and views. (Notice the two levels of groups applied to the PivotTable in Figure 34.33.) This strategy is useful if you have quantities of material grouped per week and then per month, for example. You can collapse or expand the groups just like when grouping a list on a worksheet (notice the collapsed example in Figure 34.34).

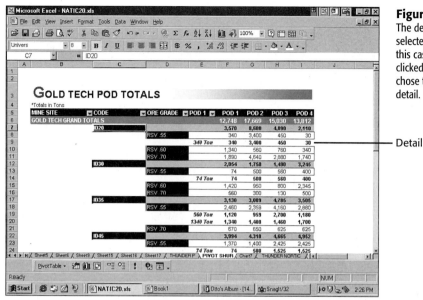

Figure 34.32.
The detail behind the
selected region. In
this case, I double-
clicked RSV .55 and
chose to view POD 1
detail.

— Detail

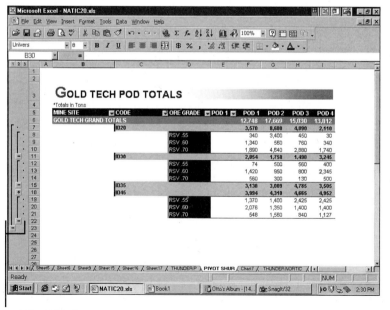

Figure 34.33.
By grouping the
PivotTable levels, you
can show detail and
then roll up the detail
as you would a
database or list.

PART

VIII

CH

34

Grouped PivotTable items

Figure 34.34.
After the groups are applied, you can roll up the PivotTable to the highest level of information.

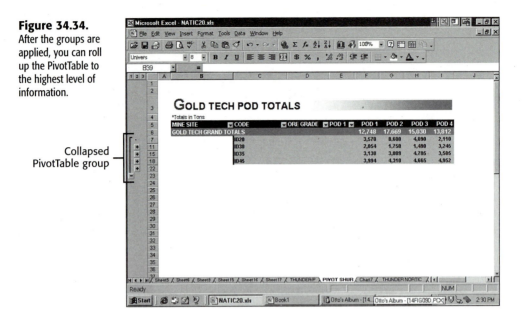

Collapsed PivotTable group

PivotTables have become seamless in that you have the flexibility to move, manage, group, and format just as you would a table, but they summarize more quickly and more efficiently than functions.

PERFORMING CALCULATIONS ON A PIVOTTABLE

You can perform calculations on a field or multiple fields within a PivotTable. Click the PivotTable button on the PivotTable toolbar. Then choose Formulas, Calculated Field from the drop-down menu.

In Figure 34.35, the name of the calculated field to be added represents the overhead for the region. The formula =sum('POD 4')*.12 calculates the percentage of overhead for the region, calculated against the current field amount ('POD 4').

Tip #438

You also can create these calculations on the worksheet and reference them to the cells in the PivotTable. Just create a simple function that references the field column and row. Please note that such calculations can't appear inside the PivotTable, but can appear just outside it (although applying AutoFormats might delete such data if the format manipulates the fields).

Notice the results in Figure 34.36 of the new calculated field in the PivotTable. It shows the percentage attributed to overhead for the region. Each time the table is refreshed, the calculations automatically update.

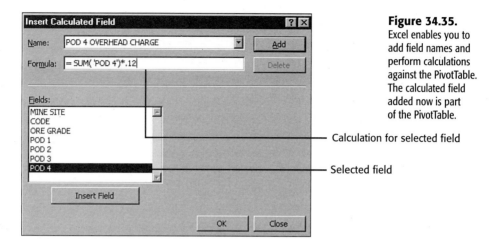

Figure 34.35.
Excel enables you to add field names and perform calculations against the PivotTable. The calculated field added now is part of the PivotTable.

Calculation for selected field

Selected field

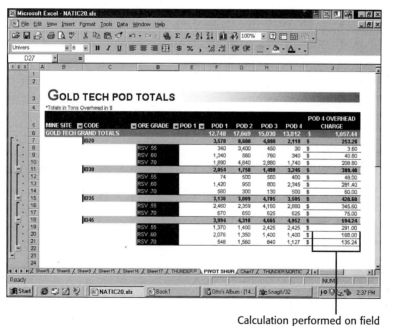

Figure 34.36.
By adding a calculated field to the PivotTable, Excel makes the addition part of the PivotTable. Each time the data is refreshed, the calculations are automatically updated.

Calculation performed on field

HIDING COLUMNS OR ROWS

For presentations or printouts, you may want to show only certain bits of information within the PivotTable. You can *hide* rows or columns that you don't want to show (see Figure 34.37) or *unhide* hidden rows or columns.

DRILLING DOWN IN A FIELD

In the PivotTable in Figure 34.38, all the information is rolled up to its highest level, without the use of grouping or hidden rows. This shows the 3D element of PivotTables. To drill up and drill down, select a field that has a subset and double-click. It's that simple. Notice the results of the product type in Figure 34.39 after you double-click the product field.

 If double-clicking doesn't allow you to drill down, this feature may be disabled. See "Enabling Drilldown" in the Troubleshooting section at the end of this chapter.

DRAGGING A FIELD FOR A PAGE VIEW

The flexibility of dragging fields in PivotTables enables you to drag fields outside the table and create what's called a *page view*. Select the field from the PivotTable and drag it above the table; the insert bar appears (see Figure 34.40). Drop the field and it becomes a drop-down list to manage the information, as shown in Figure 34.41.

Columns D through I are hidden.

Figure 34.37.
By hiding columns or rows, you can focus on newly calculated fields that point out certain pieces of information that might get lost in the original table with all data showing.

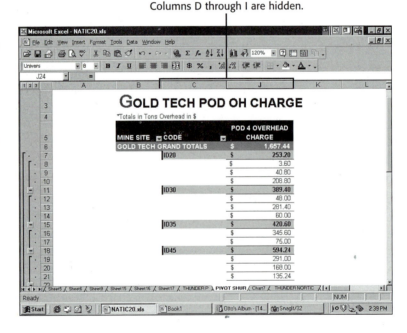

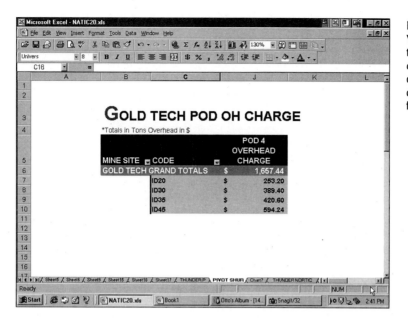

Figure 34.38.
You can hide information by using the drilldown technique on PivotTables. Just double-click the field name.

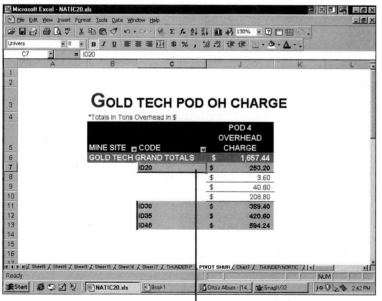

Figure 34.39.
The results of managing the view of the PivotTable by drilling down or double-clicking. Notice how the information acts as though it's collapsed or expanded, similar to grouping.

Double-click to expand detail.

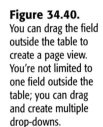

Figure 34.40.
You can drag the field outside the table to create a page view. You're not limited to one field outside the table; you can drag and create multiple drop-downs.

Select and move fields.

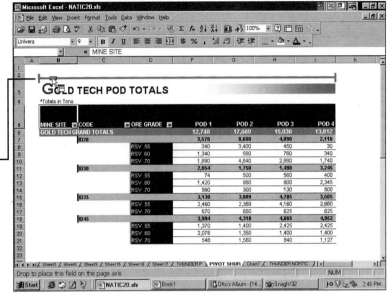

Figure 34.41.
By creating a page view with a PivotTable, you can manage the information from the PivotTable with a drop-down list.

Page drop zone

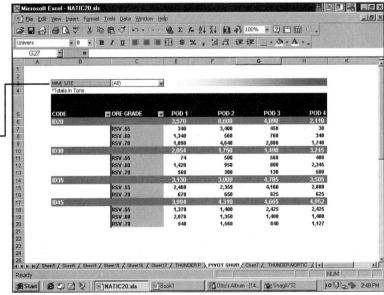

CREATING A QUICK SUMMARY

If you want a quick summary breakout of a data set, simply double-click the grand total, as shown in Figure 34.42, and Excel automatically creates an independent breakout on a separate sheet. The detail from double-clicking the grand total is shown in Figure 34.43. By double-clicking the data set, the subset of data that appears in that set will be displayed or hidden.

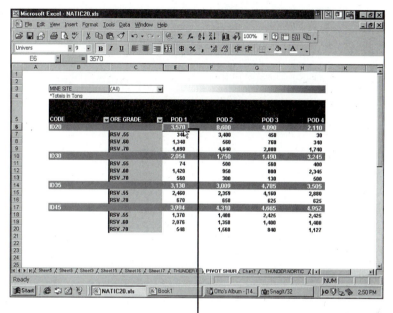

Figure 34.42.
To create an automatic summary, just double-click the grand total.

Double-click to audit.

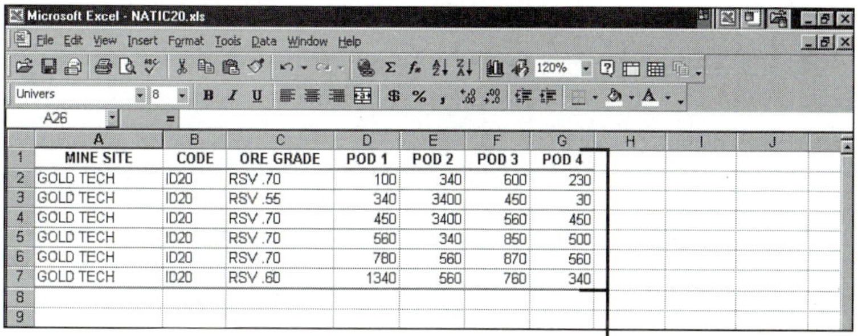

Figure 34.43.
The result of double-clicking the grand total of a set in a PivotTable is the individual records that make up the total.

Audit data behind code ID20.

WORKING WITH DATES IN PIVOTTABLES

Quite often, you'll have information from lists that contain dates. To transpose it into an understandable PivotTable, follow a few simple steps and you can create an effective summary of the information. Again, start with your list or database, like that shown in Figure 34.44.

Figure 34.44.
When working with dates, you can combine the dates to summarize by days, weeks, months, and so on.

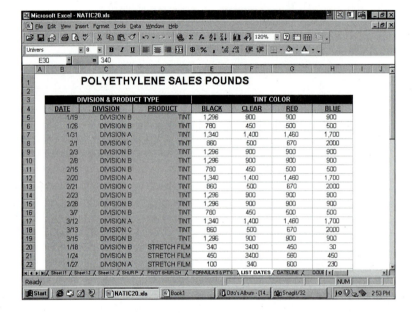

When working with dates, many times it's easier to see the information left to right rather than up and down, because most timelines are generated in this manner. Make sure to set the Page Layout setting in the PivotTable Options dialog box to Over, Then Down (see Figure 34.45).

To group dates together, select the first date field in the PivotTable and choose Data, Group and Outline, Group. The Grouping dialog box appears, enabling you to set parameters on the dates to be grouped (see Figure 34.46). Figure 34.47 shows the PivotTable grouped on a weekly basis (every seven days). You can do the same with numbers—for example, if you have average scores in a PivotTable and you want them grouped in ranges.

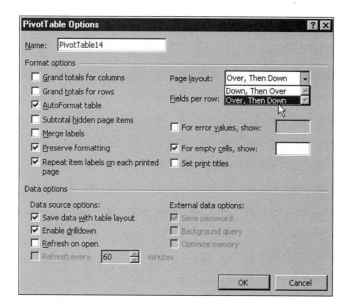

Figure 34.45.
When working with dates, many times it works well to view the information left to right rather than up and down.

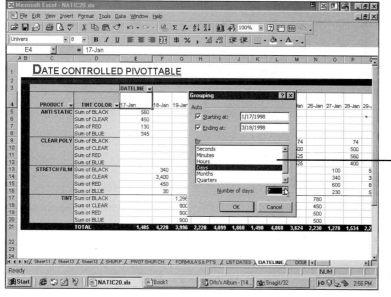

Figure 34.46.
You can set the parameters on date ranges by using the Group option. This works well with summarizing data weekly and monthly.

Set dates to group and sum data.

Dates grouped in seven-day increments

Figure 34.47.
The result of setting the number of days to seven breaks out the groups by weeks.

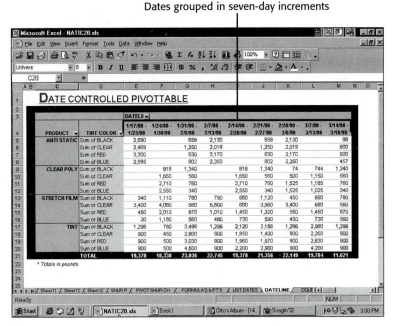

CREATING A PIVOTTABLE FROM MULTIPLE RANGES

Excel enables you to create PivotTables from multiple consolidation ranges by selecting the multiple consolidation control from Step 1 of the PivotTable Wizard. For example, if you have two companies with product sales or two divisions with product sales, you can establish separate worksheets or databases to control the list and then combine into a multiple consolidated PivotTable. (The wizard walks you through step by step.) Figure 34.48 shows Step 2b of 3 of the PivotTable Wizard, which enables you to browse through documents to find the lists or ranges. Drag over the range of data you want to consolidate and click the Add button to add it to the All Ranges section of the dialog box. If your consolidation ranges are coming from multiple files (as opposed to sheets), you can use the Browse button to select unopened files. The problem is that the Browse button doesn't actually open the files. Unless you've memorized the data ranges (addresses or range names), it's better to open the files before starting the PivotTable Wizard. The only time this could be a problem is if you have numerous files to open and restricted computer memory. In such a case, name each consolidation range so that you can manually type it in the Range box.

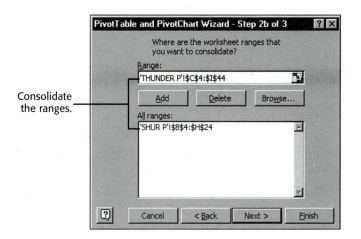

Consolidate the ranges.

Figure 34.48.
To consolidate lists into a PivotTable, select the consolidation ranges in Step 1 of the PivotTable Wizard and add the ranges together.

MANAGING EMPLOYEE HOURS AND COSTS WITH PIVOTTABLES

You can use PivotTables to manage employee hours and costs. After observing several attempts to manage employee hours and costs, I've found the easiest solution to be a combination of a table, list, VLOOKUP, and then a PivotTable. Once set up, such a table requires minimal effort to manage. If you have employee hours in one database or list, and in another area have a table that has the employee rates, use the VLOOKUP function to combine the two and then pivot the list. To build an employee cost-tracking PivotTable, first set up the information. Figure 34.49 shows a table that contains the employee base rate and overtime rate.

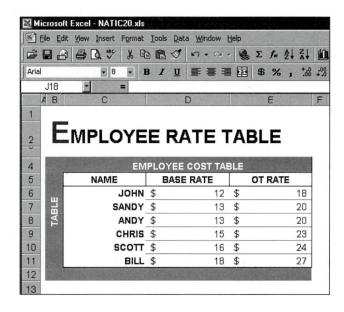

Figure 34.49.
The first step in creating an employee cost-tracking PivotTable is to create the table with rates.

Combine the employee cost table with the list of hours an employee worked by using the VLOOKUP function. In the formula in cell G16 in Figure 34.50, the VLOOKUP function looks up the employee in the list in cell D16, refers to the table range $C$5:$E$10, and then the column number of the base rate. In this case, the column number of the base rate in the cost table is in column 2. Make sure the range referring to the cost table has absolute values, because you're going to be dragging the formula down and you want the table range to remain the same. Figure 34.51 shows the VLOOKUP referring to column 3, overtime rate for the employee in cell D16.

→ For details on VLOOKUP, **see** "Using VLOOKUP to Extract Line Items," **p. 1089**

Figure 34.50.
Use a VLOOKUP function to refer to the employee in the list and the cost associated with the employee from the cost table.

Match the base rate from the table to the list with VLOOKUP.

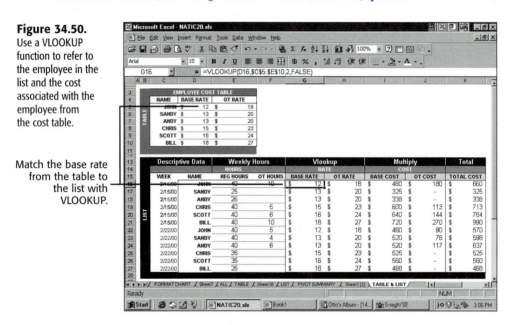

Multiply the regular hours times the base rate to find the base cost for the week for that particular employee. In Figure 34.52, cell I16, the formula reads =E16*G16. Drag the formula to the right to cell J16 to calculate the overtime costs. The total column in cell K16 adds the base cost and overtime cost in cells I16 and J16. Drag cells G16:K16 down the length of the list.

Now that you have the base of information set up, you'll want to pivot the information to summarize the employee cost for the week. In addition, if you have codes and/or projects the employee is working on, you can include that information and break out the summaries in PivotTables by employee, project, week, and so on.

There is a trick to making this PivotTable effortless. In Step 2 of the PivotTable Wizard, the range selected is C16:E2000 (see Figure 34.53). Although the current range of the list only goes down to row 27, I've selected a range that the PivotTable will never actually reach; thus, the PivotTable range will always include all the new rows of information added.

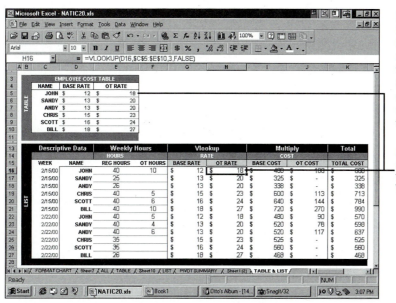

Figure 34.51.
Notice the difference in this VLOOKUP formula. It still refers to the same employee and table; but the column number from the range is 3, referring to the overtime rate.

Match the overtime rate from the table to the list with VLOOKUP.

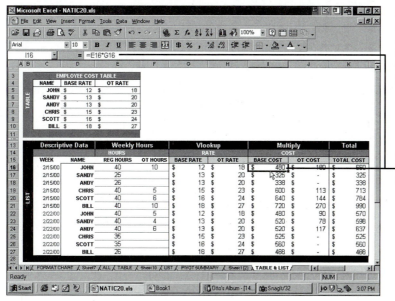

Figure 34.52.
Multiply the base rate and the regular hours to get the base cost for the employee for that week.

Multiply the base rate times the regular hours.

PART

VIII

CH

34

Note

Although highlighting extra blank rows keeps the range updated, they are nevertheless included in the PivotTable calculations, which adds to the calculation effort and the PivotTable cache (memory). It also adds a blank listing to the PivotTable, which can be hidden by using the name field drop-down list.

PivotTable list to manage hours and costs

Figure 34.53.
Select a range that the list will never grow to. This will ensure that when the PivotTable is refreshed, it's always selecting all the information in the list.

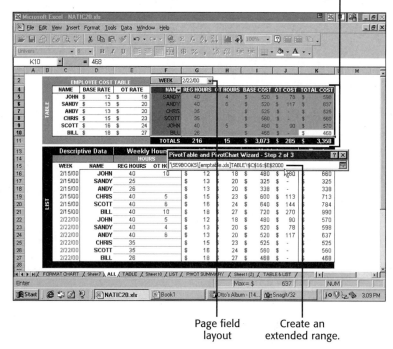

Page field layout

Create an extended range.

To arrange the PivotTable in a logical fashion, set the fields in order (see Figure 34.54): the WEEK field in the <u>P</u>AGE section of the diagram and the NAME field in the <u>R</u>OW section. Place the regular hours, overtime hours, base cost, overtime cost, and total cost in the <u>D</u>ATA section.

In the final step of the PivotTable Wizard, click the <u>O</u>ptions button and deselect <u>G</u>rand Totals for Columns and Grand <u>T</u>otals for Rows (see Figure 34.55).

The final setup of the PivotTable shows the Week pull-down at the top and the employees listed down the left column (in F6:F11), with the corresponding totals to the right. I've placed the tables on the same sheet so that you can get an understanding of how they work together (see Figure 34.56).

Week   Employee Name   Hours

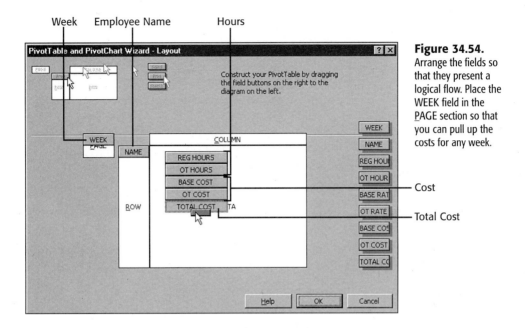

Figure 34.54.
Arrange the fields so that they present a logical flow. Place the WEEK field in the PAGE section so that you can pull up the costs for any week.

Cost

Total Cost

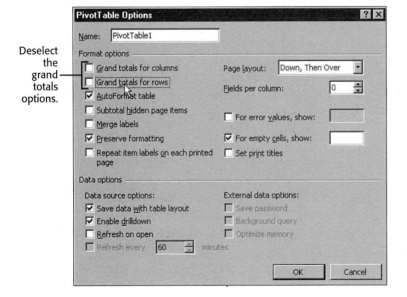

Deselect the grand totals options.

Figure 34.55.
Deselect the grand totals options to help create an easy-to-read PivotTable.

Figure 34.56.
The final result shows the cost table, the list reference to the cost table, and the PivotTable derived from the list.

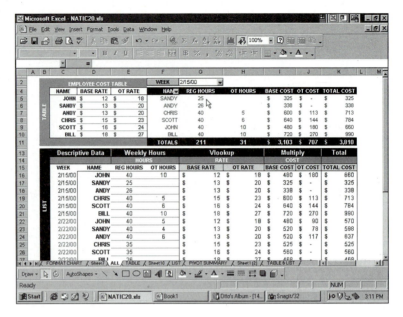

ANALYZING COSTS WITH PIVOTCHARTS

With PivotCharts, you can analyze your information from the table of employee costs. The two important characteristics to look at when analyzing costs are the base costs versus overtime costs, and the regular hours versus overtime hours. These are due to specific variables in the workplace as to why overtime occurs (but you may be able to minimize cost by implementing a checkpoint with a signoff sheet before overtime occurs, and also with proper planning and scheduling).

The PivotChart enables you to get a quick picture of your situation and also look at ratios. If you have a way to measure your company's performance in output, for example, you'll want to look at the ratio of overtime against output and see the trends that occur over time. Soon you'll be able to focus on inefficiencies that result from specific occurrences in the workplace or business environment. Notice the field placement in the PivotChart in Figure 34.57, which includes a secondary axis for the overtime. Look at your information in ratio form—how and where overtime stacks up against regular time, and why certain employees have massive amounts of overtime versus others who have minimal amounts of overtime. This is generally because of improper workload distribution and planning.

The reason for the secondary axis is to get a quick view of how the overtime stacks up against the regular time. By setting both axes to the same constraints, such as the maximum value being $800 and the minimum being $0, you can get a quick comparison of the two. Another way to compare items over weeks is to place the fields WEEK and Data at the bottom and eliminate all other fields (see Figure 34.58).

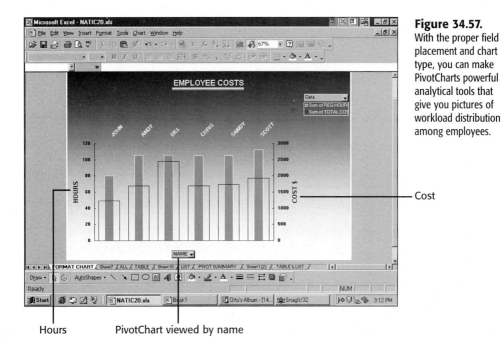

Hours   PivotChart viewed by name

Cost

Figure 34.57.
With the proper field placement and chart type, you can make PivotCharts powerful analytical tools that give you pictures of workload distribution among employees.

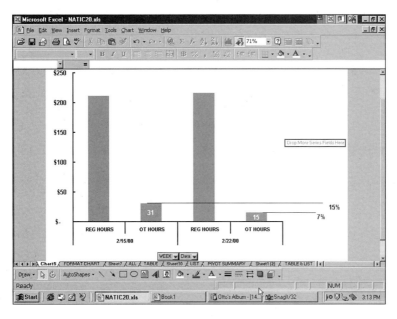

Figure 34.58.
Another way to view the information is to lay out the week and data fields at the bottom and eliminate all others. This PivotChart is viewed by week.

SAVING AND EDITING PIVOTTABLES IN HTML FORMAT

New features in Excel 2000 enable you to save a PivotTable as an HTML document and modify HTML documents posted on an Internet or intranet site.

Note

The benefit of this feature is that you can manipulate the data fields while the document is posted and then print the changes. The drawback is that you can't save the changes in Excel format; changes made to the HTML document revert to the format in which the document was posted (HTML). The data can be refreshed, but formatting changes saved must come from the source document, thus making this feature a bit cumbersome.

To save a PivotTable as a Web page, follow these steps.

1. Choose File, Save as Web Page.

2. Specify whether you want to save the whole workbook or the selected worksheet, as shown in Figure 34.59. If you select Selection: Sheet, the Add Interactivity option becomes available. Select Add Interactivity and click Publish.

Figure 34.59.
Add interactivity to your Web PivotTable by selecting Selection: Sheet and checking Add Interactivity.

3. In the Publish As Web Page dialog box, select the sheet from the Choose list. Then select the entire sheet or just the PivotTable region.

4. The Add Interactivity With option enables you to create spreadsheet functionality (formulas and so on) or PivotTable functionality (which enables you to move fields). Select PivotTable Functionality (see Figure 34.60).

5. Specify a filename for the Web page and click Publish.

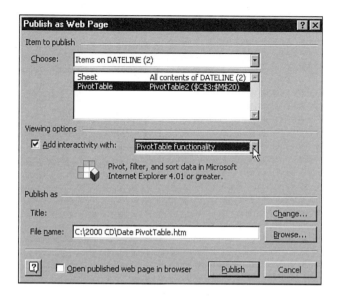

Figure 34.60.
You can choose spreadsheet functionality or PivotTable functionality from the Add Interactivity With option.

6. Select and open the HTML document from the folder where it was saved (see Figure 34.61). You can deselect field items with the drop-down list from the field just as you would in a normal PivotTable. You can also expand and collapse fields (see Figure 34.62), drag and drop fields (see Figures 20.63 and 20.64), and add or remove fields (see Figures 20.65 and 20.66).

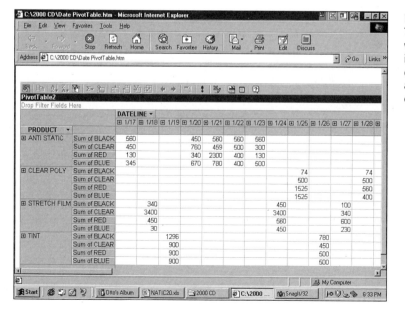

Figure 34.61.
The PivotTable saved with Web functionality enables you to drag and drop fields, and expand and collapse fields.

PART

VIII

CH

34

Figure 34.62.
Week 1/17 expanded, with the colors broken out. From here, you can use the drop-down lists to deselect line items.

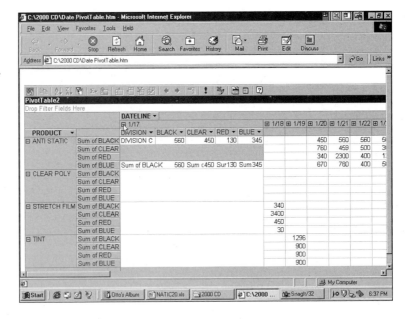

Figure 34.63.
Dragging the field item to a new drop area on the PivotTable.

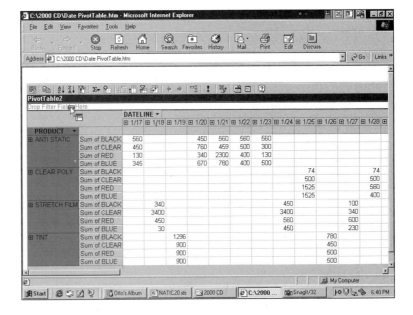

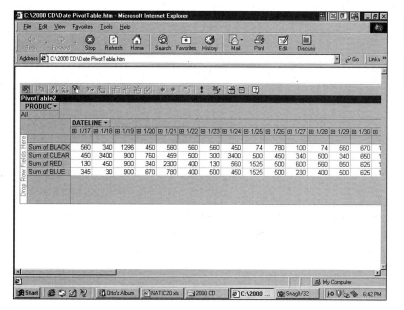

Figure 34.64.
By dropping the major field item to a page view, you can summarize line-item data for your report.

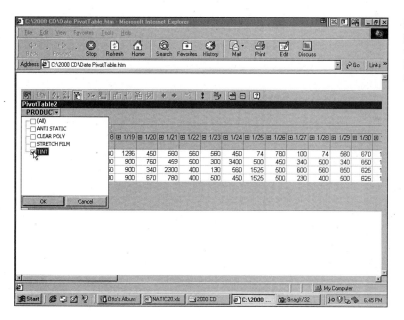

Figure 34.65.
Select the item you want to summarize. Excel will filter the data.

Figure 34.66.
The final filtered data.

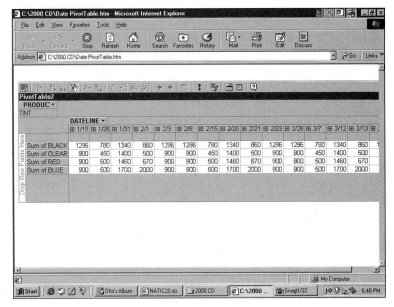

USING THE PROPERTY TOOLBOX AND FIELD LIST

When working with PivotTables in Internet Explorer, you have two special tools available. The *PivotTable Property Toolbox* allows for greater flexibility when manipulating and controlling data while on an intranet or Internet site (see Figure 34.67). From here you can modify text, display and hide the title bar or toolbar, expand and collapse indicators and drop areas, and so on. The most useful option here is the ability to change the field list. To access the Property Toolbox, click the Property Toolbox button on the PivotTable toolbar in Internet Explorer. The toolbox varies depending on what's selected when you click the button.

By clicking the Field List button on the PivotTable toolbar, you can display the *PivotTable Field List* (see Figure 34.68), from which you can add data to the PivotTable from the source document.

Formats and additions to the PivotTable Web page are interactive only while it's open; the document changes can be saved only as HTML. However, the ability to change, move, format, and print data while the PivotTable is posted to the Web is still a powerful feature. One of the most powerful features of all, of course, is that users don't need to have Excel to gain these manipulation features; they need only Internet Explorer.

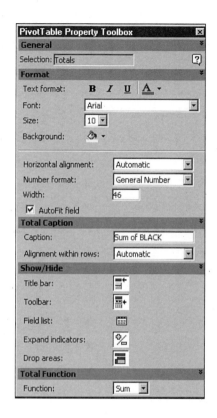

Figure 34.67.
The PivotTable
Property Toolbox.

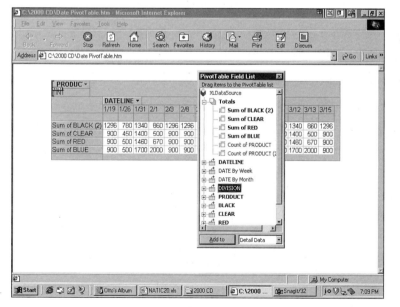

Figure 34.68.
Drag the item from
the PivotTable Field
List to the HTML
PivotTable to add it
to the PivotTable.

PART

VIII

CH

34

TROUBLESHOOTING

ENABLING DRILLDOWN

Why can't I drill down in my PivotTable?

To be able to drill down by double-clicking, the Enable Drilldown option must be selected in the Data Options section of the PivotTable Options dialog box.

GROUPING PIVOTTABLE DATES

How do I group PivotTable dates?

Select the first date cell in the PivotTable; then choose Data, Group and Outline, Group. Enter the Starting At and Ending At date. Select the time measurement under By, and adjust the Number of Days setting if necessary.

VIEWING THE DATA BEHIND PIVOTTABLE SUMMARIES

How do I see the information behind PivotTable totals?

Double-click on the total of the selected field item. Excel creates a separate sheet that lists the information that makes up the totals on the PivotTable—a powerful auditing device.

CHAPTER 35

MANAGING DATA WITH FORMULAS AND FORM CONTROLS

In this chapter

COMBINING EXCEL FEATURES TO MANAGE YOUR DATA

This chapter provides a number of suggestions for creating worksheets that help you manage your data. Some features may be familiar from other chapters. The point here is to use feature *combinations* that automate worksheets and save time and effort for the user. Although the chapter begins with some simple solutions, the particular focus of this chapter is on building more complex formulas, using database functions, and adding form controls to help the whole process work more efficiently.

Excel offers a variety of features that stand alone to accomplish specific tasks but when combined can be powerful tools to extract information from your worksheets seamlessly and almost effortlessly. Suppose that one of your job functions is to track week-to-date, month-to-date, and year-to-date costs for your company's hourly employees. With the right worksheet setup and formulas, you don't have to manually calculate this information—the worksheet will do it for you, based on the daily entries. The same principle applies whether you're tracking production quantities, inventory, sales, or any other type of information that requires some kind of consistent calculation.

Note

If you manage employee hours and costs, try a PivotTable for analyzing your data. For details on using PivotTables, see Chapter 34, "Using PivotTables and PivotCharts."

EXTRACTING DATE-BASED TOTALS FROM LISTS

When maintaining controls on a business, you'll need proper reporting procedures, and with nearly every business weekly, monthly, and yearly costs to date are standard reporting. You probably also need to know whether the business is on track with projections for the year. After extracting the totals, you'll want to show variances to analyze projections versus actual results. The following sections describe how to set up formulas for all these types of calculations.

Tip #439

The key element in extracting information effectively is consistency of the data. Formulas or functions can be case sensitive if you set them up that way; they won't return the desired results if the list isn't set up appropriately.

USING NAMED RANGES IN LONG OR COMPLEX FORMULAS

By defining *named ranges*, you can avoid certain problems that are inherent when building complex formulas. A range name works as an absolute reference in a formula. In Figure 35.1, for example, the formula in cell F9 references the TOTAL HOURS column above the formula. Dragging that formula elsewhere would change the reference. If you gave the name TOTAL_HOURS to the range F3:F7, however, you could use the formula =SUM(TOTAL_HOURS) to get the same result, as shown in Figure 35.2. You can apply named ranges to any formula by selecting the name from the Paste Name dialog box (choose Insert, Name, Paste or press F3).

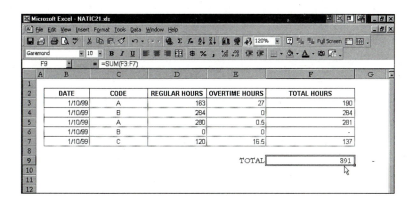

Figure 35.1.
A formula with relative references will be adjusted automatically when copied or moved.

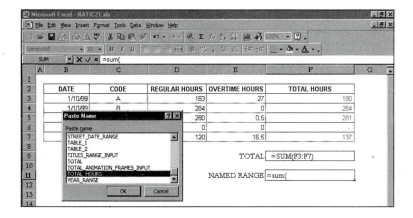

Figure 35.2.
Using a named range in a formula.

You can copy or drag formulas with range names anywhere you want, and Excel will always refer to that particular defined location when totaling the formula.

Tip #440

When creating worksheets for use by other people, remember that range names can be much easier to comprehend than row-and-column references. To understand the range F3:F7, you must look at the column and row headings and scan through the worksheet to find the referenced range, and then determine exactly what the range refers to. The range TOTAL_HOURS, on the other hand, indicates exactly what it refers to within the range name itself.

EXTRACTING WEEKLY INFORMATION

Figure 35.3 shows a simple list of weeks with employee hours broken out, including regular time, overtime, and corresponding totals. We'll use this list in this section to extract for the totals by week over a period of time.

Figure 35.3.
This week-by-week
list will be used
to extract totals.

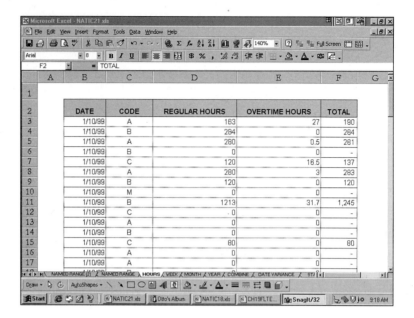

To create an extraction setup, perform the following steps:

1. Set up your worksheet with appropriate column headings, as shown in the preceding example.

2. On a separate sheet, set up a table that represents the columns in the list you want to track (see Figure 35.4). In this example, each row calculates a particular product from the HOURS sheet.

3. Create a SUM(IF formula as shown in the example, using the following syntax:

   =SUM(IF((*sheet!range*=*criteria*)*(*sheet!range*=*criteria*),*sheet!sum_range*,0))

4. Press Ctrl+Shift+Enter to enter this formula as an array.

The following table shows the ranges used in the formula in Figure 35.4.

Sheet	Range Name	Range
HOURS	DATE	B3:B93
HOURS	PRODUCT	C3:C93
HOURS	REGULAR_HOURS	D3:D93
HOURS	OVERTIME_HOURS	E3:E93
HOURS	TOTAL	F3:F93
WEEK	CODE	D5
WEEK	WEEK	G2

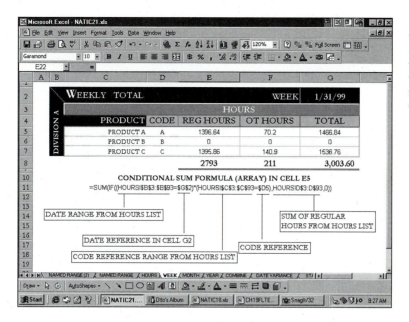

Figure 35.4.
The array formula in cell E5 extracts the total regular hours from the HOURS sheet for the week entered in cell G2.

The formula works from the following two trigger points:

- Cell D5 dictates the product or the product code.
- Cell G2 indicates the week to be used in calculations.

In essence, the conditional sum formula says, "If the date in the range B3:B93 from the HOURS sheet is equal to the date value in cell G2, and the product range C3:C93 from the HOURS sheet is equal to the product code in cell D5, then sum the total hours in the range D3:D93 from the HOURS sheet." Note the use of *mixed references* ($D5 and D$3:D$93), which allow you to properly copy the first formula to the other cells.

Please note that the IF function isn't required in the array formula. The following formula also could accomplish the goal:

`=SUM((HOURS!$B$3:$B$93=$G$2)*(HOURS!$C$3:$C$93=$D5)*(HOURS!D$3:D$93))`

The advantage of using IF is that you can specify text that you want to display for the ELSE portion of the IF (for example, displaying "N/A").

Caution

Be careful when entering ranges; the ranges must match exactly or the formula will return an error. Also, you must have exact date matches.

If the date or product code changes, the formula automatically changes to accommodate the new references. This problem is solved by using range names, as shown in Figure 35.5. It certainly is easier to understand the formula when using the defined names!

Figure 35.5.
Inserting named ranges in conditional formulas with several references can effectively communicate where each of the reference points are coming from.

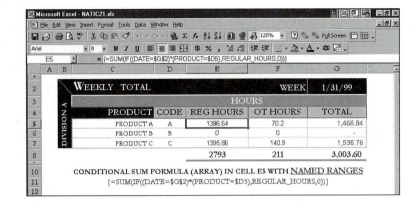

Tip #441	Copy the REGULAR_HOURS formula to the OT HOURS column, and then use Edit, Replace to change the range name.

What if you're compiling data daily instead of weekly? In other words, you have daily amounts but you want to calculate based on weeks, and the trigger cell G2 needs to indicate the week range (for example, the week of 1/10 through 1/16).

The information still falls within a specified week indicated in cell G2. The date-indicator cell should contain the week-ending date, and your list should include two columns: one with the week-ending date from which the formula will extract, and the other a date-entered column for the actual date the information was entered.

EXTRACTING MONTHLY INFORMATION

When you're tracking costs, widgets, and so on, you probably want to view your information not only by week, but also cumulative month to date. Excel lets you "roll up" the weeks into months by adding a month condition to the conditional sum formula in cell E5, as shown in Figure 35.6. (The number 1 in cell G2 is the month indicator—for example, 1 = January, 2 = February, and so on.)

To set up this table, follow these steps:

1. Set up the table similar to the weeks table in the preceding section, but change the headings in row 2 (MONTHLY TOTAL in B2 and MONTH in F2) and specify in cell G2 the number value of the month you want to track (1 through 12).

2. In cell E5, type the formula, using the following syntax:
   ```
   =SUM(IF((month(sheet!range=criteria)=month_criteria)*(sheet!range=criteria),
   ➥sheet!sum_range,0))
   ```

3. Press Ctrl+Shift+Enter to enter the formula as an array.

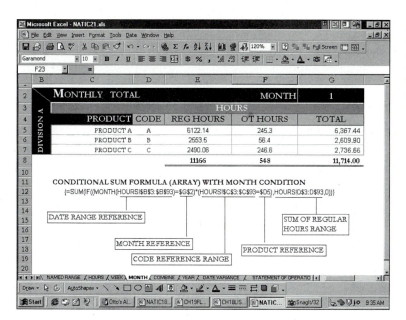

Figure 35.6.
By adding the month condition to the conditional sum formula, you can extract monthly quantity or cost data from a list.

As in the previous example, the trigger points are in cells D5 and G2. In essence, this conditional sum formula says, "If the month in the range B3:B93 from the HOURS sheet is equal to the month value in cell G2, and the product range C3:C93 from the HOURS sheet is equal to the product code in cell D5, then sum the total hours in the range D3:D93 from the HOURS sheet."

EXTRACTING YEARLY INFORMATION

To roll up the months into years, you add a year condition to the conditional sum formula, as shown in Figure 35.7.

To add a year condition to the conditional sum formula, follow these steps:

1. In the calculation worksheet, change the headings in row 2 (YEARLY TOTAL in B2 and YEAR in F2), and indicate in cell G2 the year you want to track. If you're entering the year 2000, simply enter 1/1/00, 1/1/2000, or just 2000.

Tip #442

> If possible, enter dates with four-digit years to prevent Excel from using its internal algorithm to apply the century. For example, entering 1/1/29 results in the year 2029; 1/1/30 yields 1930. Two-digit years between 00 and 29 become 2000–2029; numbers between 29–99 convert to the 20th century (1929–1999).

2. Change the formula in cell E5 to use the following syntax:

```
=SUM(IF((year(sheet!range=criteria)=year_criteria)*(sheet!range=criteria),
➥sheet!sum_range,0))
```

3. Press Ctrl+Shift+Enter to enter the formula as an array.

Figure 35.7.
By adding the year condition to the conditional sum formula, you can extract yearly quantity or cost data from a list.

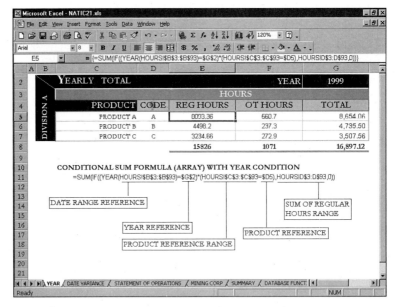

In essence, the conditional sum formula now says, "If the year in the range B3:B93 from the HOURS sheet is equal to the year value in cell G2, and the product range C3:C93 from the HOURS sheet is equal to the product code in cell D5, then sum the total hours in the range D3:D93 from the HOURS sheet."

The previous examples show the calculations being performed on separate worksheets, but you may prefer a consolidated sheet, as shown in Figure 35.8.

Figure 35.8.
Displaying the tables in hierarchical fashion enables you to get the total picture either from top down or left to right.

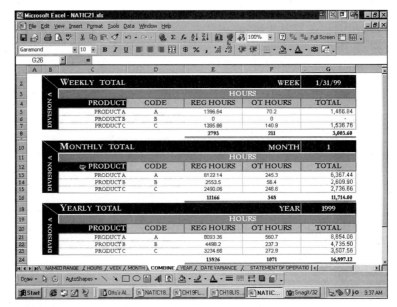

USING THE CONDITIONAL SUM WIZARD AND LOOKUP WIZARD

Not familiar with looking up or summing information with formulas? Excel makes it easy for you with the Conditional Sum Wizard and Lookup Wizard. These wizards assist you in the process of writing formulas with conditions.

Note

To use these wizards, they must be listed on the Wizard submenu of the Tools menu. To add the wizards to the menu, choose Tools, Add-Ins, select Conditional Sum Wizard and Lookup Wizard in the add-ins list, click OK, and confirm that you want to install the add-ins.

USING THE CONDITIONAL SUM WIZARD

A *conditional sum* is used when a list has several columns of data, each of which contains critical criteria for summing up information. For example, if a list has columns that specify quarter, product, sales totals, and so on, you might want to total the sales for a certain product type in a certain quarter.

Figure 35.9 shows a typical worksheet. In the following steps, I'll use the *Conditional Sum Wizard* to sum all totals for the Gold product in Q1 in this worksheet.

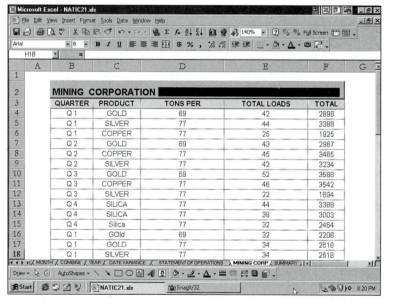

Figure 35.9.
A list containing two conditions to sum.

To use the Conditional Sum Wizard to sum values based on two or more conditions, follow these steps:

1. Select a cell somewhere in the list you want to use.

2. Choose Tools, Wizard, Conditional Sum.

3. The first dialog box of the Conditional Sum Wizard specifies the range of the list (see Figure 35.10). When the list range is defined correctly, click Next.

4. In step 2, use the first drop-down list to select the column you want to sum—in this case, the TOTAL column (see Figure 35.11).

Figure 35.10.
The first step is defining the range you want to use.

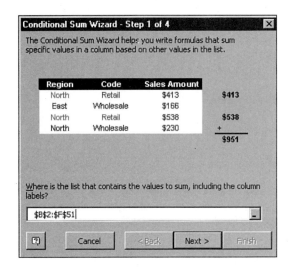

Figure 35.11.
In step 2, specify the conditions you want the formula to apply.

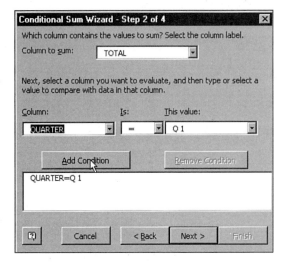

5. Now add the conditions. For this example, the first condition under Column is QUARTER. I selected = in the Is box, and under This Value selected Q1 (in other words, the value in the QUARTER column is equal to Q1). After specifying the first condition, click Add Condition. Then add the second condition—for this example, PRODUCT = GOLD.

6. Choose Next.

7. In step 3, you have two choices (see Figure 35.12):

  ▪ Copy the formula you have created to your worksheet.

  ▪ Copy the formula and its conditional values. This option creates automation in the formula—that is, when you change a condition, the formula reflects the conditional change. Use this option when you think you will want to sum different values in the same column later on.

  Make your choice and click Next.

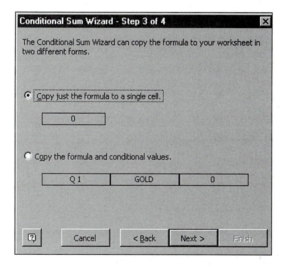

Figure 35.12.
Now that the wizard knows how to create your formula, you just need to indicate where you want it.

8. If you specified copying just the formula in the preceding step, type or select the cell address for the formula. If you're copying formula and conditions, specify the cell for the first value, click Next, specify the location of the second value, click Next, and so on until you have positioned all the conditions and the formula.

  As you click Next, the wizard positions the formula or condition in the specified cell.

9. Click Finish to place the newly created formula in the specified location.

USING THE LOOKUP WIZARD

The *Lookup Wizard* finds the point where two conditions intersect. Let's say you have different points of interest for your global business. You want to be able to pull up data for a

PART

VIII

CH

35

global business sector and find out whether the different deals in progress are complete for your business strategies. You could use the Lookup Wizard to find the intersecting points. For this example, look at Figure 35.13. I'll use the Lookup Wizard to find out whether the North America contract for bundled items is complete.

Figure 35.13.
I'll use the Lookup Wizard to look up values and text where two specified points in this worksheet intersect.

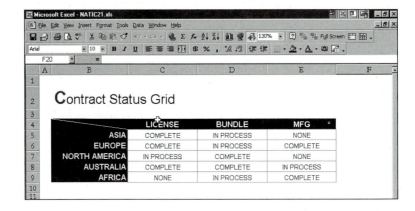

To find the text or value where two points intersect, follow these steps:

1. Click anywhere in the list you want included in your formula.

2. Choose Tools, Wizard, Lookup.

3. Confirm the range you want to use (see Figure 35.14). Be sure that the range includes the row and column headings.

4. In step 2, you indicate which row and column labels identify the value you're looking up (see Figure 35.15). In this example, the lookup column is BUNDLE, and the lookup row is NORTH AMERICA.

Tip #443

If the data doesn't include labels, or the labels in the drop-down lists don't exactly match what you want, select No row label matches exactly or No column label matches exactly in the appropriate drop-down list.

5. In the next step, you have two options (see Figure 35.16):

   ■ Copy the formula you have created to your worksheet.

   ■ Copy the formula and its lookup parameters, thus making the formula conditionally interactive. For example, if you change the cell containing the row heading to reflect a new region, the formula automatically updates to reflect the cell change.

Make your choice and click Next.

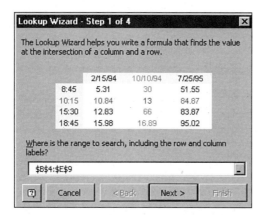

Figure 35.14.
Specify or confirm the range of the list.

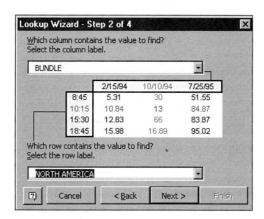

Figure 35.15.
Indicate the headings that will contain the intersecting point.

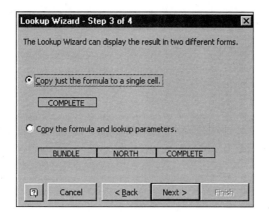

Figure 35.16.
Specify whether you want just the formula, or formula and parameters.

PART

VIII

CH

35

6. If you specified copying just the formula in the preceding step, type or select the cell address for the formula. If you're copying formula and lookup parameters, specify the cell for the first parameter, click Next, specify the location of the second parameter, click Next, and so on until you have positioned all the parameters and the formula.

   As you click Next, the wizard positions the formula or parameter in the specified cell.

   For this example, I'll place the row heading parameter in cell B12, the column heading parameter in cell C12, and the formula in cell D12.

7. Click Finish to place the newly created formula in the specified location.

The final result for this simple example is shown in Figure 35.17. The formula in the Formula bar reflects cell B12 in MATCH case 1 and cell C12 in MATCH case 2. If the value in cell D12 is changed from NORTH AMERICA to ASIA, the result in cell D12 would be IN PROCESS.

Figure 35.17.
The result of the Lookup Wizard process is an INDEX MATCH formula that matches two conditions to the Index range.

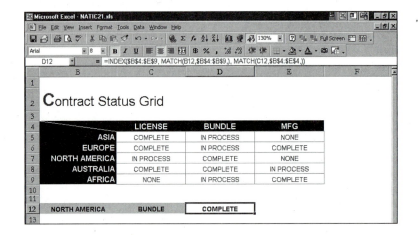

Tip #444	Unlike manually using the VLOOKUP or HLOOKUP function, the lookup row or column doesn't have to be sorted A–Z in the Lookup Wizard.

USING FUNCTIONS WITH TABLES

One of the most difficult things for people in business to understand is how to measure data. Whether you're writing a book, creating widgets, dealing with creative factors, or managing finances, each element of the process can be measured. Being able to create a variance analysis is one of the most critical factors in gauging the success of your project or process. Knowing where you are at any given point enables you to both manage your business and peer over the horizon to see potential problems before they occur.

Figure 35.18 shows a simple table that explains the critical components in measuring variance. This particular table is an *active variance table*, which responds to something in process or occurring. A *static* or *final variance table* deals with final analysis—after the fact, when the project or process is complete.

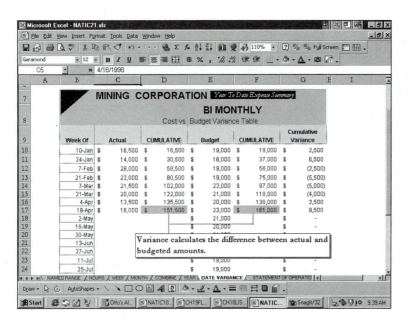

Figure 35.18.
The variance is calculated from the cumulative projected data versus the cumulative actual data.

Tip #445

Variance can be pulled from any time factor, such as seconds, minutes, weeks, months, quarters, and years. The key is to maintain the projected and actual figures.

In this example, cell G17 shows that the amount budgeted to date exceeds the amount spent to date by $9,500. The critical components for the variance table in this example are the cumulative columns for actual and budgeted dollars.

USING VLOOKUP TO EXTRACT LINE ITEMS

After you establish a variance table or list, you can use Excel's lookup functions to extract line items for variance analysis. The table in Figure 35.19 uses a formula with the VLOOKUP function (in cell D5). In this example, the formula is triggered by the week specified in cell C5. Excel looks for that week within the first column of the data table (in the range B9:B22). When it finds that week, Excel displays in the formula cell (D5) the corresponding amount in the third column of the data table (the cumulative actual amount).

If the source cell in the worksheet doesn't yet contain a cumulative amount—the number hasn't been entered yet—Excel displays a zero in the formula cell.

Figure 35.19.
The VLOOKUP function looks up the value in a selected range of cells to match the cell value and column placement.

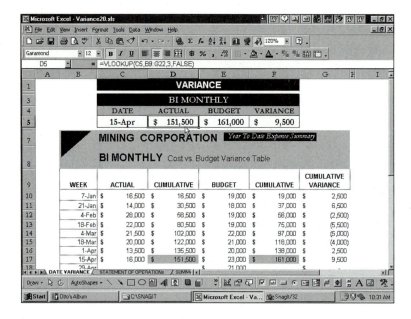

> **Note**
>
> Excel lookup functions count columns or rows only within the data table.

> **Caution**
>
> The lookup column (the Week column, in this example) must be sorted in ascending order (A–Z).

Figure 35.20 shows the VLOOKUP formula (in cell E5) that finds and displays the cumulative budgeted amount. It's identical to the formula in cell D5 except for the column number, which has been changed to indicate that the fifth column in the data table contains the value we're looking up.

LAYING OUT A VARIANCE TABLE REPORT

After you set up a list with the variance of the different categories you want to track, you can automatically extract the information with SUM(IF formulas, as discussed earlier in the chapter, or you could use the VLOOKUP function to extract data for a particular line item.

You can combine multiple variance calculations into a single worksheet, as Figure 35.21 shows. This worksheet uses the date values in cells B3, F3, and J3 to trigger the formula sum variances over time. You also can reference the text in column A to make your table completely automated. After you enter the formula, you can improve the look of the report by hiding the date reference cells in row 3 (see Figure 35.22).

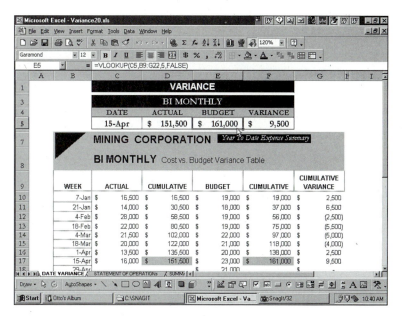

Figure 35.20.
Although you can scan by eye for totals with a simple table like this, most businesses accumulate far more data. Using lookup functions can simplify the process of finding targeted information.

This example references a list that contains the date range in column P, the project range in column Q, and the actual cost in column R. You can reference any list or sheet; in this example, the list is to the right of the summary table, on the same sheet.

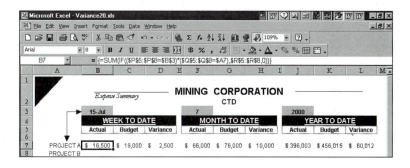

Figure 35.21.
Using absolute values means that you would need to generate this formula only once. If this formula is dragged down one row, the $A7 reference would change to refer to $A8 (Project B), because the row number is relative.

EXTRACTING DATA WITH THE DATABASE FUNCTIONS

Database functions are great for analyzing data with changing criteria. In Figure 35.23, for example, a set of database functions provides a variety of information from the data in the range B3:G9. Notice that in place of the field or cell reference, these formulas use the column heading in quotations. This is just an easier way to understand where the information is coming from. As the example shows, database functions can extract both numbers and text.

PART

VIII

CH

35

Figure 35.22.
Hide the date reference row to finish the variance report for a clear, concise presentation.

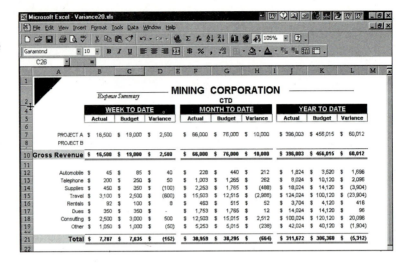

Figure 35.23.
Database functions can be powerful tools for extracting and managing information that meets specific criteria.

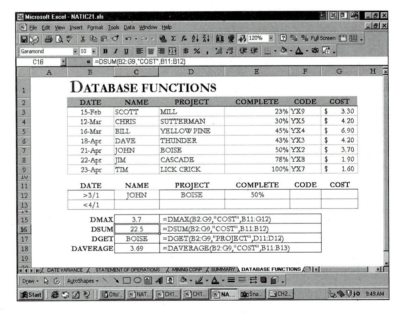

Table 35.1 describes several commonly used database functions.

TABLE 35.1. COMMON DATABASE FUNCTIONS

Function	Definition
DCOUNT	Counts the number of records that meet the specified criteria.
DMAX	Extracts the maximum value within a specified range.

Function	Definition
DSUM	Sums the values within the specified range.
DGET	Extracts a single value from the database, based on the specified criteria.
DAVERAGE	Returns the average of the values within a specified range.

You use the following syntax for database functions:

`=Dfunction(database,field,criteria)`

- The *database* argument refers to the range encompassing the entire list or database.

- The *field* argument refers to a particular column in the list. If you omit the *field* argument, the function operates on the entire list. This argument can consist of either the column heading in quotes (""), or the cell address containing that column heading.

- The *criteria* argument specifies the basis on which you want the function to select particular cells. A criteria range must include column headings, just like the criteria range in a list *filter*.

For additional information on functions, see Appendix A.

CLEANING UP DATA WITH TEXT FUNCTIONS

In an environment with multiple lists generated by several people, it's common to inherit lists that weren't set up properly and need to change the format of the list for use in extracting and manipulating data. Figure 35.24 shows several text functions used to account for many variations of text situations.

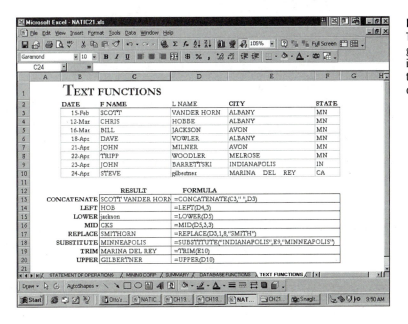

Figure 35.24.
Text functions are great tools for cleaning lists of information that have little or no consistency.

Table 35.2 describes a number of common text functions.

TABLE 35.2. TEXT FUNCTIONS

Function	Definition
CONCATENATE	Adjoins text from independent cells into one cell.
LEFT	Extracts the left character(s) of text to the number specified.
LOWER	Returns text to lowercase.
MID	Extracts the middle characters of text.
REPLACE	Replaces a portion of a text string with a different string that you specify. Use REPLACE when you want to replace any text string in a specific location.
SUBSTITUTE	Replaces specific text with other text.
TRIM	Removes extra spaces in a cell.
UPPER	Returns text to uppercase.

For additional information on functions, see Appendix A.

ADDING FORM CONTROLS TO YOUR WORKSHEETS

Form controls in Excel include check boxes, drop-down lists, spinners, and so on that you can add to charts, lists, and other areas of your worksheets to create custom forms for use in data entry and data management. There are multiple ways to use form controls, but the underlying premise is to use form controls in conjunction with formulas. Form controls link to a cell, and then you apply a formula that addresses the link to look up the information or calculate from the information. For example, suppose you're creating a standard bid sheet for different types of construction equipment. A check box on the form could be set up so that if you check the box, it automatically includes and calculates the type of equipment and rate.

You can use form controls with tables, lists, charts, and even PivotTables. The controls actually are quite simple to create and use. After you set up your worksheet, you then apply the controls from the Forms toolbar as needed to fit your situation. The form shown in Figure 35.25, for example, uses a simple drop-down list to extract an equipment number. Formulas tied to the cell link then extract the corresponding values. Some form controls can be tied to Excel macros or VBA programs to perform tasks.

Note

If you have some experience writing Visual Basic code or Web scripts, you can use ActiveX controls from the Control toolbox in Excel to create custom applications for Excel. These topics are beyond the scope of this book, but Macmillan Computer Publishing offers a wide variety of other books that specifically cover Visual Basic and ActiveX. You also can consult the Excel Help system for limited guidance on using the ActiveX controls with Excel.

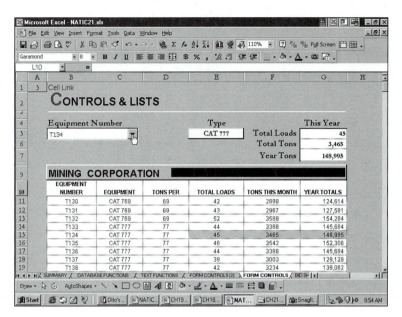

Figure 35.25.
Form controls applied to lists allow for minimal formula writing and can serve as a great analytical tool.

Table 35.3 describes the form controls available from the Forms toolbar.

TABLE 35.3. CONTROLS ON THE FORMS TOOLBAR

Button	Name	Description
Aa	Label	Places a label in the worksheet for use in naming other controls.
ab|	Edit Box	Creates a data-entry box for forms. (This control doesn't work on regular worksheets.)
[xyz]	Group Box	Groups the selected option buttons. Using two groups allows for additional cell links.
	Button	Runs a macro.
☑	Check Box	Produces a TRUE or FALSE response when selected or deselected.
◉	Option Button	Creates the number of the option button in a single group. You can add additional groups for generating a new cell link.
	List Box	Returns the number of the item selected.
	Combo Box	Combines a list box and an edit box.
	Combination List-Edit	A combined list and text box. This feature is not available on a worksheet.

PART

VIII

CH

35

continues

TABLE 35.3. CONTINUED

Button	Name	Description
	Combination Drop-Down Edit	A drop-down list with an edit box. This feature is not available on a worksheet.
	Scroll Bar	A draggable scrollbar that allows for high and low limits, as well as incremental change.
	Spinner	A counter that allows for high and low limits, as well as incremental change.
	Control Properties	Displays a dialog box of options for the selected control.
	Edit Code	Enables you to edit code associated with the control selected.
	Toggle Grid	Turns the grid lines of a worksheet on or off.
	Run Dialog	Displays the dialog box on the active dialog sheet. Used as a test or preview of the dialog box drawn. This feature is unavailable on a worksheet.

To apply form controls to a list or form, display the Forms toolbar (choose View, Toolbars, Forms), click the desired tool, and draw the control on the worksheet. After you create the control, you can format it and set its properties as desired.

The following steps describe the process of creating the Equipment Number drop-down list shown earlier (refer to Figure 35.25):

1. On the Forms toolbar, click the Combo Box tool (see Figure 35.26).

2. Draw the control on the worksheet by holding down the left mouse button and dragging the crosshair to the desired size (see Figure 35.27). To create a default-size control, just click in the worksheet.

3. Right-click the form control, and select Format Control from the context menu (see Figure 35.28). The Format Object dialog box appears.

4. In the Format Object dialog box, select the Control tab. In the Input Range box, specify the range of the data you want to display in the drop-down list in the combo box. In Figure 35.29, the range is the Equipment Number column from the list.

5. Input the cell link your formulas will reference. In the example, the cell link is in cell A1. The cell link displays the item number of the chosen value on the list. A link value of 2, for example, would refer to the second item on the drop-down list.

6. Establish the number of drop-down lines you want to display in the combo box. If the number of items in the list exceeds the number of drop-down lines displayed, Excel displays a scrollbar that the user can click to scroll the list and display the rest of the

entries. You need to use this option only if you want to restrict the number of lines shown in the drop-down list. By default, Excel automatically displays as many or as few lines as needed.

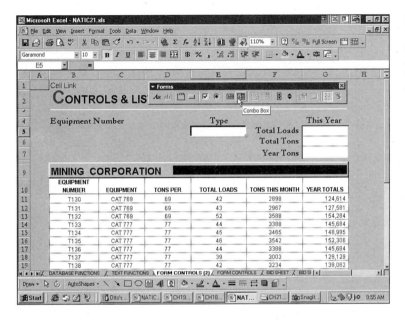

Figure 35.26.
The combo box control creates a drop-down list of entries from which you can choose.

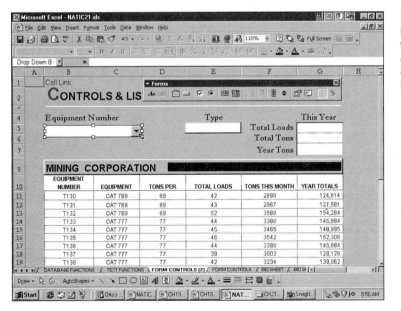

Figure 35.27.
Draw the form control to the desired size above the list. You can resize the control later, if necessary.

Figure 35.28.
Select Format Control from the context menu to establish the range and cell link for the control.

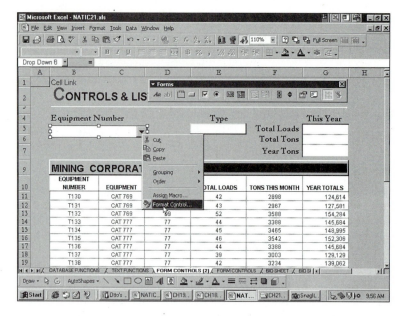

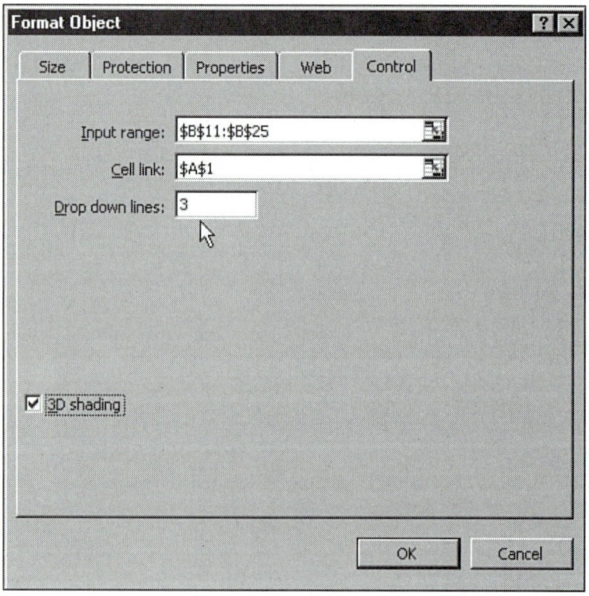

Figure 35.29.
In the Format Object dialog box, format the control and establish the cell link and list range.

7. If desired, check the <u>3</u>D Shading option to give the control a three-dimensional look.

8. Set additional options for the control as desired on other tabs in the dialog box. The following list describes some of the options:

- **Colors and Lines (option and check boxes only)**. Determines the color, line, and arrow styles used for the control.

- **Size**. Sets the control's size, scale, and so on.

- **Protection**. Locks the object or its text to prevent changes by users when the worksheet is protected.

- **Properties**. Manipulates the control's reaction to sizing of cells, as well as printing of the object with the worksheet.

- **Web**. Specifies the alternative text you want to display on Web browsers when loading the object or when pictures are not displayed.

9. Click OK when the settings are complete.

10. Click anywhere on the worksheet to deselect the control.

11. To test the control, click the down arrow and select a record so that the cell link is activated (see Figure 35.30).

Figure 35.30.
Select a record from the new control to activate the cell link.

Now that you have created the control, reference a formula to the link to activate this model. To do this, use an index formula (see Figure 35.31). In this example, the formula is =INDEX(C11:C25,A1,1). C11:C25 is the list range, the link cell is the form control's record count cell (A1), and 1 is the column number in the range.

Figure 35.31.
Attach or reference formulas to the link and the list. The control then activates the cell link and the formula extracts the values.

Tip #446

You also can use =INDEX($C$11:$G$25,$A$1,2). Specifying the entire table (minus the equipment column) for the Reference argument and making the first two arguments absolute enables you to copy the formula to the other cells (G5:G7). All you'd need to do then would be to change the Column argument in the pasted formulas.

For each item you want to pull up, select a cell and create the index formula.

USING CONTROLS WITH CALCULATION TABLES

At this point, you may find yourself thinking, "Form controls are a nice feature, but how can I really use them?" Think of it in terms of a formula that's triggered by a result. The result sets off a chain reaction that's determined by how creative you are with the formula and worksheet setup.

Figure 35.32 shows a worksheet that uses check boxes, spinners, and text boxes to create a *calculation table* that determines whether certain criteria are met. In this case, the user fills in a check box to specify the equipment to be used; the client will be charged by the number of weeks using that equipment. A spinner is applied to the number of weeks for each of the different breakouts.

In this example, the check boxes are selected by default, as shown in Figure 35.33. Thus, the check box control establishes a TRUE value in the cell link cell. Using the Unchecked option results in FALSE, and Mixed results in #NA.

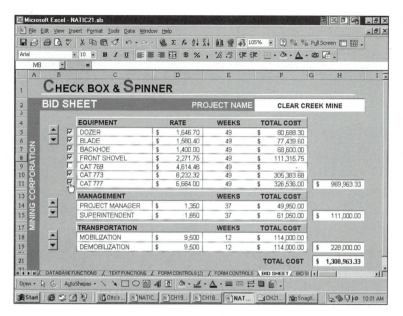

Figure 35.32.
You can use check boxes and spinners in conjunction with calculation tables to automate bid sheets or calculation tables of any kind.

Mixed isn't a value that the user can select when clicking the control. It's the shading effect that appears in the check box when #NA appears in the linked cell. It's normally used to change the appearance of the control by changing the cell link value via programming. Formulas can't directly alter the contents of other cells, so there's no way to change the value of the linked cell (to #NA) unless you manually type it in or change it using VBA code.

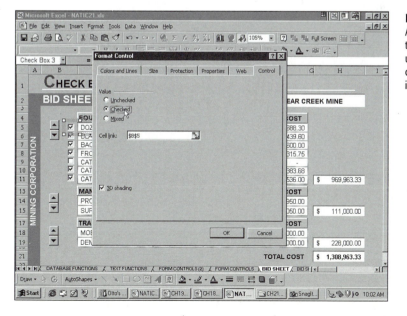

Figure 35.33.
A check box returns the result FALSE if unchecked, TRUE if checked, and #NA if mixed.

PART

VIII

CH

35

Tip #447

You can use a check box as an indicator only by placing a formula in the linked cell itself. For example, you can enter a nested IF formula in the linked cell that evaluates to TRUE, FALSE, or #NA. The formula's result then changes the look of the check box. To prevent users from using the check box (and thereby eliminating the cell link's formula), simply lock it (and its associated linked cell); then protect the worksheet.

The cell link for the row 5 check box is in cell B5, as shown in Figure 35.34. When checked, the check box returns the value TRUE, which is used by the IF statement in cell F5. Following is the syntax:

`=IF(link_cell,true_result,false_result)`

- `link_cell`. The link cell in B5 returns the result TRUE if checked, FALSE if not. The IF statement refers to the link cell looking for a match.

- `true_result`. The TRUE result is the result of the box being checked. The result returns the text in the link cell.

- `false_result`. The FALSE result in the formula is 0. So if there's no match between the statement and the link cell, the result posted is 0.

Figure 35.34.
Use an IF statement to perform a calculation if the cell link is true.

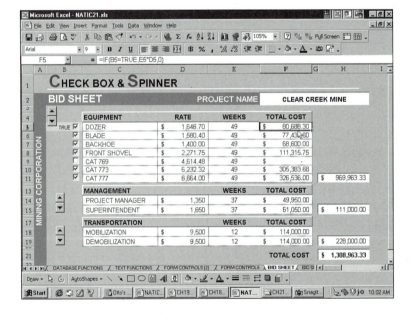

Tip #448

To hide the cell link value, format the cell so that the text color is identical to the background color. If the background is white, the text should be white. Alternatively, you can hide the column or row.

A spinner applies a number in a cell that incrementally increases or decreases, based on the specifications you provide on the Control tab in the Format Control dialog box (shown in Figure 35.35). Setting the minimum value of the spinner controls the lowest value the spinner will spin down to, and vice versa for the maximum value. The range is 0 to 30,000. Specifying an incremental change setting tells Excel to move the values up or down by the specified increment with each click of the spin arrows.

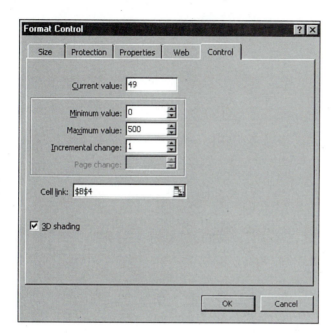

Figure 35.35.
The spinner control enables you to apply maximum and minimum values and also apply an incremental change by which the spinner will increase or decrease the linked cell value.

Setting the weeks in the example equal to the value of the link cell for the spinner changes the weeks to match the spinner (see Figure 35.36). For example, if the cell link to the spinner is in cell B1, apply **=B1** to all the cells that you want to refer to the cell link.

USING CONTROLS WITH CHARTS

You may never have thought of adding form controls to your charts, but the example in Figure 35.37 shows another way that form controls can be helpful. Here, a scrollbar controls the values displayed in the chart. The user can drag the scroll box, click in the scrollbar, or click the scroll arrows to change the quarter values displayed on the chart. The changes are incremental jumps you set when formatting the control. A drop-down list control also would work for switching between quarters.

When drawing a scrollbar control, draw from left to right for a horizontal scrollbar or top to bottom for a vertical scrollbar. Set the value options to a desired high, low, incremental, and page change (see Figure 35.38). A *page change* is just an incremental jump when you click on the scroll track.

Figure 35.36.
Make the weeks equal to the spinner cell link, so that the weeks change when the spinner is activated.

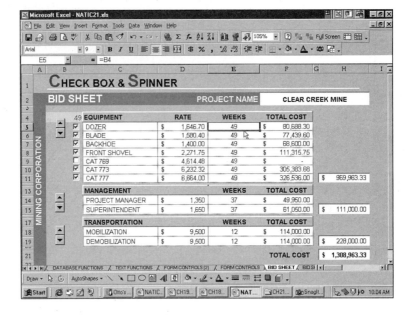

Figure 35.37.
You most often use scrollbars when you have large differences from the lowest value to the highest value. This example demonstrates scrolling through quarters.

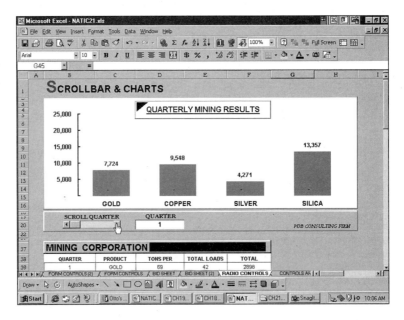

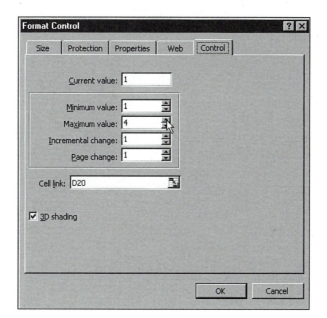

Figure 35.38.
Set the ceiling and floor to which the scroll will reach up and drop down.

To create a chart that responds to the control, you'll need to create a table that references the cell link. Following is one way to do this:

1. Create a SUM(IF formula that extracts the product by quarter from the list (see Figure 35.39). The formula shown here looks up the quarter in column B from the list against cell C$24, which is the quarter indicator 1. Then it looks up the product in column C from the list against the product indicator in cell $B25, Gold. If these conditions are met, then the sum of column F—which is the total quantity for that quarter and product—is applied to the formula cell.

   Figure 35.40 shows the formula that references the cell link in cell D20. The IF statement just states that if the cell link equals 1, apply the value in cell C25, else FALSE (0). Notice the absolute referencing. When the formula is dragged to the right, it references Q2, then Q3, and so on. This way, you have to apply the formula only one time. When it's filled to the right, the referencing corresponds accordingly.

Tip #449

If you prefer, you could compress this formula with the SUM(IF array into one nested array formula, thereby eliminating the need for the SUM table.

PART

VIII

CH

35

Figure 35.39.
Create a SUM(IF table that extracts the product and quarter. You also could use a PivotTable for this.

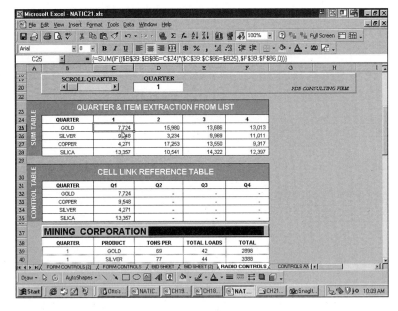

Figure 35.40.
Mirror your SUM(IF table with a table that references the cell link and equals the criteria or zero.

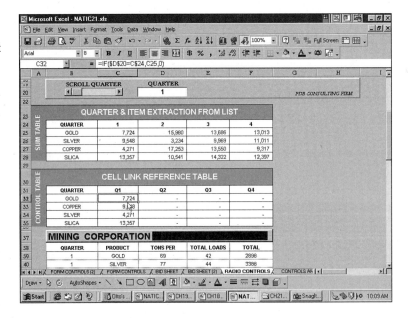

2. Create a column chart from the cell link reference table, setting the series in columns (see Figure 35.41).

You set the series in columns to display the product rather than quarters on the category (X) axis. The product will be displayed all the time, and the quarters respond to the selected quarter from the scrollbar.

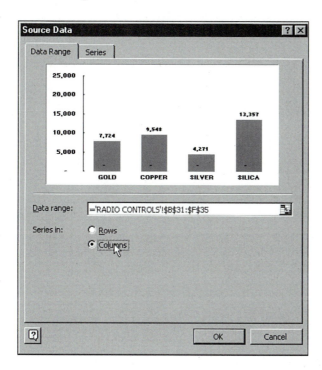

Figure 35.41.
Set the series in columns.

3. Select the data series in the chart, and choose F̲ormat, S̲elected Data Series.

4. Select the Options tab in the Format Data Series dialog box.

5. Set the overlap to 100 and the gap width to 80 (see Figure 35.42). This will place the columns over each other so that they don't move along the axis.

6. Click OK.

CONTROL CHARACTERISTICS

Figure 35.43 shows a variety of controls:

- The list box applies a cell link in the form of the number of the chosen record.
- The combo box does the same, but uses a drop-down list instead of a scrolling list.
- The scrollbar and spinner are similar controls, but the scrollbar allows for horizontal orientation, as well as page change scrolling—an incremental jump when the scroll track is clicked. You can also grab the scroll box and slide it along the scroll track.

PART

VIII

CH

35

- The check box applies the cell link result of TRUE, FALSE, or #NA.

- The option buttons create stacked numbers associated with the number of option buttons. For example, option button number 2 is stacked number 2 in the cell link. If you create a new group of option buttons, that group's cell link numbers start from 1 again.

Figure 35.42.
Set the overlap and gap width so the columns display in the same location rather than jogging on the X-axis.

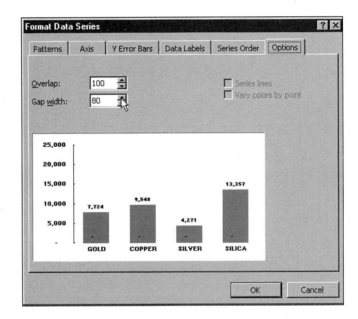

Figure 35.43.
Controls and their characteristics.

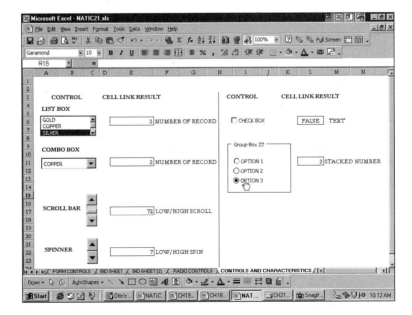

TROUBLESHOOTING

INTERSECTING POINTS IN LISTS OR TABLES

My index formula doesn't work when trying to pull up two intersecting points within a list.

Use the Lookup Wizard to help you rewrite formulas with complex INDEX(MATCH cases. (I suggest using this tool as a way to learn indexing and matching formulas as well.)

COMPLEX FORMULAS

The formula has become too long to understand.

Use named ranges to simplify formulas. (But do this only for ranges that generally don't change.) You also can apply a range that's much longer than the list; as the list grows, the new cells with data will be included in the range.

FORMULAS ARE SLOWING DOWN THE WORKBOOK

How can I increase the performance of a workbook that seems lethargic?

One option is to turn off automatic recalculation. Choose Tools, Options, click the Calculation tab in the Options dialog box, and select Manual. To then calculate the workbook, press F9. Another way to increase efficiency is to use form controls for looking up information. Finally, if possible, use *PivotTables*—the most efficient way to summarize large amounts of data in a workbook.

PARSING A LIST OF NAMES

I've inherited a list with first and last names combined and random capitalization. What's the best way to fix this problem?

To separate the combined names in a list, use the Text to Columns feature on the Data menu. To fix random capitalization, use the text function UPPER() or LOWER() in an adjacent row or column and then paste the final result back in the list as values (use Paste Special).

CHAPTER 36

USING EXCEL'S ANALYSIS TOOLS

In this chapter

USING EXCEL TO ANALYZE YOUR DATA

Many Excel users input data into a worksheet, use simple functions or formulas to calculate results, and then report those results to someone else. Although this is a perfectly legitimate use of Excel, it basically turns Excel into a calculator.

When you need to do more than just type data into a worksheet, you can use special Excel features to analyze your data and solve complex problems by employing variables and constraints. Goal Seek and Solver are two great tools included with Excel that you can use to analyze data and provide answers to simple or even fairly complex problems. Goal Seek is primarily used when there is one unknown variable, and Solver when there are many variables and multiple constraints. Although you may have used Solver in the past, primarily with complex tables for financial analysis, this chapter also shows you how to combine Solver with *Gantt charts*. Solver isn't just for financial analysis; it can be used against production, financial, marketing, and accounting models. Solver should be used when you're searching for a result and you have multiple variables that change (constraints). The more complex the constraints, the more you need to use Solver, as shown later in this chapter for resource loading.

Both Goal Seek and Solver enable you to play "what if" with the result of a formula when you know what result you're shooting for, without manually changing the cells that are being referenced in the formula.

The data tables in Excel provide a very important function: creating one- and two-variable tables for use in amortization and other tasks—allowing you to create a series of results based on one formula (such as cash flows). This chapter includes the details on how to set up your tables and shows a few tricks for these kinds of tables that can save you time and effort.

Whether you're manufacturing plastic cups, hauling quantities of material or dirt, or manufacturing digital assets in software development, Excel's powerful analytical tools combined with structured worksheet design can make your life easier and help you to manage your time more effectively.

USING GOAL SEEK

The *Goal Seek* feature in Excel uses a single variable to find a desired result. To understand Goal Seek, let's start with a simple scenario. Suppose that you're a sales representative for a packaging business. You must achieve $100,000 in sales this year to receive a bonus. Figure 36.1 shows a table that displays the current situation—you have sold 2,000 units of a product with a per-unit sales price of $3.46. How many units must you sell to achieve your $100,000 goal?

Note

The goal amount ($100,000 in this case) must be the result of a formula, not just plain data.

At this point, you've probably already set up the formula in your head: `(100000  6920)/3.46=26901.73` units remaining to be sold. What would be the advantage of using a special Excel feature to calculate something so simple? Wouldn't you just create a formula in a cell and be done with it? The advantage of Goal Seek is that you can set up your formula just once, and then substitute different amounts to get quick alternative routes to your goal.

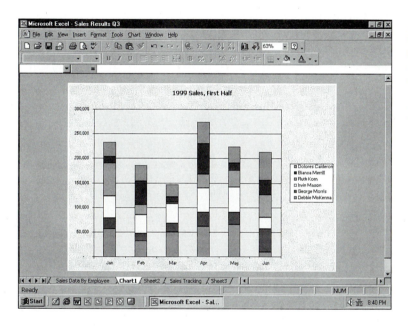

Figure 36.1.
Use Goal Seek to find the unknown variable—such as how many boxes must be sold at a unit price of $3.46 to reach $100,000 in sales.

To use Goal Seek, select the formula cell (D7 in this example) and then choose Tools, Goal Seek to display the Goal Seek dialog box (see Figure 36.2). The following list describes the entries for each of the items in the dialog box:

- Set cell specifies the location of the formula you use to get the end result. In this case, the formula is in cell D7, and simply multiplies the number of units sold by the unit price.

- Type the target value in the To Value box.

- In the By Changing Cell box, specify the cell location of the variable that you want to change to reach your goal—in this case, $100,000 in sales.

Figure 36.2.
Specify the settings in the dialog box to begin the Goal Seek process.

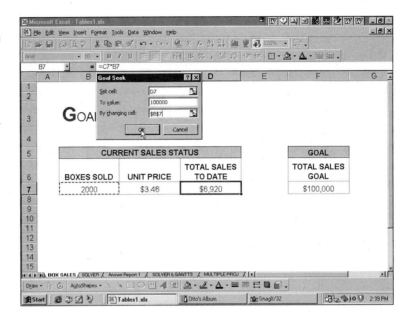

As soon as you click OK or press Enter, Excel begins seeking the specified goal. In this case, the solution indicated is 28901.7341 total units at the current price of $3.46 (see Figure 36.3). In this case, you probably would need to round the solution to the nearest integer (28,902), because units aren't generally sold in fractional amounts.

Figure 36.3.
Goal Seek found the desired result.

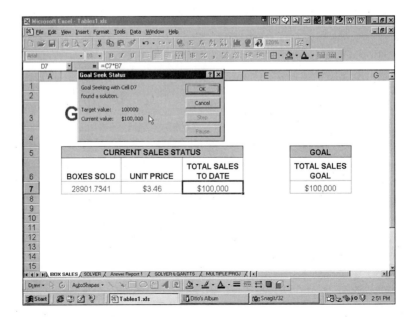

Now suppose you need to determine the unit price—the other variable in the total-sales-to-date formula. If you want to sell only 2,000 units of something, how high would the price need to be for you to reach the $100,000 target? To find out, you change the By Changing Cell setting in the Goal Seek dialog box to specify cell C7, the unit price (see Figure 36.4). Here, Goal Seek will raise the price of the boxes to a dollar value that will equal $100,000 in sales but keep the units sold at 2,000. Figure 36.5 shows the outcome: To reach $100,000 by selling only 2,000 units, each unit must cost $50.

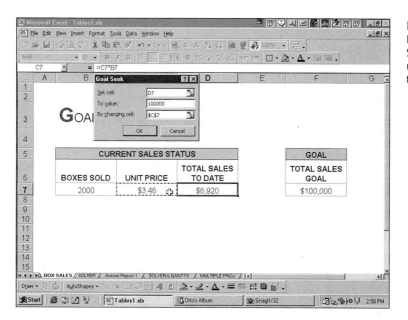

Figure 36.4.
In this case, Goal Seek is adjusting the unit price to reach the target.

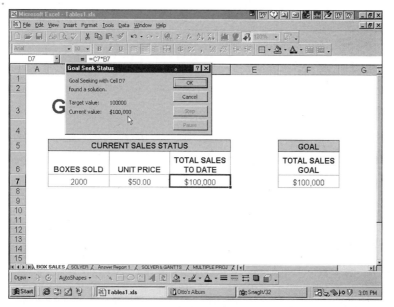

Figure 36.5.
Finding a unit price to meet the target.

Tip #450	You can use Goal Seek with complex financial models as well as with a simple solution. Link the final result cell to other cells within the model to drive the changes.

USING SOLVER

Goal Seek is an efficient feature for helping you reach a particular goal, but it deals with only a single variable. For most businesses, the variables are much more complex. How can you reach the profit goal if advertising expenses increase? What's the best mix of products to increase sales in the first quarter, when revenues traditionally decline for your business? Which suppliers give you the optimum combination of price and delivery? For problems like these, you can use *Solver*, an add-in program that comes with Excel. This powerful analysis tool uses multiple changing variables and constraints to find the optimum solution to solve a problem. Previously, Solver was a tool used primarily for financial modeling analysis; however, Solver can be used in conjunction with models of any kind that you build in Excel. Later in this section is a discussion of using Solver with Gantt charts.

Note	Solver isn't enabled by default. To add it to the Tools menu, choose Tools, Add-Ins, select Solver Add-in in the Add-Ins dialog box, and click OK. If asked to confirm, choose Yes. (You'll need the Office 2000 CD.)

Tip #451	The best way to learn how to work with Solver is to experiment with simple problems, using the Solvsamp.xls file on the Office 2000 CD. When you understand how to work with multiple variables and constraints to solve a problem, you can begin using your own data and solving real business problems.

The key to understanding complex analysis tools is to start with something relatively simple. The example in Figure 36.6 uses several variables to calculate a project's total cost. What if your total budget for the year is $500,000 (as shown in the constraints cell G20) and you were using only $375,351 (as shown in cell G16)? You want each project to have a total cost of $50,000 (G5:G14) and you want to optimize or add to your marketing and advertising dollars (columns E and F). Solver will add to the Marketing cost and Advertising cost for you, adjusting your total cost for a project to $50,000.

Quite often, companies must deal with projects that have total budget caps for the year. For this, Solver works well in adjusting variables within the projects to maximize dollar amounts in certain categories, while maintaining the budget cap.

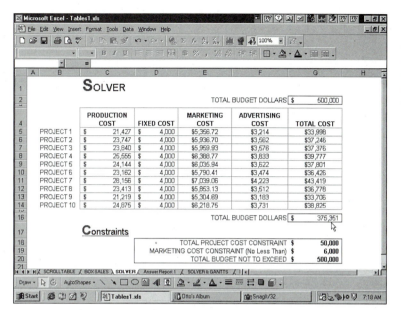

Figure 36.6.
A Solver scenario where you want all projects' total costs to equal $50,000, while optimizing marketing and advertising costs.

To set up this Solver scenario, follow these steps:

1. Set up the table. In the example, the production costs are in C5:C14, the fixed costs in D5:D14, the marketing costs in E5:E14, the advertising costs in F5:F14, and the totals in G5:G14.

2. Set up the constraints. In cell G18 in the example, the constraint is $50,000 for the maximum cost per project. In cell G19, the constraint is marketing costs of no less than $6,000 per project, and the total maximum budget in cell G20 is set at $500,000.

3. Select the target cell, G16, and choose Tools, Solver.

4. In the Solver Parameters dialog box, set the parameters you want to use for the problem (see Figure 36.7). For this example, you want the target cell to be the total dollars spent (cell G16), which you want to equal the budget maximum, $500,000 (specified in the Value of box). Solver will calculate the best dispersion to achieve the optimum result by adjusting the amounts in the range E5:F14 (the changing cells).

Tip #452

For many problems, the Guess button does a great job of selecting the cells needed to effect the result. It uses the auditing feature to locate the appropriate cells.

5. Next, you add constraints to the problem. Select Add to specify the first constraint. In this example, you want to spend exactly $50,000 total on any project. The constraint cell is G18, as shown in Figure 36.8.

Figure 36.7.
Establish the target cell, the target value, and the cells that can be changed.

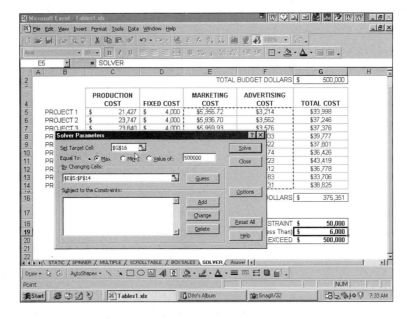

Figure 36.8.
Add variable constraints you want Solver to adhere to.

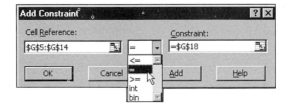

6. To add more constraints, click <u>A</u>dd and specify the constraint. In this example, add another constraint, as shown in Figure 36.9. The marketing costs in the range E5:E14 will be greater than or equal to the constraint set in cell G19, $6,000.

Figure 36.9.
The second constraint ensures that the marketing dollars allocated to each project are greater than or equal to $6,000.

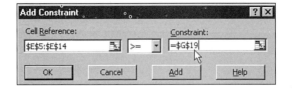

7. The last constraint is the total budget, $500,000, in cell G20 (see Figure 36.10). Don't click Add for the last constraint. Instead, when the constraints are complete, click OK to go back to the Solver Parameters dialog box. Notice that all the constraints added appear in the Su<u>b</u>ject to the Constraints list (see Figure 36.11).

Figure 36.10.
The last constraint equals $500,000, or the sum of total projects.

Figure 36.11.
All the constraints appear in the Subject to the Constraints list. You can add more, change, or delete any of the constraints.

8. Click Solve or press Enter to start Solver on the problem. As Solver works, it displays a message in the status bar, as shown in Figure 36.12.

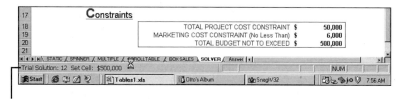

Figure 36.12.
The calculations appear in the lower left while Excel runs through all the constraints set.

At this point, Solver has tried 12 possible combinations.

9. When Solver reaches a conclusion, it displays a dialog box that indicates the result and changes the specified values in the worksheet to reach the target. In Figure 36.13, notice the changed cells when Solver has created the optimum solution for the problem. The total costs now equal $500,000 and the projects all equal $50,000.

10. From here, you can save the Solver results and create an answer report that shows the original scenario of costs and the final result. Select Answer under Reports in the Solver Results dialog box, and click the Save Scenario button to display the dialog box shown in Figure 36.14.

11. If you want to reset the worksheet to return to the original values, select the Restore Original Values option to start with the original values again.

Figure 36.13.
Solver enables you to create reports and save scenarios so that you can later view and recall scenarios you've run.

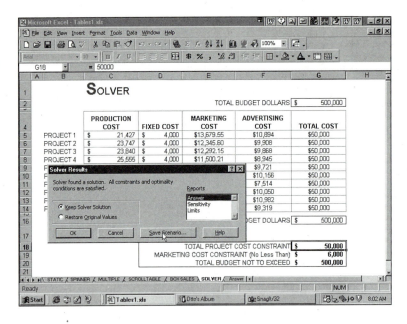

Figure 36.14.
Name the scenario.

Caution

Excel automatically changes the data in the constraint cells referenced by the formula (clearing the original data). If the finished scenario isn't what you were looking for, revert to the worksheet's original state to restore the data.

12. Click OK and Excel will restore the values and create the answer report (see Figure 36.15). The answer report compares the original values with the changed values and indicates the cells that were changed. This way, you can compare scenarios.

Tip #453

The answer report is created on a separate sheet. If you have multiple reports and scenarios, you may want to hide the report sheet(s).

The constraints are saved with the workbook, so you don't have to retype them each time the workbook is opened.

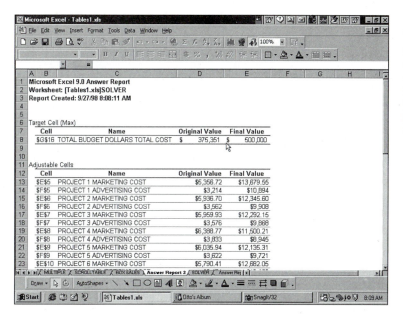

Figure 36.15.
The answer report
shows original values
against final values,
along with the cate-
gory name and the
adjusted cell. The tar-
get cell is called out,
separated at the top.

If Solver can't reach a satisfactory conclusion with the data provided, a message box will
appear. Adjust constraints or variables as needed to continue attempting to solve the problem.

> **Note**
>
> Some problems are too complex even for Solver. For problems with too many variables or
> constraints, try breaking the problem into segments, solving each segment separately, and
> then using those solutions together in Solver to reach a final conclusion.

Solver's solution for a complex problem may be correct but unrealistic. Be skeptical; check
the appropriateness of any adjusted amounts before reporting or implementing any suggestion from Solver.

Solver can be very useful, but you don't want it to run forever attempting to solve an
unsolvable problem. You can change the Solver settings before starting on the problem if
you suspect that the solution may take a long time or require too much computing power.
Clicking the Options button in the Solver Parameters dialog box displays the Solver
Options dialog box, in which you can set the number of iterations of the problem that
Solver will run to search for an answer or the amount of time it will spend searching before
giving up. Figure 36.16 shows the options available, and Table 36.1 provides descriptions of
each option.

Figure 36.16.
The Solver Options dialog box enables you to set parameters for Solver.

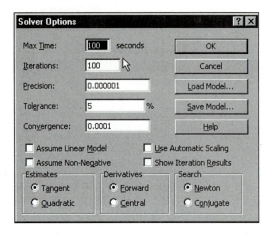

TABLE 36.1. SOLVER OPTIONS

Option	Description
Max Time	Determines the maximum amount of time Solver will search for a solution, in seconds, up to approximately nine hours.
Iterations	Determines the number of times Solver will run the parameters in search of a solution.
Precision	Determines the accuracy of the solution. The lower the number, the more accurate the solution.
Tolerance	When integer constraints are used, it's more difficult for Solver to solve the problem. Here, you can provide more tolerance and give up accuracy.
Convergence	For all nonlinear problems. Indicates the minimum amount of change Solver will use in each iteration. If the target cell is below the convergence setting, Solver will offer the best solution and stop.
Assume Linear Model	When checked, Solver will find a quicker solution, providing that the model is linear (using simple addition or subtraction). Nonlinear models would use growth factor and exponential smoothing or nonlinear worksheet functions.
Assume Non-Negative	Stops Solver from placing negative values in changing cells. (You also can apply constraints that indicate the value must be greater than or equal to zero.) The preceding example would use this option to prevent Solver from using negative amounts.
Use Automatic Scaling	Used when the changing cells and the target cell differ by very large amounts.
Show Iteration Results	Stops and enables you to view the results of each iteration in the Solver sequence.
Load Model	Loads the model to use from a stored set of parameters on the worksheet.

Option	Description
Save Model	Saves a model to a cell or set of cells and allows you to recall the model again.
Tangent	Select when the model is linear.
Quadratic	Select when the model is nonlinear.
Forward	When cells controlled by constraints change slowly for each iteration, check this box to potentially speed up the Solver.
Central	To ensure accuracy when constraint cells change rapidly and by large amounts, use this option.
Newton	Uses more memory but requires fewer iterations to provide the solution.
Conjugate	Use with large models because it requires less memory; however, it will use more iterations to provide a solution for the model.

Using Solver with Gantt Charts

Understanding the simple Solver scenario with constraints described in the preceding section can help you think in terms of combining Excel's powerful tools to solve real-world problems.

Although I've worked extensively with project-management programs, I've found that with the proper construction of workbooks in Excel, Solver can do the following:

- Forecast future costs
- Track actual costs against projected costs
- Forecast production plans
- Track actual production against projected production
- Forecast head count against production loads
- Run resource-loading models for maximum efficiency

Using Gantt charts in Excel, PivotTables, Solver, and formulas to manage production plans is the most efficient mechanism available on the market. The key here is proper worksheet format and workbook construction. If done correctly, the workbook can be completely automated to manage the most complex productions—from managing a construction site, where quantities and haul times are a factor, to the manufacture of digital assets in software development.

Figure 36.17 shows a production model, with constraints indicated on the worksheet under the project's Gantt chart. In this example, a project must start on a certain day (cell O9) and be completed by a certain day (P11), and there is an average number of units or quantities not to exceed per week (Q9:Q11). The target cell is the maximum number of units on the project (Q7), or any quantity you specify. Figure 36.18 shows the parameters for the first problem in the constraints box beneath the Gantt chart setup.

> **Note**
>
> This workbook includes special color formatting to help make the model easier to follow. You may want to open the file from the CD while reading the description in this section.

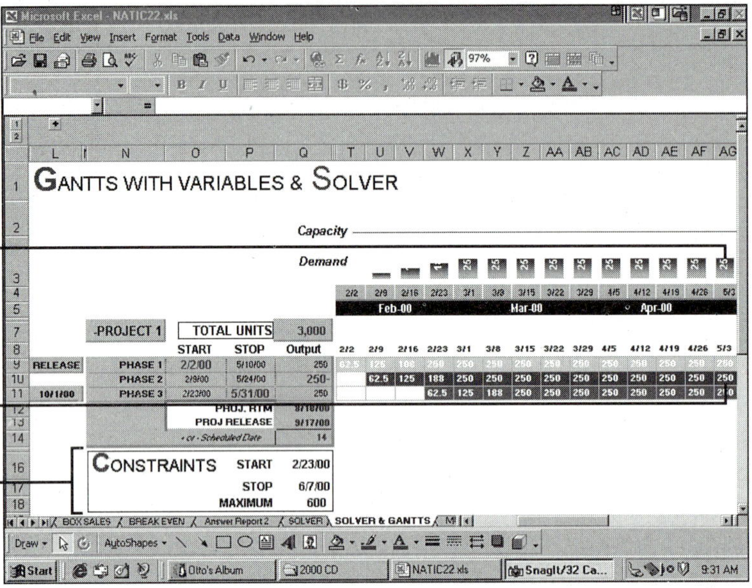

Figure 36.17.
Using Solver to optimize production models can answer questions in seconds rather than running the scenarios manually.

Current demand

Demand based on Phase 2

Constraints used with Solver parameters

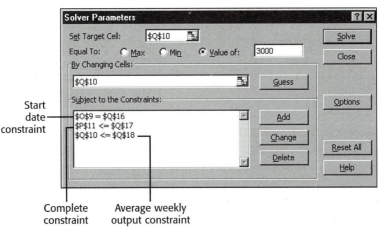

Figure 36.18.
The Solver constraints give the project a start date, stop date (or at least completed by), total quantity of units to produce, and a maximum average weekly output.

Start date constraint

Complete constraint

Average weekly output constraint

The following list describes the issues affecting the problem:

- The original planned start date was 2/2/00, but the constraint start date is 2/23/00, indicating that the project is starting later than planned.

- The original stop date was 5/10/00, but the project must be completed by the constraint set at 5/31/00.

- The current weekly output is 250 units per week per phase, and the constraint is set not to exceed 600.

Figure 36.19 shows the solution.

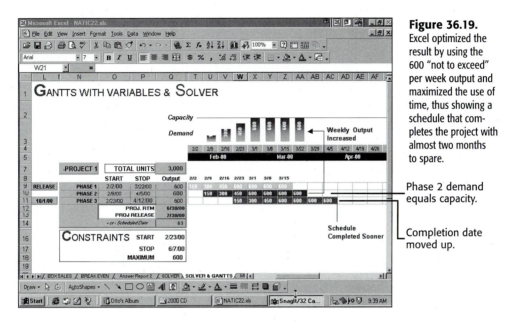

Figure 36.19.
Excel optimized the result by using the 600 "not to exceed" per week output and maximized the use of time, thus showing a schedule that completes the project with almost two months to spare.

A MULTIPLE-PROJECT SOLVER SCENARIO

Based on the previous example and understanding how to apply constraints to production models, suppose that you have teams that have to be managed and quantities and dates you must adhere to. Solver can take multiple projects and multiple constraints and determine the optimum solution to the problem. In the example in Figure 36.20, the multiple projects overlap, and Phase 2 of each project is the critical path in the production of the project. The total units of Phase 2 are summed at the bottom, starting in cell T22.

The constraints are called out at the bottom as Start and Stop dates for each project and a maximum total output per week. On any given week, your total capacity to produce equals 600 units, but the example shows several weeks in excess of 1,000 units output in row 22. By applying the constraint to the total at the bottom, it will also take into account your capacity to produce, and find a solution. If the example isn't possible, Excel will still find the optimum solution, given the parameters of the constraints.

Figure 36.20.
Excel can analyze critical-path production and cycle teams, phases, or machines by applying the right constraints with the production model.

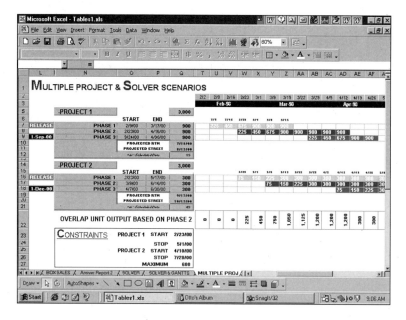

Figure 36.21 shows the parameters used for this example. Notice how many cells are going to be changed based on the parameters or constraints supplied. I've established all the start and stop dates, as well as the maximum quantity per week not to exceed—not only per project, but also based on the overlap range starting in cell T22. This means the total capacity to output cannot exceed 600 per week for the company as a whole, so the projects' time and output will have to be modified to fit all these variables into the Solver parameters.

Figure 36.21.
You can place multiple constraints of start and stop dates and quantities not to exceed, and Excel will find the optimum solution, taking all the variables into account.

The settings are as follows:

- The original start date for project 1 is set at 2/9/00 and, based on the constraints, will start on 2/23 in cell Q23. The original stop date from 4/30/00 will be constrained to 5/1/00. The maximum not to exceed per week currently is 900 and will be constrained to 600 in cell Q27.

- The original start date for project 2 is set at 2/23/00 and will be constrained to 4/10/00. The stop date from 6/30/00 will move to the constraint date of 7/28/00. The weekly not to exceed is constrained at no more than 600 per week in cell Q27.

- The last constraint placed on the model will ensure that each weekly overlap unit output for Phase 2 (row 22) will not exceed the maximum output of 600 in cell Q27.

- The change range is from T22:BB22, which is the sum of Phase 2 of both projects carried out through the length of the timeline.

Figure 36.22 shows overlap per week exceeding the weekly capacity to output in row 22. Figure 36.23 shows all the constraints placed on the project. Excel found the optimum solution.

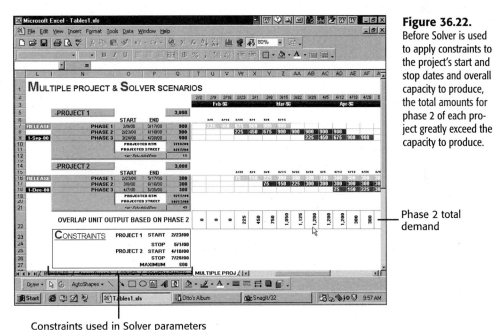

Figure 36.22.
Before Solver is used to apply constraints to the project's start and stop dates and overall capacity to produce, the total amounts for phase 2 of each project greatly exceed the capacity to produce.

Phase 2 total demand

Constraints used in Solver parameters

Figure 36.23.
After Solver applies the constraints to the production model, Excel provides the optimum solution, solving the problem and maintaining efficient project production flow.

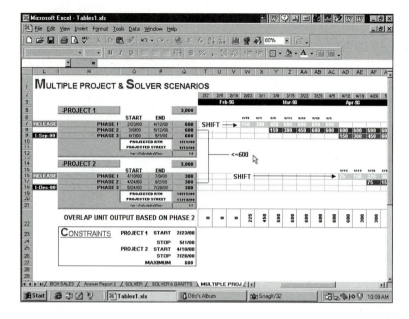

CREATING AMORTIZATION TABLES TO CALCULATE MORTGAGE PAYMENTS

Excel's Table feature helps you to create structured tables for calculating mortgage and lease payments, depreciation, and so on. Suppose that you want to purchase a house; you need to see the mortgage rate based on variable percentages and mortgage amounts. Here, you would use the PMT function to create a table to provide the mortgage rate, as shown in Figure 36.24. The schedule in cells F5:F19 is calculated based on a total loan amount of $100,000 on a 30-year mortgage, with percentage rates starting at 5 percent and increasing in .5 percent increments.

Following is the syntax for the PMT function used to create the table:

The PMT function calculates the loan payment for a loan based on constant payments and constant interest rates. This is the syntax:

```
=PMT(rate,nper,pv,fv,type)
```

- *rate*. The interest rate on the borrowed money. The percentage rate per payment period.

- *nper*. The number of payment periods of the loan. One year has 12 periods. Technically, PMT can be used to calculate a yearly payment instead of the typical monthly payment scenario. That having been said, one year could be one period.

- *pv*. The amount of money borrowed or loaned at the beginning of the transaction. A positive *pv* results in a negative payment and vice versa. (Add a negative sign to this argument to display the result as a positive number.)

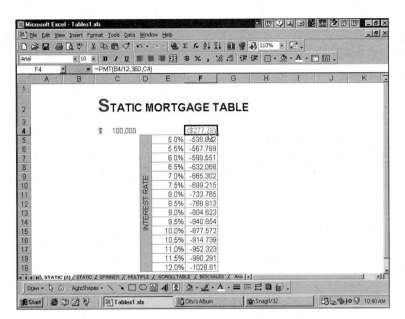

Figure 36.24.
A simple mortgage table calculates the mortgage payments based on the interest rate and the total mortgage.

- *fv*. The future value defines the amount of value remaining at the end of the loan. This might be used for a balloon payment at the end of a loan. The *fv* argument is optional; if not provided, Excel assumes it's zero.

- *type*. The *type* argument is also optional, and determines whether payments on the loan are made at the beginning of the pay period or the end of the pay period. Providing a 0 (or leaving it blank) means the payments are at the end of each period, and providing a 1 means they're at the beginning of each pay period.

To set up a single-variable table, follow these steps:

1. In the first cell in the table, type the first interest rate percentage—for this example, you would type **5%** in cell E5.

2. In the next cell down, type a formula to increase the first percentage by the increment amount. In this example, the increment is .5%, so the formula in cell E6 is =E5+0.005. This will add .5 percent to the previous percentage. Then drag the formula down to the bottom row of the table (cell E19 in this case, which will equal 12 percent, which is the maximum interest rate you're willing to pay).

3. In the trigger cell (cell C4 in this case), type the mortgage amount—for this example, $100,000.

4. In the target cell (cell F4 in this case), type the payment function. Here, the formula is =PMT(B4/12,360,C4) where B4/12 is the monthly interest rate, 360 is the term (30 years is 360 months), and C4 equals the total mortgage. Where cell B4 is a placeholder of zero (Excel assigns a value of zero to a blank cell referenced in a numeric formula), Excel uses the placeholder to calculate the payment needed to amortize the loan at zero percent.

The reason you place the mortgage in a cell rather than in the formula is that all you have to do then is change the mortgage amount. The formula references the cell and the table automatically changes, instead of your having to go into the formula and change the mortgage every time. To maximize the flexibility, you could also place the period value in a cell.

5. Select the range you want to fill. In Figure 36.25, I've deleted the previous table to rebuild the example.

Figure 36.25.
Select the total range to build the table.

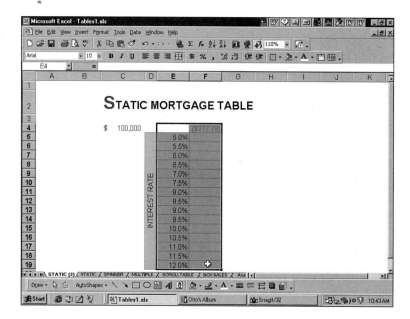

6. Choose Data, Table. Excel displays the Table dialog box shown in Figure 36.26. Because the interest rates in this example are listed down a column, we use the Column Input Cell box to look for the interest rate used in the PMT function.

7. Click OK to build the table (see Figure 36.27).

Notice that by changing the mortgage amount from $100,000 to $600,000, the table automatically responds (see Figure 36.28).

Figure 36.26.
The input cell is the payment needed to amortize a loan, at zero percent in this case.

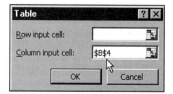

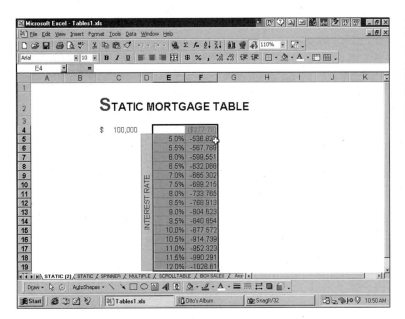

Figure 36.27.
The final result shows the mortgage payments in the body of the table, based on the corresponding percentage and mortgage amount.

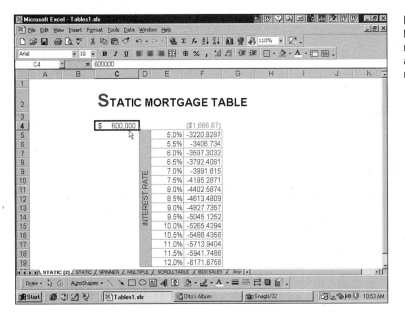

Figure 36.28.
By changing the mortgage, the table automatically responds.

The new table is in the form of an array, which means that you can't change the table, although you can move or delete the table (notice the entry in the Formula bar in Figure 36.29). You can apply tricks to get around this limitation, however. You could copy the table and paste it as values using Paste Special, or you could simply re-create the table with a mirrored table using =. Figure 36.30 shows a mirrored table. Using a simple formula that repeats the entries in the first table (starting with cell E5), you can drag the formula to pick up all the entries in the table, which you then can manipulate.

Figure 36.29.
The table formula.

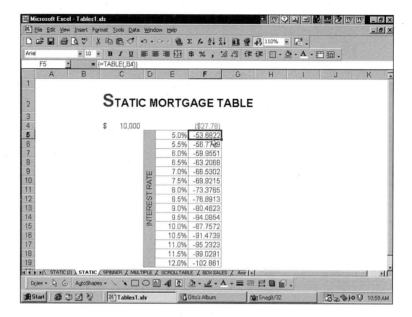

Figure 36.30.
Create a mirrored table to get around the array formula, thus allowing you to manipulate the formula.

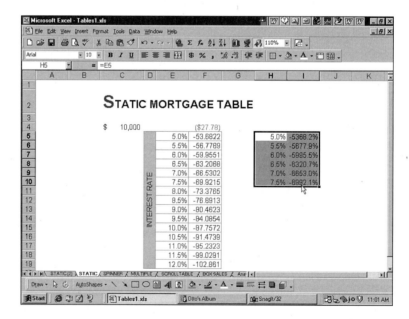

CREATING ACTIVE TABLES WITH SPINNERS AND CHARTS

If your data tables are large, you can add special features such as *form controls* to make the tables easier to read and use. I've applied a *spinner* to the mortgage table in Figure 36.31. However, because the spinner control allows for a maximum value of 30,000, I use a multiplier in a different cell (cell C4 in this example) that multiplies the cell link in cell A1 times 50, so with every incremental change to the spinner control, it multiplies the cell link by 50.

→ For details on creating form controls, **see** "Adding Form Controls to Your Worksheets," **p. 1094**

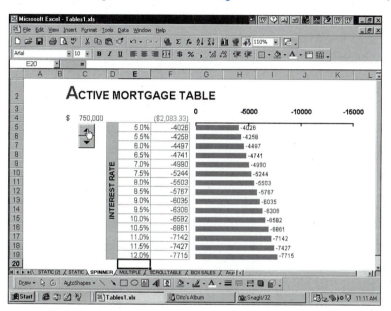

Figure 36.31.
Use spinners with multipliers to drive tables.

Tip #454

The chart could actually be used in place of the table column F by hiding column F. If you do this, be sure to plot all cells, not just visible cells.

When creating the spinner, set the cell link to cell A1 in the Format Control dialog box (see Figure 36.32). Set the maximum value to 30,000 and the minimum to 0, and the incremental change to 1000. This means the maximum value the spinner will go up to is 30,000, and the lowest value is 0. By adding the multiplier, we can make the mortgage table more flexible; with each click on the spin arrow, the mortgage change will be 1,000.

Type the multiplier formula in the table reference cell (cell C4 in this example), as shown in Figure 36.33. The formula references the cell link—the current value of the spinner—and multiplies it by 50 to give you the current principal.

Figure 36.32.
Set the cell link, minimum and maximum values, as well as the incremental change as shown.

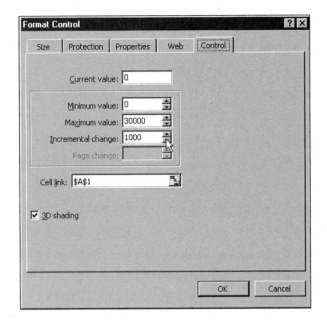

Figure 36.33.
Type the multiplier formula in cell C4, the table reference cell.

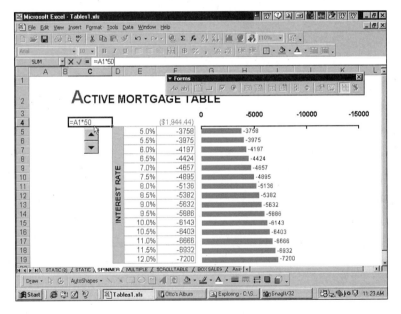

Clicking the spinner increases or decreases the mortgage amount, as shown in Figure 36.34.

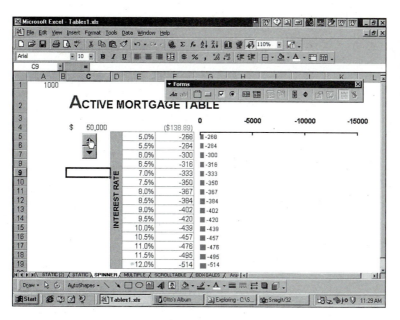

Figure 36.34.
Activate the control
by pressing the up or
down arrow to make
the table more inter-
active.

MULTIPLE-VARIABLE TABLES

After learning the basic one-variable table, you can apply multiple variables to make an
expanded table, referenced to different mortgage amounts (see Figure 36.35). In the previous examples, you typed in the new mortgage amounts. In this instance, you reference the
different cells across columns in the formula to create a broader-based table.

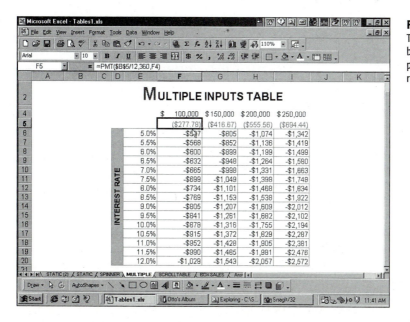

Figure 36.35.
To create a broad-
based table, the
payment formula
references cell F4.

ADDING SCROLLBARS TO THE MORTGAGE TABLE

By adding scrollbars to a table, you can span hundreds of rows and columns in a window of a few rows and columns. In the example in Figure 36.36, the interest is scrolled down to zero percent and the loan amount is scrolled back to 0 in the first column (cell F6). When you scroll up, the maximum interest rate in this example is 13.7% and the maximum mortgage is $1,150,000. It normally would take multiple rows and columns of information to span this list; however, with the proper use of scrollbars, you can create a window in which the table will scroll.

Figure 36.36.
You can span the range of hundreds of rows and columns.

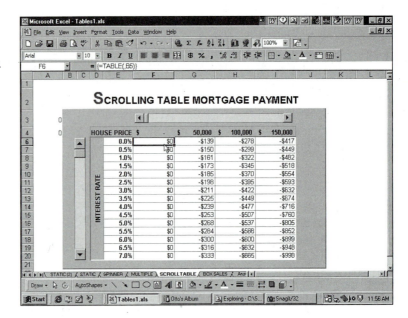

To create a scrolling window, follow these steps:

1. Create the same table setup as in the multiple-variable tables shown previously.

2. In cell E6, the beginning of the interest rate column, type the formula `=A4/150`, where A4 will equal the cell link for the vertical scrollbar form control.

3. In cell F4, type the formula `=$A$3*10,000`, where A3 is the cell link (note the absolute reference). Drag the formula to the right to I4.

4. Draw the scrollbar next to the interest rates, right-click it, and select Format Control (see Figure 36.37).

5. Format the control as follows:

Current Value = 0

Minimum Value = 0

Maximum Value = 10

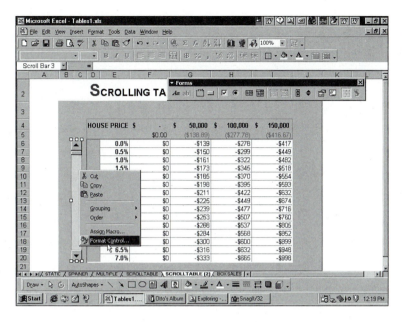

Figure 36.37.
Draw the control and then right-click and select Format Control.

Incremental Change = 1

Page Change = 10

Cell Link = A4

These settings mean that the maximum value the scrollbar will reach is 10 and the lowest value is 0; each click will change the value by 1.

6. Click OK.

7. Draw the horizontal scrollbar above the house price. Right-click it and choose Format Control. Set the format control as follows:

Current Value = 0

Minimum Value = 0

Maximum Value = 100

Incremental Change = 10

Page Change = 10

Cell Link = A3

8. Click OK to finish formatting the scrollbar.

USING THE ANALYSIS TOOLPAK ADD-IN

Excel's *Analysis ToolPak* (accessed by choosing Tools, Data Analysis) enables you to perform complex and sophisticated statistical analyses, with 17 statistical commands and 47 mathematical functions. From creating a random distribution of numbers to performing regression analysis, the tools can provide the essential calculations to solve just about any problem.

Note

You may need to enable the add-in before you can use it (choose Tools, Add-Ins, and select the Analysis ToolPak in the list of add-ins).

Table 36.2 describes the various tools.

TABLE 36.2. TOOLS IN THE ANALYSIS TOOLPAK

Tool	What It Does
ANOVA: Single Factor	Simple variance analysis
ANOVA: Two-Factor	Variance analysis that includes more than one sample of data for each group
ANOVA: Two-Factor Without Replication	Variance analysis that doesn't include more than one sample of data for each group
Correlation	Measurement—independent correlation between data sets
Covariance	Measurement—dependent covariance between data sets
Descriptive Statistics	Report of univariate statistics for sample
Exponential Smoothing	Smooths data, weighting more recent data heavier
F-Test: Two-Sample for Variance	Two-sample F-Test to compare population variances
Histogram	Counts occurrences in each of several data bins
Moving Average	Smooths data series by averaging the last few periods
Random number generation	Creates any of several types of random numbers: Uniform: Uniform random numbers between upper and lower bounds Normal: Normally distributed numbers based on the mean and the standard deviation Bernoulli: Ones and zeros with a specified probability of success Poisson: A distribution of random numbers given a desired lambda Patterned: A sequence of numbers at a specific interval Discrete: Probabilities based on the predefined percents of total
Rank and Percentile	Creates a report of ranking and percentile distribution
Regression	Creates a table of statistics that result from least-squares regression
t-Test: Paired Two Sample for Means	Paired two-sample students t-test
t-Test: Two Sample Assuming Equal Variances	Paired two-sample t-test assuming equal means

Tool	What It Does
t-Test: Two Sample Assuming Unequal Variances	Heteroscedastic t-test
z-Test: Two-Sample for Means	Two-sample z-test for means with known variances
Fourier Analysis	DFT or FFT method, including reverse transforms
Sampling	Samples a population randomly or periodically

The analysis tools all work in basically the same way. Choose Tools, Data Analysis to display the Data Analysis dialog box (see Figure 36.38). Select the tool you want to use, and click OK to display a separate dialog box for that particular tool.

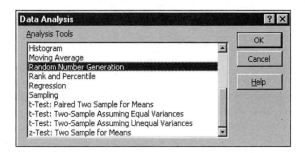

Figure 36.38.
The Data Analysis dialog box.

For example, suppose you want to generate random data sets to perform analysis of calls at your company's call center, based on historical data. By far the simplest method to achieve a random sampling is using the Random Number Generation tool, which creates realistic sample data sets between ranges that you specify.

To create a random sampling, select the Random Number Generation tool in the Data Analysis dialog box. When you click OK, Excel displays the Random Number Generation dialog box, in which you can specify the parameters for the data set you want. For the example in Figure 36.39, I want two columns of variables, each of which contains 15 random numbers in uniform distribution, between 50 and 100. (Seven different distribution generators are available; refer to Table 36.2 for descriptions.)

If you don't specify a particular number for variables or random numbers, Excel fills the cells in the output range.

Figure 36.40 shows the result. Figure 36.41 shows how you can use this data set for multiple analyses—just tie the analysis results to formulas, charts, and PivotTables.

Figure 36.39.
Use the Random
Number Generation
dialog box to set
parameters for
your data.

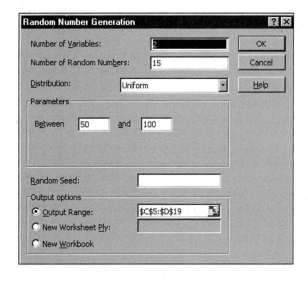

Figure 36.40.
Two sets of random
numbers between
50 and 100.

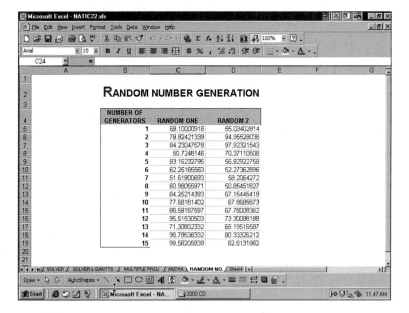

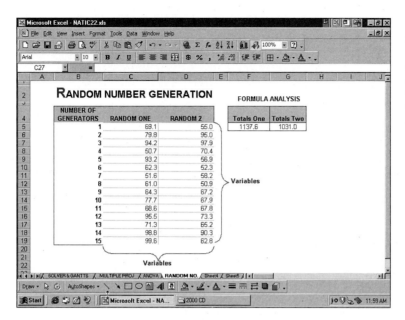

Figure 36.41.
Set up the desired range so you can create the analysis over and over, and tie the analysis to formulas, charts, and PivotTables.

INTEGRATION

CHAPTER 37

INTEGRATING WITH MICROSOFT OFFICE

In this chapter

WORD AND OFFICE: MORE TIGHTLY INTEGRATED THAN EVER

One of Word's most important strengths is its tight integration with Microsoft Excel, Access, PowerPoint, Publisher, and the rest of Office 2000. These programs extend Word's power, and knowing how to use them with Word will make you much more productive. In Office 2000, Office's main applications are more tightly integrated than ever. In this chapter, you'll learn to leverage all of Microsoft Office to make Word an even more powerful tool.

> **Note**
>
> To work with Excel, PowerPoint, Outlook, Publisher, or Access, you must first install them, either as part of Microsoft Office or as standalone applications.

Communicating with Word: Integrate

The integration tools offered by Office 2000 can be used to prevent an administrative headache. You may use a Word document on the Web to promote your company with a specific page showing your company's personnel profile and another page with the company's sales performance for the past quarter. Instead of manually updating these pages each time you use the presentation, you can use the integration tools to link the source documents to your document. That way as the information changes, you can load the page in Word and refresh the links.

INTEGRATING EXCEL AND WORD

Word 2000 can perform a surprising number of calculations all by itself, as you learned in the "Calculating with Tables" section in Chapter 5, "Tables: Organizing Your Pages." However, it's not a dedicated spreadsheet program like Microsoft Excel.

Luckily, if you've installed Excel, you can call on it whenever you need extra number-crunching power. You can insert Excel spreadsheets or charts when you need the extra number-crunching power. Or perhaps you just want to take advantage of work already completed in one program, so you can avoid redoing it in another.

This integration between Word and Excel is a two-way street. Excel offers tremendous mathematical prowess, but it's obviously more limited than Word when it comes to creating and formatting complex documents. You can use Word to present your Excel data in a format that communicates the information more effectively than Excel could alone.

Moreover, the connection between Word and Excel is as lively as you want it to be. If, for example, you link your quarterly report to sales data kept in three different files (gathered by three different sales representatives) on your company's network, every time you open or print the report, your numbers are updated. Just as importantly, you can also set the links to not update automatically, so you can always generate an accurate archival record of a project as it existed at a given point in time.

You can use several techniques to bring Excel data into Word; none are overly complicated and some are downright simple. In the next section, you'll leverage Excel's mathematical capabilities in Word by integrating a new Excel worksheet into a Word document.

INSERTING A NEW EXCEL WORKSHEET IN A WORD DOCUMENT

In Chapter 5, you learned how you can use Word to add numbers in a table or insert a field that can calculate a formula anywhere in a document, using basic arithmetic operations and functions. You may well find, however, that you need to perform calculations beyond Word's capability. Fortunately, you can tap Excel's powerful capabilities without leaving Word.

PART
IX
CH
37

Note

Of course, you need to know how to use Excel to take advantage of its features. But, as an Office application, Excel shares Word's interface—somewhat smoothing the learning curve.

INSERTING AN EXCEL WORKSHEET OF A SPECIFIC SIZE

If you need to create a new set of data that is reasonably compact, Word enables you to insert a blank Excel worksheet of specific proportions. The higher your screen resolution, the more rows and columns you can insert. To insert a worksheet using the toolbar button, click in your document where you want the worksheet to appear and click the Insert Microsoft Excel Worksheet button on the toolbar. A grid appears (see Figure 37.1). Drag the mouse pointer down and across the grid to define the size of your worksheet. The worksheet appears in your Word document.

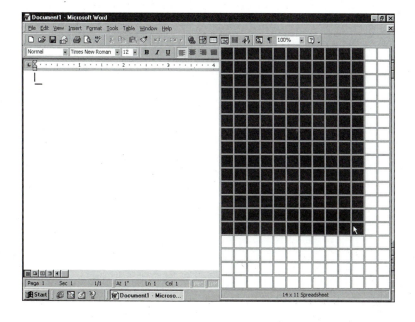

Figure 37.1
Dragging the Insert Excel Worksheet grid to insert a worksheet with specific proportions.

INSERTING AN EXCEL WORKSHEET THROUGH MENU COMMANDS

Another way to insert a new Excel worksheet is through menu commands. Choose Insert, Object to open the Object dialog box (see Figure 37.2). From the Create New tab, scroll down the Object Type list until you see Microsoft Excel Worksheet. Double-click it to insert the worksheet and close the dialog box.

The default worksheet is 7 columns wide by 10 rows high. Since this procedure can only insert a sheet of the default size, you may have to adjust the size manually afterward.

Figure 37.2
Inserting a new Excel worksheet through the Object dialog box.

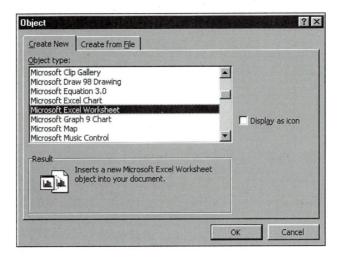

> **Note**
>
> You can use the Object dialog box to create an object corresponding to any OLE-compliant program installed on your computer. Simply choose the type of object you want to create in the Object Type scroll box.

 Inserting a new worksheet through the Object dialog box gives you one option you don't have if you use the Insert Microsoft Excel Worksheet toolbar button. You can choose to insert the worksheet as an icon, rather than display the data itself in your document (see Figure 37.3). To do so, check the Display as Icon check box.

After you insert the icon, you can double-click on it to edit the Excel worksheet in a separate Excel window.

When would you display a worksheet (or any other object) as an icon? When you won't need to print it, and when you're running Word and Excel on a relatively slow computer. You still have access to the live data, but Word runs a bit faster, because it needs to display only an icon representing the worksheet except when you are actually working with the data.

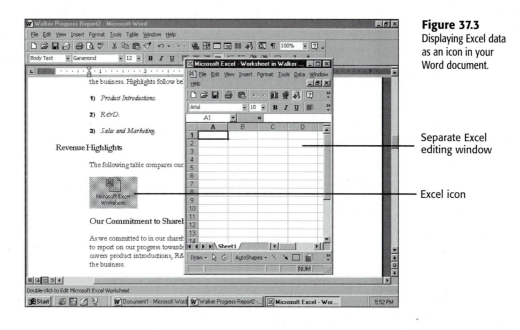

Figure 37.3
Displaying Excel data
as an icon in your
Word document.

Separate Excel
editing window

Excel icon

Tip #455

If you choose to display worksheet cells in your document, and later decide you prefer to
display an icon—or vice versa—you can easily swap between the two options. Right-click on
the object to display the shortcut menu and choose Worksheet Object, Convert. The
Convert dialog box appears (see Figure 37.4). Check or clear the Display as Icon check box
and click OK.

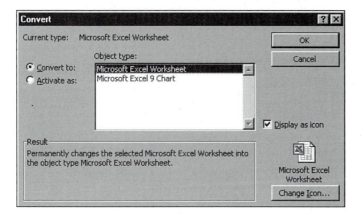

Figure 37.4
Converting worksheet
cells to an icon, or
vice versa.

 *If you open, edit, and save an Excel worksheet in Word, and then cannot reopen it in Excel, see "What
to Do If You Can't Open a Worksheet in Excel After You Edit and Save It in Word," in the
"Troubleshooting" section of this chapter.*

IMPORTING EXCEL OBJECTS

In the previous sections, you learned how to insert a blank Excel worksheet. But it's equally likely that you'll already have an Excel workbook containing the data you want to include. Many users prefer to create their data first, in Excel, before inserting the data into a Word document.

If you already have an Excel worksheet, Microsoft gives you plenty of options for incorporating it into a Word document. For example, you can

- Import a copy of an entire existing Excel workbook
- Import a linked version of an existing Excel workbook
- Insert a range of cells from Excel as a table in Word
- Insert a range of cells from Excel into Word and retain all the Excel formatting
- Insert a range of cells as a link from Excel to Word

Note

A word about terminology: An Excel file is called a *workbook*. Workbooks consist of one or more *worksheets*—individual "pages" of the spreadsheet that can be displayed separately.

When you insert a blank worksheet into your Word document, Excel creates a workbook consisting of a single worksheet. If you insert an existing workbook, you need to pay attention to whether you're inserting one worksheet or several. Later in this section, you'll learn how to control which parts of a workbook you insert.

When you insert a workbook with multiple sheets, only the active cells in the first sheet are visible, and only those cells print. However, if you double-click on the workbook to edit it, you can choose to display the active cells from a different sheet by clicking on that sheet's tab at the bottom of the Excel window.

IMPORTING AN ENTIRE WORKBOOK

To import an entire workbook that already exists, follow these steps:

1. Choose Insert, Object.
2. Click the Create from File tab (see Figure 37.5).
3. Unless you know the exact filename and path, click Browse. The Browse dialog box appears, which looks like a standard Open File dialog box. (If you do know the filename and path, you can simply enter it in the File Name text box, in place of the *.* characters that are present when you display this tab.)
4. Browse to and select your file.
5. Click Insert.
6. Click OK.

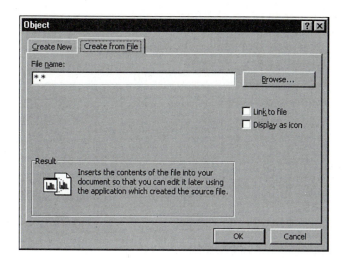

Figure 37.5
Creating an object
from an existing file.

PART

IX

Cᴴ

37

Tip #456

You've already learned how to embed a Microsoft Excel object; you can do the same thing with any kind of object, including a PowerPoint presentation, a Visio graphic, or any other file created in an OLE-compatible application–from Microsoft or anyone else.

CHOOSING HOW TO IMPORT YOUR WORKBOOK

Word gives you three options for how to import a workbook as an object:

- By default, Word embeds the workbook's contents in your document. You can edit them in Excel, but there is no connection to the original file, and if the original file changes, the change is not reflected in the Word document.

- Check the Link to File check box in the Create from File tab. This not only inserts the contents of the Excel worksheet, it also establishes a link to the source file, so that updates to the source file can be reflected in the Word document.

- Check the Display as Icon check box in the Create from File tab. You've already learned that this option displays an icon in place of the worksheet cells; you can double-click the icon to open the worksheet in a separate editing window.

After you confirm your choice by clicking OK in the Object dialog box, a copy of the entire Excel workbook is inserted in your Word document as an object.

LINKING TO THE SOURCE FILE: ADVANTAGES AND DISADVANTAGES

When you choose Link to File, you're no longer working with a copy of the original file; you're working with the actual file. When you are working in Word and double-click the Excel object to edit it, Excel opens the workbook in another window and any changes you make are incorporated into the source file. Likewise, with a linked object, any changes you make in the source file are reflected in the linked version.

Inserting a workbook as a linked file is both a blessing and a curse. The good news is that all your updates are centralized and you don't have to worry about making changes in both Excel and Word. On the other hand, sometimes you want to lock in your report data after a certain point. Luckily, Word 2000 lets you have it both ways.

> **Caution**
>
> Linking worksheets into a document creates a path to the spreadsheets on your local/networked drive. If you send a file containing links to a colleague via email or on a floppy disk, you need to send the linked files as well. If the linked files are in a different folder, you might need to place all the linked files in the same folder as the original file, and edit the links to match for your colleague to adequately use the links.

 If you cannot create a link to a worksheet you recently created, see "What to Do If You Cannot Link Cells from an Excel Worksheet," in the "Troubleshooting" section of this chapter.

MODIFYING AN OBJECT'S LINKS

After you have embedded a linked object into your Word document, the Edit, Links option becomes active. Choosing this menu option opens the Links dialog box, as seen in Figure 37.6. From here you can choose to update your link automatically, manually, or to completely lock the link.

 If the Manual option is chosen, you must select the object (or the entire document) and press F9 or the Update Now button from the Links dialog box. Locking the link deactivates the Update Now button and prevents any updates from occurring until the link is unlocked. Your original Excel file can still be edited, but the Word file cannot be updated to reflect them.

Figure 37.6
You can modify a linked object's status at any time through the Links dialog box.

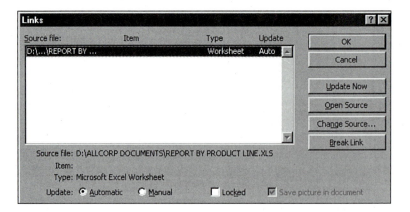

RESIZING A WORKSHEET TO FIT

Often, after you insert an Excel worksheet, you'll discover that it is larger than your Word page. If this occurs, Word will display as much of your worksheet as it can, up to the edge of the page. Remaining cells beyond the edge are cut off, and not displayed. Figure 37.7 shows an example of this.

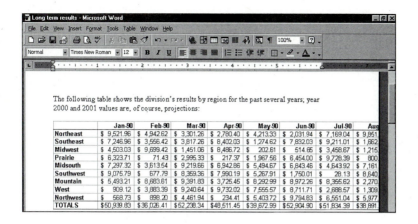

Figure 37.7
An inserted worksheet that's too wide to be read.

In some cases, making page setup adjustments can solve the problem. For example, to accommodate a worksheet that's too wide, you can change your page to Landscape mode. To change the page to Landscape, click on the worksheet object once to select it and choose File, Page Setup. Click the Paper Size tab and select the Landscape option button. Choose Selected Text in the Apply To drop-down box and then click OK.

If Page Setup changes are insufficient, Word gives you two ways to resize a worksheet object, which are covered in the next two sections.

RESIZING A WORKSHEET WITHOUT CHANGING THE NUMBER OF CELLS DISPLAYED

The first approach to resizing a worksheet retains the same number of cells, but shrinks or stretches the contents of each cell, changing font sizes if necessary. This approach is especially helpful if you need to make minor sizing adjustments, and cannot change the number of cells that appear in your document. To resize the worksheet, click on the worksheet object once to select it—black sizing handles appear (see Figure 37.8). Click and drag a sizing handle to the proportions you want and then release the mouse button.

Caution

If you need to shrink the worksheet extensively, the cells may become too small to be read comfortably.

Object borders

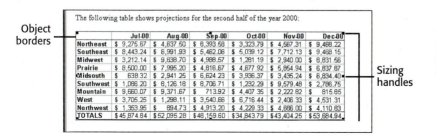

Sizing handles

Figure 37.8
When you click on an Excel object, sizing handles appear within solid line borders.

CHANGING THE NUMBER OF CELLS DISPLAYED IN YOUR DOCUMENT

Sometimes you may need to change the number of cells that appear in your Word document. For example, you may have to show fewer cells to make the information fit. Conversely, your worksheet may have changed and you need to show more cells. Perhaps you've added several new products and you need to display several additional rows of data about them in your Word document.

To adjust both the size of your worksheet object and the number of cells shown in it, follow these steps:

1. Double-click on the worksheet to edit it. Excel's menus and tools appear, and the worksheet is surrounded by diagonal cross-hatching (see Figure 37.9).

2. Drag one of the sizing handles inward or outward to adjust the proportions of the worksheet.

3. Click outside the worksheet: The new proportions appear in your Word document.

Figure 37.9
When you double-click on an Excel object, sizing handles appear within diagonal cross-hatch borders.

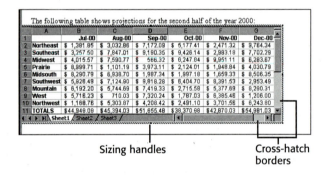

Sizing handles   Cross-hatch borders

Note

Note that when you single-click an Excel worksheet in a Word document, and drag its borders to change its shape, the existing cells are stretched or squeezed. However, when you double-click an Excel worksheet to edit its contents, you can change the number of rows and columns displayed, or the height and width of individual rows and columns.

INSERTING A RANGE OF CELLS

Most of the time, you won't need to insert an entire Excel workbook into your Word document, just a specific range of cells. The process for doing this is one you're familiar with: Cut and Paste. As noted previously, you can achieve three different results when you insert a range of Excel cells: They can appear as a Word table, as an independent Excel object, or as a linked Excel object. The following sections cover each of these alternatives.

PASTING CELLS AS A WORD TABLE   The simplest method of transferring data is to select and copy it from Excel and paste it into Word by clicking the Paste button on the Standard toolbar or pressing Ctrl+V. If you have highlighted a range of cells, the pasted entry is converted into a Word table. Numbers are right-justified, and formulas become values. Most formatting is retained, with the exception of spanned columns, which can be simulated by selecting the cells in question and choosing Table, Merge Cells. Cutting and pasting is a good alternative for simple, fixed data where there is little or no chance of the former formulas needing to be recalculated.

> **Caution**
>
> When a range of Excel cells are copied and pasted into a Word document, the table in which the data appears is formatted with borders turned on for each cell and around the entire table, whether or not the selected cells have borders in Excel. To change or eliminate the border, you must select the table in Word and choose Format, Borders and Shading and select your options.

PASTING CELLS AS A WORKSHEET OBJECT If you even think it's remotely possible that you'll need to update your numbers and recalculate your formulas, it's best to paste the Excel data as an object. The process is basically the same as regular cutting and pasting, with one little twist: You use Edit, Paste Special instead of the Paste command. Follow these steps to insert Excel information as an object:

1. From Excel, select the range of cells you want to insert.

2. Click the Copy button on the Standard toolbar.

3. Switch to your Word document.

4. Place the insertion point where you want the data to appear.

5. Choose Edit, Paste Special. (Paste Special does not normally appear on the Edit menu; you may have to open the menu and wait a second for it to show.) The Paste Special dialog box opens, as shown in Figure 37.10.

6. From the As list, select Microsoft Excel Worksheet Object.

7. If you want to establish a link to your source document, click the Paste Link option button; otherwise, leave the Paste option button selected.

8. If you want to display the worksheet as an icon, check the Display as Icon check box.

9. Click OK to insert the object.

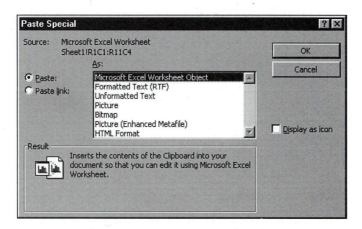

Figure 37.10
Paste Special enables you to maintain all your Excel data's formulas and formatting.

INSERTING WORKSHEET CELLS AS A WORD HYPERLINK   If you click Paste Link in the Paste Special dialog box, Word displays a new set of options for the kind of links you can create. One of these is a Word *hyperlink*.

If you paste the worksheet cells as a Word hyperlink, the worksheet cells appear in your document at your insertion point, with blue underline formatting. When you click on any of them, you're taken directly to the worksheet in Excel.

Note

To paste a spreadsheet into a document as a hyperlink, you can also select Paste as Hyperlink from the Edit menu.

WORKING IN A WORKSHEET YOU'VE INSERTED

Unless you insert your worksheet as an icon, the worksheet cells appear and are selected after you insert it. While the worksheet is selected, the standard Word menus and toolbars change to Excel menus and toolbars, as shown in Figure 37.11.

Figure 37.11
Word displays Excel's menus, toolbars, and other controls, and embeds a row-and-column worksheet within your document.

Excel menus ─

Excel Standard and Formatting toolbars

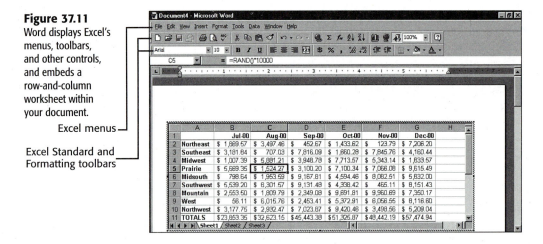

After you insert your worksheet, you'll notice the typical Excel layout with alphabetic column headings and numeric row headings. You can now enter and format your data and formulas in the worksheet's rows and columns as you would if you were working in Excel. You can also resize the columns just as you can in Excel—by moving your mouse pointer over the boundary of a column, then clicking and dragging the boundary to a new width.

Note

For all practical purposes, you are working in Excel: You just happen to be looking at it through a narrow portal provided by Word.

Tip #457

The most recent version of Excel supports multiple worksheets accessed by clicking one of the sheet tabs at the bottom of the Excel window.

When you finish editing inside the worksheet, click anywhere outside it, and your menus and toolbars return to their usual appearance, displaying Word commands. The borders of each cell are displayed in light, nonprinting gray. You can work inside the worksheet again at any time by double-clicking on it, or by right-clicking and choosing Worksheet Object, Edit from the shortcut menu.

If you've inserted the Excel worksheet cells with a link to an Excel workbook elsewhere, the changes you make to the worksheet cells are saved to the original workbook when you save your Word document. If you've inserted a new Excel workbook, the changes are saved only as part of the Word document, not as part of a separate workbook.

DELETING AN EXCEL WORKSHEET FROM A WORD DOCUMENT

To delete an Excel worksheet from your Word document, first make sure you're in Word editing mode (if the Excel layout is active, click outside of the worksheet into the regular document). Then select the object by clicking it once and press Delete.

If you have inserted a workbook with several worksheets, you can delete a single worksheet from within Word. Double-click on the worksheet to select it for editing and right-click on the worksheet tab you want to delete. Choose Delete from the Excel shortcut menu that appears.

CREATING MAPS AND CHARTS IN EXCEL

In Chapter 15, "Using Graphs to Make Sense of Your Data—Visually," you learned how to create charts in Microsoft Word, using the Microsoft Graph applet. However, you may have already built your charts in Excel. Word makes it easy to insert these charts into Word documents:

1. Starting in Excel, click on the chart to select it.

2. In Excel, click the Copy button on the Standard toolbar to copy the chart to the Clipboard.

3. Switch to Word and place your insertion point where you want the chart to appear.

4. If you don't need a link to the original chart, click the Paste button on the Standard toolbar. Otherwise, choose Edit, Paste Special.

5. If you want a link, click the Paste Link button.

6. Click OK.

In the Paste Special dialog box, Word gives you two options for the type of chart object you can create:

- **Microsoft Excel Chart Object.** This is the default setting, and it enables you to double-click on the chart to edit it in Excel.
- **Picture (Enhanced Metafile).** With this option selected, your picture is inserted as a bitmap that can be edited using tools such as Microsoft Paint or Microsoft Photo Editor.

INSERTING A MICROSOFT MAP IN YOUR WORD DOCUMENT

Both Word and Excel have access to a special program called Microsoft Map that enables you to chart data to a regional, national, or global map. Work in Excel to create your map, as follows:

1. Select the data you want to map. Make sure you're working with data that contains row or column headings corresponding to countries or states. For example, in Figure 37.12, a list of states has been selected, along with a row of data for sales of the "SweatSox" product.

2. Click the Map button in Excel's Standard toolbar, or if the button isn't present, choose Insert, Map.

Figure 37.12
Data formatted so that Excel can map it.

Mappable data —

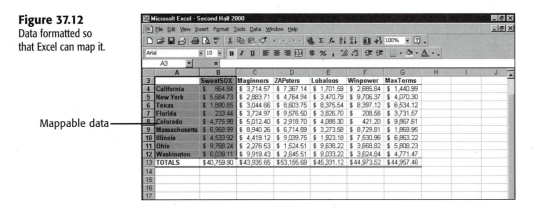

Note

If Microsoft Map does not run, you might need to run a maintenance setup to install it. Also, if the Map choice isn't available on the Insert menu, you might have to add it through Excel's Tools, Customize dialog box.

3. Click in the area of the spreadsheet where you want the map inserted.

4. If Excel asks you to choose among multiple maps, do so.

5. Excel inserts the map. Drag the mouse pointer to specify the borders of your map if necessary.

6. With the map selected, choose <u>E</u>dit, <u>C</u>opy. (There is no Copy button within Microsoft Map.)

7. Switch to Word and place your insertion point where you want the map to appear.

8. To control what kind of object Word inserts, choose <u>E</u>dit, Paste <u>S</u>pecial. (You can't insert a map with a link.)

9. By default, Word inserts a Microsoft Map Object. If you prefer to insert a Picture that can be edited with Word's drawing tools, choose Picture from the <u>A</u>s scroll box.

10. Click OK.

Figure 37.13 shows an example of a map inserted in a Word document.

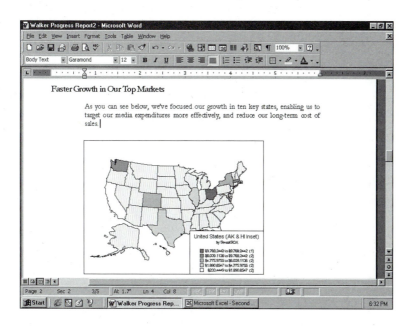

Figure 37.13
A map inserted in a Word document; the border has been added through Format, Object.

WORKING WITH ACCESS AND WORD

Increasingly, much of an office's day-to-day business involves keeping track of data. Take an overdue invoice notice, for example. Although the letter you send to your debtor is typically a word processing document, the key bits of information incorporated in it may well be stored in a database: the business name and address, invoice numbers, amount due, and so forth. Word's tight integration with Microsoft Access enables you to produce an unlimited number of reports, letters, labels, and other documents based on the same data source.

In Chapter 6, "Using Mail Merge Effectively," (see the section titled "Using an Access Database as a Data Source"), you walked step by step through creating a mail merge using a Microsoft Access database as a data source. This may be the most common scenario for using Access data in Word, but it's far from the only one. For example, you may want to

■ Incorporate specific, filtered elements of a database in a document you're creating, such as a discussion of new customers or sales opportunities

■ Create a report based entirely (or largely) on Access data, but utilize Word's more sophisticated formatting capabilities

Aside from mail merge, there are three ways to retrieve Access data for use in Word:

■ You can use Word's Database toolbar to specify which Access data you want, and manage it after you insert it. This technique often makes sense when you're incorporating Access data into a Word document that already exists.

■ You can use Access's Publish It with MS Word feature to build an RTF (Rich Text Format) file that can be edited and formatted in Word. If you're at least reasonably familiar with Access, this is the fastest way to create a Word document containing large amounts of Access data.

■ You can use Access's standard data export tools, which enable you to specify the name, placement, and type of file Access creates when it exports data.

The following sections walk you through each of these techniques. But first, the next section provides some background about databases and how Access works with Word.

→ For more information on running mail merges, **see** "An Overview of Word's Mail Merge," **p. 166**.

SOME IMPORTANT POINTS ABOUT ACCESS DATABASES

Remember that a database is made up of many records, each of which represents one business, person, or transaction. The records, in turn, are composed of a number of different fields. Each field represents one unique aspect of a record, such as a first name, a last name, a street address, a zip code, and so on. Databases are often represented as tables with each column representing a different field and each row a different record. The first row of the table is reserved for the field names and is called the header row.

In Access, you can enter field names of up to 64 characters with spaces and most special characters. However, if you're planning on using your database in Word, it's best to limit your field names to 20 or fewer characters and avoid spaces and any special characters other than the underscore. Otherwise, when you link your Word document with your Access database while setting up a mail merge, Word automatically truncates the field names to 20 characters and alters any spaces or special characters to the underscore character.

Word inserts your Access data just as it appears in Access. So if your AmountDue field isn't formatted to show dollars and cents in Access, it won't show up that way in Word. The same is true of date fields and text fields.

INTEGRATING MICROSOFT ACCESS DATA INTO AN EXISTING WORD DOCUMENT

Imagine you're writing a report to management that describes all the new sales opportunities your division has generated in the past 30 days. You've already written plenty of glowing prose about your sales team's hard work. Now it's time to get down to cases: Which companies represent the largest sales potential? The data is stored in Access. You want to include it in your Word report, in the form of a Word table. In this section, you'll learn how to make that happen.

Tip #458

If possible, it will help to familiarize yourself ahead of time with the specific Access database file you'll be using. For example, you need to know in which database tables the information you're seeking is stored, and which fields exist in those tables.

Follow these steps to import data into Word from Access:

1. Choose View, Toolbars, Database to display the Database toolbar (see Figure 37.14).

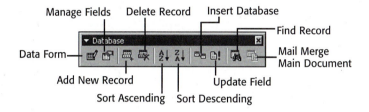

Manage Fields   Delete Record   Insert Database

Find Record

Data Form

Mail Merge
Main Document

Figure 37.14
The Database toolbar enables you to import and control database data.

Add New Record

Update Field

Sort Ascending   Sort Descending

2. Click the Insert Database button. The Database dialog box opens (see Figure 37.15).

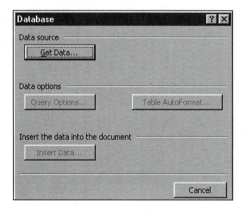

Figure 37.15
The first step in integrating Access data into a Word document is to click Get Data, and retrieve the data you need.

3. Click Get Data. The Open Data Source dialog box opens, which looks like a standard Open File dialog box.

4. In the Files of Type drop-down box, choose MS Access Databases.

Tip #459

If you wanted to insert another type of data source, such as an Excel worksheet, you would choose that option instead.

5. Browse to and select the database you want to use.

6. Click Open. The Microsoft Access dialog box opens (see Figure 37.16).

Figure 37.16
Choosing a database
table or preexisting
query.

7. Choose the table that contains the database fields you want to use. (Or, if a predefined query exists within Access that generates the data you want, click the Queries tab and choose the query instead.)

Note

If Microsoft Query does not run, you may need to run a maintenance setup to install it.

8. Click OK.

You've now connected your Access database to your Word document, but you haven't actually inserted any data yet. At this point, you have a choice:

- If you want to insert all the data in the database, or specific consecutive numbered records, you can click Insert Data in the Database dialog box, and work from there (see "Inserting Data Through the Insert Data Dialog Box," later in this chapter).

- If you want to create a more complex query, sort the information placed in your document, or choose which fields to include, click Query Options in the Database dialog box. The Query Options dialog box opens, offering options for specifying exactly which data to include in your Word document. Query Options is covered in the next section.

CREATING QUERY OPTIONS

As covered in the previous sections, you manage the process of importing data from Access through the Database dialog box. Once you've selected the file that contains your data, you specify which data you want to use by clicking Query Options in the Database dialog box.

Most of Word's database Query Options are covered at length in Chapter 6, in the section titled "Choosing the Records to Merge" Briefly, however:

- In the Filter Records tab (see Figure 37.17), you can filter which data appears, based on any field in the database table you've chosen. You can also use comparisons such as "Equal to" and "Is Not Blank" to refine the data further. Finally, you can establish six different criteria to widen or narrow the "data net" you're casting.

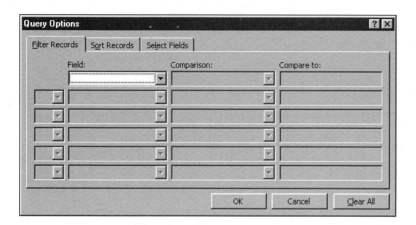

Figure 37.17
The Filter Records tab of the Query Options dialog box.

- In the Sort Records tab (see Figure 37.18), you can choose which field or fields to sort by. You can choose up to three sort fields, and specify whether each of them sort in ascending or descending order.

Figure 37.18
The Sort Records tab enables you to specify a sort order for your data, based on up to three fields.

- Finally, in the Select Fields tab—which is not available in mail merge—you can choose which fields from your data source are placed in your document. This tab is shown in Figure 37.19.

By default, every field in the data source is selected. To remove one field, highlight it in the Selected Fields scroll box, and click Remove. To remove all fields, click Remove All. You can then add fields back one at a time, by highlighting them in the Fields in Data Source scroll box and clicking Select.

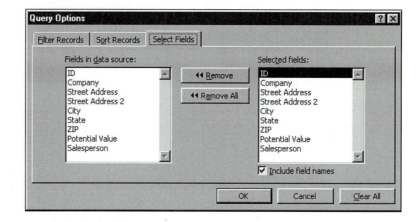

If you don't want a header row containing the field names, clear the Include Field Names check box. When you're finished, click OK.

AUTOFORMATTING YOUR DATA BEFORE YOU INSERT IT

In Chapter 9, you learned about Word's tools for AutoFormatting a table after you place it in your document. Because you might want to AutoFormat the information in the database you import, the Database dialog box (refer to Figure 37.15) enables you to choose Table AutoFormat before you place the information in your document.

After you complete the Get Data step and set Query Options (if any), click Table AutoFormat. The Table AutoFormat dialog box appears. Choose the Formats and other settings you want, and click OK to return to the Database dialog box.

INSERTING DATA THROUGH THE INSERT DATA DIALOG BOX

Now you're ready to insert the data. In the Database dialog box (refer to Figure 37.15), click Insert Data. The Insert Data dialog box opens (see Figure 37.20). Here, you have one last chance to refine your data. By default, Word searches the entire database for records that fit the query options you've already set. If you prefer to search only a specific range of numbered records, enter the range in the From and To text boxes.

Figure 37.20
In the Insert Data dia-
log box, you can
specify a range of
records, or specify
that data be inserted
as an updatable field.

Finally, if you want the data to be inserted as a { DATABASE } field that can be updated based on the source database file, check the Insert Data as Field check box. When you're finished, click OK. The information appears in your document (see Figure 37.21).

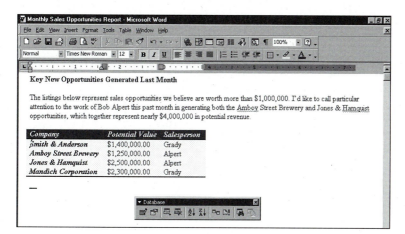

Figure 37.21
Formatted database data inserted in a Word document.

PART

IX

CH

37

→ For more information about working with fields, **see** Chapter 18, "Automating Your Documents with Field Codes," **p. 555**.

Tip #460

If you've inserted a { DATABASE } field linked to a database file, you can update the database information at any time by clicking inside the data in your document, and either pressing F9 or clicking the Update Field button on the Database toolbar.

USING THE DATABASE TOOLBAR TO MODIFY DATA PLACED IN YOUR DOCUMENT

After you've inserted database data in your document, the Database toolbar gives you tools for managing it. The following sections cover each of the tools.

VIEWING THE DATA IN A FORM

To display the data through a data form, which makes it easier for you to move among records and edit them, click Data Form. Figure 37.22 shows the navigation tools available in a data form.

→ For more information about working with data forms, **see** "Working with the Data Form," **p. 177**.

MANAGING FIELDS

To add, rename, or delete fields displayed in the table, click Manage Fields. The Manage Fields dialog box opens (see Figure 37.23).

Figure 37.22
The data form makes it easy to browse and edit the content of records you've inserted.

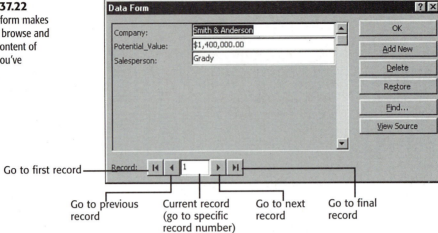

Go to first record —

Go to previous record

Current record (go to specific record number)

Go to next record

Go to final record

Figure 37.23
In the Manage Fields dialog box, you can add, rename, or remove fields from the database data in your document.

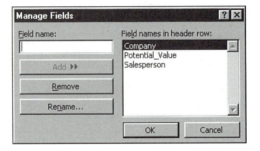

ADDING, DELETING, AND SORTING RECORDS

To add a blank line where you can enter an additional database record, click Add New Record.

To remove an existing record, click inside it, and click Delete Record.

To sort the records (excluding the header row), click Sort Ascending; or to sort in reverse order, click Sort Descending.

PUBLISHING ACCESS DATA TO WORD VIA OFFICE LINKS

Microsoft Access contains a powerful shortcut for exporting data to Word: the Publish It with MS Word feature, one of a family of "Office Links" features. To publish database information using this feature, open the Access database you want to use. You can publish to Word directly from an Access table, query, form, or report.

To publish to Word, select or display the item from which you want to publish. Then choose Tools, Office Links, Publish It with MS Word. Access creates an RTF file containing a table of database information, and immediately opens the RTF file as a table in a separate Word document window (see Figure 37.24). You can then save the RTF file as a Word document; copy the data into any other Word document; link or embed the Word file; or edit and format your file as needed.

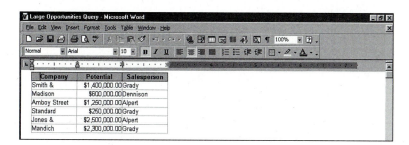

Figure 37.24
An Access query, published to Word.

Keep the following points in mind:

- If you publish to Word from a report or form, the appearance of the Word table depends on the formatting you used in the Access report or form. You may find this unsatisfactory. If so, use Table AutoFormat or Word's manual formatting techniques to reformat the data after it appears in Word.

- If you publish from an Access report, the information isn't stored in a Word table at all; rather, Access uses tabs to separate columns. You may want to immediately select the data and choose Table, Convert Text to Table to reformat the information in a Word table, which is almost always easier to manage.

- If you publish from a query or a report, you can refine the information you select using Access query and reporting tools, prior to inserting it in Word.

- Regardless of which Access source you use, you may need to adjust column widths and alignments after your data is displayed in Word.

- Access automatically names the RTF file after the table, report, form, or query on which it was based, unless it finds an RTF file in the same directory that already uses this name. In that case, you're given a chance to rename the file.

- The published data does not retain any link to Access, so it is not automatically updated if the database is updated. Often, the best way to update information you've published to Word is to simply delete it and republish it using Access's Publish It with MS Word feature again.

GETTING MORE CONTROL OVER ACCESS DATA EXPORT

Access's one-click Publish It with MS Word feature is very handy, but you may sometimes want a bit more control over how you export Access data to Word. If so, open Access, and select the form, report, table, or query you want to export. Then, from within Access, choose File, Export. The Export To dialog box appears (see Figure 37.25).

Figure 37.25
Exporting Access data through the Export To dialog box.

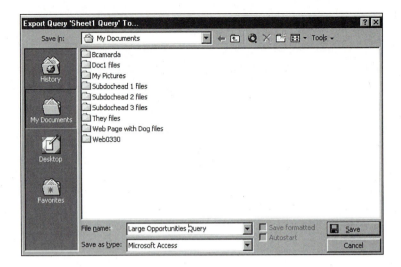

From this dialog box you can

■ Specify a File Name

■ Browse to the folder where you want the file to appear

■ Specify a file type (Save as Type); possibilities include Rich Text Format (RTF), Text Files, or HTML Documents

When you're finished, click Save. You now have a file with the name you selected, in the format and location you selected, containing all the information from the table, form, report, or query. You can open or insert this file in Word, and edit it there as you wish.

USING POWERPOINT WITH WORD

Over the years, PowerPoint has developed into the multimedia center of Office 2000. Not only can you use it to incorporate text and images in a slide format, but you can also add animation, sound, and movies to teach, explain, and persuade. Because both Word and PowerPoint are Office 2000 family members, you have a strong connection that enables you to share information in both directions.

Consider just a few of the ways you can use PowerPoint and Word together:

■ You can draft your outlines in Word and then import them into PowerPoint.

■ You can send presentation information from PowerPoint to Word, including outlines, notes, and handouts.

■ You can take quick notes and mark action items in PowerPoint while you are making a presentation in front of an audience, and then publish them to Word for editing and refinement.

- You can embed slides or an entire presentation into a Word document for inclusion in a report.

In the following section, you'll learn how you can use an outline from Word as the basis for a PowerPoint multimedia presentation.

USING WORD OUTLINES IN POWERPOINT

Quite often, the impetus for a PowerPoint presentation is a report drafted in Word. If you use Heading styles or Outline levels in Word, you can build your presentation with much less effort. The key to "no-brainer" Word-to-PowerPoint conversions is setting up your Word document using Heading styles or Outline levels.

Each paragraph or title, formatted with Heading 1 style (or Outline Level 1), becomes the title of a new slide, and each paragraph or subtitle, formatted with the Heading 2 style (or Outline Level 2), becomes the first level of text, and so on.

To export a finished Word outline to PowerPoint, open the document and choose File, Send To, Microsoft PowerPoint. You'll see a brief progress bar and then the program switches to PowerPoint, as shown in Figure 37.26.

PART

IX

CH

37

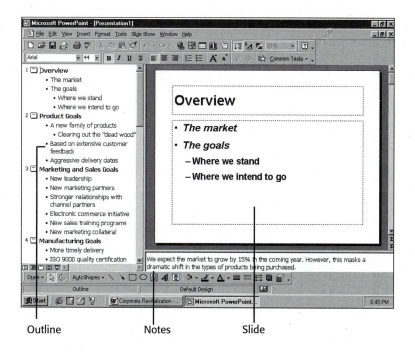

Outline   Notes   Slide

Figure 37.26
Build your presentation's "talking points" by sending your Word outline to a PowerPoint presentation.

Tip #461

If you haven't used Heading styles or Outline levels in Word, but you have used tabs to indicate headings and subheadings, save your document as a text file. Then, in PowerPoint, choose File, Open. Change the file type to All Outlines, select your text file, and choose Open. Each first non-indented paragraph becomes a slide title on a new slide; paragraphs with one indent become first-level text, and so forth.

EXPORTING POWERPOINT FILES TO WORD

The slides are the flashy part of a PowerPoint presentation, but there's also a lot of supporting material: an outline, speaker notes, and handouts, to name a few. PowerPoint makes it easy for you to export all this information and more to Word, where you can further modify it or incorporate it into an existing document. Moreover, through PowerPoint's Meeting Minder utility, you can take notes during your presentation and even assign tasks or actions; later, you can export these items to Word as well.

When giving a presentation, it's extremely useful to have a hard copy of your talk that tells you what slide comes when and what to say about it. After you've created your slide show, you can export it to Word so that you can further develop your speaker's notes. From PowerPoint's main menu, choose File, Send To, Microsoft Word. This opens the Write-Up dialog box shown in Figure 37.27.

Figure 37.27
You can send your entire slide presentation along with any speaker notes to Word for further editing through the Write-Up dialog box.

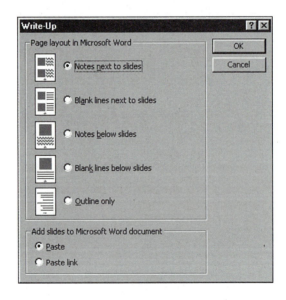

The Write-Up dialog box comes with various layout options that not only govern how your Write-Up will look, but also what you are actually exporting. You can choose from the following options:

- **Notes <u>N</u>ext to Slides.** With this option selected, Word creates a 3-column table showing the slide number, a small image of the slide, and speaker notes. Three slides appear per page.

- **Bl<u>a</u>nk Lines Next to Slides.** This option creates a 3-column table showing slide number, a small image of the slide, and a series of underscored lines for speaker notes. Three slides appear per page.

- **Notes <u>B</u>elow Slides.** When this option is selected, Word puts each slide on its own page with a slide number and the speaker text.

- **Blan<u>k</u> Lines Below Slides.** This option gives you each slide on its own page with a slide number and a series of underscored lines for speaker text.

- **<u>O</u>utline Only.** This option gives you just the outline for the presentation without a picture of the slide. The text of the presentation appears in the form of a Word outline, with each slide's main heading corresponding to a first-level heading in Word.

You'll notice that <u>P</u>aste and Paste <u>L</u>ink options are available for all but the <u>O</u>utline Only selection. As with all embedded objects in Word, choosing Paste <u>L</u>ink causes the document to be updated whenever changes are made to the source material, in this case a slide or presentation.

After you make your selections about how you want the PowerPoint presentation exported to Word, click OK. PowerPoint converts the file, and Word opens, displaying the file in the format you requested.

EXPORTING MEETING MINUTES AND ACTION ITEMS

Meeting Minder is a PowerPoint utility that enables a presenter to take notes or keep minutes during a presentation. To use it, right-click on a slide during a presentation, and select Meeting Minder from the shortcut menu (see Figure 37.28).

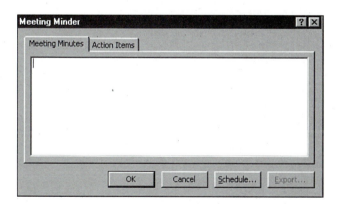

Figure 37.28
You can enter meeting minutes and action items in the Meeting Minder dialog box, and then export them to Word.

The Meeting Minder dialog box has two tabs: Meeting Minutes and Action Items. Meeting Minutes is an open-ended text area; Action Items are task-oriented to-do items. After you enter text in either tab, the Export button becomes available; click it. In the Meeting Minder Export dialog box (see Figure 37.29), make sure Send Meeting Minutes and Action Items to Microsoft Word is checked, and click Export Now.

Note	If your workgroup uses Microsoft Outlook and Microsoft Exchange, you can also export action items directly to the task lists of the individuals you want to perform them. In the Meeting Minder Export dialog box, click Post Action Items to Microsoft Outlook, and choose Export Now.

Figure 37.29
The Meeting Minder Export dialog box enables you to export Meeting Minder information to Word and Outlook.

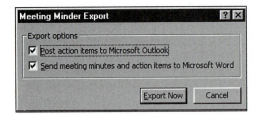

Tip #462	It's best to export these items only once at the end of the session, because Word creates a new document each time the information is sent.

EMBEDDING A NEW POWERPOINT SLIDE IN A WORD DOCUMENT

PowerPoint comes with a great number of templates and designs to give your message a professional edge. Word gives you full access to them: You can include slides in your documents at will, even if you have no intention of creating a full-fledged slide show. To insert a single PowerPoint slide as a graphic in a Word document, follow these steps:

1. In Word, position your insertion point where you want the slide inserted.

2. Choose Insert, Object to open the Object dialog box.

3. From the Create New tab, choose Microsoft PowerPoint Slide. The default slide appears as an object in your Word document.

In Word, whenever you double-click the slide, PowerPoint's menus and toolbars appear; you can now edit the slide using PowerPoint's menus and toolbars.

To quickly format the slide, right-click on it and choose Apply Design Template (see Figure 37.30). Choose the template you want to apply, and preview it in the Preview window. When you're satisfied, click Apply.

You can now enter text in the slide. Editing text in PowerPoint slides is much like editing text in Word text boxes. You simply click next to a heading or bullet. A box that resembles a Word text box appears; start typing. Figure 37.31 shows an example of a slide created in a Word newsletter.

→ For more information about text boxes, **see** "Using Text Boxes," **p. 456**.

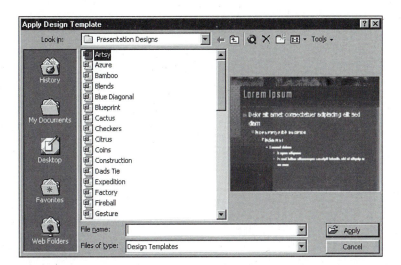

Figure 37.30
Choosing a design template with which to format the slide.

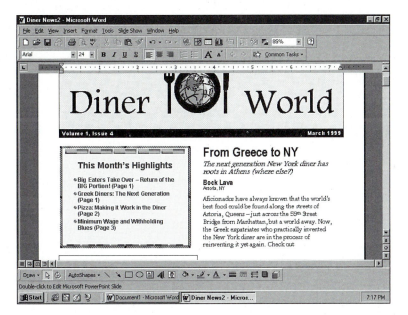

Figure 37.31
An example of a slide used in a Word newsletter.

When you're finished working in the slide, click outside it, and Word's menus reappear. You can work on the slide again by double-clicking it.

EMBEDDING AN EXISTING PRESENTATION IN A WORD DOCUMENT

You can also embed an entire PowerPoint slide presentation in a Word document. This works well for online training, manuals, and other documents that would benefit from a multimedia presence.

Choose Insert, Object, and click the Create from File tab. Next, browse to your existing presentation, select it, click Insert, and click OK. Word normally displays the first slide of the presentation in the document. To run the presentation, double-click the slide object.

Note

Of course, you can also incorporate any existing PowerPoint slide by using the Copy and Paste features. As with Excel and other objects, you can put a plain copy of your slide straight into your document by clicking the Paste button on the Standard toolbar.

You also can put a linked copy of the slide by choosing Edit, Paste Special, selecting Microsoft PowerPoint Slide Object from the list, and then selecting the Paste Link option before you click OK. Now, whenever you update your PowerPoint slide, your Word document is also updated.

Tip #463

If you want to copy an entire PowerPoint slide into your Word document, be sure you're in PowerPoint's Slide Sorter view (choose View, Slide Sorter). If you're in Slide view (rather than Slide Sorter view), only the selected portion of your slide will be copied and pasted.

This can cause problems, because you'll lose formatting stored in the slide master (in other words, most formatting is applied to the entire presentation, not just a single slide).

If you copy a slide from PowerPoint to Word, but only parts of the slide appear in Word, see "What to Do If Parts of a PowerPoint Slide Don't Appear in Word," in the "Troubleshooting" section of this chapter.

INTEGRATING WITH MICROSOFT PUBLISHER 2000

With Office 2000, Microsoft has added the surprisingly powerful Microsoft Publisher to every version of the suite—not just with Office Small Business Edition, as was the case in Office 97. Microsoft Publisher goes far beyond Word's desktop publishing capabilities, making it extremely easy to build a wide range of documents. For Word users, one of Publisher's most attractive features is its intimate integration with Word. You can use Word as your editing tool at the very same time you take advantage of Publisher's desktop publishing capabilities.

When you run Publisher, it displays the Microsoft Publisher Catalog (see Figure 37.32), which provides three approaches to building a new publication:

- From the Publications by Wizard tab, you can choose a publication and a design at the same time. Then, click Start Wizard, and walk through a Publisher Wizard that helps you build the publication:

- From the Publications by Design tab, you can choose a design from a master set of complementary designs for business stationery, fundraising, moving announcements, and other types of special events; then click Start Wizard, and walk through a Publisher Wizard that helps you build the publication.

- From the Blank Publications tab, choose a publication size and shape; click Create; and work in Publisher to insert the design and text manually.

When you finish running the wizard to create either a Publication by Wizard or a Publication by Design, a document appears, containing boilerplate text—much like the text that Word inserts when you run Word's Newsletter or Brochure Wizard.

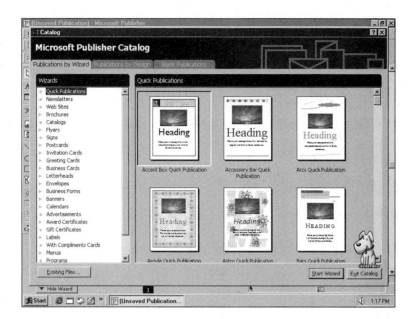

Figure 37.32
Microsoft Publisher displays a catalog of Publications by Wizard, Publications by Design, and Blank Publications.

To edit this (or any other) Publisher text using Microsoft Word, right-click in the story you want to edit. From the shortcut menu, choose Change Text, Edit Story in Microsoft Word. Word opens with the story displayed. You can now edit the story using Word's editing and formatting tools. Nearly all text and paragraph formatting you apply in Word will be readable by Publisher, and vice versa. These include boldface, italic, and underlining; styles; indents; text alignment; and bullets and numbering. There are a few exceptions, however. For instance, you can't insert images in Word and see them when you return to Publisher. Also

- Borders you apply to paragraphs in Word do not appear in Publisher.
- Publisher's built-in color schemes include some colors that may not appear accurately in Word.
- Word's animated text effects do not appear.

When you're finished editing your Publisher story in Word, choose File, Close & Return to Publication.

If you want to insert a Word file in a Publisher document, click in the text frame where you want the Word document to go. Next, choose Insert, Text File. The Insert Text File dialog box opens. Browse to and select the file you want. (Publisher directly imports Word 2000, Word 97, Word 95, Word 6, and Rich Text Format files, including Word files created on the Macintosh.)

After you select the file, click OK to insert it.

USING OUTLOOK WITH WORD

Microsoft Outlook 2000, Microsoft Office's "personal information manager," is included in every version of Microsoft Office 2000. Outlook 2000 integrates with Word in three key ways that can make you more productive:

- If you use Outlook as your email client software, you can edit your email with Word. This gives you access to Word's extensive formatting and proofing capabilities. You can also send a Word file as an attachment, using the File, Send To, Mail Recipient (as Attachment) command.

- You can track your contacts in Outlook, and use your contact information in a Word mail merge (This is covered in detail in Chapter 6 in the section "Using an Outlook Address Book as a Data Source.)

- You can track your Word documents through Outlook's Journal feature, making it easy to find out what files you worked on when, and for how long you worked on them. This is covered in the following section.

TRACKING WORD PROGRESS IN THE OUTLOOK JOURNAL

Did you ever wonder how much time you spent on a particular document over a series of days? Or maybe you're looking for a particular file you worked on sometime last Wednesday in the afternoon, but now you can't find it or remember its name. Outlook's Journal feature can keep track of all your work in Word (and Excel and PowerPoint), recording exactly what you worked on, when you worked on it, and for how long.

→ To learn how to turn on Outlook's Journal tracking feature, **see** "Controlling Whether Outlook Tracks Your Work" **p. 1178**.

Note

> A new feature in Outlook 2000, "Activity Tracking," can also be used to keep track of your work.

To see which entries, if any, are currently in your Journal, click the Journal folder in the Outlook bar on the left side of the screen. If the Journal folder doesn't appear, choose Journal from the list of options in your current view. You'll see a timeline of days at the top of the Journal window, and filenames at the bottom (see Figure 37.33).

You can choose between a daily, weekly, or monthly timeline by clicking the appropriate toolbar button. Figure 37.34 shows a daily view. Each icon has a Duration bar above it to show when and for how long the document was open. By default, if you double-click the icon, the journal entry associated with the file opens. This journal entry contains information about the file, including exactly how long it was opened. It also contains a shortcut you can double-click to open the file itself.

You can also right-click the journal entry for a list of options. For example, Open Item Referred To opens the file the journal entry refers to, without the extra step of displaying the journal entry.

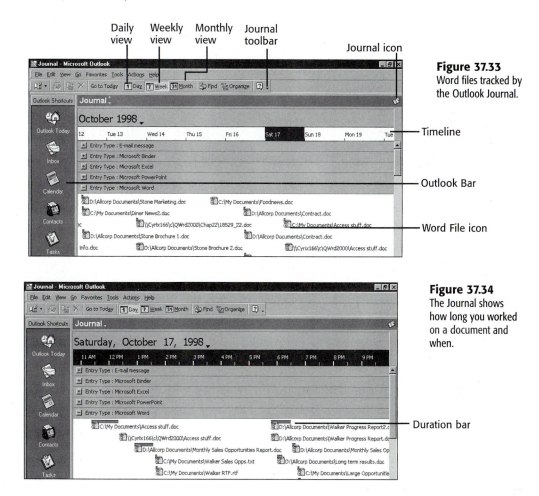

Daily view · Weekly view · Monthly view · Journal toolbar · Journal icon · Timeline · Outlook Bar · Word File icon · Duration bar

Figure 37.33
Word files tracked by the Outlook Journal.

Figure 37.34
The Journal shows how long you worked on a document and when.

WORKING WITH THE JOURNAL ENTRY

An Outlook journal entry contains much more than a filename and date. To work with the journal entry, right-click it. The shortcut menu appears. Choose Open Journal Entry. The file's journal entry appears (see Figure 37.35).

Figure 37.35
A Word file's journal entry in Outlook 2000.

Contact associated with the file

Start time

Document icon

Duration

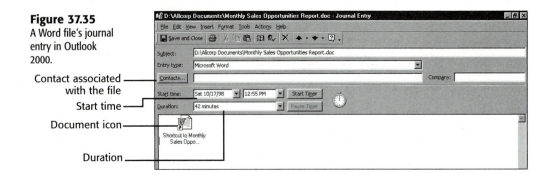

Start Time shows when you started working with the file on that day. Duration shows how long the file was open. You can assign the file to a contact by clicking Contacts and selecting a name from your Outlook contact list. When you finish reviewing or editing the journal entry, click Save and Close.

Tip #464

You can open the Word file directly from within Outlook.

From the Journal window, right-click on the journal entry, and choose Open Item Referred To from the shortcut menu. The Opening Mail Attachment dialog box appears; click Open It, and click OK.

From within the Journal Entry dialog box, double-click on the file icon. The Opening Mail Attachment dialog box appears; click Open It, and click OK.

Note

To link a document to a specific contact, enter the contact name in the document's property keywords.

CONTROLLING WHETHER OUTLOOK TRACKS YOUR WORK

By default, the Journal tracking feature in Outlook is turned off. To turn it on, or to make sure it is still turned off, follow these steps:

1. Open Outlook.
2. Choose Tools, Options.
3. If the Preferences tab isn't already open, click Preferences to display it.
4. Click Journal Options. The Journal Options dialog box appears (see Figure 37.36).
5. In the Also Record Files From box, check or clear the check boxes next to Microsoft Word and any other Office program you want Outlook to track, or to stop tracking.
6. Click OK.

Once you turn tracking on, Journal tracks your work whether you open the Outlook application or not.

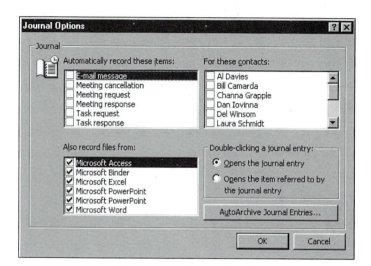

Figure 37.36
Changing the way
Outlook tracks your
work in Word.

USING BINDERS TO COMBINE MULTIPLE DOCUMENTS

An office doesn't survive on single Word documents alone. To accomplish a single task, an organization might have to create numerous documents, spreadsheets, and presentations. For instance, consider the typical product introduction, which might include

- A sales letter or internal cover letter
- A brochure and/or data sheet prepared in Word
- A customer presentation, or presentation to the sales force
- Excel workbooks with pricing and financial data
- Perhaps even a Microsoft Project file containing project management information

That's where Microsoft Binder 2000 comes in. This Office applet can help you gather disparate Word, Excel, and PowerPoint files into a cohesive, easily transportable file. Binder can even print the entire file with consecutive page numbers and consistent headers and footers for all the documents you include, regardless of their source.

Note

Microsoft Access files can't be included in a binder.

Tip #465

If all the documents you want to assemble are Word documents, you can achieve much the same results with Word's Master Documents feature. (See Chapter 8, "Master Documents: Control and Share Even the Largest Documents.")

Master documents are superior to binders in some ways: For example, you cannot create a unified table of contents for multiple Word documents through a binder, but with master documents, you can.

After you group your varied documents in a binder file, you can edit them through the same interface while retaining access to all the source applications' menus, toolbars, shortcuts, and macros.

You could, for example, pull together the last four already-published quarterly reports and create a new Excel chart that depicts the big picture especially for the binder. You can even put multiple binders together.

WORKING WITH BINDERS

To work with Binder, choose Start, Programs, Office Tools, Microsoft Binder 2000. The bare Binder interface appears (see Figure 37.37).

Figure 37.37
Microsoft Binder 2000, as it appears when you open it for the first time.

> **Note**
>
> If Microsoft Binder isn't listed in your Office Tools, run maintenance setup to install it.

As soon as you start Binder, it creates a new, blank binder. To insert an existing file as a Binder section, choose Section, Add from File. The Add from File dialog box appears. Browse to and select the file you want to include, and then click Add.

You can also insert new files based on Word (or Excel or PowerPoint) templates, and add the information to those files later. To do so, choose Section, Add. This opens the Add Section dialog box (see Figure 37.38), which enables you to choose from any installed Office 2000 template, including those for blank documents.

As you add files to your binder, they appear in the Contents pane at the left side of the binder window; accompanying icons reflect their source program (see Figure 37.39).

Each document in a binder is its own section. You can rearrange the sections at any time, as well as duplicate and delete them. A binder can consist of any combination of existing documents and new documents. The document that is currently selected appears in the document window, where it can be edited.

In the document window you see the currently selected document. The source program's toolbars and menus are available at the top of the screen, and can be used normally. Two menus are added:

- The Go menu includes Web browsing commands
- The Section menu gives you tools for managing individual sections in the binder

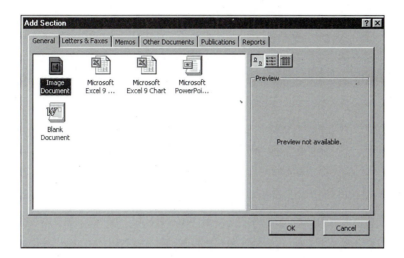

Figure 37.38
Adding a section based on a yet-to-be-created document.

Current document icon   Show/Hide Left Pane   Added Web menu   Added Section menu

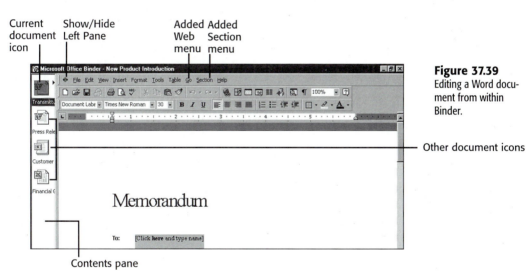

Figure 37.39
Editing a Word document from within Binder.

Other document icons

Contents pane

Binder-wide commands such as <u>P</u>rint or Page Set<u>u</u>p are located under the <u>F</u>ile menu.

You can hide (or show) the Contents pane by clicking the double-headed Show/Hide Left Pane arrow to the left of the <u>F</u>ile menu. Whenever one of the icons in the Contents pane is activated, a right-pointing arrow appears next to the icon and the document appears in the document window at the right.

Caution

It's important to note that whenever you add a file to your binder, a copy of that file is added, not the original. Unlike Office 2000 embedded objects, files added to the binder maintain no linkage to the original.

Tip #466

You can merge two or more binder files. Choose Section, Add from File and pick an existing binder file. The documents contained in the existing binder are copied to the new binder file.

SAVING A BINDER

You can save a binder much as you save any other document. Working within Microsoft Binder, click the Save button on the Standard toolbar (or choose File, Save). The Save binder As dialog box opens. Enter a name for the binder in the File Name box, and click Save.

EDITING YOUR BINDER SECTIONS

You have two choices when it comes to editing a section in the binder. You can either edit from within Binder, or edit in Word (or Excel or PowerPoint) and return to Binder when you're finished. For any work that spans more than one section, it is best to edit within Binder and take advantage of tools available there, such as Binder-wide printing. You can also cut, copy, and paste between documents in a binder.

If you need to do extensive editing within one of the sections, you can work in the application window as you normally would. Follow these steps to edit a document outside of Binder:

1. Select the document you want to edit.

2. Choose Section, View Outside.

3. A new application window opens with your document.

4. After you complete your edits, click the Document Close button or choose File, Close & Return to Binder.

MANAGING YOUR BINDER

The Section menu contains controls that enable you to Delete, Duplicate, Rename, Rearrange, and hide individual sections. You can also access most of these management commands by right-clicking the Section icon in the Contents pane.

Tip #467

You can act on more than one document at a time by using the extended selection technique. Click the first document in the Contents pane and then press Ctrl and click the other documents to add to the selection.

REARRANGING FILES IN A BINDER

You may occasionally want to rearrange the files stored in your binder—either to make their order more logical, or because binders print in the order they are arranged. You can move a section before or after any other section by choosing <u>S</u>ection, R<u>e</u>arrange. This opens the Rearrange Sections dialog box shown in Figure 37.40. Select the section you want to move, and then click the Move <u>U</u>p or the Move <u>D</u>own buttons to adjust the section's position in the binder. Click OK when you have finished.

Figure 37.40
You can rearrange sections in any order within the binder.

PART

IX

CH

37

Tip #468

You can also rearrange the sections by clicking and dragging the icons in the Contents pane.

DUPLICATING YOUR SECTIONS

At times you might want to duplicate certain sections in your binder. For example, you might want to insert a PowerPoint slide as a transition between every major section of your binder. Select the section to copy and then choose <u>S</u>ection, Dupli<u>c</u>ate. The Duplicate dialog box opens and enables you to specify the section you would like the copy to follow. Highlight that section and click OK.

HIDING SECTIONS TO AVOID PRINTING

Occasionally, you might want to print most elements of a binder, but not print one or two—such as private email messages or cover memos. To avoid printing a section, you can temporarily hide it.

When you hide a section of a binder, its icon is removed from the Contents pane so that it can't be activated or printed as part of the overall binder. Select the section (or sections) you want to hide and choose <u>S</u>ection, <u>H</u>ide. To retrieve hidden sections, choose <u>S</u>ection, U<u>n</u>hide Sections. The Unhide Sections dialog box appears (see Figure 37.41), listing all hidden sections in the binder. Choose one and click OK. The document reappears.

Caution

Although the Hide feature can help you suppress an individual file you don't want to print, the easy-to-access Unhide Section dialog box means you can't depend on Hide as a security feature.

Figure 37.41
Making a hidden section visible again.

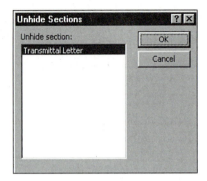

SAVING INDIVIDUAL SECTIONS

 From any open document within a binder, you can save the entire binder by clicking the Save button on the toolbar or choosing File, Save. However, what if you want to save an individual section? Choose Section, Save as File to open a standard Save File dialog box. This option comes in handy when you've made extensive changes to a copy of an existing file or when you want to isolate an original file prepared for the binder.

PRINTING A BINDER

One of the major benefits to using binders is that you can print a collection of documents as though they were one large report. Continuous page numbers and consistent headers and footers go a long way toward transforming a diverse group of documents into a cohesive publication. Follow these steps to set up the pages for the entire binder:

1. Choose File, Binder Page Setup.

2. From the Header/Footer tab of the Binder Page Setup dialog box, choose the All Supported Sections option or select the individual sections to affect (see Figure 37.42).

3. To add a preset header or footer, choose from one of the options by clicking the arrow on the right of the Header or Footer box (see Figure 37.43).

4. To add a custom header or footer, click the respective Custom button. From the Custom Header or Custom Footer dialog box (see Figure 37.44), insert text in Left, Center, and/or Right sections. From the toolbar, you can add codes that insert page number, section number, number of sections, binder name, date, or time.

5. Click OK when you're finished or click the Print button to open the Print dialog box.

Headers, footers, and page numbers you insert through the Binder Page Setup dialog box replace any corresponding headers, footers, or page numbers that you may have inserted in the original documents in Word.

After you complete your binder page setup and before you print it, it's a good idea to choose File, Binder Print Preview. Previewing the file is helpful for spotting unnecessary or incorrect page breaks. When in Print Preview mode, you have an option to skip from one section to the next.

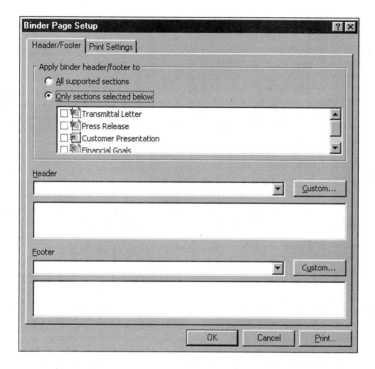

Figure 37.42
Binder Page Setup
enables you to estab-
lish headers and foot-
ers for the entire
binder.

PART

IX

CH

37

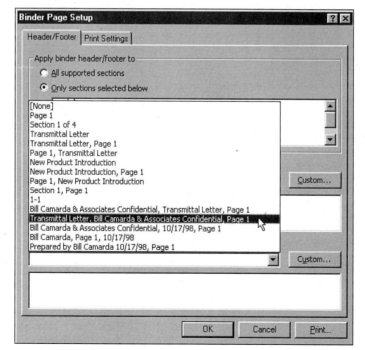

Figure 37.43
Choosing a prefor-
matted header.

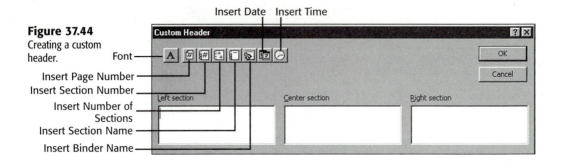

Figure 37.44
Creating a custom header.

Insert Date   Insert Time

Font

Insert Page Number

Insert Section Number

Insert Number of Sections

Insert Section Name

Insert Binder Name

When you're ready to print, choose File, Print Binder. The Print Binder dialog box (see Figure 37.45) is similar to the regular Word Print dialog box, but there are a couple of exceptions. In the Print What section, you can choose to print all the available sections or only those selected in the left (Contents) pane. In the Numbering section, you can either make the page numbers consecutive or restart the numbers with each section.

Figure 37.45
The Print Binder dialog box is similar to Word's Print dialog box, but not identical.

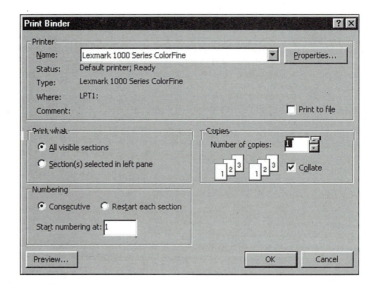

USING THE MICROSOFT OFFICE SHORTCUT BAR

The Office Shortcut Bar (see Figure 37.46) is one of the true workhorses of Office 2000. The Office Shortcut Bar is a completely customizable toolbar that enables you open the following items:

- A wide range of types of documents, from Word templates to Outlook messages
- Any folder or application on your desktop, or in any frequently accessed location
- Any Office 2000 application
- Any application at all

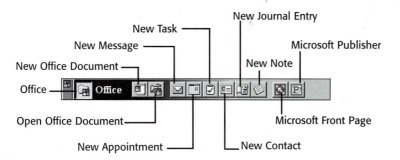

Office Shortcut Bar menu items

New Journal Entry

New Task

New Message

Microsoft Publisher

New Office Document

New Note

Office

Open Office Document

Microsoft Front Page

New Appointment

New Contact

Figure 37.46
The Office Shortcut Bar, displayed on the right edge of the Windows Desktop.

MOVING THE OFFICE SHORTCUT BAR

You can set the Office Shortcut Bar to dock along any edge of the screen. Or you can park it unobtrusively on the desktop. To move the Office Shortcut Bar, just click any area of it that is not occupied by a button and drag the bar. When you get close to the top, bottom, left, or right edges of the screen, the bar snaps into position.

> **Note**
>
> If the Office Shortcut Bar doesn't appear automatically, choose Start, Programs, Office Tools, Office Shortcut Bar.
>
> When you open the Office Shortcut Bar this way, a dialog box appears, asking if you want Office Shortcut Bar to run automatically at startup. If you want it to do so, click Yes. (If Office Shortcut Bar isn't listed in the Office Tools folder, run a maintenance setup to install it.)

CUSTOMIZING THE OFFICE SHORTCUT BAR

Many Word and Office users customize their Office Shortcut Bars to contain separate tool-bars, each with a set of related programs or documents. For example, you might create a Graphics toolbar containing shortcuts to all your graphics programs, a Forms toolbar with shortcuts to your often used forms or templates, or a Web Tools toolbar with shortcuts to your Internet applications. This is a convenient way of getting easy access to all your tools without cluttering up your desktop. The Office Shortcut Bar can also be set to appear "on top" of all applications, allowing you to access its options without minimizing all of your applications (unlike the desktop).

Customizing your Office Shortcut Bar is easy to do. Right-click on any empty part of the Office Shortcut Bar, and choose Customize from the shortcut menu. This opens the Customize dialog box with its four tabs: View, Buttons, Toolbars, and Settings.

The View tab of the Customize dialog box, shown in Figure 37.47, controls the overall set-tings for the Office Shortcut Bar. You can select the color for any of the available toolbars in the Color section. The Options area enables you to control the following options:

Figure 37.47
You can completely personalize your Office Shortcut Bar through the Customize dialog box.

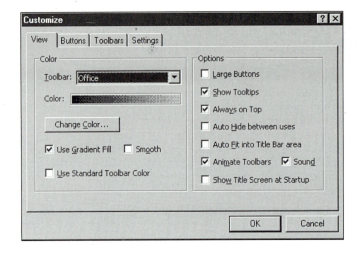

- **Large Buttons.** Controls the size of the buttons in the toolbar.
- **Show ToolTips.** Displays the name of the toolbar when touched by the mouse pointer.
- **Always on Top.** Keeps the Office Shortcut Bar always visible.
- **Auto Hide Between Uses.** Makes the Office Shortcut Bar disappear when docked at a corner of the screen, unless the mouse is near it.
- **Auto Fit into Title Bar Area.** Puts the Office Shortcut Bar in the title bar area of an application. This option has no effect if the Office Shortcut Bar is docked on either side of the screen.
- **Animate Toolbars.** Animates toolbar movement when you switch between toolbars, making the change in toolbars easier to recognize.
- **Sound.** Associates a sound effect with the Office Shortcut Bar's appearance.

Note
Additional sounds are available on Microsoft's Web site. (Choose Help, Office to automatically access the Web site.)

- **Show Title Screen at Startup.** Displays the Microsoft Office title screen when the Office Shortcut Bar starts.

The Buttons tab of the Office Shortcut Bar (see Figure 37.48) is where you select the various programs and applications that appear on the toolbar. Check any existing entry in the scrolling list or add a new one by clicking the Add File or Add Folder button. You can also control the order of the toolbar buttons by using the Move Up and Move Down buttons. Finally, you can rename or delete any button by selecting it and clicking the appropriate command.

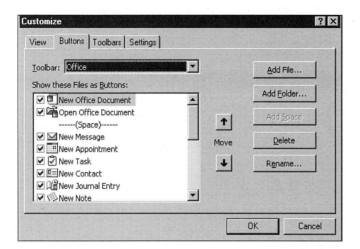

Figure 37.48
Controlling the buttons that appear on the Office Shortcut Bar.

You're not limited to only one toolbar on the Office Shortcut Bar. Add additional toolbars, either preset or custom, by clicking the Toolbars tab (see Figure 37.49). After the toolbars are enabled here, you can further customize them on the View and Buttons tabs.

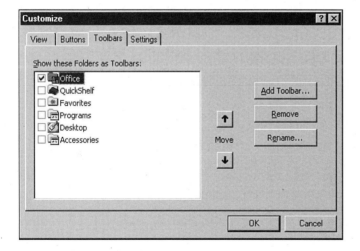

Figure 37.49
Displaying multiple toolbars on the Office Shortcut Bar.

The Settings tab (see Figure 37.50) enables you to choose the location of the template folders used by the Office Shortcut Bar. The templates available are the ones used by the generic document buttons when you click the Open Office Document button. These are the same templates available from within Word, Excel, PowerPoint, Publisher, and Outlook. By default, these settings match the settings in the individual programs, and you should rarely have to change them.

Figure 37.50
Controlling where the
Office Shortcut Bar
looks for templates.

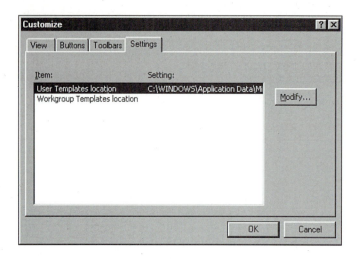

USING MICROSOFT PHOTO EDITOR 3.01

Office 2000 includes a program for retouching and altering photographs called Microsoft
Photo Editor 3.01 (see Figure 37.51). Word 97 relied on Microsoft Photo Editor to acquire
scanned images and to edit them once they were digitized. In contrast, Word 2000 has a
built-in scanning feature. However, Microsoft Photo Editor's image editing capabilities are
still very handy.

Figure 37.51
Working in Microsoft
Photo Editor.

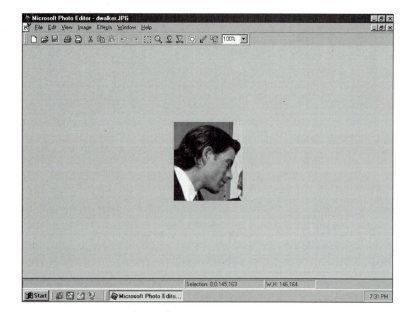

After you open an image in Microsoft Photo Editor, you have numerous options. Basic resizing, cropping, and rotation commands are found under the Image menu, as are commands for adjusting the red, green, and blue components of a color image.

The Effects menu offers 14 different possibilities that can affect the entire picture. Each effect, such as the Chalk and Charcoal shown in Figure 37.52, has its own set of parameters that enables you to vary the results. Experimentation—and copious use of the Undo button—are the order of the day.

Figure 37.52
Chalk and Charcoal is just one of 14 effects available in Microsoft Photo Editor.

When you finish editing the picture, click the Close button or choose File, Exit and Return from the Photo Editor menu. You can return for further editing by double-clicking the image at any time.

Note

Microsoft Photo Editor offers fairly rudimentary image editing capabilities. For instance, it cannot use industry-standard Photoshop-compatible image filters; it cannot handle multiple layers, a key tool for professional image editing; it has no automated tools for batch processing; it does not contain touch-up tools for fixing problems like red-eye in photographs of people; and its ability to create Web images is limited.

If you need to perform top-quality professional image editing, consider Adobe Photoshop or the less-expensive Jasc Paint Shop Pro.

If you need to touch up photos for personal use, consider Microsoft Picture-It or Adobe PhotoDeluxe.

If you need to create Web images, consider Macromedia Fireworks, Adobe ImageReady, or perhaps Microsoft PhotoDraw or Microsoft Image Composer, each of which is included with Microsoft Office Premiere Edition.

USING MICROSOFT ORGANIZATION CHART 2.0

One of the most dreaded assignments any white-collar worker can get is to draw up a new organization chart. Trying to keep all the boxes and lines straight with Word's regular drawing tools can be challenging at best. Office 2000 includes a program designed to address the problem: Organization Chart 2.0. Aside from organization charts, you can also use the program to create any diagram that requires a hierarchical structure.

From within Word, choose Insert, Object and then choose MS Organization Chart 2.0 to begin the process. Figure 37.53 shows the opening screen of the program with its beginning template. Highlight any text and replace it to begin constructing your chart. When you click in any of the existing boxes, two additional comment areas appear in the same box, <Comment 1> and <Comment 2>. You can click in either one and start typing.

Figure 37.53
Organization Chart 2.0 starts with a pre-defined template.

Select tool

Enter Text tool

Zoom

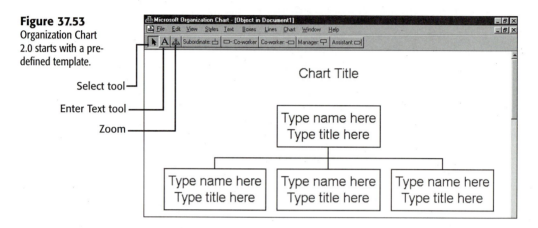

You add additional elements to the organization chart by first choosing the Select tool from the toolbar. Then pick the appropriate member button on the toolbar (Subordinate, Co-worker, Manager, or Assistant) and click the box to which you want to add. You can choose from eight different chart styles as well as a number of different box and line styles and colors.

If you need to move a box, choose the Select tool and then click and drag your box. Drop it onto any other box to connect to it. The relationship between the two boxes is determined by where you position the box prior to dropping it.

To add text, click the Enter Text tool and click anywhere in the chart. You can modify a text's font, color, and alignment by first selecting your text and then making your choice from the Text menu.

When you finish creating your chart, choose File, Exit and Return from the Organizational Chart 2.0 menu. If you embed the chart in another document, you can edit the chart by double-clicking it just as you can with any other embedded object.

USING EQUATION EDITOR 3.0

The Equation Editor is useful for creating extended mathematical expressions. A variety of mathematical symbols and templates simplify the process of constructing the most complex formulas. Begin by choosing Insert, Object, and selecting Microsoft Equation Editor from the option list. A working area, surrounded by a dotted box, opens on your screen, as does the Equation toolbar shown in Figure 37.54.

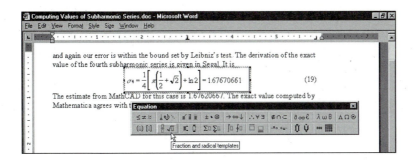

Figure 37.54
Use the Equation Editor for inserting complex formulas in your Word document.

Numbers, variables, and ordinary mathematical operators (such as =, +, -) can be typed directly from the keyboard. To enter an operator or symbol not available from the keyboard, click the appropriate button on the top row of the Equation toolbar and select from one of the options that appear in the drop-down menu. Complex expressions such as fractions, square roots, or integrals can be added by clicking the appropriate button on the bottom row of the Equation toolbar and choosing one of the drop-down options. Depending on the choice, an expression has one or more outlined boxes for inserting numbers or other symbols.

The relative spacing for the formula is handled through the Format, Spacing menu option. This opens the Spacing dialog box (see Figure 37.55), where you can control the line spacing, matrix row and column spacing, superscript height, subscript depth, and the limit height between symbols.

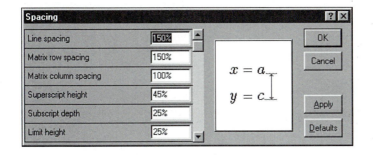

Figure 37.55
You can control a formula's overall spacing through the Spacing dialog box.

TROUBLESHOOTING

WHAT TO DO IF YOU CANNOT LINK CELLS FROM AN EXCEL WORKSHEET

Make sure you've actually saved the Excel worksheet; if the worksheet doesn't have a filename yet, the link won't work properly. Once you've done so, create the link again, specifying the filename you just created.

WHAT TO DO IF YOU CAN'T OPEN A WORKSHEET IN EXCEL AFTER YOU EDIT AND SAVE IT IN WORD

Word enables you to open an Excel worksheet directly, by choosing it in the Open dialog box and clicking Open. If you do this, the cells are placed in your document in the form of a Word table. Because Word cannot save in Excel format, when you resave the file, it is converted to a Word file, and Excel cannot read it. If you've made changes, you can copy them manually into Excel, though you'll have to reformat them. If you need to make changes that will be readable in Excel, use the techniques described elsewhere in this chapter to create a link to an Excel document, rather than opening it directly.

WHAT TO DO IF PARTS OF A POWERPOINT SLIDE DON'T APPEAR IN WORD

If you want to copy an entire PowerPoint slide into your Word document, be sure you're in PowerPoint's Slide Sorter view (choose View, Slide Sorter). If you're in Slide view (rather than Slide Sorter view), only the selected portion of your slide will be copied and pasted.

This can cause problems, because you'll lose formatting stored in the slide master (in other words, most formatting that is applied to the entire presentation, not just a single slide).

WHAT TO DO IF YOU CAN'T SEND A WORD OUTLINE TO POWERPOINT

If you use File, Send To, PowerPoint, and Word displays an error message instead of opening PowerPoint, it's possible that you've recently installed the PowerPoint Viewer for Windows 95 to view older PowerPoint files (perhaps files stored on the Internet or your intranet). You now need to reregister PowerPoint 2000 as the application you want to use with PowerPoint files. To do so, quit all Office programs, and choose Start, Run. Then, enter the following text in the Open box:

```
powerpnt /regserver
```

Click OK. If this does not work, run a maintenance install of Microsoft Office 2000 or Microsoft PowerPoint 2000.

CHAPTER 38

USING EXCEL WITH WORD AND POWERPOINT

In this chapter

USING EXCEL WITH OTHER MICROSOFT OFFICE PROGRAMS

Interoperability is probably the main reason that users purchase a suite of products rather than buying word processing programs, spreadsheet software, and presentation products individually. The pricing of suite software is generally attractive, but the capability to share content between applications easily, with predictable results, is a powerful incentive.

Office 2000's focus on Web-enabled collaboration improves upon previous versions' collaborative tools. Microsoft's vision for the workplace requires that everyone's efforts be shared, and toward that end, HTML becomes the common file format among applications. The result? Through the Clipboard and Insert menu, you can insert as much or as little as you like of one application's content into another application's file quickly and easily, retaining as much or as little as you like of the source application's formatting.

COPYING EXCEL DATA TO A WORD DOCUMENT

Why add Excel content to a Word document? To save time and effort in reentering existing text and/or numbers, and to ensure consistency between files. If your Word document discusses numbers already entered into an Excel worksheet, don't create a Word table and re-enter the numbers—copy them from Excel and paste them into the Word document. The result is an instant table, containing the numbers as they appeared in Excel.

Using Excel for tables that contain numeric data also gives you access to Excel's tools for calculation and numeric formatting, which you don't have to the same extent in Word. Therefore, you should try to create, format, and add formulas to the table in Excel—before you copy the table to a Word document.

Figure 38.1 shows the Word and Excel application windows tiled, with a selection in Excel pasted into a Word document. When Excel data is copied to a Word document, it appears in table format—the worksheet cells become table cells that match the dimensions of the selected range of cells from Excel. All of Word's formatting and table tools are at your disposal—just as though the table were originally created in Word.

Tip #477	If you can't see the table's gridlines, choose Table, Show Gridlines in Word. Nonprinting gridlines such as those in Excel will appear.

If you create charts in Excel, you can also copy those charts to a Word document (for instance, to support data presented in a written proposal). Excel provides extensive charting capabilities, whereas Word provides only limited chart features through the use of Microsoft Graph.

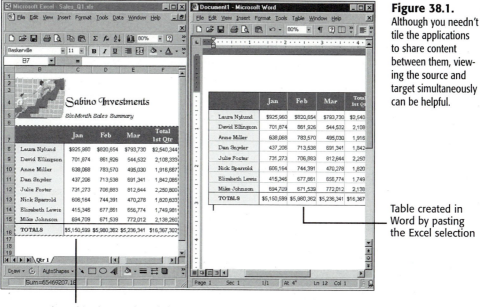

Figure 38.1.
Although you needn't tile the applications to share content between them, viewing the source and target simultaneously can be helpful.

Table created in Word by pasting the Excel selection

Source content selected in the Excel worksheet

You can add Excel content to a Word document in one of two ways:

- Copy the Excel source content (such as a range of cells or a chart) to the Clipboard, and paste it into the Word document.
- Insert an Excel workbook in its entirety or select an individual worksheet to insert.

PASTING EXCEL DATA AS A WORD TABLE

One of the simplest ways to take Excel content and place it in a Word document is to use the Clipboard. In Office 2000, the Clipboard toolbar can hold up to 12 items, making the Clipboard a much more powerful and flexible tool than in previous versions.

To paste Excel data into a Word document, follow these steps:

1. In an Excel worksheet, select the cell or range you want to copy.
2. Choose Edit, Copy, click the Copy button, or press Ctrl+C.
3. Switch to Word, and click in the document to position the insertion point where you want to place the Excel data.
4. In Word, choose Edit, Paste, click the Paste button, or press Ctrl+V.

The Excel content appears as a table, in Arial, 10-point text (or whatever default font you have set in Excel).

Tip #478	If you want to copy all the data in a worksheet, press Ctrl+A in the Excel worksheet to select all the cells. Only the range of cells that contain data will be pasted in Word.

INSERTING AN EXCEL FILE

In many cases, especially in the case of large reports developed in Word, the need arises to paste an entire Excel workbook (or an entire worksheet) into the Word document. Doing so saves you the time of selecting small sections of the worksheets one at a time and pasting them from Excel to Word individually. Inserting the workbook or worksheet saves not only time and effort, but eliminates the possibility of missing a particular section of a worksheet or pasting worksheet sections out of order in the Word document.

Note	When inserting an entire workbook or even an individual worksheet, only the portion of the worksheets that contain data will be inserted—you won't see 256 columns and thousands of rows appear in the Word document.
	Also, when you use the Insert, File command, you may need to reformat the data after you insert it in a Word document. For example, if your Excel data uses fill colors or font colors, these colors won't transfer to Word—instead, all the data appears in black and white. You may prefer to use the Clipboard to copy data if you want to retain all your Excel formats, including colors.

INSERTING AN EXCEL WORKBOOK

Before you can insert a workbook into a Word file, you must ensure that you've already saved the workbook. To insert a workbook into a Word document, follow these steps:

1. In the Word document, position the insertion point at the point where you want to insert the workbook.
2. Choose Insert, File.
3. In the resulting Insert File dialog box, change the Files of Type to All Files (*.*).
4. Using the Look In list box and/or the list of files and folders displayed, locate the workbook file you want to use (see Figure 38.2).
5. Double-click the desired file, or click it once and choose the Insert button.
6. In the Open Worksheet dialog box, leave Entire Workbook selected in the Open Document in Workbook list box, and choose OK (see Figure 38.3).

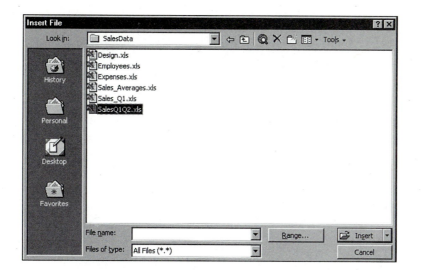

Figure 38.2.
Use the Insert File dialog box to search for the .xls file you want to insert.

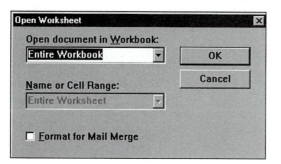

Figure 38.3.
By default, the entire workbook will be inserted into the Word document.

The entire workbook will be inserted into the Word document, appearing as a table. If you want to maintain a connection between the Excel source workbook and the data copied to the target Word document, you can insert the file as a link. To do so, in the Insert File dialog box, click the drop-down arrow beside the Insert button and choose Insert As Link. As long as your source and target files remain in the same locations and retain the same names, the link will remain intact. Each time the target file is opened, you can choose to update the link, and any changes to the source workbook will be updated in the document. You can also preserve the Word document's current content by not updating the linked content.

INSERTING AN INDIVIDUAL WORKSHEET

Perhaps your Word document doesn't require all the data in the entire workbook—maybe one or two specific sheets from a workbook contain the data you need. To insert an individual sheet from a workbook file, follow these steps:

1. In the Word document, position the insertion point where you want the inserted worksheet(s) placed.

2. Choose Insert, File.

3. In the Insert File dialog box, select All Files (*.*) from the Files of Type list box.

4. Navigate to the workbook file that contains the sheet you want to use, and double-click the filename.

5. In the Open Worksheet dialog box, click the Open Document in Workbook list box, and select the name of the sheet that you want to insert.

6. In the Name or Cell Range list box, select Entire Worksheet to insert the whole worksheet, or type a range of cell addresses (B7:F16, for example) or a named range from within the selected worksheet to insert just that range of cells (see Figure 38.4).

Figure 38.4.
If you've named any ranges in the worksheet, you can type the name to select that range of cells for insertion.

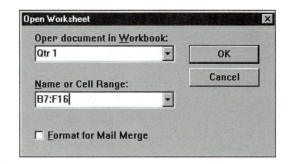

7. Choose OK to close the Open Worksheet dialog box and insert the data.

Once inserted, the data appears and functions as a Word table, and can be formatted by using Word's table, text, and paragraph formatting tools.

INSERTING A WORKSHEET RANGE

In some cases, you may want to insert just a portion of your Excel worksheet—perhaps just a few cells are of use, or you want a large section, but not the entire sheet and the inherent increase in file size for your target Word document. Whereas you could just copy and paste the range, inserting it instead frees you to add the content even if your Clipboard is full.

To insert a worksheet range in a Word document, follow these steps:

1. In the Word document, position the cursor at the point where you want to insert the Excel range.

2. Choose Insert, File.

3. In the Insert File dialog box, select All Files (*.*) from the Files of Type list box.

4. Navigate to the folder containing the workbook from which you want to insert a range, and click on the workbook file once to select it (see Figure 38.5).

5. Choose the Range button in the Insert File dialog box.

6. Enter the range addresses (such as B7:F16) in the Set Range dialog box (see Figure 38.6), and choose OK.

7. In the Insert File dialog box, choose Insert to add the specified range to your Word document.

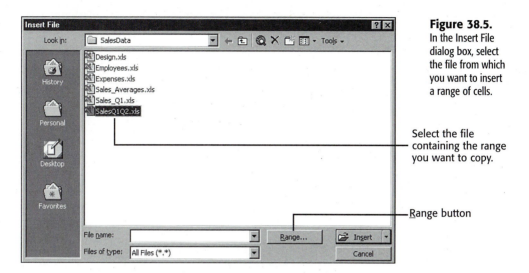

Figure 38.5.
In the Insert File dialog box, select the file from which you want to insert a range of cells.

Select the file containing the range you want to copy.

Range button

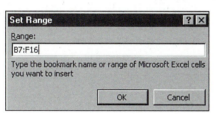

Figure 38.6.
Type your range of cells by entering two cell addresses separated by a colon.

MERGING EXCEL DATA INTO WORD MAIL MERGE DOCUMENTS

An Excel list database can be used as the data source for your Word form letters, labels, and catalogs. When a Mail Merge is performed in Word, a document (such as a letter or sheet of labels) is combined with a table of data, which provides the data called for in the document. For example, in a form letter, *merge codes* are inserted to tell Word where to place the recipient's name. When the document and the data are merged, Word goes to the cited database and extracts data from the field (or column, in Excel) that contains the requested data, such as First Name or Last Name. The data is inserted within the letter's body text, and a form letter is completed.

Your Excel list database must be set up properly. The complete set of rules for proper data entry is described in detail in Chapter 31, "Setting Up a List or Database in Excel." The basic requirements are as follows:

■ Your column labels become your field names, also known as a header row. Choose short, illustrative names such as First Name or Product Number. Each column label should be unique.

- Break down your data into as many fields as possible. For example, break your address data down into Address 1, Address 2, City, State, and Zip. A single "Address" field would be too hard to use for mailings restricted to people in a particular town or state.

- Leave no blank rows between your column labels and the first record (row) in your database. There can be no blank rows within your data, either.

- Each row (after the column labels) is a record, made up of data entered into the fields that are created by your column headings. Figure 38.7 shows an example of an employee database.

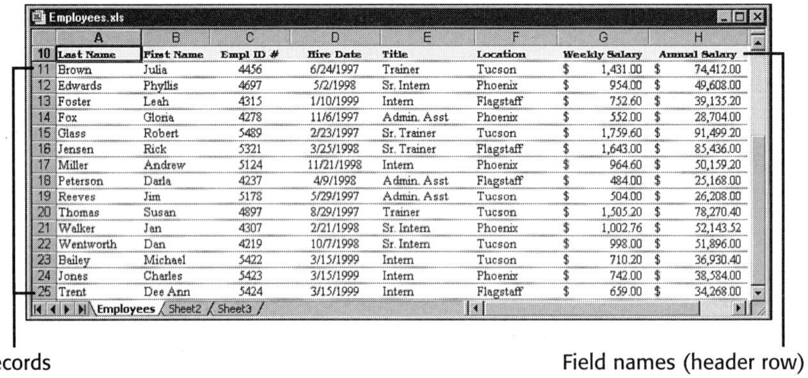

Figure 38.7.
The more care you put into the building of your Excel database, the more you'll be able to do with it.

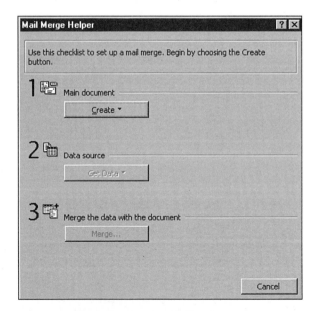

Records   Field names (header row)

After the database has been set up correctly, you can select it as the source for your mail merge data as described in the following steps:

1. In Word, choose Tools, Mail Merge. The Mail Merge Helper dialog box opens, as shown in Figure 38.8.

Figure 38.8.
The Mail Merge Helper dialog box is divided into three sections, or steps, to be followed sequentially.

2. In step 1 of the dialog box, choose the Create button, and choose the type of merged document you want to create—Form Letters, Mailing Labels, Envelopes, or Catalog.

3. Choose a new window or the current (Active) window for your new document.

4. Choose the Get Data button, and choose Open Data Source (see Figure 38.9).

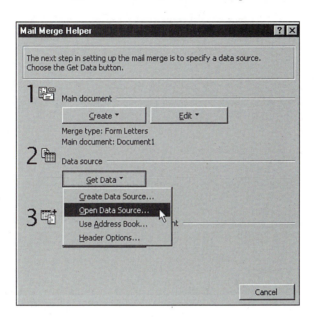

Figure 38.9.
Among other data sources, Word will accept Word documents (containing a table of data), Excel worksheets, and Access tables (.mdb files) as sources of data for your mail merge.

5. In the Open Data Source dialog box, select All Files (*.*) from the Files of Type list box.

6. Navigate to the folder containing the worksheet you want to use, and double-click the filename.

7. In the Microsoft Excel dialog box, select or type the name or cell range in the Named or Cell Range text box, and then choose OK.

8. Complete your mail merge by editing your document, which includes inserting merge codes (instructions for where to place data and which data to use), and merging the document and the selected data source.

To learn more about the complete process of merging a document and a database, consider the book *Special Edition Using Microsoft Word 2000*, published by Que (ISBN: 0-7897-1852-9).

FORMATTING EXCEL DATA IN A WORD DOCUMENT

Excel workbooks, worksheets, or cell ranges appear in Word in the form of a Word table—a collection of columns and rows, forming cells. Word provides a significant set of tools for adjusting the dimensions of table columns and rows, and visually formatting table cells and their content.

You can use Word's formatting tools to format the inserted Excel content in the Word document:

- *Change the width of columns and height of rows.* Click anywhere inside the table and choose Table, Table Properties. Using the Row and/or Column tabs, adjust the measurement of selected sections of the table.

- *Apply paragraph formatting.* If you want space above or below the cells' text, select the cells and then choose Format, Paragraph. Enter a point measurement in the Before and/or After boxes in the Spacing section of the Paragraph dialog box.

- *Format the text.* Select individual cells or columns/rows, and change alignment, fonts, font sizes, and font styles (such as Bold, Italic, and Underline). You can use the Formatting toolbar or the Font dialog box (choose Format, Font).

Unless you don't need or want any formatting of the data in Excel (perhaps the worksheet requires a plain appearance), it may be easier to format the cell content in Excel and utilize the Paste Special procedure to preserve formatting.

COPYING EXCEL DATA TO A POWERPOINT PRESENTATION

PowerPoint presentations often contain numeric data in the form of tables and charts. Charts are perhaps the more prevalent form in which numeric data is presented—they're highly graphical, and if set up properly, easy to interpret. Because presentations are generally best when they contain more pictures than words, charts are an important component.

PowerPoint presentations can display Excel data as cell blocks (which appear as tables) and as charts. You can build the chart in Excel and then copy it to the presentation slide, or you can use Excel data to build the PowerPoint datasheet, which in turn produces a PowerPoint chart.

Deciding which Excel content to use (cell ranges or an Excel chart) depends on what already exists in Excel—if you have only Excel data and haven't created a chart, you can use the data and create the chart in PowerPoint. However, keep in mind that Excel provides more extensive charting capabilities than PowerPoint. You may prefer to complete the chart in Excel and then transfer it to PowerPoint.

USING EXCEL RANGES IN A POWERPOINT SLIDE

Assuming Excel is your primary tool for storing statistical, financial, and list data, it's very likely that the information you want to use in your PowerPoint presentation already exists in an Excel worksheet. Rather than risk a typo or waste time retyping it into a PowerPoint table, why not use the Clipboard and/or Office's OLE tools for placing the Excel data into your PowerPoint slide?

It's a simple procedure to take a range of cells from your Excel worksheet and paste them into a PowerPoint slide. Somewhat more complex methods can be employed to insert the

Excel content and at the same time create a link between the worksheet and the slide, enabling you to keep the slide updated when changes are made to the worksheet. The approach you take depends on whether or not you need such a relationship between the source file (Excel worksheet) and the target file (PowerPoint slide).

Pasting Excel Ranges into a PowerPoint Slide

To paste a range of cells from an Excel worksheet into your PowerPoint slide, follow these steps:

1. In your Excel worksheet, select the contiguous range of cells that you want to use in your PowerPoint slide.

2. Choose Edit, Copy or press Ctrl+C.

3. Switch to or open your PowerPoint presentation, and go to the slide to which you want to add the Excel content. Be sure to use Slide View or Normal View.

4. In the PowerPoint window, choose Edit, Paste, or press Ctrl+V. If the Clipboard toolbar is displayed, click the icon that represents your Excel content.

Your Excel range appears as a table in your PowerPoint slide, and it can be formatted as such by moving, resizing the object as a whole, or by adjusting the dimensions of columns and rows by using PowerPoint's table tools. To find out more about PowerPoint, check out Que's *Special Edition Using Microsoft PowerPoint 2000*, ISBN: 0-7897-1904-5.

Linking Excel Data to Your PowerPoint Slide

To create a relationship between your Excel source range and the copy of it pasted on a PowerPoint slide, you must link the two files. Once linked, moving or renaming either the Excel workbook or the PowerPoint presentation severs the link. You can update and break links later should you need to.

To paste Excel content into your PowerPoint slide and establish a link between the source and target files, follow these steps:

1. In your Excel worksheet, select the contiguous range of cells that you want to use in your PowerPoint slide.

2. Choose Edit, Copy, or press Ctrl+C.

3. Open or switch to your PowerPoint presentation, and use Slide View to display the slide into which you want to paste the Excel content.

4. In the PowerPoint window, choose Edit, Paste Special.

5. In the Paste Special dialog box, choose the Paste Link option (see Figure 38.10).

6. Choose Microsoft Excel Worksheet Object from the As box, and choose OK.

Figure 38.10.
Your copied Excel content will now be linked to the PowerPoint presentation, and you can keep the data between source and target in sync as needed.

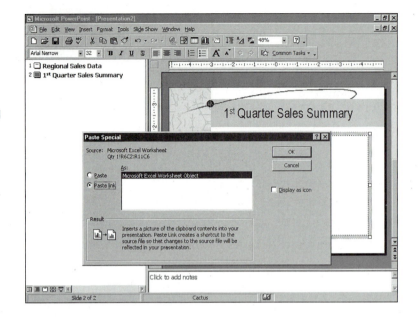

Your linked Excel content appears in the form of a table, and can be moved or resized. To edit its content, double-click it. The Excel worksheet from which it came will open, and any edits you perform there will be updated in the slide. Make your changes, and then switch back to the PowerPoint slide (use the Taskbar or Alt+Tab) and you'll see the changes reflected there.

Tip #479

Each time you open the target presentation in the future, you can choose whether or not to update the link—if changes have been made to the source Excel content, you can opt to have them reflected in the presentation. If you choose not to, you can always update them later by choosing Edit, Links and choose the Update Now button.

Excel content can also be embedded in your PowerPoint slide, which will give you not only the existing Excel content, but when the Excel object is active, the tools of Excel as well, right within your PowerPoint window.

PASTING EXCEL DATA IN A POWERPOINT DATASHEET

In addition to using existing Excel data directly on a PowerPoint slide, you can use it to fill in your PowerPoint datasheet when creating a PowerPoint chart. To use Excel data in a PowerPoint datasheet, follow these steps:

1. With both the PowerPoint presentation and Excel worksheet open, select the Excel content you want to use (see Figure 38.11).

Don't select the worksheet titles.

Select column headings that will become category axis labels.

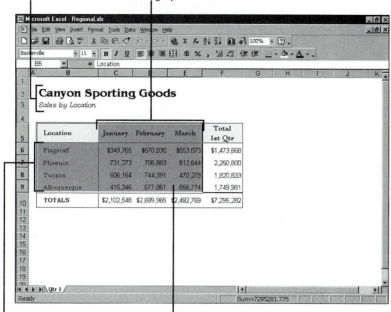

Figure 38.11.
Keep the chart's content in mind when selecting the range of cells to paste into the PowerPoint datasheet.

Select row headings that will form the legend.

Select the numeric data that will be plotted in the chart.

2. Choose Edit, Copy.

3. Switch to the PowerPoint presentation, and go to the slide in which you'll be using the data.

4. Double-click the chart placeholder to display the datasheet. The datasheet appears with sample data inside it.

5. In the PowerPoint datasheet, click the upper-left gray cell to select all the cells in the datasheet (see Figure 38.12).

6. Press Delete to remove the datasheet's sample data.

7. Click in the first cell in the datasheet (above row 1, in the blank column to the left of column A).

8. Choose Edit, Paste. The Excel content appears in the datasheet, and you see a chart form behind the datasheet (see Figure 38.13). Continue the chart-creation process in PowerPoint.

Note

You use the first blank column instead of column A in the datasheet because the first blank column contains the chart's legend data. The row above row 1 contains the category axis information. PowerPoint's charting tools will enable you to switch these two groups of data as needed.

Figure 38.12.
Selecting all cells before deletion enables you to be certain that all the sample data is removed.

Click here to select all the cells in the datasheet.

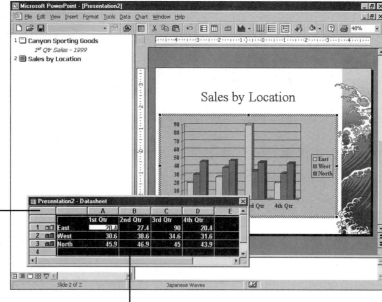

Sample data

Figure 38.13.
The Excel data is immediately used to create a PowerPoint chart.

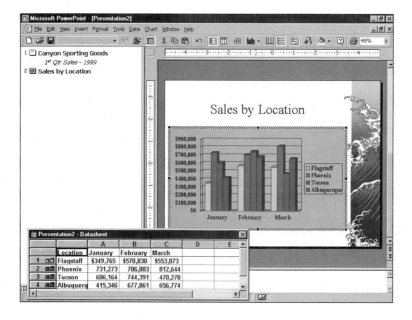

USING EXCEL CHARTS IN A POWERPOINT PRESENTATION

If you've already created a chart in Excel, why go through the process of building it again in PowerPoint? Unless you want to create a different type of chart, it's much easier to use the Excel chart in the PowerPoint presentation.

Follow these steps to paste the Excel chart into the PowerPoint slide:

1. With both the Excel worksheet that contains the chart and the target PowerPoint presentation open, click once on the Excel chart to select it.

2. Choose Edit, Copy.

3. Switch to the PowerPoint presentation, and move to the slide onto which you want to paste the chart.

4. If a chart placeholder appears on the slide, delete it.

5. In PowerPoint, choose Edit, Paste.

The chart appears in the PowerPoint presentation, exactly as it appeared in Excel. You can move and resize the chart as needed, or double-click it to access Excel's charting tools to make any adjustments to the chart's appearance.

Note

> If you want the Excel data that was used to create the chart to remain linked to this copy of the chart, use Paste Special and choose to paste link the chart. If the chart is linked and not simply pasted, changes to the Excel data will update the chart.

For more information on using Excel to create a chart, see Chapter 27, "Building Charts with Excel." To learn more about formatting Excel charts, see Chapter 29, "Formatting Charts."

COPYING WORD AND POWERPOINT DATA TO AN EXCEL WORKSHEET

Whereas Excel data can be a valuable addition to Word documents and PowerPoint presentations, the reverse also is true—you can realize significant savings of time and effort by using existing Word and PowerPoint content in Excel worksheets. Following are some examples of how you can use Word and PowerPoint content:

- If the data's first appearance is in a PowerPoint datasheet, copy it to an Excel worksheet to avail yourself of Excel's superior formatting and calculation tools. If the data is valuable beyond the scope of the presentation, you'll get much more out of it in Excel.

- If a table containing a valuable list already exists in Word, bring it into Excel for quick sorting and filtering. Whereas these features are available in Word, their Excel equivalents are much more powerful and easier to use.

- Reuse clip art or drawn objects from PowerPoint or Word in an Excel worksheet. If the graphic images you need already exist in another file, don't reinsert or redraw—paste them!

- Copy an individual PowerPoint slide into your Word document. If you've created a visually pleasing slide that conveys something valuable for your document, don't waste time re-creating it. Using slide content in your Word documents also contributes to an overall visual consistency between your files.

ADDING WORD TEXT TO AN EXCEL WORKSHEET

Word text appears in two formats that you can use in Excel—paragraph text and table text. Obviously, Word tables are a natural for placing in an Excel worksheet—the data is already arranged in cells. Paragraph text is best used when it appears in the form of short phrases or titles. Unless the Excel cells are formatted for text wrapping, a long sentence or paragraph can cause problems fitting into an existing Excel worksheet. If you insert paragraph text as an object into a worksheet, it will appear as a text box, obscuring worksheet cells.

Tip #480	Your paragraph text can be parsed (separated) into individual cells through Excel's Data, Text to Columns feature, discussed later in this chapter.

You can add Word content, regardless of form, to an Excel worksheet in one of the two following ways:

- *Use the Clipboard.* Copy the Word text and paste it into the Excel worksheet. You can use this method for tables or paragraph text. When pasting, be sure to click in the cell that should contain the text or that will serve as the first cell in the pasted range.

- *Insert a Word object.* In this case, the text is typed into the object after it's inserted (see Figure 38.14). It will be placed in a floating object window, which, when active, will cause Word's tools to take over the Excel toolbars and menus.

SORTING AND FILTERING TABLE DATA

One of the primary reasons for bringing Word table data into an Excel worksheet is to avail yourself of Excel's sorting and filtering tools. While you can perform simple sorts in Word, Excel's sorting tools are faster and easier to use, and provide additional sort options.

Sorting and filtering commands are found in the Data menu in Excel. Sorting can be performed on up to three fields, and filtering can be performed on as many fields as you desire.

Tip #481	If you still need to use the table data in a Word environment, paste it back into the Word document after you've sorted and/or filtered it in Excel.

→ For more information on sorting and filtering Excel lists, **see** "Sorting a List," **p. 981** and "Filtering a List," **p. 985**

Word tools in Excel window

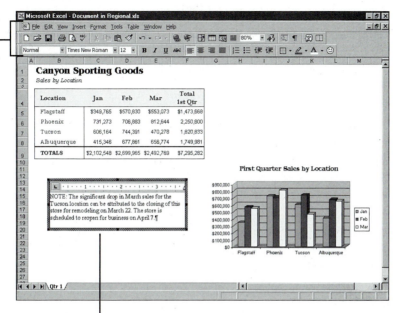

Figure 38.14.
Choose Insert, Object, and choose Microsoft Word Document. Type the text into the Word window that opens on the worksheet.

Word window on top of worksheet

PART

IX

CH

38

PARSING DATA

Because users don't expect the level of flexibility in their use of Word tables that one finds in Excel, tables designed and completed in Word don't tend to be as well planned in terms of their use as a database as those that are built from the ground up in Excel. For example, in order to have the greatest degree of sorting and filtering capability, tables should be broken down into as many fields as possible—instead of a "Name" field in a name and address list, the name should be divided into two fields, "First Name" and "Last Name." This gives you the capacity to sort the list by last name, and to use it for a mail merge wherein letters contain a salutation such as "Dear Mr. Smith" or "Dear Bob" instead of "Dear Bob Smith." Also, breaking "Address" down into "Street," "City," "State," and "Zip" makes filtering by city or zip code much easier.

So what do you do if the Word-created table isn't currently conducive to effective sorting and filtering? You parse the table in Excel. Parsing takes larger pieces and breaks them down, making more analysis possible.

Note

Parsing isn't only for Word lists. You can parse any list that you can import to Excel—including database information from Access, text-formatted lists from other programs, and so on.

To parse table data, follow these steps:

1. If the column to the right of the column you want to parse contains data, insert columns to make room for the parsed information. For example, if you're parsing a single column into three columns, insert two columns to the right of the column you're parsing. To insert a column, select the column before which to insert the column and choose Insert, Columns.

2. After pasting the table from Word into Excel, select the rightmost column that requires further breakdown (see Figure 38.15).

Figure 38.15.
Working from right to left avoids accidental overwriting of table data with the columns added through parsing. In this example, only the first column needs to be parsed.

The Name column will become two columns—First Name and Last Name.

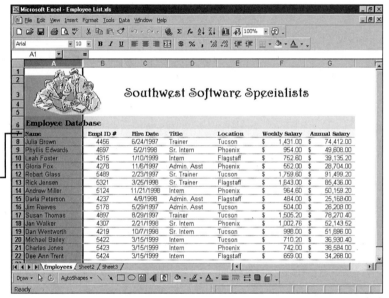

3. Choose Data, Text to Columns.

4. The Convert Text to Columns Wizard opens, as shown in Figure 38.16.

5. In the Original data type box, choose Delimited. Delimiters are characters (such as commas, spaces, or semicolons) or codes (such as tabs or hard returns) that are used to break text content into pieces.

6. Choose Next.

7. Choose the delimiters that you want Excel to use in determining where column breaks should occur (see Figure 38.17).

8. Choose Next.

9. After checking the Data Preview in the wizard's final dialog box, choose Finish to complete the wizard and apply the commands to the selected column.

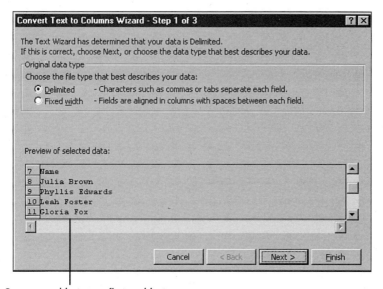

Figure 38.16.
Preview the selected data in Step 1 of 3 of the wizard.

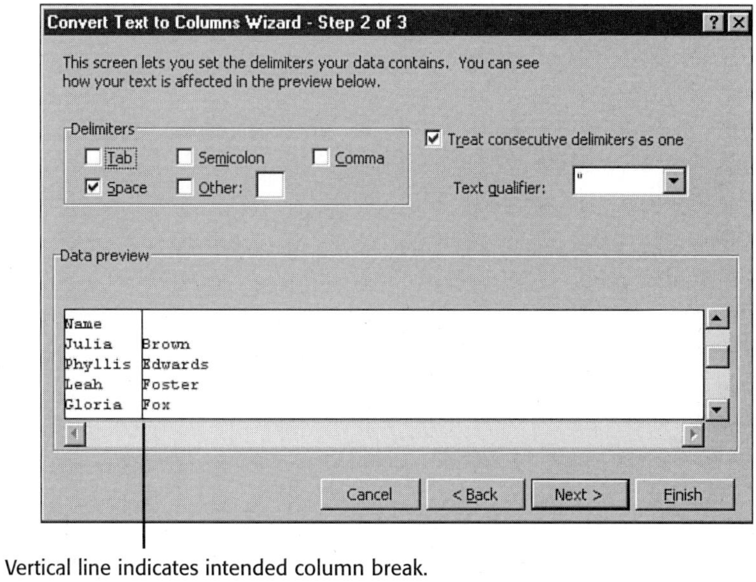

Spaces used between first and last names

Figure 38.17.
After selecting one or more delimiters, view the Data preview to see how the data will be parsed.

Vertical line indicates intended column break.

In the wizard's last step, you can also choose to apply General (the default), Text, or Date formats to the new columns. In addition, you can specify a particular Destination for the parsed cells.

You may notice the need to do subsequent parsing, especially when you've used a combination of delimiters in the text. If you didn't use consistent delimiters, you can always reparse one of the new columns and choose a different delimiter for the second conversion of text to columns.

Tip #482

Sometimes you need to combine text into one cell from separate cells, rather than the other way around. In the target cell where you want the combined data, enter the formula =CONCATENATE(*cell1*,*cell2*), where *cell1* is the first cell whose contents you want to include and *cell2* is the second. Excel will combine the text into one cell.

USING POWERPOINT DATASHEET CONTENT IN EXCEL

There may be times that your initial use of pertinent data occurs first in PowerPoint—for example, when sales figures are entered into the PowerPoint datasheet for the purpose of creating a chart for a presentation. In these cases, the creation of the PowerPoint datasheet can become the first step in later using the data in Excel, where it can be formatted and used in calculations. The datasheet data can be the start of a new worksheet or can be added to an existing worksheet.

To copy the PowerPoint datasheet content to an Excel worksheet, follow these steps:

1. In the PowerPoint slide, display the datasheet and the content you've entered.

2. Drag through the datasheet's cells or click the Select All button on the datasheet (see Figure 38.18).

Figure 38.18.
Use the Select All button to select every cell in the datasheet.

The Select All button

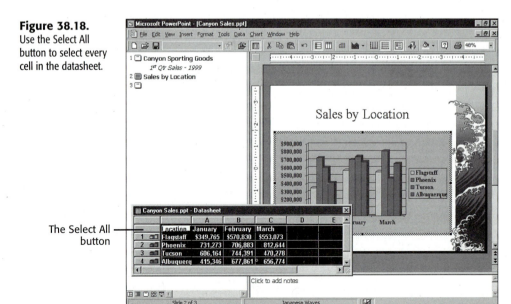

3. Choose Edit, Copy, or press Ctrl+C.

4. Switch to or open the Excel worksheet, and click in the cell where you'd like the pasted content to begin.

5. Choose Edit, Paste, or press Ctrl+V.

After pasting the datasheet content, you might need to move things around or add column/row labels to fit the desired layout for the Excel worksheet. The data is now ready for any formatting or formulas you want to apply.

Note

> While you can paste a chart from PowerPoint to Excel, it's generally not a good idea to do so. It's much better to re-create the chart in Excel so that changes and updates to the data (which are more likely to occur in Excel than PowerPoint) can easily update the chart.

COMBINING WORD, EXCEL, AND POWERPOINT FILES WITH HYPERLINKS

A powerful way to use Office 2000 applications together is to use hyperlinks. A *hyperlink* is a selection of text or a graphic image that is associated with another file, a Web page on the Internet, or your company's intranet. You can link Word, PowerPoint, and Excel files quickly and easily with hyperlinks, making it possible to open a worksheet from within a Word document, a Word document or Excel worksheet from within a PowerPoint presentation, or a PowerPoint presentation from within a Word document or an Excel worksheet. There is no limit to the number of hyperlinks you can insert into a single file, nor is there a limit to the relationships that hyperlinks can create—for example, a hyperlink in a Word document can point to a presentation that contains an Excel chart, thus combining two applications in a single link.

Following are some ideas for using hyperlinks with Office 2000:

- *Access supporting data.* Create a hyperlink in a PowerPoint presentation that opens a worksheet containing the data that a PowerPoint chart reflects. If someone asks to see the supporting data, you can get to it quickly, but you haven't wasted space on the slide displaying the data.

- *Refer to related documents.* If you're sending a memo that refers to an Excel list (database), include a link to that worksheet. This is more efficient for the memo recipients than merely telling them where the database is stored.

- *Display a chart on command.* What if you don't want to waste space on the worksheet with a chart or have a sheet within the workbook used for the chart? Copy the chart data to another workbook, create a chart from it, and then create a hyperlink in the original workbook that points to the chart. If the chart is of interest, it's accessible, but it's not taking up valuable space.

CREATING A HYPERLINK

Hyperlinks can be represented by text or graphics. The procedure you use to create hyperlinks is the same for Word, Excel, and PowerPoint.

To create a hyperlink in Word, Excel, or PowerPoint, follow these steps:

1. In the open file, select a single word, short phrase, or a graphic object that you want to use as a hyperlink.

2. Choose Insert, Hyperlink.

3. In the Insert Hyperlink dialog box, enter a folder and filename (or Web page name) for the file to which the hyperlink should point (see Figure 38.19).

The selected cell

Figure 38.19.
It's a good idea to browse for the file if you're not absolutely sure of the path and filename.

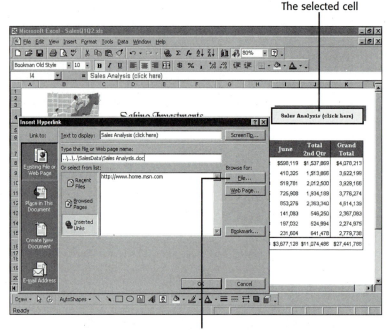

Choose File to simultaneously locate and enter the path and filename to which the hyperlink will point.

4. If you don't know the exact folder path to the file or the full filename, choose the File button on the right.

5. After entering or selecting the file for the hyperlink, choose OK.

In the file that contains the hyperlink, test it by pointing to it with the mouse—the mouse pointer should turn into a pointing hand (see Figure 38.20). The file referenced in the link appears in a ScreenTip beside the pointing hand. Click the hyperlink to verify that the link points to the appropriate file.

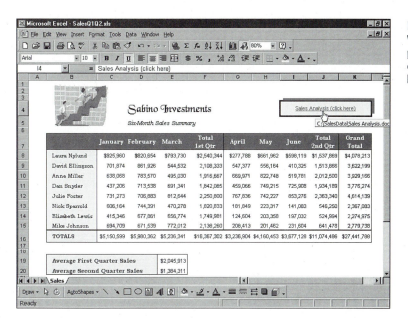

Figure 38.20.
When you see the pointing hand, click once to go to the hyperlinked file.

In the destination file (the file that the hyperlink jumps to), you may choose to include another hyperlink that returns the reader to the previous file (the source file containing the first hyperlink). Use the same procedure detailed previously to add the second hyperlink, and then reference the original file in step 3. You also could instruct readers to click the Back button in the Web toolbar (if it appears onscreen) to return to the previous file.

Caution

If others within your organization will use the file containing hyperlinks, be sure that the files to which the hyperlinks point will be available to those users. The hyperlinked files should be on network drives to which everyone has access. If the hyperlink is for your own use, the linked files can reside on your local hard drive.

If you'd like a different ScreenTip (other than the filename) to appear onscreen when you point to a hyperlink, choose the ScreenTip button in the Insert Hyperlink dialog box. Type the ScreenTip text in the resulting dialog box, and choose OK.

Tip #483

If you'd like the person reviewing the file to be able to easily email you with comments or questions, add a hyperlink that points to an email address. When the link is clicked, a new message window will open, automatically addressed to the address you specify. Choose the E-mail Address button on the left side of the Insert Hyperlink dialog box and supply all requested information.

Using Hyperlinks to Access a Range of Cells

You also can use hyperlinks to navigate within an open Excel workbook. Working similarly to named ranges, hyperlinks can be established in a worksheet, pointing to other cells within the workbook. This quick navigation/access method eliminates the need to create names for the ranges, and makes it possible to create the look and feel of a Web page within the workbook.

To create a hyperlink to access a specific range of cells, follow these steps:

1. In the open workbook, click on the cell or graphic image that will serve as the hyperlink.

2. Choose Insert, Hyperlink, and choose the Place in This Document button on the left side of the dialog box.

3. Type the cell address. It can be a single cell or a range of cells (see Figure 38.21). You also can select a named range from the Defined Names list.

This graphic will be used for the hyperlink.

Figure 38.21.
Create the feel of a Web site within the workbook by creating hyperlinks to cells within the workbook.

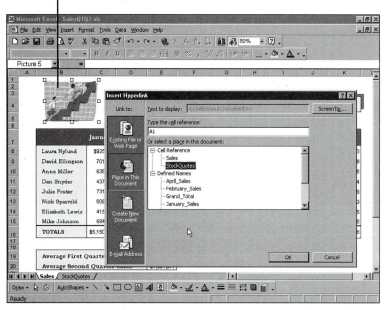

4. Choose the ScreenTip button, then type the pop-up text that will appear when pointing to the link (see Figure 38.22), and choose OK.

5. In the list box, select the worksheet that contains the specified cell or range.

6. Choose OK.

Figure 38.22.
Type the name of the cell range or a description of the information to which the hyperlink points.

Tip #484

You can nest links by creating a hyperlink in Word or PowerPoint that points to an Excel workbook that contains its own hyperlinks to important locations within its own worksheets.

UPDATING HYPERLINKS

Over time, hyperlinks can become invalid—perhaps the file to which the hyperlink points has been moved or deleted, or the information considered important enough to link to is no longer of interest. For a multitude of reasons, you'll want to update the hyperlinks.

To edit the hyperlink, follow these steps:

1. Right-click the hyperlink you want to edit.

2. From the shortcut menu, choose Hyperlink, Edit Hyperlink.

3. The Edit Hyperlink dialog box opens, looking very similar to the Insert Hyperlink dialog box (see Figure 38.23). Click the appropriate Link To button (on the left side of the dialog box) to choose the type of link.

4. Make the desired changes to the link, and choose OK.

PART
IX

CH
38

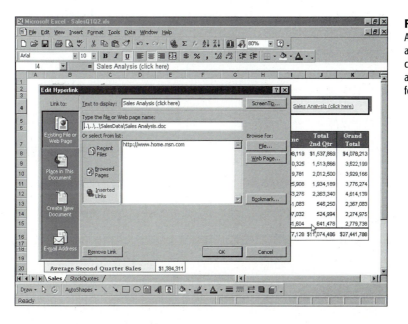

Figure 38.23.
Adjust the folder path and filename, or choose a new sheet and/or range of cells for the hyperlink.

DELETING HYPERLINKS

If a hyperlink is no longer of use, you can delete it. Deleting a hyperlink doesn't delete the text or graphic that currently serves as a hyperlink—deleting the link merely eliminates the text or graphic's role as a pointer to another file or range of cells within the worksheet.

To delete the hyperlink, follow these steps:

1. Right-click the hyperlink text or graphic.

2. From the shortcut menu, choose Hyperlink, Remove Hyperlink.

Tip #485	You also can delete a hyperlink from within the Edit Hyperlink dialog box by clicking the Remove Link button.

TROUBLESHOOTING

UPDATING LINKS BETWEEN FILES

The Excel data that I linked to a PowerPoint slide seems to be broken. Whenever I change the data in Excel, these edits aren't reflected in PowerPoint. How do I fix the link?

Switch to the application containing the link (PowerPoint, in this example), and choose Edit, Links. Then, select the link you want to reconnect from the Links list box and choose the Change Source button. In the Change Source dialog box, select the file you want the linked object to connect to (select another folder from the Look In list, if necessary). Choose the Open button. The file you chose appears in the Links dialog box; choose Close to close the dialog box. The updated link information appears in the application.

EDITING AN EXISTING HYPERLINK

I need to make changes to an existing hyperlink, but when I try to click the hyperlink to select it, I jump to the file referenced in the hyperlink. How do I edit the hyperlink?

Right-click the hyperlink. Then choose Hyperlink, Edit Hyperlink from the shortcut menu. Make the desired changes in the dialog box, and then choose OK.

If you just want to make simple formatting changes to the hyperlink (such as using a different font or adding italic), right-click the hyperlink and choose Hyperlink, Select Hyperlink. Then use the menus or toolbars to format the text, as usual. Click outside of the hyperlink to deselect it.

FIXING INVALID HYPERLINKS

The hyperlink I created in an Excel workbook no longer works. How do I fix this?

Most likely, the file referenced in the hyperlink was moved or deleted, or you moved the Excel file itself. To update the hyperlink, right-click the hyperlink and choose Hyperlink, Edit Hyperlink. Click the appropriate Link To button, edit the location of the destination file, and choose OK.

If this doesn't seem to be the source of the problem, and the hyperlink references file(s) on a network, ensure that you have access to the files on the network.

WEB PUBLISHING AND DOCUMENT CREATION

USING WORD TO DEVELOP WEB CONTENT

WEB PAGE DEVELOPMENT: WORD'S STRENGTHS AND WEAKNESSES

The Internet and its underlying technologies have become a fixture in many businesses today. The Web is now becoming integral to the operation of many businesses. The preferred method for disseminating information within many corporations is now the company intranet. An *intranet* is an internal Web site designed for use within an entire organization or departmental unit. Parts of it may be open to public consumption on the Internet, but generally access is restricted to employees or other parties important to the organization. Some intranets have grown into *extranets*, which are networks of organizations that share a common interest.

Communicating with Word: Choose the Right Tool for the Job
Choose your tools based on the job you want to do. If you plan on using a lot of flashy Java, JavaScript, VBScript, or dynamic HTML effects, then using a tool specifically designed to implement such elements would be a good idea. If you choose to provide information in a more conservative manner, then Word can do the job. Word's roundtrip HTML feature is a useful tool if you plan to mirror your pages with print communications and you will be updating both versions simultaneously.

MICROSOFT'S ANSWERS TO WEB PUBLISHING

Previously, Microsoft developed an add-on to Word 95 called the Internet Assistant. This was a very crude Web page editor, built as Microsoft's first attempt to add Internet features. With Office 97, Microsoft began the first true integration of Web technologies into Word. A new Web toolbar showed up in the product. Word 97 could now natively read, edit, save, and create HTML (Hypertext Markup Language), the language of Web pages. But Word has a much richer document type than HTML alone can express. When Word 97 documents were saved to HTML, many Word formatting conventions and features were lost. Word 97 also had the bad habit of unexpectedly changing the HTML code built using other HTML editors when these Web pages were edited in Word 97.

WORD 2000 AND THE WEB

Word 2000 represents the next evolutionary step of incorporating Web technology into an Office product. And Microsoft has done a lot of work under the hood to tune up the Web capabilities of this product. Some of the new Web-related capabilities in Word 2000 include

- A more robust translation to Web pages
- An improved wizard for building Web pages or even small Web sites
- An option to build Web pages within Word, without switching to a separate working environment
- A Web Page preview, similar to Print Preview

By far the most important change is the improvement to the HTML format. Microsoft has cleverly incorporated a wide variety of new Web technologies and languages into its Web page format. This new alphabet soup of technologies includes

- XML (eXtensible Markup Language)
- CSS (Cascading Style Sheets)
- VML (Vector Markup Language)
- JavaScript and VBScript (Visual Basic Script)

You don't need to know how to use each or any of these technologies to build or edit Web pages in Word 2000. The main effect of adding these technologies is to enhance the capability of browsers to display the data, improve formatting, and increase the scope of graphical object types that can be included in Web pages.

What this means is that, in many situations, it doesn't matter anymore whether you save a document as a .doc binary file or a Web page. Either file format looks the same in both Word 2000 and a properly equipped browser. All the information normally contained in the .doc binary file format is also included in the Web page format and vice versa. This interchangeability of file formats is called *round-tripping* by Microsoft. You can use any Web page created in Word 2000 to completely regenerate the binary .doc format. This was not possible with Word 97.

PART

X

CH

39

Note

Round-tripping applies only to Web pages created in Word. The document will look the same whether it's a Word Web page or a Word .doc file. If any other Web page is edited in Word, it may or may not look like it originally did after it has been saved from Word.

The beefed-up Web page format can now display the majority of Word features. These supplementary technologies increase the capability of HTML to display and manage more than is possible by just using HTML.

Note

So why use the .doc binary file format anymore? If communication is increasingly performed using Web technologies and Web pages, and Word pages display the same in browsers as they do in Word 2000, why bother translating back and forth between these two formats? Why not just start saving everything as Web pages? Why bother with a proprietary binary format anymore? The Web format has the same functionality. It is up to you as an Office user to decide whether the Web technologies in Word 2000 warrant discarding the .doc file format. Microsoft will be watching.

WORD 2000'S HTML SHORTCOMINGS

Word 2000 still has weaknesses in its capability to translate all its features to a Web page, though the list is far shorter than that seen in Word 97. The following Word features do not translate to a Web page:

- Versioning is lost.
- Passwords are lost.
- Word file headers/footers are not displayed in any form.
- Columns are not maintained, though the text is unaffected.

That's a total of four Word features in the Web Page format that don't display in a browser. That's a short enough list to put on a note and stick to your monitor. When the Web page is loaded back into Word, however, the columns and headers/footers are restored to their original format. So no text or formatting information is lost in the conversion to the Word 2000 Web page format. Microsoft Internet Explorer simply cannot render some information.

Tip #486	Web pages generated by Word 2000 are not easily interchangeable with those created in earlier versions of Word or other word processors or HTML editors. The new languages incorporated into Word 2000 Web pages—XML and VML especially—simply don't have equivalents in most other programs. To avoid problems with programs that don't have any or as robust support for XML and VML, save your Word documents into earlier versions of Word or other earlier, more compatible formats.

With only these few gaps remaining, Word is now ready for prime time as a tool for Web page creation. Using Word to create Web pages has three advantages:

- If documents already exist as Word .doc files, saving them as Web pages is now a one-step operation.
- You don't need to learn how to use a separate Web page editor, such as FrontPage.
- You don't have to wonder which Word features will or will not show up in a Web page; almost all Word features can now be expressed in Web pages.

Because there's more to making and maintaining a Web site than creating Web pages, there is a point at which it is more suitable to use a formal Web page authoring tool, such as FrontPage. This is discussed in more detail in the section in this chapter titled "Web Publishing in Word 2000."

CREATING A SINGLE WEB PAGE IN WORD

In Word 2000, creating a Web page is no different than creating a Word document. You do not need to open up a special environment or think differently about the contents of your page. For step-by-step instructions on building a Web page, see the section at the end of this chapter titled "Project: Building a Basic Web Page."

BUILDING A WEB PAGE FROM SCRATCH

To begin building from a blank page, just open a new page from the menu or toolbar. If you prefer a page that has some basic formatting, choose File, New, click the Web Pages tab, and choose from among some preformatted Web page types, as shown in Figure 39.1.

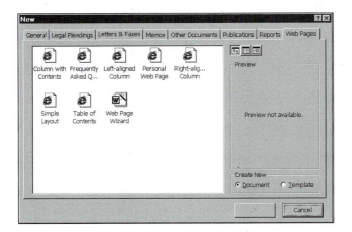

Figure 39.1
A list of preformatted Web pages.

After you open the preformatted page, just replace the placeholder text with your own content.

Tip #487	The main advantage of using template pages is that you can concentrate on content rather than worry about the formatting. To maintain the formatting, select only the placeholder text you want to replace in a given section. If you select the whole page when you intend to delete the placeholder elements, you may lose some of the other formatting elements. Also note that you can create your own templates and add them to the list of Web page templates as discussed in the section in this chapter titled "Creating Your Own Web Page Templates."

PREVIEWING THE WEB PAGE

As you are building your Web page, you can view or preview your Web pages using Web Layout view and Web Page Preview.

 Web Layout view (choose View, Web Layout from the menu or click the Web Layout icon in the status bar) presents your document like a Web page. The only difference between Normal view and Web Layout view is that the background texture or image, normally present in a Web page, is turned off in Normal view. All other items display identically.

Web Page Preview enables you to preview your Web page in a browser without first having to save the file. Click File, Web Page Preview on the menu to initiate the process. The file in Word is opened in your default browser for viewing. This ensures that what you are building in Word is indeed being displayed the same way in the browser.

Note

Remember that just because your Web page looks good in one browser doesn't mean it'll look good in all browsers. Unless you know everyone will be accessing your Web page with the same browser and version, it is a good idea to test your Web pages out with the latest versions of Microsoft and Netscape browsers as well as earlier versions, if possible. Note that if some things do not show up in one browser (the scrolling marquee, for instance, is not supported by Netscape browsers), you may need to remove that element or build browser-specific pages.

In Figure 39.2, you can see the effect of browser type on the Web page display of a table with a background color.

Figure 39.2
Table borders display differently between Netscape Navigator and Internet Explorer when a table background color is used.

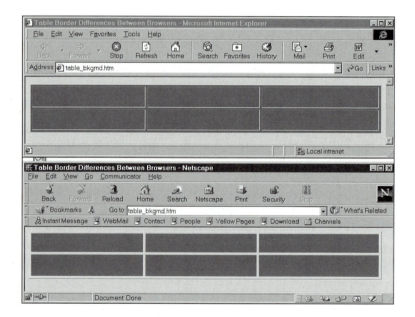

The table size and table color background (red) are the same, but the borders are different.

→ To see a list of browser-specific tags, **see** "Web Browsers and Platforms," (chapter 6) in the book *HTML 4 Unleashed* (Rick Darnell, ISBN: 1575212994, Sams Publishing.)

SAVING A WEB PAGE

With a Word .doc file, you can embed many elements, such as graphics and sounds, directly into the .doc file, so that you have only one file to worry about. Web pages, however, do not directly embed many of the items that are displayed in browsers. For a graphic, the

Web page contains only the path to the image file, not the image file itself. The same is true for sounds, videos, Java applets, and many other items. So what happens to these associated files when you save a Web page from Word 2000?

Imagine that you're saving your Web page to a local drive under the filename of HomePage.htm. First, the actual Web page, HomePage.htm, is stored in the folder you selected on your local hard drive. Next, a folder called HomePage Files is created under the folder containing HomePage.htm. In the HomePage Files folder you will find the following:

- Two files, filelist.xml and header.htm, contain information necessary for round-tripping (that is, for translating HomePage.htm back to a .doc file). These files are not used when HomePage.htm is viewed in a browser.

- All the bitmap image files are saved under image001.gif, image002.gif, image001.jpg, and so forth.

- Drawing objects are also saved as .gif files.

- Sound and video files are not moved to the HomePage Files folder. Although your Web page works on your local hard drive, anyone else accessing it will not receive any audio or video.

PART

X

CH

39

Tip #488

Save your Web page before inserting the multimedia elements. Doing so instructs Word to create the HomePage Files folder. Then copy the audio, video, and Java applets to the HomePage Files folder before inserting them in your Web page. This ensures that the files remain linked to HomePage.htm.

VIEWING HTML SOURCE CODE

When you save a file as a Web page, the file is saved as a .htm or .html file. The actual code that a browser translates into a Web page is called *HTML source code*. In Word 2000, this is not only HTML but also includes XML, CSS, VML, and the scripting languages. If you want to access this code—for instance to modify the JavaScript—you can access the code from the menu under View, HTML Source. The source code is displayed in an MDE (Microsoft Development Environment) window, as shown in Figure 39.3.

As far as the HTML source code is concerned, you can search and edit the HTML source code from within the MDE as you wish. To save your changes, just choose File, Exit from the menu.

Directly modifying the HTML source from within the MDE is not recommended unless you are an experienced programmer or Web developer.

Figure 39.3
Modifying HTML source code in the Microsoft Development Environment.

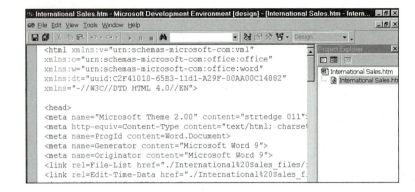

USING WEB SCRIPTING

Web pages commonly use scripting languages to define actions and objects accessible from within a browser. The most common languages in use are JavaScript (Microsoft's version is called JScript) and VBScript (Visual Basic Script). To add JavaScript or VBScript code to a new Web page:

1. Choose <u>T</u>ools, <u>M</u>acro, Microsoft Scripting <u>E</u>ditor from the menu. Or use the keyboard shortcut, Alt+Shift+F11. The MDE (Microsoft Development Environment) opens up as shown in Figure 39.4.

Note

The MDE used to view HTML source (refer to Figure 39.3) is a simpler variant of the MDE used to create or edit scripting code (see Figure 39.4).

Figure 39.4
Adding script code to a Web page using the Microsoft Scripting Editor.

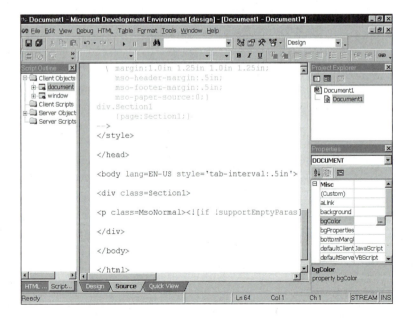

2. To choose the default language (either VBScript or JavaScript) in which to write a script, choose View, Property Pages from the menu (Shift+F4 from the keyboard). This affects scripts for which you do not explicitly specify a language. As shown in Figure 39.5, you can choose between VBScript and JavaScript for either client-side or server-side scripts.

Note

Client-side scripts execute within the browser after the Web page has loaded; they are self-contained. A server-side script requires some additional action on the part of the Web server (other than serving the Web page itself) to execute.

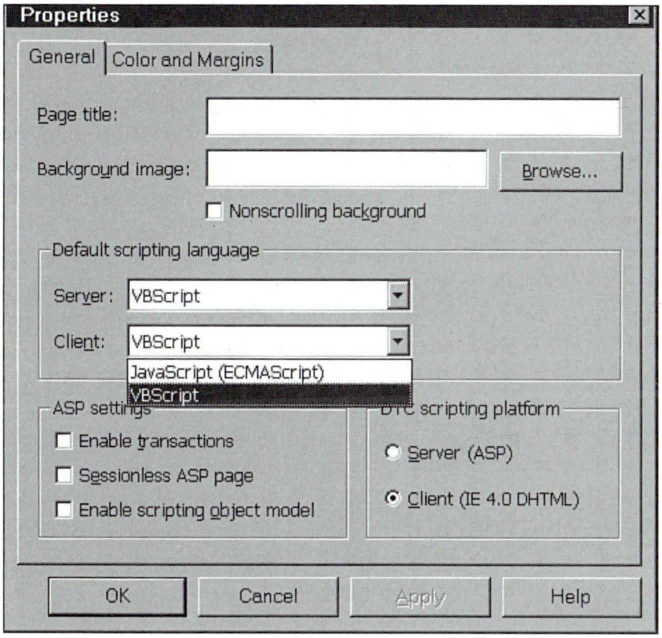

Figure 39.5
Choosing the scripting language to use in your Web page.

3. Next you have two choices for how to add code to the Web page: add a blank scripting container or insert script functions directly. A *blank scripting container* is simply the code for starting and ending the text of the script within a Web page. You fill in the middle of the container with your desired scripting functions.

   • To add a blank scripting container, choose HTML, Script Block, Client (Server is also available) from the menu. A blank scripting container is inserted into the Web page, as shown in Figure 39.6.

   • If you prefer to select scripting functions from a list, open the Script Outline by choosing View, Other Windows, Script Outline from the menu or Ctrl+Alt+S from the keyboard. From the Script Outline, you can double-click on any one of the many predefined functions to insert it into your Web page (see Figure 39.7).

Figure 39.6
Inserting a blank scripting container into a Web page.

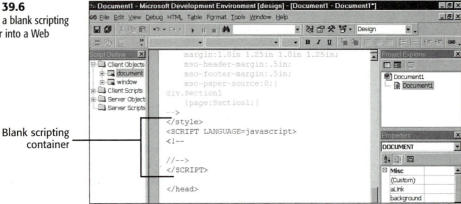

Blank scripting container ──────

Figure 39.7
Choosing script functions from the Script Outline for insertion into a Web page.

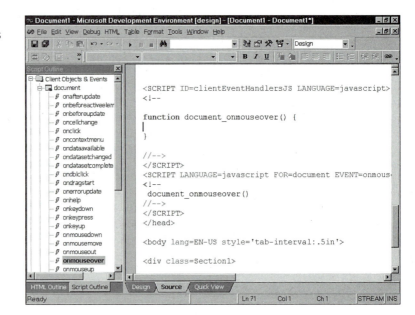

The MDE includes many of the amenities found in sophisticated programming environments such as debugging and the capability to insert breakpoints. You can completely test and debug your script from within the MDE.

When the script works to your satisfaction, save the file, and exit the MDE to return to your Office application.

THE WEB TOOLBAR

If you have used Word 97, then you are already familiar with the Web toolbar. This toolbar has not changed since its introduction in Word 97. This toolbar contains much of the same functionality as a Web browser toolbar:

- The Forward and Back arrows take you through your browsing history. Because Word documents and other files can now contain hyperlinks, you can browse through previous Word documents as well as Web pages using these arrows.

- The Stop Current Jump button stops the loading of a Web page.

- The Refresh Current Page button reloads the page into Word.

- Clicking on the Start Page button loads your Start page as it is defined under the Go button on this toolbar.

- The Search the Web button loads your Search page as it is defined under the Go button on this toolbar.

Note

The Start page and the Search the Web page are defined in the Internet browser properties and invoke the browser and connection if they are selected—these are not Word-specific features.

- The Favorites List is the same list of Internet (or other) addresses you see in the Microsoft Internet Explorer Favorites list.

PART

X

CH

39

- The Go button enables you to edit your Start and Search pages under Set Start Page and Set Search Page. You can also choose Open after clicking this button to pop up an address box. You can enter any Internet address into this address box. The functions of the Load Start Page and Load Search Page are also duplicated here.

Tip #489

If you choose the Set Start Page or Set Search Page options, you are given only the option to select the current page as your new Start page or new Search page. You cannot browse to another page or choose another file.

- The Show Only Web Toolbar button toggles the display between showing only the Web toolbar and all selected Word toolbars.

- You can enter any Internet address, network path, or filename from a local drive in the address box. Clicking the arrow to the right of this box displays your browsing history. You can also select from this list to choose a particular file or address.

Using the Web toolbar is a convenient way to browse a set of hyperlinked Word documents or to launch your browser with your Start page or Search page loaded.

Tip #490	The Web toolbar can be customized like any other toolbar in Word. If you click the Add or Remove buttons at the end of the toolbar, then Customize, and select All Commands in the Categories window, you can add anything. An especially useful addition to the Web toolbar might be the Web Page Preview button.

CREATING A WEB SITE WITH WORD'S WEB PAGE WIZARD

The Web Page Wizard has been substantially improved from the version in Word 97. This wizard enables you to

- Build a single Web page or even a small Web site using several different page types
- Apply a *template* (a consistent series of graphics and colors) across all Web pages
- Build a consistent navigation system connecting all your pages

Using the Web Page Wizard is a great way to build a small Web site with a consistent look and feel. It does, however, have two shortcomings:

- The Web Page Wizard does not have any HTML form templates. You have to build these yourself completely from scratch.
- The wizard does not have any Web site management tools for dealing with large numbers of files and hyperlinks. If your Web site grows to include more than 10 pages, you will benefit from the site management capabilities built into dedicated HTML editors such as FrontPage 2000.

Note	HTML forms are a set of form elements (text boxes, option buttons, lists, and so forth) to be filled out by a visitor and sent to the Web server for some action. The Search box you find on many Web sites is an example of a simple HTML form.

You can get to the Web Page Wizard by selecting File, New from the menu, clicking on the Web Pages tab, and double-clicking Web Page Wizard. (By default, this wizard is not installed in a standard installation. Word may prompt you to insert your installation CD to install this. If the Web Page Wizard icon is not present, you need to start the installer manually and install this optional component.)

The next few sections walk you through the creation of a Web site using the wizard.

DEFINING A TITLE AND LOCATION

After the wizard has opened, click Next> to go past the opening screen to the Title and Location screen shown in Figure 39.8.

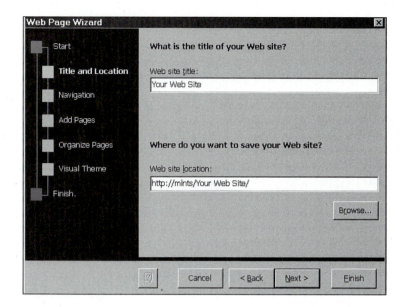

Figure 39.8
Choose the title and file storage location for your Web site in the Web Page Wizard.

Type in a title for your Web site into the Web Site Title box. Notice that this name is reflected in the default path in the Web Site Location box below it. The title will become the folder name under which all the files and subfolders for your site will be saved at the Web site location. The location for saving your Web page(s) can be any standard place you'd normally save a file, such as

- A folder on a local hard drive
- A folder on a network drive
- A Web folder

A *Web folder* is a shortcut to a Web server. A *Web server* is the underlying software and hardware platform for servicing requests for Web pages from browsers. Internet Web sites are hosted on a wide variety of Web servers. Web folders enable you to save, edit, or delete files directly on the Web server without having to use other software, such as an FTP (File Transfer Protocol) client.

DEFINING YOUR NAVIGATION MENU

After you choose a title and file storage location, click Next>. On this Navigation page, you can choose how you want to set the Navigation menu for your page(s).

The *Navigation menu* is the list of hyperlinks to all the other pages on your Web site. The Web Page Wizard builds this menu automatically. You can choose to use frames or place the Navigation menu on a separate page. Specifically, you have three options for where to display your Navigation menu:

PART

X

CH

39

- **Vertical Frame.** The Navigation menu is placed in a smaller frame on the left with the contents of the Web page displayed in the larger frame on the right.

- **Horizontal Frame.** The Navigation menu is placed in an upper, smaller frame with the contents of the Web page displayed in the lower, larger frame.

- **Separate Page.** The Navigation menu is placed on a separate Web page. Forward and Back hyperlinks are provided on each Web page.

Using frames provides a convenient and intuitive navigation system. Some old browsers do not support frames. Unless you know many of the people accessing your Web site use these older browsers (they are becoming quite rare), I recommend using frames for navigation.

ADDING PAGES TO YOUR NEW SITE

After you decide what navigation system to use, click <u>N</u>ext> to go to the Add Pages screen, as shown in Figure 39.9.

Figure 39.9
Add different types of Web pages to your Web site with the Web Page Wizard.

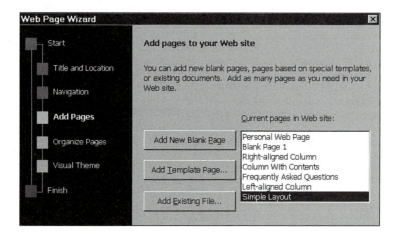

This part of the wizard enables you to add and remove pages from your new site. You can also rename your pages to something meaningful.

Note

Be careful in your selection of names for individual Web pages. These names will be used in your Navigation menu and should clearly define the page to any visitors. For instance, if a page contains the company mission statement, then it should be named "Mission Statement" or "Company Mission Statement."

You can choose from three types of Web pages, each represented by a button:

- A blank page
- A template page
- An existing file

A blank page is just that: an empty page containing only the barest HTML code to define the page as a Web page. You need to fill in all formatting and content on your own.

If you choose a template page, a selection box, shown in Figure 39.10, appears. These templates are the same ones found in the File, New, Web Pages list.

Figure 39.10
Available Web page templates.

Template pages give you some basic Web page organization. All you need to do is customize the text and graphics. As you click a template page in the Web Page Templates box, the template is displayed behind the box. If you click OK, a template page is added to your Current Pages list, as shown earlier in Figure 39.10. You can add as many of a given template page as you want. You can find more information on creating custom Web page templates in this chapter in the section titled "Creating Your Own Web Page Templates."

You can also open an existing file. This is usually a Web page with an .htm or .html file extension. You can select Web pages from your local drive, any Web server on the Internet or your intranet, or a network drive. You can also choose the Web page contained in a Favorites address (.url extension).

Tip #491

When you choose files to add to your Web site, they don't necessarily need to be Web pages. You can add any other type of file, such as an Office document. Be aware that if you do choose a non-Web page file to add to your Web site, how your machine responds to that file type and how someone else's responds may be very different. For instance, if you include an Excel worksheet, when you click on it, it will open in Excel on your computer. Someone using UNIX who clicks on that same link might be able to only download the file, and might not even be able to view it. Be aware that after you stray from the .htm or .html file format, you are no longer dealing with universally accessible file formats.

Finally, you can delete pages from your Current List by selecting a given page and clicking Remove Page.

ORGANIZING YOUR PAGES

Click Next> when you have all the Web pages you want on your site. On the Organize Pages screen, seen in Figure 39.11, you can choose the order for your navigation links.

Figure 39.11
Choosing the order for your navigational hyperlinks in the Web Page Wizard.

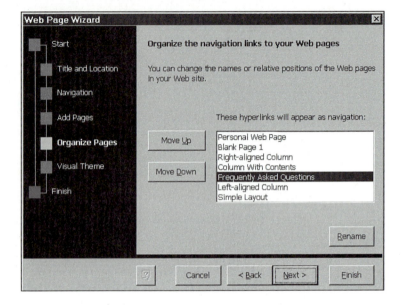

Use the Move Up and Move Down buttons to move pages within the list of pages. The file at the top of the list will be listed first in your navigation links and so on to the bottom of the list. You can also rename pages by selecting a Web page, clicking Rename, and typing in a new name. Click Next> when you have the files organized as you want.

ADDING A THEME TO YOUR SITE

On the next screen you can add a visual theme to your Web site. A *theme* is the visual topic of the Web site: a coordinated set of fonts, colors, and graphics. The theme can center around a region, set a professional tone, or have holiday overtones. The theme sets the visual mood for the entire Web site.

To add a theme, select Add a Visual Theme and click on Browse Themes. A list of themes, similar to those shown in Figure 39.12, appears.

Clicking on a theme displays a sample of a Web page using that theme. If the theme is not installed, you are given the option to install it. Also notice three additional options in the lower-left corner:

- Vivid Colors
- Active Graphics
- Background Image

Figure 39.12
The sample on the right shows the heading, bullet, line, text, and hyperlink styles for the selected theme.

PART

X

CH

39

Vivid Colors enables you to toggle the text color for sub-headings. Active Graphics enables you to choose whether the graphical elements inserted by the themes are static or animated. Deselecting the Background Image option takes the background image out of your selected theme and replaces it with a background color.

After you decide on your theme, click OK to return to the Visual Theme page. Click Finish and the wizard generates your Web page(s).

UNDERSTANDING THE FINISHED WEB SITE ORGANIZATION

Imagine that you use the Web Site Wizard to build a Web site dealing with company sales. From the wizard, you used frame navigation and a theme. The four pages in the site are

- International Sales
- National Sales
- Sales Summary
- Table of Contents

When you click the Finish button on the Web Page Wizard, you generate a file structure that looks like Figure 39.13.

Figure 39.13
The structure of a Web site built with the Web Page Wizard.

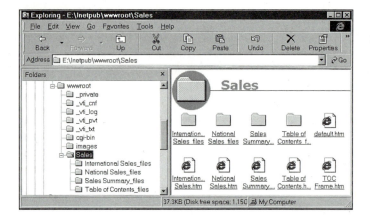

In this site, a folder corresponding to each Web page is created by the wizard. All the Web pages (.htm files) are stored in the root Sales folder. At this point each of the four folders under the root contain only filelist.xlm and the image file from the selected theme for use with the page background. Your home page, named default.htm by, well, default, is automatically loaded into Word for immediate editing.

Because this example uses frames for navigation, default.htm is only the frameset or container file for the list of links on the left (TOC Frame.htm) and the Table of Contents (Table of Contents.htm) on the right. Any images or other objects that you add as you edit your Web pages will automatically be placed into the correct folder. To edit any of the other Web pages, open them as you would any other file in Word.

CREATING YOUR OWN WEB PAGE TEMPLATES

If you don't like any of the Web templates that come with Office or need a special template for your organization, you can easily build your own.

To build a new Web page template

1. From the menu choose File, New, click the General tab, and select the Template option in the lower-right corner. Click Open.
2. Save your template immediately.

Note

Notice that when you choose File, Save As from the menu, the Save as Web Page option is not available.

To save your template with the other Web page templates that come with Word 2000, save your file to the Program Files/Microsoft Office/Templates/1033 folder on the drive where Office 2000 is installed.

This path, of course, assumes the default installation path for Office 2000 was used. The default file format is .htm. This template will now show up as a Web template in the File, New list of templates.

3. Add whatever items you need to make a basic template. These might include

- A company logo
- A background texture or color
- Font colors and styles
- A basic text outline
- Standard hyperlinks, such as one to your Web site home page

For instance, if your company has established colors and fonts, you could use those in your Web page template. You could use a company color as a background color to your Web pages. Your legal department might require you to include a hyperlink to a disclaimer in small text at the bottom of every page. These are the types of elements to include in a template to maintain consistency through all the Web pages on your site.

4. Save the template again with the items you just added.

WEB PUBLISHING IN WORD 2000

As mentioned earlier, building a Web page is no different than working on a regular Word document. There are, however, some special considerations you need to keep in mind when you're building Web pages that generally aren't important when you're dealing with .doc files. These include

- Browser compatibility
- Network bandwidth
- Streaming media
- Building hyperlinks
- Inserting horizontal lines
- Scrolling text
- Frames
- The Web palette
- The importance of a Web page title

Most of these topics are unique to Web environments and need to be discussed separately for Web authors.

PART
X

CH
39

BROWSER COMPATIBILITY

Word 2000 generates Web pages that are compatible with Microsoft Internet Explorer 5 and above. Netscape 4 and earlier do not support XML or VML; Netscape 5, however, should support both XML and VML. VBScript does not work in any Netscape browser.

If you are building Web pages for the Internet, you must consider the wide variety of browsers used around the world. You must choose a "lowest common denominator" browser and build your Web pages accordingly. Remember that Microsoft is including cutting-edge languages in its Web pages built using Word 2000. Given the large number of Office users worldwide, however, this cutting-edge may quickly become the norm and browser compatibility may be less of a concern.

NETWORK BANDWIDTH

When you build Web pages, you may be tempted to load up on multimedia: sounds, a large number of graphics, or video clips. These special effects require large amounts of network bandwidth (on either your internal network or the Internet or both). The larger your files, the more network bandwidth you consume. This increases the amount of time it takes your Web page to load in your audience's browsers. Some things you can do to reduce the bandwidth required by your Web pages include the following:

- Use graphics only when absolutely necessary. Use text as much as possible. Also keep your bitmap graphics small. Use .gif files when saving line art and use .jpg files for photographs to optimize file sizes.

- Use short background sounds or consider using none at all.

- Do not use video at all or use compressed formats, such as streaming video (see the section in this chapter, "Streaming Media," for more detail). If you must use videos, use the smallest possible size and the shortest time. Nothing uses up network bandwidth faster than video files because they are so large.

- If the content on one Web page is too great, consider splitting the content between two or more Web pages.

The people who view your Web page will thank you many times over for doing your part in saving bandwidth and not contributing to the World Wide Wait. This is also the most practical approach in a business environment where time is money.

STREAMING MEDIA

Streaming media is the process of playing a file, usually video or audio, as it is received at the browser, rather than waiting for the entire file to be downloaded before playing it. In this situation, the file is said to be "streamed" to a browser. The most common example of this is RealAudio or RealVideo, now combined into RealMedia. Microsoft NetShow also provides a compressed streaming audio and video format. Using these file formats greatly reduces the bandwidth requirements for audio and video. There is also, however, usually a loss in quality for both audio and video content.

BUILDING HYPERLINKS

One of the most powerful technologies on a Web page is the hyperlink. Through a simple click, you can be transported almost anywhere on the Internet. For now, you need to know the basics of building a hyperlink if you want to work through building a Web page at the end of this chapter.

A *hyperlink* is simply a line of text that tells a browser to load another Web page or other object. Any text or image on a Web page can hold a hyperlink. Hyperlinks most commonly point to

- Web pages
- Media objects such as sounds, video, or pictures
- An email address

BUILDING A TEXT HYPERLINK

Any text phrase, word, or part of a word can be a hyperlink. To build a hyperlink, you need some text in a document and an idea of where you want the hyperlink to lead when it is clicked:

1. From a document in Word, highlight a text phrase. For instance, highlight "Microsoft" in the phrase, "For more information, visit the Microsoft home page."

2. Click the Insert Hyperlink button on the Standard toolbar, choose Insert, Hyperlink from the menu, use the keyboard shortcut Ctrl+K, or right-click over the selected text and choose Hyperlink to open the Insert Hyperlink dialog box, shown in Figure 39.14.

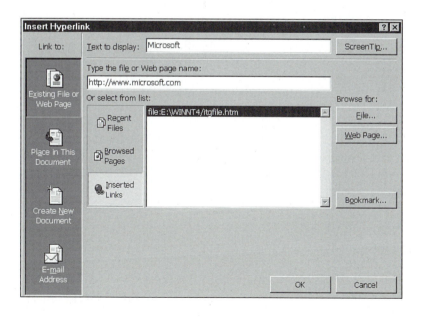

Figure 39.14
Filling in the Insert Hyperlink box.

3. In the top box, labeled <u>T</u>ext to Display, the text you highlighted is displayed. You enter the address for Microsoft in the next box, labeled Type the Fil<u>e</u> or Web Page Name, as shown in Figure 39.14.

4. Click OK. When you return to your document, the text you highlighted is now a blue color and underlined, indicating that it is now an active hyperlink.

BUILDING A HYPERLINKED IMAGE

The process for building a clickable image is very similar to building a text hyperlink:

1. Select any clipart, picture, Drawing object, or WordArt within a document.

2. Click Insert Hyperlink on the toolbar to display the Insert Hyperlink dialog box. Notice that the Text to Display line is dimmed.

3. Type the address for the link in the box labeled Type the Fil<u>e</u> or Web Page Name.

4. Clicking OK completes the hyperlink.

The picture will not look any different, but the cursor will change when it hovers over the image to indicate it is now clickable.

BUILDING AN EMAIL HYPERLINK

Besides referencing other pages, hyperlinks can open and preaddress blank email addresses:

1. Select the text or choose an image for the hyperlink.

2. Click on the Insert Hyperlink button to display the Insert Hyperlink dialog box.

3. In the lower-left corner of the Insert Hyperlink box, click on E-<u>m</u>ail Address.

4. Enter the email address, as shown in Figure 39.15.

Figure 39.15
Hyperlinking to an email address.

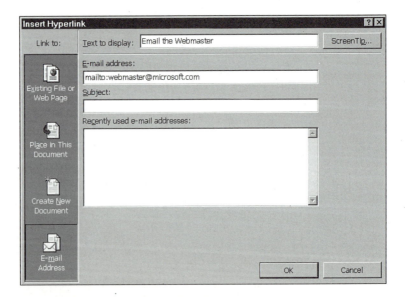

Notice how the phrase `mailto:` is automatically added to the beginning of your email address.

5. Click OK to complete the link.

The email hyperlink is a convenient means for letting your visitors send you feedback or questions.

INSERTING HORIZONTAL LINES IN A WEB PAGE

Word documents don't normally use horizontal lines to separate topical sections. This is a commonly used convention, however, in Web pages. You can add horizontal lines by going to the menu under Format, Borders and Shading, and then clicking the Horizontal Line button. A list of lines from which to choose is displayed and should look similar to Figure 39.16.

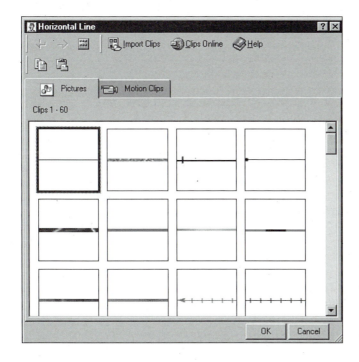

Figure 39.16
Select a horizontal line to use.

 Horizontal lines are also available from the Formatting toolbar by clicking on the Borders button and clicking the Horizontal Line Selection List.

After you find a line you like, you can gather more information by following these steps:

1. Select the image, then right-click over it and choose Properties from the menu. The Clip Properties box, shown in Figure 39.17, gives you information on the file size of the line.

Figure 39.17
Viewing the clip proper-
ties of a horizontal line.

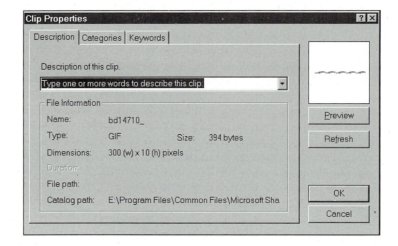

2. Clicking Preview displays the line and, if it is animated, plays the animation.

3. The next tab in this box, Categories, enables you to choose a new clip category in which to place the horizontal line, if you are not satisfied with its current category.

4. The last tab, Keywords, enables you to delete, add, or change the list of keywords associated with the clip.

5. After you make any changes, clicking OK takes you back to the Horizontal Line Selection List.

6. Clicking OK here inserts the horizontal line into your Web page.

The horizontal line can be edited like any other graphic in Word: Grab the bounding box and stretch or shrink it. You can also right-click the horizontal line, choose Format Horizontal Line, and Edit Properties from the Format Horizontal Line box that opens up, as shown in Figure 39.18.

1. From the first tab, Horizontal Line, you can change the width, height, and color of the shadow of the line (if a shadow is associated with the line). You can also choose to align the horizontal line with the left, right, or center of the page.

2. The Picture tab, seen in Figure 39.19, enables you to crop the image, change the color of the line, and adjust the contrast and brightness of the horizontal line.

3. Click OK to apply your changes to the line.

Tip #492

After you have the line looking just as you want, use the Clipboard to copy and paste the line when you want to use it again. For consistency, you should use the same horizontal line throughout your Web site or section of a Web site.

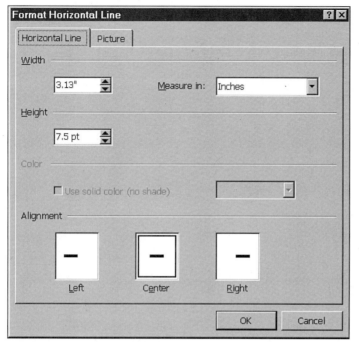

Figure 39.18
Formatting a horizontal line after it is placed into a Web page.

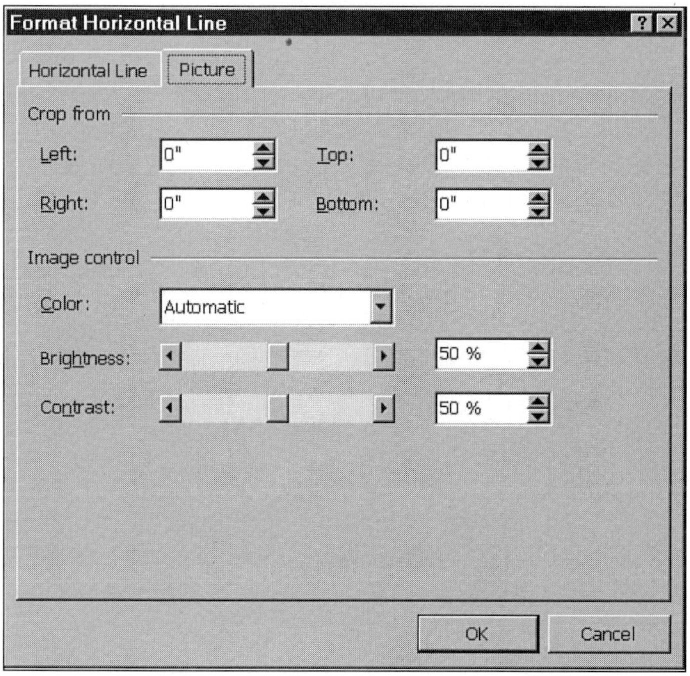

Figure 39.19
Cropping and changing the color of a horizontal line in a Web page.

INSERTING SCROLLING TEXT

Scrolling text is also called *marquee text*. Scrolling text appears stock-ticker style in a line across your Web page. Before using this feature, remember that it is not supported in Netscape browsers and displays only partially or not at all. If you expect your Web page to be viewed with Netscape browsers, either don't use this feature or don't put any critical information in it.

You can find scrolling text on the Web Tools toolbar. (Right-click on a toolbar and select Web Tools if this toolbar isn't open.)

The ScreenTip for this control is labeled Scrolling Text. When you click on it, the Scrolling Text dialog box appears, as shown in Figure 39.20.

To modify the behavior of the scrolling text:

1. Set your text behavior to Scroll (the default), Slide (which scrolls the text only once and stops on the opposite side of the screen), or Alternate (which bounces the text back and forth—like a Ping-Pong ball—between the left and right margins of your page).

2. For the Scroll and Alternate settings, you can choose how many loops to scroll or bounce with the Loop settings. Your only choices with this control are 1 through 5 times and Infinite.

3. Choose a background color for your control from the list. (Sorry, no custom colors are on this list.)

4. Choose the direction of your scroll: Left or Right.

Figure 39.20

5. The slider control in the middle of the box controls the speed of the scroll (or bounce).

6. Finally, type in the text you want to scroll. The window at the bottom of this box provides you a preview of your scrolling text as you change the various options.

7. Click OK to place the marquee in your Web page.

After the marquee is inserted into your Web page, you can make more changes to it. Make sure you are in Design mode by clicking the Design Mode button on the Web Tools toolbar. While you are in Design mode, you can make any of the following changes:

- Grab the bounding box with your mouse to change the length or height of the marquee (the text stays centered).

- Format the scrolling text using any of the standard font-formatting tools in Word.

- If you right-click over the marquee, the context menu shows three options: Stop (stops the marquee from scrolling or bouncing), Play (starts the marquee), and Properties (brings up the Scrolling Text box again).

- To make the entire marquee a clickable hyperlink, select the marquee by choosing Design Mode from the Web Tools toolbar. Choose Insert, Hyperlink from the menu. Insert the correct Web address and click OK.

Note

Marquees are great attention-grabbing devices for pointing people to new or important information. They can be irritating, however, if placed on a page where people also have to read a lot of text.

USING FRAMES

Frames enable you to display more than one Web page at a time in a Web browser, with each page in its own custom-sized frame. You can have as many frames as you like, but in practical use most people use two or three. The most common use for frames is for navigation. As you saw earlier with the Web Page Wizard, you can choose to place your navigation links in a frame (or navigation pane) above or to the left of a larger frame. Clicking a link in the navigation pane displays the page content in the main, larger frame. Some people choose to use a third frame for additional navigation choices or advertising.

Some people choose to not use frames for a number of reasons:

- Older browsers, usually version 2 or earlier, do not support frames. These browsers are becoming increasingly rare on the World Wide Web and are virtually nonexistent in intranets.

- Hyperlinking becomes more complex. You need to add some special text to your hyperlinks when working with frames, though this is done transparently in Word. If hyperlinks in frames are used improperly, you can get the dreaded "hall of mirrors" effect, where a frame is duplicated several times in a browser, making each window very small and virtually unreadable.

- Frames eat up valuable screen real estate on smaller screens such as those on laptops and mobile computing devices.

ADDING FRAMES

You can put a set of frames into a Web page, either by choosing Format, Frames, New Frame Page from the menu or by opening the Frames toolbar. From the Frames toolbar, shown in Figure 39.21, you can choose to put a frame on any side of the existing page (above, below, left, or right).

Note

A *frameset* is just a container page that tells the browser how to split the screen among the pages in the set. For instance, a browser displaying two Web pages as frames is actually using three Web pages: one Web page for display in each frame and the third frameset page, defining how the screen is split up between the other two pages.

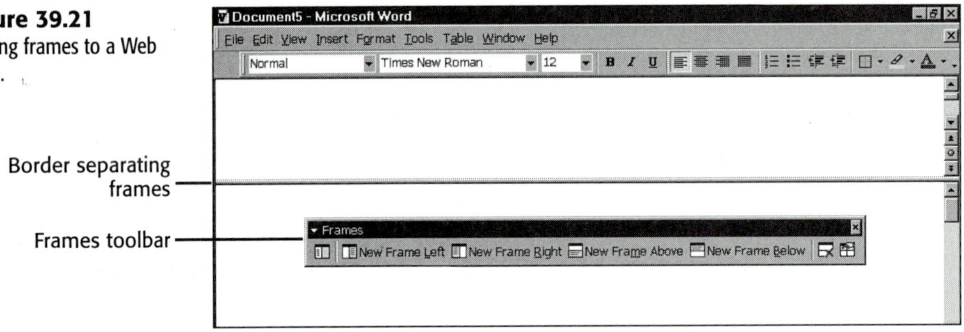

Figure 39.21
Adding frames to a Web page.

Border separating frames

Frames toolbar

MODIFYING FRAMES

After you have a frameset, you can grab the bar between frames and resize each frame manually.

You can also access the properties of each frame by right-clicking over that frame and choosing Frame Properties or choosing a same-named button from the Frames toolbar. The settings chosen in the Frame Properties dialog box are specific for one frame.

1. From the first tab, Frame, shown in Figure 39.22, you can name your frame and numerically resize it.

2. The Initial Page combo box displays the filename for that frame; you can name the frame in the Name combo box underneath. Word assigns default names to each frame also. Naming each frame based on function makes it easier for you to build hyperlinks between frames later.

3. Resize the frame based on Percent, Inches, or Relative (that is, proportionately). For example, you can define the current frame as 30%. Word resizes this window to take up 30% of the screen and automatically resizes the second frame to take up 70%. You can do the same using inches. If you choose Relative, then you are defining each frame as a fraction of one (one being the whole screen). You can define one frame as 0.3 and the second will be sized to 0.7.

The second tab of the Frame Properties box, <u>B</u>orders (shown in Figure 39.23), enables you to modify the properties of the frame border.

1. In the upper part of the Borders tab, you can choose to display or not display the border.

2. For borders left on, you can change the color of the border and its thickness in points.

3. You can also choose No Borders to eliminate the border. Turning the borders off often improves the appearance of a frameset.

4. In the lower part of the Borders tab, you can decide what to do about scrollbars. Each frame gets its own scrollbar by default, and that scrollbar is always showing. You can also decide to permanently turn the scrollbars off for a given frame or have them show up only when needed.

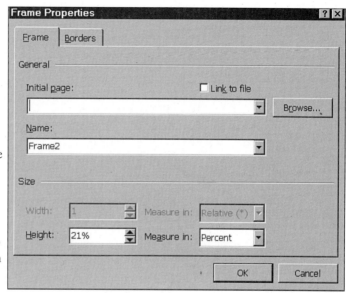

Figure 39.22

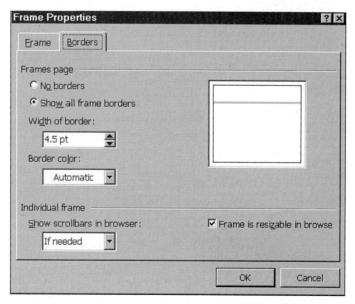

Figure 39.23

PART

X

CH

39

Caution

Be cautious about turning scrollbars completely off. Even though the contents of one frame may not change (in your navigation frame, for instance), it may not display the same in every browser, especially if you use text. Another browser may choose a larger default font. If you don't enable the scrollbars to come up in this situation, your visitor won't be able to read the contents of your frame. Visitors using laptops or mobile computing devices with small screens may need the scrollbars just to view the contents of a frame.

5. Lastly, the Borders tab has a Frame Is Resizable in Browse check box. If this is checked, users can grab the frame border and resize the frames from within their browsers. If this is unchecked, then the frame size is fixed and unchangeable from a browser. You may want to leave frames resizable so that your visitors can move them around for a better view on their monitors, if necessary.

SAVING FRAMES AND BUILDING A TABLE OF CONTENTS FOR FRAMES

If you have two frames in a Web page, you are dealing with three separate documents:

- The container page that defines the frameset contents
- A separate Web page for each of the two frames

Each of these three files must be saved as a separate Web page. To save the container page, use File, Save as Web Page from the menu. To save each frame page, right-click in any blank area of the frame and choose Save Current Frame As.

If you later decide that you don't want frames, you can select a frame in Word by clicking in it, then choose the Delete Frame button from the Frames toolbar. That frame disappears, although its file is unaffected if it was saved. The Delete Frame option also shows up on the Format Frames menu when a frameset is open.

You can automatically build a Table of Contents for your Web page containing frames. This works effectively only if you have built your Web page using heading styles (Headers 1 through 9). This feature can be accessed from the Frames toolbar or from the menu under Format, Frames, Table of Contents in Frame. The Table of Contents in Frame feature builds a navigation frame with hyperlinks to each of your headers. It is quite handy for building a simple navigation system for lengthy Web pages, with a hyperlink to each header on the page.

Tip #493

The Table of Contents built for a given frame is formatted with the default style. If your Web site is using a theme, you need to apply the theme to the Table of Contents page by choosing Format, Theme from the menu and selecting your site theme.

THE WEB PAGE PALETTE

When you are working with a video card displaying 24-bit color, all RGB combinations are available for use. In the Web world, however, many browsers use a 216-color palette called the "Web" or "Netscape" palette. Whenever possible, you should limit your .gif images to these 216 colors for optimal display.

Note

You cannot change the palette in .jpg files; they are 24-bit color by definition.

Pixels present in a .gif image that are not one of the 216 colors present in the palette are dithered. Because you want optimal control over the appearance of your image, stick with the 216-color palette rather than depend on a dithering algorithm. Many modern paint or graphics programs have the Netscape palette built into them. You can find a nice table listing all 216 colors of the Web palette and their hex and decimal equivalents at
`http://www.lynda.com/hexv.html`.

Communicating with Word: Choose Your Colors Carefully

Generally, it is a good idea to limit your colors to about three. Your background color should be one that shows your text with good contrast. You should then reserve the second color for your main text color. You can use the third color to add accents and highlight those things you want to grab the audience's attention. Using too many colors is distracting to the eye, and detracts from the overall message. This would be a good time to use the company colors if they fit the profile. If the colors are hard to work with, you can use just one or two of the colors and use a white background. If you choose to use an image as your background, use one that doesn't have contrasting colors or sharp patterns because they make it difficult to read the text.

THE IMPORTANCE OF THE WEB PAGE TITLE

When you create a Word document, you can consider giving the page a title for ease of searching. When you create a Web page, the title is important for the following reasons:

- Whenever you open a Web page in a browser, the title of the page is displayed across the top title bar of the browser. This is an important visual aid to your visitors, because it tells them what site they're on and what part of that site they're currently in.

- The search engines on the Internet (Lycos, HotBot, Excite, and so forth) often use the information in the title to index a Web page. Some search engines use the title exclusively to index the contents of a Web page. If your Web page has no title or an unremarkable title, people will have a hard time finding your Web page via search engines. This phenomenon is also true on intranets if a local search engine is used.

Word uses the document's title (from the document properties) as the HTML title. You enter the page title for a Web page by selecting File, Properties from the menu, as shown in Figure 39.24.

Notice that you can also enter keywords. Search engines also use keywords to index files.

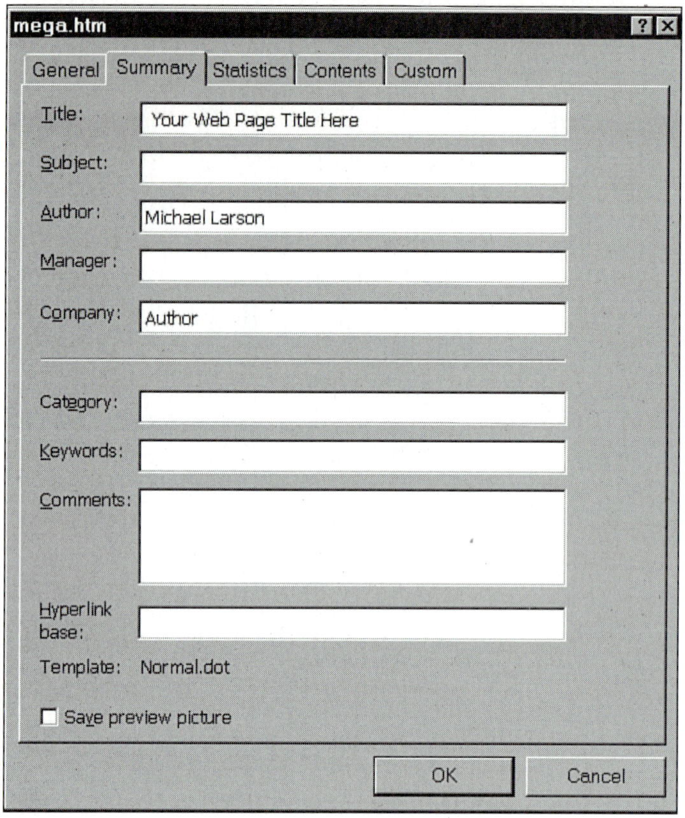

Figure 39.24
Adding a title to a Web page.

THE NEW TECHNOLOGIES USED IN WORD 2000 WEB PAGES

Whenever you save a Word document as a Web page or build a new Web page in Word 2000, you are building a page of HTML source code that can be read by a browser and interpreted by the browser to display the various elements in the Web page. As described earlier, traditional HTML code is now being supplemented by four other technologies (XML, CSSs, VML, and scripting languages) in Word 2000.

ADVANTAGES AND DISADVANTAGES

Word 2000's new scripting technologies have some advantages and disadvantages. The advantages include

- Web pages can now contain almost anything that a Word document can.
- It no longer matters whether you save a file as .doc or as .html; a document looks the same in Word 2000 as it does in a version 5.0 browser.

- XML greatly improves the organization and searchability of the Web page. (Achieving this improvement is described later in this chapter under "XML Tags and What They Do.")

- VML reduces the bandwidth required to send a graphical image from a Web server to a browser. This improves the browser page load time, improves image quality, and helps to reduce Internet or intranet network congestion.

- By implementing such a complex online document format, Microsoft is hurrying the market; that is, it is pushing the envelope of Web technologies. VML and XML are very recent additions to Internet technology. CSSs have been around longer but are only now beginning to be widely implemented. By making these technologies transparent and easily available to millions of Office users, their quick acceptance into wide usage on the Internet is almost guaranteed.

The disadvantages to these new technologies include

- If you want to edit the HTML code outside of Word 2000, you need to be a programmer (that is, be able to understand the scripting languages). Also, rather than just having to only know HTML, you need to understand VML, CSSs, and XML, as well as how these four languages interact with each other. This can be daunting even for many experienced Web designers and programmers.

- It may be several years before there is a critical mass of higher-version browsers (version 5 or later) on the Internet that can properly interpret all the code found in a Web page produced using Word 2000. Telling Word 2000 to implement only those Web page features common to version 4 browsers helps somewhat, although it reduces the effectiveness of using Word 2000 to build Web pages, especially round-tripping ones. In the meantime, this technology can be used to its fullest on an intranet or extranet where most people can be motivated or required to have version 5 or higher browsers.

PART
X

CH
39

COMPONENT OVERVIEW

Want to hear more about each component language used in a Word 2000 Web page? Below is a short overview of each of the five languages:

- **HTML.** Hypertext Markup Language is the lingua franca (medium of exchange) of the World Wide Web. Almost every Web page is built with this language. HTML, a simple formatting and organizational language, is ideal for the display of text, simple graphics, and hyperlinks. It is not suited at all for precise page layout (such as you might find in a magazine) or complex data organization. The appeal of HTML is its ease of use and universal acceptance. HTML 4 is the current version of this language.

| Caution | Do not confuse the language version of HTML, currently at 4.0, with the browser versions already mentioned. |

- **CSS.** Cascading Style Sheets are used to define the layout of a document precisely. Style sheets are more powerful than the styles found in Word because style sheets can also specify page layout. A style sheet can be a separate document or it can be embedded in each HTML page. Because browsers have different capabilities in how they interpret these styles, they interpret what they can and ignore the rest; that is, they cascade down in their interpretation and display what they are able to. Netscape Navigator 3 and Microsoft Internet Explorer 2 browsers or earlier cannot read these style sheets.

- **XML.** EXtensible Markup Language is more robust and extensible (hence its name) than HTML. You can define new tags and their uses at any time and in any way by referencing them in an associated text document. The strength of XML is its capability to use these new tags to identify specific information. For instance, if you're talking about a golf wood on a Web page, your page can include golf-specific tags. This distinguishes your page from the many others that may be dealing with carpentry; they would probably use woodworking-specific tags. People who now want to look for only golf wood Web pages can now filter out the woodworking pages or vice versa. This technology will vastly improve the users' abilities to find specific-subject Web pages and will open the Internet up to extensive data mining.

- **VML.** Vector Markup Language uses text to define geometric shapes, colors, line widths, and so forth. These words are then interpreted and displayed as graphical images in browsers that understand VML (currently only Microsoft Internet Explorer 5). No matter what size circle you want to display, you use the same amount of text to define it.

- **JavaScript or VBScript.** Both of these script-style programming languages are in common everyday use on the Web right now. They are both robust. JavaScript is supported by the vast majority of browsers; VBScript is supported by only Microsoft Internet Explorer browsers. These languages enable you to program interactivity into Web pages.

All (or most) of these languages are used to build Word 2000 Web pages. The following sections describe each language in more detail and then discuss how they are used in Web pages created with Word 2000.

Note

Do not let this plethora of languages dismay you. You do not need to understand one line of code of any language to use Word 2000 to build effective Web pages. Because the use of these languages is new, there are some concerns about backward compatibility with older browsers. Understanding the languages helps you decide whether using Word 2000 is the best way for you or your organization to build Web pages or convert existing Word documents to Web pages.

HTML TAGS AND WHAT THEY DO

HTML and browsers made the Internet accessible to everyone. Before the creation of the browser, the Internet was the playground of researchers and the military and was accessible only if you knew how to issue UNIX commands. With the advent of HTML and browsers, you didn't need to understand the underlying technology anymore to navigate through it. And the rest is history.

HTML was originally designed to give a simple hierarchical design to technical text information, such as Header 1, Header 2, and so forth, and to provide a means to link documents across a network. HTML pages are simple text pages editable by any basic text editor (such as Notepad) on any computer platform. The heart of HTML is its tags. The tags tell the browser how to interpret the data that follows them. Tags are enclosed in angle brackets and generally occur in pairs: an opening tag and a closing tag. For instance, if you want to define some text as header text, it should look like the following:

```
<H1> Some text </H1>
```

In this example <H1> and </H1> are tags. The slash in the end tag defines the closing tag. Tags can also contain attributes such as the following:

```
<font color="red"> An Important Announcement </font>
```

The text surrounded by the <font> tags would be displayed in red.

PART

X

CH

39

Note

> Which font or font size is used to display the Header 1 tag varies from platform to platform. HTML was designed this way so that its other goal of cross-platform use could be met. An unfortunate side effect is that HTML pages can look very different on different platforms.
>
> When the Internet was used to deal with strictly technical documents, this was not an issue. But now people and companies want complete control over how a Web document looks and want to know that it looks the same no matter where it is viewed. HTML was never designed with this in mind and this has led to the search for other languages that support HTML.

All Web pages begin with the <HTML> tag and end with the closing </HTML> tag. Web pages have head, title, and body sections denoted by <HEAD>, <TITLE>, and <BODY> tags. That's all. Lists of the HTML tags and their definitions can be found on the Internet in many locations. A good place to start is

```
http://www.ncsa.uiuc.edu/General/Internet/WWW/HTMLPrimer.html
```

HTML was first designed to share text-only technical documents. Tags were later added to display graphics, and the language has grown to support more multimedia. But its expandability is severely limited due to the simple goals of the original HTML specification. New tags cannot be defined unless support is built into the browsers. And the browser wars between Netscape and Microsoft have resulted in tags supported by only one or the other browser.

Though HTML has basic formatting capabilities, it cannot do precision pixel-by-pixel display of a Web page. CSS can, however, do this and more.

CSSs AND HOW THEY WORK

Cascading Style Sheets can be separate documents or defined within the body of a Web page. Style sheets can be used to define any text or page formatting that can normally be defined in HTML tags. Styles are defined between the <STYLE> and </STYLE> tags. The advantage of using a style over using just HTML tags is that after you have defined a style, you only need to reference the style name to implement the style again. This usually reduces the size of your HTML page, improving the page load time—always a desirable goal.

Style sheets use a coordinate system to give a Web page designer precise control over the elements on a page; that is, they specify horizontal and vertical position for elements on a page. Consider the following style:

```
<STYLE>
BODY {background: #FFFFFF; color: #000000; margin-top: 0.5 in; margin-left: 0.5
in}
H2 {font: 16pt arial black; color: #FF0000}
P {font: 10pt comic sans MS; text-indent: 0.25 in}
A {color: #0000FF}
</STYLE>
```

Based on this style, the Web page body will have white text on a black background with half-inch top and left margins. All text surrounded by Header 2 tags, <H2> and </H2>, will be in a red 16-point Arial Black font. Text paragraphs will be in a 10-point Comic Sans MS font and indented one-quarter of an inch. Hypertext links (or anchors) will be blue. CSSs work in Web pages just as Word styles do in documents.

Note

Colors in HTML pages are defined using hexadecimal notation (zero through F, base 16) and the RGB (Red-Green-Blue) color model. RGB is the way colors are produced on computer monitors. The first two numbers are the red component, the second two, the green component, and the last two, the blue component. For instance, yellow is FFFF00, a mixture of red and green with no contribution of blue. As noted earlier in the chapter, you can find a table listing all 216 colors of the Web palette and their hex and decimal equivalents at http://www.lynda.com/hexv.html.

After the style is set, you need only to enter your content and it will be formatted according to the style. Browsers earlier than Netscape 3 or Microsoft Internet Explorer 2 cannot read style sheets properly; they render everything according to their default settings. As these browser versions become increasingly rare, you will see style sheets used more on the World Wide Web.

Both HTML and CSS can be used to display and format information, but they give you no internal clues as to the meaning of the content. XML can be used as one tool to provide this meaning.

XML TAGS AND WHAT THEY DO

The primary job of XML is to define or give meaning to a word or document by enclosing it in a pair of tags. It is a text-based data definition language or even a simple database information language. Because there are as many definitions as there are words, it is much more powerful and complex than HTML. And it is completely extensible, hence its name. XML has nothing to do with page formatting. It is a data workhorse. And a workhorse is just what the Web needs now.

The tags can be anything. You just need to define what tags you are using and what they mean in a DTD (Document Type Definition), which can be a separate text document or embedded in an HTML page. The DTD lists the tag names and their uses.

Note

XML cannot display information. If you load an XML-only file into a browser it displays a blank page (or gibberish). XML is usually embedded in an HTML page. XML handles the data definition but there is no visual indication that XML is even there. XML handles the data organization; HTML takes care of the data display.

The XML tags can be used to give meaning to the content in an HTML page. For instance, a page about lizards might be enclosed by <REPTILE> and </REPTILE>. The next major subsections would probably be labeled <LIZARD> and </LIZARD> and include individual species such as Monitors, Iguanas, and Gila Monsters. The information about each species might be enclosed by its own tag pairs: <MONITOR> and </MONITOR>, <IGUANA> and </IGUANA>, and <GILA MONSTER> and </GILA MONSTER>. With the tags defined, any engine that can parse these tags can load the information into specific database fields and create records. Now anyone looking for information on monitor lizards does not have to wade through masses of Web pages about computer monitors.

XML is primarily used in Web pages generated by Word 2000 to define metadata for roundtripping. Word 2000 is not designed to create DTDs or to automatically use Custom DTDs.

Note

Metadata is information that is generally not directly related to the display of a Web page. It gives users a more sophisticated tool than added text comments for labeling key data in a Web page.

Word 2000 includes XML as a translation dictionary for all the Word features incorporated into a Web page. Word can correlate this XML metadata (description of data) to a particular Word capability, if the Web page is saved as a .doc file. XML is the language that makes roundtripping between .html and .doc files possible.

It is probable that standards will arise for XML DTDs for any given area or topic. For instance, mathematicians already have their own XML DTD (called MathML) with agreed-on definitions for common mathematical concepts incorporated into it. It is *not* necessary to have agreed-on standards to use XML; you just need to define your tags in a DTD. Building a DTD is not, however, a trivial matter, so it is much easier to use DTDs already in existence.

VML FOR DEFINING VECTOR GRAPHICS

Vector Markup Language is a means to define graphical images in terms of the geometric definitions of their composite parts. Graphics defined this way are called *vector graphics*. VML is actually a specialized version of XML.

Caution

Do not confuse VML with VRML (Virtual Reality Modeling Language). VRML is used to build three-dimensional objects in Web browsers. It also is a specialized language, but unrelated to VML.

The VML definition for a circle 73 pixels in diameter with no color filling is

```
</v:oval>
<span style=position: absolute;
z-index: 0; margin-left: 127px; margin-top: 93px; width: 73px; height:
73px></span>
```

The circle is 127 pixels from the left margin and 93 pixels from the top margin. The z-index is used to determine which objects are on top when multiple objects overlap on the screen. To change the size and position of this circle, all you have to do is change the numbers. Changing the size of the circle does not impact the file size. This is in contrast to how bitmap graphics (.gif and .jpg) are defined, which is with a color defined for each pixel and the total number of pixels determining the graphic's size. Increasing the size of a bitmap graphic greatly increases the file size and hence the time it takes to load. Vector graphics also retain their detail as they are resized, whereas bitmap graphics often lose information and detail if their image size is changed.

HOW HTML, CSSs, XML, VML, AND THE SCRIPT LANGUAGES ARE USED IN WORD 2000 WEB PAGES

Now that you have a basic idea of what this alphabet soup is all about, how does Microsoft use each of these pieces in its Web pages? What role does each language play and how do they work together?

- **HTML.** This language is still the basis of a Word 2000–generated Web page. All the other languages are included between the <HTML> and </HTML> tags; that is, they are all inside an HTML container. Standard HTML tags are used when needed, but Cascading Style Sheets are used to economize on the number of HTML formatting tags whenever possible.

- **CSSs.** Cascading Style Sheets are used to define text styles, such as fonts and font sizes, page margins, indents, and most other formatting required by any of the text, graphics, or table elements in the Web page.

- **XML.** This language is primarily used in Office 2000 to define which Office application a particular Web page belongs to and which parts of the page relate to specific functions within the Office application.

- **VML.** This language is used to define all Microsoft Drawing objects, including lines, geometric shapes, fills, WordArt, and so on. When a page containing a Drawing object is saved as a Web page, the object is defined as VML. A bitmap image of the object is also saved for use in browsers that don't support VML.

- **JavaScript or VBScript.** These languages are used to determine whether any given browser supports the functions in the HTML file—VML, for instance—and send the appropriate data to it. The script languages can also be used to add interactivity to a page. For instance, if you have a Drawing object of a tree, you can set the leaves to be green during the summer, turn red in the fall, be gone in the winter, and shrink to imitate buds in the spring using one of the script languages and the system clock to read the month of the year. Almost all the objects in the HTML page are available for modification by a script.

ADVANCED WEB OPTIONS

Additionally, more advanced Web options can be found in Word 2000. These Web options enable you to change the default display of your Web pages, what languages and features are supported, and how Web pages are saved.

From the menu, choose <u>T</u>ools, <u>O</u>ptions, click the General tab, and finally click the Web Options button at the bottom. The opening Web Options screen is shown in Figure 39.25.

PART
X

CH

39

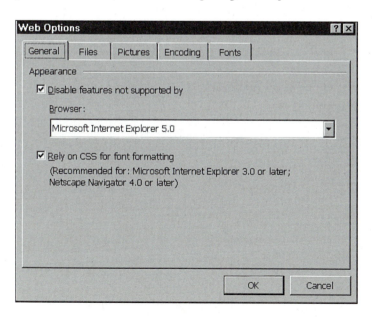

Figure 39.25
Setting Web page appearance using Web Options in Word 2000.

CUSTOMIZING THE APPEARANCE OF YOUR WEB PAGE

Under the General tab for Web Options, you can

- Set the lowest common browser version. The Disable Features Not Supported By check box is checked by default with the Microsoft Internet Explorer 5.0 browser selected. This means that Word 2000 will include Web page features that can be read by Microsoft Internet Explorer 5; that is, Microsoft Internet Explorer 5 is the lowest common denominator for browsers.

- Set the browser option in the Browser box to Microsoft Internet Explorer 4.0 or Netscape Navigator 4.0 (these are both included in a single option). If the version 4 browsers are selected, then Word 2000 will include only Web page features that can be properly interpreted by version 4 browsers. For instance, no VML would be used in Web pages generated by Word 2000 because version 4 browsers do not understand VML.

- If you clear the Disable Features Not Supported By check box, then every Web page feature built into Word 2000 will be utilized without regard for whether any browser version can support it.

- Decide whether to utilize CSSs for font formatting. Again, unless you think many older browsers will be accessing your site (CSSs are ignored by older browsers), I recommend leaving CSSs on.

SELECTING WEB PAGE FILE OPTIONS

From the Files tab of the Web Options dialog box, shown in Figure 39.26, you can change some filename options and make choices about Word 2000 being your default Web page editor.

Figure 39.26
Setting filenames and locations and default editor options using Web Options in Word 2000.

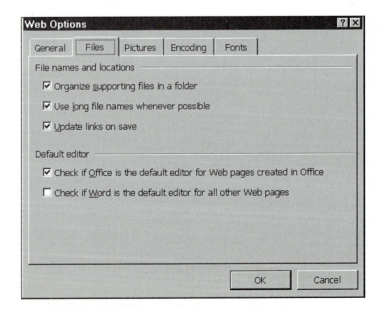

ORGANIZING FILENAMES AND LOCATIONS

The first check box in the File Names and Locations section asks whether you want to organize supporting files in a folder. When Word 2000 saves a Web page, it sends many (though not all) supporting files—such as graphics—to a separate folder. This box should be unchecked only if you already have a set of folders set up with your Web page supporting files.

CHOOSING LONG FILENAMES

The next check box, Use Long Filenames Whenever Possible, is checked by default. The only operating system that does not support long filenames is Windows 3,x running on DOS. Unless you have a large number of people using this operating system, leave this check box checked.

UPDATING HYPERLINKS ON SAVE

The final check box in this section, Update Links On Save, is one of the few Web page management features in Word 2000. With this option checked, Word 2000 checks the hyperlinks in your Web page during the file-saving process. If a link is found to be broken or missing, Word shows you an error box and gives you the option to fix it before saving.

SELECTING WORD AS YOUR DEFAULT WEB PAGE EDITOR

The Default Editor portion of the Files tab under Web Options enables you to decide whether you want

- Office to be the default editor for Web pages created in Office (checked by default)
- Word to be the default editor for all Web pages (not checked by default).

Microsoft Internet Explorer 5 can be used as a vehicle to send any Web page to Word 2000 for editing. Word 2000 is the default Web page editor for any Web pages viewed. If you choose Word 2000 as the editor for all Web pages, you can send the Web page from Microsoft Internet Explorer to Word 2000 for editing by simply pressing the Edit key on the Microsoft Internet Explorer toolbar or choosing File, Edit with Microsoft Office 2000 from the menu.

> **Note**
>
> If the Web page you are viewing in Microsoft Internet Explorer was created in another Office 2000 application, such as Excel 2000 or PowerPoint 2000, then initiating the edit sequence opens the Web page in the Office component that originally created it. If the Web page was not created in any Office 2000 application, it is sent to Word 2000 for editing.

Word 2000 does not maintain the HTML source of the original Web page completely (assuming that page was not created in Word 2000). Word 2000 immediately adds the HTML code it needs to make the Web page being edited suitable for round-tripping. This

PART
X

CH
39

means that you can save the Web page to file formats other than .htm or as a Word .doc file. This guarantees that the original Web page formatting is maintained. Any tags in a Web page that Word 2000 does not understand, however, are not changed.

If you do not want Word to add the code for round-tripping, then you should consider editing the Web page using a dedicated Web page editor, such as FrontPage 2000.

USING SPECIALTY FILE FORMATS FOR GRAPHICS

The next tab in the Web Options dialog box, Pictures (shown in Figure 39.27), gives you choices on using VML, PNG (another, newer bitmap image format), and target monitors.

Figure 39.27
Setting graphic file formats and the target monitor size using Web Options in Word 2000.

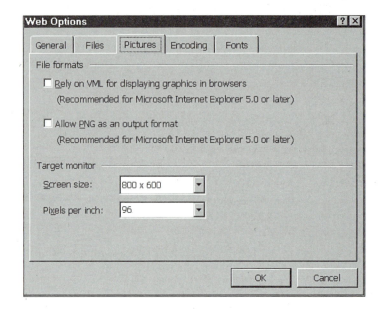

RELYING ON VML

The first option under File formats, Rely On VML for Displaying Graphics in Browsers (Recommended for Microsoft Internet Explorer 5.0 or Later), is not checked by default. Remember, as of the writing of this book, VML is supported in only Microsoft Internet Explorer 5.

USING THE NEW PNG FILE FORMAT

The next check box, Allow PNG as an Output Format, is also not checked by default. PNG (Portable Network Graphics) is a fairly new bitmap file format. It is more complex than GIF or JPG; it can use a reduced color palette such as GIF but has excellent compression capabilities similar to JPG. This format may become the dominant, single bitmap format as soon as more browsers support it. For now, only Microsoft Internet Explorer 5.0 or higher supports this new bitmap graphics file format.

OPTIMIZING THE TARGET MONITOR SCREEN SIZE

Under the Target Monitor section of this page you can choose a Screen Size from 544 × 376 up to 1920 × 1200. Pixels Per Inch supported on the monitors include 72, 96, and 120.

The target monitor screen size and pixels per inch are used in Word 2000 whenever a full page graphic (such as a chart) needs to be converted to a size that will display without being wider than the browser. The larger the screen size and the greater the number of pixels per inch, the larger the output graphic will be. Use the default screen size of 800 × 600 and 96 pixels per inch unless many people visiting your site might be using smaller monitors with a 640 × 480 screen resolution.

CHANGING LANGUAGE ENCODING

The next tab in the Web Options dialog box, Encoding (shown in Figure 39.28), enables you to choose the language code page from those installed on your machine. Choose the appropriate code page for the language you are using to build your Web page.

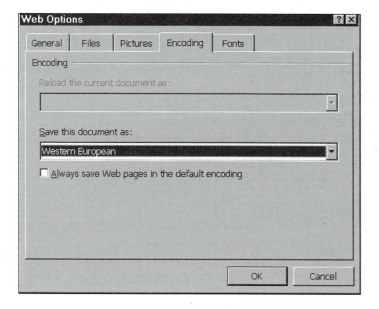

Figure 39.28
Choosing the language code page using Web Options.

SPECIFYING FONTS

The final tab in the Web Options box, Fonts (shown in Figure 39.29), enables you to choose

- The default fonts, including which default character set to choose from among those installed on your computer
- The default proportional font and size (in points)
- The default fixed-width font and size

Figure 39.29

Choosing default fonts using Web Options in Word 2000.

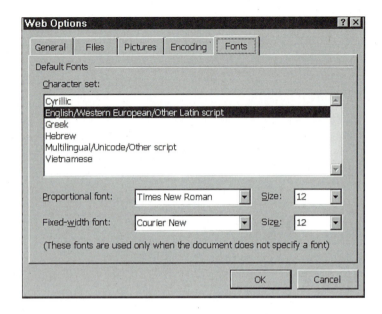

The default fonts are used only if none are specified in the Web page.

This is the final tab in the Web Options dialog box. After you make your selections, click OK to activate them.

CHANGING THE SCRIPTING LANGUAGE

If you want to change the scripting language between JavaScript and VBScript in a new Web page, you need to open the Microsoft Scripting Editor. From the menu choose Tools, Macro, Microsoft Script Editor. After the Editor opens, choose View and Property Pages. The option to change the default scripting language on the client or the server is found in the General tab of the Properties box, as shown in Figure 39.30.

You will also find several options for changing ASP (Active Server Page) settings and the choice of scripting platform. Briefly, these settings mean

- Enabling transactions tells the Microsoft Transaction Server to consider changes in the Web pages as transactions. If this is enabled, a special tag is added to the Web page.

- If you don't want session object support for your Web page, check the Sessionless ASP Page box.

- Enabling the scripting object model provides more collections (groups of addressable objects) for use.

- DTC (Design Time Control) of groups of database records can be updated by server ASP or by client (the browser) DHTML (Dynamic HTML).

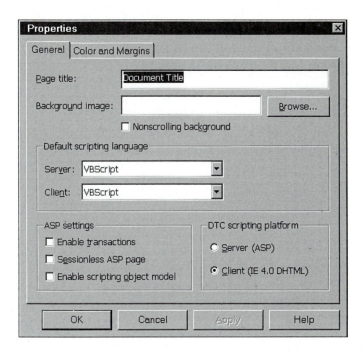

Figure 39.30
Changing the default scripting language from the Properties box in the Microsoft Scripting Editor.

Make sure that you change the default scripting language before you start building Web pages in Word 2000. After a Web page is built, the only way to change the scripting language is to manually go in and remove the old code.

TROUBLESHOOTING

WHAT TO DO IF VISITORS TO YOUR SITE CAN'T SEE YOUR ANIMATED FEATURES

I added some cool animated horizontal bars to my Web site. But visitors are complaining that the bars are irritating, making it hard to read text. What do I do?

You can either turn off the animation features in the horizontal bar or replace it with a static bar. If you have used one of the themes in Word across your site, then

1. Open the home page for your Web site (usually default.htm).
2. Choose Format, Theme from the menu.
3. Uncheck the Active Graphics check box. Click OK.

You will have to do this for each page of your Web site.

To replace the horizontal bar,

1. Select the horizontal bar you want to replace by clicking on it.
2. Delete the horizontal bar.

PART

X

CH

39

3. Choose F<u>o</u>rmat, <u>B</u>orders and Shading, and click Horizontal Bars.

4. Choose another horizontal bar. Preview it to make sure it isn't animated.

5. Click OK to add the new horizontal bar to your page.

WHAT TO DO IF YOU NEED TO REARRANGE FRAMSETS

I have a frameset composed of a smaller page on the left and a larger, main window to the right. I want to move the left frame to the top so I will have a smaller, top frame and a larger, main frame below it. How do I do this?

With your frameset open in Word,

1. Right-click in the left frame and choose Frame Properties. Make a note of the filename (it will usually have a .htm extension) listed in the Initial Page combo box. Cancel out of the Frame Properties dialog box.

2. Open the Frames toolbar.

3. Click in the main window (right frame). From the Frames toolbar, click New Frame Above to place a new frame above the main frame.

4. Click in the smaller, left window. From the Frames toolbar, click Delete Frame. The selected frame disappears.

   You should now have a two-frame window with an upper empty frame and the lower main frame.

5. Right-click in the upper, empty frame and choose Frame Properties.

6. Type the filename from step 1 (or Browse to it) into the Initial Page combo box. Click OK.

   The upper, empty frame should now contain the content formerly seen in the left frame.

7. Adjust the borders between the frames by dragging or using Frame Properties.

WHAT TO DO IF YOU ARE UNABLE TO ADD A TABLE OF CONTENTS

I have a two-page frameset. I want to have Word build an automatic table of contents for me. I added the content I wanted to index in the main frame. In the smaller frame, I clicked Table of Contents in Frame on the Frames Toolbar. The message `Error! No table of contents entries found` showed up. What happened?

The Table of Contents (TOC) is built based on any text contained in heading tags. To fix this,

1. Go back to your main page, select the text you want to see in your TOC and apply a heading (Heading 1, Heading 2, and so on) from the Style list box on the Formatting toolbar.

2. After you reapply the styles, click in the smaller frame and rebuild your TOC.

What to Do If You Need to Update Your Navigation Links

The Web Page Wizard built a series of text links for navigation when I first built my Web site.

You can't go back to the wizard. You need to manually build a text hyperlink to your page in the navigation page. To do this,

1. Open your navigation page in Word.
2. Add an extra line in your navigation menu for the new text.
3. Type the text for your new hyperlink onto this new line.
4. Right-click over the new text and click Hyperlink.
5. From the Insert Hyperlink dialog box, enter the address of your new page. Click OK.

That's it. You'll need to repeat this operation every time you create a new page.

CHAPTER 40

USING EXCEL ON THE WEB

In this chapter

EXPLORING EXCEL'S WEB CAPABILITIES

Hypertext markup language (*HTML*) format and Web compatibility are a major focus for Office 2000. One of the ways that this is demonstrated is in the improvement of Excel's tools for saving a worksheet as HTML—not only can the worksheet be posted to or used as a Web page, it can be reedited as an .xls-format worksheet in Excel, even after being saved in HTML. This is because HTML is now a companion file format to the standard .xls spreadsheet format, enabling the user to go from viewing a worksheet as a Web page to editing it as a worksheet, and back again. You don't even need to have Excel installed to edit Excel Web pages that are saved in HTML format—all you need is browser software, such as Internet Explorer.

Note

Changes to the data from the browser program can be saved only with the Save As command. Even then, each time you make changes that you want to save, you'll need to perform another Save As operation. (If you have Excel, of course, you can open the file in Excel and perform a regular save.)

Excel has simplified the Web publishing process significantly—gone is the Internet Assistant wizard, replaced by an extra step in the saving process. This simplification is yet another sign that Office 2000's applications offer complete integration with the Internet—from creating Web pages to retrieving content from the Web for use in local documents.

PUBLISHING YOUR WORKSHEET AS A WEB PAGE

Whether you or your organization have a Web site on the Internet and/or on an intranet, you'll find that Excel 2000 makes it easy to turn a workbook, worksheet, or *range* of worksheet cells into a Web page. Office 2000 has streamlined the process of saving Excel content as HTML and gives you new options for how that data will be viewed and used by those who visit your Web site:

- **Add Interactivity**. Available when publishing a range of cells, this option means that the user on the Web can actually work with the workbook—total, sort, filter, and use the Clipboard to manipulate the content. You even can view and manipulate the selection in *PivotTable* format.

- **After Saving, Open Published Web Page in Browser**. This option enables you to quickly view a new page in browser format, immediately upon saving the file as HTML.

SAVING YOUR WORKSHEET AS HTML

To begin, decide which part of your workbook will be saved as HTML—the entire workbook, a sheet within it, or cells within a single sheet. If a single sheet or cells within it are to be saved as HTML, select them before invoking the Save as Web Page command.

After selecting your desired cells (if necessary), follow these steps to save your Excel content as HTML:

1. Choose File, Save as Web Page.

2. In the Save As dialog box, type a name for your HTML file (see Figure 40.1). You don't need to type the .htm extension (Excel will insert it for you), but if you need an .html or other extension specifically, type it after the filename.

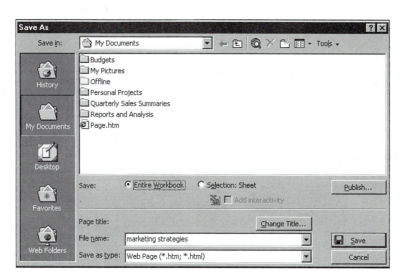

Figure 40.1.
Choose a filename for the Web page, remembering that if viewed online, the filename will be part of the address, visible to the user.

3. Choose a folder into which the file should be saved (if you want it to be saved to your local or a network drive).

4. The Save section of the dialog box indicates whether you're saving the Entire Workbook or a Selection (followed by the word Sheet, or a specific range if you highlighted a range before beginning this procedure). Change this setting if necessary.

5. Click the Publish button. This opens the Publish As Web Page dialog box (see Figure 40.2).

6. Confirm the item to publish in the Choose list box (see Figure 40.3). If you selected a range before starting the procedure, Range of cells will be selected in the Choose box. You can edit the range manually, or click the Collapse Dialog button to expose the worksheet. You can then select the desired cells and reexpand the dialog box to continue.

7. If publishing a range or single sheet, select the Add Interactivity With option, and choose Spreadsheet Functionality or PivotTable Functionality from the drop-down list.

→ For details on converting Excel PivotTables to Web pages, **see** "Saving and Editing PivotTables in HTML Format," **p. 1068**

Figure 40.2.
If you choose to publish the page (in addition to simply saving it in HTML), the options for how the page will be viewed and used are offered in the Publish As Web Page dialog box.

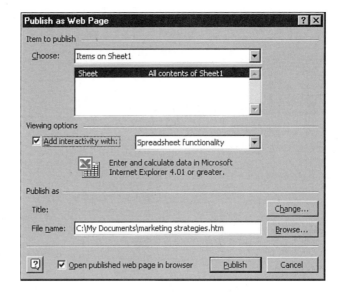

Figure 40.3.
If you want to edit a range or click on another sheet, click the Collapse Dialog button.

Collapse Dialog button ⸺

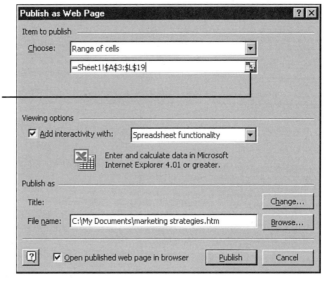

8. In the Publish as section, enter a File Name and path for the file. You can enter an HTTP or FTP address.

9. If your browser program is open, select the Open Published Web Page in Browser option. (This step is optional, but useful.)

10. If you want to add a title centered over the published selection, click the <u>C</u>hange button. The Set Title dialog box opens, as shown in Figure 40.4; type a title in the text box and then click OK to return to the Publish as Web Page dialog box.

11. Click <u>P</u>ublish.

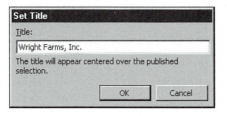

Figure 40.4.
Type a title that you want to display over the published Web content.

Note

At this point, you might receive a warning message indicating that certain Excel features included in your workbook won't be supported in the browser.

If the browser isn't open and you've turned on the <u>O</u>pen Published Web Page in Browser option, your Web browser will open automatically and display the page.

The workbook, worksheet, or specified section is now published as a Web page, saved in HTML format. Figure 40.5 shows a worksheet section published with interactivity, viewed in an Internet Explorer window.

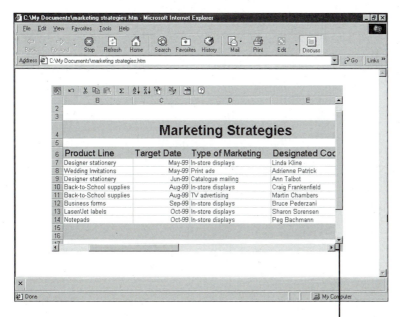

Figure 40.5.
A set of tools appropriate for the interactivity setting you choose will be displayed with the cells that you published.

PART
X

CH
40

Use the scrollbars to see the portions of the published worksheet that don't fit in the view.

Caution

> If the workbook, worksheet, or range of cells contains hyperlinks, be sure that the files to which the hyperlinks point are available to online viewers—in other words, consider publishing these files to the Web as well. If this isn't possible, delete the hyperlinks before publishing the Web page. If the hyperlinks point to Web sites, it's a good idea to check that they're still valid sites before publishing (and check them later on, too, to ensure that the hyperlinks stay updated).

VIEWING YOUR WORKSHEET AS A WEB PAGE

You can view the Excel Web page with Excel, Word, or Web browser software (Internet Explorer, Netscape, or other comparable programs). To open a previously published Web page, follow these steps:

1. In Excel, choose File, Open.

2. In the Files of type list box, select Web Pages, so that you see only HTML-formatted files.

3. Locate the folder that contains the Web page file, and double-click the Web page to open it.

The Web page will open in Microsoft FrontPage if you have that program installed. Otherwise, the file will open in Word. The display will include a toolbar if the page was saved with interactivity added. Depending on the size of your range of cells, there may also be scrollbars around the Web content, in addition to the scrollbars found in the Word window (see Figure 40.6).

Tip #494

> You can force Excel to open the Web page (thereby bypassing FrontPage and Word) by selecting the file and using the Open in Microsoft Excel command on the Open drop-down list. This leads to a drawback in the HTML feature: Even though you can open the Web file in Excel, you don't gain all of Excel's functionality. You get the same functionality you had in the browser.

Opening a Web page in Internet Explorer (while offline) is very similar—choose File, Open, and from within the Open dialog box, click the Browse button to locate the file you want to open (see Figure 40.7). After selecting the file, click OK to close the Open dialog box and view the Web page.

To preview a Web page as it will actually be seen online, type the full path to the file (such as **c:\My Documents\Web Pages\budget.htm**) in the address/URL list box in the browser's window, and the published worksheet will appear onscreen. If the Web page has already been posted to your Web site, you can use Internet Explorer's address bar to enter the Web address, such as www.yourcompany.com/travel.htm (see Figure 40.8). An address such as this will take you to your Web site, and, additionally, go to the .htm file posted at the site.

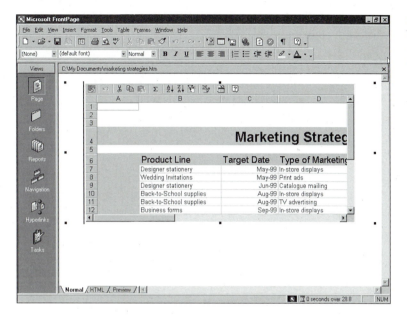

Figure 40.6.
The Web page is displayed within a FrontPage window.

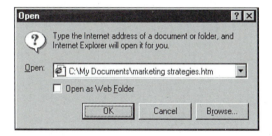

Figure 40.7.
Type the path and file-name, if you know it, or click Browse to look for an HTML file.

Tip #495

If you'll be using or updating this particular page often, add it to your Favorites list in Internet Explorer.

Figure 40.8.
Type the URL (Web address) of your posted Web page into Internet Explorer's address box.

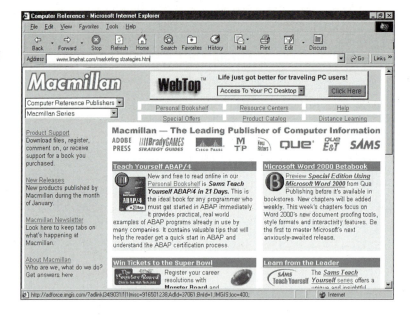

COPYING TABULAR WEB DATA TO AN EXCEL WORKSHEET

You can copy Web page content—viewed in Excel, Word, or through a browser—to an Excel worksheet by way of the *Clipboard* or drag and drop. This capability is a significant benefit to organizations and workgroups: One person can post a worksheet on the Web and other people can not only view but also copy portions of the worksheet to their local Excel workbook, and use the data there.

To copy Excel Web content to another worksheet, follow these steps:

1. With both the Web page (in a Word or browser window) and the target Excel worksheet open, switch to the Web page.

2. Select the source cells within the Web page, and copy them to the Clipboard with your favorite copying method.

3. Switch back to the target worksheet, select the target cell, and paste the data from the Clipboard.

It can be very helpful to tile the two application windows when you're copying Web content—right-click a blank space on the taskbar and choose Tile Vertically (or Horizontally). As shown in Figure 40.9, this allows you to see both the source (Web page) and target (local worksheet).

Pasted Web content in the worksheet

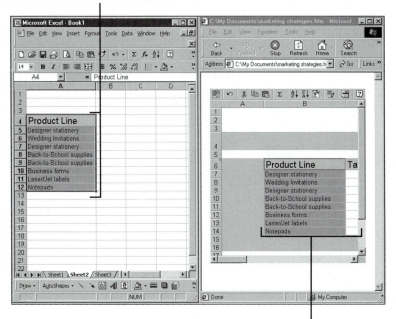

Figure 40.9.
Tile the browser and Excel windows to facilitate copying from the Web page to the worksheet.

Web content selected and copied

Using drag and drop is possible only if the application windows are tiled, as you must be able to see both the source and target locations simultaneously.

Tip #496

You may be able to drag data from the browser to Word, Excel, and PowerPoint without having to tile the windows. Drag the data from the browser down to the Office program's taskbar button. You'll see a "no drag allowed" symbol, but leave the mouse over the taskbar button for a second or two. If this feature is going to work, the program you're pointing to should activate, at which time you can drag the data up into the newly activated window and release it. (This method doesn't seem to work in all cases.)

When using drag and drop between an online view of the Web content and the local worksheet, a copy will be made by default. If you're using drag and drop between the Web page in Word and an offline view through the browser, you must press the Ctrl key while dragging in order to make a copy. If you forget to use Ctrl in this situation, you risk editing the offline Web content by removing the content that's dragged and dropped onto the worksheet. Figure 40.10 shows content being dragged from the Web page to a worksheet.

PART

X

CH

40

Plus sign on the mouse pointer indicates a copy is being dragged.

Figure 40.10.
In lieu of the Clipboard, use drag and drop to copy content from the Web page to a worksheet on a local or network drive.

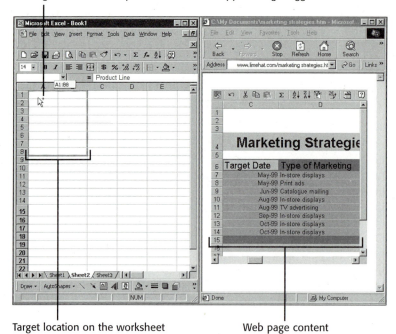

Target location on the worksheet   Web page content

COLLABORATING ONLINE WITH EXCEL

Publishing a worksheet to the Web, placing Excel content on a Web page, and using Web content in worksheets on your local drive are significant uses of the Web in relation to Excel. These features truly expand your distribution capabilities and access to Excel data. However, in each of these situations, you're operating alone in that you're not discussing or sharing information interactively. Publishing a Web page and copying Web content to a local workbook are solitary activities, and any questions or ideas that other users might have would need to be shared through an external vehicle such as email or a phone call.

To remedy this situation, Excel 2000's online tools include *online collaboration*, enabling you to communicate live with other users—people within your organization or in the outside world—via the Internet or an intranet. Meetings can be set up for immediate collaboration or scheduled for a future date, and Web discussions can be held to share ideas and information.

Note

Microsoft NetMeeting, the software used for collaborating "live" online, is beyond the scope of this book, but the following section provides a brief discussion of how it's used.

MEETING WITH COWORKERS ONLINE

To set up an immediate meeting, choose Tools, Online Collaboration, Meet Now. The Meeting dialog box opens as shown in Figure 40.11, allowing you to set up your user information—first and last name, email address, and the server to which you'll be attached for the online meeting.

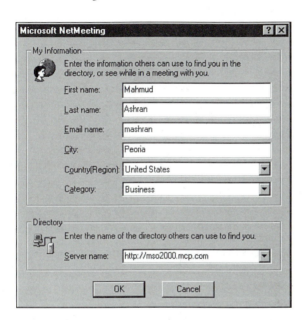

Figure 40.11.
Identify yourself and the server to which you and your collaborators will be attached for the meeting.

If you've already provided this information on a previous collaboration, this dialog box will not appear when Meet Now is selected. Rather, the Place a Call dialog box will appear, enabling you to select from a list those people with whom you'd like to have an online meeting.

Tip #497

> All the people you call must be running NetMeeting at the time you call them—otherwise, you'll just get an error message. It's a good idea to call your intended collaborators before setting up the meeting, to be sure they're on their computers, logged onto the server, and running NetMeeting.

After your meeting begins, you can use the Online Meeting toolbar to access meeting tools, as described in the following list (see Figure 40.12):

- **Participant List**. Displays a list of the people currently involved in the online collaboration.

- **Call Participant**. Reopens the Place a Call dialog box, in case you need to add a new participant.

- **Remove Participant**. If a participant logs off or exits NetMeeting, it removes him or her from the participant list.

- **Allow Others to Edit**. Gives the other participants the rights to contribute to the meeting and edit the content of the Chat and Whiteboard windows.

- **Display Chat Window**. Opens a chat-room window into which each participant can type text contributions to the meeting conversation.

- **Display Whiteboard**. Displays a window in which you can write, type, and draw, such as a whiteboard or easel in a conference room.

- **End Meeting**. Ends the online collaboration.

Figure 40.12.
Control the list of meeting members or access a chat window from the Online Meeting toolbar.

In some cases, the people with whom you'd like to collaborate aren't available right away, and you have to pick a future time to meet online. Excel gives you the ability to set up a meeting in the future, selecting the time and date for the meeting, as well as the names of the people who will be included in the meeting.

To schedule an online meeting, follow these steps:

1. Choose Tools, Online Collaboration, Schedule Meeting.

2. In the resulting Outlook Meeting dialog box shown in Figure 40.13, enter the names of the people you want in the meeting, and choose the time and date for the online collaboration.

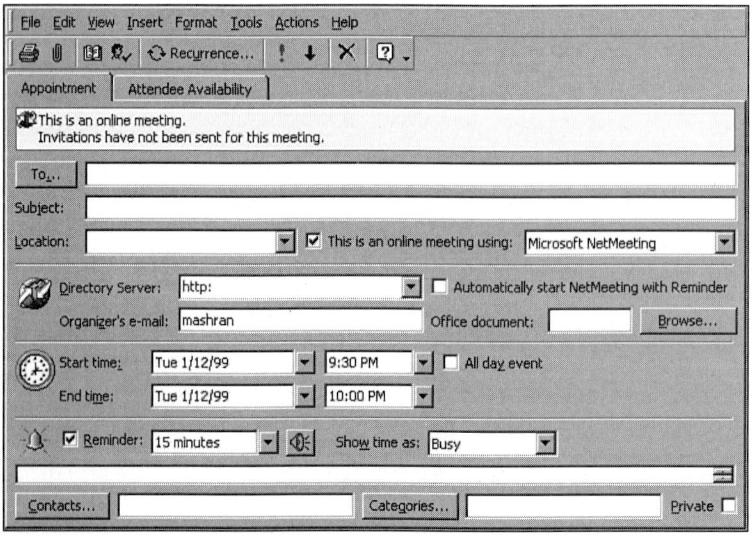

Figure 40.13.
Select the date, time, and planned duration of your online meeting.

3. If you and those whom you've invited are on a network and can view each other's schedules through Outlook, click the Attendee Availability tab (see Figure 40.14) to select a time at which everyone will be free to participate.

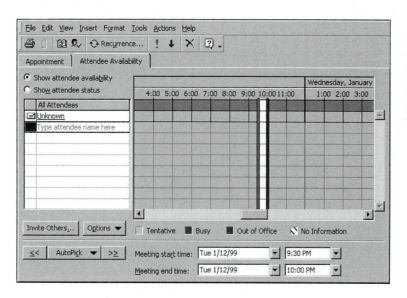

Figure 40.14.
Coworkers' schedules need to be up-to-date and available to you through your network in order to make proper use of Attendee Availability.

4. Click Send to send the invitations to your attendee list.

Note

If you're not a Microsoft Outlook user or you haven't yet set up Outlook as part of Office 2000, starting the process of scheduling an online meeting will generate a wizard that takes you through the process of setting up Outlook so that you can schedule the meeting.

DISCUSSING DOCUMENTS ONLINE

By placing Excel documents in HTML format at a central server location, you can collaborate on the design and use of those documents with other users—and no one is required to have Excel for this purpose. This feature is useful for creating new workbooks that will be used by more than one department, redesigning existing worksheets (especially if they're shared cross-country or cross-division), posting proposals or quarterly results, and so on.

Each person who logs onto the server can open the shared document(s) and provide discussion about the document as needed, replying to existing comments and creating new comments. The discussion works like that of a newsgroup, where you post a comment and other people reply to it, or you reply to other people's comments—no one else has to be online while you are commenting or replying to other users' comments.

To enter or initiate a discussion about a document, log on to the server and open the document. Click the Discussions button on the Discussions toolbar. (If the Discussions pane or toolbar isn't visible in the Internet Explorer window, choose View, Explorer Bar, Discuss.)

Then choose Insert about the Document to place a comment about the document in the discussion pane, or Insert in the Document to place a comment within the document itself. The discussion pane displays the comments made by each person, his or her user name, and the comments, along with the date and time. As the discussion continues, other users can add comments, reply to comments, add questions for the group, and so forth.

Figure 40.15 shows the Enter Discussion Text dialog box (opened by choosing to insert discussion about the document) and the text of the next comment/question that will appear in the discussion.

Figure 40.15.
Type your comment or question in the Discussion Text box, and click OK to insert it into the discussion pane.

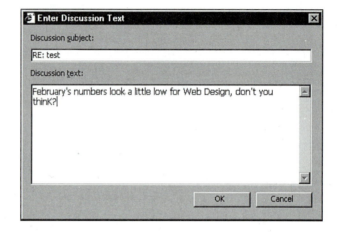

As the attendees' comments accumulate, you see them stack up in the discussion pane. Figure 40.16 shows a discussion of marketing tactics underway. To reply to a comment, edit it, or delete it, click the down arrow next to the note icon and select Reply, Edit, or Delete, as appropriate. You may be asked for additional confirmation, depending on the network setup.

Note

Changes like this undoubtedly will require you to have certain permissions or rights on the network. If you get error messages when trying to save, edit, or delete discussion comments, consult the network administrator.

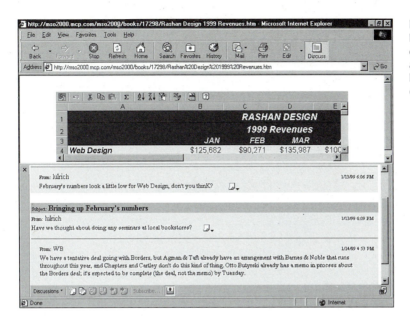

Figure 40.16.
Each comment/
question appears with
a small note icon,
helping to keep each
one visually separate.

SENDING YOUR EXCEL WORKBOOK VIA EMAIL

Excel enables you to share Excel workbooks via email by turning a single worksheet into the body of a message or by attaching your workbook file to an email message. When sending a workbook as an attachment, the recipient should also have Excel, and it's a good idea to find out which version she's running, to make sure you save the file in a format that will be compatible with that installed version. If the recipient will be receiving the worksheet as the body of the message, she doesn't need to have Excel unless she wants to take the message content and paste it into a worksheet of her own on her local drive.

Tip #498

If the recipient is a Lotus 1-2-3 user, save the Excel worksheet to a Lotus 1-2-3 format that matches that version. When in doubt, check with the recipient before sending. If that's not possible, choose the oldest version that supports all of your worksheet's content and formatting.

The exact procedure for attaching the file to the message will vary slightly with different software programs (CompuServe, America Online, Outlook, Netscape, Internet Explorer, among others) but the basic procedure consists of the following steps:

1. In the email message window, click the Attachments button. It may appear as a paper-clip button on the toolbar or as a button with the word Attach or Attachments on it.

2. In the resulting dialog box, navigate to the folder that contains the file you want to attach. Double-click the worksheet file.

3. Click OK to confirm your intention to attach the file.

The attached file will appear as an icon within the message (wherever the insertion point was when you clicked the Attach button) or listed somewhere in the window. When the recipient receives the message, double-clicking the icon in the message or clicking a Download button in the message window opens a dialog box. From there, she can choose a location to save the file or merely opt to view it onscreen without saving it to her local or network drive.

Another easy option for sending workbooks to other users via email is to use the File, Send To command from Excel. This command allows for attaching the active workbook as either body text, in which case you choose Mail Recipient from the submenu, or as an attachment to a mail message, in which case you choose Mail Recipient (as Attachment). The submenu also offers an underused but very effective Routing Recipient command, which sends the active workbook through a series of recipients either one at a time (in any order you choose) or all at once. You can even send the workbook to someone in an online meeting you're currently attending.

INDEX

Symbols

& function, using, 792-793

.doc binary file format *versus* Web page, 1225

.gif images and palette, 1252

#NAME? error, troublehsooting, 814

#NUM! error, troubleshooting, 799

#REF! error, troubleshooting, 792

24-hour clock, 624

2000 and beyond date formats, 624

2D charts, advantages of, 929

3D button (Drawing toolbar), 404, 427, 636

3D charts
   creating, 841
   creating column depth in, 929-931
   creating gradient fills in, 937-938
   cylinder, cone, and pyramid, 852
   formatting
      data series, 911-912
      floors, 911
      overview of
      views, 913-914
      walls, 911
   slicing through, 702

3D effects, adding to shapes, 427-429

3D effects, applying to drawn objects, 665-666

3D objects, generating realistic, 429

3D Settings options, 428

3D Settings tool, 666

3D surface charts, 472, 848

3D View command (Chart menu), 913

3D View dialog box, 913, 930

3D wire frame charts, 848

A

A4 paper size, 716

abbreviating column or row headings for charts, 828

absolute references and formulas, 751

Accept or Reject Changes dialog box, 518-519

Access
   data source for mail merge, using as, 184
   databases, overview of, 1160
   exporting data to Word, 1167
   inserting data into documents
      AutoFormatting before inserting, 1164
      Insert Data dialog box, using, 1164
      overview of, 1160-1162
      Query Options, using, 1162-1163
   integrating with, 1159-1160
   modifying data in documents, 1165-1166
   publishing data to Word, 1166-1167

accessibility issues with Web pages, 1237

accessing
   cell ranges using hyperlinks, 1218
   Drawing toolbar, 403
   Formula Palette, 762
   underlying data table for mail merge, 179-180

action fields, 557

Active Graphics option (Web Page Wizard), 1239

Active Server Pages settings, changing, 1266

active tables, creating using spinners and charts, 1134-1136

active variance tables, 1089

active workbook, changing default font, 615

ActiveX controls, using with Excel, 1094

adapting styles, 41

Add Clip to Clip Gallery dialog box (Clip Gallery), 375

Add Custom Chart Type dialog box (Microsoft Graph), 487

Add Interactivity option, 1272

Add New Record button (Database toolbar), 181

Add Report dialog box (Report Manager), 975

Add Section dialog box (Binder), 1180

Add Text command (shortcut menu), 409

Add Trendline dialog box (Microsoft Graph), 492, 878-879

C

G

P

Page Break Preview button (Print Preview toolbar), 711

Page Break Preview feature, 711-712

page changes, 1103

PAGE field, 503, 510

Page Layout option (PivotTable Options dialog box), 1042

Page Number button (Custom Header and Footer dialog boxes), 723

page numbering feature, 312

page numbers
formatting tables of contents, 272
indexes, 304, 311, 323
tables, 296

Page Order option (Sheet tab of Page Setup dialog box), 725

Page Setup dialog box
Header/Footer tab, 721
options, 713
Sheet tab
options, 724
Print Area option, 725
Print Titles option, 726

Page tab (Page Setup dialog box), 713

page view, dragging fields for in PivotTables, 1054

pages
adding to Web sites, 1236-1237
counting in documents, 72

painting numeric pictures, 578

palette and Web publishing issues, 1252-1253

paper size and printing worksheets, 716

paragraphs
AutoFormatting feature and, 100
formatting, 91
moving within outlines, 220
Outline view, displaying first lines of, 222

styles
creating with Style by Example feature, 41
interaction with character styles, 34

parentheses, finding missing in formulas, 748

parsing table data, 1211-1214

Participant List button (Online Meeting toolbar), 1281

passim, use in Table of Authorities, 295

password-protected documents
revising, 507

passwords
applying, 995-996
forms
adding when protecting, 550
removing, 551
reviewing documents and, 506

Paste as Hyperlink command (Edit menu), 1156

Paste command (Insert menu), 806

Paste Function box, 156-157

Paste Function dialog box, 760, 766, 807

Paste Link command (Edit menu), Microsoft Graph, 495

Paste Name dialog box, 740, 806, 812

Paste Special dialog box
charts, adding data to, 863-864
overview of, 1155
Values option, 799, 964

pasting
charts into PowerPoint presentations, 1209
conditional formats over multiple rows, 997
data
into PowerPoint datasheets, 1206-1207
into PowerPoint presentations, 1205
as Word table, 1197

footnotes and endnotes, 335
lists of named ranges, 812-813
range names into formulas, 807-808
range of cells
as Word hyperlinks, 1156
as Word tables, 1154
as worksheet objects, 1155

Pattern option (Fill Color tool), 662

Pattern tab (Fill Effects dialog box), 422

patterns
applying to cells, 612
formatting chart elements using, 484-485

Patterns tab
Format Axis dialog box, 885
Format Cells dialog box, 612

Percent Style button (Formatting toolbar), 490, 618

Percentage format, applying, 621-622

percentage tables, formatting, 692

performance and formulas, 1109

performing calculations, 1052

personalized custom charts, creating, 853

Photo Editor 3.01, 1190-1191

PhotoDraw application, 634

picas, 594

Picture command (Insert menu), 634

Picture fills and file size, 663

Picture option (Fill Color tool), 663

Picture Placeholder feature, 365

Picture tab (Fill Effects dialog box), 423-424

Picture toolbar
buttons, 922
Camera pictures and, 704
Crop button, 387
Less Brightness button, 390

X-Z

Get **FREE** books and more...when you register this book online for our Personal Bookshelf Program

http://register.quecorp.com/

 Register online and you can sign up for our *FREE Personal Bookshelf Program...*unlimited access to the electronic version of more than 200 complete computer books—immediately! That means you'll have 100,000 pages of valuable information onscreen, at your fingertips!

 Plus, you can access product support, including complimentary downloads, technical support files, book-focused links, companion Web sites, author sites, and more!

 And you'll be automatically registered to receive a *FREE subscription to a weekly email newsletter* to help you stay current with news, announcements, sample book chapters, and special events, including sweepstakes, contests, and various product giveaways!

 We value your comments! Best of all, the entire registration process takes only a few minutes to complete, so go online and get the greatest value going—absolutely FREE!

Don't Miss Out On This Great Opportunity!

QUE® is a brand of Macmillan Computer Publishing USA.

For more information, please visit *www.mcp.com*